CHILDREN

CHILDREN

FIFTH EDITION

John W. Santrock
University of Texas at Dallas

Brown & Benchmark
PUBLISHERS

Madison, WI Dubuque Guilford, CT Chicago Toronto London
Mexico City Caracas Buenos Aires Madrid Bogotá Sydney

Book Team

Executive Publisher *Edgar J. Laube*
Acquisitions Editor *Steven Yetter*
Developmental Editor *Ted Underhill*
Production Editor *Donna Nemmers*
Proofreading Coordinator *Carrie Barker*
Designer *Christopher E. Reese*
Art Editor *Miriam Hoffman*
Photo Editor *Carol Judge*
Permissions Coordinator *Karen L. Storlie*
Production Manager *Beth Kundert*
Production/Costing Manager *Sherry Padden*
Design and New Media Development Manager *Linda Meehan Avenarius*
Marketing Manager *Carla Aspelmeier*
Copywriter *Jennifer Smith*
Proofreader *Mary Svetlik Anderson*

Basal Text *10/12 Goudy*
Display Type *Goudy*
Typesetting System *Macintosh® QuarkXPress®*
Paper Stock *50# Nature Web Matte*

Executive Vice President and General Manager *Bob McLaughlin*
Vice President, Business Manager *Russ Domeyer*
Vice President of Production and New Media Development *Victoria Putman*
National Sales Manager *Phil Rudder*
National Telesales Director *John Finn*

A Times Mirror Company

To my family:
Mary Jo, Tracy, and Jennifer

BRIEF CONTENTS

CONTENTS

SECTION ONE

The Nature of Children's Development   3

John W. Santrock

CHAPTER SEVEN

Cognitive Development in Infancy   187

CHAPTER EIGHT

Socioemotional Development in Infancy   215

SECTION FOUR

Early Childhood   251

CHAPTER NINE

Physical Development in Early Childhood   253

CHAPTER TEN

Cognitive Development in Early Childhood   277

CHAPTER ELEVEN

Socioemotional Development in Early Childhood 311

SECTION FIVE

Middle and Late Childhood 351

CHAPTER TWELVE

Physical Development in Middle and Late Childhood 353

CHAPTER THIRTEEN

Cognitive Development in Middle and Late Childhood 379

CHAPTER FOURTEEN

Socioemotional Development in Middle and Late Childhood 415

SECTION SIX

Adolescence   453

Tables, Boxes, and Endpieces

Concept Tables

CRITICAL THINKING ABOUT CHILDREN'S DEVELOPMENT

HEALTH AND WELL-BEING

FAMILIES AND PARENTING

EDUCATION

CULTURE AND ETHNICITY

GENDER

PREFACE

Children are our nation's most important resource. They are the future of our society. Because they are such an important resource and the future of our society, we need to show a deep concern for helping all children reach their full potential. We can accomplish this in a number of ways. For one, by taking a course like this one on child development you can increase your knowledge of how children learn and develop. For another, we can develop a deep compassion for helping children reach their full potential. The fifth edition of *Children* continues to emphasize practical applications to the real worlds of children and ways to improve children's lives.

FIVE IMPORTANT THEMES IN CHILDREN'S LIVES AND IN CHILDREN, FIFTH EDITION

Five important themes continue to be woven throughout the fifth edition of *Children:* (1) health and well-being, (2) families and parenting, (3) education, (4) culture and ethnicity, and (5) gender. I believe that these five themes hold important keys to improving the lives of children and helping them reach their full potential.

In addition to being discussed at various points within chapters, these five themes appear at the end of each chapter in a new section called "Improving the Lives of Children." Each of the themes—health and well-being, families and parenting, education, culture and ethnicity, and gender—is connected to the chapter's content. Many of the discussions of these important topics are new to this edition of the book.

The five themes also are revisited in an Epilogue at the end of the book, which recaps the importance of health and well-being, families and parenting, education, culture and ethnicity, and gender in children's lives.

A special effort was made to provide very up-to-date coverage of these five themes. In the fourth edition of *Children*, five experts served as consultants, providing advice about these topics: Jennifer Cousins (health and well-being), Phyllis Bernstein (families and parenting), Greta Fein (education), Algea Harrison (culture and ethnicity), and Michelle Paludi (gender).

To expand the inclusion of up-to-date material on these topics, the following individuals served as consultants for the fifth edition of *Children:* Tiffany Field (health and well-being), Diana Baumrind (families and parenting), Rosalind Charlesworth (education), Sandra Graham (culture and ethnicity), and Florence Denmark (gender). These experts truly made the fifth edition of *Children* an improved portrait of what we know about children's development in these important domains.

CRITICAL THINKING

The discussion of critical thinking was expanded in the fifth edition of *Children*. In each chapter, several boxes on critical thinking stimulate students to think critically about topics related to the chapter's contents. Most of the critical-thinking discussions are new in *Children's* fifth edition. One of the nation's leading experts on critical thinking—Jane Halonen—served as a consultant for the incorporation of critical thinking into this edition.

PRACTICAL KNOWLEDGE ABOUT CHILDREN

The well-received feature "Practical Knowledge About Children," which was introduced in the book's fourth edition, has been retained in the fifth edition. These book reviews are now presented at the end of each chapter. The "Practical Knowledge About Children" section reviews recommended books, many of which provide valuable information about improving the lives of children.

SCIENCE AND RESEARCH

The fifth edition of *Children* not only provides extensive information about applications to the real world of children but also is a thorough, sound, up-to-date presentation of the science of child development. Both classic and leading-edge research are highlighted.

As part of the citation changes in the fifth edition of *Children*, I did a considerable amount of "reference house-cleaning." That is, I very carefully added appropriate new references but also removed a number of older references that were no longer necessary to include. The result is far fewer total references in the fifth edition of the book, but far more recent references—more than 350 of the citations now come from 1995, 1996, 1997, or in-press sources.

WRITING

I continue to strive to make *Children* more student-friendly. I have explored many alternative ways of presenting ideas and have asked large numbers of students to give me feedback about which strategies are the most effective. Covering the entire journey of children's development in one book is a difficult task. To incorporate the core knowledge of the field of child development, present the latest advances on the scientific front, and describe practical applications in each period of development requires careful consideration of what to include (as well as what to exclude), and how to include it.

This challenging task requires clear writing and a very usable pedagogical system. In constructing this edition of *Children,* I rewrote virtually every section—adding, subtracting, integrating, and simplifying. *Children* also has a carefully designed pedagogical system that will benefit student learning. The key features of the learning system will be presented shortly in a visual preface for students, "How the Learning System Works."

MOTIVATION

Students learn best when they are highly motivated and interested in what they are reading and experiencing. It is important to be motivated right from the start, so each chapter of *Children* begins with a high-interest piece called "Images of Children" that should motivate students to read the chapter. The increased applications to the real lives of children throughout the book should also motivate students, because they will increasingly be able to perceive how the material relates to their roles as parents, educators, and caring adults who work with children to help them reach their potential. I also have tried to communicate the discoveries about children's development with energy and enthusiasm and have provided lively examples when I introduce a new concept. I personally chose virtually every photograph in *Children* because I believe the combination of the right photograph with the right words improves student motivation and learning. I also participated extensively in the book's design and created a number of visual figures that combine photographs with figure information or summaries of concepts; I believe these also enhance student motivation and learning.

In summary, I have tried to convey the complex and exciting story of how children develop and how we have in our hands the ability to help them reach their full potential in a manner that is both informative *and* enjoyable. I will have reached the goals I set for the fifth edition of *Children*

if I have engaged students with the material, they learn effectively from it, and they feel they have more wisdom about improving children's lives.

REDESIGN OF CHAPTERS FOR A CLEARER, LESS-CLUTTERED LOOK

An important change in the fifth edition of *Children* is a clearer, less-cluttered look to the chapters. By moving the previously boxed features on culture and ethnicity, education, and parenting to the end of the chapter, as well as also moving the "Practical Knowledge About Children" discussions, to the end of the chapter, the chapter content is considerably more streamlined and clear.

In addition, the popular feature *Resources for Improving the Lives of Children* has been expanded and is now offered as an ancillary for *Children*, Fifth Edition. The *Resources* feature consists of phone numbers, addresses, books, and brochures that can be used to improve the lives of children.

B&B CourseKits™

B&B CourseKits™ are course-specific collections of for sale educational materials custom packaged for maximum convenience and value. CourseKits offer you the flexibility of customizing and combining Brown & Benchmark course materials (B&B CourseKits®, Annual Editions®, Taking Sides®, etc.) with your own or other material. Each CourseKit contains two or more instructor-selected items conveniently packaged and priced for your students. For more information on B&B CourseKits™, please contact your local Brown & Benchmark Sales Representative.

Annual Editions®

Magazines, newspapers, and journals of the public press play an important role in providing current, first-rate, relevant educational information. If in your child development course you are interested in exposing your students to a wide range of current, well-balanced, carefully selected articles from some of the most important magazines, newspapers, and journals published today, you may want to consider *Annual Editions: Child Growth and Development*, published by the Dushkin Publishing Group, a unit of Brown & Benchmark Publishers. *Annual Editions: Child Growth and Development* is a collection of over 40 articles on topics related to the latest research and thinking in child development. *Annual Editions* is updated on an annual basis, and there are a number of features designed to make it particularly useful, including a topic guide, an annotated table of contents, and unit overviews. Consult your Brown & Benchmark Sales Representative for more details.

John W. Santrock

Taking Sides®

Are you interested in generating classroom discussion? In finding a tool to more fully involve your students in their experience of your course? Would you like to encourage your students to become more active learners? To develop their critical thinking skills? Lastly, are you yourself intrigued by current controversies related to issues in childhood and development? If so, you should be aware of a new publication from The Dushkin Publishing Group, a unit of Brown & Benchmark Publishers: *Taking Sides: Clashing Views on Controversial Issues in Childhood and Society*, edited by Professors Robert L. DelCampo and Diane S. DelCampo of New Mexico State University. *Taking Sides*, a reader that takes a pro/con approach to issues, is designed to introduce students to controversies in childhood and development. The readings, which represent the arguments of leading child behaviorists and social commentators, reflect a variety of viewpoints and have been selected for their liveliness, currency, and substance. Consult your Brown & Benchmark Sales Representative for more details.

CourseMedia™

As educational needs and methods change, Brown & Benchmark adds innovative, contemporary student materials for the computer, audio, and video devices of the 1990s and beyond. These include:

- Stand-alone materials
- Study guides
- Software simulations
- Tutorials
- Exercises

CourseMedia™ also includes instructional aids you can use to enhance lectures and discussions, such as:

- Videos
- Level I and III videodiscs
- CD-ROMs

CourseWorks

CourseWorks (formerly Kinko's CourseWorks in the U.S.) is the Brown & Benchmark custom publishing service. With its own printing and distribution facility, CourseWorks gives you the flexibility to add current material to your course at any time. CourseWorks provides you with a unique set of options:

- Customizing Brown & Benchmark CourseBooks
- Publishing your own material
- Including any previously published material for which we can secure permissions
- Adding photos
- Performing copyediting
- Creating custom covers

ANCILLARY MATERIALS FOR THE INSTRUCTOR

The publisher and ancillary team have worked together to produce an outstanding integrated teaching package to accompany *Children*. The authors of the ancillaries are all experienced teachers in the child development course. The ancillaries have been designed to make it as easy as possible to customize the entire package to meet the unique needs of professors and students.

Instructor's Course Planner

The key to this teaching package was created by Allen H. Keniston and Blaine F. Peden of the University of Wisconsin–Eau Claire. Allen and Blaine are both award-winning teachers and active members of The Council of Teachers of Undergraduate Psychology. This flexible planner provides a variety of useful tools to enhance your teaching efforts, reduce your workload, and increase your enjoyment. For each chapter of the text, the planner provides an outline and overview. The planner also contains lecture suggestions, classroom activities, discussion questions, integrative essay questions, a film list, and a transparency guide. It contains an abundance of handouts and exercises for stimulating classroom discussion and encouraging critical thinking.

The **Test Item File** was constructed by Janet A. Simons. Simons is an experienced author of test item files and psychology texts. This comprehensive test bank includes over 1,800 multiple-choice test questions that are keyed to the text and learning objectives. Each item is designated as factual, conceptual, or applied as defined by the first three levels of Benjamin Bloom's *Taxonomy of Educational Objectives* (1956).

The questions in the Test Item File are available on **MicroTest III,** a powerful but easy-to-use test-generating program by Chariot Software Group. MicroTest is available for DOS, Windows, and Macintosh. With MicroTest, you can easily select questions from the Test Item File and print a test and an answer key. You can customize questions, headings, and instructions, you can add or import questions of your own, and you can print your test in a choice of fonts if your printer supports them. You can obtain a copy of MicroTest III by contacting your local Brown & Benchmark Sales Representative or by phoning Educational Resources at 1–800–338–5371.

The **Student Study Guide** was also created by Blaine F. Peden and Allen H. Keniston of the University of Wisconsin–Eau Claire. For each chapter of the text, the student is provided with learning objectives and key terms, a guided review, and two self-tests. One covers key terms and key persons, and the other entails multiple choice questions (with answers provided for self-testing). The study guide includes the section "How to Be a Better Student" to help students study more effectively and efficiently.

A **Student Study Tape** is a new supplement being offered with this edition. To further reinforce student learning, this valuable audio tape features key term recitation and a summary of the main topics presented in the text.

Guide to Life-Span Development for Future Nurses and **Guide to Life-Span Development for Future Educators** are new course supplements that help students apply the concepts of human development to the education and nursing professions. Each supplement contains information, exercises, and sample tests designed to help students prepare for certification and understand human development from these professional perspectives.

The **Brown & Benchmark Human Development Transparency/Slide Set,** Second Edition, consists of 141 newly developed acetate transparencies or slides. These full-color transparencies, selected by author John Santrock and Janet Simons, include graphics from the text and various outside sources and were expressly designed to provide comprehensive coverage of all major topic areas generally covered in life-span development. A comprehensive annotated guide provides a brief description for each transparency and helpful suggestions for use in the classroom.

The **Human Development Electronic Image Bank CD-ROM** contains more than 100 useful images and a computer projection system divided into two separate programs: The Interactive Slide Show and the Slide Show Editor. The Interactive Slide Show allows you to play a preset slide show containing selected images from Times Mirror Higher Education Group textbooks. The Slide Show Editor allows you to customize and create your own slide show. You can add slides anywhere you like in the presentation and incorporate any audio or visual files you'd like, as well as create title screens. You also may use the CD-ROM images with your own presentation software (PowerPoint, etc.). (Images are available in both PICT and BMP formats. Macintosh and Windows compatible.)

A large selection of **Videotapes,** including *Seasons of Life,* is also available to instructors, based upon the number of textbooks ordered from Brown & Benchmark Publishers by your bookstore.

The **AIDS Booklet,** Third Edition, by Frank D. Cox of Santa Barbara City College, is a brief but comprehensive introduction to the Acquired Immune Deficiency Syndrome which is caused by HIV (Human Immunodeficiency Virus) and related viruses.

The **Critical Thinker,** written by Richard Mayer and Fiona Goodchild of the University of California, Santa Barbara, uses excerpts from introductory psychology textbooks to show students how to think critically about psychology. Either this or the AIDS booklet are available at no charge to first-year adopters of our textbook or can be purchased separately.

A **Customized Transparency Program** is available to adopters for *Children,* Fifth Edition, based on the number of textbooks ordered. Consult your Brown & Benchmark representative for ordering policies.

The **Human Development Interactive Videodisc Set** produced by Roger Ray of Rollins College, brings life-span development to life with instant access to over 30 brief video segments from the highly acclaimed *Seasons of Life* series. The 2-disc set can be used alone for selecting and sequencing excerpts, or in tandem with a Macintosh computer to add interactive commentary capability, as well as extra video and search options. Consult your Brown & Benchmark Sales Representative for details.

ACKNOWLEDGMENTS

A project of this magnitude requires the effort of many individuals. I owe special thanks to Steven Yetter, Acquisitions Editor, for providing outstanding guidance and support. I also thank Ted Underhill, Developmental Editor, who showed a special enthusiasm and competence in monitoring the revision process. The numerous members of the production team did a marvelous job of editing, rearranging, and designing the book—the particular members of the book team are listed at the beginning of the book. Thanks also go to Allen Keniston and Blaine Peden, who prepared a very useful Instructor's Course Planner and Student Study Guide, and to Janet Simons for her hard work in constructing a brand-new Test Item File.

I have benefited extensively from the ideas and insights of many colleagues. I would like to thank the following individuals for their feedback on earlier editions of *Children.*

Harry H. Avis
Sierra College
Patricia J. Bence
Tompkins Cortland Community College
Michael Bergmire
Jefferson College
Ruth Brinkman
St. Louis Community College, Florissant Valley
Dan W. Brunworth
Kishwaukee College
Dixie R. Crase
Memphis State University
JoAnn Farver
Oklahoma State University
Janet Fuller
Mansfield University
Thomas Gerry
Columbia Greene Community College
Barbara H. Harkness
San Bernardino Valley College
Susan Heidrich
University of Wisconsin
Alice S. Hoenig
Syracuse University
Sally Hoppstetter
Palo Alto College
Diane Carlson Jones
Texas A&M University

Ellen Junn
Indiana University

Claire B. Kopp
UCLA

Gloria Lopez
Sacramento City College

Mary Ann McLaughlin
Clarion University

Chloe Merrill
Weber State College

Karla Miley
Black Hawk College

Sandy Osborne
Montana State University

Richard Riggle
Coe College

James A. Rysberg
California State University, Chico

Marcia Rysztak
Lansing Community College

Diane Scott-Jones
University of Illinois

Ross A. Thompson
University of Nebraska, Lincoln

Dorothy A. Wedge
Fairmont State College

William H. Zachry
University of Tennessee, Martin

John A. Addleman
Messiah College

Lori A. Beasley
University of Central Oklahoma

Kathleen Crowley-Long
The College of Saint Rose

Swen H. Digranes
Northeastern State University

Ruth H. Doyle, N.C.C., L.P.C.
Casper College

Timothy P. Eicher
Dixie Community College

Robert J. Ivy
George Mason University

Deborah N. Margolis
Boston College

Richard L. Wagner
Mount Senario College

Marilyn E. Willis
Indiana University of Pennsylvania

A final note of thanks goes to my family—Mary Jo, my wife, Tracy, and Jennifer—whose love and companionship I cherish.

CHILDREN'S CONSULTING ADVISORS

ive main content themes are woven throughout *Children*, fifth edition:

- Health and well-being
- Families and parenting
- Education
- Culture and ethnicity
- Gender

To improve the coverage of these important themes of children's development, five consulting advisors provided valuable advice and suggestions. Each of these individuals is an expert in her respective area. Their recommendations and insights have considerably improved the coverage of health and well-being, families and parenting, education, culture and ethnicity, and gender.

Dr. Tiffany M. Field is director of the Touch Research Institute and the Touch Research Institute Nursery School of the University of Miami School of Medicine, and Professor in the Department of Psychology, Pediatrics, and Psychiatry. She is a recipient of the American Psychological Association Distinguished Young Scientist Award and has had a research scientist award from NIMH for her research career. She is the author of *Infancy, Touch, and Advances in Touch Research*; the editor of a series of volumes entitled *High-Risk Infants* and *Stress and Coping*; and the author of over 200 journal papers. The mission of the Touch Research Institute is to conduct multidisciplinary and multiuniversity studies on touch as a basic sense, touch as communication, and the use of touch therapies in wellness and medical programs. Among the promising findings is that touch therapy enhances growth in premature infants, reduces stress (cortisol and norepinephrine levels) in child psychiatric patients, enhances alertness (decreases alpha waves, and increases math accuracy) in adults, and increases natural killer-cell activity in HIV men.

Dr. Diana Baumrind is a research scientist at the Institute of Human Development at the University of California in Berkeley (UCB). She received her Doctor of Philosophy in clinical, developmental, and social psychology at UCB, where for the last 30 years she has conducted her well-known longitudinal study, *The Family Socialization and Developmental Competence Project*. Dr. Baumrind is the leading authority on how contrasting patterns of parental authority affect the development of character and competence in children and adolescents. As a consequence of the author's seminal longitudinal research on the contrasting impact on children's character and competence of authoritative, authoritarian, permissive, and unengaged parenting styles, it is generally acknowledged that the authoritative pattern, which balances parental responsiveness (warmth, reciprocity, clear communication and attachment) with demandingness (firm control, monitoring, maturity demands), most successfully promotes the welfare and social-emotional adjustment of middle-class children. In addition to her seminal work on child-rearing, Dr. Baumrind is known for her work on ethics, and more recently on social policy applications of scholarly work on the family.

Dr. Rosalind Charlesworth is a leading expert in the fields of early education and child development. Dr. Charlesworth is a Professor of Child and Family Studies in the College of Education at Weber State University in Ogden, Utah. She holds a bachelor's degree in psychology from Stanford University, a master's degree in child psychology from the University of Iowa, and a Ph.D. in curriculum and instruction from the University of Toledo. Prior to receiving her doctorate, she was a laboratory and Title I preschool teacher and a primary learning disabilities teacher. Since receiving her doctorate, she has been an Assistant Professor in Educational Psychology and Home Economics at Bowling Green State University (Ohio) and a Professor at Louisiana State University; she joined the faculty at Weber State in the fall of 1993. Her major focus is connecting child development knowledge to educational practices with young children. She is an advocate for developmentally appropriate instructional practices.

Dr. Charlesworth's main research interests center on the effects of developmentally appropriate and inappropriate practice on young children's stress behaviors, academic success, and classroom social behavior, and kindergarten and primary teachers' beliefs and practices relative to developmentally appropriate and inappropriate teaching strategies. With Dr. Diane Burts of Louisiana State University and Dr. Craig Hart of Brigham Young University she has been collaborating on a longitudinal study of the long-term effects on children of developmentally appropriate and inappropriate kindergarten experiences. Another current interest is an in-depth self-study of her own teaching.

Dr. Charlesworth is the author of *Understanding Child Development: For Adults Who Work with Young Children* and coauthor with Karen K. Lind of *Math and Science for Young Children*. She has authored and coauthored numerous articles and chapters; the most recent focus on various aspects of the collaborative research on developmentally appropriate/inappropriate practice and on the relationship of early childhood mathematics instruction to developmentally appropriate practice. She is currently an editorial consultant for *Early Childhood Research Quarterly*.

Dr. Sandra Graham is a Professor in the Department of Education at the University of California–Los Angeles. She is also the Chair of the Interdepartmental Master's Program in African American Studies and the Associate Director of the Center for African American Studies at UCLA. She received her Ph.D. from UCLA and holds degrees in history from Columbia University and Barnard College.

Among her research interests are cognitive approaches to motivation, the development of attributional processes, motivation in African Americans, and peer-directed aggression. She has received grants from the National Science Foundation and the Haynes Foundation to continue her research on childhood aggression and interventions to increase social skills and academic motivation in incarcerated adolescents. Professor Graham serves on the boards of many academic journals and professional associations, and is the author of many articles and book chapters. She is also the editor, with V. S. Folkes, of *Attribution Theory: Applications to Achievement, Mental Health, and Interpersonal Conflict* (Lawrence Erlbaum, 1990).

Dr. Florence L. Denmark is an internationally recognized scholar, administrator, leader, researcher, and policy maker. She received her Ph.D. in social psychology from the University of Pennsylvania and has since made many contributions in that area, particularly to the psychology of women. However, her broad interests and distinguished accomplishments in psychology attest to her status as an eminent generalist in an age of specialization.

Denmark's impact on the field of psychology is widespread. She has authored more than 75 articles and 15 books, presented over 100 talks and invited addresses, and appeared on numerous radio and television shows. Denmark has also served as a leader in psychology in many capacities, including having been president of the American Psychological Association and president of the Council of International Psychologists. Her research and teaching achievements have earned her fellowship status in several APA distinctions. She is also the recipient of numerous other prestigious distinctions, including the APA's Distinguished Contributions to Psychology in the Public Interest/Senior Career Award as well as APA Division 35's (Psychology of Women) Carolyn Wood Sherif Award.

Denmark has been the Thomas Hunter Professor of Psychology at Hunter College of the City University of New York. At present she is the Robert Scott Pace Distinguished Professor of Psychology at Pace University, where she is Chair of the Department of Psychology.

TO THE STUDENT

How the Learning System Works

This book contains a number of learning devices, each of which presents the field of child development in a meaningful way. The learning devices in *Children* will help you learn the material more effectively.

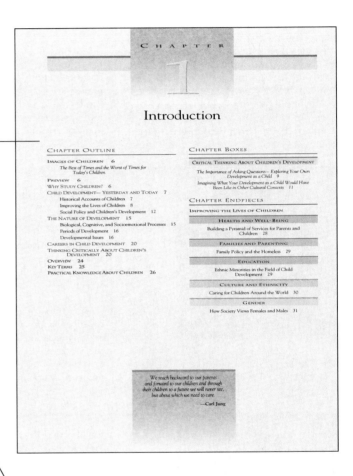

We reach backward to our parents
and forward to our children and through
their children to a future we will never see,
but about which we need to care.

—Carl Jung

Chapter Outlines

Each chapter begins with an outline, showing the organization of topics by heading levels. The outline functions as an overview to the arrangement and structure of the chapter.

Children are on a different
plane. They belong to a generation
and way of feeling properly
their own.

—George Santayana

IMAGES OF CHILDREN

The Best of Times and the Worst of Times for Today's Children

It is both the best of times and the worst of times for today's children. Their world possesses powers and perspectives inconceivable 50 years ago: computers, longer life expectancies, the ability to reach out to the entire planet through television, satellites, air travel. Children want to trust, but the world has become an untrustworthy place. The sometimes-fatal temptations of the adult world can descend upon children so early that their ideals become tarnished. Crack cocaine is a far more addictive and deadly substance than marijuana, the drug of an earlier generation. Strange depictions of violence and sex come flashing out of the television set and lodge in the minds of children. The messages are powerful and contradictory: Rock videos suggest orgiastic sex. Public health officials counsel safe sex. Oprah Winfrey and Phil Donahue conduct seminars on exotic drugs, transsexual surgery, serial murders. Television pours a bizarre version of reality into children's imaginations. In New York City, two 5-year-olds argue about whether there is a Santa Claus and what Liberace died of. In New Orleans, a first-grader shaves a piece of chalk and passes the dust around the classroom, acting as if it is cocaine.

Every stable society transmits values from one generation to the next. That is civilization's work. In today's world, the transmission of values is not easy. Parents are raising children in a world far removed from Ozzie and Harriet's era of the 1950s, when two of three American families consisted of a breadwinner (the father), a caregiver (the mother), and the children they were raising. Today fewer than one in five families fits that description. Phrases like *quality time* have found their way into the American vocabulary. A motif of absence plays in the lives of many children. It may be an absence of authority and limits or an absence of emotional commitment (Morrow, 1988).

Images of Children

Opening each chapter is an imaginative, high-interest piece, focusing on a topic related to the chapter's content.

PREVIEW

By examining the shape of childhood, we can understand it better. This book is a window into the nature of children's development— your own and that of every other child of the human species. In this first chapter, you will be introduced to some ideas about why we should study children, contemporary concerns about child development, and a historical perspective on children's development. You will learn what development is and what issues are raised by a developmental perspective on children. You will be asked to think about ways to improve the lives of children. You also will read about the nature of careers in child development and how to think critically about children's development.

Preview

This brief section describes the chapter's main points.

WHY STUDY CHILDREN?

Why study children? Perhaps you are or will be a parent or teacher. Responsibility for children is or will be a part of your everyday life. The more you learn about children, the better you can deal with them. Perhaps you hope to gain some insight into your own history— as an infant, as a child, and as an adolescent. Perhaps you just stumbled onto this course thinking that it sounded interesting and that the topic of child development would raise some provocative and intriguing issues about how human beings grow and develop. Whatever your reasons, you will discover that the study of child development is provocative, is intriguing, and is filled with information about who we are and how we grew to be this way.

6   John W. Santrock

adverse effects of maternal deprivation (mothers' neglect of their infants) became known and was interpreted to include a lack of stimulation. A number of research studies followed that indicated a "more is better" approach in the stimulation of preterm infants. Today, however, experts on infant development argue that preterm infant care is far too complex to be described only in terms of amount of stimulation.

Following are some conclusions about the situation of preterm infants (Lester & Tronick, 1990):

1. Preterm infants' responses to stimulation vary with their conceptual age, illness, and individual makeup. The immature brain of the preterm infant may be more vulnerable to excessive, inappropriate, or mistimed stimulation. The very immature infant should probably be protected from stimulation that could destabilize its homeostatic condition.
2. As the healthy preterm infant becomes less fragile and approaches term, the issue of what is appropriate stimulation should be considered. Infants' behavioral cues can be used to determine appropriate interventions. An infant's signs of stress or avoidance behaviors indicate that stimulation should be terminated. Positive behaviors indicate that stimulation is appropriate.
3. Intervention with the preterm infant should be organized in the form of an individualized developmental plan. This plan should be constructed as a psychosocial intervention to include the parents and other immediate family members and to acknowledge the socioeconomic, cultural, and home environmental factors that will determine the social context in which the infant will be reared. The developmental plan should also include assessing the infant's behavior, working with the parents to help them understand the infant's medical and behavioral status, and helping the parents deal with their own feelings.

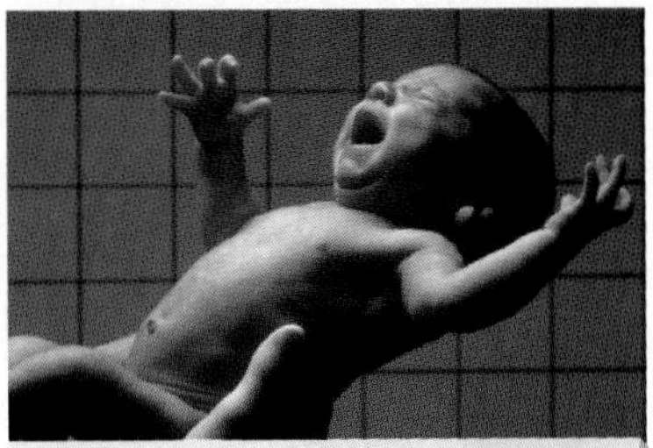

	0	1	2
Heart rate	Absent	Slow— less than 100 beats per minute	Fast— 100–140 beats per minute
Respiratory effort	No breathing for more than 1 minute	Irregular and slow	Good breathing with normal crying
Muscle tone	Limp and flaccid	Weak, inactive, but some flexion of extremities	Strong, active motion
Body color	Blue and pale	Body pink, but extremities blue	Entire body pink
Reflex irritability	No response	Grimace	Coughing, sneezing, and crying

FIGURE 5.2

The Apgar Scale

MEASURES OF NEONATAL HEALTH AND RESPONSIVENESS

The **Apgar scale** *is a method widely used to assess the health of newborns at 1 and 5 minutes after birth. The Apgar scale evaluates infants' heart rate, respiratory effort, muscle tone, body color, and reflex irritability.* An obstetrician or nurse does the evaluation and gives the newborn a score, or reading, of 0, 1, or 2 on each of these five health signs (see figure 5.2). A total score of 7 to 10 indicates that the newborn's condition is good, a score of 5 indicates there may be developmental difficulties, and a score of 3 or below signals an emergency and indicates that the baby might not survive.

Whereas the Apgar scale is used immediately after birth to identify high-risk infants who need resuscitation, the **Brazelton Neonatal Behavioral Assessment Scale** *is given shortly after birth to assess the newborn's neurological development, reflexes, and reactions to people.* Twenty reflexes are assessed, along with reactions to circumstances, such as the infant's reaction to a rattle. The examiner rates the newborn, or neonate, on each of 27 categories

146 *John W. Santrock*

Visual Figures and Tables

These include both a description of important content information and photographs that illustrate the content. They review and summarize important theories and ideas contained in the text.

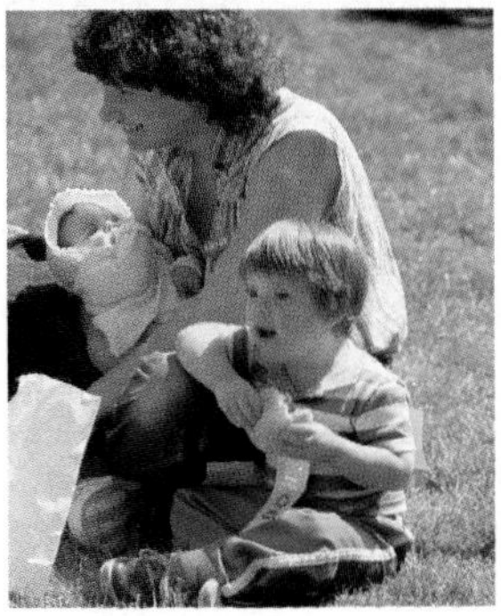

FIGURE 13.8

A Down Syndrome Child
What causes a child to develop Down syndrome? In what major classification of mental retardation does the condition fall?

and are highly sensitive to what others—both peers and adults—want from them. However, as adults, the familially retarded are usually invisible, perhaps because adult settings don't tax their cognitive skills as sorely. It may also be that the familially retarded increase their intelligence as they move toward adulthood.

Giftedness There have always been people whose abilities and accomplishments outshine others—the whiz kid in class, the star athlete, the natural musician. People who are **gifted** *have above-average intelligence (an IQ of 120 or higher) and/or superior talent for something.* When it comes to programs for the gifted, most school systems select children who have intellectual superiority and academic aptitude. Children who are talented in the visual and performing arts (arts, drama, dance), athletics, or other special aptitudes tend to be overlooked.

Until recently, giftedness and emotional distress were thought to go hand in hand. English novelist Virginia Woolf suffered from severe depression, for example, and eventually committed suicide. Sir Isaac Newton, Vincent van Gogh, Ann Sexton, Socrates, and Sylvia Plath all had emotional problems. However, these are the exception rather than the rule; in general, no relation between giftedness and mental disorder has been found. Recent studies support the conclusion that gifted people tend to be more mature and have fewer emotional problems than others (Feldman & Piirto, 1995).

Lewis Terman (1925) has followed the lives of approximately 1,500 children whose Stanford-Binet IQs averaged 150 into adulthood; the study will not be complete until the year 2010. Terman has found that this remarkable group is an accomplished lot. Of the 800 males, 78 have obtained doctorates (they include two past presidents of the American Psychological Association), 48 have earned M.D.s, and 85 have been granted law degrees. Most of these figures are 10 to 30 times greater than those found among the 800 men of the same age chosen randomly as a comparison group. These findings challenge the commonly held belief that the intellectually gifted are emotionally disordered or socially maladjusted.

The 672 gifted women studied by Terman (Terman & Oden, 1959) underscore the importance of relationships and intimacy in women's lives. Two-thirds of these exceptional women graduated from college in the 1930s, and one-fourth of them attended graduate school. Despite their impressive educational achievements, when asked to order their life's priorities, the gifted women placed families first, friendships second, and careers last. For these women, having a career often meant not having children. Of the 30 most successful women, 25 did not have any children. Such undivided commitments to the family are less true of women today. Many of the highly gifted women in Terman's study questioned their intelligence and concluded that their cognitive skills had waned in adulthood. Studies reveal that today gifted women have a stronger confidence in their cognitive skills and intellectual abilities than the gifted women in Terman's study did (Tomlinson-Keasey, 1990). Terman's gifted women represented a cohort who reached midlife prior to the women's movement and the current pervasiveness of the dual-career couple and the single-parent family (Tomlinson-Keasey, 1993).

In the most recent analysis of Terman's gifted children, two factors predicted longevity: personality and family stability (Friedman & others, 1995). With regard to personality, those who as children were conscientious and less impulsive lived significantly longer. With regard to family stability, those whose parents had divorced before the children reached age 21 faced a one-third greater mortality risk than did their counterparts whose parents had not divorced. Individuals who became divorced themselves also faced a shorter life. And not marriage itself, but rather a stable marriage history, was linked with increased longevity.

Never to be cast away are the gifts of the gods, magnificent.
—**Homer, *The Iliad*, 9th Century B.C.**

Creativity Most of us would like to be both gifted and creative. Why was Thomas Edison able to invent so many things? Was he simply more intelligent than most people? Did he spend long hours toiling away in private?

Cognitive Development in Middle and Late Childhood 395

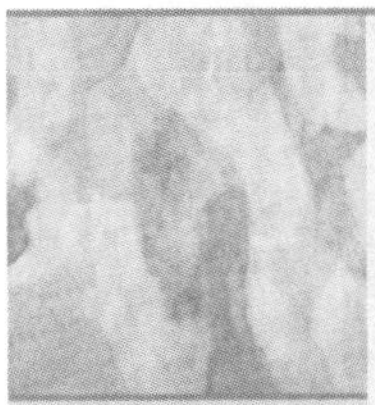

CRITICAL THINKING ABOUT CHILDREN'S DEVELOPMENT

Evaluating the Parenting Styles of Both Parents

In our discussion of parenting styles, authoritative parenting was associated with social competence in children. In some cases, though, a child's parents differ in their parenting styles. Consider all four styles of parenting— authoritarian, authoritative, neglectful, and indulgent— on the parts of the mother and the father. A best case is when both parents are authoritative. What might the effects on the child be, if the father is authoritarian and the mother is indulgent, or the father is authoritarian and the mother is authoritative, and so on? Is it better for the child if both parents have the same parenting style, even if the styles both are authoritarian, both indulgent, or both neglectful, or is it better for the child to have at least one authoritative parent when the other parent is authoritarian, indulgent, or neglectful?

In thinking about parenting styles, consider also what style or styles your father and mother used in rearing you. Were they both authoritative, one authoritarian, the other indulgent, and so on? What effects do you think their parenting styles had on your development?

By evaluating the nature of parenting styles on the part of both parents, you are learning to think critically by *applying developmental concepts to enhance personal adaptation*.

> We had just come home from the ball game. I sat down on the sofa next to the light so I could read. Sally [the sister] said, "Get up. I was sitting there first. I just got up for a second to get a drink." I told her I was not going to get up and that I didn't see her name on the chair. I got mad and started pushing her. Her drink spilled all over her. Then she got really mad; she shoved me against the wall, hitting and clawing at me. I managed to grab a handful of hair.

At this point, Sally comes into the room and begins to tell her side of the story. Sandra interrupts, "Mother, you always take her side." Sound familiar? Any of you who have grown up with siblings probably have a rich memory of aggressive, hostile interchanges; but sibling relationships have many pleasant, caring moments as well. Children's sibling relationships include helping, sharing, teaching, fighting, and playing. Children can act as emotional supports, rivals, and communication partners (Carlson, 1995). More than 80 percent of American children have one or more siblings (brothers or sisters). Because there are so many possible sibling combinations, it is difficult to generalize about sibling influences. Among the factors to be considered are the number of siblings, age of siblings, birth order, age spacing, sex of siblings, and whether sibling relationships are different from parent-child relationships.

Is sibling interaction different from parent-child interaction? There is some evidence that it is. Observations indicate that children interact more positively and in more varied ways with their parents than with their siblings (Baskett & Johnson, 1982). Children also follow their parents' dictates more than those of their siblings, and they behave more negatively and punitively with their siblings than with their parents.

In some instances, siblings may be stronger socializing influences on the child than parents are (Cicirelli, 1994). Someone close in age to the child—such as a sibling—may be able to understand the child's problems and be able to communicate more effectively than parents can. In dealing with peers, coping with difficult teachers, and discussing taboo subjects such as sex, siblings may be more influential in the socialization process than parents.

Is sibling interaction the same around the world? In industrialized societies like the United States, delegation of responsibility for younger siblings to older siblings tends to be carried out informally by parents, primarily to give the parent freedom to pursue other activities. However, in nonindustrialized countries, such as Kenya (in Africa), a much greater degree of importance is attached to the older sibling's role as a caregiver to younger siblings. In industrialized countries, the older sibling's caregiving role is often discretionary; in nonindustrialized countries it is more obligatory (Cicirelli, 1994).

Big sisters are the crab grass in the lawn of life.
—**Charles Schulz, *Peanuts***

Birth order is a special interest of sibling researchers. When differences in birth order are found, they usually are explained by variations in interactions with parents and siblings associated with the unique experiences of being in a particular position in the family. This is especially true in the case of the firstborn child (Teti & others, 1993). The oldest child is the only one who does not have to share parental love and affection with other siblings—until another sibling comes along. An infant requires more attention than an older child; this means that the firstborn

Socioemotional Development in Early Childhood 315

Key Term Definitions

Key terms appear in boldface type with their definitions immediately following in italic type. This provides you with a clear understanding of important concepts.

Critical Thinking Boxes

Critical Thinking About Children's Development boxes appear several times in every chapter. These questions will challenge you to think more deeply about the contents of the chapters.

PREVIEW

Some individuals have difficulty thinking of child development as being a science in the same way that physics, chemistry, and biology are sciences. Can a discipline that studies how babies develop, how parents nurture children, how peers interact, and how children think be equated with disciplines that investigate how gravity works and the molecular structure of a compound? Science is defined not by *what* it investigates but by *how* it investigates. Whether you are studying photosynthesis, butterflies, Saturn's moons, or human development, it is the *way* you study that makes the approach scientific or not.

In this chapter, we will study three key ingredients of child development as a science—the scientific method, theories, and methods. You will also learn about ethics and sexism in research on child development, as well as how to be a wise consumer of information about children's development.

THEORY AND THE SCIENTIFIC METHOD

According to nineteenth-century French mathematician Henri Poincaré, "Science is built of facts the way a house is built of bricks, but an accumulation of facts is no more science than a pile of bricks a house." Science *does* depend on the raw material of facts or data, as Poincaré indicated, child development's theories are more than just facts.

A **theory** *is a coherent set of ideas that helps explain data and make predictions.* A theory contains **hypotheses,** *assumptions that can be tested to determine their accuracy.* For example, a theory about children's aggression would explain our observations of aggressive children and predict why children become aggressive. We might predict that children become aggressive because of the coercive interchanges they experience and observe in their families. This prediction would help direct our observations by telling us to look for coercive interchanges in families.

The **scientific method** *is an approach that can be used to discover accurate information about behavior and development that includes the following steps: identify and analyze the problem, collect data, draw conclusions, and revise theories.* For example, suppose you decide that you want to help aggressive children control their aggression. You *identify a problem,* which does not seem like a difficult task. However, as part of the first step, you need to go beyond a general description of the problem by isolating, analyzing, narrowing, and focusing on what you hope to investigate. What specific strategies do you want to use to reduce children's aggression? Do you want to look at only one strategy, or several strategies? What aspect of aggression do you want to study—its biological, cognitive, or socioemotional characteristics? Gerald Patterson and his colleagues (Patterson, 1991; Patterson, Capaldi, & Bank, 1991) argue that parents' failure to teach reasonable levels of compliance sets in motion coercive inter-

Researchers use the scientific method to obtain accurate information about children's behavior and development. Data collection is part of the scientific method, demonstrated here by a researcher conducting a study of infant development.

changes with family members. In this first step in the scientific method, a problem is identified and analyzed.

After you have identified and analyzed the problem, the next step is to *collect information (data).* Psychologists observe behavior and draw inferences about thoughts and emotions. For example, in the investigation of children's aggression, you might observe how effectively parents teach reasonable compliance levels to their children and the extent to which coercive exchanges take place among family members.

Truth is arrived at by the painstaking process of eliminating the untrue.

—Arthur Conan Doyle

CONCEPT TABLE 8.2

Emotional and Personality Development

Concept	Processes/Related Ideas	Characteristics/Description
Emotional Development	What is emotion?	Emotion is feeling or affect that involves a mixture of physiological arousal and overt behavior. Emotions can be classified in terms of positive affectivity and negative affectivity.
	The New Functionalism in Emotions	The new functionalist view emphasizes that emotion is relational rather than intrapsychic, that there is a close link between emotion and the person's goals and effort, that emotional expressions can serve as social signals, and that the physiology of emotion is much more than homeostasis and the person's interior—it also includes the ability to regulate and be regulated by social processes.
	Affect in parent-child relationships	Emotions are the first language that parents and infants communicate with before the infant acquires speech. Infant and adult affective communicative capacities make possible coordinated infant-adult interaction.
	Emotional development in infancy	Izard developed the Maximally Discriminative Facial Coding System (MAX) for coding infants' expression of emotions. Based on this coding system, interest, distress, and disgust are present at birth, a social smile appears at about 4 to 6 weeks, anger, surprise, and sadness emerge at about 3 to 4 months, fear is displayed at about 5 to 7 months, shame and shyness emerge at about 6 to 8 months, and contempt and guilt appear at about 2 years of age.
	Crying	Crying is the most important mechanism newborns have for communicating with their world. Babies have at least three types of cries—basic cry, anger cry, and pain cry. Most parents, and adults in general, can tell whether an infant's cries signify anger or pain. Controversy still swirls about whether babies should be soothed when they cry. An increasing number of developmentalists support Ainsworth's and Bowlby's idea that infant crying should be responded to immediately in the first year of life.
	Smiling	Smiling is an important communicative affective behavior of the infant. Two types of smiling can be distinguished in infants: reflexive and social.
Personality Development	Trust	Erikson argues that the first year is characterized by the crisis of trust versus mistrust; his ideas about trust have much in common with Ainsworth's concept of secure attachment.
	Developing a sense of self and independence	At some point in the second half of the second year of life, the infant develops a sense of self. Independence becomes a central theme in the second year of life. Mahler argues that the infant separates herself from the mother and then develops individuation. Erikson stresses that the second year of life is characterized by the stage of autonomy versus shame and doubt.
	Adapting caregiving to the developmental status of the infant and toddler	From birth to 4 months of age, caregivers should respond quickly to the infant's needs with love, affection, and care. From 4 to 8 months of age, the caregiver's consistent care and emotional involvement with the infant support the development of a focused attachment. From 8 to 12 months of age, caregivers should continue to talk and play with the infant, and allow the infant access to other adults and infants. During this age period, caregivers need to monitor their infants' attentional bids. From 12 to 18 months of age, toddlers' independence needs to be promoted but their negativism needs to be dealt with firmly in the context of a loving and nurturant atmosphere. From 18 to 24 months of age, caregivers can encourage the toddler's development of self, continue monitoring their negativism, and continue giving them considerable attention.
Problems and Disorders	Child abuse	An understanding of child abuse requires information about cultural, familial, and community influences. Sexual abuse of children is now recognized as a more widespread problem than was believed in the past. Child abuse places the child at risk for a number of developmental problems.
	Infantile autism	Infantile autism is a severe disorder that first appears in infancy. It involves an inability to relate to people, speech problems, and upsets over changes in routine or environment. Autism seems to involve some form of organic brain and genetic dysfunction.

OVERVIEW

Biological beginnings raise questions of how we as a species came to be, how parents' genes are shuffled to produce a particular child, and how much experience can go against the grain of heredity.

In this chapter, we studied the Jim and Jim twins; the evolutionary perspective, in which we discussed natural selection, sociobiology, evolutionary psychology, and race and ethnicity; the nature of heredity; what genes are; how reproduction takes place; some abnormalities in genes and chromosomes; genetic principles; methods used by behavior geneticists; heredity's influence on development; and what heredity-environment interaction is like. With regard to heredity-environment interaction, behavior geneticists believe that it is important to consider passive genotype-environment, evocative genotype-environment, and active genotype-environment interactions, as well as shared and nonshared environmental experiences. Scarr's biological view has recently generated considerable controversy. Remember that you can obtain a summary of the main ideas in the entire chapter by again studying the two concept tables on pages 87 and 94.

In the next chapter, we will continue our exploration of children's biological beginnings by discussing the dramatic unfolding of prenatal development.

BIOLOGICAL BEGINNINGS

- THE EVOLUTIONARY PERSPECTIVE
  - Natural Selection
  - Sociobiology
  - Race and Ethnicity
  - Evolutionary Psychology
- HEREDITY
  - What Are Genes?
  - Reproduction
  - Abnormalities in Genes and Chromosomes
- GENETIC PRINCIPLES AND METHODS
  - Some Genetic Principles
  - Heredity's Influence on Development
  - Methods Used by Behavior Geneticists
- HEREDITY-ENVIRONMENT INTERACTION AND CHILDREN'S DEVELOPMENT
  - Genotype Environment Concepts
  - Shared and Nonshared Environmental Influences
  - The Contemporary Heredity-Environment Controversy

Key Terms

Listed at the end of each chapter are key terms that are defined throughout the chapter. They are listed with page references and are defined again in a page-referenced glossary at the end of the book.

KEY TERMS

natural selection The evolutionary process that favors individuals of a species that are best adapted to survive and reproduce. 75
sociobiology A view that relies on the principles of evolutionary biology to explain behavior. 76
evolutionary psychology A contemporary approach that emphasizes that behavior is a function of mechanisms, requires input for activation, and is ultimately related to survival and reproduction. 76
race The term for a system for classifying plants and animals into subcategories according to specific physical and structural characteristics. 77
chromosomes Threadlike structures that come in 23 pairs, one member of each pair coming from each parent. Chromosomes contain the genetic substance DNA. 80
DNA A complex molecule that contains genetic information. 80
genes Units of hereditary information composed of DNA. Genes act as a blueprint for cells to reproduce themselves and manufacture the proteins that maintain life. 80
gametes Human reproduction cells created in the testes of males and the ovaries of females. 80
meiosis The process of cell doubling and separation of chromosomes in which each pair of chromosomes in a cell separates, with one member of each pair going into each gamete. 80
reproduction The process that, in humans, begins when a female gamete (ovum) is fertilized by a male gamete (sperm). 81
zygote A single cell formed through fertilization. 81
in vitro fertilization Conception outside the body. 81
phenylketonuria (PKU) A genetic disorder in which an individual cannot properly metabolize an amino acid. PKU is now easily detected but, if left untreated, results in mental retardation and hyperactivity. 83
Down syndrome A common genetically transmitted form of mental retardation, caused by the presence of an extra (47th) chromosome. 83
sickle-cell anemia A genetic disorder that affects the red blood cells and occurs most often in African American individuals. 83
Klinefelter syndrome A genetic disorder in which males have an extra X chromosome, making them XXY instead of XY. 83
Turner syndrome A genetic disorder in which females are missing an X chromosome, making them XO instead of XX. 84
XYY syndrome A genetic disorder in which males have an extra Y chromosome. 84
amniocentesis A prenatal medical procedure in which a sample of amniotic fluid is withdrawn by syringe and tested to discover if the fetus is suffering from any chromosomal or metabolic disorders. It is performed between the 12th and 16th weeks of pregnancy. 84
ultrasound sonography A prenatal medical procedure in which high-frequency sound waves are directed into the pregnant woman's abdomen. 84
chorionic villus test A prenatal medical procedure in which a small sample of the placenta is removed at a certain point in the pregnancy between the 8th and the 11th weeks of pregnancy. 86
maternal blood test A prenatal diagnostic technique that is used to assess blood alphaprotein level, which is associated with neural-tube defects. This technique is also called the alpha-fetoprotein test (AFP). 86
dominant-recessive genes principle If one gene of a pair is dominant and one is recessive (goes back or recedes), the dominant gene exerts its effect, overriding the potential influence of the recessive gene. A recessive gene exerts its influence only if both genes in a pair are recessive. 88
polygenic inheritance The genetic principle that many genes can interact to produce a particular characteristic. 88
genotype A person's genetic heritage; the actual genetic material. 88
phenotype The way an individual's genotype is expressed in observed and measurable characteristics. 88
reaction range The range of possible phenotypes for each genotype, suggesting the importance of an environment's restrictiveness or enrichment. 89
canalization The process by which characteristics take a narrow path or developmental course. Apparently, preservative forces help to protect a person from environmental extremes. 90
behavior genetics The study of the degree and nature of behavior's heredity basis. 90
twin study A study in which the behavioral similarity of identical twins is compared with the behavioral similarity of fraternal twins. 90
identical twins Twins who develop from a single fertilized egg that splits into two genetically identical replicas, each of which becomes a person. 90
fraternal twins Twins who develop from separate eggs and separate sperm, making them genetically no more similar than ordinary siblings. 90
adoption study A study in which investigators seek to discover whether, in behavior and psychological characteristics, adopted children are more like their adoptive parents, who provided a home environment, or more like their biological parents, who contributed their heredity. Another form of the adoption study is to compare adoptive and biological siblings. 90
passive genotype-environment interactions The type of interactions that occur when parents, who are genetically related to the child, provide a rearing environment for the child. 92
evocative genotype-environment interactions The type of interactions that occur when the child's genotype elicits certain types of physical and social environments. 92
active (niche-picking) genotype-environment interactions The type of interactions that occur when children seek out environments they find compatible and stimulating. 92
shared environmental experiences Children's common environmental experiences that are shared with their siblings, such as their parents' personalities and intellectual orientation, the family's social class, and the neighborhood in which they live. 93
nonshared environmental experiences The child's own unique experiences, both within the family and outside the family, that are not shared by another sibling. Thus, experiences occurring within the family can be part of the "nonshared environment." 93

96 *John W. Santrock*

Practical Knowledge About Children

This feature, appearing at the end of each chapter, reviews recommended books that contain valuable information to help children reach their full potential.

PRACTICAL KNOWLEDGE ABOUT CHILDREN

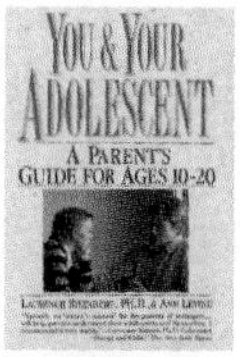

You & Your Adolescent
(1990) by Laurence Steinberg and Ann Levine.
New York: Harper Perennial.

You & Your Adolescent provides a broad, developmental overview of adolescence with parental advice mixed in along the way. Author Laurence Steinberg is a professor of psychology at Temple University and a highly respected researcher in adolescent development. The book is divided into the preteens (10–13), the teens (14–17), and toward adulthood (18–20). In Steinberg and Levine's approach, knowing how adolescents develop keeps parents from making a lot of mistakes. This is an excellent book for parents of adolescents. It serves the dual purpose of educating parents about how adolescents develop and giving them valuable parenting strategies for coping with teenagers.

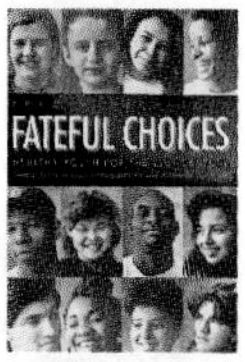

Fateful Choices
(1992) by Fred Hechinger.
New York: Hill and Wang.

The substance of this excellent book was provided by the Carnegie Council on Adolescent Development. One of the Carnegie Council's main themes comes through clearly in this book—linking health and education in the development of adolescents. The author provides valuable recommendations that can improve the health and well-being of all adolescents, especially those at risk for problems. Various chapters focus on adolescents at risk, adolescent pregnancy, drug abuse, nutrition and exercise, and youth organizations.

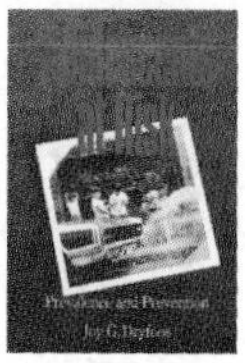

Adolescents at Risk
(1990) by Joy Dryfoos.
New York: Oxford University Press.

This is an excellent book on adolescent problems. Dryfoos describes four main problems that keep adolescents from reaching their potential: drug problems, delinquency, pregnancy, and school-related problems. She provides helpful sketches of programs that are successful in treating these problems. She argues that many at-risk adolescents have more than one problem and that treatment needs to take this interrelatedness of problems into account. School and community programs are especially highlighted.

482 *John W. Santrock*

Improving the Lives of Children

The final part of each chapter is called "Improving the Lives of Children." It contains discussions of five topics that can help children reach their full potential: Health and Well-Being, Families and Parenting, Education, Culture and Ethnicity, and Gender.

IMPROVING THE LIVES OF CHILDREN

Remember that at the end of each chapter we will examine five areas of children's development that hold opportunities for improving children's lives: health and well-being, families and parenting, education, culture and ethnicity, and gender.

HEALTH AND WELL-BEING

Protective Buffers for Children

What are some of the factors that help children be resilient in response to stressful circumstances and assaults on their health and well-being? In one large-scale study, Emmy Werner and Ruth Smith (1982) found that children greatly benefit from having a readily available support network of grandparents, neighbors, or relatives. Many children who cope effectively with stress, threats, and assaults on their health and well-being have a cluster of protective factors, not just one or two. But if forced to pick the most important factor that helps children weather problems, Werner says it is a basic, trusting relationship with an adult. In all of the protective clusters in Werner's study, there was not one that did not include that one good relationship, whether with a parent, grandparent, older sibling, teacher, or mentor— someone consistent in the child's life who could say to the child, "You count. I love you and will care for you. I will always be there for you." Even children of abusive or schizophrenic parents sometimes prove to be resilient if they have had at least one caring person nurturing and protecting them— someone who serves as sort of a beacon in their lives.

Thomas Boyce (1991), a pediatrics professor at the University of California, San Francisco, described an 8-year-old boy from an impoverished rural African American family, who had been abandoned by his mother. The boy also had "prune-belly syndrome," an abnormality of the abdominal musculature that left him with significant kidney and urinary problems, which required extensive surgery. But the boy had two nurturing, caring grandparents who had raised him from infancy. They consistently supported him and unfailingly accompanied him on his hospital visits. Despite his physical problems and the absence of his mother, the boy's school performance was superb.

Such protective factors in children's lives work best when they are long-lasting. There is no guarantee that the child will always be resilient, since families and children may experience a host of ups and downs as children develop. Children who cope well early in their development can have setbacks later because of family or school problems. In life, no child is unbreakable. Caring and supporting are needed by at least one significant person throughout the childhood years for optimal development.

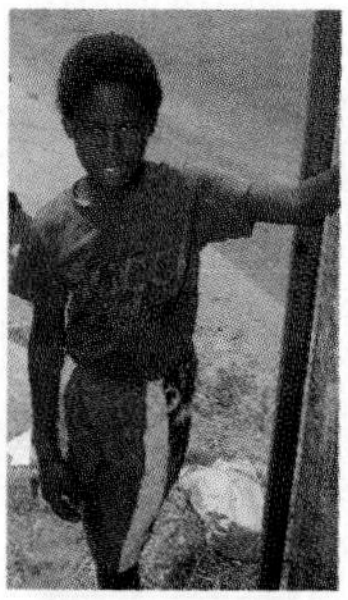

One of the most important factors that provides a protective buffering of children from stressors and problems is the long-term presence of a basic, trusting relationship with an adult.

66 *John W. Santrock*

PROLOGUE

If I Had My Child to Raise Over Again

If I had my child to raise all over again,

I'd finger paint more, and point the finger less.

I'd do less correcting, and more connecting.

I'd take my eyes off my watch, and watch with my eyes.

I would care to know less, and know to care more.

I'd take more hikes and fly more kites.

I'd stop playing serious, and seriously play.

I would run through more fields, and gaze at more stars.

I'd do more hugging, and less tugging.

I would be firm less often, and affirm much more.

I'd build self-esteem first, and the house later.

I'd teach less about the love of power,

And more about the power of love.

— Diane Loomans

CHILDREN

The Nature of Children's Development

—

*I*n every child who is born,
under no matter what
circumstances, and of no matter
what parents, the potentiality of the
human race is born again.

—James Agee

Examining the shape of childhood
allows us to understand it better.
Every childhood is distinct, the first
chapter of a new biography in the
world. This book is about children's
development—its universal
features, its individual variations, its
nature as we move ever closer to the
twenty-first century. *Children* is
about the rhythm and meaning of
children's lives, about turning
mystery into understanding, and
about weaving together a portrait of
who each of us was, is, and will be.
In Section One you will read two
chapters: "Introduction" (chapter 1)
and "The Science of Child
Development" (chapter 2).

PICASSO
Girl with a Dove, detail

Introduction

> We reach backward to our parents
> and forward to our children and through
> their children to a future we will never see,
> but about which we need to care.
>
> —Carl Jung

IMAGES OF CHILDREN

The Best of Times and the Worst of Times for Today's Children

It is both the best of times and the worst of times for today's children. Their world possesses powers and perspectives inconceivable 50 years ago: computers, longer life expectancies, the ability to reach out to the entire planet through television, satellites, air travel. Children want to trust, but the world has become an untrustworthy place. The sometimes-fatal temptations of the adult world can descend upon children so early that their ideals become tarnished. Crack cocaine is a far more addictive and deadly substance than marijuana, the drug of an earlier generation. Strange depictions of violence and sex come flashing out of the television set and lodge in the minds of children. The messages are powerful and contradictory: Rock videos suggest orgiastic sex. Public health officials counsel safe sex. Oprah Winfrey and Phil Donahue conduct seminars on exotic drugs, transsexual surgery, serial murders. Television pours a bizarre version of reality into children's imaginations. In New York City, two 5-year-olds argue about whether there is a Santa Claus and what Liberace died of. In New Orleans, a first-grader shaves a piece of chalk and passes the dust around the classroom, acting as if it is cocaine.

Every stable society transmits values from one generation to the next. That is civilization's work. In today's world, the transmission of values is not easy. Parents are raising children in a world far removed from Ozzie and Harriet's era of the 1950s, when two of three American families consisted of a breadwinner (the father), a caregiver (the mother), and the children they were raising. Today fewer than one in five families fits that description. Phrases like *quality time* have found their way into the American vocabulary. A motif of absence plays in the lives of many children. It may be an absence of authority and limits or an absence of emotional commitment (Morrow, 1988).

PREVIEW

By examining the shape of childhood, we can understand it better. This book is a window into the nature of children's development—your own and that of every other child of the human species. In this first chapter, you will be introduced to some ideas about why we should study children, contemporary concerns about child development, and a historical perspective on children's development. You will learn what development is and what issues are raised by a developmental perspective on children. You will be asked to think about ways to improve the lives of children. You also will read about the nature of careers in child development and how to think critically about children's development.

WHY STUDY CHILDREN?

Why study children? Perhaps you are or will be a parent or teacher. Responsibility for children is or will be a part of your everyday life. The more you learn about children, the better you can deal with them. Perhaps you hope to gain some insight into your own history—as an infant, as a child, and as an adolescent. Perhaps you just stumbled onto this course thinking that it sounded interesting and that the topic of child development would raise some provocative and intriguing issues about how human beings grow and develop. Whatever your reasons, you will discover that the study of child development *is* provocative, *is* intriguing, and *is* filled with information about who we are and how we grew to be this way.

As you might imagine, understanding children's development, and our own personal journey through childhood, is a rich and complicated undertaking. You will discover that various experts approach the study of children in many different ways and ask many different questions. Amid this richness and complexity we seek a simple answer: to understand how children change as they grow up and the forces that contribute to this change.

CHILD DEVELOPMENT— YESTERDAY AND TODAY

Everywhere an individual turns in contemporary society, the development and well-being of children capture public attention, the interest of scientists, and the concern of policymakers. Historically, though, interest in the development of children has been uneven.

Historical Accounts of Children

Childhood has become such a distinct period that it is hard to imagine that it was not always thought of in that way. However in medieval times, laws generally did not distinguish between child and adult offenses. After analyzing samples of art along with available publications, historian Philippe Ariès (1962) concluded that European societies did not accord any special status to children prior to 1600. In paintings, children were often dressed in smaller versions of adultlike clothing (see figure 1.1).

Were children actually treated as miniature adults with no special status in medieval Europe? Ariès' interpretation has been criticized. He primarily sampled aristocratic, idealized subjects, which led to the overdrawn conclusion that children were treated as miniature adults and not accorded any special status. In medieval times, children did often work, and their emotional bond with parents may not have been as strong as it is for many children today. However, in medieval times, childhood probably was recognized as a distinct phase of life more than Ariès believed. Also, we know that, in ancient Egypt, Greece, and Rome, rich conceptions of children's development were held.

Through history, philosophers have speculated at length about the nature of children and how they should be reared. Three such philosophical views are original sin, tabula rasa, and innate goodness. In the **original sin view,** *especially advocated during the Middle Ages, children were perceived as basically bad, being born into the world as evil beings.* The goal of child rearing was to provide salvation, to remove sin from the child's life. Toward the end of the seventeenth century, the **tabula rasa view** *was proposed by English philosopher John Locke. He argued that children are not innately bad but instead are like a "blank tablet," a tabula rasa.* Locke believed that childhood experiences are important in determining adult characteristics. He advised parents to spend time with their children and to help them become contributing members of society. In the

FIGURE 1.1

Historical Perception of Children
These artistic impressions show how children were viewed as miniature adults earlier in history. Artists' renditions of children as miniature adults may have been too stereotypical.

eighteenth century, the **innate goodness view** *was presented by Swiss-born philosopher Jean-Jacques Rousseau, who stressed that children are inherently good.* Because children are basically good, said Rousseau, they should be permitted to grow naturally, with little parental monitoring or constraint.

In the past century and a half, our view of children has changed dramatically. We now conceive of childhood as a highly eventful and unique period of life that lays an important foundation for the adult years and is highly differentiated from them. In most approaches to childhood, distinct periods are identified, in which children master special skills and confront new life tasks. Childhood is no longer seen as an inconvenient "waiting" period during which adults must suffer the incompetencies of the young. We now value childhood as a special time of growth and change, and we invest great resources in caring for and educating our children. We protect them from the excesses of the adult work world through tough child labor laws; we treat their crimes against society under a special system of juvenile justice; and we have governmental provisions for helping children when ordinary family support systems fail or when families seriously interfere with children's well-being.

Improving the Lives of Children

Consider some of the newspaper articles you might read every day on important dimensions of children's lives—such as their health and well-being, families and parenting, education, culture and ethnicity, and gender. What the experts are discovering in each of these areas has direct and significant consequences for understanding children and for improving their lives. An important theme of this book is to provide up-to-date coverage of the roles that health and well-being, families and parenting, education, culture and ethnicity, and gender play in improving children's lives.

Health and Well-Being

While we have become a nation obsessed with health and well-being, the health and well-being of our nation's children and children in many countries around the world raise serious concerns. The AIDS epidemic, starving children in Somalia, the poor quality of health care that many American families receive compared to their counterparts in other industrialized nations, inadequate nutrition and exercise, the succumbing of many teenagers to lives of alcohol and drug abuse, how children can most effectively cope with major life events such as the death of a parent or their parents' divorce, countless hassles and stressors, and the tragedy of poverty that invades too many children's lives are among the virtually unending list of issues and dilemmas that affect children's health and well-being.

Asian physicians around 2600 B.C. and Greek physicians around 500 B.C. recognized that good habits are essential for good health. They did not blame the gods for illness and think that magic would cure it. They realized that people have some control over their health and well-being. A physician's role was as guide, assisting patients in restoring a natural and emotional balance.

As we approach the twenty-first century, once again we recognize the power of lifestyles and psychological states in promoting health and well-being. We are returning to the ancient view that the ultimate responsibility for our health and well-being, both ours and our children's, rests in our hands. Parents, teachers, nurses, physicians, and other adults serve as important models of health and well-being for children. They also can communicate effective strategies for health and well-being to children and monitor how effectively children are following these strategies.

Recognizing that adolescents are not getting adequate advice about health and well-being, the editors of the *Journal of the American Medical Association* devoted an entire issue (March 1993) to encouraging doctors and nurses, who are used to curing with a stethoscope and prescription pad, to ask more personal questions of teenagers, to establish a doctor/teenager relationship instead of just having a doctor/parent relationship, and to explain that everything that goes on in the office is confidential except when the teenagers are a danger to themselves or others.

Our coverage of children's health and well-being in this book will be integrated into the discussion of children's development in every chapter. Two features also highlight their importance in every chapter: (1) "Health and Well-Being," part of the chapter-ending piece on how to improve the lives of children; and (2) "Practical Knowledge About Children," also at the end of each chapter, which briefly reviews outstanding or controversial books that will expand your understanding of how to improve children's health and well-being.

Families and Parenting

We hear a great deal from experts and popular writers about pressures on contemporary families. The number of families in which both parents work is increasing; at the same time, the number of one-parent families has risen over the past two decades as a result of a climbing divorce rate. With more children being raised by single parents or by parents who are both working, the time parents have to spend with their children is being squeezed and the quality of child care is of concern to many. Are working parents better using the decreased time with their children? Do day-care arrangements provide high-quality alternatives for parents? How troubled should we be about the increasing number of latchkey children—those at home alone after school, waiting for their parents to return from work? Answers to these questions can be formed by several different kinds of information obtained by experts in child development. This information comes from studies of the way working parents use the time with their children and the nature of their parenting approaches and behaviors, studies of the way various day-care arrangements influence children's social and intellectual growth in relation to home-care arrangements, and examination of the consequences of a child being without adult supervision for hours every day after school (Gottfried, Gottfried, & Bathurst, 1995; Lamb, 1994).

Famous playwright George Bernard Shaw once commented that although parenting is a very important profession, no test of fitness for it is ever imposed. If a test were imposed, some parents would turn out to be more fit than others. Most parents do want their children to grow into socially mature individuals, but they often are not sure about what to do as parents to help their children reach this goal (Stenhouse, 1996). One reason for the frustration of parents is that they often get conflicting messages about how to deal with their children. One "expert" might urge them to be more permissive with their children; another might tell them to place stricter controls on them or they will grow up to be spoiled brats.

Most of you taking this course will be a parent someday; some of you already are. I hope that each of you will take seriously the importance of rearing your children, because they are the future of our society. Good parenting takes a considerable amount of time. If you plan to become a parent, you should be willing to commit yourself, day after day, week after week, month after month, and year after year, to providing your children with a warm,

CRITICAL THINKING
ABOUT CHILDREN'S
DEVELOPMENT

The Importance of Asking Questions—Exploring Your Own Development as a Child

Our question asking reflects our active curiosity. Children—especially young children—are remarkable for their ability to ask questions. My granddaughter, Jordan, is 3½ years old. "Why?" is one of her favorite questions, and she uses the word *why* relentlessly. As strong as question asking is early in our life, many of us ask far fewer questions as adults.

Asking questions can help us engage in critical thinking about children's development, including our own development as children. As you go through this course, you might want to ask yourself questions about how you experienced a particular aspect of development. For example, consider your experiences in your family as you were growing up. Questions you could pose to yourself might include these: "How did my parents bring me up?" "How did the way they reared me influence what I'm like today?" "How did my relationship with my brothers or sisters affect my development?" Consider also questions about your experiences with peers and at school: "Did I have many close friends while I was growing up?" "How much time did I spend with my peers and friends at various points in childhood and adolescence compared with the time I spent with my parents?" "What were the schools I attended like?" "How good were my teachers?" "How did the schools and teachers affect my achievement orientation today?"

Be curious. Ask questions. Ask your friends or classmates about their experiences as they were growing up and compare them with yours. By asking questions about children's development, you are *applying a developmental framework to understanding behavior.*

supportive, safe, and stimulating environment that will make them feel secure and allow them to reach their full potential as human beings.

Understanding the nature of children's development can help you to become a better parent. Many parents learn parenting practices and how to care for their children from their parents—some practices they accept, some they discard. Unfortunately, when parenting practices and child care strategies are passed on from one generation to the next, both desirable and undesirable ones are usually perpetuated. This book and your instructor's lectures in this course can help you become much more knowledgeable about the nature of children's development and to sort through which practices in your own upbringing you would like to continue with your own children and which you would like to abandon. To further evaluate your development as a child, refer to Critical Thinking About Children's Development.

If a community values its children, it must cherish their parents.

—**John Bowlby,**
Child Care and the Growth of Love

An important theme of this textbook is to provide a detailed, up-to-date coverage of families and parenting. Issues involving families and parenting are integrated into discussions throughout the book, and important aspects of children's development are described at the end of each chapter as part of our evaluation of how to improve the lives of children.

Education

Like parenting, education is an extremely important dimension of children's lives (Gorman & Pollitt, 1996). When we think of education, we usually associate it with schools. Schools are an extremely important aspect of education, but education also occurs in contexts other than schools. Children learn from their parents, from their siblings, from their peers, from books, from watching television, and from computers as well.

You can probably look back on your own education and think of ways it could have been a lot better. Some, or even most, of your school years may have been spent in classrooms in which learning was not enjoyable but boring, stressful, and rigid. Some of your teachers may have not adequately considered your own unique needs and skills. On the other hand, you probably can remember some classrooms and teachers that made learning exciting, something you looked forward to each morning you got up. You liked the teacher and the subject, and you learned.

There is widespread agreement that something needs to be done to improve the education our nation's children are receiving (Holtzmann, 1992). What would you do to make the education of children more effective? What would you do to make schools more productive and enjoyable contexts for children's development? Would you make the school days longer or shorter? The school year longer or shorter? Or keep it the same and focus more on changing the curriculum itself? Would you emphasize less memorization and give more attention to the development of children's ability to process information more efficiently? Have schools become too soft and watered down? Should they make more demands and have higher expectations of children? Should schools focus only on developing the child's knowledge and cognitive skills, or should they pay more attention to the whole child and consider the child's socioemotional and physical development as well? Should more tax dollars be spent on schools and should teachers be paid more to educate our nation's children? Should schools be dramatically changed so that they serve as a locus for a wide range of services, such as primary health care, child care, preschool education, parent education, recreation, and family counseling, as well as traditional educational activities, such as learning in the classroom?

These are provocative questions, and how they are answered will influence the future of your children. Information about education and schools is integrated into chapters throughout the book, and important educational issues are highlighted in the discussion of how to improve the lives of children at the end of each chapter.

Culture and Ethnicity

The tapestry of American culture has changed dramatically in recent years. Nowhere is the change more noticeable than in the increasing ethnic diversity of America's citizens (see figure 1.2). Ethnic minority groups—African American, Latino, Native American (American Indian), and Asian, for example—made up 20 percent of all children and adolescents under the age of 17 in 1989. Projections indicate that, by the year 2000, one-third of all school-aged children will fall into this category. This changing demographic tapestry promises not only the richness that diversity produces but also difficult challenges in extending the American dream to individuals of all ethnic groups. Historically, ethnic minorities have found themselves at the bottom of the economic and social order. They have been disproportionately represented among the poor and the inadequately educated

FIGURE 1.2

Ethnic Minority Population Increases in the United States
The percentage of African American, Latino, and Asian American individuals increased far more from 1981 to 1991 than did the percentage of Whites. Shown here are two Korean-born children on the day they became U.S. citizens. Asian American children are the fastest-growing group of ethnic minority children.

(Edelman, 1995). Half of all African American children and one-third of all Latino American children live in poverty. School dropout rates for minority youth reach the alarming rate of 60 percent in some urban areas. These population trends and our nation's inability to prepare ethnic minority individuals for full participation in American life have produced an imperative for the social institutions that serve ethnic minorities (Halonen & Santrock, 1996). Schools, social services, health and mental health agencies, juvenile probation services, and other programs need to become more sensitive to ethnic issues and to provide improved services to ethnic and minority and low-income individuals.

CRITICAL THINKING
ABOUT CHILDREN'S
DEVELOPMENT

*Imagining What Your
Development as a Child
Would Have Been
Like in Other
Cultural Contexts*

Imagine what your development as a child would have been like in a culture that offered few choices compared to the Western world—Communist China during the Cultural Revolution. Young people could not choose their jobs or their mates in rural China. They also were not given the choice of migrating to the city. Imagine also another cultural context, this one in the United States. What would your life as a child have been like if you had grown up in the inner city, where most services had moved out, most schools were inferior, poverty was extreme, and crime was common? (Unfortunately, some of you did grow up in these circumstances.) By imagining what your development would have been like in these cultural contexts, you are *engaging in perspective taking and identifying the sociohistorical, cultural factors that influence children's development.*

These contexts or settings include homes, schools, peer groups, churches, cities, neighborhoods, communities, university laboratories, the United States, China, Mexico, Japan, Egypt, and many others—each with meaningful historical, economic, social, and cultural legacies (Cairns & Dawes, 1996; Kagitcibasi, 1996).

Two sociocultural contexts that many child development researchers believe merit special attention are culture and ethnicity. **Culture** *refers to the behavior patterns, beliefs, and all other products of a particular group of people that are passed on from generation to generation.* The products result from the interaction between groups of people and their environment over many years. A cultural group can be as large as the United States or as small as an African hunter-gatherer group. Whatever its size, the group's culture influences the identity, learning, and social behavior of its members (Goodnow, 1995; LeVine & Shweder, 1995). For example, the United States is an achievement-oriented culture with a strong work ethic, but recent comparisons of American and Japanese children revealed that the Japanese were better at math, spent more time working on math in school, and spent more time doing homework than Americans (Stevenson, 1995).

Our most basic link is that we all inhabit the same planet. We all breathe the same air. We all cherish our children's future.

—**John F. Kennedy**

Cross-cultural studies—*comparisons of one culture with one or more other cultures—provide information about the degree to which children's development is similar, or universal, across cultures, and to what degree it is culture-specific.* A special concern in comparing the United States with other cultures is our nation's unsatisfactory record in caring for its children, which will be discussed at the end of this chapter in the section "Improving the Lives of Children." To further evaluate children's development in different cultural contexts, refer to Critical Thinking About Children's Development.

Ethnicity (*the word* ethnic *comes from the Greek word for "nation") is based on cultural heritage, nationality characteristics, race, religion, and language.* Ethnicity is central to the development of an **ethnic identity,** *which is a sense of membership in an ethnic group, based upon shared language,*

An especially important idea in considering the nature of ethnic minority groups is that not only is there ethnic diversity within a culture such as the United States, but there is also considerable diversity within each ethnic group (Mattsumoto, 1996). Not all African American children come from low-income families. Not all Latino children are members of the Catholic church. Not all Asian American children are geniuses. Not all Native American children drop out of school. It is easy to make the mistake of stereotyping the members of an ethnic minority group as all being the same. Keep in mind, as we describe children from ethnic groups, that each group is heterogeneous.

Sociocultural contexts of development includes three important concepts: the concepts of contexts, culture, and ethnicity. These concepts are central to our discussion of children's development in this book, so we need to clearly define them. **Context** *refers to the setting in which development occurs, a setting that is influenced by historical, economic, social, and cultural factors.* To sense how important context is in understanding children's development, consider a researcher who wants to discover whether children today are more racially tolerant than they were a decade ago. Without reference to the historical, economic, social, and cultural aspects of race relations, students' racial tolerance cannot be fully understood. Every child's development occurs against a cultural backdrop of contexts (Cauce, 1996; Parke, 1996).

religion, customs, values, history, and race. Each of you is a member of one or more ethnic groups. Your ethnic identity reflects your deliberate decision to identify with an ancestor or ancestral group. If you are of Native American and African slave ancestry, you might choose to align yourself with the traditions and history of Native Americans, although an outsider might believe that your identity is African American.

Recently, some individuals have voiced dissatisfaction with the use of the term *minority* in the phrase *ethnic minority group*. Some individuals have also raised objections about using the term *Blacks* or *Black Americans*, preferring instead the term *African Americans* to emphasize their ancestry. What is the nature of such dissatisfaction and objections? The term *minority* has traditionally been associated with inferiority and deficits. Further, the concept of minority implies that there is a majority. Indeed, it can be argued that there really is no majority in the United States because Whites are actually composed of many different ethnic groups, and Whites are not a majority in the world. When we use the term *ethnic minority* in this text, the use is intentional. Rather than implying that ethnic minority children should be viewed as inferior or deficient in some way, we want to convey the impact that minority status has had on many ethnic minority children. The circumstances of any ethnic group are not solely a function of its own culture. Rather, many ethnic groups have experienced considerable discrimination and prejudice. For example, patterns of alcohol abuse among Native American adolescents cannot be fully understood unless the exploitation that has accompanied Native Americans' history is also considered.

Our discussion of culture and ethnicity is woven into the text in every chapter. In addition, as part of our overview about ways to improve children's lives, issues in culture and ethnicity will be evaluated at the end of each chapter.

We need every human gift and cannot afford to neglect any gift because of artificial barriers of sex or race or class or national origin.

—Margaret Mead,
Male and Female (1949)

Gender

Another important theme of this book is gender. Gender is receiving increased attention in studying children and in making their lives competent (Paludi, 1995; Wood, 1996). **Gender** *is the sociocultural dimension of being female or male. Sex refers to the biological dimension of being female or male.* Few aspects of children's development are more central to their identity and to their social relationships than their gender or sex. Society's gender attitudes are changing. But how much? Is there a limit to how much society can

determine what is appropriate behavior for females and males? These are among the provocative questions about gender we will explore in *Children*.

Earlier we indicated that diversity characterizes every ethnic group. Females and males are also very diverse. For example, some females excel at math, others do not. Some females have highly connected friendships, others are lonely; and the same is true for males. Diversity and individual differences exist in every ethnic, cultural, and gender group. Failure to recognize this strong diversity and individual variation results in the stereotyping of ethnic, cultural, and gender groups.

If you are going to generalize about women, you will find yourself up to here in exceptions.

—Dolores Hitchens,
In a House Unknown (1973)

An important goal of this book is to evaluate extensively the gender worlds of children and to promote gender equity in children's development. Gender is woven into the discussion of every chapter, and at the end of each chapter. We also discuss issues in gender at the end of each chapter as part of our overview of how to improve the lives of children.

Social Policy and Children's Development

Social policy *is a national government's course of action designed to influence the welfare of its citizens.* A current trend is to conduct child development research that produces knowledge that will lead to wise and effective decision making in the area of social policy (Blum, 1995; Gomby, 1995; Erwin, 1996). When more than 20 percent of all children and more than half of all ethnic minority children are being raised in poverty, when between 40 and 50 percent of all children born in a particular era can expect to spend at least 5 years in a single-parent home, when children and young adolescents are giving birth, when the use and abuse of drugs is widespread, and when the specter and spread of AIDS is present, our nation needs revised social policy related to children (Horowitz & O'Brien, 1989). Figure 1.3 vividly portrays one day in the lives of children in the United States.

The shape and scope of social policy related to children is heavily influenced by our political system, which is based on negotiation and compromise. The values held by individual lawmakers, the nation's economic strengths and weaknesses, and partisan politics all influence the policy agenda and whether the welfare of children will be improved. Periods of comprehensive social policy are often the outgrowth of concern over broad social issues. Child labor laws were established in the early twentieth century to protect children and jobs for adults as well; federal day-care

17,051 women get pregnant.
2,773 of them are teenagers.
1,106 teenagers have abortions.
372 teenagers miscarry.
1,295 teenagers give birth.
689 babies are born to women who have had inadequate prenatal care.
719 babies are born at low birthweight.
129 babies are born at very low birthweight.
67 babies die before 1 month of life.
105 babies die before their first birthday.
27 children die from poverty.
10 children die from guns.
30 children are wounded by guns.

6 teenagers commit suicide.
135,000 children bring a gun to school.
7,742 teens become sexually active.
623 teenagers get syphilis or gonorrhea.
211 children are arrested for drug abuse.
437 children are arrested for drinking or drunken driving.
1,512 teenagers drop out of school.
1,849 children are abused or neglected.
3,288 children run away from home.
1,629 children are in adult jails.
2,556 children are born out of wedlock.
2,989 see their parents divorced.
34,285 people lose jobs.

FIGURE 1.3

One Day in the Lives of Children in the United States

Marian Wright Edelman, president of the Children's Defense Fund (shown here interacting with a young child) has been a tireless advocate of children's rights and has been instrumental in calling attention to the needs of children.

funding during World War II was justified by the need for women laborers in factories; and Head Start and other War on Poverty programs in the 1960s were implemented to decrease intergenerational poverty (Zigler & Styfco, 1994).

If our American way of life fails the child, it fails us all.
—Pearl Buck,
The Child Who Never Grew

Among the groups that have worked to improve the lives of the world's children are UNICEF in New York and the Children's Defense Fund in Washington, DC. At a recent United Nations convention, a number of children's rights were declared (Cummings, Rebello, & Gardiner, 1995); a sampling of these rights appears in table 1.1. Marian Wright Edelman, president of the Children's Defense Fund, has been a tireless advocate of children's rights and has been instrumental in calling attention to the needs of children. Especially troubling to Edelman (1995) are the indicators of societal neglect that place the United States at or near the bottom of industrialized nations in the treatment of children. Edelman says that parenting and nurturing the next generation of children is our society's most important function and that we need to take it more seriously than we have in the past. She points out that we hear a lot from politicians these days about the importance of "family values," but that when we examine our nation's policies for families, they don't reflect the politicians' words.

Child developmentalists can play an important role in social policy related to children by helping to develop more positive public opinion for comprehensive child welfare legislation, by contributing to and promoting research that will benefit children's welfare, and by helping provide legislators with information that will influence their support of comprehensive child welfare legislation.

TABLE 1.1

A Partial Listing of the Declaration of Children's Rights Presented to the United Nations

Abuse and Neglect

The need to protect children from all forms of maltreatment by parents and others: In cases of abuse and neglect, the government is obligated to undertake preventive and treatment programs

Best Interests of the Child

The need for the best interests of children to prevail in all legal and administrative decisions, taking into account children's opinions

Child Labor

The need to protect children from economic exploitation and from engaging in work that is a threat to their health, education, and development

Children of Ethnic Minorities

The right of children from ethnic minority backgrounds to enjoy their own culture and to practice their own religion and language

Children Without Families

The right to receive special protection and assistance from the government when deprived of family support and to be provided with alternative care

Drug Abuse

The need of children to be protected from illegal drugs, including their production or distribution

Education

The right to education: The government should be obligated to provide free and compulsory education and to ensure that school discipline reflects children's human dignity

Aims of Education

Education that develops a child's personality and talents and fosters respect for human rights and for children's and others' cultural and national value

Sexual Exploitation

The right of children to be protected from sexual exploitation and abuse, including prostitution and pornography

Freedom From Discrimination

The need to protect children without exception from any form of discrimination

Handicapped Children

The right of handicapped children to special care and training designed to help them achieve self-reliance and a full, active life in society

Health and Health Services

The right to the highest standard of health and access to medical services: The government should be obligated to ensure preventive health care, health care for expectant mothers, health education, and the reduction of infant and child mortality

Leisure and Recreation

The right to leisure, play, and participation in cultural and artistic activities

Standard of Living

The right to an adequate standard of living: The government should have a responsibility to assist parents who cannot meet this responsibility

CONCEPT TABLE 1.1

The Reasons for Studying Children's Development and Child Development Yesterday and Today

Concept	Processes/Related Ideas	Characteristics/Description
Why Study Children?	Explanations	Responsibility for children is or will be a part of our everyday lives. The more we learn about children, the more we can better deal with them and assist them in becoming competent human beings.
Child Development— Yesterday and Today	Historical accounts of children	The history of interest in children is long and rich. In the Renaissance, philosophical views were important, including original sin, *tabula rasa,* and innate goodness. We now conceive of childhood as highly eventful.
	Improving children's lives	Five very important contemporary concerns in children's development are family issues and parenting, sociocultural contexts, education, health and well-being, and gender.
	Social policy	A current trend is to conduct child development research that is relevant to the welfare of children. The shape and scope of social policy are influenced by our political system. Child developmentalists can play an important role in social policy. Improved social policy related to children is needed to help all children reach their potential.

We believe the children are the future . . . teach them well and let them lead the way . . . show them all the beauty they possess inside . . . give them a sense of pride . . . let the children's laughter remind us how we used to be.

—**George Benson**

A summary of the main ideas we have discussed so far is presented in concept table 1.1. Next, we explore some important developmental issues in the study of children.

THE NATURE OF DEVELOPMENT

Each of us develops in certain ways like all other individuals, like some other individuals, and like no other individuals. Most of the time, our attention is directed to a person's uniqueness, but psychologists who study development are drawn to our shared as well as our unique characteristics. As humans, each of us has traveled some common paths. Each of us—Leonardo da Vinci, Joan of Arc, George Washington, Martin Luther King, Jr., and you—walked at about the age of 1, engaged in fantasy play as a young child, and became more independent as a youth.

What do psychologists mean when they speak of an individual's development? **Development** *is the pattern of change that begins at conception and continues through the life span.* Most development involves growth, although it includes decay (as in death and dying). The pattern of movement is complex because it is the product of several processes—biological, cognitive, and socioemotional.

Biological, Cognitive, and Socioemotional Processes

Biological processes *involve changes in an individual's physical nature.* Genes inherited from parents, the development of the brain, height and weight gains, motor skills, and the hormonal changes of puberty all reflect the role of biological processes in development.

The chess-board is the world. The pieces are the phenomena of the universe. The rules of the game are what we call laws of nature.

—**Thomas Henry Huxley**

Cognitive processes *involve changes in an individual's thought, intelligence, and language.* The tasks of watching a colorful mobile swinging above a crib, putting together a two-word sentence, memorizing a poem, solving a math problem, and imagining what it would be like to be a movie star all reflect the role of cognitive processes in children's development.

I think, therefore I am.

—**René Descartes**

Socioemotional processes *involve changes in an individual's relationships with other people, changes in emotions, and changes in personality.* An infant's smile in response to her mother's touch, a young boy's aggressive attack on a playmate, a girl's development of assertiveness, and an

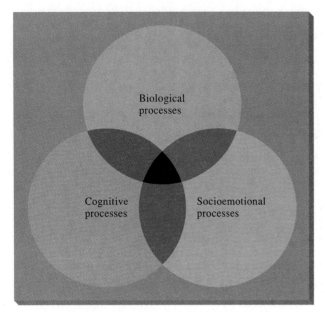

FIGURE 1.4

Biological, Cognitive, and Socioemotional Processes
Changes in development are the result of biological, cognitive, and socioemotional processes. These processes are interwoven as the child develops.

adolescent's joy at the senior prom all reflect the role of socioemotional processes in children's development.

> *Man is by nature a social animal.*
>
> **—Aristotle**

Remember as you read about biological, cognitive, and socioemotional processes that they are intricately interwoven. You will read about how socioemotional processes shape cognitive processes, how cognitive processes promote or restrict socioemotional processes, and how biological processes influence cognitive processes. Although it is helpful to study the various processes involved in children's development in separate sections of the book, keep in mind that you are studying the development of an integrated human child who has only one interdependent mind and body (see figure 1.4).

Periods of Development

For the purposes of organization and understanding, we commonly describe development in terms of periods. The most widely used classification of developmental periods involves the following sequence: the prenatal period, infancy, early childhood, middle and late childhood, and adolescence. Approximate age ranges are placed on the periods to provide a general idea of when a period first appears and when it ends.

The **prenatal period** *is the time from conception to birth*. It is a time of tremendous growth—from a single cell to an organism complete with a brain and behavioral capabilities, produced in approximately a 9-month period.

Infancy *is the developmental period that extends from birth to 18 to 24 months*. Infancy is a time of extreme dependence on adults. Many psychological activities are just beginning—language, symbolic thought, sensorimotor coordination, and social learning, for example.

Early childhood *is the developmental period that extends from the end of infancy to about 5 to 6 years; sometimes the period is called the preschool years*. During this time, young children learn to become more self-sufficient and to care for themselves, develop school readiness skills (following instructions, identifying letters), and spend many hours in play and with peers. First grade typically marks the end of this period.

Middle and late childhood *is the developmental period that extends from about 6 to 11 years of age, approximately corresponding to the elementary school years; sometimes the period is called the elementary school years*. Children master the fundamental skills of reading, writing, and arithmetic, and they are formally exposed to the larger world and its culture. Achievement becomes a more central theme of the child's world, and self-control increases.

Adolescence *is the developmental period of transition from childhood to early adulthood, entered approximately at 10 to 12 years of age and ending at 18 to 22 years of age*. Adolescence begins with rapid physical changes—dramatic gains in height and weight; changes in body contour; and the development of sexual characteristics such as enlargement of the breasts, development of pubic and facial hair, and deepening of the voice. At this point in development, the pursuit of independence and an identity are prominent. Thought is more logical, abstract, and idealistic. More and more time is spent outside of the family during this period.

Today, developmentalists do not believe that change ends with adolescence (Santrock, 1997). They describe development as a lifelong process. However, the purpose of this text is to describe the changes in development that take place from conception through adolescence.

The periods of development from conception through adolescence are shown in figure 1.5, along with the processes of development—biological, cognitive, and socioemotional. The interplay of biological, cognitive, and socioemotional processes produces the periods of development.

Developmental Issues

Major issues raised in the study of children's development include these: Is children's development due more to maturation (nature, heredity) or more to experience (nurture, environment)? Is development more continuous and smooth or more discontinuous and stagelike? Is development due more to early experience or more to later experience?

John W. Santrock

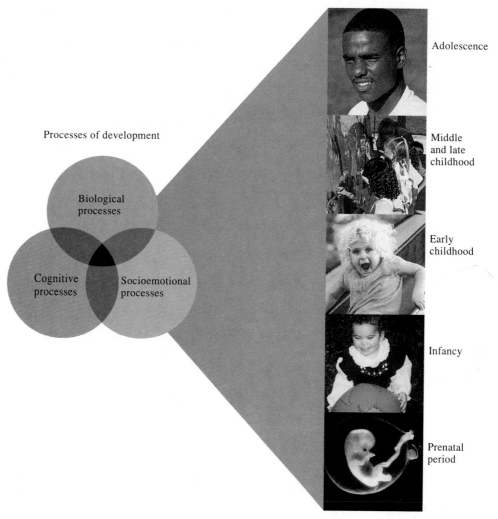

Processes of development

Biological processes

Cognitive processes

Socioemotional processes

Adolescence

Middle and late childhood

Early childhood

Infancy

Prenatal period

FIGURE 1.5

Processes and Periods of Development
Development moves through the prenatal, infancy, early childhood, middle and late childhood, and adolescence periods. These periods of development are the result of biological, cognitive, and sociemotional processes. Development is the creation of increasingly complex forms.

Maturation and Experience (Nature and Nurture)

We can think of development as produced not only by the interplay of biological, cognitive, and socioemotional processes but also by the interplay of maturation and experience. **Maturation** *is the orderly sequence of changes dictated by the genetic blueprint we each have.* Just as a sunflower grows in an orderly way—unless defeated by an unfriendly environment—so does a human being grow in an orderly way, according to the maturational view. The range of environments can be vast, but the maturational approach argues that the genetic blueprint produces commonalities in our growth and development. We walk before we talk, speak one word before two words, grow rapidly in infancy and less so in early childhood, experience a rush of sexual hormones in puberty after a lull in

childhood, reach the peak of our physical strength in late adolescence and early adulthood and then decline, and so on. The maturationists acknowledge that extreme environments—those that are psychologically barren or hostile—can depress development, but they believe that basic growth tendencies are genetically wired into human beings.

By contrast, other psychologists emphasize the importance of experiences in child development. Experiences run the gamut from individuals' biological environment (nutrition, medical care, drugs, and physical accidents) to their social environment (family, peers, schools, community, media, and culture).

The debate about whether development is primarily influenced by maturation or by experience has been a part of psychology since its beginning. This debate is often

"If you ask me, he's come too far too fast."

Drawing by Lorenz; © 1988 The New Yorker Magazine, Inc.

referred to as the **nature-nurture controversy.** *Nature refers to an organism's biological inheritance, nurture to environmental experiences.* The "nature" proponents claim biological inheritance is the most important influence on development, the "nurture" proponents that environmental experiences are the most important.

Ideas about development have been like a pendulum, swinging between nature and nurture. In the 1980s, we witnessed a surge of interest in the biological underpinnings of development, probably because the pendulum previously had swung too far in the direction of thinking that development was exclusively due to environmental experiences. In the 1990s, a heightened interest in sociocultural influences on development has emerged, again probably because the pendulum in the 1980s had swung so strongly toward the biological side.

Continuity and Discontinuity

Think about your development for a moment. Did you gradually grow to become the person you are, in the slow cumulative way a seedling grows into a giant oak? Or did you experience sudden, distinct changes in your growth, like the way a caterpillar changes into a butterfly? (See figure 1.6.) For the most part, developmentalists who emphasize experience have described development as a gradual, continuous process; those who emphasize maturation have described development as a series of distinct stages.

Some developmentalists emphasize the **continuity of development,** *the view that development involves gradual, cumulative change from conception to death.* A child's first word, while seemingly an abrupt, discontinuous event, is actually the result of months of growth and

FIGURE 1.6

Continuity and Discontinuity in Development
Is human development more like that of a seedling gradually growing into a giant oak or more like that of a caterpillar suddenly becoming a butterfly?

practice. Puberty, while also seemingly an abrupt, discontinuous occurrence, is actually a gradual process occurring over several years.

Other developmentalists focus on the **discontinuity of development,** *the view that development involves distinct stages in the life span.* This view sees each of us as passing through a sequence of stages in which change is qualitative rather than quantitative. As an oak moves from seedling to giant tree, it becomes *more* oak—its development is continuous. As a caterpillar changes into a butterfly, it does not become more caterpillar but instead becomes a *different kind* of organism—its development is discontinuous. For example, at a certain point a child moves from not being able to think abstractly about the world to being able to do so. This is a qualitative, discontinuous change in development, not a quantitative, continuous change.

John W. Santrock

What is the nature of the early and later experience issue in development?

Early and Later Experience

Another important developmental topic is the **early-later experience issue,** *which focuses on the degree to which early experiences (especially in infancy) or later experiences are the key determinants of the child's development.* That is, if infants experience negative, stressful circumstances in their lives, can those experiences be overcome by later, more-positive experiences? Or are the early experiences so critical, possibly because they are the infant's first, prototypical experiences, that they cannot be overridden by a later, more-enriched environment?

The early-later experience issue has a long history and continues to be hotly debated among developmentalists. Some believe that unless infants experience warm, nurturant caregiving in the first year or so of life, their development will never be optimal (Bowlby, 1989; Waters & others, 1995). Plato was sure that infants who were rocked frequently became better athletes. Nineteenth-century New England ministers told parents in Sunday sermons that the way they handled their infants would determine their children's future character. The emphasis on the importance of early experience rests on the belief that each life is an unbroken trail on which a psychological quality can be traced back to its origin (Kagan, 1984, 1992).

The early-experience doctrine contrasts with the later-experience view, which states that rather than statue-like permanence after change in infancy, development continues to be like the ebb and flow of an ocean. The later-experience advocates argue that children are malleable throughout development and that later sensitive caregiving is just as important as earlier sensitive caregiving. A number of life-span developmentalists, who focus on the entire life span rather than only on child development, stress that too little attention has been given to later experiences in development (Baltes, 1987). They accept that early experiences are important contributors to development, but no more important than later experiences. Jerome Kagan (1992) points out that even children who show the qualities of an inhibited temperament, which is linked to heredity, have the capacity to change their behavior. In his research, almost one-third of a group of children who had an inhibited temperament at 2 years of age were not unusually shy or fearful when they were 4 years of age (Kagan & Snidman, 1991).

People in Western cultures, especially those steeped in the Freudian belief that the key experiences in development are children's relationships with their parents in the first 5 years of life, have tended to support the idea that early experiences are more important than later experiences (Chan, 1963; Lamb & Sternberg, 1992). By contrast, the majority of people in the world do not share this belief. For example, people in many Asian countries believe that experiences occurring after about 6 to 7 years of age are more important aspects of development than earlier experiences. This stance stems from the long-standing belief in Eastern cultures that children's reasoning skills begin to develop in important ways in the middle childhood years.

Evaluating the Developmental Issues

As we consider further these three salient developmental issues—nature and nurture, continuity and discontinuity, and early and later experiences—it is important to realize that most developmentalists recognize that it is unwise to take an extreme position on these issues. Development is not all nature or all nurture, not all continuity or all discontinuity, and not all early or later experiences. Nature and nurture, continuity and discontinuity, and early and later experiences all characterize our development through the human life cycle. For example, in considering the nature-nurture issue, the key to development is the *interaction* of nature and nurture rather than either factor alone (Plomin, 1993). Thus, an individual's cognitive development is the result of heredity-environment interaction, not heredity or environment alone. Much more about the role of heredity-environment interaction appears in chapter 3.

Nonetheless, although most developmentalists do not take extreme positions on these three important issues, this consensus has not meant the absence of spirited debate about how strongly development is influenced by each of these factors. Are girls less likely to do well in math because of their "feminine" nature or because of society's masculine bias? If, as children, adolescents experienced a world of poverty, neglect by parents, and poor schooling, can enriched experiences in adolescence remove the "deficits" they encountered earlier in their development? The answers developmentalists give to such questions depends on their stance on the issue of nature and nurture, continuity and discontinuity, and early and later experience. The answers to these questions also influence public policy decisions about children and how each of us lives through the human life span.

CAREERS IN CHILD DEVELOPMENT

A career in child development is one of the most rewarding vocational opportunities you can pursue. By choosing a career in child development, you will be able to help children who might not reach their potential as productive contributors to society develop into physically, cognitively, and socially mature individuals. Adults who work professionally with children invariably feel a sense of pride in their ability to contribute in meaningful ways to the next generation of human beings.

If you decide to pursue a career related to children's development, a number of options are available to you. College and university professors teach courses in child development, education, family development, and nursing; counselors, clinical psychologists, pediatricians, psychiatrists, school psychologists, pediatric nurses, psychiatric nurses, and social workers see children with problems and disturbances or illnesses; teachers instruct children in kindergartens, elementary schools, and secondary schools. In pursuing a career related to child development, you can expand your opportunities (and income) considerably by obtaining a graduate degree, although an advanced degree is not absolutely necessary.

Most college professors in child development and its related areas of psychology, education, home economics, nursing, and social work have a master's degree and/or doctorate degree that required 2 to 5 years of academic work beyond their undergraduate degree. Becoming a child clinical psychologist or counseling psychologist requires 5 to 6 years of graduate work to obtain the necessary Ph.D.; this includes both clinical and research training. School and career counselors pursue a master's or doctoral degree in counseling, often in graduate programs in education departments; these degrees require 2 to 6 years to complete. Becoming a pediatrician or psychiatrist requires 4 years of medical school, plus an internship and a residency in pediatrics or psychiatry, respectively; this career path takes 7 to 9 years beyond a bachelor's degree. School psychologists obtain either a master's degree (approximately 2 years) or a D.Ed. degree (approximately 4 to 5 years) in school psychology. School psychologists counsel children and parents when children have problems in school, often giving psychological tests to assess children's personality and intelligence. Social work positions may be obtained with an undergraduate degree in social work or related fields, but opportunities are expanded with an M.S.W. (master's of social work) or Ph.D., which require 2 and 4 to 5 years, respectively. Pediatric and psychiatric nursing positions can also be attained with an undergraduate R.N. degree; M.A. and Ph.D. degrees in nursing, which require 2 and 4 to 5 years of graduate training, respectively, are also available. To read further about jobs and careers that involve working with children, turn to table 1.2. This list is not exhaustive but rather is meant to give you an idea of

Apply a developmental framework to understand behavior

Make accurate observations, descriptions, and inferences about children's development

Identify the sociohistorical, cultural contexts that influence children's development

Apply developmental concepts to enhance personal adaptation

Pursue alternative explanations to understand children's development comprehensively

Evaluate the quality of conclusions and strategies about children's development

Engage in perspective taking to better understand children's development

Use knowledge about development to improve human welfare

Demonstrate appreciation of individual differences in children's development

Create arguments based on developmental concepts

FIGURE 1.7

Critical Thinking About Children's Development

the many opportunities to pursue a rewarding career in child development and its related fields. Also keep in mind that majoring in child development or a related field can provide sound preparation for adult life.

THINKING CRITICALLY ABOUT CHILDREN'S DEVELOPMENT

What does it mean to think critically about children's development? Each of us uses various forms of critical thinking. However, when we learn a new discipline, like child development, we have an opportunity to refine the critical-thinking skills that the discipline emphasizes.

How should your critical-thinking skills change as a result of reading this book and taking this course on children's development? You should develop more effective critical-thinking skills in ten areas that involve children's development (see figure 1.7).

CONCEPT TABLE 1.2

The Nature of Development, Developmental Issues, Careers in Child Development, and Thinking Critically About Children's Development

Concept	Processes/Related Ideas	Characteristics/Description
The Nature of Development	What is development?	Development is the pattern of movement or change that occurs throughout the life span.
	Biological, cognitive, and socioemotional processes	Development is influenced by an interplay of biological, cognitive, and socioemotional processes.
	Periods of development	Development is commonly divided into the following periods from conception through adolescence: the prenatal period, infancy, early childhood, middle and late childhood, and adolescence.
Developmental Issues	Maturation and experience (nature and nurture)	The debate over whether development is due primarily to maturation or to experience is another version of the nature-nurture controversy.
	Continuity and discontinuity	Some developmentalists describe development as continuous (gradual, cumulative change), others as discontinuous (abrupt, sequence of stages).
	Early and later experience	This hotly debated issue focuses on whether early experiences (especially in infancy) are more important in development than later experiences are.
	Evaluating the developmental issues	Most developmentalists recognize that extreme positions on the nature-nurture, continuity-discontinuity, and early-later experience issues are unwise. Despite this consensus, spirited debate still occurs on these issues.
Careers in Child Development	Their nature	A wide range of opportunities are available to individuals who want to pursue a career related to child development. These opportunities include jobs in college and university teaching, child clinical psychology and counseling, school teaching and school psychology, nursing, pediatrics, psychiatry, and social work. A special interest is the history of ethnic minority individuals in the field of child development, and the current educational status of ethnic minority individuals.
Critical Thinking about Children's Development	Its nature	Critical thinking about children's development involves such strategies as applying a developmental framework to understand behavior, making accurate observations and inferences, identifying contextual factors, applying developmental concepts to enhance personal adaptation, pursuing alternative explanations, evaluating the quality of conclusions and strategies, engaging in perspective taking, using knowledge to improve human welfare, demonstrating appreciation of individual differences, and developing arguments based on developmental concepts.

As you read this text, you will frequently be asked to think critically about children's development. Several times in each chapter you will read boxes called "Critical Thinking About Children's Development." In this chapter, you have already been asked to imagine what your development as a child would have been like if you had grown up in a different culture, which encourages you to engage in perspective taking and identify the sociohistorical, cultural factors that influence children's development; and to ask yourself questions about your own development as a child, which helps you to apply a developmental framework to understanding behavior. Beyond the critical-thinking boxes, you will often encounter critical-thinking opportunities to enhance your ability to think like a developmentalist and to improve your grasp of the concepts and principles you are learning.

At this point, we have discussed a number of ideas about the nature of development, careers in child development, and critical thinking about children's development. A summary of these ideas is presented in concept table 1.2.

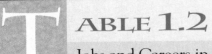

TABLE 1.2

Jobs and Careers in Child Development and Related Fields

Jobs/Careers	Degree	Education Required
Child clinical psychologist or counseling psychologist	Ph.D.	5–7 years postundergraduate
Child life specialist	Undergraduate degree	4 years of undergraduate study
Child psychiatrist	M.D.	7–9 years postundergraduate
Child welfare worker	Undergraduate degree is minimum	4 years minimum
College/university professor in child development, education, family development, nursing, social work	Ph.D. or master's degree	5–6 years for Ph.D. (or D.Ed.) postundergraduate; 2 years for master's degree postundergraduate
Day-care supervisor	Varies by state	Varies by state
Early childhood educator	Master's degree (minimum)	2 years of graduate work (minimum)
Elementary or secondary school teacher	Undergraduate degree (minimum)	4 years
Exceptional children teacher (special education teacher)	Undergraduate degree (minimum)	4 years or more (some states require a master's degree or passing a standardized exam to obtain a license to work with exceptional children)
Guidance counselor	Undergraduate degree (minimum); many have master's degree	4 years undergraduate; 2 years graduate
Pediatrician	M.D.	7–9 years of medical school
Pediatric nurse	R.N.	2–5 years
Preschool/kindergarten teacher	Usually undergraduate degree	4 years
Psychiatric nurse	R.N.	2–5 years
School psychologist	Master's or Ph.D.	5–6 years of graduate work for Ph.D. or D.Ed.; 2 years for master's degree

Nature of Training	Description of Work
Includes both clinical and research training; involves a 1-year internship in a psychiatric hospital or mental health facility.	Child clinical psychologists or counseling psychologists diagnose children's problems and disorders, administer psychological tests, and conduct psychotherapy sessions. Some work at colleges and universities where they do any combination of teaching, therapy, and research.
Many child life specialists have been trained in child development or education but undergo additional training in child life programs that includes parent education, developmental assessment, and supervised work with children and parents.	Child life specialists are employed by hospitals and work with children and their families before and after the children are admitted to the hospital. They often develop and monitor developmentally appropriate activities for child patients. They also help children adapt to their medical experiences and their stay at the hospital. Child life specialists coordinate their efforts with physicians and nurses.
Four years of medical school, plus an internship and residency in child psychiatry are required.	The role of the child psychiatrist is similar to the child clinical psychologist, but the psychiatrist can conduct biomedical therapy (for example, such as using drugs to treat clients); the child clinical or counseling psychologists cannot.
Coursework and training in social work or human services.	Child welfare workers are employed by the Child Protective Services Unit of each state to protect children's rights. They especially monitor cases of child maltreatment and abuse, and make decisions about what needs to be done to help protect the abused child from further harm and effectively cope with their prior abuse.
Take graduate courses, learn how to conduct research, attend and present papers at professional meetings.	College and university professors teach courses in child development, family development, education, or nursing; conduct research; present papers at professional meetings; write and publish articles and books; and train undergraduate and graduate students for careers in these fields.
The Department of Public Welfare in many states publishes a booklet with the requirements for a day-care supervisor.	Day-care supervisors direct day-care or preschool programs, being responsible for the operation of the center. They often make decisions about the nature of the center's curriculum, may teach in the center themselves, work with and consult with parents, and conduct workshops for staff or parents.
Coursework in early childhood education and practice in day-care or early childhood centers with supervised training.	Early childhood educators usually teach in community colleges that award associate or bachelor's degrees in early childhood education with specialization in day care. They train individuals for careers in the field of day care.
Wide range of courses with a major or concentration in education.	Elementary and secondary teachers teach one or more subjects; prepare the curriculum; give tests, assign grades, and monitor students' progress; interact with parents and school administrators; attend lectures and workshops involving curriculum planning or help on special issues, and direct extracurricular programs.
Coursework in education with a concentration in special education.	Exceptional children teachers (also called special education teachers) work with children who are educationally handicapped (those who are mentally retarded, have a physical handicap, have a learning disability, or have a behavioral disorder) or who are gifted. They develop special curricula for the exceptional children and help them to adapt to their exceptional circumstances. Special education teachers work with other school personnel and with parents to improve the adjustment of exceptional children.
Coursework in education and counseling in a school of education; counselor training practice.	The majority of guidance counselors work with secondary school students, assisting them in educational and career planning. They often give students aptitude tests and evaluate their interests, as well as their abilities. Guidance counselors also see students who are having school-related problems, including emotional problems, referring them to other professionals such as school psychologists or clinical psychologists when necessary.
Four years of medical school, plus an internship and residency in pediatrics.	Pediatricians monitor infants' and children's health and treat their diseases. They advise parents about infant and child development and the appropriate ways to deal with children.
Courses in biological sciences, nursing care, and pediatrics (often in a school of nursing); supervised clinical experiences in medical settings.	Pediatric nurses promote health in infants and children, working to prevent disease or injury, assisting children with handicaps or health problems so they can achieve optimal health, and treating children with health deviations. Some pediatric nurses specialize in certain areas (for example, the neonatal intensive care unit clinician cares exclusively for newborns; the new-parent educator helps the parents of newborns develop better parenting skills). Pediatric nurses work in a variety of medical settings.
Coursework in education with a specialization in early childhood education; state certification usually required.	Preschool teachers direct the activities of prekindergarten children, many of whom are 4-year-olds. They develop an appropriate curriculum for the age of the children that promotes their physical, cognitive, and social development in a positive atmosphere. The number of days per week and hours per day varies from one program to another. Kindergarten teachers work with young children who are between the age of preschool programs and the first year of elementary school; they primarily develop appropriate activities and curricula for 5-year-old children.
Courses in biological sciences, nursing care, and mental health in a school of nursing; supervised clinical training in child psychiatric settings.	Psychiatric nurses promote the mental health of individuals; some specialize in helping children with mental health problems and work closely with child psychiatrists to improve these children's adjustment.
Includes coursework and supervised training in school settings, usually in a department of educational psychology.	School psychologists evaluate and treat a wide range of normal and exceptional children who have school-related problems; work in a school system and see children from a number of schools; administer tests, interview and observe children, and consult with teachers, parents, and school administrators; and design programs to reduce the child's problem behavior.

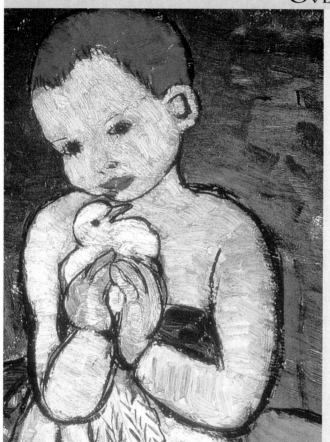

hildren should have a special place in any society, for they are the society's future. An important concern is that too many children today will not reach their full potential because of inadequate rearing conditions. Far too many children live in poverty, have parents who do not adequately care for them, and go to schools where learning conditions are far from optimal.

In this chapter, you were introduced to the field of child development. You read about how today is both the best of times and the worst of times for children and why it is important to study children. You learned about the nature of child development through history, ways to improve children's lives, and social policy issues. You also studied the nature of development by exploring biological, cognitive, and socioemotional processes; periods of development; and developmental issues. You read about a number of careers in child development and the importance of thinking critically about children's development.

To obtain a summary of the chapter, go back and again study the two concept tables on pages 15 and 21. In the next chapter, we will turn our attention to the field of child development as a science. You will learn about the importance of the scientific method, theories, and methods in studying children.

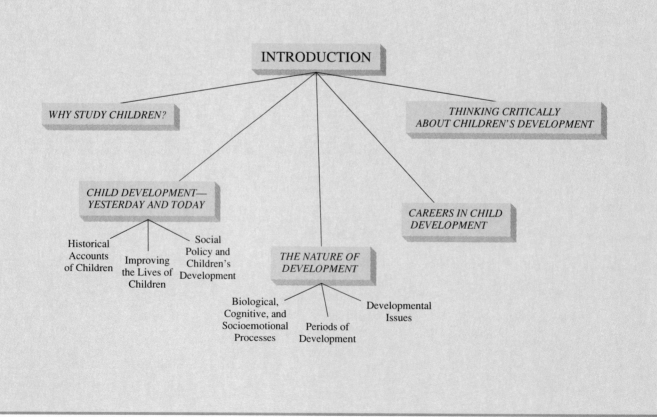

INTRODUCTION

WHY STUDY CHILDREN?

THINKING CRITICALLY
ABOUT CHILDREN'S DEVELOPMENT

CHILD DEVELOPMENT—
YESTERDAY AND TODAY

CAREERS IN CHILD
DEVELOPMENT

Historical Accounts of Children

Improving the Lives of Children

Social Policy and Children's Development

THE NATURE OF
DEVELOPMENT

Biological, Cognitive, and Socioemotional Processes

Periods of Development

Developmental Issues

John W. Santrock

original sin view Advocated during the Middle Ages, the belief that children were born into the world as evil beings and were basically bad. 7

tabula rasa view The idea, proposed by John Locke, that children are like a "blank tablet." 7

innate goodness view The idea, presented by Swiss-born philosopher Jean-Jacques Rousseau, that children are inherently good. 7

context The settings, influenced by historical, economic, social, and cultural factors, in which development occurs. 11

culture The behavior patterns, beliefs, and all other products of a group that are passed on from generation to generation. 11

cross-cultural studies Comparisons of one culture with one or more other cultures. These provide information about the degree to which children's development is similar, or universal, across cultures, and to the degree to which it is culture-specific. 11

ethnicity A characteristic based on cultural heritage, nationality characteristics, race, religion, and language. 11

ethnic identity A sense of membership in an ethnic group, based upon shared language, religion, customs, values, history, and race. 11

gender The sociocultural dimension of being male or female. 12

social policy A national government's course of action designed to influence the welfare of its citizens. 12

development The pattern of change that begins at conception and continues through the life cycle. 15

biological processes Changes in an individual's physical nature. 15

cognitive processes Changes in an individual's thought, intelligence, and language. 15

socioemotional processes Changes in an individual's relationships with other people, emotions, and personality. 15

prenatal period The time from conception to birth. 16

infancy The developmental period that extends from birth to 18 to 24 months. 16

early childhood The developmental period that extends from the end of infancy to about 5 to 6 years, sometimes called the preschool years. 16

middle and late childhood The developmental period that extends from about 6 to 11 years of age, approximately corresponding to the elementary school years, sometimes called the elementary school years. 16

adolescence The developmental period of transition from childhood to early adulthood, entered at approximately 10 to 12 years of age and ending at 18 to 22 years of age. 16

maturation The orderly sequence of changes dictated by a genetic blueprint. 17

nature-nurture controversy *Nature* refers to an organism's biological inheritance, *nurture* to environmental influences. The "nature" proponents claim biological inheritance is the most important influence on development; the "nurture" proponents claim that environmental experiences are the most important. 18

continuity of development The view that development involves gradual, cumulative change from conception to death. 18

discontinuity of development The view that development involves distinct stages in the life span. 18

early-later experience issue The issue of the degree to which early experiences (especially infancy) or later experiences are the key determinants of the child's development. 19

Familyhood
(1992) by Lee Salk.
New York: Simon & Schuster.

Familyhood is about the importance of the family in children's lives and about nurturing the family values that matter. Lee Salk was a well-known clinical psychologist who championed better lives for children for many years. He died in 1992.

Salk says that though the structure of families has changed enormously in recent years because of high divorce rates, increasing numbers of stepfamilies, and huge numbers of working mother families, the values the family cherishes most have not changed. Relying on information from a comprehensive family values survey, Salk found that parents today still have the same needs, wants, and values. They

- want family members to provide emotional support for one another.
- want children to show respect for parents.
- believe parents should also show respect for their children.
- think that parents should show mutual respect for each other.
- believe that family members should take responsibility for their own actions.
- think that family members should try to understand and listen to each other.

Salk draws on his extensive background in counseling parents to provide advice on how to make their families places where people care about each other and transmit important family values.

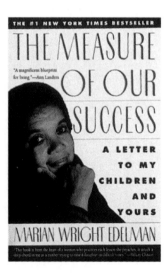

The Measure of Our Success: A Letter to My Children and Yours
(1992) by Marian Wright Edelman.
Boston: Beacon Press.

Marian Wright Edelman founded the Children's Defense Fund in 1973 and for more than two decades has been working to advance the health and well-being of America's children and parents. This slim volume begins with a message to her oldest son, Joshua, 22. In that message and throughout the book, Edelman conveys the message that parenting and nurturing the next generation is the most important function of a society and that we need to take it more seriously than we have in the past. High on her list is the belief that there is no free lunch—don't feel entitled to anything you don't sweat and struggle for. She warns against working only for money or for power, because they won't save your soul, build a decent family, or help you sleep at night. She also tells her sons to remember that their wife is not their mother or their maid. Edelman admonishes our society for not developing better safety nets for children and not being the caring community that children and parents need.

Edelman's book stimulates thought about what kind of nation we want to be, what kind of values mean the most to us, and what we can do to improve the health and well-being of our nation's children and parents.

IMPROVING THE LIVES OF CHILDREN

As the twenty-first century approaches, the well-being of children is one of America's foremost concerns. We all cherish our children, because they are the future of any society. Children who do not reach their potential, who are destined to make fewer contributions to society than it needs from them, and who do not take their place as productive adults diminish the society's future.

We need to take seriously how we can improve the lives of today's children. Of the areas in which we can make a difference in the quality of children's development, five especially stand out: health and well-being, families and parenting, education, culture and ethnicity, and gender. This section—"Improving the Lives of Children"—appears at the end of each chapter and includes discussions of the five themes related to the chapter's contents.

Children's health and well-being is enhanced when their parents have reasonable jobs, housing, and health care. And many families, especially those in low-income circumstances, need access to family services and support that will help them cope with challenges and stress that invade their lives. MaryLee Allen, Patricia Brown, and Belva Finlay (1992) recently proposed that communities need to offer a pyramid of services that range from provisions for all families to families whose children cannot be protected or treated at home (see figure 1.8). In between are families needing some extra support, families needing special assistance, and families in crisis.

There are essentially two overall types of programs that help families do a better job of nurturing and protecting their children. The first consists of programs that are variously called *family support programs, family resource programs,* or *parent education programs.* These programs offer low-intensity preventive services designed to strengthen family functioning early on to avert crises. The second, more-intensive type of program, *family preservation services,* is intended to help families already in crisis change their behavior to remove the immediate risk to the children and, if possible, avert the need to remove the children from the home.

FIGURE 1.8

A Pyramid of Services to Improve Family Health and Well-Being
When communities are able to offer a pyramid of assistance that matches the pyramid of family needs, problems are likely to be solved or alleviated at earlier stages, when they are easier and less costly to address. As family needs grow in intensity, so do services to meet those needs.

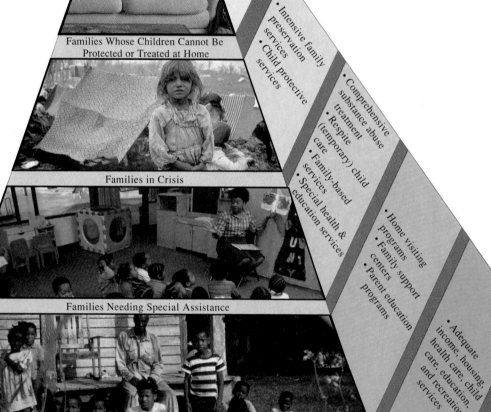

Residential treatment centers
Therapeutic group homes
Foster family homes

Families Whose Children Cannot Be Protected or Treated at Home

• Intensive family preservation services
• Child protective services

Families in Crisis

• Comprehensive substance abuse treatment
• Respite (temporary) child care
• Family-based services
• Special health & education services

Families Needing Special Assistance

• Home visiting programs
• Family support centers
• Parent education programs

Families Needing Some Extra Support

• Adequate income, housing, health care, child care, education, and recreational services

All Families

FAMILIES AND PARENTING

Family Policy and the Homeless

The last decade has been one of extremes with respect to family policy in the United States, ranging from efforts to dismantle welfare programs to modest efforts at reform (Berardo, 1990). Controversy has focused on the ability of government intervention to reduce poverty and promote family well-being. The Family Support Act was passed in 1988, linking family welfare payments to job training or work obligations and strengthening child support enforcement strategies, so that families would ultimately become economically independent.

According to social commentator Richard Louv (1990), a successful family policy will not be shaped primarily by committees and lobbyists in Washington, D.C., but by parents themselves, when they come to understand their need for each other and the interconnectedness of families, schools, and communities.

Family policies can be divided into those that help parents in their "breadwinning" roles and those that concentrate on their nurturing and caregiving roles (Kamerman & Kahn, 1978). Breadwinning family policy supports the family as a viable economic unit, either by maintaining a certain minimal family income or by providing for the care of children while parents work. Nurturing and caregiving family policy focuses on the internal life of the family by promoting positive family functioning and the

development and well-being of individual family members.

Consider the plight of the homeless. Some people maintain that homeless families only need housing. Others argue that homeless families need a broader economic package of affordable housing, decent jobs, child care, and health care. And yet others stress that homeless families need more than economic assistance, that the factors that precipitated their plight and the harmful effects of being homeless call for additional support—a "caregiving package" that includes services such as home management training, parental support groups, and parent education (Jacobs, Little, & Almeida, 1993). In the last decade, public support for caregiving and nurturing policies has increased, but less so than support for economic assistance.

The family policies of the United States are overwhelmingly treatment-oriented, with only those families and individuals already having problems being eligible; few preventive programs are available on any widespread basis. For example, families in which the children are on the verge of being placed in foster care are eligible, and often required, to receive counseling; families in which problems are brewing but are not yet full-blown usually cannot qualify for public services. Most experts on family policy believe more attention should be given to preventing family problems.

What are some family policy issues that are involved in helping the homeless?

EDUCATION

Ethnic Minorities in the Field of Child Development

Barriers have prevented the entry of African Americans, Latinos, Asian Americans, and Native Americans into the field of child development throughout most of its history. Ethnic minority individuals who obtained doctoral degrees were very dedicated and overcame extensive bias against their ethnic group. Two pioneering African American psychologists were Kenneth and Mamie Clark, who con-

ducted research on African American children's self-conceptions and identity (Clark & Clark, 1939). In 1971, Kenneth Clark became the first African American president of the American Psychological Association. In 1932, Latino psychologist George Sanchez conducted research that demonstrated the cultural bias of intelligence tests for ethnic minority children.

In the past 25 years, important movements calling for recognition of the rights and needs of ethnic minorities in higher education have surfaced (Bronstein & Quina, 1988; Stricker & others, 1990). The civil rights movement has led to social change, stimulating developmentalists—especially those who also are members of ethnic minority groups—to reexamine the existing body of knowledge about children's

Mamie and Kenneth Clark conducted pioneering research on African American children's self-conceptions and identity.

development and to question to what degree it is relevant to ethnic minority children. This questioning has formed the basis of new areas of developmental inquiry, focusing on populations who previously were omitted from subject pools of developmental research and from the theoretical ideas of mainstream child development.

Recognizing the underrepresentation of ethnic minority individuals in psychology, the American Psychological Association (APA)—the main organization of psychologists in the United States—has formed the Board of Ethnic Minority Affairs to represent the ethnic group concerns of its members. In one survey, only 5 percent of doctoral psychologists in the developmental area, 4.7 percent in the clinical, counseling, and school areas, and 7.5 percent in the educational area were members of ethnic minority groups (Stapp, Tucker, & VandenBos, 1985). The percentage of Latino and Native American individuals with doctorates in these areas is especially low. And in nursing, the percentage of those with master's and doctoral degrees who represent ethnic minorities is equally low (for example, African Americans—5 percent; Asian Americans—2 percent; Latinos—1 percent; and Native Americans—0.2 percent).

George Sanchez conducted pioneering research on cultural bias in children's intelligence tests.

Job opportunities are increasingly available to qualified applicants from every ethnic group. We need more qualified ethnic minority individuals in the field of child development.

CULTURE AND ETHNICITY

Caring for Children Around the World

According to a report by the Children's Defense Fund, the United States does not compare well with other nations in caring for children (Edelman, 1995). In this report, the Children's Defense Fund gave the United States an A for capacity to care for children but an F for performance on many key markers of children's well-being. Consider the following cross-cultural comparisons:

- United States 1-year-olds have lower immunization rates against polio than 1-year-olds in 14 other countries. Polio immunization rates for non-White infants in the United States rank behind those of 48 other countries, including Albania, Colombia, and Jamaica.

- In overall infant mortality rate, the United States lags behind 18 other countries. Our non-White infant mortality rate ranks 13th compared to other nations' overall rates. An African American child born in inner-city Boston has less chance of surviving the first year of life than does a child born in Panama, North or South Korea, or Uruguay.

- In a study of 8 industrialized nations (the United States, Switzerland, Sweden, Norway, former West Germany, Canada, England, and Australia), the United States had the highest poverty rate.

- The United States has the highest adolescent pregnancy rate of any industrialized Western nation.

- The United States and South Africa are the only industrialized countries that do not provide universal health coverage and child care to families.

- American schoolchildren know less geography than schoolchildren in Iran, less math than schoolchildren in Japan, and less science information than schoolchildren in Spain.

The United States does not compare well with other nations in caring for children. Eighteen other countries have lower infant mortality rates than the United States does. An African American child born in inner-city Boston has less chance of surviving the first year of life than does a child born in Panama, North or South Korea, or Uruguay. American schoolchildren know less science information than do their counterparts in Spain.

- The United States invests a smaller portion of its gross national product (GNP) in child health than 18 other industrialized nations do. It invests a smaller portion of its GNP in education than 6 other industrialized countries do.

In sum, the United States needs to devote more attention to caring for its children. Too many American children, from every socioeconomic and ethnic group, are neglected and are not given the opportunity to reach their full potential.

GENDER

How Society Views Females and Males

In an analysis of a course on children's development, Lynn Bond (1988) concluded that if we followed the rule of truth in advertising, we would probably have to rename the course something like "The Development of White Male Children with Mention of Variations from the 'Norm.'" The variations would be girls, children from ethnic minority groups, and children from other cultures. Too often, she says, the standard by which competence is judged in our culture is a White male standard. In far too many cases, the behavior of females is judged by male standards, the behavior of children from ethnic minority groups by White standards.

With regard to gender, Carol Tavris, writing in *The Mismeasure of Women* (1992), says that no matter how hard they try, females often can't measure up. They are criticized for being too feminine or not feminine enough. They are always judged by how well they fit into a male world. Tavris and other gender experts, such as Janet Shibley Hyde (1990; Hyde & Plant, 1995), believe that more evidence exists for similarities between the sexes than differences between them. She does not accept male superiority or female superiority. In her view, if females appear to be different, it is because of the roles they have been assigned by society, which historically has been male dominant.

For example, our society, like most other societies, has assigned mothers the role of rearing children. Consequently, when a child develops a problem, the mother is often blamed for the problem. The roles of fathers, siblings, peers, schools, the extended family, other children and adults in the community, and heredity also need to be taken into account before blaming mothers when children develop problems.

I hope that as you go through this course and read this book, you will become more aware of how pervasively gender infuses children's lives. Seek out opportunities to observe children's gender worlds—on playgrounds, in malls, at grocery stores with parents, and so on. Observe how parents, teachers, other adults, siblings, and peers react to children similarly or differently because they are girls or boys. Think about how your parents reared you—do you think they would have treated you differently if you had been of the other sex? Would they have had different expectations?

HAYWARD L. OUBRE
Pensive Family, detail

The Science of Child Development

*There is nothing quite so practical
as a good theory.*

—**Kurt Lewin,
Psychologist, 1890–1947**

The childhood shows the man, as morning shows the day.

—Milton

IMAGES OF CHILDREN

Erikson and Piaget as Children

Imagine that you have developed a major theory of child development. What would influence someone like you to construct this theory? A person interested in developing such a theory usually goes through a long university training program that culminates in a doctoral degree. As part of the training, the future theorist is exposed to many ideas about a particular area of child development, such as biological, cognitive, or socioemotional development. Another factor that could explain why someone develops a particular theory is that person's life experiences. Two important developmental theorists, whose views we will describe later in the chapter, are Erik Erikson and Jean Piaget. Let's examine a portion of their lives as they were growing up to discover how their experiences might have contributed to the theories they developed.

Erik Homberger Erikson (1902–1994) was born near Frankfort, Germany, to Danish parents. Before Erik was born, his parents separated and his mother left Denmark to live in Germany. At age 3, Erik became ill, and his mother took him to see a pediatrician named Homberger. Young Erik's mother fell in love with the pediatrician, married him, and named Erik after his new stepfather.

Erik attended primary school from the ages of 6 to 10 and then the gymnasium (high school) from 11 to 18. He studied art and a number of languages rather than science courses such as biology and chemistry. Erik did not like the atmosphere of formal schooling, and this was reflected in his grades. Rather than go to college at age 18, the adolescent Erikson wandered around Europe, keeping a diary about his experiences. After a year of travel through Europe, he returned to Germany and enrolled in art school, became dissatisfied, and enrolled in another. Later he traveled to Florence, Italy. Psychiatrist Robert Coles described Erikson at this time:

> To the Italians he was . . . the young, tall, thin Nordic expatriate with long, blond hair. He wore a corduroy suit and was seen by his family and friends as not odd or "sick" but as a wandering artist who was trying to come to grips with himself, a not unnatural or unusual struggle. (Coles, 1970, p. 15)

The second major theorist whose life we will examine is Jean Piaget. Piaget (1896–1980) was born in Neuchâtel, Switzerland. Jean's father was an intellectual who taught young Jean to think systematically. Jean's mother was also very bright. His father had an air of detachment from his mother, whom Piaget described as prone to frequent outbursts of neurotic behavior.

In his autobiography, Piaget detailed why he chose to study cognitive development rather than social or abnormal development:

> I started to forego playing for serious work very early. Indeed, I have always detested any departure from reality, an attitude which I relate to . . . my mother's poor health. It was this disturbing factor which at the beginning of my studies in psychology made me keenly interested in psychoanalytic and pathological psychology. Though this interest helped me to achieve independence and widen my cultural background, I have never since felt any desire to involve myself deeper in that particular direction, always much preferring the study of normalcy and of the workings of the intellect to that of the tricks of the unconscious. (Piaget, 1952a, p. 238)

These excerpts from Erikson's and Piaget's lives illustrate how personal experiences might influence the direction in which a particular theorist goes. Erikson's own wanderings and search for self contributed to his theory of identity development, and Piaget's intellectual experiences with his parents and schooling contributed to his emphasis on cognitive development.

John W. Santrock

THEORY AND THE SCIENTIFIC METHOD

According to nineteenth-century French mathematician Henri Poincaré, "Science is built of facts the way a house is built of bricks, but an accumulation of facts is no more science than a pile of bricks a house." Science *does* depend on the raw material of facts or data, as Poincaré indicated, child development's theories are more than just facts.

A **theory** *is a coherent set of ideas that helps explain data and make predictions.* A theory contains **hypotheses**, *assumptions that can be tested to determine their accuracy.* For example, a theory about children's aggression would explain our observations of aggressive children and predict why children become aggressive. We might predict that children become aggressive because of the coercive interchanges they experience and observe in their families. This prediction would help direct our observations by telling us to look for coercive interchanges in families.

The **scientific method** *is an approach that can be used to discover accurate information about behavior and development that includes the following steps: identify and analyze the problem, collect data, draw conclusions, and revise theories.* For example, suppose you decide that you want to help aggressive children control their aggression. You *identify a problem*, which does not seem like a difficult task. However, as part of the first step, you need to go beyond a general description of the problem by isolating, analyzing, narrowing, and focusing on what you hope to investigate. What specific strategies do you want to use to reduce children's aggression? Do you want to look at only one strategy, or several strategies? What aspect of aggression do you want to study—its biological, cognitive, or socioemotional characteristics? Gerald Patterson and his colleagues (Patterson, 1991; Patterson, Capaldi, & Bank, 1991) argue that parents' failure to teach reasonable levels of compliance sets in motion coercive inter-

Researchers use the scientific method to obtain accurate information about children's behavior and development. Data collection is part of the scientific method, demonstrated here by a researcher conducting a study of infant development.

changes with family members. In this first step in the scientific method, a problem is identified and analyzed.

After you have identified and analyzed the problem, the next step is to *collect information (data)*. Psychologists observe behavior and draw inferences about thoughts and emotions. For example, in the investigation of children's aggression, you might observe how effectively parents teach reasonable compliance levels to their children and the extent to which coercive exchanges take place among family members.

Truth is arrived at by the painstaking process of eliminating the untrue.

—**Arthur Conan Doyle**

Once data have been collected, psychologists use *statistical procedures* to understand the meaning of quantitative data. They then try to *draw conclusions*. In the investigation of children's aggression, statistics would help you determine whether your observations were due to chance. After data have been collected, psychologists compare their findings with what others have discovered about the same issue.

The final step in the scientific method is *revising theory*. Psychologists have generated a number of theories about children's development; they also have theorized about why children become aggressive. Data such as those collected by Patterson and his colleagues force us to study existing theories of aggression to see if they are accurate. Over the years, some theories of children's development have been discarded and others revised. Theories are an integral part of understanding the nature of children's development. They will be woven through our discussion of children's development in the remainder of the text.

THEORIES OF CHILD DEVELOPMENT

We will briefly explore five major theoretical perspectives on child development: psychoanalytic, cognitive, behavioral/social learning, ethological, and ecological. You will read more in-depth portrayals of these theories at different points in later chapters in the book.

The diversity of theories makes understanding children's development a challenging undertaking. Just when you think one theory correctly explains children's development, another theory crops up and makes you rethink your earlier conclusion. To keep from getting frustrated, remember that children's development is a complex, multifaceted topic, and no single theory has been able to account for all its aspects. Each theory has contributed an important piece to the child development puzzle. Although the theories sometimes disagree about certain aspects of children's development, much of their information is *complementary* rather than contradictory. Together the various theories let us see the total landscape of children's development in all its richness.

Psychoanalytic Theories

Psychoanalytic theorists describe development as primarily unconscious—that is, beyond awareness—and as heavily colored by emotion. Psychoanalytic theorists believe that behavior is merely a surface characteristic and that, to truly understand development, we have to analyze the symbolic meanings of behavior and the deep inner workings of the mind. Psychoanalytic theorists also stress that early experiences with parents extensively shape our development. These characteristics are highlighted in the main psychoanalytic theory, that of Sigmund Freud.

Sigmund Freud, the pioneering architect of psychoanalytic theory.

The passions are at once tempters and chastisers. As tempters, they come with garlands of flowers on the brows of youth; as chastisers, they appear with wreaths of snakes on the forehead of deformity. They are angels of light in their delusion; they are fiends of torment in their inflictions.

—Henry Giles

Freud's Theory

Freud (1856–1939) developed his ideas about psychoanalytic theory from work with mental patients. He was a medical doctor who specialized in neurology. He spent most of his years in Vienna, though he moved to London near the end of his career because of the Nazis' anti-Semitism. To further evaluate Freud's life in Vienna, refer to Critical Thinking About Children's Development.

Freud (1917) believed that personality has three structures: the id, the ego, and the superego. The **id** *is the Freudian structure of personality that consists of instincts, which are an individual's reservoir of psychic energy.* In Freud's view, the id is totally unconscious; it has no contact with reality. As children experience the demands and constraints of reality, a new structure of personality emerges—the **ego,** *the Freudian structure of personality that deals with the demands of reality.* The ego is called the executive branch of personality because it uses reasoning to make decisions. The id and the ego have no morality. They do not take into account whether something is right or wrong. The **superego** *is the Freudian structure of personality that is the moral branch of personality.* The superego takes into account whether something is right or wrong. Think of the superego as what we often refer to as

Arnold Schwarzenegger

If Sigmund Freud were alive today, what reactions do you think he might have to the level of violence and sexuality in contemporary action films? Conversely, how do you think Schwarzenegger might have fared in

Victorian Vienna

Freud's Victorian Viennese culture? Consideration of these questions sensitizes you to the importance of *identifying the sociohistorical, cultural factors that influence behavior.*

our "conscience." You probably are beginning to sense that both the id and the superego make life rough for the ego. Your ego might say, "I will have sex only occasionally and be sure to take the proper precautions because I don't want the intrusion of a child in the development of my career." However, your id is saying, "I want to be satisfied; sex is pleasurable." Your superego is at work too: "I feel guilty about having sex."

Remember that Freud considered personality to be like an iceberg; most of personality exists below our level of awareness, just as the massive part of an iceberg is beneath the surface of the water. Figure 2.1 illustrates this analogy.

How does the ego resolve the conflict between its demands for reality, the wishes of the id, and constraints of the superego? Through **defense mechanisms,** *the psychoanalytic term for unconscious methods the ego uses to distort reality, thereby protecting it from anxiety.* In Freud's view, the conflicting demands of the personality structures produce anxiety. For example, when the ego blocks the pleasurable pursuits of the id, inner anxiety is felt. This diffuse, distressed state develops when the ego senses that the id is going to cause harm to the individual. The anxiety alerts the ego to resolve the conflict by means of defense mechanisms.

Repression *is the most powerful and pervasive defense mechanism, according to Freud; it works to push unacceptable id impulses out of awareness and back into the unconscious mind.* Repression is the foundation from which all other defense mechanisms work; the goal of every defense mechanism is to repress or push threatening impulses out of awareness. Freud said that our early childhood experiences, many of which he believed were sexually laden, are

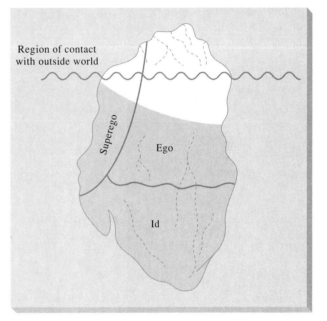

FIGURE 2.1

Conscious and Unconscious Processes: The Iceberg Analogy
This rather odd-looking diagram illustrates Freud's theory that most of the important personality processes occur below the level of conscious awareness. In examining people's conscious thoughts and their behaviors, we can see some reflections of the ego and the superego. Whereas the ego and superego are partly conscious and partly unconscious, the primitive id is the unconscious, totally submerged part of the iceberg.

too threatening and stressful for us to deal with consciously. We reduce the anxiety of this conflict through the defense mechanism of repression.

THE FAR SIDE   By GARY LARSON

"So, Mr. Fenton . . . Let's begin with your mother."

THE FAR SIDE cartoon by Gary Larson is reprinted by permission
of Chronicle Features, San Francisco, CA. All rights reserved.

As Freud listened to, probed, and analyzed his patients, he became convinced that their problems were the result of experiences early in life. Freud believed that we go through five stages of psychosexual development and that, at each stage of development, we experience pleasure in one part of the body more than in others. **Erogenous zones** *are, in Freud's theory, the parts of the body that have especially strong pleasure-giving qualities at each stage of development.*

Freud thought that the adult personality is determined by the way conflicts between the early sources of pleasure—the mouth, the anus, and then the genitals—and the demands of reality are resolved. When these conflicts are not resolved, the individual may become fixated at a particular stage of development. For example, a parent might wean a child too early, be too strict in toilet training, punish the child for masturbation, or smother the child with warmth.

The **oral stage** *is the first Freudian stage of development, occurring during the first 18 months of life, in which the infant's pleasure centers around the mouth.* Chewing, sucking, and biting are the chief sources of pleasure. These actions reduce tension in the infant.

The **anal stage** *is the second Freudian stage of development, occurring between 1½ and 3 years of age, in which the child's greatest pleasure involves the anus or the eliminative functions associated with it.* In Freud's view, the exercise of anal muscles reduces tension.

The **phallic stage** *is the third Freudian stage of development, which occurs between the ages of 3 and 6; its name comes from the Latin word* phallus, *which means "penis."* During the phallic stage, pleasure focuses on the genitals as the child discovers that self-manipulation is enjoyable.

In Freud's view, the phallic stage has a special importance in personality development because it is during this period that the Oedipus complex appears. This name comes from Greek mythology, in which Oedipus, the son of the King of Thebes, unwittingly kills his father and marries his mother. The **Oedipus complex,** *according to Freudian theory, is the young child's development of an intense desire to replace the same-sex parent and enjoy the affections of the opposite-sex parent.*

How is the Oedipus complex resolved? At about 5 to 6 years of age, children recognize that their same-sex parent might punish them for their incestuous wishes. To reduce this conflict, the child identifies with the same-sex parent, striving to be like him or her. If the conflict is not resolved, though, the individual may become fixated at the phallic stage.

The **latency stage** *is the fourth Freudian stage of development, which occurs between approximately 6 years of age and puberty; the child represses all interest in sexuality and develops social and intellectual skills.* This activity channels much of the child's energy into emotionally safe areas and helps the child forget the highly stressful conflicts of the phallic stage.

The **genital stage** *is the fifth and final Freudian stage of development, occurring from puberty on. The genital stage is a time of sexual reawakening; the source of sexual pleasure now becomes someone outside of the family.* Freud believed that unresolved conflicts with parents reemerge during adolescence. When resolved, the individual is capable of developing a mature love relationship and functioning independently as an adult.

Freud's theory has undergone significant revisions by a number of psychoanalytic theorists. Many contemporary psychoanalytic theorists place less emphasis on sexual instincts and more emphasis on cultural experiences as determinants of an individual's development. Unconscious thought remains a central theme, but most contemporary psychoanalysts believe that conscious thought makes up more of the iceberg than Freud envisioned. Next, we will explore the ideas of an important revisionist of Freud's ideas—Erik Erikson.

Erik Erikson with his wife, Joan, who is an artist. Erikson generated one of the most important developmental theories of the twentieth century.

Erikson's Theory

Erik Erikson recognized Freud's contributions but believed that Freud misjudged some important dimensions of human development. For one, Erikson (1950, 1968) says we develop in *psychosocial stages,* in contrast to Freud's psychosexual stages. For another, Erikson emphasizes developmental change throughout the human life span, whereas Freud argued that our basic personality is shaped in the first 5 years of life. In Erikson's theory, eight stages of development unfold as we go through the life span. Each stage consists of a unique developmental task that confronts individuals with a crisis that must be faced. For Erikson, this crisis is not a catastrophe but a turning point of increased vulnerability and enhanced potential. The more an individual resolves the crises successfully, the healthier development will be.

Trust versus mistrust *is Erikson's first psychosocial stage, which is experienced in the first year of life. A sense of trust requires a feeling of physical comfort and a minimal amount of fear and apprehension about the future.* Trust in infancy sets the stage for a lifelong expectation that the world will be a good and pleasant place to live.

Autonomy versus shame and doubt *is Erikson's second stage of development, occurring in late infancy and toddlerhood (1–3 years). After gaining trust in their caregivers, infants begin to discover that their behavior is their own. They start to assert their sense of independence or autonomy. They realize their will.* If infants are restrained too much or punished too harshly, they are likely to develop a sense of shame and doubt.

Initiative versus guilt *is Erikson's third stage of development, occurring during the preschool years. As preschool children encounter a widening social world, they are challenged more than when they were infants.* Active, purposeful behavior is needed to cope with these challenges. Children are asked to assume responsibility for their bodies, their behavior, their toys, and their pets. Developing a sense of responsibility increases initiative. Uncomfortable guilt feelings may arise, though, if the child is irresponsible and is made to feel too anxious. Erikson has a positive outlook on this stage. He believes that most guilt is quickly compensated for by a sense of accomplishment.

Industry versus inferiority *is Erikson's fourth developmental stage, occurring approximately in the elementary school years. Children's initiative brings them in contact with a wealth of new experiences. As they move into middle and late childhood, they direct their energy toward mastering knowledge and intellectual skills.* At no other time is the child more enthusiastic about learning than at the end of early childhood's period of expansive imagination. The danger in the elementary school years is the development of a sense of inferiority—of feeling incompetent and unproductive. Erikson believes that teachers have a special responsibility for children's development of industry. Teachers should "mildly but firmly coerce children into the adventure of finding out that one can learn to accomplish things which one would never have thought of by oneself" (Erikson, 1968, p. 127).

Identity versus identity confusion *is Erikson's fifth developmental stage, which individuals experience during the adolescent years. At this time, individuals are faced with finding out who they are, what they are all about, and where they are going in life.* Adolescents are confronted with many new roles and adult statuses—vocational and romantic, for example. Parents need to allow adolescents to explore many different roles and different paths within a particular role. If the adolescent explores such roles in a healthy manner and arrives at a positive path to follow in life, then a positive identity will be achieved. If an identity is pushed on the adolescent by parents, if the adolescent does not adequately explore many roles, and if a positive future path is not defined, then identity confusion reigns.

Intimacy versus isolation *is Erikson's sixth developmental stage, which individuals experience during the early adulthood years. At this time, individuals face the developmental task of forming intimate relationships with others.* Erikson describes intimacy as finding oneself yet losing oneself in another. If the young adult forms healthy friendships and an intimate close relationship with another individual, intimacy will be achieved; if not, isolation will result.

Generativity versus stagnation *is Erikson's seventh developmental stage, which individuals experience during middle adulthood. A chief concern is to assist the younger generation in developing and leading useful lives*—this is what Erikson means by *generativity.* The feeling of having done nothing to help the next generation is *stagnation.*

Integrity versus despair
is Erikson's eighth and final developmental stage, which individuals experience during late adulthood. In the later years of life, we look back and evaluate what we have done with our lives. Through many different routes, the older person may have developed a positive outlook in most or all of the previous stages of development. If so, the retrospective glances will reveal a picture of a life well spent, and the person will feel a sense of satisfaction—integrity will be achieved. If the older adult resolved many of the earlier stages negatively, the retrospective glances likely will yield doubt or gloom—the despair Erikson talks about.

> *Each of us stands at the heart of the earth pierced through by a ray of sunlight; and suddenly it is evening.*
> —**Salvatore Quasimodo**

Erikson does not believe that the proper solution to a stage crisis is always completely positive in nature. Some exposure or commitment to the negative end of the person's bipolar conflict is sometimes inevitable—you cannot trust all people under all circumstances and survive, for example. Nonetheless, in the healthy solution to a stage crisis, the positive resolution dominates. A summary of Erikson's stages is presented in figure 2.2.

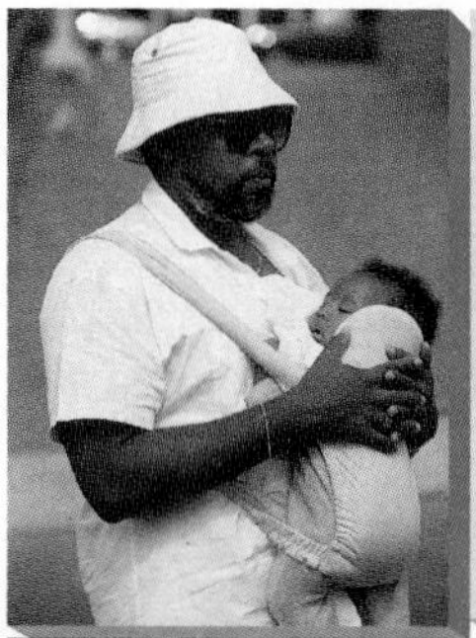

Erikson's stages	Developmental period	Characteristics
Trust versus mistrust	Infancy (first year)	A sense of trust requires a feeling of physical comfort and a minimal amount of fear about the future. Infants' basic needs are met by responsive, sensitive caregivers.
Autonomy versus shame and doubt	Infancy (second year)	After gaining trust in their caregivers, infants start to discover that they have a will of their own. They assert their sense of autonomy, or independence. They realize their will. If infants are restrained too much or punished too harshly, they are likely to develop a sense of shame and doubt.
Initiative versus guilt	Early childhood (preschool years, ages 3–5)	As preschool children encounter a widening social world, they are challenged more and need to develop more purposeful behavior to cope with these challenges. Children are now asked to assume more responsibility. Uncomfortable guilt feelings may arise, though, if the children are irresponsible and are made to feel too anxious.
Industry versus inferiority	Middle and late childhood (elementary school years, 6 years–puberty)	At no other time are children more enthusiastic than at the end of early childhood's period of expansive imagination. As children move into the elementary school years, they direct their energy toward mastering knowledge and intellectual skills. The danger at this stage involves feeling incompetent and unproductive.

FIGURE 2.2

Erikson's Stages of Childhood

Cognitive Theories

Whereas psychoanalytic theories stress the importance of children's unconscious thoughts, cognitive theories emphasize their conscious thoughts. Two important cognitive theories are Piaget's cognitive development theory and information processing.

Piaget's theory will be covered in greater detail later in this book when we discuss cognitive development in infancy, early childhood, middle and late childhood, and adolescence. Here we briefly present the main ideas of his theory.

> *Man is a reed, the weakest in nature; but he is a thinking reed.*
> —**Pascal**

John W. Santrock

Erikson's stages	Developmental period	Characteristics
Identity versus identity confusion	Adolescence (10 to 20 years)	Individuals are faced with finding out who they are, what they are all about, and where they are going in life. An important dimension is the exploration of alternative solutions to roles. Career exploration is important.
Intimacy versus isolation	Early adulthood (20s, 30s)	Individuals face the developmental task of forming intimate relationships with others. Erikson described intimacy as finding oneself yet losing oneself in another person.
Generativity versus stagnation	Middle adulthood (40s, 50s)	A chief concern is to assist the younger generation in developing and leading useful lives.
Integrity versus despair	Late adulthood (60s –)	Individuals look back and evaluate what they have done with their lives. The retrospective glances can either be positive (integrity) or negative (despair).

Piaget's Theory

The famous Swiss psychologist Jean Piaget stressed that children actively construct their own cognitive worlds; information is not just poured into their minds from the environment. Piaget believed that children adapt their thinking to include new ideas.

Two processes underlie the individual's construction of the world: organization and adaptation. To make sense of our world, we organize our experiences. For example, we separate important ideas from less important ideas. We connect one idea to another. But not only do we organize our observations and experiences, we also *adapt* our thinking to include new ideas because additional information furthers understanding. Piaget (1954) believed that we adapt in two ways: assimilation and accommodation.

Assimilation *occurs when individuals incorporate new information into their existing knowledge.* **Accommodation** *occurs when individuals adjust to new information.* Consider a circumstance in which a 9-year-old girl is given a hammer and nails to hang a picture on the wall. She has never used a hammer, but from observation and vicarious experience she realizes that a hammer is an object to be held, that it is swung by the handle to hit the nail, and that it is usually swung a number of times. Recognizing each of these things, she fits her behavior into this information she already has (assimilation). However, the hammer is heavy, so she holds it near the top. She swings too hard and the nail bends, so she adjusts the pressure of her strikes. These adjustments reveal her ability to alter her conception of the world slightly (accommodation).

Piaget thought that assimilation and accommodation operate even in the very young infant's life. Newborns reflexively suck everything that touches their lips (assimilation), but after several months of experience, they construct their understanding of the world differently. Some objects, such as fingers and the mother's breast, can be sucked, and others, such as fuzzy blankets, should not be sucked (accommodation).

Piaget also believed that we go through four stages in understanding the world. Each of the stages is age-related and consists of distinct ways of thinking. Remember, it is the *different* way of understanding the world that makes one stage more advanced than another; knowing *more* information does not make the child's thinking more advanced in the Piagetian view. This is what Piaget meant when he said the child's cognition is *qualitatively* different

Jean Piaget, the famous Swiss developmental psychologist, changed the way we think about the development of children's minds. For Piaget, a child's mental development is a continuous creation of increasingly complex forms.

in one stage compared to another. What are Piaget's four stages of cognitive development like?

The **sensorimotor stage,** *which lasts from birth to about 2 years of age, is the first Piagetian stage. In this stage, infants construct an understanding of the world by coordinating sensory experiences (such as seeing and hearing) with physical, motoric actions—hence the term* sensorimotor. At the beginning of this stage, newborns have little more than reflexive patterns with which to work. At the end of the stage, 2-year-olds have complex sensorimotor patterns and are beginning to operate with primitive symbols.

The **preoperational stage,** *which lasts from approximately 2 to 7 years of age, is the second Piagetian stage. In this stage, children begin to represent the world with words, images, and drawings.* Symbolic thought goes beyond simple connections of sensory information and physical action.

However, although preschool children can symbolically represent the world, according to Piaget, they still lack the ability to perform *operations,* the Piagetian term for internalized mental actions that allow children to do mentally what they previously did physically.

The **concrete operational stage,** *which lasts from approximately 7 to 11 years of age, is the third Piagetian stage. In this stage, children can perform operations, and logical reasoning replaces intuitive thought as long as reasoning can be applied to specific or concrete examples.* For instance, concrete operational thinkers cannot imagine the steps necessary to complete an algebraic equation, which is too abstract for thinking at this stage of development.

The **formal operational stage,** *which appears between the ages of 11 and 15, is the fourth and final Piagetian stage. In this stage, individuals move beyond concrete experiences and think in abstract and more logical terms.* As part of thinking more abstractly, adolescents develop images of ideal circumstances. They might think about what an ideal parent is like and compare their parents with this ideal standard. They begin to entertain possibilities for the future and are fascinated with what they can be. In solving problems, formal operational thinkers are more systematic, developing hypotheses about why something is happening the way it is, then testing these hypotheses in a deductive fashion. Piaget's stages are summarized in table 2.1.

Information Processing

Information processing *involves how individuals process information about their world—how information enters the mind, how it is stored and transformed, and how it is retrieved to perform such complex activities as problem solving and reasoning.* A simple model of information processing is shown in figure 2.3.

Cognition begins when children detect information from the world through their sensory and perceptual processes. Then children store, transform, and retrieve the information through the processes of memory. Notice in our model that information can flow back and forth between memory and perceptual processes. For example, children are good at remembering the faces they see, yet their memory of a person's face may differ from the way the person actually looks. Keep in mind that our information-processing model is a simple one, designed to illustrate the main cognitive processes and their interrelations. We could have drawn other arrows—between memory and language, between thinking and sensory and perceptual processes, and between language and sensory and perceptual processes, for example. Also, it is important to know that the boxes in figure 2.3 do not represent sharp, distinct stages in processing information. There is continuity and flow between the cognitive processes, as well as overlap.

Behavioral and Social Learning Theories

Behaviorists believe we should examine only what can be directly observed and measured. At approximately the

TABLE 2.1
Piaget's Stages of Cognitive Development

Stage	Description	Age Range
Sensorimotor	An infant progresses from reflexive, instinctual action at birth to the beginning of symbolic thought. The infant constructs an understanding of the world by coordinating sensory experiences with physical actions.	Birth to 2 years
Preoperational	The child begins to represent the world with words and images; these words and images reflect increased symbolic thinking and go beyond the connection of sensory information and physical action.	2 to 7 years
Concrete operational	The child can now reason logically about concrete events and classify objects into different sets.	7 to 11 years
Formal operational	The adolescent reasons in more abstract and logical ways. Thought is more idealistic.	11 to 15 years

FIGURE 2.3

A Model of Cognition

same time that Freud was interpreting his patients' unconscious minds through early childhood experiences, behaviorists such as Ivan Pavlov and John B. Watson were conducting detailed observations of behavior in controlled laboratory circumstances. Out of the behavioral tradition grew the belief that development is observable behavior, learned through experience with the environment. The two versions of the behavioral approach that are prominent today are the view of B. F. Skinner and social learning theory.

Skinner's Behaviorism

Behaviorism *emphasizes the scientific study of observable behavioral responses and their environmental determinants.* In Skinner's behaviorism, the mind, conscious or unconscious, is not needed to explain behavior and development. For him, development is behavior. For example, observations of Sam reveal that his behavior is shy, achievement-oriented, and caring. Why is Sam's behavior this way? For Skinner, rewards and punishments in Sam's environment have shaped him into a shy, achievement-oriented, and caring person. Because of interactions with family members, friends, teachers, and others, Sam has *learned* to behave in this fashion.

Since behaviorists believe that development is learned and often changes according to environmental experiences, it follows that rearranging experiences can change development. For behaviorists, shy behavior can be transformed into outgoing behavior; aggressive behavior can be shaped into docile behavior; lethargic, boring behavior can be turned into enthusiastic, interesting behavior.

Social Learning Theory

Some psychologists believe that the behaviorists basically are right when they say development is learned and is influenced strongly by environmental experiences. However, they believe that Skinner went too far in declaring that cognition is unimportant in understanding development. **Social**

B. F. Skinner was a tinkerer who liked to make new gadgets. The younger of his two daughters, Deborah, was raised in Skinner's enclosed Air-Crib, which he invented because he wanted to control her environment completely. The Air-Crib was soundproofed and temperature controlled. Some critics accused Skinner of monstrous experimentation with his children; however, the early controlled environment has not had any noticeable harmful effects. Debbie, shown here as a child with her parents, is currently a successful artist, is married, and lives in London.

learning theory *is the view of psychologists who emphasize behavior, environment, and cognition as the key factors in development.*

The social learning theorists say we are not like mindless robots, responding mechanically to others in our environment. Neither are we like weather vanes, behaving like a Communist in the presence of a Communist or like a John Bircher in the presence of a John Bircher. Rather, we think, reason, imagine, plan, expect, interpret, believe, value, and compare. When others try to control us, our values and beliefs allow us to resist their control.

American psychologists Albert Bandura (1977, 1986, 1994) and Walter Mischel (1973, 1994) are the main architects of social learning theory's contemporary version, which Mischel (1973) labeled *cognitive* social learning theory. Both Bandura and Mischel believe that cognitive processes are important mediators of environment-behavior connections. Bandura's research program has focused heavily on observational learning, learning that occurs through observing what others do. Observational learning is also referred to as imitation or modeling. What is *cognitive* about observational learning in Bandura's view? Bandura (1925–) believes that people cognitively represent the behavior of others and then sometimes adopt this behavior themselves. For example, a young boy might observe his father's aggressive outbursts

Albert Bandura has been one of the leading architects of the contemporary version of social learning theory—cognitive social learning theory.

Drawing by Opie; © 1978 The New Yorker Magazine, Inc.

and hostile interchanges with people; when observed with his peers, the young boy's style of interaction is highly aggressive, showing the same characteristics as his father's behavior. A girl might adopt the dominant and sarcastic style of her teacher. When observed interacting with her younger brother, she says, "You are so slow. How can you do this work so slow?" Social learning theorists believe that children acquire a wide range of such behaviors, thoughts, and feelings through observing others' behavior. These observations form an important part of children's development.

FIGURE 2.4

Imprinting

Konrad Lorenz, a pioneering student of animal behavior, is followed through the water by three imprinted greylag geese. Lorenz described imprinting as rapid, innate learning within a critical period that involves attachment to the first moving object seen. For goslings the critical period is the first 36 hours after birth.

Social learning theories also differ from Skinner's behavioral view by emphasizing that children can regulate and control their own behavior. For example, another girl who observes her teacher behaving in a dominant and sarcastic way toward her students finds the behavior distasteful and goes out of her way to be encouraging and supportive toward her younger brother. Someone tries to persuade an adolescent to join a particular club at school. The adolescent thinks about the offer to join the club, considers her own interests and beliefs, and makes the decision not to join. The adolescent's *cognition* (thoughts) led her to control her own behavior and resist environmental influence in this instance.

Like the behavioral approach of Skinner, the social learning approach emphasizes the importance of empirical research in studying children's development. This research focuses on the processes that explain children's development—the social and cognitive factors that influence what children are like (Mayer & Sutton, 1996).

Ethological Theories

Sensitivity to different kinds of experience varies over the life span. The presence or absence of certain experiences at particular times in the life span influences individuals well beyond the time they first occur. Ethologists believe that most psychologists underestimate the importance of these special time frames in early development and the powerful roles that evolution and biological foundations play in development (Hinde, 1992).

Ethology emerged as an important view because of the work of European zoologists, especially Konrad Lorenz (1903–1989). **Ethology** *stresses that behavior is strongly influenced by biology, is tied to evolution, and is characterized by critical or sensitive periods.*

Working mostly with greylag geese, Lorenz (1965) studied a behavior pattern that was considered to be programmed within the bird's genes (see figure 2.4). A

THE FAR SIDE   By GARY LARSON

When imprinting studies go awry . . .

newly hatched gosling seemed to be born with the instinct to follow its mother. Observations showed that the gosling was capable of such behavior as soon as it hatched. Lorenz proved that it was incorrect to assume that such behavior was programmed in the animal. In a remarkable set of experiments, Lorenz separated the eggs laid by one goose into two groups. One group he returned to the goose to be hatched by her; the other group

---

was hatched in an incubator. The goslings in the first group performed as predicted; they followed their mother as soon as they hatched. However, those in the second group, which saw Lorenz when they first hatched, followed him everywhere, as though he were their mother. Lorenz marked the goslings and then placed both groups under a box. Mother goose and "mother" Lorenz stood aside as the box was lifted. Each group of goslings went directly to its "mother". Based on such observations, Lorenz developed the ethological concept of **imprinting,** *rapid, innate learning within a limited critical period of time that involves attachment to the first moving object seen.*

The ethological view of Lorenz and the European zoologists forced American developmental psychologists to recognize the importance of the biological basis of behavior. However, the research and theorizing of ethology still seemed to lack some ingredients that would elevate it to the ranks of the other theories discussed so far in this chapter. In particular, there was little or nothing in the classical ethological view about the nature of social relationships across the human life span, something that any major theory of development must explain. Also, its concept of **critical period,** *a fixed time period very early in development during which certain behaviors optimally emerge,* seemed to be overdrawn. Classical ethological theory was weak in stimulating studies with humans. Recent expansion of the ethological view has improved its status as a viable developmental perspective.

Like behaviorists, ethologists are careful observers of behavior. Unlike behaviorists, ethologists believe that laboratories are not good settings for observing behavior; rather, they meticulously observe behavior in its natural surroundings, in homes, playgrounds, neighborhoods, schools, hospitals, and so on.

Ecological Theory

Ethological theory places a strong emphasis on the biological foundations of children's development. In contrast to ethological theory, Urie Bronfenbrenner (1917–   ) has proposed a strong environmental view of children's development that is receiving increased attention. **Ecological theory** *is Bronfenbrenner's sociocultural view of development, which consists of five environmental systems ranging from the fine-grained inputs of direct interactions with social agents to the broad-based inputs of culture. The five systems in Bronfenbrenner's ecological theory are the*

Urie Bronfenbrenner (above with his grandson) has developed ecological theory, a perspective that is receiving increased attention. His theory emphasizes the importance of both micro and macro dimensions of the environment in which the child lives.

microsystem, mesosystem, exosystem, macrosystem, and chronosystem. We will consider each in turn. Bronfenbrenner's (1979, 1986, 1995) ecological model is shown in figure 2.5.

The **microsystem,** *in Bronfenbrenner's ecological theory, is the setting in which an individual lives. This context includes the person's family, peers, school, and neighborhood.* It is in the microsystem that most of the direct interactions with social agents take place—with parents, peers, and teachers, for example. The individual is not viewed as a passive recipient of experiences in these settings, but as someone who helps construct the settings. Bronfenbrenner points out that most of the research on environmental influences has focused on microsystems.

The **mesosystem,** *in Bronfenbrenner's ecological theory, involves relationships between microsystems or connections between contexts.* Examples are the relation of family experiences to school experiences, school experiences to church experiences, and family experiences to peer experiences. For instance, a boy whose parents have rejected him may have difficulty developing positive relations with teachers. Developmentalists increasingly believe it is important to observe behavior in multiple settings—such as in family, peer, and school contexts—to obtain a more complete picture of an individual's development (Booth & Dunn, 1996).

The **exosystem,** *in Bronfenbrenner's ecological theory, is involved when experiences in a social setting in which an individual does not have an active role influence what that person experiences in an immediate context.* For example, work

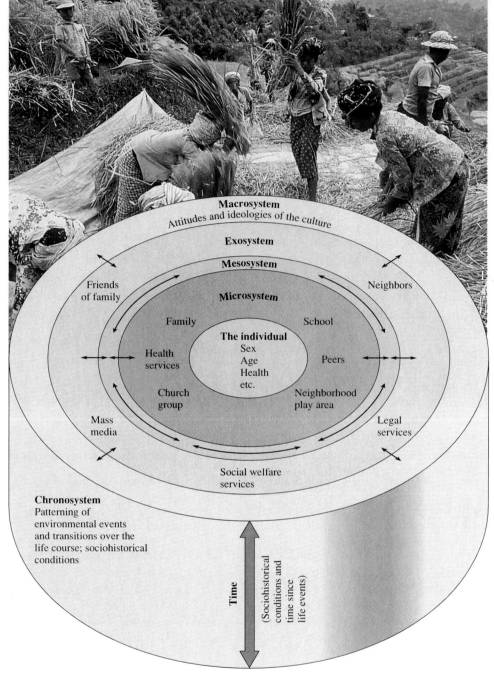

The **macrosystem,** *in Bronfenbrenner's ecological theory, involves the culture in which individuals live.* Remember from chapter 1 that *culture* refers to the behavior patterns, beliefs, and all other products of a group of people that are passed on from generation to generation. Remember also that *cross-cultural studies*—comparisons of one culture with one or more other cultures—provide information about the universality of children's development.

The **chronosystem,** *in Bronfenbrenner's ecological theory, involves the patterning of environmental events and transitions over the life course and sociohistorical circumstances.* For example, in studying the effects of divorce on children, researchers have found that the negative effects often peak in the first year after the divorce and that the effects are more negative for sons than for daughters (Hetherington, 1995; Hetherington, Cox, & Cox, 1982). By 2 years after the divorce, family interaction is less chaotic and more stable. With regard to sociocultural circumstances, girls today are much more likely to be encouraged to pursue a career than they were 20 to 30 years ago. In ways such as these, the chronosystem has a powerful impact on children's lives.

Developmental Analogies

Many analogies (which often reflect theories) have been used to describe the nature of development, including the analogies of (1) a staircase, (2) a seedling in a greenhouse, and (3) a strand of ivy in a forest. The staircase analogy is directly related to stage theories of development, such as the theories of Freud, Erikson, and Piaget. Recently, cognitive developmentalist Robbie Case (1992) even titled a book *The Mind's Staircase* to emphasize the staircase-like nature of children's cognitive development.

FIGURE 2.5

Bronfenbrenner's Ecological Theory of Development
Bronfenbrenner's ecological theory consists of five environmental systems: microsystem, mesosystem, exosystem, macrosystem, and chronosystem.

experiences may affect a woman's relationship with her husband and their child. The woman may receive a promotion that requires more travel, which might increase marital conflict and change patterns of parent-child interaction. Another example of an exosystem is a city government, which is responsible for the quality of parks, recreation centers, and library facilities for children and adolescents.

a. Staircase   b. Seedling in a greenhouse   c. Strand of ivy in a forest

FIGURE 2.6

Analogies for Development
Three developmental analogies are the analogies of (*a*) a staircase, (*b*) a seedling in a greenhouse, and (*c*) a strand of ivy in a forest.

The analogy of the seedling in a greenhouse has been popular for many years in developmental psychology (Kagan, 1992). In this view, the individual is acted upon by the environment (according to the behavioral perspective of Skinner) or the child acts on the world (in Piaget's perspective). This analogy emphasizes the individual as the primary unit of development. Thus, Piaget's theory has characteristics of both the staircase analogy and the greenhouse seedling analogy.

The contemporary analogy of the strand of ivy in a forest stresses the many different paths development can take and the importance of contextual factors in that development (Kagan, 1992). In this analogy, development is not portrayed as consistently stagelike as in the staircase analogy, and the individual is not seen as a solitary scientist as in Piaget's view. An important dimension of this analogy is its emphasis on the individual's reciprocal encounters with others and the changing symbolic construction of these relationships. Bronfenbrenner's environmental, contextual theory is allied with the strand of ivy analogy.

Which of these analogies best reflects the way development actually occurs? As with virtually all theories and analogies, each has its adherents, although the ivy analogy

has become increasingly popular in recent years. A visual image of the three analogies is shown in figure 2.6.

An Eclectic Theoretical Orientation

An **eclectic theoretical orientation** *does not follow any one theoretical approach, but rather selects and uses from each theory whatever is considered the best in it.* No single theory described in this chapter is indomitable or capable of explaining entirely the rich complexity of child development. Each of the theories has made important contributions to our understanding of children's development, but none provides a complete description and explanation. Psychoanalytic theory best explains the unconscious mind. Erikson's theory best describes the changes that occur in adult development. Piaget's theory is the most complete description of children's cognitive development. The behavioral and social learning and ecological theories have been the most adept at examining the environmental determinants of development. The ethological theories have made us aware of biology's role and the importance of sensitive periods in development. It is important to recognize that, although theories are helpful guides, relying on a single theory to explain children's development is probably a mistake.

John W. Santrock

TABLE 2.2

A Comparison of Theories and the Issues and Methods in Child Development

Theory	Issues and Methods			
	Continuity/Discontinuity, Early Versus Later Experiences	*Biological and Environmental Factors*	*Importance of Cognition*	*Research Methods*
Psychoanalytic	Discontinuity between stages—continuity between early experiences and later development; early experiences very important; later changes in development emphasized in Erikson's theory	Freud's biological determination interacting with early family experiences; Erikson's more balanced biological-cultural interaction perspective	Emphasized, but in the form of unconscious thought	Clinical interviews, unstructured personality tests, psychohistorical analyses of lives
Cognitive	Discontinuity between stages—continuity between early experiences and later development in Piaget's theory; has not been important to information-processing psychologists	Piaget's emphasis on interaction and adaptation; environment provides the setting for cognitive structures to develop; information-processing view has not addressed this issue extensively, but mainly emphasizes biological-environmental interaction	The primary determinant of behavior	Interviews and observations
Behavioral and social learning	Continuity (no stages); experience at all points of development important	Environment viewed as the cause of behavior in both views	Strongly deemphasized in the behavioral approach but an important mediator in social learning	Observation, especially laboratory observation
Ethological	Discontinuity but no stages; critical or sensitive periods emphasized; early experiences very important	Strong biological view	Not emphasized	Observation in natural settings
Ecological	Little attention to continuity/discontinuity; change emphasized more than stability	Strong environmental view	Not emphasized	Varied methods; especially stresses importance of collecting data in different social contexts

An attempt was made in this chapter to present five theoretical perspectives objectively. The same eclectic orientation will be maintained throughout the book. In this way, you can view the study of children's development as it actually exists—with different theorists making different assumptions, stressing different empirical problems, and using different strategies to discover information.

These theoretical perspectives, along with research issues that were discussed in chapter 1 and methods that will be described shortly, provide a sense of development's scientific nature. Table 2.2 compares the main theoretical perspectives in terms of how they view important developmental issues and the methods they prefer to use when they study children.

At this point we have discussed a number of ideas about the scientific method and theories of child development. A summary of these ideas is presented in concept table 2.1. Next, we explore the methods child developmentalists use to study children, beginning with the measures they use.

METHODOLOGY

Remember that in addition to the development of theories, a critical aspect of improving our knowledge about children's development involves conducting scientific research. In this section we will explore the methods child development researchers use when they conduct scientific research. Our discussion will cover measures, correlational and experimental strategies, and the time span of inquiry.

CONCEPT TABLE 2.1

Theory and the Scientific Method, and Theories of Child Development

Concept	Processes/Related Ideas	Characteristics/Description
Theory and the Scientific Method	Theory	Theories are general beliefs that help us to explain what we observe and make predictions. A good theory has hypotheses, which are assumptions to be tested.
	The scientific method	The scientific method is a series of procedures (identifying and analyzing a problem, collecting data, drawing conclusions, and revising theory) to obtain accurate information.
Theories of Child Development	Psychoanalytic theories	Two important psychoanalytic theories are Freud's and Erikson's. Freud said personality is made up of three structures—id, ego, and superego—and that most of children's thoughts are unconscious. The conflicting demands of children's personality structures produce anxiety. Defense mechanisms, especially repression, protect the child's ego and reduce anxiety. Freud was convinced that problems develop because of early childhood experiences. He said individuals go through five psychosexual stages—oral, anal, phallic, latency, and genital. During the phallic stage, the Oedipus complex is a major source of conflict. Gender-based criticisms of psychoanalytic theory have been made. Erikson developed a theory that emphasizes eight psychosocial stages of development: trust vs. mistrust, autonomy vs. shame and doubt, initiative vs. guilt, industry vs. inferiority, identity vs. identity confusion, intimacy vs. isolation, generativity vs. stagnation, and integrity vs. despair.
	Cognitive theories	Two important cognitive theories are Piaget's cognitive developmental theory and information processing. Piaget said that children are motivated to understand their world and use the processes of organization and adaptation (assimilation, accommodation) to do so. Piaget said children go through four cognitive stages: sensorimotor, preoperational, concrete operational, and formal operational. Information-processing theory is concerned with how individuals process information about their world. It includes how information gets into the child's mind, how it is stored and transformed, and how it is retrieved to allow them to think and solve problems.
	Behavioral and social learning theories	Behaviorism emphasizes that cognition is not important in understanding children's behavior. Development is observed behavior, which is determined by rewards and punishments in the environment, according to B. F. Skinner, a famous behaviorist. Social learning theory, developed by Albert Bandura and others, states that the environment is an important determinant of behavior, but so are cognitive processes. Children have the ability to control their own behavior in the social learning view.
	Ethological theories	Konrad Lorenz was one of the important developers of ethological theory. Ethology emphasizes the biological and evolutionary basis of development. Imprinting and critical periods are key concepts.
	Ecological theory	In Bronfenbrenner's ecological theory, five environmental systems are important: microsystem, mesosystem, exosystem, macrosystem, and chronosystem.
	Developmental analogies	Three such metaphors, reflecting theories, are the metaphors of (1) a staircase, (2) a seedling in a greenhouse, and (3) a strand of ivy in a forest.
	Eclectic theoretical orientation	No single theory can explain the rich, awesome complexity of children's development. Each of the theories has made a different contribution, and it probably is a wise strategy to adopt an eclectic theoretical perspective as we attempt to understand children's development.

John W. Santrock

Measures

Systematic observations can be conducted in a number of ways. For example, we can watch behavior in a laboratory or in a more natural setting such as a school, home, or neighborhood playground. We can question children using interviews and surveys, develop and administer standardized tests, conduct case studies, examine behavior cross-culturally, or carry out physiological research. To help you understand how developmentalists use these methods, we will continue to draw examples from the study of children's aggression.

Observation

Sherlock Holmes chided Watson, "You see but you do not observe." We look at things all the time; however, casually watching a mother and her infant is not scientific observation. Unless you are a trained observer and practice your skills regularly, you might not know what to look for, you might not remember what you saw, what you are looking for might change from one moment to the next, and you might not communicate your observations effectively.

For observations to be effective, we have to know what we are looking for, who we are observing, when and where we will observe, how the observations will be made, and in what form they will be recorded. That is, our observations have to be made in a *systematic* way (Martin, 1996). Consider aggression. Do we want to study verbal or physical aggression, or both? Do we want to study younger or older children, or both? Do we want to evaluate them in a university laboratory, at school, at home, at a playground, or at all of these locations? A common way to record observations is to write them down, using shorthand or symbols. However, tape recorders, video cameras, special coding sheets, one-way mirrors, and computers are increasingly used to make observations more efficient (Roberts, 1993; Rosnow & Rosenthal, 1996).

Frequently, when we observe, it is necessary to control certain factors that determine behavior but that are not the focus of our inquiry. For this reason, much psychological research is conducted in a **laboratory,** *a controlled setting in which many of the complex factors of the "real world" are removed.* For example, Albert Bandura (1965) brought children into a laboratory and had them observe an adult repeatedly hit an inflated plastic Bobo doll about 3 feet tall. Bandura wondered to what extend the children would copy the adult's behavior. After the children saw the adult attack the Bobo doll, they, too, aggressively hit the inflated toy. By conducting his experiment in a laboratory with adults the children did not know as models, Bandura had complete control over when the children witnessed aggression, how much aggression the children saw, and what form the aggression took. Bandura could not have had as much control in his experiment if other factors, such as parents, siblings, friends, television, and a familiar room, had been present.

Observation is a valuable method for obtaining information about children's development. Here a researcher observes the social interaction of young children using a one-way mirror through which the observer can see the children but the children cannot see the observer.

Laboratory research has some drawbacks, however. First, it is almost impossible to conduct the research without the participants' knowing they are being studied. Second, the laboratory setting might be *unnatural* and therefore elicit unnatural behavior from the participants. Subjects usually show less aggressive behavior in a laboratory than in a more familiar natural setting, such as in a park or at home. They also show less aggression when they are unaware they are being observed than when they are aware that an observer is studying them. Third, some aspects of child development are difficult, if not impossible, to examine in a laboratory. For instance, it would be difficult (and unethical) to recreate and study in a laboratory certain types of stress, such as the circumstances that stimulate family conflict.

Although laboratory research is a valuable tool for developmentalists, naturalistic observation provides insight we sometimes cannot achieve in a laboratory. In **naturalistic observation,** *scientists observe behavior in real-world settings and make no effort to manipulate or control the situation.* Developmentalists conduct naturalistic observations at day-care centers, hospitals, schools, parks, homes, malls, dances, and other places people live in and frequent (Pellegrini, 1996). In contrast to Bandura's observations of aggression in a laboratory, developmentalists observe the aggression of children in nursery schools, of adolescents on street corners, and of marital partners at home (Bronfenbrenner, 1995).

Interviews and Questionnaires

Sometimes the best and quickest way to get information from children is to ask them for it. Psychologists use interviews and questionnaires to find out about children's experiences and attitudes. Most interviews occur face-to-face, although they can take place over the telephone.

The types of interviews range from highly unstructured to highly structured. Examples of unstructured interview questions include these: How aggressive do you see yourself as being? and How aggressive is your child? Examples of structured interview questions include these: In the last week, how often did you yell at your spouse? and How often in the last year was your child involved in fights at school? Structure is imposed by the questions themselves, or the interviewer can categorize answers by asking respondents to choose from several options. For example, in the question about your level of aggressiveness, you might be asked to choose from "highly aggressive," "moderately aggressive," "moderately unaggressive," and "highly unaggressive." In the question about how often you yelled at your spouse in the last week, you might be asked to choose "0," "1–2," "3–5," "6–10," or "more than 10 times."

Child developmentalists also question children and adults using questionnaires or surveys. A **questionnaire** *is similar to a highly structured interview except that respondents read the questions and mark their answers on paper rather than respond verbally to the interviewer.* One major advantage of surveys and questionnaires is that they can be given to a large number of people easily. Good surveys have concrete, specific, and unambiguous questions and assessment of the authenticity of the replies.

Interviews and questionnaires are not without drawbacks. Perhaps the most critical is the "social desirability" response set, in which individuals say what they think is most socially acceptable or desirable rather than what they truly think or feel. When asked about her marital conflict, Jane might not want to disclose that arguments have been painfully tense in the past month. Her 10-year-old son might not want to divulge that he often gets in fights with his peers. Skilled interviewing techniques and questions to help eliminate such defenses are critical in obtaining accurate information. Another problem with interviews and questionnaires is that individuals also might simply lie when responding to questions.

Case Studies

A **case study** *is an in-depth look at an individual; it is used mainly by clinical psychologists when the unique aspects of a person's life cannot be duplicated, for either practical or ethical reasons.* A case study provides information about an individual's fears, hopes, fantasies, traumatic experiences, upbringing, family relationships, health, or anything that helps a psychologist understand that person's development. Some vivid case studies appear at different points in this text, among them one about a modern-day wild child named Genie, who lived in near isolation during her childhood.

Although case studies provide dramatic, in-depth portrayals of people's lives, we need to exercise caution when generalizing from this information. The subject of a case study is unique, with a genetic makeup and experiences no one else shares. In addition, case studies involve judgments of unknown reliability, in that usually no check is made to see if other psychologists agree with the observations.

Standardized Tests

Standardized tests *require people to answer a series of written or oral questions. They have two distinct features. First, psychologists usually total an individual's score to yield a single score, or set of scores, that reflects something about the individual. Second, psychologists compare the individual's score to the scores of a large group of similar people to determine how the individual responded relative to others.* Scores are often described in percentiles. For example, a child who scored in the 92nd percentile of the Stanford-Binet Intelligence Test scored higher than 92 percent of the large group of children who had taken the test previously.

To continue our look at how different measures are used to evaluate aggression, consider the Minnesota Multiphasic Personality Inventory (MMPI), which includes a scale to assess delinquency or antisocial tendencies. The items on this scale ask you whether you are rebellious, impulsive, and have trouble with authority figures. This part of the MMPI might be given to adolescents to determine their delinquent and antisocial tendencies.

Cross-Cultural Research and Research with Ethnic Minority Groups

When researchers examine the behavior and mental processes of children in different cultures and different ethnic minority groups, they must follow certain strategies. When measures are used with cultural and ethnic groups with whom the researchers are unfamiliar, it is vital that they construct the measures so that they are meaningful for all of the cultural or ethnic minority groups being studied. To accomplish this objective, cross-cultural researchers do not use one culture as the sole source for developing a measure. Rather, informants from all cultures in the investigation provide information to the researchers so they can develop a meaningful measure.

In keeping with our theme of applying different ways of obtaining information about children to aggression, what have cross-cultural psychologists discovered about aggression in different cultures? They have found that aggression is a cultural universal, appearing in all cultures studied; however, the ways in which aggression is expressed may be culture-specific. For example, in the !Kung culture of southern Africa, the members actively try to dissuade individuals from behaving aggressively, whereas the members of the Yanomamo Indian culture of South American promote aggression. Yanomamo youth are told that they cannot achieve adult status unless they are capable of killing, fighting, and pummeling others.

John W. Santrock

In conducting research on cultural and ethnic minority issues, investigators distinguish between the emic approach and the etic approach (Triandis, 1994). In the **emic approach,** *the goal is to describe behavior in one culture or ethnic group in terms that are meaningful and important to the people in that culture or ethnic group, without regard to other cultures or ethnic groups.* In the **etic approach,** *the goal is to describe behavior so that generalizations can be made across cultures.* That is, the emic approach is culture-specific; the etic approach is culture-universal. If researchers construct a questionnaire in an emic fashion, their concern is only that the questions be meaningful to the particular culture or ethnic group being studied. If, however, the researchers construct a questionnaire in an etic fashion, they want to include questions that reflect concepts familiar to all cultures involved.

How might the emic and etic approaches be reflected in the study of family processes? In the emic approach, the researchers might choose to focus only on middle-class White families, without regard for whether the information obtained in the study can be generalized to or is appropriate for ethnic minority groups. In a subsequent study, the researchers may decide to adopt an etic approach by studying not only middle-class White families, but also lower-income White families, African American families, Latino families, and Asian American families. In studying ethnic minority families, the researchers would likely discover that the extended family is more frequently a support system in ethnic minority families than in White American families. If so, the emic approach would reveal a different pattern of family interaction than would the etic approach, documenting that research with middle-class White families cannot always be generalized to all ethnic groups.

In a symposium on racism in developmental research (Lee, 1992), the participants concluded that we need to include more ethnic minority children in our research. Historically, ethnic minority children have essentially been discounted from research and viewed simply as variations from the norm or average (Coll & others, 1995; Zambrina, 1995). The development of nonmainstream children has been viewed as "confounds" or "noise" in data, and consequently researchers have deliberately excluded such children from the samples they have selected (Landrine, 1995; Stevenson, 1995). Because ethnic minority children have been excluded from research for so long, there likely is more variation in children's real lives than our research data have indicated in the past.

Cross-cultural psychologist Joseph Trimble (1989) is especially concerned about researchers' tendencies to use ethnic gloss when they select and describe ethnic groups. By **ethnic gloss,** Trimble means *using an ethnic label, such as African, Latino, Asian, or Native American, in a superficial way that makes an ethnic group seem more homogeneous than it actually is.* For example, the following is an unsuitable description of a research sample, according to Trimble: "The subjects included 28 African Americans, 22 Latinos, and 24 Whites." An acceptable description of each of the

Systematic observations in natural settings provide valuable information about behavior across cultures. For example, in one investigation, observations in different cultures revealed that American children often engage in less work and more play than children in many other cultures (Whiting & Whiting, 1975). However, conducting cross-cultural research using such methods as systematic observation in natural settings is difficult and requires attention to a number of methodological issues.

groups requires much more detail about the participants' country of origin, socioeconomic status, language, and ethnic self-identification, such as this: "The 22 subjects were Mexican Americans from low-income neighborhoods in the southwestern area of Los Angeles. Twelve spoke Spanish in the home, while 10 spoke English; 11 were born in the United States, 11 were born in Mexico; 16 described themselves as Mexican, 3 as Chicano, 2 as American, and 1 as Latino." Trimble believes that ethnic gloss can cause researchers to obtain samples of ethnic groups and cultures that are not representative of their ethnic and cultural diversity, leading to overgeneralizations and stereotypes.

Physiological Research and Research with Animals

Two additional methods that psychologists use to gather data are physiological research and research with animals. Research on the biological basis of behavior and technological advances continue to produce remarkable insights about mind and behavior. For example, researchers have found that the electrical stimulation of certain areas of the brain turn docile, mild-mannered people into hostile, vicious attackers, and higher concentrations of some hormones have been associated with anger in adolescents (Susman & others, 1995).

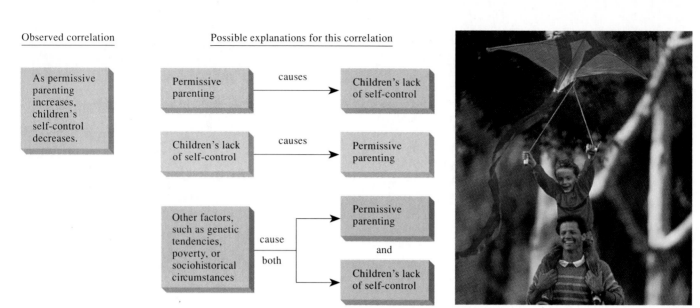

Observed correlation	Possible explanations for this correlation

As permissive parenting increases, children's self-control decreases.

Permissive parenting — causes → Children's lack of self-control

Children's lack of self-control — causes → Permissive parenting

Other factors, such as genetic tendencies, poverty, or sociohistorical circumstances — cause both → Permissive parenting — and — Children's lack of self-control

FIGURE 2.7

Possible Explanations for Correlational Data
An observed correlation between two events cannot be used to conclude that one event caused the other. Some possibilities are that the second event caused the first event or that a third, unknown event caused the correlation between the first two events.

Because much physiological research cannot be carried out with humans, psychologists sometimes use animals. Animal studies permit researchers to control their subjects' genetic background, diet, experiences during infancy, and many other factors (Drickamer, Vessey, & Miekle, 1996). In studying humans, psychologists treat these factors as random variation, or "noise," that may interfere with accurate results. In addition, animal researchers can investigate the effects of treatments (brain implants, for example) that would be unethical with humans. Moreover, it is possible to track the entire life span of some animals over a relatively short period of time. Laboratory mice, for instance, have a life span of approximately 1 year.

Multimeasure, Multisource, Multicontext Approach

The various methods have their strengths and weaknesses. Direct observations are extremely valuable tools for obtaining information about children, but there are some things we cannot observe in children—their moral thoughts, their inner feelings, the arguments of their parents, how they acquire information about sex, and so on. In such instances, other measures, such as interviews, questionnaires, and case studies, may be valuable. Because virtually every method has limitations, many investigators use multiple measures in assessing children's development. For example, a researcher studying children's aggressive behavior might interview children, check with their friends, observe them carefully at home and in their neighborhood, interview their parents, observe the children at school during recess, and ask teachers to rate the children's aggression. Researchers hope that the convergence of multimeasure, multisource, and multicontext information provides a more comprehensive and valid assessment of children's development.

Correlational and Experimental Strategies

How can we determine if a pregnant woman's cigarette smoking affects her offspring's attentional skills? How can we determine if responding nurturantly to an infant's cries increases attachment to the caregiver? How can we determine if day care is damaging to a child's development? How can we determine if listening to rock music lowers an adolescent's grades in school? When designing a research study to answer such questions, investigators must decide whether to use a correlational or an experimental strategy.

Correlational Strategy

In the **correlational strategy,** *the goal is to describe the strength of the relation between two or more characteristics.* This is a useful strategy because the more strongly events are correlated (related, or associated), the more we can predict one from the other. For example, if we find that, as parents use more permissive ways to deal with their children, the children's self-control decreases, this does not mean that the parenting style caused the lack of self-control. It could mean that, but it could also mean that the children's lack of self-control stimulated the parents to simply throw up their arms in despair and give up trying to control the obstreperous children's behavior, or it could mean that this correlation is caused by other factors, such as genetic background, poverty, and sociohistorical conditions. (Several decades ago a permissive parenting strategy was widely advocated, but today it no longer is in vogue.) Figure 2.7 portrays these possible interpretations of correlational data.

The **correlation coefficient** *is a number based on statistical analysis that is used to describe the degree of association between two variables. The correlation coefficient ranges from −1.00 to +1.00.* A negative number means an inverse relation. For example, today we often find a *negative* correlation between permissive parenting and children's self-control, and we often find a *positive* correlation between a parent's involvement in and monitoring of a child's life and the child's self-control. The higher the correlation coefficient (whether positive or negative), the stronger the association between the two variables. A correlation of 0 means that there is no association between the two variables. A correlation of −.40 is a stronger correlation than +.20 because we disregard the negative or positive nature of the correlation in determining the correlation's magnitude.

Experimental Strategy

Whereas the correlational strategy allows us to say only that two events are related, the **experimental strategy** *allows us to precisely determine behavior's causes. Developmentalists accomplish this task by performing an experiment, which is a study done in a carefully regulated setting in which one or more of the factors believed to influence the behavior being studied is manipulated and all others are held constant.* If the behavior under study changes when a factor is manipulated, we say that the manipulated factor causes the behavior to change. Experiments establish cause and effect between events, something correlational studies cannot do. *Cause* is the event being manipulated, and *effect* is the behavior that changes because of the manipulation. Remember that, in testing correlation, nothing is manipulated; in an experiment, a researcher actively changes an event to see its effect on behavior.

The following example illustrates the nature of an experiment. The problem to be studied is whether aerobic exercise during pregnancy affects infant development. We need to have one group of pregnant women engage in aerobic exercise and the other not engage in aerobic exercise. We randomly assign our subjects to these two groups. **Random assignment** *occurs when researchers assign subjects to experimental and control conditions by chance, thus reducing the likelihood the results of the experiment will be due to preexisting differences in the two groups.* For example, random assignment greatly reduces the probability that the two groups will differ on such factors as age, social class, prior aerobic exercise, intelligence, health problems, alertness, and so on.

The **independent variable** *is the manipulated, influential, experimental factor in an experiment.* The label *independent* is used because this variable can be changed independently of other factors. In the aerobic exercise experiment, the amount of aerobic exercise is the independent variable. We manipulate the amount of the aerobic exercise by having the pregnant women exercise four times a week under the direction of a trained instructor. The **dependent variable** *is the factor that is measured in an experiment; it may change because of the manipulation of the independent variable.* The label *dependent* is used because this variable depends on what happens to the subjects in

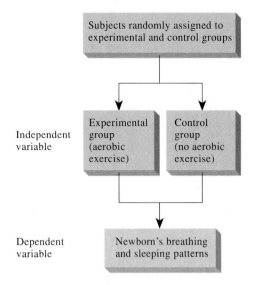

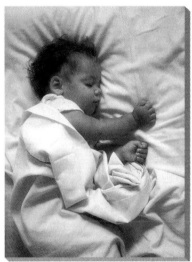

FIGURE 2.8

Principles of the Experimental Strategy
The effects of aerobic exercise by pregnant women on their newborns' breathing and sleeping patterns.

the experiment. In the aerobic exercise experiment, the dependent variable is represented by two infant measures—breathing and sleeping patterns. The subjects' responses on these measures depend on the influence of the independent variable (whether or not pregnant women engaged in aerobic exercise). An illustration of the nature of the experimental strategy, applied to the aerobic exercise study, is presented in figure 2.8. In our experiment, we test the two sets of offspring in the first week of life. We find that the experimental-group infants have more regular breathing and sleeping patterns than do their control-group counterparts; thus, we conclude that aerobic exercise by pregnant women promotes more regular breathing and sleeping patterns in newborn infants.

It might seem as if we should always choose an experimental strategy over a correlational strategy, since the experimental strategy gives us a better sense of the influence of one variable on another. Are there instances when a correlational strategy might be preferred? Three such instances are (1) when the focus of the investigation is so new that we have little knowledge of which variables to manipulate (as when AIDS first appeared), (2) when it is physically impossible to manipulate the variables (such as factors involved in suicide), and (3) when it is unethical to manipulate the variables (for example, in determining the association between illness and exposure to dangerous chemicals).

TIME SPAN OF INQUIRY

A special concern of developmentalists is the time span of a research investigation. Studies that focus on the relation of age to another variable are common in the field of child development. We have several options—we can study different children of different ages and compare them, or we can study the same individuals as they grow older.

Cross-Sectional Approach

The **cross-sectional approach** *is a research strategy in which individuals of different ages are compared all at one time.* A typical cross-sectional study might include a group of 5-year-olds, 8-year-olds, and 11-year-olds. The different groups can be compared with respect to a variety of dependent variables—IQ, memory, peer relations, attachment to parents, hormonal changes, and so on. All of this can be accomplished in a short time. In some studies, data are collected in a single day. Even in large-scale cross-sectional studies with hundreds of subjects, data collection usually does not take longer than several months to complete.

The main advantage of a cross-sectional study is that researchers do not have to wait for subjects to grow up. Despite its time efficiency, the cross-sectional approach has its drawbacks: It gives no information about how individuals change or about the stability of their characteristics. The increases and decreases—the hills and valleys—of growth and development can become obscured in the cross-sectional approach. Also, because the children studied are of different ages and different groups, they were born at different times; they may have experienced different types of parenting and schooling; and they may have been influenced by different trends in dress, television, and play materials.

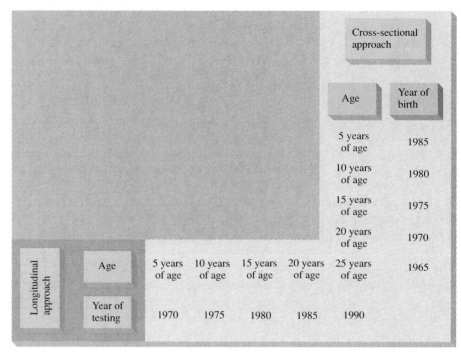

FIGURE 2.9

A Comparison of Cross-Sectional and Longitudinal Approaches

Longitudinal Approach

The **longitudinal approach** *is a research strategy in which the same individuals are studied over a period of time, usually several years or more.* In a typical longitudinal study of the same topics we discussed regarding the cross-sectional approach, we might structure a test to administer to children once a year when they are 4, 8, and 12 years old. In this example, the same children would be studied over an 8-year time span, allowing us to examine patterns of change within each child. One of the great values of the longitudinal approach is that we can evaluate how individual children change as they grow up.

Fewer longitudinal than cross-sectional studies are conducted because they are time consuming and costly. A close examination of the longitudinal approach reveals some additional problems: (1) When children are examined over a long period of time, some drop out because they lose interest or move away and cannot be recontacted by the investigator. A fairly common finding is that the remaining children represent a slightly biased sample, in that, compared to those who dropped out, they tend to be psychologically superior on almost every dimension (intelligence, motivation, and cooperativeness, for example) that the investigator checks. (2) With repeated testing, some children may become more "testwise," which may increase their ability to perform "better" or "more maturely" the next time the investigator interacts with them. For a comparison of longitudinal and cross-sectional research designs, see figure 2.9.

BY BILL HOEST

"That's my dad when he was 10 . . . . He was in some sort of cult."

© 1986; Reprinted courtesy of Bill Hoest and Parade Magazine.

Cohort Effects

Cohort effects *are effects due to a subject's time of birth or generation but not actually to age.* Today's children are living a childhood of firsts (Louv, 1990). They are the first day-care generation; the first truly multicultural generation; the first generation to grow up in the electronic bubble of an environment defined by computers and new forms of media; the first post-sexual-revolution generation; the first generation to grow up in new kinds of dispersed, deconcentrated cities, not quite urban, rural, or suburban.

> The mark of the historic is the nonchalance with which it picks up an individual and deposits him in a trend, like a house playfully moved in a tornado.
>
> —**Mary McCarthy**

Cohort effects are important because they can powerfully affect the dependent measures in a study ostensibly concerned with age. Researchers have shown that cohort effects are especially important to investigate in the assessment of intelligence (Schaie, 1994). For example, individuals born at different points in time—such as 1920, 1940, and 1960—have had varying opportunities for education, with the individuals born in earlier years having less access.

Now that we have considered the main ways that child developmentalists conduct research, it is also important to examine how child development research can become less sexist and some ethical considerations in child development research.

RESEARCH CHALLENGES

A number of issues are raised when research on children's development is conducted. Many of the issues involve the pursuit of research knowledge itself. Others involve how the research impacts the participants and how consumers can improve their understanding of the information derived from research studies.

Ethics in Research on Child Development

Increasingly, child developmentalists recognize that considerable caution must be taken to ensure the well-being of children when they are involved in a research study. Today colleges and universities have review boards that evaluate the ethical nature of research conducted at their institutions. Proposed research plans must pass the scrutiny of an ethics research committee before the research can be initiated. In addition, the American Psychological Association (APA) has developed guidelines for its members' ethics.

The code of ethics adopted by the APA instructs researchers to protect their subjects from mental and physical harm. The best interests of the subjects must be kept foremost in the researcher's mind (Kimmel, 1996). All subjects, if they are old enough, must give their informed consent to participate in a research study. This requires that subjects know what their participation will entail and any risks that might develop. For example, subjects in an investigation of the effects of divorce on children should be told beforehand that interview questions might stimulate thought about issues they might not anticipate. The subjects should also be informed that in some instances a discussion of the family's experiences might improve family relationships, but in other instances it might bring up issues that bring the children unwanted stress. After informed consent is given, the subjects reserve the right to withdraw from the study at any time.

Special ethical concerns govern the conduct of research with children (Hoagwood, Jensen, & Fisher, 1996). First, if children are to be studied, informed consent from their parents or legal guardians must be obtained. Parents have the right to a complete and accurate description of what will be done with their children and may refuse to let them participate. Second, children have rights too. Psychologists are obliged to explain precisely what the children will experience. The children may refuse to participate, even after parental permission has been given. Also, if a child becomes upset during the research study, it is the psychologist's obligation to calm the child. Third, psychologists must always weigh the potential for harming children against the prospects of contributing some clear benefits to them. If there is the chance of harm—as when drugs are used, social deception takes place, or children are treated aversively (that is, punished or reprimanded)—psychologists must convince a group of peers that the benefits of the experience clearly outweigh any chance of harm. Fourth, since children are in a vulnerable position and lack power and control when facing adults, psychologists should always strive to make a professional encounter a positive and supportive experience.

Florence Denmark (shown here talking with a group of students) has developed a number of guidelines for nonsexist research. Denmark and others believe that psychology needs to be challenged to examine the world in a new way, one that incorporates girls' and women's perspectives.

Conducting Nonsexist Research

Traditional science is presented as being value free and, thus, a valid way of studying mental processes and behavior. However, there is a growing consensus that science in general and psychology in particular are not value free (Paludi, 1995). A special concern is that the vast majority of psychological research has been male oriented and male dominated. Some researchers believe that male-dominated sciences, such as psychology, need to be challenged to examine the world in a new way, one that incorporates girls' and women's perspectives and respects their ethnicity, sexual orientation, age, and socioeconomic status. For example, Florence Denmark and her colleagues (1988) provided the following three recommendations as guidelines for nonsexist research:

1. Research methods
   Problem: The selection of research participants is based on stereotypic assumptions and does not allow for generalizations to other groups.
   Example: On the basis of stereotypes about who should be responsible for contraception, only females are studied.
   Correction: Both sexes should be studied before conclusions are drawn about the factors that determine contraception use.
2. Data analysis
   Problem: Gender differences are inaccurately magnified.

Example: "Whereas only 24 percent of the girls were found to . . . fully 28 percent of the boys were . . ."
Correction: The results should include extensive descriptions of the data so that differences are not exaggerated.
3. Conclusions
   Problem: The title or abstract (summary) of an article makes no reference to the limitations of the study participants and implies a broader scope of the study than is warranted.
   Example: A study purporting to be about "perceptions of the disabled" examines only blind White boys.
   Correction: Use more-precise titles and clearly describe the sample and its selection criteria in the abstract or summary.

Being a Wise Consumer of Information About Children's Development

We live in an information society in which there is a vast amount of information about children's development available for public consumption. The information varies greatly in quality. How can you become a wise consumer of information about children's development?

Be Cautious About What Is Reported in the Media

Research and clinical findings about children's development are increasingly talked about in the media. Television, radio, newspapers, and magazines all make it a frequent practice to report on research and clinical findings involving children that are likely to be of interest to the general public. Many professional and mental health and psychological organizations regularly supply the media with information about research and clinical findings. In many cases, this information has been published in professional journals or presented at national meetings. And most major colleges and universities have a media relations department that contacts the press about current research by their faculty.

Not all psychological and mental health information involving children that is presented for public consumption comes from professionals with excellent credentials and reputations at colleges and universities and in applied mental health settings. Journalists, television reporters, and other media personnel are not scientifically and clinically trained. It is not an easy task for them to sort through the widely varying material they come across and make sound decisions about which research and clinical information that involves children should be presented to the public.

Unfortunately, the media often focuses on sensational and dramatic psychological findings. They want you to read what they have written or stay tuned and not flip to another channel. They can capture your attention and keep it by presenting dramatic, sensational, and surprising information. As a consequence, media presentations of information about children tend to go beyond what actual research articles and clinical findings really say.

Even when excellent research and clinical findings are presented to the public, it is difficult for media personnel to adequately inform people about what has been found and the implications for their lives. For example, throughout this text you will be introduced to an entirely new vocabulary. Each time we present a new concept, we precisely define it and give examples of it as well. We have an entire book to carry out our task of carefully introducing, defining, and elaborating on key concepts and issues, research, and clinical findings about children's development. However, the media do not have the luxury of time and space to go into considerable detail and specify the limitations and qualifications of research and clinical findings. They often have only a few minutes or few lines to summarize as best they can the complex findings of a study about children's development.

Among the other ways that you can think critically about the psychological information you see, hear, or read are to understand the distinction between nomothetic research and idiographic needs, to be aware of the tendency to overgeneralize from a small sample or a unique clinical sample, to know that a single study is often not the final and definitive word about an issue or topic, to be sure you understand why causal conclusions cannot be drawn from a correlational study, and to always consider the source of the information about children and evaluate its credibility.

Know How to Make a Distinction Between Nomothetic Research and Idiographic Needs

In being a wise consumer of information about children, it is important to understand the difference between nomothetic research and idiographic needs. **Nomothetic research** is conducted at the level of the group. Most research on children's development is nomothetic research. Individual variations in how children respond is often not a major focus of the research. For example, if researchers are interested in the effects of divorce on children's ability to cope with stress, they might conduct a study of 50 children from divorced families and 50 children from intact, never-divorced families. They might find that children from divorced families, as a group, cope more poorly with stress than children from intact families do. That is a nomothetic finding that applies to children of divorce as a group. And that is what commonly is reported in the media. In this particular study, some of the children from divorced families probably were coping better with stress than some of the children from intact families were—not as many, but some. Indeed, it is entirely possible that, of the 100 children in the study, the 2 or 3 children who were coping the very best with stress might have been children from divorced families and that the findings will still be reported

as showing that children from divorced families (as a group) cope more poorly with stress than children from intact families do.

As a consumer of information, you want to know what the information means for you *individually*, not necessarily for a group of people. **Idiographic needs** *are needs that are important for the individual, not to the group.* The failure of the media to adequately distinguish between nomothetic research and idiographic needs is not entirely their fault. Researchers have not adequately done this either. The research they conduct too often fails to examine the overlap between groups and tends to present only the differences that are found. And when those differences are reported, too often they are reported as if there is no overlap between the groups being compared (in our example, children from divorced families and children from intact families), when in reality there is substantial overlap. If you read a study in a research journal or media report of a study that states that children from divorced families coped more poorly with stress than do children from intact families, it does not mean that all children from divorced families coped more poorly than all children from intact families did. It simply means that as a group intact family children coped better.

Recognize How It Is Easy to Overgeneralize from a Small or Clinical Sample

There often isn't space or time in media presentations of information about children to go into details about the nature of the sample. Sometimes you will get basic information about the sample's size—whether it is based on 10 subjects, 50 subjects, or 200 subjects, for example. In many cases, small or very small samples require that care be exercised in generalizing to a larger population of individuals. For example, if a study of children from divorced families is based on only 10 or 20 such children, what is found in the study may not generalize to all divorced children, because the sample investigated may have some unique characteristics. The sample subjects all might come from families that have substantial economic resources, are White American, live in a small southern town, and are undergoing psychotherapy. In this study, then, we clearly would be making unwarranted generalizations if we thought the findings also characterize divorced children from families who have moderate to low incomes, are from other ethnic backgrounds, live in different locations, and are not undergoing psychotherapy.

Be Aware That a Single Study Is Usually Not the Defining Word About Some Aspect of Children's Development

The media might identify an interesting piece of research or a clinical finding and claim that it is something phenomenal with far-reaching implications. While such studies and findings do occur, it is rare for a single study to provide earth-shattering and conclusive answers, especially

CRITICAL THINKING
ABOUT CHILDREN'S
DEVELOPMENT

Reading and Analyzing
Reports About
Children's Development

Information about children's development appears in research journals and in magazines and newspapers. Choose one of the topics covered in this book and course—such as day care, adolescent problems, or parenting. Find an article in a research journal (for example, *Child Development* or *Developmental Psychology*) and an article in a newspaper or magazine on the same topic. How did the research article on the topic differ from the newspaper or magazine article? What did you learn from this comparison? By comparing research journal articles and newspaper and magazine accounts, you are learning to *make accurate observations, descriptions, and inferences about children's development.*

simply correlated. We cannot say that one causes another. In the case of divorce, a headline might read "Divorce Causes Children to Have Problems in School." We read the article and find out the headline was derived from the results of a research study. Since we obviously cannot, for ethical or practical reasons, randomly assign children to families that will become divorced or stay intact, this headline is based on a correlational study, which cannot be the basis of such causal statements. At least some of the children's problems in school probably occurred prior to the divorce of their parents. Other factors, such as poor parenting practices, low socioeconomic status, a difficult temperament, and low intelligence, may also contribute to children's problems in school and not be a direct consequence of divorce itself. What we can say in such studies, if the data warrant it, is that divorce is related to or associated with problems in school. What we cannot legitimately say in such studies is that divorce causes problems in school.

answers that apply to all children. In fact, in most domains of children's development, where there are a large number of investigations, it is not unusual to find conflicting results about a particular topic or issue. Answers to questions about children's development usually emerge after many scientists and/or clinicians have conducted similar investigations or therapy has been practiced by a number of mental health professionals who have drawn similar conclusions. Thus, a report of one study or clinical observations by only one or two therapists should not be taken as the absolute, final answer to a problem.

In our example of divorce, if one study reports that a particular therapy conducted by a therapist has been especially effective with children of divorce, we should not conclude that the therapy will work as effectively with all such children and with other therapists until more studies are conducted.

Remember That Causal Conclusions Cannot Be Drawn from Correlational Studies

Drawing causal conclusions from correlational studies is one of the most common mistakes made by the media. In studies in which an experiment has not been conducted (remember that in an experiment, subjects are randomly assigned to treatments or experiences), two variables or factors might be related to each other. However, causal interpretations are unjustified when two or more factors are

Always Consider the Source of the Information and Evaluate Its Credibility

Studies are not automatically accepted by the research community. Researchers usually have to submit their findings to a research journal, where their paper is reviewed by their colleagues, who make a decision about whether to publish it or not. While the quality of research in journals is not uniform, in most cases the research has undergone far greater scrutiny and more careful consideration of the quality of the work than is the case for research or any other information that has not gone through the journal review process. And within the media, we can distinguish between what is presented in respected newspapers, such as the *New York Times* and *Washington Post,* as well as credible magazines, such as *Time* and *Newsweek,* and much less respected and less credible tabloids, such as the *National Enquirer* and *Star.* To further evaluate reports about children's development, refer to Critical Thinking About Children's Development.

Since our last review, we have discussed a number of ideas about methods and how to be a wise consumer of information about children's development. A summary of these ideas is presented in concept table 2.2.

CONCEPT TABLE 2.2

Methodology and Research Challenges

Concept	Processes/Related Ideas	Characteristics/Description
Measures	Observation	It is a key ingredient in research that includes laboratory and naturalistic observation.
	Interviews and questionnaires	They are used to assess perceptions and attitudes. Social desirability and lying are problems with their use.
	Case studies	They provide an in-depth look at an individual. Caution in generalizing is warranted.
	Standardized tests	They are designed to assess an individual's characteristics relative to those of a large group of similar individuals.
	Cross-cultural research and research with ethnic minority groups	This research focuses on the culture-universal (etic approach) and culture-specific (emic approach) nature of mind and behavior. A special concern in research with ethnic minority groups is ethnic gloss. In the past ethnic minority children have often been excluded from research because researchers wanted to reduce variation in their data. We need to include more ethnic minority children in research.
	Physiological research and research with animals	Physiological research provides information about the biological basis of behavior. Since much physiological research cannot be carried out with humans, psychologists sometimes use animals. Animal studies permit researchers to control genetic background, diet, experiences in infancy, and countless other factors. One issue is the extent to which research with animals can be generalized to humans.
	Multiple measures, sources, and contexts	Researchers are increasingly adopting a multimeasure, multisource, multicontext approach.
Strategies for Setting Up Research Studies	Correlational strategy	It describes how strongly two or more events or characteristics are related. It does not allow causal statements.
	Experimental strategy	It involves manipulation of influential factors—independent variables—and measurement of their effect on the dependent variables. Subjects are randomly assigned to experimental and control groups in many studies. The experimental strategy can reveal the causes of behavior and tell us how one event influenced another.
Time Span of Inquiry	Cross-sectional approach	Individuals of different ages are compared all at one time.
	Longitudinal approach	The same individuals are studied over a period of time, usually several years or more.
	Cohort effects	Cohort effects are due to a subject's time of birth or generation but not actually to age. The study of cohort effects underscores the importance of considering the historical dimensions of development.
Research Challenges	Ethics in research on child development	Researchers must ensure the well-being of subjects in research. The risk of mental and physical harm must be reduced, and informed consent should be obtained. Special ethical considerations are involved when children are research subjects.
	Conducting nonsexist research	A special concern is that the vast majority of psychological research has been male oriented and male dominated. Some researchers believe that developmentalists need to be challenged to examine children's worlds in a new way, one that incorporates girls' and women's perspectives. Recommendations have been made for conducting nonsexist research.
	Being a wise consumer of information about children's development	In many instances the quality of information you read about children's development, especially in the media, varies greatly. Being a wise consumer involves understanding the distinction between nomothetic research and idiographic needs, being aware of the tendency to overgeneralize from a small sample or a unique sample, knowing that a single study is often not the defining word about an issue or problem, understanding why causal conclusions cannot be drawn from a correlational study, and always considering the source of the information and evaluating its credibility.

A discipline that studies how babies develop, how parents nurture children, how peers interact, and how children think can be a science just as much as disciplines that investigate how gravity works and the molecular structure of a compound. That is because science is defined not by what it investigates but by how it investigates.

We began the study of child development as a science by examining the nature of theory and the scientific method. Then we evaluated five main theories—psychoanalytic (Freud and Erikson), cognitive (Piaget and information processing), behavioral/social learning (Skinner and Bandura), ethological (Lorenz), and ecological (Bronfenbrenner)— as well as an eclectic theoretical orientation and developmental analogies. We studied a variety of measures that can be used to collect information about children, such as observations, interviews and questionnaires, case studies, standardized tests, cross-cultural research and research with ethnic minority individuals, physiological research and research with animals, and the importance of a multimethod, multisource, multicontext approach. We also examined strategies for setting up research studies, the time span of inquiry, ethics in research on child development, conducting nonsexist research, and how to be a wise consumer of information about children's development.

To obtain a summary of this chapter, go back and again study the two concept tables on pages 50 and 61. This concludes Section One of the book. In Section Two, we will explore the beginnings of children's development, beginning with chapter 3, "Biological Beginnings."

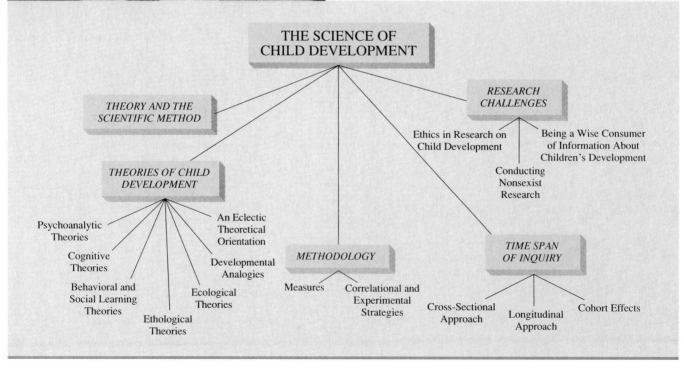

THE SCIENCE OF CHILD DEVELOPMENT

THEORY AND THE SCIENTIFIC METHOD

RESEARCH CHALLENGES

Ethics in Research on Child Development

Being a Wise Consumer of Information About Children's Development

Conducting Nonsexist Research

THEORIES OF CHILD DEVELOPMENT

Psychoanalytic Theories

Cognitive Theories

Behavioral and Social Learning Theories

Ethological Theories

Ecological Theories

Developmental Analogies

An Eclectic Theoretical Orientation

METHODOLOGY

Measures

Correlational and Experimental Strategies

TIME SPAN OF INQUIRY

Cross-Sectional Approach

Longitudinal Approach

Cohort Effects

theory A coherent set of ideas that helps explain data and make predictions. 35

hypotheses Assumptions that can be tested to determine their accuracy. 35

scientific method An approach that can be used to discover accurate information about behavior and development (includes the following steps: identify and analyze the problem, collect data, draw conclusions, and revise theories). 35

id The Freudian structure of personality that consists of instincts, which are an individual's reserve of psychic energy. 36

ego The Freudian structure of personality that deals with the demands of reality. 36

superego The Freudian structure of personality that is the moral branch of personality. 36

defense mechanisms The psychoanalytic term for unconscious methods used by the ego to distort reality in order to protect itself from anxiety. 37

repression The most powerful and pervasive defense mechanism; it pushes unacceptable id impulses out of awareness and back into the unconscious mind. 37

erogenous zones Freud's concept of the parts of the body that have especially strong pleasure-giving qualities at each stage of development. 38

oral stage The first Freudian stage of development, occurring during the first 18 months of life; the infant's pleasure centers around the mouth. 38

anal stage The second Freudian stage of development, occurring between 1½ and 3 years of age, the child's greatest pleasure involves the anus or the eliminative functions associated with it. 38

phallic stage The third Freudian stage of development, occurring between the ages of 3 and 6; its name comes from the Latin word *phallus*, which means "penis." 38

Oedipus complex In Freudian theory, the young child's development of an intense desire to replace the same-sex parent and enjoy the affections of the opposite-sex parent. 38

latency stage The fourth Freudian stage, occurring between approximately 6 years of age and puberty; the child represses all interest in sexuality and develops social and intellectual skills. 38

genital stage The fifth and final Freudian stage of development, that occurs from puberty on; a sexual reawakening in which the source of sexual pleasure now becomes someone outside of the family. 38

trust versus mistrust Erikson's first psychosocial stage, experienced in the first year of life; a sense of trust requires a feeling of physical comfort and a minimal amount of fear and apprehension about the future. 39

autonomy versus shame and doubt Erikson's second stage of development, which occurs in late infancy and toddlerhood (1–3 years). After gaining trust in their caregivers, infants begin to discover that their behavior is their own. 39

initiative versus guilt Erikson's third stage of development, which occurs during the preschool years. As preschool children encounter a widening social world, they are challenged more than they were as infants. 39

industry versus inferiority Erikson's fourth stage of development, which occurs approximately in the elementary school years. Children's initiative brings them into contact with a wealth of new experiences, and they direct their energy toward mastering knowledge and intellectual skills. 39

identity versus identity confusion Erikson's fifth stage of development, which occurs during the adolescent years. Adolescents are faced with finding out who they are, what they are all about, and where they are going in life. 39

intimacy versus isolation Erikson's sixth stage of development, which occurs during the early adulthood years. Young adults face the developmental task of forming intimate relationships with others. 39

generativity versus stagnation Erikson's seventh stage of development, which occurs during middle adulthood. A chief concern is to assist the younger generation in developing and leading useful lives. 39

integrity versus despair Erikson's eighth and final stage of development, which occurs during late adulthood. In the later years of life, we look back and evaluate what we have done with our lives. 40

assimilation Individuals' incorporation of new information into their existing knowledge. 41

accommodation Individuals' adjustment to new information. 41

sensorimotor stage The first of Piaget's stages that lasts from birth to about 2 years of age; infants construct an understanding of the world by coordinating sensory experiences (such as seeing and hearing) with motoric actions. 42

preoperational stage The second Piagetian developmental stage that lasts from about 2 to 7 years of age; children begin to represent the world with words, images, and drawings. 42

concrete operational stage Piaget's third stage, which lasts from approximately 7 to 11 years of age; children can perform operations, and logical reasoning replaces intuitive thought as long as the reasoning can be applied to specific concrete examples. 42

formal operational stage Piaget's fourth and final stage, which occurs between the ages of 11 and 15; individuals move beyond concrete experiences and think in more abstract and more logical ways. 42

information processing How individuals process information about their world; how information enters the mind, and how it is stored and transformed, and how it is retrieved to perform such complex activities as problem solving and reasoning. 42

behaviorism The scientific study of observable behavioral responses and their environmental determinants. 43

social learning theory Emphasizes a combination of behavior, environment, and cognition as the key factors in development. 43

ethology A theory that stresses that behavior is strongly influenced by biology, is tied to evolution, and is characterized by critical or sensitive periods. 45

imprinting In ethological theory, rapid, innate learning within a limited critical period of time, which involves attachment to the first moving object seen. 46

critical period A fixed time period very early in development during which certain behaviors optimally emerge. 46

ecological theory Bronfenbrenner's sociocultural view of development that consists of five environmental systems ranging from the fine-grained inputs of direct interactions with social agents to the broad-based inputs of culture. The five systems in Bronfenbrenner's ecological theory are the microsystem, mesosystem, exosystem, macrosystem, and chronosystem. 46

microsystem The setting or context in which an individual lives, including the person's family, peers, school, and neighborhood. 46

mesosystem Relationships between microsystems or connections between contexts, such as the connection between family experience and the school experience. 46

exosystem The level at which experiences in another social setting—in which the individual does not have an active role—influence what the individual experiences in an immediate context. 46

macrosystem The culture in which individuals live. 47

chronosystem The patterning of environmental events and transitions over the life course and their sociohistorical contexts. 47

eclectic theoretical orientation Not following any one theoretical approach, but rather selecting from each theory whatever is considered the best in it. 48

laboratory A controlled setting in which many of the complex factors of the "real world" are removed. 51

naturalistic observation A method in which scientists observe behavior in real-world settings and make no effort to manipulate or control the situation. 51

questionnaire Similar to a highly structured interview except that respondents read the questions and mark their answers on paper, rather than responding verbally to an interviewer. 52

case study An in-depth look at an individual; it is used mainly by clinical psychologists when the unique aspects of a person's life cannot be duplicated, for either practical or ethical reasons. 52

standardized tests Tests that require an individual to answer a series of written or oral questions. These tests have two distinct features: First, psychologists usually total an individual's score to yield a single score, or set of scores, that reflects something about the individual. Second, psychologists compare the individual's score with the scores of a large group of persons to determine how the individual responded relative to others. 52

emic approach The goal is to describe behavior in one culture or ethnic group in terms that are meaningful and important to the people in that group, without regard to other cultures or ethnic groups. 53

etic approach The goal in this approach is to describe behaviors so that generalizations can be made across cultures. 53

ethnic gloss Using an ethnic label, such as *African*, *Latino*, *Asian*, or *Native American*, in a superficial way that makes an ethnic group seem more homogeneous than it actually is. 53

correlational strategy The goal is to describe the strength of the relation between two or more events or characteristics. 54

correlation coefficient A number based on statistical analysis used to describe the degree of association between two variables. The correlation coefficient ranges from −1.00 to 1.00. 54

experimental strategy A research strategy that allows investigators to determine behavior's causes by performing an experiment that is a precisely regulated setting in which one or more of the factors believed to influence the behavior being studied are manipulated and all others are held constant. 55

random assignment The assignment of subjects to experimental and control conditions by chance, thus reducing the likelihood that the results of the experiment will be due to preexisting differences in the two groups. 55

independent variable The manipulated, influential, experimental factor in the experiment. 55

dependent variable The factor that is measured in an experiment; it may change because of the manipulation of the independent variable. 55

cross-sectional approach A research strategy in which individuals of different ages are compared all at one time. 56

longitudinal approach A research strategy in which the same individuals are studied over a period of time, usually several years or more. 56

cohort effects Effects due to an individual's time of birth or generation but not the individual's age. 57

nomothetic research Research conducted at the group level in which individual variation is not a major focus. 59

idiographic needs Needs that are important to the individual, not to the group. 59

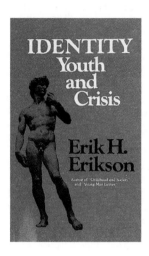

Identity: Youth and Crisis
(1968) by Erik H. Erikson.
New York: W. W. Norton.

Erik Erikson was one of the leading theorists in the field of life-span development. In *Identity: Youth and Crisis*, he outlined his eight stages of life-span development and provided numerous examples from his clinical practice to illustrate the stages. This book gives special attention to the fifth stage in Erikson's theory, identity versus identity confusion. Especially worthwhile are Erikson's commentaries about identity development in different cultures.

Two other Erikson books that are excellent reading on life-span development are *Young Man Luther* and *Gandhi's Truth*. Anyone interested in learning more about their development of an identity will find any of these three books to provide many insights about their pursuit of who they are, what they are all about, and where they are going in life.

IMPROVING THE LIVES OF CHILDREN

Remember that at the end of each chapter we will examine five areas of children's development that hold opportunities for improving children's lives: health and well-being, families and parenting, education, culture and ethnicity, and gender.

HEALTH AND WELL-BEING

Protective Buffers for Children

What are some of the factors that help children be resilient in response to stressful circumstances and assaults on their health and well-being? In one large-scale study, Emmy Werner and Ruth Smith (1982) found that children greatly benefit from having a readily available support network of grandparents, neighbors, or relatives. Many children who cope effectively with stress, threats, and assaults on their health and well-being have a cluster of protective factors, not just one or two. But if forced to pick the most important factor that helps children weather problems, Werner says it is a basic, trusting relationship with an adult. In all of the protective clusters in Werner's study, there was not one that did not include that one good relationship, whether with a parent, grandparent, older sibling, teacher, or mentor—someone consistent in the child's life who could say to the child, "You count. I love you and will care for you. I will always be there for you." Even children of abusive or schizophrenic parents sometimes prove to be resilient if they have had at least one caring person nurturing and protecting them—someone who serves as sort of a beacon in their lives.

Thomas Boyce (1991), a pediatrics professor at the University of California, San Francisco, described an 8-year-old boy from an impoverished rural African American family, who had been abandoned by his mother. The boy also had "prune-belly syndrome," an abnormality of the abdominal musculature that left him with significant kidney and urinary problems, which required extensive surgery. But the boy had two nurturing, caring grandparents who had raised him from infancy. They consistently supported him and unfailingly accompanied him on his hospital visits. Despite his physical problems and the absence of his mother, the boy's school performance was superb.

Such protective factors in children's lives work best when they are long-lasting. There is no guarantee that the child will always be resilient, since families and children may experience a host of ups and downs as children develop. Children who cope well early in their development can have setbacks later because of family or school problems. In life, no child is unbreakable. Caring and supporting are needed by at least one significant person throughout the childhood years for optimal development.

One of the most important factors that provides a protective buffering of children from stressors and problems is the long-term presence of a basic, trusting relationship with an adult.

John W. Santrock

FAMILIES AND PARENTING

Observing and Imitating Parents

Think for a moment about the thousands of hours most children spend observing their parents' behavior. Often on a daily basis, children watch and listen to their parents comment about their work and careers, observe whether they drink too much or not at all, experience their model of marital relationships and whether their mother and father argue a lot or very little, see and hear if they solve problems calmly or with great discharge of anger, view whether they are generous toward others or are more selfish, and see how male and female adults act.

Why are children motivated to imitate their parents' behaviors? Children can gain and maintain their parents' affection and avoid punishment by behaving like their parents. Children also acquire a sense of mastery over their environment by imitating the behavior of warm, competent, and powerful parents.

One issue in observational learning is whether parents can get by with telling their children, "Do what I say, not what I do," and not harm their children's development. Such parents often hope that by rewarding their children's positive behavior and/or punishing their negative behaviors, they still can engage in their own maladaptive, selfish, and inappropriate ways without jeopardizing their children's development. Imitation often occurs without parents' knowingly trying to influence their children, but when parents verbalize standards and try

Observational learning is a primary way children learn from their parents.

to get children to abide by them, they are usually consciously shaping their children's behavior.

Child developmentalists believe a "Do as I say, but not as I do" approach by parents is not a wise parenting strategy. Children who see their parents attend church regularly and hear them talk about how moral they are, but then observe them cheat on their income tax, never give any money to charity, turn down requests to help others in need, and treat others with little respect, will often imitate their parents *actions* rather than their

words. In the case of children's imitation of parents, then, a familiar saying often holds true: Actions speak louder than words.

How much children learn by observing parents also is influenced by what children see are the consequences of that behavior for the parent. If parental models are rewarded for their behavior, children are more likely to imitate their behavior than if the parents receive no reward or are punished for their behavior. The consequences to the model can be either external (someone else says or does something positive to the parent after the parent engages in a particular action) or internal (the parent engages in a self-reinforcement by showing pleasure after performing a behavior). For example, a father may give to a charity and subsequently smile and say how good it made him feel. The father's children observe these consequences and then may imitate the father's kind, generous behavior as long as it makes the children feel good. Parents may find it ineffective to exhort their children to share their toys because children will not feel good letting others share what they want themselves. However, if children see their parents derive pleasure from sharing, the self-sacrificing behavior probably will bring more joy to the children. Thus, imitation is an important part of the process in getting children to behave in kind ways toward others (Jensen & Kingston, 1986).

EDUCATION

An Important Mesosystem Connection—Family and School

In Bronfenbrenner's ecological theory, the mesosystem refers to connections between microsystems or social contexts. An important mesosystem connection is between families and schools. Researchers have consistently found that successful students often receive long-term support from parents or other adults at home, as well as strong support from teachers and others at school.

Involving parents in learning activities with their children at home is one kind of parental involvement that many educators believe is an important aspect of the child's learning. Family researcher and educator Ira Gordon (1978) concluded that parents of students in the early grades can play six key roles: volunteer, paid employee, teacher at home, audience, decision maker, and adult

learner. These roles likely influence not only parents' behavior and their children's schoolwork, but also the quality of schools and communities.

Today, after many decades of limited success, schools are beginning to put more thought into their communication with parents, recognizing that the initial contacts can make or break relationships and that first contacts

An important dimension of effective schooling is the role of families in children's education. Shown here is a parent-teacher conference in Lima, Ohio, where a systematic effort has been made to more extensively involve parents in children's education.

affect later communication (Epstein, 1992). Recognizing the importance of parental involvement in education, a number of programs are being developed to enhance communication between schools and families.

Three types of school/family programs are face-to-face, technological, and written communication (D'Angelo & Adler, 1991). In Lima, Ohio, the main goal is for each school to establish a personal relationship with every parent. At an initial parent/teacher conference, parents are given a packet that is designed to increase their likelihood of engaging in learning activities with their children at home. Conferences, regular phone calls, and home visits establish an atmosphere of mutual understanding that makes other kinds of communication (progress reports, report cards, activity calendars, or discussions about problems that arise during the year) more welcome and successful.

Many programs are discovering new ways to use electronic communication to establish contact with a wider range of parents. In McAllen, Texas, the school district has developed a community partnership with local radio stations, and it sponsors "Discusiones Escolares," a weekly program in Spanish that encourages parents to become more involved in their children's education. Family and school relationships, parent involvement at school, preventing school dropouts, creating a learning atmosphere at home, and communicating with adolescents are some of the topics the radio programs have addressed. Parents and others in the communities may check out copies of the script or a cassette tape of each program from the parent coordinators at their schools.

In Omaha, Nebraska, a monthly newsletter is sent to parents that highlights home activities that are coordinated with classroom activities. Each month's issue reports on the meeting of the parent advisory council and gives information about how parents can become more involved in their children's education. The monthly newsletters also focus on classroom themes. In addition to the newsletter, a calendar is published each year, and families are offered many opportunities for added learning. For example, during school vacations, students receive "The Sizzler"—a packet of learning materials for the entire family to use at home.

In sum, extra care in developing and maintaining channels of communication between schools and families is an important aspect of children's development (Rosenthal & Sawyers, 1996).

CULTURE AND ETHNICITY

Culture-Based Criticisms of Freud's Theory

Many psychologists believe Freud overemphasized behavior's biological determinants and did not give adequate attention to sociocultural influences and learning. In particular, his view on the differences between males and females, including their personality development, has a strong biological flavor, relying mainly on anatomical differences: that is, Freud argued that because they have a penis, boys are likely to develop a dominant, powerful personality, and that because they do not have a penis, girls are likely to develop a submissive, weak personality. In basing his view of male/female differences in personality development on anatomical differences, Freud ignored the enormous impact of culture and experience in determining the personalities of the male and the female (Cloninger, 1996).

More than half a century ago, English anthropologist Bronislaw Malinowski (1927) observed the behavior of the Trobriand islanders of the Western

Bwaitalu village carvers with children in the Trobriand islands of New Guinea. In the Trobriand islands, the authoritarian figure in the young boy's life is the maternal uncle, not the father. The young boys in this culture fear the maternal uncle, not the father. Thus, it is not sexual relations in a family that create conflict and fear for a child, a damaging finding for Freud's Oedipus complex theory.

John W. Santrock

Pacific. He found that the Oedipus complex is not universal but depends on cultural variations in families. The family pattern of the Trobriand islanders is different from that found in many cultures. In the Trobriand islands, the biological father is not the head of the household, a role reserved for the mother's brother, who acts as a disciplinarian. Thus, the Trobriand islanders tease apart the roles played by the same person in Freud's Vienna and in many other cultures. In Freud's view, this different family constellation should make no difference: The Oedipal complex should still emerge, in which the father is the young boy's hated rival for the mother's love. However, Malinowski found no indication of conflict between fathers and sons in the Trobriand islanders, though he did observe some negative feelings directed by the boy toward the maternal uncle. Thus, the young boy feared the man who was the authoritarian figure in his life, which in the Trobriand island culture was the maternal uncle, not the father. In sum, Malinowski's study documented that it was not the sexual relations within the family that created conflict and fear for a child, a damaging finding for Freud's Oedipus complex theory.

GENDER

Masculine Bias in Freud's Theory and Today's Feminist Therapies

Karen Horney developed the first feminist-based criticism of Freud's theory. Horney's model emphasizes females' positive qualities and self-evaluation.

Nancy Chodorow has developed an important contemporary feminist revision of psychoanalytic theory that emphasizes the meaningfulness of emotions for females.

The Oedipus complex was one of Freud's most influential concepts pertaining to the importance of early psychosexual relationships for later personality development. Freud's theory was developed during the Victorian era of the late nineteenth century, when the male was dominant and the female was passive, and when sexual interests, especially the female's, were repressed. According to Freud, the sequence of events in the phallic stage for the girl begins when she realizes that she has no penis. She recognizes that the penis is superior to her own anatomy, and thus develops penis *envy*. Since her desire for having a penis can never be satisfied directly, Freud said, the young girl develops a wish to become impregnated by her father. Holding her mother responsible for her lack of a penis, she renounces her love for her mother and becomes intensely attached to her father, thus forming her own version of the Oedipus complex, sometimes referred to as the Electra complex. Thus the sequence of events becomes reversed: For the boy, the Oedipal complex produces castration anxiety; whereas for the girl, penis envy—the parallel to castration anxiety—occurs first and leads to the formation of the Oedipus complex.

The first feminist-based criticism of Freud's theory was proposed by psychoanalytic theorist Karen Horney (1967). She developed a model of women with positive feminine qualities and self-evaluation. Her critique of Freud's theory included reference to a male-dominant society and culture. Rectification of the male bias in psychoanalytic theory continues today. For example, Nancy Chodorow (1989) emphasizes that many more women than men define themselves in terms of their relationships and connections to others. Her feminist revision of psychoanalytic theory also emphasizes the meaningfulness of emotions for women, as well as the belief that many men use the defense mechanism of denial in self-other connections.

Not only did Freud create a highly influential theory of development, but his approach to therapy has also had a tremendous impact on the way mental health professionals strive to help adults and children cope with problems in their lives. In Freud's psychoanalysis, and most other forms of therapy, including humanistic, the goal has been to foster autonomy, independence, freedom, and self-determination. However, therapists are taking a new look at autonomy as the ideal goal of therapy for girls and women. Should therapy with females focus more on the way most females have been socialized and place more emphasis on relationships? Can females, even with psychotherapy, achieve autonomy in a male-dominated world? Would therapy for females, as well as males, be improved if its goals were more androgynous, stressing better psychological functioning in *both* autonomy and connectedness?

Because traditional therapy often has not adequately addressed the specific concerns of girls and women in a sexist society, several nontraditional approaches have been created (Brown & Brodsky, 1992; Paludi, 1995; Worrell & Remer, 1992). These nontraditional therapies emphasize the importance of helping girls and women break free from traditional gender roles and stereotypes. The nontraditional therapies also avoid language that labels one gender as more socially desirable or valuable than the other.

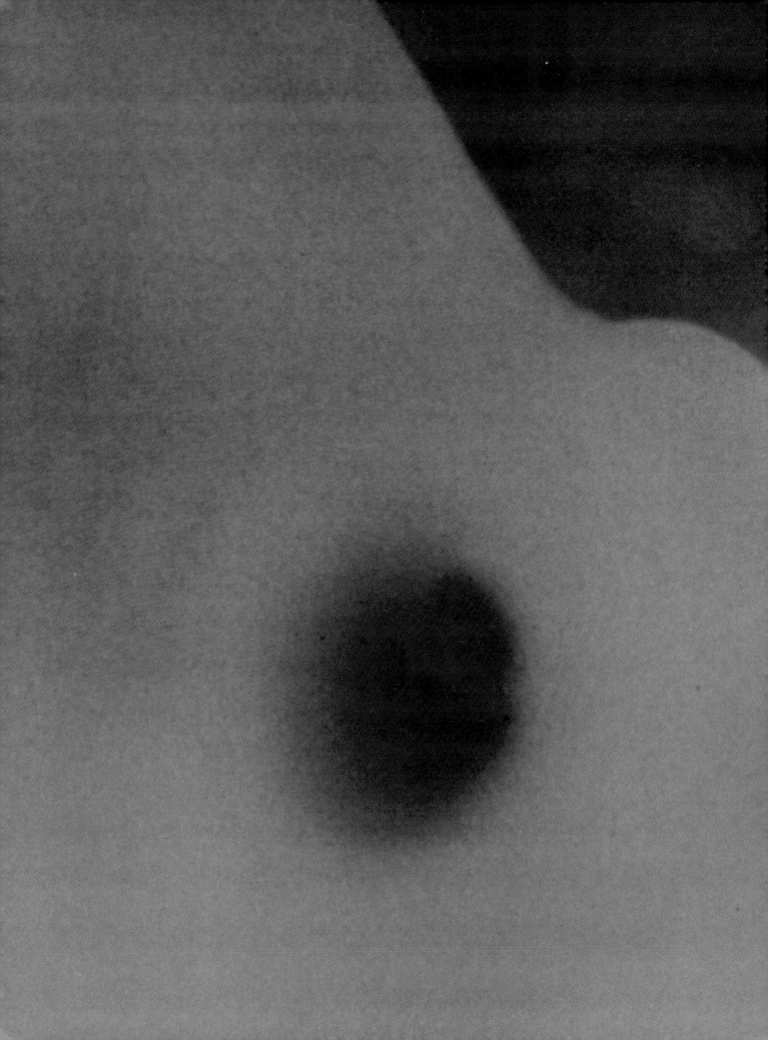

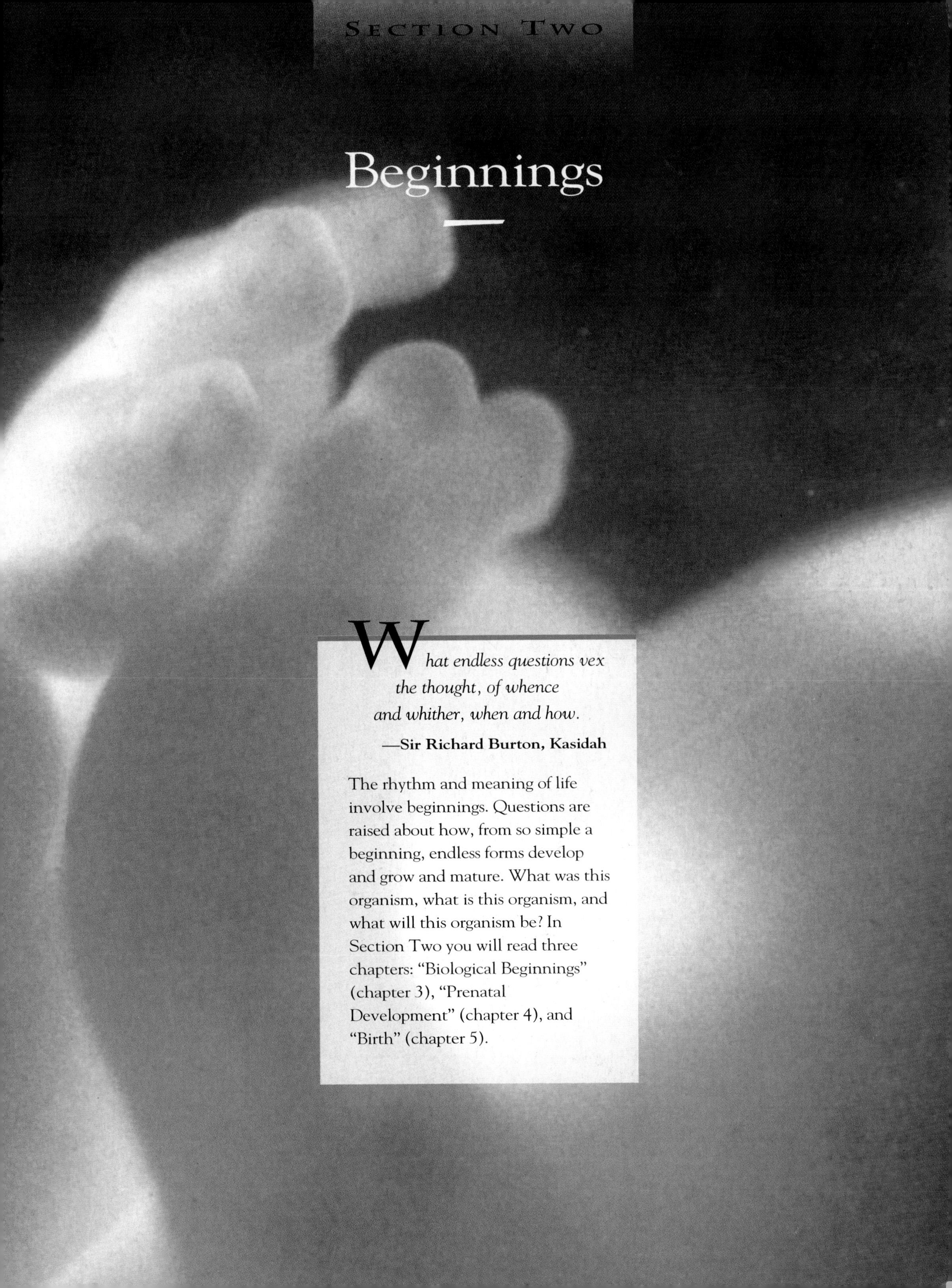

SECTION TWO

Beginnings

What endless questions vex the thought, of whence and whither, when and how.

—Sir Richard Burton, Kasidah

The rhythm and meaning of life involve beginnings. Questions are raised about how, from so simple a beginning, endless forms develop and grow and mature. What was this organism, what is this organism, and what will this organism be? In Section Two you will read three chapters: "Biological Beginnings" (chapter 3), "Prenatal Development" (chapter 4), and "Birth" (chapter 5).

WINSLOW HOMER
Three Boys and a Kitten, detail

Biological Beginnings

*There are one hundred and ninety-three
living species of monkeys and apes.
One hundred and ninety-two of them are
covered with hair. The exception is
the naked ape self-named, Homo sapiens.*

—Desmond Morris

The frightening part about heredity and environment is that we parents provide both.

—Notebook of a Printer

IMAGES OF CHILDREN

The Jim and Jim Twins

Jim Springer and Jim Lewis are identical twins. They were separated at 4 weeks of age and did not see each other again until they were 39 years old. Both worked as part-time deputy sheriffs, vacationed in Florida, drove Chevrolets, had dogs named Toy, and married and divorced women named Betty. One twin named his son James Allan, and the other named his son James Alan. Both liked math but not spelling, enjoyed carpentry and mechanical drawing, chewed their fingernails down to the nubs, had almost identical drinking and smoking habits, had hemorrhoids, put on 10 pounds at about the same point in development, first suffered headaches at the age of 18, and had similar sleep patterns.

But Jim and Jim had some differences. One wore his hair over his forehead, the other slicked it back and had sideburns. One expressed himself best orally, the other was more proficient in writing. But for the most part, their profiles were remarkably similar.

Another pair, Daphne and Barbara, were called the "giggle sisters" because they were always making each other laugh. A thorough search of their adoptive families' histories revealed no gigglers. And the identical sisters handled stress by ignoring it, avoided conflict and controversy whenever possible, and showed no interest in politics.

Two other female identical twin sisters were separated at 6 weeks and reunited in their fifties. Both had nightmares, which they describe in

Jim Lewis (left) and Jim Springer (right).

hauntingly similar ways: Both dreamed of doorknobs and fishhooks in their mouths as they smothered to death! The nightmares began during early adolescence and had stopped in the last 10 to 12 years. Both women were bed wetters until about 12 or 13 years of age, and they reported educational and marital histories that were remarkably similar.

These sets of twins are part of the Minnesota Study of Twins Reared Apart, directed by Thomas Bouchard and his colleagues. They bring identical twins (identical genetically because they come from the same fertilized egg) and fraternal twins (dissimilar genetically because they come from different fertilized eggs) from all over the world to

Minneapolis to investigate their lives. The twins are given a number of personality tests, and detailed medical histories are obtained, including information about diet, smoking, exercise habits, chest X-rays, heart stress tests, and EEGs (brain-wave tests). The twins are interviewed and asked more than 15,000 questions about their family and childhood environment, personal interests, vocational orientation, values, and aesthetic judgments. They also are given ability and intelligence tests (Bouchard & others, 1990).

Critics of the Minnesota identical twins study point out that some of the separated twins were together several months prior to their adoption, that some of the twins had been reunited prior to their testing (in some cases, a number of years earlier), that adoption agencies often place twins in similar homes, and that even strangers who spend several hours together and start comparing their lives are likely to come up with some coincidental similarities (Adler, 1991). Still, even in the face of such criticism, the Minnesota study of identical twins indicates how scientists have recently shown an increased interest in the genetic basis of human development, and that we need further research on genetic and environmental factors (Bouchard & others, 1996; Wilcox & Bouchard, 1996).

John W. Santrock

The examples of Jim and Jim, the giggle sisters, and the identical twins who had the same nightmares stimulate us to think about our genetic heritage and the biological foundations of our existence. Organisms are not like billiard balls, moved by simple, external forces to predictable positions on life's table. Environmental experiences and biological foundations work together to make us who we are. Our coverage of life's biological beginnings focuses on evolution, genetics, heredity's influence on development, and the interaction of heredity and environment.

THE EVOLUTIONARY PERSPECTIVE

In evolutionary time, humans are relative newcomers to Earth, yet we have established ourselves as the most successful and dominant species. If we consider evolutionary time as a calendar year, humans arrived here in the last moments of December (Sagan, 1977). As our earliest ancestors left the forest to feed on the savannahs, and finally to form hunting societies on the open plains, their minds and behaviors changed. How did this evolution come about?

Natural Selection

Natural selection *is the evolutionary process that favors individuals of a species that are best adapted to survive and reproduce.* To understand natural selection, let's return to the middle of the nineteenth century, when Charles Darwin was traveling around the world observing many different species of animals in their natural surroundings. Darwin (1859), who published his observations and thoughts in *On the Origin of Species,* observed that most organisms reproduced at rates that would cause enormous increases in the population of most species and yet populations remained nearly constant. He reasoned that an intense, constant struggle for food, water, and resources must occur among the many young born each generation, because many of the young do not survive. Those that do survive pass their genes on to the next generation. Darwin believed that those who do survive to reproduce are probably superior in a number of ways to those who do not. In other words, the survivors are better adapted to their world than the nonsurvivors (Enger & others, 1996). Over the course of many generations, organisms with the characteristics needed for survival would comprise a larger percentage of the population. Over many, many generations, this could produce a gradual modification of the whole population. If environmental conditions change, however, other characteristics might become favored by natural selection, moving the process in a different direction (Zubay, 1996).

Over a million species have been classified, from bacteria to blue whales, with many varieties of beetles in between. The work of natural selection produced the disappearing acts of moths and the quills of porcupines.

FIGURE 3.1

The Better an Animal Is Adapted, the More Successful It Becomes
Humans, more than any other mammal, adapt to and control most types of environments. Because of longer parental care, humans learn more complex behavior patterns, which contribute to adaptation.

And the effects of evolution produced the technological advances, intelligence, and longer parental care of human beings (see figure 3.1).

> *What seest thou else in the dark backward and*
> *abysm of time.*
>
> —William Shakespeare
>
> *I am a brother to dragons, and a companion to owls.*
>
> —Job 30:29

Generally, evolution proceeds at a very slow pace. The lines that led to the emergence of human beings and the great apes diverged about 14 million years ago! Modern humans, *Homo sapiens*, came into existence only about 50,000 years ago. And the beginning of civilization as we know it began about 10,000 years ago. No sweeping evolutionary changes in humans have occurred since then—for example, our brain is not ten times as big, we do not have a third eye in the back of our head, and we haven't learned to fly.

Although no dramatic evolutionary changes have occurred since *Homo sapiens* appeared on the fossil record 50,000 years ago, there have been sweeping cultural changes. Biological evolution shaped human beings into a culture-making species.

Sociobiology

Sociobiology *relies on the principles of evolutionary biology to explain social behavior.* Sociobiologists believe that psychologists have a limited understanding of social behavior because they primarily study one mammalian species—*Homo sapiens.* Sociobiology derives its information from the comparison of tens of thousands of animal species that have evolved some form of social life.

According to E. O. Wilson (1975, 1995), the purpose of sociobiology is not to make crude comparison among animal species or between animals and humans, such as simply comparing wolf and human aggression. Rather, sociobiology's purpose is to develop general laws of the evolution and biology of social behavior. The hope also is to extend the principles of sociobiology to help explain human behavior.

Let's consider a sociobiological inquiry. In some species of birds, the young born in one year might not breed the second year but instead help their parents rear the second year's brood. In other instances, adult birds that have lost their mates might help close relatives rear their young. These social systems that involve helping at the nest occur in Florida scrub jays (Woolfenden, 1975), African white-fronted bee-eaters (Emlen, 1984), and acorn woodpeckers in the western United States (Koenig, Mumme, & Pitelka, 1984). Nests with helpers are more successful—they fledge more young. But the energy expended in such helping behavior does not appear to directly benefit the helper's own progeny. Sociobiologists are interested in how such helping behavior evolved and what the advantages are for helping or not helping.

Sociobiology has helped to clarify the relation between animal behavior and human behavior, focused attention on the costs and benefits of behavior, directed inquiry toward individual and group differences, highlighted the role of ecology in behavior, and broadened our understanding of behavior's causes (Byrne, 1997; Crawford, 1987).

Nonetheless, sociobiology is not without its critics, especially when sociobiology is applied to human behavior. The critics argue that sociobiologists do not adequately consider human adaptability and experience, and that sociobiology portrays human beings as mere automatons in thrall to their genes. The critics also say that sociobiology explains behavior after the fact, lacking the predictive ability that characterizes any good theory, and that it promotes discrimination against women and ethnic minorities under the guise of being scientific (Paludi, 1995). As you can see, when sociobiology is applied to human behavior it is controversial.

How do sociobiologists respond to such criticisms? They argue that most psychologists have not given adequate attention to the evolutionary basis of behavior, that sociobiologists do consider both the biological and the experiential sides of behavior, that much of their work does have predictive validity, and that the use of sociobiology to discriminate against women and ethnic minorities has been inappropriate. Such misuses of sociobiology have included the work of "eugenicists," who focus on genetics as a basis for producing superior human beings or a superior race of humans. In addition, sociobiologists believe that political and ideological issues need to be clearly separated from the scientific issues; they hold that the fact that someone finds a scientific theory to be politically objectionable is irrelevant to whether the theory is true or false.

Evolutionary Psychology

Many sociobiologists have skipped the psychological level of analysis. They go directly from principles of evolution to patterns of social organization—such as the mating system (for instance, polygamy or monogamy)—without describing or investigating the psychological mechanisms involved. **Evolutionary psychology** *is a contemporary approach that emphasizes that behavior is a function of mechanisms, requires input for activation, and is ultimately related to successful survival and reproduction.*

David Buss (1995) recently described the basic principles of evolutionary psychology. In evolutionary psychology, psychological and physiological mechanisms are the product of evolution by selection. These mechanisms owe their existence to successful solutions to adaptive problems that ancestral humans faced in their environments. Adaptive problems are numerous, and they are all related to successful survival and reproduction; reproduction is the engine that drives evolution, and survival is important because it aids reproduction. Evolutionary psychology is not about genetic determinism but rather is an interactionistic framework—no human behavior can be produced without input into the evolved psychological mechanisms of humans.

John W. Santrock

The central issue for evolutionary psychologists is the nature of the psychological mechanisms created by selection and the adaptive functions they serve. According to evolutionary psychologists, human psychological mechanisms are domain-specific, or modular. Once developed, all mechanisms require particular forms of input to be activated and to function properly.

Domain-specific, or modular, psychological mechanisms that have been discovered include these:

- A highly patterned distribution of fears and phobias that correspond to hazards faced by humans in ancestral environments—for example, the fear of strangers that emerges between 8 to 24 months of age, as well as fear of snakes, spiders, heights, open spaces, and darkness (Marks, 1987)
- Children's imitation of high-status rather than low-status models (Bandura, 1977)
- The worldwide preference for mates who are kind, intelligent, and dependable (Buss, 1994)

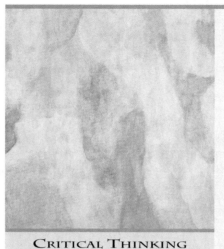

CRITICAL THINKING ABOUT CHILDREN'S DEVELOPMENT

Mate Selection: Male and Female Strategies

Evolutionary psychologists believe that the sexes have different roles to play in sexual selection because of evolution (Buss, 1994; Buss & Malamuth, 1996). They argue that males want to spread their genes to many females who have a good chance of bearing their children, whereas females want to attract the best male they can find (and therefore obtain the best genes). From the perspective of evolutionary psychology, then, the best female strategy in selecting a mate would be to find someone who is physically attractive, youthful, and sexually appealing; the best male strategy would be to develop superiority by winning competitive encounters with other males.

What do you think about evolutionary psychology's position on male selection? Does it ignore the culture-making capacity of the human species, or are we bound to biological imperatives that direct the ways we select our mates? Might an intelligent, self-supporting, and nurturant male be a better choice for the female in many cases than a physically attractive, youthful, and sexually appealing male? By thinking about biological and culture-based reasons for mate selection, you are *pursuing alternative explanations to understand children's development comprehensively.*

Thus, evolutionary psychologists believe that research increasingly supports the concept that numerous mechanisms have evolved because of the large number of diverse adaptive problems humans needed to solve in their evolutionary environments. To read further about evolutionary psychology's stance on mate selection, refer to Critical Thinking About Children's Development.

One of the applications of evolutionary psychology to development involves attachment and warmth (Bowlby, 1989; McDonald, 1992). For example, Kevin McDonald (1992) argues that warmth can be viewed as a reward system that evolved to facilitate cohesive family relationships and parental investment. According to Buss (1995), other important developmental issues in addition to the origins of attachment and warmth are the shifts from mating to parenting, and then to menopause and grandparenting. He asks questions like these: "What psychological mechanisms are triggered by the birth of a child?" "Are the same psychological mechanisms in parents activated by female and male infants, or are some of the mechanisms different?" "Is the asymmetry between the sexes in capacity for reproduction after age 50 accompanied by sex differences in effort allocation and psychological activation?"

Evolutionary psychologists believe that their approach provides a much needed emphasis on the functional properties of mental processes and behavior that can help to integrate the entire field of psychology. They believe that, in the twenty-first century, evolutionary psychology will infiltrate virtually every domain of psychology (Barkow, Cosmides, & Toomy, 1992; Buss, 1995).

Not all psychologists agree, raising criticisms of evolutionary psychology that were once reserved for sociobiology—that it does not place enough emphasis on cultural diversity, and that its explanations are developed after the fact, for example. Critics also argue that it is highly unlikely that one single metatheory—such as evolutionary psychology—will ever encompass all of psychology's complexity (Graziano, 1995). Nonetheless, the field of psychology is currently benefiting from the application of evolutionary psychology's principles to a number of adaptation problems (Daly & Wilson, 1995; Gangestad, 1995).

Race and Ethnicity

In keeping with one of the main themes of this text—exploration of sociocultural issues—let's examine the biological concept of race and see how it has taken on elaborate, often unfortunate, social meanings. **Race** *originated as a biological concept. It refers to a system for classifying plants and animals into subcategories according to specific physical and structural characteristics.* Race is one of the most misused and misunderstood words in the English

Race originated as a biological concept but has unfortunately taken on a number of negative social meanings. Ethnicity is a sociocultural concept.

John W. Santrock

language. Loosely, it has come to mean everything from a person's religion to skin color.

The three main classifications of the human race are Mongoloid, or Asian; Caucasoid, or European; and Negroid, or African. Skin color, head shape, facial features, stature, and the color and texture of body hair are the physical characteristics most widely used to determine race.

These racial classifications presumably were created to define and clarify the differences among groups of people; however, they have not been very useful. Today many people define races as groups that are socially constructed on the basis of physical differences because race is a social construction and no longer a biological fact (Van den Berghe, 1978). For example, some groups, such as Native Americans, Australians, and Polynesians, do not fit into any of the three main racial categories. Also, obvious differences *within* groups are not adequately accounted for. Arabs, Hindus, and Europeans, for instance, are physically different, yet they are all called Caucasians. Although there are some physical characteristics that distinguish "racial" groups, there are, in fact, more similarities than differences among such groups.

Too often we are socialized to accept as facts many myths and stereotypes about people whose skin color, facial features, and hair texture differ from ours. For example, some people still believe that Asians are inscrutable, Jews are acquisitive, and Latinos are lazy. What people believe about race has profound social consequences. Until recently, for instance, African Americans were denied access to schools, hospitals, churches, and other social institutions attended by Whites.

Although scientists are supposed to be a fair-minded lot, some also have used racial distinctions to further their own biases. Some even claim that one racial group has a biological inheritance that gives it an adaptive advantage over other racial groups. Nineteenth-century biologist Louis Agassiz, for example, asserted that God had created Blacks and Whites as separate species. Also, in Nazi Germany, where science and death made their grisliest alliance, Jews, homosexuals, and other "undesirables" were ascribed whatever characteristics were necessary to reinforce the conclusion that "survival of the fittest" demanded their elimination.

Unfortunately, racism cloaked in science still finds champions. Recently psychologist Philipe Rushton (1988) argued that evolution accounts for racial differences in sexual practices, fertility, intelligence, and criminality. Using these traits, he ranks Asians as superior, followed by Caucasians and people of African descent. Asians, Rushton claims, are the most intelligent, most sexually restrained, most altruistic, and least criminal of the races. Rushton ascribes a similar order to social classes: Those who are impoverished resemble African Americans; those who earn high incomes resemble Asians and Whites. Rushton's theory, according to his critics, is full of "familiar vulgar stereotypes" (Weizmann & others, 1990). His notions are stitched together with frequent misinterpretations and overgeneralizations about racial differences and evolutionary history, and the data are tailored to fit his bias. Regrettably, even flimsy theories such as Rushton's provide whole cloth for anyone intent on justifying racism.

Remember that, although race is primarily a *biological* concept, ethnicity is primarily a *sociocultural* concept. In chapter 1, you read that cultural heritage, national characteristics, religion, language, *and* race constitute *ethnicity*. Race is just one component. However, the term *race* is often mistakenly used to refer to ethnicity. Jews, for example, are thought of as a race. Most are Caucasian, but they are too diverse to group into one racial subcategory. They also share too many anatomical similarities with other Caucasians to separate them as a distinct race (Thompson & Hughes, 1958). If we think of ethnicity predominantly in terms of social and cultural heritage, then Jews constitute an ethnic group.

Although we distinguish between race and ethnicity in this book, society usually does not. *Race* is used in a much broader way than many sociocultural psychologists recommend (Brislin, 1993). Social psychologist James Jones (1993) points out that thinking in racial terms has become embedded in cultures as an important factor in human interactions. For example, people often consider what race they will associate with when they decide on such things as where to live, who will make a suitable spouse, where to go to school, and what kind of job they want. Similarly, people often use race to judge whether or not another person is intelligent, competent, responsible, or socially acceptable. Children tend to adopt their parents' attitudes about race as they grow up, often perpetuating stereotypes and prejudice.

HEREDITY

Every species must have a mechanism for transmitting characteristics from one generation to the next. This mechanism is explained by the principles of genetics. Each of us carries a genetic code that we inherited from our parents. This code is located within every cell in our bodies. Our genetic codes are alike in one important way—they all contain the human genetic code. Because of the human genetic code, a fertilized human egg cannot grow into an egret, eagle, or elephant.

What Are Genes?

Each of us began life as a single cell weighing about one twenty-millionth of an ounce! This tiny piece of matter housed our entire genetic code—information about who we would become. These instructions orchestrated growth from that single cell to a person made of trillions of cells, each containing a perfect replica of the original genetic code (Miller & Harley, 1996).

FIGURE 3.2

The Remarkable Substance Known as DNA
Genes are composed of DNA.

The nucleus of each human cell contains 46 **chromosomes,** *which are threadlike structures that come in 23 pairs, one member of each pair coming from each parent. Chromosomes contain the remarkable genetic substance deoxyribonucleic acid, or DNA.* **DNA** *is a complex molecule that contains genetic information.* DNA's "double helix" shape looks like a spiral staircase (see figure 3.2). **Genes,** *the units of hereditary information, are short segments composed of DNA. Genes act as a blueprint for cells to reproduce themselves and manufacture the proteins that maintain life.* Chromosomes, DNA, and genes can be mysterious. To help you turn mystery into understanding, see figure 3.3.

Reproduction

Gametes *are human reproduction cells, which are created in the testes of males and the ovaries of females.* **Meiosis** *is the process of cell doubling and separation of chromosomes, with*

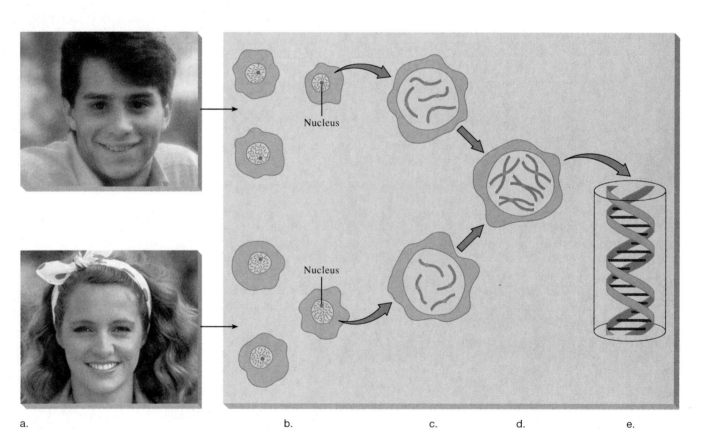

a.   b.   c.   d.   e.

FIGURE 3.3

Facts About Chromosomes, DNA, and Genes
(*a*) The body contains billions of cells that are organized into tissue and organs. (*b*) Each cell contains a central structure, the nucleus, which controls reproduction. (*c*) Chromosomes reside in the nucleus of each cell. The male's sperm and the female's egg are specialized reproductive cells that contain chromosomes. (*d*) At conception the offspring receives matching chromosomes from the mother's egg and the father's sperm. (*e*) The chromosomes contain DNA, a chemical substance. Genes are short segments of the DNA molecule. They are the units of heredity information that act as a blueprint for cells to reproduce themselves and manufacture the proteins that sustain life.

Drawing by Ziegler; © 1985 The New Yorker Magazine, Inc.

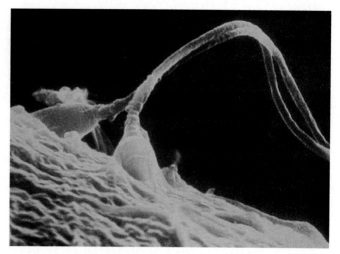

FIGURE 3.4

Union of Sperm and Egg

one member of each chromosomal pair going into each gamete, or daughter cell. Thus, each human gamete has 23 unpaired chromosomes. The process of human **reproduction** begins when a female gamete (ovum) is fertilized by a male gamete (sperm) (see figure 3.4). A **zygote** is a single cell formed through fertilization. In the zygote, two sets of unpaired chromosomes combine to form one set of paired chromosomes—one member of each pair from the mother and the other member from the father. In this manner, each parent contributes 50 percent of the offspring's heredity.

The ovum is about 90,000 times as large as a sperm. Thousands of sperm must combine to break down the ovum's membrane barrier to allow a single sperm to penetrate the membrane barrier. Ordinarily, females have two X chromosomes and males have one X and one Y chromosome. Because the Y chromosome is smaller and lighter than the X chromosome, Y-bearing sperm can be separated from X-bearing sperm in a centrifuge. This raises the possibility that the offspring's sex can be controlled. Not only are the Y-bearing sperm lighter, but they are more likely than the X-bearing sperm to coat the ovum. This results in the conception of 120 to 150 males for every 100 females. But males are more likely to die (spontaneously abort) at every stage of prenatal development, so only about 106 males are born for every 100 females.

Reproduction's fascinating moments have been made even more intriguing in recent years. **In vitro fertilization** is conception outside the body. Consider the following situation. The year is 1978. One of the most dazzling occurrences of the 1970s is about to unfold. Mrs. Brown is infertile, but her physician informs her of a new procedure that could enable her to have a baby. The procedure involves removing the mother's ovum surgically, fertilizing it in a laboratory medium with live sperm cells obtained from the father or another male donor (see figure 3.5), storing the fertilized egg in a laboratory solution that substitutes

FIGURE 3.5

In Vitro Fertilization
Egg meets sperm in a laboratory dish.

for the uterine environment, and finally implanting the egg in the mother's uterus. For Mrs. Brown, the procedure was successful, and 9 months later her daughter Louise was born.

Since the first in vitro fertilization in the 1970s, variations of the procedure have brought hope to childless couples. A woman's egg can be fertilized with the husband's sperm, or the husband and wife may contribute their sperm and egg, with the resulting embryo carried by a third party, who essentially is donating her womb. Researchers have not found any developmental deficiencies in children born through in vitro fertilization.

Approximately 10 to 15 percent of couples in the United States are estimated to experience infertility, which

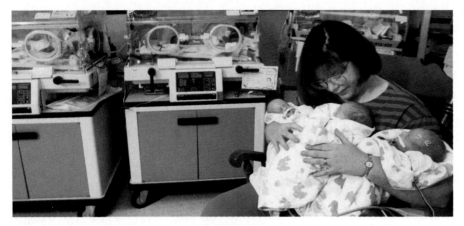

The arrival of six healthy babies—with the assistance of fertility technology—dramatically transformed the lives of Becky and Keith Dilley. The parents face extraordinary hardship and exhilaration, as their challenges of parenting are multiplied by six. To date, the Dilley babies continue to thrive; not all families experiencing multiple births are so lucky. Sometimes babies born in multiple births show birth defects, and some do not survive. Thus, technological developments in childbirth have been the source of great hope and heartbreak.

is defined as the inability to conceive a child after 12 months of regular intercourse without contraception. The cause of infertility can rest with the woman or the man. The woman may not be ovulating, she may be producing abnormal ova, her fallopian tubes may be blocked, or she may have a disease that prevents implantation of the ova. The man may produce too few sperm, the sperm may lack motility (the ability to move adequately), or he may have a blocked passageway. In one study, long-term use of cocaine by men was related to low sperm count, low motility, and a higher number of abnormally formed sperm (Bracken & others, 1990). Cocaine-related infertility appears to be reversible if users stop taking the drug for at least 1 year. In some cases of infertility, surgery may correct the problem; in others hormonal-based drugs may improve the probability of having a child. However, in some instances, fertility drugs have caused superovulation, producing as many as three or more babies at a time. A summary of some of infertility's causes and solutions is presented in table 3.1.

The creation of families by means of the new reproductive technologies raises important questions about the psychological consequences for children. In one recent study, the family relationships and socioemotional development of children were investigated in four types of families—two created by the most widely used reproductive technologies (in vitro fertilization and donor insemination) and two control groups of families (those with a naturally conceived child and adoptive families) (Golombok & others, 1995). There were no differences between the four types of families on any of the measures of children's socioemotional development. The picture of families created by the new reproductive technologies was a positive one. To read further about reproductive technology, refer to Critical Thinking About Children's Development.

While surgery and fertility drugs can solve the infertility problem in some cases, another choice is to adopt a child. Researchers have found that adopted children are often more at risk for psychological and school-related problems than nonadopted children are (Brodzinsky & others, 1984), although some adopted children adapt well to their circumstances (Marquis & Detweiler, 1985; Sharma, McGue, & Benson, 1996). Some adopted children show difficulties during adolescence, when, as part of their search for identity, they feel a void and incompleteness because they do not know their biological family's history (Brodzinsky, Lang, & Smith, 1995).

A question that virtually every adoptive parent wants answered is "Should I tell my adopted child that he

TABLE 3.1

Fertility Problems and Solutions

Females

Problem	Solution
Damaged fallopian tubes	Surgery, in vitro fertilization
Abnormal ovulation	Hormone therapy, antibiotics, in vitro fertilization
Pelvic Inflammatory Disease (PID)	Antibiotics, surgery, change in birth control methods
Endometriosis*	Antibiotics, hormone therapy, surgery, artificial insemination
Damaged ovaries	Surgery, antibiotics, hormone therapy
Hostile cervical mucus	Antibiotics, artificial insemination, hormone therapy
Fibroid tumor	Surgery, antibiotics

Males

Problem	Solution
Low sperm count	Antibiotics, hormone therapy, artificial insemination, lowered testicular temperature
Dilated veins around testicle	Surgery, lowered testicular temperature, antibiotics
Damaged sperm ducts	Surgery, antibiotics
Hormone deficiency	Hormone therapy
Sperm antibodies	Antibiotics, in vitro fertilization

*Endometriosis occurs when the uterine lining grows outside of the uterus and causes bleeding, blocking, or scarring that can interfere with conception or pregnancy.

Source: Data from A. Toth, *The Fertility Solution*, 1991.

John W. Santrock

Where do you stand with regard to access to technological advances in reproductive interventions? Should these techniques be available only to those who can pay for it? Should any woman with childbearing intentions gain access to sophisticated technology, regardless of her age? As newer and more unusual methods are developed, how will we make appropriate determinations about access? How do such investments compare to the challenge of caring for children who are already here? In times of rising taxes and health insurance costs, how much of the cost should be borne by persons not directly involved in raising the child?

Obviously these are messy ethical questions indeed. However, your pattern of responses to these questions may reveal something about your underlying values system. Are you more inclined to champion an *individual rights* stance or a *collectivist* position? Are you more likely to favor the value of *scientific progress* in support of new technologies or a *naturalistic* perspective in which any artificial methods are likely to be condemned? Does being able to *identify these values and the role they play in decisions* make your choices about these and other ethical dilemmas easier to predict? In considering access to advances in reproductive technology, you are learning to think critically about children's development by *pursuing alternative explanations to understand children's development comprehensively*.

or she is adopted? If so, when?" Most psychologists believe that adopted children should be told that they are adopted, because they will eventually find out anyway. Many children begin to ask where they came from when they are approximately 4 to 6 years of age. This is a natural time to begin to respond in simple ways to children about their adopted status. Clinical psychologists report that one problem that sometimes surfaces is the desire of adoptive parents to make life too perfect for the adoptive child and to present a perfect image of themselves to the child. The result too often is that adopted children feel that they cannot release any angry feelings and openly discuss problems in this climate of perfection (Warshak, 1996). To read further about adoption, turn to Critical Thinking About Children's Development.

Abnormalities in Genes and Chromosomes

What are some abnormalities that can occur in genes and chromosomes? What tests can be used to determine the presence of these abnormalities?

Abnormalities

Geneticists and developmentalists have identified a range of problems caused by some major gene or chromosome defect. **Phenylketonuria (PKU)** *is a genetic disorder in which the individual cannot properly metabolize an amino acid. Phenylketonuria is now easily detected, but if left untreated, mental retardation and hyperactivity result.* When detected, the disorder is treated by diet to prevent an excess accumulation of phenylalanine, an amino acid. Phenylketonuria

involves a recessive gene and occurs about once in every 10,000 to 20,000 live births. Phenylketonuria accounts for about 1 percent of institutionalized mentally retarded individuals and it occurs primarily in Whites.

Down syndrome *is a common genetically transmitted form of mental retardation, caused by the presence of an extra (47th) chromosome.* An individual with Down syndrome has a round face, a flattened skull, an extra fold of skin over the eyelids, a protruding tongue, short limbs, and retardation of motor and mental abilities. It is not known why the extra chromosome is present, but the health of the male sperm or female ovum may be involved (Vining, 1992). Women between the ages of 18 and 38 are less likely to give birth to a Down syndrome child than are younger or older women. Down syndrome appears approximately once in every 700 live births. African American children are rarely born with Down syndrome.

Sickle-cell anemia, *which occurs most often in Africans and African Americans, is a genetic disorder affecting the red blood cells.* A red blood cell is usually shaped like a disk, but in sickle-cell anemia a change in a recessive gene modifies its shape to a hook-shaped "sickle." These cells die quickly, causing anemia and early death of the individual because of their failure to carry oxygen to the body's cells. About 1 in 400 African American babies is affected. One in 10 African Americans is a carrier, as is 1 in 20 Latinos (see figure 3.6).

Other disorders are associated with sex-chromosome abnormalities. Remember that normal males have an X chromosome and a Y chromosome, and normal females have two X chromosomes. **Klinefelter syndrome** *is a genetic disorder in which males have an extra X chromosome, making*

FIGURE 3.6

Sickle-Cell Anemia
(a) Avery Hubbard's family—parents Jerry and Tami, sister Sara (age 4), and Avery. All carry the gene that causes sickle-cell anemia. (b) Avery Hubbard, age 3. She is the first in a long line of carriers to develop the painful disease. Jerry Hubbard, 32, learned he carried the gene for sickle-cell anemia during a physical examination for a college football tryout. Daughter Sara is healthy, but Avery has sickle-cell anemia. Their parents say that they won't try to have any more children.

them XXY instead of XY. Males with this disorder have undeveloped testes, and they usually have enlarged breasts and become tall. Klinefelter syndrome occurs approximately once in every 800 live male births.

Turner syndrome *is a genetic disorder in which females are missing an X chromosome, making them XO instead of XX.* These females are short in stature and have a webbed neck. They may be sexually underdeveloped. Turner syndrome occurs approximately once in every 3,000 live female births.

The XYY syndrome *is a genetic disorder in which the male has an extra Y chromosome. Early interest in this syndrome involved the belief that the Y chromosome found in males contributed to male aggression and violence.* It was then reasoned that if a male had an extra Y chromosome he would likely be extremely aggressive and possibly develop a violent personality. However, researchers subsequently found that XYY males were no more likely to commit crimes than were XY males (Witkin & others, 1976).

We have discussed six genetic disorders—phenylketonuria, Down syndrome, sickle-cell anemia, Klinefelter syndrome, Turner syndrome, and the XYY syndrome.

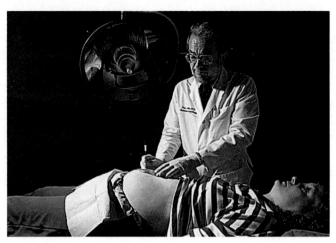

FIGURE 3.7

Amniocentesis Being Performed on a Pregnant Woman

A summary of these genetic disorders, as well as others, appears in table 3.2.

Each year in the United States, approximately 100,000 to 150,000 infants are born with a genetic disorder or malformation. These infants comprise about 3 to 5 percent of the 3 million births and account for at least 20 percent of infant deaths. Prospective parents increasingly are turning to genetic counseling for assistance, wanting to know their risk of having a child born with a genetic defect or malformation.

Tests to Determine Abnormalities

Scientists have developed a number of tests to determine whether the fetus is developing normally, among them amniocentesis, ultrasound sonography, the chorionic villus test, and the maternal blood test, each of which we will discuss in turn.

Amniocentesis *is a prenatal medical procedure in which a sample of amniotic fluid is withdrawn by syringe and tested to discover if the fetus is suffering from any chromosomal or metabolic disorders. Amniocentesis is performed between the 12th and 16th weeks of pregnancy.* The later amniocentesis is performed, the better the diagnostic potential. The earlier it is performed, the more useful it is in deciding whether a pregnancy should be terminated (see figure 3.7).

Ultrasound sonography *is a prenatal medical procedure in which high-frequency sound waves are directed into the pregnant woman's abdomen.* The echo from the sounds is transformed into a visual representation of the fetus's inner structures. This technique has been able to detect such disorders as microencephaly, a form of mental retardation involving an abnormally small brain. Ultrasound sonography is often used in conjunction with amniocentesis to determine the precise location of the fetus in the mother's abdomen (see figure 3.8).

As scientists have searched for more accurate, safe assessments of high-risk prenatal conditions, they have

TABLE 3.2

Genetic Disorders and Conditions

Name	Description	Treatment	Incidence	Prenatal Detection	Carrier Detection
Anencephaly	Neural-tube disorder that causes brain and skull malformations; most children die at birth.	Surgery	1 in 1,000	Ultrasound, amniocentesis	None
Cystic fibrosis	Glandular dysfunction that interferes with mucus production; breathing and digestion are hampered, resulting in a shortened life span.	Physical and oxygen therapy, synthetic enzymes, and antibiotics	1 in 2,000	Amniocentesis	Family history, DNA analysis
Down syndrome	Extra or altered 21st chromosome causes mild to severe retardation and physical abnormalities.	Surgery, early intervention, infant stimulation, and special learning programs	1 in 800 women; 1 in 350 women over 35	AFP, CVS, amniocentesis	Family history, chromosomal analysis
Hemophilia	Lack of the clotting factor causes excessive internal and external bleeding.	Blood transfusions and/or injections of the clotting factor	1 in 10,000 males	CVS, amniocentesis	Family history, DNA analysis
Klinefelter syndrome	An extra X chromosome causes physical abnormalities.	Hormone therapy	1 in 800 males	CVS, amniocentesis	None
Phenylketonuria (PKU)	Metabolic disorder that, left untreated, causes mental retardation.	Special diet	1 in 14,000	CVS, amniocentesis	Family history, blood test
Pyloric stenosis	Excess muscle in upper intestine causes severe vomiting and death if not treated.	Surgery	1 male in 200; 1 female in 1,000	None	None
Sickle-cell anemia	Blood disorder that limits the body's oxygen supply, it can cause joint swelling, sickle-cell crises, heart and kidney failure.	Penicillin, medication for pain, antibiotics, and blood transfusions	1 in 400 African American children (lower among other groups)	CVS, amniocentesis	Blood test
Spina bifida	Neural tube disorder that causes brain and spine abnormalities.	Corrective surgery at birth, orthopedic devices and physical/medical therapy	2 in 1,000	AFP, ultrasound, amniocentesis	None
Tay-Sachs disease	Deceleration of mental and physical development caused by an accumulation of lipids in the nervous system; few children live to age 5.	Medication and special diet	1 in 30 American Jews is a carrier	CVS, amniocentesis	Blood test
Thalassemia	Group of inherited blood disorders that causes anemic symptoms ranging from fatigue and weakness to liver failure.	Blood transfusions and antibiotics	1 in 400 children of Mediterranean descent	CVS, amniocentesis	Blood test
Turner syndrome	A missing or altered X chromosome may cause sexual underdevelopment or physical abnormalities.	Hormone therapy	1 in 3,000 females	None	Blood test

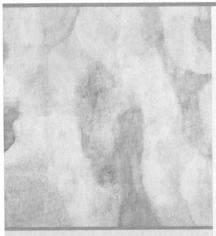birth parents are given little information about the adoptive parents (Brodzinsky, Schechter, & Henig, 1992). This strategy—followed by most adoption agencies—is thought to be in the best interest of both parties. A number of activist groups, such as the Adoptees Liberty Movement Association and Concerned United Birthmothers—challenge this strategy. These groups stress that sealing records at the time of adoption violates our basic right to know about ourselves (and our offspring, in the case of the Concerned United Birthmothers). They also argue that sealing records about parent or child identity can set the stage for potential difficulties related to the adoption experience.

Develop an argument that sealing records and giving little information at the time of adoption is a wise strategy. Now argue the opposite side of this issue. By doing so, you are *creating arguments based on developmental concepts.*

developed a new test. The **chorionic villus test** *is a prenatal medical procedure in which a small sample of the placenta is removed at some point between the 8th and 11th weeks of pregnancy.* Diagnosis takes approximately 10 days. The chorionic villus test allows a decision about abortion to be made near the end of the first trimester of pregnancy, a point when abortion is safer and less traumatic than after amniocentesis in the second trimester. These techniques provide valuable information about the presence of birth defects, but they also raise issues pertaining to whether an abortion should be obtained if birth defects are present.

The **maternal blood test** *(alpha-fetoprotein—AFP) is a prenatal diagnostic technique that is used to assess blood alphaprotein level, which is associated with neural-tube defects.* This test is administered to women 14 to 20 weeks into pregnancy only when they are at risk for bearing a child with defects in the formation of the brain and spinal cord.

So far in this chapter, we have discussed the evolutionary perspective, genes, chromosomes, and reproduction, and abnormalities in genes and chromosomes. A summary of these ideas is outlined in concept table 3.1.

GENETIC PRINCIPLES AND METHODS

What are some basic genetic principles that affect children's development? What methods do behavior geneticists use to study heredity's influence? How does heredity influence such aspects of children's development as their intelligence? And how do heredity and environment interact to produce children's development?

Some Genetic Principles

Genetic determination is a complex affair, and much is unknown about the way genes work (Tamarin, 1996). But a number of genetic principles have been discovered, among them

FIGURE 3.8

Ultrasound Sonography
A 6-month-old infant poses with the ultrasound sonography record taken 4 months into the baby's prenatal development.

John W. Santrock

CONCEPT TABLE 3.1

The Evolutionary Perspective and Genetics

Concept	Processes/Related Ideas	Characteristics/Description
The Evolutionary Perspective	Natural selection	Natural selection is the process that favors the individuals of a species that are best adapted to survive and produce. This concept was originally proposed by Charles Darwin. Although no dramatic evolutionary changes have occurred in humans since *Homo sapiens* first appeared in the fossil record 50,000 years ago, there have been sweeping cultural changes. Biological evolution shaped human beings into a culture-making species.
	Sociobiology	This approach relies on the principles of evolutionary biology to explain the social behavior of animals. Sociobiology's purpose is to develop general laws of the evolution and biology of social behavior. The hope also is that sociobiology can help explain human behavior. Sociobiology has made important contributions to our understanding of social behavior.
	Evolutionary psychology	This is a contemporary approach that emphasizes that behavior is a function of mechanisms, requires input for activation, and is ultimately related to successful survival and reproduction. Psychological mechanisms are the product of evolution. The central issue for evolutionary psychologists is the nature of the psychological mechanisms created by selection and the adaptive functions they serve. Evolutionary psychologists believe that human psychological mechanisms are domain-specific, or modular. Evolutionary psychology can be applied to developmental psychology. Evolutionary psychologists believe their approach provides a much needed integration of psychology's disparate areas, although criticisms of the approach have been made.
	Race and ethnicity	Race is a biological concept; ethnicity is a sociocultural concept. The concept of race has taken on a number of social meanings, some of which have resulted in discrimination and prejudice. Race continues to be a misunderstood and abused concept.
Heredity	What are genes?	The nucleus of each human cell contains 46 chromosomes, which are composed of DNA. Genes are short segments of DNA and act as a blueprint for cells to reproduce and manufacture proteins that maintain life.
	Reproduction	Genes are transmitted from parents to offspring by gametes, or sex cells. Gametes are formed by the splitting of cells, a process called "meiosis." Reproduction takes place when a female gamete (ovum) is fertilized by a male gamete (sperm) to create a single-celled ovum. In vitro fertilization has helped to solve some infertility problems. Approximately 10 to 15 percent of couples in the United States experience infertility problems, some of which can be corrected through surgery or fertility drugs. Another choice for infertile couples is adoption.
	Abnormalities in genes and chromosomes	A range of problems are caused by major gene or chromosome defects, among them PKU, Down syndrome, sickle-cell anemia, Klinefelter syndrome, Turner syndrome, and the XYY syndrome. Genetic counseling has increased in popularity as couples desire information about their risk of having a defective child. Amniocentesis, ultrasound sonography, the chorionic villus test, and the maternal blood test are used to determine the presence of defects after pregnancy has begun.

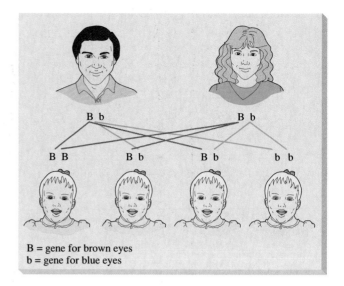

B = gene for brown eyes
b = gene for blue eyes

FIGURE 3.9

How Brown-Eyed Parents Can Have a Blue-Eyed Child
Although both parents have brown eyes, each parent can have a recessive gene for blue eyes. In this example both parents have brown eyes, but each parent carries the recessive gene for blue eyes. Therefore, the odds of their child having blue eyes is one in four—the probability the child will receive a recessive gene (b) from each parent.

those of dominant-recessive genes, sex-linked genes, polygenically inherited characteristics, reaction range, and canalization.

According to the **dominant-recessive genes principle,** *if one gene of the pair is dominant and one is recessive, the dominant gene exerts its effect, overriding the potential influence of the other, recessive gene. A recessive gene exerts its influence only if the two genes of a pair are both recessive.* If you inherit a recessive gene for a trait from each of your parents, you will show the trait. If you inherit a recessive gene from only one parent, you may never know you carry the gene. Brown eyes, farsightedness, and dimples rule over blue eyes, nearsightedness, and freckles in the world of dominant-recessive genes. Can two brown-eyed parents have a blue-eyed child? Yes, they can. Suppose that in each parent the gene pair that governs eye color includes a dominant gene for brown eyes and a recessive gene for blue eyes. Since dominant genes override recessive genes, the parents have brown eyes. But both are carriers of blueness and pass on their recessive genes for blue eyes. With no dominant gene to override them, the recessive genes can make the child's eyes blue. Figure 3.9 illustrates the dominant-recessive genes principles.

For thousands of years, people wondered what determined whether we become male or female. Aristotle believed that the father's arousal during intercourse determined the offspring's sex. The more excited the father was, the more likely it would be a son, he reasoned. Of course, he was wrong, but it was not until the 1920s that researchers confirmed the existence of human sex chromosomes, 2 of the 46 chromosomes human beings normally carry. As we saw earlier, ordinarily females have two

X chromosomes and males have an X and a Y. (Figure 3.10 shows the chromosomal makeup of a male and a female.)

Genetic transmission is usually more complex than the simple examples we have examined thus far (Weaver & Hedrick, 1996). **Polygenic inheritance** *is the genetic principle that many genes can interact to produce a particular characteristic.* Few psychological characteristics are the result of single pairs. Most are determined by the interaction of many different genes. There are as many as 50,000 or more genes, so you can imagine that possible combinations of these are staggering in number. Traits produced by this mixing of genes are said to be polygenically determined.

No one possesses all the characteristics that our genetic structure makes possible. A **genotype** *is the person's genetic heritage, the actual genetic material.* However, not all of this genetic material is apparent in our observed and measurable characteristics. A **phenotype** *is the way an individual's genotype is expressed in observed and measurable characteristics.* Phenotypes include physical traits (such as height, weight, eye color, and skin pigmentation) and psychological characteristics (such as intelligence, creativity, personality, and social tendencies).

That which comes of a cat will catch mice.

—English proverb

For each genotype, a range of phenotypes can be expressed. Imagine that we could identify all of the genes that would make a person introverted or extraverted. Would measured introversion-extraversion be predictable from knowledge of the specific genes? The answer is no,

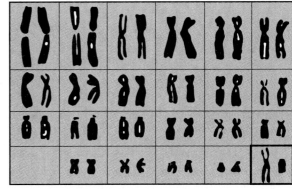

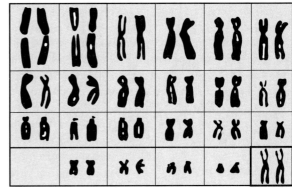

FIGURE 3.10

The Genetic Difference Between Males and Females
Set (*a*) shows the chromosome structure of a male, and set (*b*) shows the chromosome structure of a female. The last pair of 23 pairs of chromosomes is in the bottom right box of each set. Notice that the Y chromosome of the male is smaller than that of the female. To obtain this kind of chromosomal picture, a cell is removed from a person's body, usually from the inside of the mouth. The chromosomes are stained by chemical treatment, magnified extensively, and then photographed.

because even if our genetic model were adequate, introversion-extraversion is a characteristic shaped by experience throughout life. For example, parents may push an introverted child into social situations and encourage the child to become more gregarious.

To understand how introverted a person is, think about a series of genetic codes that predispose the child to develop in a particular way, and imagine environments that are responsive or unresponsive to this development. For instance, the genotype of some persons may predispose them to be introverted in an environment that promotes a turning inward of personality, yet in an environment that encourages social interaction and outgoingness, these individuals may become more extraverted. However, it would be unlikely for the individual with this introverted genotype to become a strong extravert. The **reaction range** *is the range of possible phenotypes for each genotype, suggesting the importance of an environment's restrictiveness or enrichment* (see figure 3.11).

Sandra Scarr (1984) explains reaction range this way: Each of us has a range of potential. For example, an individual with "medium-tall" genes for height who grows

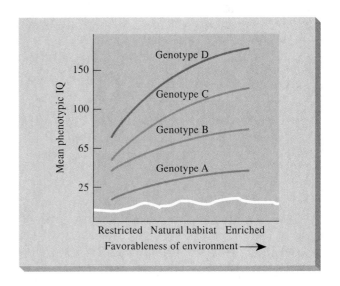

FIGURE 3.11

Responsiveness of Genotypes to Environmental Influences
Although each genotype responds favorably to improved environments, some are more responsive to environmental deprivation and enrichment than are others.

up in a poor environment may be shorter than average. But in an excellent nutritional environment, the individual may grow up taller than average. However, no matter how well fed the person is, someone with "short" genes will never be taller than average. Scarr believes that characteristics such as intelligence and introversion work the same way. That is, there is a range within which the environment can modify intelligence, but intelligence is not completely malleable. Reaction range gives us an estimate of how modifiable intelligence is.

Genotypes, in addition to producing many phenotypes, may show the opposite track for some characteristics—those that are somewhat immune to extensive changes in the environment. These characteristics seem to stay on a particular developmental course regardless of the environmental assaults on them (Waddington, 1957). **Canalization** *is the term chosen to describe the narrow path, or developmental course, that certain characteristics take. Apparently, preservative forces help to protect or buffer a person from environmental extremes.* For example, American developmental psychologist Jerome Kagan (1984) points to his research on Guatemalan infants who had experienced extreme malnutrition as infants yet showed normal social and cognitive development later in childhood. And some abused children do not grow up to be abusers themselves.

However, although the genetic influence of canalization exerts its power by keeping organisms on a particular developmental path, genes alone do not directly determine human behavior. Developmentalist Gilbert Gottlieb (1991) points out that genes are an integral part of the organism, but that their activity (genetic expression) can be affected by the organism's environment. For example, hormones that circulate in the blood make their way into the cell, where they influence the cell's activity. The flow of hormones themselves can be affected by environmental events such as light, day length, nutrition, and behavior.

Methods Used by Behavior Geneticists

Behavior genetics *is the study of the degree and nature of behavior's hereditary basis.* Behavior geneticists assume that behaviors are jointly determined by the interaction of heredity and environment (Goldsmith, 1994). To study heredity's influence on behavior, behavior geneticists often use either twin studies or adoption studies.

In a **twin study,** *the behavioral similarity of identical twins is compared with the behavioral similarity of fraternal twins.* **Identical twins** (called monozygotic twins) *develop from a single fertilized egg that splits into two genetically identical replicas, each of which becomes a person.* **Fraternal twins** (called dizygotic twins) *develop from separate eggs and separate sperm, making them genetically no more similar than ordinary siblings.* Although fraternal twins share the same womb, they are no more alike genetically than are nontwin brothers and sisters, and they may be of different sexes. By comparing groups of identical and fraternal twins, behavior geneticists capitalize on the basic knowledge that identical twins are more similar

Identical twins develop from a single fertilized egg that splits into two genetically identical organisms. Twin studies compare identical twins with fraternal twins. Fraternal twins develop from separate eggs, making them genetically no more similar than ordinary brothers and sisters.

genetically than are fraternal twins (Scarr, 1996). In one twin study, 7,000 pairs of Finnish identical and fraternal twins were compared on the personality traits of extraversion (outgoingness) and neuroticism (psychological instability) (Rose & others, 1988). On both of these personality traits, identical twins were much more similar than fraternal twins were, suggesting the role of heredity in both traits. However, several issues crop up as a result of twin studies. Adults might stress the similarities of identical twins more than those of fraternal twins, and identical twins might perceive themselves as a "set" and play together more than fraternal twins do. If so, observed similarities in identical twins could be environmentally influenced.

In an **adoption study,** *investigators seek to discover whether, in behavior and psychological characteristics, adopted children are more like their adoptive parents, who provided a home environment, or more like their biological parents, who contributed their heredity.* Another form of the adoption study is to compare adoptive and biological siblings. In one investigation, the educational levels attained by biological parents were better predictors of adopted children's IQ scores than were the IQs of children's adopted parents (Scarr & Weinberg, 1983). Because of the genetic relation between the adopted children and their biological parents, the implication is that heredity influences children's IQ scores.

John W. Santrock

By permission of Johnny Hart and NAS, Inc.

Heredity's Influence on Development

What aspects of development are influenced by genetic factors? They all are. However, behavior geneticists are interested in more precise estimates of a characteristic's variation that can be accounted for by genetic factors. Intelligence and temperament are among the most widely investigated aspects of heredity's influence on development.

Arthur Jensen (1969) sparked a lively and, at times, hostile debate when he presented his thesis that intelligence is primarily inherited. Jensen believes that environment and culture play only a minimal role in intelligence. He examined several studies of intelligence, some of which involved comparisons of identical and fraternal twins. Remember that identical twins have identical genetic endowments, so their IQs should be similar. Fraternal twins and ordinary siblings are less similar genetically, so their IQs should be less similar. Jensen found support for his argument in these studies. Studies with identical twins produced an average correlation of .82; studies with ordinary siblings produced an average correlation of .50. Note the difference of .32. To show that genetic factors are more important than environmental factors, Jensen compared identical twins reared together with those reared apart; the correlation for those reared together was .89 and for those reared apart was .78 (a difference of .11). Jensen argued that, if environmental influences were more important than genetic influences, then siblings reared apart, who experienced different environments, should have IQs much farther apart.

Many scholars have criticized Jensen's work. One criticism concerns the definition of intelligence itself. Jensen believes that IQ as measured by standardized intelligence tests is a good indicator of intelligence. Critics argue that IQ tests tap only a narrow range of intelligence. Everyday problem solving, work, and social adaptability, say the critics, are important aspects of intelligence not measured by the traditional intelligence tests used in Jensen's sources. A second criticism is that

most investigations of heredity and environment do not include environments that differ radically. Thus, it is not surprising that many genetic studies show environment to be a fairly weak influence on intelligence.

Intelligence is influenced by heredity, but most developmentalists have not found as strong a relationship as Jensen found in his work. Other experts estimate heredity's influence on intelligence to be in the 50 percent range (Plomin, DeFries, & McClearn, 1990).

The most recent controversy about heredity and intelligence focuses on the book *The Bell Curve: Intelligence and Class Structure in Modern Life* (1994) by Richard Hernstein and Charles Murray. The authors argued that America is rapidly evolving a huge underclass of intellectually deprived individuals whose cognitive abilities will never match the future needs of most employers. The authors believe that members of this underclass, a large percentage of whom are African American, might be doomed by their shortcomings to welfare dependency, poverty, crime, and lives devoid of any hope of ever reaching the American dream.

Hernstein and Murray believe that IQ can be quantitatively measured and that IQ test scores vary across ethnic groups. They point out that, in the United States, Asian Americans score several points higher than Whites, while African Americans score about 15 points lower than Whites. They also argue that these IQ differences are at least partly due to heredity, and that government money spent on education programs like Project Head Start is wasted, helping only the government's bloated bureaucracy.

Why do Hernstein and Murray call their book *The Bell Curve?* A bell curve is a normal distribution graph, which has the shape of a bell—bulging in the middle and thinning out at the edges (see figure 3.12). Normal distribution graphs are used to represent large numbers of people who are sorted according to some shared characteristic, such as weight, exposure to asbestos, taste in clothes, or IQ.

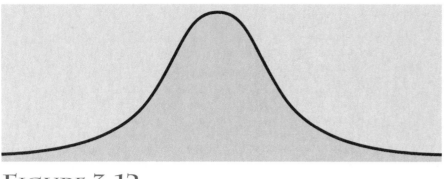

FIGURE 3.12

The Bell Curve
The term *bell curve* is used to describe a normal distribution graph, which looks like a bell—bulging in the middle and thinning out at the edges.

Hernstein and Murray often refer to bell curves to make a point: that predictions about any individual based exclusively on the person's IQ are useless. Weak correlations between intelligence and job success have predictive value only when they are applied to large groups of people. Within such large groups, say Hernstein and Murray, the pervasive influence of IQ on human society becomes apparent (Browne, 1994).

Significant criticisms have been leveled at *The Bell Curve*. Experts on intelligence generally agree that African Americans score lower than Whites on IQ tests. However, many of these experts raise serious questions about the ability of IQ tests to accurately measure a person's intelligence. Among the criticisms of IQ tests is that the tests are culturally biased against African Americans and Latinos. In 1971, the U.S. Supreme Court endorsed such criticisms and ruled that tests of general intelligence, in contrast to tests that solely measure fitness for a particular job, are discriminatory and cannot be administered as a condition of employment. Another criticism is that most investigations of heredity and environment do not include environments that differ radically. Thus, it is not surprising that many genetic studies show environment to be a fairly weak influence on intelligence (Fraser, 1995).

HEREDITY-ENVIRONMENT INTERACTION AND CHILDREN'S DEVELOPMENT

A common misconception is that behavior geneticists only analyze the effects of heredity on development. While they believe heredity plays an important role in children's development, they also carve up the environment's contribution to heredity-environment interaction.

Genotype → Environment Concepts

Parents not only provide the genes for their child's biological blueprint for development; they also play important roles in determining the types of environments their children will encounter. Behavior geneticist Sandra Scarr (1993) believes that the environments parents select for their children depend to some degree on the parents' own genotypes. Behavior geneticists believe that three ways heredity and environment interact are passively, evocatively, and actively. The arrow (→) in the heading for this section ("Genotype → Environment Concepts") expresses Scarr's emphasis that heredity drives the interactions between genotype and environment.

Passive genotype-environment interactions *occur when parents who are genetically related to the child provide a rearing environment for the child.* For example, parents may have a genetic predisposition to be intelligent and read skillfully. Because they read well and enjoy reading, they provide their child with books to read, with the likely outcome that their children will become skilled readers who enjoy reading.

Evocative genotype-environment interactions *occur because a child's genotype elicits certain types of physical and social environments.* For example, active, smiling babies receive more social stimulation than passive, quiet babies do. Cooperative, attentive children evoke more pleasant and instructional responses from the adults around them than uncooperative, distractible children do.

Active (niche-picking) genotype-environment interactions *occur when children seek out environments they find compatible and stimulating.* Niche-picking *refers to finding a niche or setting that is especially suited to the child's abilities.* Children select from their surrounding environment some aspects that they respond to, learn about, or ignore. Their active selections of certain environments are related to their particular genotype. Some children, because of their genotype, have the sensorimotor skills to perform well at sports. Others, because of their genotype, may have more ability in music. Children who are athletically inclined are more likely to actively seek out sports environments in which they can perform well, while children who are musically inclined are more likely to spend time in musical environments in which they can successfully perform their skills.

Scarr (1993) believes that the relative importance of the three genotype-environment interactions changes as children develop from infancy through adolescence. In infancy, much of the environment that children experience is provided by adults. When those adults are genetically related to the child, the environment they provide is related to their own characteristics and genotypes. Although infants are active in structuring their experiences by actively attending to what is available to them, they cannot seek out and build their own environmental niches as much as older children can. Therefore, passive genotype-environment interactions are more common in the lives of infants and

Sandra Scarr has developed a number of important theoretical ideas and conducted a number of research investigations on the roles of heredity and environment in children's development. She believes that the environments parents select for their children depend to some degree on the parents' own genotype. Critics argue that the environment plays a stronger role in children's development than Scarr acknowledges.

young children than they are for older children, who can extend their experiences beyond the family's influences and create their environments to a greater degree.

Shared and Nonshared Environmental Influences

Behavior geneticists also believe that another way the environment's role in heredity-environment interaction can be carved up is to consider the experiences that children in families have that are in common with other children living in the same home and those that are not common or shared (Finkel, Whitfield, & McGue, 1995). Behavior geneticist Robert Plomin (1993) has found that common rearing, or shared environment, accounts for little of the variation in children's personality or interests. In other words, even though two children live under the same roof with the same parents, their personalities are often very different.

Shared environmental experiences *are children's common experiences, such as their parents' personalities and intellectual orientation, the family's social class, and the neighborhood in which they live.* By contrast, **nonshared environmental experiences** *are a child's own unique experiences, both within the family and outside the family, that are not shared with another sibling. Thus, experiences occurring within the family can be part of the "nonshared environment."* Parents often do interact differently with each sibling, and siblings interact differently with parents. Siblings often have different peer groups, different friends, and different teachers at school.

The Contemporary Heredity-Environment Controversy

As we have seen, Sandra Scarr (1993, 1996) believes that heredity plays a powerful role in children's development.

Her theory of genotype → environment effects essentially states that genotypes drive experiences. Scarr also stresses that unless a child's family is harshly abusive or fails to provide what she calls "average expectable" conditions (conditions like those in which the species has evolved), parental differences in child-rearing styles, social class, and income have only small effects on differences in children's intelligence, personality, and interests. Scarr also has presented the provocative view that biology makes non-at-risk infants invulnerable to lasting, negative effects of day care. In sum, Scarr stresses that, except in extreme instances of abused and at-risk children, environmental experiences play a minimal role, if any, in determining differences in children's cognitive and socioemotional development.

Not surprisingly, Scarr's claims have generated considerable controversy in the field of child development. Among Scarr's critics, Diana Baumrind (1993), Eleanor Maccoby (1992), and Jacquelyne Jackson (1993) point to a number of loopholes in her arguments. They conclude that Scarr has not adequately defined just what an "average expectable" environment is, that good parenting optimizes both normal and vulnerable children's development, and that Scarr's interpretations of behavior genetics studies go far beyond what is justified, given the inherent limitations of such studies.

Scarr (1993) responds to such criticisms by arguing that understanding children's development requires describing it under the umbrella of evolutionary theory and that many developmentalists do not give adequate attention to the important role that biology plays in children's development. She, like other biology-oriented theorists (Goldsmith, 1994), feels that her critics often misinterpret what she says. Scarr claims that social reformers oppose her ideas because they believe that these ideas cause pessimism about social change. She responds that she is simply motivated to discover the facts about the roles of genes and environment in determining human development. According to Scarr, all children should have an opportunity to become species-normal, culturally appropriate, and uniquely themselves—their own versions of Georgia O'Keefe and Martin Luther King; many children in today's world lack those opportunities, and their needs should be addressed. However, she concludes that humanitarian concerns should not drive developmental theory and that developmental theory must have a strong biological orientation to be accurate.

Virtually all developmentalists today are interactionists in that they believe heredity and environment interact to determine children's development (George, 1996; Kendler, 1996). However, Scarr argues that heredity plays a powerful role in heredity-environment interaction, while Baumrind, Maccoby, and Jackson believe the environment is a much stronger influence on children's development than Scarr acknowledges.

In sum, both genes and environment are necessary for a child to even exist. Heredity and environment operate together—or cooperate—to produce a child's intelligence, temperament, height, weight, ability to pitch a baseball, reading talents, and so on (McGue & Carmichael, 1995; Plomin, 1996; Rose, 1995). Without genes, there is no

CONCEPT TABLE 3.2

Genetic Principles and Methods, Heredity, and Heredity-Environment Interaction

Concept	Processes/Related Ideas	Characteristics/Description
Genetic Principles and Methods	Genetic principles	Genetic transmission is complex, but some principles have been worked out, among them dominant-recessive genes, sex-linked genes, polygenic inheritance, genotype-phenotype distinction, reaction range, and canalization.
	Methods used by behavior geneticists	Behavior genetics is the field concerned with the degree and nature of behavior's heredity basis. Among the most important methods used by behavior geneticists are twin studies and adoption studies.
Heredity's Influence on Development	Its scope	All aspects of development are influenced by heredity.
	Intelligence	Like Hernstein and Murray's, Jensen's argument that intelligence is due primarily to heredity sparked a lively and, at times, bitter debate. Intelligence is influenced by heredity, but not as strongly as Jensen and Hernstein and Murray envisioned.
Heredity-Environment Interaction and Development	Genotype → environment concepts	Scarr believes that the environments parents select for their own children depend to some degree on the parents' genotypes. Three ways behavior geneticists believe heredity and environment interact in this manner are passively, evocatively, and actively. Passive genotype/environment interactions occur when parents, who are genetically related to the child, provide a rearing environment for the child. Evocative genotype/environment interactions occur because a child's genotype elicits certain types of physical and social environments. Active (niche-picking) genotype/environment interactions occur when children seek out environments they find compatible and stimulating. Scarr believes the relative importance of these three forms of genotype/environment interactions changes as children develop.
	Shared and nonshared environments	Shared environmental experiences are children's common experiences, such as their parents' personalities and intellectual orientation, the family's social class, and the neighborhood in which they live. Nonshared environmental experiences refer to the child's own unique experiences both within a family and outside the family, that are not shared by another sibling. Plomin argues that it is nonshared environmental experiences that primarily make up the environment's contribution to why one sibling's personality is different from another's.
	The contemporary heredity/ environment controversy	Scarr's genotype → environment theory has generated considerable controversy. She argues that except in extreme abusive and at-risk conditions, the environment plays a minimal role in determining differences in children's cognitive and socioemotional development. A number of criticisms of her view have been offered. In sum, without genes, there is no organism; without environment, there is no organism. Because the environment's influence depends on genetically endowed characteristics, we say that the two factors interact.

child; without environment, there is no child (Scarr & Weinberg, 1980). If an attractive, popular, intelligent girl is elected president of her senior class in high school, should we conclude that her success is due to heredity? to environment? Of course, the answer is both. Because the environment's influence depends on genetically endowed characteristics, we say the two factors *interact* (Mader, 1996).

A summary of the main ideas in our discussion of genetic principles and methods, heredity's influence on children's development, and how heredity and environment interact to produce development is presented in concept table 3.2. In the next chapter, we will continue to discuss biological beginnings, turning to the nature of prenatal development and birth.

B iological beginnings raise questions of how we as a species came to be, how parents' genes are shuffled to produce a particular child, and how much experience can go against the grain of heredity.

In this chapter, we studied the Jim and Jim twins; the evolutionary perspective, in which we discussed natural selection, sociobiology, evolutionary psychology, and race and ethnicity; the nature of heredity; what genes are; how reproduction takes place; some abnormalities in genes and chromosomes; genetic principles; methods used by behavior geneticists; heredity's influence on development; and what heredity-environment interaction is like. With regard to heredity-environment interaction, behavior geneticists believe that it is important to consider passive genotype-environment, evocative genotype-environment, and active genotype-environment interactions, as well as shared and nonshared environmental experiences. Scarr's biological view has recently generated considerable controversy. Remember that you can obtain a summary of the main ideas in the entire chapter by again studying the two concept tables on pages 87 and 94.

In the next chapter, we will continue our exploration of children's biological beginnings by discussing the dramatic unfolding of prenatal development.

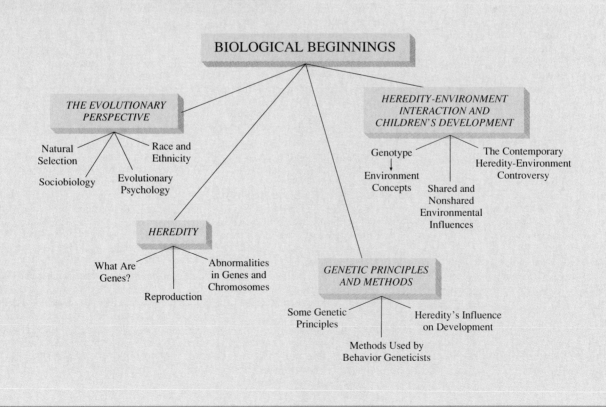

BIOLOGICAL BEGINNINGS

THE EVOLUTIONARY PERSPECTIVE

Natural Selection

Sociobiology

Race and Ethnicity

Evolutionary Psychology

HEREDITY-ENVIRONMENT INTERACTION AND CHILDREN'S DEVELOPMENT

Genotype → Environment Concepts

Shared and Nonshared Environmental Influences

The Contemporary Heredity-Environment Controversy

HEREDITY

What Are Genes?

Reproduction

Abnormalities in Genes and Chromosomes

GENETIC PRINCIPLES AND METHODS

Some Genetic Principles

Methods Used by Behavior Geneticists

Heredity's Influence on Development

natural selection The evolutionary process that favors individuals of a species that are best adapted to survive and reproduce. 75

sociobiology A view that relies on the principles of evolutionary biology to explain behavior. 76

evolutionary psychology A contemporary approach that emphasizes that behavior is a function of mechanisms, requires input for activation, and is ultimately related to survival and reproduction. 76

race The term for a system for classifying plants and animals into subcategories according to specific physical and structural characteristics. 77

chromosomes Threadlike structures that come in 23 pairs, one member of each pair coming from each parent. Chromosomes contain the genetic substance DNA. 80

DNA A complex molecule that contains genetic information. 80

genes Units of hereditary information composed of DNA. Genes act as a blueprint for cells to reproduce themselves and manufacture the proteins that maintain life. 80

gametes Human reproduction cells created in the testes of males and the ovaries of females. 80

meiosis The process of cell doubling and separation of chromosomes in which each pair of chromosomes in a cell separates, with one member of each pair going into each gamete. 80

reproduction The process that, in humans, begins when a female gamete (ovum) is fertilized by a male gamete (sperm). 81

zygote A single cell formed through fertilization. 81

in vitro fertilization Conception outside the body. 81

phenylketonuria (PKU) A genetic disorder in which an individual cannot properly metabolize an amino acid. PKU is now easily detected but, if left untreated, results in mental retardation and hyperactivity. 83

Down syndrome A common genetically transmitted form of mental retardation, caused by the presence of an extra (47th) chromosome. 83

sickle-cell anemia A genetic disorder that affects the red blood cells and occurs most often in African American individuals. 83

Klinefelter syndrome A genetic disorder in which males have an extra X chromosome, making them XXY instead of XY. 83

Turner syndrome A genetic disorder in which females are missing an X chromosome, making them XO instead of XX. 84

XYY syndrome A genetic disorder in which males have an extra Y chromosome. 84

amniocentesis A prenatal medical procedure in which a sample of amniotic fluid is withdrawn by syringe and tested to discover if the fetus is suffering from any chromosomal or metabolic disorders. It is performed between the 12th and 16th weeks of pregnancy. 84

ultrasound sonography A prenatal medical procedure in which high-frequency sound waves are directed into the pregnant woman's abdomen. 84

chorionic villus test A prenatal medical procedure in which a small sample of the placenta is removed at a certain point in the pregnancy between the 8th and the 11th weeks of pregnancy. 86

maternal blood test A prenatal diagnostic technique that is used to assess blood alphaprotein level, which is associated with neural-tube defects. This technique is also called the alpha-fetoprotein test (AFP). 86

dominant-recessive genes principle If one gene of a pair is dominant and one is recessive (goes back or recedes), the dominant gene exerts its effect, overriding the potential influence of the recessive gene. A recessive gene exerts its influence only if both genes in a pair are recessive. 88

polygenic inheritance The genetic principle that many genes can interact to produce a particular characteristic. 88

genotype A person's genetic heritage; the actual genetic material. 88

phenotype The way an individual's genotype is expressed in observed and measurable characteristics. 88

reaction range The range of possible phenotypes for each genotype, suggesting the importance of an environment's restrictiveness or enrichment. 89

canalization The process by which characteristics take a narrow path or developmental course. Apparently, preservative forces help to protect a person from environmental extremes. 90

behavior genetics The study of the degree and nature of behavior's heredity basis. 90

twin study A study in which the behavioral similarity of identical twins is compared with the behavioral similarity of fraternal twins. 90

identical twins Twins who develop from a single fertilized egg that splits into two genetically identical replicas, each of which becomes a person. 90

fraternal twins Twins who develop from separate eggs and separate sperm, making them genetically no more similar than ordinary siblings. 90

adoption study A study in which investigators seek to discover whether, in behavior and psychological characteristics, adopted children are more like their adoptive parents, who provided a home environment, or more like their biological parents, who contributed their heredity. Another form of the adoption study is to compare adoptive and biological siblings. 90

passive genotype-environment interactions The type of interactions that occur when parents, who are genetically related to the child, provide a rearing environment for the child. 92

evocative genotype-environment interactions The type of interactions that occur when the child's genotype elicits certain types of physical and social environments. 92

active (niche-picking) genotype-environment interactions The type of interactions that occur when children seek out environments they find compatible and stimulating. 92

shared environmental experiences Children's common environmental experiences that are shared with their siblings, such as their parents' personalities and intellectual orientation, the family's social class, and the neighborhood in which they live. 93

nonshared environmental experiences The child's own unique experiences, both within the family and outside the family, that are not shared by another sibling. Thus, experiences occurring within the family can be part of the "nonshared environment." 93

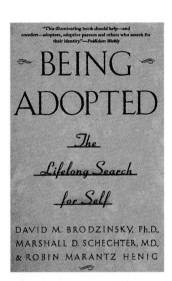

Being Adopted
(1992) by David Brodzinsky, Marshall Schechter, & Robin Henig. New York: Doubleday.

This book provides an excellent overview of how adoption influences people's lives throughout the human life span and includes a discussion of how adoption ties in with Erikson's stages of the human life span. The authors bring together a wide body of information to address the special hurdles that adoptees and adopters must manage. Adoptees, adoptive parents, professionals, and other interested individuals will find the book to be a rich source of information.

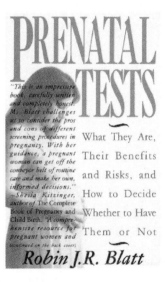

Prenatal Tests
(1988) by Robin J. R. Blatt. New York: Vintage Books.

Prenatal Tests is a comprehensive guide to what prenatal tests are available, their benefits and risks, and how to decide whether to have them. The author challenges women to consider the pros and cons of various screening procedures during pregnancy. Pregnant women are encouraged to avoid the conveyor belt of routine care and make their own, informed decisions. The book also provides valuable information for the partners of pregnant women, addressing the emotional and ethical aspects of decision making that couples face when considering prenatal testing.

How Healthy Is Your Family Tree?
(1995) by Carol Krause. New York: Simon & Schuster.

In this book, you will learn how to create a family medical tree. The author asks you to find out how any of your relatives died; how old they were when they died; what illnesses, health conditions, or surgeries they had had; what the exact diagnoses were; whether the person smoked, drank excessively, or took drugs; whether there was a history of mental disorders; and other information. She also suggests that once you put together a medical family tree, a specialist or genetic counselor can help you understand it.

IMPROVING THE LIVES OF CHILDREN

Let's further explore ways that we can improve the lives of children in the areas of health and well-being, families and parenting, education, culture and ethnicity, and gender.

HEALTH AND WELL-BEING

Prepregnancy Planning and Health Care Providers

The medical community has placed new emphasis on prepregnancy or preconception planning. Some hospitals now offer prepregnancy planning classes, and some practitioners suggest that both potential parents meet with them prior to conception to assess their health and review their personal and family histories. During this meeting, the health care provider may review immunization records, adjust any medications or medical treatments, and discuss nutrition and other aspects of health that may affect an unborn baby. This meeting can also be used to identify the chances of passing on a particular inherited disorder and to describe available genetic screening tests. The idea behind preconception planning is that early care is the best way to discover and treat a potential problem. Such programs give parents a sense of reassurance that they are doing everything possible to have a healthy baby.

Many different kinds of health care professionals are qualified to provide care for pregnant women. They include:

- Obstetrician-gynecologist (OB-GYN). This health care provider is a medical doctor, certified by the American College of Obstetricians and Gynecologists, who is trained to provide medical and surgical care to women. Obstetricians mainly provide pregnancy care, whereas gynecologists provide care for women's reproductive systems. Only licensed obstetricians are trained to perform surgical prenatal diagnostic procedures such as chorionic villus sampling and amniocentesis.

- Family practitioner (FP). This provider is a medical doctor who specializes in health care for all family members. Some general practitioners provide basic obstetric care but refer women to an obstetrician for prenatal testing.

- Nurse practitioner (NP). This person is a registered nurse with advanced training in maternal and child health care. Some nurse practitioners work independently in providing pregnancy-related care but refer women to a doctor for prenatal testing or if a complication develops. Many nurse practitioners work with doctors to provide prenatal care and education.

- Certified nurse-midwife (CNM). This provider is a registered nurse who has graduated from an accredited midwifery program and who is trained to provide comprehensive health care to women and their babies from early pregnancy through labor, delivery, and after birth. Midwives can help women understand the reasons for choosing or refusing prenatal testing. They can refer women to an obstetrician for prenatal testing or if a problem arises.

Regardless of which health care provider a woman chooses, she should try to find someone who (Blatt, 1988)

- takes time to do a thorough family history,
- encourages the woman to take responsibility,
- is not patronizing,
- is knowledgeable and stays current on prenatal testing,
- is honest about risks, benefits, and side effects of any tests or treatments, and
- inspires trust.

Genetic Counseling

In 1978, Richard Davidson was an athletic 37-year-old. A slip on an icy driveway landed him in the hospital for minor surgery for a broken foot. The day after the operation, he died. The cause of death was malignant hyperthermia (MH), a fatal allergy-like reaction to certain anesthetics. The condition is hereditary and preventable—if the anesthesiologist is aware of the patient's susceptibility, alternative drugs can be used. Richard's death inspired his parents, Owen and Jean Davidson, to search their family tree for others with the MH trait. They mailed three hundred letters to relatives, telling them of their son's death and warning about the hereditary risk. The gene, it turned out, came from Jean's side of the family. When her niece Suellen Gallamore informed the hospital where she was going to have infertility surgery about the MH in her bloodline, the doctors refused to treat her. In 1981, she cofounded the Malignant Hyperthermia Association to educate medical providers about MH so that people at risk, like her sons, would not suffer as she had. Or lose their lives, as her cousin Richard had (Adato, 1995).

Consider also Bob and Mary Sims, who have been married for several years. They would like to start a family, but they are frightened. The newspapers and popular magazines are full of stories about infants who are born prematurely and don't survive, infants with debilitating physical defects, and babies found to have congenital mental retardation. The Simses feel that to have such a child would create a social, economic, and psychological strain on them and on society.

Accordingly, the Simses turn to a genetic counselor for help. Genetic counselors are usually physicians or biologists who are well versed in the field of medical genetics. They are familiar with the kinds of problems that can be inherited, the odds for encountering them, and helpful measures for offsetting some of their effects. The Simses tell their counselor that there has been a history of mental retardation in Bob's family. Bob's younger sister was born with Down syndrome, a form of mental retardation. Mary's older brother has

Suellen Gallamore with her sons Scott and Greg Vincent. Among her immediate family, only Suellen has had the painful muscle biopsy for the MH gene. Scott, 24, and Greg, 26, assume that they carry the gene and protect against MH by alerting doctors about their family's medical history.

hemophilia, a condition in which bleeding is difficult to stop. They wonder what the chances are that a child of theirs might also be retarded or have hemophilia and what measures they can take to reduce their chances of having a mentally or physically defective child.

The counselor probes more deeply, because she understands that these facts in isolation do not give her a complete picture of the possibilities. She learns that no other relatives in Bob's family are retarded and that Bob's mother was in her late forties when his younger sister was born. She concludes that the retardation was probably due to the age of Bob's mother and not to some general tendency for members of his family to inherit retardation. It is well known that women over 40 have a

much higher probability of giving birth to retarded children than are younger women. Apparently, in women over 40, the ova (egg cells) are not as healthy as in women under 40.

In Mary's case the counselor determines that there is a small but clear possibility that Mary may be a carrier of hemophilia and might transmit that condition to a son. Otherwise; the counselor can find no evidence from the family history to indicate genetic problems.

The decision is then up to the Simses. In this case, the genetic problem will probably not occur, so the choice is fairly easy. But what should parents do if they face the strong probability of having a child with a major birth defect? Ultimately, the decision depends on the couple's ethical and religious beliefs.

EDUCATION

The Effects of Early Intervention on Intelligence

Researchers are increasingly interested in manipulating the environment early in children's lives when they are perceived to be at risk for impoverished intelligence (Burchinal & Sideeck, 1996). In a program conducted in North Carolina by Craig Ramey and his associates (1988), pregnant women with IQs averaging 80 were recruited for a study. After their babies were born, half of the infants were cared for during the day at an educational day-care center and half were reared at home by their mothers. Both groups of children were given medical care and dietary supplements, and their families were given social services if they requested them.

At the age of 3, the children who attended the educational day-care center had significantly higher IQs than did the home-reared children. This difference was likely due to the decline in the IQs of the home-reared children during the period from 12 to 18 months of age. By the time the children were 5 years old, 39 percent of the home-reared children had IQs below 85 but only 11 percent of the educational day-care children had IQs this low. In the most recent evaluation of this project, positive effects of educational day care on the intellectual development and academic achievement of the children were evident at age 12 (Campbell & Ramey, 1994).

Some parents, such as those in Ramey's study, have difficulty providing an adequate environment for the intellectual needs of their infants. Once these difficulties are a recurring part of the family system, change efforts probably will be more difficult and costly. Early intervention in the family system is directed at changing parental adaptive and responsive functioning so that permanent negative effects are minimized.

In another investigation, the Infant Health and Development

Craig Ramey's research has documented that high-quality early educational day care can significantly raise the intelligence of young children from impoverished environments.

Program, early intervention with low-birthweight children revealed that both home visitation and an educational child curriculum improved the children's IQ, decreased behavior problems, and improved the home environment (Infant Health and Development Program Staff, 1990; Liaw, Meisels, & Brooks-Gunn, 1994). The intervention was more effective with mothers with low educational attainment than those with high educational attainment, more effective for African American than White children, and effective for most at-risk children.

Intervention programs have the most positive effects on children's well-being when they (a) begin as early as possible, (b) provide services to parents as well as to the child, (c) have a low child-teacher ratio, (d) have high parental involvement, and (e) have frequent contacts. In one review of family intervention studies, intervention was more effective when there were eleven or more contacts between the intervenor and the family (Heinicke, Beckwith, & Thompson, 1988). While eleven sessions is a somewhat arbitrary number, it does indicate that a certain duration of contact is necessary for intervention success.

John W. Santrock

CULTURE AND ETHNICITY

The Human Species Is a Culture-Making Species

Unlike all other animal species, which evolve mainly in response to random changes in their environment, humans have more control over their own evolution. This change occurs through *cultural evolution*. For example, we've made astonishing accomplishments in the past 10,000 years or so, ever since we developed language. Biological (Darwinian) evolution continues in our species, but its rate, compared with cultural evolution, is so slow that its impact seems almost negligible. There is no evidence, for example, that brain size or structure has changed in our species since *Homo sapiens* appeared on the fossil record about 50,000 years ago.

As humans evolved, we acquired knowledge and passed it on from generation to generation. This knowledge, which originally instructed us in how to hunt, make tools, and communicate, became our culture. The accumulation of knowledge has gathered speed—from a slow swell to a meteoric rise. Hunter-gatherer tribes, characteristic of early human society, changed over thousands of years into small agricultural communities. With people rooted in one place, cities grew and flourished. Life within those cities remained relatively unchanged for generations. Then industrialization put a dizzying speed on cultural change. Now technological advances in communication and transportation—such as computers, fax machines, and the SST—transform everyday life at a staggering pace.

Whatever one generation learns, it can pass to the next through writing, word of mouth, ritual, tradition, and a host of other methods humans have developed to assure their culture's continuity (Gould, 1981). By creating cultures, humans have built, shaped, and carved out their own environments. The human species is no

More than 99 percent of all humans now live in a different kind of environment from that in which the species evolved. By creating cultures, humans have, in effect, built, shaped, and carved out their own environments.

longer primarily at nature's mercy. Rather, humans are capable of changing their environment to fit their needs.

GENDER

The Marital Relationship

Marriages have traditionally been based on male dominance. But the traditional pattern of employed husband, homemaker wife no longer is the norm or the ideal for many females and males. Contemporary marriages range from traditional male-dominated ones to equal role-sharing ones. Marital satisfaction is influenced by the match between the expectations of husbands and wives regarding the division of labor inside and outside the home. Although most wives are employed, they still bear main responsibility for home and children, which can weigh heavily on them. Since more men than women want a traditional male-dominated marriage, some husbands feel stress when their wife is in the labor force or when she earns as much as or more than he does. Sex typing also influences marital satisfaction. The happiest marriages are reported by couples in which both partners have strong nurturant, relationship-oriented characteristics. A nurturant, relationship orientation is especially important to wives. Traditional male-dominant marriages often fail to meet the emotional needs of wives, although men in such marriages report that they like this type of marriage.

What all of this means is that, in general, male-dominant marriages—which the majority of marriages are—satisfy husbands far more than wives. Today wives are still expected to adapt to their husband's life rather than vice versa, which can place further strain on the wife. Employed wives are especially burdened, because they tend to work "double shifts" and earn less in the labor force than husbands. The most happily married wives are those who enjoy their jobs and whose husbands share domestic responsibilities.

In sum, adherence to gender stereotypes can have negative effects on children and adults. It is encouraging that the younger generation of men is moving toward less traditional gender expectations for marriage than their fathers had. The hope is that, over time, such cultural change will result in marriage being as satisfying for wives as it now is for husbands. And the very important beneficiaries of many marriages in which both the wife and husband are satisfied are the children.

BILL RANE
Mayan Madonna, detail

Prenatal Development

> The history of man for nine months
> preceding his birth would, probably, be far
> more interesting, and contain events of
> greater moment than all three score
> and ten years that follow it.
>
> —Samuel Taylor Coleridge

What web is this
Of will be, is, and was?

—Jorge Luis Borges

IMAGES OF CHILDREN

Jim and Sara, an Expectant Couple

Although Jim and Sara did not plan to have a baby, they did not take precautions to prevent it, and it was not long before Sara was pregnant. Jim and Sara read the popular pregnancy book *What to Expect When You're Expecting* (Eisenberg, Murkoff, & Hathaway, 1991). They found a nurse-midwife they liked and invented a pet name—Bibinello—for the fetus. They signed up for birth preparation classes, and each Friday night for 8 weeks they faithfully practiced simulated contractions. They drew up a birth plan that included their decisions about such matters as the type of care provider they wanted to use, the birth setting they wanted, and various aspects of labor and birth. They moved into a larger apartment so the baby could have its own room and spent weekends browsing through garage sales and second-hand stores to find good prices on baby furniture—a crib, a high chair, a stroller, a changing table, a crib mobile, a swing, a car seat.

Jim and Sara also spent a lot of time talking about Sara's pregnancy, what kind of parents they wanted to be, and what their child might be like. They also discussed what changes in their life the baby would make. One of their concerns was that Sara's maternity leave would only last 6 weeks. If she wanted to stay home longer, she would have to quit her job, something she and Jim were not sure they could afford. These are among the many questions that expectant couples face.

PREVIEW

This chapter chronicles the truly remarkable changes that take place from conception to birth. Imagine . . . at one time you were an organism floating around in a sea of fluid in your mother's womb. Let's now explore what development is like from the time you were conceived until the time you were born.

THE COURSE OF PRENATAL DEVELOPMENT

Imagine how you came to be. Out of thousands of eggs and millions of sperm, one egg and one sperm united to produce you. Had the union of sperm and egg come a day or even an hour earlier or later, you might have been very different—maybe even of the opposite sex. Remember from chapter 3 that conception occurs when a single sperm cell from the male unites with an ovum (egg) in the female's fallopian tube in a process called fertilization. Remember also that the fertilized egg is called a zygote. By the time the zygote ends its 3- to 4-day journey through the fallopian tube and reaches the uterus, it has divided into approximately 12 to 16 cells.

The Germinal Period

The **germinal period** *is the period of prenatal development that takes place in the first 2 weeks after conception. It includes the creation of the zygote, continued cell division, and the attachment of the zygote to the uterine wall.* By approximately 1 week after conception, the zygote is composed of 100 to 150 cells. The differentiation of cells has already commenced as inner and outer layers of the organism are formed. The **blastocyst** *is the inner layer of cells that develops during the germinal period. These cells later develop into the embryo* (see figure 4.1). The **trophoblast** *is the outer layer of cells that develops during the germinal period. It later provides nutrition and support for the embryo.* **Implantation,** *the attachment of the zygote to the uterine wall, takes place about 10 days after conception.* Figure 4.2 illustrates some of the most significant developments during the germinal period.

John W. Santrock

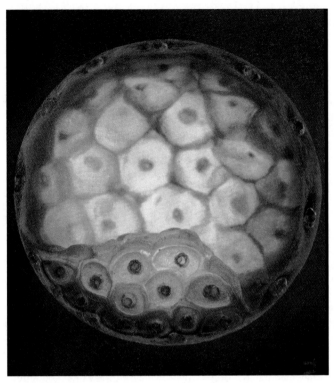

FIGURE 4.1

The Blastocyst
The blastocyst produces this mass of cells when the fertilized egg repeatedly divides after conception. The blastocyst is the inner layer of cells that develops during the germinal period. These cells later develop into the embryo.

The Embryonic Period

The **embryonic period** *is the period of prenatal development that occurs from 2 to 8 weeks after conception. During the embryonic period, the rate of cell differentiation intensifies, support systems for the cells form, and organs appear.* As the zygote attaches to the uterine wall, its cells form two layers. At this time, the name of the mass of cells changes from *zygote* to *embryo.* The embryo's **endoderm** *is the inner layer of cells, which will develop into the digestive and respiratory systems.* The outer layer of cells is divided into two parts. The **ectoderm** *is the outermost layer, which will become the nervous system, sensory receptors (ears, nose, and eyes, for example), and skin parts (hair and nails, for example).* The **mesoderm** *is the middle layer, which will become the circulatory system, bones, muscles, excretory system, and reproductive system.* Every body part eventually develops from these three layers. The endoderm primarily produces internal body parts, the mesoderm primarily produces parts that surround the internal areas, and the ectoderm primarily produces surface parts.

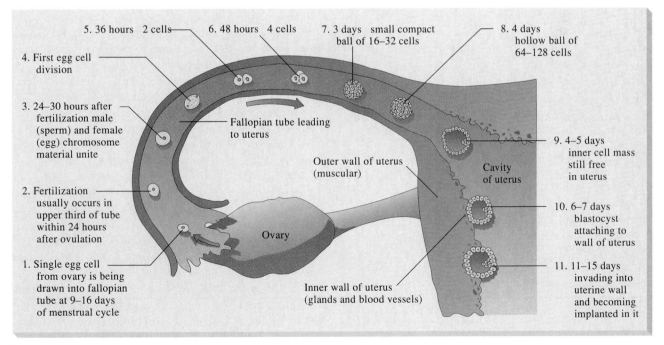

FIGURE 4.2

Significant Developments in the Germinal Period

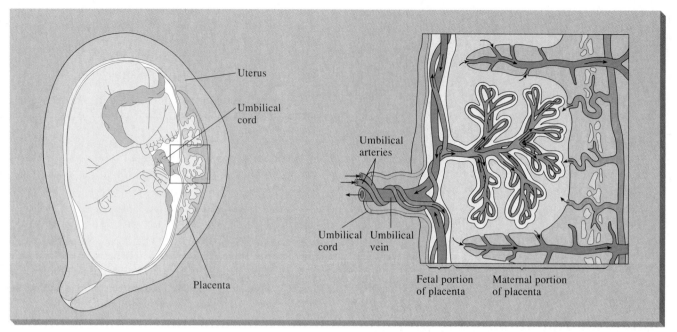

Uterus

Umbilical cord

Placenta

Umbilical arteries

Umbilical cord

Umbilical vein

Fetal portion of placenta

Maternal portion of placenta

FIGURE 4.3

The Placenta and the Umbilical Cord
Maternal blood flows through the uterine arteries to the spaces housing the placenta and returns through the uterine veins to maternal circulation. Fetal blood flows through the umbilical arteries into the capillaries of the placenta and returns through the umbilical veins to the fetal circulation. The exchange of materials takes place across the layer separating the maternal and fetal blood supplies, so the bloods never come into contact. *Note:* The area bound by the square is enlarged in the right half of the illustration. Arrows indicate the direction of blood flow.

DENNIS THE MENACE

"My Mom says I come from Heaven, My Dad says he can't remember an' Mr. Wilson is POSITIVE I came from Mars!"

As the embryo's three layers form, life-support systems for the embryo mature and develop rapidly. These life-support systems include the placenta, the umbilical cord, and the amnion. The **placenta** *is a life-support system that consists of a disk-shaped group of tissues in which small blood vessels from the mother and the offspring intertwine but do not join.* The **umbilical cord** *is a life-support system, containing two arteries and one vein, that connects the baby to the placenta.* Very small molecules—oxygen, water, salt, food from the mother's blood, and carbon dioxide and digestive wastes from the embryo's blood—pass back and forth between the mother and infant. Large molecules cannot pass through the placental wall; these include red blood cells and harmful substances such as most bacteria, maternal wastes, and hormones. The mechanisms that govern the transfer of substances across the placental barrier are complex and are still not entirely understood (Rosenblith, 1992). Figure 4.3 provides an illustration of the placenta, the umbilical cord, and the nature of blood flow in the expectant mother and developing child in the uterus. The **amnion,** *a bag or envelope that contains a clear fluid in which the developing embryo floats, is another important life-support system.* Like the placenta and umbilical cord, the amnion develops from the fertilized egg, not from the mother's own body. At approximately 16 weeks, the kidneys of the fetus begin to produce urine. This fetal urine remains the main source of the amniotic fluid until the third trimester, when some of the fluid is excreted from the lungs of the growing fetus. Although the

John W. Santrock

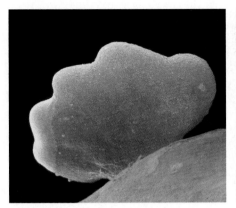

The hand of an embryo at 6 weeks.

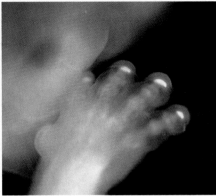

Fingers and thumb with pads seen at 8 weeks.

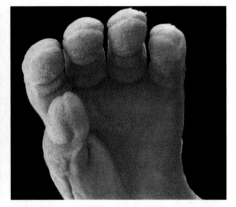

The finger pads have regressed by 13 weeks.

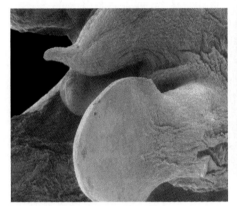

Toe ridges emerge after 7 weeks.

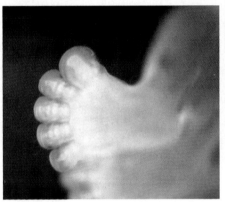

Toe pads and the emerging heel are visible by 9 weeks.

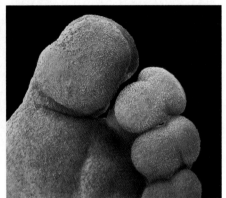

The toe pads have regressed by 13 weeks.

The fingers and toes form rapidly during the first trimester. After 13 weeks of pregnancy, the hands and feet already look remarkably similar to those of a mature human although they are still smaller than an adult's fingernail.

amniotic fluid increases in volume tenfold from the 12th to the 40th week of pregnancy, it is also removed in various ways. Some is swallowed by the fetus, and some is absorbed through the umbilical cord and the membranes covering the placenta. The amniotic fluid is important in providing an environment that is temperature and humidity controlled, as well as shockproof.

Before most women even know they are pregnant, some important embryonic developments take place. In the third week, the neural tube that eventually becomes the spinal cord forms. At about 21 days, eyes begin to appear, and at 24 days the cells for the heart begin to differentiate. During the fourth week, the first appearance of the urogenital system is apparent, and arm and leg buds emerge. Four chambers of the heart take shape, and blood vessels surface. From the fifth to the eighth week, arms and legs differentiate further; at this time, the face starts to form but still is not very recognizable. The intestinal tract develops and the facial structures fuse. At 8 weeks, the developing organism weighs about 1/30 ounce and is just over 1 inch long. **Organogenesis** *is the process of organ formation that takes place during the first 2 months of prenatal development.* When

organs are being formed, they are especially vulnerable to environmental changes. Later in the chapter, we will describe the environmental hazards that are harmful during organogenesis.

The Fetal Period

The **fetal period** *is the prenatal period of development that begins 2 months after conception and lasts for 7 months, on the average.* Growth and development continue their dramatic course during this time. Three months after conception, the fetus is about 3 inches long and weighs about 1 ounce. It has become active, moving its arms and legs, opening and closing its mouth, and moving its head. The face, forehead, eyelids, nose, and chin are distinguishable, as are the upper arms, lower arms, hands, and lower limbs, and the genitals can be identified as male or female. By the end of the fourth month, the fetus has grown to 6 inches in length and weighs 4 to 7 ounces. At this time, a growth spurt occurs in the body's lower parts. Prenatal reflexes are stronger; arm and leg movements can be felt for the first time by the mother.

By the end of the fifth month, the fetus is about 12 inches long and weighs close to a pound. Structures of

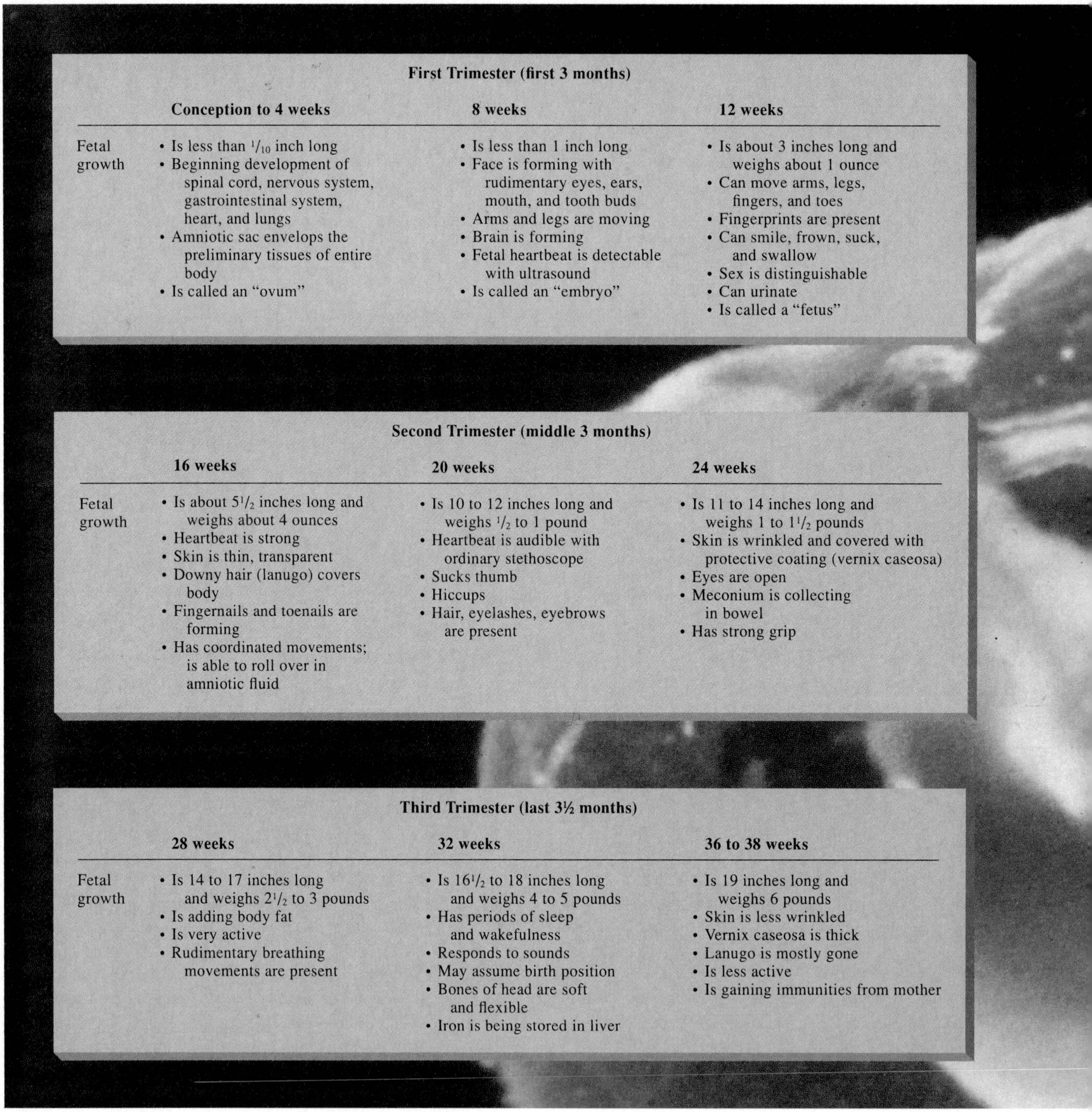

First Trimester (first 3 months)

	Conception to 4 weeks	8 weeks	12 weeks
Fetal growth	• Is less than $^{1}/_{10}$ inch long • Beginning development of spinal cord, nervous system, gastrointestinal system, heart, and lungs • Amniotic sac envelops the preliminary tissues of entire body • Is called an "ovum"	• Is less than 1 inch long • Face is forming with rudimentary eyes, ears, mouth, and tooth buds • Arms and legs are moving • Brain is forming • Fetal heartbeat is detectable with ultrasound • Is called an "embryo"	• Is about 3 inches long and weighs about 1 ounce • Can move arms, legs, fingers, and toes • Fingerprints are present • Can smile, frown, suck, and swallow • Sex is distinguishable • Can urinate • Is called a "fetus"

Second Trimester (middle 3 months)

	16 weeks	20 weeks	24 weeks
Fetal growth	• Is about $5^{1}/_{2}$ inches long and weighs about 4 ounces • Heartbeat is strong • Skin is thin, transparent • Downy hair (lanugo) covers body • Fingernails and toenails are forming • Has coordinated movements; is able to roll over in amniotic fluid	• Is 10 to 12 inches long and weighs $^{1}/_{2}$ to 1 pound • Heartbeat is audible with ordinary stethoscope • Sucks thumb • Hiccups • Hair, eyelashes, eyebrows are present	• Is 11 to 14 inches long and weighs 1 to $1^{1}/_{2}$ pounds • Skin is wrinkled and covered with protective coating (vernix caseosa) • Eyes are open • Meconium is collecting in bowel • Has strong grip

Third Trimester (last 3½ months)

	28 weeks	32 weeks	36 to 38 weeks
Fetal growth	• Is 14 to 17 inches long and weighs $2^{1}/_{2}$ to 3 pounds • Is adding body fat • Is very active • Rudimentary breathing movements are present	• Is $16^{1}/_{2}$ to 18 inches long and weighs 4 to 5 pounds • Has periods of sleep and wakefulness • Responds to sounds • May assume birth position • Bones of head are soft and flexible • Iron is being stored in liver	• Is 19 inches long and weighs 6 pounds • Skin is less wrinkled • Vernix caseosa is thick • Lanugo is mostly gone • Is less active • Is gaining immunities from mother

FIGURE 4.4

The Three Trimesters of Prenatal Development

the skin have formed—toenails and fingernails, for example. The fetus is more active, showing a preference for a particular position in the womb. By the end of the sixth month, the fetus is about 14 inches long and already has gained another half pound to a pound. The eyes and eyelids are completely formed, and a fine layer of hair covers the head. A grasping reflex is present and irregular breathing occurs. By the end of the seventh month, the fetus is about 16 inches long and has gained another pound, now weighing about 3 pounds. During the eighth and ninth months, the fetus grows longer and gains substantial weight—about another 4 pounds. At birth, the

John W. Santrock

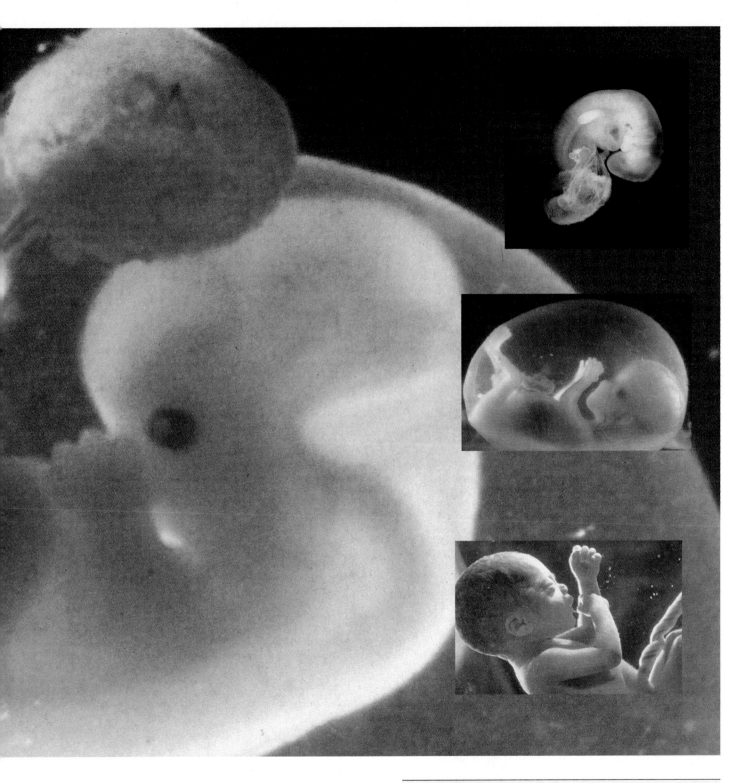

average American baby weighs 7 pounds and is about 20 inches long. In these last 2 months, fatty tissues develop and the functioning of various organ systems—heart and kidneys, for example—steps up.

We have described a number of developments in the germinal, embryonic, and fetal periods. An overview of some of the main developments we have discussed and some more specific changes in prenatal development are presented in figure 4.4.

So the riders of the darkness pass on their circuits: the luminous island of the self trembles and waits, waits for us all my friends, where the sea's big brush recolors the dying lives, and the unborn smiles.

—Lawrence Durrell

MISCARRIAGE AND ABORTION

A miscarriage, or spontaneous abortion, happens when pregnancy ends before the developing organism is mature enough to survive outside the womb. The embryo separates from the uterine wall and is expelled by the uterus. About 15 to 20 percent of all pregnancies end in a spontaneous abortion, most in the first 2 to 3 months. Many spontaneous abortions occur without the mother's knowledge, and many involve an embryo or fetus that was not developing normally. Most spontaneous abortions are caused by chromosomal abnormalities.

Early in history, it was believed that a woman could be frightened into a miscarriage by loud thunder or a jolt in a carriage. Today, we recognize that this is highly unlikely; the developing organism is well protected. Abnormalities of the reproductive tract and viral or bacterial infections are more likely to cause spontaneous abortions. In some cases, severe traumas may be at fault.

Deliberate termination of pregnancy is a complex issue, medically, psychologically, socially and legally. Carrying a baby to term can affect a woman's health, the woman's pregnancy may have resulted from rape or incest, the woman may not be married, or perhaps she is poor and wants to continue her education. Abortion is legal in the United States; in 1973, the U.S. Supreme Court ruled that any woman can obtain an abortion during the first 6 months of pregnancy, a decision that continues to generate ethical objections from antiabortion forces. The U.S. Supreme Court also has ruled that abortion in the first trimester is solely the decision of the mother and her doctor. Courts also have ruled that the baby's father and the parents of minor girls do not have any say during this time frame. In the second trimester, states can legislate the time and method of abortion for protection of the mother's health. In the third trimester, the fetus's right to live is a much stronger factor.

What are the psychological effects of having an abortion? In 1989, a research review panel appointed by the American Psychological Association examined more than 100 investigations of the psychological effects of abortion. The panel's conclusions follow: Unwanted pregnancies are stressful for most women. However, it is common for women to report feelings of relief as well as feelings of guilt after an abortion. These feelings are usually mild and tend to diminish rapidly over time without adversely affecting the woman's ability to function. Abortion is more stressful for women who have a history of serious emotional problems and who are not given support by family or friends. Only a small percentage of women fall into these high-risk categories. If an abortion is performed, it should not only involve competent medical care but care for the woman's psychological needs as well. Yet another ethical issue related to abortion has appeared recently—the medical use of tissues from aborted fetuses.

TERATOLOGY AND HAZARDS TO PRENATAL DEVELOPMENT

Some expectant mothers carefully tiptoe about in the belief that everything they do and feel has a direct effect on their unborn child. Others behave casually, assuming that their experiences will have little effect. The truth lies somewhere between these two extremes. Although living in a protected, comfortable environment, the fetus is not totally immune to the larger world surrounding the mother (McFarlane, Parker, & Soeken, 1996). The environment can affect the child in many well-documented ways. Thousands of babies born deformed or mentally retarded every year are the result of events that occurred in the mother's life, as early as one or two months before conception.

Teratology

A **teratogen** *(the word comes from the Greek word* tera *meaning "monster") is any agent that causes a birth defect. The field of study that investigates the causes of birth defects is called teratology.* A specific teratogen (such as a drug) usually does not cause a specific birth defect (such as malformation of the legs). So many teratogens exist that practically every fetus is exposed to at least some teratogens. For this reason, it is difficult to determine which teratogen causes which birth defect. In addition, it may take a long time for the effects of a teratogen to show up; only about half of all potential effects appear at birth.

Despite the many unknowns about teratogens, scientists have discovered the identity of some of these hazards to prenatal development and the particular point of fetal development at which they do their greatest damage. As figure 4.5 shows, sensitivity to teratogens begins about 3 weeks after conception. The probability of a structural defect is greatest early in the embryonic period, because this is when organs are being formed. After organogenesis is complete, teratogens are less likely to cause anatomical defects. Exposure later, during the fetal period, is more likely to stunt growth or to create problems in the way organs function. The precision of organogenesis is evident; teratologists point out that vulnerability of the brain is greatest at 15 to 25 days after conception, the eyes at 24 to 40 days, the heart at 20 to 40 days, and the legs at 24 to 36 days.

In the following sections, we will explore how certain environmental agents and contexts influence prenatal development. We will examine how maternal diseases and conditions, the mother's age, nutrition, emotional states and stress, drugs, and environmental hazards can influence prenatal development.

Maternal Characteristics

Maternal characteristics that can affect prenatal development include maternal diseases and conditions and the mother's age, nutrition, emotional states, and stress.

John W. Santrock

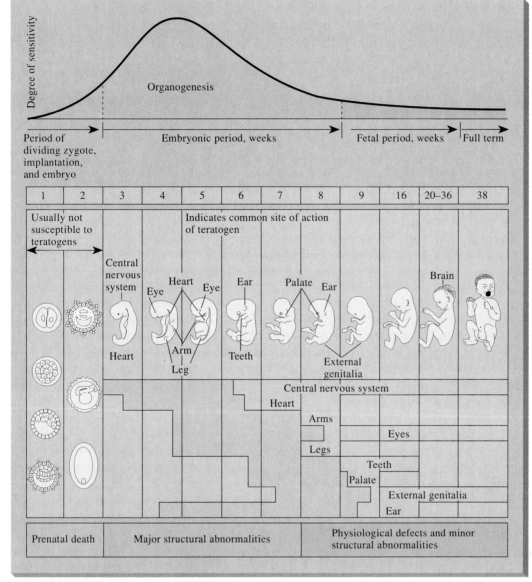

Figure 4.5

Teratogens and the Timing of Their Effects on Prenatal Development
The danger of structural defects caused by teratogens is greatest early in embryonic development. This is the period of organogenesis, and it lasts for several months. Damage caused by teratogens during this period is represented by the dark-colored bars. Later assaults by teratogens typically occur during the fetal period and, instead of structural damage, are more likely to stunt growth or cause problems of organ function.

Maternal Diseases and Conditions

Maternal diseases or infections can produce defects by crossing the placental barrier, or they can cause damage during the birth process itself. Rubella (German measles) is a maternal disease that can cause prenatal defects. A rubella outbreak in 1964–1965 resulted in 30,000 prenatal and neonatal (newborn) deaths, and more than 20,000 affected infants were born with malformations, including mental retardation, blindness, deafness, and heart problems. The greatest damage occurs when mothers contract rubella in the third and fourth weeks of pregnancy, although infection during the second month is also damaging. Elaborate preventive efforts ensure that rubella will never again have the disastrous effects it had in the mid 1960s. A vaccine that prevents German measles is now routinely administered to children, and women who plan to have children should have a blood test before they become pregnant to determine if they are immune to the disease.

Syphilis (a sexually transmitted disease) is more damaging later in prenatal development—4 months or more after conception. Rather than affecting organogenesis, as rubella does, syphilis damages organs after they have formed. Damage includes eye lesions, which can cause blindness, and skin lesions. When syphilis is present at birth, other problems involving the central nervous system and gastrointestinal tract can develop. Most states require that pregnant women be given a blood test to detect the presence of syphilis.

Another infection that has received widespread attention recently is genital herpes. Newborns contract this virus when they are delivered through the birth canal of a mother with genital herpes. About one-third of babies delivered through an infected birth canal die; another one-fourth become brain damaged. If an active case of genital herpes is detected in a pregnant woman close to her delivery date, a cesarean section can be performed (in which the infant is delivered through an incision in the mother's abdomen) to keep the virus from infecting the newborn.

AIDS   The importance of women's health to the health of their offspring is nowhere better exemplified than when the mother has acquired immune deficiency syndrome

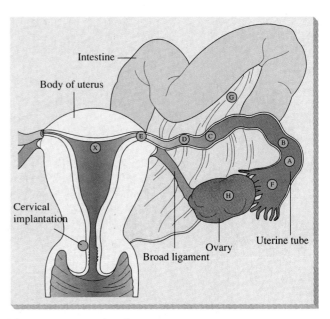

FIGURE 4.6

Locations of Ectopic Pregnancies
The X marks the normal site of ectopic pregnancies. Abnormal sites are indicated by the other letters in order of their frequency of occurrence.

(AIDS). As the number of women with HIV grows, more children are born exposed to and infected with AIDS (Cohen & others, 1996). Through the end of 1993, 3,265 children younger than 5 had been diagnosed with AIDS. The number of pediatric AIDS cases does not include as many as 10,000 children infected with HIV who have not yet developed AIDS. African American and Latino children make up 83 percent of all pediatric AIDS cases. The majority of mothers who transmit HIV to their offspring were infected through intravenous drug use or heterosexual contact with injecting drug users.

A mother with AIDS can infect her offspring in three ways: (1) during gestation across the placenta; (2) during delivery through contact with maternal blood or fluids; and (3) postpartum through breast-feeding. Approximately one-third of infants born to infected mothers will ultimately become infected with HIV themselves (Caldwell & Rogers, 1991). Babies born to HIV-infected mothers can be (1) infected and symptomatic (show AIDS symptoms), (2) infected but asymptomatic (not show AIDS symptoms), and (3) not infected at all. An infant who is infected and asymptomatic may still develop HIV symptoms up until 15 months of age. One recent study documented a rare instance of the AIDS virus subsequently disappearing in an infant who was born infected with HIV (Bryon & others, 1995). This might have been an unusual transient or defective form of HIV.

Ectopic Pregnancy Ectopic pregnancy *is the presence of a developing embryo or fetus outside the normal location in the uterus.* Figure 4.6 illustrates the possible locations of

ectopic pregnancies. More than 90 percent of ectopic pregnancies occur in the fallopian tubes. The incidence of ectopic pregnancy has more than tripled in recent years. Most of the increase is due to the increase in sexually transmitted tubal infections, such as genital chlamydia, and the tendency of women to delay childbearing until later in life, when the risk of ectopic pregnancy is greatest. Tubal ectopic pregnancies usually result in a rupture of the fallopian tube during the first 8 weeks, resulting in the death of the embryo and hemorrhaging into the abdominal cavity. If a tubal pregnancy is detected prior to tubal rupture, it can be surgically terminated to avoid this dangerous event, which can be fatal to the mother because of the hemorrhaging.

The Mother's Age

When the mother's age is considered in terms of possible harmful effects on the fetus and infant, two time periods are of special interest: adolescence and the thirties and beyond. Approximately 1 of every 5 births is to an adolescent; in some urban areas, the figure reaches as high as 1 in every 2 births. Infants born to adolescents are often premature. The mortality rate of infants born to adolescent mothers is double that of infants born to mothers in their twenties. Although such figures probably reflect the mother's immature reproductive system, they also may involve poor nutrition, lack of prenatal care, and low socioeconomic status. Prenatal care decreases the probability that a child born to an adolescent girl will have physical problems. However, adolescents are the least likely of women in all age groups to obtain prenatal assistance from clinics, pediatricians, and health services.

Increasingly, women are seeking to establish their careers before beginning a family, delaying childbearing until their thirties. Down syndrome, a form of mental retardation, is related to the mother's age. A baby with Down syndrome rarely is born to a mother under the age of 30, but the risk increases after the mother reaches 30. By age 40, the probability is slightly over 1 in 100, and by age 50 it is almost 1 in 10. The risk also is higher before age 18.

Women also have more difficulty becoming pregnant after the age of 30. In one study, the clients of a French fertility clinic all had husbands who were sterile (Schwartz & Mayaux, 1982). To increase their chances of having a child, the women were artificially inseminated once a month for 1 year. Each women has twelve chances to become pregnant. Seventy-five percent of the women in their twenties became pregnant, 62 percent of the women 31 to 35 years old became pregnant, and only 54 percent of the women over 35 years old became pregnant.

We still have much to learn about the role of the mother's age in pregnancy and childbirth. As women remain active, exercise regularly, and are careful about their nutrition, their reproductive systems may remain healthier at older ages than was thought possible in the past. Indeed, as we will see next, the mother's nutrition influences prenatal development.

Nutrition

A developing fetus depends completely on its mother for nutrition, which comes from the mother's blood. Nutritional status is not determined by any specific aspect of diet; among the important factors are the total number of calories and appropriate levels of protein, vitamins, and minerals. The mother's nutrition even influences her ability to reproduce. In extreme instances of malnutrition, women stop menstruating, thus precluding conception. Children born to malnourished mothers are more likely to be malformed.

One investigation of Iowa mothers documents the important role of nutrition in prenatal development and birth (Jeans, Smith, & Stearns, 1995). The diets of 400 pregnant women were studied and the status of their newborns was assessed. The mothers with the poorest diets were more likely to have offspring who weighed the least, had the least vitality, were born prematurely, or died. In another investigation, diet supplements given to malnourished mothers during pregnancy improved the performance of their offspring during the first 3 years of life (Werner, 1979).

Emotional States and Stress

Tales abound about how a pregnant woman's emotional state affects the fetus. For centuries it was thought that frightening experiences—such as a severe thunderstorm or a family member's death—would leave birthmarks on the child or affect the child in more serious ways. Today we believe that the mother's stress can be transmitted to the fetus, but we have gone beyond thinking that this transmission is somehow magically produced (Parker & Barrett, 1992). We now know that when a pregnant woman experiences intense fears, anxieties, and other emotions, physiological changes occur—among them, respiration and glandular secretions. For example, producing adrenaline in response to fear restricts blood flow to the uterine area and may deprive the fetus of adequate oxygen.

The mother's emotional state during pregnancy can influence the birth process too. An emotionally distraught mother might have irregular contractions and a more difficult labor, which can cause irregularities in the baby's oxygen supply or tend to produce irregularities after birth. Babies born after extended labor also may adjust more slowly to their world and be more irritable.

A number of researchers have found that maternal anxiety during pregnancy is related to less than optimal outcomes (Stechler & Halton, 1982). In one study, maternal anxiety during pregnancy was associated with infants who were more hyperactive and irritable, and who had more feeding and sleeping problems (Stanley, Soule, & Copens, 1979). Stresses during pregnancy that have been linked with maternal anxiety include marital discord, the death of a husband, and unwanted pregnancy (Field, 1990).

In one study, Tiffany Field and her colleagues (1985) attempted to reduce anxiety about pregnancy by giving video and verbal feedback during ultrasound assessments to assure the mother of the fetus's well-being. Compared to infants whose mothers did not receive such feedback, infants whose mothers got the intervention were less active in utero and had higher birthweights. As newborns, they were less irritable and their performance on neonatal behavior assessments was superior. Thus, reassuring the mother of fetal well-being had positive outcomes for infants in this study.

Drugs

How do drugs affect prenatal development? Some pregnant women take drugs, smoke tobacco, and drink alcohol without thinking about the possible effects on the fetus. Occasionally, a rash of deformed babies are born, bringing to light the damage drugs can have on a developing fetus. This happened in 1961, when many pregnant women took a popular tranquilizer, thalidomide, to alleviate their morning sickness. In adults, the effects of thalidomide are mild; in embryos, however, they are devastating. Not all infants were affected in the same way. If the mother took thalidomide on day 26 (probably before she knew she was pregnant), an arm might not grow. If she took the drug 2 days later, the arm might not grow past the elbow. The thalidomide tragedy shocked the medical community and parents into the stark realization that the mother does not have to be a chronic drug user for the fetus to be harmed. Taking the wrong drug at the wrong time is enough to physically handicap the offspring for life.

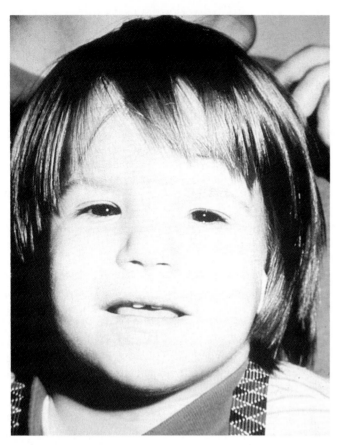

FIGURE 4.7

Fetal Alcohol Syndrome
Notice the wide-set eyes, flat bones, and thin upper lip.

Heavy drinking by pregnant women can also be devastating to offspring. **Fetal alcohol syndrome (FAS)** *is a cluster of abnormalities that appears in the offspring of mothers who drink alcohol heavily during pregnancy.* The abnormalities include facial deformities and defective limbs, face, and heart. Most of these children are below average in intelligence and some are mentally retarded (Olson & Burgess, 1996). Although many mothers of FAS infants are heavy drinkers, many mothers who are heavy drinkers do not have children with FAS, or might have one child with FAS and other children who do not have it. Figure 4.7 shows a child with fetal alcohol syndrome. Although no serious malformations such as those produced by FAS are found in infants born to mothers who are moderate drinkers, in one study, infants whose mothers drank moderately (one to two drinks a day) during pregnancy were less attentive and alert, with the effects still present at 4 years of age (Streissguth & others, 1984).

Expectant mothers are becoming more aware that alcohol and pregnancy do not mix. In one study of 1,712 pregnant women in 21 states, the prevalence of alcohol consumption by pregnant women declined from 32 percent in 1985 to 20 percent in 1988 (Serdula & others, 1991). The declines in drinking were greatest among the oldest and most educated pregnant women—19 percent

of pregnant college graduates drank in 1988, a decline from the 41 percent rate in 1985. However, no decline in drinking was found among the least educated and youngest pregnant women. The proportion of drinkers among pregnant women with only a high school education stayed at 23 percent from 1985 to 1988.

Cigarette smoking by pregnant women can also adversely influence prenatal development, birth, and postnatal development (Johnson & others, 1993). Fetal and neonatal deaths are higher among smoking mothers; also prevalent are a higher incidence of preterm births and lower birthweights (see figure 4.8). In one study, prenatal exposure to cigarette smoking was related to poorer language and cognitive development at 4 years of age (Fried & Watkinson, 1990). In another study, mothers who smoked during pregnancy had infants who were awake more on a consistent basis—a finding one might expect, since the active ingredient in cigarettes is the stimulant nicotine (Landesman-Dwyer & Sackett, 1983). Respiratory problems and sudden infant death syndrome (also known as crib death) are also more common among the offspring of mothers who smoked during pregnancy (Schoendorf & Kiely, 1992). Intervention programs designed to get pregnant women to stop smoking can be successful in reducing some of smoking's negative effects on offspring, especially in raising their birthweights (Chomitz, Cheung, & Lieberman, 1995). To further evaluate smoking by pregnant women, refer to Critical Thinking About Children's Development.

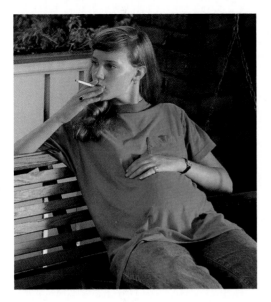

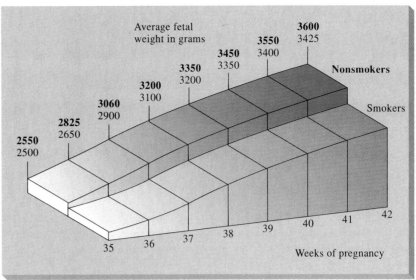

FIGURE 4.8

The Effects of Smoking by Expectant Mothers on Fetal Weight
Throughout prenatal development, the fetuses of expectant mothers who smoke weigh less than the fetuses of expectant mothers who do not smoke.

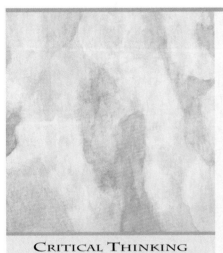

CRITICAL THINKING
ABOUT CHILDREN'S
DEVELOPMENT

*Intervention to Stop
Pregnant Women
from Smoking*

Scientists have known about the negative consequences of smoking for more than three decades, but they have made little progress in developing effective interventions to help pregnant women quit smoking or to keep young women from becoming addicted to smoking. What needs to be done to get pregnant women to not smoke? Consider the role of health care providers and their training, the role of insurance companies, and specific programs targeted at pregnant women. By considering ways to intervene in the lives of pregnant women to get them to stop smoking, you are learning to think critically by *using knowledge to improve human welfare*.

(Hans, 1989). The young infants of these mothers are addicted and show withdrawal symptoms characteristic of opiate abstinence, such as tremors, irritability, abnormal crying, disturbed sleep, and impaired motor control. Behavioral problems are still often present at the first birthday, and attention deficits may appear later in the child's development. The most common treatment for heroin addicts, methadone, is associated with very severe withdrawal symptoms in newborns.

With the increased use of cocaine in the United States, there is growing concern about its effects on the embryos, fetuses, and infants of pregnant cocaine users. Cocaine use during pregnancy has recently attracted considerable attention because of possible harm to the developing embryo and fetus (Dow-Edwards, 1995; Zelazo, Potter, & Valiante, 1995). The most consistent finding is that infants born to cocaine abusers have reduced birthweight and length (Chasnoff & others, 1992). There are increased frequencies of congenital abnormalities in the offspring of cocaine users during pregnancy, but other factors in the drug addict's lifestyle, such as malnutrition and other substance abuse, might be responsible for the congenital abnormalities (Eyler, Behnke, & Stewart, 1990).

Marijuana use by pregnant women also has detrimental effects on a developing fetus. Marijuana use by pregnant women is associated with increased tremors and startles among newborns and poorer verbal and memory development at 4 years of age (Fried & Watkinson, 1990).

It is well documented that infants whose mothers are addicted to heroin show several behavioral difficulties

---

Prenatal Development

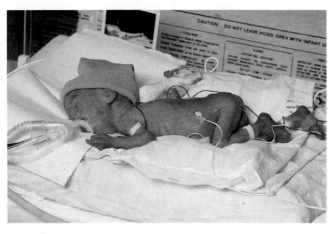

This baby was born addicted to cocaine because its mother was a cocaine addict. Researchers have found that the offspring of women who use cocaine during pregnancy often have hypertension and heart damage. Many of these infants face a childhood full of medical problems.

For example, cocaine users are more likely to smoke cigarettes and marijuana, drink alcohol, and take amphetamines than are cocaine nonusers. Teasing apart these potential influences from the effects of cocaine use itself has not yet been adequately accomplished (Lester, Frier, & LaGasse, 1995). Obtaining valid information about the frequency and type of drug use by mothers is also complicated, since many mothers fear prosecution or loss of custody because of their drug use.

Each year, 375,000 babies are born to women who used drugs during pregnancy; in recent years, an increasing number have been cocaine babies. Although some of the babies born to mothers who take drugs during pregnancy will suffer little or no long-term effects, many of the drug-affected infants will require extra attention. One intervention effort aimed at helping drug-abusing mothers and their young children is Operation PAR (Parental Awareness and Responsibility), which serves 28,000 people a year in Florida. Operation PAR includes a day-care center, which in St. Petersburg serves 31 children 2 to 6 years old. Much of what goes on in this day-care center is indistinguishable from any good day-care center. For example, the staff-to-child ratio is low, teachers are warm and friendly to the children, and there is an abundance of attractive and interesting toys and play areas. What is different are the anti-drug cartoons that become an early fixture in the children's experience at the center. Also, the parents whose children are in the center must seek drug treatment and attend parenting-skill groups.

A list of the effects of cocaine and of various other drugs, on offspring, and some guidelines for safe use of these drugs, are presented in table 4.1.

Environmental Hazards

Radiation, chemicals, and other hazards in our modern industrial world can endanger the fetus. For instance, radiation can cause a gene mutation, an abrupt but permanent change in genetic material. Chromosomal abnormalities are higher among the offspring of fathers exposed to high levels of radiation in their occupations (Schrag & Dixon, 1985). Radiation from X rays also can affect the developing embryo and fetus, with the most dangerous time being the first several weeks after conception, when women do not yet know they are pregnant. It is important for women and their physicians to weigh the risk of an X ray when an actual or potential pregnancy is involved.

Environmental pollutants and toxic wastes are also sources of danger to unborn children. Researchers have found that various hazardous wastes and pesticides cause defects in animals exposed to high doses. Among the dangerous pollutants and wastes are carbon monoxide, mercury, and lead. Some children are exposed to lead because they live in houses where lead-based paint flakes off the walls, or near busy highways, where there are heavy automobile emissions from leaded gasoline. Researchers believe that early exposure to lead affects children's mental development. For example, in one study, 2-year-olds who prenatally had high levels of lead in their umbilical-cord blood performed poorly on a test of mental development (Bellinger & others, 1987).

Researchers also have found that the manufacturing chemicals known as PCBs are harmful to prenatal development. In one investigation, the extent to which pregnant women ate PCB-polluted fish from Lake Michigan was examined, and subsequently their newborns were observed (Jacobson & others, 1984). Women who had eaten more PCB-polluted fish were more likely to have smaller, preterm infants who were more likely to react slowly to stimuli. And in another study, prenatal exposure to PCBs was associated with problems in visual discrimination and short-term memory in 4-year-old children (Jacobson & others, 1992).

A current environmental concern involves women who spend long hours in front of computer monitors. The fear is that low-level electromagnetic radiation from the monitors might adversely affect their offspring should these women become pregnant. In one study of 2,430 women telephone operators (Schnorr & others, 1991), half of the women worked at computer monitors (or video display terminals), half did not. During the 4 years of the study, 730 of the women became pregnant, some more than once, for a total of 876 pregnancies. Over the 4 years, there was no significant difference in miscarriage rates between the two groups. The researchers concluded that working at a computer monitor does not increase miscarriage risk. Critics point out that there was no check for early fetal loss and that all of the women were younger than 34 years of age, so whether the findings hold for early fetal loss and older women will have to await further research. In this study, miscarriages were higher among women who had more than 8 alcoholic drinks per month or smoked more than 20 cigarettes a

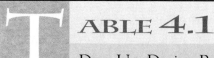

Drug Use During Pregnancy

Drug	Effects on Fetus and Offspring	Safe Use of the Drug
Alcohol	Small amounts increase risk of spontaneous abortion. Moderate amounts (1–2 drinks a day) are associated with poor attention in infancy. Heavy drinking can lead to fetal alcohol syndrome. Some experts believe that even low to moderate amounts, especially in the first 3 months of pregnancy, increase the risk of FAS.	Avoid use.
Nicotine	Heavy smoking is associated with low-birthweight babies, which means the babies may have more health problems than other infants. Smoking may be especially harmful in the second half of pregnancy.	Avoid use.
Tranquilizers	Taken during the first 3 months of pregnancy, they may cause cleft palate or other congenital malformations.	Avoid use if you might become pregnant and during early pregnancy. Use only under a doctor's supervision.
Barbiturates	Mothers who take large doses may have babies who are addicted. Babies may have tremors, restlessness, and irritability.	Use only under a doctor's supervision.
Amphetamines	They may cause birth defects.	Use only under a doctor's supervision.
Cocaine	Cocaine may cause drug dependency and withdrawal symptoms at birth, as well as physical and mental problems, especially if the mother uses cocaine in the first 3 months of pregnancy. There is a higher risk of hypertension, heart problems, developmental retardation, and learning difficulties.	Avoid use.
Marijuana	It may cause a variety of birth defects and is associated with low birthweight and height.	Avoid use.

Source: Modified from the National Institute on Drug Abuse.

day. While computer monitors might not be related to miscarriage, they are associated with an increase in a variety of problems involving eye strain and the musculoskeletal system.

Another environmental concern is **toxoplasmosis,** *a mild infection that causes coldlike symptoms or no apparent illness in adults. However, toxoplasmosis can be a teratogen for the unborn baby, causing possible eye defects, brain defects, and premature birth.* Cats are common carriers of toxoplasmosis, especially outdoor cats who eat raw meat, such as rats and mice. The toxoplasmosis organism passes from the cat in its feces and lives up to 1 year. The expectant mother may pick up these organisms by handling cats or cat litter boxes, or by working in soil where cats have buried their feces. Eating raw or undercooked meat is another way of acquiring the disease. To avoid getting toxoplasmosis, expectant mothers need to wash their hands after handling cats, litter boxes, and raw meat. In addition, pregnant women should make sure that all meats are thoroughly cooked before eating them.

Yet another recent environmental concern for expectant mothers is prolonged exposure to heat in saunas or hot tubs that may raise the mother's body temperature,

creating a fever that endangers the fetus. The high temperature of a fever may interfere with cell division and may cause birth defects or even fetal death if the fever occurs repeatedly for prolonged periods of time. If the expectant mother wants to take a sauna or bathe in a hot tub, prenatal experts recommend that she take her oral temperature while she is exposed to the heat. When the expectant mother's body temperature rises a degree or more, she should get out and cool down. Ten minutes is a reasonable length of time for expectant mothers to spend in a sauna or a hot tub, since the body temperature does not usually rise in this length of time. If the expectant mother feels uncomfortably hot in a sauna or a hot tub, she should get out even if she has only been there for a short time.

Fetal Surgery and Therapy

Unborn fetuses have become medicine's tiniest patients. Consider the following circumstance. At 8 weeks into prenatal development, the diaphragm of the fetus had failed to close as it should have. The abdominal organs had grown up into the left lung's cavity and the left lung had hardly developed at all. The abdomen had shrunk and the heart had shifted to the center of the chest. This condition is called *diaphragmatic hernia,* which affects 1 in 2,200 babies. These fetuses have a 75 percent chance of dying before or soon after birth. To repair the hernia in the diaphragm, an incision is made through the mother's abdomen and uterus. Grasping the arm of the fetus, the surgeon gently rotates the tiny patient into position, then makes another incision under the fetus's rib cage. Next, the abdominal organs are moved out of the chest so the lungs will have room to grow. Then the diaphragm is rebuilt to keep the organs in their proper places. Wires connecting the fetus to a heart monitor make the surgical maneuvers especially difficult (see figure 4.9).

In addition to prenatal treatment of diaphragmatic hernia, surgeons have begun to prenatally treat such serious problems and diseases as hydrocephaly (a congenital malformation causing enlargement of the skull and compression of the brain), blocked bladder, and diseases now treated by bone marrow transplant—such as sickle-cell anemia, enzyme deficiencies, and various liver diseases. Also, drugs that might not pass through the placenta can be injected directly through the umbilical cord.

An important concern about fetal surgery is its risk. Before fetal surgery to correct a specific problem or disease is tried on the human fetus, it is tested on many animals. Still, any surgery involves considerable risk, especially in an organism as delicate and tiny as the human fetus. The advantages of prenatal surgery and therapy—such as rapid postoperative healing and the possible prevention of irreversible damage—always have to be weighed against the surgical risks to the expectant mother and the fetus.

At this point we have discussed a number of ideas about the course of prenatal development, miscarriage and abortion, and teratology and hazards to prenatal development. A summary of these ideas is presented in concept table 4.1.

EXPECTANT PARENTS

For many people, becoming parents is one of the greatest life changes they will experience. Parenthood is permanent, and the physical and emotional nurturing of a child is both a time-intensive responsibility and a wonderful opportunity. So far most of our discussion has focused on the embryo and the fetus, but it is also important to examine the effects of pregnancy on the expectant parents. An important first consideration is to confirm the pregnancy, and then to calculate the due date. Then as the pregnancy proceeds, a number of family issues emerge in the first, second, and third trimesters of pregnancy.

Confirming the Pregnancy and Calculating the Due Date

Although pregnancy can be detected soon after conception, a woman might not suspect she is pregnant until she has missed a menstrual period. A pregnancy test checks the woman's urine or blood for human chorionic gonadotropin

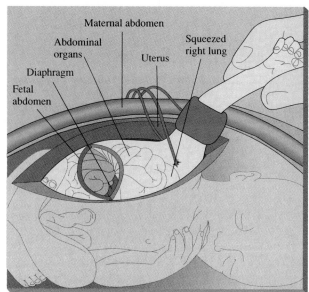

a.

b.

FIGURE 4.9

Fetal Surgery
(*a*) The repair of a hernia in the diaphragm of a fetus.
(*b*) Dr. Michael Harrison, the pioneering surgeon who developed the prenatal surgical techniques for correcting diaphragmatic hernia.

John W. Santrock

CONCEPT TABLE 4.1

The Course of Prenatal Development, Miscarriage and Abortion, and Teratology and Hazards to Prenatal Development

Concept	Processes/Related Ideas	Characteristics/Description
The Course of Prenatal Development	Germinal period	This period is from conception to about 10 to 14 days later. A fertilized egg is called a zygote. The period ends when the zygote attaches to the uterine wall.
	Embryonic period	The embryonic periods lasts from about 2 to 8 weeks after conception. The embryo differentiates into three layers, life-support systems develop, and organ systems form (organogenesis).
	Fetal period	The fetal period lasts from about 2 months after conception until 9 months or when the infant is born. Growth and development continue their dramatic course, and organ systems mature to the point where life can be sustained outside the womb.
Miscarriage and Abortion	Their nature and ethical issues	A miscarriage, or spontaneous abortion, happens when pregnancy ends before the developing organism is mature enough to survive outside the womb. Estimates indicate that about 15 to 20 percent of all pregnancies end this way, many without the mother's knowledge. Induced abortion is a complex issue—medically, psychologically, ethically, and socially. An unwanted pregnancy is stressful for the woman regardless of how it is resolved. A recent ethical issue focuses on the use of fetal tissue in transplant operations.
Teratology and Hazards to Prenatal Development	Teratology	This field investigates the causes of congenital (birth) defects. Any agent that causes birth defects is called a teratogen.
	Maternal characteristics	Maternal diseases and infections can cause damage by crossing the placental barrier, or they can be destructive during the birth process. Among the maternal diseases and conditions believed to be involved in possible birth defects are rubella, syphilis, genital herpes, AIDS, the mother's age, nutrition, and emotional state and stress. An ectopic pregnancy is the presence of a developing embryo or fetus outside the normal location in the uterus.
	Drugs	Thalidomide was a tranquilizer given to pregnant women to alleviate their morning sickness. In the early 1960s, thousands of babies were malformed as a consequence of their mother having taken this drug. Alcohol, tobacco, marijuana, heroin, and cocaine are some of the other drugs that can adversely affect prenatal and infant development.
	Environmental hazards	Among the environmental hazards that can endanger the fetus are radiation in jobs sites and X rays, environmental pollutants, toxic wastes, toxoplasmosis, and prolonged exposure to heat in saunas and hot tubs.
	Fetal surgery and therapy	Recently developed medical treatment of the unborn fetus has focused on diaphragmatic hernia, hydrocephaly, sickle-cell anemia, and other diseases that have usually been treated by bone marrow transplants after birth. The advantages of prenatal surgery and therapy—such as rapid postoperative healing and the possible prevention of permanent damage—always have to be weighed against the surgical risks to the expectant mother and the fetus.

TABLE 4.2

Early Signs and Symptoms of Pregnancy

- Missed menstrual period
- Breast changes—a heavy and full feeling, tenderness, tingling in the nipple area, and a darkened areola
- Fullness or aching in the lower abdomen
- Fatigue and drowsiness; faintness
- Nausea, vomiting, or both
- Frequent urination
- Increased vaginal secretions
- Positive pregnancy test

(HCG), a hormone produced during pregnancy. If a woman thinks she is pregnant, she should have her pregnancy confirmed early so she can obtain prenatal care, avoid environmental hazards, and give special attention to nutritional needs. Table 4.2 describes the early signs and symptoms of pregnancy.

Fetal life begins with the fertilization of the ovum, which occurs about 2 weeks after the woman's last menstrual period. However, the length of the pregnancy is calculated from the first day of the woman's last menstrual period and lasts an average of 280 days or 40 weeks. When a doctor or midwife says that a woman is 8 weeks pregnant, it means that the fetus is 6 weeks old. The method of dating confuses many parents who are certain they know just when conception occurred. When they are informed that the expectant mother is 8 weeks pregnant, they might know that the pregnancy is only just 6 weeks along, and they are correct. Birth is likely to occur anytime between 2 weeks before or after the so-called "due date." Approximately two-thirds of all babies are born within 10 days of their due dates.

The Three Trimesters and Preparing for the Baby's Birth

A common way of thinking about issues that arise during pregnancy is in terms of pregnancy's trimesters.

The First Trimester

Earlier in this chapter we learned that the first 3 calendar months of pregnancy (the first trimester) is a time when prenatal organ systems are being formed and begin to function. For the pregnant woman, the first trimester is a time of physical and emotional adjustment to her pregnant state.

The expectant mother may feel extraordinarily tired and require more sleep because of the new demands on her

energy and because of the subsequent shift in her metabolism rate, especially in the second and third month of pregnancy. She also may experience nausea and vomiting during the early months of pregnancy. Although this is usually referred to as "morning sickness," it can occur at any time of day and is believed to be caused by human chorionic gonadotropin, produced by the developing placenta.

Although the female's breasts develop in puberty, the glandular tissue that produces milk does not completely develop until the woman becomes pregnant. As the levels of estrogen and other hormones change during pregnancy, the expectant mother's breasts change. They enlarge, veins are often more prominent, and a tingling sensation is often felt in the nipples. The expectant mother may also need to urinate more frequently as the enlarging uterus puts increased pressure on the bladder. In addition, her vagina and cervix becomes bluish in color, the cervix becomes softer, and vaginal secretions increase.

Emotional changes accompany physical changes in the early months of pregnancy. It is not unusual for the expectant mother to experience emotional ups and downs. The thought of motherhood may at times be pleasing, and at others, disturbing. She may cry easily. Such mood swings may be difficult to understand, both for the expectant mother and her partner.

Finding out that she is pregnant may not only bring about a mixture of emotions in the expectant mother, but also in her partner: pride in the ability to produce a child; fear of losing independence; apprehension about changes in the marital relationship; doubts about one's ability to parent; and happiness about becoming parents. Sharing thoughts and feelings with each other can help expectant couples develop a closer relationship during the transition of parenthood.

A couple's sexual relationship may change during the first trimester. The expectant mother may experience an increased interest in spontaneous sexual activity because she no longer has to worry about trying to become pregnant or about avoiding pregnancy. Or, an expectant mother's sexual interest may decrease because of fatigue, nausea, breast changes, or fear of miscarriage. In a normal pregnancy, the expectant couple should discuss their feelings about sexual intercourse and do what is mutually desired.

Might expectant parents benefit from a parent education class on pregnancy and prenatal development in the first trimester of pregnancy? It is important for expectant parents to become knowledgeable about the nature of pregnancy and prenatal development. To further evaluate the nature of prenatal care, refer to Critical Thinking About Children's Development.

The Second Trimester

During the middle months of pregnancy, the expectant mother will probably feel better than she did earlier or than she will later. Nausea and fatigue usually lessen or disappear. As the baby's growth continues, the expectant

Prenatal care is an important set of services for the pregnant woman. However, not enough is known about the effectiveness of the various components of the care. The content of prenatal care visits is highly variable, and little is known about how well that content corresponds to the needs of pregnant women. Consider such content as early risk assessment, continuing risk assessment, health promotion, medical intervention, psychosocial intervention, and follow-up. Should the content of prenatal care depend on the risk status of the pregnant woman and her fetus? Should more visits occur early in the pregnancy rather than in the third trimester? How should access to quality prenatal care be improved? By thinking about the content of prenatal care, you are learning to think critically by *creating arguments based on developmental concepts.*

and his interest in the pregnancy and the baby. He may or may not like the changing appearance of the expectant mother. In a normal pregnancy, the expectant couple can continue to have sexual intercourse without harming the fetus, which is believed to be adequately protected from penetrations and the strong contractions that sometimes accompany orgasm.

The Third Trimester

During the third trimester, the expectant mother's uterus expands to a level just below her breast bone (figure 4.10 shows the space taken up by the developing fetus in the first, second, and third trimesters of pregnancy). Crowding by the uterus, in addition to high levels of progesterone, may give the expectant mother heartburn and indigestion. She may also experience shortness of breath as her uterus presses upward on her diaphragm and ribs. Varicose veins in the legs, hemorrhoids, and swollen ankles sometimes appear because of the increased pressure within the abdomen, the decreased blood return from the lower limbs, and the effect of progesterone, which relaxes the walls of the blood vessels.

By the ninth month, the expectant mother often looks forward to the end of the pregnancy, relief from

mother's uterus expands into the abdominal cavity. By the end of the fifth month of pregnancy, the top of the uterus (called the fundus) reaches the navel. During monthly visits, the physician or caregiver measures the height of the fundus to ensure that the fetus is growing adequately and to estimate the length of the pregnancy. The expectant mother's breasts do not increase much in size during the second trimester, but colostrum (a yellowish fluid produced before breast milk) is usually present in the milk glands by the middle of pregnancy. This is the time for expectant mothers to begin preparing their breasts for breast-feeding if they have decided to breast-feed the baby.

Accompanying physical changes in the second trimester are psychological changes in response to advancing pregnancy and a changing body. Some expectant mothers enjoy how they look, others consider themselves unattractive, inconvenienced, and restricted. If the expectant mother has not yet read books about child care in the first few years of life, this is a good time to purchase one or more of them. Later in this book, we will recommend some of the books as we discuss infants' physical, cognitive, and social development. This also is a good time to begin preparing the nursery for the baby's arrival.

During the second trimester, pregnancy becomes more of a reality for the expectant mother's partner. He can feel the baby move when he puts his hand on her abdomen or when she is in close contact with him. This contact with the baby increases his feelings of closeness

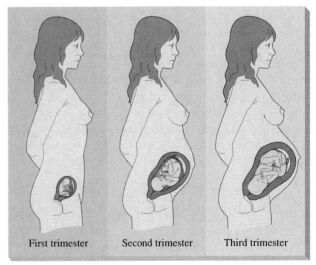

First trimester   Second trimester   Third trimester

FIGURE 4.10

**The Changing Shape and Size of the Expectant Mother
and the Fetus During the First, Second, and Third Trimesters
of Pregnancy**

In the third trimester of pregnancy, the expectant couple may feel protective of the developing baby. Lines of communication should be open between the expectant mother and her partner about their needs, feelings, and desires.

Among the important information for the expectant mother to know about is the best nutrition for her and her developing fetus. The expectant mother should eat regularly, three meals a day, with nutritious snacks of fruits, cheese, milk, or other foods between meals if desired.

physical restrictions, and the long-awaited joy of having the baby. She may become more introspective and, at times, worry about labor, birth, and the baby. Through childbirth classes, the expectant couple can learn more about labor, birth, and how to cope with the stress of the latter part of pregnancy. In the next chapter we will discuss different types of childbirth and childbirth classes.

In the third trimester of pregnancy, the expectant couple may feel protective of the developing baby. Adjustments in sexual activity continue as the expectant mother's abdomen enlarges. Lines of communication should be open between the expectant mother and her partner about their needs, feelings, and desires.

Preparing for the Baby's Birth

About 2 weeks before the baby's birth, the expectant mother's profile may change as the fetus descends into the pelvic cavity. The expectant mother may now feel less pressure on her diaphragm and thus find it easier to breathe and eat. However, because the head of the fetus can press on the expectant mother's bladder, she may need to urinate more frequently.

Toward the end of the pregnancy, noticeable contractions of the uterus (called Braxton Hicks contractions) increase in frequency. These contractions, which have occurred intermittently throughout pregnancy and which may or may not be felt by the expectant mother, help increase the efficiency of uterine circulation. Though usually not directly associated with labor, these contractions prepare the uterine muscles for labor. As the pregnancy comes to an end and the baby's head presses against the expectant mother's pelvis, her cervix becomes softer and thinner. This thinning is a sign of readiness for labor and birth.

Awkwardness and fatigue may add to the expectant mother's motivation for the pregnancy to end. She may feel as if she has been and will be pregnant forever. At the same time, the expectant mother may feel a "nesting urge" in the form of a spurt of energy that often results in preparations for the arrival of the new baby. She now visits her physician or midwife more often as these physical changes signal that her body is preparing for labor and birth.

The Expectant Mother's Nutrition, Weight Gain, and Exercise

Earlier we indicated that the mother's nutrition can have a strong influence on the development of the fetus. Here we further discuss the mother's nutritional needs and optimal nutrition during pregnancy, as well as the role of exercise in the expectant mother's health.

Nutrition and Weight Gain

The best assurance of an adequate caloric intake during pregnancy is a satisfactory weight gain over time. The optimal weight gain depends on the expectant mother's height, bone structure, and prepregnant nutritional state. However, maternal weight gains that average from 25 to 35

John W. Santrock

pounds are associated with the best reproductive outcomes. The pattern of weight gain is also important. The ideal pattern of weight gain during pregnancy is 2 to 4.4 pounds during the first trimester, followed by an average gain of 1 pound per week during the last two trimesters. In the second trimester, most of the weight gain is due to increased blood volume, the enlargement of breasts, uterus, and associated tissue and fluid, and the deposit of maternal fat. In the third trimester, weight gain mainly involves the fetus, placenta, and amniotic fluid. A 25-pound weight gain during pregnancy is generally distributed in the following way:

- 11 lb Fetus, placenta, and amniotic fluid
- 5 lb Maternal stores
- 4 lb Increased blood volume
- 3 lb Tissue fluid
- 2 lb Uterus and breasts

During the second and third trimesters, inadequate gains of less than 2.2 pounds per month or excessive gains of more than 6.6 pounds per month should be evaluated and the need for nutritional counseling considered. Inadequate weight gain has been associated with low-birthweight infants. Sudden sharp increases in weight of 3 to 5 pounds in a week may result from fluid retention and may require evaluation.

The recommended daily allowance (RDA) for all nutrients increases during pregnancy. The expectant mother should eat three meals a day, with nutritious snacks of fruits, cheese, milk, or other foods between meals if desired. More frequent, smaller meals also are recommended. Four to six glasses (8 ounces) of water and a total of eight to ten cups (8 ounces) total fluid should be consumed daily. Water is an essential nutrient. The amount of the increase in nutrients depends on the nutrient. The need for protein, iron, vitamin D, calcium, phosphorous, and magnesium increase by 50 percent or more. Recommended increases for other nutrients range from 15 to 50 percent (see figure 4.11).

Exercise

How much and what type of exercise is best during pregnancy depend to some degree on the course of the pregnancy, the expectant mother's fitness, and her customary activity level. Normal participation in exercise can continue throughout an uncomplicated pregnancy. In general, the skilled sportswoman is no longer discouraged from participating in sports she has participated in prior to her pregnancy. However, pregnancy is not the appropriate time to begin strenuous activity.

Because of the increased emphasis on physical fitness in our society, more women routinely jog as part of a physical fitness program prior to pregnancy. There are few concerns about continuing to jog during the early part of pregnancy, but in the latter part of pregnancy there is some concern about the jarring effect of jogging on breasts and abdomen. As pregnancy progresses, low-impact activities

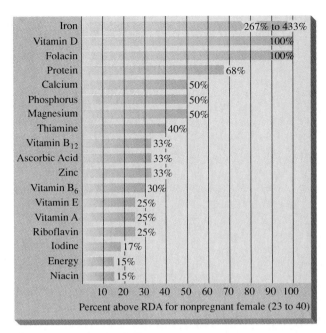

FIGURE 4.11

Recommended Nutrient Increases for Expectant Mothers

such as swimming and bicycling are safer and provide fitness as well as greater comfort, eliminating the bouncing associated with jogging.

The following guidelines for exercise are recommended for expectant mothers (Olds, London, & Ladewig, 1988):

- Exercise for shorter time intervals. Exercising for 10 to 15 minutes, resting for a few minutes, and then exercising for another 10 to 15 minutes decreases potential problems associated with the shunting of blood to the musculoskeletal system and away from organs such as the uterus.
- As pregnancy proceeds, expectant mothers should decrease the intensity of the exercise. The decreased intensity helps to compensate for decreased cardiac reserve, increased respiratory effort, and increased weight gain of the expectant mother.
- Avoid prolonged overheating. Strenuous exercise, especially in a humid environment, can raise the body temperature and increase the risk of fetal problems. Remember also our earlier comments about avoiding overheating in saunas and hot tubs.
- As pregnancy increases, the expectant mother should avoid high-risk activities such as skydiving, mountain climbing, racquetball, and surfing. An expectant mother's changed center of gravity and softened joints may decrease her coordination and increase the risk of falls and injuries in such sports.
- Warm up and stretch to help prepare the joints for activity, and cool down with a period of mild activity to help restore circulation.

How much and what type of exercise is best during pregnancy?

- After exercising, lie on the left side for 10 minutes to rest. This improves circulation from the extremities and promotes placental function.
- Wear supportive shoes and a supportive bra.
- Stop exercising and contact the physician or caregiver if dizziness, shortness of breath, tingling, numbness, vaginal bleeding, or abdominal pain occur.
- Reduce exercise in the last 4 weeks of pregnancy because there is some evidence that strenuous exercise near term increases the risk of low birthweight, stillbirth, and infant death.

Exercise during pregnancy helps to prevent constipation, conditions the body, and is associated with a more positive mental state. However, it is important to remember to not overdo it. Pregnant women should always consult their physician before starting any exercise program.

Cultural Beliefs About Pregnancy and Prenatal Development

Specific actions in pregnancy are often determined by cultural beliefs. Certain behaviors are expected if a culture views pregnancy as a medical condition, whereas other behaviors are expected if pregnancy is viewed as a natural occurrence. Prenatal care may not be a priority for expectant mothers who view pregnancy as a natural occurrence. It is important for health care providers to become aware of the health practices of various cultural groups, including health beliefs about pregnancy and prenatal development. Cultural assessment is an important dimension of providing adequate health care for expectant mothers from various cultural groups. Cultural assessment includes identifying the main beliefs, values, and behaviors related to pregnancy and childbearing. Among the important cultural dimensions are: ethnic background, degree of affiliation with the ethnic group, patterns of decision making, religious preference, language, communication style, and common etiquette practices.

Health care practices during pregnancy are influenced by numerous factors, including the prevalence of traditional home care remedies and folk beliefs, the importance of indigenous healers, and the influence of professional health care workers. Many Mexican American mothers are strongly influenced by their mothers and older women in their culture, often seeking and following their advice during pregnancy. In Mexican American culture, the indigenous healer is called a *curandero*. In some Native American tribes the medicine woman or man fulfills the healing role. Herbalists are often found in Asian cultures, and faith healers, root doctors, and spiritualists are sometimes found in African American culture. When health care providers come into contact with expectant mothers, they need to assess whether such cultural practices pose a threat to the expectant mother and the fetus. If they pose no threat, there is no reason to try to change them. On the other hand, if certain cultural practices do pose a threat to the health of the expectant mother or the fetus, the health care provider should consider a culturally sensitive way to handle the problem. For example, some Philippinos will not take any medication during pregnancy. To read further about some cultural beliefs about pregnancy, see table 4.3.

At this point we have discussed a number of ideas about expectant parents. A summary of these ideas is presented in concept table 4.2.

John W. Santrock

TABLE 4.3

Cultural Beliefs About Pregnancy

Culture	Activity	Cultural Meaning or Belief	Health Care Provider Intervention
Mexican American	Certain clothing worn (munecocord worn beneath the breasts and knotted over the umbilicus)	Ensures a safe delivery	If practice does not cause any danger, do not interfere with it.
	Use of spearmint or sassafras tea or benedictine	Eases morning sickness	Assess use of herbs and determine safety of their use.
	Use of cathartics during the last month of pregnancy	Ensures a good delivery of a healthy boy	Assess use of cathartics. Provide teaching about dangers of the practice and explore culturally acceptable means of resolving constipation (high-fiber foods).
African American	Use of self-medication for many discomforts of pregnancy (Epsom salts, castor oil for constipation; herbs for nausea and vomiting; vinegar and baking soda for heartburn)	Improves health and builds resistance	Assess use of self-medication; discourage those practices that may present problems.
Native American (selected examples)	*Navajo* Meeting with medicine man two months prior to delivery	Prayers ensure safe delivery and healthy baby	Encourage the use of support systems.
	Exercise during pregnancy; concentrating on good thoughts, and being joyful	Produces efficiency and promotes "joy"	Encourage exercise as tolerated.
	Muckeshoot Indians Keeping busy and walking a lot	Makes baby be born earlier, and labor and delivery easier	Encourage walking as tolerated.
	Tonawanda Seneca Eating sparingly and exercising freely	Makes delivery easier	Assess nutritional patterns and provide teaching if needed.
Vietnamese	Consuming ginseng tea	Gives strength	Assess use and be certain it is not taken to the exclusion of necessary nutrients.
	Conversing with and counseling fetus		
Anglo-American	Certain clothing worn	Promotes comfort	
	Self-medication for discomforts of pregnancy	Improves health	Counsel regarding effect of drugs on fetus
	Seeks obstetric care	Ensures safe pregnancy and delivery	
	Attends classes, reads books, attempts to gain more knowledge	Increases knowledge	Assist with pertinent books and topics.
	Concerned that maternity clothes make her look fat	Self-image	
	Oils and creams applied to avoid stretch marks	Self-image	Provide information regarding skin care.

From *Maternal Newborn Nursing*, Third Edition, by Olds, et al. Copyright © 1988 by Addison-Wesley Publishing Company. Reprinted by permission.

CONCEPT TABLE 4.2

Expectant Parents

Concept	Processes/Related Ideas	Characteristics/Description
Confirming the Pregnancy and Calculating the Due Date	Confirming the pregnancy	A pregnancy test checks the woman's urine or blood for human chorionic gonadotropin (HCG), a hormone produced during pregnancy.
	Calculating the due date	Fetal life begins with the fertilization of the ovum, which occurs about two weeks after the woman's last menstrual period. However, the length of the pregnancy is calculated from the first day of the woman's last menstrual period and lasts an average of 280 days or 40 weeks.
The Three Trimesters of Pregnancy and Preparing for the Baby's Birth	The first trimester	The expectant mother may feel especially tired and require more sleep in the second and third months of pregnancy. She also may experience nausea and vomiting. The expectant mother's breasts enlarge and she may need to urinate more often. Many expectant mothers experience emotional ups and downs about their pregnancy. Her partner also may experience mixed feelings about the pregnancy. It is important for expectant parents to become well educated about the nature of pregnancy and prenatal development.
	The second trimester	During the middle months of pregnancy, the expectant mother often feels better than she did earlier or than she will later. Her uterus expands and by the fifth month of pregnancy the top of her uterus reaches the navel. When colostrum appears in the milk glands, expectant mothers who plan to breast-feed should begin preparing their breasts for the breast-feeding. Psychological changes also occur in the second trimester. Some expectant mothers worry a lot about their body image, others enjoy their pregnant appearance. If the expectant mother and father have not read books about child care, this is a good time to purchase one or more of them. In a normal pregnancy, the expectant couple can continue to have sexual intercourse without harming the fetus.
	The third trimester	The expectant mother's uterus expands to a level just below her breast bone. At this time she may experience indigestion and heartburn. She also may experience shortness of breath. Through childbirth classes, the expectant couple can learn more about labor, birth, and how to cope with the latter part of pregnancy.

John W. Santrock

Concept	Processes/Related Ideas	Characteristics/Description
	Preparing for the baby's birth	Two weeks prior to the baby's birth, the expectant mother's profile may change as the fetus descends into the pelvic cavity. She now feels less pressure on her diaphragm and may find it easier to breathe and eat. She often has to urinate more because of bladder pressure from the fetus's head. Toward the end of pregnancy, noticeable contractions of the uterus increase in frequency, which help increase the efficiency of uterine circulation and prepare the uterine muscles for labor. Her cervix becomes softer and thinner; the thinning is a sign of readiness for labor and birth.
The Expectant Mother's Nutrition, Weight Gain, and Exercise	Nutrition and weight gain	The best assurance of an adequate caloric intake during pregnancy is a satisfactory weight gain over time. Maternal weight gains that average 25 to 35 pounds are associated with the best reproductive outcomes. The pattern of the weight gain is also important. Inadequate and excessive weight gains suggest a need for nutritional counseling. The recommended daily allowances for all nutrients increase during pregnancy. The amount of the recommended increase in the nutrients depends on the nutrient.
	Exercise	How much and what type of exercise may be undertaken during pregnancy depends to some extent on the course of pregnancy, the expectant mother's fitness, and her customary activity level. Normal participation in exercise can continue throughout an uncomplicated pregnancy. A number of guidelines for exercise were described. Exercise during pregnancy helps to prevent constipation, conditions the body, and is associated with a more positive mental state.
Cultural Beliefs about Pregnancy and Prenatal Development	Their nature	Specific actions in pregnancy are often determined by cultural beliefs. Certain behaviors are expected if a culture views pregnancy as a medical condition or a natural occurrence. It is important for health care providers to become aware of the health practices of various cultural groups, including health beliefs about pregnancy and prenatal development. Health care practices during pregnancy are influenced by many factors, including the prevalence of traditional home care remedies and folk beliefs, the importance of indigenous healers, and the influence of professional health care workers.

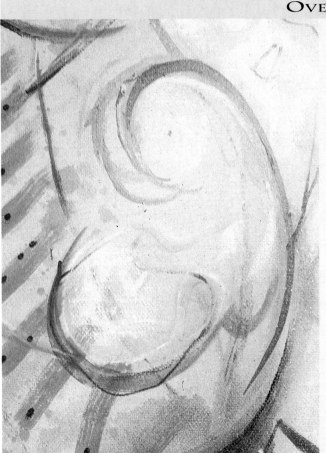

When a species reproduces itself, life comes from life. Much of this chapter was about a state of becoming. Pregnancy is a state of becoming. An unborn baby is becoming a person capable of life outside the mother's body. And a woman and a man are becoming parents.

In this chapter you read about the course of prenatal development, which includes the germinal, embryonic, and fetal periods. We also discussed the complexities of abortion. We studied teratology and hazards to prenatal development, focusing on such topics as maternal diseases and conditions (AIDS, for example), the mother's age, nutrition, emotional states and stress, drugs, environmental hazards, and fetal surgery and therapy. Our coverage of expectant parents examined confirming the pregnancy, calculating the due date, the three trimesters of pregnancy, preparing for the baby's birth, the expectant mother's nutrition, weight gain, and exercise, and cultural beliefs about pregnancy and prenatal development.

Remember that you can obtain an overall summary of the chapter by again reading the two concept tables on pages 119 and 126. In the next chapter we turn our attention to the birth process itself.

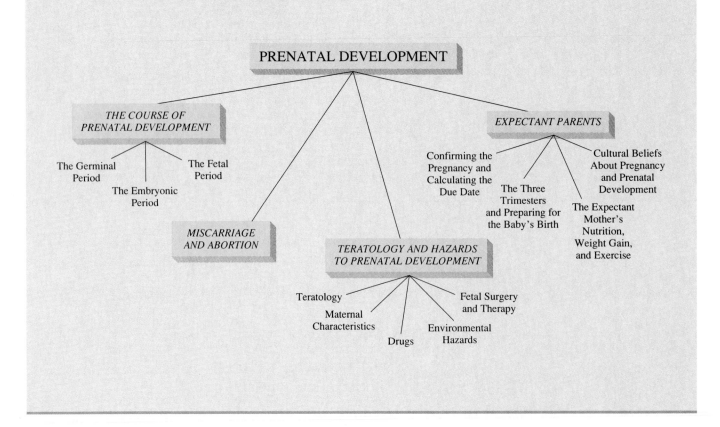

PRENATAL DEVELOPMENT

THE COURSE OF PRENATAL DEVELOPMENT

The Germinal Period

The Embryonic Period

The Fetal Period

MISCARRIAGE AND ABORTION

TERATOLOGY AND HAZARDS TO PRENATAL DEVELOPMENT

Teratology

Maternal Characteristics

Drugs

Environmental Hazards

Fetal Surgery and Therapy

EXPECTANT PARENTS

Confirming the Pregnancy and Calculating the Due Date

The Three Trimesters and Preparing for the Baby's Birth

Cultural Beliefs About Pregnancy and Prenatal Development

The Expectant Mother's Nutrition, Weight Gain, and Exercise

John W. Santrock

germinal period The period of prenatal development that takes place in the first 2 weeks after conception. It includes the creation of the zygote, continued cell division, and the attachment of the zygote to the uterine wall. 104

blastocyst The inner layer of cells that develops during the germinal period. These cells later develop into the embryo. 104

trophoblast The outer layer of cells that develops in the germinal period. These cells provide nutrition and support for the embryo. 104

implantation The attachment of the zygote to the uterine wall, which takes place about 10 days after conception. 104

embryonic period The period of prenatal development that occurs 2 to 8 weeks after conception. During the embryonic period, the rate of cell differentiation intensifies, support systems for the cells form, and organs appear. 105

endoderm The inner layer of cells that develops into digestive and respiratory systems. 105

ectoderm The outermost layer of cells, which becomes the nervous system, sensory receptors (ears, nose, and eyes, for example), and skin parts (hair and nails, for example). 105

mesoderm The middle layer of cells, which becomes the circulatory system, bones, muscles, excretory system, and reproductive system. 105

placenta A life-support system that consists of a disk-shaped group of tissues in which small blood vessels from the mother and offspring intertwine. 106

umbilical cord A life-support system containing two arteries and one vein that connects the baby to the placenta. 106

amnion The life-support system that is a bag or envelope that contains a clear fluid in which the developing embryo floats. 106

organogenesis Organ formation that takes place during the first 2 months of prenatal development. 107

fetal period The prenatal period of development that begins 2 months after conception and lasts for 7 months, on the average. 107

teratogen From the Greek word *tera*, meaning "monster." Any agent that causes a birth defect. The field of study that investigates the causes of birth defects is called teratology. 110

ectopic pregnancy The presence of a developing embryo or fetus outside the normal location in the uterus. 112

fetal alcohol syndrome (FAS) A cluster of abnormalities that appears in the offspring of mothers who drink alcohol heavily during pregnancy. 114

toxoplasmosis A mild infection that causes coldlike symptoms in adults but can be a teratogen for the unborn baby. 117

What to Expect When You're Expecting
(1991) (rev. 2nd ed.)
by Arlene Eisenberg, Heidi Murkoff, and Sandee Hathaway.
New York: Workman.

What to Expect When You're Expecting is a month-by-month, step-by-step guide to pregnancy and childbirth. The authors are a mother-daughter team and the book was the result of the second author's (Heidi Eisenberg Murkoff) unnecessarily worry-filled pregnancy. The book tries to put expectant parents' normal fears into perspective by giving them comprehensive information and helping them to enjoy this transition in their lives.

This is an excellent book for expectant parents. It is reassuring and thorough. The book is filled with charts and lists that make understanding pregnancy an easier task for expectant parents. One of the book's enthusiasts said that it is like having an experienced mother nearby whom you can always call with questions like, "Hey, did you get leg cramps in the fifth month of pregnancy?"

Will It Hurt the Baby?
(1990) by Richard Abrams.
Reading, MA: Addison-Wesley.

Will It Hurt the Baby? examines the safe use of medication during pregnancy and breast feeding. The author is a professor of medicine and pediatrics at the University of Colorado School of Medicine. Abrams describes the trend in eliminating medicine during pregnancy, but he believes that in some cases a drug's benefits outweighs its risks. He discusses fifteen common medical problems women face during pregnancy, their symptoms, and special concerns about them. He also describes nine environmental and occupational hazards during pregnancy, such as food additives, pesticides, and physical exertion. In a final section of almost 300 pages, hundreds of drugs from acetaminophen (Tylenol) to zidovudine (AZT) are evaluated.

This is a good reference guide for expectant mothers and breast-feeding mothers. Respected pediatrician T. Berry Brazelton (1990) commented that the book is very timely and useful.

What to Eat When You're Expecting
(1986) by Arlene Eisenberg, Heidi Murkoff, and Sandee Hathaway.
New York: Workman.

What to Eat When You're Expecting focuses on a special aspect of pregnancy: diet and nutrition. The book was written by the authors of *What to Expect When You're Expecting*. It is based on more than 20 years of practical applications in the Eisenberg family. They present the "best odds" diet, which they believe increases the probability of having a healthy baby by controlling the factors that can be influenced and minimizing the risk and worry about those factors that cannot be controlled. Daily recommended portions are given. Pregnant women learn how to gauge their current eating habits and how to alter them if they are bad. The book is well-written and the nutritional plan for expectant mothers is sound.

IMPROVING THE LIVES OF CHILDREN

Improving the lives of children involves attention to such factors as prenatal care; teenage pregnancy programs; prenatal education classes; poverty, empowerment, and the community; and educating about reproductive rights and freedom.

HEALTH AND WELL-BEING

Prenatal Care

Prenatal care varies enormously but usually involves a package of medical care services in a defined schedule of visits. In addition to medical care, prenatal care programs often include comprehensive educational, social, and nutritional services (Shiono & Behrman, 1995).

Prenatal care usually includes screening that can reveal manageable conditions and/or treatable diseases that could affect both the baby's life and the pregnant woman's. The education the mother receives about pregnancy, labor and delivery, and caring for the newborn can be extremely valuable, especially for first-time mothers. Prenatal care is also very important for women in poverty because it links them with other social services. The legacy of prenatal care continues after the birth because women who experience this type of care are more likely to get preventive care for their infants (Bates & others, 1994).

Women sometimes receive inadequate prenatal care for reasons related to the health care system, provider practices, and their own individual and social characteristics (Alexander & Korenbrot, 1995). In one national study, 71 percent of low-income women experienced a problem in getting prenatal care (U.S. General Accounting Office, 1987). They cited finances, transportation, and child care as barriers. Motivating positive attitudes toward pregnancy is also important. Women who do not want to be pregnant, who have negative attitudes about being pregnant, or who unintentionally become pregnant are more likely to delay prenatal care or to miss appointments (Joseph, 1989).

FAMILIES AND PARENTING

Teenage Pregnancy Programs

Adolescents who become pregnant represent a high-risk population, with increased risk to the health of both the child and the mother (Chase-Lansdale & Brooks-Gunn, 1994). Teenage pregnancy programs are often a mix of health care, education, and social services coordinated with local agencies. Services include prenatal, postpartum, and pediatric health care, remedial education, employment training and counseling, family planning services, life-planning assistance, and life skills training (Alexander & Korenbrot, 1995).

Teenage pregnancy programs are usually based in schools, health facilities, or the adolescent's home. In addition to providing psychological, nutritional, medical, and health education services, these programs often offer parenting education, encourage the continuation of schooling, urge adolescents to delay subsequent pregnancies, prepare them for further employment, and assist them with legal, family, and financial problems.

EDUCATION

The Prenatal Education Class

Early prenatal classes may include couples in both early pregnancy and prepregnancy (Olds, London, & Ladewig, 1988). The classes often focus on topics like these:

- Changes in the development of the embryo and the fetus
- Self-care during pregnancy
- Fetal development concerns and environmental dangers for the fetus
- Sexuality during pregnancy
- Birth setting and types of care providers
- Nutrition, rest, and exercise
- Common discomforts of pregnancy and relief measures
- Psychological changes in both the expectant mother and her partner
- Information needed to get the pregnancy off to a good start

Early prenatal education classes focus on such topics as changes in the development of the fetus, while later classes often focus on preparation for the birth and care of the newborn.

Early classes also may include information about factors that place the expectant mother at risk for preterm labor and recognition of the possible signs and symptoms of preterm labor. And prenatal education classes may include information on the advantages and disadvantages of breast- and bottle-feeding. Most expectant mothers (50 to 80 percent) have made this infant feeding decision prior to the sixth month of pregnancy. Therefore, information about the issues involved in breast-versus bottle-feeding in an early prenatal education class is helpful.

So far, the prenatal education classes we have described focus on expectant couples in the first trimester of pregnancy. The later classes—those when the expectant mother is in the second or third trimester of pregnancy—often focus on preparation for the birth, infant care and feeding, postpartum self-care, and birth choices. Much more about these topics appears in the next chapter.

CULTURE AND ETHNICITY

Poverty, Empowerment, and the Community

To improve prenatal development, it is critical to improve socioeconomic conditions (Alexander & Korenbrot, 1995). One strategy is to develop culturally competent outreach and prenatal care programs for disadvantaged populations.

Community empowerment involves enabling groups to act, control, or influence consequences that are important for their members. Since the beginning of the development of prenatal care programs, it has been recognized that community conditions such as poverty and racism create contexts in people's lives that discourage the use of preventive resources and services. The concept of neighborhood empowerment has led to an increased interest in the use of community health workers, community health centers, and family-life community centers.

Nurses and lay health workers can be used as home visitors in low-income contexts. Home visiting is routine in European countries, where it is usually conducted by midwives, although it has only been used sparingly in North America.

GENDER

Educating About Reproductive Rights and Freedoms

According to gender expert Michele Paludi (1995), abortion, adoption, and motherhood all have problems associated with them. What contributes to the least problems is to prevent unwanted pregnancies. Table 4.4 lists a number of methods of contraception. Notice that most of the methods are intended for females. Paludi says that this fact has been explained by the nature of a female's reproductive cycle—females are fertile only a few days a month whereas males are always fertile. Thus, it may be easier to intervene in a female's reproductive cycle. Some individuals have commented that contraceptive methods have been developed primarily by males who believe females should be responsible for controlling reproduction. Paludi concludes that females do want to control reproduction, but she wonders whether it is equitable that only females must take responsibility and risk every time they have intercourse. Especially important is educating adolescent females and males about birth control and sexuality.

In New York City, the Children's Aid Society's Teen Pregnancy Prevention Program provides youth with information about the following: family life and sex education, medical and health services, job club and career awareness program, academic assessment and homework help program, self-esteem enhancement through the performing arts, and lifetime individual sports. In addition, all participants—adolescents and their parents—are guaranteed admission to Hunter College of the City University of New York upon completion of high school, participation in the Teen Pregnancy Prevention Program, and the recommendation of the director of the program. The philosophy of this program is rooted in a broad-based conception of sexuality as involving many dimensions of a person's life.

TABLE 4.4

Methods of Contraception

Forms of Contraception	Effectiveness	Side Effects
Natural family planning	Fair to poor	Intercourse must be reduced
Withdrawal	Fair to poor	Sexual pleasure reduced due to anxiety
Abstinence	100%	
Spermicidal foam	Good to fair	Irritation of genital area
Condoms	Good	
Intrauterine device	Very good	Cramping, pelvic infections
Birth control pills	Excellent	Blood-clotting disorders
Vasectomy	Excellent	
Tubal ligation	Excellent	

MORISOT
The Cradle, detail

CHAPTER

5

Birth

There was a star danced,
and under that I was born.

—William Shakespeare

No single event can awaken within us a stranger totally unknown to us. To live is to be slowly born.

—Saint-Exupéry, *Flight to Arras,* 1942

Images of Children

Teresa Block's Pregnancy and Her Son Robert

Teresa Block's second pregnancy was difficult. Her amniotic sac ruptured, she contracted an infection that sent her temperature skyrocketing, and she had an exhausting breech delivery. Her son Robert weighed just less than 2 pounds at birth. Teresa said she had never imagined a baby looking so tiny. The first time she saw Robert, he was lying on his back attached to a respirator, and wires were connected all over his body. Robert stayed at the hospital until two weeks before his originally projected birth date, at which time he weighed 4 pounds, 8 ounces. Teresa and her husband lived in a small town 60 miles from the hospital; they commuted each day to spend time with Robert and brought their other child with them whenever it was practical.

A decade later, Robert is still at the bottom of the weight chart, but he is about average in height, and the only physical residue of his early birth difficulties is a "lazy eye." He is 20/20 in his good eye but 20/200 in the other. He is doing special exercises for the bad eye, and his doctor thinks he is not far from the day he can go without glasses. Robert is on the soccer team and the swim team.

Considering his circumstances, Robert had a relatively uncomplicated stay at the hospital. Not all children born so frail survive, and sometimes those who do show the consequences many years in the future.

Preview

The birth of a baby creates changes in a family—it is an event with long-lasting consequences. While there are many ways to have a baby, the goal should always be to ensure the health of the mother and the baby. In this chapter we will explore many different dimensions of birth, including children such as Robert, who was a low-birthweight baby. To begin, we will study the stages of birth, delivery complications, and the use of drugs during childbirth.

Exploring the Birth Process

What are the normal stages of birth? What kind of delivery complications can take place? Should drugs be used during childbirth?

Stages of Birth

The birth process occurs in three stages. For a woman having her first child, the first stage lasts an average of 12 to 24 hours; it is the longest of the three stages. In the first stage, uterine contractions are 15 to 20 minutes apart at the beginning and last up to a minute. These contractions cause the woman's cervix to stretch and open. As the first stage progresses, the contractions come closer together, appearing every 2 to 5 minutes. Their intensity increases too. By the end of the first birth stage, contractions dilate the cervix to an opening of about 4 inches so that the baby can move from the uterus to the birth canal.

Children sweeten labors . . .

—Frances Bacon, *Essays,* 1625

The second birth stage begins when the baby's head starts to move through the cervix and the birth canal. It terminates when the baby completely emerges from the mother's body. This stage lasts approximately 1½ hours.

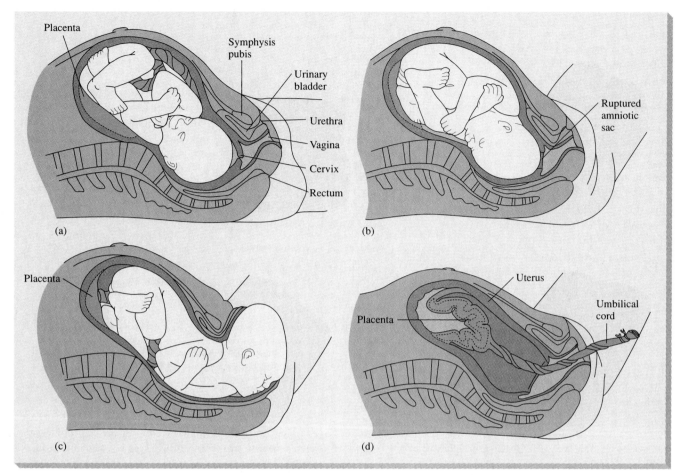

FIGURE 5.1

The Stages of Labor
(a) First stage: cervix is dilating; *(b)* Late first stage (transition stage): cervix is fully dilated, and the amniotic sac has ruptured, releasing amniotic fluid; *(c)* Second stage: birth of the infant; *(d)* Third stage: delivery of the placenta (afterbirth).

With each contraction, the mother bears down hard to push the baby out of her body. By the time the baby's head is out of the mother's body, the contractions come almost every minute and last for about a minute.

Afterbirth *is the third stage, at which time the placenta, umbilical cord, and other membranes are detached and expelled.* This final stage is the shortest of the three birth stages, lasting only minutes (see figure 5.1).

Delivery Complications

Complications can accompany the baby's delivery. A **precipitate delivery** *is a delivery that takes place too rapidly; the baby squeezes through the birth canal in less than 10 minutes.* This deviation in delivery can disturb the infant's normal flow of blood, and the pressure on the infant's head can cause hemorrhaging. On the other hand, **anoxia,** *the insufficient supply of oxygen to the infant,* can develop if the delivery takes too long. Anoxia can cause brain damage.

The **breech position** *is the baby's position in the uterus that causes the buttocks to be the first part to emerge from the vagina.* Normally, the crown of the baby's head comes

through the vagina first, but in 1 of every 25 babies, the head does not come through first. Breech babies' heads are still in the uterus when the rest of their bodies are out, which can cause respiratory problems. Some breech babies cannot be passed through the cervix and must be delivered by cesarean section.

A **cesarean section** *is the surgical removal of the baby from the uterus.* A cesarean section is usually performed if the baby is in a breech position, if it is lying crosswise in the uterus, if the baby's head is too large to pass through the mother's pelvis, if the baby develops complications, or if the mother is bleeding vaginally. The benefits and risks of cesarean section delivery are debated. Cesarean section deliveries are safer than breech deliveries, but they involve the higher infection rate, longer hospital stay, and greater expense and stress that accompany any surgery.

Some critics believe that, in the United States, too many babies are delivered by cesarean section. More cesarean sections are performed in the United States than in any other industrialized nation. From 1979 to 1987, the cesarean section rate increased almost 50 percent in the United States alone, to an annual rate of 24 percent. However, a growing use of vaginal birth after a previous cesarean, greater public awareness, and peer pressure in the medical community are beginning to slow the rate of increase.

The Use of Drugs During Childbirth

Drugs can be used to relieve pain and anxiety and to speed delivery during the birth process. The widest use of drugs during delivery is to relieve the expectant mother's pain or anxiety. A variety of tranquilizers, sedatives, and analgesics are used for this purpose. Researchers are interested in the effects of these drugs because they can cross the placental barrier, and because their use is so widespread.

Oxytocin, *a hormone that stimulates and regulates the rhythmicity of uterine contractions, has been widely used as a drug to speed delivery.* Controversy surrounds the use of this drug. Some physicians argue that it can save the mother's life or keep the infant from being damaged. They also stress that using the drug allows the mother to be well rested and prepared for the birth process. Critics argue that babies born to mothers who have taken oxytocin are more likely to have jaundice; that induced labor requires more painkilling drugs; and that greater medical care is required after the birth, resulting in the separation of the infant and mother.

Recently, prostaglandins have been used both to replace oxytocin and to precede its use. An accumulation of research suggests prostaglandins are as effective as, or more effective than, oxytocin. They are also more acceptable to women and easier for hospital personnel to administer (Rosenblith, 1992).

The following conclusions can be reached, based on research about the influence of drugs during delivery.

1. Few research studies have been done, and many that have been completed have had methodological problems. However, not all drugs have similar effects. Some—tranquilizers, sedatives, and analgesics, for example—do not seem to have long-term effects. Other drugs—oxytocin, for example—are suspected of having long-term effects.
2. The degree to which a drug influences the infant is usually small. Birthweight and social class, for instance, are more powerful predictors of infant difficulties than are drugs.
3. A specific drug may affect some infants but not others. In some cases the drug may have a beneficial effect, whereas in others it may be harmful.
4. The overall amount of medication may be an important factor in understanding drug effects on delivery.

CRITICAL THINKING ABOUT CHILDREN'S DEVELOPMENT

The Use of Drugs During Childbirth

Given the information you have just read about the use of drugs during childbirth, what considerations would be foremost in your mind if your offspring were about to be born? What questions about the use of drugs during delivery would you want to ask the individuals responsible for delivering the baby? Considering the use of drugs during your own child's birth encourages you to think critically by *evaluating the quality of conclusions about children's development.*

To further evaluate the use of drugs during childbirth, see Critical Thinking About Children's Development.

Next, we will discuss some of the increasing numbers of childbirth strategies. In the last several decades, more expectant mothers have chosen to have a prepared, or natural, childbirth. One aspect of prepared childbirth is an attempt to minimize the use of medication.

CHILDBIRTH STRATEGIES

In the past two decades, the nature of childbirth has changed considerably. Where heavy medication was once the norm, now natural, or prepared, childbirth has become increasingly popular. Today husbands much more frequently participate in childbirth. Alternative birthing centers and birthing rooms have become standard in many maternity units, and the acceptance of midwives has increased. Before we explore some of these contemporary trends in childbirth strategies, let's examine the nature of standard childbirth.

Standard Childbirth

In the standard childbirth procedure that has been practiced for many years—and the way you probably were delivered—the expectant mother is taken to a hospital, where a doctor is responsible for the baby's delivery. To prepare the pregnant woman for labor, her pubic hair is shaved and she is given an enema. She is then placed in a labor room often filled with other pregnant women, some of whom are screaming. When she is ready to deliver, she is taken to the delivery room, which looks like an operating room. She is laid on a table, and the physician, along with an anesthetist and a nurse, delivers the baby.

What could be wrong with this procedure? Critics list three things: (1) Important individuals related to the

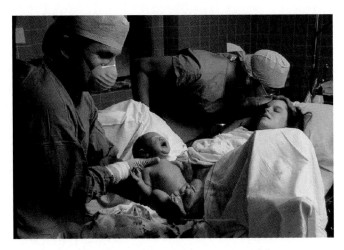

A more homelike institutional environment is one of the current changes in childbirth. Shown here is a husband helping with the birth in a birthing room at a hospital.

mother are excluded from the birth process. (2) The mother is separated from her infant in the first minutes and hours after birth. (3) Giving birth is treated like a disease, and a woman is thought of as a sick patient (Rosenblith, 1992). As we will see next, some alternatives differ radically from this standard procedure.

The Leboyer Method

The **Leboyer method,** *developed by French obstetrician Frederick Leboyer, intends to make the birth process less stressful for infants. Leboyer's procedure is referred to as "birth without violence."* He describes standard childbirth as torture (Leboyer, 1975). He vehemently objects to holding newborns upside down and slapping or spanking them, putting silver nitrite into their eyes, separating them immediately from their mothers, and scaring them with bright lights and harsh noises in the delivery room. Leboyer also criticizes the traditional habit of cutting the umbilical cord as soon as the infant is born, a situation that forces the infant to immediately take in oxygen from the air to breathe. Leboyer believes that the umbilical cord should be left intact for several minutes to allow the newborn a chance to adjust to a world of breathing air. In the Leboyer method, the baby is placed on the mother's stomach immediately after birth so the mother can caress the infant. Then the infant is placed in a bath of warm water to relax. Although most hospitals do not use the soft lights and warm baths that Leboyer suggests, they sometimes do place the newborn on the mother's stomach immediately after birth, believing that it will stimulate mother-infant bonding.

Prepared, or Natural, Childbirth

Prepared, or natural, childbirth, *includes being informed about what will happen during the procedure, knowing about comfort measures for childbirth, anticipating that little or no medication will be used, and, if complications arise, expecting to participate in decisions made to resolve the problems.* Medical treatment is used when there is a reason, but it should always

be done with care and concern for the expectant mother and the offspring. Prepared childbirth assumes the presence and support of a partner or friend, and in some cases, a labor-support person identified through local childbirth education groups. At least two persons, including the laboring woman, are needed to work with each contraction.

> *We must respect this instant of birth, this fragile moment. The baby is between two worlds, on a threshold, hesitating . . .*
>
> —**Frederick Leboyer**
> ***Birth Without Violence***

Prepared childbirth includes a number of variations. Consider the following three instances of prepared childbirth. The first woman in labor lies awake under light medication with an intravenous needle in her arm into which a nearby pump introduces a labor stimulant. She is attached to electronic monitoring devices and confined to the bed. A second woman is wearing her own clothes, sitting in a rocking chair in a birthing room, relaxing, attending to her breathing, and sipping a glass of cider with none of the above medications or equipment being used. At her infant's birth there will be no gowns or masks and she will give birth in the birthing room instead of being moved to the delivery room. An older child who has learned about childbirth may even be in the room, preparing to welcome the new sibling. The third woman and her husband are "prepared" parents, who may or may not have attended cesarean preparation classes, but agree that cesarean birth is required. Both parents are in the delivery room and she is awake. Despite obvious involvement of the couple in the decision to have the cesarean birth, no one has yet described a cesarean birth as a natural one.

A basic philosophy of prepared childbirth is that information and teaching methods should support parent confidence, provide the knowledge required to carry out normal childbirth, and explain how the medical system functions in childbirth. Professional disciplines involved in childbirth now go beyond obstetrics (with its main emphasis on pathology rather than normal birth) and also include nursing, public health, education, physical therapy, psychology, sociology, and physiology. Each of these areas has contributed to teaching programs and provided increased knowledge about childbirth. But never to be overlooked is the input to health professionals from parents themselves.

Childbirth Today

Among the current changes in childbirth are shifts in emphases, new choices, and an understanding of obstetrical terminology (Tappero, 1996). And an increasing number of instructors report that they are now using a more eclectic approach to childbirth, drawing information from several different methods (Bean, 1990). Let's examine some of these trends in more detail:

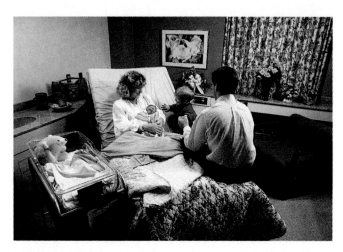

How is this scene in a hospital recovery room in the 1990s different from the childbirth scenes that were typical earlier in this century?

- Breathing methods continue to be important but are more flexible in accord with the individual needs of the expectant mother. In general, breathing is becoming less active and less vigorous, with more attention given to other methods of providing comfort. However, some prepared childbirth instructors believe that the importance of breathing should not be downplayed too much.
- New ways of teaching relaxation are offered, including guided mental imagery, massage, and meditation.
- The use of warm water for comfort is recognized, and many hospitals have showers in their labor and delivery areas. Some hospitals have introduced Jacuzzis.
- A more homelike institutional environment is believed to be important.
- Stress from intense lighting and an intrusive environment can inhibit uterine contraction, possibly slowing labor and even making the introduction of medication necessary. Hospitals are moving in the direction of having most nonsurgical births, including anesthetized births, in homelike birthing rooms that are quiet, peaceful, and less intensely lit.
- Walking during labor and the use of varied body positions during labor and birth are encouraged. For many women, the squatting position is the most comfortable and effective position.
- The "nothing by mouth" policy during labor is being seriously questioned and reexamined. Light food was initially introduced in home birth and freestanding birthing centers. It is now beginning to be offered in some hospitals.
- The use of midwife-assisted birth is becoming more widespread, allowing longer and more informative prenatal visits, labor support, and less use of medication.

- Parent-infant bonding, which we will discuss later in the chapter, is widely available and encouraged. Even if the baby is premature or ill, parents go to the intensive care nursery to see, touch, and talk to their newborn.
- Siblings and grandparents are welcome to touch and hold the baby in the hospital.
- Hospital stays have been shortened to 3 days or less, mainly because of recent government reimbursement regulations. Approximately 5 days are allowed for cesarean births.
- Increased amounts of time are spent discussing the pros and cons of various obstetrical and birthing options.

Most current methods, including the Bradley method, the Gamper method, and the Kitzinger, Simkin, and Noble approaches, as well as most of the classes that use an eclectic approach to childbirth, are based on Grantly Dick-Read's concepts. Included is a wide range of choices and comfort techniques; parents are encouraged to select what they believe will work best for them. The emphasis is placed on becoming attuned and responsive to individual prenatal and birthing needs. The current belief is that when information and support are provided, and anxieties and fears are allayed, women *know* how to give birth.

> *The strongest principle of human growth lies in human choice.*
>
> —Alexander Chase
> *Perspectives*, **1966**

The **Lamaze method** *has become a widely used childbirth strategy; it is a form of prepared or natural childbirth developed by Fernand Lamaze, a pioneering French obstetrician.* It has become widely accepted by the medical profession and involves helping the expectant mother to cope actively with the pain of childbirth and to avoid or reduce medication. Lamaze training for parents is available on a widespread basis in the United States and usually consists of six weekly classes. In these classes, the pregnant woman learns about the birth process and is trained in breathing and relaxation exercises. As the Lamaze method has grown in popularity, it has become more common for the father to participate in the exercises and to assist in the birth process.

Lamaze exercises and breathing have much in common with the other methods of prepared childbirth, with the exception that breathing techniques are more central to the method; Lamaze breathing is very active. Whatever the method of prepared childbirth that expectant couples choose, each will provide information about birth, ways of relaxing and releasing muscle tension, breathing patterns to relieve anxiety and bring adequate oxygen to the contracting uterine muscle, ways to avoid hyperventilation (overbreathing), and basic physical conditioning exercises.

John W. Santrock

Birth Strategies

There are many birth strategies available to parents today. We have discussed standard childbirth, the Leboyer method, prepared or natural childbirth, and the Lamaze method. Which method do you think is best—for the mother, the father, and the offspring? Might there be individual differences in what works best? Evaluating different birth strategies encourages you to think critically about children's development by *using knowledge about development to improve human welfare.*

Not all expectant parents in the United States participate in prepared, or natural, childbirth. Expectant parents from middle-income backgrounds are more likely to be educated about variations in childbirth methods and to choose prepared childbirth than are expectant parents from low-income backgrounds. To further evaluate birth strategies, refer to Critical Thinking About Children's Development.

Doula is a Greek word that means "a woman who helps other women." In contemporary perinatal care, **doula** *means a caregiver who provides continuous physical, emotional, and educational support to the mother before, during, and just after childbirth.* Doulas remain with the mother throughout labor, assessing and responding to her needs. In one recent study, mothers who received doula support reported less labor pain than mothers who did not receive doula support (Klaus, Kennell, & Klaus, 1993).

A doula is a layperson, usually a woman, who understands the biological and medical processes involved in labor and obstetrics, and who usually has assisted in at least five or six deliveries supervised by another doula. Doulas typically function as part of a "birthing team," serving as an adjunct to the midwife or the hospital obstetric staff.

In the United States, most doulas work as independent providers hired by the expectant woman. Managed care organizations are increasingly offering doula support as part of regular obstetric care. In some European countries, doula support is offered as standard care by midwives or nursing students. In many cultures, the practice of a knowledgeable woman helping a mother in labor is not officially labeled as "doula" support but is simply an ingrained, centuries-old custom.

Fathers and Siblings

How should fathers participate in their child's birth? How should siblings participate in the child's birth?

The Father's Participation

In the past several decades, fathers increasingly have participated in childbirth. Fathers-to-be are now more likely to go to at least one meeting with the obstetrician or caregiver during the pregnancy, attend childbirth preparation classes, learn about labor and birth, and be more involved in the care of the young infant. The change is consistent with our culture's movement toward less rigid concepts of "masculine" and "feminine."

For many expectant couples today, the father is trained to be the expectant mother's coach during labor,

Many husbands, or coaches, take childbirth classes with their wives or friends as part of prepared, or natural, childbirth. This is a Lamaze training session. Lamaze training is available on a widespread basis in the United States and usually consists of six weekly classes.

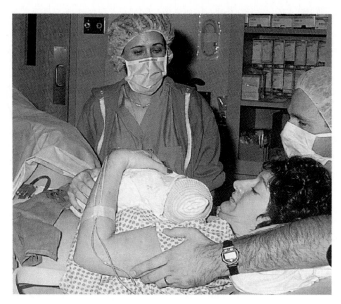

The father of a newborn is shown in the delivery room. The father's participation in the birth process strengthens his sense of involvement in and commitment to the family.

helping her to learn relaxation methods and special breathing techniques for labor and birth. Most health professionals now believe that, just as with pregnancy, childbirth should be an intimate, shared moment between two people who are creating a new life together. Nonetheless, some men do not want to participate in prepared childbirth, and some women also still prefer that he not have a very active role. In such cases, other people can provide support for childbirth—mother, sister, friend, midwife, or physician, for example.

Husbands who are motivated to participate in childbirth have an important role at their wife's side. In the long stretches when there is no staff attendant present, a husband can provide companionship, support, and encouragement. In difficult moments of examination or medication, he can be comforting. Initially, he may feel embarrassed to use the breathing techniques he learned in preparation classes, but he usually begins to feel more at home when he realizes he is performing a necessary function for his wife during each contraction.

Some individuals question whether the father is the best coach during labor. He may be nervous and feel uncomfortable in the hospital, and never having gone through labor himself, he might not understand the expectant mother's needs as well as another woman. There is no universal answer to this issue. Some laboring women want to depend on another woman, someone who has been through labor herself; others want their husband to intimately share the childbirth experience. Many cultures exclude men from births, just as the American culture did until the last several decades. In some cultures, the woman's mother, or occasionally a daughter, serves as her assistant.

Siblings

If parents have a child and are expecting another, it is important for them to prepare the older child for the birth of a sibling. Sibling preparation includes providing the child with information about pregnancy, birth, and life with a newborn that is realistic and appropriate for the child's age.

Parents can prepare their older child for the approaching birth at any time during pregnancy. The expectant mother might announce the pregnancy early to explain her tiredness and vomiting. If the child is young and unable to understand waiting, parents may want to delay announcing the pregnancy until later, when the expectant mother's pregnancy becomes obvious and she begins to look "fat" to the child.

Parents may want to consider having the child present at the birth. Many family-centered hospitals, birth centers, and home births make this option available. Some parents wish to minimize or avoid separation from the older child, so they choose to give birth where sibling involvement is possible. These parents feel that if there is no separation, the child will not develop separation anxiety and will not see the new baby as someone who took the mother away. Sibling involvement in the childbirth may enhance the attachment between the older child and the new baby. On the other hand, some children may not want to participate in the birthing process and should not be forced into it. Some preschool children may be overwhelmed by the whole process and older children may feel embarrassed.

If the birth will be in a hospital with a typical stay of 3 to 5 days, parents need to consider the possibility that the child will feel separation anxiety, which can result from the child's being separated from one or both parents. To ease the child's separation anxiety, the expectant mother should let the child know approximately when she will be going to the hospital, tour the hospital with the child if possible, and, when labor begins, tell the child where she is going. Before birth, the expectant mother can increase the father's role as a caregiver if he is not already responsible for much of the child's daily care. Parents can ask about the regulations at the hospital or birth setting, and, if possible, have the child visit the mother there. As sibling visitation has become recognized as a positive emotional experience for the entire family, hospitals are increasingly allowing children to visit their mothers after the birth of the baby. Some hospitals even allow siblings in the recovery room to see both the mother and the newborn.

In addition to being separated from the mother, the child now has to cope with another emotionally taxing experience: the permanent presence of a crying newborn who requires extensive care and attention from the mother. Life is never the same for the older child after the newborn arrives. Parents who once might have given extensive attention to the child now suddenly have less time available for the child—all because of the new sibling. It is not unusual for a child to ask a parent, "When are you going to take it

When parents have a child and are expecting another, they can provide the child with information about pregnancy, birth, and life with a newborn that is realistic and appropriate for the child's age. This information helps the child cope with the birth of a sibling. As part of the sibling preparation process, some parents choose to have the child present at the sibling's birth.

back to the hospital?" Many children engage in a number of regressive and attention-seeking behaviors after a new sibling arrives such as sucking their thumb, directing anger at their parents or the baby (hitting, biting, or throwing things), wanting a bottle or the mother's breasts for themselves, or bed-wetting. Such behaviors are natural and represent the child's way of coping with stress. Parents should not act like they are disappointed because the child is behaving in such ways and should worry about such behaviors only if they persist after the child has had a reasonable amount of time to adjust to the new baby. To help the child cope with the arrival of the new baby, parents can (Simkin, Whalley, & Keppler, 1984)

- before and after the birth, read books to the child about living with a new baby.
- plan for time alone with the older child and do what he or she wants to do.
- use the time when the baby is asleep and the parent is rested to give special attention to the older child.
- give a gift to the older child in the hospital or at home.
- "tell" the baby about his or her special older brother or sister when the older sibling is listening.

At this point, we have discussed a number of ideas about stages of birth, delivery complications, the use of drugs during childbirth, and childbirth strategies. A summary of these ideas is presented in concept table 5.1.

PRETERM INFANTS AND AGE-WEIGHT CONSIDERATIONS

How can we distinguish between a preterm infant and a low-birthweight infant? What are the developmental outcomes for low-birthweight infants? Do preterm infants have a different profile from that of full-term infants? What conclusions can we reach about preterm infants?

Preterm and Low-Birthweight Infants

An infant is full-term when it has grown in the womb for a full 38 to 42 weeks between conception and delivery. A **preterm infant** *is one who is born prior to 38 weeks after conception.* A **low-birthweight infant** *is born after a regular gestation period (the length of time between conception and birth) of 38 to 42 weeks, but weighs less than 5½ pounds.* Both preterm and low-birthweight infants are considered high-risk infants.

A short gestation period does not necessarily harm an infant. It is distinguished from retarded prenatal growth, in which the fetus has been damaged (Kopp, 1992). The neurological development of a short-gestation infant continues after birth on approximately the same timetable as if the infant still were in the womb. For example, consider an infant born after a gestation period of 30 weeks. At 38 weeks, approximately 2 months after birth, this infant shows the same level of brain development as a 38-week fetus who is yet to be born.

CONCEPT TABLE 5.1

Exploring the Birth Process and Childbirth Strategies

Concept	Processes/Related Ideas	Characteristics/Description
Exploring the Birth Process	Stages of birth	Three stages of birth have been defined. The first lasts about 12 to 24 hours for a woman having her first child. The cervix dilates to about 4 inches. The second stage begins when the baby's head moves through the cervix and ends with the baby's complete emergence. The third stage is afterbirth.
	Delivery complications	A baby can move through the birth canal too rapidly or too slowly. A delivery that is too fast is called precipitate; when delivery is too slow, anoxia may result. A cesarean section is the surgical removal of the baby from the uterus.
	The use of drugs during childbirth	A wide variety of tranquilizers, sedatives, and analgesics are used to relieve the expectant mother's pain and anxiety, and oxytocin is sometimes used to speed delivery. Birthweight and social class are more powerful predictors of problems than are medications. A drug can have mixed effects and the overall amount of medication needs to be considered.
Childbirth Strategies	Standard childbirth	The expectant mother is taken to he hospital, where a doctor is responsible for the baby's delivery. The birth takes place in a delivery room, which looks like an operating room, and medication is used in the procedure. Criticisms of the standard childbirth procedure have been made.
	The Leboyer method	This was developed by French obstetrician Frederick Leboyer; the method intends to make the birth process less stressful for infants. Leboyer's method is referred to as "birth without violence."
	Prepared, or natural, childbirth	Prepared, or natural, childbirth includes being informed about what will happen during the procedure, knowing about comfort measures for childbirth, anticipating that little or no medication will be used, and if complications arise, expecting to participate in decisions made to resolve the problems. Prepared childbirth includes a number of variations. A basic philosophy of prepared childbirth is that teaching methods are designed to support parent confidence, provide the self-help tools needed for normal childbirth, and explain how the medical system functions in childbirth.
	Doula	There is increasing use of doulas, caregivers who provide continuous physical, emotional, and educational support to the mother before, during, and just after childbirth.
	Today's methods	Among the current changes in childbirth are shifts in emphases, new choices, and an understanding of obstetrical terminology. More instructors also are using an eclectic approach to childbirth, drawing information from several different methods. Most current methods are based on Dick-Read's concepts; they include a wide range of choices and comfort techniques. Parents are encouraged to select what they believe will work best for them. The current belief is that when information, support, and anxiety reduction are provided, women *know* how to give birth. The Lamaze method has become a widely used childbirth strategy; it is a prepared, or natural, method that helps the expectant mother to cope actively with pain and to avoid or reduce medication. Active breathing is central to the Lamaze method.
	Fathers and siblings	In the past several decades, fathers increasingly have participated in childbirth. Fathers-to-be are more likely to go to at least one meeting with the obstetrician or caregiver during pregnancy, attend childbirth preparation classes, learn about labor and birth, and be more involved in the care of the young infant. Husbands who are motivated to participate in childbirth have an important role at their wife's side. In some cultures the father is excluded from childbirth, as was the case in the American culture until several decades ago. If parents have a child and are expecting another, it is important for them to prepare the older child for the birth of a sibling. Sibling preparation includes providing the child with information about the pregnancy, birth, and life with a newborn that is realistic and appropriate for the child's age.

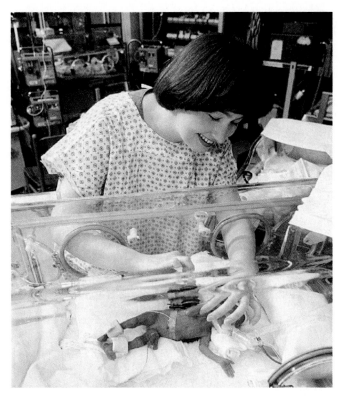

A "kilogram kid," weighing less than 2.3 pounds at birth. In the neonatal intensive care unit, banks of flashing lights, blinking numbers, and beeping alarms stand guard over kilogram kids, who are extreme preterm infants. They often lie on a water bed that gently undulates; the water bed is in an incubator that is controlled for temperature and humidity by the baby's own body. Such vital signs as brain waves, heartbeat, blood gases, and respiratory rate are constantly monitored. All of this care can be very expensive. Though the cost can usually be kept within five figures, 5 or 6 months of neonatal intensive care can result in expenses of as much as a million dollars or more.

Some infants are born very early and have a precariously low birthweight. "Kilogram kids" weigh less than 2.3 pounds (which is 1 kilogram, or 1,000 grams) and are very premature. The task of saving such a baby is not easy. At the Stanford University Medical Center in Palo Alto, California, 98 percent of the preterm babies survive; however, 32 percent of those between 750 and 1,000 grams do not, and 76 percent of those below 750 grams do not. Approximately 250,000 preterm babies are born in the United States each year, and more than 15,000 of these weigh less than 1,000 grams.

Equal opportunity for life is an American ideal that is not fulfilled at birth (Paneth, 1995). African American babies are twice as likely as White babies to be born low-birthweight, to be born preterm, or to die at birth. Seventeen percent of all births are to African American families, yet 33 percent of all low-birthweight infants and 38 percent of all very-low-birthweight infants are born to African American families.

Long-Term Outcomes for Low-Birthweight Infants

Although most low-birthweight infants are normal and healthy, as a group they have more health and developmental problems than normal-birthweight infants (Hack, Klein, & Taylor, 1995). The number and severity of these problems increase as birthweight decreases. With the improved survival rates for infants who are born very early and very small come increases in severe brain damage. Cerebral palsy and other forms of brain injury are highly correlated with brain weight—the lower the brain weight, the greater the likelihood of brain injury. Approximately 7 percent of moderately low birthweight infants (3 pounds 5 ounces to 5 pounds 8 ounces) have brain injuries. This figure increases to 20 percent for the smallest newborns (1 pound 2 ounces to 3 pounds 5 ounces). Low-birthweight infants are also more likely than normal-birthweight infants to have lung or liver diseases.

At school age, children who were born low in birthweight are more likely than their normal-birthweight counterparts to have a learning disability, attention deficit disorder, or breathing problems such as asthma (Taylor, Klein, & Hack, 1994). Children born very low in birthweight have more learning problems and lower levels of achievement in reading and math than moderately low birthweight children. These problems are reflected in much higher percentages of low-birthweight children being enrolled in special education programs. Approximately 50 percent of all low-birthweight children are enrolled in special education programs.

Not all of these adverse consequences can be attributed solely to being born low in birthweight. Some of the less severe but more common developmental and physical delays are consequences of the fact that a disproportionate number of low-birthweight children come from disadvantaged environments.

Some of the devastating effects of being born low in birthweight can be reversed (Blair & Ramey, 1996; Shiono & Behrman, 1995). Intensive enrichment programs that provide medical and educational services for both the parents and the child have been shown to improve short-term developmental outcomes for low-birthweight children. Federal laws mandate that services for school-age disabled children (which include medical, educational, psychological, occupational, and physical care) be expanded to include family-based care for infants. At present, these services are aimed at children born with severe congenital disabilities. The availability of services for moderately low birthweight children who do not have severe physical problems varies from state to state, but generally these services are not available.

Stimulation of Preterm Infants

Just three decades ago, preterm infants were perceived to be too fragile to cope well with environmental stimulation, and the recommendation was to handle such infants as little as possible. The climate of opinion changed when the adverse effects of maternal deprivation (mothers' neglect of their infants) became known and was interpreted to include a lack of stimulation. A number of research studies followed that indicated a "more is better" approach in the stimulation of preterm infants. Today, however, experts on infant development argue that preterm infant care is far too complex to be described only in terms of amount of stimulation.

Following are some conclusions about the situation of preterm infants (Lester & Tronick, 1990):

1. Preterm infants' responses to stimulation vary with their conceptual age, illness, and individual makeup. The immature brain of the preterm infant may be more vulnerable to excessive, inappropriate, or mistimed stimulation. The very immature infant should probably be protected from stimulation that could destabilize its homeostatic condition.

2. As the healthy preterm infant becomes less fragile and approaches term, the issue of what is appropriate stimulation should be considered. Infants' behavioral cues can be used to determine appropriate interventions. An infant's signs of stress or avoidance behaviors indicate that stimulation should be terminated. Positive behaviors indicate that stimulation is appropriate.

3. Intervention with the preterm infant should be organized in the form of an individualized developmental plan. This plan should be constructed as a psychosocial intervention to include the parents and other immediate family members and to acknowledge the socioeconomic, cultural, and home environmental factors that will determine the social context in which the infant will be reared. The developmental plan should also include assessing the infant's behavior, working with the parents to help them understand the infant's medical and behavioral status, and helping the parents deal with their own feelings.

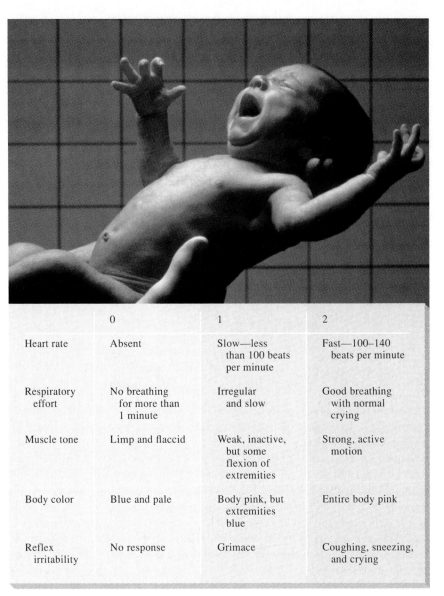

	0	1	2
Heart rate	Absent	Slow—less than 100 beats per minute	Fast—100–140 beats per minute
Respiratory effort	No breathing for more than 1 minute	Irregular and slow	Good breathing with normal crying
Muscle tone	Limp and flaccid	Weak, inactive, but some flexion of extremities	Strong, active motion
Body color	Blue and pale	Body pink, but extremities blue	Entire body pink
Reflex irritability	No response	Grimace	Coughing, sneezing, and crying

FIGURE 5.2

The Apgar Scale

MEASURES OF NEONATAL HEALTH AND RESPONSIVENESS

The **Apgar scale** *is a method widely used to assess the health of newborns at 1 and 5 minutes after birth. The Apgar scale evaluates infants' heart rate, respiratory effort, muscle tone, body color, and reflex irritability.* An obstetrician or nurse does the evaluation and gives the newborn a score, or reading, of 0, 1, or 2 on each of these five health signs (see figure 5.2). A total score of 7 to 10 indicates that the newborn's condition is good, a score of 5 indicates there may be developmental difficulties, and a score of 3 or below signals an emergency and indicates that the baby might not survive.

Whereas the Apgar scale is used immediately after birth to identify high-risk infants who need resuscitation, the **Brazelton Neonatal Behavioral Assessment Scale** *is given shortly after birth to assess the newborn's neurological development, reflexes, and reactions to people.* Twenty reflexes are assessed, along with reactions to circumstances, such as the infant's reaction to a rattle. The examiner rates the newborn, or neonate, on each of 27 categories

John W. Santrock

1. Response decrement to repeated visual stimuli
2. Response decrement to rattle
3. Response decrement to bell

4. Response decrement to pinprick
5. Orienting response to inanimate visual stimuli
6. Orienting response to inanimate auditory stimuli

7. Orienting response to inanimate visual and auditory stimuli
8. Orienting response to animate visual stimuli—examiner's face
9. Orienting response to animate auditory stimuli—examiner's voice
10. Orienting response to animate visual and auditory stimuli
11. Quality and duration of alert periods
12. General muscle tone—in resting and in response to being handled, passive, and active

13. Motor activity
14. Traction responses as the infant is pulled to sit
15. Cuddliness—responses to being cuddled by examiner

16. Defensive movements—reactions to a cloth over the infant's face
17. Consolability with intervention by examiner
18. Peak of excitement and capacity to control self
19. Rapidity of buildup to crying state
20. Irritability during examination
21. General assessment of kind and degree of activity

22. Tremulousness
23. Amount of startling
24. Lability of skin color—measuring autonomic lability

25. Lability of states during entire examination
26. Self-quieting activity—attempts to console self and control state
27. Hand-to-mouth activity

FIGURE 5.3

The 27 Categories on the Brazelton Neonatal Behavioral Assessment Scale (NBAS)

(see figure 5.3). As an indication of how detailed the ratings are, consider item 15: "cuddliness." Nine categories are involved in assessing this item, with infant behavior scored on a continuum that ranges from the infant's being very resistant to being held to the infant's being extremely cuddly and clinging. The Brazelton scale not only is used as a sensitive index of neurological competence in the week after birth, but it also is used widely as a measure in many research studies on infant development. In recent versions of scoring the Brazelton scale, Brazelton and his colleagues (Brazelton, Nugent, & Lester, 1987) categorize the 27 items into four categories—physiological, motoric, state, and interaction. They also classify the baby in global terms, such as "worrisome," "normal," or "superior," based on these categories.

A very low Brazelton score can indicate brain damage or it can reflect stress to the brain that may heal in time. However, if an infant merely seems sluggish in responding to social circumstances, parents are encouraged to give the infant attention and become more sensitive to the infant's needs. Parents are shown how the newborn can respond to people and how to stimulate such responses. Researchers have found that the social interaction skills of both high-risk infants and healthy, responsive infants can be improved through such communication with parents (Worobey & Belsky, 1982).

THE POSTPARTUM PERIOD

Many health professionals believe that the best postpartum care is family centered, using the family's resources to support an early and smooth adjustment to the newborn by all family members. What is the postpartum period? What physical changes does it involve? What emotional and psychological changes are encountered?

The Nature of the Postpartum Period

The **postpartum period** *is the period after childbirth or delivery. It is a time when the woman's body adjusts, both physically and psychologically, to the process of childbearing. It lasts for about 6 weeks or until the body has completed its adjustment and has returned to a near prepregnant state.* Some health professionals refer to the postpartum period as the "fourth trimester." While the time span of the postpartum period does not necessarily cover 3 months, the terminology of "fourth trimester" demonstrates the idea of continuity and the importance of the first several months after birth for the mother.

The postpartum period is influenced by what preceded it. During pregnancy the woman's body gradually adjusted to physical changes, but now it is forced to respond quickly. The method of delivery and circumstances surrounding the delivery affect the speed with which the woman's body readjusts during the postpartum period.

The postpartum period involves a great deal of adjustment and adaptation. The baby has to be cared for; the mother has to recover from childbirth; the mother has to learn how to take care of the baby; the mother needs to learn to feel good about herself as a mother; the father needs to learn how to take care of his recovering wife; the father needs to learn how to take care of the baby; and the father needs to learn how to feel good about himself as a father.

Physical Adjustments

The woman's body makes numerous physical adjustments in the first days and weeks after childbirth. She may have a great deal of energy or feel exhausted and let down. Most new mothers feel tired and need rest. Though these changes are normal, the fatigue can undermine the new mother's sense of well-being and confidence in her ability to cope with a new baby and a new family life.

Involution *is the process by which the uterus returns to its prepregnant size 5 or 6 weeks after birth.* Immediately following birth, the uterus weighs 2 to 3 pounds and the fundus can be felt midway between the naval and the pubic bone. By the end of 5 or 6 weeks, the uterus weighs 2 to 3½ ounces and it has returned to its prepregnancy size. Nursing the baby helps to contract the uterus at a rapid rate.

After delivery, a woman's body undergoes sudden and dramatic changes in hormone production. When the placenta is delivered, estrogen and progesterone levels drop steeply and remain low until the ovaries start producing

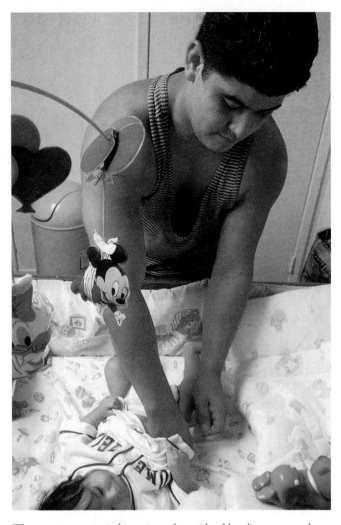

The postpartum period is a time of considerable adjustment and adaptation for both the mother and the father. Fathers can provide an important support system for mothers, especially in helping mothers care for young infants.

hormones again. The woman will probably begin menstruating again in 4 to 8 weeks if she is not breast-feeding. If she is breast-feeding, she might not menstruate for several months, though ovulation can occur during this time. The first several menstrual periods following delivery may be heavier than usual, but periods soon return to normal.

Some women and men want to resume sexual intercourse as soon as possible after the birth. Others feel constrained or afraid. A sore perineum (the area between the anus and vagina in the female), a demanding baby, lack of help, and extreme fatigue affect a woman's ability to relax and to enjoy making love. Physicians often recommend that women refrain from having sexual intercourse for approximately 6 weeks following the birth of the baby. However, it is probably safe to have sexual intercourse when the stitches heal, vaginal discharge stops, and the woman feels like it.

If the woman regularly engaged in conditioning exercises during pregnancy, exercise will help her to recover her former body contour and strength during the postpartum period. With a caregiver's approval, the woman can begin some exercises as soon as 1 hour after delivery. In addition to recommending exercise in the postpartum period for women, health professionals also increasingly recommend that women practice the relaxation techniques they used during pregnancy and childbirth. Five minutes of slow breathing on a stressful day in the postpartum period can relax and refresh the new mother as well as the new baby.

Emotional and Psychological Adjustments

Emotional fluctuations are common on the part of the mother in the postpartal period. These emotional fluctuations may be due to any of a number of factors: hormonal changes, fatigue, inexperience or lack of confidence with newborn babies, or the extensive time and demands involved in caring for a newborn. For some women, the emotional fluctuations decrease within several weeks after the delivery and are a minor aspect of their motherhood. For others, they are more long-lasting and may produce feelings of anxiety, depression, and difficulty in coping with stress. Mothers who have such feelings, even when they are getting adequate rest, may benefit from professional help in dealing with their problems. Following are some of the signs that may indicate a need for professional counseling about postpartum adaptation:

- Excessive worrying
- Depression
- Extreme changes in appetite
- Crying spells
- Inability to sleep

Another adjustment for the mother and for the father is the time and thought that go into being a competent parent of a young infant. It is important for both the mother and the father to become aware of the young infant's developmental needs—physical, psychological, and emotional. Both the mother and the father need to develop a comfortable relationship with the young infant.

A special interest in the parent-infant relationship is **bonding,** *the occurrence of close contact, especially physical, between parents and newborn in the period shortly after birth.* Some physicians believe that this period shortly after birth is critical in development; during this time, the parents and child need to form an important emotional attachment that provides a foundation for optimal development in years to come. Special interest in bonding came about when some pediatricians argued that the circumstances surrounding delivery often separate mothers and their infants, preventing or making difficult the development of a bond. The pediatricians further argued that giving the mother drugs to make her delivery less painful may contribute to the lack of bonding. The drugs may make the mother drowsy, thus interfering with her ability to respond to and stimulate the newborn. Advocates of bonding also

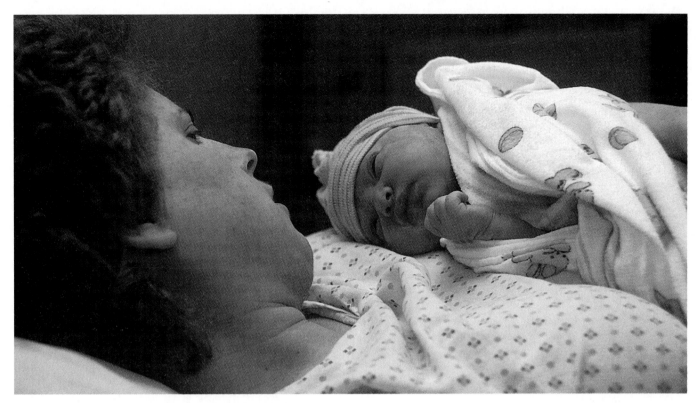

A mother bonds with her infant moments after the baby is born. How critical is bonding for the development of social competence later in childhood?

assert that preterm infants are isolated from their mothers to an even greater degree than full-term infants, thereby increasing their difficulty in bonding.

Is there evidence that such close contact between mothers and newborns is absolutely critical for optimal development later in life? Although some research supports the bonding hypothesis (Klaus & Kennell, 1976), a body of research challenges the significance of the first few days of life as a critical period (Bakeman & Brown, 1980; Rode & others, 1981). Indeed, the extreme form of the bonding hypothesis—that the newborn must have close contact with the mother in the first few days of life to develop optimally—simply is not true.

Nonetheless, the weakness of the maternal-infant bonding research should not be used as an excuse to keep motivated mothers from interacting with their infants in the postpartum period, because such contact brings pleasure to many mothers. In some mother-infant pairs—including preterm infants, adolescent mothers, or mothers from disadvantaged circumstances—the practice of bonding may set in motion a climate for improved interaction after the mother and infant leave the hospital.

The new baby also changes a mother's and father's relationship with each other. Among the questions that have to be dealt with are these: How will we share the housework and baby care? How can we find enough time for each other when the baby takes up so much of our time? How can we arrange to get out of the house so we can enjoy some of the things we did before the baby came? At some point, new parents have to figure out which of their commitments are the most important, and which have to get less time, or be dropped. Support from relatives, friends, and babysitters can help new parents find time to renew some of these activities they enjoyed earlier.

A special concern of many new mothers is whether they should stay home with the baby or go back to work. Some mothers want to return to work as soon as possible after the infant is born, others want to stay home with the infant for several months, then return to work, others want to stay home for a year before they return to work, and yet others, of course, did not work outside the home prior to the baby's arrival and do not plan to do so in the future.

Many women, because of a variety of pressures—societal, career, financial—do not have the option of staying at home after their babies are born (Eisenberg, Murkoff, & Hathaway, 1989). However, for women who have to make the choice, the process of decision making is often difficult and agonizing.

At this point we have discussed a number of ideas about preterm infants and age-weight considerations, measures of neonatal health and responsiveness, and the postpartum period. A summary of these ideas is presented in concept table 5.2.

Preterm Infants and Age-Weight Considerations, Measures of Neonatal Health and Responsiveness, and the Postpartum Period

Concept	Processes/Related Ideas	Characteristics/Description
Preterm Infants and Age-Weight Considerations	Types	Preterm infants are those born after an abnormally short time period in the womb. Infants who are born after a regular gestation period of 38 to 42 weeks but who weigh less than 5½ pounds are called low-birthweight infants.
	Long-term outcomes for low-birthweight infants	Although most low-birthweight infants are normal and healthy, as a group they have more health and developmental problems than normal-birthweight infants. The number and severity of the problems increase as birthweight decreases.
	Stimulation	Preterm infant care is much too complex to be described only in terms of amount of stimulation. Preterm infants' responses vary according to their conceptual age, illness, and individual makeup. Infant behavioral cues can be used to indicate the appropriate stimulation. Intervention should be organized in the form of an individualized developmental plan.
Measures of Neonatal Health and Responsiveness	Types	For many years the Apgar scale has been used to assess the newborn's health. A more recently developed test—the Brazelton Neonatal Behavioral Assessment Scale—is used for long-term neurological assessment. It assesses not only the newborn's neurological integrity but also social responsiveness.
The Postpartum Period	Its nature	The postpartum period is the period after childbirth or delivery. It is a time when the woman's body adjusts, both physically and psychologically, to the process of childbearing. It lasts for about 6 weeks or until the body has completed its adjustment.
	Physical adjustments	These include fatigue, involution (the process by which the uterus returns to its prepregnant size 5 or 6 weeks after birth), hormone changes that include a dramatic drop in estrogen and progesterone, consideration of when to resume sexual intercourse, and participation in exercises to recover former body contour and strength.
	Emotional and psychological adjustments	Emotional fluctuations on the part of the mother are common in the postpartum period. They may be due to hormonal changes, fatigue, inexperience or lack of confidence with newborn babies, or the extensive time and other demands involved in caring for a newborn. For some, the emotional fluctuations are minimal and disappear in several weeks; for others, they are more long-lasting. Another adjustment for both the mother and the father is the time and thought that go into being a competent parent of a young infant. A special interest in parent-infant relationships is bonding, which has not been found to be critical in the development of a competent infant or child, but which may stimulate positive interaction between some mother-infant pairs. The new baby also changes the mother's and father's relationship with each other. A special concern of many new mothers is whether they should go back to work, or whether they should stay home with the infant.

The event of giving birth is a tremendous and unforgettable experience. Childbirth, with its personal drama and significance for the survival of the family, is an event that every society views as something special.

We began this chapter by describing Teresa Block's pregnancy and her son Robert, then turned to a discussion of stages of birth, delivery complications, and the use of drugs during childbirth. Our coverage of childbirth strategies focused on standard childbirth, the Leboyer method, prepared or natural childbirth, what is new for the nineties, and today's methods, including the popular Lamaze method as well as the roles of the father and siblings in childbirth. We explored the nature of preterm infants and age-weight considerations and also examined measures of neonatal health and responsiveness. Our description of the postpartum period included information about physical adjustments, as well as psychological and emotional adjustments.

Don't forget that you can obtain an overall summary of the chapter by again reading the two concept tables on pages 144 and 150. This concludes our discussion in Section Two, "Beginnings." In Section Three we will turn our attention to the nature of infant development, beginning with chapter 6, "Physical Development in Infancy."

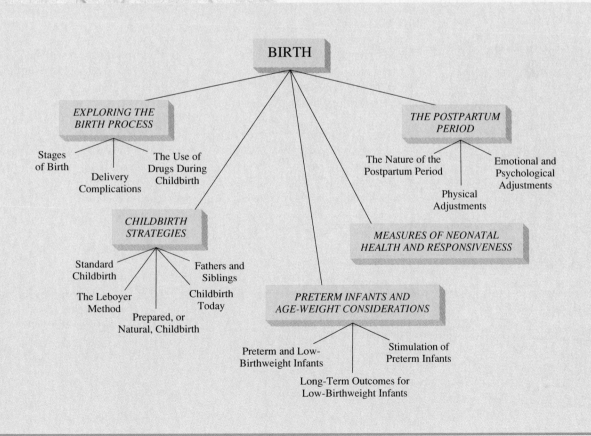

BIRTH

EXPLORING THE BIRTH PROCESS
- Stages of Birth
- Delivery Complications
- The Use of Drugs During Childbirth

CHILDBIRTH STRATEGIES
- Standard Childbirth
- The Leboyer Method
- Prepared, or Natural, Childbirth
- Fathers and Siblings
- Childbirth Today

PRETERM INFANTS AND AGE-WEIGHT CONSIDERATIONS
- Preterm and Low-Birthweight Infants
- Long-Term Outcomes for Low-Birthweight Infants
- Stimulation of Preterm Infants

MEASURES OF NEONATAL HEALTH AND RESPONSIVENESS

THE POSTPARTUM PERIOD
- The Nature of the Postpartum Period
- Physical Adjustments
- Emotional and Psychological Adjustments

afterbirth The third stage of birth, when the placenta, umbilical cord, and other membranes are detached and expelled. 137

precipitate delivery A delivery that takes place too quickly; the baby squeezes through the birth canal in less than 10 minutes. 137

anoxia The insufficient availability of oxygen to the infant. 137

breech position The baby's position in the uterus that causes the buttocks to be the first part to emerge from the vagina. 137

cesarean section The surgical removal of the baby from the uterus. 137

oxytocin A hormone that stimulates and regulates the rhythmicity of uterine contractions. It has been widely used as a drug to speed delivery. 138

Leboyer method A birth process, developed by French obstetrician Frederick Leboyer, that intends to make birth less stressful for infants. The procedure is referred to as "birth without violence." 139

prepared, or natural, childbirth Being informed about what will happen during the procedure, knowing about comfort measures for childbirth, anticipating that little or no medication will be used, and, if complications arise, expecting to participate in decisions made to resolve the problem. 139

Lamaze method A form of prepared childbirth developed by Fernand Lamaze, a pioneering French obstetrician; it involves helping pregnant women cope actively with the pain of childbirth to avoid or reduce medication. 140

doula A caregiver who provides continuous physical, emotional, and educational support to the mother before, during, and just after childbirth. 141

preterm infant An infant born prior to 38 weeks after conception. 143

low-birthweight infant An infant born after a regular period of gestation (the length of time between conception and birth) of 38 to 42 weeks but who weigh less than 5½ pounds. 143

Apgar scale A widely used method to assess the health of newborns at 1 and 5 minutes after birth. The Apgar scale evaluates infants' heart rate, respiratory effort, muscle tone, body color, and reflex irritability. 146

Brazelton Neonatal Behavioral Assessment Scale A test given several days after birth to assess newborns' neurological development, reflexes, and reactions to people. 146

postpartum period The period after childbirth when the mother adjusts, both physically and psychologically, to the process of childbirth. This period lasts for about 6 weeks, or until her body has completed its adjustment and returned to a near prepregnant state. 147

involution The process by which the uterus returns to its prepregnant size. 147

bonding Close contact, especially physical, between parents and their newborn in the period shortly after birth. 148

PRACTICAL KNOWLEDGE ABOUT CHILDREN

Methods of Childbirth
(rev. ed.) (1990)
by Constance Bean.
New York: William Morrow.

Methods of Childbirth is a comprehensive guide to prepared childbirth, including discussion of the Lamaze, Bradley, Dick-Read, Kitzinger, and other methods. Also covered are topics such as conditioning exercises; the pros and cons of medication; fitness;

how to reduce the chance of having a cesarean section; working and breast-feeding; home birth, alternative birth centers, and midwives; and how to have a meaningful dialogue with a doctor and hospital staff.

This is a good resource for learning about a wide variety of childbirth methods and for information about how to make a baby's birth as safe and worry-free as possible.

IMPROVING THE LIVES OF CHILDREN

Improving the lives of children involves consideration of the power of touch and massage in development, the mother's decision to work or not to work after her baby's birth, teaching and taking childbirth classes, care for low-birthweight infants and prenatal care around the world, and moving beyond the "mommy track."

HEALTH AND WELL-BEING

The Power of Touch and Massage in Development

There has been a recent surge of interest in the roles of touch and massage in improving the growth, health, and well-being of infants and children. The interest has especially been stimulated by a number of research investigations by Tiffany Field (1995), director of the Touch Research Institute at the University of Miami School of Medicine. In one study, forty preterm infants who had just been released from an intensive care unit and placed in a transitional nursery were studied (Field, Scafidi, & Schanberg, 1987). Twenty of the preterm babies were given special stimulation with massage and exercise for three 15-minute periods at the beginning of three consecutive hours every morning for 10 weekdays. For example, each infant was placed on its stomach and gently stroked. The massage began with the head and neck and moved downward to the feet. It also moved from the shoulders down to the hands. The infant was then rolled over. Each arm and leg was flexed and extended; then both legs were flexed and extended. Next, the massage was repeated.

The massaged and exercised preterm babies gained 47 percent more weight than their preterm counterparts who were not massaged and exercised, even though both groups had the same

Shown here is Dr. Tiffany Field massaging a newborn infant. Dr. Field's research has clearly demonstrated the power of massage in improving the developmental outcome of at-risk infants. Under her direction, the Touch Research Institute in Miami, Florida, was recently developed to investigate the role of touch in a number of domains of health and well-being.

number of feedings per day and averaged the same intake of formula. The increased activity of the massaged, exercised infants would seem to work against weight gain. However, similar findings have been discovered with animals. The increased activity may increase gastrointestinal and metabolic efficiency. The massaged infants were more active and alert, and they performed better on developmental tests. Also, their hospital stay was about 6 days shorter than that of the nonmassaged, nonexercised group, which saved about $3,000 per preterm infant. Field has recently replicated these findings with preterm infants in another study.

In a more recent study, Field (1992) gave the same kind of massage (firm stroking with the palms of the hands) to preterm infants who were exposed to cocaine in utero. The infants also showed significant weight gain and improved scores on developmental tests. Currently, Field is using massage therapy with HIV-exposed preterm infants with the hope that their immune system functioning will be improved. Others she has targeted include infants of depressed mothers, infants with colic, infants and children with sleep problems, as well as children who have diabetes, asthma, and juvenile arthritis.

In another recent study, Field and her colleagues (in press) investigated 1- to 3-month-old infants born to depressed adolescent mothers. The infants were given 15 minutes of either massage or rocking for 2 days per week for a 6 week period. The infants who received massage therapy had lower stress, as well as improved emotionality, sociability, and soothability, when compared with the rocked infants.

Field (1995) also reports that touch has been helpful with children and adolescents who have touch aversions, such as children who have been sexually abused, autistic children, and adolescents with eating disorders. Field also is studying the amount of touch a child normally receives during school activities. She hopes that positive forms of touch will return to school systems where touching has been outlawed because of potential sex abuse lawsuits.

FAMILIES AND PARENTING
To Work or Not to Work

If a mother of a newborn is pondering the question of whether to work or not to work, asking herself the following questions may help her sort out which choice to make (Eisenberg, Murkoff, & Hathaway, 1989):

What are my priorities? The new mother can carefully consider what is most important in her life and rank order these on paper. Priorities might include her baby, her family, her career, financial security, and luxuries of life (such as vacations and entertainment). Her list may be different from that of a woman next door or a woman at the next desk. After charting her priorities, she can consider whether returning to employment or staying at home will best meet the most important of them.

Which full-time role suits my personality best? The woman might ask herself whether she is at her best at home with the baby or whether staying at home would make her feel impatient and tense. Will she be able to leave worries about her baby at home when she goes to her work? Will she worry about not being employed when she stays home with the baby? Or will an inability to compartmentalize her life keep her from doing her best at either job?

Would I feel comfortable having someone else take care of my baby? Does she feel no one else can do the job of caring for the baby as well as she can herself? Or does she feel secure that she can find (or has found) a person (or small-group situation) that can substitute well for her during the hours she is away from home?

How much energy do I have? Considerable physical and emotional stamina are needed to rise with a baby, get ready for work, put in a full day on the job, then return to the demands of the baby, home, and husband. What often suffers most when energy is lacking in the two-paycheck family with infants is the husband-wife relationship.

How do I feel about missing my baby's milestones? Will the mother mind hearing about some of the baby's milestones secondhand—the first time the baby laughs, sits alone, crawls, or walks? Will the mother feel hurt if the baby runs to the sitter instead of her when the baby is frightened or hurt? Does the mother feel that she can be synchronized with the baby's needs by just spending evenings and weekends together?

How stressful is the combination of my employment and the baby? If the mother's employment involves little stress and her baby is an easy baby to care for, then the employment may not present much of a problem. But if the mother's job is very stressful and her baby is difficult to care for (has physical problems, cries a lot, and so on), then she may have difficulty coping with both the job and the baby.

If I return to work, will I get adequate support from my husband or from some other source? Even superwomen can't, and should not be expected to, do everything alone. Will her husband be willing to do his share of babysitting, shopping, cooking, cleaning, and laundry? Is the couple able to afford outside help?

What is our financial situation? If she decides not to work, will it threaten the family's economic survival or just mean cutting down on some extras the couple has been enjoying? Are there ways of cutting back so that the mother's lack of income won't hurt so much? If the mother does go back to work, how much of a dent in her income will job-related costs such as clothes, travel, and child care make?

How flexible is my job? Will the mother be able to take time off if her baby or her sitter becomes sick? Will she be able to come in late or leave early if there is an emergency at home? Does her job require long hours, weekends, or travel? Is the mother willing to spend extended time away from the baby?

If I don't return to my job, how will it influence my career? Putting a career on hold can sometimes set the woman back when she eventually does return to employment. If the mother suspects this may happen, is she willing to make this sacrifice? Are there ways to keep in touch professionally during her at-home months (or years) without making a full-time commitment?

Whatever choice the woman makes, it is likely to require some sacrifices and misgivings. Such sacrifices and misgivings are normal; since we do not live in a perfect world, we have to learn to live and cope with some of them. However, if they begin to multiply and the mother finds her dissatisfaction outweighing her satisfaction, she may want to reassess the choice she made. A choice that seemed right in theory may not work out in practice.

John W. Santrock

Teaching and Taking Childbirth Classes

Who teaches childbirth classes? It is often assumed that a qualified childbirth instructor is a nurse, but this is only a requirement of the American Society for Psychoprophylaxis in Obstetrics (Lamaze classes). Because childbirth classes involve no medical treatment, skills other than nursing are important and may include knowledge about physical therapy, psychology, biology, health education, and other areas. Except in rare instances, being a parent is perceived to be essential for

being a childbirth instructor. A childbirth instructor needs to have a thorough understanding of birth and the techniques used in childbirth. Also necessary are educational and discussion skills that improve parent self-confidence. A warm, personal approach helps to counteract some of the inevitable depersonalization of medical care.

What happens in childbirth classes? The format is often a six-part, 2-hour session with 1 hour of discussion

and 1 hour of practicing techniques and exercises. Instructors, working with each couple in turn, teach fathers or other partners (often called coaches) how to assist the woman in labor. One or more couples from previous classes may return for a visit, with their babies, to describe their childbirth experiences. This provides a valuable and interesting opportunity for expectant parents. Birth slides and films help make childbirth more real and less frightening. *The Birth Atlas*, a series of detailed, life-sized photographs of pregnancy, labor, and delivery from the Maternity Center in New York City, is another educational tool widely used in childbirth classes throughout the United States. The purpose of the Birth Atlas is to show in precise detail how birth takes place and to help demystify birth.

The International Childbirth Education Association guide for childbirth educators endorses the concept of a health care *circle* rather than a health care *team*. The key person in the center of the health care circle is the person seeking care, in this case the expectant mother. She selects the people around her for advice, information, care, and support. The circle may include family, friends, other expectant couples, obstetrician, midwife, nurse, or others. Communication, shared decision making, and her right to make informed choices are central to effective childbirth education.

At the Maternity Center in New York City, The Birth Atlas *is being used in a childbirth class. The purpose of* The Birth Atlas *is to show in precise detail how birth takes place and to help demystify birth.*

Low-Birthweight Infants and Prenatal Care Around the World

As advanced as the United States has become economically and technologically, it still has more low-birthweight infants than many other countries (Grant, 1996). As indicated in table 5.1, only 4 percent of the infants born in Sweden, Finland, the Netherlands, and Norway are low-birthweight, and only 5 percent of those born in New Zealand, Australia, France, and Japan are low-birthweight. In the United States, 7 percent of all infants are low-birthweight. However, as also indicated in table 5.1, in some developing countries, such as Bangladesh, where poverty is rampant and the health and nutrition of mothers are poor, as many as 50 percent of all infants are low-birthweight.

In many of the countries with a lower percentage of low-birthweight infants than the United States, either free or very low-cost prenatal and postnatal care is available to mothers. This care includes paid maternity leave from work that ranges from 9 to 40 weeks. In Norway and the Netherlands, prenatal care is coordinated with a general practitioner, an obstetrician, and a midwife.

Pregnant women in the United States do not receive the uniform prenatal care that women in many Scandinavian and Western European countries receive. The United States does not have a national policy of health care that assures high-quality assistance for pregnant women. The cost of giving birth is approximately $4,000 in the United States (more than $5,000 for a cesarean birth), and more than 25 percent of all American women of prime childbearing age do not have insurance that will pay for hospital costs. More than one-fifth of all White mothers and one-third of all African American mothers do not receive prenatal care in the first trimester of their pregnancy. Five percent of White mothers and 10 percent of African American mothers receive no prenatal care at all. Many infant-development researchers believe that the United States needs more comprehensive medical and educational services to improve the quality of prenatal care and reduce the percentage of low-birthweight infants.

TABLE 5.1

Percentage of Low-Birthweight Infants

Country	Low-Birthweight Infants (Percentage)
Bangladesh	50
India	30
Guatemala	18
Iran	14
Mexico	12
USSR	9
United States, Great Britain, Israel, Egypt	7
Canada, China	6
New Zealand, Australia, France, Japan	5
Sweden, Finland, the Netherlands, Norway	4

Source: Data from J. Grant, *State of the World's Children*, 1986.

Beyond the Mommy Track

One proposed work schedule that appeared in the news a few years ago was the "mommy track," which was designed as a solution for the problem of combining careers and families (Tavris, 1992). The "mommy track" concept permits career women to choose one of two paths: a "mommy track" in which work is done at a slower pace in exchange for having more time at home with a baby and a "fast track" in which women devote their energy exclusively to a career. Many career women objected to the "mommy track" concept because of its potentially unequal outcomes: Women who choose to have families, unlike men who choose to have families, would eventually pay the price in career achievement and income.

Some gender experts believe that mothers are not taken seriously in the way the current work/career system is set up. Therefore, they argue, any proposal that sets them apart is likely to be detrimental to them. What needs to be accomplished is to begin thinking about how to reshape work, including the work mothers do, so that it won't be a burden on women to have families. What might the changes look like? They might include increased benefits and security for part-time workers; an arrangement of work for reduced income now, in exchange for the possibility of expanded opportunities and more income later; and permanent part-time arrangements with health and other benefits. In careers that are incompatible with daily child care, because they require traveling, long hours, or inconsistent schedules, individuals can press for the right to reenter the occupation.

All of these solutions and many others can be generated if we rethink our priorities, say some gender authorities. And once they are rethought, men as well as women are likely to take advantage of them.

Infancy

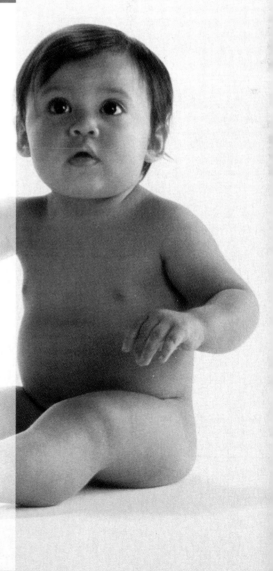

Babies are such a nice
way to start people.

—Don Herold

As newborns, we were not empty-
headed organisms. We had some
basic reflexes, among them crying,
kicking, and coughing. We slept a
lot and occasionally we smiled,
although the meaning of our first
smiles was not entirely clear. We
ate and we grew. We crawled and
then we walked, a journey of a
thousand miles beginning with a
single step. Sometimes we
conformed, sometimes others
conformed to us. Our development
was a continuous creation of more
complex forms. Our helpless kind
demanded the meeting eyes of love.
We juggled the necessity of curbing
our will with becoming what we
could will freely. Section Three
includes three chapters: "Physical
Development in Infancy" (chapter
6), "Cognitive Development in
Infancy" (chapter 7), and
"Socioemotional Development in
Infancy" (chapter 8).

DIEGO RIVERA
Mother and Child, detail

Physical Development
in Infancy

Growth is the only evidence of life.

—John Henry,
Cardinal Newman

IMAGES OF CHILDREN

Studying Newborns

The creature has poor motor coordination and can move itself only with great difficulty. Its general behavior appears to be disorganized, and although it cries when uncomfortable, it uses few other vocalizations. In fact, it sleeps most of the time, about 16 to 17 hours a day. You are curious about this creature and want to know more about what it can do. You think to yourself, "I wonder if it can see. How could I find out?"

You obviously have a communication problem with the creature. You must devise a way that will allow the creature to "tell" you that it can see. While examining the creature one day, you make an interesting discovery. When you move a large object toward it, it moves its head backward, as if to avoid a collision with the object. The creature's head movement suggests that it has at least some vision.

In case you haven't already guessed, the creature you have been reading about is the human infant, and the role you played is that of a developmentalist interested in devising techniques to learn about the infant's visual perception. After years of work, scientists have developed research tools and methods sophisticated enough to examine the subtle abilities of infants and to interpret their complex actions. Videotape equipment allows researchers to investigate elusive behaviors, and high-speed computers make it possible to perform complex data analysis in minutes instead of months and years. Other sophisticated equipment is used to closely monitor respiration, heart rate, body movement, visual fixation, and sucking behavior, which provide clues to what is going on inside the infant.

PREVIEW

Among the first things developmentalists were able to demonstrate was that infants have highly developed perceptual motor systems. Until recently, even some nurses in maternity hospitals believed that newborns are blind at birth, and they told this to mothers. Most parents were also told that their newborns could not taste, smell, or feel pain. As you will discover later in this chapter, we now know that newborns can see (albeit fuzzily), taste, smell, and feel pain. Before we turn to the fascinating world of the infant's perception, we will discuss a number of ideas about infants' and toddlers' physical development.

PHYSICAL GROWTH AND DEVELOPMENT IN INFANCY

Infants' physical development in the first 2 years of life is extensive. At birth, neonates have a gigantic head (relative to the rest of the body) that flops around in an uncontrollable fashion; they also possess reflexes that are dominated by evolutionary movements. In the span of 12 months, infants become capable of sitting anywhere, standing, stooping, climbing, and usually walking. During the second year, growth decelerates, but rapid increases in such activities as running and climbing take place. Let's now examine in greater detail the sequence of physical development in infancy by studying the infant's reflexes.

Reflexes

What is the nature of the infant's reflexes? The newborn is not an empty-headed organism. Among other things, it has some basic reflexes that are genetically carried survival mechanisms. For example, the newborn has no fear of

John W. Santrock

water; when placed underwater, it will naturally hold its breath and contract its throat to keep water out.

Reflexes govern the newborn's movements, which are automatic and beyond the newborn's control. They are built-in reactions to certain stimuli and provide young infants with adaptive responses to their environment before they have had the opportunity to learn. The **sucking reflex** *occurs when newborns automatically suck an object placed in their mouth. The sucking reflex enables newborns to get nourishment before they have associated a nipple with food.* The sucking reflex is an example of a reflex that is present at birth but later disappears. The **rooting reflex** *occurs when the infant's cheek is stroked or the side of the mouth is touched. In response, the infant turns its head toward the side that was touched, in an apparent effort to find something to suck.* The sucking and rooting reflexes disappear when the infant is about 3 to 4 months old. They are replaced by the infant's voluntary eating. The sucking and rooting reflexes have survival value for newborn mammals, who must find the mother's breast to obtain nourishment.

The **Moro reflex** *is a neonatal startle response that occurs in response to a sudden, intense noise or movement. When startled, the newborn arches its back, throws its head back, and flings out its arms and legs. Then the newborn rapidly closes its arms and legs to the center of its body.* The Moro reflex is a vestige from our primate ancestry and it too has survival value. This reflex, which is normal in all newborns, also tends to disappear at 3 to 4 months of age. Steady pressure on any part of the infant's body calms the infant after it has been startled. Holding the infant's arm flexed at the shoulder will quiet the infant.

The experiences of the first three years of life are almost entirely lost to us, and when we attempt to enter into a small child's world, we come as foreigners who have forgotten the landscape and no longer speak the native tongue.

—Selma Fraiberg

Some reflexes present in the newborn—coughing, blinking, and yawning, for example—persist throughout life. They are as important for the adult as they are for the infant. Other reflexes, though, disappear several months following birth as the infant's brain functions mature and voluntary control over many behaviors develops. The movements of some reflexes eventually become incorporated into more complex, voluntary actions. One important example is the **grasping reflex**, *which occurs when something touches the infant's palms. The infant responds by grasping tightly.* By the end of the third month, the grasping reflex diminishes and the infant shows a more voluntary grasp, which is often produced by visual stimuli. For example, when an infant sees a mobile whirling above its crib, it may reach out and try to grasp it. As its motor development becomes smoother, the infant will grasp objects, carefully manipulate them, and explore their qualities.

An overview of the main reflexes we have discussed, along with others, is provided in figure 6.1.

Sucking is an especially important reflex: It is the infant's route to nourishment. The sucking capabilities of newborns vary considerably. Some newborns are efficient at forceful sucking and obtaining milk, others are not so adept and get tired before they are full. Most newborns take several weeks to establish a sucking style that is coordinated with the way the mother is holding the infant, the way milk is coming out of the bottle or breast, and the infant's sucking speed and temperament.

One study by pediatrician T. Berry Brazelton (1956) involved observations of infants for more than a year to determine the incidence of their sucking when they were nursing and how their sucking changed as they grew older. More than 85 percent of the infants engaged in considerable sucking behavior unrelated to feeding. They sucked their fingers, their fists, and pacifiers. By the age of 1 year, most had stopped the sucking behavior.

Parents should not worry when infants suck their thumbs, fist, or even a pacifier. Many parents, though, do begin to worry when thumb sucking persists into the preschool and elementary school years. As many as 40 percent of children continue to suck their thumbs after they have started school (Kessen, Haith, & Salapatek, 1970). Most developmentalists do not attach a great deal of significance to this behavior and are not aware of parenting strategies that might contribute to it. Individual differences in children's biological makeup may be involved to some degree in the continuation of sucking behavior.

Nonnutritive sucking, *sucking behavior unrelated to the infant's feeding,* is used as a measure in a large number of research studies with young infants because young infants quit sucking when they attend to something, such as a picture or a vocalization. Nonnutritive sucking, then, is one of the ingenious ways developmentalists study the young infant's attention and learning.

Growth Patterns

Among the prominent growth patterns in infancy are those involving cephalocaudal and proximodistal sequences, height and weight, the brain, and gross and fine motor skills.

Cephalocaudal and Proximodistal Sequences

The **cephalocaudal pattern** *is the sequence in which the greatest growth always occurs at the top—the head—with physical growth in size, weight, and feature differentiation gradually working its way down from top to bottom (to neck, shoulders, middle trunk, and so on).* This same pattern occurs in the head area; the top parts of the head (the eyes and brain) grow faster than the lower parts (such as the jaw). An extraordinary proportion of the total body is occupied by the head during prenatal development and early infancy.

The **proximodistal pattern** *is the sequence in which growth starts at the center of the body and moves toward the*

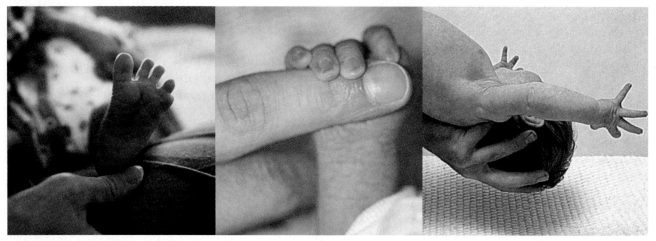

| Babinski reflex | Grasping reflex | Moro reflex |

Reflex	Stimulation	Infant's Response	Developmental Pattern
Blinking	Flash of light, puff of air	Closes both eyes	Permanent
Babinski	Sole of foot stroked	Fans out toes, twists foot in	Disappears after 9 months to 1 year
Grasping	Palms touched	Grasps tightly	Weakens after 3 months, disappears after 1 year
Moro (startle)	Sudden stimulation, such as hearing loud noise or being dropped	Startles, arches back, throws head back, flings out arms and legs and then rapidly closes them to center of body	Disappears after 3 to 4 months
Rooting	Cheek stroked or side of mouth touched	Turns head, opens mouth, begins sucking	Disappears after 3 to 4 months
Stepping	Infant held above surface and feet lowered to touch surface	Moves feet as if to walk	Disappears after 3 to 4 months
Sucking	Object touching mouth	Sucks automatically	Disappears after 3 to 4 months
Swimming	Infant put face down in water	Makes coordinated swimming movements	Disappears after 6 to 7 months
Tonic neck	Infant placed on back	Forms fists with both hands and usually turns head to the right (sometimes called the "fencer's pose" because the infant looks like it is assuming a fencer's position)	Disappears after 2 months

FIGURE 6.1

Infant Reflexes

extremities. An example of this is the early maturation of muscular control of the trunk and arms compared to that of the hands and fingers.

Height and Weight

The average North American newborn is 20 inches long and weighs 7½ pounds. Ninety-five percent of full-term newborns are 18 to 22 inches long and weigh between 5½ and 10 pounds. In the first several days of life, most newborns lose 5 to 7 percent of their body weight before they learn to adjust to neonatal feeding. Once infants adjust to sucking, swallowing, and digesting, they grow rapidly, gaining an average of 5 to 6 ounces per week during the first month. By 4 months, they have doubled their birthweight, and they have nearly tripled it by their first birthday. Infants grow about 1 inch per month during the first year, reaching approximately 1½ times their birth length by their first birthday.

Infant's rate of growth is considerably slower in the second year of life. By 2 years of age, infants weigh approximately 26 to 32 pounds, having gained a quarter to half a pound per month during the second year; now they have reached about one-fifth of their adult weight. At 2 years of age, the average infant is 32 to 35 inches in height, which is nearly one-half of their adult height. A summary of changes in height and weight during the first 18 months of life is shown in figure 6.2.

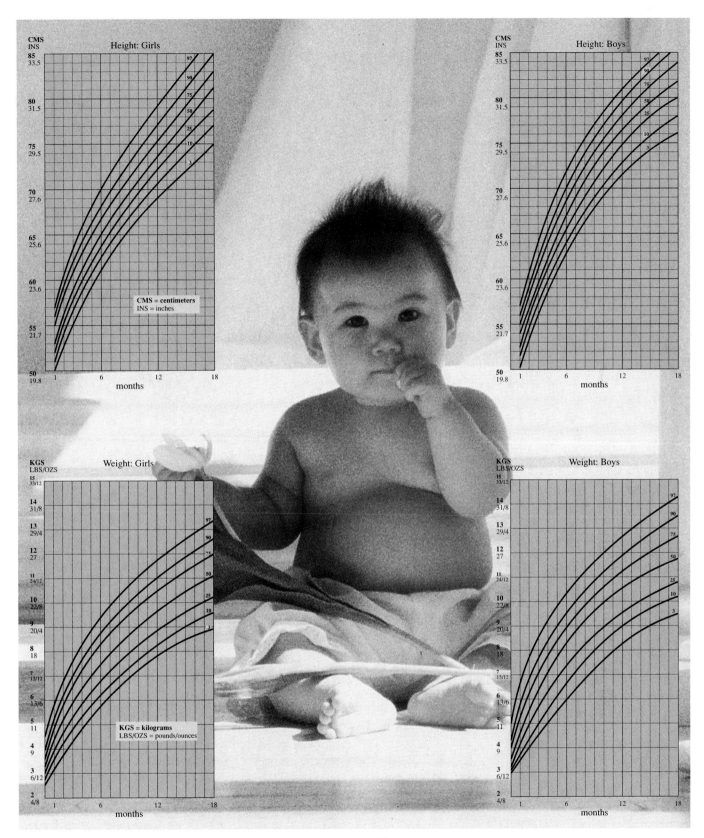

FIGURE 6.2

Developmental Changes in Height and Weight from Birth to 18 Months
The numbers on the curved lines in the charts refer to the percentiles for infants' height and weight at different months of age compared with other infants of the same age. The 50th percentile indicates that half of the infants of a particular age are taller and half are shorter. The 10th percentile tells us that 10 percent of the infants of that age are shorter and 90 percent are taller.

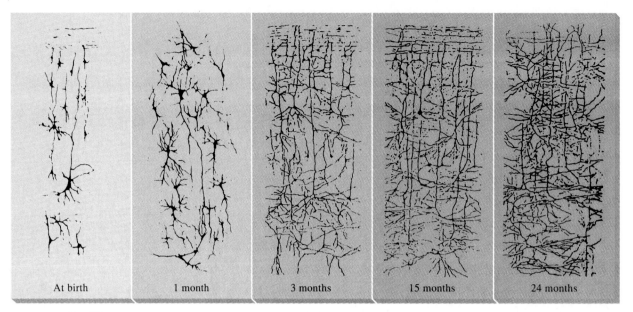

Figure 6.3

The Development of Dendritic Spreading
Note the increase in connectedness between neurons over the course of the first 2 years of life.

| At birth | 1 month | 3 months | 15 months | 24 months |

The Brain

As an infant walks, talks, runs, shakes a rattle, smiles, and frowns, changes in its brain are occurring. Consider that the infant began life as a single cell and 9 months later was born with a brain and nervous system that contained approximately 100 billion nerve cells. Indeed, at birth the infant probably has all of the nerve cells (neurons) it is going to have in its entire life. However, at birth and in early infancy, these neurons are poorly interconnected. As the infant ages from birth to 2 years, the interconnection of neurons increases dramatically as the dendrites (the receiving parts) of the neurons branch out (see figure 6.3).

At birth, the newborn's brain is about 25 percent of its adult weight, and by the second birthday it is about 75 percent of its adult weight.

Gross and Fine Motor Skills

Gross motor skills *involve large muscle activities such as moving one's arms and walking.* **Fine motor skills** *involve more finely tuned movements, such as finger dexterity.* Let's examine the changes in gross and fine motor skills in the first 2 years of life.

Gross Motor Skills At birth, the infant has no appreciable coordination of the chest or arms, but in the first month the infant can lift its head from a prone position. At about 3 months, the infant can hold its chest up and use its arms for support after being in a prone position. At 3 to 4 months, infants can roll over, and at 4 to 5 months they can support some weight with their legs. At about 6 months, infants can sit without support, and by 7 to 8 months they can crawl and stand without support.

At approximately 8 months, infants can pull themselves up to a standing position, at 10 to 11 months they can walk using furniture for support (this is called "cruising"), and at 12 to 13 months the average infant can walk without assistance. A summary of the developmental accomplishments in gross motor skills during the first year is shown in figure 6.4. The actual month at which the milestones occur varies by as much as 2 to 4 months, especially among older infants. What remains fairly uniform, however, is the sequence of accomplishments. An important implication of these infant motor accomplishments is the increasing degree of independence they bring. Older infants can explore their environment more extensively and initiate social interaction with caregivers and peers more readily than when they were younger.

> *A baby is an angel whose wings decrease as his legs increase.*
> —**French Proverb**

In the second year of life, toddlers become more motorically skilled and mobile. They are no longer content with being in a playpen and want to move all over the place. Child development experts believe that motor activity during the second year is vital to the child's competent development and that few restrictions, except for safety purposes, should be placed on their motoric adventures (Fraiberg, 1959).

By 13 to 18 months, toddlers can pull a toy attached to a string, use their hands and legs to climb up a number of steps, and ride four-wheel wagons. By 18 to 24 months, toddlers can walk fast or run stiffly for a short

John W. Santrock

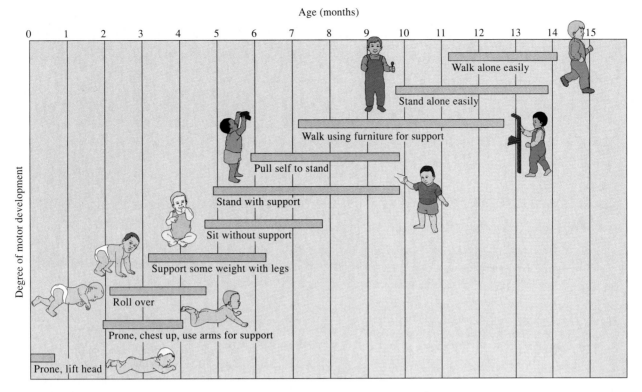

Age (months)

Walk alone easily

Stand alone easily

Walk using furniture for support

Pull self to stand

Stand with support

Sit without support

Support some weight with legs

Roll over

Prone, chest up, use arms for support

Prone, lift head

Degree of motor development

FIGURE 6.4

Developmental Milestones in Gross Motor Development

distance, balance on their feet in a squat position while playing with objects on the floor, walk backward without losing their balance, stand and kick a ball without falling, stand and throw a ball, and jump in place.

Fine Motor Skills   Infants have hardly any control over fine motor skills at birth, although they have many components of what later become finely coordinated arm, hand, and finger movements. The onset of reaching and grasping marks a significant achievement in infants' functional interactions with their surroundings. For many years it was believed that reaching for an object is visually guided—that is, that the infant has to continuously have sight of the hand and the target (White, Castle, & Held, 1964). However, in a recent study Rachel Clifton and her colleagues (1993) demonstrated that infants do not have to see their own hands when reaching for an object. They concluded that because infants could not see their hand or arm in the dark in the experiment, proprioceptive (muscle, tendon, joint sense) cues, not sight of limb, guided the early reaching of the 4-month-old infants. The development of reaching and grasping becomes more refined during the first 2 years of life. Initially, infants show only crude shoulder and elbow movements, but later show wrist movements, hand rotation, and coordination of the thumb and forefinger. The maturation of hand-eye coordination

over the first 2 years of life is reflected in the improvement of fine motor skills. Figure 6.5 provides an overview of the development of fine motor skills in the first 2 years of life.

Developmental Biodynamics

Traditional views of motor development have chronicled the stagelike changes in posture and movement that characterize the first several years of life (Gesell, 1928; Shirley, 1933). In the last decade, advances in a number of domains have led to a new perspective on the infant's motor development (Thelan, 1995). Rather than just describing the ages at which various motor achievements are reached and explaining them as a result of brain and nervous-system maturation, the new perspective—**developmental biodynamics**—*seeks to explain how motor behaviors are assembled for perceiving and acting. This new perspective is an outgrowth of developments in the neurosciences, biomechanics, and behavioral sciences.* The research of Rachel Clifton and her colleagues (1993) that was described earlier illustrates the new developmental biodynamics perspective. Recall that they found that proprioceptive cues play an important role in guiding early reaching. Their research shows *how* perception and action are linked in early manual skill development. Other researchers also are finding that perception depends more on action than once was believed (Bushnell & Boudreau, 1993).

Birth to 6 months

2 mo.	Holds rattle briefly
2 1/2 mo.	Glances from one object to another
3–4 mo.	Plays in simple way with rattle; inspects fingers; reaches for dangling ring; visually follows ball across table
4 mo.	Carries object to mouth
4–5 mo.	Recovers rattle from chest; holds two objects
5 mo.	Transfers object from hand to hand
5–6 mo.	Bangs in play; looks for object while sitting

6–12 months

6 mo.	Secures cube on sight; follows adult's movements across room; immediately fixates on small objects and stretches out to grasp them; retains rattle
6 1/2 mo.	Manipulates and examines an object; reaches for, grabs, and retains rattle
7 mo.	Pulls string to obtain an object
7 1/2–8 1/2 mo.	Grasps with thumb and finger
8–9 mo.	Persists in reaching for toy out of reach on table; shows hand preference, bangs spoon; searches in correct place for toys dropped within reach of hands; may find toy hidden under cup
10 mo.	Hits cup with spoon; crude release of object
10 1/2–11 mo.	Picks up raisin with thumb and forefinger; pincer grasp; pushes car along
11–12 mo.	Puts three or more objects in a container

12–18 months

	Places one 2-inch block on top of another 2-inch block (in imitation)
	Scribbles with a large crayon on large piece of paper
	Turns 2-3 pages in a large book with cardboard pages while sitting in an adult's lap
	Places three 1-inch cube blocks in a 6-inch diameter cup (in imitation)
	Holds a pencil and makes a mark on a sheet of paper
	Builds a 4-block tower with 2-inch cube blocks (in imitation)

18–24 months

	Draws an arc on piece of unlined paper with a pencil after being shown how
	Turns a doorknob that is within reach using both hands
	Unscrews a lid put loosely on a small jar after being shown how
	Places large pegs in a pegboard
	Connects and takes apart a pop bead string of five beads
	Zips and unzips a large-sized zipper after being shown how

FIGURE 6.5

The Development of Fine Motor Skills in Infancy

In another study from this new perspective, crawlers' and walkers' perception of the locomotor affordances (the fit between physical properties of actor and environment that is required to perform a given action) of sloping walkways was investigated (Adolph, Eppler, & Gibson, 1993). Infants learned the affordances of ascending and descending slopes through exploratory activity. The detected affordances varied depending on whether the infant was crawling or walking. This study illustrates the inseparability of perception and action in motor development and highlights the importance of exploratory activity in the development of skills.

Infant States

To chart and understand the infant's development, developmentalists have constructed classifications of infants'

John W. Santrock

states. *States* is a term for states of consciousness, or an individual's level of awareness. The following is one classification scheme, describing seven infant states (Brown, 1964):

1. *Deep sleep.* The infant lies motionless with eyes closed, has regular breathing, makes no vocalization, and does not respond to outside stimulation.
2. *Regular sleep.* The infant moves very little, breathing might be raspy or involve wheezing, and respirations may be normal or move from normal to irregular.
3. *Disturbed sleep.* There is a variable amount of movement, the infant's eyelids are closed but might flutter, breathing is irregular, and there may be some squawks, sobs, and sighs.
4. *Drowsy.* The infant's eyes are open or partly open and appear glassy, there is little movement (although startles and free movement may occur), vocalizations are more regular than in disturbed sleep, and some transitional sounds may be made.
5. *Alert activity.* This is the state most often viewed by parents as one of being awake. The infant's eyes are open and bright. The infant makes a variety of free movements, it may fret, and its skin may redden. There may be irregular breathing when the infant feels tension.
6. *Alert and focused.* This kind of attention is often seen in older children but is unusual in the neonate. The child's eyes are open and bright. Some motor activity may occur, but it is integrated around a specific activity. This state may occur when focusing on a sound or visual stimulus.
7. *Inflexibly focused.* In this state, the infant is awake but does not react to external stimuli; two examples are sucking and wild crying. During wild crying, the infant may thrash about, but the eyes are closed as screams pour out.

Using classification schemes such as the one just described, researchers have identified many different aspects of infant development. One such aspect is the sleeping-waking cycle. When we were infants, sleep consumed more of our time than it does now. Newborns sleep for 16 to 17 hours a day, although some sleep more, and others less. The range is from a low of about 10 hours to a high of about 21 hours. The longest period of sleep is not always between 11 P.M. and 7 A.M. Although total sleep remains somewhat consistent for young infants, their sleep during the day does not always follow a rhythmic pattern. An infant might change from sleeping several long bouts of 7 or 8 hours to sleeping three or four shorter sessions only several hours in duration. By about 1 month of age, most infants have begun to sleep longer at night, and by about 4 months of age they usually have moved closer to adultlike sleep patterns, spending their longest span of sleep at night and their longest span of waking during the day.

> *Sleep that knits up the ravelled sleave of care . . . Balm of hurt minds, nature's second course. Chief nourisher in life's feast.*
>
> —**William Shakespeare**

A special concern about infant sleep is **sudden infant death syndrome (SIDS),** *a condition that occurs when an infant stops breathing, usually during the night, and suddenly dies without apparent cause.* Approximately 13 percent of infant deaths are due to SIDS; for infants between 10 days after birth and 1 year of age, SIDS results in more deaths than any other factor. While we do not know exactly what causes SIDS, as a group, infants who die from the condition have biological vulnerabilities early in their development, including a greater incidence of prematurity, low birthweight, low Apgar scores, and respiratory problems (Woolsey, 1992). In one recent study, the greater the total number of cigarettes the infant was passively exposed to after birth, the higher was the infant's risk of SIDS (Klonoff-Cohen & others, 1995).

Health

The important dimensions of health in infancy include nutrition, immunization, and accident prevention.

Nutrition

Four-month-old Robert lives in Bloomington, Indiana, with his middle-class parents. He is well nourished and healthy. By contrast, 4-month-old Nikita and his parents live in Ethiopia in impoverished conditions. Nikita is so poorly nourished that he has become emaciated and lies near death. The lives of Robert and Nikita reveal the vast diversity in nutritional status among today's children. Our coverage of infant nutrition begins with information about nutritional needs and eating behavior, then turns to the issue of breast- versus bottle-feeding, and concludes with an overview of malnutrition.

Nutritional Needs and Eating Behavior The importance of adequate energy and nutrient intake consumed in a loving and supportive environment during the infant years cannot be overstated (Grantham & McGregor, 1995; Yip, 1995). From birth to 1 year of age, human infants triple their weight and increase their length by 50 percent. Individual differences of infants in nutrient reserves, body composition, growth rates, and activity patterns make defining actual nutrient needs difficult. However, because parents need guidelines, nutritionists recommend that infants consume approximately 50 calories per day for each pound they weigh—more than twice an adult's requirement per pound.

Breast- Versus Bottle-Feeding Human milk, or an alternative formula, is the baby's source of nutrients and energy for the first 4 to 6 months. For years, developmentalists

Human milk, or an alternative formula, is a baby's source of nutrients for the first 4 to 6 months. The growing consensus is that breast-feeding is better for the baby's health, although controversy still swirls about the issue of breast- versus bottle-feeding.

and nutritionists have debated whether breast-feeding an infant has substantial benefits over bottle-feeding. The growing consensus is that breast-feeding is better for the baby's health (Eiger, 1992). Breast-feeding provides milk that is clean and digestible and helps immunize the newborn from disease. Breast-fed babies gain weight more rapidly than do bottle-fed babies. However, only about one-half of mothers nurse newborns, and even fewer continue to nurse their infants after several months. Most mothers who work outside the home find it impossible to breast-feed their young infants for many months. Even though breast-feeding provides more ideal nutrition, some researchers argue that there is no long-term evidence of physiological or psychological harm to American infants when they are bottle-fed (Ferguson, Harwood, & Shannon, 1987). Despite these researchers' claims that no long-term negative consequences of bottle-feeding have been documented in American children, the American Academy of Pediatrics, the majority of physicians and nurses, and two leading publications for parents—the *Infant Care Manual* and *Parents* magazine—endorse breast-feeding as having physiological and psychological benefits (Young, 1990).

There is a consensus among experts that breast-feeding is the preferred practice, especially in developing countries where inadequate nutrition and poverty are common. In 1991, the Institute of Medicine, part of the National Academy of Sciences, issued a report that women should be encouraged to breast-feed their infants exclusively for the first 4 to 6 months of life. According to the report, the benefits of breast-feeding are protection against some gastrointestinal infections and food allergies for infants, and possible reduction of osteoporosis and breast cancer for mothers. Nonetheless, while the majority of experts recommend breast-feeding, the issue of breast- versus bottle-feeding continues to be hotly debated. Many parents, especially working mothers, are now following a sequence of breast-feeding in the first several months and bottle-feeding thereafter. This strategy allows the mother's natural milk to provide nutritional benefits to the infant early in development and permits mothers to return to work after several months. Working mothers are also increasingly using "pumping," in which they use a pump to extract breast milk that can be stored for later feeding of the infant when the mother is not present.

Malnutrition in Infancy *Marasmus is a wasting away of body tissues in the infant's first year, caused by severe deficiency of protein and calories.* The infant becomes grossly underweight, and its muscles atrophy. The main cause of marasmus is early weaning from breast milk to inadequate nutrients such as unsuitable and unsanitary cow's milk formula. Something that looks like milk, but is not (usually a form of tapioca or rice) also might be used. In many of the world's developing countries, mothers used to breast-feed their infants for at least 2 years. To become more modern, they stopped breast-feeding much earlier and replaced it with bottle-feeding. Comparisons of breast-fed and bottle-fed infants in such countries as Afghanistan, Haiti, Ghana, and Chile document that the rate of infant death is much greater among bottle-fed than among breast-fed infants, with bottle-fed infants sometimes dying at a five times higher rate than breast-fed infants (Grant, 1996). So far our discussion of malnutrition has focused on developing countries, but hunger is also a problem in some areas of the United States.

Immunization

One of the most dramatic advances in infant health has been the decline of infectious diseases over the last four decades because of the widespread immunization for preventable diseases. Though many presently available immunizations can be given to individuals of any age, the recommended schedule is to begin in infancy. The recommended age for various immunizations is shown in table 6.1.

Accident Prevention

Accidents are a major cause of death in infancy, especially in the age range of 6 to 12 months. Infants need to be closely monitored as the infant gains increased locomotor

TABLE 6.1

Recommended Immunization Schedule of Normal Infants and Children

Age	Immunization
2 months	Diphtheria Polio Influenza
4 months	Diphtheria Polio Influenza
6 months	Diphtheria Influenza
1 year	TB test
15 months	Measles Mumps Rubella Influenza
18 months	Diphtheria Polio
4–6 years	Diphtheria Polio
11–12 years	Measles Mumps Rubella
14–16 years	Tetanus-Diphtheria

Falls are most common after 4 months of age when the infant has learned to roll over, although they can occur at any age. The best advice is to never leave an infant unattended on a raised surface that has no guardrails. Changing tables, infant seats, high chairs, walkers, and swings are other locations of accidental falls.

Accidental poisoning is one of the main causes of death in children under the age of 5. The highest incidence occurs in the 2-year-old age group, with the second highest incidence in the 1-year-old group. Once locomotion begins, danger from poisoning is present almost everywhere in the infant's environment. There are more than 500 toxic substances in the average home. About one-third of all infant poisonings occur in the kitchen.

Burns are often not perceived to be a particular danger to infants, but several hazards exist such as scalding from water that is too hot, excessive sunburn, and burns from electrical wires, sockets, and floor furnaces. One of the best burn safety measures is a smoke detector; parents are advised to have one in their homes.

Automobile accidents are the leading cause of accidental deaths in children over 1 year of age. The major danger for the infant is improper restraint within the motor vehicle. All infants, newborns included, should be secured in special car restraints rather than being held or placed on the car seat.

Accidents can also cause bodily damage to infants in other ways. For example, sharp, jagged objects can cause skin wounds and long, pointed objects can be poked in the eye. Thus, a fork should not be given for self-feeding until the child has mastered the spoon, which usually happens by 18 months of age. Another often unrecognized danger to infants is attacks by young siblings and pets, especially dogs and cats.

Toilet Training

Being toilet trained is a physical and motor skill that is expected to be attained in the North American culture by 3 years of age. By the age of 3, 84 percent of children are dry throughout the day and 66 percent are dry throughout the night. The ability to control elimination depends both on muscular maturation and on motivation. Children must be able to control their muscles to eliminate at the appropriate time, and they must also want to eliminate in the toilet or potty rather than in their pants.

There are no data on the optimal time of toilet training. Developmentalists argue that, whenever it is initiated, it should be accomplished in a warm, relaxed, supportive manner. Many of today's parents begin toilet training of their infants at about 20 months to 2 years of age.

One argument being made today against late toilet training is that it is best to accomplish it before onset of the "terrible twos". The 2-year-old's strong push for autonomy can lead to confrontations for parents trying to toilet train the 2-year-old. Late toilet training can become such a battleground that it can extend to 4 or 5 years of age.

and manipulative skills combined with a strong curiosity to explore the environment. Among the most common accidents in infancy are aspiration of foreign objects, suffocation, falls, poisoning, burns, motor vehicle accidents, and bodily damage. Asphyxiation by foreign material in the respiratory tract is the leading cause of fatal injury in infants under 1 year of age. Toys need to be carefully inspected for potential danger. An active infant can grab a low-hanging mobile and rapidly chew off a piece. Balloons, whether partially inflated, uninflated, or popped, cause more deaths in infants than any other kind of small object and should be kept away from infants and young children.

Suffocation can cause infant deaths; infants get caught under sheets or blankets, caregivers roll over and smother the infant when they sleep together, large plastic bags become wrapped around the infant's head, strings on toys become wrapped around the infant's neck, the infant strangles if its head gets caught between the crib slats and mattress or object close to the crib, and the infant drowns when left unsupervised in a bathtub or near a source of water, such as a swimming pool, toilet, or bucket.

Another argument against late toilet training is that many toddlers go to day care and a child in diapers or training pants can be stigmatized by peers.

At this point we have discussed a number of ideas about physical growth and development in infancy. A summary of those ideas is presented in concept table 6.1.

SENSORY AND PERCEPTUAL DEVELOPMENT

At the beginning of this chapter, you read about how newborns come into the world equipped with sensory capacities. What are sensation and perception? Can a newborn see, and, if so, what can it perceive? What about the other senses—hearing, smell, taste, touch, and pain? What are they like in the newborn, and how do they develop in infancy? What kind of visual, auditory, and tactile stimulation is appropriate for infants? These are among the intriguing questions we will now explore.

What Are Sensation and Perception?

How does a newborn know that her mother's skin is soft rather than rough? How does a 5-year-old know what color his hair is? How does an 8-year-old know that summer is warmer than winter? How does a 10-year-old know that a firecracker is louder than a cat's meow? Infants and children "know" these things because of their senses. All information comes to the infant through the senses. Without vision, hearing, touch, taste, smell, and other senses, the infant's brain would be isolated from the world; the infant would live in dark silence, a tasteless, colorless, feelingless void.

Sensation *occurs when information contacts sensory receptors—the eyes, ears, tongue, nostrils, and skin.* The sensation of hearing occurs when waves of pulsating air are collected by the outer ear and transmitted through the bones of the inner ear to the auditory nerve. The sensation of vision occurs as rays of light contact the two eyes and become focused on the retina. **Perception** *is the interpretation of what is sensed.* The information about physical events that contacts the ears may be interpreted as musical sounds, for example. The physical energy transmitted to the retina may be interpreted as a particular color, pattern, or shape.

Visual Perception

How do we see? Anyone who has ever taken pictures while on vacation appreciates the miracle of perception. The camera is no match for it. Consider a favorite scenic spot that you visited and photographed sometime in the past. Compare your memory of this spot to your snapshot. Although your memory may be faulty, there is little doubt that the richness of your perceptual experience is not captured in the picture. The sense of depth that you felt at this spot probably is not conveyed by the snapshot. Neither is the subtlety of the colors you perceived nor the intricacies of textures and shapes. Human vision is complex, and its development is complex too.

The Newborn's Vision

Psychologist William James (1890/1950) called the newborn's perceptual world a "blooming, buzzing confusion." Was James right? A century later we can safely say that he was wrong. Infants' perception of visual information is *much* more advanced than previously thought (Bahrick, 1992; Bower, 1996).

Our tour of visual perception begins with the pioneering work of Robert Fantz (1963). Fantz placed infants in a "looking chamber" that had two visual displays on the ceiling above the infant's head. An experimenter viewed the infant's eyes by looking through a peephole. If the infant was fixating on one of the displays, the experimenter could see the display's reflection in the infant's eyes. This allowed the experimenter to determine how long the infant looked at each display. In figure 6.6, you can see Fantz's looking chamber and the results of his experiment. The infants preferred to look at patterns rather than at color or brightness. For example, they preferred to look at a face, a piece of printed matter, or a bull's-eye longer than at red, yellow, or white discs. In another experiment, Fantz found that younger infants—only 2 days old—looked longer at patterned stimuli, such as faces and concentric circles, than at red, white or yellow discs. Based on these results, pattern perception likely has an innate basis, or at least is acquired after only minimal environmental experience. The newborn's visual world is not the blooming, buzzing confusion William James imagined.

Just how well can infants see? The newborn's vision is estimated to be 20/200 to 20/600 on the well-known Snellen chart that you are tested with when you have your eyes examined. This is about 10 to 30 times lower than normal adult vision (20/20). By 6 months of age, however, vision is 20/100 or better.

Infants' Perception of Faces

The human face is perhaps the most important visual pattern for the newborn to perceive. The infant masters a sequence of steps in progressing toward full perceptual appreciation of the face (Gibson, 1969). At about 3½ weeks, the infant is fascinated with the eyes, perhaps because the infant notices simple perceptual features such as dots, angles, and circles. At 1 to 2 months of age, the infant notices and perceives contour. At 2 months and older, the infant begins to differentiate facial features; the eyes are distinguished from other parts of the face, the mouth is noticed, and movements of the mouth draw attention to it. By 5 months of age, the infant has detected other features of the face—its plasticity, its solid, three-dimensional surface, the oval shape of the head, and the orientation of the eyes and the mouth. Beyond 6 months of age, the infant distinguishes familiar faces from unfamiliar faces—mother from stranger, masks from real faces, and so on.

John W. Santrock

CONCEPT TABLE 6.1

Physical Growth and Development in Infancy

Concept	Processes/Related Ideas	Characterististics/Description
Reflexes	Their nature	We no longer view the newborn as a passive, empty-headed organism. Reflexes (automatic movements) govern the newborn's behavior. For infants, sucking is an important means of obtaining nutrition. Nonnutritive sucking is of interest to researchers, especially to assess attention.
Growth Patterns	Cephalocaudal and proximodistal patterns	The cephalocaudal pattern is growth from the top down; the proximodistal pattern is growth from the center out.
	Height and weight	The average North American newborn is 20 inches long and weighs 7½ pounds. Infants grow about 1 inch per month during the first year and nearly triple their weight by their first birthday. Infants' rate of growth is slower in the second year.
	The brain	Considerable brain development occurs during the first 2 years of life. Dendritic spreading increases dramatically in this time frame. At birth the newborn's brain is about 25 percent of its adult weight, and by the second birthday it is about 75 percent of its adult weight.
	Gross and fine motor skills	Gross motor skills involve large muscle activities such as moving one's arms and walking. A number of gross motor milestones occur in infancy. Fine motor skills involve more finely tuned movements than gross motor skills, and include such skills as finger dexterity. A number of fine motor milestones occur in infancy.
	Developmental biodynamics	This new perspective on infant motor development seeks to explain how motor behaviors are assembled for perceiving and acting.
Infant States	Their nature	Researchers have put together different classification systems; one involves seven infant state categories, including deep sleep, drowsy, alert and focused, and inflexibly focused. Newborns usually sleep 16 to 17 hours a day. By 4 months, they approach adultlike sleeping patterns. Sudden infant death syndrome (SIDS) is a condition that occurs when an infant stops breathing and suddenly dies without apparent cause.
Health	Nutrition	Infants need to consume approximately 50 calories per day for each pound they weigh. The growing consensus is that breast-feeding is superior to bottle-feeding, but the increase in working mothers has meant fewer breast-fed babies. Severe infant malnutrition is still prevalent in many parts of the world. Severe protein-calorie deficiency can cause marasmus, a wasting away of body tissues. It is mainly caused by early weaning from breast milk.
	Immunization	One of the most dramatic advances in infant health has been the decline of infectious diseases over the last four decades because of widespread immunization.
	Accident prevention	Accidents are a major cause of death in infancy, especially in the 6- to 12-month age period. Among the most common accidents in infancy are aspiration of foreign objects, suffocation, falls, poisoning, burns, motor vehicle accidents, and bodily damage.
Toilet Training	Its nature	In North America, being toilet trained is expected to be attained by about 3 years of age. There are no data on the optimal time for toilet training, but when initiated it should be done in a relaxed, supportive manner. Late toilet training can lead to confrontations with the autonomy-seeking toddler.

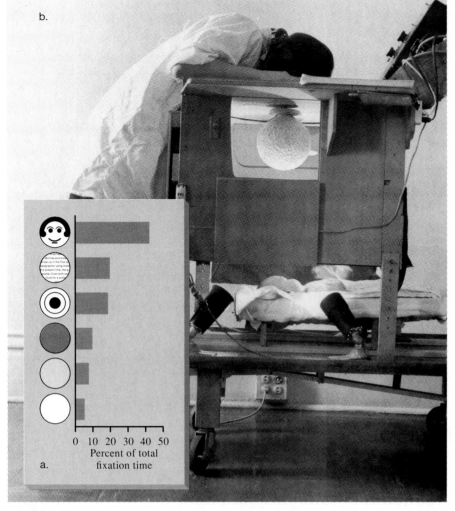

a.

0 10 20 30 40 50
Percent of total
fixation time

FIGURE 6.6

Fantz's Experiment on Infants' Visual Perception
(*a*) Infants 2 to 3 months old preferred to look at some stimuli more than others. In Fantz's experiment, infants preferred to look at patterns rather than at color or brightness. For example, they looked longer at a face, a piece of printed matter, or a bull's eye than at red, yellow, or white discs. (*b*) Fantz used a "looking chamber" to study infants' perception of stimuli.

Depth Perception

How early can infants perceive depth? To investigate this question, infant perception researchers Eleanor Gibson and Richard Walk (1960) conducted a classic experiment. They constructed a miniature cliff with a drop-off covered by glass. The motivation for this experiment arose when Gibson was eating a picnic lunch on the edge of the Grand Canyon. She wondered whether an infant looking over the canyon's rim would perceive the dangerous dropoff and back up. In their laboratory, Gibson and Walk placed infants on the edge of a visual cliff and had their mothers coax them to crawl onto the glass (see figure 6.7). Most infants would not crawl out on the glass, choosing instead to remain on the shallow side, indicating that they could perceive depth. However,

because the 6- to 14-month-old infants had extensive visual experience, this research did not answer the question of whether depth perception is innate.

Exactly how early in life does depth perception develop? Since younger infants do not crawl, this question is difficult to answer. Research with 2- to 4-month-old infants shows differences in heart rate when these infants are placed directly on the deep side of the visual cliff instead of on the shallow side (Campos, Langer, & Krowitz, 1970). However, an alternative interpretation is that young infants respond to differences in some visual characteristics of the deep and shallow cliffs, with no actual knowledge of depth.

The Young Infant's Built-In Knowledge of How the Perceptual World Works

Infant perception researcher Elizabeth Spelke (1991) has revealed that babies as young as 4 months of age have a rudimentary knowledge of the way the perceptual world works, or should work (see figure 6.8). She places babies before a puppet stage, where she shows them a series of unexpected actions—for example, a ball seems to roll through a solid barrier, another seems to leap between two platforms, and a third appears to hang in midair. Spelke measures the babies' looking time and records longer intervals for unexpected than expected actions. She concludes that babies must have some basic knowledge about the way physical objects work in the perceptual world. Spelke says that at such young ages, when infants can't yet talk about objects, move around objects, manipulate objects, or even see objects with high resolution, they seem to be able to recognize where a moving object is when it has left their visual field and make inferences about where it should be when it comes into their sight again.

Spelke and an increasing number of other infant perception researchers believe that young infants have a biologically programmed core knowledge about the way the perceptual world works.

Other Senses

Considerable development also occurs in other infant sensory systems. We will explore development in hearing, touch and pain, smell, and taste.

FIGURE 6.7

Examining Infants' Depth Perception on the Visual Cliff
Eleanor Gibson and Richard Walk (1960) found that most infants would not crawl out on the glass, which indicated that they had depth perception.

Hearing

What is the nature of hearing in newborns? Can the fetus hear? What types of auditory stimulation should be used with infants at different points in the first year? We will examine each of these questions.

Immediately after birth, infants can hear, although their sensory thresholds are somewhat higher than those of adults (Werner & Marean, 1996). That is, a stimulus must be louder to be heard by a newborn than it must be to be heard by an adult. Also, in one study, as infants aged from 8 to 28 weeks, they became more proficient at localizing sounds (Morrongiello, Fenwick, & Chance, 1990). Not only can newborns hear, but the possibility has been raised that the fetus can hear as it nestles within its mother's womb. Let's examine this possibility further.

The fetus can hear sounds in the last few months of pregnancy: the mother's voice, music, and so on (Kisilevsky, 1995; LeCanuet, Granier-Deferre, & Busnel, 1995). Given that the fetus can hear sounds, two psychologists wanted to find out if listening to Dr. Seuss' classic story *The Cat in the Hat* while still in the mother's womb would produce a preference for hearing the story after birth (DeCasper & Spence, 1986). Sixteen pregnant women read *The Cat in the Hat* to their fetuses twice a day over the last 6 weeks of their pregnancies. When the babies were born, they were given a choice of listening to either *The Cat in the Hat* or a story with a different rhyme and pace, *The King, the Mice, and the Cheese*. They made their choices by varying their sucking rate. Sucking at

FIGURE 6.8

The Young Infant's Knowledge of the Perceptual World
Above, a four-month-old in Elizabeth Spelke's infant perception laboratory is tested to determine if it knows that an object in motion will not stop in midair. Spelke believes the young infant's knowledge about how the perceptual world works is innate.

one rate (slowly, for example) resulted in their hearing a recording of one of the stories, and sucking at another rate resulted in hearing a recording of the other story. The newborns preferred listening to *The Cat in the Hat*, which they had heard frequently as a fetus (see figure 6.9).

Two important conclusions can be drawn from this investigation. First, it reveals how ingenious scientists have become at assessing the development not only of infants but of fetuses as well, in this case discovering a way to "interview" newborn babies who cannot yet talk. Second, it reveals the remarkable ability of an infant's brain to learn even before birth.

Touch and Pain

Do newborns respond to touch? What activities can adults engage in that involve tactile (touch) stimulation at various points in the infant's development? Can newborns feel pain?

Touch in the Newborn   Newborns do respond to touch. A touch to the cheek produces a turning of the head, whereas a touch to the lips produces sucking movements. An important ability that develops in infancy is to connect information about vision with information about touch. One-year-olds clearly can do this, and it appears that 6-month-olds can too (Acredolo & Hake, 1982). Whether still-younger infants can coordinate vision and

CRITICAL THINKING
ABOUT CHILDREN'S
DEVELOPMENT

*Devising Age-Appropriate
Activities to Stimulate
Infants' Different
Sensory Modalities*

Devise a list of age-appropriate activities for the two sensory modalities we have just discussed—hearing and touch. For each modality, think about stimulation in the first 6 months and from 6 months to 1 year. Hints: Think about auditory activities like listening to music boxes, musical mobiles, musical animals and dolls, and records, as well as about tactile activities like touching stuffed animals and books with textures.

By developing lists of age-appropriate activities to stimulate infants' different sensory modalities, you are learning to think critically by *creating arguments based on developmental concepts.*

FIGURE 6.9

Hearing in the Womb

(*a*) Pregnant mothers read *The Cat in the Hat* to their fetuses during the last few months of pregnancy. (*b*) When they were born, the babies preferred listening to a recording of their mothers reading *The Cat in the Hat*, as evidenced by their sucking on a nipple that produced this recording.

touch is yet to be determined. To further evaluate touch and hearing, refer to Critical Thinking About Children's Development.

Pain   If and when you have a son and need to consider whether he should be circumcised, the issue of an infant's pain perception probably will become important to you.

Circumcision is usually performed on young boys about the third day after birth. Will your young son experience pain if he is circumcised when he is 3 days old? Increased crying and fussing occur during the circumcision procedure, suggesting that 3-day-old infants experience pain (Gunnar, Malone, & Fisch, 1987).

In the study by Megan Gunnar and her colleagues (1987), the healthy newborn's ability to cope with stress was evaluated. The newborn infant males cried intensely during the circumcision, indicating that it was stressful. The researchers pointed out that it is rather remarkable that the newborn infant does not suffer serious consequences from the surgery. Rather, the circumcised infant displays amazing resiliency and ability to cope. Within several minutes after the surgery, the infant can nurse and interact in a normal manner with his mother. And, if allowed to, the newly circumcised newborn drifts into a deep sleep that seems to serve as a coping mechanism. In this experiment, the time spent in deep sleep was greater in the 60 to 240 minutes after the circumcision than before it.

For many years, doctors have performed operations on newborns without anesthesia. This accepted medical practice was followed because of the dangers of anesthesia and the supposition that newborns do not feel pain. Recently, as researchers have convincingly demonstrated that newborns can feel pain, the long-standing practice of operating on newborns without anesthesia is being challenged.

CRITICAL THINKING ABOUT CHILDREN'S DEVELOPMENT

Evaluating Gender Differences and Similarities in Infant Perceptual Development

Gender comparisons in infancy are especially important because they help to clarify whether gender differences can be traced to biological explanations (nature) or environmental explanations (nurture) (Matlin, 1993). Suppose that, in 1-day-old infants, females respond more to human faces than males do. Is this difference likely a biological one or an environmental one? Explain your answer.

What kind of gender differences in perception do you think might exist in infancy? It turns out that girls and boys have quite similar perceptual development. There is an activity level difference (boys are more active than girls). However, the gender differences that do exist are not very large, and many investigators report gender similarities.

By evaluating gender differences and similarities in infant development, you are learning to think critically by *applying a developmental framework to understand behavior.*

Smell

Newborn infants can differentiate odors. For example, by the expressions on their faces, they seem to indicate that they like the way vanilla and strawberry smell but do not like the way rotten eggs and fish smell. In one study, young infants who were breast-fed showed a clear preference for smelling their mother's breast pad when they were 6 days old (MacFarlane, 1975). However, when they were 2 days old, they did not show this preference (compared to a clean breast pad), indicating that they require several days of experience to recognize this odor (see figure 6.10).

Taste

Sensitivity to taste may be present before birth. When saccharin was added to the amniotic fluid of a near-term fetus, increased swallowing was observed (Windle, 1940). Sensitivity to sweetness is clearly present in the newborn. When sucks on a nipple are rewarded with a sweetened solution, the amount of sucking increases (Lipsitt & others, 1976). In another study, newborns showed a smilelike expression after being given a sweetened solution but pursed their lips after being given a sour solution (Steiner, 1979). And in one study, 1-to 3-day-old infants cried much less when they were given sucrose through a pacifier (Smith, Fillion, & Blass, 1990). To further evaluate infant perception, see Critical Thinking About Children's Development.

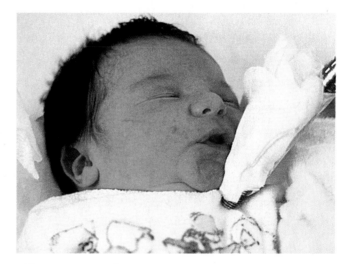

FIGURE 6.10

Newborns' Preference for the Smell of Their Mother's Breast Pad
In the experiment by MacFarlane (1975), 6-day-old infants preferred to smell their mother's breast pad over a clean one that had never been used, but 2-day-old infants did not show this preference, indicating that this odor preference requires several days of experience to develop.

Intermodal Perception

Are young infants so competent that they can relate and integrate information through several senses? **Intermodal perception** *is the ability to relate and integrate information about two or more sensory modalities, such as vision and hearing.* An increasing number of developmentalists believe

CONCEPT TABLE 6.2

Sensory and Perceptual Development in Infancy

Concept	Processes/Related Ideas	Characteristics/Description
What Are Sensation and Perception?	Sensation	When information contacts sensory receptors—eyes, ears, tongue, nostrils, and skin—sensation occurs.
	Perception	Perception is the interpretation of what is sensed.
Visual Perception	The newborn's visual world	William James said it is a blooming, buzzing confusion; he was wrong. The newborn's perception is more advanced than we previously thought.
	Visual preferences	Fantz's research—showing that infants prefer striped to solid patches—demonstrated that newborns can see.
	Quality of vision	The newborn's vision is about 20/600 on the Snellen chart; by 6 months, vision has improved to at least 20/100.
	The human face	The face is an important visual pattern for the newborn. The infant gradually masters a sequence of steps in perceiving the human face.
	Depth perception	A classic study by Gibson and Walk (1960) demonstrated, through the use of a visual cliff, that 6-month-old infants can perceive depth.
	Built-in perceptual knowledge	An increasing number of researchers, such as Spelke, believe the young infant has a built-in knowledge about how the perceptual world works.
Other Senses	Hearing in the fetus and newborn	The fetus can hear several weeks before birth; immediately after birth, newborns can hear, although their sensory threshold is higher than that of adults.
	Touch and pain	Newborns do respond to touch. Newborns can feel pain. Research on circumcision shows that 3-day-old males experience pain and can adapt to stress.
	Smell and taste	Both of these senses are present in the newborn.
Intermodal Perception	Its nature	There is considerable interest today in the infant's ability to relate information across perceptual modalities; the coordination and integration of perceptual information across two or more modalities—such as the visual and auditory senses—is called "intermodal perception." Research indicates that infants as young as 4 months of age have intermodal perception. The direct-perception and constructivist views are two important views of perception that make predictions about intermodal perception.

that young infants experience related perceptual worlds, such as auditory and visual, and tactile and visual (Gibson & Spelke, 1983; Rose, 1995). Keep in mind, though, that intermodal perception in young infants remains a controversial concept. For example, in one study of 6-month-old infants, the auditory sense dominated the visual sense, restricting intermodal perception (Lewkowicz, 1988).

The claim that the young infant can relate information from several senses has been addressed by two important theoretical perspectives. The **direct-perception view** *states that infants are born with intermodal perception abilities that enable them to display intermodal perception early in infancy.* In this view, infants only have to attend to the appropriate sensory information; they do not have to build up an internal representation of the information through months of sensorimotor experiences. In contrast, the **constructivist view** *advocated by Piaget states that the*

main perceptual abilities—visual, auditory, and tactile, for example—are completely uncoordinated at birth and that young infants do not have intermodal perception. According to Piaget, only through months of sensorimotor interaction with the world is intermodal perception possible. For Piaget, infant perception involves a representation of the world that builds up as the infant constructs an image of experiences.

Although the intermodal perception and direct-perception/constructivist arguments have not completely been settled, most developmental experts agree that young infants know a lot more than used to be thought (Lewkowicz & Lickliter, 1995). They see and hear more than we used to think was possible for them.

At this point, we have discussed a number of ideas about sensory and perceptual development in infancy. A summary of these ideas is presented in concept table 6.2.

John W. Santrock

The Right Sensory Stimulation

Some parents don't interact with their infants often enough and don't provide them with adequate experiences to stimulate their senses. Other well-meaning parents may actually over-stimulate their baby.

Infants do need a certain amount of stimulation to develop their perceptual skills. Infants should not be unattended for long stretches of time in barren environments. Many babies born into impoverished families, as well as babies in day-care centers that are like "warehouses" where there are many babies per caregiver and few appropriate stimuli or toys, are at risk for receiving inadequate sensory stimulation.

Caregivers should play with infants, give them toys, and periodically provide them with undivided attention during the course of a day. Some infant experts, however, worry that parents who want to have a "superbaby" may give their infant too much stimulation, which can cause the infant to become confused, irritated, or withdrawn (Bower, 1977). Such parents likely place too much pressure on the infant's developing sensory systems and cause more damage than good.

In thinking about what the "right" amount and type of stimulation is, it is important to recognize that what is "right" may differ from one baby to another. Some infants have a low threshold for sensory stimulation—that is, they can't handle a heavy load of stimulation. They become overwhelmed and cry and fuss when they are frequently exposed to sensory stimulation. Other infants have a high threshold for sensory stimulation—that is, they like a lot of sensory stimulation and can benefit from it (Zuckerman, 1979).

Another important point about sensory stimulation is that when infants can control a display they gain more pleasure from it and show more persistence in using it. That is, infants should be active rather than passive participants while observing and manipulating displays.

In sum, it is important for parents to be sensitive to their infant's stimulation needs and monitor when the infant "senses" too little or too much stimulation.

At 4 to 6 months, infants can be positioned to see in a mirror and they can be given brightly colored toys to hold (toys that are small enough to grasp).

I t once was believed that the newborn infant was a virtually empty-headed organism that experienced the world as a "blooming, buzzing confusion." Today, child developmentalists believe the young infant has far more advanced capabilities.

In this chapter, you initially learned how newborns can be studied, and then you read about physical growth and development in infancy. Among the topics you studied were the nature of the infant's reflexes, growth patterns, health, and toilet training. Then you learned about the nature of sensation and perception, how the infant's visual perception changes, as well as what the infant's hearing, touch and pain, smell, and taste are like. You also read about the infant's intermodal perception abilities.

Remember that you can obtain an overall summary of the chapter by again reading the two concept tables on pages 173 and 178. Of course, the infant's development involves more than physical, motor, and perceptual development. In the next chapter, we will study how infants develop cognitively.

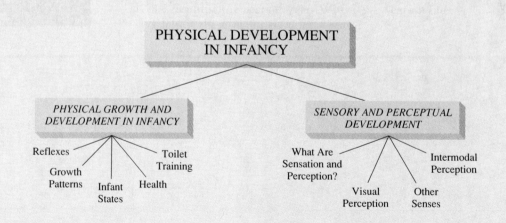

Children Living Hungry in America

Harlingen, Texas, is a heavily Chicano city of approximately 40,000 near the Rio Grande. At Su Clinica ("Your Clinic"), which serves many Chicano residents, poverty and unemployment are evident in the waiting list of 800 families needing low-cost care. Many of the Chicanos working in Texas agriculture receive no health care benefits, and few make even the minimum wage. Farm workers usually get less than $1.50 an hour for working long days in the pesticide-infected fields. The infant mortality rate for the region is listed as good by the U.S. government, but this description is wrong. Many of the deaths are not counted. A baby dies and is buried. People outside the family seldom know. Many infants and young children experience growth problems because they do not get enough to eat. This is not unique to Harlingen, Texas; many other locations in the United States have their share of impoverished families who have difficulty making ends meet and putting food on the table. Hunger and poverty are seen in the children of

Many locations in the United States, including the ghettos of many large American cities, have impoverished families that have difficulty making ends meet and putting food on the table.

poor Mississippi tenant farmers, in the children of laid-off coal miners in West Virginia, in neglected children in the ghettos of New York and Chicago, and in the increasing number of homeless families across the nation. In many instances, these children are the victims of silent undernutrition, less dramatic than in Africa or Bangladesh, but no less real.

Breast-Feeding While Working Outside the Home

Researchers have found physiological benefits, such as decreased risk of allergies and fewer illnesses, for infants when they are fed breast milk rather than formula. If a mother works outside the home and still wants to breast-feed her infant, what challenges does she face and how can she overcome any obstacles? Following are some suggestions (Eisenberg, Murkoff, & Hathaway, 1989):

- *Enlist Support at the Workplace.* Try to arrange a time and a place for expressing milk, and refrigeration for storage if needed. If there is no way to express and store her breast milk at work, the mother will have to depend on breast milk she pumped and stored at home. Breast milk can remain fresh for as long as 6 hours at room temperature, but, to be safe, breast milk should be stored in sterilized bottles or containers and refrigerated.

- *When arranging for a caregiver for the baby, be sure the person understands and supports the mother's plan to continue breast-feeding.* Otherwise the mother might find her baby recently fed and fully satiated when she arrives home eager to nurse. The mother can leave instructions not to give bottles of milk (or juice or water) for at least 2 hours before the mother is expected to come home to nurse.

- *Enlist the support of the husband.* The husband can share some of the household duties so that the mother can spend the necessary time nursing.

- *Arrange a schedule that maximizes the number of feedings.* The mother can do two feedings before she goes to work and possibly several more in the evening. If she works near home, she might be able to either return during lunch for nursing or have the sitter meet her somewhere with the baby.

- *Ensure that the baby gets proper nutrition.* If the mother needs to use formula supplements for home feeding, it is best to breast-feed before giving formula feedings.

THOMAS EAKINS
Baby at Play, detail

Cognitive Development
in Infancy

*I wish I could travel by the road that
crosses the baby's mind, and out beyond all
bounds; where messengers run errands for
no cause between the kingdoms of kings of
no history; where Reason makes kites of
her laws and flies them, and Truth sets
Fact free from its fetters.*

—Rabindranath Tagore, 1913

IMAGES OF CHILDREN

Piaget's Observations of His Children

Jean Piaget, the famous Swiss psychologist, was a meticulous observer of his three children—Lucienne, Jacqueline, and Laurent. His books on cognitive development are filled with these observations. The following provide a glimpse of Piaget's observations of his children's cognitive development in infancy (Piaget, 1952).

- At 21 days of age, Laurent finds his thumb after three attempts; once he finds his thumb, prolonged sucking begins. But when he is placed on his back, he doesn't know how to coordinate the movement of his arms with that of his mouth; his hands draw back even when his lips seek them.
- During the third month, thumb sucking becomes less important to Laurent because of new visual and auditory interests. But when he cries, his thumb goes to the rescue.
- Toward the end of Lucienne's fourth month, while she is lying in her crib, Piaget hangs a doll over her feet. Lucienne thrusts her feet at the doll and makes it move. Afterward she looks at her motionless foot for a second, then kicks at the doll again. She has no visual control of her foot because her movements are the same whether she only looks at the doll or whether it is placed over her head. By contrast, she does have tactile control of her foot; when she tries to kick the doll and misses, she slows her foot movements to improve her aim.

- At 11 months, while seated, Jacqueline shakes a little bell. She then pauses abruptly so she can delicately place the bell in front of her right foot; then she kicks the bell hard. Unable to recapture the bell, she grasps a ball and places it in the same location where the bell was. She gives the ball a firm kick.
- At 1 year, 2 months, Jacqueline holds in her hands an object that is new to her: a round, flat box that she turns over and shakes; then she rubs it against her crib. She lets it go and tries to pick it up again. She only succeeds in touching it with her index finger, being unable to fully reach and grasp it. She keeps trying to grasp it and presses to the edge of her crib. She makes the box tilt up, but it nonetheless falls again.

Jacqueline shows an interest in this result and studies the fallen box.

- At 1 year, 8 months, Jacqueline arrives at a closed door with a blade of grass in each hand. She stretches her right hand toward the doorknob but detects that she cannot turn it without letting go of the grass. So she puts the grass on the floor, opens the door, picks up the grass again, and then enters. But when she wants to leave the room, things get complicated. She puts the grass on the floor and grasps the doorknob. Then she perceives that by pulling the door toward her she simultaneously chases away the grass that she had placed between the door and the threshold. She then picks up the grass and places it out of the door's range of movement.

For Piaget, these observations reflect important changes in the infant's cognitive development. Later in the chapter, you will learn that Piaget believed that infants go through six substages of development and that the behaviors you have just read about characterize those substages.

PREVIEW

The current excitement and enthusiasm about infant cognition have been fueled by an interest in what an infant knows at birth and soon after, by continued fascination with innate and learned factors in the infant's cognitive development, and by controversies about whether infants construct their knowledge (as Piaget believed) or whether they know their world more directly. In this chapter we will study Piaget's theory of infant development, the new look in infant cognitive development, individual differences in intelligence, and language development.

PIAGET'S THEORY OF INFANT DEVELOPMENT

The poet Noah Perry once asked, "Who knows the thoughts of a child?" Piaget knew as much as anyone. Through careful, inquisitive interviews and observations of his own three children—Laurent, Lucienne, and Jacqueline—Piaget changed the way we think about children's conception of the world. Remember that we studied a general outline of Piaget's theory in chapter 2. It may be helpful for you to review the basic features of his theory at this time.

Piaget believed that the child passes through a series of stages of thought from infancy to adolescence. Passage through the stages results from biological pressures to *adapt* to the environment (through assimilation and accommodation) and to organize structures of thinking. The stages of thought are *qualitatively* different from one another; the way children reason at one stage is very different from the way they reason at another stage. This contrasts with the quantitative assessments of intelligence made through the use of standardized intelligence tests, where the focus is on what the child knows, or how many questions the child can answer correctly. According to Piaget, the mind's development is divided into four such quantitatively different stages: sensorimotor, preoperational, concrete operational, and formal operational. Here our concern is with the stage that characterizes infant thought—the sensorimotor stage.

We are born capable of learning.

—Jean-Jacques Rousseau

The Stage of Sensorimotor Development

Piaget's sensorimotor stage lasts from birth to about 2 years of age, corresponding to the period of infancy. During this time, mental development is characterized by considerable progression in the infant's ability to organize and coordinate sensations with physical movements and actions—hence the name *sensorimotor* (Piaget, 1952).

At the beginning of the sensorimotor stage, the infant has little more than reflexive patterns with which to work. By the end of the stage, the 2-year-old has complex sensorimotor patterns and is beginning to operate with a primitive system of symbols. Unlike other stages, the sensorimotor stage is subdivided into six substages, each of which involves qualitative changes in sensorimotor organization. The term **scheme (or schema)** *refers to the basic unit (or units) for an organized pattern of sensorimotor functioning.*

As we learned in the chapter introduction, Piaget was a masterful observer of his three children. The following observation of his son, Laurent, provides an excellent example of the infant's emerging coordination of visual and motor schemes, and eloquently portrays how infants learn about their hands.

At 2 months, Laurent by chance discovers his right index finger and looks at it briefly. Several days later, he briefly inspects his open right hand, which he perceived by chance. About a week later, he follows its spontaneous movement for a moment, then he holds his two fists in the air and looks at the left one. Then he slowly brings it toward his face and rubs his nose with it, then his eye. A moment later the left hand again approaches his face. He looks at it and touches his nose. He does that again and laughs five or six times while moving the left hand to his face. He seems to laugh before the hand moves, but looking has no influence on its movement. Then he rubs his nose. At a given moment, he turns his head to the left, but looking has no effect on the direction of the hand's movement. The next day, the same reaction occurs. And then, another day later, he looks at his right hand, then at his clasped hands. Finally, on the day after that, Piaget says, Laurent's looking acts on the orientation of his hands, which tend to remain in the visual field.

Within a given substage, there may be different schemes—sucking, rooting, and blinking in substage 1, for example. In substage 1, the schemes are basically reflexive in nature. From substage to substage, the schemes change in organization. This change is at the heart of Piaget's description of the stages. The six substages of sensorimotor development are (1) simple reflexes; (2) first habits and primary circular reactions; (3) secondary circular reactions; (4) coordination of secondary circular reactions; (5) tertiary circular reactions, novelty, and curiosity; and (6) internalization of schemes.

Simple reflexes *is Piaget's first sensorimotor substage, which corresponds to the first month after birth. In this substage, the basic means of coordinating sensation and action is through reflexive behaviors, such as rooting and sucking, which the infant has at birth.* In substage 1, the infant exercises these reflexes. More importantly, the infant develops an ability to produce behaviors that resemble reflexes in the absence of obvious reflexive stimuli. The newborn may suck when a bottle or nipple is only nearby, for example. When the baby was just born, the bottle or nipple would have produced the sucking pattern only when placed directly in its mouth or touched to the lips. Reflexlike actions in the absence of a triggering stimulus are evidence that the infant is initiating action and is actively structuring experiences in the first month of life.

First habits and primary circular reactions *is Piaget's second sensorimotor substage, which develops between 1 and 4 months of age. In this substage, the infant learns to coordinate sensation and types of schemes or structures—that is, habits and primary circular reactions.* A *habit* is a scheme based upon a simple reflex, such as sucking, that has become completely divorced from its eliciting stimulus. For example, an infant in substage 1 might suck when orally stimulated by a bottle or when visually shown the bottle, but an infant in substage 2 might exercise the sucking scheme even when no bottle is present.

A **primary circular reaction** *is a scheme based upon the infant's attempt to reproduce an interesting or pleasurable event that initially occurred by chance.* In a popular Piagetian example, a child accidentally sucks his fingers when they are placed near his mouth; later, he searches for his fingers to suck them again, but the fingers do not cooperate in the search because the infant cannot coordinate visual and manual actions. Habits and circular reactions are stereotyped, in that the infant repeats them the same way each time. The infant's own body remains the center of attention; there is no outward pull by environmental events.

Secondary circular reactions *is Piaget's third sensorimotor substage, which develops between 4 and 8 months of age. In this substage, the infant becomes more object-oriented or focused on the world, moving beyond preoccupation with the self in sensorimotor interactions.* The chance shaking of a rattle, for example, may fascinate the infant, and the infant will repeat this action for the sake of experiencing fascination. The infant imitates some simple actions of others, such as the baby talk or burbling of adults, and some physical gestures. However, these imitations are limited to actions the infant is already able to produce. Although directed toward objects in the world, the infant's schemes lack an intentional, goal-directed quality.

Coordination of secondary circular reactions *is Piaget's fourth sensorimotor substage, which develops between 8 and 12 months of age. In this substage, several significant changes take place involving the coordination of schemes and*

intentionality. Infants readily combine and recombine previously learned schemes in a *coordinated way.* They may look at an object and grasp it simultaneously, or visually inspect a toy, such as a rattle, and finger it simultaneously in obvious tactile exploration. Actions are even more outwardly directed than before. Related to this coordination is the second achievement—the presence of *intentionality,* the separation of means and goals in accomplishing simple feats. For example, infants might manipulate a stick (the means) to bring a desired toy within reach (the goal). They may knock over one block to reach and play with another one.

Tertiary circular reactions, novelty, and curiosity *is Piaget's fifth sensorimotor substage, which develops between 12 and 18 months of age. In this substage, infants become intrigued by the variety of properties that objects possess and by the multiplicity of things they can make happen to objects.* A block can be made to fall, spin, hit another object, slide across the ground, and so on. Tertiary circular reactions are schemes in which the infant purposely explores new possibilities with objects, continually changing what is done to them and exploring the results. Piaget says that this stage marks the developmental starting point for human curiosity and interest in novelty. Previous circular reactions have been devoted exclusively to reproducing former events, with the exception of imitation of novel acts, which occurs as early as substage 4. The tertiary circular act is the first to be concerned with novelty.

Internalization of schemes *is Piaget's sixth and final sensorimotor substage, which develops between 18 and 24 months of age. In this substage the infant's mental functioning shifts from a purely sensorimotor plane to a symbolic plane, and the infant develops the ability to use primitive symbols.* For Piaget, a *symbol* is an internalized sensory image or word that represents an event. Primitive symbols permit the infant to think about concrete events without directly acting them out or perceiving them. Moreover, symbols allow the infant to manipulate and transform the represented events in simple ways. In a favorite Piagetian example, Piaget's young daughter saw a matchbox being opened and closed; sometime later, she mimicked the event by opening and closing her mouth. This was an obvious expression of her image of the event. In another example, a child opened a door slowly to avoid disturbing a piece of paper lying on the floor on the other side. Clearly, the child had an image of the unseen paper and what would happen to it if the door opened quickly. However, developmentalists have debated whether 2-year-olds really have such representations of action sequences at their command (Corrigan, 1981).

Object Permanence

Object permanence *is the Piagetian term for one of an infant's most important accomplishments: understanding that objects and events continue to exist even when they cannot directly be seen, heard, or touched.* Imagine what thought would be like if you could not distinguish between yourself and your world. Your thought would be chaotic, disorganized, and

John W. Santrock

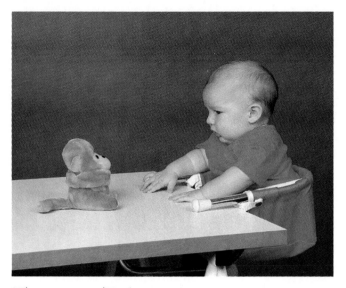

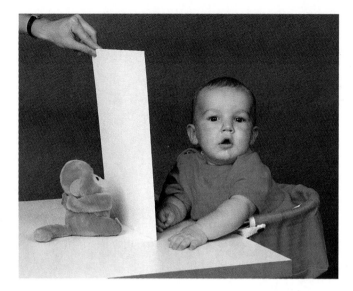

Figure 7.1

Object Permanence
Piaget thought that object permanence was one of infancy's landmark cognitive accomplishments. For this 5-month-old boy, "out-of-sight" is literally out of mind. The infant looks at the toy monkey *(left)*, but, when his view of the toy is blocked *(right)*, he does not search for it. Several months later, he will search for the hidden toy monkey, reflecting the presence of object permanence.

unpredictable. This is what the mental life of a newborn is like, according to Piaget. There is no self-world differentiation and no sense of object permanence. By the end of the sensorimotor period, however, both are present.

The principal way that object permanence is studied is by watching an infant's reaction when an interesting object or event disappears (see figure 7.1). If infants show no reaction, it is assumed they believe the object no longer exists. By contrast, if infants are surprised at the disappearance and search for the object, it is assumed they believe it continues to exist.

At this point we have discussed a number of characteristics of Piaget's stage of sensorimotor thought. To help you remember the main characteristics of sensorimotor thought, turn to figure 7.2.

Although Piaget's stage sequence is the best summary of what might happen as the infant fathoms the permanence of things in the world, some contradictory findings have emerged (Baillargeon, 1995). Piaget's stages broadly describe the interesting changes reasonably well, but the infant's life is not so neatly packaged into distinct stages as Piaget believed. Some of Piaget's explanations for the causes of change are debated.

THE NEW LOOK IN INFANT COGNITIVE DEVELOPMENT

In the past decade, a new understanding of infants' cognitive development has been arising. The new look attacks Piaget's theory of sensorimotor development and emphasizes the importance of exploring how infants process information.

Figure 7.2

The Main Characteristics of Sensorimotor Thought According to Piaget

CRITICAL THINKING
ABOUT CHILDREN'S
DEVELOPMENT

Comparing Piaget's
Methodological Strategy
with a More Rigorous
Experimental Strategy

What are the advantages and disadvantages of basing theoretical ideas on natural observations of and interviews with one's own children, as Piaget did? Why do Piaget's critics believe that such methodology is flawed? How might developmental psychology benefit from both Piaget's strategy and more precise experiments with larger numbers of children?

By comparing Piaget's methodological approach with a more rigorous experimental approach, you are learning to think critically by *evaluating the quality of conclusions about children's development.*

The Attacks on Piaget's Theory of Sensorimotor Development

For many years, Piaget's ideas were so widely known and respected that, to many psychologists, one aspect of development seemed certain: Human infants go through a long, protracted period during which they cannot think (Mandler, 1992). They can learn to recognize things and smile at them, to crawl, and to manipulate objects, but they do not yet have concepts and ideas. Piaget believed that only near the end of the sensorimotor stage of development, at about 1½ to 2 years of age, do infants learn how to represent the world in a symbolic, conceptual manner.

Piaget constructed his view of infancy mainly by observing the development of his own three children. Very few laboratory techniques were available at the time. Recently, however, sophisticated experimental techniques have been devised to study infants, and there is now a large number of research studies on infant cognitive development. Much of the new research suggests that Piaget's theory of sensorimotor development will have to be modified substantially (Gounin-Decarie, 1996). To further evaluate Piaget's theory, refer to Critical Thinking About Children's Development.

Piaget's theory of sensorimotor development has been attacked from two sources. First, extensive research in the area of infant perceptual development suggests that a stable and differentiated perceptual world is established much earlier in infancy than Piaget envisioned. Second, researchers recently have found that memory and other forms of symbolic activity occur by at least the second half of the first year (Gelman & Au, 1996).

Perceptual Development

In chapter 6, we described research on infants' perceptual development, indicating that a number of theorists, such as Eleanor Gibson (1989), Elizabeth Spelke (1991), and Tom Bower (1996), believe that infants' perceptual abilities are highly developed very early in development. For example, Spelke has demonstrated that infants as young as 4 months of age have intermodal perception—the ability to coordinate information from two or more sensory modalities, such as vision and hearing. Other research by Renée Baillargeon (1995) documents that infants as young as 4 months expect objects to be substantial (in the sense that other objects cannot move through them) and permanent (in the sense that they assume objects to continue to exist when they are hidden). In sum, the perceptual development researchers believe that infants see objects as bounded, unitary, solid, and separate from their background, possibly at birth or shortly thereafter, but definitely by 3 to 4 months of age. Young infants still have much to learn about objects, but the world appears both stable and orderly to them, and, thus, capable of being conceptualized.

Conceptual Development

It is more difficult to study what infants are thinking about than what they see. Still, researchers have devised ways to assess whether or not infants are thinking. One strategy is to look for symbolic activity, such as using a gesture to refer to something. Piaget (1952) used this strategy to document infants' motor recognition. For example, he observed his 6-month-old daughter make a gesture when she saw a familiar toy in a new location. She was used to kicking at the toy in her crib. When she saw it across the room, she made a brief kicking motion. However, Piaget did not consider this to be true symbolic activity because it was a motor movement, not a purely mental act. Nonetheless, Piaget suggested that his daughter was referring to, or classifying, the toy through her actions (Mandler, 1992). In a similar way, infants whose parents use sign language have been observed to start using conventional signs at about 6 to 7 months of age (Bonvillian, Orlansky, & Novack, 1983).

In summary, the recent research on infants' perceptual and conceptual development suggests that infants have more sophisticated perceptual abilities and can begin to think earlier than Piaget envisioned. These researchers believe that infants either are born with or acquire these abilities early in their development (Mandler, 1990, 1992). Information-processing psychologists have made important contributions to the new perspective on infant cognition.

John W. Santrock

Researchers use a variety of ingenious techniques to study infant development. In researcher Mark Johnson's laboratory at Carnegie Mellon University, babies have shown an ability to organize their world and to anticipate future events by learning and remembering sequences of colorful images on TV monitors.

The Information-Processing Perspective

Unlike Piaget, information-processing psychologists do not describe infancy as a stage or a series of substages. Rather, they emphasize the importance of such cognitive processes as attention, memory, and thinking in the way the infant processes information about the world (Rose, 1995).

Piaget believed that the infant's ability to construct sensorimotor schemas, establish a coherent world of objects and events suitable to form the content of ideas, imitate, and form images that can stand for things is completed in the second half of the second year. However, many information-processing psychologists believe the young infant is more competent than Piaget believed, with attentional, symbolic, imitative, and conceptual capabilities present earlier in infant development than Piaget envisioned (Meltzoff, 1992).

Habituation and Dishabituation

If a stimulus—a sight or sound—is presented to infants several times in a row, they usually pay less attention to it each time, suggesting they are bored with it. This is the process of **habituation**—*repeated presentation of the same stimulus that causes reduced attention to the stimulus.* **Dishabituation** *is an infant's renewed interest in a stimulus.* Among the measures infant researchers use to study whether habituation is occurring are sucking behavior

(sucking behavior stops when the young infant attends to a novel object), heart and respiration rates, and the length of time the infant looks at an object. Newborn infants can habituate to repetitive stimulation in virtually every stimulus modality—vision, hearing, touch, and so on (Rovee-Collier, 1987). However, habituation becomes more acute over the first 3 months of life. The extensive assessment of habituation in recent years has resulted in its use as a measure of an infant's maturity and well-being. Infants who have brain damage or have suffered birth traumas such as lack of oxygen do not habituate well and may later have developmental and learning problems.

> *Man is the only animal that can be bored.*
> —**Erich Fromm, The Sane Society, 1955**

A knowledge of habituation and dishabituation can benefit parent-infant interaction. Infants respond to changes in stimulation. If stimulation is repeated often, the infant's response will decrease to the point that the infant no longer responds to the parent. In parent-infant interaction, it is important for parents to do novel things and to repeat them often until the infant stops responding. The wise parent senses when the infant shows an interest and that many repetitions of the stimulus may be necessary for the infant to process the information. The parent stops or changes behaviors when the infant redirects her attention (Rosenblith, 1992).

Memory

Memory is a central feature of cognitive development, pertaining to all situations in which an individual retains information over time. Sometimes information is retained for only a few seconds, and at other times it is retained for a lifetime. Memory is involved when we look up a telephone number and dial it, when we remember a telephone number and dial it, when we remember the name of our best friend from elementary school, when an infant remembers who her mother is, and when an older adult remembers to keep a doctor's appointment.

> *Life is all memory, except for the one present moment that goes by you so quick you hardly catch it going.*
> —Tennessee Williams,
> ***The Milk Train Doesn't Stop Here Anymore, 1963***

Popular child-rearing expert Penelope Leach (1990) tells parents that 6- to 8-month-old babies cannot hold in their mind a picture of their mother or father. And historically psychologists have believed that infants cannot store memories until they have the language skills required to form them and retrieve them. Recently, though, child development researchers have revealed that infants as young as three months of age show memory skills (Grunwald & others, 1993).

In one study, infants were placed in large black boxes where they lay looking up at TV screens, viewing a sequence of colorful objects that appeared repeatedly on the screens (Canfield & Haith, 1991). The babies' eye movements were monitored with a infrared camera linked to a computer. After viewing the sequence only five times, the babies could anticipate where the next object in the sequence would appear. With just a little more practice, they predicted a four-step sequence, and most could still remember it up to 2 weeks later.

Carolyn Rovee-Collier (1987) has found that infants can remember surprisingly intricate material. In a characteristic experiment, she places a baby in a crib underneath an elaborate mobile, ties one end of a ribbon to the baby's ankle and the other end to the mobile, and observes as the baby kicks and makes the mobile move. Weeks later the baby is returned to the crib but its foot is not tied to the mobile. The baby kicks, apparently trying to make the mobile move (see figure 7.3). However, if the mobile's makeup is changed even slightly, the baby doesn't kick. If the mobile is then restored to being exactly like it was when the baby's ankle was originally tied to it, the baby will begin kicking again. According to Rovee-Collier, even by 2½ months the baby's memory is incredibly detailed.

Nancy Myers and her colleagues (Myers, Clifton, & Clarkson, 1987) have found that 2-year-olds can remember experiences they had at 6 months of age. They placed

FIGURE 7.3

The Technique Used in Rovee-Collier's Investigation of Infant Memory
The mobile is connected to the infant's ankle by the ribbon and moves in direct proportion to the frequency and vigor of the infant's kicks. This infant is in a reinforcement period. During this period the infant can see the mobile, but because the ribbon is attached to a different stand, she cannot make the mobile move. Baseline activity is assessed during a nonreinforcement period prior to training, and all retention tests are also conducted during periods of nonreinforcement. As can be seen, this infant has already learned and is attempting to make the mobile move by kicking her leg with the ribbon attachments.

sixteen 6-month-old babies in a dark room with objects that made different sounds. Using infrared cameras they observed how and when the infants reached for objects. Two years later, the same children were brought back into the laboratory, along with a control group of sixteen other 2½-year-old children (Perris, Myers, & Clifton, 1990). The experimental group revealed the same behavior they had shown at 6 months, reaching for the objects and displaying no fear, but fewer control group children reached for the objects and many of them cried. The experiment demonstrates that young children can remember experiences up to 2 years earlier when put in the same context.

In summary, the capacity for memory appears much earlier in infancy than we used to believe, and is also more precise than earlier conclusions suggested.

Imitation

Can infants imiate someone else's emotional expressions? If an adult smiles, will the baby follow with a smile? If an adult protrudes her lower lip, wrinkles her forehead, and frowns, will the baby show a saddened look? If an adult

FIGURE 7.4

Infant Imitation
Infant development researcher Andrew Meltzoff displays
tongue protrusion in an attempt to get the infant to imitate
his behavior. Researchers have demonstrated that young
infants can imitate adult behaviors far earlier than
traditionally believed.

opens his mouth, widens his eyes, and raises his eyebrows,
will the baby follow suit? Could infants only a few days old
do these things?

> *We are, in truth, more than half what we are by imitation.*
> —Lord Chesterfield, *Letters to His Son,* 1750

Infant development researcher Andrew Meltzoff
(1992) has conducted numerous studies of the imitative
abilities of infants. He believes infants' imitative abilities
are biologically based, because infants can imitate a facial
expression within the first few days after birth, before they
have had the opportunity to observe social agents in their
environment engage in tongue protrusion and other behaviors. He also emphasizes that the infant's imitative abilities are not like what ethologists conceptualize as a
hardwired, reflexive, innate releasing mechanism, but
rather involve flexibility, adaptability, and intermodal perception. In Meltzoff's observations of infants in the first 72
hours of life, the infants gradually displayed a full imitative
response of an adult's facial expression, such as tongue protrusion or opening the mouth wide (see figure 7.4).
Initially, the young infant may only get its tongue to the
edge of its lips, but after a number of attempts and observations of the adult behavior, the infant displays a more full-
blown response.

Meltzoff has also studied **deferred imitation,** *which is
imitation that occurs after a time delay of hours or days.* In one
study, Meltzoff (1988) demonstrated that 9-month-old infants could imitate actions they had seen performed 24
hours earlier. Each action consisted of an unusual gesture—such as pushing a recessed button in a box (which
produced a beeping sound). Piaget believed that deferred

imitation does not occur until about 18 months of age;
Meltzoff's research suggests that it occurs much earlier in
infant development.

In sum, rather than assuming that infants' conceptual functioning—involving such important cognitive processes as memory and deferred imitation—can
occur only as an outcome of a lengthy sensorimotor
stage, information-processing psychologists believe that infants either are born with these capabilities or acquire
them much earlier in infancy than Piaget believed. As we
will see next, a third perspective on infant cognition also
differs from Piaget's approach.

INDIVIDUAL DIFFERENCES IN INTELLIGENCE

So far we have stressed general statements about how the
cognitive development of infants progresses, emphasizing
what is typical of the largest number of infants or the average infant. But the results obtained for most infants do not
apply to all infants. Individual differences in infant cognitive development have been studied primarily through the
use of developmental scales or infant intelligence tests.

It is advantageous to know whether an infant is advancing at a slow, a normal, or an advanced pace of development. In chapter 4, we discussed the Brazelton Neonatal
Behavioral Assessment Scale, which is widely used to evaluate newborns. Developmentalists also want to know how
development proceeds during the course of infancy. If an
infant advances at an especially slow rate, then some form
of enrichment may be necessary. If an infant develops at an
advanced pace, parents may be advised to provide toys that
stimulate cognitive growth in slightly older infants.

The infant testing movement grew out of the tradition of IQ testing with older children. However, the measures that assess infants are necessarily less verbal than IQ
tests that assess the intelligence of older children. The infant developmental scales contain far more items related to
perceptual motor development. They also include measures
of social interaction.

The most important early contributor to the developmental testing of infants was Arnold Gesell (1934). He
developed a measure that was used as a clinical tool to help
sort out potentially normal babies from abnormal ones.
This was especially useful to adoption agencies who had
large numbers of babies awaiting placement. Gesell's examination was used widely for many years and is still frequently used by pediatricians in their assessment of normal
and abnormal infants. The current version of the Gesell
test used has four categories of behavior: motor, language,
adaptive, and personal-social. The **developmental quotient
(DQ)** *is an overall developmental score that combines subscores
in motor, language, adaptive, and personal-social domains in
the Gesell assessment of infants.* However, overall scores on
tests like the Gesell do not correlate highly with IQ scores
obtained later in childhood. This is not surprising, because

the items on the developmental scales are considerably less verbal in nature than the items on intelligence tests given to older children.

The **Bayley Scales of Infant Development,** *developed by Nancy Bayley (1969), are widely used in the assessment of infant development. The current version has three components: a mental scale, a motor scale, and an infant behavior profile.* Unlike Gesell, whose scales were clinically motivated, Bayley wanted to develop scales that could document infant behavior and predict later development. The early version of the Bayley scales covered only the first year of development; in the 1950s, the scales were extended to assess older infants. In 1993, the Bayley-II was published with updated norms for diagnostic assessment at a younger age.

Because our discussion centers on the infant's cognitive development, our primary interest is in Bayley's mental scale, which includes assessment of the following:

- Auditory and visual attention to stimuli
- Manipulation, such as combining objects or shaking a rattle
- Examiner interaction, such as babbling and imitation
- Relation with toys, such as banging spoons together
- Memory involved in object permanence, as when the infant finds a hidden toy
- Goal-directed behavior that involves persistence, such as putting pegs in a board
- Ability to follow directions and knowledge of objects' names, such as understanding the concept of "one"

How well should a 6-month-old perform on the Bayley mental scale? The 6-month-old infant should be able to vocalize pleasure and displeasure, persistently search for objects that are just out of immediate reach, and approach a mirror that is placed in front of the infant by the examiner. How well should a 12-month-old perform? By 12 months of age, the infant should be able to inhibit behavior when commanded to do so, imitate words the examiner says (such as *Mama*), and respond to simple requests (such as "Take a drink"). To further evaluate the individual differences approach, see Critical Thinking About Children's Development.

Tests of infant intelligence have been valuable in assessing the effects of malnutrition, drugs, maternal deprivation, and environmental stimulation on the development of infants. They have met with mixed results in predicting

CRITICAL THINKING ABOUT CHILDREN'S DEVELOPMENT

Comparing Piaget's Approach with the Individual Differences Approach

Piaget worked in the Paris laboratory of Alfred Binet, who, with Theophile Simon, developed the first intelligence test. Piaget was more intrigued by children's incorrect responses to items than by their correct responses. For Piaget, studying *what* children *know* was merely a beginning to discovering developmental changes in *how* children *think.*

In thinking about Piaget's theory and the individual differences approach, consider whether an older infant's intelligence is just quantitatively different from a younger infant's intelligence or qualitatively different. How would Piaget have answered this question?

By comparing Piaget's cognitive developmental approach with the individual differences approach, you are learning to think critically by *pursuing alternative explanations to understand development comprehensively.*

later intelligence. Global developmental quotient or IQ scores for infants have not been good predictors of childhood intelligence. However, specific aspects of infant intelligence are related to specific aspects of childhood intelligence. For example, in one study, infant language abilities as assessed by the Bayley test predicted language, reading, and spelling ability at 6 to 8 years of age (Siegel, 1989). Infant perceptual motor skills predicted visuospatial, arithmetic, and fine motor skills at 6 to 8 years of age. These results indicate that an item analysis of infant scales like Bayley's can provide information about the development of specific intellectual functions.

The explosion of interest in infant development has produced many new measures, especially tasks that evaluate the way infants process information. Evidence is accumulating that measures of habituation and dishabituation predict intelligence in childhood (McCall & Carriger, 1993). Less cumulative attention in the habituation situation and greater amounts of attention in the dishabituation situation reflect more efficient information processing. Both types of attention—decrement and recovery—when measured in the first 6 months of infancy, are related to higher IQ scores on standardized intelligence tests given at various times between infancy and adolescence. In sum, more-precise assessments of the infant's cognition with information-processing tasks involving attention have led to the conclusion that continuity between infant and childhood intelligence is greater than was previously believed.

It is important, however, not to go too far and think that the connections between early infant cognitive development and later childhood cognitive development are so strong that no discontinuity takes place. Rather than asking whether cognitive development is continuous *or* discontinuous, perhaps we should be examining the ways cognitive development is both continuous *and* discontinuous. Some important changes in cognitive development take place after infancy, changes that underscore the discontinuity of cognitive development. We will describe these changes in cognitive development in subsequent chapters that focus on later periods of development.

So far we have discussed a number of ideas about cognitive development in infancy. A summary of these ideas is presented in concept table 7.1. Next we will study another key dimension of the infant's development—language.

FIGURE 7.5

Infants' Recognition of Speech Sounds
In Patricia Kuhl's research, babies at 7 months show an ability to read lips, connecting vowel sounds with lip movements. In the insert, a 6-month-old baby is being tested in Kuhl's laboratory to determine if she recognizes the sounds of her native language.

LANGUAGE DEVELOPMENT

In 1799, a nude boy was observed running through the woods in France. The boy was captured when he was approximately 11 years old. It was believed he had lived in the wild for at least 6 years. He was called the "Wild Boy of Aveyron" (Lane, 1976). When the boy was found, he made no effort to communicate. Ever after a number of years he never learned to communicate effectively. The Wild Boy of Aveyron raises an important issue in language, namely, what are the biological, environmental, and cultural contributions to language? Later in the chapter we will describe a modern-day wild child named Genie, who will shed some light on this issue. Indeed, the contributions of biology, environment, and culture figure prominently into our discussion of language.

What Is Language?

Every human culture has language. Human languages number in the thousands, differing so much on the surface that many of us despair at learning more than even one. Yet all human languages have some common characteristics. A **language** *is a system of symbols used to communicate with others. In humans, language is characterized by infinite generativity and rule systems.* **Infinite generativity** *is an individual's ability to generate an infinite number of meaningful sentences using a finite set of words and rules, which makes language a highly creative enterprise.* Language's rule systems include phonology, morphology, syntax, semantics, and pragmatics, each of which we will discuss in turn.

Language is made up of basic sounds, or *phonemes*. In the English language there are approximately 36 phonemes. **Phonology** *is the study of a language's sound system*. Phonological rules ensure that certain sound sequences occur (for example, *sp, ba,* or *ar*) and others do not (for example, *zx* or *qp*). A good example of a phoneme in the English language is /k/, the sound represented by the letter *k* in the word *ski* and the letter *c* in the word *cat*. While the /k/ sound is slightly different in these two words, the variation is not distinguished, and the /k/ sound is described as a single phoneme. In some languages, such as Arabic, this kind of variation represents separate phonemes. An increasing number of researchers believe that speech is an infant's gateway to language (Eimas, 1995; Morgan & Demuth, 1995).

What phonology does is provide a basis for constructing a large and expandable set of words—all that are or ever will be in that language—out of two or three dozen phonemes. We do not need 500,000. We need only two or three dozen.

Patricia Kuhl (1993) has conducted research that reveals that long before they actually begin to learn words, infants can sort through a number of spoken sounds in search of the ones that have meaning. Kuhl argues that from birth to about 4 months of age, infants are "universal linguists" who are capable of distinguishing each of the 150 sounds that make up human speech. But by about 6 months of age, they have started to specialize in the speech sounds of their native language (see figure 7.5). By 8 or 9 months of age, comprehension is more noticeable.

CONCEPT TABLE 7.1

Infant Cognitive Development

Concept	Processes/Related Ideas	Characteristics/Description
Piaget's Theory of Infant Development	Sensorimotor stage	This stage lasts from birth to about 2 years of age and involves progression in the infant's ability to organize and coordinate sensations with physical movements. The sensorimotor stage has six substages: simple reflexes; first habits and primary circular reactions; secondary circular reactions; coordination of secondary circular reactions; tertiary circular reactions, novelty, and curiosity; and internalization of schemes.
	Object permanence	Object permanence refers to the development of the ability to understand that objects and events continue to exist even though the infant no longer is in contact with them. Piaget believed that this ability develops over the course of the six substages.
The New Look in Infant Cognitive Development	The attacks on Piaget's theory of sensorimotor development; perceptual and cognitive development	In the past decade, a new understanding of infants' cognitive development has been emerging. Piaget's theory has been attacked from two sources. First, extensive research in perceptual development suggests that a stable and differentiated perceptual world is established much earlier than Piaget envisioned. Second, researchers recently have found that memory and other forms of symbolic activity occur by at least the second half of the first year.
The Information-Processing Perspective and Infant Development	Its nature	Unlike Piaget, information-processing psychologists do not describe infancy as a stage or series of substages of sensorimotor development. Rather, they emphasize the importance of cognitive processes such as attention, memory, and thinking. The information-processing psychologists believe that the young infant is more competent than Piaget envisioned, with attentional, symbolic, imitative, and conceptual abilities occurring much earlier in development than Piaget thought.
	Habituation and dishabituation	Habituation is the repeated presentation of the same stimulus, causing reduced attention to the stimulus. If a different stimulus is presented and the infant pays attention to it, dishabituation is occurring. Newborn infants can habituate, but habituation becomes more acute over the first 3 months of infancy.
	Memory	Memory is the retention of information over time. Memory develops much earlier in infancy than once was believed and is more specific than earlier conclusions suggested.
	Imitation	Infants can imitate the facial expressions of others in the first few days of life. Meltzoff demonstrated that deferred imitation occurs at about 9 months of age, much earlier than Piaget believed.
Individual Differences in Intelligence	History	Developmental scales for infants grew out of the tradition of IQ testing with older children. These scales are less verbal than IQ tests. Gesell was an early developer of an infant test. His scale is still widely used by pediatricians; it provides a developmental quotient (DQ).
	Bayley scales	The developmental scales most widely used today, developed by Nancy Bayley, consist of a motor scale, a mental scale, and an infant behavior profile.
	Conclusions about infant tests and continuity in mental development	Global infant intelligence measures are not good predictors of childhood intelligence. However, specific aspects of infant intelligence, such as information-processing tasks involving attention, have been better predictors of childhood intelligence, especially in a specific area. There is both continuity and discontinuity between infant cognitive development and cognitive development later in childhood.

For example, babies look at a ball when their mothers say "ball." Language experts say that it is impossible to determine how many words babies understand at this point in their development, but research with slightly older children suggests that comprehension might outpace expression by a factor of as much as 100 to 1. Researchers also have found that although some babies are slow in beginning to talk, comprehension is often about equal between early and late talkers (Bates & Thal, 1991).

Morphology *is the study of what language users know about the units of meaning and the rules of combining morphemes.* A morpheme *is a meaningful string of phonemes (sounds) that has no smaller meaningful parts.* Every word in the English language is made up of one or more morphemes. Some words consist of a single morpheme (for example, *help*), whereas others are made up of more than one morpheme (for example, *helper*, which has two morphemes, *help* + *-er*, with the morpheme *-er* meaning "one who"—in this case "one who helps"). However, not all morphemes are words (for example, *pre-*, *-tion*, and *-ing*). Just as the rules that govern phonemes ensure that certain sound sequences occur, the rules that govern morphemes ensure that certain strings of sounds occur in meaningful sequences. For example, we would not reorder *helper* as *erhelp*.

Syntax *involves the ways words are combined to form acceptable phrases and sentences.* For example, *He didn't stay, did he?* is a grammatical sentence, but *He didn't stay, didn't he?* is unacceptable and ambiguous. Similarly, if I say to you, "Bob slugged Tom" and "Bob was slugged by Tom," you know who did the slugging and who was slugged in each case because we share the same syntactic understanding of sentence structures. This concept of "who does what to whom" is called *grammatical relations*, and it is an important type of syntactic information.

The adjective is the banana peel of the parts of speech.
—**Clifton Fadiman**

The term **semantics** *refers to the meanings of words and sentences.* Every word has a set of semantic features. *Girl* and *woman*, for instance, both have some of the semantic features of the words *female* and *human*, but they also differ in meaning (for instance, regarding age). Words have semantic restrictions on how they can be used in sentences. The sentence *The bicycle talked the boy into buying a candy bar* is syntactically correct but semantically incorrect. The sentence violates our semantic knowledge that bicycles do not talk.

A person gets from a symbol the meaning he puts into it, and what is one man's comfort and inspiration is another's jest and scorn.

—**Justice Robert Jackson**

"If you don't mind my asking how much does a sentence diagrammer pull down a year?"

© Reprinted by permission of Bob Thaves.

A final set of language rules involves **pragmatics**—*the use of appropriate conversation, and knowledge underlying the use of language in context.* The domain of pragmatics is broad, covering such circumstances as (a) taking turns in discussions instead of everyone talking at once; (b) using questions to convey commands ("Why is it so noisy in here?" "What is this, Grand Central Station?"); (c) using words like *the* and *a* in a way that enhances understanding ("I read *a* book last night. *The* plot was boring."); (d) using polite language in appropriate situations (for example, when talking to one's teacher); and (e) telling stories that are interesting, jokes that are funny, and lies that convince.

Do we learn this ability to generate rule systems for language and then use them to create an almost infinite number of words, or is it the product of biology and evolution?

Biological Influences

The strongest evidence for the biological basis of language is that children all over the world reach language milestones at about the same time developmentally and in about the same order, despite the vast variation in the language input they receive. For example, in some cultures adults never talk to children under 1 year of age, yet these infants still acquire language. Also, there is no other convincing way to explain how *quickly* children learn language than through biological foundations.

With these thoughts in mind, let's now explore these questions about biological influences on language: How strongly is language influenced by biological evolution? Are humans biologically wired to learn language? Do animals have language? Is there a critical period for language acquisition?

Biological Evolution

A number of experts stress the biological foundations of language (Chomsky, 1957; Miller, 1981). They believe it is undeniable that biological evolution shaped humans into linguistic creatures (Scott, 1997). In terms of biological evolution, the brain, nervous system, and vocal system changed over hundreds of thousands of years. Prior to

---

Homo sapiens, the physical equipment to produce language was not present. *Homo sapiens* went beyond the groans and shrieks of their predecessors with the development of abstract speech. Estimates vary as to how long ago humans acquired language—from about 20,000 to 70,000 years ago. In evolutionary time, then, language is a very recent acquisition.

Biological Prewiring

Linguist Noam Chomsky (1957) believes humans are biologically prewired to learn language at a certain time and in a certain way. He said that children are born into the world with a **language acquisition device (LAD),** *a biological endowment that enables the child to detect certain language categories, such as phonology, syntax, and semantics.* The LAD is a theoretical construct that flows from evidence about the biological basis of language.

Is there evidence for the existence of a LAD? Supporters of the LAD concept cite the uniformity of language milestones across languages and cultures, biological substrates for language, and evidence that children create language even in the absence of well-formed input. With regard to the last argument, most deaf children are the offspring of hearing parents. Some of these parents choose not to expose their deaf child to sign language, in order to motivate the child to learn speech while providing the child with a supportive social environment. Susan Goldin-Meadow (1979) has found that these children develop spontaneous gestures that are not based on their parents' gestures.

Do Animals Have Language?

Many animal species have complex and ingenious ways to signal danger and to communicate about basic needs, such as food and sex. For example, in one species of firefly, the females have learned to imitate the flashing signal of another species to lure the aliens into their territory. Then they eat the aliens. However, is this language in the human sense? What about higher animals, such as apes? Is ape language similar to human language? Can we teach human language to apes?

Some researchers believe that apes can learn language. One celebrity in this field is the chimp Washoe, who was adopted when she was about 10 months old (Gardner & Gardner, 1971). Since apes do not have the vocal apparatus to speak, the researchers tried to teach Washoe American Sign Language, which is one of the sign languages of the deaf. Washoe used sign language during everyday activities, such as meals, play, and car rides. In 2 years, Washoe learned 38 signs, and by the age of 5 she had a vocabulary of 160 signs. Washoe learned how to put signs together in novel ways, such as "you drink" and "you me tickle." A number of other efforts to teach language to chimps have had similar results (Premack, 1986).

The debate about chimpanzees' ability to use language focuses on two key issues. Can apes understand the meaning of symbols (that is, can they comprehend that

FIGURE 7.6

Sue Savage-Rumbaugh with a Chimp in Front of a Board with Languagelike Visual Geometric Symbols
The Rumbaughs (Sue and Duane) claim that these pygmy chimpanzees have a communication system in which they can come up with novel combinations of words.

one thing stands for another) and can apes learn syntax (that is, can they learn the mechanics and rules that give human language its creative productivity)? The first of these issues may have been settled recently by Sue Savage-Rumbaugh and her colleagues (1993). They claim that pygmy chimpanzees have a communication system that can combine a set of visual geometric symbols and responses to English words (see figure 7.6). They state that these animals often come up with novel combinations of words and that their language is broader than that of common chimpanzees.

The debate over whether or not animals can use language to express thoughts is far from resolved. Researchers agree that animals can communicate with each other and that some can be trained to manipulate languagelike symbols. However, although such accomplishments may be

John W. Santrock

remarkable, they fall far short of human language, with its infinite number of novel phrases to convey the richness and subtleties of meaning that are the foundation of human relationships.

Is There a Critical Period for Learning Language?

Have you ever encountered young children serving as unofficial "translators" for their non-English-speaking parents? Doctors and nurses sometimes encounter this when treating patients. Does this indicate that young children are able to easily learn language, while their parents have lost this ability? Such an explanation would fit the view that there is a **critical period,** *a period in which there is a learning readiness; beyond this period learning is difficult or impossible.* The concept of a critical period applies nicely to certain varieties of songbirds. For example, baby white-crowned sparrows learn the song of their species quite well if they are exposed to it during a specific time as a chick; after this time they can never develop a fully formed song pattern. But whether this notion can be extended to humans learning language is much less certain.

Almost all children learn one or more languages during their early years of development, so it is difficult to determine whether there is a critical period for language development (Obler, 1993). In the 1960s, Eric Lenneberg (1967) proposed a biological theory of language acquisition. He said that language is a maturational process and that there is a critical period between about 18 months of age and puberty during which a first language must be acquired. Central to Lenneberg's thesis is the idea that language develops rapidly and with ease during the preschool years as a result of maturation. Lenneberg provided support for the critical-period concept from studies of several atypical populations, including children with left-hemisphere brain damage, deaf children, and children with mental retardation (Tager-Flusberg, 1994). With regard to brain damage, Lenneberg believed that adults had already passed the critical period during which plasticity of brain function allows reassignment and relearning of language skills.

The stunted language development of a modern "wild child" supports the idea that there is a critical period for language acquisition (see figure 7.7). In 1970, a California social worker made a routine visit to the home of a partially blind woman who had applied for public assistance. The social worker discovered that the woman and her husband had kept their 13-year-old daughter, Genie, locked away in almost total isolation during her childhood. Genie could not speak or stand erect. She had spent every day bound naked to a child's potty seat, able to move only her hands and feet. At night she was placed in a kind of straightjacket and caged in a crib with wire mesh sides and a cover. Whenever Genie made a noise, her father beat her. He never communicated with her in words but growled and barked at her instead (Rymer, 1992).

FIGURE 7.7

What were Genie's experiences like, and what implications do her experiences have for language acquisition?

After she was rescued from her parents, Genie spent a number of years in extensive rehabilitation programs such as speech and physical therapy (Curtiss, 1977). She eventually learned to walk, though with a jerky motion, and to use the toilet. Genie also learned to recognize many words and to speak in rudimentary sentences. At first she spoke in one-word utterances. Later she was able to string together and create two-word combinations, such as "Big teeth," "Little marble," and "Two hand." Consistent with the language development of most children, three-word combinations (such as "Small two cup") followed. Unlike normal children, Genie never learned to ask questions, and she never understood grammar. She was never able to distinguish among pronouns or between passive and active verbs. Four years after she began stringing words together, Genie's speech still sounded like a garbled telegram. As an adult she speaks in short, mangled sentences, such as "Father hit leg," "Big wood," and "Genie hurt."

Children like Genie, "Wild" Peter of Germany, and Kamala (the wolf-girl), who are abandoned, abused, and not exposed to language for many years, rarely speak normally. Such tragic evidence supports the critical-period hypothesis in language development. However, because these children also suffer severe emotional trauma and possible neurological deficits, the issue is still far from clear.

Let's go back to our "child translator" example. Why is it that children seem to do better than older people in learning language? Many researchers have proposed that the preschool years (until age 5) may be a critical period for language acquisition. Evidence for this notion comes from studies of brain development in young children, and from the amount of language learned by preschool children. However, other evidence suggests that we do not have a critical period for language learning. First of all, although much language learning takes place during the preschool years, learning continues well into the later school years and adulthood. Also, with respect to second-language learning, adults can do as well as or better than young children, provided they are motivated and spend equivalent amounts of time. In other words, young children's proficiency in language, while impressive, does not seem to involve a biologically salient critical period that older children and adults have passed.

Behavioral and Environmental Influences

Behaviorists view language as just another behavior, like sitting, walking, or running. They argue that language represents chains of responses (Skinner, 1957) or imitation (Bandura, 1977). But many of the sentences we produce are novel; we have not heard them or spoken them before. For example, a child hears the sentence "The plate fell on the floor" and then says, "My mirror fell on the blanket," after dropping the mirror on the blanket. The behavioral mechanisms of reinforcement and imitation cannot completely explain this.

While spending long hours observing parents and their young children, child language researcher Roger Brown (1973) searched for evidence that parents reinforce their children for speaking in grammatical ways. He found that parents sometimes smiled and praised their children for sentences they liked, but that they also reinforced sentences that were ungrammatical. Brown concluded that no evidence exists to document that reinforcement is responsible for language's rule systems.

Another criticism of the behavioral view is that it fails to explain the extensive orderliness of language. The behavioral view predicts that vast individual differences should appear in children's speech development because of each child's unique learning history. But as we have seen, a compelling fact about language is its structure and ever-present rule systems. All infants coo before they babble. All toddlers produce one-word utterances before two-word utterances, and all state sentences in the active form before they state them in a passive form.

However, we do not learn language in a social vacuum. Most children are bathed in language from a very early age (Hart & Risley, 1995). We need this early exposure to language to acquire competent language skills. The Wild Boy of Aveyron did not learn to communicate effectively after being reared in social isolation for years. Genie's language was rudimentary even after years of extensive training.

Today most language acquisition researchers believe that children from a wide variety of cultural contexts acquire their native language without explicit teaching, in some cases without apparent encouragement. Thus, there appear to be very few aids that are necessary for learning a language. However, the support and involvement of caregivers and teachers greatly facilitate a child's language learning. Of special concern are children who grow up in poverty-infested areas and are not exposed to guided participation in language.

Recently, John Locke (1993) argued that one reason why social interactionist aspects have been underplayed recently in explaining language development is that linguists concentrate on language's complex, structural properties, especially the acquisition of grammar, and give inadequate attention to the communicative aspects of language. Locke reminds us that language learning occurs in the very real context of physical and social maturation, and that children are neither exclusively young biological linguists nor exclusively social beings. An interactionist view emphasizes the contributions of both biology and experience in language—that is, that children are biologically prepared to learn language as they and their caregivers interact (Huttenlocher, 1995; Nelson & Réger, 1995).

One intriguing role of the environment in the young child's acquisition of language is called **motherese,** *the kind of speech often used by mothers and other adults to talk to babies—in a higher pitch than normal and with simple words and sentences.* It is hard to talk in motherese when not in the presence of a baby. But as soon as you start talking to a baby, you immediately shift into motherese. Much of this is automatic and something most parents are not aware they are doing. Motherese has the important functions of capturing the infant's attention and maintaining communication. When parents are asked why they use baby talk, they point out that it is designed to teach their baby to talk. Older peers also talk baby talk to infants, but observations of siblings indicate that the affectional features are dropped when sibling rivalry is sensed (Dunn & Kendrick, 1982).

Are there strategies other than motherese that adults use to enhance the child's acquisition of language? Four candidates are recasting, echoing, expanding, and labeling. **Recasting** *is rephrasing something the child has said in a different way, perhaps turning it into a question.* For example, if the child says, "The dog was barking," the adult can respond by asking, "When was the dog barking?" The effects of recasting fit with suggestions that "following in order to lead" helps a child to learn language. That is, letting a child initially indicate an interest and then proceeding to elaborate that interest—commenting, demonstrating, and explaining—enhance communication and help language acquisition. In contrast, an overly active, directive approach to communicating with the child may be harmful.

Echoing *is repeating what a child says, especially if it is an incomplete phrase or sentence.* **Expanding** *is restating, in a linguistically sophisticated form, what a child has said.* **Labeling** *is identifying the names of objects.* Young children are forever

Around the world, young children learn to speak in two-word utterances, in most cases at about 18 to 24 months of age.

being asked to identify the names of objects. Roger Brown (1986) identified this as "the great word game" and claimed that much of the early vocabulary acquired by children is motivated by this adult pressure to identify the words associated with objects.

The strategies we have just described—recasting, echoing, expanding, and labeling—are used naturally and in meaningful conversations. Parents do not (and should not) use any deliberate method to teach their children to talk. Even for children who are slow in learning language, the experts agree that intervention should occur in natural ways, with the goal of being able to convey meaning.

It is important to recognize that children vary in their ability to acquire language and that this variation cannot be readily explained by differences in environmental input alone (Rice, 1996). For children who are slow in developing language skills, opportunities to talk and be talked with are important, but remember that encouragement of language development, not drill and practice, is the key (de Villiers, 1996; Snow, 1996). Language development is not a simple matter of imitation and reinforcement, a fact acknowledged even by most behaviorists today.

How Language Develops

In describing language, we have touched on language development many times. You just read about the motherese that parents use with their infants. Earlier we

discussed the Wild Boy of Aveyron, Genie, and Washoe. Now let's examine in greater detail the developmental changes in language that take place in infancy.

In the first few months of life, infants show a startle response to sharp noises. Then, at 3 to 6 months, infants begin to show an interest in sounds, play with saliva, and respond to voices. During the next 3 to 6 months, infants begin to babble, emitting such sounds as "goo-goo" and "ga-ga." The start of babbling is determined mainly by biological maturation, not reinforcement, hearing, or caregiver-infant interaction. Even deaf babies babble for a time (Lenneberg, Rebelsky, & Nichols, 1965). The purpose of the baby's earliest communication is to attract attention from parents and others in the environment. Infants engage the attention of others by making or breaking eye contact, by vocalizing sounds, or by performing manual actions such as pointing. All of these behaviors involve the aspect of language we have called pragmatics.

At approximately 6 to 9 months, infants begin to understand their first words. **Receptive vocabulary** *refers to the words an individual understands.* While infants' receptive vocabulary begins to develop in the second half of the first year, its growth increases dramatically in the second year from an average of 12 words understood at the first birthday to an estimated 300 words or more understood at the second birthday. At approximately 9 to 12 months, infants first begin to understand instructions, such as "Wave bye-bye."

Children pick up words as pigeons peas.
—**John Ray, *English Proverbs*, 1670**

So far we have not mentioned *spoken* vocabulary, which begins when the infant utters its first word, a milestone anticipated by every parent. This event usually occurs at about 10 to 15 months of age. Many parents view the onset of language development as coincident with this first word, but, as we have seen, some significant language milestones have already occurred. The infant's spoken vocabulary rapidly increases once the first word is spoken, reaching an average of 200 to 275 words by the age of 2.

A child's first words include those that name important people (*dada*), familiar animals (*kitty*), vehicles (*car*), toys (*ball*), food (*milk*), body parts (*eye*), clothes (*hat*), household items (*clock*), or greeting terms (*bye*). These were the first words of babies 50 years ago, and they are the first words of babies today. At times it is hard to tell what these one-word utterances mean. One possibility is that they stand for an entire sentence in the infant's mind. Because of the infant's limited cognitive or linguistic skills, possibly only one word comes out instead of the whole sentence. The **holophrase hypothesis** *is the hypothesis that a single word can be used to imply a complete sentence; infants' first words characteristically are holophrastic.*

By the time children are 18 to 24 months of age, they usually utter two-word statements. During this two-word stage, they quickly grasp the importance of expressing concepts and of the role that language plays in communicating with others. To convey meaning with two-word utterances, the child relies heavily on gesture, tone, and context. The wealth of meaning children can communicate with a two-word utterance includes (Slobin, 1972):

- Identification: See doggie.
- Location: Book there.
- Repetition: More milk.
- Nonexistence: Allgone thing.
- Negation: Not wolf.
- Possession: My candy.
- Attribution: Big car.
- Agent-action: Mama walk.
- Action-direct object: Hit you.
- Action-indirect object: Give papa.
- Action-instrument: Cut knife.
- Question: Where ball?

These examples are from children whose first language was English, German, Russian, Finnish, Turkish, or Samoan. Although these two-word sentences omit many parts of speech, they are remarkably succinct in conveying many messages. In fact, in every language, a child's first combinations of words have this economical quality. **Telegraphic speech** *is the use of short and precise words to communicate; young children's two- and three-word utterances characteristically are telegraphic.* When we send a telegram,

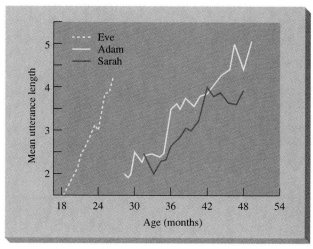

FIGURE 7.8

An Examination of MLU in Three Children
Shown here is the average length of utterances generated by three children who range in age from 1½ to just over 4 years.

we try to be short and precise, excluding any unnecessary words. As a result, articles, auxiliary verbs, and other connectives usually are omitted. Of course telegraphic speech is not limited to two-word phrases. "Mommy give ice cream" and "Mommy give Tommy ice cream" also are examples of telegraphic speech. As children leave the two-word stage, they move rather quickly into three-, four-, and five-word combinations.

In expanding this concept of classifying children's language development in terms of number of utterances, Roger Brown (1973) proposed that **mean length of utterance (MLU),** *an index of language development based on the number of morphemes per sentence a child produces in a sample of about 50 to 100 sentences,* is a good index of language maturity. Brown identified five stages based on MLU:

Stage	MLU
1	1 + 2.0
2	2.5
3	3.0
4	3.5
5	4.0

The first stage begins when a child generates sentences consisting of more than one word, such as the examples of two-word utterances mentioned earlier. The 1 + designation suggests that the average number of morphemes in each utterance is greater than one but not yet two, because some of the child's utterances are still holophrases. This stage continues until the child averages two morphemes per utterance. Subsequent stages are marked by increments of 0.5 in mean length of utterance. Figure 7.8 shows Roger Brown's examination of MLU in three children.

As we have just seen, language unfolds in a sequence. At every point in development, the child's

John W. Santrock

CONCEPT TABLE 7.2

Language Development

Concept	Processes/Related Ideas	Characteristics/Description
What Is Language?	Its nature	Language involves a system of symbols we use to communicate with each other. The system is characterized by infinite generativity and rule systems. The rule systems include phonology, morphology, syntax, semantics, and pragmatics.
Biological Influences	Strongest evidence	Children all over the world acquire language milestones at about the same time developmentally and in about the same order, despite the vast variation in input they receive.
	Biological evolution	The fact that biological evolution shaped humans into linguistic creatures is undeniable.
	Biological prewiring	Chomsky argues that humans are biologically prewired to learn language and have a language acquisition device.
	Do animals have language?	Animals clearly can communicate, and pygmy chimpanzees and sea lions can be taught to use symbols. Whether animals have all of the properties of human language is debated.
	Is there a critical period for learning language?	A critical period is a period when there is a learning readiness; beyond this period, learning is difficult or impossible. The stunted growth of "wild children" like Genie supports the notion that there is a critical period for language acquisition. However, the critical-period concept is still controversial.
Behavioral and Environmental Influences	The behavioral view	Language is just another behavior. Behaviorists believe language is learned primarily through reinforcement and limitation, although these probably play a facilitative rather than a necessary role.
	Environmental influences	Most children are bathed in language early in their development. Among the ways adults teach language to infants are motherese, recasting, echoing, expanding, and labeling. Parents should talk to infants extensively, especially about what the baby is attending to at the moment. Talk should be primarily live talk, not mechanical talk.
How Language Develops	Some developmental milestones	Among the milestones in infant language development are babbling (3 to 6 months), first words understood (6 to 9 months), the growth of receptive vocabulary (reaches 300 or more words at age 2), first instructions understood (9 months to 1 year), first word spoken (10 to 15 months), and the growth of spoken vocabulary (reaches 200 to 275 words at age 2).
	Holophrase, telegraphic speech, and mean length of utterance	The holophrase hypothesis states that a single word is often used to imply a complete sentence; it characterizes infants' first words. At 18 to 24 months of age, infants often speak in two-word utterances. Telegraphic speech is the use of short and precise words to communicate—this characterizes toddlers' two-word utterances. Brown developed the concept of mean length of utterance (MLU). Five stages of MLU have been identified, providing a valuable indicator of language maturity.

linguistic interaction with parents and others obeys certain principles. Not only is the development strongly influenced by the child's biological wiring, but the language environment the child is bathed in from an early age is far more intricate than was imagined in the past. The main ideas we have discussed about language development are summarized in concept table 7.2. In the next chapter, we will continue our discussion of infant development, turning to information about the infant's social worlds.

O ur knowledge of infant cognitive development has greatly expanded in the last two decades. We now know that infants have more sophisticated cognitive skills than we used to think.

We began this chapter with a glimpse at Piaget's observations of his own children. We studied Piaget's theory of infant development, focusing on the stage of sensorimotor development and object permanence. The new look in infant cognitive development involves an attack on Piaget's theory of sensorimotor development, evidence that infants have more advanced perceptual and conceptual development than Piaget envisioned, and the information-processing perspective. We also studied individual differences in intelligence in infancy, with special emphasis on the developmental testing of infants. Our coverage of language development focused on what language is, biological influences, behavioral and environmental influences, and how language develops.

Don't forget that you can obtain an overall summary of the chapter by again reading the two concept tables on page 198 and 205. In the next chapter, we turn our attention to the study of socioemotional development in infancy.

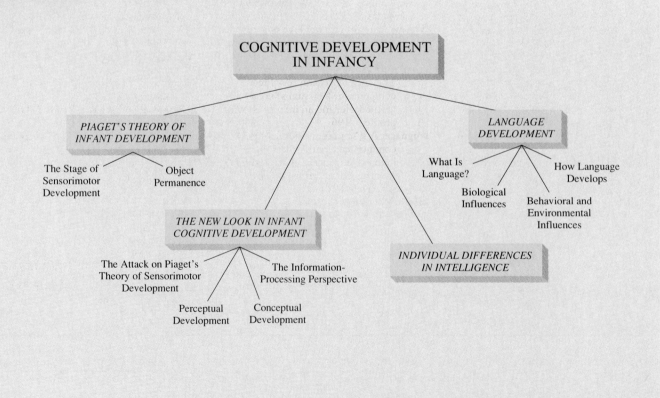

John W. Santrock

scheme (or schema) The basic unit (or units) for an organized pattern of sensorimotor functioning. 189

simple reflexes Piaget's first sensorimotor substage, which corresponds to the first month after birth. In this substage, the basic means of coordinating sensation and action is through reflexive behaviors, such as rooting and sucking, which the infant has at birth. 190

first habits and primary circular reactions Piaget's second sensorimotor substage, which develops between 1 and 4 months of age. In this substage, the infant learns to coordinate sensation and types of schemes or structures—that is, habits and primary circular reactions. 190

primary circulation reaction A scheme based upon the infant's attempt to reproduce an interesting or pleasurable event that initially occurred by chance. 190

secondary circular reactions Piaget's third sensorimotor substage, which develops between 4 and 8 months of age. In this substage, the infant becomes more object-oriented or focused on the world, moving beyond preoccupation with the self in sensorimotor interactions. 190

coordination of secondary circular reactions Piaget's fourth sensorimotor substage, which develops between 8 and 12 months of age. In this substage, several significant changes take place involving the coordination of schemes and intentionality. 190

tertiary circular reactions, novelty, and curiosity Piaget's fifth sensorimotor substage, which develops between 12 and 18 months of age. In this substage, infants become intrigued by the variety of properties that objects possess and by the multiplicity of things they can make happen to objects. 190

internalization of schemes Piaget's sixth and final sensorimotor substage, which develops between 18 and 24 months of age. In this substage, the infant's mental functioning shifts from a purely sensorimotor plane to a symbolic plane, and the infant develops the ability to use primitive symbols. 190

object permanence The Piagetian term for one of an infant's most important accomplishments: understanding that objects and events continue to exist even when they cannot directly be seen, heard, or touched. 190

habituation Repeated presentation of the same stimulus that causes reduced attention to the stimulus. 193

dishabituation An infant's renewed interest in a stimulus. 193

memory A central feature of cognitive development, pertaining to all situations in which an individual retains information over time. 194

deferred imitation Imitation that occurs after a time delay of hours or days. 195

developmental quotient (DQ) An overall developmental score that combines subscores in motor, language, adaptive, and personal-social domains in the Gesell assessment of infants. 195

Bayley Scales of Infant Development Scales developed by Nancy Bayley that are widely used in the assessment of infant development. The current version has three components: a mental scale, a motor scale, and an infant behavior profile. 196

language A system of symbols used to communicate with others. In humans language is characterized by infinite generativity and rule systems. 197

infinite generativity An individual's ability to generate an infinite number of meaningful sentences using a finite set of words and rules, which makes language a highly creative enterprise. 197

phonology The study of a language's sound system. 197

morphology The study of the rules for combining morphemes; morphemes are the smallest meaningful units of language. 199

syntax The ways words are combined to form acceptable phrases and sentences. 199

semantics The meanings of words and sentences. 199

pragmatics The use of appropriate conversation, and knowledge underlying the use of language in context. 199

language acquisition device (LAD) A biological endowment that enables the child to detect certain language categories, such as phonology, syntax, and semantics. 200

critical period A period in which there is a learning readiness; beyond this period, learning is difficult or impossible. 201

motherese The kind of speech often used by mothers and other adults to talk to babies—in a higher pitch than normal and with simple words and sentences. 202

recasting Rephrasing something a child has said, perhaps turning it into a question. 202

echoing Repeating what a child says, especially if it is an incomplete phrase or sentence. 202

expanding Restating, in a linguistically sophisticated form, what a child has said. 202

labeling Identifying the names of objects. 202

receptive vocabulary The words an individual understands. 203

holophrase hypothesis The hypothesis that a single word can be used to imply a complete sentence; infants' first words characteristically are holophrastic. 204

telegraphic speech The use of short and precise words to communicate; young children's two- and three-word utterances characteristically are telegraphic. 204

mean length of utterance (MLU) An index of language development based on the number of morphemes per sentence a child produces in a sample of about 50 to 100 sentences; a good index of language maturity. 204

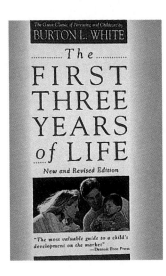

The First Three Years of Life
(1990, rev. ed.) by Burton White.
New York: Prentice-Hall.

The First Three Years of Life presents a broad-based approach to how parents can optimally rear their infants and young children. White strongly believes that most parents in America fail to provide an adequate intellectual and social foundation for their child's development, especially between the ages of 8 months and 3 years of age. White provides in-depth portrayals of motor, sensory, emotional, sociability, and language milestones at different points in the first 3 years of life. He gives specific recommendations for how parents should interact with their children, as well as criticisms of inappropriate strategies.

White's book is controversial. Some educational, parenting, and child clinical experts praise the book. Others fault White for his rigid emphasis on critical periods and time frames for certain learning to occur, for failing to capture at least some variability in recommended parenting practices, and for recommending that mothers should spend most of their waking hours in the infant's and child's life, stimulating and monitoring the infant's and child's learning and development.

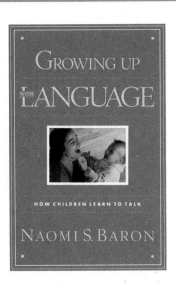

Growing Up With Language
(1992) by Naomi Baron.
Reading, MA: Addison-Wesley.

Dr. Naomi Baron is a professor of linguistics at American University in Washington, D.C. In this book, she presents an excellent portrayal of the appropriate role of parents in children's language development. Baron focuses on three representative children and their families, exploring how children put their first words together, how they struggle to understand meaning, and how they come to use language as a creative tool. She shows parents how their own attitudes about language are extremely important in the child's language development. Baron especially advocates that parents need to instill an enduring love of language in children by asking them interactive questions, using humor in conversation and other aspects of language through the use of books, computers, and even television. Concerns about gender differences, birth order, raising bilingual children, and adults' use of baby talk are evaluated. Katherine Nelson, an expert in language development, commented that Baron's book provides an insightful analysis of how children become skilled language users.

IMPROVING THE LIVES OF CHILDREN

Improving the lives of children involves reducing malnutrition in infancy to elevate intelligence, parents' facilitating their child's language development, developing a day-care curriculum based on Piaget's theory of infant development, providing more family and community supports in low-income inner-city areas, and discouraging negative expectations for infants based on their sex.

HEALTH AND WELL-BEING

Malnutrition in Infancy and Children's Intelligence

In this chapter we explored the nature of infant cognitive development. Might there be some aspects of infants' health and well-being that undermine optimal cognitive growth and development? Nutritional intake, prenatal and postnatal factors, infections, accidents, and other assorted trauma can influence the infant's and child's intelligence. Recognizing that nutrition is important for the child's growth and development, the government provides money for school lunch programs. When we think about how nutrition affects development, we usually think of physical development, such as skeletal growth, body shape, and susceptibility to disease. What we often fail to recognize is that nutrition can also affect cognitive and social development. In recent years, developmentalists have shown a special concern about malnutrition in infancy and how it can restrict the child's cognitive development.

In one study, two groups of extremely malnourished 1-year-old South African infants were studied (Bayley, 1970). The children in one group were given adequate nourishment during the next 6 years; no intervention took place in the lives of the other group of children. After the seventh year, the poorly nourished group of children performed much worse on tests of intelligence than did the adequately nourished group.

In another study, George Gutherie and his coworkers (Gutherie, Masangkay, & Gutherie, 1976) evaluated a group of severely underweight, malnourished infants in a rural area of the Philippines. They found that a combination of malnutrition, infection, and inadequate social stimulation from caregivers was associated with very low scores on the Bayley Scales of Mental Development.

In the most recent research on early supplementary feeding and children's cognitive development, Ernesto Pollitt and his colleagues (1993) conducted a longitudinal investigation over two decades in rural Guatemala. They found that early nutritional supplements in the form of protein and increased calories can have positive long-term consequences for cognitive development. The researchers also found that the relation of nutrition to cognitive performance was moderated both by the time period during which the supplement was given and by the sociodemographic context. For example, children in the lowest socioeconomic groups benefited more than did children in the higher socioeconomic groups. And, although there still was a positive nutritional influence when supplementation began after 2 years of age, the effect on cognitive development was less powerful.

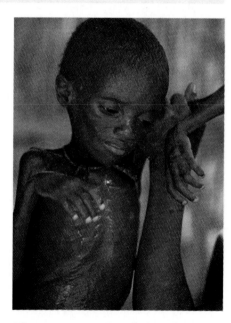

The recent crisis in Somalia brought to light how extensive malnutrition is in some developing countries. Both moderate and severe malnutrition in infancy can have detrimental effects not only on children's physical growth and development but also on their cognitive and social growth and development.

In sum, good nutrition in infancy is important not only for the child's physical growth and development, but for cognitive development as well.

How Parents Can Facilitate Their Children's Language Development

In Growing Up With Language, linguist Naomi Baron (1992) provides a number of helpful ideas about ways that parents can facilitate their child's language development. A summary of her ideas follows:

Infants

- *Be an active conversational partner.* Initiate conversation with the infant. If the infant is in a daylong child-care program, ensure that the baby gets adequate language stimulation from adults.

- *Talk as if the infant understands what you are saying.* Parents can generate self-fulfilling prophecies by addressing their young children as if they understand what is being said. The process may take 4 to 5 years, but children gradually rise to match the language model presented to them.

- *Use a language style with which you feel comfortable.* Don't worry about how you sound to other adults when you talk with your child. Your effect, not your content, is more important when talking with an infant. Use whatever type of baby talk you feel comfortable with.

Toddlers

- *Continue to be an active conversational partner.* Engaging toddlers in conversation, even one-sided conversation, is the most important thing a parent can do to nourish a child linguistically.

- *Remember to listen.* Since toddlers' speech is often slow and laborious, parents are often tempted to supply words and thoughts for them. Be patient and let toddlers express themselves, no matter how painstaking the process is or how great a hurry you are in.

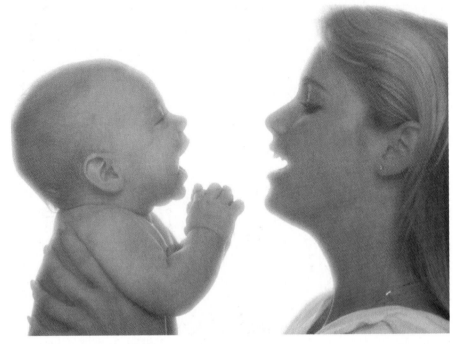

It is unquestionably a good idea for parents to begin talking to their babies right at the start. The best language teaching occurs when the talking is begun before the infant becomes capable of its first intelligible speech.

- *Use a language style with which you are comfortable, but consider ways of expanding your child's language abilities and horizons.* For example, using long sentences need not be problematic; don't be afraid to use ungrammatical language to imitate the toddlers' novel forms (such as "No eat"); use rhymes; ask questions that encourage answers other than "Yes"; actively repeat, expand, and recast the child's utterances; introduce new topics; and use humor in your conversation.

- *Adjust to your child's idiosyncrasies instead of working against them.* Many toddlers have difficulty pronouncing words and making themselves understood. Whenever possible, make toddlers feel that they are being understood.

- *Avoid sexual stereotypes.* Don't let the toddler's sex unwittingly determine your amount or style of conversation. Many American mothers are more linguistically supportive of girls than of boys, and many fathers talk less with their children than mothers do. Active and cognitively enriching initiatives from both mothers and fathers benefit both boys and girls.

- *Resist making normative comparisons.* Be aware of the ages at which your child reaches specific milestones (first word, first fifty words, first grammatical combination), but be careful not to measure this development rigidly against children of neighbors or friends. Such social comparisons can bring about unnecessary anxiety.

EDUCATION

Suggestions for a Day-Care Curriculum Based on Piaget's Theory

As more infants spend much of their day in day-care centers, it is important for the caregivers to interact in effective ways with the infants and for the day-care center to develop a curriculum that is appropriate for infant cognitive development. Following is a developmentally appropriate curriculum for infant cognitive development that was proposed by educator and developmentalist LaVisa Wilson (1990):

Piagetian Substage	Materials	Examples of Caregiver Strategies
Substage 1: Simple reflexes (birth–1 month)	Visually attractive crib and walls next to crib, objects near crib; occasional music, singing, talking, chimes	Provide nonrestrictive clothes, uncluttered crib, to allow freedom of movement; provide environment that commands attention during the infant's periods of alertness.
Substage 2: First habits and primary circular reactions (1–4 months)	Face and voice, musical toys, musical mobile, rattle; objects infant can grasp and are safe to go in the infant's mouth; objects the infant can grasp and lift	Provide change in infant's environment; carry infant around, hold infant, place infant in crib; observe, discuss, record changes in the infant; turn on musical toys and place where the infant can see them; place objects in the infant's hands or within the infant's reach; provide clothes that allow freedom of movement; provide time and space for repetition of behaviors.
Substage 3: Secondary circular reactions (4–8 months)	Objects that attract attention (of contrasting colors, that change in sounds, have a variety of textures or designs); toys; balls	Watch movements the infant repeats, as when a waving arm hits the crib gym and then this action is repeated; provide materials that facilitate such repetitions (new items on the crib gym, for example); place blocks, dolls, ball, and other toys near the infant so they can be reached; initiate action, wait for the infant to imitate it, then repeat the action (smile, open mouth, for example).
Substage 4: Coordination of secondary circular reactions (8–12 months)	Toys, visually attractive objects	Place objects near the infant; play hide-the-doll-under-the-blanket; place the block behind you; verbalize your own actions, such as "I put the ball behind me"; introduce new copy games; allow time and space for the infant to play.
Substage 5: Tertiary circular reactions, novelty, and curiosity (12–18 months)	Blanket, paper, toys, dolls, spoon, interesting objects; water toys, water basin; narrow-neck milk carton and different sizes and shapes of objects	Play game of hide-the-object with infant—hide the object while the infant watches, let infant watch you move the object to a different place under the blanket, and ask, "Where is it?" "Can you find it?"; observe and allow infant to find the object, praise infant for good watching and thinking; allow infant to play with water and toys to discover different actions of water and of the objects in the water; provide time and materials that stimulate infant to think and try out new ideas; ask questions but do not tell answers or show infant; encourage infant to pretend—to drink from a pretend bottle like baby Gwen, to march like Pearl, to pick up toys; allow infant to repeat own play and develop own preferences.
Substage 6: Internalization of schemes (18–24 months)		Allow toddler time to figure out solutions; allow toddler time to think and search for objects; observe toddler's representations and identify the ideas that seem important to the toddler; allow the toddler to act out conflict in play with toys and materials; observe toddler's play and identify consistent themes; provide clothes and materials that help the toddler pretend to be someone else.

CULTURE AND ETHNICITY

Lack of Family and Community Supports in Low-Income, Inner-City Areas

The structure of low-income families, many of which are single-parent families, often provides little verbal stimulation for children. One mother in such a family agreed to let language researcher Shirley Heath tape-record her interactions with her children over a 2-year period and to write notes about her activities with them. In the interactions recorded in 500 hours of tape and more than a thousand lines of notes, the mother initiated talk with her three preschool children on only eighteen occasions (other than giving them a brief directive or asking a quick question). Few of the mother's conversations involved either planning or executing actions with or for her children.

Heath (1989) points out that the lack of family and community supports is widespread in urban housing projects, especially among African Americans. The deteriorating, impoverished conditions of these inner-city areas severely impede the ability of young children to develop the cognitive and social skills they need to function competently.

Children who grow up in low-income, poverty-ridden neighborhoods of large cities often experience a lack of family and community support, which can seriously undermine the development of their language skills.

John W. Santrock

Infant Girls and Boys—Responses to Them and Expectations for Them

Once the label *girl* or *boy* is assigned by the obstetrician, virtually everyone from parents to siblings to strangers begins treating the infant differently (Matlin, 1993). Look at the photograph of the baby in figure 7.9. Imagine that it is a girl. What characteristics would you attribute to the baby since it is a girl? What expectations might you have for her? Now replace the image of the baby as a girl with an image of the baby as a boy. What characteristics do you attribute to the baby boy? What expectations do you have for him? Probably very different ones. Possibly you said that the baby girl is soft, nice, and very cuddly, and that the baby boy is strong, solid, and will be adventuresome.

In one study, an infant girl, Avery, was dressed in a neutral outfit of overalls and a T-shirt (Brooks-Gunn & Matthews, 1979). People responded to her differently if they thought she was a girl rather than a boy. People who thought she was a girl made such comments as "Isn't she cute. What a sweet little, innocent thing." By contrast, people who thought the baby was a boy made remarks like "I bet he is a tough little customer. He will be running around all over the place and causing trouble in no time."

In general, parents even hope that their offspring will be a boy. In one study, 90 percent of the men and 92 percent of the women wanted their first child to be a boy (Peterson & Peterson, 1973). In a more recent study, parents still preferred a boy as the firstborn child—75 percent of the men and 79 percent of the women (Hamilton, 1991).

FIGURE 7.9

Gender Expectations
Would you respond differently to this baby depending on whether it is a boy or a girl? If so, how?

In some countries, a male child is so preferred over a female child that many mothers will abort a female offspring once its sex is learned through fetal testing procedures such as amniocentesis and a sonogram. For example, in South Korea, where fetal testing to determine sex is common, male births exceed female births by 14 percent, in contrast with a worldwide average of 5 percent. To help counteract this trend, in 1990 Asian nations designated that year as the Year of the Girl Child.

PICASSO
Mother and Child on Beach,
detail

Socioemotional Development
in Infancy

> *We never know the love of our parents
> until we have become parents.*
>
> —Henry Ward Beecher, 1887

IMAGES OF CHILDREN

The Newborn Opossum, Wildebeest, and Human

The newborns of some species function independently in the world; other species are not so independent. At birth, the opossum is still considered fetal and is capable of finding its way around only in its mother's pouch, where it attaches itself to her nipple and continues to develop. This protective environment is similar to the uterus. By contrast, the newborn wildebeest must run with the herd moments after birth. The behavior often is far more adult than the opossum's, although the wildebeest does have to obtain food through suckling. The maturation of the human infant lies somewhere between these two extremes; much learning and development must take place before the infant can sustain itself (Maccoby, 1980).

Variations in the dependency of newborns of different species. (a) The newborn opossum is fetal, capable of finding its way around only in its mother's pouch, where it attaches itself to her nipple and continues to develop. (b) By contrast, the wildebeest runs with the herd moments after birth. (c) The human newborn's maturation lies somewhere in between that of the opossum and that of the wildebeest.

John W. Santrock

Because it cannot sustain itself, the human infant requires extensive care. What kind of care is needed and how does the infant start down the road to social maturity? Much of the interest in infant care focuses on attachment and parent-infant interaction, although the roles of day care and temperament in infant development are also important considerations. Among the other topics we will address are emotional development, personality development, adapting caregiving to the developmental status of the infant and toddler, and problems and disorders, but to begin we explore some basic aspects of family processes.

FAMILY PROCESSES

Most of us began our lives in families and spent thousands of hours during our childhood interacting with our parents. Some of you are already parents; others of you may become parents. What is the transition to parenthood like? What is the parental role? What is the nature of family processes? What is the family life cycle?

The Transition to Parenthood

When people become parents through pregnancy, adoption, or stepparenting, they face disequilibrium and must adapt. Parents want to develop a strong attachment with their infant, but they still want to maintain strong attachments to their spouse and friends, and possibly continue their careers. Parents ask themselves how this new being will change their lives. A baby places new restrictions on partners; no longer will they be able to rush out to a movie on a moment's notice, and money may not be readily available for vacations and other luxuries. Dual-career parents ask, "Will it harm the baby to place her in day care? Will we be able to find responsible babysitters?"

The excitement and joy that accompany the birth of a healthy baby are often followed by "postpartum blues" in mothers—a depressed state that lasts as long as nine months into the infant's first year (Osofsky, 1989). The early months of the baby's physical demands may bring not only the joy of intimacy but also the sorrow of exhaustion. Pregnancy and childbirth are demanding physical events that require recovery time for the mother.

Many fathers are not sensitive to these extreme demands placed on the mother. Busy trying to make enough money to pay the bills, fathers may not be at home much of the time. A father's ability to sense and adapt to the stress placed on his wife during the first year of the infant's life has important implications for the success of the marriage and the family. In sum, becoming a father is both wonderful *and* stressful.

In a longitudinal investigation of couples from late pregnancy until 3½ years after the baby was born, Carolyn Cowan and her colleagues (1995) found that the couples enjoyed more positive marital relations before the baby was born than after. Still, almost one-third showed an increase in marital satisfaction. Some couples said that the baby had both brought them closer together *and* moved them farther apart. They commented that being parents enhanced their sense of themselves and gave them a new, more stable identity as a couple. Babies opened men up to a concern with intimate relationships, and the demands of juggling work and family roles stimulated women to manage family tasks more efficiently and pay attention to their personal growth.

At some point during the early years of the child's life, parents do face the difficult task of juggling their roles as parents and as self-actualizing adults. Until recently in our culture, nurturing our children and having a career were thought to be incompatible. Fortunately, we have come to recognize that the balance between caring and achieving, nurturing and working—although difficult to manage—can be accomplished.

The Parental Role

In chapter 1, we described the nature of the parental role. We concluded that for many adults, the parental role is well planned and coordinated with other roles in life and is developed with the individual's economic situation in mind. For others, the discovery that they are about to become parents is a startling surprise. In either event, the prospective parents may have mixed emotions and romantic illusions about having a child. Parenting consists of a number of interpersonal skills and emotional demands, yet there is little in the way of formal education for this task. Most parents learn parenting practices from their own parents, and husbands and wives may bring different viewpoints of parenting practices to the marriage.

The needs and expectations of parents have stimulated many myths about parenting:

- The birth of a child will save a failing marriage.
- As a possession or extension of the parent, the child will think, feel, and behave like the parents did in their childhood.
- Children will take care of parents in old age.
- Parents can expect respect and get obedience from their children.

- Having a child means that the parents will always have someone who loves them and is their best friend.
- Having a child gives the parents a "second chance" to achieve what they should have achieved.
- If parents learn the right techniques, they can mold their children into what they want.
- It's the parents fault when children fail.
- Mothers are naturally better parents than fathers.
- Parenting is an instinct and requires no training.

For years we have given scientific attention to the care and rearing of plants and animals, but we have allowed babies to be raised chiefly by tradition.

—**Edith Belle Lowry, *False Modesty*, 1912**

Reciprocal Socialization

For many years, socialization between parents and children was viewed as a one-way process: Children were considered to be the products of their parents' socialization techniques. Today, however, we view parent-child interaction as reciprocal (Schaffer, 1996). **Reciprocal socialization** *is socialization that is bidirectional; children socialize parents just as parents socialize children.* For example, the interaction of mothers and their infants is symbolized as a dance or a dialogue in which successive actions of the partners are closely coordinated. This coordinated dance or dialogue can assume the form of mutual synchrony (each person's behavior depends on the partner's previous behavior). Or, it can be reciprocal in a more precise sense; the actions of the partners can be matched, as when one partner imitates the other or when there is mutual smiling.

When reciprocal socialization has been investigated in infancy, mutual gaze or eye contact plays an important role in early social interaction. In one investigation, the mother and infant engaged in a variety of behaviors while they looked at each other; by contrast, when they looked away from each other, the rate of such behaviors dropped considerably (Stern & others, 1977). In sum, the behaviors of mothers and infants involve substantial interconnection, mutual regulation, and synchronization.

Scaffolding *refers to parental behavior that serves to support children's efforts, allowing them to be more skillful than they would be if they relied only on their own abilities.* Caregivers provide a positive, reciprocal framework in which they and their children interact. Parent's efforts to time interactions in such a way that the infant experiences turn-taking with the parent illustrates an early parental scaffolding behavior. For example, in the game peek-a-boo, mothers initially cover their babies, then remove the covering, and finally register "surprise" at the reappearance. As infants become more skilled at peek-a-boo, pat-a-cake, and so big there are other caregiver games that exemplify scaffolding and turn-taking sequences. In one study, infants

FIGURE 8.1

Interaction Between Children and Their Parents: Direct and Indirect Effects

who had more extensive scaffolding experiences with their parents, especially in the form of turn-taking, were more likely to engage in turn-taking when they interacted with their peers (Vandell & Wilson, 1988). Scaffolding is not just confined to parent-infant interaction but can be used by parents to support children's achievement-related efforts in school by adjusting and modifying the amount and type of support that best suits the child's level of development.

The Family as a System

As a social system, the family can be thought of as a constellation of subsystems defined in terms of generation, gender, and role (Davis, 1996). Divisions of labor among family members define particular subunits, and attachments define others. Each family member is a participant in several subsystems—some dyadic (involving two people), some polyadic (involving more than two people). The father and child represent one dyadic subsystem, the mother and father another; the mother-father-child represent one polyadic subsystem, the mother and two siblings another.

An organizational scheme that highlights the reciprocal influences of family members and family subsystems is shown in figure 8.1 (Belsky, 1981). As the arrows in the figure show, marital relations, parenting, and infant behavior

John W. Santrock

can have both direct and indirect effects on each other. An example of a direct effect is the influence of the parents' behavior on the child; an example of an indirect effect is how the relationship between the spouses mediates the way a parent acts toward the child. For example, marital conflict might reduce the efficiency of parenting, in which case marital conflict would be an indirect effect on the child's behavior.

The Family Life Cycle

As we go through life, we are at different points in the family life cycle. The stages of the family cycle include leaving home and becoming a single adult; the joining of couples through marriage—the new couple; becoming parents and families with children; families with adolescents; families at midlife; and the family in later life. A summary of these stages in the family life cycle is shown in figure 8.2, along with key aspects of emotional processes involved in the transition from one stage to the next, and changes in family status required for developmental change to take place (Carter & McGoldrick, 1989).

Leaving Home and Becoming a Single Adult

Leaving home and becoming a single adult *is the first stage in the family life cycle and it involves launching, the process in which the youth moves into adulthood and exits his or her family of origin.* Adequate completion of launching requires that the young adult separate from the family of origin without cutting off ties completely or fleeing in a reactive way to find some form of substitute emotional refuge. The launching period is a time for the youth and young adult to formulate personal life goals, to develop an identity, and to become more independent before joining with another person to form a new family. This is a time for young people to sort out emotionally what they will take along from the family of origin, what they will leave behind, and what they will create themselves.

Complete cutoffs from parents rarely or never resolve emotional problems. The shift to adult-to-adult status between parents and children requires a mutually respectful and personal form of relating, in which young adults can appreciate parents as they are, needing neither to make them into what they are not nor to blame them for what they could not be. Neither do young adults need to comply with parental expectations and wishes at their own expense.

The Joining of Families Through Marriage: The New Couple

The **new couple** *is the second stage in the family life cycle, in which two individuals from separate families of origin unite to form a new family system.* This stage not only involves the development of a new marital system, but also a realignment with extended families and friends to include the spouse. Women's changing roles, the increasingly frequent marriage of partners from divergent cultural backgrounds, and the increasing physical distances between family members are placing a much stronger burden on couples to define their relationship for themselves than was true in the past. Marriage is usually described as the union of two individuals, but in reality it is the union of two entire family systems and the development of a new, third system. Some experts on marriage and the family believe that marriage represents such a different phenomenon for women and men that we need to speak of "her" marriage and "his" marriage (Bernard, 1972). In the American society, women have anticipated marriage with greater enthusiasm and more positive expectations than men have, although statistically it has not been a very healthy system for women.

Becoming Parents and Families with Children

Becoming parents and families with children *is the third stage in the family life cycle. Entering this stage requires that adults now move up a generation and become caregivers to the younger generation.* Moving through the lengthy stage successfully requires a commitment of time as a parent, understanding the role of parents, and adapting to developmental changes in children. Problems that emerge when a couple first assumes the parental role are struggles with each other about taking responsibility, as well as refusal or inability to function as competent parents to children.

> *I looked on childrearing not only as a work of love and duty but as a profession that was fully as interesting and challenging as any honorable profession in the world and one that demanded the best that I could bring to it.*
> —**Rose Kennedy**

The Family with Adolescents

The **family with adolescents** *represents the fourth stage of the family life cycle. Adolescence is a period of development in which individuals push for autonomy and seek to develop their own identity.* The development of mature autonomy and identity is a lengthy process, transpiring over at least 10 to 15 years. Compliant children become noncompliant adolescents. Parents tend to adopt one of two strategies to handle noncompliance—clamp down and put more pressure on the adolescent to conform to parental values or become more permissive and let the adolescent have extensive freedom. Neither is a wise overall strategy; rather, a more flexible, adaptive approach is best.

> *The generations of living things pass in a short time, and like runners hand on the torch of life.*
> —**Lucretius, 1st Century B.C.**

Midlife Families

Family at midlife *is the fifth stage in the family cycle. It is a time of launching children, playing an important role in linking*

Family Life Cycle Stage	Emotional Process of Transition: Key Principles	Changes in Family Status Required to Proceed Developmentally
1. Leaving home: Single young adults	Accepting emotional and financial responsibility for self	a. Differentiation of self in relation to family of origin b. Development of intimate peer relationships c. Establishment of self in relation to work and financial independence
2. The joining of families through marriage: The new couple	Commitment to new system	a. Formation of marital system b. Realignment of relationships with extended families and friends to include spouse
3. Becoming parents and families with children	Accepting new members into the system	a. Adjusting marital system to make space for child(ren) b. Joining in childrearing, financial, and household tasks c. Realignment of relationships with extended family to include parenting and grandparenting roles
4. Families with adolescents	Increasing flexibility of family boundaries to include children's independence and grandparents' frailties	a. Shifting of parent-child relationships to permit adolescent to move in and out of system b. Refocus on mid-life marital and career issues c. Beginning shift toward joint caring for older generation
5. Mid-life families	Accepting a multitude of exits from and entries into the family system	a. Renegotiation of marital system as a dyad b. Development of adult to adult relationships between grown children and their parents c. Realignment of relationships to include in-laws and grandchildren d. Dealing with disabilities and death of parents (grandparents)
6. Families in later life	Accepting the shifting of generational roles	a. Maintaining own and/or couple functioning and interests in face of physiological decline; exploration of new familial and social role options b. Support for a more central role of middle generation c. Dealing with loss of spouse, siblings, and other peers and preparation for own death. Life review and integration

FIGURE 8.2

The Stages of the Family Life Cycle

From B. Carter and M. McGoldrick, *The Changing Family Life Cycle: A Framework for Family Therapy.* Coyright © 1989 by Allyn and Bacon. Reprinted by permission.

John W. Santrock

generations, and adapting to midlife changes in development. Several generations ago, most families were involved in raising their children for much of their adult lives until old age. Because of the lower birth rate and longer life of most adults, parents now launch their children much earlier, which frees many midlife parents to pursue other activities.

For the most part, family members maintain considerable contact across generations. Parent-child similarity is most noticeable in religious and political areas, least in gender roles, lifestyle, and work orientation. Intergenerational relationships also differ by gender. In one study, mothers and their daughters had much closer relationships during their adult years than mothers and sons, fathers and daughters, and fathers and sons (Rossi, 1989). Also, in this same investigation, married men were more involved with their wives' kin than with their own. These findings underscore the significance of the woman's role in monitoring access to and feelings toward kin.

The Family in Later Life

The **family in later life** *is the sixth and final stage in the family life cycle. Retirement alters a couple's lifestyle, requiring adaptation. Grandparenting also characterizes many families in later life.* The greatest changes occur in the traditional family, in which the husband works and the wife is a homemaker. The husband may not know what to do with his time, and the wife may feel uneasy having him around the house all of the time. In traditional families, both partners may need to move toward more expressive roles. The husband must adjust from being the good provider to being a helper around the house; the wife must change from being only a good homemaker to being even more loving and understanding. Marital happiness as an older adult is also affected by each partner's ability to deal with personal conflicts, including aging, illness, and eventual death.

> *Grow old with me!*
> *The best is yet to be,*
> *The last of life,*
> *For which the first was made.*
>
> **—Browning**

About three of every four adults over the age of 65 has at least one living grandchild, and most grandparents have some regular contact with their grandchildren. About 80 percent of grandparents say they are happy in their relationships with their grandchildren, and a majority of grandparents say that grandparenting is easier than parenthood and enjoy it more than parenthood (Brubaker, 1985).

ATTACHMENT, FATHERS, AND DAY CARE

A small curly-haired girl named Danielle, age 11 months, begins to whimper. After a few seconds, she begins to wail.

The psychologist observing Danielle is conducting a research study on the nature of attachment between infants and their mothers. Subsequently, the mother reenters the room, and Danielle's crying ceases. Quickly, Danielle crawls over to where her mother is seated and reaches out to be held. This scenario is one of the main ways that psychologists study the nature of attachment during infancy.

Attachment

What exactly is attachment? What individual differences occur in attachment? How is attachment measured? How has the attachment concept been criticized? We will explore each of these questions in turn.

What Is Attachment?

In everyday language, *attachment* refers to a relationship between two individuals who feel strongly about each other and do a number of things to continue the relationship. Many pairs of people are attached: relatives, lovers, a teacher and a student. In the language of developmental psychology, though, attachment is often restricted to a relationship between particular social figures and a particular phenomenon that is thought to reflect unique characteristics of the relationship. In this case, the developmental period is infancy, the social figures are the infant and one or more adult caregivers, and the phenomenon is a bond (Bowlby, 1969, 1989). To summarize, **attachment** *is a close emotional bond between the infant and the caregiver.*

There is no shortage of theories about infant attachment. Freud believed that infants become attached to the person or object that provides oral satisfaction; for most infants, this is the mother, since she is most likely to feed the infant.

Is feeding as important as Freud thought? A classic study by Harry Harlow and Robert Zimmerman (1959) reveals that the answer is no. These researchers evaluated whether feeding or contact comfort was more important to infant attachment. Infant monkeys were removed from their mothers at birth and reared for 6 months by surrogate (substitute) "mothers." As shown in figure 8.3, one of the mothers was made of wire, the other of cloth. Half of the infant monkeys were fed by the wire mother, half by the cloth mother. Periodically, the amount of time the infant monkeys spent with either the wire or the cloth monkey was computed. Regardless of whether they were fed by the wire or the cloth mother, the infant monkeys spent far more time with the cloth mother. This study clearly demonstrated that feeding is not the crucial element in the attachment process and that contact comfort is important.

Most toddlers develop a strong attachment to a favorite soft toy or a particular blanket. Toddlers may carry the toy or blanket with them everywhere they go, just as Linus does in the "Peanuts" cartoon strip, or they may run for the toy or blanket only in moments of crisis, such as after an argument or a fall. By the time they have outgrown the security object, all that may be left is a small fragment

FIGURE 8.3

Harlow's Classic "Contact Comfort" Study
Regardless of whether they were fed by a wire mother or by a cloth mother, the infant monkeys overwhelmingly preferred to be in contact with the cloth mother, demonstrating the importance of contact comfort in attachment.

of the blanket, or an animal that is hardly recognizable, having had a couple of new faces and all its seams resewn half a dozen times. If parents try to replace the security object with something newer, the toddler will resist. There is nothing abnormal about a toddler carrying around a security blanket. Children know that the blanket or teddy bear is not their mother, and yet they react affectively to these objects and derive comfort from them as if they were their mother. Eventually, they abandon the security object as they grow up and become more sure of themselves.

Might familiarity breed attachment? The famous study by ethologist Konrad Lorenz (1965) reveals that the answer is yes. Remember from our description of this study in chapter 2 that newborn goslings became attached to "father" Lorenz rather than to their mother because he was the first moving object they saw. The time period during which familiarity is important for goslings is the first 36 hours after birth; for human beings, it is more on the order of the first year of life.

Erik Erikson (1968) believes that the first year of life is the key time frame for the development of attachment. Recall his proposal—also discussed in chapter 2—that the first year of life represents the stage of trust versus mistrust.

Attachment theorists argue that early experiences play an important role in a child's later social development. For example, Bowlby and Ainsworth argue that secure attachment to the caregiver in infancy is related to the development of social competence during the childhood years.

A sense of trust requires a feeling of physical comfort and a minimal amount of fear and apprehension about the future. Trust in infancy sets the stage for a lifelong expectation that the world will be a good and pleasant place to be. Erikson also believes that responsive, sensitive parenting contributes to an infant's sense of trust.

> *I am what I hope and give.*
>
> **—Erik Erikson**

The ethological perspective of British psychiatrist John Bowlby (1969, 1989) also stresses the importance of attachment in the first year of life and the responsiveness of the caregiver. Bowlby believes that an infant and its mother instinctively form an attachment. He argues that the newborn is biologically equipped to elicit the mother's attachment behavior. The baby cries, clings, coos, and smiles. Later, the infant crawls, walks, and follows the mother. The infant's goal is to keep the mother nearby. Research on attachment supports Bowlby's view that, at about 6 to 7 months of age, the infant's attachment to the caregiver intensifies (Sroufe, 1985).

Individual Differences

Although attachment to a caregiver intensifies midway through the first year, isn't it likely that some babies have a more positive attachment experience than others? Mary Ainsworth (1979) thinks so and says that, in **secure attachment,** *infants use the caregiver, usually the mother, as a secure base from which to explore the environment. Ainsworth believes that secure attachment in the first year of life provides an important foundation for psychological development later in life.* The caregiver's sensitivity to the infant's signals increases secure attachment (Coffman, Levitt, & Guacci-Franco, 1996).

The securely attached infant moves freely away from the mother but processes her location through periodic glances. The securely attached infant responds positively to being picked up by others and, when put back down, freely moves away to play. An insecurely attached infant, by contrast, avoids the mother or is ambivalent toward her, fears strangers, and is upset by minor, everyday separations.

> A child forsaken, waking suddenly,
> Whose gaze affeared on all things round doth rove,
> And seeth only that it cannot see
> The meeting eyes of love.
>
> —George Eliot

Ainsworth believes that insecurely attached infants can be classified as either anxious-avoidant or anxious-resistant, making three main attachment categories: secure (type B), anxious-avoidant (type A), and anxious-resistant (type C). **Type B babies** *use the caregiver as a secure base from which to explore the environment.* **Type A babies** *exhibit insecurity by avoiding the mother (for example, ignoring her, averting their gaze, and failing to seek proximity).* **Type C babies** *exhibit insecurity by resisting the mother (for example, clinging to her but at the same time fighting against the closeness, perhaps by kicking and pushing away).*

The mothers of Type A babies are insensitive to their infant's signals, rarely have close body contact with the infant, and, rather than being affectionate, interact with the infant in an angry and irritable manner. The mothers of Type C babies are insensitive and awkward in their interaction with their infants, and they are low in affection but not as rejecting as the Type A "avoidant" mothers.

If early attachment to a caregiver is important, it should relate to a child's social behavior later in development (Bretherton, 1996; Teti & Teti, 1996). Research by Alan Sroufe (1985) documents this connection. In one study, infants who were securely attached to their mothers early in infancy were less frustrated and happier at 2 years of age than were insecurely attached infants (Matas, Arend, & Sroufe, 1978). In another study, securely attached infants were more socially competent and had better grades in the third grade (Egeland, 1989). Linkages between secure attachment and many other aspects of children's competence have been found (Waters & others, 1995).

Attachment, Temperament, and the Wider Social World

Not all developmentalists believe that a secure attachment in infancy is the only path to competence in life. Indeed, some developmentalists believe that too much emphasis is placed on the importance of the attachment bond in infancy. Jerome Kagan (1987), for example, believes that infants are highly resilient and adaptive; he argues that they are evolutionarily equipped to stay on a positive developmental course even in the face of wide

In the Hausa culture, siblings and grandmothers provide a significant amount of care for infants.

variations in parenting. Kagan and others stress that genetic and temperament characteristics play more important roles in a child's social competence than the attachment theorists, such as Bowlby, Ainsworth, and Sroufe, are willing to acknowledge (Young & Shahinfar, 1995). For example, infants may have inherited a low tolerance for stress; this, rather than an insecure attachment bond, may be responsible for their inability to get along with peers.

Another criticism of attachment theory is that it ignores the diversity of socializing agents and contexts that exist in an infant's world. In some cultures, infants show attachments to many people. Among the Hausa, both grandmothers and siblings provide a significant amount of care to infants (Harkness & Super, 1995). Infants in agricultural societies tend to form attachments to older siblings who are assigned a major responsibility for younger siblings' care. The attachments formed by infants in group care in Israeli kibbutzim provide another challenge to the singular attachment thesis.

Researchers recognize the importance of competent, nurturant caregivers in an infant's development—at issue, though, is whether or not secure attachment, especially to a single caregiver, is critical.

Episode	Persons Present	Duration of Episode	Description of Setting
1	Caregiver, baby, and observer	30 seconds	Observer introduces caregiver and baby to experimental room, then leaves. (Room contains many appealing toys scattered about.)
2	Caregiver and baby	3 minutes	Caregiver is nonparticipant while baby explores; if necessary, play is stimulated after 2 minutes.
3	Stranger, caregiver, and baby	3 minutes	Stranger enters. First minute: stranger is silent. Second minute: stranger converses with caregiver. Third minute: stranger approaches baby. After 3 minutes caregiver leaves unobtrusively.
4	Stranger and baby	3 minutes or less	First separation episode. Stranger's behavior is geared to that of baby.
5	Caregiver and baby	3 minutes or more	First reunion episode. Caregiver greets and/or comforts baby, then tries to settle the baby again in play. Caregiver then leaves, saying "bye-bye."
6	Baby alone	3 minutes or less	Second separation episode.
7	Stranger and baby	3 minutes or less	Continuation of second separation. Stranger enters and gears behavior to that of baby.
8	Caregiver and baby	3 minutes	Second reunion episode. Caregiver enters, greets baby, then picks baby up. Meanwhile stranger leaves unobtrusively.

FIGURE 8.4

The Ainsworth Strange Situation
Mary Ainsworth (*right*) developed the Strange Situation to assess whether infants are securely or insecurely attached to their caregiver.

Measuring Attachment

Much of the early research on attachment relied on caregivers' impressions rather than on direct observation of caregivers interacting with their infant. However, interview data might be flawed and unreliably related to what actually takes place when parents interact with their infant. In the last several decades, researchers have increasingly observed infants with their caregivers. The main setting that has been used to observe attachment in infancy is the Strange Situation developed by attachment researcher Mary Ainsworth (1967). The **Strange Situation** *is an observational measure of infant attachment that requires the infant to move through a series of introductions, separations, and reunions with the caregiver and an adult stranger in a prescribed order* (see figure 8.4).

Although the Strange Situation has been used in a large number of studies of infant attachment, some critics believe that the isolated, controlled events of the setting might not necessarily reflect what would happen if infants were observed with their caregiver in a natural environment. The issue of using controlled, laboratory assessments versus naturalistic observations is widely debated in child development circles.

Fathers as Caregivers for Infants

Can fathers take care of infants as competently as mothers can? Observations of fathers and their infants suggest that fathers have the ability to act sensitively and responsively with their infants (McHale & others, 1995; Parke, 1995). Probably the strongest evidence of the plasticity of male caregiving abilities is derived from information about male primates who are notoriously low in their interest in offspring but are forced to live with infants whose female caregivers are absent. Under these circumstances, the adult male competently rears the infants. Remember, however, that although fathers can be active, nurturant, involved caregivers with their infants, many do not choose to follow this pattern.

Do fathers behave differently toward infants than mothers do? Whereas maternal interactions usually center around child-care activities—feeding, changing diapers, bathing—paternal interactions are more likely to include play. Fathers engage in more rough-and-tumble play, bouncing infants, throwing them up in the air, tickling them, and so on (Lamb, 1986). Mothers do play with infants, but their play is less physical and arousing than that of fathers.

In stressful circumstances, do infants prefer their mother or father? In one study, twenty 12-month-olds were observed interacting with their parents (Lamb, 1977). With both parents present, the infants preferred neither their mother nor their father. The same was true when the infants were alone with the mother or the father. However the entrance of a stranger, combined with boredom and fatigue, produced a shift in the infants' social

John W. Santrock

Can fathers take care of infants as competently as mothers can? Do fathers interact differently than mothers do?

The father's role in China has been slow to change, but it is changing. Traditionally in China, the father has been expected to be strict, the mother kind. The father is characterized as a stern disciplinarian; the child is expected to fear the father. The notion of the strict father has ancient roots. The Chinese character for father (fu) evolved from a primitive character representing a hand holding a cane, which symbolizes authority. However, the twentieth century has witnessed a decline in the father's authority. Younger fathers are more inclined to allow children to express their opinions and be more independent. Influenced to a degree by the increased employment of mothers, Chinese fathers are becoming more involved in caring for their children. In some instances, intergenerational tension has developed between fathers and sons, as younger generations behave in less traditional ways.

behavior toward the mother. In stressful circumstances, then, infants show a stronger attachment to the mother.

Might the nature of parent-infant interaction be different in families that adopt nontraditional gender roles? This question was investigated by Michael Lamb and his colleagues (1982). They studied Swedish families in which the fathers were the primary caregivers of their firstborn, 8-month-old infants. The mothers were working full-time. In all observations, the mothers were more likely to discipline, hold, soothe, kiss, and talk to the infants than were the fathers. These mothers and fathers dealt with their infants differently, along the lines of American fathers and mothers following traditional gender roles. Having fathers assume the primary caregiving role did not substantially alter the way they interacted with their infants. This may be for biological reasons or because of deeply ingrained socialization patterns in cultures.

Day Care

Each weekday at 8 A.M., Ellen Smith takes her 1-year-old daughter Tanya to the day-care center at Brookhaven College in Dallas. Then Mrs. Smith goes to work and returns in the afternoon to take Tanya home. After 3 years, Mrs. Smith reports that her daughter is adventuresome and interacts confidently with peers and adults. Mrs. Smith believes that day care has been a wonderful way to raise Tanya.

In Los Angeles, however, day care has been a series of horror stories for Barbara Jones. After 2 years of unpleasant experiences with sitters, day-care centers, and day-care homes, Mrs. Jones has quit her job as a successful real estate agent to stay home and take care of her 2½-year-old daughter Gretchen. "I didn't want to sacrifice my baby for my job," said Mrs. Jones, who was unable to find good substitute day-care homes. When she put Gretchen into a day-care center, she said that she felt her daughter was being treated like a piece of merchandise—dropped off and picked up.

Many parents worry whether day care will adversely affect their children. They fear that day care will reduce their infants' emotional attachment to them, retard the infants' cognitive development, fail to teach them how to control anger, and allow them to be unduly influenced by their peers. How extensive is day care? Are the worries of these parents justified?

In the 1990s, far more young children are in day care than at any other time in history; about 2 million children currently receive formal, licensed day care, and more than 5 million children attend kindergarten. Also, uncounted millions of children are cared for by unlicensed baby-sitters. Day care clearly has become a basic need of the American family.

The type of day care that young children receive varies extensively (Burchinal & others, 1996). Many day-care centers house large groups of children and have elaborate facilities. Some are commercial operations, others are nonprofit centers run by churches, civic groups, and employers. Child

CRITICAL THINKING ABOUT CHILDREN'S DEVELOPMENT

Characteristics of Competent Caregivers

Much of the health and well-being of infants is in the hands of caregivers.

Whether the caregivers are parents or day-care personnel, these adults play significant roles in children's lives. What are the characteristics of competent caregivers? For one thing, competent caregivers enjoy caregiving. They reflect these positive feelings as they interact with infants and children. Try to come up with a list of five other characteristics of competent caregivers. Toward the end of this chapter, in the "Health and Well-Being" section of "Improving Children's Lives," you will read further about the personal characteristics of competent caregivers. Compare the list you develop here with the list discussed later in the text. By considering the characteristics of competent caregivers, you are engaging in critical thinking by *using knowledge about development to enhance personal adaptation.*

Provision of day care in most developing countries has improved, but this often has been in a form that denies access to the poorest children. In some locations in India, mobile day-care centers have provided intensive integrated child services to young children in slum settlements within large cities and rural villages.

care is frequently provided in private homes, at times by child-care professionals, at others by mothers who want to earn extra money.

A special contemporary interest of researchers who study day care is the role of poverty, (Huston, McLoyd, & Coll, 1994). In one study, day-care centers that served high-income children delivered better-quality care than did centers that served middle- and low-income children (Phillips & others, 1994). The indices of quality (such as teacher–child ratios) in subsidized centers for the poor were fairly good, but the quality of observed teacher–child interaction was lower than in high-income centers. To further evaluate the characteristics of competent caregivers, refer to Critical Thinking About Children's Development.

The quality of care children experience in day care varies extensively. Some caregivers have no training, others have extensive training; some day-care centers have a low caregiver–child ratio, others have a high caregiver–child ratio. Some experts have recently argued that the quality of day care most children receive in the United States is poor. Infant researcher Jay Belsky (1989) not only believes that the quality of day care children experience is generally poor, but he also argues that this translates into negative developmental outcomes for children. Belsky concludes that extensive day-care experience during the first 12 months of life—as is typical in the United States—is associated with insecure attachment as well as increased aggression, noncompliance, and possibly social withdrawal during the preschool and early elementary school years.

One study supports Belsky's beliefs (Vandell & Corasaniti, 1988). Extensive day care in the first year of life was associated with long-term negative outcomes. In contrast to children who began full-time day care later, children who began full-time day care (defined as more than 30 hours per week) as infants were rated by parents and teachers as being less compliant and as having poorer peer relations. In the first grade, they received lower grades and had poor work habits by comparison.

Belsky's conclusions about day care are controversial. Other respected researchers have arrived at a different conclusion; their review of the day-care research suggest no ill effects of day care (Clarke-Stewart, Alhusen, & Clements, 1995; Scarr, Lande, & McCartney, 1989).

What can we conclude? Does day care have adverse effects on children's development? Trying to combine the

John W. Santrock

results into an overall conclusion about day-care effects is a problem because of the different types of day care children experience and the different measures used to assess outcome (Honig, 1995). Belsky's analysis does suggest that parents should be very careful about the quality of day care they select for their infants, especially those 1 year of age or less. Even Belsky agrees, though, that day care itself is not the culprit; rather it is the quality of day care that is problematic in this country. Belsky acknowledges that no evidence exists to show that children in high-quality day care are at risk in any way.

What constitutes a high-quality day-care program for infants? The demonstration program developed by Jerome Kagan and his colleagues (1978) at Harvard University is exemplary. The day-care center included a pediatrician, a nonteaching director, and an infant-teacher ratio of 3 to 1. Teachers' aides assisted at the center. The teachers and aides were trained to smile frequently, to talk with the infants, and to provide them with a safe environment that included many stimulating toys. No adverse effects of day care were observed in this project. Carolee Howes (1988) discovered that children who entered low-quality child care as infants were least likely to be socially competent in early childhood; such children were less compliant, less self-controlled, less task-oriented, more hostile, and have more problems in peer interaction. Unfortunately, children who come from families with few resources (psychological, social, and economic) are more likely to experience poor-quality day care than are children from more-advantaged backgrounds.

Edward Zigler (1987) proposed a solution to the day-care needs of families. Zigler says that we should think of school not as an institution, but rather as a building, one that is owned by tax-paying parents who need day care for their children. Part of the school building would be for teaching and part would be for child care and supervision. This system could provide parents with competent developmental child-care services. Zigler believes it should be available to every child over the age of 3. He does not think children should start formal schooling at age 3; they would be in the schools only for day care. At the age of 5, children would start kindergarten, but only for half days. If the child has a parent at home, the child would spend the remainder of the day at home. If the parents are working, the child would spend the second half of the day in the day-care part of the school. For children aged 6 to 12, after-school and vacation care would be available to those who need it.

Zigler does not believe that teachers should provide day care; they are trained as educators and are too expensive. What we need, he says, is a child development associate, someone who is trained to work with children, someone we can afford to pay. This is a large vision, one that involves a structural change in society and a new face for our school system. As Zigler remembers, between the fall of 1964 and the summer of 1965, we managed to put 560,000 children into Head Start programs, an educational program for impoverished children. He believes we can do the same thing with day care. Despite the efforts of Zigler and others, the child-care bills currently being introduced in Congress still do not adequately address the quality of child care and the low pay of child-care workers.

We have all the knowledge necessary to provide absolutely first-rate child care in the United States. What is missing is the commitment and the will.

—**Edward Zigler, 1987**

In our discussion of attachment, we learned that some developmentalists believe temperament plays a more important role in infant development than many attachment enthusiasts take it to play. Next we look more closely at temperament's effects on children's development.

TEMPERAMENT

What is the nature of temperament? Should parenting strategies vary depending on the child's temperament?

Temperament's Nature

Temperament *is an individual's behavioral style and characteristic way of responding.* Developmentalists are especially interested in the temperament of infants. Some infants are extremely active, moving their arms, legs, and mouths incessantly. Others are tranquil. Some children explore their environment eagerly for great lengths of time. Others do not. Some infants respond warmly to people. Others fuss and fret. All of these behavioral styles represent a person's temperament.

A widely debated issue in temperament research is just what the key dimensions of temperament are. Psychiatrists Alexander Chess and Stella Thomas (Chess & Thomas, 1977; Thomas & Chess, 1991) believe there are three basic types, or clusters, of temperament—easy, difficult, and slow to warm up.

1. An **easy child** *is generally in a positive mood, quickly establishes regular routines in infancy, and adapts easily to new experiences.*
2. A **difficult child** *tends to react negatively and cry frequently, engages in irregular daily routines, and is slow to accept new experiences.*
3. A **slow-to-warm-up child** *has a low activity level, is somewhat negative, shows low adaptability, and displays a low intensity of mood.*

Different dimensions make up these three basic clusters of temperament. The three basic clusters and their dimensions are shown in table 8.1. In their longitudinal investigation, Chess and Thomas found that 40 percent of the children they studied could be classified as easy, 10 percent

TABLE 8.1

Chess and Thomas's Dimensions and the Basic Clusters of Temperament

This table identifies those dimensions that were critical in spotting a basic cluster of temperament and the level of responsiveness for each critical feature. A blank space indicates that the dimension was not strongly related to a basic cluster of temperament.

Temperament Dimension	Description	Temperament Cluster		
		Easy Child	*Difficult Child*	*Slow-to-Warm-Up Child*
Rhythmicity	Regularity of eating, sleeping, toileting	Regular	Irregular	
Activity level	Degree of energy movement		High	Low
Approach-withdrawal	Ease of approaching new people and situations	Positive	Negative	Negative
Adaptability	Ease of tolerating change in routine plans	Positive	Negative	Negative
Sensory threshold	Amount of stimulation required for responding			
Predominant quality of mood	Degree of positive or negative affect	Positive	Negative	
Intensity of mood expression	Degree of affect when pleased, displeased, happy, sad	Low to moderate	High	Low
Distractibility/attention span/persistence	Ease of being distracted			

as difficult, and 15 percent as slow to warm up. Researchers have found that these three basic clusters of temperament are moderately stable across the childhood years.

Other researchers suggest that temperament is composed of different basic components. Personality psychologist Arnold Buss and behavior geneticist Robert Plomin (1987) believe that infants' temperament falls into three basic categories: emotionality, sociability, and activity level. **Emotionality** *is the tendency to be distressed.* It reflects the arousal of a person's sympathetic nervous system. During infancy, distress develops into two separate emotional responses: fear and anger. Fearful infants try to escape something that is unpleasant; angry ones protest it. Buss and Plomin argue that children are labeled "easy" or "difficult" on the basis of their emotionality. **Sociability** *is the tendency to prefer the company of others to being alone.* It matches a tendency to respond warmly to others. **Activity level** *involves tempo and vigor of movement.* Some children walk fast, are attracted to high-energy games, and jump or bounce around a lot; others are more placid.

Some experts on temperament believe there should be even further differentiation of certain domains of temperament (Eisenberg, 1992). For example, in the general domain of social withdrawal, researchers are beginning to distinguish between shyness (inhibited and awkward behavior with strangers or acquaintances, accompanied by feelings of tension and a desire to escape), introversion (a nonfearful preference for not affiliating with others), sociability (a preference for affiliating with others), and extraversion (the tendency to seek social interaction as a source of stimulation rather than out of true social interest in others).

A number of scholars conceive of temperament as a stable characteristic of newborns that comes to be shaped and modified by the child's later experiences. This raises the question of heredity's role in temperament (Lemery & Buss, 1995). Twin and adoption studies have been conducted to answer this question (Plomin & others, 1994; Schmitz & others, 1996). The researchers find a heritability index in the range of .50 to .60, suggesting a moderate influence of heredity on temperament. However, the strength of the association usually declines as infants become older. This finding supports the belief that temperament becomes more malleable with experience. Alternatively, it may be that, as a child becomes older, behavior indicators of temperament are more difficult to spot.

The consistency of temperament depends, in part, on the "match" or "fit" between the child's nature and the parent's nature (Sanson & Rothbart, 1995). Imagine a high-strung parent with a child who is difficult and sometimes slow to respond to the parent's affection. The parent may begin to feel angry or rejected. A father who does not need much face-to-face social interaction will find it easy to manage a similarly introverted baby, but he may not be able to provide an extraverted baby with sufficient stimulation. Parents influence infants, but infants also influence parents. Parents may withdraw from difficult children, or they may become critical and punish them; these responses may make the difficult child even more difficult. A more

John W. Santrock

Parents' responsiveness to their infant is an important part of the "match" or "fit" between parent and infant.

easygoing parent may have a calming effect on a difficult child or may continue to show affection even when the child withdraws or is hostile, eventually encouraging more competent behavior.

In sum, heredity does seem to influence temperament. However, the degree of influence depends on parents' responsiveness to their children and on other environmental childhood experiences.

Parenting and the Child's Temperament

Many parents don't become believers in temperament's importance until the birth of their second child. The first child's behavior is often viewed by parents as being solely a result of how they socialized the child. However, management strategies that worked with the first child might not be as effective with the second child. Problems experienced with the first child (such as those involved in feeding, sleeping, and coping with strangers) might not exist with the second child, but new problems might arise. Such experiences strongly suggest that "nature" as well as "nurture" influence the child's development, that children differ from each other from very early in life, and that these differences have important implications for parent-child interaction.

What are the implications of temperamental variations for parenting? Although answers to this question necessarily are speculative because of the incompleteness of the research literature, the following conclusions were recently reached by temperament experts Ann Sanson and Mary Rothbart (1995):

- *Attention to and respect for individuality.* An important implication of taking children's individuality seriously is that it becomes difficult to generate prescriptions for "good parenting," other than possibly specifying that parents need to be sensitive and flexible. Parents need to be sensitive to the infant's signals and needs. A goal of parenting might be accomplished in one way with one child and in another way with another child, depending on the child's temperament.

Some temperament characteristics pose more parenting challenges than others, at least in modern Western societies. Children's proneness to distress, as exhibited by frequent crying and irritability, can contribute to the emergence of avoidant or coercive parent responses. In one research study, though, extra support and training for mothers of distress-prone infants improved the quality of mother-infant interaction (van den Boom, 1989).

Parents might react differently to a child's temperament depending on whether the child is a girl or a boy and on the culture in which they live. For example, in one study, mothers were more responsive to the crying of irritable girls than to the crying of irritable boys (Crockenberg, 1986). Also, an active temperament might be valued in some cultures (such as the United States) but not in other cultures (such as China). Parents should respect each child's temperament rather than try to fit all children into the same mold.

- *Structuring the child's environment.* Crowded, noisy environments can pose greater problems for some children (such as a "difficult child") than others (such as an "easygoing" child). We might also expect that a fearful, withdrawing child would benefit from slower entry into new contexts.

- *The "difficult child" and packaged parenting programs.* Some books and programs for parents focus specifically on temperament (Cameron, Hansen, & Rosen, 1989; Turecki & Tonner, 1989). These programs usually focus on children with "difficult" temperaments. Acknowledgment that some children are harder to parent is often helpful, and advice on how to handle particular difficult temperament characteristics can also be useful.

However, weighing against these potential advantages are several disadvantages. Whether a particular characteristic is difficult depends on its fit with the environment, whereas the notion of "difficult temperament" suggests that the problem rests with the child. To label a child "difficult" also has the danger of becoming a self-fulfilling prophecy. The stability of temperament is somewhat low from infancy to late childhood, and moderate after infancy. If a child is identified as "difficult," the labeling may serve to maintain that categorization.

Children's temperament needs to be taken into account when considering caregiving behavior. Research evidence does not yet allow for many highly specific recommendations, but in general, caregivers should (1) be sensitive to the individual characteristics of the child, (2) be flexible in responding to these characteristics, and (3) avoid negative labeling of the child.

At this point we have discussed a number of ideas about family processes, attachment, fathers as caregivers for infants, day care, and temperament. A summary of these ideas is presented in concept table 8.1. Next we turn our attention to the study of children's emotional development.

Family Processes, Attachment, Fathers as Caregivers for Infants, Day Care, and Temperament

Concept	Processes/Related Ideas	Characteristics/Description
Family Processes	The transition to parenthood	This requires considerable adjustment and adaptation on the part of parents.
	The parental role	There is little in the way of formal training for the parental role. Some individuals have mixed emotions and romantic illusions about having a child. There are many myths about parenting.
	Reciprocal socialization	Children socialize their parents just as parents socialize their children. Scaffolding, synchronization, and mutual regulation are important dimensions of reciprocal socialization.
	The family as a system	The family is a system of individuals interacting with different subsystems, some dyadic, others polyadic. Belsky's model describes direct and indirect effects.
	The family life cycle	As we go through life, we are at different points in the family life cycle. The stages of the family life cycle include: leaving home and becoming a single adult, the joining of families through marriage—the new couple, becoming parents and families with children, families with adolescents, families at midlife, and the family in later life.
Attachment, Fathers, and Day Care	Attachment	Attachment is a relationship between two people in which each person feels strongly about the other and does a number of things to ensure the relationship's continuation. In infancy, attachment refers to the bond between the caregiver and the infant. Feeding is not the critical element in attachment, although contact comfort, familiarity, and trust are important. Bowlby's ethological theory stresses that the caregiver and infant instinctively trigger attachment. Attachment to the caregiver intensifies at about 6 to 7 months. Ainsworth believes that individual differences in attachment can be classified into secure, avoidant, and resistant categories. Ainsworth believes that securely attached babies have sensitive and responsive caregivers. In some investigations, secure attachment is related to social competence later in childhood. The main way infant attachment has been assessed is through the use of Ainsworth Strange Situation, although this measure has been criticized for being unnatural. Some developmentalists believe that too much emphasis is placed on the role of attachment; they believe that genetics and temperament, on the one hand, and the diversity of social agents and contexts, on the other, deserve more credit.
	Fathers as caregivers for infants	Fathers have increased their interaction with their children, but they still lag far behind mothers, even when mothers are employed. Fathers can act sensitively to the infant's signals, but in many cases they do not. The mother's role in the infant's development is primarily caregiving. That of the father involves playful interaction. Infants generally prefer their mother under stressful circumstances. Even in nontraditional families, as when the father is the main caregiver, the behaviors of mothers and fathers follow traditional gender lines.
	Day care	Day care has become a basic need of the American family; more children are in day care today than at any other time in history. The quality of day care is uneven. Belsky concluded that most day care is inadequate and that extensive day care in the first 12 months of an infant's life has negative developmental outcomes. Other experts disagree with Belsky. Day care remains a controversial topic. Quality day care can be achieved, and it seems to have few adverse effects on children.
Temperament	Its nature	Temperament is behavioral style; temperament has been studied extensively. Chess and Thomas described three temperamental clusters—easy, difficult, and slow to warm up. Temperament is influenced strongly by biological factors in early infancy but becomes more malleable with experience. An important consideration is the fit of the infant's temperament with the parents' temperament.
	Parenting and the child's temperament	Although research evidence is sketchy at this point in time, some general recommendations are that caregivers should (1) be sensitive to the individual characteristics of the child, (2) be flexible in responding to these characteristics, and (3) avoid negative labeling of the child.

EMOTIONAL AND PERSONALITY DEVELOPMENT

Infants have emotions and emotional experiences, and their personality is also developing. In this section, we also will explore several problems and disorders that can emerge.

Emotional Development

What is the nature of children's emotions? How do emotions develop in infancy?

The Nature of Children's Emotions

What is an emotion? What are the functions of emotion in children? What is the role of emotion in parent-infant relationships?

Defining Emotion   Defining emotion is difficult because it is not easy to tell when a child or an adult is in an emotional state. Is a child in an emotional state when her heart beats fast, her palms sweat, and her stomach churns? Or is she in an emotional state when she smiles or grimaces? The body and face play important roles in understanding children's emotion, although psychologists debate how important each is in determining whether a child is in an emotional state. For our purposes, we will define **emotion** as *feeling or affect that involves a mixture of physiological arousal (a fast heartbeat, for example) and overt behavior (a smile or grimace, for example).*

Blossoms are scattered by the wind
And the wind cares nothing, but
The blossoms of the heart
No wind can touch.

—**Youshida Kenko,**
***The Harvest of Leisure,* 1330**

When we think about children's emotions, a few dramatic feelings, such as rage, fear, and glorious joy, usually spring to mind. But emotions can be subtle as well—the feeling a mother has when she holds her baby, the mild irritation of boredom, and the uneasiness of being in a new situation.

Psychologists have classified emotions in many different ways, but one characteristic of almost all classifications is whether an emotion is positive or negative. **Positive affectivity (PA)** *refers to the range of positive emotions, from high energy, enthusiasm, and excitement to being calm, quiet, and withdrawn. Joy, happiness, and laughter involve positive affectivity.* **Negative affectivity (NA)** *refers to emotions that are negatively toned, such as anxiety, anger, guilt, and sadness.* PA and NA are independent dimensions, in that a child can be high along both dimensions at the same time (for example, in a high-energy state and enthusiastic yet angry).

The New Functionalism in Emotion   A number of developmentalists view the nature of emotion differently today than their predecessors did (Campos, 1994). The new view proposes that emotion is relational rather than intrapsychic, that there is a close link between emotion and the person's goals and effort, that emotional expressions can serve as social signals, and that the physiology of emotion involves much more than homeostasis and the person's interior—it also incudes the ability to regulate and be regulated by social processes.

The new approach is called "functionalist"—not because it focuses on evolutionary survival, but because it links emotion with what the person is trying to do. In this view, the person and an environmental event constitute a whole. Emotion, thus, involves person-event transactions, in this perspective (see figure 8.5).

The new functionalist approach does not diminish the importance of feelings, or of the autonomic nervous system, but deals with such aspects of emotion differently than traditional theories do (Magai & McFadden, 1995). What is new is the nesting of these factors—feelings and the body's physiology—within the description of the striving person's adaptation to the environment (Barrett, 1995).

To learn how the new functionalists assess emotions, let's examine the concept of attachment discussed earlier in this chapter. Advances in understanding attachment were made when researchers such as Alan Sroufe (1985) argued that "proximity seeking" and "felt security" could not be measured by concrete, observable behaviors like physical distance in meters. Sroufe instead proposed that researchers should investigate the functional dimensions of behaviors. For example, a child can show proximity-seeking not only through a physical approach measured by actual distance but also through her or his attempts to be picked up, ease of soothing by the parent when distressed, or smiles of delight when reunited with the parent. The extensive research literature on attachment in the last several decades contains many studies in which observers reliably made inferences about such functional properties of attachment instead of relying on discrete, concrete, observable behaviors (Posada, Lord, & Waters, 1995; Sroufe, 1996).

More needs to be said about goals and emotion. Goals are related to emotion in a variety of ways. Regardless of what the goal is, an individual who overcomes an obstacle to attain a goal experiences happiness. By contrast, a person who must relinquish a goal as unattainable experiences sadness. And a person who faces difficult obstacles in pursuing a goal often experiences anger. The specific nature of the goal can affect the experience of a given emotion. For example, avoidance of threat is linked with fear, desire to atone is related to guilt, and the wish to avoid the scrutiny of others is associated with shame. Many of the new functionalists focus their work on goal-related emotions (Hakim-Larson, 1995).

FIGURE 8.5

The New Functionalism in Emotions
Infant researcher Nathan Fox (in press) measured the brain waves of infants, like this 4-month-old, who have been stimulated with toys to elicit different emotional states. Fox demonstrated that very inhibited babies show a distinctive brain-wave pattern (as measured by the electroencephalogram [EEG] helmet in the photograph). Fox's research fits within the new functionalist view of emotion, which argues that the physiology of emotion involves much more than homeostasis or an internal milieu. In the new functionalism, emotions are modes of adaptation to the environment.

Affect in Parent-Child Relationships Emotions are the first language that parents and infants communicate with before the infant acquires speech (Maccoby, 1992). Infants react to their parents' facial expressions and tones of voice. In return, parents "read" what the infant is trying to communicate, responding appropriately when their infants are either distressed or happy.

The initial aspects of infant attachment to parents are based on affectively toned interchanges, as when an infant cries and the caregiver sensitively responds to the infant. By the end of the first year, a mother's facial expression—either smiling or fearful—influences whether an infant will explore an unfamiliar environment. And when children hear their parents quarreling, they often react with distressed facial expressions and inhibited play (Cummings, 1987). Exceptionally well-functioning families often include humor in their interactions, sometimes making each other laugh and developing light, pleasant mood states to defuse conflicts. And when a positive mood has been induced in the child, the child is more likely to comply with a parent's directions.

Infant and adult affective communicative capacities make possible coordinated infant-adult interactions. The face-to-face interactions of even 3-month-old infants and their adults are bidirectional (mutually regulated). That is, infants modify their affective displays and behaviors on the basis of their appreciation of their parents' affective displays and behaviors. This coordination has led to characterizations of the mother-infant interaction as "reciprocal" or "synchronous." These terms are attempts to capture the quality of interaction when all is going well.

Emotional Development in Infancy

Infants express some emotions earlier than others. Let's examine the developmental timetable for the expression of emotions, and then explore in detail two important emotionally expressive behaviors—crying and smiling.

Developmental Timetable of Emotions To determine whether infants are actually expressing a particular emotion, we need some system for measuring emotions.

John W. Santrock

Emotional expression	Approximate time of emergence
Interest, neonatal smile (a sort of half smile that appears spontaneously for no apparent reason),* startled response,* distress,* disgust	Present at birth
Social smile	4 to 6 weeks
Anger, surprise, sadness	3 to 4 months
Fear	5 to 7 months
Shame/shyness	6 to 8 months
Contempt, guilt	2 years

* These expressions are precursors of the social smile and the emotions of surprise and sadness, which appear later. No evidence exists to suggest that they are related to inner feelings when they are observed in the first few weeks of life.

FIGURE 8.6

The Developmental Course of Facial Expression of Emotions

Carroll Izard (1982) developed such a system. The **Maximally Discriminative Facial Movement Coding System (MAX)** *is Izard's system of coding infants' facial expressions related to emotion. Using MAX, coders watch slow-motion and stop-action videotapes of infants' facial reactions to stimuli.* Among the stimulus conditions are giving an infant an ice cube, putting tape on the backs of the infant's hands, handing the infant a favorite toy and then taking it away, separating the infant from the mother and then reuniting them, having a stranger approach the infant, restraining the infant's head, placing a ticking clock next to the infant's ear, popping a balloon in front of the infant's face, and giving the infant camphor to sniff and lemon rind and orange juice to taste. To give just one example of how an emotion is coded, anger is indicated when the infant's brows are sharply lowered and drawn together, eyes are narrowed or squinted, and mouth is open in an angular, square shape. Based on Izard's classification system, interest, distress, and disgust are present at birth, a social smile appears at about 4 to 6 weeks, anger, surprise, and sadness emerge at about 3 to 4 months, fear is displayed at about 5 to 7 months, shame and shyness are displayed at about 6 to 8 months, and contempt and guilt don't appear until 2 years of age. A summary of the approximate timetable for the emergence of facial expressions of emotions is shown in figure 8.6.

Crying Crying is the most important mechanism newborns have for communicating with their world (Gustafson, Green, & Kalinowski, 1993). This is true for the first cry, which tells the mother and doctor the baby's lungs have filled with air. Cries also may tell physicians or researchers something about the central nervous system.

Babies don't have just one type of cry. They have at least three (Wolff, 1969). The **basic cry** *is a rhythmic pattern that usually consists of a cry, followed by a briefer silence,* then a shorter inspiratory whistle that is somewhat higher in pitch than the main cry, then another brief rest before the next cry. Some infancy experts believe that hunger is one of the conditions that incites the basic cry. The **anger cry** *is a variation of the basic cry. However, in the anger cry more excess air is forced through the vocal cords.* The **pain cry,** *which is stimulated by high-intensity stimuli, differs from other types of cries in that there is a sudden appearance of loud crying without preliminary moaning, and a long initial cry followed by an extended period of breath holding.*

Most parents, and adults in general, can determine whether an infant's cries signify anger or pain (Zeskind, Klein, & Marshall, 1992). Parents also can distinguish the cries of their own baby better than those of a strange baby. There is little consistent evidence to support the idea that mothers or females, but not fathers or males, are innately programmed to respond nurturantly to an infant's crying.

To soothe or not to soothe? Should a crying baby be given attention and soothed, or does this spoil the infant? Many years ago the famous behaviorist John Watson (1928) argued that parents spend too much time responding to infant crying. As a consequence, he said, parents are actually rewarding infant crying and increasing its incidence. More recently, by contrast, infant experts Mary Ainsworth (1979) and John Bowlby (1989) stress that you can't respond too much to infant crying in the first year of life. They believe that the caregiver's quick, comforting response to the infant's cries is an important ingredient in the development of secure attachment. In one of Ainsworth's studies, mothers who responded quickly to their infants when they cried at 3 months of age had infants who cried less later in the first year of life (Bell & Ainsworth, 1972). On the other hand, behaviorist Jacob Gerwirtz (1977) found that a caregiver's quick, soothing response to crying increased subsequent crying.

Controversy, then, still swirls about the issue of whether parents should respond to an infant's cries. However, many developmentalists increasingly argue that an infant cannot be spoiled in the first year of life, which suggests that parents should soothe a crying infant rather than be unresponsive: In this manner infants will likely develop a sense of trust and secure attachment to the caregiver in the first year of life.

Smiling Smiling is another important communicative affective behavior of the infant. Two types of smiling can be distinguished in infants—one reflexive, the other social. A **reflexive smile** *does not occur in response to external stimuli. It appears during the first month after birth, usually during irregular patterns of sleep, not when the infant is in an alert state.* By contrast, a **social smile** *occurs in response to an external stimulus, which, early in development, typically is in response to a face.* Social smiling does not occur until 2 to 3 months of age (Emde, Gaensbauer, & Harmon, 1976), although some researchers believe that infants grin in response to voices as early as 3 weeks of age (Sroufe &

Reprinted with special permission of North America Syndicate.

Waters, 1976). The power of the infant's smiles was appropriately captured by British attachment theorist John Bowlby (1960): "Can we doubt that the more and better an infant smiles the better he is loved and cared for? It is fortunate for their survival that babies are so designed by nature that they beguile and enslave mothers."

He who binds himself to joy
Does the winged life destroy;
But he who kisses the joy as it
Flies lives in eternity's sun rise.

—**William Blake**

Personality Development

The individual characteristics of the infant that are often thought of as central to personality development are trust, the self, and independence.

Trust

According to Erik Erikson (1968), the first year of life is characterized by the trust-versus-mistrust stage of development. Following a life of regularity, warmth, and protection in the mother's womb, the infant faces a world that is less secure. Erikson believes that infants learn trust when they are cared for in a consistent, warm manner. If the infant is not well fed and kept warm on a consistent basis, a sense of mistrust is likely to develop.

Earlier we briefly described Erikson's ideas about the role of trust in attachment. His thoughts have much in common with Mary Ainsworth's concept of secure attachment. The infant who has a sense of trust is likely to be securely attached and to have confidence to explore new circumstances; the infant who has a sense of mistrust is likely to be insecurely attached and to not have such confidence and positive expectations.

Trust versus mistrust is not resolved once and for all in the first year of life; it arises again at each successive stage of development. There is both hope and danger in this. Children who enter school with a sense of mistrust may trust a particular teacher who has taken the time to make herself trustworthy. With this second chance children overcome their early mistrust. By contrast, children who leave infancy with a sense of trust can still have their sense of mistrust activated at a later stage, perhaps if their parents are separated or divorced under conflicting circumstances. An example is instructive (Elkind, 1970). A 4-year-old boy was being seen by a clinical psychologist at a court clinic because his adoptive parents, who had had him for 6 months, now wanted to give him back to the agency. They said he was cold and unloving, stole things, and could not be trusted. He was indeed a cold and apathetic boy, but with good reason. One year after his illegitimate birth, he was taken away from his mother, who had a drinking problem, and was shuttled back and forth among several foster homes. At first he tried to relate to people in the foster homes, but the relationships never had an opportunity to develop, because he was moved so frequently. In the end, he gave up trying to reach out to others, because the inevitable separations hurt too much. Like the burned child who dreads the flame, this emotionally burned child shunned the pain of close relationships. He had trusted his mother, but now he trusted no one. Only years of devoted care and patience could now undo the damage to this child's sense of trust.

The Developing Sense of Self and Independence

Individuals carry with them a sense of who they are and what makes them different from everyone else. They cling to this identity and begin to feel secure in the knowledge that this identity is becoming more stable. Real or imagined, this sense of self is a strong motivating force in life. When does the individual begin to sense a separate existence from others?

Children begin to develop a sense of self by learning to distinguish themselves from others. To determine whether infants can recognize themselves, psychologists have used mirrors. In the animal kingdom, only the great

Erikson believes that autonomy versus shame and doubt is the key developmental theme of the toddler years.

Erikson (1968), like Mahler, believes that independence is an important issue in the second year of life. Erikson describes the second stage of development as the stage of autonomy versus shame and doubt. Autonomy builds on the infant's developing mental and motor abilities. At this point in development, not only can infants walk, but they can also climb, open and close, drop, push and pull, hold and let go. Infants feel pride in these new accomplishments and want to do everything themselves, whether it is flushing a toilet, pulling the wrapping off a package, or deciding what to eat. It is important for parents to recognize the motivation of toddlers to do what they are capable of doing at their own pace. Then they can learn to control their muscles and their impulses themselves. But when caregivers are impatient and do for toddlers what they are capable of doing themselves, shame and doubt develop. Every parent has rushed a child from time to time. It is only when parents consistently overprotect toddlers or criticize accidents (wetting, soiling, spilling, or breaking, for example) that children develop an excessive sense of shame and doubt about their ability to control themselves and their world.

I am what I can will freely.

—Erik Erikson, 1968

Erikson also believes that the stage of autonomy versus shame and doubt has important implications for the development of independence and identity during adolescence. The development of autonomy during the toddler years gives adolescents the courage to be independent individuals who can choose and guide their own future.

Too much autonomy, though, can be as harmful as too little. A 7-year-old boy who had a heart condition learned quickly how afraid his parents were of any signs of his having cardiac problems. It was not long before he ruled the household. The family could not go shopping or for a drive if the boy did not approve. On the rare occasions his parents defied him, he would get angry, and his purple face and gagging would frighten them into submission. This boy actually was scared of his power and eager to relinquish it. When the parents and the boy realized this, and recognized that a little shame and doubt were a healthy opponent of an inflated sense of autonomy, the family began to function much more smoothly (Elkind, 1970).

Consider also Robert, age 22 months, who has just come home from watching his 5-year-old brother, William, take a swimming lesson. Their mother has gone in the kitchen to get dinner ready when she hears a scream. She hurries into the living room and sees Robert's teeth sunk into William's leg. The next day, Robert is playing with a new game and he can't get it right. He hurls it across the room and just misses his mother. That night his mother tells him it is time for bed. Robert's response: "No."

apes learn to recognize their reflection in the mirror, but human infants accomplish this feat by about 18 months of age. How does the mirror technique work? The mother puts a dot of rouge on her infant's nose. The observer watches to see how often the infant touches his nose. Next, the infant is placed in front of a mirror and observers detect whether nose touching increases. Researchers have found that in the second half of the second year of life, infants recognized their own image and coordinated the image they saw with the actions of touching their own body (Lewis & Brooks-Gunn, 1979).

Not only does the infant develop a sense of self in the second year of life, but independence becomes a more central theme in the infant's life as well. The theories of Margaret Mahler and Erik Erikson have important implications for both self-development and independence. Mahler (1979) believes that the child goes through a separation and then an individuation process. Separation involves the infant's movement away from the mother, and individuation involves the development of self.

We learn to curb our will and keep our overt actions within the bounds of humanity, long before we can subdue our sentiments and imaginations in the same mild tone.

—**William Hazlitt, 1826**

Sometimes the world of 2-year-olds becomes very frustrating. Much of their frustration stems from their inability to control the adult world. Things are too big to manage, to push around, or to make happen. Toddlers want to be in the driver's seat of every car and to push every cart by themselves. Two-year-olds want to play the dominant role in almost every situation. When things don't go their way, toddlers can become openly defiant, even though they were placid as babies earlier in life. Called the "terrible twos" by Arnold Gesell, this developmental time frame can try the patience of the most even-tempered parents. Nonetheless, calm, steady affection and firm patience can help to disperse most of toddlerhood's tensions. Fortunately, the defiance is only temporary in most children's development.

Adapting Caregiving to the Developmental Status of the Infant and Toddler

In our discussion of infant socioemotional development, the themes of attachment, independence, emotional development, and the development of self have been predominant. We have examined developmental changes in attachment and seen that the push for independence is stronger in the second than in the first year of life. We have observed that different emotions emerge at different points in infancy, and we have seen that the second year is an important point in the emergence of a sense of self. Let's now examine some of these social developmental changes in infancy and evaluate the importance of adapting caregiving to the developmental changes. The following recommendations are based on LaVisa Wilson's (1990) development of a curriculum for people who care for infants and toddlers.

Birth to 4 Months

Caregivers can use several strategies to enhance the young infant's social development. The caregiver should respond quickly to the infant's needs and can initiate social interaction by looking at, holding, stroking, talking with, playing with, carrying, and rocking the infant. Caregivers must become emotionally involved with the infant. Caregivers need to frequently look at and touch the infant, which contributes to the development of an emotional relationship. Caregivers should arrange time and select materials that help infants to learn about themselves. For example, mirrors fascinate infants. Dots on bare feet and hands extend infants' interest in their bodies. Caregivers need to arrange for infants to interact with other people and with playthings.

4 to 8 Months

Infants are now developing a focused attachment to a primary caregiver; the primary caregiver's presence, consistent care, and emotional involvement with the infant support the development of an attachment. If the infant is in day care, a specific caregiver should be assigned to the infant; one caregiver can be a significant other for several infants. The caregiver should share the infant's pleasure and calm, as well as soothe, stroke, and sing to the infant during the infant's frustrating periods.

Infants now express a wider range of emotions in more elaborate ways. Pleasure, happiness, fear, and frustration are shown through a variety of sounds, such as gurgles, coos, wails, and cries, along with physical movements, such as rapid kicking, arm waving, rocking, and smiling. Many infants show a fear of strangers, or what has been called stranger anxiety. Stranger anxiety often emerges between 5 and 7 months of age. Therefore, strangers should be introduced carefully, and the stranger should not hover close to the infant. Give the infant time to become adjusted to the stranger from a distance.

8 to 12 Months

Social interaction with others is often increasing. Infants' increased mobility in this age period allows them to socially interact with and move away from other people. Caregivers should talk and play with the infant and allow the infant access to other adults and infants. Infants often continue to fear strangers at this age, so strangers should not be forced on infants immediately. A number of turn-taking games should be initiated with the infant, such as pat-a-cake. Infants are egocentric and want their own pleasure, usually not considering others' needs. Caregivers can begin to verbalize limits and help the infant choose other activities and materials. Infants at this age are very possessive of the caregiver, thus it is important for the caregiver to verbally assure the infant that she will come back to talk and play with the infant again.

External controls like a verbal "no" or a firm look may be needed to help infants limit or change their behavior at this age. Restrictive words should be followed by an explanation. For example, if an infant throws food on the floor, the caregiver can say, "No. You need the carrots up here on your plate. Can you put a carrot in your mouth?" Sometimes infants will stop their own negative behaviors, and if so, caregivers should praise the infant for their self-restriction. When infants at this age show anger or frustration, caregivers can determine and remove the causes of the anger or frustration if possible. Use calm talking, and sometimes hold and soothe the infant. Help the infant start a new activity. Tantrums may need to be ignored so they will not be reinforced and will eventually decrease in frequency and intensity.

12 to 18 Months

Toddlers push for independence, but at the same time they are very dependent on their caregivers, needing help for many tasks. Toddlers need emotional support, which affirms their importance as individuals who make some

John W. Santrock

choices and accomplish some tasks all by themselves. Toddlers' negativism may be expressed by "No!" or in tantrums. Their pursuit of independence may lead them to sometimes do the opposite of what the caregiver does.

As toddlers seek independence, allow them to attempt activities by themselves. Don't take over if toddlers can be successful alone. When toddlers express negativism, provide workable alternatives, such as "Do you want to walk or run to the table?" Toddlers also increasingly behave differently toward different people, adjusting their interactions with them. They may be eager and excited with a caregiver and quiet and shy with an adult stranger. Caregivers need to recognize these different responses and accept the toddler's choices. Don't force the toddler to interact with everyone.

18 to 24 Months

The development of self is especially important during this time period, as toddlers begin to use words that identify them as separate people—*I, mine, me,* and *you,* for example. Caregivers can verbally respond to the toddler's use of pronouns referring to the self, reinforcing the distinction the toddler makes between self and others. Toddlers at this age continue to expand their social relationships. Caregivers should encourage children to interact with others and provide support when they do.

Toddlers' behavior often moves to extremes, from lovable to demanding and stubborn. Caregivers need to allow the toddler to express swings in behavior. Show acceptance of the toddler as a person. Help toddlers work on their demands and stubbornness by suggesting alternatives in behavior. And, even though toddlers sometimes reject their caregivers, caregivers should continue to express to toddlers how much they love them and continue to show them a great deal of affection.

The experiences of the first three years of life are almost entirely lost to us, and when we attempt to enter into a small child's world, we come as foreigners who have forgotten the landscape and no longer speak the native tongue.

—Selma Fraiberg, *The Magic Years,* 1959

Problems and Disorders

Problems and disorders in infancy can arise for a number of reasons. All development—normal and abnormal—is influenced by the interaction of heredity and environment. In a comprehensive study of children at risk, a variety of biological, social, and developmental characteristics were identified as predictors of problems and disturbances at age 18 (Werner & Smith, 1982). They included moderate to severe perinatal (at or near birth) stress and birth defects, low socioeconomic status at 2 to 10 years of age, level of maternal education below 8 years, low family stability between 2 and 8 years, very

Dante Cicchetti has significantly advanced our knowledge of maltreated children. He and his colleagues at Mount Hope Family Center in Rochester, New York, have developed a model of intervention with maltreated children that is receiving increased attention.

low or very high infant responsiveness at 1 year, a Cattell score below 80 at age 2 (the Cattell is one of the early measures of infant intelligence), and the need for long-term mental health services or placement in a learning-disability class at age 10. When four or more of these factors were present, the stage was set for serious coping problems in the second decade of life. Among the problems in infancy that deserve special consideration are child abuse and autism.

Child Abuse

Unfortunately, parental hostility toward children in some families escalates to the point where one or both parents abuse the children. Child abuse is an increasing problem in the United States. Estimates of its incidence vary, but some authorities say that as many as 500,000 children are physically abused every year. Laws in many states now require doctors and teachers to report suspected cases of child abuse, yet many cases go unreported, especially those of battered infants.

Child abuse is such a disturbing circumstance that many people have difficulty understanding or sympathizing

---

with parents who abuse or neglect their children. Our response is often outrage and anger directed at the parent. This outrage focuses our attention on parents as bad, sick, monstrous, sadistic individuals who cause their children to suffer. Experts on child abuse believe that this view is too simple and deflects attention away from the social context of the abuse and parents' coping skills. It is especially important to recognize that child abuse is a diverse condition, that it is usually mild to moderate in severity, and that it is only partially caused by individual personality characteristics of parents.

The Multifaceted Nature of Child Maltreatment
Whereas the public and many professionals use the term *child abuse* to refer to both abuse and neglect, developmentalists increasingly are using the term *child maltreatment*. This term does not have quite the emotional impact of the term *abuse* and acknowledges that maltreatment includes several different conditions. Among the different types of maltreatment are physical and sexual abuse; fostering delinquency; lack of supervision; medical, educational, and nutritional neglect; and drug or alcohol abuse. In one large survey, approximately 20 percent of the reported cases involved abuse alone, 46 percent neglect alone, 23 percent both abuse and neglect, and 11 percent sexual abuse (American Association for Protecting Children, 1986). Abused children are more likely to be angry or wary than neglected children, who tend to be passive.

Severity of Abuse   The concern about child abuse began with the identification of the "battered child syndrome" and has continued to be associated with severe, brutal injury for several reasons. First, the media tend to underscore the most bizarre and vicious incidents. Second, much of the funding for child abuse prevention, identification, and treatment depends on the public's perception of the horror of child abuse and the medical professions's lobby for funds to investigate and treat abused children and their parents. The emphasis is often on the worst cases. These horrific cases do exist, and are indeed terrible, but they make up only a small minority of maltreated children. Less than 1 percent of maltreated children die, and another 11 percent suffer life-threatening, disabling injuries (American Association for Protecting Children, 1986). By contrast, almost 90 percent suffer temporary physical injuries. These milder injuries, though, are likely to be experienced repeatedly in the context of daily hostile family exchanges. Similarly, neglected children, who suffer no physical injuries, often experience extensive, long-term psychological harm.

The Cultural Context of Maltreatment   The extensive violence that takes place in the American culture is reflected in the occurrence of violence in the family. A regular diet of violence appears on television screens, and parents often resort to power assertion as a disciplinary technique. In China, where physical punishment is rarely used to discipline children, the incidence of child abuse is reported to be very low. In the United States, many abusing parents report that they do not have sufficient resources or help from others. This may be a realistic evaluation of the situation experienced by many low-income families, who do not have adequate preventive and supportive services.

Community support systems are especially important in alleviating stressful family situations, thereby helping to prevent child abuse. An investigation of the support systems in 58 counties in New York State revealed a relation between the incidence of child abuse and the absence of support systems available to the family (Garbarino, 1976). Both family resources—relatives and friends, for example—and such formal community support systems as crisis centers and child abuse counseling were associated with a reduction in child abuse.

Family Influences   To understand abuse in the family, the interactions of all family members need to be considered, regardless of who actually performs the violent acts against the child (Margolin, 1994). For example, even though the father may be the one who physically abuses the child, contributions by the mother, the child, and siblings also should be evaluated. Many parents who abuse their children come from families in which physical punishment was used. These parents view physical punishment as a legitimate way of controlling the child's behavior, and physical punishment may be a part of this sanctioning. Children themselves may unwittingly contribute to child abuse: An unattractive child may receive more physical punishment than an attractive child, and a child from an unwanted pregnancy may be especially vulnerable to abuse (Harter, Alexander, & Neimeyer, 1988). Husband-wife violence and financial problems may result in displaced aggression toward a defenseless child. Displaced aggression is commonly involved in child abuse. To further evaluate child abuse, refer to Critical Thinking About Children's Development.

Developmental Consequences of Child Maltreatment   Among the developmental consequences of child maltreatment are poor emotion regulation, attachment problems, problems in peer relations, difficulty in adapting to school, and other psychological problems (Rogosch & others, 1995).

Emotion Regulation. Difficulties in initiating and modulating positive and negative affect have been observed in maltreated infants (Cicchetti, Ganiban, & Barnett, 1991). Maltreated infants also may show excessive negative affect or blunted positive affect.

Attachment. Not only do maltreated infants show insecure patterns of attachment, they also might show a form of attachment not often found in normal samples of children. Maltreated children tend to display an inconsistent attachment pattern referred to as *disorganized*, which involves high

John W. Santrock

CRITICAL THINKING
ABOUT CHILDREN'S
DEVELOPMENT

*Developing a Model of
Intervention for
Maltreating Families*

What is the best way to help maltreated children? Intervention with maltreating families is difficult because of the multiple risk factors involved and the difficulty in getting such families to deal with the chaos in their lives. Poverty, intellectual and educational limitations, social isolation, and mental disorders are but a few of the factors that make it difficult to involve these families in effective treatment. With these limitations in mind, develop a model of intervention that you believe would benefit maltreated children and their families. Think about ways that therapists could assist families, about educational programs, and about recreational and activity possibilities. By developing a model for intervening in the lives of maltreating families, you are learning to think critically by *using knowledge about development to improve human welfare.*

avoidance and high resistance (Main & Solomon, 1990). In one study, the disorganized attachment pattern was found in 80 percent of the maltreated infants observed (Carlson & others, 1989).

Peer Relations. Maltreated children appear to be poorly equipped to develop successful peer relations, due to their aggressiveness, avoidance, and aberrant responses to both distress and positive approaches from peers (Mueller & Silverman, 1989). Two patterns of social behavior are common in maltreated children. Sometimes maltreated children show excessive physical and verbal aggression, while at other times maltreated children show a pattern of avoidance. These patterns have been described in terms of "fight or flight."

Adaptation to School. Maltreated children's difficulties in establishing effective relationships may show up in interactions with teachers. Maltreated children might expect teachers to be unresponsive or unavailable, based on their relationships with their parents. For maltreated children, dealing with fears about abuse and searching for security in relationships with adults can take precedence over performing competently at academic tasks.

Psychopathology. Being physically abused has been linked with children's anxiety, personality problems, depression, conduct disorder, and delinquency (Toth, Manley, & Cicchetti, 1992). Later, during the adult years, maltreated children show increased violence toward other adults, dating partners, and marital partners, as well as increased substance abuse, anxiety, and depression (Malinosky-Rummell & Hansen, 1993). In sum,

child maltreatment places children at risk for the development of a wide range of problems and disorders.

Infantile Autism

As its name suggests, **infantile autism** *has its onset in infancy. It is a severe developmental disorder that includes deficiencies in social relationships, abnormalities in communication, and restricted, repetitive, and stereotyped patterns of behavior.* Social deficiencies include a failure to use an eye-to-eye gaze to regulate social interaction, rarely seeking others for comfort or affection, rarely initiating play with others, and having no peer relations involving mutual sharing of interests and emotions. As babies, these children require very little from their parents. They do not demand much attention, and they do not reach out (literally or figuratively) for their parents. They rarely smile. When someone tries to hold them, they usually withdraw by arching their backs and pushing away. In their cribs or playpens, they appear oblivious to what is going on around them, often sitting and staring into space for long periods of time.

In addition to these social deficiencies, autistic children also show communication abnormalities that focus on the problems of using language for social communication: poor synchrony and lack of reciprocity in conversation, and stereotyped, repetitive use of language. As many as one of every two autistic children never learns to speak. **Echolalia** *is a speech disorder associated with autism in which children echo what they hear.* For example, if you ask, "How are you, Chuck?" Chuck responds, "How are you, Chuck?" Autistic children also confuse pronouns, inappropriately substituting *you* for *I*, for example.

Stereotyped patterns of behavior by autistic children include compulsive rituals, repetitive motor mannerisms, and distress over changes in small details of the environment (Wicks-Nelson & Israel, 1996). Rearrangement of a sequence of events or even furniture in the course of a day may cause autistic children to become extremely upset, suggesting that they are not flexible in adapting to new routines and changes in their daily lives.

What causes autism? Autism seems to involve some form of organic brain dysfunction and may also have a hereditary basis. There has been no satisfactory evidence developed to document that family socialization causes autism (Rutter & Schopler, 1987).

At this point we have studied a number of ideas about children's emotions, emotional development, personality development, and problems and disorders. A summary of these ideas is presented in concept table 8.2.

CONCEPT TABLE 8.2

Emotional and Personality Development

Concept	Processes/Related Ideas	Characteristics/Description
Emotional Development	What is emotion?	Emotion is feeling or affect that involves a mixture of physiological arousal and overt behavior. Emotions can be classified in terms of positive affectivity and negative affectivity.
	The New Functionalism in Emotions	The new functionalist view emphasizes that emotion is relational rather than intrapsychic, that there is a close link between emotion and the person's goals and effort, that emotional expressions can serve as social signals, and that the physiology of emotion is much more than homeostasis and the person's interior—it also includes the ability to regulate and be regulated by social processes.
	Affect in parent-child relationships	Emotions are the first language that parents and infants communicate with before the infant acquires speech. Infant and adult affective communicative capacities make possible coordinated infant-adult interaction.
	Emotional development in infancy	Izard developed the Maximally Discriminative Facial Coding System (MAX) for coding infants' expression of emotions. Based on this coding system, interest, distress, and disgust are present at birth, a social smile appears at about 4 to 6 weeks, anger, surprise, and sadness emerge at about 3 to 4 months, fear is displayed at about 5 to 7 months, shame and shyness emerge at about 6 to 8 months, and contempt and guilt appear at about 2 years of age.
	Crying	Crying is the most important mechanism newborns have for communicating with their world. Babies have at least three types of cries—basic cry, anger cry, and pain cry. Most parents, and adults in general, can tell whether an infant's cries signify anger or pain. Controversy still swirls about whether babies should be soothed when they cry. An increasing number of developmentalists support Ainsworth's and Bowlby's idea that infant crying should be responded to immediately in the first year of life.
	Smiling	Smiling is an important communicative affective behavior of the infant. Two types of smiling can be distinguished in infants: reflexive and social.
Personality Development	Trust	Erikson argues that the first year is characterized by the crisis of trust versus mistrust; his ideas about trust have much in common with Ainsworth's concept of secure attachment.
	Developing a sense of self and independence	At some point in the second half of the second year of life, the infant develops a sense of self. Independence becomes a central theme in the second year of life. Mahler argues that the infant separates herself from the mother and then develops individuation. Erikson stresses that the second year of life is characterized by the stage of autonomy versus shame and doubt.
	Adapting caregiving to the developmental status of the infant and toddler	From birth to 4 months of age, caregivers should respond quickly to the infant's needs with love, affection, and care. From 4 to 8 months of age, the caregiver's consistent care and emotional involvement with the infant support the development of a focused attachment. From 8 to 12 months of age, caregivers should continue to talk and play with the infant, and allow the infant access to other adults and infants. During this age period, caregivers need to monitor their infants' attentional bids. From 12 to 18 months of age, toddlers' independence needs to be promoted but their negativism needs to be dealt with firmly in the context of a loving and nurturant atmosphere. From 18 to 24 months of age, caregivers can encourage the toddler's development of self, continue monitoring their negativism, and continue giving them considerable affection.
Problems and Disorders	Child abuse	An understanding of child abuse requires information about cultural, familial, and community influences. Sexual abuse of children is now recognized as a more widespread problem than was believed in the past. Child abuse places the child at risk for a number of developmental problems.
	Infantile autism	Infantile autism is a severe disorder that first appears in infancy. It involves an inability to relate to people, speech problems, and upsets over changes in routine or environment. Autism seems to involve some form of organic brain and genetic dysfunction.

John W. Santrock

F rom birth, babies are wrapped in a socioemotional world with their caregivers. Babies and their caregivers communicate with each other through emotions, their senses, and their words. Through interaction with their caregivers, infants learn to adapt to their world.

We began this chapter by briefly examining how the human infant cannot sustain itself and therefore requires extensive care. Next we described some basic ideas about family processes. Much of the interest in the infant's social world has focused on attachment—we considered what attachment is, individual differences in attachment (secure and insecure), how attachment is measured, and the relation of attachment to temperament and the wider social world. We evaluated fathers as caregivers for infants and the role of day care in children's lives and how it affects their development. We learned that temperament is an important aspect of the infant's development, and explored the important worlds of infants' emotional and personality development. And we discussed two problems and disorders—child abuse and infantile autism.

Remember that by again studying the two concept tables on pages 230 and 240 you can obtain an overall summary of the chapter. This chapter concludes our coverage of infant development. Next, we will turn our attention to Section Four "Early Childhood," beginning with chapter 9, "Physical Development in Early Childhood."

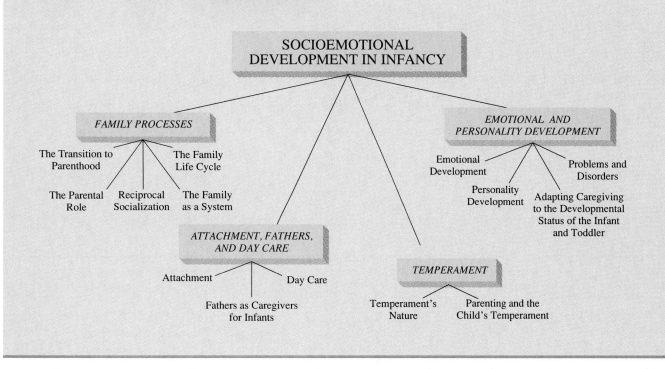

SOCIOEMOTIONAL DEVELOPMENT IN INFANCY

FAMILY PROCESSES

The Transition to Parenthood   The Family Life Cycle

The Parental Role   Reciprocal Socialization   The Family as a System

ATTACHMENT, FATHERS, AND DAY CARE

Attachment   Day Care

Fathers as Caregivers for Infants

TEMPERAMENT

Temperament's Nature   Parenting and the Child's Temperament

EMOTIONAL AND PERSONALITY DEVELOPMENT

Emotional Development   Problems and Disorders

Personality Development   Adapting Caregiving to the Developmental Status of the Infant and Toddler

reciprocal socialization Socialization that is bidirectional; children socialize parents just as parents socialize children. 218

scaffolding Parental behavior that supports children's efforts, allowing them to be more skillful than they would be if they relied only on their own abilities. 218

leaving home and becoming a single adult The first stage in the family life cycle, in which the child is launched (or exits his or her family of origin) into adulthood. 219

new couple The second stage in the family life cycle, in which two individuals from separate families of origin unite to form a new family system. 219

becoming parents and families with children The third stage in the family life cycle, in which the adults move up a generation and become caregivers to the next generation. 219

family with adolescents The fourth stage in the family life cycle, in which adolescent children push for autonomy and seek to develop their own identity. 219

family at midlife The fifth stage in the family life cycle, an important time of launching children, linking generations, and adapting to midlife changes in development. 219

family in later life The sixth and final stage in the family life cycle, in which retirement and, for many, grandparenting alter the couple's lifestyle. 221

attachment A close emotional bond between an infant and a caregiver. 221

secure attachment The infant uses a caregiver as a secure base from which to explore the environment. Ainsworth believes that secure attachment in the first year of life provides an important foundation for psychological development later in life. 222

type B babies Infants who use a caregiver as a secure base from which to explore the environment. 223

type A babies Infants who exhibit insecurity by avoiding their mother (for example, ignoring her, averting their gaze, and failing to seek proximity). 223

type C babies Infants who exhibit insecurity by resisting the mother (for example, clinging to her but at the same time kicking and pushing away). 223

Strange Situation An observational measure of infant attachment that requires the infant to move through a series of introductions, separations, and reunions with the caregiver and an adult stranger in a prescribed order. 224

temperament An individual's behavioral style and characteristic way of responding. 227

easy child A child who is generally in a positive mood, who quickly establishes regular routines in infancy, and who adapts easily to new experiences. 227

difficult child A child who tends to react negatively and cry frequently, who engages in irregular daily routines, and who is slow to accept new experiences. 227

slow-to-warm-up child A child who has a low activity level, is somewhat negative, shows low adaptability, and displays a low intensity mood. 227

emotionality The tendency to be distressed. 228

sociability The tendency to prefer the company of others to being alone. 228

activity level The tempo and vigor of movement. 228

emotion Feeling or affect that involves a mixture of physiological arousal and overt behavior. 231

positive affectivity (PA) The range of positive emotions from high energy, enthusiasm, and excitement to being calm, quiet, and withdrawn. Joy, happiness, and laughter involve positive affectivity. 231

negative affectivity (NA) Emotions that are negatively toned, such as anger, anxiety, guilt, and sadness. 231

Maximally Discriminative Facial Movement Coding System (MAX) Izard's system of coding infants' facial expressions related to emotions. Using MAX, coders watch slow-motion and stop-action videotapes of infants' facial reactions to stimuli. 233

basic cry A rhythmic pattern usually consisting of a cry, a briefer silence, a shorter inspiratory whistle that is higher pitched than the main cry, and then a brief rest before the next cry. 233

anger cry Similar to the basic cry, with more excess air forced through the vocal chords (associated with exasperation or rage by mothers). 233

pain cry A sudden appearance of loud crying without preliminary moaning and a long initial cry followed by an extended period of breath holding. 233

reflexive smile A smile that does not occur in response to external stimuli. It happens during the month after birth, usually during irregular patterns of sleep, not when the infant is in an alert state. 233

social smile A smile in response to an external stimulus, which, early in development, typically is in response to a face. 233

infantile autism A severe developmental disorder that has its onset in infancy and includes deficiencies in social relationships; abnormalities in communication; and restricted, repetitive, and stereotyped patterns of behavior. 239

echolalia An autistic condition in which children echo what they hear. 239

Daycare
(1993, rev. ed.) by Alison Clarke-Stewart.
Cambridge, MA: Harvard University Press.

This book draws on extensive research to survey the social, political, and economic contexts of day care. The author discusses options and consequences to help parents make informed choices. She provides a broad overview of day care's role in contemporary society, and evaluates the emergence and current state of institutional day care in schools and businesses. The book includes a checklist parents can use to assess their own arrangements.

Touchpoints
(1992) by T. Berry Brazelton.
Reading, MA: Addison-Wesley.

Touchpoints is pediatrician T. Berry Brazelton's most recent book. Covering the period from pregnancy to first grade, Brazelton focuses on the concerns and questions that parents have about the child's feelings, behavior, and development. The book's title derives from Brazelton's belief that there are universal spurts of development, and trying times of adaptation that accompany them, throughout childhood. Section 1 chronicles development from pregnancy through 3 years; section 2 describes a number of challenges to development, from allergies to toilet training; and section 3 focuses on important figures in the child's development, such as fathers, mothers, grandparents, friends, caregivers, and the child's doctor.

IMPROVING THE LIVES OF CHILDREN

Improving the lives of children involves ensuring that children have competent caregivers with positive personal characteristics, increasing the number of parent-educators, developing better-quality day care, enacting a more competent child-care policy, and understanding the mother's role.

HEALTH AND WELL-BEING

The Personal Characteristics of Competent Caregivers

Much of the health and well-being of infants is in the hands of caregivers. Whether the caregivers are parents or day-care personnel, these adults play significant roles in infants' lives. What are the personal characteristics of competent caregivers?

That question was recently addressed by child-care expert LaVisa Wilson (1990). She believes the following personal characteristics define a competent caregiver:

- *Competent caregivers are physically healthy.* Good health is necessary to provide the high level of energy required for competent caregiving. In day care, good health is required to resist the variety of illnesses to which caregivers are exposed.
- *Competent caregivers are mentally healthy.* In daily interactions with infants, caregivers need to provide physical closeness and nurturance for an extended period of time, to give emotionally more than they

often receive, and to be patient longer than they would like. Emotionally stable caregivers who have learned how to cope with a variety of emotional demands in their daily experiences are often able to encourage mental health in others.

- *Competent caregivers have a positive self-image.* Feelings of self-confidence and positive self-worth show that caregivers believe in themselves. Caregivers who have positive self-images are people who infants and toddlers want to approach rather than avoid.
- *Competent caregivers are flexible.* Competent caregivers do not get upset if they have to change the daily schedule, daily plans, or responsibilities.
- *Competent caregivers are patient.* Infants and toddlers are very demanding and require considerable attention and monitoring, which can stretch the

caregiver's patience. However, competent caregivers show patience as they respond to the infants' and toddlers' needs.

- *Competent caregivers are positive models for infants.* Caregivers' behaviors are observed and imitated by infants and toddlers. Competent caregivers monitor their own behavior, knowing it is a model for infants and toddlers.
- *Competent caregivers are open to learning.* Competent caregivers seek to develop additional skills and are open to new insights, understanding, and skills.
- *Competent caregivers enjoy caregiving.* Competent caregivers gain considerable enjoyment and satisfaction in providing effective, high-quality care for infants and toddlers. Competent caregivers reflect these positive feelings as they interact with infants and toddlers.

John W. Santrock

FAMILIES AND PARENTING

A Parent-Educator Program

The National City, California, school district established a program called Parents As Teachers (Louv, 1990). It hired a number of parent-educators to visit new parents once a month to support them emotionally and provide them with educational strategies for working with their infants. The parents participate voluntarily.

One of the parent-educators said that parents are a child's first teachers. Let's follow her on one of her family visits to see what a parent-educator does in a program like this.

The parent-educator sits down on the worn carpet and pulls out from her purse a coffee can filled with clothespins. The smallest child in the room reaches in and takes one out and begins to pull at the spring. The parent-educator comments that he is interested in taking things apart. The child's

mother responds that he is a real handful, opening up the dressers, the trash, and getting into just about everything. The parent-educator tells the mother that he does these things because he is curious and not because he is a trouble-maker. She suggests that the mother designate a lower drawer in the kitchen as "his" drawer and make sure that he can pull things out of it.

One of the enrolled mothers in the parent-educator program said that her parents thought good parenting just meant providing good food, a roof, and a ride to school. She further commented that she herself believed this was all there was to parenting until the parent-educator came into her life.

The National City program teaches parents to monitor their infant's and toddler's world and to look for educational moments. For example,

if a toddler happens to be playing with blocks on the floor, the parent-educator might suggest that the parent get down on the floor and count the blocks or talk about the blocks rather than pull the toddler away from them. She explains that peek-a-boo actually is an educational game that helps the infant's short-term memory. She also tactfully discourages parents from using playpens to corral their infants for any length of time, instead encouraging them to get their infants to explore their world.

One important side effect of parent-educator programs is that they help to prevent child abuse. For isolated, stressed-out parents, any kind of positive support from someone like a parent-educator can make a difference. In ways such as these, parent-educators can help parents weave a more curious, competent, gentler next generation.

EDUCATION

What Is Quality Day Care?

What constitutes quality child care? The following recommendations were made by the National Association for the Education of Young Children (1986). They are based on a consensus arrived at by experts in early childhood education and child development. It is especially important to meet the adults who will care for their child. They are responsible for every aspect of the program's operation.

1. The adult caregivers.
   - The adults should enjoy and understand how infants and young children grow.
   - There should be enough adults to work with a group and to care for the individual needs of children. More specifically, there should be no more than four infants for each adult caregiver, no more than eight 2- to 3-year-old children for each caregiver, and no more

   than ten 4- to 5-year-old children for each adult caregiver.
   - Caregivers should observe and record each child's progress and development.
2. The program activities and equipment.
   - The environment should foster the growth and development of young children working and playing together.
   - A good center should provide appropriate and sufficient equipment and play materials and make them readily available.
   - Infants and children should be helped to increase their language skills and to expand their understanding of the world.
3. The relation of staff to families and the community.

Quality day care includes having adult caregivers who enjoy being with infants and young children. The adult caregivers also should be knowledgeable about how infants and young children grow.

- A good program should consider and support the needs of the entire family. Parents should be welcome to observe, discuss policies, make suggestions, and work in the activities of the center.
- The staff in a good center should be aware of and contribute to community resources. The staff should share information about community recreational and learning opportunities with families.

4. The facility and the program should be designed to meet the varied demands of infants and young children, their families, and the staff.
   - The health of children, staff, and parents should be protected and promoted. The staff should be alert to the health of each child.
   - The facility should be safe for children and adults.

- The environment should be spacious enough to accommodate a variety of activities and equipment. More specifically, there should be a minimum of 35 square feet of usable playroom floor space indoors per child and 75 square feet of play space outdoors per child.

CULTURE AND ETHNICITY

Child-Care Policy Around the World

Sheila Kamerman (1989) surveyed the nature of child-care policies around the world with special attention given to European countries. Maternity and paternity policies for working parents include paid, job-protected leaves which are sometimes supplemented by additional unpaid, job-protected leaves. Child-care policy packages also often include full health insurance. An effective child-care policy is designed to get an infant off to a competent start in life and to protect maternal health while maintaining income. More than a hundred countries around the world have such child care policies, including all of Europe, Canada, Israel, and many developing countries. Infants are assured of at least 2 to 3 months of maternal/paternal care, and in most European countries 5 to 6 months.

The maternity policy as now implemented in several countries involves a paid maternity leave that begins 2 to 6 weeks prior to expected childbirth and lasts from 8 to 20 or even 24 weeks after birth. This traditional maternal policy stems from an effort to protect the health of pregnant working women, new mothers, and their infants. Only since the 1960s has the maternity policy's link with employment become strong. A second child-care policy emphasizes the importance of parenting and recognizes the potential of fathers as well as mothers to care for their infants. In Sweden a parent insurance benefit provides protection to the new mother before birth and for 6 to 12 weeks after birth but then allows the father to participate in the postchildbirth leave. Approximately one-fourth of Swedish fathers take at least part of the postchildbirth leave, in addition to the 2 weeks of paid leave all fathers are entitled to at the time of childbirth. In a typical pattern in Sweden, the working mother might take off 3 months, after which she and her husband might share child care between them, each working half-time for 6 months. In addition, Swedish parents have the option of taking an unpaid but fully protected job leave until their child is 18 months old and working a 6-hour day (without a reduction in pay) from the end of the parental leave until their child is 8 years old.

In sum, almost all the industrialized countries other than the United States have recognized the importance of developing maternity/paternity policies that allow working parents some time off after childbirth to physically recover, to adapt to parenting, and to improve the well-being of the infant. These policies are designed to let parents take maternity/paternity leave without losing employment or income.

John W. Santrock

The Mother's Role

What do you think of when you hear the word *motherhood?* If you are like most people, you associate motherhood with a number of positive characteristics, such as warmth, selflessness, dutifulness, and tolerance (Matlin, 1993). And though most women expect that motherhood will be happy and fulfilling, the reality is that motherhood has been accorded relatively low prestige in our society. When stacked up against money, power, and achievement, motherhood unfortunately doesn't fare too well, and mothers rarely receive the appreciation they warrant. When children don't succeed or develop problems, our society has had a tendency to attribute the lack of success or the development of problems to a single source—mothers. One of psychology's most important lessons is that behavior is multiply determined. So it is with children's development; when development goes awry, mothers are not the single cause of the problems even though our society stereotypes them in this way.

The reality of motherhood in the 1990s is that although fathers have increased their childrearing responsibilities somewhat, the main responsibility for childrearing still falls on the mother's shoulders (Paludi, 1995). Mothers do far more family work than fathers do—two to three times more. A few "exceptional" men do as much family work as their wives; in one study the figure was 10 percent of the men (Berk, 1985). Not only do women do more family work than men, the family work most women do is unrelenting, repetitive, and routine, often involving cleaning, cooking, child care, shopping, laundry, and straightening up. The family work most men do is infrequent, irregular, and nonroutine, often involving household repairs, taking out the garbage, and yard work. Women report that they often have to do several tasks at once, which helps to explain why they find domestic work less relaxing and more stressful than men do (Shaw, 1988).

Because family work is intertwined with love and embedded in family relations, it has complex and contradictory meanings. Most women feel that family tasks are mindless but essential. They usually enjoy tending to the needs of their loved ones and keeping the family going, even if they do not find the activities themselves enjoyable and fulfilling. Family work is both positive and negative for women. They are unsupervised and rarely criticized, they plan and control their own work, and they have only their own standards to meet. However, women's family work is often worrisome, tiresome, menial, repetitive, isolating, unfinished, inescapable, and often unappreciated. It is not surprising that more men than women report that they are satisfied with their marriage.

In sum, the role of the mother brings with it benefits as well as limitations. Although motherhood is not enough to fill most women's entire lives, for most mothers, it is one of the most meaningful experiences in their lives.

Earlier in the chapter we discussed the father's role. Father-mother cooperation and mutual respect helps the child to develop positive attitudes toward both males and females (Biller, 1993). It is much easier for working parents to cope with changing family circumstances and day-care issues when the father and mother equitably share childrearing responsibilities. Mothers feel less stress and have more positive attitudes toward their husbands when they are supportive partners.

REVIEW OF CHILDREN'S DEVELOPMENT
Infancy
—

PHYSICAL DEVELOPMENT

Physical development in the first 2 years of life is extensive. Infants are born into the world equipped with a number of survival reflexes, such as coughing, blinking, yawning, and grasping. Cephalocaudal (top-down) and proximodistal (center-out) patterns characterize infant physical growth. Infants' rate of growth is much faster in the first year of life than in the second year. Both gross motor skills (such as walking) and fine motor skills (such as finger dexterity) make significant advances during infancy. As the infant ages from birth to 2 years, the interconnection of neurons increases dramatically. Newborns usually sleep 16 to 17 hours a day, but by 4 months they approach adultlike sleeping patterns. With regard to nutrition, infants need to consume about 50 calories per day for each pound they weigh. Breast- versus bottle-feeding continues to be a hotly debated issue. Many parents begin toilet training their toddlers at about 20 months to 2 years of age and conclude it by 3 years of age. The newborn's perception is much more advanced than we previously thought. Newborn vision is about 20/600, but by 6 months it has improved to at least 20/100. The visual cliff study demonstrated that depth perception is present at least by 6 months of age. Newborns, and even the fetus, can hear. Newborns also can feel pain, smell, and taste. Infants as young as 4 months of age have intermodal perception.

COGNITIVE DEVELOPMENT

Piaget proposed that infant cognitive development involves the sensorimotor stage, or progression in the infant's ability to organize and coordinate sensations with physical movements. Piaget divided the sensorimotor stage into six substages, ranging from simple reflexes (birth to first month) to internalization of schemes (18–24 months). Piaget also found that object permanence is an important accomplishment in the first year. A number of contemporary developmentalists believe that Piaget underestimated some of the infant's competencies, especially competencies in developing a more stable and differentiated perceptual world and engaging in symbolic activity. The information-processing perspective emphasizes the infant's development of cognitive processes—such as attention and memory—rather than stages. Developmental scales that evaluate individual differences among infants have been developed. Milestones in infant language development include babbling (3–6 months), first words understood (6–9 months), the growth of receptive vocabulary (reaches 300 or more words by age 2), and the growth of spoken vocabulary (reaches 200–275 words by age 2). An infant's first words characteristically are holophrastic; at about 18–24 months, infants speak in two-word utterances. Mean length of utterance (MLU) has been used as an indicator of language maturity; five stages of MLU have been identified.

SOCIOEMOTIONAL DEVELOPMENT

Attachment to the caregiver intensifies at about 6 to 7 months of age. Ainsworth believes that attachment can be classified as secure, avoidant, or resistant, with optimal development occurring for secure attachment. Some critics believe that too much emphasis is placed on secure attachment's ability to predict later competence. Fathers have increased their interaction with infants but still lag far behind mothers. Day care has become a basic need of the American family. Too much of American day care is low-quality. The infant's temperament (such as easy, difficult, or slow to warm up) is strongly influenced by biological factors but becomes more malleable with experience. Emotions are the first language that parents and infants communicate with before the infant acquires language. Various emotions emerge at different ages—for instance, a social smile at about 4 to 6 weeks, surprise at 3 to 4 months, and shame at 6 to 8 months. Erikson argues that the first year is the stage of trust versus mistrust, and that the second year is the stage of autonomy versus shame and doubt. At some point in the second year of life, the infant develops a sense of self. Caregiving needs to be adapted to the developmental status of the infant and toddler. Of special concern are developmental problems, such as child abuse and infantile autism.

Early Childhood

You are troubled at seeing him spend his early years doing nothing. What! Is it nothing to be happy? Is it nothing to skip, to play, to run about all day long? Never in his life will he be so busy as now.

—Jean-Jacques Rousseau

In early childhood, our greatest untold poem was being only 4 years old. We skipped and ran and played all the sun long, never in our lives so busy, busy being something we had not quite grasped yet. Who knew our thoughts, which we worked up into small mythologies all our own? Our thoughts and images and drawings took wings. The blossoms of our heart, no wind could touch. Our small world widened as we discovered new refuges and new people. When we said, "I," we meant something totally unique, not to be confused with any other. Section Four consists of three chapters: "Physical Development in Early Childhood" (chapter 9), "Cognitive Development in Early Childhood" (chapter 10), and "Socioemotional Development in Early Childhood" (chapter 11).

GRACE CARPENTER
HUDSON
Indian Girl with Kachina, detail

Physical Development in Early Childhood

*That energy which makes a child hard to
manage is the energy which afterward
makes him a manager of life.*

—Henry Ward Beecher,
Proverbs from Plymouth Pulpit, 1887

> $\mathcal{A}$*ll the sun long I was running . . .*
>
> —Dylan Thomas

IMAGES OF CHILDREN

Tony's Physical Development

$\mathcal{A}$t 2 years of age, Tony is no saint. Tony's growing demand for autonomy keeps his mother busy hour after hour. Only a year earlier, he had learned to walk. Now he is running away from her into neighbors' yards and down the aisles of grocery stores. Trying out his new skills, he is constantly testing his parents and finding out the limits of his behavior.

By about his third birthday, Tony's behavior takes a slightly different turn. His temper tantrums have not entirely disappeared—the "terrible twos" can last into the fourth year—but much of his negative behavior has gone away. Every week produces a palate of new words and new tricks of climbing, skipping, and jumping. Tony is beginning to be able to make his body do what he wants it to do. As he moves through the preschool years, he learns how to draw and how to play different ball games. He is boastful, too, about his newly developed competencies. Tony says, "I'm bigger now, aren't I?" "I'm not a little baby anymore am I?" Tony is right. He is not a baby anymore. His babyhood is gone.

By 4 years of age, Tony has become even more adventuresome, exploring his world with fascination and abandon. By age 5, Tony is a self-assured child. He has good coordination and he delights at alarming his parents with his hair-raising stunts on any object suitable for climbing.

PREVIEW

As poet Dylan Thomas artfully observed, young children do "run all the sun long." And as their physical development advances, children's small worlds widen. Our coverage of early childhood's physical development focuses on body growth and change, motor development, sleep and sleep problems, nutrition, and health and illness.

BODY GROWTH AND CHANGE

Remember from chapter 6 that the infant's growth in the first year is extremely rapid and follows cephalocaudal and proximodistal patterns. At some point around the first birthday, most infants have begun to walk. During the infant's second year, the growth rate begins to slow down, but both gross and fine motor skills progress rapidly. The infant develops a sense of mastery through increased proficiency in walking and running. Improvement in fine motor skills—such as being able to turn the pages of a book one at a time—also contributes to the infant's sense of mastery in the second year. The growth rate continues to slow down in early childhood; otherwise we would be a species of giants.

> *Passing hence from infancy, I came to boyhood, or rather it came to me, displacing infancy, nor did that depart—and yet it was no more.*
>
> —**Confessions of St. Augustine**

Height and Weight

The average child grows 2½ inches in height and gains between 5 and 7 pounds a year during early childhood. As the preschool child grows older, the percentage of increase in height and weight decreases with each additional year. Figure 9.1 shows the average height and weight of children as they age from 2 to 6 years. Girls are only slightly smaller and lighter than boys during these years, a difference that continues until puberty. During the preschool years, both boys and girls slim down as the trunk of their bodies lengthens. Although their heads are still somewhat large for their bodies, by the end of the preschool years most children have lost their top-heavy look. Body fat also shows a slow, steady decline during the preschool years, so that the chubby baby often looks much leaner by the end of early childhood. Girls have more fatty tissue than boys, and boys have more muscle tissue.

Most preschool children are fascinated by bodies—especially their own, but also the bodies of family members and friends. Children have lots of questions about how their bodies work. Jonathan, age 4, says, "You know, I sometimes wonder about what is inside me. I bet it is all wet with blood and other stuff moving around. Outside of me it is all dry. You wouldn't know my inside by looking at the outside part." Jason, age 5, asks "How does my brain work?" Jennifer, age 5, asks, "Why do we eat food? What happens to the food after we eat it?" Budding 4-year-old biologists like Jonathan, Jason, and Jennifer are telling us they want to know more about their body's machinery. Two recommended books to help answer some of children's curious questions about their bodies are *The Body Book* by Claire Raynor and *Blood and Guts* by Linda Allison.

Growth patterns vary individually. Think back to your preschool years. This was probably the first time you noticed that some children were taller than you, some shorter; that some were fatter, some thinner; that some were stronger, some weaker. Much of the variation is due to heredity, but environmental experiences are involved to some extent. A review of the heights and weights of children around the world concluded that the two most important contributors to height differences are ethnic origin and nutrition (Meredith, 1978). Urban, middle-class, and firstborn children were taller than rural, lower-class, and later-born children. Children whose mothers smoked during pregnancy were half an inch shorter than children whose

FIGURE 9.1

Average Height and Weight of Girls and Boys from 2 to 6 Years of Age

mothers did not smoke during pregnancy. In the United States, African American children are taller than White children.

Why are some children unusually short? The culprits are congenital factors (genetic or prenatal problems), a physical problem that develops in childhood, or an emotional difficulty. In many cases, children with congenital growth problems can be treated with hormones. Usually this treatment is directed at the pituitary, the body's master gland, located at the base of the brain. This gland secretes growth-related hormones. With regard to physical problems that develop during childhood, malnutrition and chronic infections can stunt growth, although if the problems are properly treated, normal growth usually is attained. **Deprivation dwarfism** *is a type of growth retardation caused by emotional deprivation; children are deprived of affection, which causes stress and alters the release of hormones by the pituitary gland.* Some children who are not dwarfs may also show the effects of an impoverished emotional environment, although most parents of these children say they are small and weak because they have a poor body structure or constitution (Gardner, 1972).

The Brain

One of the most important physical developments during early childhood is the continuing development of the brain and nervous system. While the brain continues to grow in early childhood, it does not grow as rapidly as in infancy. By the time children have reached 3 years of age, the brain is three-quarters of its adult size. By age 5, the brain has reached about nine-tenths its adult size.

The brain and the head grow more rapidly than any other part of the body. The top parts of the head, the eyes, and the brain grow faster than the lower portions, such as the jaw. Figure 9.2 reveals how the growth curve for the head and brain advances more rapidly than the growth curve for height and weight. At 5 years of age, when the brain has attained approximately 90 percent of its adult weight, the 5-year-old's total body weight is only about one-third of what it will be when the child reaches adulthood.

Some of the brain's increase in size is due to the increase in the number and size of nerve endings within and between areas of the brain. These nerve endings continue to grow at least until adolescence. Some of the brain's increase in size also is due to the increase in **myelination,** *a process in which nerve cells are covered and insulated with a layer of fat cells. This process has the effect of increasing the speed of information traveling through the nervous system.* Some developmentalists believe myelination is important in the maturation of a number of children's abilities. For example, myelination in the areas of the brain related to hand-eye coordination is not complete until about 4 years of age. Myelination in the areas of the brain related to focusing attention is not complete until the end of the middle or late childhood.

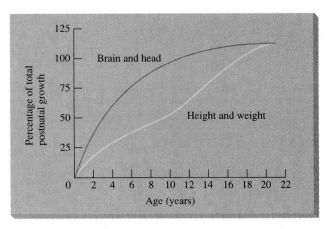

FIGURE 9.2

Growth Curves for the Head and Brain and for Height and Weight
The more rapid growth of the brain and head can be easily seen. Height and weight advance more gradually over the first two decades of life.

The increasing maturation of the brain, combined with opportunities to experience a widening world, contribute enormously to children's emerging cognitive abilities. Consider a child who is learning to read and is asked by the teacher to read aloud to the class. Input from the child's eyes is transmitted to the child's brain, then passed through many brain systems, which translate (process) the patterns of black and white into codes for letters, words, and associations. The output occurs in the form of messages to the child's lips and tongue. The child's own gift of speech is possible because brain systems are organized in ways that permit language processing.

Swiftly the brain becomes an enchanted loom, where millions of flashing shuttles weave a dissolving pattern— always a meaningful pattern—though never an abiding one.
—**Sir Charles Sherrington, 1906**

Visual Perception

Visual maturity increases during the early childhood years. Only toward the end of early childhood are most children's eye muscles adequately developed to allow them to move their eyes efficiently across a series of letters. And preschool children are often farsighted, not being able to see up close as well as they can far away. By the time they enter the first grade, though, most children can focus their eyes and sustain their attention quite well.

Depth perception continues to mature during the preschool years. However, because of young children's lack of motor coordination, they may trip and spill drinks, fall from a jungle gym, or produce poor artwork.

Some children develop **functional amblyopia,** *or "lazy eye," which usually results from not using one eye enough to avoid the discomfort of double vision produced by imbalanced* *eye muscles*. Children with a lazy eye have no way of knowing that they are not seeing adequately, even though their vision is decreased because one eye is doing most of the work. Treatment may include patching the stronger eye for several months to encourage the use of the affected eye, wearing glasses, or doing eye exercises. Occasionally, surgery may be required on the muscles of the eye.

What signs suggest that a child might be having vision problems? These include rubbing of the eyes, excessive blinking, squinting, appearing irritable when playing games that require good distance vision, shutting or covering one eye, and tilting the head or thrusting it forward when looking at something. A child who shows any of these behaviors should be examined by an ophthalmologist.

MOTOR DEVELOPMENT

Running as fast as you can, falling down, getting right back up and running just as fast as you can . . . building towers with blocks . . . scribbling, scribbling, and more scribbling . . . cutting paper with scissors. During your preschool years you probably developed the ability to perform all of these activities.

Gross and Fine Motor Skills

Considerable progress is made in both gross and fine motor skills during early childhood. First let's explore changes in gross motor skills.

Gross Motor Skills

The preschool child no longer has to make an effort simply to stay upright and to move around. As children move their legs with more confidence and carry themselves more purposefully, the process of moving around in the environment becomes more automatic (Poest & others, 1990).

At 3 years of age, children are still enjoying simple movements such as hopping, jumping, and running back and forth, just for the sheer delight of performing these activities. They take considerable pride in showing how they can run across a room and jump all of six inches. The run-and-jump will win no Olympic gold medals, but for the 3-year-old the activity is a source of considerable pride and accomplishment.

By 4 years of age, children are still enjoying the same kind of activities, but they have become more adventurous. They scramble over low jungle gyms as they display their athletic prowess. Although they have

been able to climb stairs with one foot on each step for some time now, they are just beginning to be able to come down the same way. They still often revert to marking time on each step.

By 5 years of age, children are even more adventuresome than when they were 4. As our description of Tony at the beginning of the chapter indicated, it is not unusual for self-assured 5-year-olds to perform hair-raising stunts on practically any climbing object. Five-year-olds run hard and enjoy races with each other and their parents. A summary of development in gross motor skills during early childhood is shown in figure 9.3.

You probably have arrived at one important conclusion about preschool children: They are very, very active. Indeed, researchers have found that 3-year-old children have the highest activity level of any age in the entire human life span. They fidget when they watch television. They fidget when they sit at the dinner table. Even when they sleep, they move around quite a bit. Because of their activity level and the development of large muscles, especially in the arms and legs, preschool children need daily exercise. To further evaluate gross motor skills in young children, see Critical Thinking About Children's Development.

It is important for preschool and kindergarten teachers to develop programs that encourage young children's gross motor skills. Catherine Poest and her colleagues (1990) provided some valuable suggestions for such programs. One set of their recommendations involves developing fundamental movement skills. Careful planning is

CRITICAL THINKING ABOUT CHILDREN'S DEVELOPMENT

Explaining to Parents Why Most 3-Year-Olds Should Not Participate in Sports

Assume that you are the director of a preschool program and the parents ask you to develop a program to teach the children how to participate in sports. Think through how you would explain to the parents why most 3-year-olds are not ready for participation in sports programs. Include in your answer information about 3-year-olds' limited motor skills as well as the importance of learning basic motor skills first. By developing a rationale for why most 3-year-olds should not participate in sports, you are learning to think critically by *applying a developmental framework to understand behavior.*

37–48 months	49–60 months	61–72 months
Throws ball underhanded (4´) Pedals tricycle 10´ Catches large ball Completes forward somersault (aided) Jumps to floor from 12´´ Hops three hops with both feet Steps on footprint pattern Catches bounced ball	Bounces and catches ball Runs 10´ and stops Pushes/pulls a wagon/doll buggy Kicks 10´´ ball toward target Carries 12-pound object Catches ball Bounces ball under control Hops on one foot four hops	Throws ball (44´ boys; 25´ girls) Carries a 16-pound object Kicks rolling ball Skips alternating feet Roller skates Skips rope Rolls ball to hit object Rides two-wheel bike with training wheels

Figure 9.3

The Development of Gross Motor Skills in Early Childhood
The skills are listed in the approximate order of difficulty within each age period.

needed to ensure that a variety of motor activities appropriate to the ages and individual skills of children are provided. Beam walking is one activity that can be used. The variety of balance beam pathways help meet the individual motor needs of young children. Challenge children to walk the beams in different directions or walk balancing bean bags on different body parts. Decrease the width of the beams, raise the height, or set up the beams on an incline.

Competent teachers of young children also plan daily fitness activities. Include a daily run or gallop to music on the bike path. Children love to run and too infrequently get to do so in early childhood education centers and at home. Several fast-paced fitness activities can be planned over the school year. Combine fitness with creative movement, music, and children's imaginations. Children enjoy moving like snakes, cats, bears, elephants, dinosaurs, frogs, kangaroos, seals, conductors and trains, police and police cars, pilots and airplanes, washing machines, and teeter-totters. Avoid recordings or activities that "program" children or that include group calisthenics and structured exercise routines that are not appropriate for young children.

Developing young children's gross motor skills also includes perceptual-motor activities. Teachers can ask children to copy their movements, such as putting hands on toes, hands on head, or hands on stomach. These activities help children to learn body awareness and visual awareness. As the year progresses, teachers can gradually increase the difficulty of these exercises by touching body parts more difficult to name and locate (like shoulders and elbows) (Weikart, 1987). Also provide children with many opportunities to move to a steady beat. They can tap and march to the tune of nursery rhymes, chants, songs, and parades, for example. Obstacle courses are enjoyable activities for children and help them to understand such directions in space as "over," "under," "around," and "through" as well as to practice moving through space without touching any of the obstacles.

In sum, designing and implementing a developmentally appropriate movement curriculum takes time and effort. But while time consuming, such a curriculum facilitates the development of children's gross motor skills. To further evaluate physical instruction

John W. Santrock

programs for young children, see Critical Thinking About Children's Development.

Fine Motor Skills

At 3 years of age, children are still emerging from the infant ability to place and handle things. Although they have had the ability to pick up the tiniest objects between their thumb and forefinger for some time now, they are still somewhat clumsy at it. Three-year-olds can build surprisingly high block towers, each block being placed with intense concentration but often not in a completely straight line. When 3-year-olds play with a form board or a simple jigsaw puzzle, they are rather rough in placing the pieces. Even when they recognize the hole a piece fits into, they are not very precise in positioning the piece. They often try to force the piece in the hole or pat it vigorously.

At 4 years of age, children's fine motor coordination has improved substantially and become much more precise. Sometimes 4-year-old children have trouble building high towers with blocks because in their desire to place each of the blocks perfectly they may upset those already stacked. By age 5, children's fine motor coordination has improved further. Hand, arm, and body all move together under better command of the eye. Mere towers no longer interest the 5-year-old, who now wants to build a house or a church complete with steeple, though adults may still need to be told what each finished project is meant to be. A summary of the development of fine motor skills in early childhood is shown in figure 9.4.

How do developmentalists measure children's motor development? The **Denver Developmental Screening Test** *is a simple, inexpensive, fast method of diagnosing developmental delay in children from birth through 6 years of age. The test is individually administered and includes separate assessments of gross and fine motor skills, as well as language and personal-social ability.* Among the gross motor skills this test measures are the child's ability to sit, walk, long jump, pedal a tricycle, throw a ball overhand, catch a bounced ball, hop on one foot, and

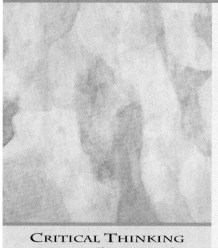

CRITICAL THINKING ABOUT CHILDREN'S DEVELOPMENT

Planning a Physical Instruction Program for 3- and 4-Year-Olds

Imagine that you have just become a teacher and are faced with developing a physical instruction program for 3- and 4-year-olds. What kind of guidelines will you want to use? Keep in mind the characteristics of 3- and 4-year-old children and that instruction should probably be brief and to the point. Also keep in mind that the children will need to practice their physical skills. Above all else, the activities should be fun for them. In developing your program, you might want to include visual cues to help children improve their motor skills. You also might want to work with the young children on their balance, spatial orientation, throwing and kicking, jumping, and many other movement activities. By planning a physical instruction program for 3- to 4-year-olds, you are learning to think critically by *using knowledge about development to promote human welfare.*

37–48 months

Approximates circle
Cuts paper
Pastes using pointer finger
Builds three-block bridge
Builds eight-block tower
Draws *0* and +
Dresses and undresses doll
Pours from pitcher without spilling

49–60 months

Strings and laces shoelace
Cuts following line
Strings ten beads
Copies figure *X*
Opens and places clothespins (one-handed)
Builds a five-block bridge
Pours from various containers
Prints first name

61–72 months

Folds paper into halves and quarters
Traces around hand
Draws rectangle, circle, square, and triangle
Cuts interior piece from paper
Uses crayons appropriately
Makes clay object with two small parts
Reproduces letters
Copies two short words

Note: The skills are listed in the approximate order of difficulty within each age period.

FIGURE 9.4

The Development of Fine Motor Skills in Early Childhood

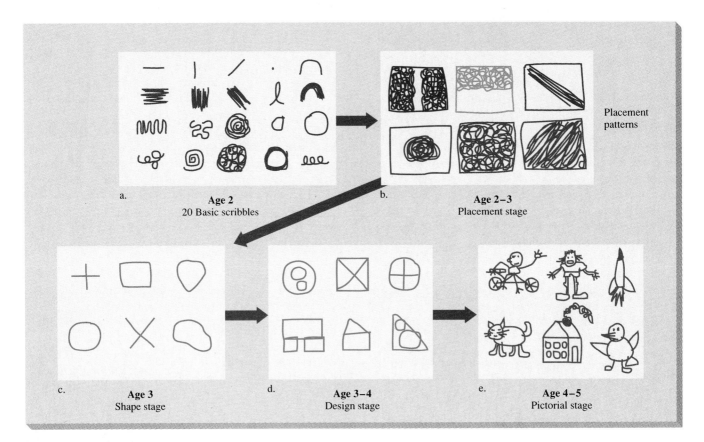

FIGURE 9.5

The Stages of Young Children's Artistic Drawings

"You moved."

Drawing by Lorenz; © 1987 The New Yorker Magazine, Inc.

balance on one foot. Fine motor skills measured by the test include the child's ability to stack cubes, reach for objects, and draw a person (Frankenburg & others, 1992).

Young Children's Artistic Drawings

The development of fine motor skills in the preschool years allows children to become budding artists. There are dramatic changes in how children depict what they see. Art provides unique insights into children's perceptual worlds—what they are attending to, how space and distance are viewed, how they experience patterns and forms.

Rhoda Kellogg is a creative teacher of preschool children who has been observing and guiding young children's artistic efforts for many decades. She has assembled an impressive array of tens of thousands of drawings produced by more than 2,000 preschool children. Adults who are unfamiliar with young children's art often view the productions of this age group as meaningless scribbles. Kellogg (1970) has tried to change this perception by showing that young children's artistic productions are orderly, meaningful, and structured.

By their second birthday, children can scribble. Scribbles represent the earliest form of drawing. Every form of graphic art, no matter how complex, contains the lines found in children's artwork, which Kellogg calls the twenty basic scribbles. These include vertical, horizontal, diagonal, circular, curving, waving or zigzag lines, and dots. As young children progress from scribbling to picture making, they go through four distinguishable stages: placement, shape, design, and pictorial (see figure 9.5).

The **placement stage** *is Kellogg's term for 2- to 3-year-olds' drawings, drawn on a page in placement patterns.* One example of these patterns is the spaced border pattern shown in figure 9.5b. The **shape stage** *is Kellogg's term for 3-year-olds' drawings consisting of diagrams in different shapes* (figure 9.5c). Young children draw six basic shapes: circles, squares or rectangles, triangles, crosses, Xs, and forms. The **design**

FIGURE 9.6

Children's Cat Drawings
The first two cats are typical of a young child's early efforts at drawing animals. They are humanlike, standing upright. As children become more aware of the nature of cats, they draw them more catlike, standing on all four feet, as shown in the cat on the right.

stage *is Kellogg's term for 3- to 4-year-olds' drawings in which young children mix two basic shapes into a more complex design* (figure 9.5d). This stage occurs rather quickly after the shape stage. The **pictorial stage** *is Kellogg's term for 4- to 5-year-olds' drawings which consist of objects that adults can recognize* (figure 9.5e). In the next chapter, we will look further at young children's art, paying special attention to the role of cognitive development in their art.

> *The youth of an art is like the youth of anything else—its most interesting period.*
>
> —Samuel Butler, *Note-Books*, 1912

Young children often use the same formula for drawing different things. Though modified in small ways, one basic form can cover a range of objects. When children begin to draw animals, they portray them in the same way they portray humans: standing upright with a smiling face, legs, and arms (see figure 9.6). Pointed ears may be the only clue adults have as to the nature of the particular beast. As children become more aware of the nature of a cat, their drawings acquire more catlike features and the cat is shown on all four feet, tail in the air.

Not all children embrace art with equal enthusiasm, and the same child may want to draw one day but have no interest in it the next day. For most children, however, art is an important vehicle for conveying feelings and ideas that are not easily expressed in words (Schiller, 1995; Seefeldt, 1995). Drawing and constructing also provide children with a hands-on opportunity to use their problem-solving skills to develop creative ways to represent scale, space, or motion. Parents can provide a context for artistic exploration in their children by giving children a work space where they are not overly concerned about messiness or damage, making supplies available, having a bulletin board display space for the child's art, and supporting and encouraging the child's art activity.

Today, most teachers let children write with the hand they favor.

Handedness

For centuries left-handers have suffered unfair discrimination in a world designed for the right-hander. Even the devil himself was portrayed as a left-hander. For many years, teachers forced all children to write with their right hand even if they had a left-hand tendency. Fortunately, today most teachers let children write with the hand they favor.

Some children are still discouraged from using their left hand, even though many left-handed individuals have become very successful. Their ranks include Leonardo da Vinci, Benjamin Franklin, and Pablo Picasso. Each of these famous men was known for his imagination of spatial layouts, which may be stronger in left-handed individuals. Left-handed athletes also are often successful; since there are fewer left-handed athletes, the opposition is not as accustomed to the style and approach of "lefties." Their serve in tennis spins in the opposite direction, their curve ball in baseball swerves the opposite way, and their left foot in soccer is not the one children are used to defending against. Left-handed individuals also do well intellectually. In an analysis of the Scholastic Aptitude Test (SAT) scores of more than 100,000 students, 20 percent of the top-scoring group was left-handed, which is twice the rate of left-handedness found in the general population (Bower, 1985). Quite clearly, many left-handed people are competent in a wide variety of human activities, ranging from athletic skills to intellectual accomplishments.

When does hand preference develop? Adults usually notice a child's hand preference during early childhood, but researchers have found handedness tendencies in the infant years. Even newborns have some preference for one side of their body over the other. In one study, 65 percent of infants turned their head to the right when they were lying on their stomachs in the crib (Michel, 1981). Fifteen percent preferred to face toward the left. These preferences for the right or left were related to later handedness. By about 7 months of age, infants prefer grabbing with one hand or the other, and this is also related to later handedness (Ramsay, 1980). By 2 years of age, about 10 percent of children favor their left hand. Many preschool children, though, use both hands, with a clear hand preference not completely distinguished until later in development. Some children use one hand for writing and drawing, and the other hand for throwing a ball. My oldest daughter, Tracy, confuses the issue even further. She writes left-handed and plays tennis left-handed, but she plays golf right-handed. During early childhood, her handedness was still somewhat in doubt. My youngest daughter, Jennifer, was left-handed from early in infancy. Their left-handed orientation has not handicapped them in their athletic and academic pursuits, although Tracy once asked me if I would buy her a pair of left-handed scissors.

What is the origin of hand preference? Genetic inheritance and environmental experiences have been proposed as causes. In one investigation, a genetic interpretation was favored. The handedness of adopted children was not related to the handedness of their adoptive parents but was related to the handedness of their biological parents (Carter-Saltzman, 1980).

SLEEP AND SLEEP PROBLEMS

Most young children sleep through the night and also have one daytime nap. Sometimes, though, it is difficult to get young children to go to sleep as they drag out their bedtime routine. Helping the child to slow down before bedtime often contributes to less resistance in going to bed. Reading the child a story, playing with the child in the bath, or letting the child sit on the caregiver's lap while listening to music are quieting activities.

Many young children want to take a soft, cuddly object, such as a favorite blanket, teddy bear, or other stuffed animal, to bed with them. **Transitional objects** *are those that are repeatedly used by children as bedtime companions; they usually are soft and cuddly, and most developmentalists view them as representing a transition from being a dependent person to being a more independent one.* Therefore, using transitional objects at bedtime is normal behavior for young children. In one study, children who relied on transitional objects at age 4 showed the same level of emotional adjustment at ages 11 and 16 as children who had not relied on transitional objects (Newson, Newson, & Mahalski, 1982).

Among the sleep problems that children may develop are nightmares, night terrors, sleepwalking, and sleeptalking. **Nightmares** *are frightening dreams that awaken the sleeper, more often toward the morning than just after the child has gone to bed at night.* Caregivers should not worry about young children having occasional nightmares because almost every child has them. If children have nightmares on a persistent basis, it many indicate that they are feeling too much stress during their waking hours.

REM

Stage 4

Night terrors *are characterized by a sudden arousal from sleep and an intense fear, usually accompanied by a number of physiological reactions such as rapid heart rate and breathing, loud screams, heavy perspiration, and physical movement.* In most instances, the child has little or no memory of what happened during the night terror. Night terrors are less common than nightmares and occur more often in deep sleep than nightmares. Many children who experience night terrors return to sleep rather quickly after the night terror. Caregivers tend to be especially worried when children have night terrors, although they are usually not a serious problem and are not believed to reflect any emotional problems in children.

Somnambulism *(sleepwalking) occurs during the deepest stage of sleep.* Approximately 15 percent of children sleepwalk at least once, and from 1 to 5 percent do it regularly. Most children outgrow the problem without professional intervention. Except for the danger of accidents while walking around asleep in the dark, there is nothing abnormal about sleepwalking. It is safe to awaken sleepwalking children, and it is a good idea to do so because they might harm themselves. If children sleepwalk regularly, parents need to make the bedroom and house as safe from harm as possible. Sleeptalkers are soundly asleep as they speak, although occasionally they make fairly coherent statements for a brief period of time. Most of the time, though, you can't understand what children are saying during sleeptalking. There is nothing abnormal about sleeptalking and there is no reason to try to stop it from occurring.

At this point we have discussed a number of ideas about young children's body growth and change, motor development, and sleep. A summary of these ideas is presented in concept table 9.1.

NUTRITION

Four-year-old Bobby is on a steady diet of double cheeseburgers, french fries, and chocolate milkshakes. Between meals he gobbles up candy bars and marshmallows. He hates green vegetables. Only a preschooler, Bobby already has developed poor nutrition habits. What are a preschool child's energy needs? What is a preschooler's eating behavior like?

Energy Needs

Feeding and eating habits are important aspects of development during early childhood. What children eat affects their skeletal growth, body shape, and susceptibility to disease. Recognizing that nutrition is important for the child's growth and development, the federal government provides money for school lunch programs. An average preschool child requires 1,700 calories per day. Figure 9.7 shows the increasing energy needs of children as they move from infancy through the childhood years. Energy

John W. Santrock

CONCEPT TABLE 9.1

Body Growth and Change, Motor Development, and Sleep

Concept	Processes/Related Ideas	Characteristics/Description
Body Growth and Change	Height and weight	The average child grows 2½ inches in height and gains between 5 and 7 pounds a year during early childhood. Growth patterns vary individually, though. Some children are unusually short because of congenital problems, a physical problem that develops in childhood, or emotional problems.
	The brain	The brain is a key aspect of growth. By age 5, the brain has reached nine-tenths of its adult size. Some of its increase in size is due to increases in the number and size of nerve endings, some to myelination. Increasing brain maturation contributes to improved cognitive abilities.
	Visual perception	Visual maturity increases in early childhood. Some children develop functional amblyopia, or "lazy eye."
Motor Development	Gross motor skills	They increase dramatically during early childhood. Children become increasingly adventuresome as their gross motor skills improve. Young children's lives are extremely active, more active than at any other point in the life span. Rough-and-tumble play often occurs, especially in boys, and it can serve positive educational and developmental functions. It is important for preschool and kindergarten teachers to design and implement developmentally appropriate activities for young children's gross motor skills. Such activities include fundamental movement, daily fitness, and perceptual-motor opportunities.
	Fine motor skills	They also improve substantially during early childhood. The Denver Developmental Screening Test is one widely used measure of gross and fine motor skills.
	Young children's artistic drawings	The development of fine motor skills in the preschool years allows young children to become budding artists. Scribbling begins by 2 years of age and is followed by four stages of drawing, culminating in the pictorial stage at 4 to 5 years of age.
	Handedness	At one point, all children were taught to be right-handed. In today's world, the strategy is to allow children to use the hand they favor. Left-handed children are as competent in motor skills and intellect as right-handed children. Both genetic and environmental explanations of handedness have been given.
Sleep and Sleep Problems	Their nature	Most young children sleep through the night and also have one daytime nap. Helping the child slow down before bedtime often contributes to less resistance in going to bed. Many young children want to take transitional objects to bed with them; these objects represent a transition from being dependent to being more independent. Among the problems in sleep that may develop are nightmares, night terrors, somnambulism (sleepwalking), and sleeptalking.

requirements for individual children are determined by the **basal metabolism rate (BMR),** *which is the minimum amount of energy a person uses in a resting state.* Energy needs of individual children of the same age, sex, and size vary. Reasons for these differences remain unexplained. Differences in physical activity, basal metabolism, and the efficiency with which children use energy are among the candidates for explanation.

Eating Behavior

Among the most important considerations for improving young children's eating behavior are knowing about basic

Age	Weight (kg)	Height (cm)	Energy Needs (calories)	Calorie Ranges
1–3	13	90	1,300	900–1,800
4–6	20	112	1,700	1,300–2,300
7–10	28	132	2,400	1,650–3,300

FIGURE 9.7

Recommended Energy Intakes for Children Ages 1 through 10

Eating habits become ingrained early in development. Especially in the early childhood years, parents need to monitor the amount of fat and sugar in their children's diets. These Asian children are developing a better diet than many American children, who too often eat fast-food meals high in fat content.

daily routines, understanding the implications of fat and sugar intake, and recognizing a number of problems in eating behavior that may appear through the course of development.

Daily Routines

What are the daily routines of eating for most 3-year-olds, 4-year-olds, and 5-year-olds (Allen & Marotz, 1989)?

3-year-olds

- Their appetite is fairly good and they prefer small servings.
- They usually like only a few cooked vegetables, but often eat about everything else.
- They feed themselves independently if they are hungry, using a spoon in a semiadult fashion; they may even spear with a fork.
- They dawdle over their food when they are not hungry.
- They can pour milk and juice and serve individual portions from a serving dish with prompts such as "fill it up to the line."
- They often begin to drink a lot of milk, so it is important to ensure that the 3-year-old does not fill up on milk to the exclusion of other needed foods.

4-year-olds

- Their appetite fluctuates from very good to fair.
- They may develop dislikes of certain foods and refuse to eat them to the point of tears if pushed.
- They use all eating utensils and become skilled at spreading jelly or peanut butter or cutting soft foods such as bread.
- Their eating and talking get in the way of each other; talking usually dominates eating.
- They like to help in the preparation of a meal, engaging in such activities as dumping premeasured ingredients, washing vegetables, and setting the table.

Spinach: Divide into little piles. Rearrange again into new piles. After five or six maneuvers, sit back and say you are full.

—Delia Ephron

John W. Santrock

TABLE 9.1

The Fat and Calorie Content of Selected Fast Foods

Food	Calories	% of Calories from Fat
Burger King Whopper, fries, vanailla shake	1,250	43
Big Mac, fries, chocolate shake	1,100	41
McDonald's Quarter-Pounder with Cheese	418	52
Pizza Hut 10-inch pizza with sausage, mushrooms, pepperoni, and green pepper	1,035	35
Arby's roast beef sandwich, two potato patties, coleslaw, chocolate shake	1,200	30
Kentucky Fried Chicken dinner (three pieces chicken, mashed potatoes and gravy, coleslaw, roll)	830	50
Arthur Treacher's fish and chips (two pieces breaded and fried fish, french fries, cola drink)	900	43
Typical restaurant "diet plate" (hamburger patty, cottage cheese, etc.)	638	63

Source: From Virginia DeMoss, "Good, the Bad, and the Edible" in *Runner's World,* June 1980. © Virginia DeMoss. Reprinted by permission.

5-year-olds

- They usually eat well, but not at every meal.
- They like familiar foods.
- They become aware of other family members' food dislikes and declare that they too dislike these foods.
- They like to make their breakfast (pouring cereal, getting out milk and juice) and lunch (spreading peanut butter and jam on bread).

Fat and Sugar

Special concerns of caregivers involve the appropriate amount of fat and sugar in young children's diets. While some health-conscious mothers may be providing too little fat in their infant's and children's diets, other parents are raising their children on diets in which the percentage of fat is far too high. Our changing lifestyles, in which we often eat on the run and pick up fast-food meals, probably contribute to the increased fat levels in children's diets. Most fast-food meals are high in protein, especially meat and dairy products. But the average American child does not need to be concerned about getting enough protein. What must be of concern is the vast number of young children who are being weaned on fast foods that are not only high in protein but also high in fat. Eating habits become ingrained very early in life, and unfortunately, it is during the preschool years that many people get their first taste of fast food (Poulton & Sexton, 1996). The American Heart Association recommends that the daily limit for calories from fat should be approximately 35 percent. Compare this figure with the figures in table 9.1. Clearly, many fast-food meals contribute to excess fat intake by children.

Being overweight can be a serious problem in early childhood. Consider Ramón, a kindergartner who always begged to stay inside to help during recess. His teacher noticed that Ramón never joined the running games the small superheroes played as they propelled themselves around the playground. Ramón is an overweight 4-year-old boy. Except for extreme cases of obesity, overweight preschool children are usually not encouraged to lose a great deal of weight, but to slow their rate of weight gain so that they will grow into a more normal weight for their height by thinning out as they grow taller. Prevention of obesity in children includes helping children and parents see food as a way to satisfy hunger and nutritional needs, not as proof of love or as a reward for good behavior. Snack foods should be low in fat, simple sugars, and salt, and high in fiber. Routine physical activity should be a daily occurrence. The child's life should be centered around activities, not meals.

There is concern not only about excessive fat in children's diets but also about excessive sugar. Consider Robert, age 3, who loves chocolate. His mother lets him have three chocolate candy bars a day. He also drinks an average of four cans of caffeine cola a day, and he eats sugar-coated cereal each morning at breakfast. It is estimated that the average American child consumes almost 2 pounds of sugar per week (Riddle & Prinz, 1984). How does sugar consumption influence the health and behavior of young children?

The association of sugar consumption and children's health problems—dental cavities and obesity, for example—has been widely documented (Rogers & Morris, 1986). In recent years, a growing interest in the influence of sugar on children's behavior has surfaced. In one study, eight preschool children on separate mornings each received 6 ounces of juice, sweetened one morning with sucrose and on the other with an artificial sweetener (Goldman & others, 1986). The children were observed for 90 minutes following the drinks. After the sucrose drink, the young children exhibited more inappropriate behavior. They were less attentive and overly active, for example. Other findings support the belief that sugar consumption by young children increases their aggression, especially in unstructured circumstances and when the child is bored (Goldman & others, 1987).

The jury is still out on how extensively sugar affects children's behavior. Some reviews conclude that we do not have good evidence for claiming that sugar promotes aggressive or hyperactive behavior (Pipes, 1988). However, investigations such as the one described here argue for a closer look at the contribution of sugar to children's behavior.

In sum, although there is individual variation in appropriate nutrition for children, their diets should be well-balanced and should include fats, carbohydrates, protein, vitamins, and minerals. An occasional candy bar does not hurt and can even benefit a growing body, but a steady diet of hamburgers, french fries, milkshakes, and candy bars should be avoided.

In general, my children refused to eat anything that had not danced on TV.

—**Erma Bombeck**

Sweets, Snacks, and "Fussy Eaters"

Eating too many sweets is often a contributing factor in eating problems during early childhood. When young children eat too many sweets—candy bars, cola, and sweetened cereals, for example—they can spoil their appetite and then not want to eat more nutritious foods when they are served at mealtime. Thus, it is important for caregivers to be firm in limiting the amount of sweets young children eat. Another reason sweets should be limited is that tooth decay is directly related to the consumption of sugar.

Most preschool children genuinely need to eat more often than the adults in the family because preschool children use up so much energy. It is a long time from breakfast to lunch and from lunch to dinner for the active young child. Thus, a midmorning and midafternoon snack are recommended routines. A good strategy is to early on avoid giving sweets to young children during these snacktimes.

This would be a better world for children if parents had to eat the spinach.

—**Groucho Marx**

Many eating problems are carryovers from the toddler years. To avoid eating problems and "fussy eaters" in the preschool years, the following caregiver practices are recommended in the toddler and preschool years (Leach, 1991):

- Encourage the child's independence in eating.
- Let the child eat in any order or combination.
- Let the meal end when the child has had enough.

- Try to keep mealtimes enjoyable.
- Don't use food as a reward, punishment, bribe, or threat (that is, try to keep the child's eating completely separate from discipline).

Many young children get labeled as "fussy" or "difficult eaters" when they are only trying to exercise the same rights to personal taste and appetite adults take for granted. Allow for the child's developing tastes in food.

Malnutrition in Young Children from Low-Income Families

One of the most common nutritional problems in early childhood is iron deficiency anemia, which results in chronic fatigue. This is a problem that results from the failure to eat adequate amounts of quality meats and dark green vegetables. Young children from low-income families are most likely to develop iron deficiency anemia.

Poor nutrition is a special concern in lives of young children from low-income families. In a review of hunger in the United States, it was estimated that approximately 11 million preschool children are malnourished (Brown & Allen, 1988). Many of these preschool children do not get essential iron, vitamins, or protein. A report by the Children's Defense Fund (1990) documented that despite the proven effectiveness of the Special Supplemental Food Program for Women, Infants, and Children (WIC) in improving maternal and child health and in spite of the dramatic cost-effectiveness, only nine states and the District of Columbia supplement their federal WIC allotment to provide food and nutrition services to additional women, infants, and children. Only slightly more than half of all eligible women and children receive federal WIC funds.

ILLNESS AND HEALTH

What is the nature of young children's illness and health in the United States? What is the status of young children's illness and health around the world? What are some important developmental concerns for young children's illness and health? We will consider each of these questions in turn.

Young Children's Illness and Health in the United States

Fortunately in the United States the dangers of many diseases such as measles, rubella (German measles), mumps, whooping cough, diphtheria, and polio are no longer present. The vast majority of children in the United States have been immunized against such major childhood diseases. It is important, though, for parents to recognize that these diseases, though no longer afflicting our nation's children, do require a sequence of vaccinations. Without the vaccinations, children can still get the diseases.

The disorders most likely to be fatal during the preschool years are birth defects, cancer, and heart disease.

Death rates from these problems have been reduced in recent years because of improved treatments and health care.

A special concern in the United States is the poor health status of many young children from low-income families. As we saw earlier in our discussion of nutrition and eating behavior, it is estimated that about 11 million preschool children in the United States are malnourished. Their malnutrition places their health at risk. They often have less resistance to diseases, including minor ones such as colds and major ones such as influenza.

The State of Illness and Health in the World's Children

Of every three deaths in the world, one is a child under the age of 5. Every week, more than a quarter of a million young children still die in developing countries in a quiet carnage of infection and undernutrition (Grant, 1996).

What are the main causes of death and child malnutrition in the world?

- *Diarrhea* is the leading cause of childhood death. However, approximately 70 percent of the more than 4 million children killed by diarrhea in 1990 could have been saved if all parents had available a low-cost breakthrough known as **oral rehydration therapy (ORT).** *This treatment encompasses a range of techniques designed to prevent dehydration during episodes of diarrhea by giving the child fluids by mouth.* When a child has diarrhea, dehydration can often be prevented by giving the child a large volume of water and other liquids.
- More than 3 million children were killed in 1990 by *measles, tetanus,* and *whooping cough.* Another 200,000 have been permanently disabled by polio. The efforts in the 1980s made immunization widely available, and the lives of many children have been saved by vaccination costing only about $5 a child. What is needed is improved communication to inform parents in developing countries and around the world of the importance of a course of vaccinations for their children.
- *Acute respiratory infections,* mainly *pneumonias,* killed 2 to 3 million children under the age of 5 in 1990. Most of these children could have been saved by 50 cents worth of antibiotics administered by a community health worker with a few months of training. Most of the children's parents could have sought out the low-cost help if they had known how to distinguish between a bad cough and a life-threatening lung infection.

A simple child
That lightly draws its breath,
What should it know of death?
　　　—William Wordsworth, "We Are Seven," 1798

- *Undernutrition* was a contributing cause in about one-third of the 14 million child deaths in the world in 1990. While not having enough to eat is still a fundamental problem in some of the world's poorest countries, the major cause of undernutrition in the world is not a shortage of food in the home. Rather, it is a lack of basic services and a shortage of information about preventing infection and using food to promote growth. Making sure that parents know that they can protect their children's nutritional health by such means as birth spacing, care during pregnancy, breast-feeding, immunization, preventing illness, special feeding before and after illness, and regularly checking the child's weight gain can overcome many cases of malnutrition and poor growth in today's world.
- A contributing factor in at least one-fourth of today's child deaths is the *timing of births.* Births that are too numerous or too close, or mothers who are too young or too old, carry a much higher risk for both the mother and the child. Using this knowledge and today's low-cost ways of timing births is one of the most powerful and least expensive means for raising the child survival rate and improving children's health around the world.
- Also, more than half of all illnesses and deaths among children are associated with inadequate *hygiene.* In communities without a safe water supply and sanitation, it is very difficult to prevent the contamination of food and water. Some low-cost methods can prevent the spread of germs, and all families should be informed of these sanitation measures.

In summary, most child malnutrition, as well as most child deaths, could now be prevented by parental actions that are almost universally affordable and are based on knowledge that is already available.

Nations with the highest mortality rate for children under age 5 include African nations such as Angola and Asian nations such as Afghanistan. In Angola in 1991, for every 1,000 children born alive, 292 died before the age of 5; in Afghanistan, the figure was 257 per 1,000.

The countries with the lowest mortality rates for children under age 5 include Scandinavian countries, such as Sweden, where in 1991 only 5 of every 1,000 children under the age of 5 died. The U.S. mortality rate for children under the age of 5 is better than that of most countries, but of the 129 countries for which figures were available in 1991, 22 countries had better rates than the United States. In 1991, the U.S. mortality rate for children under the age of 5 was 11 per 1,000.

Health, Illness, and Development

Although there has been great national interest in the psychological aspects of adult health, only recently has a developmental perspective on psychological aspects of children's health been proposed. The uniqueness of young children's health-care needs is evident when we consider their motor, cognitive, and social development (Maddux & others, 1986). For example, think about the infant's and preschool child's motor development—inadequate to ensure personal safety while riding in an automobile. Adults must take preventive measures to restrain infants and young children in car seats. Young children may lack the intellectual skills—including reading ability—to discriminate between safe and unsafe household substances. And they may lack the impulse control to keep from running out into a busy street while chasing after a ball or a toy.

Playgrounds for young children need to be designed with the child's safety in mind. The initial steps in ensuring children's safety are to walk with children through the existing playground or the site where the playground is to be developed, talk with them about possible safety hazards, let them assist in identifying hazards, and indicate how they can use the playground safely. The outdoor play environment should enhance the child's motor, cognitive, and social development. The inadequate attention to the safety of children on playgrounds is evident in the following statistic: More than 305,000 preschool children were treated in emergency rooms with playground-related injuries from 1983 through 1987. One of the major problems is that playground equipment—superstructures incorporating climbers, swings, slides, clatter bridges, and sliding poles—is not constructed over impact-absorbing surfaces, such as wood chips and sand. A 1-foot fall, headfirst into concrete, or a 4-foot fall headfirst onto packed earth can be fatal. The wood chips and sand under equipment should be kept at a minimum of 8 inches deep.

Health-education programs for preschool children need to be cognitively simple. There are three simple but important goals for health-education programs for preschool children (Parcel & others, 1979): (1) be able to identify feelings of wellness and illness and be able to express them to adults; (2) be able to identify appropriate sources of assistance for health-related problems; and (3) be able to independently initiate the use of sources of assistance for health problems.

Caregivers play an important role in the health of young children. For example, by controlling the speed of the vehicles they drive, by decreasing their drinking—especially before driving—and by not smoking around children, caregivers enhance children's health. In one

study, if the mother smoked, her children were twice as likely to have respiratory ailments (Etzel, 1988). The young children of single, unemployed, smoking mothers are also three times more likely to be injured. Smoking may serve as a marker to identify mothers less able to supervise young children. In sum, caregivers can actively affect young children's health and safety by training and monitoring children on recreational safety, self-protection skills, proper nutrition, and dental hygiene (Hoot & Robertson, 1994).

Illnesses, especially those that are not life threatening, provide an excellent opportunity for the young children to expand their development. The preschool period is a peak time for illnesses such as respiratory infections (colds, flu) and gastrointestinal upsets (nausea, diarrhea). The illnesses usually are of short duration and are often handled outside the medical community through the family, day care, or school. Such minor illnesses can increase the young child's knowledge of health and illness and sense of empathy.

Young children may confuse terms such as *feel bad* with bad behavior and *feel good* with good behavior. Examples include the following:

- "I feel bad. I want aspirin."
- "I feel bad. My tummy hurts."
- "Bobby hurt me."
- "I bad girl. I wet my pants."
- "Me can do it. Me good girl."
- "I'm hurting your feeling, 'cause I was mean to you."
- "Stop, it doesn't feel good."

Young children often attribute their illness to what they view as a transgression, such as having eaten the wrong food or playing outdoors in the cold when told not to. In illness and wellness situations, adults have the potential to help children sort out distressed feelings resulting from emotional upsets and from physical illness. For example, a mother might say to her young daughter, "I know you feel bad because you are sick like your sister was last week, but you will be well soon just as she is now." Or a mother might comment, "I know you feel bad because I am going on a trip and I can't take you with me, but I will be back in a few days" (Parmalee, 1986).

Thus far, we have discussed a number of ideas about nutrition, health, and illness in early childhood. These ideas are summarized in concept table 9.2.

John W. Santrock

CONCEPT TABLE 9.2

Nutrition, Illness, and Health

Concept	Processes/Related Ideas	Characteristics/Description
Nutrition	Energy needs	They increase as children go through the childhood years. Energy requirements vary according to basal metabolism, rate of growth, and level of activity.
	Eating behavior	There are a number of daily routines in eating behaviors that 3-, 4-, and 5-year-old children follow. Many parents are raising children on diets that are too high in fat and sugar. Children's diets should include well-balanced proportions of fats, carbohydrates, protein, vitamins, and minerals. Eating too many sweets is often a contributing factor to eating problems in early childhood. Midmorning and midafternoon snacks are recommended for young children because children have high energy expenditures. Many eating problems are carryovers from the toddler years. Parents should try to keep the child's eating completely separate from discipline. A special concern is the poor nutrition of young children from low-income families. One problem these children may develop is iron deficiency anemia. Approximately 11 million preschool children are estimated to be malnourished in the United States.
Illness and Health	Young children's illness and health in the United States	Fortunately, in the United States the dangers of many diseases such as diphtheria and polio are no longer present, but it is important for parents to keep children on an immunization schedule. The disorders most likely to be fatal during the preschool years are birth defects, cancer, and heart disease. A special concern is the poor health status of many young children in low-income families—they often have less resistance to diseases, including colds and influenza, than their middle-class counterparts.
	The state of illness and health in the world's children	One death of every three in the world is the death of a child under age 5. Every week, more than a quarter of a millon children die in developing countries. The main causes of death and child malnutrition in the world are diarrhea, measles, tetanus, whooping cough, acute respiratory infections (mainly pneumonias), and undernutrition. Contributing factors include the timing of births and hygiene. Most child malnutrition and child deaths could be prevented by parental actions that are affordable and based on knowledge that is available today. The United States has a relatively low rate of child deaths compared to other countries, although the Scandinavian countries have the best rates.
	Health, illness, and development	Children's health care needs are related to their motor, cognitive, and social development.

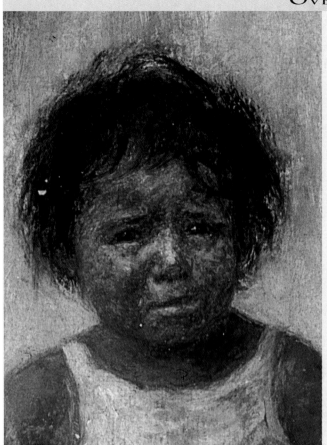

A lthough young children's physical growth and development is slower than in infancy, their lives are very active—the most active of any period in the human life span.

We began this chapter by evaluating young children's body growth and change, including height and weight, the brain, and visual perception. Then we studied motor development, focusing on gross motor skills, fine motor skills, young children's artistic drawings, and handedness. We also examined sleep and sleep problems. Our coverage of young children's nutrition involved energy needs and eating behavior, and our discussion of illness and health explored these topics in the United States and around the world, as well as health, illness, and development.

Don't forget that you can obtain an overall summary of the chapter by again reading the two concept tables on pages 263 and 269. In the next chapter, we will turn our attention to the young child's cognitive development.

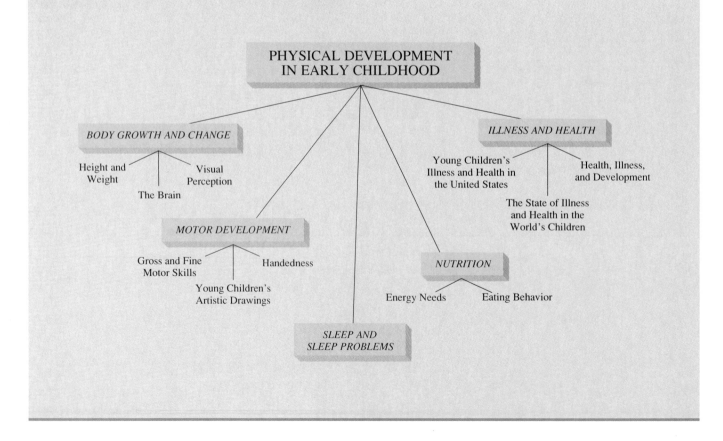

PHYSICAL DEVELOPMENT
IN EARLY CHILDHOOD

BODY GROWTH AND CHANGE

Height and Weight

The Brain

Visual Perception

MOTOR DEVELOPMENT

Gross and Fine Motor Skills

Young Children's Artistic Drawings

Handedness

SLEEP AND SLEEP PROBLEMS

NUTRITION

Energy Needs

Eating Behavior

ILLNESS AND HEALTH

Young Children's Illness and Health in the United States

The State of Illness and Health in the World's Children

Health, Illness, and Development

deprivation dwarfism Growth retardation caused by emotional deprivation; children who are deprived of affection experience stress that affects the release of hormones by the pituitary gland.   256

myelination The process in which the nerve cells are covered and insulated with a layer of fat cells, which increases the speed at which information travels through the nervous system.   256

functional amblyopia An eye defect that results from not using one eye enough to avoid the discomfort of double vision produced by imbalanced eye muscles; "lazy eye."   256

Denver Developmental Screening Test A test used to diagnose developmental delay in children from birth to 6 years of age; includes separate assessments of gross and fine motor skills, language, and personal-social ability.   259

placement stage Kellogg's terms for 2- to 3-year-olds' drawings that are drawn in placement patterns.   260

shape stage Kellogg's terms for 3-year-olds' drawings consisting of diagrams in different shapes.   260

design stage Kellogg's terms for 3- to 4-year-olds' drawings that mix two basic shapes into more complex designs.   260

pictorial stage Kellogg's terms for 4- to 5-year-olds' drawings depicting objects that adults can recognize.   261

transitional objects Objects that are repeatedly used by children as bedtime companions. These usually are soft and cuddly, and probably mark the child's transition from being dependent to being more independent.   262

nightmares Frightening dreams that awaken the sleeper.   262

night terrors Sudden arousal from sleep characterized by intense fear, usually accompanied by the physiological reactions such as rapid heart rate and breathing, loud screams, heavy perspiration, and physical movement.   262

somnambulism Sleepwalking; occurs in the deepest stage of sleep.   262

basal metabolism rate (MBR) The minimum amount of energy a person uses in a resting state.   263

oral rehydration therapy (ORT) Treatment to prevent dehydration during episodes of diarrhea by giving fluids by mouth.   267

PRACTICAL KNOWLEDGE ABOUT CHILDREN

Solve Your Child's Sleep Problems
(1985) by Richard Ferber.
New York: Simon & Schuster.

Solve Your Child's Sleep Problems helps parents recognize when their infant or child has a sleep problem and tells them what to do about the problem. Author Richard Ferber is director of the Center for Pediatric Sleep Disorders at Children's Hospital in Boston. Among the topics covered are basic information about normal and abnormal sleep patterns in infants and children, the sleepless child, sleep rhythm disorders, interruptions during sleep, and other problems such as snoring and headbanging. An appendix provides suggestions for further reading, such as children's books on bedtime, sleep, and dreams, as well as information about organizations that might help parents who have infants or children with sleep disorders.

This is an excellent self-help book for parents who have an infant or child with a sleep disorder. It is clearly written and the author's prescriptions are humane and wise.

IMPROVING THE
LIVES OF CHILDREN

Improving the lives of children includes overcoming poverty-related impediments to young children's health care, teaching children to use seat belts, supporting young children's motor development, carrying out oral rehydration therapy in countries where child death rates are high, and including fathers and other men more in early childhood education.

HEALTH AND WELL-BEING
Poverty and Children's Health

Children from low-income families are especially prone to illness and health problems. Children from low-income families:

- Have health problems that are compounded because of difficulty in obtaining medical care.
- Are less likely than their more affluent peers to receive physical examinations, vision testing, immunizations, and dental care.
- Experience about the same number of medical visits as other children, but the amount of care they receive is not proportional to their greater incidence of health problems. Emergency rooms, where counseling, anticipatory guidance, and routine preventive care are unlikely, are often the only available sources of care for low-income families.

Medicaid, the public insurance program for children who live in poverty, finances extensive preventive benefits through the Early Periodic Screening, Diagnosis, and Treatment (EPSDT) program, but less than one-third of all eligible children participate. In one study, low-income families with Medicaid were far more likely to have children who benefited from frequent use of preventive services than their non-Medicaid counterparts (Newacheck & Halfon, 1988). Project Head Start, which we will discuss extensively in the next chapter, has been very successful in providing health services to children from low-income families, but like the Early Periodic Screening, Diagnosis, and Treatment program, it reaches too few eligible children.

Other poverty-related impediments to preventive health care include limited health care resources in regions with clusters of low-income families, lack of knowledge of the benefits of prevention, inadequate public transportation, apathy and despair, and the understandable preoccupation with the pressing priorities of survival.

John W. Santrock

FAMILIES AND PARENTING

Buckle Up for Safety

Each year more American children are injured or die as a result of automobile accidents than as a result of any other type of accident or disease. According to recent statistics from the National Safety Council, about 1,500 deaths and 125,000 injuries occur each year in children 14 years of age and under. There is a strong consensus that safety belts and child safety seats, if used properly, could eliminate about half of these deaths and injuries.

In the face of such evidence, one natural question is, How can we get children to use safety belts consistently? For those children old enough to understand and take responsibility for themselves, how can we make "buckling up" a high-frequency behavior when children get into a car?

A study by Karen Sowers-Hoag, Bruce Thyer, and Jon Bailey (1987) offers a simple, but powerful, answer. The authors reviewed what other experts had tried. Many of these efforts, not unexpectedly, were directed toward adults. Typical intervention programs included reminder flyers placed on automobile windshields, safety-belt lotteries, dashboard reminder stickers, and "flash-for-life" cards used as prompts for unbuckled drivers. Only modest gains were observed in the number of individuals buckling up in these programs.

The researchers thought that it was important to direct efforts at children themselves—to try to invent a program that would get large numbers of children to buckle up and to demonstrate the lasting effects of behavior change. They identified 16 children ranging from 4 to 7 years of age, all of whom attended an afterschool program and none of whom buckled up when they drove home with their parents at the end of the school day.

Following a baseline period of observing the children, the behavior modification consisted of four parts. First, one of the authors presented educational facts about the use of safety belts and discussed famous role models known to use safety belts, such as airline and jet fighter pilots, race car drivers, and well-known movie stars. Second, the same author taught children how to be assertive about the

Safety belts and child safety seats, if used properly, can eliminate about half of the 1,500 deaths and 125,000 injuries that occur each year to children under 14 years of age. How can we get children to "buckle up" consistently?

use of seat belts by role-playing a number of situations children might encounter. Third, the children engaged in behavioral rehearsal during which they went to the school parking lot and practiced getting into and out of the front and back seats of several cars, buckling the seat belts in the cars and practicing how to accomplish this quickly. Finally, a lottery was set up and any child observed buckling up on the afterschool trip home was eligible to win a prize in the next day's lottery. Half of the children won prizes in the lottery, including stickers, toy cars, and coloring books. The results of the

study were impressive. On many of the days, all of the children buckled up. And in follow-up observations through approximately 100 days, a high percentage of the children were still buckling up. Even when the children were not being observed, interviews with the parents indicated that the children were consistently buckling up in other situations as well. These findings are important because they report a relatively simple educational technique that takes only a few hours to implement and because the results may save a child's life one day.

EDUCATION

Supporting Young Children's Motor Development

Young children frequently engage in such activities as running, jumping, throwing, and catching. These activities form the basis for advanced, often sports-related, skills. For children to progress to effective, coordinated, and controlled motor performance, interaction with and instruction from supportive adults can be beneficial.

How can early childhood educators support young children's motor development? When planning physical instruction for young children, it is important to keep in mind that their attention span is rather short, so instruction should be brief and to the point. Young children need to practice skills in order to learn them, so

instruction should be followed with ample time for practice.

Fitness is an important dimension of people's lives, and it is beneficial to develop a positive attitude toward it early in our lives (Benelli & Yongue, 1995). Preschoolers need vigorous activities for short periods of time. They can be encouraged to rest or change to a quieter activity as needed. Movement, even within the classroom, can improve a child's stamina. Such movement activities might be as basic as practicing locomotor skills or as complex as navigating an obstacle course. It is recommended that a number of locomotor skills (such as walking, running, jumping,

sliding, skipping, and leaping) be practiced forward and backward. And it is very important to keep practice fun, allowing children to enjoy movement for the sheer pleasure of it.

There can be long-term negative effects for children who fail to develop basic motor skills. These children will not be as able to join in group games or participate in sports during their school years and in adulthood. The positive development of motor skills has other benefits besides participation in games and sports. Engaging in motor skills fulfills young children's needs and desires for movement, and exercise builds muscles, strengthens the heart, and enhances aerobic capacity.

CULTURE AND ETHNICITY

Oral Rehydration Therapy in Bangladesh

Bangladesh is where much of the pioneering work on oral rehydration therapy has been carried out. Still, 10 percent of all children born in Bangladesh die before the age of 5 from dehydration and malnutrition brought about by diarrhea. The majority of Bangladesh women are illiterate, so health workers must go to considerable lengths to contact families and instruct them in how to give oral rehydration therapy. A homemade solution was needed that every household could afford. The solution that was decided upon was a three-finger pinch of salt and a four-finger scoop of molasses dissolved in water, a solution that has been very effective. Close to 1,000 oral rehydration workers have been trained to go from door to door in villages. More than 5 million mothers have had half an hour's instruction with an oral rehydration worker. Mothers are taught that it is a mistake to stop giving food and drink to the child because this only increases the danger of dehydration. The worker shows the mother how to prepare the solution and then watches the

Although oral rehydration therapy is being used in Bangladesh, 10 percent of all children born in Bangladesh die before reaching the age of 5 from dehydration and malnutrition brought about by diarrhea.

mother make it. Although average usage rates have yet to rise above 60 percent, the technique is being promoted in

posters and leaflets and on television and radio.

John W. Santrock

Fathers and Other Men in Early Childhood Education

Very few males teach in preschools, kindergartens, or the lower elementary school grades. The ratio of female teachers to male teachers is more than 50 to 1 in the first few grades of elementary school and much higher than that in preschool and kindergarten. Many young children have been deprived of interaction with adult males not only outside of school but also in school during their early education.

Researchers have found that boys generally do better in societies where there are more male teachers, although research in the United States is inconsistent on this topic. However, some studies have revealed that many young children, especially those who have been paternally deprived, improve their attitude toward school when they interact with supportive male teachers (Biller, 1993).

More fathers should become knowledgeable about the early education of their children. Fathers as well as mothers should be involved in the family-school partnership. Early childhood education programs should seek to bring fathers to the school. Men can be invited to come as guest speakers and share something about their lives or be asked to host a field trip, perhaps to their place of work. Teachers might also set up a special event, such as an evening play session for men and children consisting of typical activities and games in which men and children can participate together. A Saturday breakfast and play session is another option.

In many programs, some of the children do not know their fathers or have very little contact with them. To be sensitive to the needs of these children, teachers can discuss men who can serve as their psychological fathers (Cunningham, 1994). The psychological father might be a supportive friend, a male relative, the mother's boyfriend, a male teacher, or a participant in organized activities such as a Big Brother program or a sports program. When teachers include these other men in their discussions of fathers, most children will be able to identify with at least one male in their lives.

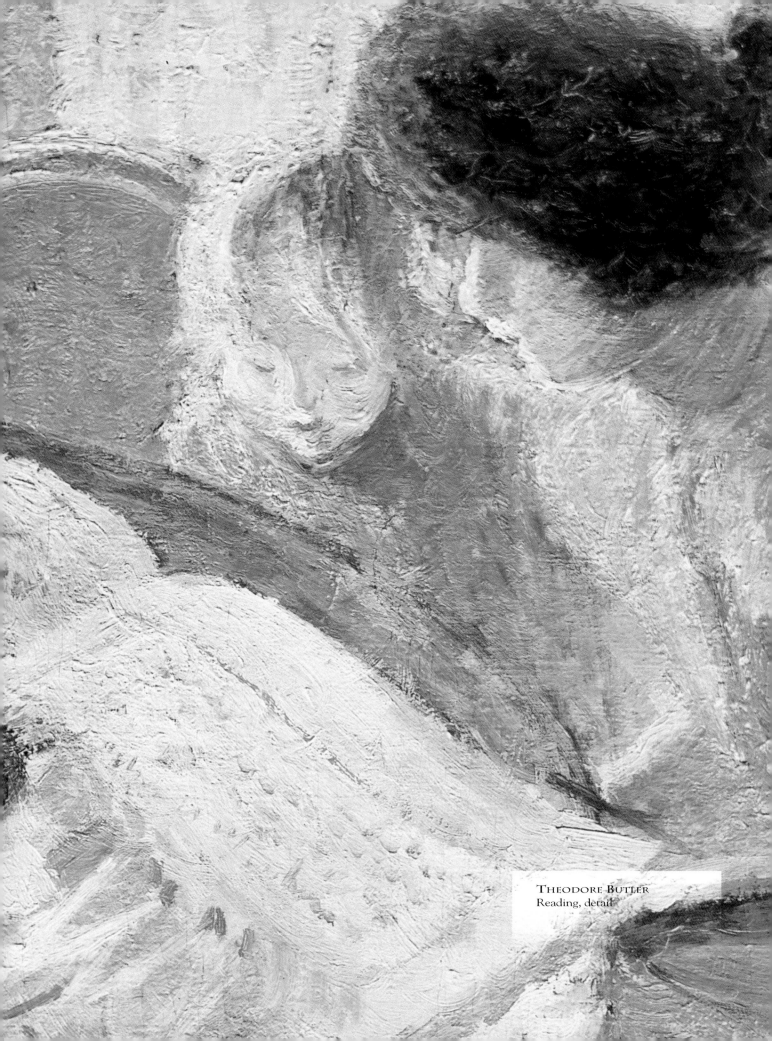

THEODORE BUTLER
Reading, detail

CHAPTER 10

Cognitive Development
in Early Childhood

*Learning is an ornament in prosperity,
a refuge in adversity.*

—Aristotle

> T*he mind is an enchanting thing.*
>
> **—Marianne Moore,**
> **Collected Poems, 1951**

IMAGES OF CHILDREN

Reggio Emilia

The Reggio Emilia approach is an educational program for young children that was developed in the northern Italian city of Reggio Emilia. Children of single parents and children with disabilities have priority in admission; other children are admitted according to a scale of needs. Parents pay on a sliding scale based on income.

The children are encouraged to learn by investigating and exploring topics that interest them. A wide range of stimulating media and materials are available for children to use as they learn—music, movement, drawing, painting, sculpting, making collages, using puppets and disguises, and photography, for example.

In this program, children often explore topics in a group, which fosters a sense of community, respect for diversity, and a collaborative approach to problem solving. Two co-teachers are present to serve as guides for children. The Reggio Emilia teachers consider a project as an adventure, which can start from an adult's suggestion, from a child's idea, or from an event such as a snowfall or something else unexpected. Every project is based on what the children say and do. The teachers allow children enough time to think and craft a project.

At the core of the Reggio Emilia approach is the image of children who are competent and have rights, especially the right to outstanding care and education (Bredekamp, 1993). Parent participation is considered essential, and cooperation is a major theme in the schools (Gandini, 1993). Many early childhood education experts believe the Reggio Emilia approach provides a supportive, stimulating context in which children are motivated to explore their world in a competent and confident manner.

PREVIEW

The cognitive world of the young child is creative, free, and fanciful. In the symbolic world of the young child's art, sometimes cars float on clouds, the sun is green, the sky is yellow, pelicans kiss seals, and people look like tadpoles. Young children's imaginations work overtime and their mental grasp of the world improves. Our coverage of cognitive development in early childhood focuses on cognitive development and information processing, language development, and early childhood education.

COGNITIVE DEVELOPMENTAL CHANGES

How do young children's minds change as they age through early childhood? Piaget had some thoughts about these changes, as did Lev Vygotsky. We will explore Piaget's ideas about the preoperational stage of development, Vygotsky's theory, the information-processing perspective, and the young child's theory of mind.

Piaget's Preoperational Stage of Development

What characterizes preoperational thought? What happens during the substages of symbolic function and intuitive thought?

The Nature of Preoperational Thought

Remember from chapter 7 that, during Piaget's sensorimotor stage of development, the infant progresses in the ability to

John W. Santrock

"Mrs. Hammond! I'd know you anywhere from little Billy's portrait of you."

Drawing by Frascino; © 1988 The New Yorker Magazine, Inc.

organize and coordinate sensations and perceptions with physical movements and actions. What kinds of changes take place in the preoperational stage?

> There are no days in life so memorable as those which vibrated to some stroke of imagination.
>
> —Ralph Waldo Emerson,
> **The Conduct of Life,** 1860

Since this stage of thought is called preoperational, it would seem that not much of importance occurs until full-fledged operational thought appears. Not so! The preoperational stage stretches from approximately 2 to 7 years of age. It is a time when stable concepts are formed, mental reasoning emerges, egocentrism begins strongly and then weakens, and magical beliefs are constructed. Preoperational thought is anything but a convenient waiting period for concrete operational thought, although the label *preoperational* emphasizes that the child at this stage does not yet think in an operational way. What are operations? **Operations** *are internalized sets of actions that allow the child to do mentally what before she did physically.* Operations are highly organized and conform to certain rules and principles of logic. The operations appear in one form in concrete operational thought and in another form in formal operational thought. Thought in the preoperational stage is flawed and not well organized. Preoperational thought is the beginning of the ability to reconstruct at the level of thought what has been established in behavior. Preoperational thought also involves a transition from primitive to more sophisticated use of symbols. Preoperational thought can be divided into two substages: the symbolic function substage and the intuitive thought substage.

Young children's art reflects the growth in their symbolic thought. Art can be a very enjoyable activity for young children.

Symbolic Function Substage

The **symbolic function substage** *is the first substage of preoperational thought, occurring roughly between the ages of 2 and 4. In this substage, the young child gains the ability to mentally represent an object that is not present.* The ability to engage in such symbolic thought is called symbolic function, and it vastly expands the child's mental world. Young children use scribbled designs to represent people, houses, cars, clouds, and so on. Other examples of symbolism in early childhood are language and the prevalence of pretend play. In sum, the ability to think symbolically and represent the world mentally predominates in this early substage of preoperational thought. However, although young children make distinct progress during this substage, their thought still has several important limitations, two of which are egocentrism and animism.

Egocentrism *is a salient feature of preoperational thought. It is the inability to distinguish between one's own perspective and someone else's perspective.* The following telephone conversation between 4-year-old Mary, who is at home, and her father, who is at work, typifies Mary's egocentric thought:

Father: Mary, is Mommy there?
Mary: (Silently nods.)
Father: Mary, may I speak to Mommy?
Mary: (Nods again silently.)

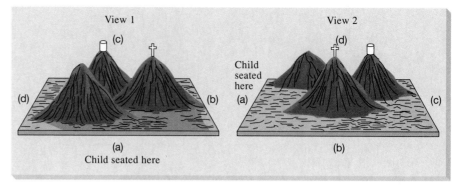

FIGURE 10.2

The Three Mountains Task
View 1 shows the child's perspective from where he or she is sitting. View 2 is an example of the photograph the child would be shown mixed in with others from different perspectives. To correctly identify this view, the child has to take the perspective of a person sitting at spot (b). Invariably, a preschool child who thinks in a preoperational way cannot perform this task. When asked what a view of the mountains looks like from position (b), the child selects a photograph taken from location (a), the child's view at the time.

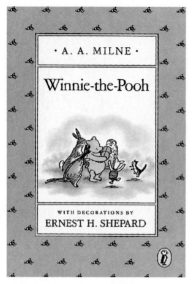

FIGURE 10.1

Piaget and *Winnie-the-Pooh*
If Piaget had opened the pages of *Winnie-the-Pooh,* he would have discovered that A. A. Milne's descriptions of egocentrism were strikingly similar to his own. Milne's psychological insight breathes life and meaning into a little story about an imaginary forest, peopled with animals from the nursery. We first meet Edward Bear as he is being dragged down the stairs on the back of his head. "It is, as far as he knows, the only way of coming down the stairs." This example of egocentrism sets the tone for the rest of the book. The narrator tells us that Edward's name is Winnie-the-Pooh. When asked if Winnie is not a girl's name, Christopher replies with a second example of egocentrism. "He's Winnie-ther-Pooh. Don't you know what *ther* means?" Again, an example of egocentrism. Christopher knows, so no further explanation is necessary, or forthcoming. Piglet, an egocentric friend of Pooh, is a weak and timid pig, and is certain that everyone knows when he is in distress, but Pooh is just as egocentric when he interprets a note. Pooh only recognizes the letter *P* and each *P* convinces him further that *P* means "Pooh" so "it's a very important Missage to me."

Mary's response is egocentric in that she fails to consider her father's perspective before replying. A nonegocentric thinker would have responded verbally. Piaget's concept of egocentrism appeared in A. A. Milne's wonderful story *Winnie-the-Pooh* (see figure 10.1).

> *False would be a picture which insisted on the brutal egocentrism of the child, and ignored the physical beauty which softens it.*
>
> —A. A. Milne

Piaget and Barbel Inhelder (1969) initially studied young children's egocentrism by devising the three mountains task (see figure 10.2). The child walks around the model of the mountains and becomes familiar with what the mountains look like from different perspectives and can see that there are different objects on the mountains. The child is then seated on one side of the table on which the mountains are placed. The experimenter moves a doll to different locations around the table, at each location asking the child to select, from a series of photos, the one photo that most accurately reflects the view the doll is seeing. Children in the preoperational stage often pick their view from where they are sitting rather than the doll's view. Perspective-taking does not develop uniformly in preschool children, who frequently show perspective skills on some tasks but not others.

Animism, *another facet of preoperational thought, is the belief that inanimate objects have "lifelike" qualities and are capable of action.* A young child might show animism by saying, "That tree pushed the leaf off, and it fell down," or "The sidewalk made me mad; it made me fall down." A young child who uses animism fails to distinguish the appropriate occasions for using human and nonhuman perspectives.

Possibly because young children are not very concerned about reality, their drawings are fanciful and inventive. Suns are blue, skies are yellow, and cars float on clouds in their symbolic, imaginative world. One 3½-year-old looked at a scribble he had just drawn and described it as a pelican kissing a seal (see figure 10.3a). The symbolism is simple but strong, like abstractions found in some modern art. As Picasso commented, "I used to draw like Raphael but it has taken me a lifetime to draw like young children." In the elementary school years, a child's drawings become more realistic, neat, and precise (see figure 10.3b). Suns are yellow, skies are blue, and cars travel on roads (Winner, 1986).

Intuitive Thought Substage

Tommy is 4 years old. Although he is starting to develop his own ideas about the world he lives in, his ideas are still simple and he is not very good at thinking things out. He has difficulty understanding events he knows are taking

John W. Santrock

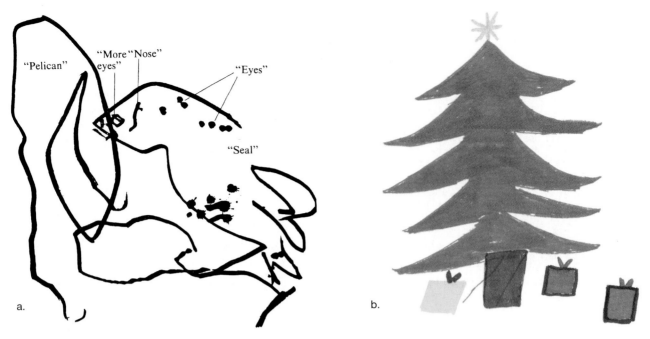

FIGURE 10.3

The Symbolic Drawings of Young Children
(*a*) A 3½-year-old's symbolic drawing. Halfway into this drawing, the 3½-year-old artist said it was "a pelican kissing a seal."
(*b*) This 11-year-old's drawing is neater and more realistic but also less inventive.

place but cannot see. His fantasized thoughts bear little resemblance to reality. He cannot yet answer the question, "What if . . . ?" in any reliable way. For example, he has only a vague idea of what would happen if a car hit him. He also has difficulty negotiating traffic because he cannot do the mental calculations necessary to estimate whether an approaching car will hit him when he crosses the road.

The **intuitive thought substage** *is the second substage of preoperational thought, occurring between approximately 4 and 7 years of age. In this substage, children begin to use primitive reasoning and want to know the answers to all sorts of questions.* Piaget called this time period *intuitive* because, on the one hand, young children seem so sure about their knowledge

and understanding, yet are so unaware of how they know what they know. That is, they say they know something but know it without the use of rational thinking.

An example of young children's reasoning ability is the difficulty they have putting things into correct categories. Faced with a random collection of objects that can be grouped together on the basis of two or more properties, preoperational children are seldom capable of using these properties consistently to sort the objects into appropriate groupings. Look at the collection of objects in figure 10.4a. You would respond to the direction, "Put the things together that you believe belong together" by sorting the characteristics of size and shape together. Your

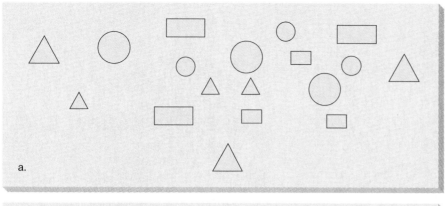

FIGURE 10.4

Arrays

(*a*) A random array of objects. (*b*) An ordered array of objects.

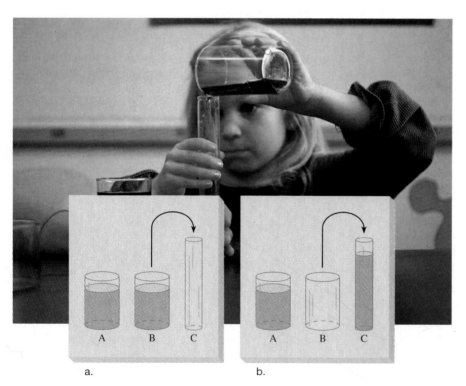

FIGURE 10.5

Piaget's Conservation Task

The beaker test is a well-known Piagetian test to determine whether a child can think operationally—that is, can mentally reverse actions and show conservation of the substance. (*a*) Two identical beakers are presented to the child. Then, the experimenter pours the liquid from B into C, which is taller and thinner than A or B. (*b*) The child is asked if these beakers (A and C) have the same amount of liquid. The preoperational child says no. When asked to point to the beaker that has more liquid, the preoperational child points to the tall, thin beaker.

sorting might look something like that shown in figure 10.4b. In the social realm, the 4-year-old girl might be given the task of dividing her peers into groups according to whether they are friends and whether they are boys or girls. She would be unlikely to arrive at the following classification: friendly boys, friendly girls, unfriendly boys, unfriendly girls. Another example of classification shortcomings involves the preoperational child's understanding of religious concepts (Elkind, 1976). When asked, "Can you be a Protestant and an American at the same time?" 6- and 7-year-olds usually say no; 9-year-olds are likely to say yes, understanding that objects can be cross-classified simultaneously.

Many of these examples show a characteristic of preoperational thought called **centration**—*the focusing, or centering, of attention on one characteristic to the exclusion of all others*. Centration is most clearly evidenced in young children's lack of **conservation**—*the idea that an amount stays the same regardless of how its container changes*. To adults, it is obvious that a certain amount of liquid stays the same regardless of a container's shape. But this is not obvious at all to young children; instead, they are struck by the height of the liquid in the container. In the conservation task—Piaget's most famous—a child is presented with two identical beakers, each filled to the same level with liquid (see figure 10.5). The child is asked if these beakers have the same amount of liquid, and she usually says yes. Then the liquid from one beaker is poured into a third beaker, which is taller and thinner than the first two. The child is then asked if the amount of liquid in the tall, thin beaker is equal to that which remains in one of the original beakers. Children who are less than 7 or 8 years old usually say no and justify their answers in terms of the differing height or width of the beakers. Older children usually answer yes and justify their answers appropriately ("If you poured the milk back, the amount would still be the same").

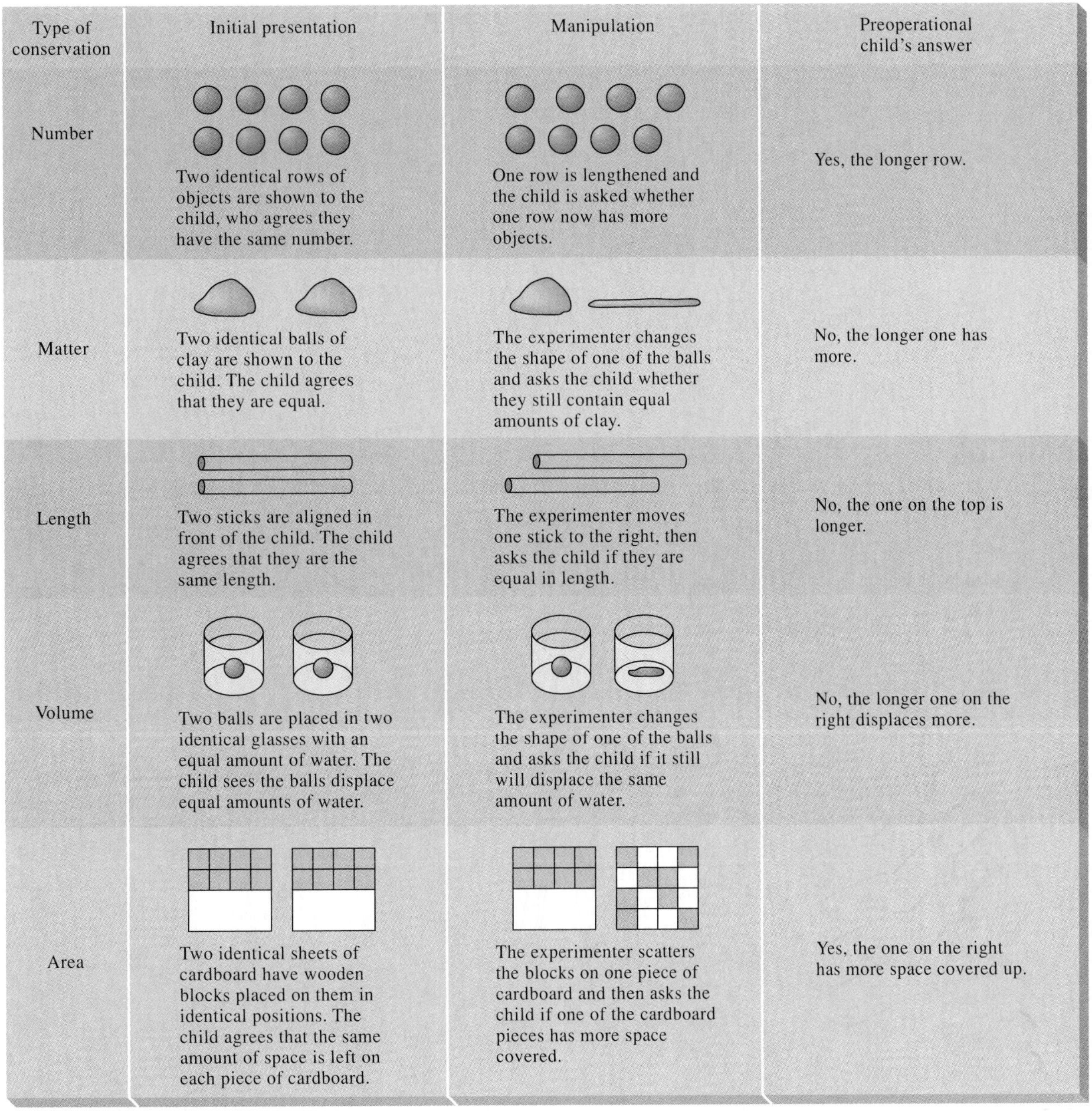

Type of conservation	Initial presentation	Manipulation	Preoperational child's answer
Number	Two identical rows of objects are shown to the child, who agrees they have the same number.	One row is lengthened and the child is asked whether one row now has more objects.	Yes, the longer row.
Matter	Two identical balls of clay are shown to the child. The child agrees that they are equal.	The experimenter changes the shape of one of the balls and asks the child whether they still contain equal amounts of clay.	No, the longer one has more.
Length	Two sticks are aligned in front of the child. The child agrees that they are the same length.	The experimenter moves one stick to the right, then asks the child if they are equal in length.	No, the one on the top is longer.
Volume	Two balls are placed in two identical glasses with an equal amount of water. The child sees the balls displace equal amounts of water.	The experimenter changes the shape of one of the balls and asks the child if it still will displace the same amount of water.	No, the longer one on the right displaces more.
Area	Two identical sheets of cardboard have wooden blocks placed on them in identical positions. The child agrees that the same amount of space is left on each piece of cardboard.	The experimenter scatters the blocks on one piece of cardboard and then asks the child if one of the cardboard pieces has more space covered.	Yes, the one on the right has more space covered up.

FIGURE 10.6

Some Dimensions of Conservation: Number, Matter, Length, Volume, and Area

In Piaget's theory, failing the conservation of liquid task is a sign that children are at the preoperational stage of cognitive development, while passing this test is a sign that they are at the concrete operational stage. In Piaget's view, the preoperational child not only fails to show conservation of liquid, but also of number, matter, length, volume, and area (see figure 10.6). The child's inability to mentally reverse actions is an important characteristic of preoperational thought. For example, in the conservation of matter shown in figure 10.6, preoperational children say that the longer shape has more clay because they assume that "longer is more." Preoperational children cannot mentally reverse the clay-rolling process to see that the amount of clay is the same in both the shorter ball shape and the longer stick shape.

Some developmentalists do not believe Piaget was entirely correct in his estimate of when children's conservation skills emerge. For example, Rochel Gelman (1969) showed that by improving the child's attention to relevant aspects of the conservation task, the child is more likely to conserve. Gelman has also demonstrated that attentional training on one type of task, such as number, improves the

FIGURE 10.7

Preoperational Thought's Characteristics

*"I still don't have all the answers, but I'm
beginning to ask the right questions."*

Drawing by Lorenz; © 1989 The New Yorker Magazine, Inc.

preschool child's performance on another type of task, such as mass. Thus, Gelman believes that conservation appears earlier than Piaget thought and that the process of attention is especially important in explaining conservation.

Yet another characteristic of the preoperational child is that they ask a barrage of questions. Children's earliest questions appear around the age of 3, and by the age of 5 they have just about exhausted the adults around them with "Why" questions. The child's questions yield clues about mental development and reflect intellectual curiosity. These questions signal the emergence of the child's interest in reasoning and figuring out why things are the way they are. Following are some samples of the questions children ask during the questioning period of 4 to 6 years of age (Elkind, 1976):

- "What makes you grow up?"
- "What makes you stop growing?"
- "Why does a lady have to be married to have a baby?"
- "Who was the mother when everybody was a baby?"
- "Why do leaves fall?"
- "Why does the sun shine?"

At this point we have discussed a number of characteristics of preoperational thought. To help you remember these characteristics, turn to figure 10.7.

Earlier we mentioned that Gelman's research demonstrated that children may fail a Piagetian task because they do not attend to relevant dimensions of the task—length, shape, density, and so on. Gelman and other developmentalists also believe that many of the tasks used to assess cognitive development may not be sensitive to the child's cognitive abilities. Thus, any apparent limitations on cognitive development may be due to the tasks used to assess that development. Gelman's research reflects the

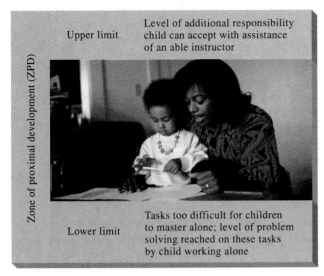

FIGURE 10.8

Vygotsky's Zone of Proximal Development
Vygotsky's zone of proximal development has a lower limit and
an upper limit. Tasks in the ZPD are too difficult for the child
to perform alone. They require assistance from an adult or a
skilled child. As children experience the verbal instruction or
demonstration, they organize the information in their existing
mental structures so they can eventually perform the skill or
task alone.

*Lev Vygotsky (1896–1934), shown here with his daughter,
believed that children's cognitive development is advanced through
social interaction with skilled individuals embedded in a
sociocultural backdrop.*

thinking of information processing psychologists who place
considerable importance on the tasks and procedures involved in assessing children's cognition.

Vygotsky's Theory of Development

Children's cognitive development and language development do not develop in a social vacuum. Lev Vygotsky
(1896–1934), a Russian psychologist, recognized this important point about children's minds more than half a century ago. Vygotsky's theory is receiving increased attention
as we move toward the close of the twentieth century.
Before we turn to Vygotsky's ideas on language and
thought, and culture and society, let's examine his important concept called the zone of proximal development.

The Zone of Proximal Development

The **zone of proximal development (ZPD)** *is Vygotsky's
term for tasks too difficult for children to master alone, but that
can be mastered with the guidance and assistance of adults or
more skilled children.* Thus, the lower limit of the ZPD is the
level of problem solving reached by a child working independently. The upper limit is the level of additional responsibility the child can accept with the assistance of an
able instructor (see figure 10.8). Vygotsky's emphasis on
the ZPD underscored his belief in the importance of social
influences on cognitive development and the role of instruction in children's development.

The ZPD is conceptualized as a measure of learning potential. IQ is also a measure of learning potential. However,
IQ emphasizes that intelligence is a property of the child,
whereas ZPD emphasizes that learning is interpersonal, a

dynamic social event that depends on a minimum of two
minds, one better informed or more drilled than the other. It
is inappropriate to say that the child *has* a ZPD; rather, a
child *shares* a ZPD with an instructor.

The practical teaching involved in ZPD begins toward the zone's upper limit, where the child is able to
reach the goal only through close collaboration with the
instructor. With adequate continuing instruction and practice, the child organizes and masters the behavioral sequences necessary to perform the target skill (DiPardo,
1996). As the instruction continues, the performance
transfers from the instructor to the child as the teacher
gradually reduces the explanations, hints, and demonstrations until the child is able to adequately perform alone.
Once the goal is achieved, it may become the foundation
for the development of a new ZPD.

Learning by toddlers provides an example of how the
ZPD works. The toddler has to be motivated and must be
involved in activities that involve the skill at a reasonably
high level of difficulty—that is, toward the zone's upper
end. The teacher must have the know-how to exercise the
target skill at any level required by the activity and must be
able to locate and stay in the zone. The teacher and the
child have to adapt to each other's requirements. The reciprocal relationship between the toddler and the teacher
adjusts dynamically as the division of labor is negotiated
and aimed at increasing the weaker partner's share of the
goal attainment.

In one study of toddler/mother dyads, the pair was
put to work on a number of problems with arrays of various numbers (few versus many objects) and varying complexity (simple counting versus number reproduction)

(Saxe, Guberman, & Gearhart, 1987). The mothers were told to treat this as an opportunity to encourage learning and understanding in their children. Based on videotaped interactions of the mothers and their toddlers, the mothers adjusted their task goals to meet their children's abilities. Importantly, the mothers also adjusted the quality of their assistance during the problem-solution period in direct response to the children's successes and failures. Vygotsky's concept of the zone of proximal development is also being effectively applied to teaching children math and how to read (Glassman, 1995; Steward, 1995).

Language and Thought

In Vygotsky's view, the child's mental or cognitive structures are made of relations between mental functions. The relation between language and thought is believed to be especially important in this regard. Vygotsky (1962) said that language and thought initially develop independently of each other but eventually merge.

Two principles govern the merging of thought and language. First, all mental functions have external or social origins. Children must use language and communicate with others before they focus inward on their own mental processes. Second, children must communicate externally and use language for a long period of time before the transition from external to internal speech takes place. This transition period occurs between 3 and 7 years of age and involves talking to oneself. After a while, the self-talk becomes second nature to children and they can act without verbalizing. When this occurs, children have internalized their egocentric speech in the form of inner speech, which becomes the thoughts of the child. Vygotsky believed that children who engage in a large amount of private speech are more socially competent than those who do not use it extensively. He argued that private speech represents an early transition in becoming more socially communicative.

Vygotsky's theory challenges Piaget's ideas on language and thought. Vygotsky argued that language, even in its earliest forms, is socially based, whereas Piaget emphasized young children's egocentric and nonsocially oriented speech. Vygotsky believed young children talk to themselves to govern their behavior and to guide themselves. By contrast, Piaget stressed that young children's egocentric speech reflects social and cognitive immaturity.

Culture and Society

Many developmentalists who work in the field of culture and development find themselves comfortable with Vygotsky's theory, which focuses on the sociocultural context of development (Rogoff & Morelli, 1989). Vygotsky's theory offers a portrayal of human development that is inseparable from social and cultural activities. Vygotsky emphasized how the development of higher mental processes, such as memory, attention, and reasoning, involves learning to use the inventions of society, such as language, mathematical systems, and memory devices. He also emphasized how children are aided in development by the guidance of individuals who are already skilled in these tools. Vygotsky's emphasis on the role of culture and society in cognitive development contrasts with Piaget's description of the solitary little scientist.

Vygotsky stressed both the institutional and the interpersonal levels of social contexts. At the institutional level, cultural history provides organizations and tools useful to cognitive activity through institutions such as schools, inventions such as computers, and literacy. Institutional interaction gives children broad behavioral and societal norms to guide their lives. The interpersonal level has a more direct influence on the child's mental functioning. According to Vygotsky (1962), skills in mental functioning develop through immediate social interaction. Information about cognitive tools, skills, and interpersonal relations are transmitted through direct interaction with people. Through the organization of these social interactional experiences embedded in a cultural backdrop, children's mental development matures.

Information Processing

Not only can we study the stages of cognitive development that young children go through, as Piaget did, but we can also study the different cognitive processes of young children's mental worlds. Two limitations on preschool children's thoughts are in attention and memory, important domains involved in the way young children process information. Advances in these two domains are made during early childhood. What are the limitations and advances in attention and memory during the preschool years?

Attention

In chapter 6 we discussed attention in the context of habituation, which is something like being bored, in that the infant becomes disinterested in a stimulus and no longer attends to it. Habituation can be described as a decrement in attention, while dishabituation is the recovery of attention. The importance of these aspects of attention in infancy for the preschool years was underscored by research showing that both decrement and recovery of attention, when measured in the first 6 months of infancy, were associated with higher intelligence in the preschool years (Bornstein & Sigman, 1986).

Although the infant's attention has important implications for cognitive development in the preschool years, the child's ability to pay attention changes significantly during the preschool years. The toddler wanders around, shifting attention from one activity to another, generally seeming to spend little time focused on any one object or event. By comparison, the preschool child might be observed watching television for a half hour. In one study, young children's attention to television in the natural setting of the home was videotaped (Anderson & others, 1985). Ninety-nine families comprising 460 individuals were observed for 4,672 hours. Visual attention to television dramatically increased during the preschool years.

One deficit in attention during the preschool years concerns those dimensions that stand out, or are *salient*, compared to those that are relevant to solving a problem or performing well on a task. For example, a problem might have a flashy, attractive clown that presents the directions for solving a problem. Preschool children are influenced strongly by the features of the task that stand out, such as the flashy, attractive clown. After the age of 6 or 7, children attend more efficiently to the dimensions of the task that are relevant, such as the directions for solving a problem. Developmentalists believe this change reflects a shift to cognitive control of attention so that children act less impulsively and reflect more.

Memory

Memory is a central process in children's cognitive development; it involves the retention of information over time. Conscious memory comes into play as early as 7 months of age, although children and adults have little or no memory of events experienced before the age of 3. Among the interesting questions about memory in the preschool years are those involving short-term memory.

> I come into the fields and spacious palaces of my memory, where are treasures of countless images of things in every manner.
>
> **—St. Augustine**

In **short-term memory,** *individuals retain information for up to 15 to 30 seconds, assuming there is no rehearsal.* Using rehearsal, we can keep information in short-term memory for a much longer period. One method of assessing short-term memory is the memory-span task. If you have taken an IQ test, you were probably exposed to one of these tasks. You simply hear a short list of stimuli—usually digits—presented at a rapid pace (one per second, for example). Then you are asked to repeat the digits. Research with the memory-span task suggests that short-term memory increases during early childhood. For example, in one investigation, memory span increased from about 2 digits in 2- to 3-year-old children to about 5 digits in 7-year-old children; yet between 7 and 13 years of age, memory span increased only by 1½ digits (Dempster, 1981). Keep in mind, though, the individual differences in memory span, which is why IQ and various aptitude tests are used.

Why are there differences in memory span because of age? Rehearsal of information is important; older children rehearse the digits more than younger children. Speed and efficiency of processing information are important, too, especially the speed with which memory items can be identified. For example, in one study, children were tested on their speed at repeating words presented orally (Case, Kurland, & Goldberg, 1982). Speed of repetition was a powerful predictor of memory span. Indeed, when the speed of repetition was controlled, the 6-year-olds' memory spans were equal to those of young adults!

"Can we hurry up and get to the test? My short-term memory is better than my long-term memory."

© 1985; reprinted courtesy of Bill Hoest and Parade Magazine.

The speed-of-processing explanation highlights an important point in the information-processing perspective. That is, the speed with which a child processes information is an important aspect of the child's cognitive abilities.

Task Analysis

Another major emphasis in the information-processing perspective is identifying the components of the task the child is performing. Information-processing psychologists are intrigued by the possibility that if tasks are made interesting and simple, children may display greater cognitive maturity than Piaget realized. This strategy was followed to determine if preschool children could reason about a *syllogism*—a type of reasoning problem consisting of two premises, or statements assumed to be true, plus a conclusion (Hawkins & others, 1984). To simplify problems, words such as *some* and *all* were made implicit rather than explicit. The problems focused on fantasy creatures alien to practical knowledge. Imagine how wide a child's eyes become when told stories about purple bangas who sneeze at people and merds who laugh don't like mushrooms. The following are two syllogisms that were read to children:

Every banga is purple.
Purple animals always sneeze at people.
Do bangas sneeze at people?

Merds laugh when they're happy.
Animals that laugh don't like mushrooms.
Do merds like mushrooms?

By simplifying the problem and making its dimensions more understandable to young children, the researchers demonstrated that preschool children can reason about syllogisms.

The Young Child's Theory of Mind

Children are very curious about the nature of the human mind and developmentalists have shown a flurry of recent interest in children's thoughts about what the human mind is like (Flavell, Green, & Flavell, 1995; Wellman, 1990).

As the following account of children's developing knowledge of the mind indicates, children are aware that the mind exists, has connections to the physical world, is separate from the physical world, can represent objects and events accurately or inaccurately, and actively mediates the interpretation of reality and the emotions experienced (Flavell, Miller, & Miller, 1993).

A first developmental acquisition is knowing that such a thing as a mind exists. By the age of 2 or 3, children refer to needs, emotions, and mental states—"I need my Mommy," "Tom feels bad," and "I forgot my doll." They also use intentional action or desire words, such as "wants to." Cognitive terms such as know, remember, and think usually appear after perceptual and emotional terms, but often are used by the age of 3. Later children make finer distinctions between such mental phenomena as guessing versus knowing, believing versus fantasizing, and intending versus not on purpose.

At about 2 or 3 years of age, children develop the knowledge that people can be "cognitively connected" to objects and events in the external world in such ways as seeing them, hearing them, liking them, wanting them, fearing them, and so on. By their awareness of the connections among stimuli, mental states, and behavior, young children possess a rudimentary mental theory of human action. On the input side, 2-year-olds sometimes hide objects so that another person cannot see them, which involves manipulating stimuli to produce a certain perceptual state in another person. On the output side (mind to behavior), older 2-year-old children can predict action and emotional expression based on desires, as when comprehending that a child wants a cookie, tries to get one, and is happy if successful. However, 2-year-olds cannot predict actions based on beliefs. For instance, if Ann wants to find her toy but can't find it in one location, children predict she would be sad and look for it in another location. But they don't know that Ann's beliefs about possible locations influence where she will look.

In addition to inferring connections from stimuli to mental states, or from mental states to behavior or emotion, 3-year-olds also can often infer mental states from behavior. When children use spontaneous language, they sometimes explain action by referring to mental causes. For example, a 3-year-old explains that he has paint on his hands because he thought his hands were paper, which gives new meaning to the term *finger painting!* In sum, children acquire knowledge about links between stimuli, mental states, and behavior fairly early in their development.

Young children also develop an understanding that the mind is separate from the physical world. They know that the mind is different from rocks, roller skates, and even the head. For example, a 3-year-old who is told that one boy has a cookie and that another boy is thinking about cookie knows which cookie can be seen by others, touched, eaten, shared, and saved for later. Three-year-olds also know that they can fantasize about things that don't exist, such as Martians, ghosts, or dragons.

Children develop an understanding that the mind can represent objects and events accurately or inaccurately. Understanding of false beliefs usually appears in 4- or 5-year-old children, but not 3-year-olds. Consider the following story acted out for children with dolls. A boy places some chocolate in a blue cupboard and then goes out to play. While he is outside, his mother moves the chocolate to a green cupboard. When the boy returns and wants the chocolate, the subject is asked where the boy will look for it. Three-year-olds usually say "The green cupboard," where the chocolate actually is, even though the boy had no way of knowing the chocolate was moved. Thus, 3-year-olds do not understand that a person acts on the basis of what he or she believes to be true rather than what they themselves know to be true. By contrast, 4- and 5-year-old children usually understand false beliefs.

Finally, children also develop an understanding that the mind actively mediates the interpretation of reality and the emotion experienced. The shift from viewing the mind as passive to viewing it as active appears in children's knowledge that prior experiences influence current mental states, which in turn affect emotions and social inferences. In the elementary school years, children change from viewing emotions as caused by external events without any mediation by internal states, to viewing emotional reactions to an external event as influenced by a prior emotional state, experience, or expectations. For example, 6-year-old children do not understand that a child would be sad or scared when his friends suggest they ride bikes if that child previously was almost hit by a car when she could not stop her bike because her legs were too short.

In summary, young children are very curious about the human mind. By the age of 3, they turn some of their thoughts inward and understand that they and others have internal mental states. Beginning at about 3 years of age, children also show an understanding that the internal desires and beliefs of a person can be connected to that person's actions. Young children also know that they cannot physically touch thoughts, believe that a person has to see an object to know it, and grasp that their mental image of an object represents something that exists in the world.

At this point we have discussed a number of ideas about cognitive developmental changes and early childhood. A summary of these ideas is presented in concept table 10.1.

LANGUAGE DEVELOPMENT

Young children's understanding sometimes gets way ahead of their speech. One 3-year-old, laughing with delight as an abrupt summer breeze stirred his hair and tickled his skin, commented, "It did winding me!" Adults would be understandably perplexed if a young child ventured, "Anything is not to break, only plates and glasses," when she meant, "Nothing is breaking except plates and glasses." Many of the oddities of young children's language sound like mistakes to adult listeners. But from the children's

CONCEPT TABLE 10.1

Cognitive Developmental Changes

Concept	Processes/Related Ideas	Characteristics/Description
Piaget's Stage of Preoperational Thought	Its nature	This is the beginning of the ability to reconstruct at the level of thought what has been established in behavior, and a transition from primitive to more sophisticated use of symbols. The child does not yet think in an operational way.
	Symbolic function substage	This substage occurs roughly between 2 and 4 years of age and is characterized by symbolic thought, egocentrism, and animism.
	Intuitive thought substage	This substage stretches from approximately 4 to 7 years of age. It is called intuitive because, on the one hand, children seem so sure about their knowledge yet, on the other hand, they are so unaware of how they know what they know. The preoperational child lacks conservation and asks a barrage of questions.
Vygotsky's Theory	The zone of proximal development	Has a lower and an upper limit. The lower limit is the level of problem solving reached by a child working independently; the upper limit is the level of additional responsibility a child can accept with assistance of an able instructor.
	Language and thought	Language and thought develop independently and then merge. The merging of language and thought takes place between 3 and 7 years of age and involves talking to oneself.
	Culture and society	Vygotsky's theory stresses how the child's mind develops in the context of the sociocultural world. Cognitive skills develop through social interaction embedded in a cultural backdrop.
Information Processing	Attention	The child's attention dramatically improves during early childhood. One deficit in attention in early childhood is that the child attends to the salient rather than the relevant features of a task.
	Memory	Significant improvement in short-term memory occurs during early childhood. For example, memory span increases substantially in early childhood. Increased use of rehearsal and increased speed of processing are related to young children's memory improvement.
	Task analysis	Information-processing advocates believe a task's components should be analyzed. By making tasks more interesting and simple, some aspects of children's cognitive development have been shown to occur earlier than thought possible.
The Young Child's Theory of Mind	Its nature	Young children are very curious about the human mind. By about 3 years of age, they turn some of their thoughts inward and understand that they and others have internal mental states. Beginning at about 3, they also show an understanding that the internal beliefs and desires of another person can be connected to that person's actions. Young children also know that they cannot physically touch thoughts, believe that a person has to see an object to know it, and grasp that their mental image of an object represents something that exists in the world.

Roger Brown, shown talking with a young girl, has been a pioneer in providing rich insights about children's language development. Among his contributions is the concept of MLU, or mean length of utterance, which has been documented as a good index of a child's language maturity.

"No, Timmy, not 'I sawed the chair'; it's 'I saw the chair' or 'I have seen the chair.'"

© Glenn Bernhardt.

point of view, they are not mistakes; they represent the way young children perceive and understand their world at that point in their development.

Stages and Rule Systems

What stages are involved in young children's language development? How do young children's rule systems for language change in early childhood?

Elaboration of Brown's Stages

In chapter 6, we briefly described Roger Brown's five stages of language development. Remember that Brown (1973) believes that mean length of utterance (MLU) is a good index of a child's language maturity. He identified five stages of a child's language development based on MLU.

In stage 1, occurring from 12 to 26 months of age, the MLU is 1.00 to 2.00. Vocabulary consists mainly of nouns and verbs, with several adjectives and adverbs. Word order is preserved. Typical sentences are "Mommy bye-bye" and "Big doggie."

In stage 2, occurring from 27 to 30 months, MLU is 2.00 to 2.50. Plurals are correctly formed, past tense is used, *be* is used, definite articles (*the*) and indefinite

John W. Santrock

articles (*a, an*) are used, and so are some prepositions. Typical sentences are "Dolly in bed," "Them pretty," and "Milk's all gone."

In stage 3, occurring from 31 to 34 months of age, MLU is 2.50 to 3.00. Yes-no questions appear, *wh*-questions (*who, what, where*) proliferate, negatives (*no, not, non*) are used, and so are imperatives (commands or requests). Typical sentences are "Daddy come home?" and "Susie no want milk."

In stage 4, occurring from 35 to 40 months, MLU is 3.00 to 3.75. One sentence is sometimes embedded in another. Typical sentences include "I think it's red" and "Know what I saw."

In stage 5, occurring from 41 to 46 months, MLU is 3.75 to 4.50. Simple sentences and propositional relations are coordinated. Typical sentences are "I went to Bob's and had ice cream" and "I like bunnies 'cause they're cute."

But whatever the process, the result is wonderful, gradually from naming an object we advance step-by-step until we have traversed the vast difference between our first stammered syllable and the sweep of thought in a line of Shakespeare.

—**Helen Keller**

Rule Systems

Remember from our discussion of language development in chapter 6 that language consists of rule systems such as those involving morphology, syntax, semantics, and pragmatics. What kinds of changes take place in these rule systems during early childhood?

As children move beyond two-word utterances, there is clear evidence that they know morphology rules. Children begin using the plurals and possessive forms of nouns (such as *dogs* and *dog's*), putting appropriate endings on verbs (such as *-s* when the subject is third-person singular, *-ed* for the past tense, and *-ing* for the present progressive tense), using prepositions (such as *in* and *on*), articles (such as *a* and *the*), and various forms of the verb *to be* (such as "I *was going* to the store"). Some of the best evidence for changes in children's use of morphological rules occur in their overgeneralizations of the rules. Have you ever heard a preschool child say "foots" instead of "feet," or "goed" instead of "went"? If you do not remember having heard such oddities, talk to some parents who have young children, or to the young children themselves. You will hear some interesting errors in the use of morphological rule endings.

In a classic experiment, Jean Berko (1958) presented preschool children and first-grade children with cards such as the one shown in figure 10.9. Children were asked to look at the card while the experimenter read the words on the card aloud. Then the children were asked to supply the missing word. This might sound easy, but

This is a wug.

Now there is another one.
There are two of them.
There are two_____.

FIGURE 10.9

Stimuli in Berko's Study of Young Children's Understanding of Morphological Rules
In Jean Berko's (1958) study, young children were presented cards such as this one with a "wug" on it. Then the children were asked to supply the missing word; in supplying the missing word, they had to say it correctly, too. "Wugs" is the correct response here.

Berko was interested not just in the children's ability to recall the right word, but also in their ability to say it "correctly" (with the ending that was dictated by morphological rules). "Wugs" would be the correct response for the card in figure 10.9. Although the children's answers were not perfect, they were much better than chance. Moreover, the children demonstrated their knowledge of morphological rules not only with the plural forms of nouns ("There are two wugs"), but with possessive forms of nouns and the third-person singular and past-tense forms of verbs. What makes the study by Berko impressive is that most of the words were fictional, created for the experiment. Thus, the children could not base their responses on remembering past instances of hearing the words. Instead they were forced to rely on *rules*.

Similar evidence that children learn and actively apply rules can be found at the level of syntax. After advancing beyond two-word utterances, children speak word sequences that show a growing mastery of complex rules for how words should be ordered. Consider the case of *wh*-questions: "Where is Daddy going?" and "What is that boy doing?" for example. To ask these questions properly, the

---

How do children's language abilities develop during early childhood?

child has to know two important differences between *wh-* questions and simple affirmative statements (such as "Daddy is going to work" and "That boy is waiting on the school bus"). First, a *wh-* word must be added at the beginning of the sentence. Second, the auxiliary verb must be "inverted"—that is, exchanged with the subject of the sentence. Young children learn quite early where to put the *wh-* word, but they take much longer to learn the auxiliary-inversion rule. Thus, it is common to hear preschool children asking such questions as "Where daddy is going?" and "What that boy is doing?"

As children move into the elementary school years, they become skilled at using syntactical rules to construct lengthy and complex sentences. Sentences such as "The man who fixed the house went home" and "I don't want you to use my bike" are impressive demonstrations of how the child can use syntax to combine ideas into a single sentence. How young children achieve the mastery of such complex rules and yet struggle with relatively simple arithmetic rules is a mystery we must still solve.

Regarding semantics, as children move beyond the 2-word stage, their knowledge of meanings also rapidly advances (Rice, 1991). The speaking vocabulary of a 6-year-old child ranges from 8,000 to 14,000 words. Assuming that word learning began when the child was 12 months old, this translates into a rate of 5 to 8 new word meanings a day between the ages of 1 and 6. After 5 years of word learning, the 6-year-old child does not slow down.

According to some estimates, the average child of this age is moving along at the awe-inspiring rate of 22 words a day! How would you fare if you were given the task of learning 22 new words every day? It is truly miraculous how quickly children learn language.

Although there are many differences between a 2-year-old's language and a 6-year-old's language, none are more important than those pertaining to pragmatics—rules of conversation (Ninio & Snow, 1996). A 6-year-old is simply a much better conversationalist than a 2-year-old. What are some of the improvements in pragmatics that are made in the preschool years? At about 3 years of age, children improve in their ability to talk about things that are not physically present; that is, they improve their command of the characteristic of language known as "displacement." One way displacement is revealed is in games of pretend. Although a 2-year-old might know the word *table,* he is unlikely to use this word to refer to an imaginary table that he pretends is standing in front of him. But a child over 3 probably has this ability, even if he does not always use it. There are large individual differences in preschoolers' talk about imaginary people and things.

Literacy and Early Childhood Education

The concern about our nation's literacy—the ability to read and write—has led to a careful examination of preschool and kindergarten children's experiences with the hope that a positive orientation toward reading and writing can be developed early in life. Literacy begins in infancy. Reading and writing skills in young children should build on their existing understanding of oral and written language. Learning should occur in a supportive environment, one in which children can generate a positive perception of themselves and develop a positive attitude toward reading and writing (Stone, 1994).

Unfortunately, in the push to develop a nation of literate people by emphasizing the early development of reading and writing skills, some dangers have emerged (Early Childhood and Literacy Development Committee, 1986). Too many preschool children are being subjected to rigid, formal prereading programs with expectations and experiences that are too advanced for children of their levels of development. Too little attention is being given to the individual development of young children's learning styles and skills. Too little attention is being placed on reading for pleasure and this may keep children from associating reading with enjoyment. The pressure to achieve high scores on standardized tests that often are inappropriate for preschool children has resulted in a curriculum that is too advanced and too intense. Such programs frequently restrict curiosity, critical thinking, and creative expression.

What should a literacy program for preschool children be like? Instruction should be built on what children already know about oral language, reading, and writing. All young children should experience feelings of success and pride in their early reading and writing exercises. Teachers need to help them perceive themselves as people who can enjoy exploring oral and written language. Reading should be integrated into the broad communication process, which includes speaking, listening, and writing, as well as other communication systems such as art, math, and music (Neuman & Roskos, 1993). Children's early writing attempts should be encouraged without concern for the proper formation of letters or correct conventional spelling. Children should be encouraged to take risks in reading and writing, and errors should be viewed as a natural part of the child's growth. Teachers and parents should take time to regularly read to children from a wide variety of poetry, fiction, and nonfiction. Teachers and parents should present models for young children to emulate by using language appropriately, listening and responding to children's talk, and engaging in their own reading and writing. And children should be encouraged to be active participants in the learning process rather than passive recipients of knowledge. This can be accomplished by using activities that stimulate experimentation with talking, listening, writing, and reading.

EARLY CHILDHOOD EDUCATION

Our coverage of early childhood education focuses on variations in the education of young children, whether preschool is necessary, and school readiness.

Variations in Early Childhood Education

There are many variations in the way young children are educated. In the "Images" section that opened this chapter, you read about the Reggio Emilia program in northern Italy, a promising strategy that is receiving increased attention. First we will explore the nature of the child-centered kindergarten, then turn our attention to Maria Montessori's approach. Next we will examine the important concepts of developmentally appropriate and inappropriate education, followed by a discussion of what early childhood education's effects are.

The Child-Centered Kindergarten

Kindergarten programs vary a great deal. Some approaches place more emphasis on young children's social development, others on their cognitive development. Some experts on early childhood education believe that the curriculum of too many of today's kindergarten and preschool programs place too much emphasis on achievement and success, putting pressure on young children too early in their development (Charlesworth, 1996; Elkind, 1988). Placing such heavy emphasis on success is not what kindergartens were originally intended to do. In the 1840s, Friedrich Froebel's concern for quality education for young children led to the founding of the kindergarten, literally "a garden for children." The founder of the kindergarten understood that, like growing plants, children require careful nurturing. *Unfortunately, too many of today's kindergartens have forgotten the importance of careful nurturing for our nation's young children.*

Learning is an ornament of prosperity, a refuge in adversity.
—**Aristotle**

In the **child-centered kindergarten,** *education involves the whole child and includes concern for the child's physical, cognitive, and social development.* Instruction is organized around the child's needs, interests, and learning styles. The process of learning, rather than what is learned, is emphasized. Each child follows a unique developmental pattern, and young children learn best through firsthand experiences with people and materials. Play is extremely important in the child's total development. *Experimenting, exploring, discovering, trying out, restructuring, speaking,* and *listening* are all words that describe excellent kindergarten programs. Such programs are closely attuned to the developmental status of 4- and 5-year-old children. They are based on a state of being, not on a state of becoming.

The Montessori Approach

Montessori schools are patterned after the educational philosophy of Maria Montessori, an Italian physician-turned-educator, who crafted a revolutionary approach to young children's education at the beginning of the twentieth century. Her work began with a group of mentally retarded

Maria Montessori (1870–1952), the Italian physician and educator who developed the Montessori approach to educating young children.

deemphasized. Montessori's critics also argue that imaginative play is restricted.

Developmentally Appropriate and Inappropriate Practices in the Education of Young Children

It is time for number games in a kindergarten class at the Greenbrook School in South Brunswick, New Jersey. With little prodding from the teacher, twenty-three 5- and 6-year-old children fetch geometric puzzles, playing cards, and counting equipment from the shelves lining the room. At one round table, some young children fit together brightly colored shapes. One girl forms a hexagon out of triangles. Other children gather around her to count up how many parts were needed to make the whole. After about half an hour the children prepare for story time. They put away their counting equipment and sit in a circle around one young girl. She holds up a giant book about a character named Mrs. Wishywashy, who insists on giving the farm animals a bath. The children recite the whimsical lines, clearly enjoying one of their favorite stories. The hallway outside the kindergarten is lined with drawings depicting the children's own interpretations of the book. After the first reading, volunteers act out various parts of the book. There is not one bored face in the room.

This is not reading, writing, and arithmetic the way most individuals remember it. A growing number of educators and psychologists believe that preschool and young elementary school children learn best through active, hands-on teaching methods like games and dramatic play. They know that children develop at varying rates and that schools need to allow for these individual differences. They also believe that schools should focus on improving children's social development as well as their cognitive development. Educators refer to this type of schooling as **developmentally appropriate practice,** *which is based upon knowledge of the typical development of children within an age span (age appropriateness) as well as the uniqueness of the child (individual appropriateness). Developmentally appropriate practice contrasts with developmentally inappropriate practice, which ignores the concrete, hands-on approach to learning. Direct teaching largely through abstract, paper-and-pencil activities presented to large groups of young children is believed to be developmentally inappropriate.*

children in Rome. She was successful in teaching them to read, write, and pass examinations designed for normal children. Some time later, she turned her attention to poor children from the slums of Rome and had similar success in teaching them. Her approach has since been adopted extensively in private nursery schools in the United States.

The **Montessori approach** *is a philosophy of education in which children are given considerable freedom and spontaneity in choosing activities and are allowed to move from one activity to another as they desire.* The teacher acts as a facilitator rather than a director of learning. The teacher shows the child how to perform intellectual activities, demonstrates interesting ways to explore curriculum materials, and offers help when the child requests it.

Some developmentalists favor the Montessori approach, but others believe that it neglects children's social development (Chattin-McNichols, 1992). For example, while Montessori fosters independence and the development of cognitive skills, verbal interaction between the teacher and child and peer interaction are

John W. Santrock

These preschool children are attending a Head Start program, a national effort to provide children from low-income families the opportunity to experience an enriched environment.

One of the most comprehensive documents addressing the issue of developmentally appropriate practice in early childhood programs is the position statement by the NAEYC (National Association for the Education of Young Children, 1986; Bredekamp, 1987). This document represents the expertise of many of the foremost experts in the field of early childhood education. By turning to figure 10.10, you can examine some of the NAEYC recommendations for developmentally appropriate practice. In one study, children who attended developmentally appropriate kindergartens displayed more appropriate classroom behavior, had better conduct records, and better work and study habits in the first grade than children who attended developmentally inappropriate kindergartens (Hart & others, 1993).

A special worry of early childhood educators is that the back-to-basics movement that has recently characterized educational reform is filtering down to kindergarten. Another worry is that many parents want their children to go to school earlier than kindergarten for the purpose of getting a "head

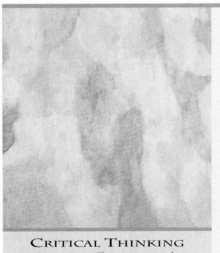

CRITICAL THINKING
ABOUT CHILDREN'S
DEVELOPMENT

Giving Advice to Parents About Selecting a Good Preschool Program

Imagine that you are a preschool educational consultant. What kind of advice would you give parents about selecting a good preschool program? In developing your recommendations, consider what you would tell parents about the following:

· The relationship between the teacher-caregiver and the child
· Activities
· Teacher-caregiver development
· Staffing and group size
· The physical environment
· Health, safety, and nutrition
· The relationship between the parent and the teacher-caregiver

By developing guidelines for recommending a good preschool to parents, you are learning to think critically by *applying developmental concepts to enhance personal adaptation.*

start" in achievement. To further evaluate early childhood education, see Critical Thinking About Children's Development.

Component	Appropriate practice	Inappropriate practice
Curriculum goals	Experiences are provided in all developmental areas—physical, cognitive, social, and emotional.	Experiences are narrowly focused on cognitive development without recognition that all areas of the child's development are interrelated.
	Individual differences are expected, accepted, and used to design appropriate activities.	Children are evaluated only against group norms, and all are expected to perform the same tasks and achieve the same narrowly defined skills.
	Interactions and activities are designed to develop children's self-esteem and positive feelings toward learning.	Children's worth is measured by how well they conform to rigid expectations and perform on standardized tests.
Teaching strategies	Teachers prepare the environment for children to learn through active exploration and interaction with adults, other children, and materials.	Teachers use highly structured, teacher-directed lessons almost exclusively.
	Children select many of their own activities from among a variety the teacher prepares.	The teacher directs all activity, deciding what children will do and when.
	Children are expected to be mentally and physically active.	Children are expected to sit down, be quiet, and listen, or do paper-and-pencil tasks for long periods of time. A major portion of time is spent passively sitting, watching, and listening.
Guidance of socioemotional development	Teachers enhance children's self-control by using positive guidance techniques such as modeling and encouraging expected behavior, redirecting children to a more acceptable activity, and setting clear limits.	Teachers spend considerable time enforcing rules, punishing unacceptable behavior, demeaning children who misbehave, making children sit and be quiet, or refereeing disagreements.
	Children are provided many opportunities to develop social skills such as cooperating, helping, negotiating, and talking with the person involved to solve interpersonal problems.	Children work individually at desks and tables most of the time and listen to the teacher's directions to the total group.

FIGURE 10.10

Developmentally Appropriate and Inappropriate Practice in Early Childhood—NAEYC Recommendations

John W. Santrock

Component	Appropriate practice	Inappropriate practice
Language development, literacy, and cognitive development	Children are provided many opportunities to see how reading and writing are useful before they are instructed in letter names, sounds, and word identification. Basic skills develop when they are meaningful to children. An abundance of these activities is provided to develop language and literacy: listening to and reading stories and poems, taking field trips, dictating stories, participating in dramatic play; talking informally with other children and adults; and experimenting with writing.	Reading and writing instruction stresses isolated skill development, such as recognizing single letters, reading the alphabet, singing the alphabet song, coloring within predefined lines, or being instructed in correct formation of letters on a printed line.
	Children develop an understanding of concepts about themselves, others, and the world around them through observation, interacting with people and real objects, and seeking solutions to concrete problems. Learning about math, science, social studies, health, and other content areas is integrated through meaningful activities.	Instruction stresses isolated skill development through memorization. Children's cognitive development is seen as fragmented in content areas such as math or science, and times are set aside for each of these.
Physical development	Children have daily opportunities to use large muscles, including running, jumping, and balancing. Outdoor activity is planned daily so children can freely express themselves.	Opportunity for large muscle activity is limited. Outdoor time is limited because it is viewed as interfering with instructional time, rather than as an integral part of the children's learning environment.
	Children have daily opportunities to develop small muscle skills through play activities, such as puzzles, painting, cutting, and similar activities.	Small motor activity is limited to writing with pencils, coloring predrawn forms, or engaging in similar structured lessons.
Aesthetic development and motivation	Children have daily opportunities for aesthetic expression and appreciation through art and music. A variety of art media is available.	Art and music are given limited attention. Art consists of coloring predrawn forms or following adult-prescribed directions.
	Children's natural curiosity and desire to make sense of their world are used to motivate them to become involved in learning.	Children are required to participate in all activities to obtain the teacher's approval, to obtain extrinsic rewards like stickers or privileges, or to avoid punishment.

Education for Disadvantaged Children

For many years, children from low-income families did not receive any education before they entered the first grade. In the 1960s, an effort was made to try to break the cycle of poverty and poor education for young children in the United States through compensatory education. **Project Head Start** *is a compensatory education program designed to provide children from low-income families the opportunity to acquire the skills and experiences important for success in school.* Project Head Start began in the summer of 1965, funded by the Economic Opportunity Act, and it continues to serve disadvantaged children today.

Initially, Project Head Start consisted of many different types of preschool programs in different parts of the country. Little effort was made to find out whether some programs worked better than others, but it became apparent that some programs did work better than others. **Project Follow Through** *was implemented in 1967 as an adjunct to Project Head Start. In Project Follow Through, different types of educational programs were devised to determine which programs were the most effective. In the Follow Through programs, the enriched programs were carried through the first few years of elementary school.*

Were some Follow Through programs more effective than others? Many of the variations were able to produce the desired effects in children. For example, children in academically oriented, direct-instruction approaches did better on achievement tests and were most persistent on tasks than were children in the other approaches. Children in affective education approaches were absent from school less often and showed more independence than children in other approaches. Thus, Project Follow Through was important in demonstrating that variation in early childhood education does have significant effects in a wide range of social and cognitive areas (Stallings, 1975).

The effects of early childhood compensatory education continue to be studied, and recent evaluations support the positive influence on both the cognitive and the social worlds of disadvantaged young children (Campbell & Taylor, 1996; Gaines, Blair, & Cluett, 1995; Klein & Starkey, 1995). Of special interest are the long-term effects such intervention might produce. Model preschool programs lead to lower rates of placement in special education, dropping out of school, grade retention, delinquency, and use of welfare programs. Such programs might also lead to higher rates of high school graduation and employment. For every dollar invested in high-quality, model preschool programs, taxpayers receive about $1.50 in return by the time the participants reach the age of 20. The benefits include savings on public school education (such as special-education services), tax payments on additional earnings, reduced welfare payments, and savings in juvenile justice system costs. Predicted benefits over a lifetime are much greater to the taxpayer, a return of $5.73 on every dollar invested.

One long-term investigation of early childhood education was conducted by Irving Lazar, Richard Darlington,

and their colleagues (1982). They pooled their resources into what they called a "consortium for longitudinal studies," developed to share information about the long-term effects of preschool programs so that better designs and methods could be created. When the data from the eleven different early education studies were analyzed together, the children ranged in age from 9 to 19 years. The early education models varied substantially, but all were carefully planned and executed by experts in early childhood education. Outcome measures included indicators of school competence (such as special education and grade retention), abilities (as measured by standardized intelligence and achievement tests), attitudes and values, and impact on the family. The results indicated substantial benefits of competent preschool education with low-income children on all four dimensions investigated. In sum, ample evidence indicates that well-designed and well-implemented early childhood education programs with low-income children are successful.

Although educational intervention in impoverished children's lives is important, Head Start programs are not all created equal. One estimate is that 40 percent of the 1,400 Head Start programs are of questionable quality (Zigler & Styfco, 1994). More attention needs to be given to developing consistently high-quality Head Start programs (Bronfenbrenner, 1995; Parker & others, 1995). One high-quality early childhood education program (although not a Head Start program) is the Perry Preschool program in Ypsilanti, Michigan, designed by David Weikart (1982). The Perry Preschool program is a 2-year preschool program that includes weekly home visits from program personnel. In a recent analysis of the long-term effects of the program, as young adults the Perry Preschool children had higher high school graduation rates, more are in the workforce, fewer need welfare, crime rates are lower among them, and there are fewer teen pregnancies than in a control group from the same background who did not get the enriched early childhood education experience (Weikart, 1993).

The Effects of Early Childhood Education

Because kindergarten and preschool programs are so diverse, it is difficult to draw overall conclusions about their effects on children's development. Nonetheless, in one review of early childhood education's influence (Clarke-Stewart & Fein, 1983), it was concluded that children who attend preschool or kindergarten

- interact more with peers, both positively and negatively
- are less cooperative with and responsive to adults than home-reared children
- are more socially competent and mature in that they are more confident, extraverted, assertive, self-sufficient, independent, verbally expressive, knowledgeable about the social world, comfortable in social and stressful circumstances, and better adjusted

CRITICAL THINKING
ABOUT CHILDREN'S
DEVELOPMENT

_Observing Children
in Preschool
and Kindergarten_

To learn about children, there is no substitute for interacting with them and observing them. Try to visit at least one preschool and one kindergarten. When I (your author) was trying to develop a meaningful idea for a master's thesis some years ago, my advisor suggested that I spend several weeks at different Head Start programs in Miami, Florida. The experience was invaluable and contributed significantly to my further pursuing a career in the field of child development.

When you conduct your observations, consider whether the programs meet the criteria of developmentally appropriate education. Are the programs play- and child-centered or academics-centered? By visiting early childhood education programs and evaluating whether they are developmentally appropriate, you are learning to think critically by _making accurate observations, descriptions, and inferences about children's development._

have the commitment, the time, the energy, and the resources to provide young children with an environment that approximates a good early childhood program, then it _does_ matter whether a child attends preschool. In this case, the issue is not whether preschool is important, but whether home schooling can closely duplicate what a competent preschool program can offer.

We should always keep in mind the unfortunate idea of early childhood education as an early start to ensure the participants will finish early or on top in an educational race. Elkind (1988) points out that perhaps the choice of the phrase _head start_ for the education of disadvantaged children was a mistake. "Head Start program" does not imply a race. Not surprisingly, when middle-class parents heard that low-income children were getting a "head start," they wanted a head start for their own young children. In some instances, starting children in formal academic training too early can produce more harm than good. In Denmark, where reading instruction follows a language experience approach and formal instruction is delayed until the age of 7, illiteracy is virtually nonexistent. By contrast, in France, where state-mandated formal instruction in reading begins at age 5, 30 percent of the children have reading problems. Education should not be stressful for young children. Early childhood education should not be solely an academic prep school.

Preschool is rapidly becoming a norm in early childhood education. Twenty-three states already have legislation pending to provide schooling for 4-year-old children, and there are already many private preschool programs. The increase in public preschools underscores the growing belief that early childhood education should be a legitimate component of public education. There are dangers, though. According to child developmentalist David Elkind (1988), early childhood education is often not well understood at higher levels of education. The danger is that public preschool education for 4-year-old children will become little more than a downward extension of traditional elementary education. This is already occurring in preschool programs in which testing, workbooks, and group drill are imposed on 4- and 5-year-old children.

Elkind believes that early childhood education should become a part of public education, but on its own terms. Early childhood should have its own curriculum, its own methods of evaluation and classroom management,

when they go to school (exhibiting more task persistence, leadership, and goal direction, for example)

- are less socially competent in that they are less polite, less compliant to teacher demands, louder, and more aggressive and bossy, especially if the school or family supports such behavior

In sum, early childhood education generally has a positive effect on children's development, since the behaviors just mentioned—while at times negative—seem to be in the direction of developmental maturity, in that they increase as the child ages through the preschool years. To further evaluate children's development in early childhood, see Critical Thinking About Children's Development.

Does Preschool Matter?

According to child developmentalist David Elkind (1988), parents who are exceptionally competent and dedicated and who have both the time and the energy can provide the basic ingredients of early childhood education in their home. If parents have the competence and resources to provide young children with a variety of learning experiences and exposure to other children and adults (possibly through neighborhood play groups), along with opportunities for extensive play, then home schooling may sufficiently educate young children. However, if parents do not and its own teacher-training programs. Although there may be some overlap with the curriculum, evaluation, classroom management, and teacher training at the upper levels of schooling, they certainly should not be identical.

Researchers are already beginning to document some of the stress that increased academic pressure can bring to young children. In one study, Diane Burts and her colleagues (1989) compared the frequencies of stress-related behaviors observed in young children in classrooms with developmentally appropriate and developmentally inappropriate instructional practices. They found that children in the developmentally inappropriate classrooms exhibited more stress-related behaviors than children in the developmentally appropriate classrooms. In another study, children in a high academically oriented early childhood education program were compared with children in a low academically oriented early childhood education program (Hirsch-Pasek & others, 1989). No benefits appeared for children in the high academically oriented early childhood education program, but some possible harmful effects were noted. Higher test anxiety, less creativity, and a less positive attitude toward school characterized the children who attended the high academic program more than the low academic program.

School Readiness

Educational reform has prompted considerable concern about children's readiness to enter kindergarten and first grade. The issue gained national attention when the president and the nation's governors adopted school readiness as a national educational goal, vowing that by the year 2000 all children will start school ready to learn. The concept of school readiness is based on the assumption that all children need to possess a predetermined set of capabilities before they enter school. Thus, any discussions of school readiness should consider three important factors:

- The diversity and inequity of children's early life experiences.
- The wide range of variation in young children's development and learning.
- The degree to which school expectations for children entering kindergarten are reasonable, appropriate, and supportive of individual differences in children.

The National Association for the Education of Young Children (1990) stresses that government officials and educators who promote universal school readiness should commit to the following:

- Addressing the inequities in early life experiences so that all children have access to the opportunities that promote success in school.

- Recognizing and supporting individual differences in children.
- Establishing reasonable and appropriate expectations for children's capabilities upon school entry.

The National Association for the Education of Young Children believes that every child, except in the most severe instances of abuse, neglect, or disability, enters school ready to learn. However, not all children succeed in school. Inadequate health care and economic difficulties place many children at risk for academic failure before they enter school. Families who lack emotional resources and support also are not always capable of preparing their children to meet school expectations.

Therefore, according to the NAEYC, it is important to provide families with access to the services and support necessary to prepare children to succeed in school. Such services include basic health care, economic support, basic nutrition, adequate housing, family support services, and high-quality early childhood education programs.

Expectations for young children's skills and abilities need to be based on knowledge of child development and how children learn. A basic principle of child development is that *there is tremendous normal variability both among children of the same chronological age and within an individual child.* Children's social skills, physical skills, cognitive skills, and emotional adjustment are equally important areas of development, and each contributes to how well children do in school. Within any group of children, one child may possess advanced language and cognitive skills, but show poor social skills and emotional adjustment; another child may have advanced social skills, be well adjusted emotionally, and have good physical skills, but have poor language skills, and so on. Readiness expectations should not be based on a narrow checklist focusing on only one or two dimensions of development. Such a narrow focus—only considering language or cognitive skills, for example—ignores the complexity and multidimensionality of children's development.

Wide variability also occurs in the rate of children's development. The precise time at which children will achieve a certain level of development or acquire specific skills is difficult to predict. Learning and development often do not occur in rigid, uniform ways. Thus, raising the legal entry age for school or holding a child out of school for a year may not be wise but could be misdirected efforts that only serve to impose a rigid schedule on the child's development despite their normal differences from other children.

At this point we have discussed a number of ideas about language development and early childhood education. These ideas are summarized in concept table 10.2.

CONCEPT TABLE 10.2

Language Development and Early Childhood Education

Concept	Processes/Related Ideas	Characteristics/Description
Language Development	Elaboration of Brown's stages	Roger Brown's five stages represent a helpful model for describing young children's language development. They involve mean length of utterance, age ranges, characteristics of language, and sentence variations.
	Rule systems	Rule systems involve changes in phonology, morphology, syntax, semantics, and pragmatics during the early childhood years.
	Literacy and early childhood	There has been increased interest in teaching young children reading and writing skills. Unfortunately, this had led to some dangers, with too many preschool children subjected to rigid, intense programs too advanced for their development. Young children need to develop positive feelings about their reading and writing skills through a supportive environment. Children should be active participants and be immersed in a wide range of interesting and enjoyable listening, talking, writing, and reading experiences.
Early Childhood Education	Variations	Child-centered kindergarten involves education of the whole child, with emphasis on individual variation, the process of learning, and the importance of play in development. The Montessori approach is another well-known early-childhood education strategy. Developmentally appropriate practice is based on knowledge of the typical development of children within an age span (age appropriateness) as well as the uniqueness of the child.(individual appropriateness). Developmentally appropriate practice contrasts with developmentally inappropriate practice, which ignores the concrete, hands-on approach to learning. Direct teaching largely through abstract, paper-and-pencil activities presented to large groups of young children is believed to be developmentally inappropriate. The National Association for the Education of Young Children has been a strong proponent of developmentally appropriate practice and has developed extensive recommendations for its implementation. Compensatory education has tried to break through the poverty cycle with programs like Head Start and Follow Through. Long-term studies reveal that model preschool programs have positive effects on development. The overall effects of early childhood education seem to be positive. However, outcome measures reveal areas in which social competence is more positive, others in which it is less positive.
	Does preschool matter?	Parents can effectively educate their young children just as schools can. However, many parents do not have the commitment, time, energy, and resources needed to provide young children with an environment that can compare with a competent early childhood education program. Too often, parents see education as a race, and preschool as a chance to get ahead in the race. However, education is not a race and it should not be stressful for young children. Public preschools are appearing in many states. A concern is that they should not become merely simple versions of elementary school. Early childhood education has some issues that overlap with upper levels of schooling, but in many ways the agenda of early childhood is different.
	School readiness	Educational reform has prompted considerable concern about children's readiness to enter kindergarten and first grade. The National Association for the Education of Young Children believes that the proposed guidelines for school readiness often do not adequately take into account the diversity and inequity of children's early life experiences and the opportunities needed to succeed in school, do not recognize and support individual differences in children, and do not establish reasonable and appropriate expectations of children's capabilities upon school entry.

Y oung children make significant advances in cognitive development during early childhood. Their imagination soars and their mental grasp of the world improves.

We began this chapter by describing the excellent early childhood education program Reggio Emilia. Our coverage of cognitive developmental changes focused on Piaget's preoperational thought stage, Vygotsky's theory of development, information processing, and the young child's theory of mind. Then we turned our attention to changes in language development. We also studied numerous aspects of early childhood education, including variations of early childhood education, whether preschool matters, and school readiness.

Don't forget that you can obtain an overall summary of the chapter by again studying the two concept tables on pages 289 and 301. In the next chapter we will continue our exploration of early childhood, focusing on socioemotional development.

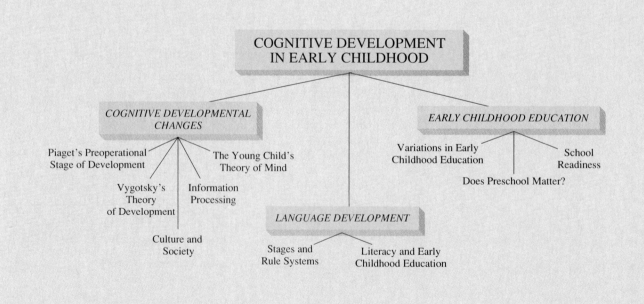

COGNITIVE DEVELOPMENT IN EARLY CHILDHOOD

COGNITIVE DEVELOPMENTAL CHANGES

Piaget's Preoperational Stage of Development

Vygotsky's Theory of Development

Information Processing

The Young Child's Theory of Mind

Culture and Society

LANGUAGE DEVELOPMENT

Stages and Rule Systems

Literacy and Early Childhood Education

EARLY CHILDHOOD EDUCATION

Variations in Early Childhood Education

Does Preschool Matter?

School Readiness

John W. Santrock

operations In Piaget's theory, internalized set of actions that allow a child to do mentally what she formerly did physically. 279

symbolic function substage Piaget's first substage of preoperational thought, in which the child gains the ability to mentally represent an object that is not present (between 2 and 4 years of age). 279

egocentrism The inability to distinguish between one's own perspective and someone else's (salient feature of the first substage of preoperational thought). 279

animism The belief that inanimate objects have "lifelike" qualities and are capable of action. 280

intuitive thought substage Piaget's second substage of preoperational thought, in which children begin to use primitive reasoning and want to know the answers to all sorts of questions (between 4 and 7 years of age). 281

centration The focusing of attention on one characteristic to the exclusion of all others. 282

conservation The idea that an amount stays the same regardless of how its container changes. 282

zone of proximal development (ZPD) Vygotsky's term for tasks too difficult for children to master alone, but can be mastered with assistance. 285

short-term memory The memory component in which individuals retain information for 15–30 seconds, assuming there is no rehearsal. 287

child-centered kindergarten Education that involves the whole child by considering both the child's physical, cognitive, and social development and the child's needs, interests, and learning styles. 293

Montessori approach An educational philosophy in which children are given considerable freedom and spontaneity in choosing activities and are allowed to move from one activity to another as they desire. 294

developmentally appropriate practice Education that focuses on the typical developmental patterns of children (age appropriateness) and the uniqueness of each child (individual appropriateness). Such practice contrasts with developmentally inappropriate practice, which ignores the concrete, hands-on approach to learning. Direct teaching largely through abstract, paper-and-pencil activities presented to large groups of young children is believed to be developmentally inappropriate. 294

Project Head Start Compensatory education designed to provide children from low-income families the opportunity to acquire the skills and experiences important for school success. 298

Project Follow Through An adjunct to Project Head Start in which the enrichment programs are carried through the first few years of elementary school. 298

PRACTICAL KNOWLEDGE ABOUT CHILDREN

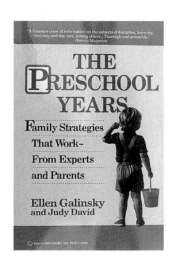

"A treasure chest of information on the subjects of discipline, learning, routines, and day care, among others...Thorough and accessible."
Parents Magazine

THE PRESCHOOL YEARS

Family Strategies
That Work–
From Experts
and Parents

Ellen Galinsky
and Judy David

The Preschool Years
(1988) by Ellen Galinsky and Judy David.
New York: Times Books.

The Preschool Years describes normal child development in the 2- to 5-years age period and provides recommendations to parents for how to cope with specific problems in this period of development. *The Preschool Years* presents a wealth of information about children's development in early childhood and is an excellent resource guide for children's growth and development during this time frame. The authors sort through what researchers have found out about young children's development and make practical suggestions for parents based on the research. They present a wide range of helpful strategies for solving children's everyday problems in the preschool years. All of the chapters include examples of young children's interchanges with people, including parents, teachers, and peers. The chapters focus on discipline, learning and growth, at-home and away-from-home routines, happy and sad times, family relationships, family work, work and family life, and schools and child care. This is an outstanding book for the parents of preschool children.

Reaching Potentials: Appropriate Curriculum and Assessment for Young Children, vol. 1 (1992)
edited by Sue Bredekamp and Teresa Rosegrant.
Washington, DC: National Association for the Education of Young Children.

This excellent book addresses how to help young children reach their full potential—not only their academical and vocational potential, but, just as importantly, their full potential as healthy, sensitive, caring, and contributing members of society. The authors argue that curriculum, assessment, and teaching practices help to determine whether these potentials are reached. The book closely follows the guidelines for appropriate curriculum content and assessment developed by the National Association for the Education of Young Children (NAEYC), a highly respected organization of early childhood educators. Bredekamp is the editor of NAEYC's position statements on accreditation, developmentally appropriate education, and standardized testing.

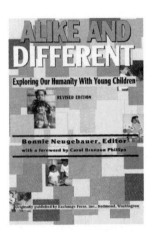

Alike and Different
(1992) edited by Bonnie Neugebauer.
Washington, DC: National Association for the Education of Young Children.

This collection of practical essays addresses the many complex issues involved in educating young children from diverse ethnic backgrounds as well as those with special needs. The essays cover many useful activities that promote an antibias atmosphere for early childhood education, criteria for selecting antibiased books and materials, resources for diversity, the interface between families and schools, and a variety of excellent multicultural programs.

John W. Santrock

IMPROVING THE LIVES OF CHILDREN

Improving the lives of children includes developing early interventions that work, increasing the partnership of parents and schools in the young child's education, using computers and technology in positive ways in early childhood programs, learning about early childhood education in other cultures, and developing nonsexist early childhood education programs.

HEALTH AND WELL-BEING

Early Interventions That Work

Children's health expert Lisbeth Schorr (1989) discussed society's stake in improving services to young children, especially poor children, and considered the attributes of early interventions that work. Investment in improved services to young children is increasingly recognized as essential to the welfare of every American (Crnic & Stormshak, 1996; Edelman, 1996; McIntosh, 1996). Connections have been made between early interventions and later outcomes such as the incidence of welfare dependence, crime, adolescent pregnancy, and dropping out of school.

According to Schorr, a number of early-intervention programs do work. How and why do they work? Schorr says there are four reasons.

1. *Successful programs are comprehensive and intensive.* They provide access to a wide array of services. Low-income families usually don't have the energy or the skills to wend their way through the maze of eligibility determinations and other hoops they must jump through to obtain support. Flexible access to a wide range of programs is more important for them than for middle-class families.

2. *In successful programs, staff have the time, training, and skills that are needed to build relationships of trust and respect with children and families.* The leaders and workers in successful programs know that *how* services are provided is just as important as *what* is provided. Such programs emphasize the importance of listening to parents, exchanging information rather than lecturing, and helping parents gain greater control over their own lives and act more effectively on behalf of their children.

3. *Successful programs deal with the child as part of the family, and the family as part of the neighborhood and community.* For instance, the nurse in a high-quality program not only responds to a child's recurrent diarrhea, but goes beyond that problem and asks whether the child's health is threatened by circumstances for which the family needs support and services it is not getting. The successful school also enlists parents as collaborators in giving children reasons to learn.

Whether they focus on children or on parents, successful programs usually follow a *two-generational approach.* They might offer support to parents who need help with their lives as adults before they can effectively use services that are directed at children. They take into account the world inhabited by those they serve—rural health clinics deliver clean water, home visitors help young mothers plan their return to school or employment while teaching them about effective child rearing, and the Head Start teacher knows when a family is threatened by eviction.

4. *Successful programs cross long-standing professional and bureaucratic boundaries.* They are prepared to provide a wide range of services in nontraditional settings, including homes, and at nontraditional hours. Nurses may offer family support, social workers might collaborate with teachers and physicians, and psychologists might listen to a mother's anxieties about her children in the course of taking her to the market. No one says, "This may be what you need, but helping you get it is not part of my job or in my jurisdiction."

Brief sketches of two programs illustrate how these characteristics can be implemented. The first is a Head Start program in Baltimore, Maryland, that serves children who have a history of lead poisoning. The children's breakfast and lunch are planned around their special nutritional needs, and their activities stress the structure, stimulation, and verbal exchange that are absent from many of their lives. Next door, the mothers meet with staff who assist them in developing better parenting skills and new approaches to nutrition. The pediatric department that sponsors the program works with local health and housing agencies to get the lead paint out of the homes.

The second successful early intervention, Homebuilders, was started by a small Catholic family-service agency in Tacoma, Washington, and now is spreading to other parts of the country. Homebuilders work to keep families together that are threatened with the removal of a child because of abuse or neglect. The staff works with families, mainly in the family's own home, during crises, for a period of as much as 2 months. Its master's-level professionals have caseloads of no more than two or three families at a time.

FAMILIES AND PARENTING

Parents and Schools as Partners in the Young Child's Education

Mothers and fathers play important roles in the development of young children's positive attitudes toward learning and education (Cowan, Heming, & Shuck, 1993). In one study, mothers and their preschool children were evaluated and then the children's academic competence was assessed when they were in sixth grade (Hess & others, 1984). Maternal behavior in the preschool years was related to the children's academic competence in sixth grade. The best predictors of academic competence in sixth grade were the following maternal behaviors shown during the preschool years: effective communication with the child, a warm relationship with the child, positive expectations for achievement, use of rule-based rather than authority-based discipline, and not believing that success in school was based on luck.

The father's involvement with the child can also help to build positive attitudes toward school and learning. Competent fathers of preschool children set aside regular time to be with the child, listen to the child and respond to questions, become involved in the child's play, and show an interest in the child's preschool and kindergarten activities. Fathers can help with the young child's schooling in the following ways:

- Supporting their children's efforts in school and their children's unique characteristics
- Helping children with their problems when the children seek advice
- Communicating regularly with teachers
- Participating in school functions

The relationship between the school and the parents of young children is an important aspect of preschool and kindergarten education (Stipek, Rosenblatt, & DiRocco, 1994). Schools and parents can cooperate to provide young children with the best possible preschool and kindergarten experience, and a positive orientation toward learning. In one study, the most important factor in contributing to the success of the preschool program was the positive involvement of the parents in their young children's learning and education (Lally, Mangione, & Honig, 1987).

An important question that most parents of young children ask is: How can I evaluate whether or not a preschool program is a good one? Ellen Galinsky and Judy David (1988) provided some helpful guidelines for parents faced with choosing a preschool program; the guidelines include the relationship between the teacher-caregiver and the child, activities, teacher-caregiver development, staffing/group size, physical environment, and the relationship between parents and the teacher-caregiver. Some of their suggestions for selecting a good preschool follow:

- Ask the teacher to describe another child she has cared for and see whether the description is warm and enthusiastic or judgmental and punitive.
- Ask the teacher "what if" questions, such as "What would you do if my child were fussy?" or "What would you do if my child refused to cooperate?"
- Listen to the tone of the room—is it pleasant and filled with happy, busy voices?
- Ask yourself if there are enough adults to have time to talk to and care for each child.
- Ask yourself if you would like to spend time there.
- Observe whether the space is childproof.
- Ask the teacher to describe other parents she has worked with—are the descriptions positive or negative?
- Ask for names of other parents with children in the program and call them as references—ask them what are the best and the worst aspects of the preschool.

John W. Santrock

Early Childhood Programs and Computers

Technology is coming to the education of young children. The Writing to Read program, developed by IBM, is a computer-based reading and writing program for kindergarten and first-grade students. The program is based on the concept that children can effectively learn to read by being taught how to write. Five learning stations are coordinated to provide an active learning environment: computer, work journal, writing/typing, listening library, and making words. Thus, the computer and software are an integral part of the Writing to Read program.

In another approach, "The computer-enriched kindergarten," computers are seen as a way of providing open-ended discovery learning, problem solving, and computer competence (Morrison, 1995). An important goal is to get young children to feel as comfortable using computers as they do using pencils and crayons. Computers are a versatile resource for the early childhood education classroom. They can provide activities that promote language development, math skills, problem-solving skills, social skills, and many other domains of the child's development.

Most educational experts now believe that it is important to include computers in early childhood education programs and to help children develop a positive attitude toward them. Children gain confidence in using computers when their computer activities are appropriate for their age.

In the Writing to Read program, developed by IBM, kindergarten and first-grade students use computers and software as they learn to read by learning how to write.

Early Childhood Education in Japan

At a time of low academic achievement by children in the United States, many Americans are turning to Japan, a country of high academic achievement and economic success, for possible answers. However, the answers provided by Japanese preschools are not the ones Americans expected to find. In most Japanese preschools, surprisingly little emphasis is put on academic instruction. In one study, 300 Japanese and 210 American preschool teachers, child development specialists, and parents were asked about various aspects of early childhood education (Tobin, Wu, & Davidson, 1989). Only 2 percent of the Japanese respondents listed "to give children a good start academically" as one of their top three reasons for a society to have preschools. In contrast, over half the American respondents chose this as one of their top three choices. To prepare children for successful careers in first grade and beyond, Japanese schools do not teach reading, writing, and mathematics but rather skills like persistence, concentration, and the ability to function as a member of a group. The vast majority of young Japanese children are taught to read at home by their parents.

In the comparison of Japanese and American preschool education, 91 percent of Japanese respondents chose providing children with a group experience as one of their top three reasons for a society to have preschools. Sixty-two percent of the more individually oriented Americans listed group experience as one of their top three choices. An emphasis on the importance of the group seen in Japanese early childhood education continues into elementary school education.

Lessons in living and working together grow naturally out of the Japanese culture. In many Japanese kindergartens, children wear the same uniforms, including caps, which are of different colors to indicate the classrooms to which they belong. They have identical sets of equipment, kept in identical drawers and shelves. This is not intended to turn the young children into robots, as some Americans

In Japan, learning how to cooperate and participating in group experiences are viewed as extremely important reasons for the existence of early childhood education.

have observed, but to impress on them that other people, just like themselves, have needs and desires that are equally important (Hendry, 1986).

Like in America, there is diversity in Japanese early childhood education. Some Japanese kindergartens have specific aims, such as early musical training or the practice of Montessori strategies. In large cities, some kindergartens are attached to

universities that have elementary and secondary schools. Some Japanese parents believe that, if their young children attend a university-based program, it will increase the children's chances of eventually being admitted to top-rated schools and universities. Several more progressive programs have introduced free play as an antidote for the heavy intellectualizing in some Japanese kindergartens.

Nonsexist Early Childhood Education

An important goal of nonsexist early childhood education is to free children from constraining stereotypes of gender roles so that no aspect of their development will be closed off because of their sex. Another important goal is to promote equality for both sexes by facilitating each child's participation in activities necessary for optimal cognitive and socioemotional development. Yet another important goal is to help children develop skills that will enable them to challenge sexist stereotypes and behaviors.

Young children's awareness of equitable gender roles can be expanded by having them participate in a number of activities, such as these (Derman-Sparks and the ABC Task Force, 1989):

- Reading books about girls and boys that contradict gender stereotypes. Examples of such books are *William's Doll* (Zolotow, 1972), *Stephanie and the Coyote* (Crowder, 1969), and *Everybody Knows That* (Pearson, 1978).

- Getting children to find and cut out magazine pictures of girls and boys, women and men, with a diversity of looks, dress, activities, and emotions.

- Creating a display of photographs and pictures of women and men performing the same kind of tasks in the home and in the world of work. Use the display to talk with children about the tasks that family members do and what kinds of tasks the children will do when they grow up.

- Being a nonsexist role model as a teacher, helping children learn new skills and sharing tasks in a nonsexist manner.

- Inviting members of children's families (including extended family relatives) who have nontraditional jobs (such as a male flight attendant, nurse, or secretary; a female construction worker, engineer, or doctor) to come and talk with the class about their work.

- Supporting children's dramatic play that involves nontraditional gender roles.

- Telling stories about nonstereotyped dolls that support nontraditional behaviors and describing the conflicts they sometimes have when acting in ways that challenge stereotypic gender roles.

Socioemotional Development in Early Childhood

*Let us play, for it is yet day
'And we cannot go to sleep;
'Besides, in the sky the little birds fly
'And the hills are all covered with sheep.'*

—William Blake, "Nurse's Song"

IMAGES OF CHILDREN

The Diversity of Families and Parenting

Children grow up in a diversity of families. Some children live in families that have never experienced divorce, some live virtually their entire childhood in single-parent families, and yet others live in stepfamilies. Some children live in poverty, others in economically advantaged families. Some children's mothers work full-time and place them in day care, while some mothers stay home with their children. Some children grow up in a White culture, others in ethnic minority cultures. Some children have siblings, others don't. Some children's parents treat them harshly and abuse them, other children have parents who nurture and support them.

In thinking about the diversity of families and parenting, consider the following two circumstances and predict how they might influence the child's development:

A young mother is holding an infant in her arms and trying to keep track of two boys walking behind her. The younger boy, who is about 3, clutches an umbrella but seems to be having trouble with it. He drags its curved handle along the ground, and that irritates his mother. She tells him to carry the umbrella right or she will knock the (expletive) out of him. "Carry it right, I said," she says, and then she slaps him in the face, knocking him off balance. She rarely nurtures her son and has beaten him so hard that at times he has bruises that don't go away for days. The mother lives in the poverty of an inner city and she is unemployed. She is unaware of how her own life stress affects her parenting behavior.

Now consider another child, who is growing up in a very different family environment:

A 28-year-old mother is walking along the street with her 4-year-old daughter. They are having a conversation about her daughter's preschool. As the conversation continues, they smile back and forth several times as the daughter describes some activities she did. As they reach home, the mother tells her daughter that she loves her and gives her a big hug. This mother also lives in a poverty-stricken area. She has received considerable support from her extended family in raising her daughter, and the preschool her daughter attends has high ratings. The mother reports that she sincerely enjoys being with her daughter and loves to plan enjoyable things for her to do.

PREVIEW

The two children you just read about are growing up in very different family atmospheres. In this chapter we will study different types of parenting styles and how they influence children's development. We also will explore other dimensions of families in young children's lives, along with peer relations, play, television, the self, gender, and moral development.

FAMILIES

In chapter 7, we learned that attachment is an important aspect of family relationships during infancy. Remember that some experts believe attachment to a caregiver during the first several years of life is the key ingredient in the child's social development, increasing the probability the child will be socially competent and well adjusted in the preschool years and beyond. We also learned that other experts believe secure attachment has been overemphasized and that the child's temperament, other social agents and contexts, and the complexity of the child's social world are

Calvin and Hobbes

by Bill Watterson

WHAT ASSURANCE DO I HAVE THAT YOUR PARENTING ISN'T SCREWING ME UP?

also important in determining the child's social competence and well-being. Some developmentalists also emphasize that the infant years have been overdramatized as determinants of life-span development, arguing that social experiences in the early childhood years and later deserve more attention than they have sometimes been given.

In this chapter, we will discuss early childhood experiences beyond the attachment process as we explore the different types of parenting styles to which children are exposed, sibling relationships, and how more children are now experiencing socialization in a greater variety of family structures than at any other point in history. Keep in mind, as we discuss these aspects of families, the importance of viewing the family as a system of interacting individuals who reciprocally socialize and mutually regulate each other.

Parenting

Two important dimensions of parenting are parenting styles and adapting parenting to the child's developmental status.

Parenting Styles

Parents want their children to grow into socially mature individuals, and they may feel frustrated in trying to discover the best way to accomplish this. Developmentalists have long searched for the ingredients of parenting that promote competent social development in children. For example, in the 1930s, John Watson argued that parents were too affectionate with their children. In the 1950s, a distinction was made between physical and psychological discipline, with psychological discipline, especially reasoning, emphasized as the best way to rear a child. In the 1970s and beyond, the dimensions of competent parenting have become more precise.

Especially widespread is the view of Diana Baumrind (1971), who believes parents should be neither punitive nor aloof, but should instead develop rules for their children and be affectionate with them. She emphasizes three types of parenting that are associated with different aspects

of the child's social behavior: authoritarian, authoritative, and laissez-faire (permissive). More recently, developmentalists have argued that permissive parenting comes in two different forms: neglectful and indulgent. What are these forms of parenting like?

Authoritarian parenting *is a restrictive, punitive style in which parents exhort the child to follow their directions and to respect work and effort. The authoritarian parent places firm limits and controls on the child and allows little verbal exchange. Authoritarian parenting is associated with children's social incompetence.* For example, an authoritarian parent might say, "You do it my way or else. There will be no discussion!" Children of authoritarian parents are often anxious about social comparison, fail to initiate activity, and have poor communication skills. And in one study, early harsh discipline was associated with child aggression (Weiss & others, 1992).

> There's no vocabulary for love within a family, love that's lived in but not looked at, love within the light of which all else is seen, the love within which all other love finds speech. This love is silent.
>
> —**T. S. Eliot, *The Elder Statesman***

Authoritative parenting *encourages children to be independent but still places limits and controls on their actions. Extensive verbal give-and-take is allowed, and parents are warm and nurturant toward the child. Authoritative parenting is associated with children's social competence.* An authoritative parent might put his arm around the child in a comforting way and say "You know you should not have done that; let's talk about how you can handle the situation better next time." Children whose parents are authoritative are socially competent, self-reliant, and socially responsible.

Permissive parenting comes in two forms: neglectful and indulgent (Maccoby & Martin, 1983). **Neglectful parenting** *is a style in which the parent is very uninvolved in the child's life; it is associated with children's social incompetence,*

---

especially a lack of self-control. This parent cannot answer the question "It is 10 P.M.—do you know where your child is?" Children whose parents are neglectful develop the sense that other aspects of the parents' lives are more important than they are. These children tend to be socially incompetent, showing poor self-control and not handling independence well.

Indulgent parenting *is a style of parenting in which parents are highly involved with their children but place few demands or controls on them. Indulgent parenting is associated with children's social incompetence, especially a lack of self-control*. Such parents let their children do what they want, and the result is that the children never learn to control their own behavior and always expect to get their way. Some parents deliberately rear their children in this way because they believe the combination of warm involvement with few restraints will produce a creative, confident child. One boy I knew whose parents deliberately reared him in an indulgent manner moved his parents out of their bedroom suite and took it over for himself. He is now 18 years old and has not learned to control his behavior; when he can't get something he wants, he still throws temper tantrums. As you might expect, he is not very popular with his peers. Children whose parents are indulgent rarely learn respect for others and have difficulty controlling their behavior.

FIGURE 11.1

Classification of Parenting Styles
The four types of parenting styles (authoritative, authoritarian, indulgent, and neglectful) involve the dimensions of acceptance and responsiveness, on the one hand, and demand and control, on the other. For example, authoritative parenting involves being both accepting/responsive and demanding/controlling.

Parenting is a very important profession, but no test of fitness for it is ever imposed in the interest of children.
—George Bernard Shaw,
Everybody's Political About What, 1944

The four classifications of parenting just discussed involve combinations of acceptance and responsiveness, on the one hand, and demand and control, on the other. How these dimensions combine to produce authoritarian, authoritative, neglectful, and indulgent parenting is shown in figure 11.1. To further evaluate parenting styles, refer to Critical Thinking About Children's Development.

Adapting Parenting to Developmental Changes in the Child

Parents also need to adapt their behavior to the child, based on the child's developmental maturity. Parents

should not treat the 5-year-old the same as the 2-year-old. The 5-year-old and the 2-year-old have different needs and abilities. In the first year, parent-child interaction moves from a heavy focus on routine caretaking—feeding, changing diapers, bathing, and soothing—to later include more noncaretaking activities like play and visual-vocal exchanges. During the child's second and third years, parents often handle disciplinary matters by physical manipulation: They carry the child away from a mischievous activity to the place they want the child to go; they put fragile and dangerous objects out of reach; they sometimes spank. But as the child grows older, parents turn increasingly to reasoning, moral exhortation, and giving or withholding special privileges. As children move toward the elementary school years, parents show them less physical affection.

Sibling Relationships and Birth Order

Sandra describes to her mother what happened in a conflict with her sister:

John W. Santrock

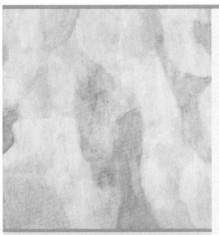

*Evaluating the Parenting
Styles of Both Parents*

In our discussion of parenting styles, authoritative parenting was associated with social competence in children. In some cases, though, a child's parents differ in their parenting styles. Consider all four styles of parenting—authoritarian, authoritative, neglectful, and indulgent—on the parts of the mother and the father. A best case is when both parents are authoritative. What might the effects on the child be, if the father is authoritarian and the mother is indulgent, or the father is authoritarian and the mother is authoritative, and so on? Is it better for the child if both parents have the same parenting style, even if the styles both are authoritarian, both indulgent, or both neglectful, or is it better for the child to have at least one authoritative parent when the other parent is authoritarian, indulgent, or neglectful?

In thinking about parenting styles, consider also what style or styles your father and mother used in rearing you. Were they both authoritative, one authoritarian, the other indulgent, and so on? What effects do you think their parenting styles had on your development?

By evaluating the nature of parenting styles on the part of both parents, you are learning to think critically by *applying developmental concepts to enhance personal adaptation.*

siblings, and whether sibling relationships are different from parent-child relationships.

Is sibling interaction different from parent-child interaction? There is some evidence that it is. Observations indicate that children interact more positively and in more varied ways with their parents than with their siblings (Baskett & Johnson, 1982). Children also follow their parents' dictates more than those of their siblings, and they behave more negatively and punitively with their siblings than with their parents.

In some instances, siblings may be stronger socializing influences on the child than parents are (Cicirelli, 1994). Someone close in age to the child—such as a sibling—may be able to understand the child's problems and be able to communicate more effectively than parents can. In dealing with peers, coping with difficult teachers, and discussing taboo subjects such as sex, siblings may be more influential in the socialization process than parents.

Is sibling interaction the same around the world? In industrialized societies like the United States, delegation of responsibility for younger siblings to older siblings tends to be carried out informally by parents, primarily to give the parent freedom to pursue other activities. However, in nonindustrialized countries, such as Kenya (in Africa), a much greater degree of importance is attached to the older sibling's role as a caregiver to younger siblings. In industrialized countries, the older sibling's caregiving role is often discretionary; in nonindustrialized countries it is more obligatory (Cicirelli, 1994).

We had just come home from the ball game. I sat down on the sofa next to the light so I could read. Sally [the sister] said, "Get up. I was sitting there first. I just got up for a second to get a drink." I told her I was not going to get up and that I didn't see her name on the chair. I got mad and started pushing her. Her drink spilled all over her. Then she got really mad; she shoved me against the wall, hitting and clawing at me. I managed to grab a handful of hair.

At this point, Sally comes into the room and begins to tell her side of the story. Sandra interrupts, "Mother, you always take her side." Sound familiar? Any of you who have grown up with siblings probably have a rich memory of aggressive, hostile interchanges; but sibling relationships have many pleasant, caring moments as well. Children's sibling relationships include helping, sharing, teaching, fighting, and playing. Children can act as emotional supports, rivals, and communication partners (Carlson, 1995). More than 80 percent of American children have one or more siblings (brothers or sisters). Because there are so many possible sibling combinations, it is difficult to generalize about sibling influences. Among the factors to be considered are the number of siblings, age of siblings, birth order, age spacing, sex of

Big sisters are the crab grass in the lawn of life.

—**Charles Schulz, *Peanuts***

Birth order is a special interest of sibling researchers. When differences in birth order are found, they usually are explained by variations in interactions with parents and siblings associated with the unique experiences of being in a particular position in the family. This is especially true in the case of the firstborn child (Teti & others, 1993). The oldest child is the only one who does not have to share parental love and affection with other siblings—until another sibling comes along. An infant requires more attention than an older child; this means that the firstborn

What socializing roles do siblings play in children's development?

The one-child family is becoming much more common in China because of the strong motivation to limit population growth in the People's Republic of China. The policy is still new, and its effects on children have not been fully examined.

sibling now gets less attention than before the newborn arrived. Does this result in conflict between parents and the firstborn? In one research study, mothers became more negative, coercive, and restraining and played less with the firstborn following the birth of a second child (Dunn & Kendrick, 1982). Even though a new infant requires more attention from parents than does an older child, an especially intense relationship is often maintained between parents and firstborns throughout the life span. Parents have higher expectations for firstborn children than for later-born children; they put more pressure on them for achievement and responsibility, and interfere more with their activities (Rothbart, 1971).

Birth order is also associated with variations in sibling relationships. The oldest sibling is expected to exercise self-control and show responsibility in interacting with younger siblings. When the oldest sibling is jealous or hostile, parents often protect the younger sibling. The oldest sibling is more dominant, competent, and powerful than the younger siblings; the oldest sibling is also expected to assist and teach younger siblings. Indeed, researchers have shown that older siblings are both more antagonistic—hitting, kicking, and biting—and more nurturant toward their younger siblings than vice versa (Abramovitch & others, 1986). There is also something unique about same-sex sibling relationships. Aggression and dominance occur more in same-sex relationships than in opposite-sex sibling relationships (Minnett, Vandell, & Santrock, 1983).

Given the differences in family dynamics involved in birth order, it is not surprising that firstborns and later-borns have different characteristics. Firstborn children are more adult oriented, helpful, conforming, anxious, and self-controlled than their siblings. Parents give more attention to first-borns and this is related to first-borns' nurturant behavior (Stanhope & Corter, 1993). Parental demands and high standards established for first-borns result in these children excelling in academic and professional endeavors. Firstborns are overrepresented in *Who's Who* and Rhodes scholars, for example. However, some of the same pressures placed on firstborns for high achievement may be the reason they also have more guilt, anxiety, difficulty in coping with stressful situations, and higher admission to child guidance clinics.

What is the only child like? The popular conception is that the only child is a "spoiled brat" with such undesirable characteristics as dependency, lack of self-control, and self-centered behavior. But researchers present a more positive portrayal of the only child, who often is achievement oriented and displays a desirable personality, especially in comparison to later-borns and children from large families (Falbo & Poston, 1993; Jiao, Ji, & Jing, 1996).

So far our consideration of birth-order effects suggests that birth order might be a strong predictor of behavior. However, an increasing number of family researchers believe that birth order has been overdramatized and overemphasized. The critics argue that, when all of the factors that influence behavior are considered, birth order itself shows limited ability to predict behavior. Consider just sibling relationships alone. They vary not only in birth order, but also in number of siblings, age of siblings, age spacing of siblings, and sex of siblings.

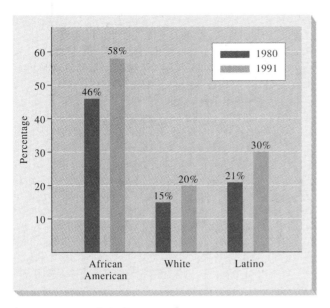

FIGURE 11.2

Percentage of Children Under 18 Living with One Parent in 1980 and 1991
Shown here is the breakdown for African American, White, and Latino families. Note the substantially higher percentage of African American single-parent families.

Consider also the temperament of siblings. Researchers have found that siblings' temperamental traits ("easy" and "difficult," for example), as well as differential treatment of siblings by parents, influence how siblings get along (Stocker & Dunn, 1991). Siblings with "easy" temperaments who are treated in relatively equal ways by parents tend to get along with each other the best, whereas siblings with "difficult" temperaments, or whose parents have given one of them preferential treatment, get along the worst.

Beyond temperament and differential treatment of siblings by parents, think about some of the other important factors in children's lives that influence their behavior beyond birth order. They include heredity, models of competency or incompetency that parents present to children on a daily basis, peer influences, school influences, socioeconomic factors, sociohistorical factors, cultural variations, and so on. When someone says firstborns are always like this, but last-borns are always like that, you now know that they are making overly simplistic statements that do not adequately take into account the complexity of influences on a child's behavior. Keep in mind, though, that, although birth order itself may not be a good predictor of children's behavior, sibling relationships and interaction are important dimensions of family processes.

The Changing Family in a Changing Society

Children are growing up in a greater variety of family structures than ever before in history. Many mothers spend the greatest part of their day away from their children, even their infants. More than one of every two mothers with a child under the age of 5 is in the labor force; more than two of every three with a child from 6 to 17 years of age is. And the increasing number of children growing up in single-parent families is staggering. As shown in figure 11.2, a substantial increase in the number of children under the age of 18 who live in a single-parent family occurred between 1980 and 1991. Also note that a much higher percentage of African American families than White families or Latino families are single-parent families. If current trends continue, by the year 2000 one in every four children will also have lived a portion of their lives in a step-parent family. And, as we saw in chapter 8, fathers perform more child-rearing duties than in the past.

Working Mothers

Because household operations have become more efficient and family size has decreased in America, it is not certain that children with mothers working outside the home actually receive less attention than children in the past whose mothers were not employed. Outside employment—at least for mothers with school-age children—may simply be filling time previously taken up by added household burdens and more children. It also cannot be assumed that if the mother did not go to work, the child would benefit from the time freed up by streamlined household operations and smaller families. Mothering does not always have a positive effect on the child. The educated, nonworking mother may overinvest her energies in her children, fostering an excess of worry and discouraging the child's independence. In such situations, the mother may give more parenting than the child can profitably handle.

As Lois Hoffman (1989) commented, maternal employment is a part of modern life. It is not an aberrant aspect of it, but a response to other social changes, one that meets needs that cannot be met by the previous family ideal of a full-time mother and homemaker. Not only does it meet the parent's needs, but in many ways it may be a pattern better suited to socializing children for the adult roles they will occupy. This is especially true for daughters, but it is also true for sons. The broader range of emotions and skills that each parent presents is more consistent with this adult role. Just as his father shares the breadwinning role and the child-rearing role with his mother, so the son, too, will be more likely to share these roles. The rigid gender stereotyping perpetuated by the divisions of labor in the traditional family is not appropriate for the demands that will be made on children of either sex as adults. The needs of the growing child require the mother to loosen her hold on the child, and this task may be easier for the working woman whose job is an additional source of identity and self-esteem. Overall, researchers have found no detrimental effects of maternal employment on children's development (Gottfried, Gottfried, & Bathurst, 1995; Richards & Duckett, 1994).

A common experience of working mothers (and working fathers) is feeling guilty about being away from their children. The guilt may be triggered by parents missing their child, worrying that their child is missing them, being concerned about the implications of working (such as whether the child is receiving good child-care), and worrying about the long-term effects of working (such as whether they are jeopardizing the child's future). To reduce guilt, the guilt needs to be acknowledged. Pediatrician T. Berry Brazelton (1983) believes that parents respond to guilt either by admitting it and working through it or by denying it and rationalizing it away. The latter tendency is not recommended. Working parents' guilt can also be reduced if they begin paying closer attention to how their children are doing.

Effects of Divorce on Children

Two main models have been proposed to explain how divorce affects children's development: the family structure model and the multiple-factor model. The **family structure model** *states that any differences in children from different family structures are due to the family structure variations, such as the father's being absent in one set of the families*. However, family structure (such as father-present versus father-absent) is only one of many factors that influence children's development and adjustment in single-parent families. Even when researchers compare the development of children in more precise family structures (such as divorced versus widowed), there are many factors other than family structure that need to be examined to explain the child's development. As we see next, a second model of the effects of divorce on children's development goes beyond the overly simplistic family structure model.

The **multiple-factor model of divorce** *takes into account the complexity of the divorce context and examines a number of influences on the child's development, including not only family structure, but also the strengths and weaknesses of the child prior to the divorce, the nature of the events surrounding the divorce itself, the type of custody involved, visitation patterns, socioeconomic status, and postdivorce family functioning*. Researchers are finding that the availability and use of support systems (relatives, friends, housekeepers), an ongoing positive relationship between the custodial parent and the ex-spouse, authoritative parenting, financial resources, and the child's competencies at the time of the divorce are important factors in how successfully the adolescent adapts to the divorce of her or his parents (Forgatch, Patterson, & Ray, 1996; Hetherington, 1995; Stevenson & Black, 1996). Thus, just as the family structure factor of birth order by itself is not a good predictor of children's development, neither is the family structure factor of father absence. In both circumstances—birth order and father absence—there are many other factors that always have to be taken into consideration when explaining the child's development is at issue. Let's further examine what some of those complex factors are in the case of children whose parents divorce.

Age and Developmental Changes The age of the child at the time of the divorce needs to be considered. Young children's responses to divorce are mediated by their limited cognitive and social competencies, their dependency on their parents, and possibly inferior day care (Hetherington & Stanley-Hagan, 1995). The cognitive immaturity that creates considerable anxiety for children who are young at the time of their parents' divorce may benefit the children over time. Ten years after the divorce of their parents, adolescents had few memories of their own earlier fears and suffering or their parents' conflict (Wallerstein, Corbin, & Lewis, 1988). Nonetheless, approximately one-third of these children continued to express anger about not being able to grow up in an intact, never-divorced family. Those who were adolescents at the time of their parents' divorce were more likely to remember the conflict and stress surrounding the divorce some 10 years later, in their early adult years. They, too, expressed disappointment at not being able to grow up in an intact family and wondered if their life would not have been better if they had been able to do so.

Evaluations of children and adolescents 6 years after the divorce of their parents by E. Mavis Hetherington (1995) found that living with a mother who did not remarry had long-term negative effects on boys, with deleterious outcomes appearing consistently from kindergarten to adolescence. No negative effects on preadolescent girls were found. However, at the onset of adolescence, early-maturing girls from divorced families engaged in frequent conflict with their mothers, behaved in noncompliant ways, had lower self-esteem, and experienced more problems in heterosexual relationships.

Conflict Many separations and divorces are highly emotional affairs that immerse the child in conflict. Conflict is a critical aspect of family functioning that often outweighs the influence of family structure on the child's development. For example, children in divorced families low in conflict function better than children in intact, never-divorced families high in conflict (Black & Pedro-Carroll, 1993). Although the escape from conflict that divorce provides may be a positive benefit for children, in the year immediately following the divorce, the conflict does not decline but increases. At this time, children—especially boys—in divorced families show more adjustment problems than children in intact families with both parents present. During the first year after the divorce, the quality of parenting the child experiences is often poor; parents seem to be preoccupied with their own needs and adjustment—experiencing anger, depression, confusion, and emotional instability—which inhibits their ability to respond sensitively to the child's needs. During the second year after the divorce, parents are more effective in their child-rearing duties, especially with daughters (Hetherington, 1995; Hetherington, Cox, & Cox, 1982).

John W. Santrock

Sex of the Child and the Nature of Custody The sex of the child and the sex of the custodial parent are important considerations in evaluating the effects of divorce on children. One research study directly compared 6- to 11-year-old children living in father-custody and mother-custody families (Santrock & Warshak, 1986). On a number of measures, including videotaped observations of parent-child interaction, children living with the same-sex parent were more socially competent—happier, more independent, with higher self-esteem, and more mature—than children living with the opposite-sex parent.

Most studies have found support for the same-sex parent-child custodial arrangement, but in one study adolescents were better adjusted in mother-custody or joint-custody families than in father-custody families (Buchanan, Maccoby, & Dornbusch, 1992). In this study, the best predictors of positive adolescent outcomes were the closeness of the adolescent to the custodial parent and the custodial parent's monitoring of the adolescent.

The Mexican American family reunion of the Limon family in Austin, Texas. Latino American children often grow up in families with a network of relatives that runs into scores of individuals. Large and extended families are more common among Latino Americans than among Anglo-Americans.

Income and Economic Stress An increasing number of studies reveal that income is a significant factor in the adjustment of parents and children in divorced families (Bronstein & others, 1994). Income usually drops dramatically following divorce for mothers with custody of their children, whereas postdivorce income for fathers with custody does not (Santrock & Warshak, 1986). Today, women are far less likely than in the past to receive alimony or child-support payments. Even when alimony or child-support payments are awarded to a woman, they are poorly enforced.

Conclusions About Children in Divorced Families In sum, large numbers of children are growing up in divorced families. Most children initially experience considerable stress when their parents divorce, and they are at risk for developing problem behaviors. However, divorce can also remove children from conflicted marriages. Many children emerge from divorce as competent individuals. In recent years, developmentalists have moved away from the view that single-parent families are atypical or pathological, focusing more on the diversity of children's responses to divorce and the factors that facilitate or disrupt children's development and adjustment (Chase-Lansdale, 1996; Hetherington, 1995).

Cultural, Ethnic, and Social Class Variations in Families

Cultures vary on a number of issues involving families, such as what the father's role in the family should be, the extent to which support systems are available to families, and how children should be disciplined. Although there are cross-cultural variations in parenting (Whiting & Edwards, 1988), in one study of parenting behavior in 186 cultures around the world, the most common pattern was a warm and controlling style, one that was neither permissive nor restrictive (Rohner & Rohner, 1981). The investigators commented that the majority of cultures have discovered, over many centuries, a "truth" that only recently emerged in the Western world—namely, that children's healthy social development is most effectively promoted by love and at least some moderate parental control.

Ethnic minority families differ from White American families in their size, structure, and composition, their reliance on kinship networks, and their levels of income and education. Large and extended families are more common among ethnic minority groups than among White Americans. For example, more than 30 percent of Latino families consist of five or more individuals. African American and Latino children interact more with grandparents, aunts, uncles, cousins, and more-distant relatives than do White American children.

Single-parent families are more common among African Americans and Latinos than among White Americans. In comparison with two-parent households, single parents often have more limited resources of time, money, and energy. This shortage of resources may prompt them to encourage early autonomy among their children. Also, ethnic minority parents are less well educated and engage in less joint decision making than White American parents. And ethnic minority children are more likely to come from low-income families than are White American children. Although impoverished families often raise competent youth, poor parents may have a diminished capacity for supportive and involved parenting.

Some aspects of home life can help to protect ethnic minority children from social patterns of injustice. The community and family can filter out destructive racist messages, parents can provide alternate frames of reference than those presented by the majority, and parents can also provide competent role models and encouragement. And the extended family system in many ethnic minority families provides an important buffer to stress (Wakschlag, Chase-Lansdale, & Brooks-Gunn, 1996).

In America and most Western cultures, social class differences in child-rearing have been found. Working class and low-income parents often place a high value on external characteristics such as obedience and neatness, whereas middle-class families often place a high value on internal characteristics, such as self-control and delay of gratification. There are social class differences not only in child-rearing values but also in parenting behaviors. Middle-class parents are more likely to explain something, use verbal praise, use reasoning to accompany their discipline, and ask their children questions. By contrast, parents in low-income and working-class households are more likely to discipline their children with physical punishment and criticize their children more (Hoff-Ginsberg & Tardif, 1995).

A children's peer group in Indonesia. What roles do peers play in children's development?

PEER RELATIONS, PLAY, AND TELEVISION

Children's development is influenced by a number of factors. Three important ones are peers, play, and television.

Peer Relations

As children grow older, peer relations consume increasing amounts of their time. What is the function of a child's peer group? Although children spend increasingly more time with peers as they become older, are there ways in which family and peer relations are coordinated?

Peer Group Functions

Peers *are children of about the same age or maturity level.* Same-age peer interaction fills a unique role in our culture. Age grading would occur even if schools were not age graded and children were left alone to determine the composition of their own societies. One of the most important functions of the peer group is to provide a source of information and comparison about the world outside the family. Children receive feedback about their abilities from their peer group. Children evaluate what they do in terms of whether it is better than, as good as, or worse than what other children do. It is hard to do this at home because siblings are usually older or younger.

Are peers necessary for development? When peer monkeys who have been reared together are separated, they become depressed and less advanced socially (Suomi, Harlow, & Domek, 1970). The human development literature contains a classic example of the importance of peers in social development. Anna Freud (Freud & Dann, 1951) studied six children from different families who banded together after their parents were killed in World War II. Intensive peer attachment was observed; the children formed a tightly knit group, dependent on one another and aloof with outsiders. Even though deprived of parental care, they neither became delinquent nor developed serious mental disorders.

Thus, good peer relations may be necessary for normal social development (Prinstein, Fetter, & La Greca, 1996; Ryan & Patrick, 1996). Social isolation, or the inability to "plug in" to a social network, is linked with many problems and disorders ranging from delinquency and problem drinking to depression (Kupersmidt & Coie, 1990). In one study, poor peer relations in childhood was associated with a tendency to drop out of school and delinquent behavior in adolescence (Roff, Sells, & Golden, 1972). In another

John W. Santrock

Rejecting, authoritarian, permissiveness toward aggression; discord

Anxious, overprotective parenting; take special care to avoid aggression

Bullies ←→ Whipping boys

FIGURE 11.3

Peer Aggression: The Influence of the Relationship Histories of Each Peer

study, harmonious peer relations in adolescence was related to positive mental health at midlife (Hightower, 1990).

The Distinct but Coordinated Worlds of Parent-Child and Peer Relations

What are some of the similarities and differences between peer and parent-child relationships? Children touch, smile, frown, and vocalize when they interact with parents and peers. However, rough-and-tumble play occurs mainly with other children, not with adults, and, in times of stress, children often move toward their parents rather than toward their peers.

A number of theorists and researchers argue that parent-child relationships serve as emotional bases for exploring and enjoying peer relations (Allen & Bell, 1995; Posada, Lord, & Waters, 1995). In one study, the relationship history of each peer helped to predict the nature of peer interaction (Olweus, 1980; see figure 11.3). Some boys were highly aggressive ("bullies") and other boys were the recipients of aggression ("whipping boys") throughout their preschool years. The bullies and the whipping boys had distinctive relationship histories. The bullies' parents frequently rejected them, were authoritarian, and were permissive about their sons' aggression, and the bullies' families were characterized by discord. By contrast, the whipping boys' parents were anxious and overprotective, taking special care to have their sons avoid aggression. The well-adjusted boys in the study were much less likely to be involved in aggressive peer interchanges than were the bullies and whipping boys. Their parents did

not sanction aggression, and the parents' responsive involvement with their sons promoted the development of self-assertion rather than aggression or wimpish behavior.

Parents also may model or coach their children in the ways of relating to peers. In one study, parents indicated they recommended specific strategies to their children regarding peer relations (Rubin & Sloman, 1984). For example, parents told their children how to mediate disputes or how to become less shy with others. They also encouraged them to be tolerant and to resist peer pressure. In another study, parents who frequently initiated peer contacts for their preschool children had children who were more accepted by their peers and who had higher levels of prosocial behavior (Ladd & Hart, 1992).

A key aspect of peer relations can be traced to basic life-style decisions by parents (Cooper & Ayers-Lopez, 1985). Parents' choices of neighborhoods, churches, schools, and their own friends influence the pool from which their children might select possible friends. For example, the chosen schools can lead to specific grouping policies, as well as particular academic and extracurricular activities. In turn, such factors affect which students their children meet, their purposes in interacting, and eventually who become friends. Classrooms in which teachers encourage more cooperative peer interchanges, for instance, have fewer isolates.

In sum, parent-child and peer worlds are coordinated and connected (Ladd & LeSieur, 1995; Maccoby, 1996; Silbereisen, 1995). But they are also distinct. Earlier we indicated that rough-and-tumble play occurs mainly with other children and not in parent-child interaction, and that children often turn to parents, not peers, for support in times of stress. Peer relations also are more likely to consist of interaction on a much more equal basis than are parent-child relations. Because parents have greater knowledge and authority, children must often learn how to conform to rules and regulations laid down by parents. With peers, children learn to formulate and assert their own opinions, appreciate the perspective of peers, cooperatively negotiate solutions to disagreements, and evolve standards of conduct that are mutually acceptable.

Play

An extensive amount of peer interaction during childhood involves play. But although peer interaction can involve play, social play is but one type of play. Just what is play? **Play** *is a pleasurable activity that is engaged in for its own sake.*

Our coverage of play includes its functions, Parten's classic study of play, and types of play.

Play's Functions

Play is essential to the young child's health. As today's children move into the twenty-first century and continue to experience pressure in their lives, play becomes even more crucial. Play increases affiliation with peers, releases tension, advances cognitive development, increases exploration, and provides a safe haven in which to engage in potentially dangerous behavior. Play increases the probability that children will converse and interact with each other. During this interaction, children practice the roles they will assume later in life.

For Freud and Erikson, play was an especially useful form of human adjustment, helping the child master anxieties and conflicts. Because tensions are relieved in play, the child can cope with life's problems. Play permits the child to work off excess physical energy and to release pent-up tensions. **Play therapy** *allows the child to work off frustrations and is a medium through which the therapist can analyze the child's conflicts and ways of coping with them. Children may feel less threatened and be more likely to express their true feelings in the context of play.*

Piaget (1962) saw play as a medium that advances children's cognitive development. At the same time, he said that children's cognitive development *constrains* the way they play. Play permits children to practice their competencies and acquired skills in a relaxed, pleasurable way. Piaget believed that cognitive structures need to be exercised, and play provides the perfect setting for this exercise. For example, children who have just learned to add or multiply begin to play with numbers in different ways as they perfect these operations, laughing as they do so.

Vygotsky (1962), whose developmental theory was discussed in chapter 8, also believed that play is an excellent setting for cognitive development. He was especially interested in the symbolic and make-believe aspects of play, as when a child substitutes a stick for a horse and rides the stick as if it were a horse. For young children, the imaginary situation is real. Parents should encourage such imaginary play, because it advances the child's cognitive development, especially creative thought.

And that park grew up with me; that small world widened as I learned its secret boundaries, as I discovered new refuges in the woods and jungles: hidden homes and lairs for the multitudes of imagination, for cowboys and Indians. . . .
I used to dawdle on half holidays along the bent and devon-facing seashore, hoping for gold watches or the skull of a sheep or a message in a bottle to be washed up by the tide.

—Dylan Thomas

Daniel Berlyne (1960) described play as being exciting and pleasurable in itself because it satisfies the exploratory drive each of us possesses. This drive involves curiosity and a desire for information about something new or unusual. Play is a means whereby children can safely explore and seek out new information—something they might not otherwise do. Play encourages this exploratory behavior by offering children the possibilities of novelty, complexity, uncertainty, surprise, and incongruity.

Parten's Classic Study of Play

Many years ago, Mildred Parten (1932) developed an elaborate classification of children's play. Based on observations of children in free play at nursery school, Parten arrived at these play categories:

1. **Unoccupied play** *occurs when the child is not engaging in play as it is commonly understood and may stand in one spot, look around the room, or perform random movements that do not seem to have a goal.* In most nursery schools, unoccupied play is less frequent than other forms of play.
2. **Solitary play** *occurs when the child plays alone and independently of others.* The child seems engrossed in the activity and does not care much about anything else that is happening. Two- and 3-year-olds engage more frequently in solitary play than older preschoolers do.
3. **Onlooker play** *occurs when the child watches other children play.* The child may talk with other children and ask questions but does not enter into their play behavior. The child's active interest in other children's play distinguishes onlooker play from unoccupied play.
4. **Parallel play** *occurs when the child plays separately from others, but with toys like those the others are using or in a manner that mimics their play.* The older children are, the less frequently they engage in this type of play, although even older preschool children engage in parallel play quite often.
5. **Associative play** *occurs when play involves social interaction with little or no organization.* In this type of play children seem to be more interested in each other than in the tasks they are performing. Borrowing or lending toys and following or leading one another in line are examples of associative play.
6. **Cooperative play** *involves social interaction in a group with a sense of group identity and organized activity.* Children's formal games, competition aimed at winning, and groups formed by the teacher for doing things together are examples of cooperative play. Cooperative play is the prototype for the games of middle childhood. Little cooperative play is seen in the preschool years.

John W. Santrock

Mildred Parten classified play into six categories. Study this photograph and determine which of her categories are reflected in the behavior of the children.

Types of Play

Parten's categories represent one way of thinking about the different types of play. However, today researchers and practitioners who are involved with children's play believe other types of play are important in children's development. Whereas Parten's categories emphasize the role of play in the child's social world, the contemporary perspective on play emphasizes both the cognitive and the social aspects of play. Among the most widely studied types of children's play today are sensorimotor/practice play, pretense/symbolic play, social play, constructive play, and games (Bergen, 1988). We will consider each of these types of play in turn.

Sensorimotor/Practice Play
Sensorimotor play *is behavior engaged in by infants to derive pleasure from exercising their existing sensorimotor schemas.* The development of sensorimotor play follows Piaget's description of sensorimotor thought, which we discussed in chapter 8. Infants initially engage in exploratory and playful visual and motor transactions in the second quarter of the first year of life. By 9 months of age, infants begin to select novel objects for exploration and play, especially those that are responsive, such as toys that make noise or bounce. By 12 months of age, infants enjoy making things work and exploring cause and effect. At this point in development, children like toys that perform when they act on them.

In the second year, infants begin to understand the social meaning of objects, and their play reflects this awareness. And 2-year-olds may distinguish between exploratory play that is interesting but not humorous, and "playful" play, which has incongruous and humorous dimensions. For example, a 2-year-old might "drink" from a shoe or call a dog a "cow." When 2-year-olds find these deliberate incongruities

funny, they are beginning to show evidence of symbolic play and the ability to play with ideas.

Practice play *involves the repetition of behavior when new skills are being learned or when physical or mental mastery and coordination of skills are required for games or sports. Sensorimotor play, which often involves practice play, is primarily confined to infancy, while practice play can be engaged in throughout life.* During the preschool years, children often engage in play that involves practicing various skills. Estimates indicate that practice play constitutes about one-third of the preschool child's play activities, but less than one-sixth of the elementary school child's play activities (Rubin, Fein, & Vandenberg, 1983). Practice play contributes to the development of coordinated motor skills needed for later game playing. While practice play declines in the elementary school years, practice play activities such as running, jumping, sliding, twirling, and throwing balls or other objects are frequently observed on the playgrounds at elementary schools. These activities appear similar to the earlier practice play of the preschool years, but practice play in the elementary school years differs from earlier practice play because much of it is ends rather than means related. That is, elementary school children often engage in practice play for the purpose of improving motor skills needed to compete in games or sports.

Pretense/Symbolic Play
Pretense/symbolic play *occurs when the child transforms the physical environment into a symbol.* Between 9 and 30 months of age, children increase their use of objects in symbolic play. They learn to transform objects—substituting them for other objects and acting toward them as if they were these other objects. For example, a preschool child treats a table as if it is a car and says, "I'm fixing the car," as he grabs a leg of the table.

Many experts on play consider the preschool years the "golden age" of symbolic/pretense play that is dramatic or sociodramatic in nature (Fein, 1986). This type of make-believe play often appears at about 18 months of age and reaches a peak at 4 to 5 years of age, then gradually declines. In the early elementary school years, children's interests often shift to games. In one observational study of nine children, at 4 years of age the children spent more than 12 minutes per hour in pretend play (Haight & Miller, 1993). In this study, a number of parents agreed with Piaget and Vygotsky that pretending helps to develop children's imagination.

Catherine Garvey (1977) has spent many years observing young children's play. She indicates that three elements are found in almost all of the pretend play she has observed: props, plot, and roles. Children use objects as *props* in their pretend play. Children can pretend to drink from a real cup or from a seashell. They can even create a make-believe cup from thin air, if nothing else is available. Most pretend play also has a story line, though the *plot* may be quite simple. Pretend play themes often reflect what children see going on in their lives, as when they play family, school, or doctor. Fantasy play can also take its theme from a story children have heard, or a show they have seen. In pretend play, children try out many different *roles*. Some roles, like mother or teacher, are derived from reality. Other roles, like cowgirls or Superman, come from fantasy.

Carolee Howes (1992) believes that the function of pretend play from 3 to 36 months is the mastery of the communication of meaning. As social pretend play becomes possible through increases in cognitive and language abilities, children engage in pretend play with parents, older siblings, and peers. During the earliest period, the scaffold provided by the parent or older sibling increases the child's ability to engage in more-complex social pretend play. As children become able to self-regulate their pretenses, their social pretend play with their peers becomes more complex.

Social Play

Social play *is play that involves social interaction with peers.* Parten's categories, which we described earlier, are oriented toward social play. Social play with peers increases dramatically during the preschool years. In addition to general social play with peers and group pretense or sociodramatic play, another form of social play is rough-and-tumble play. The movement patterns of rough-and-tumble play are often similar to those of hostile behavior (running, chasing, wrestling, jumping, falling, hitting), but in rough-and-tumble play these behaviors are accompanied by signals such as laughter, exaggerated movement, and open rather than closed hands that indicate that this is play.

Constructive Play

Constructive play *combines sensorimotor/practice repetitive activity with symbolic representation of ideas. Constructive play occurs when children engage in self-regulated creation or construction of a product or a problem solution.* Constructive play increases in the preschool years as symbolic play increases and sensorimotor play decreases. In the preschool years, some practice play is replaced by constructive play. For example, instead of moving their fingers around and around in finger paint (practice play), children are more likely to draw the outline of a house or a person in the paint (constructive play). Some researchers have found that constructive play is the most common type of play during the preschool years (Rubin, Maioni, & Hornung, 1976). Constructive play is also a frequent form of play in the elementary school years, both in and out of the classroom. Constructive play is one of the few playlike activities allowed in work-centered classrooms. For example, having children create a play about a social studies topic involves constructive play. Whether such activities are considered play by children usually depends on whether they get to choose whether to do it (it is play) or whether the teacher imposes it (it is not play), and also whether it is enjoyable (it is play) or not (it is not play) (King, 1982).

Constructive play can also be used in the elementary school years to foster academic skill learning, thinking skills, and problem solving. Many educators plan classroom activities that include humor, encourage playing with ideas, and promote creativity (Bergen, 1988). Educators also often support the performance of plays, the writing of imaginative stories, the expression of artistic abilities, and the playful exploration of computers and other technological equipment. However, distinctions between work and play frequently become blurred in the elementary school classroom.

Games

Games *are activities engaged in for pleasure that include rules and often competition with one or more individuals.* Preschool children may begin to participate in social game play that involves simple rules of reciprocity and turn taking, but games take on a much more salient role in the lives of elementary school children. In one study, the highest incidence of game playing occurred between 10 and 12 years of age (Eiferman, 1971). After age 12, games decline in popularity, often being replaced by practice play, conversations, and organized sports (Bergin, 1988).

In the elementary years, games feature the meaningfulness of a challenge. This challenge is present if two or more children have the skills required to play and understand the rules of the game. Among the types of games children engage in are steady or constant games, such as tag, which are played consistently; recurrent or cyclical games, such as marbles or hopscotch, which seem to follow cycles of popularity and decline; sporadic games, which are rarely played; and one-time games, such as hula hoop contests, which rise to popularity once and then disappear.

In sum, play is a multidimensional, complex concept. It ranges from an infant's simple exercise of a newfound sensorimotor talent to a preschool child's riding a tricycle to an older child's participation in organized games. It is also important to note that children's play can involve a combination of the play categories we have described. For example, social play can be sensorimotor (rough-and-tumble), symbolic, or constructive.

Television

Few developments in society in the second half of the twentieth century have had a greater impact on children than television has. Many children spend more time in front of the television set than they do with their parents. Although it is only one of the many mass media that affect children's behavior, television is the most influential. The persuasion capabilities of television are staggering; the 20,000 hours of television watched by the time the average American adolescent graduates from high school are greater than the number of hours spent in the classroom.

Television's Many Roles

Although television can have a negative influence on children's development by taking them away from homework, making them passive learners, teaching them stereotypes, providing them with violent models of aggression, and presenting them with unrealistic views of the world, television can have a positive influence on children's development by presenting motivating educational programs, increasing children's information about the world beyond their immediate environment, and providing models of prosocial behavior (Clifford, Gunter, & McAleer, 1995).

Television is a medium of entertainment which permits millions of people to listen to the same joke at the same time, and yet remain lonesome.

—**T. S. Eliot**

Television has been called many things, not all of them good. Depending on one's point of view, it may be a "window on the world," the "one-eyed monster," or the "boob tube." Television has been attacked as one of the reasons why scores on national achievement tests in reading and mathematics are lower now than in the past. Television, it is claimed, attracts children away from books and schoolwork. In one study, children who read printed materials, such as books, watched television less than those who did not read (Huston, Seigle, & Bremer, 1983). Furthermore, critics argue that television trains children to become passive learners: rarely, if ever, does television require active responses from the observer.

Television also is said to deceive; that is, it teaches children that problems are resolved easily and that everything always comes out right in the end. For example, TV detectives usually take only 30 to 60 minutes to sort through a complex array of clues to reveal the killer—and they *always* find the killer! Violence is a way of life on many shows, where it is all right for police to use violence and to break moral codes in their fight against evildoers. The lasting results of violence are rarely brought home to the viewer. A person who is injured suffers for only a few seconds; in real life, the person might need months or years to recover, or might not recover at all. Yet one out of every two first-grade children says that the adults on television are like adults in real life.

"Mrs. Horton, could you stop by school today?"
© Martha F. Campbell

A special concern is how ethnic minorities are portrayed on television (Greenberg & Brand, 1994). Ethnic minorities have historically been underrepresented and misrepresented on television. Ethnic minority characters—whether African American, Latino, Asian American, or Native American—have traditionally been presented as less dignified and less positive than White characters. In one study, character portrayals of ethnic minorities were examined during heavy children's viewing hours (weekdays 4–6 P.M. and 7–11 P.M.) (Williams & Condry, 1989). The percentage of White characters far exceeded the actual percentage of Whites in the United States; the percentage of African American, Latino, and Asian American characters fell short of the population statistics. Latino characters were especially underrepresented—only 0.6 percent of the characters were Latino, while the Latino population in the United States is 6.4 percent of the total U.S. population. Minorities tended to hold lower-status jobs and were more likely than Whites to be cast as criminals or victims.

There are some positive aspects to television's influence on children. For one, television presents children with a world that is different than the one in which they live. It exposes children to a wider variety of viewpoints and information than they might get from only their parents, teachers, and peers. And some television programs have educational and developmental benefits. One of television's major programming attempts to educate children is "Sesame Street," which is designed to teach children both cognitive and social skills. The program began in 1969 and is still going strong.

"Sesame Street" demonstrates that education and entertainment can work well together (Green, 1995;

Wright, 1995). Through "Sesame Street," children experience a world of learning that is both exciting and entertaining. "Sesame Street" also follows the principle that teaching can be accomplished in both direct and indirect ways. Using the direct way, a teacher might tell children exactly what they are going to be taught and then teach them. However, in real life, social skills are often communicated in indirect ways. Rather than merely telling children, "You should cooperate with others," TV can show children so that children can figure out what it means to be cooperative and what the advantages are.

Amount of Television Watching by Children

Just how much television do young children watch? They watch a lot, and they seem to be watching more all the time. In the 1950s, 3-year-old children watched television for less than 1 hour a day; 5-year-olds watched just over 2 hours a day. But in the 1970s, preschool children watched television for an average of 4 hours a day; elementary school children watched for as long as 6 hours a day (Friedrich & Stein, 1973). In the 1980s, children averaged 11 to 28 hours of television per week, which is more than for any other activity except sleep. Of special concern is the extent to which children are exposed to violence and aggression on television. Up to 80 percent of the prime-time shows include violent acts, including beatings, shootings, and stabbings. The frequency of violence increases on the Saturday morning cartoon shows, which average more than 25 violent acts per hour.

Effects of Television on Children's Aggression and Prosocial Behavior

What are the effects of television violence on children's aggression? Does television merely stimulate a child to go out and buy a Star Wars ray gun, or can it trigger an attack on a playmate? When children grow up, can television violence increase the likelihood they will violently attack someone?

In one longitudinal study, the amount of violence viewed on television at age 8 was significantly related to the seriousness of criminal acts performed as an adult (Huesmann, 1986). In another study, long-term exposure to television violence was significantly related to the likelihood of aggression in 1,565 12- to 17-year-old boys (Belson, 1978). Boys who watched the most aggression on television were the most likely to commit a violent crime, swear, be aggressive in sports, threaten violence toward another boy, write slogans on walls, or break windows. These investigations are *correlational* in nature, so we cannot conclude from them that television violence causes children to be more aggressive, only that watching television violence is *associated* with aggressive behavior. In one experiment, children were randomly assigned to one of two groups: One watched television shows taken directly from violent Saturday morning cartoon offerings on

11 different days; the second group watched television cartoon shows with all of the violence removed (Steur, Applefield, & Smith, 1971). The children were then observed during play at their preschool. The preschool children who saw the TV cartoon shows with violence kicked, choked, and pushed their playmates more than the preschool children who watched nonviolent TV cartoon shows. Because children were randomly assigned to the two conditions (TV cartoons with violence versus nonviolent TV cartoons), we can conclude that exposure to TV violence *caused* the increased aggression in children in this investigation.

Although some critics have argued that the effects of television violence do not warrant the conclusion that TV violence causes aggression (Freedman, 1984), many experts argue that TV violence can induce aggressive or antisocial behavior in children (Strasburger, 1995). Of course, television is not the *only* cause of aggression. There is no *one* single cause of any social behavior. Aggression, like all other social behaviors, has a number of determinants.

Children need to be taught critical viewing skills to counter the adverse effects of television violence. In one study, elementary school children were randomly assigned to either an experimental or a control group (Huesmann & others, 1983). In the experimental group, children assisted in making a film to help children who had been fooled or harmed by television. The children also composed essays that focused on how television is not like real life and why it is bad to imitate TV violence or watch too much television. In the control group, children received no training in critical viewing skills. The children who were trained in critical viewing skills developed more negative attitudes about TV violence and reduced their aggressive behavior.

Television can also teach children that it is better to behave in positive, prosocial ways than in negative, antisocial ways. Aimee Leifer (1973) demonstrated that television is associated with prosocial behavior in young children. She selected a number of episodes from the television show "Sesame Street" that reflected positive social interchanges. She was especially interested in situations that taught children how to use their social skills. For example, in one interchange, two men were fighting over the amount of space available to them; they gradually began to cooperate and to share the space. Children who watched these episodes copied these behaviors, and in later social situations they applied the prosocial lessons they had learned. To read about ways television could be improved to be more developmentally appropriate, turn to table 11.1.

Television and Cognitive Development

Children bring various cognitive skills and abilities to their television viewing experience (Doubleday & Droege, 1993; Lorch, 1995; Rabin & Dorr, 1995). Compared to older children, preschoolers and young children attend to television more, comprehend less central

TABLE 11.1

Television and Children's Development

Developmental Issues	What Children See on TV	What Children Should See on TV
To establish a sense of *trust and safety*.	The world is dangerous; enemies are everywhere; weapons are needed to feel safe.	A world where people can be trusted and help each other, where safety and predictability can be achieved, where fears can be overcome.
To develop a sense of *autonomy with connectedness*.	Autonomy is equated with fighting and weapons. Connectedness is equated with helplessness, weakness, and altruism.	A wide range of models of independence within meaningful relationships and of autonomous people helping each other.
To develop a sense of *empowerment and efficacy*.	Physical strength and violence equals power and efficacy. Bad guys always return, and a range of ways to have an impact are *not* shown.	Many examples of people having a positive effect on their world without violence.
To establish *gender identity*.	Exaggerated, rigid gender divisions—boys are strong, violent, and save the world; girls are helpless, victimized and irrelevant to world events.	Complex characters with wide-ranging behaviors, interests, and skills; commonalities between the sexes overlapping in what both can do.
To develop an *appreciation of diversity* among people.	Racial and ethnic stereotyping. Dehumanized enemies. Diversity is dangerous. Violence against those who are different is justified.	Diverse peoples with varied talents, skills, and needs, who treat each other with respect, work out problems nonviolently, and enrich each others' lives.
To construct the foundations *of morality and social responsibility*.	One-dimensional characters who are all good or bad. Violence is the solution to interpersonal problems. Winning is the only acceptable outcome. Bad guys deserve to be hurt.	Complex characters who act responsibly and morally toward others—showing kindness and respect, working out moral problems, taking other people's points of view.
To have opportunities for *meaningful play*.	Program content is far removed from children's experience or level of understanding. Toys are linked to programs promoting imitative, not creative play.	Meaningful content to use in play, which resonates deeply with developmental needs; shows not linked to realistic toys so that children can create their own unique play.

Source: From Diane Levin and Nancy Carlsson, "Developmentally Appropriate Television: Putting Children First" in *Young Children,* 49(5):43. Copyright © 1994 National Association for the Education of Young Children. Reprinted by permission.

content and more incidental content, and have difficulty making inferences about content. These youngest viewers have difficulty representing television content and often fill in their incomplete representations with stereotypes and familiar scripts derived from their limited general knowledge of television and the world. They usually are not aware that some content is intended to sell them toys and breakfast cereal rather than to entertain and inform them. Older children have a better understanding in all of these areas, but they still process television information less effectively than adults do. Children's greater attention to television and their less complete and more distorted understanding of what they view suggest that they may miss some of the positive aspects of television and be more vulnerable to its negative aspects.

How does television influence children's creativity and verbal skills? Television is negatively related to children's creativity (Williams, 1986). Also, because television is primarily a visual modality, verbal skills—especially expressive language—are enhanced more by aural or print exposure (Beagles-Roos & Gat, 1983). Educational programming for young children can promote creativity and imagination, possibly because it has a slower pace and auditory and visual modalities are better coordinated. Newer technologies, especially interactive television, hold promise for motivating children to learn and become more exploratory in solving problems (Singer, 1993). To further evaluate television and children's development, refer to Critical Thinking About Children's Development.

So far we have studied a number of ideas about families, peers, play, and television. A summary of these ideas is presented in concept table 11.1.

Families, Peers, Play, and Television

Concept	Processes/Related Ideas	Characteristics/Description
Families	Parenting	Authoritarian, authoritative, neglectful, and indulgent are four main parenting styles; authoritative parenting is the style most often associated with children's social competence. Parents need to adapt their interaction strategies as the child grows older. Authoritative parenting is the most widely used style around the world.
	Sibling relationships and birth order	Siblings interact with each other in more negative and less varied ways than parents and children interact. Birth order is related in certain ways to child characteristics, but some critics argue that birth order is not a good predictor of behavior.
	The changing family	There is no indication that a mother's working full-time outside the home has negative long-term effects on children. The effects of divorce on children are complex—the multiple-factor model takes this complexity into account. Cultures vary on a number of issues regarding families. Ethnic minority families generally differ from White families in their size, structure and composition, reliance on kinship networks, and levels of income and education. Working-class parents value external characteristics more, middle-class parents value internal characteristics more.
Peers, Play, and Television	Peers	Peers are powerful socialization agents. Peers are children who are of about the same age or maturity level. Peers provide a source of information and comparison about the world outside the family. Parent-child and peer relations represent distinct but coordinated worlds. Healthy family relations usually promote healthy peer relations.
	Play	Play's functions include affiliation with peers, tension release, advances in cognitive development, exploration, and provision of a safe haven. Parten developed the categories of unoccupied, solitary, onlooker, parallel, associative, and cooperative play. The contemporary perspective on play emphasizes both the cognitive and the social aspects of play. Among the most widely studied aspects of children's play today are sensorimotor/play, practice play, pretense/symbolic play, social play, constructive play, and games.
	Television	Television can have both negative influences (such as turning children into passive learners and presenting them with aggressive models) and positive influences (such as presenting motivating educational programs and providing models of prosocial behavior) on children's development. Children watch huge amounts of television. TV violence is not the only cause of children's aggression, but it can induce aggression. Prosocial behavior on TV is associated with increased positive behavior by children. Children's cognitive skills influence their TV-viewing experiences. Television viewing is negatively related to children's creativity and verbal skills.

John W. Santrock

Many parents do not carefully monitor their children's TV viewing and do not discuss the content of TV shows with them. Develop a series of guidelines that you would recommend to parents that you believe would help them make television a more positive influence in their children's lives. Consider such factors as the child's age, the child's activities other than TV, parents' patterns of interaction with their children, and types of television shows. By developing guidelines for parents to help them make television a more positive influence on their children's development, you are learning to think critically by *applying developmental concepts to enhance personal adaptation.*

THE SELF, GENDER, AND MORAL DEVELOPMENT

Three important dimensions of children's socioemotional development are the self, gender, and moral development. We will consider each of these in turn.

The Self

We learned in chapter 7 that toward the end of the second year of life children develop a sense of self. During early childhood, some important developments in the self take place. Among these developments are facing the issue of initiative versus guilt and enhanced self-understanding.

Initiative Versus Guilt

According to Erikson (1968), the psychosocial stage that characterizes early childhood is *initiative versus guilt.* By now, children have become convinced that they are a person of their own; during early childhood, they must discover what kind of person they will become. They intensely identify with their parents, who most of the time appear to them to be powerful and beautiful, although often unreasonable, disagreeable, and sometimes even dangerous. During early childhood, children use their perceptual, motor, cognitive, and language skills to make things happen. They have a surplus of energy that permits them to forget failures quickly and to approach new areas that seem desirable—even if they seem dangerous—with undiminished zest and some increased sense of direction. On their own *initiative*, then, children at this stage exuberantly move out into a wider social world.

The great governor of initiative is *conscience.* Children now not only feel afraid of being found out, but they also begin to hear the inner voice of self-observation, self-guidance, and self-punishment. Their initiative and enthusiasm may bring them not only rewards, but also punishments. Widespread disappointment at this stage leads to an unleashing of guilt that lowers the child's self-esteem.

Whether children leave this stage with a sense of initiative that outweighs their sense of guilt depends in large part on how parents respond to their self-initiated activities. Children who are given freedom and opportunity to initiate motor play such as running, bike riding, sledding, skating, tussling, and wrestling have their sense of initiative supported. Initiative is also supported when parents answer their children's questions and do not deride or inhibit fantasy or play activity. In contrast, if children are made to feel that their motor activity is bad, that their questions are a nuisance, and that their play is silly and stupid, then they often develop a sense of guilt over self-initiated activities that may persist through life's later stages (Elkind, 1970).

Self-Understanding

Self-understanding *is the child's cognitive representation of self, the substance and content of the child's self-conceptions.* For example, a 5-year-old girl understands that she is a girl, has blond hair, likes to ride her bicycle, has a friend, and is a swimmer. An 11-year-old boy understands that he is a student, a boy, a football player, a family member, a video-game lover, and a rock music fan. A child's self-understanding is based on the various roles and membership categories that define who children are. Though not the whole of personal identity, self-understanding provides its rational underpinnings (Damon & Hart, 1992).

The rudimentary beginning of self-understanding begins with self-recognition, which takes place by approximately 18 months of age. Since children can verbally communicate their ideas, research on self-understanding in childhood is not limited to visual self-recognition, as it was during infancy. Mainly by interviewing children, researchers have probed children's conceptions of many aspects of self-understanding, including mind and body, self in relation to others, and pride and shame in self. In early childhood, children usually conceive of the self in physical terms. Most young children think the self is part of their body, usually their head. Young children usually confuse self, mind, and body. Because the self is a body part for them, they describe it along many material dimensions, such as size, shape, and color. Young children distinguish themselves from others through many different physical and material attributes. Says 4-year-old Sandra, "I'm different from Jennifer because I have brown hair and she has blond hair." Says 4-year-old Ralph, "I am different from Hank because I am taller, and I am different from my sister because I have a bicycle."

Researchers also believe that the *active dimension* is a central component of the self in early childhood (Keller, Ford, & Meacham, 1978). If we define the category *physical* broadly enough, we can include physical actions as well as body image and material possessions. For example, preschool children often describe themselves in terms of activities like play. In sum, in early childhood, children frequently think of themselves in terms of a physical self or an active self.

Gender

Few aspects of children's social development are more central to their identity and to their social relationships than their sex or gender. What exactly do we mean by gender? What are the biological, cognitive, and social influences on gender?

What Is Gender?

While sex refers to the biological dimension of being male or female, **gender** *refers to the social dimension of being male or female.* Two aspects of gender bear special mention—gender identity and gender role. **Gender identity** *is the sense of being male or female, which most children acquire by the time they are 3 years old.* **Gender role** *is a set of expectations that prescribe how females or males should think, act, and feel.*

Biological Influences

It was not until the 1920s that researchers confirmed the existence of human sex chromosomes, the genetic material that determines our sex. In chapter 3, you learned that humans normally have 46 chromosomes arranged in pairs. The 23rd pair may have two X chromosomes to produce a female, or it may have an X and a Y chromosome to produce a male.

In the first few weeks of gestation, female and male embryos look alike. Male sex organs start to differ from female sex organs when XY chromosomes in the male embryo trigger the secretion of **androgen,** *the main class of male sex hormones.* Low levels of androgen in a female embryo allow the normal development of female sex organs.

Although rare, an imbalance in this system of hormone secretion can occur during fetal development. If there is insufficient androgen in a male embryo or an excess of androgen in a female embryo, the result is an individual with both male and female sex organs, a hermaphrodite. When genetically female (XX chromosomes) infants are born with masculine-looking genitals, surgery at birth can achieve a genital/genetic match.

Estrogen *is the main class of female sex hormones.* At puberty, the production of estrogen begins to influence both physical development and behavior, but before then these females often behave in a "tomboyish" manner, acting more aggressively than most girls. They also dress and play in ways that are more characteristic of boys than girls (Ehrhardt, 1987).

Is the behavior of these surgically corrected girls due to their prenatal hormones, or is it the result of their social experiences? Experiments with various animal species reveal that when male hormones are injected into female embryos, the females develop masculine physical traits and behave more aggressively (Hines, 1982). However, in humans, hormones exert less control over behavior. Perhaps because these girls look more masculine, they are treated more like boys and so adopt their boyish ways.

Although prenatal hormones may or may not influence gender behavior, psychoanalytic theorists, such as Sigmund Freud and Erik Erikson, have argued that an individual's genitals do play a pivotal role. Freud argued that human behavior and history are directly influenced by sexual drives and suggested that gender and sexual behavior are essentially unlearned and instinctual. Erikson went even further: He argued that, because of genital structure, males are more intrusive and aggressive, females more inclusive and passive. Erikson's critics contend that he has not given enough credit to experience, and they argue that women and men are more free to choose their behavior than Erikson allowed. In response, Erikson has clarified his view, pointing out that he never said that biology is the sole determinant of differences between the sexes. Biology, he said, interacts with both cultural and psychological factors to produce behavior.

No one argues about the presence of genetic, biochemical, and anatomical differences between the sexes. Even child developmentalists with a strong environmental orientation acknowledge that boys and girls are treated differently because of their physical differences and their different roles in reproduction. The importance of biological factors is not at issue. What is at issue is the directness or indirectness of their effects on social behavior (Huston, 1983). For example, if a high androgen level directly influences the central nervous system, which in turn increases activity level, then the biological effect on behavior is direct. By contrast, if a child's high level of androgen produces strong muscle development, which in turn causes others to expect the child to be a good athlete and, in turn, leads the child to participate in sports, then the biological effect on behavior is indirect.

Although virtually everyone thinks that children's behavior as males or females is due to an interaction of biological and environmental factors, an interactionist position means different things to different people (Bailey, 1995). For some, it suggests that certain environmental conditions are required before preprogrammed dispositions appear. For others, it suggests that a particular

John W. Santrock

environment will have different effects depending on the child's predispositions. For still others, it means that children shape their environments, including their interpersonal environment, and vice versa. The processes of influence and counterinfluence unfold over time. Throughout development, males and females actively construct their own versions of acceptable masculine and feminine behavior patterns.

Social Influences

In our culture, adults discriminate between the sexes shortly after the infant's birth. The "pink and blue" treatment may be applied to boys and girls before they leave the hospital. Soon afterward, differences in hairstyles, clothes, and toys become obvious. Adults and peers reward these differences throughout development. And boys and girls learn gender roles through imitation or observational learning by watching what other people say and do. In recent years, the idea that parents are the critical socializing agents in gender-role development has come under fire. Parents are only one of many sources through which the individual learns gender roles (Beal, 1994). Culture, schools, peers, the media, and other family members are others. Yet it is important to guard against swinging too far in this direction because—especially in the early years of development—parents are important influences on gender development.

Identification and Social Learning Theories

Two prominent theories address the way children acquire masculine and feminine attitudes and behaviors from their parents. **Identification theory** *stems from Freud's view that the preschool child develops a sexual attraction to the opposite-sex parent, then by approximately 5 or 6 years of age renounces this attraction because of anxious feelings, and subsequently identifies with the same-sex parent, unconsciously adopting the same-sex parent's characteristics.* However, today many child developmentalists do not believe gender development proceeds on the basis of identification, at least not in terms of Freud's emphasis on childhood sexual attraction. Children become gender-typed much earlier than 5 or 6 years of age, and they become masculine or feminine even when the same-sex parent is not present in the family.

Children need models rather than critics.

—Joseph Joubert

The **social learning theory of gender** *emphasizes that children's gender development occurs through observation and imitation of gender behavior, and through the rewards and punishments children experience for gender appropriate and inappropriate behavior.* Unlike identification theory, social learning theory argues that sexual attraction to parents is not involved in gender development. (A comparison of identification and social learning views is presented in

Theory	Processes	Outcome
Freud's identification theory	Sexual attraction to opposite-sex parent at 3–5 years of age; anxiety about sexual attraction and subsequent identification with same-sex parent at 5–6 years of age	Gender behavior similar to that of same-sex parent
Social learning theory	Rewards and punishments of gender-appropriate and inappropriate behavior by adults and peers; observation and imitation of models' masculine and feminine behavior	Gender behavior

FIGURE 11.4

A Comparison of Identification and Social Learning Views of Gender Development
Parents influence their children's development by action and example.

figure 11.4.) Parents often use rewards and punishments to teach their daughters to be feminine ("Karen, you are being a good girl when you play gently with your doll") and their sons to be masculine ("Keith, a boy as big as you is not supposed to cry"). Peers also extensively reward and punish gender behavior. And by observing adults and peers at home, at school, in the neighborhood, and on television, children are widely exposed to a myriad of models who display masculine and feminine behavior. Critics of the social learning view argue that gender development is

As reflected in this tug-of-war battle between boys and girls, the playground in elementary school is like going to "gender school." Elementary school children show a clear preference for being with and liking same-sex peers. Eleanor Maccoby (inset) has studied children's gender development for many years. She believes peers play a powerful role in the development of gender behavior.

not as passively acquired as it indicates. Later we will discuss the cognitive views on gender development, which stress that children actively construct their gender world.

Parental Influences   Parents, by action and by example, influence their children's gender development. Both mothers and fathers are psychologically important in children's gender development. Mothers are more consistently given responsibility for nurturance and physical care; fathers are more likely to engage in playful interaction and be given responsibility for ensuring that boys and girls conform to existing cultural norms. And whether or not they have more influence on them, fathers are more involved in socializing their sons than their daughters. Fathers seem to play an especially important part in gender-role development—they are more likely than mothers to act differently toward sons and daughters and thus contribute more to distinctions between the genders (Huston, 1983).

Many parents encourage boys and girls to engage in different types of play and activities (Fagot, Leinbach, & O'Boyle, 1992). Girls are more likely to be given dolls to play with during childhood and, when old enough, are more likely to be assigned baby-sitting duties. Girls are encouraged to be more nurturant and emotional than boys, and their fathers are more likely to engage in aggressive play with their sons than with their daughters. As adolescents increase in age, parents permit boys more freedom than girls, allowing them to be away from home and stay

out later without supervision. When parents place severe restrictions on their adolescent sons, it has a negative effect on the sons' development (Baumrind, 1989).

Peer Influences   Parents provide the earliest discrimination of gender roles in development, but, before long, peers join the societal process of responding to and modeling masculine and feminine behavior. Children who play in sex-appropriate activities tend to be rewarded for doing so by their peers. Those who play in cross-sexed activities tend to be criticized by their peers or left to play alone. Children show a clear preference for being with and liking same-sex peers (Maccoby, 1993), and this tendency usually becomes stronger during the middle and late childhood years. After extensive observations of elementary school playgrounds, two researchers characterized the play settings as "gender school," pointing out that boys teach one another the required masculine behavior and enforce it strictly (Luria & Herzog, 1985). Girls also pass on the female culture and mainly congregate with one another. Individual "tomboy" girls can join boys' activities without losing their status in the girls' groups, but the reverse is not true for boys, reflecting our society's greater sex-typing pressure for boys.

Peer demands for conformity to gender role become especially intense during adolescence. Although there is greater social mixing of males and females during early adolescence, in both formal groups and in dating, peer pressure is strong for the adolescent boy to be the very best male possible and for the adolescent girl to be the very best female possible.

School and Teacher Influences   In certain ways, both girls and boys might receive an education that is not fair (Sadker & Sadker, 1994). For example:

- Girls' learning problems are not identified as often as boys' are.
- Boys are given the lion's share of attention in schools.
- Girls start school testing higher in every academic subject than boys, yet graduate from high school scoring lower on the SAT exam.
- Boys are most often at the top of their classes, but they also are most often at the bottom as well—more likely to fail a class, miss promotion, or drop out of school.
- Pressure to achieve is more likely to be heaped on boys than on girls.

Consider the following research study (Sadker & Sadker, 1986). Observers were trained to collect data in more than a hundred fourth-, sixth-, and eighth-grade classrooms. At all three grade levels, males were involved in more interactions than female students were, and male students were given more attention than their female counterparts. Male students were also given more remediation, more criticism, and more praise than female students. Girls with strong math abilities are given lower-quality instruction than their male counterparts are (Eccles, MacIver, & Lange, 1986).

Myra Sadker and David Sadker (1994), who have been studying gender discrimination in schools for more than two decades, believe that many educators are unaware of the subtle ways that gender infiltrates the school's environment. Their hope is that sexism can be eradicated in the nation's schools.

Media Influences   As we have described, children encounter masculine and feminine roles in their everyday interactions with parents, peers, and teachers. The messages carried by the media about what is appropriate or inappropriate for males and for females are important influences on gender development as well.

A special concern is the way females are pictured on television. In the 1970s, it became apparent that television was portraying females as less competent than males. For example, about 70 percent of the prime-time characters were males, men were more likely to be shown in the work force, women were more likely to be shown as housewives and in romantic roles, men were more likely to appear in higher-status jobs and in a greater diversity of occupations, and men were presented as more aggressive and constructive (Sternglanz & Serbin, 1974).

In the 1980s, television networks became more sensitive to how males and females were portrayed on television shows. Consequently, many programs now focus on divorced families, cohabitation, and women in high-status roles. Even with the onset of this type of programming researchers continue to find that television portrays males as more competent than females (Durkin, 1985). In one investigation, young adolescent girls indicated that television occupations are more extensively stereotyped than real-life occupations (Wroblewski & Huston, 1987).

Gender stereotyping also appears in the print media. In magazine advertising, females are shown more often in advertisements for beauty products, cleaning products, and home appliances, while males are shown more often in advertisements for cars, liquor, and travel. As with television programs, females are being portrayed as more competent in advertisements than in the past, but advertisers have not yet given them equal status with males.

So far in our discussion of gender, we have seen that both biological and social factors play important roles in children's gender development. Recently, many child developmentalists have also recognized the important role that cognitive factors play.

Cognitive Influences

What is the cognitive developmental view of gender? What is the gender schema theory of gender development? What role does language play in gender development? We will consider each of these questions in turn.

Cognitive Developmental Theory   In the **cognitive developmental theory of gender,** *children's gender typing occurs after they have developed a concept of gender. Once they consistently conceive of themselves as male or female, children often organize their world on the basis of gender.* Initially developed by psychologist Lawrence Kohlberg (1966), this theory argues that gender development proceeds in the following way: A child realizes, "I am a girl; I want to do girl things; therefore, the opportunity to do girl things is rewarding." Having acquired the ability to categorize, children then strive toward consistency in the use of categories and behavior. Kohlberg based his ideas on Piaget's cognitive developmental theory. As children's cognitive development matures, so does their understanding of gender. Although 2-year-olds can apply the labels *boy* and *girl* correctly to themselves and others, their concept of gender is simple and concrete. Preschool children rely on physical features, such as dress and hairstyle, to decide who falls into which category. Girls are people with long hair, they think, whereas boys are people who never wear dresses. Many preschool children believe that people can change their own gender at will by getting a haircut or a new outfit. They do not yet have the cognitive machinery to think of gender as adults do. According to Kohlberg, all the reinforcement in the world won't modify that fact. However, by the concrete operational stage (the third stage in Piaget's theory, entered at about 6 or 7 years of age), children understand gender constancy—that a male is still a male regardless of whether he wears pants or a skirt, or his hair is short or long (Tavris & Wade, 1984). When their concept of gender constancy is clearly established, children are then motivated to become a competent, or "proper" girl or boy. Consequently, she or he finds female or male activities rewarding and imitates the behavior of same-sex models.

Childhood decides.

—Jean-Paul Sartre

Gender Schema Theory *A* **schema** *is a cognitive structure, a network of associations that organizes and guides an individual's perceptions. A* **gender schema** *organizes the world in terms of female and male.* **Gender schema theory** *states that an individual's attention and behavior are guided by an internal motivation to conform to gender-based sociocultural standards and stereotypes.* Gender schema theory suggests that "gender typing" occurs when individuals are ready to encode and organize information along the lines of what is considered appropriate or typical for males and females in a society. Whereas Kohlberg's cognitive developmental theory argues that a particular cognitive prerequisite—gender constancy—is necessary for gender typing, gender schema theory states that a general readiness to respond to and categorize information on the basis of culturally defined gender roles fuels children's gender-typing activities. A comparison of the cognitive developmental and gender schema theories is presented in figure 11.5.

While researchers have shown that the appearance of gender constancy in children is related to their level of cognitive development, especially the acquisition of conservation skills (which supports the cognitive developmental theory of gender) (Serbin & Sprafkin, 1986), they have also shown that young children who are pre-gender-constant have more gender-role knowledge than the cognitive developmental theory of gender predicts (which supports gender schema theory) (Carter & Levy, 1988). Today, gender schema theorists acknowledge that gender constancy is one important aspect of gender role development, but stress that other cognitive factors—such as gender schema—are also very important.

The Role of Language in Gender Development

Gender is present in the language children use and encounter. The language that children hear most of the time is sexist. That is, the English language contains sex bias, especially through the use of *he* and *man* to refer to everyone. For example, in one study, mothers and their 1- and 3-year-old children looked at popular children's books, such as *The Three Bears*, together (DeLoache,

Theory	Processes	Outcome
Cognitive developmental theory	Development of gender constancy, especially around 6–7 years of age, when conservation skills develop; after children develop ability to consistently conceive of themselves as male or female, children often organize their world on the basis of gender, such as selecting same-sex models to imitate	Gender-typed behavior
Gender schema theory	Sociocultural emphasis on gender-based standards and stereotypes; children's attention and behavior are guided by an internal motivation to conform to these gender-based standards and stereotypes, allowing children to interpret the world through a network of gender-organized thoughts	Gender-typed behavior

FIGURE 11.5

A Comparison of Cognitive Developmental and Gender Schema Theories of Gender Development

Cassidy, & Carpenter, 1987). The three bears were almost always referred to as boys; 95 percent of all characters of indeterminate gender were referred to by mothers as males.

John W. Santrock

Moral Development

People are hardly neutral about moral development. Many parents worry that their children are growing up without traditional values. Teachers complain that their students are unethical. What is moral development? What is Piaget's view of how children's moral reasoning develops? What is the nature of children's moral behavior? How do children's feelings contribute to their moral development?

What Is Moral Development?

Moral development *concerns rules and conventions about what people should do in their interactions with other people*. In studying these rules, developmentalists examine three different domains. First, how do children *reason* or *think* about rules for ethical conduct? For example, consider cheating. The child can be presented with a story in which someone has a conflict about whether or not to cheat in a particular situation, such as taking a test in school. The child is asked to decide what is appropriate for the character to do and why. The focus is on the *reasoning* children use to justify their moral decisions.

Second, how do children actually *behave* in moral circumstances? In our example of cheating, the emphasis is on observing the child's cheating and the environmental circumstances that produced and maintained the cheating. Children might be shown some toys and then be asked to select the one they believe is the most attractive. The experimenter then tells the young child that that particular toy belongs to someone else and is not to be played with. Observations of different conditions under which the child deviates from the prohibition or resists temptation are then conducted.

Third, how does the child *feel* about moral matters? In the example of cheating, does the child feel enough guilt to resist temptation? If children do cheat, do feelings of guilt after the transgression keep them from cheating the next time they face temptation? In the remainder of this section, we will focus on these three facets of moral development: thought, action, and feeling. Then we will evaluate the positive side of children's moral development: altruism.

Piaget's View of How Children's Moral Reasoning Develops

Interest in how the child thinks about moral issues as stimulated by Piaget (1932), who extensively observed and interviewed children from the ages of 4 to 12. He watched them play marbles, seeking to learn how they used and thought about the game's rules. He also asked children questions about ethical rules—theft, lies, punishment, and justice, for example. Piaget concluded that children think in two distinctly different ways about morality, depending on their developmental maturity. **Heteronomous morality** *is the first stage of moral development, in Piaget's theory, occurring from approximately 4 to 7 years of age. Justice and rules are conceived of as unchangeable properties of the world, removed from the control of people.* **Autonomous morality** *is*

the second stage of moral development, in Piaget's theory, displayed by older children (about 10 years of age and older). The child becomes aware that rules and laws are created by people and that, in judging an action, one should consider the actor's intentions as well as the consequences. Children 7 to 10 years of age are in a transition between the two stages, evidencing some features of both.

Let's consider Piaget's two stages of moral development further. The heteronomous thinker judges the rightness or goodness of behavior by considering the consequences of the behavior, not the intentions of the actor. For example, the heteronomous thinker says that breaking twelve cups accidentally is worse than breaking one cup intentionally while trying to steal a cookie. For the moral autonomist, the reverse is true. The actor's intentions assume paramount importance. The heteronomous thinker also believes that rules are unchangeable and are handed down by all-powerful authorities. When Piaget suggested that new rules be introduced into the game of marbles, the young children resisted. They insisted that the rules had always been the same and could not be altered. By contrast, older children—who were moral autonomists—accept change and recognize that rules are merely convenient, socially agreed-upon conventions, subject to change by consensus.

The heteronomous thinker also believes in **immanent justice,** *the concept that if a rule is broken, punishment will be meted out immediately*. The young child believes that the violation is connected in some automatic way to the punishment. Thus, young children often look around worriedly after committing a transgression, expecting inevitable punishment. Older children, the moral autonomists, recognize that punishment is socially mediated and occurs only if a relevant person witnesses the wrongdoing and that, even then, punishment is not inevitable.

Piaget argued that, as children develop, they become more sophisticated in thinking about social matters, especially about the possibilities and conditions of cooperation. Piaget believed that this social understanding comes about through the mutual give-and-take of peer relations. In the peer group, where all members have similar power and status, plans are negotiated and coordinated, and disagreements are reasoned about and eventually settled. Parent-child relations, in which parents have the power and the child does not, are less likely to advance moral reasoning, because rules are often handed down in an authoritarian way.

Moral Behavior

The study of moral behavior has been influenced by social learning theory. The processes of reinforcement, punishment, and imitation are used to explain children's moral behavior. When children are rewarded for behavior that is consistent with laws and social conventions, they are likely to repeat that behavior. When models who behave morally are provided, children are likely to adopt their actions.

And when children are punished for immoral behavior, those behaviors are likely to be reduced or eliminated. However, because punishment may have adverse side effects, it needs to be used judiciously and cautiously.

Another important point needs to be made about the social learning view of moral development: Moral behavior is influenced extensively by the situation. What children do in one situation is often only weakly related to what they do in other situations. A child may cheat in math class, but not in English class; a child may steal a piece of candy when others are not present, and not steal it when they are present; and so on. More than half a century ago, morality's situational nature was observed in a comprehensive study of thousands of children in many different situations—at home, at school, and at church, for example. The totally honest child was virtually nonexistent; so was the child who cheated in all situations (Hartshorne & May, 1928–1930).

Social learning theorists also believe that the ability to resist temptation is closely tied to the development of self-control. Children must overcome their impulses toward something they want that is prohibited. To achieve this self-control, they must learn to be patient and to delay gratification. Today, social learning theorists believe that cognitive factors are important in the child's development of self-control. For example, in one investigation, children's cognitive transformations of desired objects helped children to become more patient (Mischel & Patterson, 1976). Preschool children were asked to do a boring task. Close by was an exciting mechanical clown who tried to persuade the children to come play with him. The children who had been trained to say to themselves "I'm not going to look at Mr. Clown when Mr. Clown says to look at him" controlled their behavior and continued working on the dull task much longer than those who did not instruct themselves.

Moral Feelings

In chapter 2, we discussed Sigmund Freud's psychoanalytic theory, which describes the *superego* as one of the three main structures of personality—the id and ego being the other two. In Freud's classical psychoanalytic theory, the child's superego—the moral branch of personality—develops as the child resolves the Oedipus conflict and identifies with the same-sex parent in the early childhood years. Among the reasons why children resolve the Oedipus conflict is the fear of losing their parents' love and of being punished for their unacceptable sexual wishes toward the opposite-sex parent. To reduce anxiety, avoid punishment, and maintain parental affection, children form a superego by identifying with the same-sex parent. Through their identification with the same-sex parent, children internalize the parents' standards of right and wrong that reflect societal prohibitions. And the child turns inward the hostility that was previously aimed externally at the same-sex parent. This inwardly directed hostility is now felt self-punitively as guilt, which is experienced unconsciously (beyond the child's awareness). In the psychoanalytic account of moral development, the self-punitiveness of guilt is responsible for keeping the child from committing transgressions. That is, children conform to societal standards to avoid guilt.

What is moral is what you feel good after and what is immoral is what you feel bad after.
—**Ernest Hemingway, *Death in the Afternoon,* 1932**

Positive feelings such as empathy contribute to the child's moral development. **Empathy** *is reacting to another's feelings with an emotional response that is similar to the other's feelings.* Although empathy is experienced as an emotional state, it often has a cognitive component. The cognitive component is the ability to discern another's inner psychological states, or what is called "perspective taking." Young infants have the capacity for some purely empathic responses, but for effective moral action children need to learn how to identify a wide range of emotional states in others, and they need to learn to anticipate what kinds of action will improve another person's emotional state.

We have seen that classical psychoanalytic theory emphasizes the power of unconscious guilt in moral development. However, other theorists, such as Martin Hoffman and William Damon, emphasize the role of empathy. Today, many child developmentalists believe that both positive feelings, such as empathy, sympathy, admiration, and self-esteem, as well as negative feelings, such as anger, outrage, shame, and guilt, contribute to the child's moral development (Eisenberg & others, in press; Roberts & Strayer, 1996). When strongly experienced, these emotions influence children to act in accord with standards of right and wrong. Emotions such as empathy, shame, guilt, and anxiety over other people's violation of standards are present early in development and undergo developmental change throughout childhood and beyond (Damon & Hart, 1992). These emotions provide a natural base for the child's acquisition of moral values, both orienting children toward moral events and motivating children to pay close attention to such events. But moral emotions do not operate in a vacuum to build the child's moral awareness, and they are not sufficient in themselves to generate moral responsiveness. They do not give the "substance" of moral regulation—the actual rules, values, and standards of behavior that children need to understand and act on. Moral emotions are inextricably interwoven with the cognitive and social aspects of children's development.

Thus far, we have discussed a number of ideas about the self, gender, and moral development in young children. These ideas are summarized in concept table 11.2.

John W. Santrock

CONCEPT TABLE 11.2

The Self, Gender, and Moral Development

Concept	Processes/Related Ideas	Characteristics/Description
The Self	Initiative vs. guilt	Erikson believed that early childhood is a period when development involves resolving the conflict between initiative versus guilt.
	Self-understanding	While a rudimentary form of self-understanding occurs at about 18 months in the form of self-recognition, in early childhood the physical and active self emerges.
Gender	What is gender?	Gender is the social dimension of being male or female. Gender identity is acquired by 3 years of age for most children. A gender role is a set of expectations that prescribe how females or males should think, act, and feel.
	Biological influences	Freud's and Erikson's ideas promote the idea that anatomy is destiny. Hormones influence gender development more in animals than in humans. Today's developmentalists are all interactionists when biological and environmental influences on gender are considered.
	Social influences	Both identification theory and social learning theory emphasize the adoption of parents' gender characteristics. Peers are especially adept at rewarding gender-appropriate behavior. There is still concern about gender imbalance in education. Despite improvements, TV still portrays males as being more competent than females.
	Cognitive influences	Both cognitive developmental and gender schema theories emphasize the role of cognition in gender development. Gender is present in the language children use and encounter. Much of the language children hear is sexist.
Moral Development	What is It?	Moral development concerns rules and regulations about what people should do in their interactions with others. Developmentalists study how children think, behave, and feel about such rules and regulations.
	Piaget's view	Piaget distinguished between the heteronomous morality of younger children and the autonomous morality of older children.
	Moral behavior	Moral behavior is emphasized by social learning theorists. They believe there is considerable situational variability in moral behavior and that self-control is an important aspect of understanding children's moral behavior.
	Moral feelings	Freud's psychoanalytic theory emphasizes the importance of feelings with regard to the development of the superego, the moral branch of personality, which develops through the Oedipus conflict and identification with the same-sex parent. In Freud's view, children conform to societal standards to avoid guilt. Positive emotions, such as empathy, also are an important aspect of understanding moral feelings. In Damon's view, both positive and negative emotions contribute to children's moral development.

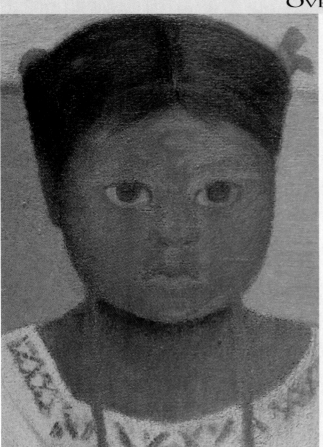

I n early childhood, children's socioemotional worlds expand to include more time spent with peers and in play. Their small worlds widen as they discover new refuges and new people, although parents continue to play an important role in their lives.

We began this chapter by considering the diversity of families and parenting, then evaluated two important dimensions of parenting—parenting styles and adapting parenting to the child's developmental status. Our coverage of the changing family in a changing social world focused on working mothers; divorce; and cultural, social class, and ethnic dimensions of parenting. We also discussed sibling relationships and birth order. Other important dimensions we read about included peers, play, and television, as well as the self, gender, and moral development.

Don't forget that you can obtain an overall summary of the chapter by again studying the concept tables on pages 328 and 337. This concludes our discussion of early childhood. In Section Five, we will continue our journey through childhood by focusing on the middle and late childhood years, beginning with physical development in this period.

authoritarian parenting A restrictive punitive style in which parents exhort the child to follow their directions and to respect work and effort. The authoritarian parent places firm limits and controls on the child and allows little verbal exchange. Authoritarian parenting is associated with children's social incompetence. 313

authoritative parenting A parenting style in which parents encourage their children to be independent but still place limits and controls on their actions. Extensive verbal give-and-take is allowed, and parents are warm and nurturant toward the child. Authoritative parenting is associated with children's social competence. 313

neglectful parenting A style of parenting in which the parent is very uninvolved in the child's life; it is associated with children's social incompetence, especially a lack of self-control. 313

indulgent parenting A style of parenting in which parents are highly involved with their children but place few demands or controls on them. Indulgent parenting is associated with children's social incompetence, especially lack of self-control. 314

family structure model A model according to which any differences in children from different family structures are due to the family structure variations, such as the father's being absent in one set of the families. 318

multiple-factor model of divorce Takes into account the complexity of the divorce context and examines a number of influences on the child's development, including not only family structure, but also the strengths and weaknesses of the child prior to the divorce, the nature of the events surrounding the divorce itself, the type of custody involved, visitation patterns, socioeconomic status, and postdivorce family functioning. 318

peers Children of about the same age or maturity level. 320

play A pleasurable activity that is engaged in for its own sake. 321

play therapy Therapy that allows the child to work off frustrations and is a medium through which the therapist can analyze the child's conflicts and ways of coping with them. Children may feel less threatened and be more likely to express their true feelings in the context of play. 322

unoccupied play Play in which the child is not engaging in play as it is commonly understood and might stand in one spot, look around the room, or perform random movements that do not seem to have a goal. 322

solitary play Play in which the child plays alone and independently of others. 322

onlooker play Play in which the child watches other children play. 322

parallel play Play in which the child plays separately from others, but with toys like those the others are using or in a manner that mimics their play. 322

associative play Play that involves social interaction with little or no organization. 322

cooperative play Play that involves social interaction in a group with a sense of group identity and organized activity. 322

sensorimotor play Behavior engaged in by infants to derive pleasure from exercising their existing sensorimotor schemas. 323

practice play Play that involves repetition of behavior when new skills are being learned or when physical or mental mastery and coordination of skills are required for games or sports. Sensorimotor play, which often involves practice play, is primarily confined to infancy, while practice play can be engaged in throughout life. 323

pretense/symbolic play Play in which the child transforms the physical environment into a symbol. 323

social play Play that involves social interactions with peers. 324

constructive play Play that combines sensorimotor/practice repetitive activity with symbolic representation of ideas. Constructive play occurs when children engage in self-regulated creation or construction of a product or a problem solution. 324

games Activities engaged in for pleasure that include rules and often competition with one or more individuals. 324

self-understanding The child's cognitive representation of self, the substance and content of the child's self-conceptions. 329

gender The social dimension of being female or male. 330

gender identity The sense of being male or female, which most children acquire by the time they are 3 years old. 330

gender role A set of expectations that prescribe how females or males should think, act, and feel. 330

androgen The main class of male sex hormones. 330

estrogen The main class of female sex hormones. 330

identification theory A theory deriving from Freud's view that the preschool child develops a sexual attraction to the opposite-sex parent, then by approximately 5 or 6 years of age renounces this attraction because of anxious feelings, and subsequently identifies with the same-sex parent, unconsciously adopting the same-sex parent's characteristics. 331

social learning theory of gender A theory that emphasizes that children's gender development occurs through observation and imitation of gender behavior, and through the rewards and punishments children experience for gender appropriate and inappropriate behavior. 331

cognitive developmental theory of gender The theory that children's gender typing occurs after they have developed a concept of gender. Once they consistently conceive of themselves as male or female, children often organize their world on the basis of gender. 333

schema A cognitive structure, a network of associations that organizes and guides an individual's perceptions. 334

gender schema A schema that organizes the world in terms of female and male. 334

gender schema theory The theory that an individual's attention and behavior are guided by an internal motivation to conform to gender-based sociocultural standards and stereotypes. 334

moral development Development regarding rules and conventions about what people should do in their interactions with other people. 335

African American Families

Although African American children are more likely than White children to be poor and live with a parent who has been separated from a spouse, it is important to keep in mind that millions of African American families are not on welfare, have considerable family support, and find ways to effectively cope with stress. The family, especially grandmothers, plays an especially important role in African American children's development.

In 1967, Martin Luther King, Jr., reflected on the American family and cautioned, "As public awareness of the Black family increases, there will be opportunity and danger. The opportunity will be to deal fully rather than haphazardly with the problem as a whole, as a social catastrophe brought on by many years of opposition. The danger is that the problems will be attributed to innate weaknesses and used to justify further neglect and to rationalize continued oppression."

Along with traditional demands of parenthood, today's parents must deal with such issues as drugs, AIDS, violence, and educational pressures. But African American and other ethnic minority parents must also face the challenging task of actively combating negative messages of racism while teaching their children to succeed in a White-dominated culture.

According to James Comer and Alvin Poussaint (1992), African American parents need to raise well-educated, confident children. Good child-rearing practices are a crucial element in assuring a positive future for African American children. Children raised in an atmosphere of love, security, and support, even in very-low-income circumstances, are more prepared to face tomorrow's challenges.

However, extended family and community support are also critical aspects of developing a competent African American child. The extended family—grandparents and other relatives—plays an important role in many African American families. With a high percentage of African American children growing up in single-parent families, the extended family provides an extremely important support system. Researchers have found that the extended family helps to reduce the stress of poverty and single parenting through emotional support, sharing of income and responsibility, and surrogate parenting (McAdoo, 1988).

Gender and Children's Books

How are females and males portrayed in children's books? The problem of gender bias in children's books first began receiving widespread attention in the early 1970s. In 1972, a report on 134 elementary school textbooks indicated that girls and women were more invisible than boys and men (Women on Words & Images, 1972). In the real world, less than 50 percent of the population are males, but in the children's readers more than 70 percent were males. Not only were females underrepresented in the books, but they also were misrepresented. Few women were portrayed in work outside of the home; when they were, they were shown in traditionally female occupations.

Females and males are portrayed with different personalities and perform different tasks in children's books (Matlin, 1993). Males are described and pictured as clever, industrious, and brave. They acquire skills, earn fame and fortune, and explore. By contrast, females tend to be passive, dependent, and kind. They cook and clean up.

The biased presentation of females is not confined to English-language books. In an analysis of textbooks used in Puerto Rico and in bilingual programs in the United States, girls were generally portrayed as passive, weak, and dependent, boys as courageous, creative, and persistent (Picó, 1983).

Are children's books becoming less biased than they were a decade or two ago? Some hopeful signs give reason for having a degree of optimism. An analysis of the winners of the prestigious Newbery Medal Award for children's books revealed several examples of competent, nonstereotypical girls. Further, an interview with a 10-year-old African American girl indicated that on her own she had been able to find and read a number of books about African American girls (Sims, 1983). One of her favorites is shown in figure 11.6.

In one study, 150 children's picture books were analyzed for gender-role content (Kortenhaus & Demarest, 1993). The frequency of depictions of females and males in the stories had become more evenly distributed over the past 50 years. The roles played by female and males have changed in a more subtle way. Girls are now being pictured in more instrumental activities (behavior that is instrumental in attaining a goal), but in their depictions they are still as passive and dependent as they were 50 years ago! Boys are occasionally shown as passive and dependent today, but no less instrumental than they were 50 years ago.

Today, with effort, parents and teachers can locate interesting books in which girls and women are presented as appropriate models. And it is worth the effort.

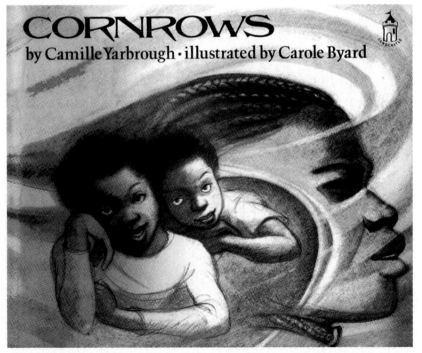

FIGURE 11.6

Camille Yarbrough's Book *Cornrows* Includes Appropriate Images of People of Color and Females

Review of Children's Development
Early Childhood

PHYSICAL DEVELOPMENT

The average child grows 2½ inches in height and gains 5 to 7 pounds a year during early childhood. Growth patterns vary individually, though. By age 5, the brain has reached nine-tenths of its adult size. Some of its size increase is due to the number and size of nerve endings, some to myelination. Gross motor skills increase dramatically during early childhood. Young children are more active than at any other period in the life span. Fine motor skills also increase substantially during early childhood. Energy needs increase as children go through the childhood years. One of every three deaths in the world is that of a child under 5. The most frequent cause of children's death is diarrhea. The United States has a relatively low mortality rate for children, although the Scandinavian countries have the lowest rates. The disorders most likely to be fatal for American children in early childhood are birth defects, cancer, and heart disease.

COGNITIVE DEVELOPMENT

Piaget's stage of preoperational thought is the stage when children begin to be able to reconstruct at the level of thought what they have already learned to do in behavior, and a transition from a primitive to a more sophisticated use of symbols. The child does not yet think in an operational way. Preoperational thought consists of two substages: symbolic function (2–4 years) and intuitive thought (4–7 years). Vygotsky's theory emphasizes the zone of proximal development, the merging of language and thought from 3 to 7 years of age, and the sociocultural contexts of cognitive development. The child's attention improves dramatically during the early childhood years, as does short-term memory. Young children develop a curiosity about the nature of the human mind. Advances in language development also occur during early childhood. Child-centered kindergarten and developmentally appropriate education are important dimensions of early childhood education, as are quality Head Start programs. A current concern is that too many preschool and early childhood education programs place too much emphasis on academic achievement.

SOCIOEMOTIONAL DEVELOPMENT

Authoritative parenting is associated with children's social competence. Parents need to adapt their parenting strategies as their child grows older, using less physical manipulation and more reasoning. In some cases, siblings are stronger socialization agents than parents. Children live in changing families; more children today grow up in working-mother and divorced families. Cross-cultural, social class, and ethnic variations in parenting exist. Peers are powerful socializing agents who provide a source of information and social comparison outside the family. Play also is an important aspect of the young child's development. Parten developed a number of categories of social play. Among the most important types of children's play are sensorimotor play, practice play, pretense/symbolic play, social play, constructive play, and games. Television is another socializing influence in children's development. Children watch huge amounts of television; preschool children watch an average of 4 hours a day. A special concern is the violence children see on television. Erikson believes that early childhood is a period when development involves resolving the conflict between initiative versus guilt. In early childhood, the physical and active self becomes a part of the child's self-understanding. Gender identity is the sense of being female or male, which most children acquire by 3 years of age. Identification, social learning, cognitive developmental, and gender schema theories have been proposed to explain children's gender development. Peers are especially adept at rewarding gender-appropriate behavior. Piaget distinguished between the heteronomous morality of younger children and the autonomous morality of older children. In addition to moral thought, moral behavior and moral feelings are important dimensions of children's moral development.

Middle and Late Childhood

> **B**lessed be childhood, which brings something of heaven into the midst of our rough earthliness.
>
> —Henri Frédéric Amiel, Journal, 1868

In middle and late childhood, children are on a different plane, belonging to a generation and feeling all their own. It is the wisdom of the human life span that at no time are children more ready to learn than during the period of expansive imagination at the end of early childhood. Children develop a sense of wanting to make things—and not just to make them, but to make them well and even perfectly. Their thirst is to know and to understand. They are remarkable for their intelligence and for their curiosity. Their parents continue to be important influences in their lives, but their growth also is shaped by successive choirs of friends. They don't think much about the future or about the past, but they enjoy the present moment. Section Five consists of three chapters: "Physical Development in Middle and Late Childhood" (chapter 12), "Cognitive Development in Middle and Late Childhood" (chapter 13), and "Socioemotional Development in Middle and Late Childhood" (chapter 14).

RENOIR
Girl with Watering Can, detail

Physical Development
in Middle and Late Childhood

*Every forward step we take we leave some
phantom of ourselves behind.*

—John Lancaster Spalding

*O*nly child life is real life.
—George Orwell

IMAGES OF CHILDREN

Training Children for the Olympics in China

S tanding on the balance beam at a sports school in Beijing, China, 6-year-old Zhang Liyin stretches her arms outward as she gets ready to perform a backflip. She wears the bright-red gymnastic suit of the elite—a suit given to only the best ten girls in her class of 6- to 8-year-olds (see figure 12.1). But her face wears a dreadful expression; she can't drum up enough confidence to do the flip. Maybe it is because she has had a rough week; a purple bruise decorates one leg, and a nasty gash disfigures the other. Her coach, a woman in her twenties, makes Zhang jump from the beam and escorts her to the high bar, where she is instructed to hang for 3 minutes. If Zhang falls, she must pick herself up and try again. But she does not fall, and she is escorted back to the beam, where her coach puts her through another tedious routine.

Zhang attends the sports school in the afternoon. The sports school is a privilege given to only 260,000 of China's 200 million students of elementary to college age. The Communist party has decided that sports is one avenue China can pursue to prove that China has arrived in the modern world. The sports schools designed to produce Olympic champions were the reason for China's success in the last three Olympics. These schools are the only road to Olympic stardom in China. There are precious few neighborhood playgrounds. And there is only one gymnasium for every 3.5 million people.

FIGURE 12.1

The Training of Future Olympians in the Sports Schools of China
Six-year-old Zhang Liyin (*third from the left*) hopes someday to become an Olympic gymnastics champion. Attending the sports school is considered an outstanding privilege; only 260,000 of China's 200 million children are given this opportunity.

Many of the students who attend the sports schools in the afternoon live and study at the schools as well. Only a few attend a normal school and then come to a sports school in the afternoon. Because of her young age, Zhang stays at home during the mornings and goes to the sports school from noon until 6 P.M. A part-timer like Zhang can stay enrolled until she no longer shows potential to move up to the next step. Any child who seems to lack potential is asked to leave.

Zhang was playing in a kindergarten class when a coach from a sports school spotted her. She was selected because of her broad shoulders, narrow hips, straight legs, symmetrical limbs, open-minded attitude, vivaciousness, and outgoing personality. If Zhang continues to show progress, she could be asked to move to full-time next year. At age 7, she would then go to school there and live in a dorm 6 days a week. If she becomes extremely competent at gymnastics, Zhang could be moved to Shishahai, where the elite gymnasts train and compete (Reilly, 1988).

John W. Santrock

PREVIEW

By American standards, Zhang's life sounds rigid and punitive. While achievement in sports has a lofty (some critics think too lofty) status in American society, children here are not trained with the intensity now being witnessed in China. Later in the chapter, we will discuss children's sports and physical fitness, as well as children's health, stress, and coping. But to begin, we turn to the nature of children's body changes in middle and late childhood.

BODY CHANGES IN MIDDLE AND LATE CHILDHOOD

The period of middle and late childhood involves slow, consistent growth. This is a period of calm before the rapid growth spurt of adolescence. Among the important aspects of body change in this development period are those involving the skeletal system, the muscular system, and motor skills.

The Skeletal and Muscular Systems

During the elementary school years, children grow an average of 2 to 3 inches a year until, at the age of 11, the average girl is 4 feet, 10¾ inches tall and the average boy is 4 feet, 9 inches tall. Children's legs become longer and their trunks slimmer. During the middle and late childhood years, children gain about 5 to 7 pounds a year. The weight increase is due mainly to increases in the size of the skeletal and muscular systems, as well as the size of some body organs.

Muscle mass and strength gradually increase as "baby fat" decreases. The loose movements and knock knees of early childhood give way to improved muscle tone. The increase in muscular strength is due to heredity and to exercise. Children double their strength capabilities during these years. Because of their greater number of muscle cells, boys are usually stronger than girls. A summary of changes in height and weight in middle and late childhood appears in table 12.1.

Motor Skills

During middle and late childhood, children's motor development becomes much smoother and more coordinated than it was in early childhood. For example, only one child in a thousand can hit a tennis ball over the net at the age

TABLE 12.1

Changes in Height and Weight in Middle and Late Childhood

	Height (inches)					
	Female Percentiles			Male Percentiles		
Age	25th	50th	75th	25th	50th	75th
6	43.75	45	46.50	44.25	45.75	47
7	46	47.50	49	46.25	48	49.25
8	48	49.75	51.50	48.50	50	51.50
9	50.25	53	53.75	50.50	52	53.50
10	52.50	54.50	56.25	52.50	54.25	55.75
11	55	57	58.75	54.50	55.75	57.25

	Weight (pounds)					
6	39.25	43	47.25	42	45.50	49.50
7	43.50	48.50	53.25	46.25	50.25	55
8	49	54.75	61.50	51	55.75	61.50
9	55.75	62.75	71.50	56	62	69.25
10	63.25	71.75	82.75	62	69.25	78.50
11	71.75	81.25	94.25	69	77.75	89

Note: The percentile tells how the child compares to other children of the same age. The 50th percentile tell us that half of the children of a particular age are taller (heavier) or shorter (lighter). The 25th percentile tells us that 25 percent of the children of that age are shorter (lighter) and 75 percent are taller (heavier).
Source: Data from R. E. Behman and V. C. Vaughan (eds.), *Nelson Textbook of Pediatrics.* W. B. Saunders, Philadelphia, PA, 1987.

As children move through the elementary school years, they gain greater control over their bodies. Physical action is essential for them to refine their developing skills.

Age in Years	Motor Skills
6	Can skip Can throw with proper weight shift and step Girls can throw a small ball 19 feet, boys 34 feet Girls and boys can vertically jump 7 inches Girls can perform a standing long jump 33 inches, boys 36 inches Children are more aware of their hands as tools Children like to draw, paint, and color Children can cut, paste paper toys, and sew crudely if needle is threaded Children enjoy making simple figures in clay Children can use a knife to spread butter or jam on bread
7	Balances on one foot without looking Can walk 2-inch wide balance beams Can hop and jump accurately into small squares Can participate in jumping-jack exercise Girls can throw a ball 25 feet, boys 45 feet Girls can vertically jump 8 inches, boys 9 inches Girls can perform standing long jump 41 inches, boys 43 inches Children are able to maintain posture for a longer period of time Children repeat physical performances to master them Children brush and comb their hair usually in an acceptable manner Children use a table knife for cutting meat
8	Children can engage in alternate rhythmic hopping in different patterns Girls can throw a ball 34 feet, boys 59 feet Girls can vertically jump 9 inches, boys 10 inches Girls can perform standing long jump 50 inches, boys 55 inches Grip strength increases Children can use common tools such as a hammer Children can help with routine household tasks such as dusting and sweeping
9	Girls can throw a ball 41 feet, boys 71 feet Girls can vertically jump 10 inches, boys 11 inches Girls can perform standing long jump 53 inches, boys 57 inches Perceptual-motor coordination becomes smoother
10–11	Children can judge and intercept pathways of small balls thrown from distance Girls can throw a small ball 49 feet, boys 94 feet at age 10; girls 58 feet and boys 106 feet at age 11 Girls can vertically jump 10 inches, boys 11 inches at age 10; girls 11 inches and boys 12 inches at age 11 Girls can perform standing long jump 57 inches, boys 61 inches at age 10; girls 62 inches and boys 66 inches at age 11 Children can make useful articles or do easy repair work Children can cook or sew in small ways Children can wash and dry their own hair

FIGURE 12.2

Changes in Motor Skills During Middle and Late Childhood

As children move through the elementary school years, they gain greater control over their bodies and can sit and attend for longer periods of time. However, elementary school children are far from having physical maturity, and they need to be active. Elementary school children become more fatigued by long periods of sitting than by running, jumping, or bicycling. Physical action is essential for these children to refine their developing skills, such as batting a ball, skipping rope, or balancing on a beam. An important principle of practice for elementary school children, therefore, is that they should be engaged in *active*, rather than passive, activities.

Increased myelinization of the central nervous system is reflected in the improvement of fine motor skills during middle and late childhood. Children's hands are used more adroitly as tools. Six-year-olds can hammer, paste, tie shoes, and fasten clothes. By 7 years of age, children's hands become steadier. At this age, children prefer a pencil to a crayon for printing, and reversal of letters is less common. Printing becomes smaller. Between 8 to 10 years of age, the hands can be used independently with more ease and precision. Fine motor coordination develops to the point where children can write rather than print words. Letter size becomes smaller and more even. By 10 to 12 years of age, children begin to show manipulative skills similar to the abilities of adults. The complex, intricate, and rapid movements needed to produce fine-quality crafts or play a difficult piece on a musical instrument can be mastered. One final point: Girls usually outperform boys in fine motor skills. A summary of changes in motor skills in middle and late childhood appears in figure 12.2.

of 3, yet by the age of 10 or 11 most children can learn to play the sport. Running, climbing, skipping rope, swimming, bicycle riding, and skating are just a few of the many physical skills elementary school children can master. And when mastered, these physical skills are a source of great pleasure and accomplishment for children. In gross motor skills involving large muscle activity, boys usually outperform girls rather handily.

John W. Santrock

HEALTH

Although we have become a health-conscious nation, many children as well as adults do not practice good health habits. Too much junk food and too much couch-potato behavior describes all too many children. Our exploration of elementary school children's health focuses on children's health status, children's understanding of health, and the relation of nutrition, exercise, and sports to children's health.

Children's Health Status and Understanding of Health

Among the most common ailments of children in the elementary school years are respiratory infections. Children in this age range may get as many as six to seven respiratory infections a year, although the average is 3.5 per year. Colds, gastrointestinal infections, and pneumonia account for more than 70 percent of school absenteeism.

CRITICAL THINKING ABOUT CHILDREN'S DEVELOPMENT

Developing a Health Program for Elementary Schools

Imagine that you have been hired as a consultant to plan the health program for an elementary school system. Consider three key components of health: nutrition, exercise, and stress. How would you go about implementing these components in schools? What would be the nature of the nutrition program? the exercise program? the stress program? Toward the end of this chapter, in the section "Improving the Lives of Children," you will read about a program called Heart Smart, one effort to improve children's health through educational intervention. Hold on to your guidelines so you can compare them with those of Heart Smart. By thinking about what would constitute a competent health program in elementary schools, you are learning to think critically by *using knowledge about development to improve children's welfare.*

Dental problems also are common in middle and late childhood. Permanent teeth are developing so rapidly in this time frame that children should have their teeth checked every 6 months. Primary teeth begin to fall out around the age of 6. These are replaced by permanent teeth at the rate of about four per year. Children's dental problems continue at a high rate in the United States. By age 12, the majority of children have more than four decayed or filled surfaces in their permanent teeth, and by age 17 more than 11 such dental problems. But there is some positive news: More than one-third of children have no tooth decay. Fluoride supplements either in the local water supply or in tablet form seem to be responsible for the reduction in children's cavities we are now witnessing.

Vision problems also are common for children. Visual maturity is usually reached between the ages of 6 to 7. Although vision screening tests are recommended during the preschool years, all children should have a visual examination when they enter school. Only one-third of the children who need visual correction are identified during the preschool years. Children with vision problems usually do not complain of poor vision because they do not know how accurately they are supposed to see their world. By age 11, 17 percent of children have poor distance vision and 10 percent have poor vision at close range, but many of these children have not yet been fitted with eyeglasses.

Hearing problems in children are frequently overlooked. Parents often believe that the hearing-impaired child is just not paying attention, doesn't understand, or

easily forgets. Recurrent or chronic ear infections, fluid in the middle ear, frequent exposure to loud noises, and illnesses such as measles or mumps can produce hearing problems. Five percent of children tested do not pass auditory screening tests.

When elementary school children are asked about their health, they seem to understand that good health is something they have to work at on a regular basis. Early positive attitudes toward health and exercise are important in the child's ability to maintain a healthy lifestyle. But while elementary school children and adolescents may recognize the contributions of nutrition and exercise to health, their behavior does not always follow suit. To further evaluate children's health, see Critical Thinking About Children's Development. Adolescents seem to have an especially difficult time applying health information and knowledge to their own personal lives. For example, in one study, adolescents reported that they probably would never have a heart attack or a drinking problem but that other adolescents would (Weinstein, 1984). The adolescents also said that no relation existed between their risk of heart attack and how much they exercised, smoked, or ate red meat or high-cholesterol foods such as eggs, even though they correctly recognized that factors such as family history influence risk. Many adolescents appear to have unrealistic, overly optimistic beliefs about their immunity from health risks.

Nutrition and Children's Obesity

In the middle and late childhood years, children's average body weight doubles. And children exert considerable energy as they engage in many different motor activities. To support their growth and active lives, children need to consume more food than they did in the early childhood years. From 1 to 3 years of age, infants and toddlers only need to consume 1,300 calories per day on the average and only 1,700 calories per day at 4 to 6 years of age. However, at 7 to 10 years of age, children need to consume 2,400 calories per day on the average (the range being 1,650 to 3,300 calories depending on the child's size).

A special concern during middle and late childhood is the development of **obesity,** *weighing 20 percent or more above the ideal weight for a particular age taking both age and sex into account.* Some obese children do not become obese adolescents and adults, but approximately 40 percent of children who are obese at age 7 also are obese as adults. Understanding why children become obese is complex, involving genetic inheritance, physiological mechanisms, cognitive factors, and environmental influences. Some children inherit a tendency to be overweight. Only 10 percent of children who do not have obese parents become overweight themselves, whereas 40 percent of children who have one obese parent become obese, and 70 percent of children who have two obese parents become obese. The extent to which this is due to genes or experience with parents cannot be determined in research with humans, but animals can be bred to have a propensity for fatness.

Another factor in the weight of children is **set point,** *the weight maintained when no effort is made to gain or lose weight.* Exercise can lower the body's set point for weight, making it much easier to maintain a lower weight. Indeed, exercise is an important aspect of helping overweight children lose weight and maintain weight loss.

A child's insulin level is another important factor in eating behavior and obesity. Judy Rodin (1984) argues that what children eat influences their insulin levels. When children eat complex carbohydrates like cereals, bread, and pasta, insulin levels go up and fall off gradually. When children consume simple sugars like candy bars and Cokes, insulin levels rise and then fall sharply—producing the sugar low with which many of us are all too familiar. Glucose levels in the blood are affected by these complex carbohydrates and simple sugars. Children are more likely to eat within the next several hours after eating simple sugars than after eating complex carbohydrates. And the food children eat at one meal influences what they will eat at the next meal. So consuming doughnuts and candy bars, in addition to providing minimal nutritional value, sets up an ongoing sequence of what and how much children crave the next time they eat.

Obesity is related to children's self-esteem. In one study, obese children in the third, fourth, and fifth grades had more negative self-concepts than average-weight children (Sallade, 1973).

What can parents do if their child is obese? A medical checkup is the first step to determine if the child has a metabolic disorder. If a metabolic disorder is present, the physician may be able to effectively treat the disorder with a revised diet or drugs. Next, parents need to ensure that the child is getting a well-balanced diet that especially includes complex carbohydrates, such as pasta, potatoes, and cereals. A regular program of physical exercise should be part of the weight loss plan. And every effort should be made to encourage children's motivation to lose weight so that they feel they are responsible for their weight loss rather than that parents have imposed the weight loss program on them and are controlling their activity (Epstein, Klein, & Wisniewski, 1994).

Exercise and Sports

How much exercise do children get? What are children's sports like?

Exercise

Many of our patterns of health and illness are long-standing. Our experiences as children contribute to our health practices as adults. Did your parents seek medical help at your first sniffle, or did they wait until your temperature reached 104 degrees? Did they feed you heavy doses of red meat and sugar or a more rounded diet with vegetables and fruit? Did they get you involved in sports or exercise programs, or did you lie around watching television all the time?

The quality of life is determined by its activities.
                                    —**Aristotle, 4th century B.C.**

Are children getting enough exercise? The 1985 School Fitness Survey tested 18,857 children aged 6 to 17 on nine fitness tasks. Compared to a similar survey in 1975, there was virtually no improvement on the tasks. For example, 40 percent of the boys 6 to 12 years of age could not do more than one pull-up, and a full 25 percent could not do any. Fifty percent of the girls aged 6 to 17 and 30 percent of the boys aged 6 to 12 could not run a mile in less than 10 minutes. In the 50-yard dash, the adolescent girls in 1975 were faster than the adolescent girls in 1985.

Some experts suggest that television is at least partially to blame for the poor physical condition of our nation's children. In one study, children who watched little television were significantly more physically fit than their heavy-television-viewing counterparts (Tucker, 1987). The more children watch television, the more they are likely to be overweight. No one is quite sure whether this is because children spend their leisure time in front of the television set instead of chasing each other around the neighborhood or whether they tend to eat a lot of junk food they see advertised on television.

Some of the blame also falls on the nation's schools, many of which fail to provide physical education classes on a daily basis. In the 1985 School Fitness Survey, 37 percent of the children in the first through the fourth grades took gym classes only once or twice a week. The investigation also revealed that parents are poor role models when it comes to physical fitness. Less than 30 percent of the parents of children in grades 1 through 4 exercised three days a week. Roughly half said they never get any vigorous exercise. In another study, observations of children's behavior in physical education classes at four elementary schools revealed how little vigorous exercise is done in these classes (Parcel & others, 1987). Children moved through space only 50 percent of the time they were in the class, and they moved continuously an average of only 2.2 minutes. In summary, not only do children's school weeks not include adequate physical education classes, but the majority of children do not exercise vigorously even when they are in such classes. Furthermore, most children's parents are poor role models for vigorous physical exercise.

Does it make a difference if we push children to exercise more vigorously in elementary school? One study says yes (Tuckman & Hinkle, 1988). One hundred fifty-four elementary school children were randomly assigned either to three 30-minute running programs per week or to regular attendance in physical education classes. Although the results sometimes varied according to sex, for the most part, the cardiovascular health as well as the creativity of children in the running program were enhanced. For example, the boys in this program had less body fat and the girls had more creative involvement in their classrooms.

In addition to the school, the family plays an important role in a child's exercise program. A wise strategy is for the family to take up activities involving vigorous physical exercise that parents and children can enjoy together. Running, swimming, cycling, and hiking are especially recommended. In encouraging children to exercise more, parents should not push them beyond their physical limits or expose them to competitive pressures that take the fun out of sports and exercise. For example, long-distance running may be too strenuous for young children and could result in bone injuries. Recently, there has been an increase in the number of children competing in strenuous athletic events such as marathons and triathalons. Doctors are beginning to see some injuries in children that they previously saw only in adults. Some injuries, such as stress fractures and tendonitis, stem from the overuse of young, still-growing bodies. If left to their own devices, how many 8-year-old children would want to prepare for a marathon? It is recommended that parents downplay cutthroat striving and encourage healthy sports that children can enjoy, a topic we discuss further in our examination of children's competitive sports.

Little league baseball, basketball, soccer, tennis, dance—as children's motor development becomes smoother and more coordinated, they are able to master these activities more competently in middle and late childhood than in early childhood.

Sports

Sports have become an increasingly integral part of American culture. Thus, it is not surprising that more and more children become involved in sports every year. Both in public schools and in community agencies, children's sports programs that involve baseball, soccer, football, basketball, swimming, gymnastics, and other activities have grown to the extent that they have changed the shape of many children's lives.

Participation in sports can have both positive and negative consequences for children. Children's participation in sports can provide exercise, opportunities to learn how to compete, increased self-esteem, and a setting for developing peer relations and friendships. However, sports also can have negative outcomes for children: too much pressure to achieve and win, physical injuries, a distraction from academic work, and unrealistic expectations for success as an athlete. Few people challenge the value of sports for children when conducted as part of a school physical education or intramural program, but some question the appropriateness of highly competitive, win-oriented sports teams in schools and communities.

There is a special concern for children in high-pressure sports settings involving championship play with accompanying media publicity. Some clinicians and child developmentalists believe such activities not only put undue stress on the participants, but also teach children the

> We are underexercised as a nation. We look instead of play. We ride instead of walk. Our existence deprives us of the minimum of physical activity essential for healthy living.
> —**John F. Kennedy, 1961**

CONCEPT TABLE 12.1

Body Changes and Health in Middle and Late Childhood

Concept	Processes/Related Ideas	Characteristics/Description
Body Changes	The skeletal and muscular systems	During the elementary school years, children grow an average of 2 to 3 inches a year. Muscle mass and strength gradually increase. Legs lengthen and trunks slim down as "baby fat" decreases. Growth is slow and consistent.
	Motor skills	During the middle and late childhood years, children's motor development becomes much smoother and more coordinated. Children gain greater control over their bodies and can sit and attend for longer frames of time. However, their lives should be activity oriented and very active. Increased myelinization of the central nervous system is reflected in improved fine motor skills. Improved fine motor development is reflected in children's handwriting skills over the course of middle and late childhood. Boys are usually better at gross motor skills, girls at fine motor skills.
Health	Children's health status and their understanding of health	Among the common ailments of the elementary school years are respiratory, dental, vision, and hearing problems. Elementary school children seem to understand that health is something that has to be worked at on a regular basis, but many of them do not adopt good health habits.
Nutrition and Children's Obesity	Their nature	In the middle and late childhood years, children's average body weight doubles. And children exert considerable energy as they engage in different motor activities. To support their growth and active lives, children need to consume more food than they did in the early childhood years. However, a special concern during the middle and late childhood years is the development of obesity. Why children become obese is complex, involving genetic inheritance, physiological mechanisms, cognitive factors, and environmental influences.
Exercise and Sports	Their nature	Every indication suggests that our nation's children are not getting enough exercise. Television viewing, parents being poor role models for exercise, and the lack of adequate physical education classes in schools may be the culprits. Children's participation in sports can have both positive and negative consequences.

wrong values—namely, a win-at-all costs philosophy. The possibility of exploiting children through highly organized, win-oriented sports programs is an ever present danger. Overly ambitious parents, coaches, and community boosters can unintentionally create a highly stressful atmosphere in children's sports. When parental, agency, or community prestige becomes the central focus of the child's participation in sports, the danger of exploitation is clearly present. Programs oriented toward such purposes often require long and arduous training sessions over many months and years, frequently leading to sports specialization at too early an age. In such circumstances, adults often transmit a distorted view of the role of the sport in the child's life, communicating to the child that the sport is the most important aspect of the child's existence.

At this point we have discussed a number of ideas about children's body changes and health during middle and late childhood. A summary of these ideas is presented in concept table 12.1. In our discussion of children's sports, we addressed the problem of increased stress that unfortunately accompanies some children's participation in organized sports. Next, we will examine more extensively the nature of stress and coping in children's development.

STRESS AND COPING

Stress is a sign of the times. No one really knows whether today's children experience more stress than their predecessors, but it does seem that their stressors have increased.

What Is Stress?

Stress is not an easy term to define. Initially the term *stress* was loosely borrowed from physics. Humans, it was thought, are in some ways similar to physical objects such as metals that resist moderate outside forces but lose their resiliency at some point of greater pressure. But, unlike metal, children can think and reason; they experience a myriad of social circumstances that make defining stress more complex in psychology than in physics.

Is stress the threats and challenges that the environment places on us (as when we say, "Sally's world is so stressful, it is overwhelming her")? Is stress our response to such threats and challenges (as when we say, "Bob is not coping well with the problems in his life; he is experiencing a lot of stress and his body is falling apart")? While there is continuing debate on whether stress is the threatening event or the response to those demands, we will define it broadly. **Stress** *is the response of individuals to the circumstances and events (called* stressors) *that threaten them and tax their coping abilities.*

Factors in Stress

What are some of the factors that contribute to stress in children? They include cognitive factors, life events and daily hassles, sociocultural factors, and personality factors.

Cognitive Factors in Stress

Most of us think of stress as environmental events that place demands on an individual's life, events such as an approaching test, being in a car wreck, or losing a friend. Although there are some common ways children and adults experience stress, not everyone perceives the same events as stressful. For example, one child may perceive an approaching test as threatening, another child may perceive it as challenging. To some degree, then, what is stressful for children depends on how they cognitively appraise and interpret events. This view has been presented most clearly by stress researcher Richard Lazarus (1993). **Cognitive appraisal** *is Lazarus' term for children's interpretations of events in their lives as harmful, threatening, or challenging, and their determination of whether they have the resources to effectively cope with the event.*

In Lazarus' view, events are appraised in two steps: primary appraisal and secondary appraisal. In **primary appraisal,** *children interpret whether an event involves harm or loss that has already occurred, a threat to some future danger, or a challenge to be overcome. Harm* is the child's appraisal of the damage the event has already inflicted. For example, if a child failed a test in school yesterday the harm has already been done. *Threat* is the child's appraisal of potential future damage an event may bring. For example, failing the test may lower the teacher's opinion of the child and increase the probability the child will get a low grade at the end of the year. *Challenge* is the child's appraisal of the potential to overcome the adverse circumstances of an event

and ultimately profit from the event. In the case of the child failing a test in school, the child may develop a commitment to never get into that situation again and become a better student.

After children cognitively appraise an event for its harm, threat, or challenge, Lazarus says they subsequently engage in secondary appraisal. In **secondary appraisal,** *children evaluate their resources and determine how effectively they can cope with the event.* This appraisal is called *secondary* because it comes after primary appraisal and depends on the degree to which the event has been appraised as harmful, threatening, or challenging. Coping involves a wide range of potential strategies, skills, and abilities for effectively managing stressful events. In the example of failing the exam, if the child learns that his or her parents will get a tutor to help him or her, then the child likely will be more confident in coping with the stress than if the parents provide no support.

Lazarus believes that a child's experience of stress is a balance of primary and secondary appraisal. When harm and threat are high, and challenge and resources are low, stress is likely to be high; when harm and threat are low, and challenge and resources are high, stress is more likely to be moderate or low.

Life Events and Daily Hassles

Children can experience a spectrum of stresses, ranging from ordinary to severe. At the ordinary end are experiences that occur in most children's lives and for which there are reasonably well-defined coping patterns. For example, most parents are aware that siblings are jealous of each other and that when one sibling does well at something the other sibling(s) will be jealous. They know how jealousy works and know ways to help children cope with it. More severe stress occurs when children become separated from their parents. Healthy coping patterns for this stressful experience are not as well spelled out. Some children are well cared for; others are ignored when there is a separation caused by divorce, death, illness, or foster placement. Even more severe are the experiences of children who have lived for years in situations of neglect or abuse (Pfeffer, 1996). Victims of incest also experience severe stress, with few coping guidelines.

Recently, psychologists have emphasized that life's daily experiences as well as life's major events may be the culprits in stress (Crnic, 1996). Enduring a tense family life and living in poverty do not show up on scales of major life events in children's development, yet the everyday pounding children take from these living conditions can add up to a highly stressful life and eventually psychological disorder or illness (Folkman & Lazarus, 1991; Pillow, Zautra, & Sandler, 1996).

Sociocultural Factors

The sociocultural factors involved in stress include acculturative stress and poverty.

To help buffer the stress in their lives, many ethnic minority groups have developed their own social structures, which include Mexican American kin systems, African American churches, Chinese American family associations, and Native American tribal associations. Shown above are members of a Chinese American family association.

Acculturative Stress **Acculturation** *is cultural change that results from continuous, firsthand contact between two distinct cultural groups.* Acculturative stress is the negative consequence of acculturation. Members of ethnic minority groups have historically encountered hostility, prejudice, and lack of effective support during crises, which contributes to alienation, social isolation, and heightened stress (Knight, Virdin, & Roosa, 1994). As upwardly mobile ethnic minority families attempt to penetrate all-White neighborhoods, interracial tensions often mount. Similarly, racial tensions and hostility often emerge among the various ethnic minorities as they each struggle for limited housing and employment opportunities, seeking a fair share of a limited market. Clashes become inevitable as Latino family markets spring up in African American urban neighborhoods; as Vietnamese extended families displace Puerto Rican apartment dwellers; as the increasing enrollment of Asian students on college campuses is perceived as a threat to affirmative action policies by other non-White ethnic minority students. Although race relations in the United States have historically been conceptualized as Black/White, this is no longer the only combination producing ethnic animosity.

As the numbers of Latinos and Asian Americans have increased dramatically, and as Native Americans have crossed the boundaries of their reservations, the visibility of these groups has brought them in contact not only with the mainstream White society, but with one another as well. Depending on the circumstances, this contact has sometimes been harmonious, sometimes antagonistic.

Although the dominant White society has tried on many occasions to enslave or dispossess entire populations, these ethnic minority groups have survived and flourished. In the face of severe stress and oppression, these ethnic minority groups have shown remarkable resilience and adaptation

(Phinney, Chavira, & Williamson, 1992). Confronted with overt or convert attempts at segregation, they have developed their own communities and social structures, which include African American churches, Vietnamese mutual assistance associations, Chinese American family associations, Japanese-language schools, American Indian "bands" and tribal associations, and Mexican American kin systems; at the same time they have learned to negotiate with the dominant White culture in America. They essentially have mastered two cultures and have developed impressive competencies and coping strategies for adapting to life in America. The resilience and adaptation shown by ethnic minority groups can teach us much about coping and survival in the face of overwhelming adversity.

Poverty In a recent report on the state of America's children, the Children's Defense Fund (1996) described what life is like for all too many children. When sixth-graders in a poverty-stricken area of St. Louis were asked to describe a perfect day, one boy said he would erase the world, then he would sit and think. Asked if he wouldn't rather go outside and play, the boy responded, "Are you kidding, out there?"

The world is dangerous and unwelcome for too many of America's children, especially those whose families, neighborhoods, and schools are low-income (Leffert & Blyth, 1996; Roberts, Jacobsen, & Taylor, 1996). Some children are resilient and cope with the challenges of poverty without any major setbacks, but too many struggle unsuccessfully. Each child of poverty who reaches adulthood unhealthy, unskilled, or alienated keeps our nation from being as competent and productive as it can be (Children's Defense Fund, 1996).

More than 20 percent of children in the United States live in poverty. This figure is about twice as high as

John W. Santrock

for other industrialized nations; for example, the child poverty rates in Canada and Sweden are about 9 percent and 2 percent, respectively.

Poverty in the United States is demarcated along ethnic lines (Huston, 1995). Almost one-half of African American children and 40 percent of Latino children live in poverty. Compared to White American children, ethnic minority children are also more likely to experience persistent poverty and to live in isolated poor urban neighborhoods where social supports are minimal and threats to positive development are abundant (Jarrett, 1995). Figure 12.3 profiles further dimensions of children's poverty in the United States.

Like their parents, children from low-income backgrounds are at high risk for experiencing mental health problems (Anderson, 1996; Chase-Lansdale & Brooks-Gunn, 1996; McLoyd & Ceballo, 1995). Social maladaptation and psychological problems, such as depression, low self-confidence, peer conflict, and juvenile delinquency, are more prevalent among poor adolescents than among economically advantaged adolescents (Gibbs & Huang, 1989).

When children from low-income backgrounds are achieving well in school, it is not unusual to find a parent or parents making special sacrifices to provide the necessary living conditions and support that contribute to school success. In one recent study, although positive times occurred in the lives of ethnically diverse young adolescents growing up in poverty, many of their negative experiences were worse than those of their middle-class counterparts (Richards & others, 1994). These adversities involved physical punishment and lack of structure at home, violence in the neighborhood, and domestic violence in their buildings.

Why are poverty rates for American children so high? Three reasons are apparent (Huston, McLoyd, & Coll, 1994): (1) Economic changes have eliminated many blue-collar jobs that paid reasonably well; (2) the percentage of children living in single-mother families has increased; and (3) government benefits declined during the 1970s and 1980s.

Personality Factors— Type A Behavior Pattern

Are there aspects of children's personality that are associated with the children's stress and health? In recent years, researchers have focused the most attention in this area on the **Type A behavior pattern,** *a cluster of characteristics— being excessively competitive, hard-driven, impatient, irritable, and hostile—thought to be related to coronary problems.* Most of the research on Type A behavior pattern has been conducted with adults (Friedman & Rosenman, 1974; Siegman & Dembrowski, 1989). Recently, researchers have examined the different components of Type A behavior to determine a more precise link with coronary risk. People who are hostile or consistently turn anger inward are more likely to develop heart disease (Williams, 1994). Hostile, angry individuals have been labeled "hot reactors,"

OUT OF 100 POOR CHILDREN IN AMERICA:

40 are White, non-Latino.
34 are African American.
22 are Latino.
5 are Asian, Pacific Islander, Native American, or Alaskan Native.

37 live in married-couple families.
59 live in female-headed families.
4 live in male-headed families.

62 live in families with at least one worker.
17 live in families with two or more workers.
22 live in families with at least one full-time, year-round worker.

45 live in central cities.
32 live in suburban areas.
24 live in rural areas.

44 live in families with incomes of less than half the poverty level ($6,962 for a family of four).

40 are younger than 6.

11 live in families headed by a person younger than 25.

FIGURE 12.3

A Profile of Poor Children in the United States

Poverty is related to threatening and uncontrollable events in children's lives. Poverty also undermines sources of social support that play a role in buffering the effects of stress.

Vonnie McLoyd (right) has conducted a number of important investigations of the roles of poverty, ethnicity, and unemployment in children's and adolescents' development. She has found that economic stressors often diminish children's and adolescents' belief in the utility of education and their achievement strivings.

meaning they have intense physiological reactions to stress—their hearts race, their breathing hurries, and their muscles tense up, all of which could contribute to heart disease. Behavioral medicine researcher Redford Williams (1994) believes everyone has the ability to control anger and develop more trust in others, which he believes reduces the risk of heart disease.

Researchers have examined the Type A behavior pattern in children and adolescents and found that Type A children and adolescents have more illnesses, cardiovascular symptoms, muscle tension, and sleep disorders (Thoresen & others, 1985). Some researchers have found that Type A children and adolescents are more likely to have Type A parents—this association is strongest for fathers and sons (Weidner & others, 1988).

When studying children, as with adults, it is important to examine which components of the Type A behavior pattern are associated more strongly than others with coronary-prone behavior and competence. In one study of 990 adolescents, the components of Type A behavior pattern that were associated with a low level of competent functioning (low self-esteem, low achievement standard, and external locus of control) were being impatient and aggressively competitive (Keltikangas-Järvinen & Raikkonen, 1990).

Children's Depression and Depressed Parents

A special concern is children who become depressed. We next evaluate some ideas about what causes children to become depressed and then study the growing interest in the effects of depressed parents on children's development.

Children's Depression

Depression is a mood disorder in which the individual is unhappy, demoralized, self-derogatory, and bored. The individual does not feel well, loses stamina easily, often has a poor appetite, is listless, and unmotivated. In childhood, the features of depression are often mixed with a broader array of behaviors than in adulthood. During childhood, aggression, school failure, anxiety, antisocial behavior, and poor peer relations are frequently associated with depression, which makes its diagnosis more difficult. Depression is more likely to occur during adolescence than childhood and is a more pervasive problem for females than for males (Petersen & Ding, 1994).

Why does depression occur in childhood? Biogenetic, cognitive, and environmental causes have been proposed. Among the views that are currently being given special attention: Bowlby's developmental, Beck's cognitive, and Seligman's learned helplessness.

John Bowlby (1989) believes that insecure attachment, a lack of love and affection in child rearing, or the actual loss of a parent in childhood leads to a negative cognitive schema. The schema that is built up during early experiences causes children to interpret later losses as yet other failures in producing enduring and close positive relationships. From Bowlby's view, early experiences, especially those involving loss, create cognitive schema that are carried forward to influence the way later experiences are interpreted. When these new experiences involve further loss, the loss precipitates depression.

In Aaron Beck's (1973) cognitive view, individuals become depressed because early in their development they acquire cognitive schema that are characterized by self-devaluation

John W. Santrock

and lack of confidence about the future. These habitual negative thoughts magnify and expand a depressed person's negative experiences. Depressed children blame themselves far more than is warranted in Beck's view. Expanding on Beck's cognitive view, developmentalist Nancy Quiggle and her colleagues (1992) presented a social information-processing view of children's depression. They argue that depressed children attend to negative cues in their environment and identify the source of negative outcomes as being within themselves.

Yet another theory of depression is **learned helplessness,** *Martin Seligman's view that when individuals are exposed to negative experiences, such as prolonged stress or pain, over which they have no control, they are likely to become depressed* (Seligman, 1975). In a reformulation of the learned helplessness view, depression follows the experience of a negative event when the individual explains the event with negative, self-blaming attributions (Abramson, Metalsky, & Alloy, 1989). This explanatory study results in the expectation that no action will control the outcome of similar events in the future, resulting in helplessness, hopelessness, passivity, and depression.

Depressed Parents

Though depression has traditionally been perceived as a problem of the individual, today we believe that this view is limited. Researchers have found an interdependence between depressed persons and their social contexts—this is especially true in the case of parents' depression and children's adjustment (Sameroff & others, 1993). Depression is a highly prevalent disorder—so prevalent it has been called the common cold of mental disorders. It occurs often in the lives of women of childbearing age—about 8 percent of these women are depressed, and about 12 percent for women who have recently given birth are depressed. As a result, large numbers of children are exposed to depressed parents.

Research on the children of depressed parents clearly documents that depression in parents is associated with problems of adjustment and disorders, especially depression, in their children (Downey & Coyne, 1990). Depressed mothers show lower rates of behavior and show constricted affect, adopt less-effortful control strategies with their children, and sometimes act hostile and negative toward them as well. In considering the effects of parental depression on children it is important to evaluate the social context of the family. For example, marital discord and stress might precede, precipitate, or co-occur with maternal depression. In such instances, it may be marital turmoil that is the key factor that contributes to children's adjustment problems, not parental depression per se.

Resilience

Even when faced with adverse conditions, such as poverty, are there characteristics of children that help to buffer them and make them resilient to negative developmental ties (Masten & Hubbard, 1995)? Norman Garmezy (1985, 1993) has studied resilience amid adversity and disadvantage for a number of years. He concludes that three factors often appear in helping children become resilient to stress, adversity, and disadvantage: (1) Reflectiveness, cognitive skills (including attention), and positive responsiveness to others; (2) families, including those in poverty, marked by warmth, cohesion, and the presence of some caring adult such as a grandparent who takes responsibility in the absence of responsive parents or in the presence of intense marital discord; and (3) the presence of some source of external support as when a strong maternal substitute in the form of a teacher, a neighbor, parents of peers, or even an institutional structure such as a caring agency or a church is available. These three factors characterized the developmental course of resilient individuals in a longitudinal study in Kuaia (Werner, 1989).

Coping

How can children cope with stress? How can they cope with death? Garmezy (1993) describes a setting in a Harlem neighborhood of New York City to illustrate resilience. In the foyer of a walkup apartment building is a large frame on the wall within the entrance way. The photographs of children who live in the apartment building are pasted on the frame with a written request that if anyone sees any of the children endangered on the street to bring them back to the apartment house. Garmezy says this is an excellent example of adult competence and concern for the safety and well-being of children.

Coping with Stress

Certain coping techniques might be used more at one developmental level than another (Brenner, 1984). For example, 3-year-old children are more likely to cope with loneliness by inventing imaginary companions than are 10-year-olds. Yet most coping mechanisms can be used effectively throughout the childhood years. As part of coping with stress, children usually call on more than one strategy at a time. For example, on the day when Brian's kitten died, he constructed a shoe box coffin for it, which he ceremonially buried in the backyard. A favorite television show helped him to keep his mind off the loss for a while, he spoke sadly of the kitten at supper, was distracted by a game of cards with his older brother, then returned to his grieving at bedtime, crying himself to sleep. Most of the time, children are not conscious of their coping strategies. They simply act without thinking when they are under stress. For example, when his brother went away to college, Kevin responded by spending hours perfecting minute details on his model airplanes. The concentration made him feel better, but he was not aware that this was a way of coping with sadness and loss.

It is important to determine whether children's coping modes are a way of avoiding or facing stress (Ebata & Moos, 1994). Strategies that allow children to go on with their lives without confronting the causes of the tension are usually believed to be more useful over the short term. Adaptations that acknowledge and accept the stress are usually believed to be more useful over the long term.

What are some of the ways children avoid stress? Denial, regression, withdrawal, and impulsive acting out are the most common responses. When children use *denial*, they act as if the stress does not exist. For example, a 7-year-old girl goes on playing with her toys while being told that her father has died. Denial can relieve pain and can help to preserve a child's equilibrium. Children also may deny by using fantasy to mask reality. For example, 3-year-old Bob constructs an imaginary friend to keep him company. When children act younger than their years and engage in earlier behaviors, they are using *regression*. For example, children may become dependent and demanding. This may lead to more physical comforting and affection than usual, thus reducing stress. *Withdrawal* is when children remove themselves either physically or mentally from the stress. They might run away from the stressful environment or become very quiet or almost invisible. To escape mentally, they might focus on their pet or lose themselves in daydreams. These efforts afford them temporary refuge from the stress. *Impulsive acting out* occurs when children act impulsively and sometimes flamboyantly to avoid thinking either of the past or of the consequences of their current actions. They conceal their pain by making others angry at them, seeking easy and quick solutions to reduce their misery. By doing so, they draw attention to themselves, and momentarily their tension is eased. However, in the long run this coping strategy is almost guaranteed to be self-destructive.

In contrast to these evasive strategies, there are ways children accept and face stress. These include altruism, humor, suppression, anticipation, and sublimation. As with the evasive strategies, each of these strategies has both positive and negative aspects. When children use *altruism*, they forget their own troubles by helping others, especially their parents and siblings. They feel good about their helper role. However, sometimes children who use altruism as a coping strategy do not let themselves be carefree. Their seriousness may push them into adultlike behavior too early in their development. Children also sometimes joke about their difficulties, using *humor* to express anger and tension. However, if this is taken to its extreme, children may lose the ability to cry and to reach out to others for help. *Suppression* allows children to set aside their tensions temporarily. For hours they may forget their cares, yet they are not afraid to go back to them when their free time is over. When a family death occurs, preschool children may unconsciously suppress the knowledge. They may cry for a while, then go and play as if nothing happened. The negative side is that children may suppress feelings to the point of denial. Children who use *anticipation* are able to foresee and plan for their next stressful episode. When the stress appears, they are better prepared to protect themselves and to accept what they cannot avoid. Anticipation can be a strong coping mechanism. It becomes negative when children become too fearful and develop compulsive needs to know and plan in rigid, overly compulsive ways. With *sublimation*, children discover ways to vent their anger, overcome their fears, or express their sadness by becoming absorbed in games, sports, or hobbies. These activities are enjoyable and compensate for their stress. Sublimation becomes negative when children become so engrossed in these activities that they ignore other pleasures or family needs.

How can parents, teachers, and helping professionals most effectively work with children in stressful circumstances? Avis Brenner (1984) proposed three intelligent strategies: removing at least one stressor; teaching new coping strategies; and showing children ways they can transfer existing coping strategies to other, more appropriate life circumstances.

Based on Michael Rutter's (1979) research on the multiple effects of stress, it makes sense that removing one stress or hassle can help children feel stronger and more competent. For example, consider Lisa, who had been coming to school hungry each morning. Her teacher arranged for Lisa to have a hot breakfast at school each morning, which improved her concentration in school. This in turn helped Lisa to suppress for a time her anxieties about her parents' impending divorce.

Children who have a number of coping techniques have the best chance of adapting and functioning competently in the face of stress. By learning new coping techniques, children might no longer feel as incompetent, and their self-confidence may improve. For example, Kim was relieved when a clinical psychologist helped her to anticipate what it would be like to visit her seriously ill sister. She had been frightened by the hospital and used withdrawal as part of her coping, saying she did not want to see her sister, even though she missed her a great deal. Children tend to apply their coping strategies only in the situations in which stress develops. Adults can show children how to use these coping skills to their best advantage in many other situations as well. For example, Jennifer used altruism to cope when her mother was hospitalized for cancer. She coped with the separation by mothering her father, her little brother, and her classmates. Her classmates quickly became annoyed with her and began to tease her. Jennifer's teacher at school recognized the problem and helped Jennifer express her altruism by taking care of the class's pet animals and by being responsible for some daily cleanup chores. Her mothering of the children stopped, and so did the teasing. By following such guidelines, both professionals and laypeople can help children cope more effectively with stress.

Coping with Death

Children who have healthy and positive relationships with their parents before a parent dies cope with the death more effectively than children with unhappy prior relationships

John W. Santrock

TABLE 12.2

Estimates of the Percentage and Number of Children with Disabilities in the United States

Handicap	% of U.S. Child Population	Number of Children, Ages 5 to 18
Visual impairment (includes blindness)	0.1	55,000
Hearing impairment (includes deafness)	0.5–0.7	275,000–385,000
Speech handicap	3.0–4.0	1,650,000–2,200,000
Orthopedic and health impairments	0.5	275,000
Emotional disorder	2.0–3.0	1,100,000–1,650,000
Mental retardation	2.0–3.0	1,100,000–1,650,000
Learning disabilities	2.0–3.0	1,100,000–1,650,000
Multiple handicaps	0.5–0.7	275,000–385,000
Total	10.6–15.0	5,830,000–8,250,000

Source: Reprinted with the permission of Macmillan College Publishing Company from *The Exceptional Student in the Regular Classroom*, 4th edition, by Bill R. Gearheart and Mel W. Weishahn. Copyright © 1988 by Macmillan College Publishing Company, Inc.

with the parent. The years of warmth and caring have probably taught the child effective ways of coping with such a traumatic event. Also, children who are given high-quality care by surviving family members during the mourning period, or who are effectively helped by care-givers in other contexts, experience less separation distress.

Sometimes the death of a sibling is even more difficult for children to understand and accept than the loss of a parent. Many children believe that only old people die, so the death of a child may stimulate children to think about their own immortality. The majority of children, though, seem to be able to cope with a sibling's death effectively if they are helped through a mourning period.

Knowing what children think about death can help adults to understand their behavior in the period following the loss of a parent or sibling. When a 3-year-old boy creeps from his bed every night and runs down the street searching for his mother who has just died, is he mourning for her? When a 6-year-old girl spends an entire afternoon drawing pictures of graveyards and coffins, is she grieving? When a 9-year-old boy can't wait to go back to school after the funeral so he can tell his classmates about how his sister died, is he denying grief? All of these are ways in which children cope with death. And all follow children's logic.

Children 3 to 5 years old think that dead people continue to live, but under changed circumstances. The missing person is simply missing, and young children expect the person to return at some point. When the person does not come back, they might feel hurt or angry at being abandoned. They might declare that they want to go to heaven to bring the dead person home. They might ask their care-givers where the dead person's house is, where the dead person eats, and why the dead person won't be cold if the person is buried without a coat and hat in winter.

Though children vary somewhat in the age at which they begin to understand death, the limitations of preoperational thought make it difficult for a child to comprehend death before the age of 7 or 8. Young children blame themselves for the death of someone they knew well, believing that the event may have happened because they disobeyed the person who died. Children under 6 rarely understand that death is universal, inevitable, and final. Instead, young children usually think that only people who want to die, or who are bad or careless, actually do die. At some point around the middle of elementary school years, children begin to grasp the concept that death is the end of life and is not reversible. They come to realize that they too will die someday.

Coping with death is a difficult circumstance for children. So is coping with a disability.

CHILDREN WITH A DISABILITY

The elementary school years are a time when children with a disability become more sensitive about their differentness and how it is perceived by others. One articulate 6-year-old described how her premature birth was the cause of her cerebral palsy: "I was a teensy-weensy baby. They put me in an incubator and I almost died." A 7-year-old physically disabled boy commented how he had successfully completed a rocket-making course during the summer: "For the first time, somebody liked me."

Life is not always fair for children with a disability. Adjusting to school and to peers is often difficult for them. Our coverage of children with special needs focuses on the number of children with a disability and their education, learning disabilities, and attention-deficit hyperactivity disorder.

Scope and Education

An estimated 10 to 15 percent of the U.S. population of children between the ages of 5 and 18 are classified as children with a disability. Table 12.2 shows the percentage and number of children with a disability in different areas.

Get together with some other students and visit several public schools to learn how they are providing individualized and appropriate programs for children with a disability. Do they have a resource room for children with a disability? What efforts are they making to involve parents? Also think about what special skills are needed to work with a child with a disability. Would you want to become a teacher of children with a disability? By evaluating different dimensions of educating children with a disability, you are learning to think critically by *making accurate observations, descriptions, and inferences about children's development.*

Public Law 94-142 *is the federal government's mandate to provide a free and appropriate education for all children. A key provision of the bill is the development of individualized education programs for children with special needs.* The individualized educational plan should meet with the approval of the child's parents, counselors, educational authorities, and, when feasible, the children themselves.

Many children with a disability are taught in the regular classroom today. This used to be called mainstreaming, but today it is more often called **inclusion,** *which refers to educating children in their natural environments, such as typical kindergarten and elementary school classrooms.* More than a decade ago it was considered appropriate to educate children with a disability outside the regular classroom. The trend today, though, is to fully include all students with a disability in the regular classroom.

Some of the education of children with a disability also often takes place in a resource room in addition to the regular classroom. The resource room is an instructional classroom for students with a disability and the professionals who work with them. The resource professional has training in working with children who have a disability. To further evaluate children with a disability, see Critical Thinking About Children's Development.

Learning Disabilities

Paula doesn't like kindergarten and can't seem to remember the names of her teacher or classmates. Bobby's third-grade teacher complains that his spelling is awful and that he is always reversing letters. Ten-year-old Tim hates to read. He says it is too hard for him and the words just don't make any sense to him. Each of these children is

learning disabled. Children with **learning disabilities** *(1) are of normal intelligence or above, (2) have difficulties in several academic areas but usually do not show deficits in others, and (3) are not suffering from some other conditions or disorders that could explain their learning problems.* The breadth of definitions of learning disabilities has generated controversy about just what learning disabilities are.

The global concept of learning disabilities includes problems in listening, thinking, memory, reading, writing, spelling, and math (Spear-Swerling & Sternberg, 1994). Attention deficits involving an inability to sit still, pay attention, and concentrate are also classified as learning disabilities. Estimates of the percentage of U.S. children who have a learning disability are as wide-ranging as the definition, ranging from 1 to 30 percent. The U.S. Department of Education reports that there are approximately 2 million such individuals in the United States between the ages of 3 and 21.

Improvement in the lives of children with a learning disability will come through (1) recognizing the complex, multifaceted nature of learning disabilities (biological, cognitive, and social aspects of learning need to be considered) and (2) becoming more precise in our analysis of the environments in which children learn (Gerber, Reiff, & Ginsberg, 1996; Kavale & Forness, 1996). The following discussion of one subtype of learning disability, attention-deficit hyperactivity disorder, provides an example of what such complexity and preciseness involve.

Attention-Deficit Hyperactivity Disorder

Matthew failed the first grade. His handwriting was messy. He did not know the alphabet and never attended very well to the lessons the teacher taught. Matthew is almost always in motion. He can't sit still for more than a few minutes at a time. His mother describes him as very fidgety. Matthew has **attention-deficit hyperactivity disorder,** *the technical term for what is commonly called hyperactivity. This disorder is characterized by a short attention span, distractibility, and high levels of physical activity.* In short, these children do not pay attention and have difficulty concentrating on what they are doing (Wodrich, 1994). Estimates of the number of children with attention-deficit hyperactivity disorder vary from less than 1 percent to 5 percent. Although young children or even infants show characteristics of this disorder, the vast majority of hyperactive children are

Public Law 94-142 mandates free, appropriate education for all children. A key provision of the bill is the development of individualized education programs for children with a disability.

What makes Jimmy so impulsive, Sandy so distractible, and Harvey so excitable? Possible causes include heredity, prenatal damage, diet, family dynamics, and the physical environment (O'Connell, 1996). As we saw in chapter 3, the influence of heredity on temperament is increasingly considered, with activity level being one aspect of temperament that differentiates one child from another very early in development. Approximately four times as many boys as girls are hyperactive. This sex difference may be due to differences in the brains of boys and girls determined by genes on the Y chromosome. The prenatal hazards we discussed in chapter 4 may also produce hyperactive behavior. Excessive drinking by women during pregnancy is associated with poor attention and concentration by their offspring at 4 years of age, for example (Streissguth & others, 1984). With regard to diet, severe vitamin deficiencies can lead to attentional problems. Vitamin B deficiencies are of special concern. Caffeine and sugar may also contribute to attentional problems.

A wide range of psychotherapies and drug therapy has been used to improve the lives of hyperactive children. For unknown reasons, some drugs that stimulate the brains and behaviors of adults have a quieting effect on the brains and behaviors of children. The drugs most widely prescribed for hyperactive children are amphetamines, especially Ritalin. Amphetamines work effectively for some hyperactive children, but not all. As many as 20 percent of hyperactive children treated with Ritalin do not respond to it. Even when Ritalin works, it is also important to consider the social world of the hyperactive child. The teacher is especially important in this social world, helping to monitor the child's academic and social behavior to determine whether the drug works and whether the prescribed dosage is correct.

identified in the first three grades of elementary school when teachers recognize that they have great difficulty paying attention, sitting still, and concentrating on their schoolwork.

At this point we have discussed a number of ideas about children's stress and about children with a disability. A summary of these ideas is presented in concept table 12.2.

CONCEPT TABLE 12.2

Stress and Children with a Disability

Concept	Processes/Related Ideas	Characteristics/Description
Stress	What is stress?	Stress is the response of individuals to the circumstances and events, called stressors, that threaten them and tax their coping abilities.
	Factors in stress	Lazarus proposed that stress depends on how individuals cognitively appraise and interpret events. Coping with stress involves primary and secondary appraisal. Both life events—such as divorce, incest, death of a parent—and daily hassles, such as living in an impoverished world, can cause stress. *Acculturation* refers to culture change that results from continuous, first-hand contact between two distinctive cultural groups. *Acculturative stress* refers to the negative consequences of acculturation. Members of ethnic minority groups have historically encountered hostility, prejudice, and lack of effective support during crises, which contribute to alienation, social isolation, and heightened stress. Poverty also imposes considerable stress on children and their families. Chronic life conditions such as inadequate housing, dangerous neighborhoods, burdensome responsibilities, and economic uncertainties are potent stresses in the lives of the poor. The incidence of poverty is especially pronounced among ethnic minority children and their families. The Type A behavior pattern is a cluster of characteristics—being excessively competitive, hard-driven, impatient, irritable, and hostile—thought to be related to coronary problems. The Type A behavior pattern is controversial among some researchers who argue that only specific components of the cluster, such as hostility, are associated with coronary risk.
	Children's depression and depressed parents	Depression is a mood disorder in which the individual is unhappy, demoralized, self-derogatory, and bored. In childhood, the features of depression are often mixed with a broader array of behaviors than in adulthood. Depression is more likely to occur in adolescence than in childhood, and is more frequent among females than males. Bowlby's developmental view, Beck's cognitive view, and Seligman's learned helplessness view are three perspectives on children's depression. Depression is especially prominent in women of childbearing age. Depression in parents is associated with problems of adjustment and disorders, especially depression, in their children. In considering the role of depressed parents in children's problems it is important to evaluate the social context of the family, especially marital discord.
	Resilience	Garmezy concludes that three sets of characteristics are reflected in the lives of children who show resilience amidst adversity and disadvantage: (1) temperament factors; (2) families marked by warmth, cohesion, and the presence of a caring adult; and (3) the presence of some source of external support.
	Coping	Avoiding stress is wiser as a short-term strategy than as a long-term strategy. Avoiding stress can be accomplished by denial, regression, withdrawal, and impulsive acting out. Accepting and facing stress include altruism, humor, suppression, anticipation, and sublimation. Adults can help children deal with stress by removing at least one stressor, teaching new coping strategies, and showing the children how to transfer feelings of stress to other circumstances. A positive close relationship with a parent before the death of the parent and high-quality care by surviving individuals help a child to cope. Young children do not understand the nature of death, believing that it is not final. By the middle of the elementary school years, they comprehend its final, irreversible nature.
Children with a Disability	Scope and education	An estimated 10 to 15 percent of the U.S. population of children from 5 to 18 years old are classified as children with a disability. Public Law 94-142 mandates a free and appropriate education for all children. A key provision for children with special needs is an individualized education program. The term *inclusion,* which refers to educating children in their natural environments, is replacing the term *mainstreaming.* Many children with a disability are also taught in a resource room in addition to the regular classroom.
	Learning disabilities	Children with a learning disability have normal or above-normal intelligence, have difficulties in some areas but not others, and do not suffer from some other disorder that could explain their learning problems. Learning disabilities are complex and multifaceted, and require precise analysis.
	Attention-deficit hyperactivity disorder	This is the technical term for what is commonly called hyperactivity. This disorder is characterized by a short attention span, distractibility, and high levels of physical activity. Possible causes include heredity, prenatal damage, diet, family dynamics, and physical environment. Amphetamines have been used with some success in treatment, but they do not work with all hyperactive children.

John W. Santrock

I n middle and late childhood, healthy and competent children lead active lives. Their physical skills become more rhythmic and smoothly coordinated than they were in early childhood.

We began this chapter by reading about the training of future Olympians in the sports schools of China, then chronicled the body changes of middle and late childhood—those involving the skeletal and muscular system, and motor skills. Our coverage of children's health focused on their health status, understanding of health, nutrition and obesity, exercise, and sports. We studied children's stress and coping by evaluating what stress is, cognitive factors, sociocultural factors, personality factors, children's depression and depressed parents, resilience, coping with stress, and coping with death. We discussed children with a disability by examining the scope and education of these children, learning disabilities, and attention-deficit hyperactivity disorder.

Remember that you can obtain an overall summary of the chapter by again studying the two concept tables on pages 360 and 370. In the next chapter, we turn our attention to children's cognitive development in middle and late childhood.

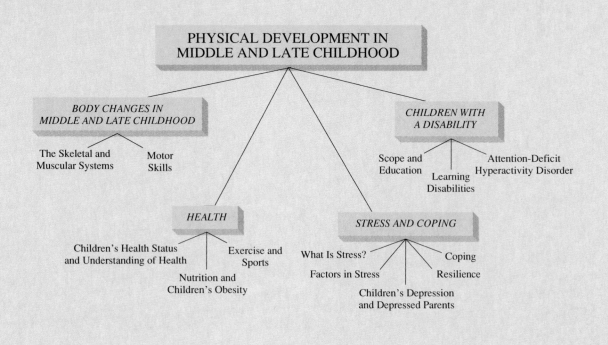

PHYSICAL DEVELOPMENT IN MIDDLE AND LATE CHILDHOOD

BODY CHANGES IN MIDDLE AND LATE CHILDHOOD

The Skeletal and Muscular Systems

Motor Skills

CHILDREN WITH A DISABILITY

Scope and Education

Learning Disabilities

Attention-Deficit Hyperactivity Disorder

HEALTH

Children's Health Status and Understanding of Health

Nutrition and Children's Obesity

Exercise and Sports

STRESS AND COPING

What Is Stress?

Factors in Stress

Children's Depression and Depressed Parents

Coping

Resilience

obesity Weighing 20 percent or more above the ideal weight for a particular age and sex.   358

set point The weight maintained when no effort is made to lose or gain weight.   358

stress The response of individuals to circumstances and events, called stressors, that threaten or tax an individual's coping ability.   361

cognitive appraisal Lazarus' term for children's interpretations of events in their lives as harmful, threatening, or challenging, and their determination of whether they have the resources to effectively cope with the event.   361

primary appraisal Determining whether an event involves harm or loss that has already occurred, a threat of some future danger, or a challenge to be overcome.   361

secondary appraisal Children's evaluating their resources and determining how effectively they can be used to cope with the event.   361

acculturation Cultural change that results from continuous, firsthand contact between two distinctive cultural groups.   362

Type A behavior pattern A cluster of characteristics (being excessively competitive, hard-driven, impatient, irritable, and hostile) thought to be related to coronary problems.   363

depression A mood disorder in which the individual is unhappy, demoralized, self-derogatory, and bored. The individual does not feel well, loses stamina easily, often has a poor appetite, is listless, and unmotivated.   364

learned helplessness Seligman's term for the development of depression in individuals who are exposed to prolonged negative experiences over which they have no control.   365

Public Law 94-142 The federal government's mandate that all children must be given a free and appropriate education. A key provision of the bill is the development of individualized education programs for children with special needs.   368

inclusion Educating children in their natural environments, such as typical kindergarten and elementary school classrooms.   368

learning disabilities Disabilities in which individuals with normal intelligence are having academic difficulties in several areas but are not suffering from an overt condition that explains their difficulty.   368

attention-deficit hyperactivity disorder A disorder characterized by a short attention span, distractibility, and high levels of physical activity; also called hyperactivity.   368

To Listen to a Child
(1984) by T. Berry Brazelton.
Reading, MA: Addison-Wesley.

The focus in *To Listen to a Child* is primarily on problematic events that arise in the lives of children. Fears, feeding, sleeping problems, stomachaches, and asthma are among the normal problems of growing that Brazelton evaluates. He assures parents that it is only when parents let their own anxieties interfere that these problems (such as bed-wetting) become chronic and guilt-laden. Each chapter closes with practical guidelines for parents. A final chapter focuses on the hospitalized child, including how to prepare the child for a hospital stay and how to interact with the child at the hospital.

To Listen to a Child includes clearly explained examples and is warm, personal, and entertaining. It is a good resource book for parents to hold on to as their child ages through the childhood years and to consult when physical problems develop.

Kid Fitness
(1992) by Kenneth Cooper.
New York: Random House.

Author Kenneth Cooper developed the concept of aerobic fitness. In this book he adapts his ideas that have helped millions of adults become more physically fit to children. Cooper describes a total program of diet and exercise designed to improve children's physical fitness and foster healthy eating habits.

Customized programs are presented for children of all fitness levels from the physically unfit to the average child to the athletically gifted. The book includes a comprehensive checklist of tests to help gauge the child's level of physical fitness. Standard fitness levels for children and adolescents from 5 to 16+ are provided. This is an excellent book for improving children's physical fitness and eating habits.

Helping Children Grieve
(1991) by Theresa Huntley.
Minneapolis, MN: Augsburg Press.

Helping Children Grieve addresses how to help children cope with either their own death or the death of a loved one. The author presents a developmental approach to helping children cope with death, focusing on the 3 to 7, 6 to 10, 10 to 12, and early and late adolescent periods. Advice is given on how to talk about death with children and common behaviors and feelings children show when faced with death. Among these common reactions are denial, panic, anger, guilt, regression, hyperactivity, and withdrawal. Adults are encouraged to get children to ask questions about death, and to answer those questions as honestly as possible. Fears of the dying child are covered, as are ways to care for the dying child's basic needs.

IMPROVING THE LIVES OF CHILDREN

Improving the lives of children involves adopting family-centered and culture-centered approaches in working with a disabled child, developing appropriate parenting strategies in children's sports, creating better health education programs in schools, making a difference in the lives of children in poverty, and decreasing the feminization of poverty.

HEALTH AND WELL-BEING

Family-Centered and Culture-Centered Approaches to Working with a Disabled Child

Best practices in service delivery to children who are disabled or at risk for disabilities are moving toward a family-focused or family-centered approach (Lynch & Hanson, 1993). This approach emphasizes the importance of partnerships between parents and disability professionals and shared decision making in assessment, intervention, and evaluation. It also underscores the belief that services for children must be offered in the context of the entire family and that the entire family system is the partner and the client, not just the child (Lyytinen & others, 1994).

At the same time as services are becoming more family focused, the families served by many intervention programs are becoming increasingly diverse. Many families are characterized by attitudes, beliefs, values, customs, languages, and behaviors that are unfamiliar to interventionists. It is not uncommon for interventionists in some locations to work with families from as many as ten different cultures or more. In a large school district, as many as fifty languages may be spoken.

Who are these interventionists who work with children who have a disability or are at risk for one? They include educators, nurses, speech and language specialists, audiologists, occupational and physical therapists, physicians, social workers, and psychologists. Regardless of the agency, program, service, setting, or professional discipline, having the attitudes and skills that facilitate effective cross-cultural interactions is needed for competent intervention.

Ideally, families in need of services for their children receive assistance from professionals who are knowledgeable and competent in their discipline, who speak the same language as family members, and have the ability to establish rapport and work in partnership with family members to implement interventions for the child and family. However, the current match between many professionals and the families whom they serve is not perfect. This does not mean, though, that families cannot receive high-quality assistance. It simply means that interventionists need to be especially sensitive to the importance of developing cross-cultural competence and learning how to respond in sensitive and appropriate ways.

FAMILIES AND PARENTING

Parents and Children's Sports

Most sports psychologists believe it is important for parents to show an interest in their children's sports participation. Most children want their parents to watch them perform in sports. Many children whose parents do not come to watch them play in sporting events feel that their parents do not adequately support them. However, some children become extremely nervous when their parents watch them perform, or get embarrassed when their parents cheer too loudly or make a fuss. If children request that their parents not watch them perform, parents should respect their children's wishes (Schreiber, 1990).

Parents should compliment their children for their sports performance. In

Children's participation in sports can have both positive and negative consequences. On the positive side, sports can provide children with exercise, opportunities to learn how to compete, increased self-esteem, and a setting for developing peer relations and friendships. However, on the negative side, sports sometimes involves too much pressure to achieve and win, physical injuries, distractions from academic work, and unrealistic expectations for success as an athlete.

the course of a game there are dozens of circumstances when the child has done something positive—parents should stress a child's good performance, even if the child has limited abilities. Parents can tell their children how much the children hustled in the game and how enthusiastically they played. Even if the child strikes out in a baseball game, a parent can say, "That was a nice swing."

One of the hardest things for parents to do is to watch their children practicing or performing at a sport without helping them, to let their children make mistakes without interfering. Former Olympic swimmer Donna de Varona commented that the best way parents can help children in sports is to let them get to know themselves, and the only way they can do this is by having experiences in life. Naturally parents want to provide their children with support and encouragement, but there is a point at which parental involvement becomes overinvolvement.

I (your author) have coached a number of young tennis players and seen many parents who handled their roles as a nurturant, considerate parent well, but observed others who became overinvolved in their children's sport. Some parents were aware of their tendency to become overinvolved and backed off from pushing their children too intensely. However, some were not aware of their overintrusiveness and did not back off. The worst parent I had to deal with had a daughter who, at the age of 9, was already nationally ranked and showed great promise. Her father went to every lesson, every practice session, every tournament. Her tennis began to consume *his* life. At one tournament, he stormed onto the court during one of her matches and accused his daughter's 10-year-old opponent of cheating, embarrassing his daughter and himself. I called him the next day, told him I no longer could coach his daughter because of his behavior, and recommended that he seek counseling or not go to any more of her matches.

If parents do not become overinvolved, they can help their children build their physical skills and help them emotionally—discussing with them how to deal with a difficult coach, how to cope with a tough loss, and how to put in perspective a poorly played game. Parents need to carefully monitor their children as they participate in sports for signs of developing stress. If the problems appear to be beyond the intuitive skills of a volunteer coach or a parent, a consultation with a counselor or clinician may be needed. Also, the parent needs to be sensitive to whether the sport in which the child is participating is the best one for the child and whether the child can handle its competitive pressures.

Some guidelines provided by the Women's Sports Foundation in its booklet *Parent's Guide to Girls' Sports* can benefit both parents and coaches of all children in sports:

The Dos

Make sports fun; the more children enjoy sports, the more they will want to play.

Remember that it is OK for children to make mistakes; it means they are trying.

Allow children to ask questions about the sport and discuss the sport in a calm, supportive manner.

Show respect for the child's sports participation.

Be positive and convince the child that he or she is making a good effort.

Be a positive role model for the child in sports.

The Don'ts

Yell or scream at the child.

Condemn the child for poor play or continue to bring up failures long after they happen.

Point out the child's errors in front of others.

Expect the child to learn something immediately.

Expect the child to become a pro.

Ridicule or make fun of the child.

Compare the child to siblings or to more talented children.

Make sports all work and no fun.

EDUCATION

A Model School Health Program: Heart Smart

Exercise is an important component in the Bogalusa Heart Study, a large-scale investigation of children's health that involves an ongoing evaluation of 8,000 boys and girls in Bogalusa, Louisiana (Nicklas & others, 1995). Observations show that the precursors of heart disease begin at a young age, with many children already possessing one or more clinical risk factors, such as hypertension or obesity. Based on the Bogalusa Heart Study, a cardiovascular health intervention model for children has been developed. The model is called "Heart Smart."

The school is the focus of the Heart Smart intervention. Since 95 percent of children and adolescents aged 5 to 18 are in school, schools are an efficient context in which to educate individuals about health. Special attention is given to teachers, who serve as role models. Teachers who value the role of health in life and who engage in health-enhancing behavior present children and adolescents with positive models for health. Teacher in-service education is conducted by an interdisciplinary team of

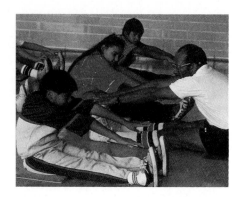

A gymnastics class for third and fourth grades at the Govalle School in Austin, Texas. One of the most important components of heart disease prevention programs is regular, vigorous exercise.

specialists, including physicians, psychologists, nutritionists, physical educators, and exercise physiologists. The school's staff is introduced to heart health education, the nature of cardiovascular disease, and risk factors for heart disease. Coping behavior, exercise behavior, and eating behavior are discussed with the staff, and a Heart Smart curriculum is explained. For example, the Heart Smart curriculum for grade 5 includes the content areas of cardiovascular health (such as risk factors associated with heart disease), behavior skills (for example, self-assessment and monitoring), eating behavior (for example, the effects of food on health), and exercise behavior (for example, the effects of exercise on the heart).

The physical education component of Heart Smart involves two to four class periods each week to incorporate a "Superkids-Superfit" exercise program. The physical education instructor teaches skills required by the school system plus aerobic activities aimed at cardiovascular conditioning, including jogging, racewalking, interval workouts, rope skipping, circuit training, aerobic dance, and games. Classes begin and end with 5 minutes of walking and stretching.

The school lunch program serves as an intervention site, where sodium, fat, and sugar levels are decreased. Children and adolescents are given reasons why they should eat healthy foods, such as a tuna sandwich, and why they should not eat unhealthy foods, such as a hot dog with chili. The school lunch program includes a salad bar, where children and adolescents can serve themselves. The amount and type of snack foods sold on the school premises is monitored.

High-risk children—those with elevated blood pressure, cholesterol, and weight—are identified as part of Heart Smart. A multidisciplinary team of physicians, nutritionists, nurses, and behavioral counselors work with the high-risk boys and girls and their parents through group-oriented activities and individual-based family counseling. High-risk boys and girls and their parents receive diet, exercise, and relaxation prescriptions in an intensive 12-session program, followed by long-term monthly evaluations.

Extensive assessment is a part of this ongoing program. Short-term and long-term changes in children's knowledge about cardiovascular disease and changes in their behavior are assessed.

In the most recent analysis of the Bogalusa Heart Study, more than half of the children exceed the recommended intake of salt, fat, cholesterol, and sugar (Nicklas & others, 1995). Families with a history of heart disease have children with more risk factors than other families. Also, African American children have hormonal and renal factors that predispose them to develop hypertension.

Other school health programs that are currently being evaluated include the Minnesota Heart Health Program (Kelder & others, 1995) and the Southwest Cardiovascular Curriculum Project (Davis & others, 1995).

CULTURE AND ETHNICITY

Making a Difference in North Philadelphia: Madeline Cartwright

Madeline Cartwright was formerly the principal of the James G. Blaine public school in a neighborhood enshrouded in poverty and rocked by violence. Cartwright became the principal of Blaine school in 1979. She grew up in Pittsburgh's poor Hill District, and she was determined to make a difference in north Philadelphia, one of America's most drug-ridden, devastated inner-city areas.

One of the first things Cartwright did when she became principal was to install a washer and dryer in the school's kitchen, where each morning she and her staff personally washed much of the children's clothing. A Philadelphia chemical company provided her with free soap powder. Cartwright said this is the only way many of the children in her school will know what it is like to have clean clothes. She is proud that

the kids in her school "looked good and had clean clothes," and she knows it made them feel better about themselves.

The most important thing Cartwright did when she became the principal was to, as she said, "browbeat" parents into getting involved in the school. She told them that she came from the same circumstances they did and that, here at Blaine school, the children were going to get a better education and have a better life than most children who attended her elementary school when she was growing up. But she told the parents that this was only going to happen if they worked with her and became partners with the school in educating and socializing the children.

When she came to Blaine school, she told the parents, "This place is dirty! How can your kids go to school in a

Madeline Cartwright (above) is an elementary school principal who has made a powerful difference in many impoverished children's lives. Especially important is Cartwright's persistence and persuasiveness in getting parents more involved in their children's education.

place like this!" One of the parents commented, "You must think you are in the suburbs." The parent expected the neighborhood and the school to be dirty. Cartwright told the parent, "The dirt in the suburbs is the same as the dirt in North Philadelphia—if you don't *move* it. And the same detergents work here." Cartwright rounded up eighteen parents and scrubbed the building until it was clean.

Blaine school's auditorium overflowed with parents when parent meetings were scheduled. Cartwright made children bring their parents to the meetings. She told the children, "Your parents need to know what we are doing in school." She gave the children a doughnut or a pretzel the next day if one of their parents came. She told the parents they could come to her if they had problems—that she could direct them to places and people who would help them solve their problems. Because of Cartwright's efforts, parents now feel comfortable at Blaine school.

Cartwright believes that a very important aspect of intervening in children's lives who come from low-income families is increasing the positive role models they see and with whom they can interact. She wants the state of Pennsylvania to set up "mentor houses," into which salvageable families can be moved. These vacant houses are located in better neighborhoods and a family with positive values is appointed or paid to be a mentor or role model for the family. Says Cartwright, "I would like to be a mentor."

Some people would say that Cartwright's dreams are naive, but maybe not. One safe and clean school, one set of clean clothes, one clean toilet, one safe house—and then another safe school, and another, and another. Concludes Cartwright, "I'm telling you; there are things you can do!" (Louv, 1990).

GENDER

Gender, Stress, and the Feminization of Poverty

Although fathers are becoming increasingly involved as caregivers for children, mothers at home and women outside the home (in day care and schools) are still the adults who interact with children the most on a daily basis. How much stress the caregivers experience, how they cope with it, and their health affects their ability to effectively rear children.

When women go to work outside the home and take on demanding jobs, how does it affect their stress and health? In almost all studies, employed women are healthier than nonemployed women. Women who stay at home and who perceive their lives as stressful and unhappy, who feel extremely vulnerable, and who engage in little physical activity or exercise are especially at risk for health problems. However, figuring out the causality in these associations is like the old chicken-and-egg question. It may be that employment directly promotes health and reduces risk for women, or it may be that women in poor health are unable to obtain or keep jobs.

Women and men have always had multiple roles, but women experience more conflict between roles and overload than men do (McBride, 1990). An important difference in women and men is women's family responsibilities. Even when both spouses work, wives perform a disproportionate share of child care and household tasks. In spite of all the strain, though, the more roles women juggle, the healthier they seem to be. Women who take on varied roles benefit from the new sources of self-esteem, control, and social support, which in turn may improve both their mental and physical health (Rodin & Ickovics, 1990).

The nature and quality of a woman's experiences within a role are also important considerations in understanding her stress and health. Roles with time constraints, irregular schedules, and little autonomy, such as a factory worker, may jeopardize health. Female clerical workers, in particular, are especially prone to health problems, such as eye strain and back pains. However, contrary to the belief that a high-powered career is more stressful to a woman's well-being, the more authority and autonomy a woman has on the job, the greater her sense of well-being (Verbrugge, 1987).

Earlier in our discussion of social class and stress, we found that poverty is associated with increased stress and poor health. Women are disproportionately among the poor. What's more, poor women face the double jeopardy of poverty and sexism. For example, women are paid less than men and, at the same time, may be denied opportunities to work because of their sex. The term *feminization of poverty* refers to the fact that far more women than men live in poverty. Women's low income, divorce, and disadvantaged status in the resolution of divorce cases by the judicial system—which leave women with less money than they and their children need to adequately function—are the likely causes of the feminization of poverty. Approximately one of every two marriages will end in a divorce, meaning that far more women today than in the past must support themselves and, in many cases, one or more children as well. Further, women today are far less likely to receive alimony or spousal support than in the past. Even when alimony or child-support payments are awarded to a woman, they are poorly enforced. An important agenda is to pay more attention to the physical and mental health risks that poverty heaps on women, how that burden affects children's development, and what can be done about it.

PAUL KLEE
The Gifted Boy, detail

Cognitive Development
in Middle and Late Childhood

*The thirst to know and understand . . .
these are the goods in life's rich hand.*

—Sir William Watson, 1905

> *Children are remarkable for their intelligence and ardor, for their curiosity, their intolerance of shams, the clarity . . . of their vision.*
>
> —Aldous Huxley

IMAGES OF CHILDREN

Children's Intelligence and IQ Tests

Intelligence and intelligence tests frequently make the news. The following story appeared in the *Los Angeles Times*:

> IQ testing that leads to the placement of an unusually large number of Black children in so-called mentally retarded classes has been ruled unconstitutional by a federal judge. On behalf of five Black children, Chief District Court Judge Robert Peckham said the use of standardized IQ tests to place children in educable mentally retarded (EMR) classes violated recently enacted federal laws and the state and federal constitutions. . . . Peckham said the history of IQ testing and special education in California "revealed an unlawful discriminatory intent . . . not necessarily to hurt Black children, but it was an intent to assign a grossly disproportionate number of Black children to the special, inferior and dead-end EMR classes." (October 18, 1979)

As you might expect, this story sparked impassioned debate. The use of IQ tests to selectively place children in special classes continues to be debated.

Robert Sternberg recalls being terrified of taking IQ tests as a child. He says that he froze when the time came to take such tests. When he was in the sixth grade, he was sent to take an IQ test with the fifth-graders; he still talks about how embarrassing and humiliating the experience was. Sternberg recalls that maybe he was dumb, but knows that he wasn't *that* dumb. He finally overcame his anxieties about IQ tests and performed much better on them. Sternberg became so fascinated with IQ tests that he devised his own at the age of 13 and began assessing the intellectual abilities of his classmates until the school psychologist scolded him. Later in the chapter, you will see that Sternberg recently has developed a provocative theory of intelligence.

PREVIEW

Intellectual performance and achievement are prized by our society and promoted by parents who enthusiastically encourage their charges to become brighter and achieve more. In middle and late childhood, children became more aware of the push for intellectual competence and achievement than earlier in their development. Now, they spend far more time in the achievement setting of school and are placed in circumstances that require them to display their intellectual skills under more pressure than they were under in early childhood. Our coverage of children's cognitive development in middle and late childhood focuses on Piaget's theory and concrete operational thought, Piaget's contributions, criticisms, and neo-Piagetian theory, information processing, intelligence, language, achievement, and computers.

COGNITION

How does children's cognition—their mental processes, such as thinking, reasoning, and memory—change during middle and late childhood? To answer this question, we will explore three dimensions of cognition—Piaget's theory and concrete operational thought, information processing, and intelligence.

Piaget's Theory

According to Piaget (1967), the preschool child's thought is preoperational. Preoperational thought involves the formation of stable concepts, the emergence of mental reasoning, the prominence of egocentrism, and the construction of magical belief systems. Thought during the preschool years is still flawed and not well organized. Piaget believed that concrete operational thought does not appear until about the age of 7, but as we learned in chapter 10, Piaget may have underestimated some of the cognitive skills of preschool children. For example, by carefully and cleverly designing experiments on understanding the concept of number, Rochel Gelman (1972) demonstrated that some preschool children show conservation, a concrete operational skill. In chapter 10, we explored concrete operational thought by describing the preschool child's flaws in thinking about such concrete operational skills as conservation and classification; here we will cover the characteristics of concrete operational thought again, this time emphasizing the competencies of elementary schoolchildren. We will also consider applications of Piaget's ideas to children's education and an evaluation of Piaget's theory.

Concrete Operational Thought

Remember that, according to Piaget, concrete operational thought is made up of operations—mental actions that allow children to do mentally what they had done physically before. Concrete operations are also mental actions that are reversible. In the well-known test of reversibility of thought involving conservation of matter, the child is presented with two identical balls of clay. The experimenter rolls one ball into a long, thin shape; the other remains in its original ball shape. The child is then asked if there is more clay in the ball or in the long, thin piece of clay. By the time children reach the age of 7 or 8, most answer that the amount of clay is the same. To answer this problem correctly, children have to imagine that the clay ball is rolled out into a long, thin strip and then returned to its original round shape. This type of imagination involves a reversible mental action. Thus, a concrete operation is a reversible mental action on real, concrete objects. Concrete operations allow the child to coordinate several characteristics rather than focus on a single property of an object. In the clay example, the preoperational child is likely to focus on height *or* width. The concrete operational child coordinates information about both dimensions.

Many of the concrete operations identified by Piaget focus on the way children reason about the properties of objects. One important skills that characterizes the concrete operational child is the ability to classify or divide things into different sets or subsets and to consider their interrelationships. An example of the concrete operational child's classification skills involves a family tree of four generations (see figure 13.1). (Furth & Wachs, 1975). This

Piaget was especially intrigued with the points of transition in development as children improve in their ability to understand principles in the physical world. For example, when on a trip with the family that involves crossing the "state line," preoperational children will literally expect a line to be observable on the ground. They discover that the line is an abstract concept rather than a real physical descriptor. Can you think of examples from your past or from your interactions with children that could also illustrate a shift from the preoperational to the concrete operational stages? For example, consider childhood superstitions or cultural rituals that involve magical forces. By evaluating transitions in Piaget's stages, you are learning to think critically by *applying a developmental perspective to understand behavior.*

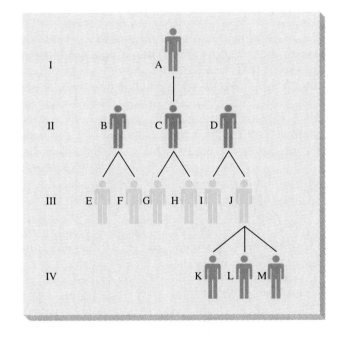

FIGURE 13.1

Classification: An Important Ability in Concrete Operational Thought
A family tree of four generations (*I to IV*): The preoperational child has trouble classifying the members of the four generations; the concrete operational child can classify the members vertically, horizontally, and obliquely (up and down and across). For example, the concrete operational child understands that a family member can be a son, a brother, and father all at the same time.

| Can use operations, mentally reversing action; shows conservation skills | Logical reasoning replaces intuitive reasoning, but only in concrete circumstances | Not abstract (can't imagine steps in algebraic equation, for example) | Classification skills—can divide things into sets and subsets and reason about their interrelations |

FIGURE 13.2

Characteristics of Concrete Operational Thought

family tree suggests that the grandfather (A) has three children (B, C, & D), each of whom has two children (E through J), and that one of these children (J) has three children (K, L, & M). A child who comprehends the classification system can move up and down a level (vertically), across a level (horizontally), and up and down and across (obliquely) within the system. The concrete operational child understands that person J can at the same time be father, brother, and grandson, for example. A summary of concrete operational thought's characteristics is shown in figure 13.2. To further evaluate Piaget's stages, see Critical Thinking About Children's Development.

Piaget and Education

Piaget was not an educator and never pretended to be. But he did provide a sound conceptual framework from which to view educational problems. What are some of the principles in Piaget's theory of cognitive development that can be applied to children's education? David Elkind (1976) described three. First, the foremost issue in education is *communication*. In Piaget's theory, the child's mind is not a blank slate; to the contrary, the child has a host of ideas about the physical and natural world, but these ideas differ from those of adults. We must learn to comprehend what children are saying and to respond in the same mode of discourse that children use. Second, the child is always unlearning and relearning in addition to acquiring knowledge. Children come to school with their own ideas about space, time, causality, quantity, and number. Third, the child is by nature a knowing creature,

motivated to acquire knowledge. The best way to nurture this motivation for knowledge is to allow the child to spontaneously interact with the environment; education needs to ensure that it does not dull the child's eagerness to know by providing an overly rigid curriculum that disrupts the child's own rhythm and pace of learning.

Piagetian Contributions and Criticisms

We have spent considerable time outlining Piaget's theory of cognitive development in chapters 2, 7, 10, and this chapter, 13. Let's briefly summarize some of Piaget's main contributions, and then enumerate criticisms of his theory.

Contributions   We owe Piaget the present field of cognitive development. We owe him a long list of masterful concepts of enduring power and fascination, such as object permanence, conservation, assimilation, and accommodation. We also owe Piaget the currently accepted vision of children as active, constructive thinkers who, through their commerce with the environment, make them manufacturers of their own development (Flavell, 1992; Lourenco & Machado, 1996).

Piaget was a genius when it came to observing children; his astute observations showed us inventive ways to discover how children, and even infants, act on and adapt to their world. Piaget showed us some important things to look for in children's cognitive development, including the shift from preoperational to concrete operational thought. He also showed us how we must make experiences fit our cognitive framework, yet simultaneously adapt our cognitive orientation to experience. Piaget also revealed how cognitive change is likely to occur if the situation is structured to allow gradual movement to the next higher level.

Criticisms   Piaget's theory has not gone unchallenged, however. Questions are raised about the following areas: estimates of the child's competence at different developmental levels; stages; training of children to reason at higher levels; and culture and education.

Estimates of Children's Competence   Some cognitive abilities emerge earlier than Piaget thought, and their subsequent development is more prolonged than he believed. As we saw earlier in the chapter, some aspects of object permanence merge much earlier in infancy than Piaget believed. Even 2-year-olds are nonegocentric in some

Piaget is shown sitting on a bench observing children. Piaget was a genius at observing children. By carefully observing and interviewing children, he constructed a comprehensive theory of children's cognitive development.

contexts—when they realize that another person will not see an object, they see if the person is blindfolded or is looking in a different direction. Conservation of number has been demonstrated in children as young as 3 years of age, although Piaget did not think it came about until 7 years of age. Young children are not as "pre" this and "pre" that (precausal, preoperational) as Piaget thought. Some aspects of formal operational thinking that involve abstract reasoning do not consistently emerge in early adolescence as Piaget envisioned. And adults often reason in far more irrational ways than Piaget believed (Siegler, 1995). In sum, recent trends highlight the cognitive competencies of infants and young children and the cognitive shortcomings of adolescents and adults.

Stages Piaget conceived of stages as unitary structures of thought, so his theory assumes synchrony in development. That is, various aspects of a stage should emerge at about the same time. However, several concrete and operational concepts do not appear in synchrony. For example, children do not learn to conserve at the same time as they learn to cross-classify.

Most contemporary developmentalists agree that children's cognitive development is not as grand-stage-like as Piaget thought. **Neo-Piagetians** *are developmentalists who have elaborated on Piaget's theory, believing children's cognitive*

development is more specific in many respects than he thought. Neo-Piagetians don't believe that all of Piaget's ideas should be junked. They argue, however, that a more accurate vision of the child's cognitive development involves fewer references to grand stages and more emphasis on the roles of strategies, skills, how fast and automatically children can process information, the task-specific nature of children's cognition, and the importance of dividing cognitive problems into smaller, more precise steps (Case, 1987).

Neo-Piagetians still believe that children's cognitive development has some general properties (Flavell, 1992). They stress that there is a regular, maturation-based increase with age in some aspects of the child's information-processing capacity, such as how fast or efficiently the child processes information. As the child's information-processing capacity increases with increasing age, new and more complex forms of cognition in all content domains are possible because the child can now hold more information in mind and think about more things at once. For example, Canadian developmentalist Robbie Case argues that adolescents have increasingly more available cognitive resources than they did as children because they can process information more automatically, they have more information-processing capacity, and they are more familiar with a range of content knowledge.

Training Children to Reason at a Higher Level Some children who are at one cognitive stage, such as preoperational thought, can be trained to reason at a higher cognitive stage, such as concrete operational thought. This poses a problem for Piaget, who argued that such training works only on a superficial level and is ineffective unless the child is at a transitional point from one stage to the next.

Culture and Education Culture and education exert stronger influences on children's development than Piaget believed (Gelman & Brenneman, 1994). The age at which individuals acquire conservation skills is associated to some extent with the degree to which their culture provides relevant practice. And in many developing countries, formal operational thought is a rare occurrence. In chapter 10, we learned about the wave of interest in how the child's cognitive development progresses through interaction with skilled adults and peers, and how children's embeddedness in a culture influences their cognitive growth. Such views, advocated by Vygotsky and his followers, stand in stark contrast to Piaget's view of the child as a solitary young scientist.

Information Processing

Among the highlights of changes in information processing during middle and late childhood are improvements in memory, schemas, scripts, and scientific thinking. Remember also, from chapter 8, that the attention of most children improves dramatically during middle and late childhood, and that at this time children attend more to the task-relevant features of a problem than to the salient features.

An outstanding teacher and education in the logic of science and mathematics are important cultural experiences that promote the development of operational thought. Schooling and education likely play more important roles in the development of operational thought than Piaget envisioned.

> *Our life is what our thoughts make it.*
> —Marcus Aurelius, *Meditations,* 2nd Century B.C.

Memory

In chapter 10, we concluded that short-term memory increases considerably during early childhood, but after the age of 7 does not show as much increase. Is the same pattern found for **long-term memory**, *a relatively permanent and unlimited type of memory?* Long-term memory increases with age during middle and late childhood. Two aspects of memory related to improvement in long-term memory are control processes and learner characteristics.

If we know anything at all about long-term memory, it is that long-term memory depends on the learning activities individuals engage in when learning and remembering information (Inton-Peterson, 1996; Pressley, 1996). **Control processes** *are cognitive processes that do not occur automatically but require work and effort. They are under the learner's conscious control and they can be used to improve memory. They are also appropriately called strategies.* Three important control processes involved in children's memory are rehearsal, organization, and imagery.

Rehearsal is a control process that improves memory. It is the repetition of information after it has been presented. An example of rehearsal occurs when children hear a phone number, then repeat the number several times to improve their memory of it. Children's spontaneous use of rehearsal increases between 5 and 10 years of age. The use of *organization* also improves memory. As with rehearsal, children in middle and late childhood are more likely to spontaneously organize information to be remembered than are children in early childhood.

Another control process that develops as children move through middle and late childhood is *imagery.* A powerful imagery strategy is the *keyword method,* which has been used to practical advantage by teaching elementary schoolchildren how to quickly master new information such as foreign vocabulary words, the states and capitals of the United States, and the names of U.S. presidents. For example, in remembering that Annapolis is the capital of Maryland, children were taught the keywords for the states, such that when a state was named (*Maryland*), they could supply the keyword (*marry*) (Levin, 1980). Then, children were given the reverse type of keyword practice with the capitals. That is, they had to respond with the capital (*Annapolis*) when given a keyword (*apple*). Finally, an illustration was provided. The keyword strategy's use of vivid mental imagery was effective in increasing children's memory of state capitals. Developmentalists today encourage the use of imagery in our nation's schools, believing that it helps to increase the child's memory.

In addition to these control processes, characteristics of the child influence memory. Apart from the obvious variable of age, many characteristics of the child determine the effectiveness of memory. These characteristics include attitude, motivation, and health. However, the characteristic that has been examined the most thoroughly is the child's previously acquired knowledge. What the child knows has a tremendous effect on what the child remembers. In one investigation, 10-year-old children who were chess experts remembered chessboard positions much better than adults who did not play much chess (Chi, 1978). However, the children did not do as well as the adults when both groups were asked to remember a group of random numbers; the children's expertise in chess gave them superior memories, but only in chess.

Children's memory is currently a topic of considerable interest in the nation's courtrooms. An emotional battle is being waged about the credibility of children's testimony (Brewer, 1996; Ceci, 1993). Listening to one side, it would seem that everything a child tells a therapist or social worker must be believed. For example, it is argued that it is hard for children to reveal the details of their victimization, so when they do talk about it, we should believe them. On the other side, critics argue that because children, especially young children, are vulnerable to erroneous suggestions and social demands, they should not be believed when they claim they have been molested.

What are we to believe? There are reliable age differences in suggestibility, with preschool children's reports

John W. Santrock

Children's content knowledge is an important factor in their memory. In areas where children are experts, their memory can sometimes exceed that of adults. How was this demonstrated in Chi's (1978) study of child chess experts?

being influenced more by the suggestibility of an interviewer's questioning and probing than older children or adults. However, the majority of children are neither as hypersuggestible or coachable as some prodefense advocates have alleged, nor are they as resistant to suggestions about their own bodies as some proprosecution advocates have claimed. Children can be led to incorporate false suggestions into their memories of even intimate body touching, if the suggestions are made by powerful adult authority figures and offered repeatedly over a long period of time. They also can be resistant to false suggestions and able to provide highly detailed and accurate reports of events that happened weeks or months ago. These findings underscore the need for considerable care in accepting claims by those who are eager to put a one-sided "spin" on the issue of children's memory accuracy and suggestibility.

Cognitive Monitoring

Cognitive monitoring *is the process of taking stock of what you are currently doing, what you will do next, and how effectively the mental activity is unfolding.* When children engage in an activity like reading, writing, or solving a math problem, they are repeatedly called on to take stock of what they are doing and what they plan to do next. For example, when children begin to solve a math problem—especially one that might take awhile to finish—they must

figure out what kind of problem they are working on and what would be a good approach in solving it. Once they undertake a problem solution, it is helpful to check whether the solution seems to be working or whether some other approach would be better.

Instructional programs in reading comprehension, writing, and mathematics have been designed to foster the development of cognitive monitoring. Ann Brown and Annemarie Palincsar's (1989) program for reading comprehension is an excellent example of a cognitive monitoring instructional program. Students in the program acquire specific knowledge and also learn strategies for monitoring their understanding. **Reciprocal teaching** *is an instructional procedure used by Brown and Palincsar to develop cognitive monitoring; it requires that students take turns in leading the group in the use of strategies for comprehending and remembering text content that the teacher models for the class.* The instruction involves a small group of students, often working with an adult leader, actively discussing a short text, with the goal of *summarizing* it, asking *questions* to promote understanding, offering *clarifying* statements for difficult or confusing words and ideas, and *predicting* what will come next. The procedure involves children in an active way, it teaches them some techniques to use for reflecting about their own understanding, and the group interaction is highly motivating and engaging.

Schemas and Scripts

In chapter 11, we described gender schema theory and defined a *schema* as a cognitive structure, a network of associations that organizes and guides an individual's perceptions. Schema is an important cognitive concept in memory and information processing. Schemas come from prior encounters with the environment and influence the way children encode, make inferences about, and retrieve information. Children have schemas for stories, scenes, spatial layouts (a bathroom or a park, for example), and common events (such as going to a restaurant, playing with toys, or practicing soccer).

Children frequently hear and tell stories. And as they develop the ability to read, they are exposed to many kinds of stories in print. Simple stories have a structure to them and after hearing enough stories, children develop a strong expectation about what kind of information will be contained in a story. This expectation is a *story schema*. For example, a story tells about what happens in a particular place and circumstance. This content is called the setting. A story will also have at least one main character, the protagonist, who attempts to achieve some purposeful goal for some clear reason. The protagonist's actions are usually captured in one or more episodes of a story, which can be further broken down, depicting a fairly simple, one-episode story (see figure 13.3).

A **script** *is a schema for an event.* Children's first scripts appear very early in development, perhaps as early as the first year of life. Children clearly have scripts by the time they enter school. As they develop, their scripts become less crude and more sophisticated. For example, a 4-year-old's script for a restaurant might include information only about sitting down and eating food. By middle and late childhood, the child adds information to the restaurant script about the types of people who serve food, paying the cashier, and so on.

Scientific Reasoning

Children's problem solving is often compared to that of scientists (Siegler, 1996). Both children and scientists ask fundamental questions about the nature of reality. Both also seek answers to problems that seem utterly trivial or unanswerable to other people (such as, Why is the sky blue?). Both also are granted by society the time and freedom to pursue answers to the problems they find interesting. This "child as scientist" metaphor has led researchers to ask whether children generate hypotheses, perform experiments, and reach conclusions concerning the meaning of their data in ways resembling those of scientists (Amsel, 1995; Fay, 1995).

Scientific reasoning often is aimed at identifying causal relations. In some ways, children's causal inferences are similar to those of scientists. For example, like scientists, they place a great deal of emphasis on causal mechanisms. Their understanding of how events are caused weighs more heavily in their causal inferences than do

Setting	1	Once there was a big gray fish named Albert.
	2	He lived in a pond near the edge of a forest.
Initiating event	3	One day Albert was swimming around the pond.
	4	Then he spotted a big juicy worm on top of the water.
Internal response	5	Albert knew how delicious worms tasted.
	6	He wanted to eat that one for his dinner.
Attempt	7	So he swam very close to the worm.
	8	Then he bit into him.
Consequence	9	Suddenly, Albert was pulled through the water into a boat.
	10	He had been caught by a fisherman.
Reaction	11	Albert felt sad.
	12	He wished he had been more careful.

FIGURE 13.3

"Albert, the Fish," A Representative Story

even such strong influences as whether the cause happened immediately before the effect.

There also are important differences between the reasoning of children and the reasoning of scientists, however. This is true even of preadolescents who have had some instruction in school regarding the scientific method. One difference comes in the preadolescents' much greater difficulty in separating their prior theories from the evidence that they have obtained. Often, when they try to learn about new phenomena, they maintain their old theories regardless of the evidence. Another difference is that they are more influenced by happenstance events than by the overall pattern of occurrences. They also have difficulty designing new experiments that can distinguish conclusively among alternative causes. Instead, they tend to bias the experiments in favor of whichever hypothesis they began with, and sometimes they will see the results as supporting their original hypothesis even when the results directly contradict it. Thus, although there are important similarities between children and scientists, in their basic curiosity and in the kinds of questions they ask, there are also important differences in their ability to design conclusive experiments and in the degree to which they can separate theory and evidence.

Critical Thinking

Much of the knowledge children are exposed to in the course of their education passes through their minds like grains of sand washed through a sieve. Children need to do more than just memorize or passively absorb new information. They must learn how to think critically. Currently, a number of psychologists and educators are

John W. Santrock

How does children's scientific reasoning improve? How do adult scientists reason differently than children?

studying children's critical-thinking skills (Halonen, 1995), although it is not a new idea. Educator John Dewey (1933) was working with a similar concept when he contrasted "reflective thinking" with "nonreflective thinking" in the use of formulas or rules to achieve goals. So was Gestalt psychologist Max Wertheimer (1945) when he distinguished between "productive thinking" and "blind induction." Although today's definitions vary, they all have in common the notion that **critical thinking** *involves grasping the deeper meaning of problems, keeping an open mind about different approaches and perspectives, and thinking reflectively rather than accepting statements and carrying out procedures without significant understanding and evaluation.* Another, often implicit, assumption is that critical thinking is an important aspect of everyday reasoning. Critical thinking can and should be used not just in the classroom, but outside it as well.

How can we cultivate the ability to think critically and clearly in children? According to a leading cognitive psychologist, Robert J. Sternberg (1987), we need to teach children to use the right thinking processes, to develop problem-solving strategies, to improve their mental representation, to expand their knowledge base, and to become motivated to use their newly learned thinking skills.

To think critically—or to solve any problem or learn any new knowledge—children need to take an active role in learning. This means that children need to call on a variety of active thinking processes, such as these:

- Listening carefully
- Identifying or formulating questions
- Organizing their thoughts
- Noting similarities and differences
- Deducing (reasoning from the general to the specific)
- Distinguishing between logically valid and invalid inferences

Children also need to learn how to ask questions of clarification, such as "What is the main point?" "What do you mean by that?" and "Why?"

Good thinkers use more than just the right thinking processes. They also know how to combine them into workable strategies for solving problems. Rarely can a problem be solved by a single type of thought process used in isolation. Children need to learn how to combine thinking processes to master a new task. Critical thinking involves combining thought processes in a way that makes sense, not just by jumbling them together.

Children need to learn to see things from multiple points of view. Unless children can interpret information from more than one point of view, they may rely on an inadequate set of information. If children are not encouraged to seek alternative explanations and interpretations of problems and issues, their conclusions may be based solely on their own expectations, prejudices, stereotypes, and personal experiences, which may lead to erroneous conclusions.

It is important to keep in mind that thinking does not occur in the absence of knowledge. Children need something to think *about*. It is a mistake, however, to concentrate only on information to the exclusion of thinking skills, because children simply would become individuals who have a lot of knowledge but are unable to evaluate and apply it. It is equally a mistake to concentrate only on thinking skills, because children would become individuals who know how to think but have nothing to think about.

Finally, all of the thinking skills children could possibly master would be irrelevant if they were not actually put to use. Critical thinking is both a matter for academic study *and* a part of living. Children need to be motivated to put their critical thinking skills to practical use. To further evaluate critical thinking, refer to Critical Thinking About Children's Development.

Intelligence

Intelligence is an abstract concept that is difficult to define. Although many psychologists and laypeople equate intelligence with verbal ability and problem-solving skills, others prefer to define it as the individual's ability to learn from and adapt to the experiences of everyday life. If we were to settle on a definition of intelligence based on these criteria, it would be that **intelligence** *is verbal ability, problem-solving skills, and the ability to learn from and adapt to the experiences of everyday life.* (see figure 13.4).

As many men, as many minds; everyone his own way.
—**Terence**

The components of intelligence are very close to the information processing and language skills we have discussed at various points in children's development. The difference between how we discuss information processing skills and language and how we discuss intelligence lies in

Too often elementary school children are simply asked to memorize acceptable responses and are not taught to think critically. Instead of just asking to recall information, teachers can ask them to reflect about information, examine evidence and arguments carefully, and solve problems.

Imagine that you have been asked to develop a critical-thinking curriculum for first-graders. Review what we have said in this chapter about the nature of critical thinking. Also consider how you have been challenged in the critical-thinking boxes that have appeared in each chapter. What would be the curriculum's main themes? By developing a critical-thinking curriculum for first-graders, you are *applying a developmental framework to understand behavior*.

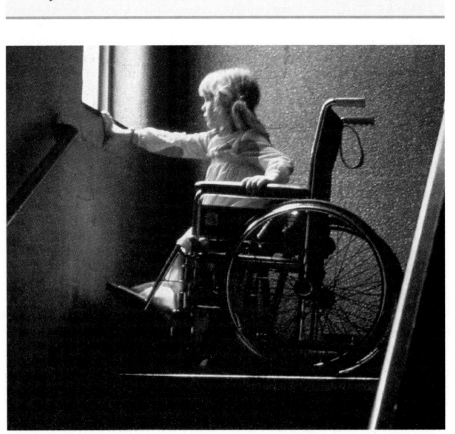

FIGURE 13.4

Defining Intelligence
Intelligence is an abstract concept that has been defined in various ways. The three most commonly agreed-upon aspects of intelligence are the following: (*a*) verbal ability, (*b*) problem-solving skills, and (*c*) an ability to learn from and adapt to experiences of everyday life, as reflected in this child's adaptation to her inability to walk.

the concepts of individual differences and assessment. Individual differences are simply the consistent, stable ways we differ from each other (Blades, 1997). The history of the study of intelligence has focused extensively on individual differences and their assessment (Cohen, Swerdlik, & Phillips, 1996). For example, an intelligence test will inform us whether a child can reason more logically than most other children who have taken the test. Our coverage of intelligence focuses on the components of intelligence, cultural bias, the use and misuse of intelligence tests, and the extremes of intelligence. As you think about intelligence, keep in mind our discussion of intelligence in chapter 3, in which we concluded that intelligence is influenced by the interaction of heredity and environment, rather than either factor alone.

One Face or Many?

Is it more appropriate to think of intelligence as an individual's general ability or as a number of specific abilities? As we explore different approaches to what intelligence is and how it should be measured, you will discover that intelligence is probably *both*.

In 1904, the French Ministry of Education asked psychologist Alfred Binet to devise a method that would determine which students did not profit from typical school instruction. School officials wanted to reduce overcrowding by placing those who did not benefit from regular classroom teaching in special schools. To meet this request, Binet and his student Theophile Simon developed an intelligence test. The test, referred to as the 1905 Scale, consisted of thirty items, ranging from the ability to touch one's nose or ear when asked to the ability to draw designs from memory and define abstract concepts.

Binet developed the concept of **mental age (MA)**—*an individual's level of mental development relative to others.* Binet reasoned that mentally retarded children would perform like normal children of a younger age. He developed norms for intelligence by testing

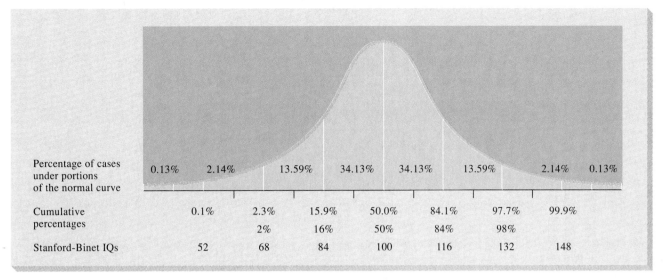

Percentage of cases under portions of the normal curve	0.13%	2.14%		13.59%	34.13%	34.13%	13.59%	2.14%	0.13%
Cumulative percentages	0.1%	2.3%		15.9%	50.0%	84.1%	97.7%	99.9%	
		2%		16%	50%	84%	98%		
Stanford-Binet IQs	52	68		84	100	116	132	148	

FIGURE 13.5

The Normal Curve and Stanford-Binet IQ Scores
The distribution of IQ scores approximates a normal curve. Most of the population falls in the middle range of scores. Notice that extremely high and extremely low scores are very rare. Slightly more than two-thirds of the scores fall between 84 and 116. Only about 1 in 50 individuals has an IQ of more than 132 and only about 1 in 50 individuals has an IQ of less than 68.

fifty nonretarded children from 3 to 11 years of age. Children suspected of mental retardation were tested, and their performance was compared with children of the same chronological age in the normal sample. Average mental-age scores (MA) correspond to chronological age (CA), which is age since birth. A bright child has an MA above CA, a dull child has an MA below CA.

The term **intelligence quotient (IQ)** *was devised by William Stern. IQ is the child's mental age divided by chronological age multiplied by 100:*

$$IQ = \frac{MA}{CA} \times 100$$

If mental age is the same as chronological age, then the child's IQ is 100; if mental age is above chronological age, the IQ is more than 100; if mental age is below chronological age, the IQ is less than 100.

Over the years extensive effort has been expended to standardize the Binet test, which has been given to thousands of children and adults of different ages selected at random from different parts of the United States. By administering the test to large numbers of individuals and recording the results, it has been found that intelligence measured by the Binet approximates a normal distribution (see figure 13.5). A **normal distribution** *is symmetrical with a majority of cases falling in the middle of the possible range of scores and few scores appearing toward the extremes of the range.*

The current Stanford-Binet (named after Stanford University, where revisions of the test were constructed) is given to persons from the age of 2 through adulthood. It includes a wide variety of items, some requiring verbal responses, others nonverbal responses. For example, items that characterize a 6-year-old's performance on the test

include the verbal ability to define at least six words such as *orange* and *envelope,* and the nonverbal ability to trace a path through a maze. Items that reflect the average adult's intelligence include defining words such as *disproportionate* and *regard,* explaining a proverb, and comparing idleness and laziness.

The fourth edition of the Stanford-Binet was published in 1985. One important addition to this version is the analysis of responses in four content areas: verbal reasoning, quantitative reasoning, abstract/visual reasoning, and short-term memory. A general composite score is also obtained to reflect overall intelligence. The Stanford-Binet continues to be one of the most widely used individual tests of children's intelligence.

Besides the Stanford-Binet, the other most widely used individual intelligence tests are the *Wechsler scales,* developed by David Wechsler. They include the Wechsler Adult Intelligence Scale–Revised (WAIS-R); the Wechsler Intelligence Scale for Children–Third Edition (WISC-III), for use with children between the ages of 6 and 16; and the Wechsler Preschool and Primary Intelligence Scale of Intelligence–Revised (WPPSI-R), for use with children from the ages of 4 to 6½.

The Wechsler scales not only provide an overall IQ, but the items are grouped according to twelve subscales, six verbal and six nonverbal. This allows the examiner to obtain separate verbal and nonverbal IQ scores and to see quickly in which areas of mental performance the child is below average, average, or above average. The inclusion of a number of nonverbal subscales makes the Wechsler test more representative of verbal *and* nonverbal intelligence; the Binet test incudes some nonverbal items but not as many as the Wechsler scales. Several

Verbal subscales

Similarities

An individual must think logically and abstractly to answer a number of questions about how things might be similar.

For example, "In what ways are boats and trains the same?"

Comprehension

This subtest is designed to measure an individual's judgment and common sense.

For example, "Why do individuals buy automobile insurance?"

Performance subscales

Picture arrangement

A series of pictures out of sequence is shown to an individual, who is asked to place them in their proper order to tell an appropriate story. This subtest evaluates how individuals integrate information to make it logical and meaningful.

For example, "The pictures below need to be placed in an appropriate order to tell a story."

Block design

An individual must assemble a set of multicolored blocks to match designs that the examiner shows. Visual-motor coordination, perceptual organization, and the ability to visualize spatially are assessed.

For example, "Use the four blocks on the left to make the pattern at the right."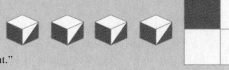

FIGURE 13.6

Sample Subscales of the Wechsler Adult Intelligence Scale for Children—Revised
Remember that the Wechsler includes 11 subscales, 6 verbal and 5 nonverbal. Four of the subscales are shown here.

of the subscales on the Wechsler Intelligence Scale for Children–Revised are shown in figure 13.6, along with examples of each subscale.

The contemporary theory of Robert J. Sternberg (1986) states that intelligence has three factors. **Triarchic theory** *is Sternberg's theory that intelligence consists of componential intelligence, experiential intelligence,* *and contextual intelligence.* Consider Ann, who scores high on traditional intelligence tests like the Stanford-Binet and is a star analytical thinker; Todd, who does not have the best test scores but has an insightful and creative mind; and Art, a street-smart person who has learned to deal in practical ways with his world, although his scores on traditional IQ tests are low.

John W. Santrock

"You're wise, but you lack tree smarts."

Drawing by D. Reilly; © 1988 The New Yorker Magazine, Inc.

Sternberg calls Ann's analytical thinking and abstract reasoning *componential intelligence*; it is the closest to what we call intelligence in this chapter and what is commonly measured by intelligence tests. Sternberg calls Todd's insightful and creative thinking *experiential intelligence,* and he calls Art's street smarts and practical know-how *contextual intelligence.*

In Sternberg's view of componential intelligence, the basic unit in intelligence is a *component,* simply defined as a basic unit of information processing. Sternberg believes such components include the ability to acquire or store information; to retain or retrieve information; to transfer information; to plan, make decisions, and solve problems; and to translate our thoughts into performance.

The second part of Sternberg's model focuses on experience. According to Sternberg, intellectual individuals have the ability to solve new problems quickly, but they also learn how to solve familiar problems in an automatic, rote way so their minds are free to handle other problems that require insight and creativity.

The third part of the model involves practical intelligence—such as how to get out of trouble, how to replace a fuse, and how to get along with people. Sternberg describes this practical or contextual intelligence as all of the important information about getting along in the real world that you are not taught in school. He believes contextual intelligence is sometimes more important than the "book knowledge" that is often taught in school.

Yet another developmental psychologist, Howard Gardner (1983), believes there are seven types of intelligence: verbal, mathematical, ability to spatially analyze the world, movement skills, insightful skills for analyzing ourselves, insightful skills for analyzing others, and musical skills. Gardner believes that each of the seven types of

Howard Gardner, here working with a young child, developed the view that intelligence comes in seven different forms: verbal, mathematical, ability to spatially analyze the world, movement skills, insightful skills for analyzing ourselves, insightful skills for analyzing others, and musical skills.

intelligence can be destroyed by brain damage, that each involves unique cognitive skills, and that each shows up in exaggerated fashion in both the gifted and idiots savants (individuals who are mentally retarded but who have unbelievable skill in a particular domain, such as drawing, music, or computing). I remember vividly an individual from my childhood who was mentally retarded but could instantaneously respond with the correct day of the week (say Tuesday or Saturday) when given any date in history (say June 4, 1926, or December 15, 1746).

Gardner is especially interested in musical intelligence, particularly when it is exhibited at an early age. He points out that musically inclined preschool children not only have the remarkable ability to learn musical patterns easily, but that they rarely forget them. He recounts a story about Stravinsky, who as an adult could still remember the musical patterns of the tuba, drums, and piccolos of the fife-and-drum band that marched outside his home when he was a young child.

To measure musical intelligence in young children, Gardner might ask a child to listen to a melody and then ask the child to re-create the tune on some bells he provides. He believes such evaluations can be used to develop a profile of a child's intelligence. He also believes that it is during this early time in life that parents can make an important difference in how a child's intelligence develops.

Critics of Gardner's approach point out that we have geniuses in many domains other than music. There are outstanding chess players, prizefighters, writers, politicians, physicians, lawyers, preachers, and poets, for example; yet we do not refer to chess intelligence, prizefighter intelligence, and so on.

Culture and Ethnicity

Are there cultural and ethnic differences in intelligence? Are standard intelligence tests biased, and, if so, can we develop culture-fair tests?

Cultural and Ethnic Comparisons   There are cultural and ethnic differences in performance on intelligence tests. For example, in the United States, children from African American and Latino families score below children from White families on standardized intelligence tests. Most research has focused on comparisons of African Americans and Whites. On the average, African American schoolchildren score 10 to 15 points lower on standardized intelligence tests than do White American schoolchildren (Anastasi, 1988; Neisser & others, 1996). Keep in mind, though, that we are talking about average scores. Many African American children score higher than many White American children. Estimates indicate that 15 to 25 percent of African American schoolchildren score higher than half of all White schoolchildren.

Many research investigations that compare African American and White American children do not take into account the diversity that exists within these groups (Jones, 1994; McLoyd & Ceballo, 1995). Critics argue that when ethnic groups are compared, researchers often document the way ethnic groups, especially African Americans and Latinos, *do not* behave rather than how they *do* behave. Further, the critics stress that studies of ethnic groups often fail to examine the underlying processes or mechanisms that explain behavioral outcomes. Such research has the unfortunate result of fostering ethnic-group stereotypes and ignoring ethnic-group diversity. Consequently, we know little about individual differences among ethnic minority children.

How extensively are ethnic differences in intelligence influenced by heredity and environment? The consensus is that the available data do not support a genetic interpretation (Brooks-Gunn, Klebanov, & Duncan, 1996). For example, in recent decades, as African Americans have experienced improved social, economic, and educational opportunities, the gap between White and African American children on standardized intelligence tests has begun to diminish (Jones, 1984). Also, when children from disadvantaged African American families are adopted by more-advantaged, middle-class families, their scores on intelligence tests are closer to the national average for middle-class children than to the national average for lower-class children (Scarr & Weinberg, 1983).

Cultural Bias and Culture-Fair Tests   Many of the early intelligence tests were culturally biased, favoring urban children over rural children, middle-class children over lower-class children, and White children over minority children (Miller-Jones, 1989). The norms for the early tests were based almost entirely on White middle-class children. And some of the items themselves were culturally biased. For example, one item on an early test asked what you should do if you find a 3-year-old child in the street; the correct answer was "Call the police." Children from impoverished inner-city families might not choose this answer if they have had bad experiences with the police; rural children might not choose it, because they may not have police nearby. Such items do not measure the knowledge necessary to adapt to one's environment or to be "intelligent" in an inner-city minority neighborhood or in rural America. The contemporary versions of intelligence tests attempt to reduce cultural bias.

Even if the content of test items is appropriate, another problem may exist with intelligence tests. Since many questions are verbal in nature, minority groups may encounter problems in understanding the language of the questions (Gibbs & Huang, 1989). Minority groups often speak a language that is very different from standard English. Consequently, they may be at a disadvantage when they take intelligence tests oriented toward middle-class whites.

Cultural bias is also dramatically underscored in the life of Gregory Ochoa. When Gregory was a high school student, he and his classmates were given an IQ test. School authorities informed them the test would allow the school to place them in classes appropriate for their skills. Gregory looked at the test questions and didn't understand many of the words. Spanish was spoken at his home, and his English was not very good. Several weeks later, Gregory was placed in a "special" class. Many of the other students in the class had last names like Ramirez and Gonzales. The special class was for mentally retarded students. Gregory lost interest in school and dropped out, eventually joining the Navy, where he took high school courses and earned enough credits to attend college. He graduated from San Jose City College as an honor student, continued his education, and wound up as a professor of social work at the University of Washington in Seattle.

Culture-fair tests *are tests of intelligence that attempt to be free of cultural bias.* Two types of culture-fair tests have been devised. The first includes items that are familiar to individuals from all socioeconomic and ethnic backgrounds, or items that at least are familiar to the individuals taking the test. For example, a child might be asked how a bird and a dog are different, on the assumption that virtually all children have been exposed to dogs and birds. The second type of culture-fair test has all the verbal items removed. Even though such tests are designed to be culture-fair, individuals with more education score higher on them than do those with less education.

John W. Santrock

FIGURE 13.7

Iatmul and Caroline Islander Intelligence
(a) The intelligence of the Iatmul people of Papua, New Guinea, involves the ability to remember the names of many clans.
(b) The Caroline Islands number 680 in the Pacific Ocean east of the Philippines. The intelligence of their inhabitants incudes the ability to navigate by the stars.

One test that takes into account the socioeconomic backgrounds of children is SOMPA, which stands for System of Multicultural Pluralistic Assessment. This test can be given to children from 5 to 11 years of age. SOMPA was designed for children from low-income families. Instead of relying on a single test, SOMPA is based on information about four different areas of a child's life: (1) verbal and nonverbal intelligence in the traditional intelligence test mold, assessed by the WISC-R; (2) social and economic background of the family, obtained through a one-hour parent interview; (3) social adjustment to school, evaluated by an adaptive behavior inventory completed by parents; and (4) physical health, determined by a medical examination.

The Kaufman Assessment Battery for Children (K-ABC) has been trumpeted as an improvement over past culture-fair tests. It can be given to children from 2½ to 12½ years of age. This test is standardized on a more representative sample, which includes more minority and handicapped children, than are most tests. The intelligence portion focuses less on language than the Stanford-Binet, and the test includes an achievement section with subtests for arithmetic and reading. Nonetheless, like other culture-fair tests, the K-ABC has its detractors. On three main criteria for evaluating tests, the K-ABC fares better on reliability and standardization, but not as well on validity.

These attempts to produce culture-fair tests remind us that traditional intelligence tests are probably culturally biased, yet the effort to develop a truly culture-fair test has not yielded a satisfactory alternative. Constructing a culture-fair intelligence test, one that rules out the role of experience emanating from socioeconomic and ethnic background, has been difficult and may be impossible. Consider, for example, that the intelligence of the Iatmul people of Papua, New Guinea, involves the ability to remember the names of 10,000 to 20,000 clans; by contrast, the intelligence of inhabitants of the widely dispersed Caroline Islands involves the talent of navigating by the stars (see figure 13.7).

The Use and Misuse of Intelligence Tests

Psychological tests are tools. Like all tools, their effectiveness depends on the knowledge, skill, and integrity of the user. A hammer can be used to build a beautiful kitchen cabinet or it can be used as a weapon of assault. Like a hammer, intelligence tests can be used for a positive purpose or they can be abusive. It is important for both the test constructor and the test examiner to be familiar with the current state of scientific knowledge about intelligence and intelligence tests.

Even though they have limitations, intelligence tests are among psychology's most widely used tools. To be effective, though, intelligence tests must be viewed realistically. They should not be thought of as a fixed, unchanging indicator of a person's intelligence. They should also be used in conjunction with other information about a person and should not be relied upon as the sole indicator of intelligence. For example, an intelligence test should not be used as the sole indicator of whether a child should be placed in a special education or gifted class. The child's developmental history, medical background, performance in school, social competencies, and family experiences should be taken into account, too.

The single number provided by many IQ tests can easily lead to stereotypes and expectations about a person. Many people do not know how to interpret the results of an intelligence test, and sweeping generalizations about a person are too often made on the basis of an IQ score. Imagine, for example, that you are a teacher sitting in the teacher's lounge the day after school has started in the fall. You mention a student—Johnny Jones—and a fellow teacher remarks that she had Johnny in class last year, and goes on to say that he was a real dunce, pointing out that his IQ is 78. You cannot help but remember this information, and it might lead you to think that Johnny Jones is not very bright so it is useless to spend much time teaching him. In this way, IQ scores are misused and stereotypes are formed (Rosenthal & Jacobsen, 1968).

We have a tendency in our culture to consider intelligence or a high IQ as the ultimate human value. It is important to keep in mind that our value as people includes other matters: consideration of others, positive close relationships, and competence in social situations, for example. The verbal and problem-solving skills measured on traditional intelligence tests are only one part of human competence.

Despite their limitations, when used judiciously by a competent examiner, intelligence tests provide valuable information about people. There are not many alternatives to intelligence tests. Subjective judgments about individuals simply reintroduce the biases the tests were designed to eliminate.

The Extremes of Intelligence

Intelligence tests have been used to discover indications of mental retardation or intellectual giftedness, the extremes of intelligence. At times intelligence tests have been misused for this purpose. Keeping in mind the theme that an intelligence test should not be used as the sole indicator of mental retardation or giftedness, we explore the nature of these intellectual extremes, as well as children's creativity.

Mental Retardation   The most distinctive feature of mental retardation is inadequate intellectual functioning. Long before formal tests were developed to assess intelligence, the mentally retarded were identified by a lack of age-appropriate skills in learning and caring for themselves. Once intelligence tests were developed, numbers were assigned to indicate degree of mental retardation. It is not unusual to find two retarded people with the same low IQ, one of whom is married, employed, and involved in the community and the other requiring constant supervision in an institution. These differences in social competence led psychologists to include deficits in adaptive behavior in their definition of mental retardation. **Mental retardation** *is a condition of limited mental ability in which an individual has a low IQ, usually below 70 on a traditional intelligence test, and has difficulty adapting to everyday life.* About 5 million Americans fit this definition of mental retardation.

There are several classifications of mental retardation. About 89 percent of the mentally retarded fall into the mild category, with IQs of 55 to 70. About 6 percent are classified as moderately retarded, with IQs of 40 to 54; these people can attain a second-grade level of skills and may be able to support themselves as adults through some types of labor. About 3.5 percent of the mentally retarded are in the severe category, with IQs of 25 to 39; these individuals learn to talk and engage in very simple tasks but require extensive supervision. Less than 1 percent have IQs below 25; they fall into the profoundly mentally retarded classification and need constant supervision.

Mental retardation can have an organic cause, or it can be social and cultural in origin. **Organic retardation** *is mental retardation caused by a genetic disorder or by brain damage; organic refers to the tissues or organs of the body, so there is some physical damage in organic retardation.* Down syndrome, one form of mental retardation, occurs when an extra chromosome is present in an individual's genetic makeup (see figure 13.8). It is not known why the extra chromosome is present, but it may involve the health or age of the female ovum or male sperm. Most people who suffer from organic retardation have IQs that range between 0 and 50.

Cultural-familial retardation *is a mental deficit in which no evidence of organic brain damage can be found; individuals' IQs range from 50 to 70.* Psychologists suspect that such mental deficits result from the normal variation that distributes people along the range of intelligence scores above 50, combined with growing up in a below-average intellectual environment. As children, those who are familially retarded can be detected in schools, where they often fail, need tangible rewards (candy rather than praise),

John W. Santrock

Figure 13.8

A Down Syndrome Child
What causes a child to develop Down syndrome? In what major classification of mental retardation does the condition fall?

and are highly sensitive to what others—both peers and adults—want from them (Feldman, 1996). However, as adults, the familially retarded are usually invisible, perhaps because adult settings don't tax their cognitive skills as sorely. It may also be that the familially retarded increase their intelligence as they move toward adulthood.

Giftedness There have always been people whose abilities and accomplishments outshine others—the whiz kid in class, the star athlete, the natural musician. People who are **gifted** *have above-average intelligence (an IQ of 120 or higher) and/or superior talent for something.* When it comes to programs for the gifted, most school systems select children who have intellectual superiority and academic aptitude. Children who are talented in the visual and performing arts (arts, drama, dance), athletics, or other special aptitudes tend to be overlooked.

Until recently, giftedness and emotional distress were thought to go hand in hand. English novelist Virginia Woolf suffered from severe depression, for example, and eventually committed suicide. Sir Isaac Newton, Vincent van Gogh, Ann Sexton, Socrates, and Sylvia Plath all had emotional problems. However, these are the exception rather than the rule; in general, no relation between giftedness and mental disorder has been found. Recent studies support the conclusion that gifted people tend to be more

mature and have fewer emotional problems than others (Feldman & Piirto, 1995).

Lewis Terman (1925) has followed the lives of approximately 1,500 children whose Stanford-Binet IQs averaged 150 into adulthood; the study will not be complete until the year 2010. Terman has found that this remarkable group is an accomplished lot. Of the 800 males, 78 have obtained doctorates (they include two past presidents of the American Psychological Association), 48 have earned M.D.s, and 85 have been granted law degrees. Most of these figures are 10 to 30 times greater than those found among the 800 men of the same age chosen randomly as a comparison group. These findings challenge the commonly held belief that the intellectually gifted are emotionally disordered or socially maladjusted.

The 672 gifted women studied by Terman (Terman & Oden, 1959) underscore the importance of relationships and intimacy in women's lives. Two-thirds of these exceptional women graduated from college in the 1930s, and one-fourth of them attended graduate school. Despite their impressive educational achievements, when asked to order their life's priorities, the gifted women placed families first, friendships second, and careers last. For these women, having a career often meant not having children. Of the 30 most successful women, 25 did not have any children. Such undivided commitments to the family are less true of women today. Many of the highly gifted women in Terman's study questioned their intelligence and concluded that their cognitive skills had waned in adulthood. Studies reveal that today gifted women have a stronger confidence in their cognitive skills and intellectual abilities than the gifted women in Terman's study did (Tomlinson-Keasey, 1990). Terman's gifted women represented a cohort who reached midlife prior to the women's movement and the current pervasiveness of the dual-career couple and the single-parent family (Tomlinson-Keasey, 1993).

In the most recent analysis of Terman's gifted children, two factors predicted longevity: personality and family stability (Friedman & others, 1995). With regard to personality, those who as children were conscientious and less impulsive lived significantly longer. With regard to family stability, those whose parents had divorced before the children reached age 21 faced a one-third greater mortality risk than did their counterparts whose parents had not divorced. Individuals who became divorced themselves also faced a shorter life. And not marriage itself, but rather a stable marriage history, was linked with increased longevity.

Never to be cast away are the gifts of the gods, magnificent.
—**Homer, *The Iliad*, 9th Century B.C.**

Creativity Most of us would like to be both gifted and creative. Why was Thomas Edison able to invent so many things? Was he simply more intelligent than most people? Did he spend long hours toiling away in private?

ABLE 13.1

Comparison of Approaches to Children's Learning and Cognition

	Piagetian/ Cognitive Development	Vygotsky's Theory	Learning	Cognitive Social Learning
Maturation/ environment	Strong maturational view, but maturation does interact with environmental experiences	Interactionist, but much stronger role for culture than in Piaget's view; interaction with skilled people	Strong emphasis on environment; little contribution by heredity/maturation	Strong environmental emphasis
Stages	Strong emphasis; cognitive stages are core of this approach	No stages emphasized	No stages	No stages
Individual differences	No emphasis	Moderately strong emphasis	No emphasis	No emphasis
Cognitive processes/ mechanisms	Assimilation, accommodation, equilibration, organization, conservation, and hypothetical-deductive reasoning skills	Discussion and reasoning through social interaction with skilled others	None	Attention, memory, plans, expectancies, problem-solving skills; self-efficacy; imitation
Model of child	Active, cognitive constructivist, solitary little scientist	Active, interactive, sociocultural constructivist	Passive, environmental determinist; empty vessicle	Interactive, reciprocal determinist

Surprisingly, when Edison was a young boy, his teacher told him he was too dumb to learn anything. Other famous people whose creative genius went unnoticed when they were young include Walt Disney, who was fired from a newspaper job because he did not have any good ideas; Enrico Caruso, whose music teacher told him that his voice was terrible; and Winston Churchill, who failed one year of secondary school.

Disney, Edison, Caruso, and Churchill were intelligent and creative men; however, experts on creativity believe that intelligence is not the same as creativity. One common distinction is between **convergent thinking,** *which produces one correct answer and is characteristic of the kind of thinking on standardized intelligence tests,* and **divergent thinking,** *which produces many answers to the same question and is more characteristic of creativity* (Guilford, 1967). For example, the following is a typical problem on an intelligence test that requires convergent thinking: "How many quarters will you get in return for 60 dimes?" The following question, though, has many possible answers: "What image comes to mind when you hear the phrase 'sitting alone in a dark room'?" (Barron, 1989). Such responses as "the sound of a violin with no strings" and "patience" are considered creative answers. Conversely, common answers, such as "a person in a crowd" or "insomnia" are not very creative.

Creativity *is the ability to think about something in novel and unusual ways and to come up with unique solutions to problems.* When creative people, such as artists and scientists, are asked what enables them to solve problems in novel ways, they say that the ability to find affinities between seemingly unrelated elements plays a key role. They also say they have the time and independence in an enjoyable setting to entertain a wide range of possible solutions to a problem. How strongly is creativity related to intelligence? Although most creative people are quite intelligent, the reverse is not necessarily true. Many highly intelligent people (as measured by IQ tests) are not very creative.

The artist finds a greater pleasure in painting than in having completed the picture.

—Seneca

Some experts remain skeptical that we will ever fully understand the creative process. Others believe that a psychology of creativity is in reach. Most experts agree, however, that the concept of creativity as spontaneously bubbling up from a magical well is a myth. Momentary flashes of insight, accompanied by images, make up only a small part of the creative process. At the heart of the creative process are ability and experience that shape an

John W. Santrock

Information Processing	Psychometric
Interactionist, but little attention given to this, except by Neo-Piagetians who emphasize age-related changes	Little attention to this issue, although age-related emphasis implies maturational emphasis
No stages	No stages
No emphasis, although recently some information-processing researchers have started to investigate	Strong emphasis; at core of the approach
Processing speed, capacity, and automaticity; attention; memory; problem solving, cognitive monitoring; critical thinking; knowledge and expertise	General intelligence and a number of specific forms of intelligence that vary with the theory
Cognitive constructivist	Individual difference

individual's intentional and sustained effort, often over the course of a lifetime.

Comparison of Learning and Cognitive Approaches

In chapters 2, 7, and 10, and so far in this chapter, we have studied a number of different approaches to learning, cognitive development, and intelligence. This is a good time to review some of the basic ideas of these approaches to get a feel for how they conceptualize children's development. So far we have examined six different approaches to learning, cognitive development, and intelligence: Piaget's cognitive developmental theory, Vygotsky's theory, learning theory, social learning theory, information-processing theory, and psychometric theory. Let's explore how these approaches view some important aspects of children's development: maturation/environmental influences, stages, individual differences, cognitive processes/mechanisms, and model of the child.

With regard to maturation/environmental influences, Piaget's theory is the strongest maturational approach; Vygotsky's theory also emphasizes maturation but to a lesser degree. Both Piaget's and Vygotsky's theories are interactionist in the sense that they emphasize maturation/environment interaction. The psychometric approach doesn't deal with this issue extensively, but its age-related emphasis implies a maturational underpinning. The

information-processing approach also does not focus on this issue to any degree, but is also best conceptualized as interactionist. The learning and cognitive social learning views are primarily environmental.

With regard to stages, only the Piagetian cognitive view has a strong stage emphasis. Indeed, stages of cognitive development—sensorimotor, preoperational, concrete operational, and formal operational—are at the heart of Piaget's theory. The neo-Piagetians, who combine some of Piaget's ideas with an emphasis on more precise aspects of information processing, place some emphasis on age-changes in cognition. The Vygotskian, learning, social learning, and psychometric approaches do not emphasize stages at all.

With regard to individual differences, only the psychometric approach and Vygotsky's theory emphasize them. In this chapter we have seen that individual differences are at the heart of the psychometric approach. Vygotsky's concept of the zone of proximal development also addresses individual differences. Recently, some information-processing researchers have begun to study individual differences in information processing, but the information-processing approach does not give individual differences a high priority. The Piagetian, learning, and social learning approaches do not emphasize individual differences at all.

With regard to cognitive processes/mechanisms, Piaget's cognitive developmental approach stresses the importance of assimilation, accommodation, equilibration, organization, conservation, and hypothetical-deductive reasoning. Vygotsky's theory stresses the importance of discussion and reasoning through interaction with skilled others. The learning approach does not emphasize cognitive processes/mechanisms at all, but rather the environmental processes of reinforcement, punishment, and classical conditioning. The cognitive social learning approach places importance on the cognitive processes of attention, memory, plans, expectancies, problem-solving skills, and self-efficacy. The information-processing approach emphasizes a large number of cognitive processes/mechanisms, among them: processing speed, capacity, and automaticity, attention; memory; problem solving; cognitive monitoring; critical thinking; knowledge and expertise. The psychometric approach focuses on general intelligence and/or a number of specific forms of intelligence, such as Sternberg's three forms—componential, experiential, and contextual.

With regard to conceptualization of the basic nature of the child or a model of how the child develops, Piagetian theory emphasizes a model of the child as an active, cognitive constructivist, and a solitary little scientist. Vygotsky's theory describes the child as an active, interactive, and sociocultural constructivist. The learning approach focuses on the child as passive, environmentally determined, and as an empty vessel. Cognitive social learning portrays the child as interactive and reciprocal determinist (behavior, cognition, and environment reciprocally interact). The information-processing

CONCEPT TABLE 13.1

Cognition in Middle and Late Childhood

Concept	Processes/Related Ideas	Characteristics/Description
Piaget's Theory	Concrete operational thought and education	Concrete operational thought involves operations, conservation, and classification skills. Thought is not as abstract as later in development. Piaget's ideas have been applied extensively to education.
	Contributions and criticisms	We owe Piaget the field of cognitive development; he was a genius at observing children. Critics question his estimates of competence at different developmental levels, his stages concept, and other ideas. Neo-Piagetians believe that children's cognition is more specific than Piaget thought.
Information Processing	Its nature	Long-term memory improves in middle and late childhood. Strategies are involved in this improvement. Schemas and scripts help children to interpret their cognitive world. Cognitive monitoring can benefit school learning. Children's scientific reasoning improves in middle and late childhood, but it is still flawed compared to that of adult scientists. There has been an increased interest in getting children to think more critically in recent years.
Intelligence	Its nature	Verbal ability, problem-solving skills, and the ability to learn from and adapt to everyday life are involved in intelligence. Psychologists debate whether intelligence has one face or many. The Binet and Wechsler tests are the most widely used individual tests of intelligence. A special concern is cultural bias in intelligence tests. There are both uses and misuses of intelligence tests.
	Extremes of intelligence and creativity	Mental retardation involves having a low IQ and difficulty in adapting to everyday life. One way of classifying mental retardation is as organic or cultural-familial. A gifted child has above-average intelligence and/or superior talent for something.
Comparison of Learning and Cognitive Approaches	Nature of differences	We compared six approaches to children's learning and cognition with regard to the following issues: maturation/environment, stages, individual differences, cognitive processes/mechanisms, and model of the child. The approaches we evaluated were Piaget's, Vygotsky's, learning, cognitive social learning, information processing, and psychometrics. For example, only Piaget's approach is a strong maturational approach and a strong stage theory, while the psychometric approach and Vygotsky's theory are the only ones that underscore the importance of individual differences.

approach conceptualizes the child as cognitive constructivist, and the psychometric approach in terms of individual differences.

A summary of how the six different approaches we have discussed in the last three chapters portray children's development is presented in table 13.1.

At this point we have discussed a number of ideas about cognition in middle and late childhood. A summary of these ideas is presented in concept table 13.1.

LANGUAGE DEVELOPMENT

As children develop during middle and late childhood, changes in their vocabulary and grammar take place. Reading assumes a prominent role in their language world. An increasingly important consideration is bilingualism.

Vocabulary and Grammar

During middle and late childhood, a change occurs in the way children think about words. They become less tied to

John W. Santrock

the actions and perceptual dimensions associated with words, and they become more analytical in their approach to words. For example, when asked to say the first thing that comes to mind when they hear a word, such as *dog*, preschool children often respond with a word related to the immediate context of a dog. A child might associate *dog* with a word that indicates its appearance (*black, big*) or to an action associated with it (*bark, sit*). Older children more frequently respond to *dog* by associating it with an appropriate category (*animal*) or to information that intelligently expands the context (*cat, veterinarian*). The increasing ability of elementary school children to analyze words helps them understand words that have no direct relation to their personal experiences. This allows children to add more abstract words to their vocabulary. For example, *precious stones* can be understood by understanding the common characteristics of *diamonds* and *emeralds*. Also, children's increasing analytic abilities allow them to distinguish between such similar words as *cousin* and *nephew* or *city, village,* and *suburb.*

Children make similar advances in grammar. The elementary school child's improvement in logical reasoning and analytical skills helps in the understanding of such constructions as the appropriate use of comparatives (*shorter, deeper*) and subjectives ("If you were president, ..."). By the end of the elementary school years, children can usually apply many of the appropriate rules of grammar.

Children's reading is a complex process. What kinds of information-processing skills are involved?

Reading

Reading is a complex ability that involves a number of different processes. What are the main ways children are taught to read?

Education and language experts continue to debate how children should be taught to read. The debate focuses on the whole-language approach versus the basic-skills-and-phonetics approach. The **whole-language approach** *stresses that reading instruction should parallel children's natural language learning. Reading materials should be whole and meaningful.* That is, in early reading instruction, children should be presented with materials in their complete form, such as stories and poems. In this way, say the whole-language enthusiasts, children can appreciate language's

communicative function. By contrast, the **basic-skills-and-phonetics approach** *advocates that reading instruction should stress phonetics and its basic rules for translating written symbols into sounds. Early reading instruction should involve simplified materials.* Only after they have learned phonological rules should children be given complex reading material such as books and poems.

Which approach is best? Researchers have not been able to successfully document that one approach is superior to the other. Some language experts believe that a combination of the two approaches should be followed (Spear-Swirling & Sternberg, 1994).

Reading is more than the sum of whole-word and phonics methods. Information-processing skills are also involved in successful reading. When children read, they process information and interpret it, so reading serves as a practical example to illustrate the information-processing approach we have talked about at various other times in this book. Remember that information processing is concerned with how children analyze the many different sources of information available to them in the environment and how they make sense of those experiences. When children read, for example, a rich and complex set of visual symbols is available to their senses. The symbols are associated with sounds, the sounds are combined to form words, and the words and large units that contain them (phrases, sentences, paragraphs) have conventional meanings. To read effectively, children must perceive and attend to words and sentences. They must also hold information in memory while processing new information. A number of information-processing skills, then, are involved in children's ability to read effectively.

What are the arguments for and against bilingual education?

Bilingualism

Octavio's Mexican parents moved to the United States 1 year before Octavio was born. They do not speak English fluently and have always spoken to Octavio in Spanish. At 6 years of age, Octavio has just entered the first grade at an elementary school in San Antonio, Texas, and he speaks no English. What is the best way to teach Octavio? How much easier would elementary school be for Octavio if his parents had been able to speak to him in Spanish *and* English when he was an infant?

Well over 6 million children in the United States come from homes in which English is not the primary language. Often, like Octavio, they live in a community in which English as a second language is the main means of communication. These children face a more difficult task than most of us: They must master the native tongue of their family to communicate effectively at home, and they must also master English to make their way in the larger society. The number of bilingual children is expanding at such a rapid rate in our country (some experts predict a tripling of their number early in the twenty-first century) that they constitute an important subgroup of language learners that society must deal with. Although the education of such children in the public schools has a long history, only recently has a national policy evolved to guarantee a high-quality language experience for them (Anderson, 1996; NAEYC, 1996).

Bilingual education *refers to programs for students with limited proficiency in English that instruct students in their own language part of the time while they learn English.* The rationale for bilingual education was provided by the United States Commission on Civil Rights (1975): Lack of English proficiency is the main reason language minority students do poorly in school; bilingual education should keep students from falling far behind in a subject while they are learning English. Bilingual programs vary extensively in content and quality. At a minimum, they include instruction in English as a second language for students with limited English proficiency. Bilingual programs often include some instruction in Spanish as well. The largest number of bilingual programs in the United States are in Spanish, so our examples refer to Spanish, although the principles also apply to bilingual programs in other languages. Bilingual programs differ in the extent to which Latino culture is taught to all students, and some bilingual programs teach Spanish to all students, regardless of whether their primary language is Spanish.

Most bilingual education programs are simply transitional programs developed to support students in Spanish until they can understand English well enough to function in the regular classroom, which is taught in English. A typical bilingual program begins teaching students with limited English proficiency in their primary language in kindergarten and then changes to English-only classes at the end of the first or second grade.

Research evaluation of bilingualism has led to the conclusion that bilingualism does not interfere with performance in either language (Hakuta & Garcia, 1989). There is no evidence that the native language should be eliminated as early as possible because it might interfere with learning a second language. Instead, higher degrees of bilingualism are associated with cognitive flexibility and improved concept formation (Diaz, 1983). These findings are based primarily on research in additive

John W. Santrock

bilingual settings—that is, in settings where the second language is added as an enrichment to the native language and not at its expense. Causal relations between bilingualism and cognitive or language competence are difficult to establish, but, in general, positive outcomes are often noted in communities where bilingualism is not socially stigmatized.

In one recent study, Kimbrough Oller (1995) compared a group of children from bilingual families, where they grew up speaking both English and Spanish, with a group of children from families that spoke only English. Virtually no differences in language development were found between the bilingual and monolingual children. As infants, both groups began making simple speech sounds, such as *da* and *ba,* at about the same age. At 3 years of age, bilingual children performed as well in Spanish as children who spoke only that language, and they actually performed better at English than English-only children. The results apply only to children who learn English and Spanish simultaneously from a young age. Latino children who do not begin learning English until kindergarten might be handicapped in U.S. schools because they have not yet developed needed English skills.

In another investigation, Grace Yeni-Komshian (1995) studied individuals who moved from Korea to the United States between 2 and 24 years of age. She found that those who began speaking English at about 6 to 8 years of age were proficient in neither Korean nor English. One recommendation for teaching kindergarten and school-age children living in the United States who have not yet learned English is a two-way bilingual program in which children learn in their native language half a day and in English the other half. There are about 200 two-way programs in the United States, and these usually continue through elementary school.

Increasingly, researchers are recognizing the complexity of bilingualism's effects. For example, as indicated earlier, the nature of bilingualism programs varies enormously—some are of excellent quality; others are of poor quality. Some teachers in bilingual education programs are completely bilingual; others are not. Some programs begin in kindergarten, others in elementary school. Some programs end in the first or second grade; others continue through the fifth or sixth grade. Some include instruction in Latino culture; others focus only on language instruction. Some researches select outcome measures that include only proficiency in English; others focus on cognitive variables such as cognitive flexibility and concept formation; and still others include more social variables such as integration into the school, self-esteem, and attitude toward school. In sum, there is more to understanding the effects of bilingual education than simple language proficiency.

One final point about bilingualism deserves attention. The United States is one of the few countries in the world in which most students graduate from high school knowing only their own language. For example, in Russia, schools have 10 grades, called forms, which correspond roughly to the 12 grades in American schools. Children begin school at age 7. In the third form, Russian students begin learning English. Because of the emphasis on teaching English in their schools, most Russian citizens today under the age of 35 speak at least some English.

ACHIEVEMENT

Yet another important dimension of cognitive development in middle and late childhood is children's achievement. We are a species motivated to do well at what we attempt, to gain mastery over the world in which we live, to explore with enthusiasm and curiosity unknown environments, and to achieve the heights of success. We live in an achievement-oriented world with standards that tell children success is important. The standards suggest that success requires a competitive spirit, a desire to win, a motivation to do well, and the wherewithal to cope with adversity and persist until an objective is reached. Some developmentalists, though, believe that we are becoming a nation of hurried, "wired" people who are raising our children to become the same way—uptight about success and failure and far too worried about what we accomplish in comparison to others. It was in the 1950s that an interest in achievement began to flourish. The interest initially focused on the need for achievement.

> *The trouble with being in the rat race is that even when you win you are still a rat.*
>
> —Lily Tomlin

Need for Achievement

Think about yourself and your friends for a moment. Are you more achievement oriented than they are, or are you less so? If we asked you and your friends to tell stories about achievement-related themes, could we accurately determine which of you is the most achievement oriented?

Some individuals are highly motivated to succeed and expend a lot of effort striving to excel. Other individuals are not as motivated to succeed and don't work as hard to achieve. These two types of individuals vary in their **achievement motivation (need for achievement),** *the desire to accomplish something, to reach a standard of excellence, and to expend effort to excel.* David McClelland (1955) assessed achievement by showing individuals ambiguous pictures that were likely to stimulate achievement-related responses. The individuals were asked to tell a story about the picture, and their comments were scored according to how strongly they reflected achievement.

A host of studies have correlated achievement-related responses with different aspects of the individual's experiences and behavior. The findings are diverse, but they do suggest that achievement-oriented individuals have a stronger hope for success than a fear of failure, are moderate rather than high or low in risk taking, and persist for appropriate lengths of time in solving difficult problems. Early research indicted that independence training by parents promoted children's achievement, but more-recent research reveals that parents, to increase achievement, need to set high standards for achievement, model achievement-oriented behavior, and reward their children for their achievements. And in one recent study, the middle school students who had the highest grades were those whose parents, teachers, and schools were authoritative (Paulson, Marchant, & Rothlisberg, 1995).

Intrinsic and Extrinsic Motivation

Our achievement motivation—whether in school, at work, or in sports—can be divided into two main types: **intrinsic motivation,** *the internal desire to be competent and to do something for its own sake;* and **extrinsic motivation,** *the influence of external rewards and punishments.* If you work hard in college because a personal standard of excellence is important to you, intrinsic motivation is involved. But if you work hard in college because you know it will bring you a higher-paying job when you graduate, extrinsic motivation is at work.

An important consideration when motivating a child to do something is whether or not to offer an incentive. If a child is not doing competent work, is bored, or has a negative attitude, it may be worthwhile to consider incentives to improve motivation. However, there are times when external rewards can get in the way of motivation. In one investigation, children with a strong interest in art spent more time in a drawing activity when they expected no reward than their counterparts who knew they would be rewarded (Lepper, Greene, & Nisbett, 1973).

Intrinsic motivation implies that internal motivation should be promoted and external factors deemphasized. In this way, children learn to attribute to themselves the cause of their success and failure, and especially how much effort they expend. But in reality, achievement is motivated by both internal and external factors; children are never divorced from their external environment. Some of the most achievement-oriented children are those who have a high personal standard for achievement and are also highly competitive. In one study, low-achieving boys and girls who engaged in individual goal setting (intrinsic motivation) and were given comparative information about peers (extrinsic motivation) worked more math problems and got more of them correct than their counterparts who experienced either condition alone (Schunk, 1983). Other research suggests that social comparison by itself is not a wise strategy (Nicholls, 1984). The argument is that social comparison puts the child in an ego-involved, threatening, self-focused state rather than in a task-involved, effortful, strategy-focused state.

The reward of a thing well done is to have done it.
—Ralph Waldo Emerson, *Essays: Second Series,* 1844

Another important consideration is the role of the child's home environment in promoting internal motivation. In one study, Adele Gottfried and Allen Gottfried (1989) found that greater variety of home experiences, parental encouragement of competence and curiosity, and home emphasis on academically related behaviors are related to children's internal motivation for achievement.

An extremely important aspect of internal causes of achievement is *effort.* Unlike many causes of success, effort is under the child's control and is amenable to change. The importance of effort in achievement is recognized by most children. In one study, third- through sixth-grade students felt that effort was the most effective strategy for good school performance (Skinner, Wellborn, & Connell, 1990).

Mastery Orientation Versus Helpless and Performance Orientations

Closely related to an emphasis on intrinsic motivation, attributions of internal causes of behavior, and the importance of effort in achievement is a mastery orientation. Developmental psychologists Valanne Henderson and Carol Dweck (1990) have found that children show two distinct responses to difficult or challenging circumstances. Individual with a **helpless orientation** *seem trapped by the experience of difficulty, and they attribute their difficulty to lack of ability.* They frequently say things like "I'm not very good at this," even though they might earlier have demonstrated their ability through many successes. And once they view their behavior as failure, they often feel anxious, and their performance worsens even further. Individuals with a **mastery orientation** *are task oriented; instead of focusing on their ability, they are concerned about their learning strategies and the process of achievement rather than outcomes.* Mastery-oriented children often instruct themselves to pay attention, to think carefully, and to remember strategies that have worked for them in previous situations. They frequently report feeling challenged and excited by difficult tasks rather than being threatened by them (Anderman, Maehr, & Midgley, 1996).

Another issue in motivation involves whether to adopt a mastery or a performance orientation. We have already described what a mastery orientation is like. A **performance orientation** *involves being concerned with the achievement outcome; winning is what matters, and happiness is thought to result from winning.*

What sustains mastery-oriented individuals is the self-efficacy and satisfaction they feel from effectively dealing with the world in which they live. By contrast, what sustains performance-oriented individuals is winning. Although skills can be, and often are, involved in winning, performance-oriented individuals do not necessarily view themselves as having skills. Rather, they see themselves as using tactics, such as undermining others, to get what they want.

John W. Santrock

Asian grade schools intersperse studying with frequent periods of activities. This approach helps children maintain their attention and likely makes learning more enjoyable. Shown here are Japanese fourth-graders making wearable masks.

Does all of this mean that mastery-oriented individuals do not like to win and that performance-oriented individuals are not motivated to experience the self-efficacy that comes from being able to take credit for one's accomplishments? No. A matter of emphasis or degree is involved, though. For mastery-oriented individuals, winning isn't everything; for performance-oriented individuals, skill development and self-efficacy take a back seat to winning.

In sum, we have seen that a number of psychological and motivational factors influence children's achievement. Especially important in the child's ability to adapt to new academic and social pressures are achievement motivation, internal attributions of causes of behavior, intrinsic motivation, and a mastery orientation. Next we will explore the roles of ethnicity and culture in achievement.

Ethnicity and Culture

What is the nature of achievement in ethnic minority children? How does culture influence children's achievement?

Ethnicity

Too often the findings of research on minority groups are presented as "deficits" in terms of middle-class White standards. Instead of characterizing individuals as *culturally different*, many research conclusions are stated in terms that characterize African Americans, Latinos, and other minority groups as deficient in some way.

Much of the research on minority-group children is plagued by a failure to consider socioeconomic status (determined by some combination of education, occupation, and income). In many instances, when ethnicity *and* socioeconomic status (also called "social class") are investigated in the same study, social class is a far better predictor of achievement orientation than is ethnicity. Middle-class individuals fare better than their lower-class counterparts in a variety of achievement-oriented circumstances—expectations for success, achievement aspirations, and recognition of importance of effort, for example.

Educational psychologist Sandra Graham (1986, 1990) has conducted a number of investigations that reveal not only stronger social class than ethnic group differences, but also the importance of studying minority group motivation in the context of general motivation theory. Her inquiries focus on the causes African Americans give for their achievement orientations—why they succeed or fail, for example. She is struck by how consistently middle-class African American children do not fit our stereotypes of either deviant or special populations. Rather, like their middle-class White counterparts, they have high expectations and understand that failure often is due to lack of effort rather than to luck.

It is always important to keep in mind the diversity that exists within any ethnic group (Fletcher, 1995; Swanson, 1995). Consider Asian American children.

Many Asian American children fit the "whiz kid, super-achiever" image, but there are still many Asian American children who are struggling just to learn English. The "whiz kid" image fits many of the children of Asian immigrant families who arrived in the United States in the late 1960s and early 1970s. Many of these immigrants came from Hong Kong, South Korea, India, and the Philippines. The image also fits many of the more than 100,000 Indochinese (primarily Vietnamese) immigrants who arrived in the United States after the end of the Vietnam War in 1975. Both groups included mostly middle- and upper-income professional people who were reasonably well educated and who passed along a strong interest in education and a strong work ethic to their children. For thousands of other Asian Americans, including a high percentage of the 600,000 Indochinese refugees who fled Vietnam, Laos, and Cambodia in the late 1970s, the problems are legion. Many in this wave of refugees lived in poor surroundings in their homelands. They came to the United States with few skills and little education. They speak little English and have a difficult time finding decent jobs. They often share housing with relatives. Adjusting to school is difficult for their children; some drop out, and some are attracted to gangs and drugs. Better school systems use a variety of techniques to help these Asian Americans, including classes in English as a second language, as well as a range of social services.

Culture

In the last decade, the poor performance of American children in math and science has become well publicized. For example, in one recent cross-national comparison of the math and science achievement of 9- to 13-year-old students, the United States finished 13th (out of 15) in science and 15th (out of 16) in math achievement (Educational Testing Service, 1992). In this study, Korean and Taiwanese students placed first and second, respectively.

Harold Stevenson and his colleagues (Hofer, Carlson, & Stevenson, 1996; Stevenson, 1995; Stevenson, Chen, & Lee, 1993) have conducted a series of cross-national studies of children's learning and achievement in various Asian countries and the United States over a period of about 15 years. Rather than just describe the deficiencies of the American children's achievement in comparison to children from other nations, Stevenson has sought to answer the all-important question: Why? He has found that, contrary to popular stereotypes, Asian children's high level of achievement does not result from rote learning and repeated drilling in tension-filled schools. Rather, children are motivated to learn, and teaching is innovative and interesting in many Asian schools. Knowledge is not force-fed to children, but rather children are encouraged to construct their own ways of representing the knowledge. Long school days in Asia are punctuated by extended recess periods. Asian schools embrace many of the ideals Americans have for their own schools, but they are more successful in implementing them in interesting and productive ways that make learning more enjoyable for children.

These conclusions were reached by Stevenson and his colleagues following five different cross-national studies of children in the United States, China, Taiwan, and Japan. In these studies, Asian children consistently outperformed U.S. children in math. And the longer the children were in school, the wider the gap between the Asian and the American children's math scores became, with the lowest differential being in the first grade, the biggest in the eleventh grade.

To learn more about the reasons for these large cross-cultural differences in achievement, the researchers spent hundreds of hours observing in classrooms, interviewing teachers, children, and mothers, and giving questionnaires to the fathers. They found that American parents' satisfaction with their children's achievement and education is high but that their standards are low in comparison with those of their Asian counterparts. And American parents emphasize that their children's math achievement is primarily determined by innate ability; Asian parents believe their children's math achievement is mainly the result of effort and training.

In 1990, President Bush and the nation's governors adopted a well-publicized goal: to change American education in ways that will help students to lead the world in math achievement by the year 2000. Stevenson (1995) says that is unlikely to happen, because American standards and expectations for children's math achievement are too low by international standards.

Even though Asian students are doing so well in math achievement, might there be a dark underside of too much stress and tension in the students and their schools? Stevenson and his colleagues (1993) have not found that to be the case. They asked eleventh-grade students in Japan and the United States how often in the past month they had experienced feelings of stress, depression, aggression, and other problems, such as not being able to sleep well. They also asked the students how often they felt nervous when they took tests. On all of these characteristics, the Japanese students expressed less distress and reported fewer problems than did the American students. Such findings do not support the Western stereotype that Asian students are tense, wired individuals driven by relentless pressures for academic excellence.

Critics of cross-national studies say that such comparisons are flawed because countries vary greatly in the percentage of children who go to school, the curricula, and so forth. Even in face of such criticisms, there is a growing consensus, based on information collected by different research teams, that American children's achievement is very low, that American educators' and parents' expectations for children's math achievement are too low, and that American schools are long overdue for an extensive overhaul.

John W. Santrock

The influence of computer use on children's learning, motivation, and social behavior continues to be a source of debate and controversy.

CHILDREN AND COMPUTERS

At the middle of the twentieth century, commercial television had barely made its debut and IBM had yet to bring its first computer to market. Now as we move toward the close of the twentieth century, both television *and* computers are important influences in children's lives. For some, the computer is a positive tool with the power to transform our schools and revolutionize children's learning. For others, the computer is a menacing force, more likely to undermine than to improve children's education and learning. Let's examine some of the possible positive and negative influences of computers in children's lives.

Positive Influences of Computers on Children

Among the potential positive influences of computers on children's development are its usefulness as a personal tutor, its function as a multipurpose tool, and its motivational and social effects (Lepper & Gurtner, 1989).

Computer-assisted instruction *uses the computer as a tutor to individualize instruction. The concept behind computer-assisted instruction is to use the computer to present information, give students practice, assess their level of understanding, and provide additional instruction if needed.* Computer-assisted instruction requires the active participation of the student, and in giving immediate feedback to students is patient and nonjudgmental. Over the past two decades, more than 200 research studies involving computer-assisted instruction have been conducted. In general, the effects of computer-assisted instruction are positive. More precisely, the effects are more positive with programs involving tutorials rather than drill and practice, with younger rather than older students, and with students with lower than average ability or unselected populations.

The computer also serves as an important influence in children's lives through the role it can play in experiential learning (Samaras, 1996). Some experts view the computer as an excellent medium for open-ended and exploratory learning. The most widely studied activity has been the use of the Logo computing language, especially its simplified "turtle graphics" programming environment, as a way to improve children's planning and problem-solving abilities (Papert, 1980). The turtle graphics involve moving a small triangular cursor, called a "turtle," on the screen. However, the research on the effects of Logo are mixed. Although the early studies of Logo essentially found no benefits for children's learning, more recent studies have been supportive of Logo. In the successful recent studies, more favorable adult-child ratios are present, prepared support materials and explicit task requirements are included, younger children are studied, and a wider array of dependent variable measures are used (such as creativity, cognitive monitoring, and solution checking).

The computer can function in children's lives as a multipurpose tool in helping children achieve academic goals and become more creative. The computer is especially helpful in improving children's writing and communication skills. Word-processing programs diminish the drudgery of writing, increasing the probability that children will edit and revise their work. Programs that assist students in outlining a paper may help students organize their thoughts before they write.

Several other themes appear in the discussion of the computer's positive influence on children's development. For one, computer adherents argue that the computer makes learning more intrinsically motivating. Computer enthusiasts also argue that the computer can make learning more fun. And, lessons can often be embedded in instructional "games" or puzzles that encourage children's curiosity and sense of challenge. Some computer adherents also argue that expanded computer use in schools will increase cooperation and collaboration on the part of students, as well as increase intellectual discussion among students. And if the computer does increase student's interest, it may free teachers to spend more time working individually with students. Finally, computer adherents hope that the computer can increase the equality of educational opportunity. Since the computer allows students to work at their own pace, it may help students who do not normally succeed in schools. Because the computer is fair and impartial, it should minimize the adverse influences of teacher prejudice and stereotyping.

Negative Influences of Computers on Children

Among the potential negative influences of computers on children's development are those involving regimentation and dehumanization of the classroom, unwarranted "shaping" of the curriculum, and generalization and limitations of computer-based teaching (Lepper & Gurtner, 1989), each of which we discuss in turn.

Skeptics worry that rather than increased individualization of instruction, computers will bring a much greater regimentation and homogenization of classroom learning experiences. Whereas some students may prefer to work autonomously and may learn most effectively when they are allowed to progress on their own, other students may rely on social interaction with guidance by the teacher for effective learning. And, some computer skeptics worry that the computer will ultimately increase inequality, rather than equality, in educational outcomes. School funding in middle-class neighborhoods is usually better than in low-income areas, and homes of children in middle-class neighborhoods are more likely to have computers than those in low-income neighborhoods. Thus, an increasing emphasis on computer literacy may be inequitable for children from low-income backgrounds because they have likely had less opportunity to use computers. Some critics also worry about the dehumanization of the classroom. They argue that school is a social world as well as a cognitive, learning world. From this perspective, children plugged into a computer all day long have little opportunity to engage in social interaction.

A further concern is that computers may inadvertently and inappropriately shape the curriculum. Some subjects, such as mathematics and science, seem to be more easily and successfully adapted to computers than subjects such as art and literature. Consequently, there is concern that the computer may eventually shape the curriculum in the direction of science and math because these areas are more easily computerized.

Yet another concern is the transfer of learning and motivation outside the computer domain. If the instructional effectiveness and motivational appeal of computer-based education depends on the use of impressive technical devices such as color, animation, and sound effects, how effectively will student learning or motivation transfer to other contexts without these technical supports? Will children provided with the editorial assistance of the computer still learn the basic skills needed to progress to more complex forms of creative writing later in their careers? Will children using computers in math gain the proficiency to deal with more complicated math in the future or will their ability to solve complex conceptual problems in the absence of the computer have atrophied? Presently, we do not know the answers to these important questions, but they do raise some important concerns about the computer's role in children's development.

At this point we have studied a number of ideas about language development, achievement, and computers. A summary of these ideas is presented in concept table 13.2.

CONCEPT TABLE 13.2

Language Development, Achievement, and Computers

Concept	Processes/Related Ideas	Characteristics/Description
Language Development	Vocabulary and grammar	In middle and late childhood, children become more analytical and logical in their approach to words and grammar.
	Reading	Reading is a complex ability that involves a number of processes. The two main ways that children are taught to read are through the whole-language approach, which stresses that reading instruction should parallel the child's natural language learning, and the basic-skills-and-phonetics approach, which advocates that reading instruction stress phonetics and its basic rules for translating written symbols into sounds. Debate continues about which approach is best; some experts believe that a combination of the two should be followed. Information-processing skills are involved in successful reading.
	Bilingualism	Bilingualism has become a major issue in our nation's schools; debate rages over the best way to conduct bilingual education. No negative effects of bilingualism have been found. Bilingualism is often associated with positive outcomes, although causal relations are difficult to establish. Increasingly researchers recognize the complexity of bilingual education.
Achievement	Need for achievement	Achievement motivation (need for achievement) is the desire to accomplish something, to reach a standard of excellence, and to expend effort to excel. Researchers have found correlations between parenting practices and children's achievement motivation.
	Intrinsic and extrinsic motivation	An important dimension of achievement is whether the motivation is internal (intrinsic) or external (extrinsic). An extremely important dimension of internal causes of achievement is effort.
	Mastery orientation versus helpless and performance orientations	Children who have a mastery orientation are task oriented and concerned with their learning strategies rather than ability. They are interested in the process of achievement rather than its outcomes. By contrast, children who have a helpless orientation seem trapped by the experience of difficulty and attribute their problems to lack of ability. The performance orientation involves being concerned with achievement outcomes rather than achievement processes. To those with a performance orientation, winning is what matters and happiness is thought to result from winning. Experts recommend a mastery rather than a helpless or performance orientation in achievement contexts.
	Ethnic and cross-cultural comparisons	Too often, research has characterized minority groups in terms of deficits. In addition to ethnic minority considerations, it is also important to determine whether socioeconomic status is a factor in achievement circumstances. It is always important to consider the diversity within an ethnic minority group. American children are more achievement oriented than children in many countries, but in recent years they have not fared well in achievement comparisons with children from Asian countries such as China, Japan, and Korea.
Computer and Children's Development	Positive influences	Among the potential positive effects of computers on children's development are those involving the computer as a personal tutor (computer-assisted instruction), its use as a multipurpose tool, and the motivational and social aspects of its use.
	Negative influences	Among the potential negative effects of computers on children's development are regimentation and dehumanization of the classroom, unwarranted "shaping" of the curriculum, and limitations of computer-based teaching.

I n middle and late childhood, competent children seek to know and understand, and they enjoy learning. They also are remarkable for their curiosity.

We began this chapter by evaluating Piaget's theory and concrete operational thought, in the process describing his contributions as well as criticisms of his theory. Our coverage of information processing focused on memory, cognitive monitoring, schemas and scripts, scientific thinking, and critical thinking. Our exploration of children's intelligence involved whether intelligence has one face or many, culture and ethnicity, and the use and misuse of intelligence tests. We also compared a number of learning and cognitive approaches. We examined children's language development by considering the nature of vocabulary and grammar development, reading, and bilingualism. To better understand children's achievement, we learned about the need for achievement, intrinsic and extrinsic motivation, mastery versus helpless orientation, and culture and ethnicity. We also studied the role of computers in children's lives.

Don't forget that you can obtain an overall summary of the chapter by again reading the two concept tables on pages 398 and 407. In the next chapter we continue our journey through middle and late childhood by exploring socioemotional development.

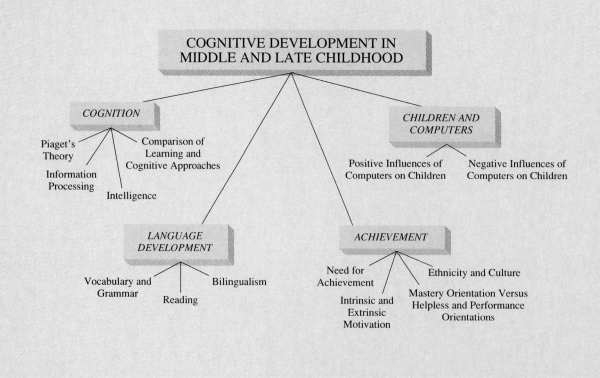

neo-Piagetians Developmentalists who have elaborated on Piaget's theory, believing that children's cognitive development is more specific in many respects than Piaget thought. 383

long-term memory A relatively permanent type of memory that holds huge amounts of information for a long period of time. 384

control processes Cognitive processes that do not occur automatically but require work and effort. These processes are under the learner's conscious control and they can be used to improve memory. They are also appropriately called strategies. 384

cognitive monitoring The process of taking stock of what you are currently doing, what you will do next, and how effectively the mental activity is unfolding. 385

reciprocal teaching An instructional procedure used by Brown and Palincsar to develop cognitive monitoring; it requires that students take turns leading a study group in the use of strategies for comprehending and remembering text content. 385

script A schema for events. 386

critical thinking Grasping the deeper meaning of problems, keeping an open mind about different approaches and perspectives, and thinking reflectively rather than merely accepting others' claims or carrying out procedures without significant understanding or evaluation. 387

intelligence Verbal ability, problem-solving skills, and the ability to learn from and adapt to the experiences of everyday life. 387

mental age (MA) Binet's measure of an individual's level of mental development compared to that of others. 388

intelligence quotient (IQ) A person's mental age divided by chronological age, multiplied by 100. 389

normal distribution A distribution that is symmetrical with most cases falling in the middle of the possible range of scores and a few scores appearing toward the extremes of the range. 389

triarchic theory Sternberg's theory that intelligence consists of componential intelligence, experiential intelligence, and contextual intelligence. 390

culture-fair tests Tests that are designed to be free of cultural bias. 392

mental retardation A condition of limited mental ability in which an individual has a low IQ, usually below 70 on a traditional test of intelligence, and has difficulty adapting to everyday life. 394

organic retardation Mental retardation that involves some physical damage and is caused by a genetic disorder or brain damage. 394

cultural-familial retardation Retardation that is characterized by no evidence of organic brain damage, but the individual's IQ is between 50 and 70. 394

gifted Having above-average intelligence, usually an IQ of 120 or higher, and a superior talent for something. 395

convergent thinking Thinking that produces one correct answer and is characteristic of the kind of thinking tested by standardized intelligence tests. 396

divergent thinking Thinking that produces many answers to the same question and is characteristic of creativity. 396

creativity The ability to think in novel and unusual ways and to come up with unique solutions to problems. 396

whole-language approach An approach to teaching reading that stresses that reading instruction should parallel children's natural language learning. 399

basic-skills-and-phonetics approach An approach to teaching reading that stresses phonetics and its basic rules for translating written symbols into sounds. 399

bilingual education Programs for students with limited proficiency in English that instruct students in their own language part of the time while they learn English. 400

achievement motivation (need for achievement) The desire to accomplish something, to reach a standard of excellence, and to expend effort to excel. 401

intrinsic motivation The desire to be competent and to do something for its own sake. 402

extrinsic motivation Motivation produced by external rewards and punishments. 402

helpless orientation An orientation in which one seems trapped by the experience of difficulty and attributes one's difficulty to a lack of ability. 402

mastery orientation An orientation in which one is task oriented and, instead of focusing on one's ability, is concerned with learning strategies. 402

performance orientation An orientation in which one focuses on achievement outcomes; winning is what matters most, and happiness is thought to result from winning. 402

computer-assisted instruction The teaching strategy that involves using computers as tutors to individualize instruction. Computers are used to present information, give students practice, assess student levels of understanding, and provide additional information when needed. 405

Parents' Guide to Raising a Gifted Child

(1985) by James Alvino.
New York: Ballantine.

This is a practical, informative book on how to raise and educate gifted children. How to assess whether a child is gifted or not is covered, along with how to select a day-care center, a school, and a home reference library. A recommended reading list is included, as well as sections on the roles of computers and television in gifted children's lives.

The New York Times Parents' Guide to the Best Books for Children

(1991) by Eden Lipson.
New York: Random House.

This revised and updated edition includes book recommendations for children of all ages. More than 1,700 titles are evaluated. The six sections are organized according to reading level: wordless, picture, story, early reading, middle reading, and young adult. Each entry provides the essential information needed to become acquainted with the book's content and know where to find it in a local library or a bookstore. More than 55 indexes make it easy to match the right book to the right child. This is an extensive, thorough, competent guide to selecting children's books.

The Hurried Child

(1988, rev. ed.) by David Elkind.
Reading, MA: Addison-Wesley.

The Hurried Child describes a pervasive and harmful circumstance that all too many American children face—that of growing up too fast and too soon. Author David Elkind is a highly respected expert on children's and adolescents' lives. Elkind says that today's American parents too often push their children to be "superkids" who are competent to deal with all of life's ups and downs. He thinks parents invented the "superkid" to alleviate their own anxiety and guilt. But he doesn't just fault parents, also pointing the finger of blame at schools and media. According to Elkind, many parents' expectations for their children are unrealistic, not just about their children's academic journeys, but about their performance on athletic fields as well. Elkind recommends that parents respect children's own developmental timetables and needs, encourage children to play and fantasize, and make sure that their expectations and support are in reasonable balance.

IMPROVING THE LIVES OF CHILDREN

Improving the lives of children involves being sensitive to the needs of gifted disadvantaged children, developing better parenting skills with gifted children, using more effective teaching strategies to encourage creativity, improving the English and computer literacy of immigrant children, and encouraging achievement in girls.

HEALTH AND WELL-BEING

Against All Odds—Gifted Disadvantaged Children

Disadvantaged children in the United States come from diverse cultural backgrounds and are often the victims of social discrimination. These children live in environments that fail to challenge their creativity and do not provide them with the resources needed to develop their creativity.

When gifted disadvantaged children learn to adapt their behavior to the values and demands of school, they begin to accomplish required tasks successfully, their achievements start to attract teachers' attention, and more opportunities are made available to them. This "snowball effect" has crucial implications for the child's personal and motivational development (Arroyo & Sternberg, 1993).

Parents in low-income families can help their children develop the self-management skills required to function well in a school setting, but in many instances they do not. For gifted disadvantaged children, teachers and other influential persons within the school can compensate for the lack of appropriate direction these children have received at home. Alternative socialization agents can expose gifted disadvantaged children to wide-ranging experiences that influence their emerging view of themselves and their future.

Especially important in the case of gifted disadvantaged children is the development of measures to identify who they are. Traditionally, giftedness has been assessed in one dimension—intellectual exceptionality. However, to adequately identify gifted disadvantaged children, it is necessary to widen the assessment procedure to include not only intellectual abilities but also behavior, motivation, and personality attributes. Researchers have found that high-achieving disadvantaged children are self-confident, industrious, tough-minded, individualistic, and raceless (Comer, 1988; Fordham & Ogbu, 1986). These same characteristics often appear in children high in creativity that come from advantaged backgrounds.

FAMILIES AND PARENTING

Parenting and Gifted Children

Though the parents of gifted children are blessed in many ways, they must deal with a number of issues related to their children's giftedness or talent (Keirouz, 1990). Parents often feel ambivalent about having their child labeled "gifted," proud that their child is talented but worried about how it will affect the child and whether the child will have a normal life. Parents of gifted children express concern over how to find the proper level of encouragement, fearing that they will over-stimulate or understimulate the child. Parents want their gifted children to be able to reach their full potential. Some parents over-indulge their gifted child, which often increases the child's self-confidence, but unfortunately carries with it the potential for having a spoiled and egocentric child. Heaping too much attention on a gifted child also has negative repercussions for nongifted siblings.

Siblings often do suffer from negative social comparison with the gifted sibling, have lower self-esteem than the gifted sibling, and show poorer emotional adjustment than the gifted sibling. Friction between siblings is the greatest when the gifted child is the oldest.

In addition to concerns about sibling issues, parents of gifted children also may worry about the education of their gifted child. Parents of gifted children may become critical of the school's efforts, or lack of efforts, to provide a positive, stimulating education for the gifted child. No matter how competent the efforts of the school or the teacher, some parents still criticize the education their gifted child is receiving.

Another important issue for parents to consider is that the gifted child's social and emotional growth may lag behind his or her intellectual growth and that the gifted child often does not have the same abilities in different domains of development. Parents should not expect the gifted child to be perfect; even in the domain of their gifted talent, gifted children have "bad days" when they don't perform at their gifted level. Not recognizing these variations in gifted children can lead parents to place unrealistic expectations on their gifted children and harm their development.

EDUCATION

The Snowflake Model of Creativity and Its Application to Education

Daniel Perkins (1984) developed the *snowflake model of creativity*. Like the six sides of a snowflake, each with its own complex structure, Perkins' model consists of six characteristics common to highly creative individuals (figure 13.9). Children and adults who are creative may not have all six characteristics, but the more they have, the more creative they tend to be, says Perkins.

First, creative thinking involves aesthetics as much as practical standards. Aesthetics involves beauty. Outside of literature and the arts, conventional schooling pays little attention to the aesthetics of human inquiry. For example, the beauty of scientific theories, mathematical systems, and historical syntheses is rarely addressed by teachers, and how often do teachers comment on the aesthetics of students' work in math and science?

Second, creative thinking involves an ability to excel in finding problems. Creative individuals spend an unusual amount of time thinking about problems. They also explore a number of options in solving a particular problem before choosing a solution to pursue. Creative individuals value good questions because they can produce discoveries and creative answers. A student once asked Nobel laureate Linus Pauling how he came up with good ideas. Pauling said he developed a lot of ideas

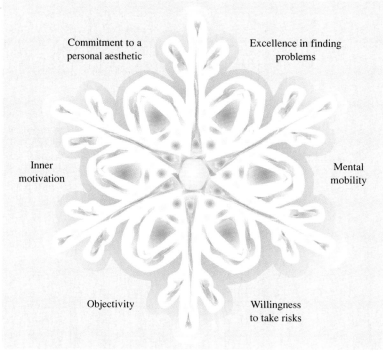

FIGURE 13.9

Snowflake Model of Creativity
Like a snowflake, Perkins' model of creativity has six parts: commitment to a personal aesthetic, excellence in finding problems, mental mobility, willingness to take risks, objectivity, and inner motivation.

and threw away the bad ones. Most assignments in school are so narrow that students have little opportunity to generate or even select among different ideas, according to Perkins.

Third, creative thinking involves mental mobility, which allows individuals to find new perspectives and approaches to problems. One example of mental mobility is being able to think in terms of opposites and contraries while seeking a new solution. According to Perkins, most problems students work on in school are convergent, not divergent. For the most part, the learning problems students face in school lack the elbow room for exercising mental mobility.

Fourth, creative thinking involves the willingness to take risks. Accompanying risk is the acceptance of failure as part of the creative quest and the ability to learn from failures. Creative geniuses don't always produce masterpieces. For example, Picasso produced more than 20,000 works of art, but much of it was mediocre. The more children produce, the better is their chance of creating something unique. According to Perkins, most schools do not challenge students to take the risk necessary to think creatively and to produce creative work.

John W. Santrock

Fifth, creative thinking involves objectivity. The popular image of creative individuals usually highlights their subjective, personal insights and commitments; however, without some objectivity and feedback from others, they would create a private world that is distant from reality and could not be shared or appreciated by others. Creative individuals not only criticize their own work but they also seek criticism from others. Schools typically do highlight objectivity, although usually not in the arts.

Sixth, creative thinking involves inner motivation. Creative individuals are motivated to produce something for its own sake, not for school grades or for money. Their catalyst is the challenge, enjoyment, and satisfaction of the work itself. Researchers have found that individuals ranging from preschool children through adults are more creative when they are internally rather than externally motivated. Work evaluation, competition for prizes, and supervision tend to undermine internal motivation and diminish creativity.

CULTURE AND ETHNICITY

Improving the English and Computer Literacy of Latino Children

Technological literacy is an issue that affects all children, but especially Latino children, who are less likely than non-Latino children to have access to computers.

One program that is designed to improve the technological literacy of Latino children is VistaKids, a project sponsored by VISTA magazine in collaboration with SER-Jobs for Progress, an educational and employment training organization that serves Latinos. The VistaKids program is located at Shenandoah Elementary School in Miami, Florida. The school serves many recently arrived families from Cuba, Nicaragua, Guatemala, and El Salvador. When the children enter, they speak little, if any, English.

VistaKids was created to address the academic problems that many Latino children face. VistaKids manages to be entertaining while teaching children the alphabet, numbers, vocabulary, pronunciation, and other academic skills. Familiar Walt Disney characters and other animated creatures interact in this vividly colored, richly detailed computer environment.

The VistaKids program is an after-school program in which children use computers to improve their English skills. It runs from 2 P.M. to 5 P.M. on weekdays and from 10 A.M. to noon on Saturdays. Parents are actively involved. They assist in the program, learn the value that English fluency plays in their children's lives, and support their children's use of English.

The teachers, children, and parents report that the VistaKids program is working extremely well. One child, Carlos, said, "I want to come all the time"; another child, Katrine, commented, "I want my parents to get me a computer so I can work at home."

GENDER

Encouraging Achievement in Girls

In the 1992 report by the American Association of University Women, it was concluded that teachers in elementary and secondary schools tend to keep girls dependent on them for help with their schoolwork while praising boys for their independence. In addition, the report noted that girls are not asked for their opinions or answers to questions as often as boys are. And girls more frequently have to raise their hands to get to say something, while boys are more likely to be rewarded for shouting out an answer or a statement.

Girls also are taught to think that when they don't succeed it is because of

their lack of intellectual ability, whereas when boys don't succeed they are often taught that it is because of their lack of effort (Dweck, 1975). This fits with our discussion of a helpless orientation earlier in the chapter—in this case, girls are given feedback that encourages a helpless orientation rather than a mastery orientation.

A special concern in achievement is the stereotyping of educational and occupational options. Many professions, especially those that are math-related and involve scientific or technical careers, are generally thought of as male activities. By contrast, teaching below the college level, working in clerical and

related support jobs, and excelling in language-related courses are thought to be female activities (Eccles & Midgley, 1987). Because the math and scientific/technical activities and careers are so stereotyped in a male's favor, girls often have little confidence in their ability to do well in them, and so they tend to avoid them.

In summary, girls' achievement orientation can be improved by encouraging girls to be independent and assertive, emphasizing their effort rather than their ability when they don't succeed at tasks, and decreasing the gender stereotyping of activities and careers.

MAURICE BRAZIL
PRENDERGAST
West Church, detail

Socioemotional Development in Middle and Late Childhood

*Children know nothing about childhood
and have little to say about it. They are too
busy becoming something they have not
quite grasped yet, something which keeps
changing. . . . Nor will they realize what
is happening to them until they are too far
beyond it to remember how it felt.*

—**Alistair Reed**

families. But there are several other major shifts in the composition of family life that especially affect children in middle and late childhood. Parents are divorcing in greater numbers than ever before, but many of them remarry. It takes time for parents to marry, have children, get divorced, and then remarry. Consequently, there are far more elementary and secondary school children than infant or preschool children living in stepfamilies. In addition, an increasing number of elementary and secondary school children are latchkey children.

Stepfamilies

The number of remarriages involving children has steadily grown in recent years, although both the rate of increase in divorce and stepfamilies slowed in the 1980s. Stepfather families, in which a woman has custody of children from a previous marriage, make up 70 percent of stepfamilies. Stepmother families make up almost 20 percent of stepfamilies, and a small minority are blended, with both partners bringing children from a previous marriage. A substantial percentage of stepfamilies produce children of their own.

Like divorce, remarriage has also become commonplace in American society. The United States has the highest remarriage rate in the world, and Americans tend to remarry soon after divorce. Younger women remarry more quickly than older women, and childless women, divorced prior to the age of 25, have higher remarriage rates than women with children. The more money a divorced male has, the more likely he is to remarry, but for women the opposite is true. Remarriage satisfaction, similar to satisfaction in first marriages, often decreases over time. In fact, few differences have been found between the factors that predict marital satisfaction in first marriages and remarriage (Coleman & Ganong, 1990).

Just as couples who are first married, remarried individuals often have unrealistic expectations about their stepfamily. Thus, an important adjustment for remarried persons is to develop realistic expectations. Money and the complexities of family structure in the remarried family often contribute to marital conflict.

Many variations in remarriage have the potential for what is called **boundary ambiguity**—*the uncertainty in stepfamilies about who is in or out of the family and who is performing or responsible for certain tasks in the family system*. The uncertainty of boundaries likely increases stress for the family system and the probability of behavior problems in children.

Research on stepfamilies has lagged behind research on divorced families, but a number of investigators have turned their attention to this increasingly common family structure (Hetherington, 1995; Santrock & Sitterle, 1987). In one recent study, entrance of a stepfather when children were 9 years or older was associated with more problems than when the stepfather family was formed earlier (Hetherington, 1995). Following remarriage of their parents, children of all ages show a resurgence of behavior problems (Freeman, 1993). Younger children seem to eventually form an attachment to a stepparent and accept the stepparenting role. However, the developmental tasks facing adolescents make them especially vulnerable to the entrance of a stepparent. At the time when they are searching for an identity and exploring sexual and other close relationships outside the family, a nonbiological parent may increase the stress associated with these important tasks.

Following the remarriage of the custodial parent, an emotional upheaval usually occurs in girls, and problems in boys often intensify (Henderson & others, 1996). Over time, preadolescent boys seem to improve more than girls in step father families. Sons who frequently are involved in conflicted or coercive relations with their custodial mothers probably have much to gain from living with a warm, supportive step father. In contrast, daughters who have a close relationship with their custodial mothers and considerable independence frequently find a stepfather both disruptive and constraining.

Children's relationships with their biological parents are more positive than with their stepparents, regardless of whether a stepmother or stepfather family is involved. However, stepfathers are often distant and disengaged from their stepchildren. As a rule, the more complex the stepfamily, the more difficult the child's adjustment. Families in which both parents bring children from a previous marriage have the highest level of behavioral problems.

In the recent investigation by E. Mavis Hetherington (1994, 1995), both parenting techniques and the school environment were associated with whether children coped effectively both with living in a divorced family and a stepfamily. From the first grade on, an authoritative environment (an organized predictable environment with clearly defined standards, and a responsive, nurturant environment) was linked with greater achievement and fewer problems in children than three other environments—authoritarian (coercive, power assertive, punitive, more criticism than praise, little responsiveness to individual children's needs, and low nurturance), permissive (low structure, disorganized, and high warmth), and chaotic/neglecting (disorganized, ineffective, erratic though usually harsh control, unstructured, low expectations, and hostile relationships). In divorced families, when only one parent was authoritative, or when neither parent was authoritative, an authoritative school improved the child's adjustment. A chaotic/neglecting school environment had the most adverse effects on children, which were most marked when there was no authoritative parent in the home.

Latchkey Children

We concluded in chapter 11 that the mother's working outside the home does not necessarily have negative outcomes for her children. However, a certain subset of children from working-mother families deserve further scrutiny: latchkey children. These children typically do not see their parents from the time they leave for school in the morning until about 6 or 7 P.M. They are called "latchkey" children because they are given the key to their home, take the key to school, and then use it to let themselves into the home while their parents are still at work. Latchkey children are largely unsupervised for 2 to 4 hours a day during each school week. During the summer months, they might be unsupervised for entire days, 5 days a week.

Thomas and Lynette Long (1983) interviewed more than 1,500 latchkey children. They concluded that a slight majority of these children had had negative latchkey experiences. Some latchkey children may grow up too fast, hurried by the responsibilities placed on them. How do latchkey children handle the lack of limits and structure during the latchkey hours? Without limits and parental supervision, latchkey children find their way into trouble more easily, possibly stealing, vandalizing, or abusing a sibling. The Longs point out that 90 percent of the juvenile delinquents in Montgomery County, Maryland, are latchkey children. Joan Lipsitz (1983), in testifying before the Select Committee on Children, Youth, and Families, called the lack of adult supervision of children in the after-school hours one of today's major problems. Lipsitz calls it the "three-to-six o'clock problem" because it is during this time that the Center for Early Adolescence in North Carolina, of which Lipsitz is director, experiences a peak of referrals for clinical help. And in a 1987 national poll, teachers rated the latchkey children phenomenon the number one reason that children have problems in schools (Harris, 1987).

But while latchkey children may be vulnerable to problems, the experiences of latchkey children vary enormously, as do the experiences of all children with working mothers. Parents need to give special attention to the ways in which their latchkey children's lives can be effectively monitored. Variations in latchkey experiences suggest that parental monitoring and authoritative parenting help the child cope more effectively with latchkey experiences, especially in resisting peer pressure (Galambos & Maggs, 1989; Steinberg, 1986). In one recent study, attending a formal after-school program that included academic, recreational, and remedial activities was associated with better academic achievement and social adjustment in comparison to other types of after-school care (such as informal adult supervision or self-care) (Posner & Vandell, 1994). The degree of developmental risk to latchkey children remains undetermined. One positive sign is that researchers are beginning to conduct more-precise analyses of children's latchkey experiences to determine which aspects of latchkey circumstances are the most detrimental.

PEER RELATIONS

During middle and late childhood, children spend an increasing amount of time in peer interaction. In one investigation, children interacted with peers 10 percent of their day at the age of 2, 20 percent at age 4, and more than 40 percent between the ages of 7 and 11 (Barker & Wright, 1951). Episodes with peers totaled 299 per typical school day.

What do children do when they are with their peers? In one study, sixth graders were asked what they do when they are with their friends (Medrich & others, 1982). Team sports accounted for 45 percent of boys' activities but only 26 percent of girls'. General play, going places, and socializing were common listings for both sexes. Most peer interactions occur outside the home (although close to home), occur more often in private than in public places, and occur more between children of the same sex than between children of different sexes.

Peer Popularity, Rejection, and Neglect

Children often think, "What can I do to get all of the kids at school to like me?" or "What's wrong with me? Something must be wrong or I would be more popular." What makes a child popular with peers? Children who give out the most reinforcements are often popular. So is a child who listens carefully to other children and maintains open lines of communication. Being themselves, being happy, showing enthusiasm and concern for others, and being self-confident but not conceited are characteristics that serve children well in their quest for peer popularity (Hartup, 1983). In one study, popular children were more likely to communicate clearly with their peers, elicit their peers' attention, and maintain conversation with peers than were unpopular children (Kennedy, 1990).

Recently, developmentalists have distinguished between two types of children who are not popular with their peers: those who are neglected and those who are rejected (Coie & Koeppl, 1990). **Neglected children** *receive little attention from their peers but they are not necessarily disliked by their peers.* **Rejected children** *are disliked by their peers. They are more likely to be disruptive and aggressive than neglected children.* Rejected children often have more serious adjustment problems later in life than do neglected children (Dishion & Spacklen, 1996). For example, in one study, 112 fifth-grade boys were evaluated over a period of 7 years until the end of high school (Kupersmidt & Coie, 1990). The key factor in predicting whether rejected children would engage in delinquent behavior or drop out of schoo later during adolescence was aggression toward peers in elementary school.

Not all rejected children are aggressive. Although aggression and its related characteristics of impulsiveness and disruptiveness underlie rejection about half the time, approximately 10 to 20 percent of rejected children are shy.

An important question to ask is how neglected children and rejected children can be trained to interact more effectively with their peers. The goal of training programs with neglected children is often to help them attract attention from their peers in positive ways and to hold their attention by asking questions, by listening in a warm and friendly way, and by saying things about themselves that relate to the peers' interests. They also are taught to enter groups more effectively.

The goal of training programs with rejected children is often to help them listen to peers and "hear what they say" instead of trying to dominate peer interactions. Rejected children are trained to join peers without trying to change what is taking place in the peer group. Children may need to be motivated to use these strategies by being persuaded that they work effectively and are satisfying. In some programs, children are shown videotapes of appropriate peer interaction; then they are asked to comment on them and to draw lessons from what they have seen. In other training programs, popular children are taught to be more accepting of neglected or rejected peers.

Social Cognition

Earlier we found that the mutual cognitions of children and parents become increasingly important in family relationships during middle and late childhood. Children's social cognitions about their peers also become increasingly important for understanding peer relationships in middle and late childhood. Of special interest are how children process information about peer relations and their social knowledge (Crick & Dodge, 1994).

A boy accidentally trips and knocks a peer's soft drink out of his hand. The peer misinterprets the encounter as hostile, which leads him to retaliate aggressively against the boy. Through repeated encounters of this kind, other peers come to perceive the aggressive boy as habitually acting in inappropriate ways. Kenneth Dodge (1983) argues that children go through five steps in processing information about their social world: decoding social cues, interpreting, searching for a response, selecting an optimal response, and enacting. Dodge has found that aggressive boys are more likely to perceive another child's actions as hostile when the child's intention is ambiguous. And when aggressive boys search for cues to determine a peer's intention, they respond more rapidly, less efficiently, and less reflectively than nonaggressive children. These are among the social cognitive factors believed to be involved in the nature of children's conflicts.

Social knowledge is also involved in children's ability to get along with peers. An important part of children's social life involves knowing what goals to pursue in poorly defined or ambiguous situations. Social relationship goals are also important, such as how to initiate and maintain a social bond. Children need to know what scripts to follow to get other children to be their friends. For example, as part of the script for getting friends, it helps to know that saying nice things, regardless of what the peer does or says, will make the peer like the child more.

From a social cognitive perspective, children who are maladjusted do not have adequate social cognitive skills to effectively interact with others. One investigation explored the possibility that children who are maladjusted do not have the social cognitive skills necessary for positive social interaction (Asarnow & Callan, 1985). Boys with and without peer adjustment difficulties were identified, and their social cognitive skills were assessed.

Boys without peer adjustment problems generated more alternative solutions to problems, proposed more assertive and mature solutions, gave less-intense aggressive solutions, showed more adaptive planning, and evaluated physically aggressive responses less positively than boys with peer adjustment problems.

The world of peers is one of varying acquaintances; children interact with some children they barely know and with friends for hours every day. It is to the latter type—friends—that we now turn.

Friends

"My best friend is nice. She is honest and I can trust her. I can tell her my innermost secrets and know that nobody else will find out about them. I have other friends, but she is my best friend. We consider each other's feelings and don't want to hurt each other. We help each other out when we have problems. We make up funny names for people and laugh ourselves silly. We make lists of which boys we think are the ugliest, which are the biggest jerks, and so on. Some of these things we share with other friends, some we don't." This is a description of a friendship by a 10-year-old girl. It reflects the belief that children are interested in specific peers—in Barbara and Tommy—not just any peers. They want to share concerns, interests, information, and secrets with them (Hartup, 1996).

A man's growth is seen in the successive choirs of his friends.
                                        —**Ralph Waldo Emerson, 1841**

Why are children's friendships important? They serve six functions: companionship, stimulation, physical support, ego support, social comparison, and intimacy/affection (Gottman & Parker, 1987). Concerning companionship, friendship provides children with a familiar partner and playmate, someone who is willing to spend time with them and join in collaborative activities. Concerning stimulation, friendship provides children with interesting information, excitement, and amusement. Concerning physical support, friendship provides time, resources, and assistance. Concerning ego support, friendship provides the expectation of support, encouragement, and feedback that helps children maintain an impression of themselves as competent, attractive, and worthwhile individuals. Concerning social comparison, friendship provides information about where the child stands vis-à-vis others and whether the child is doing OK. Concerning intimacy and affection, friendship provides children with a warm, close, trusting relationship with another individual in which self-disclosure takes place (see figure 14.1).

Hold a true friend with both hands.
                                        —**Nigerian proverb**

In contrast to other psychoanalytic theorists' narrow emphasis on the importance of parent-child relationships, Sullivan contended that friends also play important roles in shaping children's and adolescents' well-being and development. In terms of well-being, he argued that all people have a number of basic social needs, including the need for tenderness (secure attachment), playful companionship, social acceptance, intimacy, and sexual relations. Whether or not these needs are fulfilled largely determines our emotional well-being. For example, if the need for playful companionship goes unmet, then we become bored and depressed; if the need for social acceptance is not met, we suffer a lowered sense of self-worth. Developmentally, friends become increasingly depended upon to satisfy these needs during adolescence, and thus the ups and downs of experiences with friends increasingly shape adolescents' state of well-being. In particular, Sullivan believed that the need for intimacy intensifies during early adolescence, motivating teenagers to seek out close friends. He felt that if adolescents failed to forge such close friendships, they would experience painful feelings of loneliness coupled with a reduced sense of self-worth.

FIGURE 14.1

Functions of Children's Friendships

Two of friendship's most common characteristics are intimacy and similarity. **Intimacy in friendships** *is defined as self-disclosure and the sharing of private thoughts.* Research reveals that intimate friendships may not appear until early adolescence (Berndt & Perry, 1990). Also, throughout childhood, friends are more similar than dissimilar in terms of age, sex, race, and many other factors (Berndt, 1996). Friends often have similar attitudes toward school, similar educational aspirations, and closely aligned achievement orientations. Friends like the same music, the same kind of clothes, and the same kind of leisure activities.

Harry Stack Sullivan (1953) was the most influential theorist to discuss the importance of friendships. He argued that there is a dramatic increase in the psychological importance and intimacy of close friends during early adolescence.

SCHOOLS

It is justifiable to be concerned about the impact of schools on children: By the time students graduate from high school, they have spent 10,000 hours in the classroom. Children spend many years in schools as members of a small society in which there are tasks to be accomplished, people to be socialized and socialized by, and rules that define and limit behavior, feelings, and attitudes.

The world rests on the breath of the children in the schoolhouse.

— **The Talmud**

The Transition to Elementary School

For most children, entering the first grade signals a change from being a "homechild" to being a "schoolchild" in which new roles and obligations are experienced. Children take up a new role (being a student), interact and develop relationships with new significant others, adopt new reference groups, and develop new standards by which to judge themselves. School provides children with a rich source of new ideas to shape their sense of self.

A special concern about children's early school experiences is emerging. Evidence is mounting that early schooling proceeds mainly on the basis of negative feedback. For example, children's self-esteem in the latter part of elementary school is lower than it is in the earlier part, and older children rate themselves as less smart, less good, and less hardworking than do younger ones (Blumenfeld & others, 1981).

In school as well as out of school, children's learning, like children's development, is *integrated* (National Association for the Education of Young Children, 1988). One of the main pressures on elementary teachers has been the need to "cover the curriculum." Frequently, teachers have tried to do so by tightly scheduling discrete time segments for each subject. This approach ignores the fact that children often do not need to distinguish learning by subject area. For example, they advance their knowledge of reading and writing when they work on social studies projects; they learn mathematical concepts through music and physical education (Katz & Chard, 1989). A curriculum can be facilitated by providing learning areas in which children plan and select their activities. For example, the classroom may include a fully equipped publishing center, complete with materials for writing, illustrating, typing, and binding student-made books; a science area with animals and plants for observation and books to study; and other similar areas. In this type of classroom, children learn reading as they discover information about science; they learn writing as they work together on interesting projects. Such classrooms also provide opportunities for spontaneous play, recognizing that elementary school children continue to learn in all areas through unstructured play, either alone or with other children.

Knowledge which is acquired under compulsion obtains no hold on the mind.

—**Plato**

Education experts Lillian Katz and Sylvia Chard (1989) described two elementary school classrooms. In one, children spent an entire morning making identical pictures of traffic lights. The teacher made no attempt to get the children to relate the pictures to anything else the class was doing. In the other class, children were investigating a school bus. They wrote to the district's school superintendent and asked if they could have a bus parked at their school for a few days. They studied the bus, discovered the functions of its parts, and discussed traffic rules. Then, in the classroom, they built their own bus out of

cardboard. The children had fun, but they also practiced writing, problem solving, and even some arithmetic. When the class had their parents' night, the teacher was ready with reports on how each child was doing. However, all the parents wanted to see was the bus, because their children had been talking about it at home for weeks. Many contemporary education experts believe that this is the kind of education all children deserve. That is, they believe that children should be taught through concrete, hands-on experience.

Teachers

Teachers have a prominent influence in middle and late childhood. Teachers symbolize authority and establish the classroom's climate, conditions of interaction among students, and the nature of group functioning.

Almost everyone's life is affected in one way or another by teachers. You were influenced by teachers as you grew up; you may become a teacher yourself or work with teachers through counseling or psychological services; and you may one day have children whose education will be guided by many different teachers through the years. You can probably remember several of your teachers vividly: Perhaps one never smiled, another required you to memorize everything in sight, and yet another always appeared happy and vibrant and encouraged verbal interaction. Psychologists and educators have tried to create a profile of a good teacher's personality traits, but the complexity of personality, education, learning, and individual differences make the task difficult. Nonetheless, some teacher traits are associated with positive student outcomes more than others: enthusiasm, ability to plan, poise, adaptability, warmth, flexibility, and awareness of individual differences are a few (Gage, 1965).

Erik Erikson (1968) believes that good teachers should be able to produce a sense of industry, rather than inferiority, in their students. Good teachers are trusted and respected by the community and know how to alternate work and play, study and games, says Erikson. They know how to recognize special efforts and to encourage special abilities. They also know how to create a setting in which children feel good about themselves and how to handle those children to whom school is not important. In Erikson's (1968) own words, children should be "mildly but firmly coerced into the adventure of finding out that one can learn to accomplish things which one would never have thought of by oneself" (p. 127).

Teacher characteristics and styles are important, but they need to be considered in concert with what children bring to the school situation. Some children may benefit more from structure than others, and some teachers may be able to handle a flexible curriculum better than others. **Aptitude-treatment interaction (ATI)** *stresses the importance of children's aptitudes or characteristics and the treatments or experiences they are given in classrooms. Aptitude* refers to such characteristics as academic potential and personality characteristics on which students differ; *treatment* refers to educational techniques, such as structured versus flexible classrooms (Cronbach & Snow, 1977). Researchers have found that children's achievement level (aptitude) interacts with classroom structure (treatment) to produce the best learning (Peterson, 1977). For example, students who are highly achievement oriented usually do well in a flexible classroom and enjoy it; low-achievement-oriented students usually fare worse and dislike the flexibility. The reverse often appears in structured classrooms.

Social Class and Ethnicity in Schools

Sometimes it seems as though the major function of schools has been to train children to contribute to a middle-class society. Politicians who vote on school funding have been from middle-class or elite backgrounds, school board members have often been from middle-class backgrounds, and principals and teachers also have had middle-class upbringing. Critics argue that schools have not done a good job of educating lower-class and ethnic minority children to overcome the barriers that block the enhancement of their positions (Falbo & Romo, 1994; Scott-Jones, 1996).

My country is the world; My countrymen are mankind.
—William Lloyd Garrison, 1803

Teachers have lower expectations for children from low-income families than for children from middle-income families. A teacher who knows that a child comes from a lower-class background may spend less time trying to help the child solve a problem and may anticipate that the child will get into trouble. The teacher may believe that the parents in low-income families are not interested in helping the child, so she may make fewer efforts to communicate with them. There is evidence that teachers with lower-class origins may have different attitudes toward lower-class students than do teachers from middle-class origins (Gottlieb, 1966). Perhaps because they have experienced many inequities themselves, teachers with lower-class origins may be more empathetic to problems that lower-class children encounter. When asked to rate the most outstanding characteristics of their lower-class students, middle-class teachers checked lazy, rebellious, and fun-loving; lower-class teachers checked happy, cooperative, energetic, and ambitious. The teachers with lower-class backgrounds perceived the lower-class children's behaviors as adaptive; the middle-class teachers viewed the same behaviors as falling short of middle-class standards.

In his famous "I Have a Dream" speech, Martin Luther King said, "I have a dream that my four little children will one day live in a nation where they will not be judged by the color of their skin but by the content of their character." Children from lower-class backgrounds are not the only students who have had difficulties in school; so

have children from different ethnic backgrounds. In most American schools, African Americans, Mexican Americans, Puerto Ricans, Native Americans, Japanese, and Asian Americans are minorities. Many teachers have been ignorant of the different cultural meanings non-Anglo children have learned in their communities (Huang & Gibbs, 1989). The social and academic development of children from minority groups depends on teacher expectations, the teacher's experience in working with children from different backgrounds, the curriculum, the presence of role models in the schools for minority students, the quality of relations between school personnel and parents from different ethnic, economic, and educational backgrounds, and the relations between the school and the community (Minuchin & Shapiro, 1983).

School segregation is still a factor in the education of African American and Latino children and adolescents (Simons, Finlay, & Yang, 1991). Almost one-third of African American and Latino students attend schools in which 90 percent or more of the students are from ethnic minority groups. In the last two decades, the percentage of Latino children who attend predominantly minority schools has increased, while the percentage of African American children in this type of schooling has decreased somewhat.

The school experiences of children and adolescents from different ethnic groups vary considerably (DeBlassie & DeBlassie, 1996; Mare, 1996). African American and Latino students are much less likely than White or Asian students to be enrolled in academic, college preparatory programs, and much more likely to be enrolled in remedial and special education programs. African American children are twice as likely as children from other ethnic groups to be enrolled in educable mentally retarded programs. Asian children are the least likely of any ethnic group to be in any special education program for students with disabilities. Asian students are much more likely than any other ethnic group to take advanced math and science courses in high school. Almost 25 percent of all Asian students take advanced-placement calculus, compared with less than 3 percent of all other students, and Asian students are three times as likely as students in any other ethnic groups to take advanced-placement chemistry or physics. African Americans are twice as likely as Latinos, Native Americans, or Whites to be suspended from school or to be corporally punished.

American anthropologist John Ogbu (1986, 1989) proposed the controversial view that ethnic minority children are placed in a position of subordination and exploitation in the American educational system. He believes that ethnic minority children, especially African American and Latino children, have inferior educational opportunities, are exposed to teachers and administrators who have low academic expectations for them, and encounter negative stereotypes about ethnic minority groups. Ogbu states that ethnic minority opposition to the middle-class White educational system stems from a lack of trust because of years

---

of discrimination and oppression. Says Ogbu, it makes little sense for ethnic minority youth to do well academically if occupational opportunities are often closed to them.

> *Our most basic common link is that we all inhabit this planet. We all breathe the same air. We all cherish our children's future.*
>
> **—John F. Kennedy, address, The American University, 1963**

Completing high school, or even college, does not always bring the same job opportunities for many ethnic minority youth as for White youth (Entwisle, 1990). In terms of earnings and employment rates, African American high school graduates do not do as well as their White counterparts. Many Latino youth also give up in school, because, given the inadequate job opportunities awaiting them, they don't perceive any rewards for doing well in school.

According to Margaret Beale Spencer and Sanford Dornbusch (1990), a form of institutional racism prevails in many American schools. That is, well-meaning teachers, acting out of misguided liberalism, often fail to challenge ethnic minority students. Knowing the handicaps these children face, some teachers accept a low level of performance from them, substituting warmth and affection for academic challenge and high standards of performance. Ethnic minority students, like their White counterparts, learn best when teachers combine warmth with challenging standards.

One person who is trying to do something about the poor quality of education for inner city children is African American psychiatrist James Comer (1988, 1993). He has devised an intervention model that is based on a simple principle: Everyone with a stake in a school should have a say in how it's run. Comer's model calls for forming a school-governance team, made up of the principal, psychologists, and even cafeteria workers. The team develops a comprehensive plan for operating the school, including a calendar of academic and social events that encourage parents to come to school as often as possible. Comer is convinced that a strong family orientation is a key to educational success, so he tries to create a familylike environment in schools and also make parents feel comfortable in coming to their children's school. Among the reasons for Comer's concern about the lack of parental involvement in African American and Latino children's education is the high rate of single-parent families in these ethnic minority groups. A special concern is that 70 percent of the African American and Latino single-parent families headed by mothers are in poverty. Poor school performance among many ethnic minority children is related to this pattern of single parenting and poverty (Spencer & Dornbusch, 1990).

James Comer (left) is shown with some of the inner-city African American children who attend a school that became a better learning environment because of Comer's intervention. Comer is convinced that a strong, familylike atmosphere is a key to improving the quality of inner-city schools.

Thus far, we have discussed many ideas about families, peers, and schools in middle and late childhood. These ideas are summarized in concept table 14.1.

THE SELF, GENDER, AND MORAL DEVELOPMENT

In chapter 11, we discussed the development of the self, gender, and moral development in early childhood. Here we focus on these important dimensions of children's development in middle and late childhood.

The Self

What is the nature of the child's self-understanding in the elementary school years? What is the role of perspective taking in self-understanding? What is the nature of children's self-esteem? What issue does Erikson believe children face in middle and late childhood?

The Development of Self-Understanding

In middle and late childhood, self-understanding increasingly shifts from defining oneself through external characteristics

Families, Peers, and Schools

Concept	Processes/Related Ideas	Characteristics/Description
Families	Parent-child issues	Parents spend less time with children during middle and late childhood, including less time in caregiving, instruction, reading, talking, and playing. Nonetheless, parents still are powerful and important socializing agents during this period. New parent-child issues emerge, and discipline changes. Control is more coregulatory, children and parents label each other more, and parents mature just as children do.
	Societal changes in families	During middle and late childhood, two major changes in many children's lives are movement into a stepfamily and becoming a latchkey child. Just as divorce produces disequilibrium and stress for children, so does the entrance of a stepparent. An authoritative orientation in families and schools is associated with positive outcomes for children from divorced and stepfamily homes. Latchkey children may become vulnerable when they are not monitored by adults in the after-school hours.
Peers	Peer interaction	Children spend considerably more time with peers in middle and late childhood.
	Popularity, rejection, and neglect	Listening skills and effective communication, being yourself, being happy, showing enthusiasm and concern for others, and having self-confidence, but not being conceited, are predictors of peer popularity. The risk status of neglected children is unclear. Rejected children are at risk for the development of problems. A special interest focuses on improving the peer relations of neglected and rejected children.
	Social cognition	Social information-processing skills and social knowledge are two important dimensions of social cognition in peer relations.
	Friends	Children's friendships serve six functions: companionship, stimulation, physical support, ego support, social comparison, and intimacy/affection. Intimacy and similarity are common characteristics of friendships. Harry Stack Sullivan was the most influential theorist to discuss the importance of friendships. He argued that there is a dramatic increase in the psychological importance and intimacy of close friends in early adolescence.
Schools	The transition to elementary school	Children spend more than 10,000 hours in the classroom as members of a small society in which there are tasks to be accomplished, people to be socialized and socialized by, and rules that define and limit behavior. A special concern is that early schooling proceeds mainly on the basis of negative feedback to children.
	Teachers	Teachers have prominent influences in middle and late childhood. Aptitude-treatment interaction is an important consideration.
	Social class and ethnicity	Schools have a stronger middle-class than lower-class orientation. Many lower-class children have problems in schools, as do children from ethnic minorities. Ogbu proposed a controversial view that ethnic minority children are placed in a position of subordination and exploitation in the American education system.

Selman's Stages of Perspective Taking

Stage	Perspective-Taking Stage	Ages	Description
0	Egocentric viewpoint	3–5	Child has a sense of differentiation of self and other but fails to distinguish between the social perspective (thoughts, feelings) of other and self. Child can label other's overt feelings but does not see the cause-and-effect relation of reasons to social actions.
1	Social-informational perspective taking	6–8	Child is aware that other has a social perspective based on other's own reasoning, which may or may not be similar to child's. However, child tends to focus on one perspective rather than coordinating viewpoints.
2	Self-reflective perspective taking	8–10	Child is conscious that each individual is aware of the other's perspective and that this awareness influences self and other's view of each other. Putting self in other's place is a way of judging other's intentions, purposes, and actions. Child can form a coordinated chain of perspectives but cannot yet abstract from this process to the level of simultaneous mutuality.
3	Mutual perspective taking	10–12	Adolescent realizes that both self and other can view each other mutually and simultaneously as subjects. Adolescent can step outside the two-person dyad and view the interaction from a third-person perspective.
4	Social and conventional system perspective taking	12–15	Adolescent realizes mutual perspective taking does not always lead to complete understanding. Social conventions are seen as necessary because they are understood by all members of the group (the generalized other), regardless of their position, role, or experience.

Source: From R. L. Selman, "Social-Cognitive Understanding" in T. Lickona (ed.), *Moral Development and Behavior*, 1976. Reprinted by permission of Thomas Lickona.

to defining oneself through internal characteristics. Elementary school children are also more likely to define themselves in terms of social characteristics and social comparisons.

In middle and late childhood, children not only recognize differences between inner and outer states, but are also more likely to include subjective inner states in their definition of self. For example, in one study, second-grade children were much more likely than younger children to name psychological character- istics (such as preferences or personality traits) in their self-definition and less likely to name physical charac- teristics (such as eye color or possessions) (Aboud & Skerry, 1983). For example, 8-year-old Todd includes in his self-description, "I am smart and I am popular." Ten-year-old Tina says about herself, "I am pretty good about not worrying most of the time. I used to lose my temper but I'm better about that now. I also feel proud when I do well in school."

In addition to the increase of psychological charac- teristics in self-definition during the elementary school years, the *social aspects* of the self also increase at this point in development. In one investigation, elementary school children often included references to social groups in their self-descriptions (Livesly & Bromsley, 1973). For example, some children referred to themselves as Girl Scouts, as Catholics, or as someone who has two close friends.

Children's self-understanding in the elementary school years also includes increasing reference to *social comparison*. At this point in development, children are more likely to distinguish themselves from others in com- parative rather than in absolute terms. That is, elementary- school-age children are no longer as likely to think about what *I* do or do not do, but are more likely to think about what *I* can do *in comparison with others*. This developmen- tal shift provides an increased tendency of establishing one's differences from others as an individual.

The Role of Perspective Taking in Self-Understanding

Many child developmentalists believe that perspective tak- ing plays an important role in self-understanding. **Perspective taking** *is the ability to assume another person's perspective and understand his or her thoughts and feelings.* Robert Selman (1980) has proposed a developmental the- ory of perspective taking that has been given considerable attention. He believes perspective taking involves a series of five stages, ranging from 3 years of age through adoles- cence (see table 14.1). These stages begin with the egocen- tric viewpoint in early childhood and end with in-depth perspective taking in adolescence.

To study children's perspective taking, Selman indi- vidually interviews the child, asking the child to comment on such dilemmas as the following:

Holly is an 8-year-old girl who likes to climb trees. She is the best tree climber in the neighborhood. One day while climbing down from a tall tree, she falls . . . but does not hurt herself. Her father sees her fall. He is upset and asks her to promise not to climb trees any more. Holly promises.

Later that day, Holly and her friends meet Shawn. Shawn's kitten is caught in a tree and can't get down. Something has to be done right away or the kitten may fall. Holly is the only one who climbs trees well enough to reach the kitten and get it down but she remembers her promise to her father. (Selman, 1976, p. 302)

Subsequently, Selman asks the child a series of questions about the dilemma, such as:

- Does Holly know how Shawn feels about the kitten?
- How will Holly's father feel if he finds out she climbed the tree?
- What does Holly think her father will do if he finds out she climbed the tree?
- What would you do in this situation?

After analyzing children's responses to these dilemmas, Selman (1980) concluded that children's perspective taking follows the developmental sequence described in table 14.1.

Children's perspective taking not only can increase their self-understanding, but it can also improve their peer group status and the quality of their friendships. For example, in one study, the most popular children in the third and eighth grades had competent perspective-taking skills (Kurdek & Krile, 1982). Children who are competent at perspective taking are better at understanding the needs of their companions, so they are likely to communicate more effectively with them (Hudson, Forman, & Brion-Meisels, 1982).

Self-Esteem and Self-Concept

What are self-esteem and self-concept? How are they measured? How do parent-child relationships contribute to self-esteem? How is group identity involved in children's self-esteem? And, how can children's self-esteem be enhanced?

What Are Self-Esteem and Self-Concept?   Self-esteem *refers to global evaluations of the self. Self-esteem is also referred to as self-worth or self-image.* For example, a child may perceive that she is not merely a person, but a *good* person. Of course, not all children have an overall positive image of themselves. **Self-concept** *refers to domain-specific evaluations of the self.* Children can make self-evaluations in many domains of their lives—academic, athletic, appearance, and so on. In sum, *self-esteem* refers to global self-evaluations, *self-concept* to more domain-specific evaluations.

Investigators have not always made clear distinctions between self-esteem and self-concept, sometimes using the terms interchangeably or not precisely defining them. As you read the remaining discussion of self-esteem and self-concept, the distinction between self-esteem as global self-evaluation and self-concept as domain-specific self-evaluation should help you to keep the terms straight.

> *It is difficult to make people miserable when they feel worthy of themselves.*
>
> **—Abraham Lincoln**

Measuring Self-Esteem and Self-Concept

Measuring self-esteem and self-concept hasn't always been easy. Recently, different measures have been developed to assess children and adolescents.

Susan Harter's (1985) Self-Perception Profile for Children is a revision of her original measure, the Perceived Competence Scale for Children (Harter, 1982). The **Self-Perception Profile for Children** *taps five specific domains of self-concept—scholastic competence, athletic competence, social acceptance, physical appearance, and behavioral conduct—plus general self-worth.* Harter's scale does an excellent job of separating children's self-evaluations in different skill domains, and when general self-worth is assessed, questions focus on the overall self evaluations rather than in specific skill domains.

The Self-Perception Profile for Children is designed to be used with third-grade through sixth-grade children. Harter also has developed a separate scale for adolescents, recognizing important developmental changes in self-perceptions. The Self-Perception Profile for Adolescents (Harter, 1989) taps eight domains—scholastic competence, athletic competence, social acceptance, physical appearance, behavioral conduct, close friendship, romantic appeal, and job competence—plus global self-worth. Thus, the adolescent version has three skill domains not present in the children's version—job competence, romantic appeal, and close friendship.

Parent-Child Relationships and Self-Esteem   In the most extensive investigation of parent-child relationships and self-esteem, a measure of self-esteem was given to elementary school boys, and the boys and their mothers were interviewed about their family relationships (Coopersmith, 1967). Based on these assessments, the following parenting attributes were associated with boys' high self-esteem:

- Expression of affection
- Concern about the child's problems
- Harmony in the home
- Participation in joint family activities
- Availability to give competent, organized help to the boys when they need it
- Setting clear and fair rules
- Abiding by these rules
- Allowing the children freedom within well-prescribed limits

Remember that these findings are correlational, so we cannot say that these parenting attributes *cause* children's high self-esteem. Such factors as parental acceptance and allowing children freedom within well-prescribed limits probably are important determinants of children's self-esteem, but we still must say that *they are related to* rather than that *they cause* children's self-esteem, based on the available research data.

Group Identity and Self-Esteem   Children's group identity is also related to their self-esteem. **Social identity theory** *is social psychologist Henry Tajfel's (1978) theory that, when individuals are assigned to a group, they invariably think of that group as an in-group for them. This occurs because individuals want to have a positive self-image.* According to Tajfel, self-image consists of both a personal identity and many different social identities. Tajfel argues that individuals can improve their self-image by enhancing either their personal or their social identity. Tajfel believes that social identity is especially important. When children or adults compare the social identity of their group with the social identity of another group, they often maximize the distinctions between the two groups. For example, think of an adolescent's identity with the school's football or basketball team. When the school's teams win, students' self-images are enhanced, regardless of whether they play on the teams or not. Why? Because they have a social identity with the school and the school's teams.

As children and adults strive to promote their social identities, it is not long before proud, self-congratulatory remarks are interspersed with nasty comments about the opposing group(s). In a capsule, the theme becomes, "My group is good and I am good. Your group is bad and you are bad." So it goes with the sexes, ethnic groups, teams, social classes, religions, and countless other groups, all seeking to improve their respective self-images through social identity with the group and comparison of the group with other groups. These comparisons can easily lead to competition, conflict, and even a perception that discrimination against other groups is legitimate.

Tajfel showed that it does not take much to get children or adults to think in terms of "we" and "they," or in-group and out-group. He assigned children to two groups based on a trivial task. For example, one individual was assigned to one group because she overestimated the number of dots on a screen, and another individual was assigned to another group because he underestimated the number. Once assigned to the two groups, the members were asked to award amounts of money to pairs of other subjects. Those eligible to receive the money were anonymous except for their membership in one of the two groups Tajfel created. Invariably, the children acted favorably toward (awarded money to) members of their own group. It is no wonder, then, that if we favor our own group based on such trivial criteria, we will show intense in-group favoritism when differences are not as trivial.

Closely related to group identity and self-esteem is **ethnocentrism,** *the tendency to favor one's own group over other groups.* Ethnocentrism's positive side appears in the sense of in-group pride that fulfills our strong urge to attain and maintain a positive self-image. In-group pride has mushroomed as we approach the end of the twentieth century. Children observe and listen to their parents speak about Black pride, Hispanic pride, Native American pride, Irish pride, Italian pride, and so on. Unfortunately, sometimes prejudice develops. **Prejudice** *is an unjustified negative attitude toward an individual because of that person's membership in a group.* People can be prejudiced against groups of people made up of a particular ethnic group, sex, age, religion, or other detectable difference.

Many of the early attempts to assess the nature of self and self-concept in various ethnic groups compared African African and White individuals (Clark & Clark, 1939; Coopersmith, 1967). These reports indicated that African Americans, especially African American children, have a more negative self-concept than Whites. However, more-recent research suggests that African Americans, Mexican Americans, and Puerto Ricans have equally positive self-concepts and perhaps even higher self-esteem than Whites (Allen & Majidi-Ahi, 1989). A generation of ethnic awareness and pride appears to have advanced the self-esteem of ethnic minority group members.

Increasing Children's Self-Esteem   Four ways children's self-esteem can be improved are through (1) identifying the causes of low self-esteem and the domains of competence important to the self, (2) emotional support and social approval, (3) achievement, and (4) coping (see figure 14.2).

Identifying children's sources of self-esteem—that is, competence in domains important to the self—is critical to improving self-esteem. Self-esteem theorist and researcher Susan Harter (1990) points out that the self-esteem enhancement programs of the 1960s, in which self-esteem itself was the target and individuals were encouraged to simply feel good about themselves, were ineffective. Rather, Harter believes that intervention must occur at the level of the *causes* of self-esteem if the individual's self-esteem is to improve significantly. Children have the highest self-esteem when they perform competently in domains important to the self. Therefore, children should be encouraged to identify and value areas of competence.

Emotional support and social approval in the form of confirmation from others also powerfully influence children's self-esteem. Some children with low self-esteem come from conflicted families or conditions in which they experienced abuse or neglect—situations in which support is unavailable. In some cases, alternative sources of support can be implemented, either informally through the encouragement of a teacher, a coach, or other significant adult, or more formally, through programs such as Big Brothers and Big Sisters. While peer

John W. Santrock

Identifying the causes of low self-esteem and which domains of competence are important to the self

Emotional support and social approval

Achievement

Coping

FIGURE 14.2

Four Key Aspects of Improving Self-Esteem

approval becomes increasingly important during adolescence, both adult and peer support are important influences on the adolescent's self-esteem.

Achievement also can improve children's self-esteem (Bednar, Wells, & Peterson, 1995). For example, the straightforward teaching of real skills to children often results in increased achievement and, thus, in enhanced self-esteem. Children develop higher self-esteem because they know the important tasks to achieve goals, and they have experienced performing them or similar behaviors. The emphasis on the importance of achievement in improving self-esteem has much in common with Bandura's cognitive social learning concept of *self-efficacy*, which refers to individuals' beliefs that they can master a situation and produce positive outcomes.

Self-esteem also is often increased when children face a problem and try to cope with it rather than avoid it. If coping rather than avoidance prevails, children often face problems realistically, honestly, and nondefensively. This produces favorable self-evaluative thoughts, which lead to the self-generated approval that raises self-esteem. The converse is true of low self-esteem. Unfavorable self-evaluations trigger denial, deception, and avoidance in an attempt to disavow that which has already been glimpsed as true. This process leads to self-generated disapproval as a form of feedback to the self about personal adequacy.

Industry Versus Inferiority

Erikson's fourth stage of the human life span, industry versus inferiority, appears during middle and late childhood. The term *industry* expresses a dominant theme of this period: Children become interested in how things are made and how they work. It is the Robinson Crusoe age, in that the enthusiasm and minute detail Crusoe uses to describe his activities appeal to the child's budding sense of industry. When children are encouraged in their efforts to make and build and work—whether building a model airplane, constructing a tree house, fixing a bicycle, solving an addition problem, or cooking—their sense of industry increases. However, parents who see their children's efforts at making things as "mischief" or "making a mess" encourage children's development of a sense of inferiority.

Children's social worlds beyond their families also contribute to a sense of industry. School becomes especially important in this regard. Consider children who are slightly below average in intelligence. They are too bright to be in special classes but not bright enough to be in gifted classes. They fail frequently in their academic efforts, developing a sense of inferiority. By contrast, consider children whose sense of industry is derogated at home. A series of sensitive and committed teachers may revitalize their sense of industry (Elkind, 1970).

Gender

In chapter 11, we discussed the biological, cognitive, and social influences on gender development. Gender is such a pervasive aspect of an individual's identity that we further consider its role in children's development here. Among the gender-related topics we examine are gender stereotypes, similarities, and differences; gender-role classification; and gender and ethnicity.

Gender Stereotyping

Gender stereotypes *are broad categories that reflect our impressions and beliefs about females and males.* All stereotypes, whether they are based on gender, ethnicity, or other groupings, refer to an image of what the typical member of a particular social category is like. The world is extremely complex. Every day we are confronted with thousands of different stimuli. The use of stereotypes is one way we simplify this complexity. If we simply assign a label (such as *soft*) to someone, we then have much less to consider when we think about the individual. However, once labels are assigned, they are remarkably difficult to abandon, even in the face of contradictory evidence.

What are little boys made of?
Frogs and snails
And puppy dogs' tails.

What are little girls made of?
Sugar and spice
And all that's nice

—J. O. Halliwell,
Nursery Rhymes of England (1844)

Many stereotypes are so general they are very ambiguous. Consider the stereotypes of "masculine" and "feminine." Diverse behaviors can be called on to support each stereotype, such as scoring a touchdown or growing facial hair for "masculine" and playing with dolls or wearing lipstick for "feminine." The stereotype may be modified in the face of cultural change. At one point in history, muscular development may be thought of as masculine; at another point, it may be a more lithe, slender physique. The behaviors popularly agreed upon as reflecting a stereotype may also fluctuate according to socioeconomic circumstances. For example, lower socioeconomic groups might be more likely than higher socioeconomic groups to include "rough and tough" as part of a masculine stereotype.

Even though the behaviors that are supposed to fit the stereotype often do not, the label itself can have significant consequences for the individual. Labeling a male "feminine" and a female "masculine" can produce significant social reactions to the individuals in terms of status and acceptance in groups, for example.

How widespread is feminine and masculine stereotyping? According to a far-ranging study of college students in thirty countries, stereotyping of females and males is pervasive (Williams & Best, 1982). Males were widely believed to be dominant, independent, aggressive, achievement oriented, and enduring, while females were widely believed to be nurturant, affiliative, less esteemed, and more helpful in times of distress.

In a subsequent study, women and men who lived in more highly developed countries perceived themselves as more similar than women and men who lived in less-developed countries (Williams & Best, 1989). In the more highly developed countries, women were more likely to attend college and be gainfully employed. Thus, as sexual equality increases, male and female stereotypes, as well as actual behavioral differences, may diminish. In this study, women were more likely to perceive similarity between the sexes than men were (Williams & Best, 1989). And the sexes were perceived more similarly in Christian than in Muslim societies.

If you are going to generalize about women, you will find yourself up to here in exceptions.

—Dolores Hitchens,
In a House Unknown (1973)

Gender stereotyping also changes developmentally. Stereotypical gender beliefs increase during the preschool years, peak in the early elementary school years, and then decrease in the middle and late elementary school years (Bigler, Liben, & Yekel, 1992). Next we go beyond stereotyping and examine the similarities and differences between the sexes.

Gender Similarities and Differences

Let's now examine some of the differences between the sexes, keeping in mind that (a) the differences are averages—not all females versus all males; (b) even when differences are reported, there is considerable overlap between the sexes; and (c) the differences may be due primarily to biological factors, sociocultural factors, or both. First, we examine physical differences, and then we turn to cognitive and socioemotional differences.

Physical Similarities and Differences From conception on, females are less likely than males to die, and females are less likely than males to develop physical or mental disorders. Estrogen strengthens the immune system, making females more resistant to infection, for example. Female hormones also signal the liver to produce more "good" cholesterol, which makes their blood vessels more elastic than males'. Testosterone triggers the production of low-density lipoprotein, which clogs blood vessels. Males have twice the risk of coronary disease as females. Higher levels of stress hormones cause faster clotting in males, but also higher blood pressure than in females. Adult females have about twice the body fat of their male counterparts,

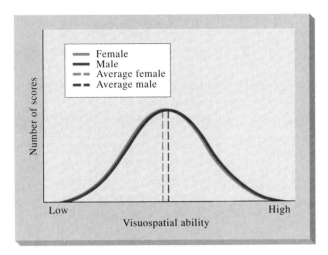

FIGURE 14.3

Visuospatial Ability of Males and Females
Notice that, although an average male's visuospatial ability is higher than an average female's, the overlap between the sexes is substantial. Not all males have better visuospatial ability than all females—the substantial overlap indicates that, although the average score of males is higher, many females outperform many males on such tasks.

most concentrated around breasts and hips. In males, fat is more likely to go to the abdomen. On the average, males grow to be 10 percent taller than females. Male hormones promote the growth of long bones; female hormones stop such growth at puberty.

Similarity was the rule rather than the exception in a recent study of metabolic activity in the brains of females and males (Gur & others, 1985). The exceptions involved areas of the brain that involve emotional expression and physical expression (which are more active in females). However, there are many physical differences between females and males. Are there as many cognitive differences?

Cognitive Similarities and Differences   In a classic review of gender differences, Eleanor Maccoby and Carol Jacklin (1974) concluded that males have better math and visuospatial skills (the kinds of skills an architect needs to design a building's angles and dimensions), while females have better verbal abilities. More recently, Maccoby (1987) revised her conclusion about several gender dimensions. She said that the accumulation of research evidence now suggests that verbal differences between females and males have virtually disappeared, but that the math and visuospatial differences still exist. Another recent analysis found that males outperform females in spatial tasks (Voyer, Voyer, & Bryden, 1995).

Some experts in gender, such as Janet Shibley Hyde (1994), believe that the cognitive differences between females and males have been exaggerated. For example, Hyde points out that there is considerable overlap in the distributions of female and male scores on math and visuospatial tasks. Figure 14.3 shows that although males outperform females on visuospatial tasks, female and male

"So according to the stereotype, you can put two and two together, but I can read the handwriting on the wall.

© 1986 Joel Pett, Phi Delta Kappan.

scores overlap substantially. Thus, while the *average* difference favors males, many females have higher scores on visuospatial tasks than most males do. The claim that "males outperform females in math" does not mean that all males outperform all females. Rather, it means that the average scores for males are higher than the average scores of females (Hyde & Plant, 1995).

> *There is more difference within the sexes than between them.*
>
> —**Ivy Compton-Burnett**

Socioemotional Similarities and Differences
Most males are more active and aggressive than most females (Maccoby & Jacklin, 1974). The consistent difference in aggressiveness often appears in children's development as early as 2 years of age.

Females and males also differ in their social connectedness. Boys often define themselves apart from their caregivers and peers, while girls emphasize their social ties. As adults, females often become more caring, supporting, and empathic, while males become more independent, self-reliant, and unexpressive.

Unless you've been isolated on a mountaintop away from people, television, magazines, and newspapers, you probably know the master stereotype about gender and emotion: She is emotional, he is not. This stereotype is a powerful and pervasive image in our culture (Shields, 1991).

Is this stereotype confirmed when researchers study the nature of emotional experiences in females and males? Researchers have found that females and males are often more alike in the way they experience emotion than the master stereotype would lead us to believe. Females and males often use the same facial expressions, adopt the same

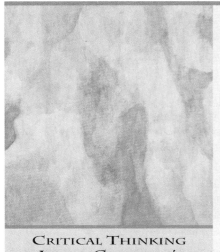

*Rethinking the Words
We Use in
Gender Worlds*

Several decades ago the word *dependency* was used to describe the relational orientation of femininity. Dependency took on negative connotations for females—such as, that females can't take of themselves and males can. In the 1990s, the term *dependency* is being replaced by the term *relational abilities*, which has much more positive connotations. Rather than being thought of as dependent, women are now more often described as skilled in forming and maintaining relationships. Make up a list of words that you associate with masculinity and a list of words you associate with femininity. Do these words have any negative connotations for males or females? For the words that do have negative connotations, think about replacements for them that have more positive connotations. By rethinking the words we use to describe people as masculine or feminine, you are learning to think critically about development by *making accurate observations and descriptions.*

stated that this belief came about because of a feminist commitment to gender similarity as a route to political equality and from piecemeal and inadequate interpretations of relevant empirical research. Many feminists express a fear that differences will be interpreted as deficiencies on the part of females and as biologically based, which could revive the stereotype that women are innately inferior to men (Unger & Crawford, 1992). Eagly (1995,1996) argues that contemporary psychology has produced a large body of research that reveals that behavior is sex-differentiated to varying extents.

Evolutionary psychologist David Buss (1995, 1996) argues that men and women differ in those psychological domains in which they have faced different adaptive problems across their evolutionary history. In all other domains, predicts Buss, the sexes are psychologically similar. He cites a sex difference in the cognitive domain that favors males—spatial rotation. Spatial rotation skills are essential for hunting, in which the trajectory of a projectile

language, and describe their emotional experiences similarly when they keep diaries about their life experiences. Thus, the master stereotype that females are emotional and males are not is simply that—a stereotype. Given the complexity and vast territory of emotion, we should not be surprised that this stereotype is not supported when actual emotional experiences are examined. Thus, for many emotional experiences, researchers do not find differences between females and males—both sexes are equally likely to feel love, jealousy, anxiety in new social situations, anger when they are insulted, grief when close relationships end, and embarrassment when they make mistakes in public (Tavris & Wade, 1984). To further evaluate children's gender worlds, refer to Critical Thinking About Children's Development.

For some areas of achievement, gender differences are so large they can best be described as nonoverlapping. For example, no major league baseball players are female, and 96 percent of all registered nurses are female. In contrast, many measures of achievement-related behaviors do not reveal gender differences. For example, girls show just as much persistence at tasks. The question of whether males and females differ in their expectations for success at various achievement tasks is not yet settled.

Gender Controversy

Not all psychologists agree that sex differences between females and males are rare or small. Alice Eagly (1995, 1996)

must anticipate the trajectory of the prey as each moves through space and time. Buss also cites a sex difference in casual sex, with men engaging in this behavior more than women. In one study, men said that ideally they would like to have more than eighteen sex partners in their lifetime, whereas women stated that ideally they would like to have only four or five (Buss & Schmitt, 1993). In another study, 75 percent of the men but none of the women approached by an attractive stranger of the opposite sex consented to a request for sex (Clark & Hatfield, 1989). Such sex differences, says Buss, are of exactly the type predicted by evolutionary psychology.

In sum, there is great controversy about the issue of whether sex differences are rare and small or frequent and large (Derry, 1996; Hyde & Plant, 1995; Maracek, 1995). Negotiating the science and politics of gender is not an easy task (Eagly, 1995).

Gender in Context

When thinking about gender similarities and differences, keep in mind that the context in which females and males are thinking, feeling, and behaving should be taken into account (Harter, Waters, & Whitesell, 1996). To see how context affects gender, let's further explore gender in relation to helping behavior and emotion.

With regard to helping, males are more likely to help in situations in which a perceived danger is present and in which males feel most competent to help (Eagly & Crowley,

1986). For example, males are more likely than females to help someone standing by the roadside with a flat tire, a context (automobile problems) in which many males feel a sense of competence. By contrast, females are more likely to volunteer time to help a child with a personal problem; there is little danger in such a context, and females generally feel competent at nurturing. In many cultures, girls show more caregiving behavior than boys do (Blakemore, 1993). However, in the few cultures where boys and girls both care for younger siblings on a regular basis, they are similar in their tendencies to nurture (Whiting, 1989).

Gender differences in the display of emotion are related to context (Anderson & Leaper, 1996; Shields, 1991). Consider anger. Males are more likely to show anger toward strangers, especially other males, when they feel that they have been challenged. Males also are more likely than females to turn their anger into aggressive action (Tavris & Wade, 1984). The most common emotional differences between females and males are related to contexts that highlight social roles and relationships. For example, females are more likely than males to see emotion as a part of interpersonal relationships (Saarni, 1988). And females are more likely than males to express fear and sadness, especially when communicating with their friends and family.

Gender-Role Classification

How were gender roles classified in the past? What is androgyny? What is gender-role transcendence?

The Past   Not too long ago, it was accepted that boys should grow up to be masculine and that girls should grow up to be feminine, that boys are made of frogs and snails and puppy dogs' tails, and that girls are made of sugar and spice and all that's nice. Today, there is more diversity in gender roles and the feedback individuals receive from their culture. A girl's mother might promote femininity, the girl might be close friends with a tomboy, and the girl's teachers at school might encourage her assertiveness.

In the past, the well-adjusted male was expected to be independent, aggressive, and power oriented. The well-adjusted female was expected to be dependent, nurturant, and uninterested in power. Further, masculine characteristics were considered to be healthy and good by society; female characteristics were considered to be undesirable. A classic study in the early 1970s summarized the traits and behaviors that college students believed were characteristic of males and those they believed were characteristic of females (Broverman & others, 1972). The traits clustered into two groups that were labeled "instrumental" and "expressive." The instrumental traits paralleled the male's purposeful, competent entry into the outside world to gain goods for his family; the expressive traits paralleled the female's responsibility to be warm and emotional in the home. Such stereotypes are more harmful to females than to males because the characteristics assigned to males are more valued than those assigned to females. The beliefs

and stereotypes have led to the negative treatment of females because of their sex, or what is called *sexism*. Females receive less attention in schools, are less visible in leading roles on television, are rarely depicted as competent, dominant characters in children's books, are paid less than males even when they have more education, and are underrepresented in decision-making roles throughout our society, from corporate executive suites to Congress.

Androgyny   In the 1970s, as both males and females became dissatisfied with the burdens imposed by their strictly stereotyped roles, alternatives to "masculinity" and "femininity" were explored. Instead of thinking of masculinity and femininity as a continuum, with more of one meaning less of the other, it was proposed that individuals could show both expressive *and* instrumental traits. This thinking led to the development of the concept of **androgyny,** *the presence of desirable masculine and feminine characteristics in the same individual* (Bem, 1977; Spence & Helmreich, 1978). The androgynous individual might be a male who is assertive (masculine) and nurturant (feminine), or a female who is dominant (masculine) and sensitive to others' feelings (feminine).

Measures have been developed to assess androgyny. One of the most widely used gender measures, the Bem Sex-Role Inventory, was constructed by a leading early proponent of androgyny, Sandra Bem. To see what the items on Bem's measure are like, see table 14.2. Based on their responses to the items in the Bem sex-role inventory, individuals are classified as having one of four gender-role orientations: masculine, feminine, androgynous, or undifferentiated (see figure 14.4). The androgynous individual is simply a female or a male who has a high degree of both feminine (expressive) and masculine (instrumental) traits. No new characteristics are used to describe the androgynous individual. A feminine individual is high on feminine (expressive) traits and low on masculine (instrumental) traits; a masculine individual shows the reverse of these traits. An undifferentiated person is not high on feminine or masculine traits.

Androgynous individuals are described as more flexible and more mentally healthy than either masculine or feminine individuals. Individuals who are undifferentiated are the least competent. To some degree, though, the context influences which gender role is most adaptive. In close relationships, a feminine or androgynous gender role may be more desirable because of the expressive nature of close relationships. However, a masculine or androgynous gender role may be more desirable in academic and work settings because of the instrumental nature of these settings. And the culture in which individuals live also plays an important role in determining what is adaptive. On the one hand, increasing numbers of children in the United States and other modernized countries such as Sweden are being raised to behave in androgynous ways. On the other hand, traditional gender roles continue to dominate the cultures of many countries around the world.

TABLE 14.2

The Bem Sex-Role Inventory: Are You Androgynous?

The following items are from the Bem Sex-Role Inventory. To find out whether you score as androgynous, first rate yourself on each item, on a scale from 1 (never or almost never true) to 7 (always or almost always true).

1. self-reliant	16. strong personality	31. makes decisions easily	46. aggressive
2. yielding	17. loyal	32. compassionate	47. gullible
3. helpful	18. unpredictable	33. sincere	48. inefficient
4. defends own beliefs	19. forceful	34. self-sufficient	49. acts as a leader
5. cheerful	20. feminine	35. eager to soothe hurt feelings	50. childlike
6. moody	21. reliable	36. conceited	51. adaptable
7. independent	22. analytical	37. dominant	52. individualistic
8. shy	23. sympathetic	38. soft-spoken	53. does not use harsh language
9. conscientious	24. jealous	39. likable	54. unsystematic
10. athletic	25. has leadership abilities	40. masculine	55. competitive
11. affectionate	26. sensitive to the needs of others	41. warm	56. loves children
12. theatrical	27. truthful	42. solemn	57. tactful
13. assertive	28. willing to take risks	43. willing to take a stand	58. ambitious
14. flatterable	29. understanding	44. tender	59. gentle
15. happy	30. secretive	45. friendly	60. conventional

SCORING
(a) Add up your ratings for items 1, 4, 7, 10, 13, 16, 19, 22, 25, 28, 31, 34, 37, 40, 43, 46, 49, 55, and 58. Divide the total by 20. That is your masculinity score.
(b) Add up your ratings for items 2, 5, 8, 11, 14, 17, 20, 23, 26, 29, 32, 35, 38, 41, 44, 47, 50, 53, 56, and 59. Divide the total by 20. That is your femininity score.
(c) If your masculinity score is above 4.9 (the approximate median for the masculinity scale) and your femininity score is above 4.9 (the approximate femininity median) then you would be classified as androgynous on Bem's scales.

From Janet S. Hyde, *Half the Human Experience: The Psychology of Women,* 5th ed. Copyright © 1995 by D. C. Heath and Company, Lexington, MA. Used by permission of Houghton Mifflin Company.

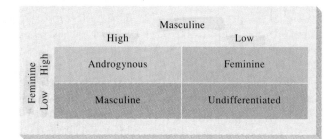

FIGURE 14.4

Gender-Role Classification

Gender-Role Transcendence Although the concept of androgyny was an improvement over exclusive notions of femininity and masculinity, it has turned out to be less of a panacea than many of its early proponents envisioned (Paludi, 1995). Some theorists, such as Joseph Pleck (1981), believe that the idea of androgyny should be replaced with the idea of **gender-role transcendence,** *the belief that, when an individual's competence is at issue, it should be conceptualized not on the basis of masculinity, femininity, or androgyny, but rather on a person basis.* Thus, rather than merging gender roles, or stereotyping people as masculine or feminine, Pleck believes, we should begin to think about people as people. However, the concepts of androgyny and gender-role transcendence both draw attention away from women's unique needs and the power imbalance between women and men in most cultures.

> *To be meek, patient, tactful, modest, honorable, brave, is not to be either manly or womanly; it is to be humane.*
> —**Jane Harrison (1850–1928), English writer**

Ethnicity and Gender

Are gender-related attitudes and behavior similar across different ethnic groups? All ethnic minority females are females, and all ethnic minority males are males, so there are many similarities in the gender-related attitudes of females across different ethnic minority groups and of males across different ethnic minority groups. Nevertheless, the different ethnic and cultural experiences of African American, Latino, Asian American, and Native American females and males need to be considered in understanding their gender-related attitudes and behavior, because in some instances even small differences can be important (Ballou, 1996; Houston & Wood, 1996). For example, the socialization of males and females in other cultures who subsequently migrate to America often reflects a stronger gap between the status of males and females than is experienced in America. Keeping in mind that there are many similarities between females in all ethnic minority groups and between males in all ethnic minority groups, we first examine information about females from specific ethnic minority groups and then discuss males from specific ethnic minority groups.

Ethnic Minority Females Let's now consider the behavior and psychological orientations of females from

Developmentalists have become increasingly interested in the roles that ethnicity and gender play in children's lives. How might gender roles be similar or different for Anglo-American boys and girls, compared to gender roles for (a) this African American boy in Philadelphia, (b) these Mexican American boys in Los Angeles, (c) this Chinese American girl in San Francisco, and (d) these Native American children in the Sierra Madre Mountains?

specific ethnic minority groups, beginning with African American females, and then, in turn, Latino females, Asian American females, and Native American females.

Researchers in psychology have only begun to focus on the behavior of African American females. For too long, African American females were treated only as a comparison for White females on selected psychological dimensions, or as the subjects of studies in which the primary research interests related to factors like poverty and unwed motherhood. Such narrow research approaches could be viewed as attributing no personal characteristics to African American females beyond the labels given to them as a group by society.

The nature and focus of psychological research on African American females has begun to change—to some extent paralleling societal changes (Hall, Evans, & Selice, 1989). In the last decade, more individualized, positive dimensions of African American females—such as self-esteem, achievement, motivation, and self-control—have been studied. In the 1980s, psychological studies of African American females began to shift away from studies focused only on the problems of African American females and toward research on the positive aspects of African American females in a pluralistic society.

Like other ethnic minority females, African African females have experienced the double jeopardy of racism and sexism. The ingenuity and perseverance shown by ethnic minority females as they have survived and grown against the odds is remarkable. For example, 499 African American women earned doctoral degrees in 1986. This represents only 2 percent of the Ph.D.'s awarded that year (and African American females were 6.4 percent of the general population). However, the positive side of these figures is that the Ph.D.'s earned by African American women in 1986 represented an increase of almost 16 percent over the number earned in 1977. Despite such gains, our society needs to make a strong commitment to providing African American and other ethnic minority females with the opportunities they deserve.

Traditionally in Latino families, women assumed the expressive role of homemaker and caretaker of children. This continues to be the norm, although less so than in the past (Chow, Wilkinson, & Baca Zinn, 1996). Historically, the Latina female's role was one of self-denial, and her needs were considered to be subordinate to those of other family members. Joint decision making and greater equality of males' and females' roles are becoming more characteristic of Latino families. Of special significance is the increased frequency of Latina women's employment outside the home, which in many instances has enhanced a wife's status in the family and in decision making.

Asian females are often expected to carry on domestic duties, to marry, to become obedient helpers of their mothers-in-law, and to bear children, especially males. In China, the mother's responsibility for the emotional nurturance and well-being of the family, and for raising children, derives from Confucian ethics (Huang & Ying, 1989). However, as China has become modernized, these roles have become less rigid. Similarly, in acculturated Chinese families in the United States, only derivatives of these rigidly defined roles remain. For example, Chinese American females are not entirely relegated to subservient roles.

For Native Americans, the amount of social and governing control exhibited by women or men depends on the tribe (LaFromboise, 1993; LaFromboise & Trimble, 1996). For example, in the traditional matriarchal Navajo family, an older woman might live with her husband, her unmarried children, her married daughter, and the daughter's husband and children (Ryan, 1980). In patriarchal tribes, women function as the central "core" of the family, maintaining primary responsibility for the welfare of children. Grandmothers and aunts often provide child care. As with other ethnic minority females, Native American females who have moved to urban areas experience the cultural conflict of traditional ethnic values and the values of the American society.

Ethnic Minority Males Just as ethnic minority females have experienced considerable discrimination and have had to develop coping strategies in the face of adversity, so have ethnic minority males (Coleman, 1996; Parham, 1996). As with ethnic minority females, our order of discussion will be African American males, Latino males, Asian American males, and Native American males.

Some statistics provide a portrayal of the difficulties many African American males have faced (Parham & McDavis, 1993). African American males of all ages are three times as likely as White males to live below the poverty line. African American males aged 20 to 44 are twice as likely to die as White males are. African American male heads of household earn 70 percent of the income of their White male counterparts. Although they make up only 6.3 percent of the U.S. population, African American males constitute 42 percent of jail inmates and more than 50 percent of men executed for any reason in the last 50 years. Murder by gun is the leading cause of death among African American males aged 15 to 19, and the rates are escalating. From 1979 to 1989, the rate of death by guns among this age group of African American males increased by 71 percent. In one recent study, the problem of inadequate male role models in African American boys' development surfaced (Browne & others, 1993).

Such statistics do not tell the complete story (Evans & Whitfield, 1988). The sociocultural aspects of historical discrimination against an ethnic minority group must be taken into account to understand these statistics (Neighbors & Jackson, 1996). Just as with African American females, researchers are beginning to focus on some of the more positive dimensions of African American males. For example, researchers are finding that African American males are especially efficient at the use of body language in communication, decoding nonverbal cues, multilingual/multicultural expression, and improvised problem solving.

In Latino families, men traditionally assume the instrumental role of provider and protector of the family. The concept of machismo—being a macho man—continues to influence the role of the male and the patriarchal orientation of Latino families, though less so than in the past. Traditionally, this orientation required men to be forceful and strong, and also to withhold affectionate emotions. Ideally, it involved a strong sense of personal honor, family, loyalty, and care for children. However, it also has involved exaggerated masculinity and aggression

(Trankina, 1983). The concepts of machismo and absolute patriarchy are currently diminishing in influence. Adolescent males are still given much more freedom than adolescent females in Latino families (Arrendondo, 1996).

Asian cultural values are reflected in traditional patriarchal Chinese and Japanese families (Copeland, Hwang, & Brody, 1996; Leong, 1996). The father's behavior in relation to other family members is generally dignified, authoritative, remote, and aloof. Sons are generally valued over daughters. Firstborn sons have an especially high status. As with Asian American females, the acculturation experienced by Asian American males has eroded some of the rigid gender roles that characterized Asian families in the past. Fathers still are often the figurative heads of families, especially when dealing with the public, but in private, they have relinquished some of their decision-making powers to their wives.

Some Native American tribes are also patriarchal, with the male being the head of the family and primary decision maker. In some tribes, though, child care is shared by men. For example, Mescalero Apache men take responsibility for children when not working away from the family (Ryan, 1980). Autonomy is highly valued among the male children in many Native American tribes, with the males operating semi-independently at an early age (La Fromboise, 1993). As with Native American females, increased movement to urban areas has led to modifications in the values and traditions of some Native American males.

At this point we have discussed a number of ideas about gender. Another important topic in children's development that requires further discussion is moral development.

Moral Development

Remember from chapter 11 our description of Piaget's view of moral development. Piaget believed that younger children are characterized by heteronomous morality, but that by 10 years of age they have moved into a higher stage called "autonomous" morality. According to Piaget, older children consider the intentions of the individual, believe that rules are subject to change, and are aware that punishment does not always follow a wrongdoing. A second major cognitive perspective on moral development was proposed by Lawrence Kohlberg.

Kohlberg's Theory of Moral Development

Kohlberg stressed that moral development is based primarily on moral reasoning and unfolds in stages (Kohlberg, 1958, 1976, 1986). Kohlberg arrived at his view after some 20 years of using a unique interview with children. In the interview, children are presented with a series of stories in which characters face moral dilemmas. The following is the most popular Kohlberg dilemma:

> In Europe a woman was near death from a special kind of cancer. There was one drug that the doctors thought might save her. It was a form of radium that a druggist in the same town had recently discovered. The drug was expensive to make, but the druggist was charging ten times what the drug cost him to make. He paid $200 for the radium and charged $2,000 for a small dose of the drug. The sick woman's husband, Heinz, went to everyone he knew to borrow the money, but he could only get together $1,000 which is half of what it cost. He told the druggist that his wife was dying and asked him to sell it cheaper or let him pay later. But the druggist said, "No, I discovered the drug, and I am going to make money from it." So Heinz got desperate and broke into the man's store to steal the drug for his wife. (Kohlberg, 1969, p. 379).

This story is one of eleven devised by Kohlberg to investigate the nature of moral thought. After reading the story, the interviewee answers a series of questions about the moral dilemma. Should Heinz have stolen the drug? Was stealing it right or wrong? Why? Is it a husband's duty to steal the drug for his wife if he can get it no other way? Would a good husband steal? Did the druggist have the right to charge that much when there was no law setting a limit on the price? Why or why not?

Based on the reasons interviewees gave in response to this and other moral dilemmas, Kohlberg believed three levels of moral development exist, each of which is characterized by two stages. A key concept in understanding moral development, especially Kohlberg's theory, is **internalization,** *the developmental change from behavior that is externally controlled to behavior that is internally controlled.*

Level One: Preconventional Reasoning

Preconventional reasoning *is the lowest level in Kohlberg's theory of moral development. At this level, the child shows no internalization of moral values—moral reasoning is controlled by external rewards and punishments.*

Stage 1. **Punishment and obedience orientation** *is the first stage in Kohlberg's theory of moral development. At this stage, moral thinking is based on punishment.* Children obey because adults tell them to obey.

Stage 2. **Individualism and purpose** *is the second stage in Kohlberg's theory of moral development. At this stage, moral thinking is based on rewards and self-interest.* Children obey when they want to obey and when it is in their best interest to obey. What is right is what feels good and what is rewarding.

Level Two: Conventional Reasoning

Conventional reasoning *is the second or intermediate level in Kohlberg's theory of moral development. At this level, the individual's internalization is intermediate. The person abides by certain standards (internal), but they are the standards of others (external), such as parents or the laws of society.*

Stage 3. **Interpersonal norms** *is the third stage in Kohlberg's theory of moral development. At this stage, the person values trust, caring, and loyalty to others as the basis of moral judgments.* Children often adopt their parents' moral standards at this stage, seeking to be thought of by their parents as a "good girl" or a "good boy."

Stage 4. **Social system morality** *is the fourth stage in Kohlberg's theory of moral development. At this stage, moral judgments are based on understanding the social order, law, justice, and duty.*

Level Three: Postconventional Reasoning

Postconventional reasoning *is the highest level in Kohlberg's theory of moral development. At this level, morality is completely internalized and not based on others' standards.* The person recognizes alternative moral courses, explores the options, and then decides on a personal moral code.

Stage 5. **Community rights versus individual rights** *is the fifth stage in Kohlberg's theory of moral development. At this stage, the person understands that values and laws are relative and that standards may vary from one person to another.* The person recognizes that laws are important for society but knows that laws can be changed. The person believes that some values, such as liberty, are more important than the law.

Stage 6. **Universal ethical principles** *is the sixth and highest stage in Kohlberg's theory of moral development. At this stage, persons have developed a moral standard based on universal human rights.* When faced with a conflict between law and conscience, the person will follow conscience, even though the decision might involve personal risk.

Kohlberg believed that these levels and stages occur in a sequence and are age related: Before age 9, most children reason about moral dilemmas in a preconventional way; by early adolescence, they reason in more conventional ways; and by early adulthood, a small number of people reason in postconventional ways. In a 20-year longitudinal investigation, the uses of stages 1 and 2 decreased (Colby & others, 1983). Stage 4, which did not appear at all in the moral reasoning of the 10-year-olds, was reflected in 62 percent of the moral thinking of the 36-year-olds. Stage 5 did not appear until the age of 20 to 22 and never characterized more than 10 percent of the individuals. Thus, the moral stages appeared somewhat later than Kohlberg initially envisioned, and the higher stages, especially stage 6, were extremely elusive. Recently, stage 6

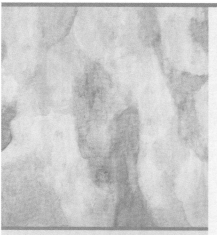

CRITICAL THINKING ABOUT CHILDREN'S DEVELOPMENT

Moral Decision Making

Fortunately, we don't have to regularly face decisions as difficult as Heinz's dilemma of whether to steal a drug to save his wife's life. However, our everyday lives involve many decisions about right and wrong. Evaluate the moral dilemmas described below and tell how you think you would respond to them. Which of Kohlberg's six moral stages are involved in your decision making?

- You meet someone that you think is very attractive, and the attraction is reciprocal. You are married, but your marriage has run into some difficulties lately. Should you go out with the person and have sex? Explain your choice.
- You see your best friend driving a car that sideswipes a parked car. Your friend drives away without reporting the accident. What should you do? Explain your choice.

By evaluating your responses to moral dilemmas from Kohlberg's perspective, you are learning to think critically by *creating arguments based on developmental concepts.*

was removed from the Kohlberg scoring manual, but it is still considered to be theoretically important in the Kohlberg scheme of moral development. To further evaluate moral thinking, refer to Critical Thinking About Children's Development.

Kohlberg's Critics

Kohlberg's provocative theory of moral development has not gone unchallenged (Lapsley, 1996). The criticisms involve the link between moral thought and moral behavior, the quality of the research, inadequate consideration of culture's role and the family's role in moral development, and underestimation of the care perspective.

Moral Thought and Moral Behavior Kohlberg's theory has been criticized for placing too much emphasis on moral thought and not enough emphasis on moral behavior. Moral reasons can sometimes be a shelter for immoral behavior. Bank embezzlers and presidents endorse the loftiest of moral virtues when commenting about moral dilemmas, but their own behavior may be immoral. No one wants a nation of cheaters and thieves who can reason at the postconventional level. The cheaters and thieves may know what is right, yet still do what is wrong.

John W. Santrock

The main concerns of adolescent Buddhist monks in Nepal do not focus on the issue of justice (as Kohlberg's theory argues); rather, they focus on the prevention of suffering and the importance of compassion.

Culture and Moral Development

Yet another criticism of Kohlberg's view is that it is culturally biased (Banks, 1993; Miller, 1995). A review of research on moral development in 27 countries concluded that moral reasoning is more culture-specific than Kohlberg envisioned and that Kohlberg's scoring system does not recognize higher-level moral reasoning in certain cultural groups (Snarey, 1987). Examples of higher-level moral reasoning that would not be scored as such by Kohlberg's system are values related to communal equity and collective happiness in Israel, the unity and sacredness of all life forms in India, and the relation of the individual to the community in New Guinea. These examples of moral reasoning would not be scored at the highest level in Kohlberg's system because they do not emphasize the individual's rights and abstract principles of justice. One study assessed the moral development of 20 adolescent male Buddhist monks in Nepal (Huebner, Garrod, & Snarey, 1990). The issue of justice, a basic theme in Kohlberg's theory, was not of paramount importance in the monks'

moral views, and their concerns about prevention of suffering and the role of compassion are not captured by Kohlberg's theory. In sum, moral reasoning is shaped more by the values and beliefs of a culture than Kohlberg acknowledged.

Family Processes and Moral Development

Kohlberg believed that family processes are essentially unimportant in the children's moral development. He argued that parent-child relationships are usually power-oriented and provide children little opportunity for mutual give and take or perspective taking. Rather, Kohlberg said that such opportunities are more likely to be provided by children's peer relations.

A number of developmentalists now believe that Kohlberg likely underestimated the contribution of family relationships to moral development. They emphasize that inductive discipline, which involves the use of reasoning and focuses children's attention on the consequences of their actions for others, positively influences moral

Carol Gilligan is shown with some of the students she has interviewed about the importance of relationships in a female's development. According to Gilligan (center), the sense of relationships and connectedness is at the heart of female development.

communication, relationships with others, and concern for others. Gilligan's theory is a care perspective. According to Gilligan, Kohlberg greatly underplayed the care perspective in moral development. She believes that this may have happened because he was a male, because most of his research was with males rather than females, and because he used male responses as a model for his theory.

In extensive interviews with girls from 6 to 18 years of age, Gilligan and her colleagues found that girls consistently interpret moral dilemmas in terms of human relationships and base these interpretations on listening and watching other people (Gilligan, 1992, 1996). According to Gilligan, girls have the ability to sensitively pick up different rhythms in relationships and often are able to follow the pathways of feelings. Gilligan believes that girls reach a critical juncture in their development when they reach adolescence. Usually around 11 to 12 years of age, girls become aware that their intense interest in intimacy is not prized by the male-dominated culture, even though society values women as caring and altruistic. The dilemma is that girls are presented with a choice that makes them look either selfish or selfless. Gilligan believes that, as adolescent girls experience this dilemma, they increasingly silence their "distinctive voice." Researchers have found support for Gilligan's claim that females' and males' moral reasoning often centers around different concerns and issues (Galotti, Kozberg, & Farmer, 1990).

However, one of Gilligan's initial claims—that traditional Kohlbergian measures of moral development are biased against females—has been extensively disputed. For example, most research studies using the Kohlberg stories and scoring system do not find sex differences (Walker, 1991). Thus, the strongest support for Gilligan's claims comes from studies that focus on items and scoring systems pertaining to close relationships, pathways of feelings, sensitive listening, and the rhythm of interpersonal behavior.

While females often articulate a care perspective and males a justice perspective, the gender difference is not absolute, and the two orientations are not mutually exclusive

development (Hoffman, 1970). They also stress that parents' moral values influence children's developing moral thoughts (Gibbs, 1993).

Gender and the Care Perspective   Carol Gilligan (1982, 1992, 1996) believes that Kohlberg's theory of moral development does not adequately reflect relationships and concern for others. The **justice perspective** *is a moral perspective that focuses on the rights of the individual; individuals stand alone and independently make moral decisions. Kohlberg's theory is a justice perspective.* By contrast, the **care perspective** *is a moral perspective that views people in terms of their connectedness with others and emphasizes interpersonal*

(Lyons, 1990). For example, in one study, 53 of 80 females and males showed either a care or a justice perspective, but 27 subjects used both orientations, with neither predominating (Gilligan & Attanucci, 1988).

Altruism

Altruism *is an unselfish interest in helping someone else.* Human acts of altruism are plentiful—the hardworking laborer who places $5 in a Salvation Army kettle; rock concerts to feed the hungry, help farmers, and fund AIDS research; and the child who takes in a wounded cat and cares for it. How do psychologists account for such acts of altruism?

Reciprocity and exchange are involved in altruism. Reciprocity is found throughout the human world. Not only is it the highest moral principle in Christianity, but it is also present in every widely practiced religion in the world—Judaism, Hinduism, Buddhism, and Islam. Reciprocity encourages children to do unto others as they would have others do unto them. Human sentiments are wrapped up in this reciprocity. Trust is probably the most important principle over the long run in altruism. Guilt surfaces if the child does not reciprocate, and anger may result if someone else does not reciprocate. Not all altruism is motivated by reciprocity and exchange, but self-other interactions and relationships help us understand altruism's nature. The circumstances most likely to involve altruism are empathic emotion for an individual in need or a close relationship between benefactor and recipient.

William Damon (1988) described a developmental sequence of children's altruism, especially of sharing. Most sharing during the first 3 years of life is done for nonempathic reasons, such as for the fun of the social play ritual or out of mere imitation. Then, at about 4 years of age, a combination of empathic awareness and adult encouragement produces a sense of obligation on the part of the child to share with others. This obligation forces the child to share, even though the child may not perceive this as the best way to have fun. Most 4-year-olds are not selfless saints, however. Children believe they have an obligation to share but do not necessarily think they should be as generous to others as they are to themselves. Neither do their actions always support their beliefs, especially when the object of contention is a coveted one. What is important developmentally is that the child has developed an internal belief that sharing is an obligatory part of a social relationship and that this involves a question of right and wrong. However, a preschool child's sense of reciprocity constitutes not a moral duty but, rather, a pragmatic means of getting one's way. Despite their shortcomings, these ideas about justice formed in early childhood set the stage for giant strides that children make in the years that follow.

> *Every man takes care that his neighbor shall not cheat him. But a day comes when he begins to care that he does not cheat his neighbor. Then all goes well.*
>
> **—Ralph Waldo Emerson**

By the start of the elementary school years, children genuinely begin to express more objective ideas about fairness. These notions about fairness have been used throughout history to distribute goods and to resolve conflicts. They involve the principles of equality, merit, and benevolence. *Equality* means that everyone is treated the same. *Merit* means giving extra rewards for hard work, a talented performance, or other laudatory behavior. *Benevolence* means giving special consideration to individuals in a disadvantaged condition. Equality is the first of these principles used regularly by elementary school children. It is common to hear 6-year-old children use the word *fair* as synonymous with *equal* or *same*. By the mid to late elementary school years, children also believe that equity means special treatment for those who deserve it—the principles of merit and benevolence.

Missing from the factors that guide children's altruism is one that many adults might expect to be the most influential of all: the motivation to obey adult authority figures. Surprisingly, a number of studies have shown that adult authority has only a small influence on children's sharing. For example, when Nancy Eisenberg (1982) asked children to explain their own altruistic acts, they mainly gave empathic and pragmatic reasons for their spontaneous acts of sharing. Not one of the children referred to the demands of adult authority. Parental advice and prodding certainly foster standards of sharing, but the give-and-take of peer requests and arguments provides the most immediate stimulation of sharing. Parents may set examples that children carry into peer interaction and communication, but parents are not present during all of their children's peer exchanges. The day-to-day construction of fairness standards is done by children in collaboration and negotiation with each other. Over the course of many years and thousands of encounters, children's understanding of altruism deepens. With this conceptual elaboration, which involves such notions as equality, merit, benevolence, and compromise, come a greater consistency and generosity in children's sharing behavior (Damon & Hart, 1992).

> *Without civic morality communities perish; without personal morality their survival has no value.*
>
> **—Bertrand Russell**

At this point we have discussed a number of ideas about the self, gender, and moral development in children's lives. A summary of these ideas is presented in concept table 14.2.

CONCEPT TABLE 14.2

The Self, Gender, and Moral Development

Concept	Processes/Related Ideas	Characteristics/Description
The Self	Self-understanding and perspective taking	The internal self, the social self, and the socially comparative self become more prominent in middle and late childhood. Selman proposed a model of perspective taking with five stages.
	Self-esteem and self-concept	Self-esteem refers to global evaluations of the self; self-esteem is also referred to as self-worth or self-image. Self-concept refers to domain-specific self-evaluations. Harter has developed separate measures of self-evaluation, for children and adolescents; these measures assess skill domain perceptions as well as general self-worth. Self-esteem and parenting, group identity and self-esteem, increasing self-esteem, and Erikson's stage of industry versus inferiority are other important dimensions of self in middle and late childhood.
Gender	Stereotypes, similarities, and differences	Gender stereotypes are widespread around the world. A number of physical differences exist between females and males. Some experts, such as Hyde, argue that cognitive differences between females and males have been exaggerated. In terms of socioemotional differences, males are more aggressive and active than females, while females emphasize their social ties. Currently, there is controversy about how similar or different females and males are in a number of areas. Context is important for understanding gender.
	Gender-role classification	The old view of gender was a dichotomy of masculinity and femininity. In the 1970s, the concept of androgyny was developed, which stresses that the most competent individuals have both masculine and feminine desirable traits. Gender-role measures often categorize individuals as masculine, feminine, androgynous, or undifferentiated. Gender-role transcendence is an alternative to androgyny.
	Ethnicity and gender	There are many gender similarities across various ethnic minority groups, but sometimes even small differences can be important. A special concern is the discrimination that ethnic minority females and males have experienced.
Moral Development	Kohlberg's theory	Kohlberg developed a provocative theory of moral reasoning with three levels—preconventional, conventional, and postconventional—and six stages (two at each level). Increased internalization characterizes movement to levels 2 and 3. Criticisms of Kohlberg's theory include the claims that Kohlberg overemphasizes cognition and underemphasizes behavior, underestimates culture's role as well as the family's role, and inadequately considers the care perspective. Gilligan advocates giving greater attention to the care perspective in moral development and believes that early adolescence is a critical juncture in female development.
	Altruism	Altruism is an unselfish interest in helping someone else. Damon described a developmental sequence of altruism.

John W. Santrock

C hildren's socioemotional development changes in many ways during the middle and late childhood years. These changes involve the self, gender, and moral development as the child interacts with others in the contexts of families, peers, and schools.

We began the chapter by exploring parent-child issues and societal changes in families; peer popularity, rejection, and neglect, social cognition, and friends; and the transition to school, teachers, and social class and ethnicity in schools. We then learned about the development of self-understanding, self-esteem, and self-concept; gender stereotyping, similarities, and differences, gender-role classification, and ethnicity and gender; and Kohlberg's theory of moral development, Kohlberg's critics, especially Carol Gilligan and other advocates of the care perspective, and altruism.

Remember that you can obtain a summary of the entire chapter by again reading the two concept tables on pages 425 and 442. This concludes our discussion of middle and late childhood. In Section Six, we will follow children's development into adolescence, beginning with chapter 15, "Physical Development in Adolescence."

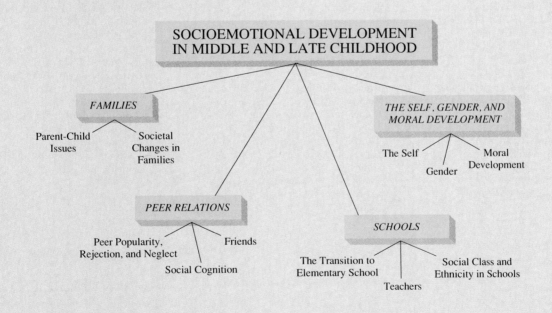

boundary ambiguity The uncertainty in stepfamilies about who is in or out of the family and who is performing or responsible for certain tasks in the family system. 418

neglected children Children who receive little attention from their peers but are not necessarily disliked by their peers. 419

rejected children Children who are more likely than neglected children to be disruptive and aggressive, and are often disliked by their peers. 419

intimacy in friendships Self-disclosure and the sharing of private thoughts. 421

aptitude-treatment interaction (ATI) The interaction between children's aptitudes or characteristics and the treatments or experiences they are given in classrooms. 422

perspective taking The ability to assume another person's perspective and understand his or her thoughts and feelings. 426

self-esteem The global evaluative dimension of the self. Self-esteem is also referred to as self-worth or self-image. 427

self-concept Domain-specific evaluations of the self. 427

Self-Perception Profile for Children A self-concept measure that has five specific domains—scholastic competence, athletic competence, social acceptance, physical appearance, and behavioral conduct—plus general self-worth. 427

social identity theory Social psychologist Henry Tajfel's (1978) theory that, when individuals are assigned to a group, they invariably think of that group as an in-group for them. This occurs because individuals want to have a positive image. 428

ethnocentrism The tendency to favor one's own group over other groups. 428

prejudice An unjustified negative attitude toward an individual because of that person's membership in a group. 428

gender stereotypes Broad categories that reflect our impressions and beliefs about females and males. 430

androgyny The presence of desirable masculine and feminine characteristics in the same individual. 433

gender-role transcendence The belief that, when an individual's competence is at issue, it should be conceptualized not on the basis of masculinity, femininity, or androgyny, but rather on a person basis. 434

internalization The developmental change from behavior that is externally controlled to behavior that is internally controlled. 437

preconventional reasoning The lowest level in Kohlberg's theory of moral development. At this level, the child shows no internalization of moral values—moral reasoning is controlled by external rewards and punishments. 437

punishment and obedience orientation The first stage in Kohlberg's theory of moral development. At this stage, moral thinking is based on punishment. 437

individualism and purpose The second stage in Kohlberg's theory of moral development. At this stage, moral thinking is based on rewards and self-interest. 437

conventional reasoning The second or intermediate level in Kohlberg's theory of moral development. At this level, the individual's internalization is intermediate. The person abides by certain standards (internal), but they are the standards of others (external), such as parents or the laws of society. 437

interpersonal norms The third stage in Kohlberg's theory of moral development. At this stage, the person values trust, caring, and loyalty to others as the basis of moral judgments. 437

social system morality The fourth stage in Kohlberg's theory of moral development. At this stage, moral judgments are based on understanding the social order, law, justice, and duty. 438

postconventional reasoning The highest level in Kohlberg's theory of moral development. At this level, morality is completely internalized and not based on others' standards. 438

community rights versus individual rights The fifth stage in Kohlberg's theory of moral development. At this stage, the person understands that values and laws are relative and that standards may vary from one person to another. 438

universal ethical principles The sixth and highest stage in Kohlberg's theory of moral development. At this stage, persons have developed a moral standard based on universal human rights. 438

justice perspective A moral perspective that focuses on the rights of the individual; individuals stand alone and independently make moral decisions. Kohlberg's theory is a justice perspective. 440

care perspective A moral perspective that views people in terms of their connectedness with others and emphasizes interpersonal communication, relationships with others, and concern for others. Gilligan's theory is a care perspective. 440

altruism An unselfish interest in helping someone else. 441

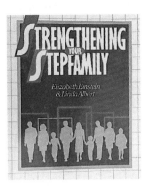

Strengthening Your Stepfamily

(1986) by Elizabeth Einstein and Linda Albert.
Circle Pines, MN: American Guidance Service.

This book covers many types of stepfamilies. It highlights myths and unrealistic expectations that are common in stepfamilies, and emphasizes strategies for developing positive relationships between stepparents and stepchildren. The authors discuss children's feelings and behaviors in stepfamilies and provide parent guidelines for helping children cope more effectively. Recommendations for dealing with stepfamily issues range from daily routines to holiday celebrations.

Smart Schools, Smart Kids

(1992) by Edward Fiske.
New York: Touchstone.

This book tours dozens of pioneering schools in the United States and describes how successful programs work, problems they have encountered, and the results they have achieved. Fiske says that too many of America's schools are put together on the outdated nineteenth-century factory-model school. He addresses how to develop learning communities, incorporate new technologies into classrooms, and how to go beyond testing. The book also tackles the learning crisis in children's education, providing many vivid examples of the tragedies of poor schools and the victories of competent schools.

Failing at Fairness

(1994) by Myra and David Sadker.
New York: Touchstone.

This book, the result of two decades of research, reveals how gender bias makes it unlikely that girls can receive an education equal to that given to boys. Among the Sadkers' conclusions are that girls' learning problems are not identified as often as boys' are; boys are given more attention by teachers; and girls start school testing higher in every academic subject, yet graduate from high school scoring 50 points lower on the SAT.

The hope is that sexism can be eradicated in the nation's schools. The authors believe that most educators are unaware of the subtle ways in which gender biases infiltrate the school environment.

The Sadkers also argue that the sexism present in schools is damaging to boys as well. Boys are most likely to be at both the top *and* the bottom of their classes—more likely to fail a class, miss promotion, or drop out of school. While girls often experience silent losses, boys' problems are usually out in the open.

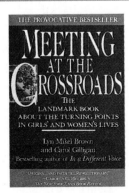

Meeting at the Crossroads

(1992) by Lyn Mikel Brown and Carol Gilligan.
Cambridge, MA: Harvard University Press.

This book provides a vivid portrayal of how adolescent girls are often ignored and misunderstood because our culture has tried to disconnect and disassemble the passage of females through adolescence. Brown and Gilligan developed a listener's guide, a method of following the pathways of girls' thoughts and feelings. Girls' voices at many different points in adolescence are revealed and recommendations for how to listen more sensitively to their needs are given.

IMPROVING THE LIVES OF CHILDREN

Improving the lives of children involves increasing parent involvement both at home and school, competent parenting in stepfamilies, cooperative learning, increased gender equity in male-dominant cultures, and developing a society free of gender barriers and discrimination.

HEALTH AND WELL-BEING

Parent-Involvement Activities at Home and School

Parent involvement is a broad concept that includes different types of activities that encourage parents to participate in nonacademic and academic activities that support their children's education (Simich-Dudgeon, 1993). Education expert Joyce Epstein (1986) believes that parent involvement activities take five different forms:

- Supporting children's learning at home
- Maintaining communication with the school
- Assisting in school activities
- Becoming involved in governance and advocacy
- Assuming the role of tutor at home

With regard to supporting children's learning at home, a basic obligation of parenting is to provide for a child's well-being (food, clothing, safety, health, and shelter) and to foster a home environment that is a good climate for learning. Children need to have an appropriate study area, the required school supplies, and parental support that values learning.

With regard to maintaining communication with the school, parents should attend parent-teacher conferences and other school functions, which conveys to children that their parents are interested in their school performance and activities.

With regard to assisting in school activities, parents can serve as volunteers at their child's school by assisting the teacher or the librarian, and by assisting during class trips and parties. Schools welcome this type of involvement, but only a small percentage of parents participate fully. In one study, only 4 percent of parents were active in school-based assistance (Epstein, 1986). In this same study, 70 percent of parents had never been involved in activities at their child's school.

With regard to becoming involved in governance and advocacy, parents can belong to a PTA/PTO organization, serve on advisory committees, or lobby the school board.

With regard to assuming the role of tutor at home, parents can be most effective if they learn the most competent tutoring strategies and support the work of the school.

FAMILIES AND PARENTING

Parenting and Children in Stepfamilies

What are some problems frequently encountered by stepfamilies? What are some ways to build a strong, positive stepfamily? William Gladden (1991) recently provided the following guidelines that address these questions:

Frequently encountered problems in stepfamilies

- Adapting to multiple viewpoints, attitudes, and personalities.
- Arranging to comply with the visitation and other custodial rights granted by a court to the absent natural parent—holidays and vacations can pose special problems, for example.

John W. Santrock

- Conflicting ideas about how to discipline children and differing expectations about children.
- Continuing battles over child custody issues.
- Disagreements over expenses and how family finances are to be allocated.
- Feelings of anger, hurt, mistrust, or guilt regarding the ex-spouse that may be transferred to the new mate.
- Interference by in-laws, especially grandparents, who have an interest in the children.
- Reduced space, privacy, and personal time.
- Refusal of the children to follow the rules or wishes of the stepparent.
- Unwillingness of the children to accept the stepparent, with possible outright rejection of the stepparent.
- Rivalry between children for attention and affection, especially when stepsiblings are involved.

- Unresolved emotional problems of the children because of the disequilibrium they have experienced in their lives.
- Unresolved personal problems of parents, such as psychological or behavioral problems, that may accompany them into the newly created family.

Strategies for building a strong, positive stepfamily

- Communicate about and come to an agreement on rules of conduct.
- Try to develop and maintain a cooperative relationship with the absent natural parent who still has legal rights to the children.
- Develop good communications between family members and learn to communicate clearly.
- Provide the children with age-appropriate responsibilities.
- Make a commitment to talk about and resolve disagreements based on mutual respect and kindness.

- Don't avoid dealing with the personal problems that create stress in the stepfamily; find positive ways to cope with them.
- Openly express affection.
- Plan for at least one mealtime per day that includes all the stepfamily members.
- Plan for family group entertainment and recreation.
- Respect the individual privacy rights of each member of the stepfamily.
- Support each stepfamily member's interests, hobbies, and goals.
- If family conflicts seem irreconcilable, or if the behavior of a child poses serious problems, it is usually wise to seek professional help. Most communities also have stepfamily support groups whose members may share problems encountered by many stepfamilies. Such support groups can be especially beneficial for coping with stepfamily issues and problems.

EDUCATION

The Jigsaw Classroom

Eliot Aronson stressed that the reward structure of elementary school classrooms needed to be changed from a setting of unequal competition to one of cooperation among equals, without making any curriculum changes. To accomplish this, he put together the *jigsaw classroom*. How might this work? Consider a class of thirty students, some White, some African American, some Latino. The lesson to be learned in the class focuses on the life of Joseph Pulitzer. The class might be broken up into five groups of six students each, with the groups being as equal as possible in terms of ethnic composition and academic achievement level. The lesson about Pulitzer's life could be divided into six parts, with one part given to each member of each six-person group. The parts might be paragraphs from Pulitzer's biography, such as how the Pulitzer family came to the United States, Pulitzer's childhood, his early work, and so on. The components are like parts of a jigsaw

puzzle. They have to be put together to form the complete puzzle.

All students in each group are given an allotted time to study their parts. Then the groups meet and each member tries to teach a part to her group. After an hour or so, each member is tested on the entire life of Pulitzer, with each member receiving an individual rather than a group score. Each student, therefore, must learn the entire lesson; learning depends on the cooperation and effort of the other members. Aronson (1986) believes that this type of learning increases the student's interdependence through cooperatively reaching the same goal.

The strategy of emphasizing cooperation rather than competition and the jigsaw classroom have been widely used in classrooms in the United States. A number of research studies reveal that this type of cooperative learning is associated with increased self-esteem, better academic performance, friendships

among classmates, and improved interethnic perceptions (Slavin, 1989).

Although the cooperative classroom strategy has many merits, it may have a built-in difficulty that restricts its effectiveness. Academic achievement is as much an individual as a team "sport" (Brown, 1986). It is individuals, not groups, who enter college, take jobs, and follow careers. Parents with advantaged children in the jigsaw classroom might react with increased ethnic hostility when their children bring home lower grades than they had been used to getting before the jigsaw classroom was introduced. A child may tell his father, "The teacher is getting us to teach each other. In my group, we have a kid named Carlos, who can barely speak English." Although the jigsaw classroom can be an important strategy for reducing ethnic hostility, caution needs to be exercised in its use because of the unequal status of the participants and the individual nature of achievement.

Gender Roles in Egypt and China

In recent decades, roles assumed by males and females in the United States have become increasingly similar—that is, androgynous. In many countries, though, gender roles have remained more gender-specific. For example, in Egypt, the division of labor between Egyptian males and females is dramatic. Egyptian males are socialized to work in the public sphere, females in the private world of home and child rearing. Islam dictates that the man's duty is to provide for his family, the woman's duty to care for her family and household. Any deviations from this traditional gender-role orientation are severely disapproved of.

Egypt is not the only country in which males and females are socialized to behave, think, and feel in strongly gender-specific ways. Kenya and Nepal are two other cultures in which children are brought up under very strict gender-specific guidelines (Munroe, Himmin, & Munroe, 1984). In the People's Republic of China, the female's status has historically been lower than the male's. The teachings of the fifth-century B.C. Chinese philosopher Confucius were used to reinforce the concept of females as inferior beings. Beginning with the 1949 revolution in China, women began to achieve more economic freedom and more equal status in marital relationships. However, even with the sanctions of a socialist government, the old patriarchal traditions of male supremacy in China have not been completely uprooted. Chinese women still make considerably less money than Chinese men in comparable positions, and in rural China, a tradition of male supremacy still governs many women's lives.

Thus, while in China, females have made considerable strides, complete equality remains a distant objective. And in many cultures, such as Egypt and other countries where the Muslim religion predominates, gender-specific behavior is pronounced, and females are not given access to high-status positions.

In China, females and males are usually socialized to behave, feel, and think differently. The old patriarchal traditions of male supremacy have not been completely uprooted. Chinese women still make considerably less money than Chinese men, and, in rural China (such as here in the Lixian village of Sichuan), male supremacy still governs many women's lives.

In Egypt near the Aswan Dam, women are returning from the Nile River where they have filled their water jugs. How might gender role socialization for girls in Egypt compare to that in the United States?

Tomorrow's Gender Worlds of Today's Children

Controversy swirls around today's females and males. Females increasingly struggle to gain influence and change the worlds of business, politics, and relationships with males. The changes are far from complete, but social reformers hope that, a generation from now, the struggles of the last decades of the twentieth century will have generated more freedom, influence, and flexibility for females. Possibly a decade or two from now, today's children will live in a world in which equal pay, child care, abortion, rape, and domestic violence will no longer be discussed as "women's issues" but rather as economic issues, family issues, and ethical issues—reflecting equal concern of females and males. Possibly a 10-year-old girl today will head a major corporation in thirty years and the circumstance will not make

headlines by virtue of her gender. Half the presidential candidates may be women and nobody will notice.

What would it take to get from here to there? The choices are not simple ones. When Barbara Bush went to Wellesley College to celebrate motherhood and wifely virtues, she stimulated a national debate on what it means to be a successful woman. The debate was further fueled by TV anchorwoman Connie Chung's announcement that she would abandon the fast track at CBS in a final drive to become a mother at 44. At the same time, children's male role models are also in a state of flux. Wall Street star Peter Lynch, the head of Fidelity Investment's leading mutual fund, resigned to have more time with his family and pursue humanitarian projects (Gibbs, 1990). Today though, both Chung and Lynch are back at work.

When asked to sketch their futures, many of today's college students say they want good careers, good marriages, and two or three children, but they don't want their children to be raised by strangers. Idealistic? Maybe. Some of you will reach these goals, whereas others of you will make other choices. Some women will choose to remain single as they pursue their career goals, others will become married but not have children, and yet others will balance the demands of family and work. In a word, not all females have the same goals; neither do all males. What is important for us is to develop a society free of barriers and discrimination, one that allows today's children—whether female or male—to choose freely, to meet their expectations, and to realize their potentials.

REVIEW OF CHILDREN'S DEVELOPMENT

Middle and Late Childhood

PHYSICAL DEVELOPMENT

During the elementary school years, children grow an average of 2 to 3 inches a year. Muscle mass and strength gradually increase. Legs lengthen and trunks slim down. Growth is slow and consistent. Motor development becomes smoother and more coordinated. Boys are usually better at gross motor skills, girls at fine motor skills. Our nation's children are not getting enough exercise. A special concern is stress in children's lives—both life events and daily hassles can cause stress. Sociocultural factors, such as poverty, can place considerable stress on children. One of children's important buffers against stress is the long-term presence of a basic trusting relationship with at least one adult. A readily available support network is also important. Of special concern are children with a disability, including children with a learning disability or attention-deficit hyperactivity disorder.

COGNITIVE DEVELOPMENT

According to Piaget, the cognitive development of children 7 to 11 years old is characterized by concrete operational thought. Concrete operations are mental actions that are reversible. We owe Piaget the present field of cognitive development. However, Piaget's theory, especially his stage concept, has not gone uncriticized. Neo-Piagetians believe children's cognitive development is more specific than Piaget proposed. Children's long term-memory, scientific reasoning, and cognitive monitoring improve during middle and late childhood. It is important for children to engage in critical thinking. One issue in intelligence is whether it is a general ability or a number of specific abilities. Concerns include the cultural bias of intelligence tests and the misuses of the tests. The extremes of intelligence involve mental retardation and giftedness. Children's creativity should be encouraged. In middle and late childhood, children become more analytical and logical in their approach to words and grammar. Reading is a more central aspect of language in the middle and late childhood years. No negative effects of bilingualism have been found. Contemporary ideas about achievement focus on the distinction between intrinsic and extrinsic motivation, a mastery versus a helpless or performance orientation, and ethnic minority children's achievement.

SOCIOEMOTIONAL DEVELOPMENT

Parents spend less time with children in middle and late childhood, but parents are still very important socializing agents in this period. New parent-child issues emerge, and discipline changes. Control is more coregulatory. In middle and late childhood, two major changes in many children's lives are movement into a stepfamily and becoming a latchkey child. Children spend considerably more time with peers in this period. Distinctions in peer relations are made between popular children, rejected children, and neglected children. Friendships become more important in middle and late childhood. A special concern about early elementary education is that it proceeds mainly on the basis of negative feedback to children. Schools have a stronger middle-class than lower-class orientation. A special concern is the education of ethnic minority children. The internal self, the social self, and the socially comparative self become more prominent in self-understanding in middle and late childhood. Perspective taking increases in this period. Self-concept and self-esteem are important dimensions of the child's socioemotional development. Gender is an important aspect of elementary school children's development, especially gender stereotypes, similarities and differences, gender-role classification, and ethnicity and gender. Kohlberg developed a provocative theory of moral reasoning, which involves three levels (preconventional, conventional, and postconventional) and six stages. Kohlberg's theory has been criticized, especially by Gilligan, who believes he underestimated the importance of the care perspective. Children's altruism changes developmentally.

Adolescence

*In no order of things is
adolescence the simple time of life.*

—Jean Erskine Stewart

Adolescents feel like they will live forever. At times, they are sure that they know everything. They clothe themselves with rainbows and go brave as the zodiac, flashing from one end of the world to the other both in mind and body. In many ways, today's adolescents are privileged, wielding unprecedented economic power. At the same time, they move through a seemingly endless preparation for life. They try on one face after another, seeking to find a face of their own. In their most pimply and awkward moments, they become acquainted with sex. They play furiously at "adult games" but are confined to a society of their own peers. They want their parents to understand them and hope that their parents give them the privilege of understanding them. Their generation of young people is the fragile cable by which the best and the worst of their parents' generation is transmitted to the present. In the end, there are only two lasting bequests parents can leave youth, one being roots, the other wings. Section six contains three chapters: "Physical Development in Adolescence" (chapter 15), "Cognitive Development in Adolescence" (chapter 16), and "Socioemotional Development in Adolescence" (chapter 17).

CARL LARRSON
In the Pawthorn Hedge, detail

Physical Development
in Adolescence

*In youth, we clothe ourselves with
rainbows, and go brave as the zodiac.*

—Ralph Waldo Emerson,
The Conduct of Life, 1860

IMAGES OF CHILDREN

Puberty's Mysteries and Curiosities

I am pretty confused. I wonder whether I am weird or normal. My body is starting to change, but I sure don't look like a lot of my friends. I still look like a kid for the most part. My best friend is only 13, but he looks like he is 16 or 17. I get nervous in the locker room during PE class because when I go to take a shower, I'm afraid somebody is going to make fun of me since I'm not as physically developed as some of the others.

Robert, age 12

I don't like my breasts. They are too small, and they look funny. I'm afraid guys won't like me if they don't get bigger.

Angie, age 13

I can't stand the way I look. I have zits all over my face. My hair is dull and stringy. It never stays in place. My nose is too big. My lips are too small. My legs are too short. I have four warts on my left hand, and people get grossed out by them. So do I. My body is a disaster!

Ann, age 14

I'm short and I can't stand it. My father is six feet tall, and here I am only five foot four. I'm 14 already. I look like a kid, and I get teased a lot, especially by other guys. I'm always the last one picked for sides in basketball because I'm so short. Girls don't seem to be interested in me either because most of them are taller than I am.

Jim, age 14

The comments of these four adolescents underscore the dramatic upheaval in our bodies following the calm, consistent growth of middle and late childhood. Young adolescents develop an acute concern about their bodies. When columnist Bob Greene (1988) dialed a party line called Connections in Chicago to discover what young adolescents were saying to each other, the first things the boys and girls asked for—after first names—were physical descriptions. The idealism of the callers was apparent. Most of the girls described themselves as having long blond hair, being 5 feet, 5 inches tall, and weighing about 110 pounds. Most of the boys said that they had brown hair, lifted weights, were 6 feet tall, and weighed 170 pounds.

PREVIEW

Puberty's changes are perplexing to adolescents as they go through them. Although the changes are perplexing and generate self-doubts, questions, fears, and anxieties, most of us effectively make it through this transition from childhood to adulthood we call adolescence. In this chapter we explore the nature of adolescence, puberty, sexuality, and some problems and disorders.

THE NATURE OF ADOLESCENCE

As in the development of children, genetic, biological, environmental, and social factors interact in adolescent development. Also, continuity and discontinuity characterize adolescent development. The genes inherited from parents still influence thought and behavior during adolescence, but inheritance now interacts with the social conditions of the adolescent's world—with family, peers, friendships, dating, and school experiences. An adolescent has experienced thousands of hours of interaction with parents, peers, and teachers in the past 10 to 13 years of development. Still new experiences and developmental tasks appear during adolescence. Relationships with parents take a different form, moments with peers become more intimate, dating occurs for the first time as does sexual exploration

John W. Santrock

and possibly intercourse. The adolescent's thoughts are more abstract and idealistic. Biological changes trigger a heightened interest in body image. Adolescence, then, has both continuity and discontinuity with childhood.

The Biological and Sociohistorical Nature of Adolescence

Is adolescence a biologically based period, or is it a sociohistorical invention? Both views have been proposed. First, we will examine G. Stanley Hall's biological view that emphasizes the storm and stress of adolescence, and second, we will study the inventionist view of adolescence.

G. Stanley Hall's View

Historians label G. Stanley Hall (1844–1924) the father of the scientific study of adolescence. Hall's ideas were first published in 1904 in a two-volume set titled *Adolescence* (Hall, 1904). Hall was strongly influenced by Charles Darwin, the famous evolutionary theorist and applied the scientific and biological dimensions of Darwin's view to the study of adolescent development. He believed that all development is controlled by genetically determined physiological factors and argued that environment plays a minimal role in development, especially during infancy and childhood. Hall did acknowledge that environment accounts for more change in development in adolescence than in earlier periods. Thus, at least with regard to adolescence, Hall believed—as we do today—that heredity interacts with environmental influences to determine the individual's development.

Jeanne Brooks-Gunn has been a pioneer in the study of puberty's role in adolescent development. Her far-ranging research interests include the psychological accompaniments of menarche, adaptive and maladaptive responses to pubertal growth, and adolescent health and well-being.

Adolescence is like cactus.

—Anaïs Nin,
A Spy in the House of Love, 1959

Hall said that adolescence is filled with storm and stress. The **storm-and-stress view** *is Hall's concept that adolescence is a turbulent time charged with conflict and mood swings.* He borrowed the "storm and stress" label from the *Sturm und Drang* descriptions of German writers such as Goethe and Schiller, who wrote novels full of idealism, commitment to goals, passion, feeling, and revolution. Hall sensed there was a parallel between the themes of the German authors and the psychological development of adolescents. In Hall's view, adolescents' thoughts, feelings, and actions oscillate between conceit and humility, good and temptation, happiness and sadness. The adolescent

may be nasty to a peer one moment, kind the next moment. At one time the adolescent may want to be alone but seconds later seek companionship.

The Inventionist View

While adolescence has a biological base, as G. Stanley Hall believed, adolescence also has a sociohistorical base. Indeed, sociohistorical conditions contributed to the emergence of the concept of adolescence. At a point not too long ago, the teenager had not yet been invented. The **inventionist view** *states that adolescence is a sociohistorical creation. Especially important in the invention of the concept of adolescence were the sociohistorical circumstances at the beginning of the twentieth century, a time when legislation was enacted that ensured the dependency of youth and helped to make their move into the economic sphere more manageable.* The sociohistorical circumstances included a decline in apprenticeship; increased mechanization during the Industrial Revolution, which also involved upgraded skills requirements of labor and specialized divisions of labor; the separation of home and work; the writings of G. Stanley Hall; urbanization; the appearance of youth groups such as the YMCA and Boy Scouts; and age-segregated schools.

Schools, work, and economics are important dimensions of the inventionist view of adolescence (Lapsley, Enright, & Serlin, 1985). Some scholars of adolescence argue that the invention of the concept of adolescence was mainly a by-product of the motivation to create a system of compulsory public education. In this view, the function of secondary schools is to transmit intellectual skills to youth. However, other scholars of adolescence

---

argue that the primary purpose of secondary schools is to deploy youth within the economic sphere and to serve as an important cog in the authority structure of the culture. In this view, the American society "inflicted" the status of adolescence on its youth through child-saving legislation. By developing laws for youth, the adult power structure placed youth in a submissive position that restricted their options, encouraged their dependency, and made their move into the world of work more manageable.

> *A few years ago it occurred to me that when I was a teenager, in the early depression years, there were no teenagers! The teenager has sneaked up on us in our own lifetime, and yet it seems he has always been with us. . . . The teenager had not yet been invented, though, and there did not yet exist a special class of beings, bounded in a certain way—not quite children and certainly not adults.*
>
> —A. K. Cohen, Foreword, in P. Musgrove, ***Youth and the Social Order***

Stereotyping Adolescents

It is easy to stereotype a person, groups of people, or classes of people. A **stereotype** *is a broad category that reflects our impressions and beliefs about people. All stereotypes refer to an image of what the typical member of a particular group is like.* We live in a complex world and want to simplify this complexity. Stereotyping people is one way we do this. We simply assign a label to a group of people—for example, "Youths are promiscuous." Then we have much less to consider when we think about this set of people. Once we assign the labels, though, it is difficult to abandon them, even in the face of contradictory evidence.

Stereotypes about adolescents are plentiful: "They say they want a job, but when they get one, they don't want to work"; "They are all lazy"; "They are all sex fiends"; "They are all into drugs, every last one of them"; "Kids today don't have the moral fiber of my generation"; "The problem with adolescents today is that they all have it too easy"; "They are a bunch of egotistical, smart-alecks"; and so it goes.

Two studies illustrate just how widespread the stereotyping of adolescents is. In the first study, pollster Daniel Yankelovich (1974) compared the attitudes of adolescents with those of their parents about different values, lifestyles, and codes of personal conduct. There was little or no difference between the attitudes of the adolescents and their parents toward self-control, hard work, saving money, competition, compromise, legal authority, and private property. There was a substantial difference, however, between the adolescents and their parents when their attitudes toward religion were sampled (89 percent of the parents said that religion was important to them, compared to only 66 percent of the adolescents). Note, though, that a majority of the adolescents still subscribed to the belief that religion is important.

A second study that contradicts the stereotypical view of adolescence as highly stressful and disturbed was conducted by adolescent researcher Daniel Offer and his colleagues (1988). The self-images of adolescents around the world were sampled—in the United States, Australia, Bangladesh, Hungary, Israel, Italy, Japan, Taiwan, Turkey, and West Germany. A healthy self-image characterized at least 73 percent of the adolescents studied. They appeared to be moving toward adulthood with a healthy integration of previous experiences, self-confidence, and optimism about the future. Although there were some differences among the adolescents, they were happy most of the time, they enjoyed life, they perceived themselves as able to exercise self-control, they valued work and school, they expressed confidence about their sexual selves, they expressed positive feelings toward their families, and they felt they had the capability to cope with life's stresses: not exactly a storm and stress portrayal of adolescence.

Beginning with G. Stanley Hall's (1904) portrayal of adolescence as a period of storm and stress, for much of this century in the United States and other Western cultures, adolescence has unfortunately been perceived as a problematic period of the human life span that youths, their families, and society had to endure. As we just saw in two studies, however, a large majority of adolescents are not nearly as disturbed and troubled as the popular stereotype of adolescence suggests. According to adolescent researchers Shirley Feldman and Glenn Elliott (1990), public attitudes about adolescence emerge from a combination of personal experience and media portrayals, neither of which produce an objective picture of how normal adolescents develop. Some of the readiness to assume the worst about adolescents likely involves the short memories of adults. Many adults measure their current perceptions of adolescents by their memories of their own adolescence. Adults may portray today's adolescents as more troubled, less respectful, more self-centered, more assertive, and more adventurous than they were.

However, in matters of taste and manners, the young people of every generation have seemed radical, unnerving, and different from adults—different in how they look, in how they behave, in the music they enjoy, in their hairstyles, and in the clothing they choose. It is an enormous error, though, to confuse adolescents' enthusiasm for trying on new identities and enjoying moderate amounts of outrageous behavior with hostility toward parental and societal standards. Acting-out and boundary testing are time-honored ways in which adolescents move toward accepting, rather than rejecting, parental values.

Stereotypes of adolescents are also generated by media portrayals. The media often present sensational and "newsworthy" material, which means that they are far more likely to focus on troubled adolescents than on normal adolescents. The impact of such media coverage conveys the impression that a majority of young people engage in deviant behaviors, when, in fact, only a small minority do. As we will see next in our consideration of today's adolescents, not only do the messages of the media convey an image of adolescents as highly troubled, but the messages to adolescents from both adults and the media are often ambivalent.

Today's Youth

What is the current status of adolescents compared to the status of their counterparts earlier in history? How complex is adolescent development today?

The Current Status of Adolescents

Today's adolescents face demands and expectations, as well as risks and temptations, that appear to be more numerous and complex than those faced by adolescents only a generation ago. Nonetheless, contrary to the popular stereotype of adolescents as highly stressed and incompetent, the vast majority of adolescents successfully negotiate the path from childhood to adulthood. By some criteria, today's adolescents are doing better than their counterparts from a decade or two earlier. Today, more adolescents complete high school, especially African American adolescents. The majority of adolescents today have positive self-conceptions and positive relationships with others. As indicated earlier, such contemporary findings do not reveal a portrayal of adolescence as a highly disturbed, overly stressful time period in the life span. Rather, the majority of adolescents find the transition from childhood to adulthood to be a time of physical, cognitive, and socioemotional development that provides considerable challenge, opportunities, and growth.

Although the majority of adolescents experience the transition from childhood to adulthood more positively than is portrayed by many adults and the media, too many adolescents today are not provided with adequate opportunities and support to become competent adults. In many ways, today's adolescents are presented with a less stable environment than adolescents of a decade or two ago. High divorce rates, high adolescent pregnancy rates, and increased geographic mobility of families contribute to this lack of stability in adolescents' lives. Today's adolescents are exposed to a complex menu of lifestyle options through the media, and, although the adolescent drug rate is beginning to show signs of decline, the rate of adolescent drug use in the United States is higher than that of any other country in the industrialized Western world. Many of today's adolescents face these temptations, as well as sexual activity, at increasingly young ages.

Our discussion underscores an important point about adolescents: They do not make up a homogeneous group (Galambos & Tilton-Weaver, 1996). The majority of adolescents negotiate the lengthy path to adult maturity successfully, but too large a group does not. Ethnic, cultural, gender, socioeconomic, age, and lifestyle differences influence the actual life trajectory of every adolescent. Different portrayals of adolescence emerge, depending on the particular group of adolescents being described.

The Complexity of Adolescent Development

As researchers more carefully examine the lives of adolescents, they are recognizing that a single developmental model may not accurately characterize all adolescents (Feldman & Elliott, 1990). The most widely described general model of adolescent development states that adolescence is a transition from childhood to adulthood during which individuals explore alternatives and experiment with choices as part of developing an identity. Although this model may accurately fit many White middle-class adolescents, it is less well suited to adolescents from low-income families, school dropouts, and unemployed adolescents (Carnegie Council on Adolescent Development, 1995). For many of these youths, development often is more chaotic and restricted. For them, social and ethnic barriers too frequently signal the presence of discrimination and prejudice (McLoyd & Ceballo, 1995).

PUBERTY

Imagine a toddler displaying all the features of puberty. Think about a 3-year-old girl with fully developed breasts or a boy just slightly older with a deep voice. That is what we would see by the year 2250 if the age at which puberty arrives were to continue to decrease at its present pace (Petersen, 1979).

In Norway, **menarche,** *first menstruation,* occurs at just over 13 years of age, as opposed to 17 years of age in the 1840s. In the United States—where children mature up to a year earlier than children in European countries—the average age of menarche has declined from 14.2 in 1900 to about 12.45 today. The age of menarche has been declining at an average of about four months per decade for the past century.

Fortunately, however, we are unlikely to see pubescent toddlers, since what has characterized the past century is special—most likely, a higher level of nutrition and health. The available information suggests that menarche began to occur earlier at about the time of the Industrial Revolution, a period associated with increased standards of living and advances in medical science.

> *What is formed for long duration arrives slowly to its maturity.*
>
> —Samuel Johnson,
> **The Rambler, 1750**

Menarche is one event that characterizes puberty, but there are others. What are puberty's markers? What are the psychological accompaniments of puberty's changes? What health care issues are raised by early and late maturation?

Pubertal Change

Puberty *is a period of rapid skeletal and sexual maturation that occurs mainly in early adolescence.* However, puberty is not a

---

single, sudden event. It is part of a gradual process. We know when a young person is going through puberty, but pinpointing its beginning and its end is difficult. Except for menarche, which occurs rather late in puberty, no single marker heralds puberty. For boys, the first whisker or first wet dream are events that could mark its appearance, but both may go unnoticed.

Behind the first whisker in boys and widening of hips in girls is a flood of hormones, powerful chemical substances secreted by the endocrine glands and carried through the body by the bloodstream. The concentrations of certain hormones increase dramatically during adolescence. **Testosterone** *is a hormone associated in boys with the development of genitals, an increase in height, and a change in voice.* **Estradiol** *is a hormone associated in girls with breast, uterine, and skeletal development.* In one study, testosterone levels increased eighteenfold in boys but only twofold in girls during puberty; estradiol increased eightfold in girls but only twofold in boys (Nottelmann & others, 1987).

The same influx of hormones that puts hair on a male's chest and imparts curvature to a female's breast may contribute to psychological development in adolescence (Dorn & Lucas, 1995). In one study of 108 normal boys and girls ranging in age from 9 to 14, a higher concentration of testosterone was present in boys who rated themselves more socially competent (Nottelmann & others, 1987). In another study of sixty normal boys and girls in the same age range, girls with higher estradiol levels expressed more anger and aggression (Inoff-Germain & others, 1988). However, hormonal effects by themselves may account for only a small portion of the variance in adolescent development. For example, in one study, social factors accounted for two to four times as much variance as hormonal factors in young adolescent girls' depression and anger (Brooks-Gunn & Warren, 1989).

These hormonal and body changes occur, on the average, about two years earlier in females (10½ years of age) than in males (12½ years of age) (see figure 15.1). Four of the most noticeable areas of body change in females are height spurt, menarche, breast growth, and growth of pubic hair; four of the most noticeable areas of body change in males are height spurt, penile growth, testes growth, and growth of pubic hair. The normal range and average age of these characteristics are shown in figures 15.2 and 15.3. Among the most remarkable normal variations is that two boys (or two girls) may be the same chronological age, yet one may complete the pubertal sequence before the other has begun it. For most girls, the first menstrual period may occur as early as the age of 10 or as late as the age of 15½ and still be considered normal, for example.

Puberty is not simply an environmental accident; genetic factors are also involved. As indicated earlier, although nutrition, health, and other factors affect puberty's timing and variations in its makeup, the basic genetic program is wired into the nature of the species.

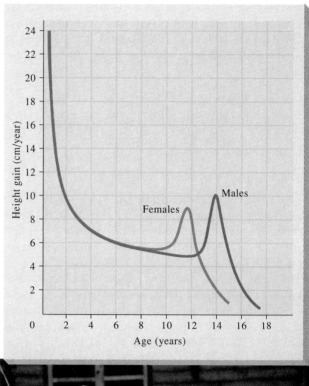

FIGURE 15.1

Pubertal Growth Spurt
On the average, the growth spurt that characterizes pubertal change occurs 2 years earlier for girls (10½) than for boys (12½).

Another key factor in puberty's occurrence is body mass. For example, menarche occurs at a relatively consistent weight in girls. A body weight of approximately 103 to 109 pounds signals menarche and the end of the adolescent growth spurt. For menarche to begin and continue, fat must make up 17 percent of a girl's total body weight.

Psychological Accompaniments of Pubertal Change

A host of psychological changes accompanies an adolescent's physical development (Graber, Petersen, & Brooks-Gunn, 1996). Imagine yourself as you were beginning puberty. Not only did you probably think about yourself differently, but your parents and peers probably began

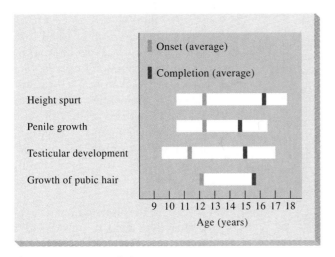

FIGURE 15.2

Normal Range and Average Age of Male Sexual Development

Adapted from "Growing Up" by J. M. Tanner. Copyright © 1973 by Scientific American, Inc. All rights reserved.

FIGURE 15.3

Normal Range and Average Age of Female Sexual Development

Adapted from "Growing Up" by J. M. Tanner. Copyright © 1973 by Scientific American, Inc. All rights reserved.

acting differently toward you. Maybe you were proud of your changing body even though you were perplexed about what was happening. Perhaps your parents no longer perceived you as someone with whom they could sit in bed and watch television or as someone who should be kissed goodnight.

One thing is certain about the psychological aspects of physical change in adolescence: Adolescents are preoccupied with their bodies and develop individual images of what their bodies are like.

Perhaps you looked in the mirror daily or even hourly to see if you could detect anything different about your changing body. Preoccupation with one's body image is strong throughout adolescence, but it is especially acute during puberty, a time when adolescents are more dissatisfied with their bodies than in late adolescence.

Being physically attractive and having a positive body image are associated with an overall positive conception of one's self. In one study, girls who were judged as being physically attractive and who generally had a positive body image had higher opinions of themselves in general (Lerner & Karabenick, 1974). In another study, breast growth in girls 9 to 11 years old was associated with a positive body image, positive peer relationships, and superior adjustment (Brooks-Gunn & Warren, 1988).

Some of you entered puberty early, others late, and yet others on time. When adolescents mature earlier or later than their peers, might they perceive themselves differently? Some years ago, in the California Longitudinal Study, early-maturing boys perceived themselves more positively and had more successful peer relations than did their late-maturing counterparts (Jones, 1965). The findings for early-maturing girls were similar but not as strong as for boys. When the late-maturing boys were in their thirties, however, they had developed a stronger sense of identity than the early-maturing boys (Peskin, 1967). Possibly this occurred because the late-maturing boys had more time to explore life's options or

Harvey Peskin's (1967) study on early- and late-maturing boys established that late maturity in adolescence benefited identity development in early adulthood. Peskins's explanation for this finding is that late-maturing boys have more time to explore a wide variety of career and lifestyle options. Can you think of other explanations? For example, consider what aspects of their development early- and late-maturing boys are likely to receive positive feedback about during their early adolescent years. By developing explanations for advantageous identity development in late-maturing boys, you are learning to think critically by *pursuing alternative explanations to understand development comprehensively*.

earlier sexual experiences. In one study, early-maturing girls had lower educational and occupational attainment in adulthood (Stattin & Magnusson, 1990). Apparently as a result of their social and cognitive immaturity, combined with early physical development, early-maturing girls are easily lured into problem behaviors, not recognizing the possibly long-term effects on their development (Petersen, 1993).

Some researchers now question whether the effects of puberty are as strong as once believed (Montemayor, Adams, & Gulotta, 1990). Puberty affects some adolescents more strongly than others and some behaviors more strongly than others. Body image, dating interest, and sexual behavior are affected by pubertal change. The recent questioning of puberty's effects suggests that, if we look at overall development and adjustment in the human life span, pubertal variations (such as early and late maturation) are less dramatic than is commonly thought. In thinking about puberty's effects, keep in mind that an adolescent's world involves cognitive and socioemotional changes as well as physical changes. As with all periods of development, these processes work in concert to produce who we are in adolescence.

because the early-maturing boys continued to focus on their advantageous physical status instead of on career development and achievement. To further evaluate the identity development of late-maturing boys, refer to Critical Thinking About Children's Development.

More recent research confirms, though, that at least during adolescence it is advantageous to be an early-maturing rather than a late-maturing boy (Simmons & Blythe, 1987). The more recent findings for girls suggest that early maturation is a mixed blessing: These girls experience more problems in school but also more independence and popularity with boys. The time that maturation is assessed also is a factor. In the sixth grade, early-maturing girls showed greater satisfaction with their figures than late-maturing girls, but, by the tenth grade, late-maturing girls were more satisfied. The reason for this is that, by late adolescence, early-maturing girls are shorter and stockier, whereas late-maturing girls are taller and thinner. Late-maturing girls in late adolescence have bodies that more closely approximate the current American ideal of feminine beauty—tall and thin.

In the last decade an increasing number of researchers have found that early maturation increases the vulnerability of girls to a number of problems (Brooks-Gunn & Paikoff, 1993). Early-maturing girls are more likely to smoke, drink, be depressed, and have an eating disorder; to request earlier independence from their parents and have older friends; and their bodies are more likely to elicit responses from males that lead to earlier dating and

Pubertal Timing and Health Care

What can be done to identify off-time maturers who are at risk for health problems? Many adolescents whose development is extremely early or extremely late are likely to come to the attention of a physician—such as a boy who has not had a spurt in height by the age of 16 or a girl who has not menstruated by the age of 15. Girls and boys who are early or late maturers but are well within the normal range are less likely to be taken to a physician because of their maturational status. Nonetheless, these boys and girls may have fears and doubts about being normal that they do not raise unless a physician, counselor, or other health care provider takes the initiative. A brief discussion outlining the sequence and timing of events and the large individual variations in them may be all that is required to reassure many adolescents who are maturing very early or very late.

Health care providers may want to discuss the adolescent's off-time development with the adolescent's parents as well. Information about the peer pressures of off-time development can be beneficial. Especially helpful to early-maturing girls is a discussion of peer pressures to date and to engage in adultlike behavior at an early age. The transition to middle school, junior high school, or high school may be more stressful for girls and boys who are in the midst of puberty than for those who are not (Brooks-Gunn & Reiter, 1990).

If pubertal development is extremely late, a physician may recommend hormonal treatment. In one study of extended pubertal delay in boys, hormonal treatment worked to increase the height, dating interest, and peer relations in several boys but resulted in little or no improvement in other boys (Lewis, Money, & Bobrow, 1977).

In sum, most early- and late-maturing individuals weather puberty's challenges and stresses competently. For those who do not, discussions with sensitive and knowledgeable health care providers and parents can improve the off-time maturing adolescent's coping abilities.

At this point we have discussed a number of ideas about the nature of adolescence and pubertal development. A summary of these ideas is presented in concept table 15.1. Next, we will examine the nature of adolescent sexuality.

SEXUALITY

I am 16 years old and I really like this one girl. She wants to be a virgin until she marries. We went out last night and she let me go pretty far, but not all the way. I know she really likes me too, but she always stops me when things start getting hot and heavy. It is getting hard for me to handle. She doesn't know it but I'm a virgin too. I feel I am ready to have sex. I have to admit I think about having sex with other girls too. Maybe I should be dating other girls.

—Frank C.

I'm 14 years old. I have a lot of sexy thoughts. Sometimes just before I drift off to sleep at night I think about this hunk who is 16 years old and plays on the football team. He is so gorgeous and I can feel him holding me in his arms and kissing and hugging me. When I'm walking down the hall between classes at school, I sometimes start daydreaming about guys I have met, and wonder what it would be like to have sex with them. Last year I had this crush on the men's track coach. I'm on the girls' track team so I saw him a lot during the year. He hardly knew I thought about him the way I did, although I tried to flirt with him several times.

—Amy S.

If we listen to boys and girls at the very moment they seem most pimply, awkward and disagreeable, we can partly penetrate a mystery most of us once felt heavily within us, and have now forgotten. This mystery is the very process of creation of man and woman.

—Colin Macinnes,
The World of Children

During adolescence, the lives of males and females become wrapped in sexuality (Brooks-Gunn & Paikoff, in press). Adolescence is a time of sexual exploration and experimentation, of sexual fantasies and sexual realities, of incorporating sexuality into one's identity. At a time when sexual identity is an important developmental task of adolescence, the adolescent is confronted with conflicting sexual values and messages. The majority of adolescents eventually manage to develop a mature sexual identity, but most have periods of vulnerability and confusion along life's sexual journey. Our coverage of adolescent sexuality focuses on sexual attitudes and behavior, sexually transmitted diseases, and adolescent pregnancy.

Sexual Attitudes and Behavior

How extensively have heterosexual attitudes and behaviors changed in the twentieth century? What sexual scripts do adolescents follow? How extensive is homosexual behavior in adolescence?

Adolescent Heterosexual Behavior— Trends and Incidence

Had you been in high school or college in 1940, you probably would have had a different attitude toward many aspects of sexuality than you do today, especially if you are a female. A review of students' sexual practices and attitudes from 1900 to 1980 revealed two important trends (Darling, Kallen, & VanDusen, 1984). First, the percentage of youth reporting that they had had sexual intercourse increased dramatically. Second, the percentage of females reporting that they had had sexual intercourse increased more rapidly than for males, although the initial base for males was greater. These changes suggest movement away from a double standard that says it is more appropriate for males than females to have sexual intercourse.

Large numbers of American adolescents are sexually active (Crump & others, 1996). Figure 15.4 reveals that by age 17, 66 percent of males and 50 percent of females have had sexual intercourse; by age 19, 86 percent of males and 75 percent of females have had sexual intercourse (Alan Guttmacher Institute, 1993). According to the Alan Guttmacher Institute, which periodically surveys adolescent sexual behavior, sexual intercourse among adolescents is increasing with fewer youth saving sex for adulthood, much less marriage. Among the other findings recently reported by the Institute:

- Both males and females report dramatic increases in condom use, undoubtedly due to AIDS education. However, only one-third of male adolescents use condoms all of the time.
- Nearly two-thirds of the sexually experienced girls have had at least two partners; the average, sexually active 17- to 19-year-old urban male claims he has had six partners.

CONCEPT TABLE 15.1

The Nature of Adolescence and Pubertal Development

Concept	Processes/Related Ideas	Characteristics/Description
The Nature of Adolescence	The biological and sociohistorical nature of adolescence	G. Stanley Hall is the father of the scientific study of adolescence. His storm-and-stress view emphasizes the biological basis of adolescence. In contrast, the inventionist view states that adolescence is a sociohistorical creation; the concept of adolescence emerged at the beginning of the twentieth century when the enactment of legislation ensured the dependency of youth and made their move into the economic sphere more manageable.
	Stereotyping adolescents	A stereotype is a broad category reflecting our impressions about people. Many stereotypes about adolescents are inaccurate. Stereotypes about adolescence often arise from a blend of personal experiences and media portrayals.
Today's Youth	The current status of adolescents	The majority of adolescents today successfully negotiate the path from childhood to adulthood. By some criteria, today's adolescents also are doing better than their counterparts from a decade or two earlier. However, too many of today's adolescents are not provided with adequate opportunities and support to become competent adults. In many ways, today's adolescents are presented with a less stable environment. It is important to view adolescents as a heterogeneous group because a different portrayal emerges depending on the particular set of adolescents being described.
	The complexity of adolescent development	As researchers carefully examine adolescents' lives, they recognize the complexity of adolescent development. Because of this complexity, no single developmental model fits all adolescents.
Puberty	Pubertal change	Puberty is a period of rapid skeletal and sexual maturation that occurs mainly in early adolescence. Testosterone plays an important role in male pubertal development, estradiol in female pubertal development. The growth spurt occurs about two years later for boys than for girls; 12½ is the average age of onset for boys, 10½ for girls. Individual maturation in pubertal change is extensive.
	Psychological accompaniments of physical change	Adolescents show a heightened interest in their body image. Early maturation favors boys, at least during adolescence. As adults, though, late-maturing boys achieve more positive identities than early-maturing boys. Researchers are increasingly finding that early-maturing girls are vulnerable to a number of problems. Some researchers now question whether puberty's effects are as strong as once believed.
	Pubertal timing and health care	Most early- and late-maturing adolescents weather puberty's challenges competently. For those who do not, discussions with sensitive and knowledgeable health care providers and parents can improve the off-time maturing adolescent's coping abilities.

- An adolescent girl having sex in 1988 was less likely to get pregnant than one having sex in 1982, probably due to increased use of contraceptives. However, because a larger number of girls had sex in 1988, overall pregnancy rates remained constant at 127 per 1,000 girls each year—a level far above that of other industrialized countries.

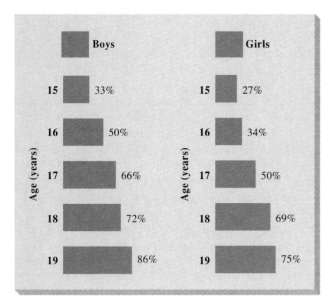

FIGURE 15.4

Percentage of U.S. Adolescents (by Sex and Age) Who Say They Have Had Sexual Intercourse

Female adolescents, more than male adolescents, report being in love as the main reason for being sexually active.

Recent data indicate that, in some areas of the country, sexual experiences of young adolescents may be even greater than these figures suggest (Forrest, 1990). In inner-city Baltimore, 81 percent of 14-year-old males said they had already engaged in sexual intercourse. Other surveys in inner-city, low-income areas also reveal a high incidence of early sexual intercourse (Clark, Zabin, & Hardy, 1984).

Adolescent Sexual Scripts

As adolescents explore their sexual identities, they engage in sexual scripts. A **sexual script** *is a stereotyped pattern of role prescriptions for how individuals should behave sexually.* Differences in the way females and males are socialized are wrapped up in the sexual scripts adolescents follow. Discrepancies in male/female scripting can cause problems and confusion for adolescents as they work out their sexual identities. Adolescent girls have learned to link sexual intercourse with love. Female adolescents often rationalize their sexual behavior by telling themselves that they were swept away by love. A number of investigators have reported that adolescent females, more than adolescent males, report being in love as the main reason for being sexually active (Cassell, 1984). Far more females than males have intercourse with partners they love and would like to marry. Other reasons for females having sexual intercourse include giving in to male pressure, gambling that sex is a way to get a boyfriend, curiosity, and sexual desire unrelated to loving and caring. Adolescent males may be aware that their female counterparts have been socialized into a love ethic. They also may understand the pressure many of them feel to have a boyfriend. A classic male line shows how males understand female thinking about sex and love: "If you really loved me, you would have sex with

me." The female adolescent who says, "If you really loved me, you would not put so much pressure on me," reflects her insight about male sexual motivation.

Some experts on adolescent sexuality believe that we are moving toward a new norm suggesting that sexual intercourse is acceptable, but mainly within the boundary of a loving and affectionate relationship (Dreyer, 1982). As part of this new norm, promiscuity, exploitation, and unprotected sexual intercourse are more often perceived as unacceptable by adolescents. One variation of the new norm is that intercourse is acceptable in a nonlove relationship, but physical or emotional exploitation of the partner is not. The new norm suggests that the double standard that previously existed does not operate as it once did. That is, physical and emotional exploitation of adolescent females by males is not as predominant today as in prior decades.

Other experts on adolescent sexuality are not so sure that the new norm has arrived (Gordon & Gilgun, 1987). They argue that remnants of the double standard are still flourishing. In most investigations, about twice as many boys as girls report having positive feelings about sexual intercourse. Females are more likely to report guilt, fear, and hurt. Adolescent males feel considerable pressure from their peers to have experienced sexual intercourse and to be sexually active. As one young adolescent recently remarked, "Look, I feel a lot of pressure from my buddies to go for the score." Further evidence for males' physical and emotional exploitation of females was found in a survey of 432 14- to 18-year-olds (Goodchilds & Zellman, 1984). Both male and female adolescents accepted the right of the male adolescent to be sexually aggressive but left matters up to the female to set the limits for the male's sexual overtures. Another attitude related to the double standard was the belief that females should not plan ahead to have sexual intercourse but should be swept up in the passion of the moment, not taking contraceptive precautions. Unfortunately, although we may have chipped away at some parts of the sexual double standard, other aspects still remain.

Homosexual Attitudes and Behavior

Although the development of gay or lesbian identity has been widely studied in adults, few researchers have investigated the gay or lesbian identity (often referred to as the coming-out process) in adolescents. In one recent study of gay male adolescents, coming out was conceptualized in three stages: sensitization; awareness with confusion, denial, guilt, and shame; and acceptance (Newman & Muzzonigro, 1993). The majority of the gay adolescents said they felt different from other boys as children. The average age at having their first crush on another boy was 12.7 years, and the average age at realizing they were gay was 12.5 years. Most of the boys said they felt confused when they first became aware that they were gay. About half of the boys said they initially tried to deny their identity as a gay. Parents who had strong traditional family values (belief in the importance of religion, emphasis on marriage and having children) were less accepting of their gay sons than were parents who had weaker traditional family values.

Both the early (Kinsey) and more recent (Hunt) surveys indicate that about 4 percent of males and 3 percent of females are exclusively homosexual (Hunt, 1974; Kinsey, Pomeroy, & Martin, 1948). In a recent comprehensive survey of adolescent sexual orientation in almost 35,000 junior and senior high school students in Minnesota, 4.5 percent reported predominantly homosexual attractions (Remafedi & others, in press). Homosexual identities, attractions, and behaviors increased with age. More than 6 percent of the 18-year-olds said they had predominantly homosexual attractions. How many of these youths later become gay is not known, although it is widely accepted that many adolescents who engage in homosexual behavior in adolescence do not continue the practice into adulthood.

An individual's sexual orientation—heterosexual or homosexual—is most likely determined by a combination of genetic, hormonal, and environmental factors (Savin-Williams & Rodriguez, 1993). Most experts on homosexuality believe that no one factor alone causes homosexuality and that the relative weight of each factor may vary from one individual to the next. In truth, no one knows *exactly*

what causes an individual to be homosexual. Scientists have a clearer picture of what does *not* cause homosexuality. For example, children raised by gay or lesbian parents or couples are no more likely to be homosexual than are children raised by heterosexual parents. There also is no evidence that male homosexuality is caused by a dominant mother or a weak father, or that female homosexuality is caused by girls choosing male role models. Among the biological factors believed to be involved in homosexuality are prenatal hormone conditions (Ellis & Ames, 1987). In the second to fifth months after conception, exposure to hormone levels characteristic of females is speculated to cause an individual (male or female) to become attracted to males. If this "prenatal critical period hypothesis" turns out to be correct, it would explain why researchers and clinicians have found it difficult to modify a homosexual orientation.

Adolescence may play an important role in the development of homosexuality (Gruskin, 1994). In one study, participation in homosexual behavior and sexual arousal by same-sex peers in adolescence was strongly related to an adult homosexual orientation (Bell & others, 1981). When interest in the same sex is intense and compelling, an adolescent often experiences severe conflict. American culture stigmatizes homosexuality; negative labels, such as *fag* and *queer*, are given to male homosexuals, and *lezzie* and *dyke* to female homosexuals. The sexual socialization of adolescent homosexuals becomes a process of learning to hide. Some gay males wait out their entire adolescence, hoping that heterosexual feelings will develop. Many female adolescent homosexuals have similar experiences. Many adult females who identify themselves as homosexuals considered themselves predominantly heterosexual during adolescence.

Sexually Transmitted Diseases

Tammy, age 15, has just finished listening to a lecture in her health class. We overhear her talking to one of her girlfriends as she walks down the school corridor. "That was a disgusting lecture. I can't believe all the diseases you can get by having sex. I think she was probably trying to scare us. She spent a lot of time talking about AIDS, which I've heard that normal people don't get. Right? I've heard that only homosexuals and drug addicts get AIDS, and I've also heard that gonorrhea and most other sexual diseases can be cured, so what's the big deal if you get something like that?" Tammy's view of sexually transmitted diseases (formerly called venereal disease, or VD) is common among adolescents. Teenagers tend to believe that sexually transmitted diseases always happen to someone else, can be easily cured without any harm done, and are too disgusting for a nice young person to even hear about, let alone get. This view is wrong. Adolescents who are having sex *do* run a risk of getting sexually transmitted diseases. Sexually transmitted diseases are fairly common among today's adolescents.

John W. Santrock

Chlamydia

Sexually transmitted diseases are primarily transmitted through sexual intercourse, although they can be transmitted orally. **Chlamydia** *is a sexually transmitted disease named for the bacteria that cause it.* Chlamydia affects as many as 10 percent of all college males and females. Males experience a burning sensation during urination and a mucoid discharge. Females experience painful urination or a vaginal discharge. These signs often mimic gonorrhea. However, when penicillin is prescribed for gonorrhealike symptoms, the problem does not go away as it would if gonorrhea were the culprit. If left untreated, the disease can affect the entire reproductive tract. This can lead to problems left by scar tissue, which can prevent the female from becoming pregnant. Effective drugs are available to treat this common sexually transmitted disease.

Herpes Simplex Virus II

An alarming increase in another sexually transmitted disease, herpes simplex virus II, has occurred in recent years. **Herpes simplex virus II** *is a sexually transmitted disease whose symptoms include irregular cycles of sores and blisters in the genital area.* Although this disease is more common among young adults (estimates range as high as 1 in 5 sexually active adults), as many as 1 in 35 adolescents have genital herpes. The herpes virus is potentially dangerous. If babies are exposed to the active virus during birth, they are vulnerable to brain damage or even death, and women with herpes are eight times more likely than unaffected women to develop cervical cancer. At present, herpes is incurable.

Syphilis

Sexual problems have plagued human beings throughout history. Hipprocrates wrote about syphilis in 460 B.C. The first major recorded epidemic of syphilis appeared in Naples, Italy, two years after Columbus' first return. It is believed that millions of people died of the disease, which is sexually transmitted through intercourse, kissing, or intimate body contact. The cause of syphilis is a tiny bacterium that requires warm, moist surfaces to penetrate the body. It was not until 400 years after the Italian outbreak that penicillin, a successful treatment for syphilis, was discovered.

AIDS

Today, we harbor the same fear of sexually transmitted disease as in Columbus' time, but, instead of syphilis it is AIDS, a major sexually related problem, that has generated considerable fear in today's world.

AIDS (acquired immune deficiency syndrome) *is caused by the human immunodeficiency virus (HIV), which destroys the body's immune system.* Many germs that usually would not harm a person with a healthy immune system can produce devastation and death in persons with AIDS.

The AIDS advertisement indicates how vulnerable our nation's population is to the epidemic of AIDS, and the disease's lethal consequences.

In 1981, when AIDS was first recognized in the United States, there were fewer than 60 reported cases. Beginning in 1990, we began losing as many Americans each year to AIDS as died in the Vietnam War, almost 60,000 people. According to federal health officials, 1 to 1.5 million Americans are now asymptomatic carriers of AIDS—those who are infected with the virus and presumably capable of infecting others but who show no clinical symptoms of AIDS. In 1989, the first attempt to assess AIDS among college students was made. Testing of 16,861 students found 30 students infected with the virus (American College Health Association, 1989). If the 12.5 million students attending college were infected at the same rate, 25,000 students would have the AIDS virus.

Currently, the incidence of AIDS in adolescence is reasonably low. For example, in 1992 there were 159 new reports of AIDS in the 13- to 19-year-old age group (compared with 7,982 new cases in the 20- to 29-year-old age group) (CDC National AIDS Clearinghouse, 1993). However, the average latency time from viral infection to time of illness is about 5 to 7 years. Thus, most infected adolescents would not become ill until they are adults. Thus, most individuals in their early twenties with an AIDS diagnosis likely were infected with HIV during adolescence—the early-twenties age group accounts for 17 percent of all AIDS cases in the United States.

There are some differences in AIDS cases in adolescents, compared to AIDS cases in adults:

1. A higher percentage of adolescent AIDS cases are acquired by heterosexual transmission.
2. A higher percentage of adolescents are asymptomatic (they will become symptomatic in adulthood).
3. A higher percentage of African American and Latino cases occur in adolescence.

TABLE 15.1

Understanding AIDS: What's Risky, What's Not

The AIDS virus is not transmitted like colds or the flu, but by an exchange of infected blood, semen, or vaginal fluids. This usually occurs during sexual intercourse, in sharing drug needles, or to babies infected before or during birth.

You Won't Get AIDS from:

- Everyday contact with individuals around you at school or the workplace, parties, child-care centers, or stores.
- Swimming in a pool, even if someone in the pool has the AIDS virus.
- A mosquito bite, or from bedbugs, lice, flies, or other insects.
- Saliva, sweat, tears, urine, or a bowel movement.
- A kiss.
- Clothes, telephones, or toilet seats.
- Using a glass or eating utensils that someone with the virus has used.
- Being on a bus, train, or crowded elevator with an individual who is infected with the virus or who has AIDS.

Blood Donations and Transfusions:

- You will not come into contact with the AIDS virus by donating blood at a blood bank.
- The risk of getting AIDS from a blood transfusion has been greatly reduced. Donors are screened for risk factors, and donated blood is tested.

Risky Behavior:

- Having a number of sex partners.
- Sharing drug needles and syringes.
- Engaging in anal sex with or without a condom.
- Performing vaginal or oral sex with someone who shoots drugs or engages in anal sex.
- Engaging in sex with someone you don't know well or with someone who has several sexual partners.
- Engaging in unprotected sex (without a condom) with an infected individual.

Safe Behavior:

- Not having sex.
- Sex with one mutually faithful, uninfected partner.
- Sex with proper protection.
- Not shooting drugs.

Source: U.S. Government educational pamphlet: *America Responds to AIDS,* 1988.

4. A special set of ethical and legal issues are involved in testing and informing partners and parents of adolescents.
5. There is less use and availability of contraceptives in adolescence.

In one study, condom use among adolescents who are at the greatest risk of contracting AIDS—for example, intravenous drug users—was significantly below average (Sonenstein, Pleck, & Ku, 1989). Only 21 percent of the adolescents who had used intravenous drugs or whose partners had used intravenous drugs used condoms. Among adolescents who reported having sex with prostitutes, only 17 percent said that they used condoms. And among adolescents who reported having sex with five or more partners in the last year, only 37 percent reported using condoms. Adolescents who reported homosexual intercourse reported the highest condom use—66 percent.

Experts say that AIDS can be transmitted only by sexual contact, the sharing of needles, or blood transfusion (which in the last few years has been tightly monitored) (Kalichman, 1996). Although 90 percent of AIDS cases continue to occur among homosexual males and intravenous drug users, a disproportionate increase among females who are heterosexual partners of bisexual males or of intravenous drug users has been recently noted. This increase suggests that the risk of AIDS may be increasing among heterosexual individuals who have multiple sex partners (Jones, 1996). Table 15.1 describes what's risky and what's not, regarding AIDS.

Adolescent Pregnancy

Angela is 15 years old and pregnant. She reflects, "I'm 3 months pregnant. This could ruin my whole life. I've made all of these plans for the future and now they are down the drain. I don't have anybody to talk to about my problem. I can't talk to my parents. There is no way they can understand." Pregnant adolescents were once practically invisible and unmentionable, but yesterday's secret has become today's national dilemma.

They are of different ethnic groups and from different places, but their circumstances have a distressing sameness. Each year more than 1 million American teenagers become pregnant, four out of five of them unmarried. Like Angela, many become pregnant in their early or middle adolescent years, 30,000 of them under the age of 15. In all, this means that one of every ten adolescent females in the United States becomes pregnant each year, with eight of the ten pregnancies unintended. As one 17-year-old Los Angeles mother of a 1-year-old boy said, "We are children having children." The only bright spot in the adolescent pregnancy statistics is that the adolescent pregnancy rate, after increasing during the 1970s, has recently declined, but only slightly.

The adolescent pregnancy rate in the United States is still the highest of any in the Western world. It is more than twice the rate in England, France, or Canada; almost three times the rate in Sweden; and seven times the rate in the Netherlands (Jones & others, 1985). Although American adolescents are no more sexually active than their counterparts in these other nations, they are many times more likely to become pregnant.

In Holland and Sweden, as well as in other European countries, sex does not carry the mystery and conflict it does in American society. Holland does not have a mandated sex-education program, but adolescents can obtain contraceptive counseling at government-sponsored clinics for a small fee. The Dutch media also have played an important role in educating the public about sex through frequent broadcasts focused on birth control, abortion, and related matters. Most Dutch adolescents do not consider having sex without birth control.

Swedish adolescents are sexually active at an earlier age than American adolescents, and they are exposed to even more explicit sex on television. However, the Swedish National Board of Education has developed a curriculum that ensures that every child in the country, beginning at age 7, will experience a thorough grounding in reproductive biology and, by the ages of 10 or 12, will have been introduced to information about various forms of contraceptives. Teachers are expected to handle the subject of sex whenever it becomes relevant, regardless of the subject they are teaching. The idea is to dedramatize and demystify sex so that familiarity will make individuals less vulnerable to unwanted pregnancy and sexually transmitted diseases. American society is not nearly so open about sex education.

Adolescent pregnancy is a complex American problem, one that strikes many nerves (East & Felice, 1996). The subject of adolescent pregnancy touches on many explosive social issues: the battle over abortion rights, contraceptives and the delicate question of whether adolescents should have easy access to them, and the perennially touchy subject of sex education in the public schools.

Dramatic changes involving sexual attitudes and social morals have swept through the American culture in the last three decades. Adolescents actually gave birth at a

Our society has not handled adolescent sex very effectively. We tell adolescents that sex is fun, harmless, adult, and forbidden. Adolescents 13 years old going on 21 want to try out new things and take risks. They see themselves as unique and indestructible—pregnancy couldn't happen to them, they think. Add to this the adolescent's increasing need for love and commitment, and the result all too often is social dynamite.

higher rate in 1957 than they do today, but that was a time of early marriage, when almost 25 percent of 18- and 19-year-olds were married. The overwhelming majority of births to adolescent mothers in the 1950s occurred within a marriage and mainly involved females 17 years of age and older. Two or three decades ago, if an unwed adolescent girl became pregnant, in most instances her parents swiftly married her off in a shotgun wedding. If marriage was impractical, the girl would discreetly disappear, the child would be put up for adoption, and the predicament would never be discussed again. Abortion was not an option for most adolescent females until 1973, when the Supreme Court ruled it could not be outlawed.

In today's world of adolescent pregnancies, a different scenario unfolds. If the girl does not choose to have an abortion (45 percent of pregnant adolescent girls do), she usually keeps the baby and raises it without the traditional involvement of marriage. With the stigma of illegitimacy largely absent, girls are less likely to give up their babies for adoption. Fewer than 5 percent do, compared with about 35 percent in the early 1960s. However, although the stigma of illegitimacy has waned, the lives of most pregnant teenagers are anything but rosy.

The consequences of our nation's high adolescent pregnancy rate are of great concern (Brooks-Gunn & Chase-Lansdale, 1995; Luster & others, 1995). Pregnancy in adolescence increases the health risks of both the child and the mother. Infants born to adolescent mothers are more likely to have low birthweights (a prominent cause of infant mortality), as well as neurological problems and childhood illnesses. Adolescent mothers often drop out of school, fail to gain employment, and become dependent on welfare. Although many adolescent mothers resume their education later in life, they generally do not catch up with women who postpone childbearing. In the National Longitudinal Survey of Work Experience of Youth, it was found that only half of the women 20 to 26 years old who first gave birth at age 17 had completed high school by their twenties. The percentage was even lower for those who gave birth at a younger age (Mott & Marsiglio, 1985). By contrast, among females who waited until age 20 to have a baby, more than 90 percent had obtained a high school education. Among the younger adolescent mothers, almost half had obtained a general equivalency diploma (GED), which does not often open up good employment opportunities.

These educational deficits have negative consequences for the young women themselves and for their children. Adolescent parents are more likely than those who delay childbearing to have low-paying, low-status jobs or to be unemployed. The mean family income of White females who give birth before age 17 is approximately half that of families in which the mother delays birth until her mid or late twenties.

Serious, extensive efforts need to be developed to help pregnant adolescents and young mothers enhance their educational and occupational opportunities (Murray, 1996). Adolescent mothers also need extensive help in obtaining competent day care and in planning for the future. Experts recommend that, to reduce the high rate of teen pregnancy, adolescents need improved sex-education and family-planning information, greater access to contraception, and broad community involvement and support (Conger, 1988). Another very important consideration, especially for young adolescents, is abstention, which is increasingly being included as a theme in sex-education classes.

PROBLEMS AND DISORDERS

In addition to the increase in adolescent pregnancy, other problems that may arise in adolescence are drug abuse, juvenile delinquency, depression, suicide, and eating disorders.

Drugs

The 1960s and 1970s were a time of marked increase in the use of illicit drugs. During the social and political unrest of those years, many youth turned to marijuana, stimulants, and hallucinogens. Increases in alcohol consumption by adolescents also were noted. More-precise data about drug use by adolescents have been collected in recent years. Each year since 1975, Lloyd Johnston, Patrick O'Malley, and Gerald Bachman (1995), working at the Institute of Social Research at the University of Michigan, have carefully monitored drug use by America's high school seniors in a wide range of public and private high schools. From time to time, they also sample the drug use of younger adolescents and adults.

In the 1993 survey, drug use among American youth increased for the first time in a number of years. A sharp rise in the use of marijuana, as well as increases in the use of stimulants, LSD, and inhalants, occurred among high school students in 1993. Johnston and his colleagues (1994) concluded that there had recently been a decrease in knowledge about the dangers associated with these drugs; when such knowledge decreases, an increase in drug use usually occurs. In addition, of the world's industrialized nations, the United States has the highest rate of drug use by adolescents. In 1994, 36 percent of the nation's high school seniors tried an illicit drug, up from 27 percent in 1992. The rise in illicit drug use has been especially pronounced for marijuana. From 1991 to 1994, annual use of marijuana (any use during the 12 months prior to the survey) doubled among eighth graders (to 13 percent), grew by two-thirds among tenth graders (to 25 percent), and increased by 40 percent among high school seniors (to 31 percent).

According to Lloyd Johnston and his colleagues (1995), considerable progress was made in the 1980s in reducing the number of adolescents who use drugs—in particular marijuana and cocaine. However, we may now be in danger of losing some of the hard-won ground as a new, more naive generation of children enters adolescence and as society decreases its communication to adolescents about the danger of drugs.

Alcohol

Some mornings, 15-year-old Annie was too drunk to go to school. Other days, she'd stop for a couple of beers or a screwdriver on the way to school. She was tall, blonde, and good looking, and no one who sold her liquor, even at 8 A.M., questioned her age. Where did she get her money? She got it from baby-sitting and from what her mother gave her to buy lunch. Annie used to be a cheerleader, but no longer; she was kicked off the squad for missing practice so often. Soon, she and several of her peers were drinking almost every morning. Sometimes, they skipped school and went to the woods to drink. Annie's whole life began to revolve around her drinking. This routine went on for 2 years. After a while, Annie's parents discovered her problem. Even though they punished her, it did not stop her drinking. Finally, this year, Annie started dating a boy she really liked who would not put up with her drinking. She agreed to go to Alcoholics

John W. Santrock

What is the pattern of alcohol consumption among adolescents?

1992, 41 percent of college students reported that they engaged in binge drinking, about the same percentage as in 1980 (Johnston, O'Malley, & Bachman, 1994).

Cocaine

Did you know that cocaine was once an ingredient in Coca-Cola? Of course, it has long since been removed from the soft drink. Cocaine comes from the coca plant, native to Bolivia and Peru. For many years, Bolivians and Peruvians chewed the plant to increase their stamina. Today, cocaine is usually snorted, smoked, or injected in the form of crystals or powder. The effect is a rush of euphoric feelings, which eventually wear off, followed by depressive feelings, lethargy, insomnia, and irritability.

Cocaine is a highly controversial drug. Users claim it is exciting, makes them feel good, and increases their confidence. It is clear, however, that cocaine has potent cardiovascular effects and is potentially addictive. When the drug's effects are extreme, it can produce a heart attack, stroke, or brain seizure. The increase in cocaine-related deaths is traced to very pure or tainted forms of the drug.

In the late 1980s and early 1990s, adolescents' use of crack declined (from 4.1 percent in 1986 to 1.5 percent in 1993—for use in the last year). However, in 1994, an increase in adolescents' use of crack occurred—to 1.8 percent.

The Roles of Parents, Peers, and Schools in Drug Use

Most adolescents become drug users at some point in their development, whether their use is limited to alcohol, caffeine, and cigarettes or is extended to marijuana, cocaine, and hard drugs. A special concern occurs when adolescents use drugs as a way of coping with stress, a practice that can interfere with their development of competent coping and decision-making skills. Researchers have found that, when drug use occurs initially in childhood or in early adolescence, it has more detrimental, long-term effects on the development of responsible, competent behavior than when drug use occurs initially in late adolescence. By using drugs to cope with stress, young adolescents often enter adult roles of marriage and work prematurely without adequate socioemotional growth, and they experience greater failure in adult roles.

A special concern in the use of drugs by adolescents is the roles parents, peers, and schools play in preventing and reducing drug use (Brook & others, 1990; Peters & McMahon, 1996; Stephenson, Henry, & Robinson, 1996). Families play an important role in adolescent drug use. In one longitudinal study, boys' poor self-control at age 4 was related to their drug use in adolescence, and permissive parenting in the families of girls at age 4 was related to their drug use in adolescence (Block & Block, 1988). In another investigation, social support during adolescence substantially reduced drug use (Newcomb & Bentler, 1989). In this study, social support included good relationships with parents, other adults, siblings, and peers. Another researcher found that the greatest use of drugs by

Anonymous and has just successfully completed treatment. She has been off alcohol for 4 consecutive months now, and she hopes that her abstinence will continue.

Alcohol is the drug most widely used by adolescents in our society. For them, it has produced many enjoyable moments and many sad ones as well. Alcoholism is the third-leading killer in the United States, with more than 13 million people classified as alcoholics, many of whom established their drinking habits during adolescence. Each year, approximately 25,000 people are killed and 1.5 million injured by drunk drivers. In 65 percent of the aggressive male acts against females, the offender is under the influence of alcohol (Goodman & others, 1986). In numerous instances of drunken driving and assaults on females, the offenders are adolescents.

How extensive is alcohol use by adolescents? Alcohol use by high school seniors has gradually declined. Monthly use declined from 72 percent in 1980 to 50 percent in 1994. The prevalence of drinking five or more drinks in a row in a 2-week interval fell from 41 percent in 1980 to 31 percent in 1994. There remains a substantial gender difference in heavy adolescent drinking: 20 percent for females versus 36 percent for males in 1992, although the gender difference was much greater before the 1980s. There has been much less change in binge drinking among college students. In

"Just tell me where you kids get the idea to take so many drugs."

© 1990 by Sidney Harris.

adolescents takes place when both the adolescent's parents take drugs (such as tranquilizers, amphetamines, alcohol, or nicotine) and the adolescent's peers take drugs (Kandel, 1974).

Schools frequently are the place where peers initiate and maintain drug use. Schools can play an important role in preventing or reducing drug use; there are few other settings where the adolescent population congregates on such a frequent basis. Although most schools have established policies on drug use, some have gone further and developed drug prevention or intervention programs. The most effective school-based programs are often part of community-wide prevention efforts that involve parents, peers, role models, media, police, courts, businesses, youth-serving agencies, as well as schools.

Juvenile Delinquency

Arnie is 13 years old. His history includes a string of thefts and physical assaults. The first theft occurred when Arnie was 8; he stole a SONY walkman from an electronics store. The first physical assault took place a year later when he shoved his 7-year-old brother up against the wall, bloodied his face, and then threatened to kill him with a butcher knife. Recently, the thefts and physical assaults have increased. In the last week, he stole a television set and struck his mother repeatedly and threatened to kill her. He also broke some neighborhood streetlights and threatened some youths with a wrench and a hammer. Arnie's father left home when Arnie was 3 years old. Until the father left, his parents argued extensively and his father often beat up his mother. Arnie's mother indicates that when Arnie was younger, she was able to control his behavior; but in the last several years she has not been able to enforce any sanctions on his antisocial behavior. Because of Arnie's volatility and dangerous behavior, it was recommended that he be placed in a group home with other juvenile delinquents.

The label **juvenile delinquent** *is applied to an adolescent who breaks the law or engages in behavior that is considered illegal.* Like other categories of disorders, juvenile delinquency is a broad concept; legal infractions range from littering to murder. Because the adolescent technically only becomes a juvenile delinquent after being judged guilty of a crime by a court of law, official records do not accurately reflect the number of illegal acts juvenile delinquents commit. Estimates regarding the number of juvenile delinquents in the United States are sketchy, but FBI statistics indicate that at least 2 percent of all youths are involved in juvenile court cases. The number of girls found guilty of juvenile delinquency has increased substantially in recent years. Delinquency rates among African Americans, other minority groups, and the lower class are especially high in proportion to the overall population of these groups. However, such groups have less influence over the judicial decision-making process in the United States and therefore may be judged delinquent more readily than their White, middle-class counterparts.

What causes delinquency? Many causes have been proposed, including heredity, identity problems, community influences, and family experiences. Erik Erikson (1968), for example, believes that adolescents whose development has restricted them from acceptable social roles or made them feel that they cannot measure up to the demands placed on them may choose a negative identity. Adolescents with a negative identity may find support for their delinquent image among peers, reinforcing the negative identity. For Erikson, delinquency is an attempt to establish an identity, although it is a negative identity.

Although delinquency is less exclusively a lower-class phenomenon than it was in the past, some characteristics of the lower-class culture may promote delinquency. The norms of many lower-class peer groups and gangs are antisocial, or counterproductive, to the goals and norms of society at large. Getting into and staying out of trouble are prominent features of life for some adolescents in low-income neighborhoods. Adolescents from low-income backgrounds may sense that they can gain attention and status by performing antisocial actions. Being "tough" and "masculine" are high-status traits for lower-class boys, and these traits are often measured by the adolescent's success in performing and getting away with delinquent acts. A community with a high crime rate also lets the adolescent observe many models who engage in criminal activities. These communities may be characterized by poverty, unemployment, and feelings of alienation toward the middle class. Quality schooling, educational funding, and organized neighborhood activities may be lacking in these communities.

Family support systems are also associated with delinquency (Feldman & Weinberger, 1994). Parents of delinquents are less skilled in discouraging antisocial behavior and in encouraging skilled behavior than are parents of nondelinquents. Parental monitoring of adolescents is especially important in determining whether an adolescent becomes a delinquent (Patterson, DeBarsyhe, & Ramsey, 1989). "It's

Antecedent	Association with delinquency	Description
Identity	Negative identity	Erikson believes delinquency occurs because the adolescent fails to resolve a role identity.
Self-control	Low degree	Some children and adolescents fail to acquire the essential controls that others have acquired during the process of growing up.
Age	Early initiation	Early appearance of antisocial behavior is associated with serious offenses later in adolescence. However, not every child who acts out becomes a delinquent.
Sex	Males	Boys engage in more antisocial behavior than girls do, although girls are more likely to run away. Boys engage in more violent acts.
Expectations for education and school grades	Low expectations and low grades	Adolescents who become delinquents often have low educational expectations and low grades. Their verbal abilities are often weak.
Parental influences	Monitoring (low), support (low), discipline (ineffective)	Delinquents often come from families in which parents rarely monitor their adolescents, provide them with little support, and ineffectively discipline them.
Peer influences	Heavy influence, low resistance	Having delinquent peers greatly increases the risk of becoming delinquent.
Socioeconomic status	Low	Serious offenses are committed more frequently by lower-class males.
Neighborhood quality	Urban, high crime, high mobility	Communities often breed crime. Living in a high-crime area, which also is characterized by poverty and dense living conditions, increases the probability that a child will become a delinquent. These communities often have grossly inadequate schools.

FIGURE 15.5

The Antecedents of Juvenile Delinquency

10 P.M.; do you know where your children are?" seems to be an important question for parents to answer affirmatively. Family discord and inconsistent and inappropriate discipline are also associated with delinquency. Peer relations also are involved in delinquency. Having delinquent peers greatly increases the risk of becoming delinquent. A summary of the antecedents of delinquency is presented in figure 15.5.

Violence and Youth

An increasing concern is the high rate of violence displayed by adolescents. According to the United States Department of Education (1993), 16 percent of seniors reported that they had been threatened with a weapon at school; 7 percent said they had been injured with a weapon. One of every five high school students routinely carries a firearm, knife, or club. Many teachers say they have been verbally abused, physically threatened, or actually attacked by students. And homicide remains the leading cause of death among African Americans, regardless of gender or age.

Intervening with children before they develop ingrained antisocial behaviors is an important dimension of reducing violence in youth (Staub, 1996; in press). Slogan campaigns and scare tactics do not work. In one successful intervention, Positive Adolescents Choices Training (PACT), African American 12- to 15-year-olds learn to manage their anger and resolve conflicts peacefully (Hammond, 1993). Through the use of culturally sensitive videotapes, students learn to give and receive feedback, control their anger, and negotiate and compromise. The videotapes show peer role models demonstrating these skills, along with adult role models who encourage the participants to practice the techniques. Over the past 3 years, students in the program have spent less time in juvenile court for violence-related offenses than have nonparticipants in a control group. The program students also have shown a drop in violence-related school suspensions and have improved their social and conflict-resolution skills.

The Safe Schools Act can help to foster programs such as PACT. Under the bill, schools can receive grants up to $3 million a year over 2 years to develop their own violence prevention programs. The initiatives could include comprehensive school safety strategies, coordination with community programs and agencies, and improved security to keep weapons out of the schools. To ensure that programs focus on prevention more than on enforcement, the grants allow only 33 percent of the funds to be used for metal detectors and security guards.

Prevention and Intervention

Brief descriptions of the varied attempts to reduce delinquency would fill a large book. These attempts include forms of individual and group psychotherapy, family therapy, behavior modification, recreation, vocational training, alternative schools, survival camping and wilderness canoeing,

A recent, special concern in low-income areas is escalating gang violence.

incarceration and probation, Big Brothers and Big Sisters, community organizations, and Bible reading. However, surprisingly little is known about what actually does help to reduce delinquency, and in many instances prevention and intervention have not been successful.

Although few successful models of delinquency prevention and intervention have been identified, many experts on delinquency agree that the following points deserve closer examination as prevention and intervention possibilities (Dryfoos, 1990):

1. Programs should be broader than just focusing on delinquency (O'Donnell, Manos, & Chesney-Lind, 1987). For example, it is virtually impossible to improve delinquency prevention without considering the quality of education available to high-risk youth.
2. Programs should have multiple components because no one component has been found to be the "magic bullet" that decreases delinquency.
3. Programs should begin early in the child's development to prevent learning and conduct problems (Berrueta-Clement & others, 1986).
4. Schools play an important role. Schools with strong governance, fair discipline policies, student participation in decision making, and high investment in school outcomes by both students and staff have a better chance of curbing delinquency (Hawkins & Lam, 1986; Hawkins & Lishner, 1987).
5. Efforts should often be directed at institutional rather than individual change. Especially important is upgrading the quality of education for disadvantaged children.
6. While point 5 is accurate, researchers have found that intensive individual attention and personalized

planning also are important factors in working with children at high risk for becoming delinquent.

7. Program benefits often "wash out" after the program stops. Thus, maintenance programs and continued effort are usually necessary.

In her review of delinquency prevention, Joy Dryfoos (1990) also outlined what has *not* worked in preventing delinquency. Ineffective attempts include preventive casework, group counseling, pharmacological interventions (except for extremely violent behavior), work experience, vocational education, "scaring straight" efforts, and the juvenile justice system. Current school practices that are ineffective in reducing delinquency include suspension, detention, expulsion, security guards, and corporal punishment.

Depression and Suicide

What is the nature of depression in adolescence? What causes an adolescent to commit suicide?

Depression in Adolescence

Increasingly, in the study of adolescent depression, distinctions are made between depressed mood, depressive syndromes, and clinical depression (Petersen & others, 1993). **Depressed mood** *refers to periods of sadness or unhappy mood that can last for a brief or an extended period of time. These periods may occur as a result of the loss of a significant relationship or failure on an important task.* The term **depressive syndromes** *refers to a cluster of behaviors and emotions that include both anxiety and depression; symptoms include feeling lonely, crying, fear of doing bad things, feeling the need to be perfect, feeling unloved, feeling worthless, nervous, guilty, or sad, and worrying.* **Clinical depression** *involves being diagnosed as experiencing major depressive disorder (MDD) or dysthymic disorder.*

Major depressive disorder is present when the adolescent has experienced five or more of the following symptoms for at least a 2-week period at a level that differs from previous functioning: (a) depressed mood or irritable most of the day, (b) decreased interest in pleasurable activities, (c) changes in weight or failure to make necessary weight gains in adolescence, (d) sleep problems, (e) psychomotor agitation or retardation, (f) fatigue or loss of energy, (g) feelings of worthlessness or abnormal amounts of guilt, (h) reduced concentration and decision-making ability, and (i) repeated suicidal ideation, suicide attempts, or plans of suicide.

Dysthymic disorder *occurs when adolescents have a period of at least 1 year in which they have shown depressed or irritable mood every day without more than 2 symptom-free months. Further, dysthymic disorder requires the presence of at least two of the following symptoms: (a) eating problems, (b) sleeping problems, (c) lack of energy, (d) low self-esteem, (e) reduced concentration or decision-making ability, and (f) feelings of hopelessness.*

How many adolescents have depressed mood, depressive syndromes, or clinical depression? Although no nationally representative study of adolescent depression has been conducted, an increasing number of studies focus on adolescent depression and allow estimates to be made. With regard to depressed mood, 25 to 40 percent of adolescent girls report having been in a depressed mood in the previous 6 months; the figure for boys is 15 to 20 percent. The figures for clinical depression have a wide range, but nonclinical samples reveal an average of 7 percent of adolescents with clinical depression; the rates for clinical samples are naturally much higher, averaging 42 percent of adolescents.

Depression is more likely to occur in adolescence than in childhood, and female adolescents are more likely than male adolescents to be depressed.

Adolescent girls consistently show higher rates of depressive disorders and mood problems than adolescent boys do. Among the reasons given for the sex difference are: Females tend to ruminate on their depressed mood and amplify it, while males tend to distract themselves from the mood; girls' self-images, especially their body images, are often more negative than for boys during adolescence; and societal bias against females.

Certain family factors have been determined to be risk factors in adolescent depression (Lasko & others, 1996; Mamorstein & Shiner, 1996; Petersen & Ding, 1994). Having a depressed parent is a major risk factor for depression in childhood, and this experience may carry through into adolescence. Parents who are emotionally unavailable, are immersed in marital conflict, and have economic problems often set the stage for the emergence of depression in their adolescent children (Galambos & Sears, 1995).

Poor peer relationships also are associated with adolescent depression. Not having a close relationship with a best friend, having less contact with friends, and peer rejection all increase depressive tendencies in adolescents.

The experience of difficult changes or challenges is associated with depressive symptoms in adolescence (Compas & Grant, 1993). Parental divorce increases depressive symptoms in adolescents. Also, when adolescents go through puberty at the same time as they move from elementary school to middle or junior high school, they report being depressed more than do adolescents who go through puberty after the school transition.

Suicide

Suicide is a common problem in our society. Its rate has tripled in the past 30 years in the United States; each year, about 25,000 people take their own lives. Beginning with the 15-year-old age group or so, the suicide rate begins to rise rapidly. Suicide accounts for about 12 percent of the mortality in the adolescent and young adult age group. Males are about three times as likely to commit suicide as females are; this may be because of their more active methods for attempting suicide—shooting, for example. By contrast, females are more likely to use passive methods, such as sleeping pills, which are less likely to produce death. Although males commit suicide more frequently, females attempt it more frequently (Forshaun, 1996).

Estimates indicate that, for every successful suicide in the general population, 6 to 10 attempts are made. For adolescents, the figure is as high as 50 attempts for every life taken. As many as two in every three college students has thought about suicide on at least one occasion; their methods range from overdosing on drugs to crashing into the White House in an airplane.

Why do adolescents attempt suicide? There is no simple answer to this important question. It is helpful to think of suicide in terms of proximal and distal factors. Proximal, or immediate, factors can trigger a suicide attempt. Highly stressful circumstances, such as the loss of a boyfriend or girlfriend, poor grades at school, or an unwanted pregnancy, can trigger a suicide attempt. Drugs have been involved more often in recent suicide attempts than in attempts in the past (Wagner, Cole, & Schwartzman, 1993).

Distal, or earlier, experiences often are involved in suicide attempts as well. A long-standing history of family instability and unhappiness may be present (Reinherz & others, 1994). Just as a lack of affection and emotional support, high control, and pressure for achievement by parents during childhood are related to adolescent depression, such combinations of family experiences are also likely to show up as distal factors in suicide attempts. The adolescent might also lack supportive friendships. In a study of suicide among gifted women, previous suicide attempts, anxiety, conspicuous instability in work and in relationships, depression, or alcoholism also were present in the women's lives (Tomlinson-Keasey, Warren, & Elliot, 1986). These factors are similar to those found to predict suicide among gifted men.

Just as genetic factors are associated with depression, they are also associated with suicide. The closer the genetic relationship a person has to someone who has committed suicide, the more likely that person is to commit suicide.

What is the psychological profile of the suicidal adolescent like? Suicidal adolescents often have depressive symptoms (Gadpaille, 1996). Although not all depressed adolescents are suicidal, depression is the most frequently cited factor associated with adolescent suicide. A sense of hopelessness, low self-esteem, and high self-blame are also associated with adolescent suicide (Harter & Marold, 1992).

Table 15.2 lists the early-warning signs of suicide in adolescents. Table 15.3 provides valuable information about what to do and what not to do when you suspect someone is contemplating suicide.

TABLE 15.2

The Early Warning Signs of Suicide in Adolescents

1. The adolescent makes suicide threats, such as: "I wish I was dead"; "My family would be better off without me"; "I don't have anything to live for."
2. A prior suicide attempt, no matter how minor. Four out of five people who commit suicide have made at least one previous attempt.
3. Preoccupation with death in music, art, and personal writing.
4. Loss of a family member, pet, or boyfriend/girlfriend through death, abandonment, breakup.
5. Family disruptions, such as unemployment, serious illness, relocation, divorce.
6. Disturbances in sleeping and eating habits, and in personal hygiene.
7. Declining grades and lack of interest in school or activities that previously were important.
8. Dramatic changes in behavior patterns, such as a very gregarious adolescent's becoming very shy and withdrawn.
9. Pervasive sense of gloom, helplessness, and hopelessness.
10. Withdrawal from family members and friends; feelings of alienation from significant others.
11. Giving away prized possessions and otherwise getting affairs in order.
12. Series of accidents or impulsive, risk-taking behaviors; drug or alcohol abuse; disregard for personal safety; taking dangerous dares. (With regard to drug or alcohol abuse, there has been a dramatic increase in recent years in the number of adolescent suicides committed while the adolescent is under the influence of alcohol or drugs.)

TABLE 15.3

What to Do and What Not to Do When You Suspect Someone Is Likely to Commit Suicide

What to Do

1. Ask direct, straightforward questions in a calm manner: "Are you thinking about hurting yourself?"
2. Assess the seriousness of the suicidal intent by asking questions about feelings, important relationships, who else the person has talked with, and the amount of thought given to the means to be used. If a gun, pills, rope, or other means has been obtained and a precise plan developed, clearly the situation is dangerous. Stay with the person until help arrives.
3. Be a good listener and be very supportive without being falsely reassuring.
4. Try to persuade the person to obtain professional help and assist him or her in getting this help.

What Not to Do

1. Do not ignore the warning signs.
2. Do not refuse to talk about suicide if a person approaches you about it.
3. Do not react with horror, disapproval, or repulsion.
4. Do not give false reassurances by saying such things as "Everything is going to be OK." Also do not give out simple answers or platitudes, such as "You have everything to be thankful for."
5. Do not abandon the individual after the crisis has passed or after professional help has commenced.

Source: From *Living with 10- to 15-Year-Olds: A Parent Education Curriculum*, edited by Robin Pulver, second edition, 1992. Center for Early Adolescence, University of North Carolina at Chapel Hill, D-2 Carr Mill Town Center, Carrboro, NC. Reprinted with permission.

Eating Disorders

Fifteen-year-old Jane gradually eliminated foods from her diet to the point where she subsisted by eating *only* applesauce and eggnog. She spent hours observing her body, wrapping her fingers around her waist to see if it

Anorexia nervosa has become an increasing problem for adolescent girls.

was getting any thinner. She fantasized about becoming a beautiful fashion model who would wear designer bathing suits. Even when she reached 85 pounds, Jane still felt fat. She continued to lose weight, eventually emaciating herself. She was hospitalized and treated for **anorexia nervosa,** *an eating disorder that involves the relentless pursuit of thinness through starvation.* Eventually, anorexia nervosa can lead to death, as it did for popular singer Karen Carpenter.

Anorexia nervosa afflicts primarily females during adolescence and early adulthood (only about 5 percent of anorexics are male) (Worrell & Todd, 1996). Most individuals with this disorder are White and from well-educated, middle- and upper-income families. Although anorexics avoid eating, they have an intense interest in food; they cook for others, they talk about food, and they insist on watching others eat. Anorexics have a distorted

body image, perceiving that they will look better even if they become skeletal (Stormer & Thompson, 1996; Thompson, 1996). As self-starvation continues and the fat content of the body drops to a bare minimum, menstruation usually stops and behavior often becomes hyperactive.

Numerous causes of anorexia nervosa have been proposed. They include societal, psychological, and physiological factors (Smolak, Levine, & Striegel-Moore, 1996). The societal factor most often held responsible is the current fashion of thinness. Psychological factors include a motivation to get attention, a desire for individuality, a denial of sexuality, and a way of coping with overcontrolling parents. Anorexics sometimes have parents who place high demands for achievement on them. Unable to meet their parents' high standards, anorexics feel unable to control their own lives. By limiting their food intake, anorexics gain a sense of self-control. Physiological causes focus on the hypothalamus, which becomes abnormal in a number of ways when an individual becomes anorexic. At this time, however, we are not exactly certain what causes anorexia nervosa.

Bulimia *is an eating disorder that involves a binge-and-purge sequence on a regular basis.* Bulimics binge on large amounts of food and then purge by self-induced vomiting or the use of a laxative. The binges sometimes alternate with fasting; at other times, they alternate with normal eating behavior. Like anorexia nervosa, bulimia is primarily a female disorder, and it has become prevalent among college women. Some estimates suggest that 50 percent of college women binge and purge at least some of the time. However, recent estimates suggest that true bulimics—those who binge and purge on a regular basis—make up less than 2 percent of the college female population. Whereas anorexics can control their eating, bulimics can not. Depression is a common characteristic of bulimics. Many of the same causes proposed for anorexia nervosa are offered for bulimia (Pomeroy, 1996).

The Interrelation of Problems and Programs That Prevent or Reduce Adolescent Problems

So far we have described some of the major problems adolescents are at risk for developing. In the next chapter, we will discuss another major problem in adolescence—school dropouts. In many instances, adolescents have more than one problem. Researchers are increasingly finding that problem behaviors in adolescence are interrelated (Tubman, Windle, & Windle, 1996). For example, heavy substance abuse is related to early sexual activity, lower grades, dropping out of school, and delinquency. Early initiation of sexual activity is associated with the use of cigarettes and alcohol, use of marijuana and other illicit drugs, lower grades, dropping out of school, and delinquency. Delinquency is related to early sexual activity, early pregnancy, substance abuse, and dropping out of school. As many as 10 percent of the adolescent population in the

Why Is a Course of Risk Taking in Adolescence Likely to Have More Serious Consequences Today Than in the Past?

The world is dangerous and unwelcoming for too many of America's teenagers, especially those from low-income families, neighborhoods, and schools. Many adolescents are resilient and cope with the challenges of adolescence without too many setbacks, but other adolescents struggle unsuccessfully to find jobs, are written off as losses by their schools, become pregnant before they are ready to become parents, or risk their health through drug abuse. Adolescents in virtually every era have been risk-takers, testing limits and making shortsighted judgments. But why are the consequences of choosing a course of risk-taking possibly more serious today than they have ever been? By evaluating the consequences of pursuing a course of risk taking today, you are learning to think critically by *identifying the sociocultural, historical contexts of development.*

1. *Intensive individualized attention.* In successful programs, high-risk children are attached to a responsible adult who gives the child attention and deals with the child's specific needs. This theme occurred in a number of different programs. In a successful substance-abuse program, a student assistance counselor was available full-time for individual counseling and referral for treatment.

2. *Community-wide multiagency collaborative approaches.* The basic philosophy of community-wide programs is that a number of different programs and services have to be in place. In one successful substance-abuse program, a community-wide health promotion campaign was implemented that used local media and community education in concert with a substance-abuse curriculum in the schools.

3. *Early identification and intervention.* Reaching children and their families before children

United States have serious multiple-problem behaviors (adolescents who have dropped out of school, or are behind in their grade level, are users of heavy drugs, regularly use cigarettes and marijuana, and are sexually active but do not use contraception). Many, but not all, of these very high-risk youth "do it all." Another 15 percent of adolescents participate in many of these same behaviors but with slightly lower frequency and less-deleterious consequences. These high-risk youth often engage in two- or three-problem behaviors (Dryfoos, 1990). To further evaluate adolescent problems, refer to Critical Thinking About Children's Development.

> *There is no easy path leading out of life, and few are the easy ones that lie within it.*
>
> —Walter Savage Landor,
> ***Imaginary Conversations***, 1824

In addition to understanding that many adolescents engage in multiple-problem behaviors, it also is important to develop programs that reduce adolescent problems. In a recent review of the programs that have been successful in preventing or reducing adolescent problems, adolescent researcher Joy Dryfoos (1990) described the common components of these successful programs. The common components include these:

develop problems, or at the beginning of their problems, is a successful strategy. One preschool program serves as an excellent model for the prevention of delinquency, pregnancy, substance abuse, and dropping out of school. Operated by the High Scope Foundation in Ypsilanti, Michigan, the Perry Preschool has had a long-term positive impact on its students. This enrichment program, directed by David Weikart, services disadvantaged African American children. They attend a high-quality 2-year preschool program and receive weekly home visits from program personnel. Based on official police records, by age 19 individuals who had attended the Perry Preschool program were less likely to have been arrested and reported fewer adult offenses than a control group. The Perry Preschool students also were less likely to drop out of school, and teachers rated their social behavior as more competent than that of a control group who did not receive the enriched preschool experience.

At this point we have studied a number of ideas about adolescent sexuality and problems and disorders. A summary of these ideas is presented in concept table 15.2.

CONCEPT TABLE 15.2

Adolescent Sexuality, and Problems and Disorders

Concept	Processes/Related Ideas	Characteristics/Description
Sexuality	Heterosexual attitudes and behavior	In the twentieth century, there has been a major increase in the number of adolescents reporting intercourse. The number of females reporting intercourse has increased more rapidly than the proportion of males. As we develop our sexual attitudes, we follow certain sexual scripts, which often are different for females and males.
	Homosexual attitudes and behavior	Rates of homosexuality have remained constant in the twentieth century. Homosexuality is no longer classified as a disorder. No definitive conclusions about the causes of homosexuality have been reached.
	Sexually transmitted diseases	Any adolescent who has sex runs the risk of getting a sexually transmitted disease, formerly called venereal disease, although many adolescents underestimate their own risk. Among the sexually transmitted diseases adolescents may get are chlamydia, herpes simplex virus II, syphilis, and AIDS.
	Adolescent pregnancy	More than 1 million American adolescents become pregnant each year. The U.S. adolescent pregnancy rate is the highest in the Western world. The consequences of adolescent pregnancy include health risks for the mother and the offspring.
Adolescent Problems and Disorders	Drugs	The United States has the highest adolescent drug-use rate of any industrialized nation. The 1960s and 1970s were times of marked increase in adolescent drug use. An increase in drug use by high school seniors occurred in 1993; this was the first such increase in a number of years. Alcohol is the drug most widely used by adolescents; alcohol abuse by adolescents is a major problem. Heavy drinking is common. Cocaine use is another concern. Parents, peers, and schools play important roles in adolescent drug use.
	Juvenile delinquency	A juvenile delinquent is an adolescent who breaks the law or engages in conduct that is considered illegal. Heredity, identity problems, community influences, and family experiences have been proposed as causes of delinquency. Parents' failure to discourage antisocial behavior and encourage skilled behavior, as well as parents' lack of monitoring of the adolescent's whereabouts, are related to delinquency. An increasing concern is the high rate of violence among youth. Intervening with children before they develop ingrained antisocial behaviors is an important dimension of reducing violence in youth. Successful programs for delinquents do not focus on delinquency alone, but rather include multiple components.
	Depression and suicide	Increasingly distinctions are being made among depressed mood, depressed syndromes, and clinical depression (major depressive disorder and dysthymia). Female adolescents are more likely to have mood and depressive disorders than male adolescents are. Adolescent suicide has tripled since the 1950s. Both proximal and distal factors are involved in suicide's causes.
	Eating disorders	Anorexia nervosa and bulimia increasingly have become problems for adolescent females. Societal, psychological, and physiological causes of these disorders have been proposed.
	Interrelation of problems and programs that prevent or reduce adolescent problems	Researchers are increasingly finding that problem behaviors in adolescence are interrelated. Dryfoos found a number of common components in programs designed to prevent or reduce adolescent problems; they include providing individual attention to high-risk children, developing community-wide intervention, and early identification and intervention.

A dolescents do often flash from one end of the world to the other as they move through a seemingly endless preparation for life. In fragile moments, they often become acquainted with sex and many other at-risk behaviors.

We began this chapter by describing the mysteries and curiosities of puberty, and then discussed the nature of adolescence by addressing the biological and sociohistorical dimensions of adolescence, stereotyping adolescents, and what today's youth are like. Our coverage of puberty focused on pubertal change, psychological accompaniments of pubertal change, and pubertal timing and health care. Our examination of sexuality involved sexual attitudes and behavior, sexually transmitted diseases, and adolescent pregnancy. We then evaluated drugs, juvenile delinquency, depression, suicide, eating disorders, and the interrelation of problems and programs that prevent or reduce adolescent problems.

Don't forget that you can obtain an overall summary of the chapter by again studying the two concept tables on pages 464 and 479. In the next chapter, we will continue our journey through adolescence by exploring the nature of cognitive development during this period.

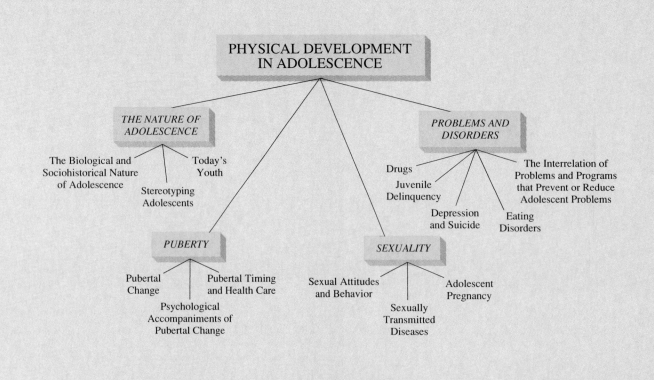

PHYSICAL DEVELOPMENT
IN ADOLESCENCE

THE NATURE OF
ADOLESCENCE

The Biological and
Sociohistorical Nature
of Adolescence

Today's
Youth

Stereotyping
Adolescents

PROBLEMS AND
DISORDERS

Drugs

Juvenile
Delinquency

The Interrelation of
Problems and Programs
that Prevent or Reduce
Adolescent Problems

Depression
and Suicide

Eating
Disorders

PUBERTY

Pubertal
Change

Pubertal Timing
and Health Care

Psychological
Accompaniments of
Pubertal Change

SEXUALITY

Sexual Attitudes
and Behavior

Adolescent
Pregnancy

Sexually
Transmitted
Diseases

storm-and-stress view   Hall's view that adolescence is a turbulent time charged with conflict and mood swings. 457

inventionist view   The belief that adolescence is a sociohistorical creation. Especially important in the development of the inventionist view of adolescence were the sociohistorical circumstances at the beginning of the twentieth century, a time when legislation was enacted that ensured the dependency of youth and made their move into the economic sphere more manageable. 457

stereotype   The broad category that reflects our impressions and beliefs about people. All stereotypes refer to an image of what the typical member of a particular group is like. 458

menarche   First menstruation. 459

puberty   A period of rapid skeletal and sexual maturation that occurs mainly in early adolescence. 459

testosterone   A hormone associated in boys with the development of genitals, an increase in height, and a change in voice. 460

estradiol   A hormone associated in girls with breast, uterine, and skeletal development. 460

sexual script   A stereotyped pattern of role prescriptions for how individuals should behave sexually. 465

chlamydia   A sexually transmitted disease named for the bacteria that cause it. 467

herpes simplex virus II   A sexually transmitted disease whose symptoms include irregular cycles of sores and blisters in the genital area. 467

AIDS (acquired immune deficiency syndrome)   A syndrome caused by the human immunodeficiency virus (HIV), which destroys the body's immune system. 467

juvenile delinquent   An adolescent who breaks the law or engages in behavior that is considered illegal. 472

depressed mood   Periods of sadness or unhappy mood that can last for a brief or an extended period of time. They may occur as a result of the loss of a significant relationship or failure on an important task. 474

depressive syndromes   A cluster of behaviors and emotions that includes feeling lonely, crying, fear of doing bad things, feeling the need to be perfect, feeling unloved, feeling worthless, nervous, guilty, or sad, and worrying. 474

clinical depression   This involves being diagnosed as experiencing major depressive disorder or dysthymic disorder. 474

major depressive disorder   This is present when the adolescent has experienced five or more of the following symptoms for at least a 2-week period at a level that differs from previous functioning: depressed mood or irritable most of the day; decreased interest in pleasurable activities; changes in weight or failure to make necessary weight gains in adolescence; sleep problems; psychomotor agitation or retardation; fatigue or loss of energy; feelings of worthlessness or abnormal amounts of guilt; reduced concentration and decision-making ability; and repeated suicidal ideation, suicide attempts, or plans of suicide. 474

dysthymic disorder   This occurs when adolescents have a period of at least 1 year in which they have shown depressed or irritable mood every day without more than 2 symptom-free months. Further, dysthymic disorder requires the presence of at least two of the following symptoms: eating problems; sleeping problems; lack of energy; low self-esteem; reduced concentration or decision-making ability; and feelings of hopelessness. 475

anorexia nervosa   An eating disorder that involves the relentless pursuit of thinness through starvation. 477

bulimia   An eating disorder in which the individual consistently follows a binge-purge eating pattern. 477

You & Your Adolescent
(1990) by Laurence Steinberg and Ann Levine.
New York: Harper Perennial.

You & Your Adolescent provides a broad, developmental overview of adolescence with parental advice mixed in along the way. Author Laurence Steinberg is a professor of psychology at Temple University and a highly respected researcher in adolescent development. The book is divided into the preteens (10–13), the teens (14–17), and toward adulthood (18–20). In Steinberg and Levine's approach, knowing how adolescents develop keeps parents from making a lot of mistakes. This is an excellent book for parents of adolescents. It serves the dual purpose of educating parents about how adolescents develop and giving them valuable parenting strategies for coping with teenagers.

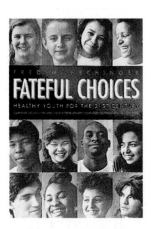

Fateful Choices
(1992) by Fred Hechinger.
New York: Hill and Wang.

The substance of this excellent book was provided by the Carnegie Council on Adolescent Development. One of the Carnegie Council's main themes comes through clearly in this book—linking health and education in the development of adolescents. The author provides valuable recommendations that can improve the health and well-being of all adolescents, especially those at risk for problems. Various chapters focus on adolescents at risk, adolescent pregnancy, drug abuse, nutrition and exercise, and youth organizations.

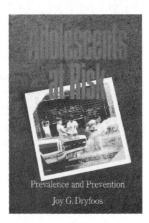

Adolescents at Risk
(1990) by Joy Dryfoos.
New York: Oxford University Press.

This is an excellent book on adolescent problems. Dryfoos describes four main problems that keep adolescents from reaching their potential: drug problems, delinquency, pregnancy, and school-related problems. She provides helpful sketches of programs that are successful in treating these problems. She argues that many at-risk adolescents have more than one problem and that treatment needs to take this interrelatedness of problems into account. School and community programs are especially highlighted.

IMPROVING THE LIVES OF CHILDREN

Improving the lives of children involves improving the imbalance between risk and opportunity, learning about guidelines for seeking therapy when an adolescent shows problem behaviors, implementing programs like the Life Skills Training program, counselors and community workers turning around the lives of children and adolescents involved in drug-related gang violence, and reducing the incidence of rape.

HEALTH AND WELL-BEING
Improving the Balance Between Risk and Opportunity

Today's world holds experiences for adolescents unlike those encountered by their parents and grandparents. Today's adolescents face greater risks to their health than ever before. Drug and alcohol abuse, depression, violence, pregnancy, sexually transmitted diseases, and school-related problems place far too many of today's adolescents at risk for not reaching their full potential. Recent estimates suggest that as many as one-fourth of American adolescents are in the high-risk category.

Adolescent expert Ruby Takanishi (1993) recently described the importance of improving the opportunity side of the adolescent risk-opportunity equation. Increased clinical and research knowledge suggests a viable approach away from remediation of single problems, such as drug abuse or delinquency or adolescent pregnancy, to the promotion of adolescent health or a cluster of health-enhancing behaviors. This approach recognizes that targeting only one problem behavior, such as drug abuse, may overlook its link to other problems, such as school failure or delinquency.

Because the adolescent interventions of the past have been so targeted, we are only beginning to unravel the clues to multiple adolescent problems that characterize many at-risk youth. For example, does improving peer resistance skills to combat smoking or other drug abuse also reduce at-risk sexual behavior in adolescents?

A special concern is that just providing information and teaching skills to adolescents is not sufficient to improve their health and well-being. Like people at other points in the human life span, adolescents have to be motivated to use information, skills, and services.

Networks of support from families, peers, and caring adults are crucial for improving the lives of at-risk youth. And social policymakers need to target improved economic opportunities for youth and their families.

Each of us who comes in contact with adolescents—as adults, parents, youth workers, professionals, and educators—can help to make a difference in improving their health and well-being. I hope this book and this course improve your knowledge of adolescent

Ruby Takanishi (right) *has worked diligently to improve the adolescent-risk-opportunity equation.*

development and motivate you to contribute to the health and well-being of today's adolescents.

Some Guidelines for Seeking Therapy When an Adolescent Shows Problem Behaviors

Determining whether adolescents need professional help when they engage in problem behaviors is not an easy task. Adolescents, by nature, tend to have mercurial moods and engage in behaviors that are distasteful to adults and run counter to their values. In many cases, though, such behaviors are only part of the adolescent's search for identity, are very normal, and do not require professional help. Too often when an adolescent first shows a problem behavior, such as drinking or stealing, parents panic and fear that their adolescent is going to turn into a drug addict or a hardened criminal. Such fears are usually not warranted—virtually every adolescent drinks alcohol at some point in their transition from childhood to adulthood, and likewise, virtually every adolescent engages in at least one or more acts of juvenile delinquency. By overreacting to such initial occurrences of adolescent problem behaviors, parents can exacerbate their relationship with the adolescent and thereby contribute to increased parent-adolescent conflict.

What are the circumstances under which parents should seek professional help for their adolescent's problems? Laurence Steinberg and Ann Levine (1990) recently developed five guidelines for determining when to get professional help if an adolescent is showing problem behaviors:

- If the adolescent is showing severe problem behaviors, such as depression, anorexia nervosa, drug addiction, repeated delinquent acts, or serious school-related problems, parents should not try to treat these problems alone and probably should seek professional help for the adolescent.

- If the adolescent has a problem, but the parents do not know what the problem is, they may want to seek professional help for the adolescent. An example is an adolescent who is socially withdrawn and doesn't have many

Among the times when parents might think about seeking professional help for their adolescent are when the adolescent engages in frequent truancy, chronic running away, or repeated, hostile opposition to authorities. Family therapy (shown here), in which the adolescent as well as other family members, especially one or both parents, participate, is often recommended in such circumstances.

friends, which could be due to extreme shyness, depression, stress at school, drug involvement, or any of a number of other reasons. If parents do not know what the adolescent's problem is, how can they help the adolescent? Professionals can often make specific diagnoses and provide recommendations for helping the adolescent.

- If parents have tried to solve the adolescent's problem but have not been successful and the problem continues to disrupt the adolescent's life, then parents may wish to seek professional help for the adolescent. Frequent truancy, chronic running away, or repeated, hostile opposition to authority are examples of such problems.

- If parents realize they are part of the adolescent's problem, they may wish to seek professional help for the family. Constant, intense, bitter fighting that disrupts the everyday living of the family is a good example. Rarely is one individual the single cause of extensive family dissension. A therapist can objectively analyze the family's problems and help the family members to see why they are fighting so much and to find ways to reduce the fighting.

- When the family is under extensive stress (from the death of a family member or a divorce, for example) and the adolescent is not coping well (for example, becomes depressed or drinks a lot), professional help may be needed.

The Life Skills Training Program

Gilbert Botvin's Life Skills Training program was selected as one of fourteen showcase programs by the American Psychological Association's Task Force on Promotion, Prevention, and Intervention Alternatives in Psychology. Botvin's (1986) program was the only drug prevention/intervention program selected out of a field of 300 nominees.

In Botvin's approach, substance abuse is a socially learned, purposive, and functional behavior. The approach involves an attempt to reduce pressure to smoke, develop general personal competence, and learn specific skills to resist peer pressure. The Life Skills Training curriculum consists of five main components:

1. Information is given to youth about the short-term and long-term consequences of substance abuse; biofeedback demonstrates the immediate effects of cigarette smoking.

2. Decision-making skills are taught to students to foster their critical thinking. Formulation of counterarguments to advertising appeals are discussed.

3. Coping skills are taught to students so they deal with stress more effectively.

4. Social skills training for resisting peer pressure is implemented. The training sessions include such topics as dealing with shyness, coping with dating, and assertiveness skills.

5. Self-improvement is emphasized by helping students develop a positive self-image using learning principles.

The Life Skills Training program consists of twenty sessions and is designed primarily for middle school and junior high school students. It is directed by a classroom teacher using a Teacher's Manual after the teacher receives one day of inservice training. Older peers (eleventh- and twelfth-graders) are also used as teachers after extensive training and on-site monitoring by the Life Skills Training staff.

Botvin has conducted a number of evaluations of the Life Skills Training program and demonstrated that the program is effective in reducing cigarette smoking, alcohol use, and marijuana use. The greatest success has occurred when the sessions are led by older peers.

Frog and Dolores

He goes by the name of Frog. He is the cocky prince of the barrio in East Los Angeles. He has street smarts. Frog happily smiles as he talks about raking in $200 a week selling crack cocaine. He proudly details his newly acquired membership in a violent street gang, the Crips. Frog brags about using his drug money to rent a convertible on weekends, even though at less than 5 feet in height, he can barely see over the dashboard. Frog is 13 years old.

With the advent of crack, juvenile arrests in New York City tripled from 1983 to 1987 and almost quadrupled in the same time frame in Washington, D.C. Adults who founded the crack trade recognized early on that young adolescents do not run the risk of mandatory jail sentences that courts hand out to adults. Being a lookout is the entry-level position for 9- and 10-year-olds. They can make as much as $100 a day warning dealers that police are in the area. The next step up the ladder is as a runner, a job that can pay as much as $300 a day. A runner transports drugs to the dealers on the street from makeshift factories where cocaine powder is cooked into rock-hard crack. And, at the next level, older adolescents can reach the status of dealer. In a hot market like New York City, they can make over $1,000 a day.

The escalating drug-related gang violence is difficult to contain or reduce. Police crackdowns across the country seem to have had a minimal impact. In a recent weekend-long raid on drug-dealing gangs in Los Angeles, police arrested 1,453 individuals, including 315 adolescents. Half had to be released for lack of evidence. The Los Angeles County juvenile facilities are designed to house 1,317. Today more than 2,000 adolescents are overflowing their facilities.

Counselors, school officials, and community workers report that turning around the lives of children and adolescents involved in drug-related

Dolores Bennett, volunteer in a low-income area of Detroit, Michigan, talks with and listens to one of her "children."

gang violence is extremely difficult. When impoverished children can make $100 a day, it is hard to wean them away from gangs. Federal budgets for training and employment programs, which provide crucial assistance to disadvantaged youth, have been reduced dramatically.

However, in Detroit, Michigan, Dolores Bennett has made a difference. For twenty-five years, she has worked long hours trying to find things to keep children from low-income families busy. Her activities have led to the creation of neighborhood sports teams, regular fairs and picnics, and an informal job-referral

service for the children and youth in the neighborhood. She also holds many casual get-togethers for the youth in her small, tidy, yellow frame house. The youth talk openly and freely about their problems and their hopes, knowing that Dolores will listen. Dolores says that she has found being a volunteer to be priceless. On the mantel in her living room are hundreds of pictures of children and adolescents with whom she has worked. She points out that most of them did not have someone in their homes who would listen to them and give them love. America needs more Dolores Bennetts.

Rape

Rape is forcible sexual intercourse with a person who does not give consent. Nearly 200,000 rapes are reported each year in the United States. According to most estimates, this figure is far below the actual number of rapes because of the fears and problems associated with reporting a rape. Approximately one-third of all rape victims are between 11 to 17 years of age. Most rapes are committed by someone known to the victim, with many of the rape attacks occurring during the course of a date. Females account for approximately 95 percent of all rape victims.

Why is rape so pervasive in our culture? Feminist writers believe that males are socialized to be sexually aggressive, to regard females as inferior beings, and to view their own pleasure as the most important objective. Researchers have found the following characteristics common among rapists: Aggression enhances the offender's sense of power or masculinity; rapists are angry at females in general; and rapists want to hurt their victims.

An increasing concern is date or acquaintance rape, which is coercive sexual activity directed at someone with whom the individual is at least casually acquainted. Date rape is recognized as a major problem among adolescents and college students (Flanagan, 1996). In one group of college males, 15 percent admitted that they had had sexual intercourse against their date's will. A survey of college females found that 24 percent had experienced unwanted attempts at intercourse and 31 percent had been subjected to unwanted fondling of their genitals (Kavin & Parcell, 1977).

Rape is a traumatic experience for the victim and those close to her. The rape victim initially feels shock and numbness and is often acutely disorganized. Some victims show their distress through words and tears; others suffer more internally. As victims strive to get their life back to normal, they may experience depression, fear, and anxiety for months or years. Sexual dysfunctions, such as reduced sexual desire and the inability to reach orgasm, occur in 50 percent of all rape victims. A victim's recovery depends on both her coping abilities and her psychological adjustment prior to the assault. Social support from parents, friends, and others are important to recovery, as is the availability of professional counseling, which sometimes is obtained through a rape crisis center.

Experts on rape and sexuality believe that improved sex education and the promotion of more egalitarian relationships between females and males are important in reducing the incidence of rape of adolescent females (Kershner, 1996; Rickel & Hendren, 1993).

PICASSO
Young Boy with Dog, detail

Cognitive Development
in Adolescence

*I remember my youth and that feeling
that never came back to me anymore—
the feeling that I could last forever,
outlast the sea, the earth, and all men.*

—**Joseph Conrad**

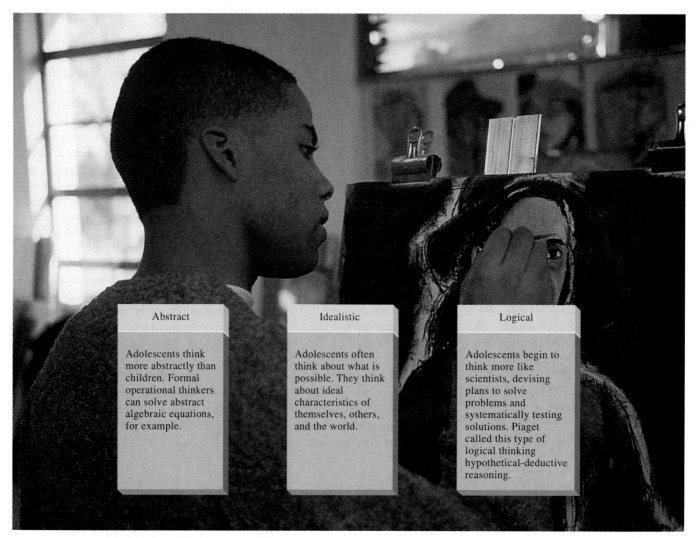

FIGURE 16.1

Characteristics of Formal Operational Thought
Adolescents begin to think more as scientists think, devising plans to solve problems and systematically testing solutions. Piaget gave this type of thinking the imposing name of hypothetical-deductive reasoning.

which considerably narrows the field of choices. The most effective plan is a "halving" strategy (Q: Is it in the right half of the array? A: No. Q: OK: Is it in the top half? And so on.) Used correctly, the halving strategy guarantees the questioner the correct solution in seven questions or less, no matter where the correct picture is located in the array. Even if adolescents use a less elegant strategy than "halving," those who are deductive hypothesis testers understand that when the experimenter answers no to one of their questions, several possibilities are immediately eliminated.

By contrast, the concrete thinker may persist with questions that continue to test some of the same possibilities that previous questions should have eliminated. For example, these adolescents may ask whether the correct picture is in row 1 and receive the answer no, but later ask whether the picture is x, which is in row 1.

Thus, formal operational thinkers test their hypotheses with judiciously chosen questions and tests.

Often a single question or test will help them to eliminate an untenable hypothesis. By contrast, concrete operational thinkers often fail to understand the relation between a hypothesis and a well-chosen test of it—stubbornly clinging to the idea despite clear, logical disconfirmation of it.

> *The error of youth is to believe that intelligence is a substitute for experience, while the error of age is to believe that experience is a substitute for intelligence.*
>
> — **Slyman Bryson**

Piaget believed that formal operational thought is the best description of how adolescents think. A summary of formal operational thought's characteristics is shown in figure 16.1. As we see next, though, formal operational thought is not a homogeneous stage of development.

John W. Santrock

The colorful attire of this skateboarder reflects adolescent egocentrism. Attention-getting behavior reflects the desire to be on stage and noticed. The risk-taking behavior of skateboarding, as well as racing cars, taking drugs, and many other behaviors, reflects adolescents' sense of indestructibility. Joseph Conrad once commented, "I remember my youth and the feeling that never came back anymore—the feeling that I could last forever, outlast the sea, the earth, and all men."

Early and Late Formal Operational Thought

Not all adolescents are full-fledged formal operational thinkers. Some developmentalists believe formal operational thought consists of two subperiods: early and late. In **early formal operational thought,** *adolescents' increased ability to think in hypothetical ways produces unconstrained thoughts with unlimited possibilities. In this early period, the world is perceived too subjectively and idealistically.* **Late formal operational thought** *involves a restoration of intellectual balance. Adolescents now test out the products of their reasoning against experience and a consolidation of formal operational thought takes place. An intellectual balance is restored, as the adolescent accommodates to the cognitive upheaval that has taken place.* Late formal operational thought may appear during the middle adolescent years. In this view, assimilation of formal operational thought marks the transition to

adolescence; accommodation to formal operational thought marks a later consolidation.

Piaget's (1952) early writings indicated that the onset and consolidation of formal operational thought is completed during early adolescence, from about 11 to 15 years of age. Later, Piaget (1972) revised his view and concluded that formal operational thought is not completely achieved until later in adolescence, between approximately 15 and 20 years of age. As we see next, many developmentalists believe there is considerable individual variation in adolescent cognition.

Individual Variation in Adolescent Cognition

Piaget's theory emphasizes universal and consistent patterns of formal operational thought. His theory does not adequately account for the unique, individual differences that characterize the cognitive development of adolescents. These individual variances in adolescents' cognitive development have been documented in a number of investigations (Bart, 1971; Kaufmann & Flaitz, 1987).

Some individuals in early adolescence are formal operational thinkers; others are not. A review of formal operational thought investigations revealed that only about one of every three eighth-grade students is a formal operational thinker (Strahan, 1983). Many college students and adults do not think in formal operational ways either. For example, investigators have found that from 17 percent to 67 percent of college students think in formal operational ways (Tomlinson-Keasey, 1972).

Many young adolescents are at the point of consolidating their concrete operational thought, using it more consistently than in childhood. At the same time, many young adolescents are just beginning to think in a formal operational manner. By late adolescence, many adolescents are beginning to consolidate their formal operational thought, using it more consistently. And there often is variation across the content areas of formal operational thought, just as there is in concrete operational thought in childhood. A 14-year-old adolescent may reason at the formal operational level when analyzing algebraic equations but not do so in verbal problem solving or when reasoning about interpersonal relations.

Adolescent Egocentrism

"Oh my gosh! I can't believe it. Help! I can't stand it!" Tracy desperately yells. "What is wrong? What is the matter?" her mother asks. Tracy responds, "Everyone in here is looking at me." The mother queries, "Why?" Tracy says, "Look, this one hair just won't stay in place," as she rushes to the rest room of the restaurant. Five minutes later she returns to the table in the restaurant after she has depleted an entire can of hair spray. During a conversation between two 14-year-old girls, the one named Margaret says, "Are you kidding, I won't get pregnant." And, 13-year-old Adam describes himself, "No one understands me, particularly my parents. They have no idea of what I am feeling."

These comments of Tracy, Margaret, and Adam represent the emergence of egocentrism in adolescence. **Adolescent egocentrism** *refers to the heightened self-consciousness of adolescents that is reflected in their belief that others are as interested in them as they themselves are, and in their sense of personal uniqueness.*

Developmental psychologist David Elkind (1978) believes adolescent egocentrism can be dissected into two types of social thinking—the imaginary audience and the personal fable. The term **imaginary audience** *refers to the heightened self-consciousness of adolescents that is reflected in their belief that others are as interested in them as they themselves are. The imaginary audience involves attention-getting behavior in the desire to be noticed, visible, and "on stage."* Tracy's comments and behavior reflect the imaginary audience. Another adolescent may think that others are as aware of a small spot on his trousers as he is, possibly knowing that he has masturbated. Another adolescent, an eighth-grade girl, walks into her classroom and thinks that all eyes are riveted on her complexion. Adolescents especially sense that they are "on stage" in early adolescence, believing they are the main actors and all others are the audience.

According to Elkind, the **personal fable** *is the part of adolescent egocentrism involving an adolescent's sense of uniqueness.* The comments of Margaret and Adam, mentioned earlier, reflect the personal fable. Adolescents' sense of personal uniqueness makes them feel that no one can understand how they really feel. For example, an adolescent girl thinks that in no way can her mother sense the hurt that she feels because her boyfriend broke up with her. As part of their effort to retain a sense of personal uniqueness, adolescents may craft a story about the self that is filled with fantasy, immersing themselves in a world that is far removed from reality. Personal fables frequently show up in adolescent diaries.

Developmentalists have increasingly studied adolescent egocentrism in recent years. The research interest focuses on what the components of egocentrism really are, the nature of self-other relationships, why egocentric thought emerges in adolescence, and the role of egocentrism in adolescent problems. For example, Elkind believes that adolescent egocentrism is brought about by formal operational thought. Others, however, argue that adolescent egocentrism is not entirely a cognitive phenomenon. Rather, they think the imaginary audience is due both to the ability to think hypothetically (formal operational thought) and the ability to step outside one's self and anticipate the reactions of others in imaginative circumstances (perspective taking) (Lapsley, 1991).

Some developmentalists believe that egocentrism may account for some of the seemingly reckless behavior of adolescents including drug use, suicidal thoughts, and failure to use contraceptives during intercourse (Dolcini & others, 1989). The reckless behavior may stem from the egocentric characteristics of uniqueness and invulnerability. In one study, eleventh- and twelfth-grade females who were high in adolescent egocentrism estimated they were less likely to get pregnant if they engaged in sex without contraception than their counterparts who were low in adolescent egocentrism (Arnett, 1990).

Adolescent Decision Making

Adolescence is a time of increased decision making. Adolescence is a time when individuals make decisions about the future, which friends to choose, whether to go to college, which person to date, whether to have sex, whether to take drugs, whether to buy a car, and so on. How competent are adolescents at making decisions? Older adolescents are more competent than younger adolescents, who in turn are more competent than children (Keating, 1990). Young adolescents are more likely than children to generate options, to examine a situation from a variety of perspectives, to anticipate the consequences of decisions, and to consider the credibility of sources. However, young adolescents are less competent at these decision-making skills than are older adolescents.

Transitions in decision making appear at approximately 11 to 12 years of age and at 15 to 16 years of age. For example, in one study eighth-, tenth-, and twelfth-grade students were presented with dilemmas involving the choice of a medical procedure (Lewis, 1981). The oldest students were most likely to spontaneously mention a variety of risks, to recommend consultation with an outside specialist, and to anticipate future consequences. For example, when asked a question about whether to have cosmetic surgery, a twelfth-grader said that different aspects of the situation need to be examined along with its effects on the individual's future, especially relationships with other people. By contrast, an eighth-grader provided a more limited view, commenting on the surgery's effects on getting turned down for a date, the money involved, and being teased at school by peers.

However, the decision-making skills of older adolescents and adults is often far from perfect. And the ability to make decisions does not guarantee that such decisions will be made in everyday life, where breadth of experience often comes into play (Ganzel & Jacobs, 1992). For example, driver training courses improve the adolescent's cognitive and motor skills to levels equal to, or sometimes superior to, those of adults. However, driver training has not been effective in reducing adolescents' high rate of traffic accidents. Thus, an important research agenda is to study the ways adolescents make decisions in practical situations.

Adolescents need more opportunities to practice and discuss realistic decision making. Many real-world decisions occur in an atmosphere of stress, involving such factors as time constraints and emotional involvement. One strategy to improve adolescent decision making about real-world choices involving such matters as sex, drugs, and daredevil driving is for schools to develop more opportunities for adolescents to engage in role playing and group problem solving related to such circumstances.

John W. Santrock

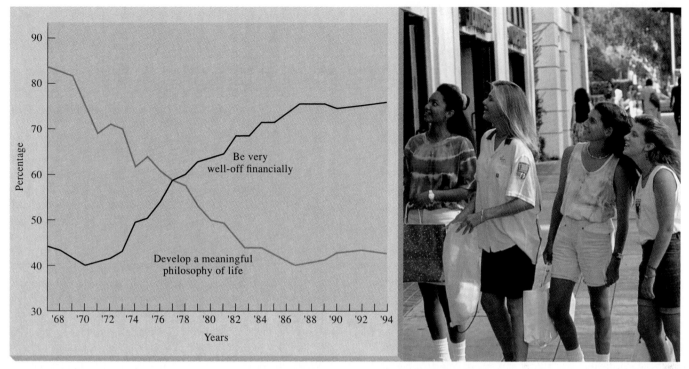

FIGURE 16.2

Changing Freshman Life Goals, 1968–1994
The percentages indicated are in response to the question of identifying a life goal as "essential" or "very important." There has been a significant reversal in freshman life goals in the last two decades, with a far greater percentage of today's college freshmen stating that a "very important" life goal is to be well-off financially, and far fewer stating that developing a meaningful philosophy of life is a "very important" life goal.

In some instances, adolescents' decision making may be blamed, when in reality the problem involves society's orientation toward adolescents and its failure to provide adolescents with adequate choices (Keating, 1990). For example, a mathematically precocious ninth-grade girl may abandon mathematics not because of poor decision-making skills but because of a stronger motivation to maintain positive peer relations that would be threatened if she stayed in the math tract. The decision of an adolescent in a low-income, inner-city area to engage in drug trafficking even at considerable risk may not be a consequence of the adolescent's failure to consider all of the relevant information but may be the outcome of quite sophisticated thinking about risk-benefit ratios in oppressive circumstances offering limited or nonexistent options. As cognitive developmentalist Daniel Keating observes, if we dislike adolescents' choices, perhaps we need to provide them with better options from which to choose.

VALUES AND RELIGION

What are adolescents' values like today? How powerful is religion in adolescents' lives?

Values

Adolescents carry with them a set of values that influences their thoughts, feelings, and actions. What were your values when you were an adolescent? Are the values of today's adolescents changing?

Over the past two decades, adolescents have shown an increased concern for personal well-being and a decreased concern for the well-being of others, especially for the disadvantaged (Astin & others, 1994). As shown in figure 16.2, today's college freshmen are more strongly motivated to be well off financially and less motivated to develop a meaningful philosophy of life than were their counterparts of 20 or even 10 years ago. Student commitment to becoming very well-off financially as a "very important" reason for attending college has reached a record high in the 1990s.

However, two values that increased during the 1960s continue to be important to many of today's youth: self-fulfillment and self-expression (Conger, 1988). As part of their motivation for self-fulfillment, many adolescents show great interest in their physical health and well-being. Greater self-fulfillment and self-expression can be laudable goals, but if they become the only goals, self-destruction, loneliness, or alienation may result. Young people also need to develop a corresponding sense of commitment to others' welfare. Encouraging adolescents to have a strong commitment to others, in concert with an interest in self-fulfillment, is an important task for America at the close of the twentieth century.

There are some signs that today's adolescents are shifting toward a stronger interest in the welfare of society, as evidenced by the volunteer work these adolescents are doing on Earth Day.

Without civic morality communities perish; without personal morality their survival has no value.

—**Bertrand Russell**

Some signs indicate that today's students are shifting toward a stronger interest in the welfare of society (Yates, 1996). For example, between 1986 and 1994, there was an

increase in the percentage of freshmen who said that they were strongly interested in participating in community action programs (28 percent in 1994, compared to 18 percent in 1986) and in helping promote racial understanding (40 percent in 1994, compared to 27 percent in 1986). In one recent study, students' participation in community service stimulated them to reflect on society's political organization and moral order (Yates, 1995). More students are showing an active interest in the problems of the homeless, child abuse, hunger, and poverty (Conger, 1988). The percentage of students who believe that it is desirable to work for a social service organization rose from 11 percent in 1980 to 17 percent in 1989 (Johnston, Bachman, & O'Malley, 1990). Whether these small incremental increases in concern for the community and society will continue is difficult to predict.

Religion

Many children and adolescents show an interest in religion, and religious institutions created by adults are designed to introduce certain beliefs and ensure that children will carry on a religious tradition. Societies have invented, for example, Sunday schools, parochial education, tribal transmission of religious traditions, and home schooling.

Does this indoctrination work? In many cases it does (Paloutzian, 1996). In general, adults tend to adopt the religious teachings of their upbringing. For instance, if individuals are Catholics by the time they are 25 years of age, and were raised as Catholics, they likely will continue to be Catholics throughout their adult years. If a religious change or reawakening occurs, it is most likely to take place during adolescence (Argyle & Beit-Hallahmi, 1975).

Religious issues are important to adolescents (Paloutzian & Santrock, 1997). In one recent survey, 95 percent of 13- to 18-year-olds said that they believe in God or a universal spirit (Gallup & Bezilla, 1992). Almost three-fourths of adolescents said that they pray, and about one-half indicated that they had attended

John W. Santrock

Many children and adolescents show an interest in religion, and many religious institutions created by adults, such as this Muslim school in Malaysia, are designed to introduce them to certain beliefs and ensure that they will carry on a religious tradition.

religious services in the past week. Almost one-half said that it is very important for a young person to learn religious faith.

Developmental Changes

Adolescence might be an especially important juncture for religious development. Even if children have been indoctrinated into a religion by their parents, because of advances in their cognitive development they begin to question what their own religious beliefs truly are.

During adolescence, especially in late adolescence and the college years, identity development becomes a central focus (Erikson, 1968). Youth want to find answers to these kinds of questions: "Who am I?" "What am I all about as a person?" "What kind of life do I want to lead?" As part of their search for identity, adolescents begin to grapple in more sophisticated, logical ways with such questions as these: "Why am I on this planet?" "Is there really a God or higher spiritual being, or have I just been believing what my parents and the church imprinted in my mind?" "What really are my religious views?"

Piaget's (1962) cognitive developmental theory provides a theoretical backdrop for understanding religious development in children and adolescents. For example, in one study, children were asked about their understanding of certain religious pictures and Bible stories (Goldman, 1964). The children's responses fell into three stages closely related to Piaget's theory.

In the first stage (up until 7 or 8 years of age)—*preoperational intuitive religious thought*—children's religious thoughts were unsystematic and fragmented. The children often either did not fully understand the material in the stories or did not consider all of the evidence. For example, one child's response to the question "Why was Moses afraid to look at God?" (Exodus 3:6) was "Because God had a funny face!"

In the second stage (occurring from 7 or 8 to 13 or 14 years of age)—*concrete operational religious thought*—children focused on particular details of pictures and stories. For example, in response to the question about why Moses was afraid to look at God, one child said, "Because it was a ball of fire. He thought he might burn him." Said another child, "It was a bright light and to look at it might blind him."

In the third stage (age 14 through the remainder of adolescence)—*formal operational religious thought*—adolescents revealed a more abstract, hypothetical religious understanding. For example, one adolescent said that Moses was afraid to look at God because "God is holy and the world is sinful." Another youth responded, "The awesomeness and almightiness of God would make Moses feel like a worm in comparison."

Other researchers have found similar developmental changes in children and adolescents. For example, in one study, at about 17 or 18 years of age adolescents increasingly commented about freedom, meaning, and hope—abstract concepts—when making religious judgments (Oser & Gmunder, 1991).

How do their religious thought and behavior change as children develop? How are children's religious conceptions influenced by their cognitive development?

Religiousness and Sexuality in Adolescence

One area of religion's influence on adolescent development involves sexual activity. Although variability and change in church teachings make it difficult to characterize religious doctrines simply, most churches discourage premarital sex. Thus, the degree of adolescents' participation in religious organizations may be more important than religious affiliation as a determinant of premarital sexual attitudes and behavior. Adolescents who attend religious services frequently may hear messages about abstaining from sex. Involvement of adolescents in religious organizations also enhances the probability that they will become friends with adolescents who have restrictive attitudes toward premarital sex. In one study, adolescents who attended church frequently and valued religion in their lives were less experienced sexually and had less permissive attitudes toward premarital sex than their counterparts who attended church infrequently and said that religion did not play a strong role in their lives (Thornton & Camburn, 1989). However, while religious involvement is associated with a lower incidence of sexual activity among adolescents, adolescents who are religiously involved and sexually active are less likely to use medical methods of contraception (especially the pill) than their sexually active counterparts with low religious involvement.

Fowler's Developmental Theory

James Fowler (1981) proposed a theory of religious development that focuses on the motivation to discover meaning in life, either within or outside of organized religion. Fowler proposed six stages of religious development that are related to Erikson's, Piaget's, and Kohlberg's theories of development (Torney-Purta, 1993).

Stage 1. Intuitive-projective faith (early childhood). After infants learn to trust their caregiver (Erikson's formulation), they invent their own intuitive images of what good and evil are. As children move into Piaget's preoperational stage, their cognitive worlds open up a variety of new possibilities. Fantasy and reality are taken as being the same thing. Right and wrong are seen in terms of consequences to the self.

Stage 2. Mythical-literal faith (middle and late childhood). As children move into Piaget's concrete operational stage, they begin to reason in a more logical, but not abstract, way. They see the world as more orderly. Grade-school-age children interpret religious stories literally, and they perceive God as being much like a parent figure who rewards the good and punishes the bad. What is right is often perceived as fair exchange.

Stage 3. Synthetic-conventional faith (transition between childhood and adolescence, early adolescence). Adolescents

John W. Santrock

start to develop formal operational thought (Piaget's highest stage) and begin to integrate what they have learned about religion into a coherent belief system. According to Fowler, although the synthetic-conventional faith stage is more abstract than the previous two stages, young adolescents still mainly conform to the religious beliefs of others (analogous to Kohlberg's conventional level of morality) and have not yet adequately analyzed alternative religious ideologies. Behavior that involves a question of right and wrong is seen in terms of the harm it does to a relationship or what others might say. Fowler believes that most adults become locked into this stage and never move on to higher stages of religious development.

Stage 4. Individuating-reflexive faith (transition between adolescence and adulthood, early adulthood). Fowler believes that at this stage, for the first time, individuals are capable of taking full responsibility for their religious beliefs. Often as a response to their leaving-home experience, young people begin to take responsibility for their lives. Young adults now start to realize that they can choose the course of their life and that they must expend effort to follow a particular life course. Individuals come face-to-face with decisions about whether to consider themselves or the welfare of others first, and whether the religious doctrines they were taught when they were growing up are absolute or relative. Fowler believes that both formal operational thought and the intellectual challenges to an individual's values and religious ideologies that often take place in college are essential to developing individuating-reflexive faith.

Stage 5. Conjunctive faith (middle adulthood). Fowler believes that only a small number of adults ever move on to this stage, which involves being more open to paradox and opposing viewpoints. This openness stems from people's awareness of their finiteness and limitations. One woman Fowler (1981, p. 192) placed at this stage revealed the following complex religious understanding: "Whether you call it God or Jesus or Cosmic Flow or Reality or Love, it doesn't matter what you call it. It is there."

Stage 6. Universalizing faith (middle adulthood or late adulthood). Fowler says that the highest stage in religious development involves transcending specific belief systems to achieve a sense of oneness with all being and a commitment to breaking down the barriers that are divisive to people on this planet. Conflictual events are no longer seen as paradoxes. Fowler argues that very, very few people ever achieve this elusive, highest stage of religious development. Three who he says have are Mahatma Gandhi, Martin Luther King, and Mother Teresa. Figure 16.3 describes the six stages in Fowler's theory of religious development.

As with other stage theories of development—such as Erikson's, Piaget's, and Kohlberg's—Fowler's theory does not adequately take into account individual variation in development. Not everyone goes through the stages as coherently as Fowler portrays them.

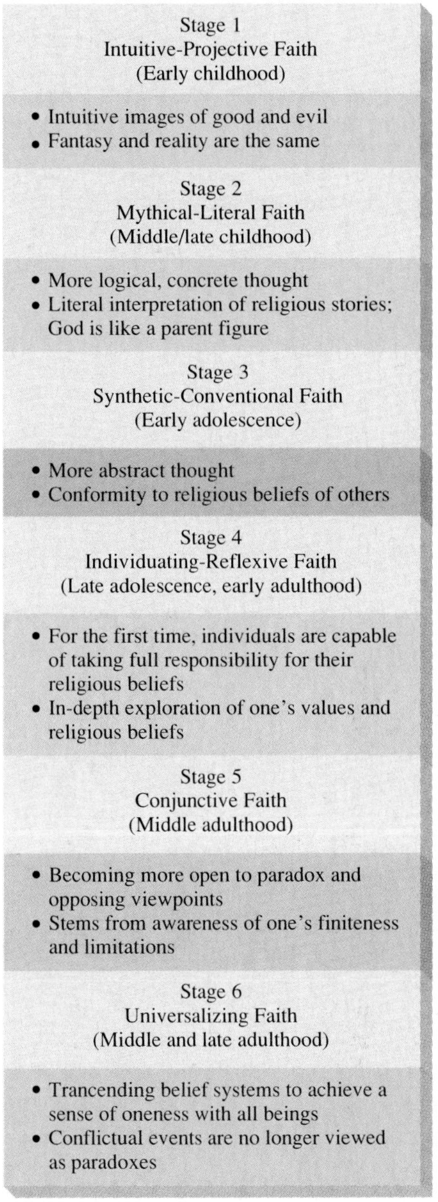

FIGURE 16.3

Fowler's Stage Theory of Religious Development

At this point we have studied a number of ideas about cognition and values and religion in adolescence. A summary of these ideas is presented in concept table 16.1.

SCHOOLS

What is the nature of schooling for adolescents? How many adolescents drop out of school?

Schools for Adolescents

The impressive changes in adolescents' cognition lead us to examine the nature of schools for adolescents. In chapter 14, we discussed different ideas about the effects of schools on children's development. Here we focus

CONCEPT TABLE 16.1

Adolescent Cognition, Values, and Religion

Concept	Processes/Related Ideas	Characteristics/Description
Adolescent Cognition	Piaget's theory	Abstractness and idealism, as well as hypothetical-deductive reasoning, are highlighted in formal operational thought. Formal operational thought involves the ability to reason about what is possible and hypothetical, as opposed to what is real, and the ability to reflect on one's own thoughts. Formal operational thought occurs in two phases—an assimilation phase in which reality is overwhelmed (early adolescence) and an accommodation phase in which intellectual balance is restored through a consolidation of formal operational thought (middle years of adolescence). Individual variation is extensive, and Piaget did not give this adequate attention. Many young adolescents are not formal operational thinkers but rather are consolidating their concrete operational thought.
	Adolescent egocentrism	Elkind proposed that adolescents, especially young adolescents, develop an egocentrism that involves both the construction of an imaginary audience (the belief that others are as preoccupied with the adolescent as the adolescent is) and a personal fable (a sense of personal uniqueness). Elkind believes that egocentrism appears because of formal operational thought. Others argue that perspective taking also is involved.
	Adolescent decision making	Adolescence is a time of increased decision making. Older adolescents are more competent at decision making than younger adolescents, who in turn are more competent than children. The ability to make decisions does not guarantee they will be made in practice because in real life, breadth of experience comes into play. Adolescents need more opportunities to practice and discuss realistic decision making. In some instances, adolescents' faulty decision making may be blamed when in reality the problem is society's orientation toward adolescents and failure to provide them with adequate choices.
Values and Religion	Values	Over the last two decades adolescents have shown an increased concern for personal well-being and a decreased concern for the welfare of others. Recently, adolescents have shown a slight increase in concern for community and societal issues.
	Religion	Many children and adolescents show an interest in religion, and religious institutions are designed to introduce them to religious beliefs. Adolescence may be a special juncture in religious development for many individuals. Piaget's theory provides a cognitive background for understanding religious development. Linkages between religiousness and sexuality occur in adolescence. Fowler proposed a life-span theory of religious development.

more exclusively on the nature of secondary schools. Among the questions we try to answer are the following: What should be the function of secondary schools? What is the nature of the transition from elementary to middle or junior high school? What are effective schools for young adolescents?

In youth we learn, in age we understand.
—**Marie Ebner von Eschenbach,** *Aphorism,* 1904

John W. Santrock

The Controversy Surrounding Secondary Schools

During the twentieth century, schools have assumed a more prominent role in the lives of adolescents. From 1890 to 1920, virtually every state developed laws that excluded youth from work and required them to attend school. In this time frame, the number of high school graduates increased 600 percent (Tyack, 1976). By making secondary education compulsory, the adult power structure placed adolescents in a submissive position and made their move into the adult world of work more manageable. In the nineteenth century, high schools were mainly for the elite, with the main educational emphasis being on classical liberal arts courses. By the 1920s, educators perceived that the secondary school curriculum needed to be changed. Schools for the masses, it was thought, should not just involve intellectual training, but should also involve training for work and citizenship. The curriculum of secondary schools became more comprehensive and grew to include general education, college preparatory, and vocational education courses. As the twentieth century unfolded, secondary schools continued to expand their orientation, adding courses in music, art, health, physical education, and other topics. By the middle of the twentieth century, schools had moved further toward preparing students for comprehensive roles in life. Today, secondary schools have retained their comprehensive orientation, designed to train adolescents intellectually, but in many other ways as well, such as vocationally and socially.

Although there has been a consistent trend of increased school attendance for more than 150 years, the distress over alienated and rebellious youth led some educators and social scientists to question whether secondary schools actually benefit adolescents. During the early 1970s, these experts agreed that high schools contribute to adolescent alienation and interfere with the transition to adulthood (Martin, 1976). They said that adolescents should be given educational alternatives to the comprehensive high school, such as on-the-job community work, to increase their exposure to adult roles and to decrease their sense of isolation from adults. To some degree in response to these critics, a number of states lowered from 16 to 14 the age at which adolescents could leave school.

In the last decade of the twentieth century, the back-to-basics movement has gained momentum, with proponents arguing that the main function of schools should be rigorous training of intellectual skills through subjects like English, math, and science. Advocates of the back-to-basics movement point to the excessive fluff in secondary school curricula, with students being allowed to select from many alternatives that will not give them a basic education in intellectual subjects. Some critics also point to the extensive time students spend in extracurricular activities. They argue that schools should be in the business of imparting knowledge to adolescents and not be so concerned about their social and emotional lives. Related to the proverbial dilemma of schools' functions is whether schools should include a vocational curriculum in addition to training in basic subjects such as English, math, and science. Some critics of the fluff in secondary schools argue that the school day should be longer and that the school year should be extended into the summer months. Such arguments are made by critics who believe that the main function of schools should be the training of intellectual skills. Little concern for adolescents' social and emotional development appears in these arguments.

Should the main—and perhaps only—major goal of schooling for adolescents be the development of an intellectually mature individual? Or should schools also focus on the adolescent's maturity in social and emotional development? Should schools be comprehensive, providing a multifaceted curriculum that includes many electives and alternative subjects to basic core courses? These are provocative questions that continue to be heatedly debated in educational and community circles.

The Transition to Middle or Junior High School

The emergence of junior high schools in the 1920s and 1930s was justified on the basis of physical, cognitive, and social changes that characterize early adolescence, as well as the need for more schools for the growing student population. Old high schools became junior high schools and new regional high schools were built. In most systems, the ninth grade remained a part of the high school in content, although physically separated from it in a 6-3-3 system. Gradually, the ninth grade has been restored to the high school as many school systems have developed middle schools that include the seventh and eighth grades, or sixth, seventh, and eighth grades. The creation of middle schools has been influenced by the earlier onset of puberty in recent decades.

One worry of educators and psychologists is that junior high and middle schools have simply become watered-down versions of high schools, mimicking their curricular and extracurricular schedules. The critics argue that unique curricular and extracurricular activities reflecting a wide range of individual differences in biological and psychological development in early adolescence should be incorporated into our junior high and middle schools. The critics also stress that many high schools foster passivity rather than autonomy, and that schools should create a variety of pathways for students to achieve an identity.

The transition to middle school or junior high school from elementary schools interests developmentalists because, even though it is a normative experience for virtually all children, the transition can be stressful. Why? Because the transition takes place at a time when many changes—in the individual, in the family, and in school—are taking place simultaneously. These changes include puberty and related concerns about body image; the emergence of at least some aspects of formal operational

The transition from elementary to middle or junior high school occurs at the same time a number of other changes take place in development. Biological, cognitive, and socioemotional changes converge with this schooling transition to make it a time of considerable adaptation.

thought, including accompanying changes in social cognition; increased responsibility and independence in association with decreased dependency on parents; change from a small, contained classroom structure to a larger, more impersonal school structure; change from one teacher to many teachers and a small, homogeneous set of peers to a larger, more heterogeneous set of peers; and increased focus on achievement and performance, and their assessment. This list includes a number of negative, stressful features, but there can be positive aspects to the transition. Students are more likely to feel grown up, have more subjects from which to select, have more opportunities to spend time with peers and to locate compatible friends, and enjoy increased independence from direct parental monitoring, and they may be more challenged intellectually by academic work.

When students make the transition from elementary school to middle or junior high school, they experience the **top-dog phenomenon,** *the circumstance of moving from the top position (in elementary school, being the oldest, biggest, and most powerful students in the school) to the lowest position (in middle or junior high school, being the youngest, smallest, and least powerful students in the school).* Researchers who have charted the transition from elementary to middle or junior high school find that the first year of middle or junior high

school can be difficult for many students (Hawkins & Berndt, 1985). For example, in one study of the transition from sixth grade in an elementary school to the seventh grade in a junior high school, adolescents' perceptions of the quality of their school life plunged in the seventh grade (Hirsch & Rapkin, 1987). In the seventh grade, the students were less satisfied with school, were less committed to school, and liked their teachers less. The drop in school satisfaction occurred regardless of how academically successful the students were.

Effective Schools for Young Adolescents

What makes a successful middle school? Joan Lipsitz (1984) and her colleagues searched the nation for the best middle schools. Extensive contacts and observations were made. Based on the recommendations of education experts and observations in schools in different parts of the United States, four middle schools were chosen for their outstanding ability to educate young adolescents. What were these middle schools like? The most striking feature was their willingness and ability to adapt all school practices to the individual differences in physical, cognitive, and social development of their students. The schools took seriously the knowledge we have developed about young adolescents. This seriousness was reflected in the decisions about different aspects of school life. For example, one middle school fought to keep its schedule of minicourses on Friday so that every student could be with friends and pursue personal interests. Two other middle schools expended considerable energy on a complex school organization so that small groups of students worked with small groups of teachers who could vary the tone and pace of the school day, depending on the students' needs. Another middle school developed an advisory scheme so that each student had daily contact with an adult who was willing to listen, explain, comfort, and prod the adolescent. Such school policies reflect thoughtfulness and personal concern about individuals who have compelling developmental needs.

What does education often do? It makes a straight-cut ditch of a free, meandering brook.

—**Henry David Thoreau**

Another aspect of the effective middle schools was that early in their existence—the first year in three of the schools and the second year in the fourth school—they emphasized the importance of creating an environment that was positive for adolescents' social and emotional development. This goal was established not only because such environments contribute to academic excellence, but also because social and emotional development are valued as intrinsically important in adolescents' schooling.

Recognizing that the vast majority of middle schools do not approach the excellent schools described by Joan Lipsitz (1984), in 1989 the Carnegie Corporation issued an extremely negative evaluation of our nation's middle schools. In the report, "Turning Points: Preparing American Youth for the 21st Century," the conclusion was put forth that most young adolescents attend massive, impersonal schools, learn from seemingly irrelevant curricula, trust few adults in school, and lack access to health care and counseling. The Carnegie report (1989) recommended the following:

- Develop smaller "communities" or "houses" to lessen the impersonal nature of large middle schools.
- Lower student-to-counselor ratios from several hundred-to-1 to 10-to-1.
- Involve parents and community leaders in schools.
- Develop curricula that produce students who are literate, understand the sciences, and have a sense of health, ethics, and citizenship.
- Have teachers team teach in more flexibly designed curriculum blocks that integrate several disciplines instead of presenting students with disconnected, rigidly separated 50-minute segments.
- Boost students' health and fitness with more in-school programs and help students who need public health care to get it.

Many of these same recommendations were echoed in a report from the National Governors' Association (*America in Transition*, 1989), which stated that the very structure of middle school education in America neglects the basic developmental needs of young adolescents. Many educators and psychologists strongly support these recommendations (Wigfield & Eccles, 1994, 1995). The Edna McConnell Clark Foundation's Program for Disadvantaged Youth is an example of a multiyear, multisite effort designed to implement many of the proposals for middle school improvement. The foundation has engaged the Center for Early Adolescence at the University of North Carolina to guide five urban school districts in their middle school reform (Scales, 1992). In sum, middle schools throughout the nation need a major redesign if they are to be effective in educating adolescents for becoming competent adults in the twenty-first century.

Through its Middle Grade School State Policy Initiative, Carnegie Foundation of New York is implementing the *Turning Points* recommendations in nearly 100 schools and 15 states nationwide. A national evaluation of this initiative is currently underway. Data from the state of Illinois already show that in 42 schools participating in at least one year of the study since 1991, enactment of the *Turning Points* recommendations was associated with significant improvements in students' reading, math, and language arts achievement. In 31 schools with several years of data, the same pattern of positive results was found within schools over time. That is, as schools continued to implement the *Turning Points* recommendations, students' achievement continued to improve (Carnegie Council on Adolescent Development, 1995).

High School Dropouts

For many decades, dropping out of high school has been viewed as a serious educational and societal problem. By leaving high school before graduating, many dropouts take with them educational deficiencies that severely curtail their economic and social well-being throughout their adult lives. We will study the scope of the problem, the causes of dropping out, and ways to reduce dropout rates. While dropping out of high school has negative consequences for youth, the picture is not entirely bleak. Over the last 40 years, the proportion of adolescents who have not finished high school has decreased considerably. In 1940, more than 60 percent of all individuals 25 to 29 years of age had not completed high school. By 1986, this proportion had dropped to less than 14 percent. From 1973 to 1983, the annual dropout rate nationwide fell by almost 20 percent, from 6.3 to 5.2 percent.

Despite the decline in overall high school dropout rates, a major concern is the higher dropout rate of minority-group and low-income students, especially in large cities (Cohen, 1994; Evans & others, 1995). The student dropout rates of most minority groups have been declining, but they remain substantially above those of white adolescents. The proportion of Latino youth who finish high school is not keeping pace with the gains by African Americans. High school completion rates for Latino youth dropped from 63 percent in 1985 to 56 percent in 1989; the completion rate was 52 percent in 1972. In contrast, the high school graduation rate for African American youth increased from 67 percent in 1972 to 76 percent in 1989. The comparable rates for White youth remained the same—82 percent in both 1972 and 1989.

Dropout rates are also high for Native Americans (fewer than 10 percent graduate from high school). In some inner-city areas the dropout rate for ethnic minority students is especially high, reaching more than 50 percent in Chicago, for example.

Students drop out of schools for many reasons (Jacobs, Garnier, & Weisner, 1996; McDougall, Schonert-Reichel, & Hymel, 1996). In one study, almost 50 percent of the dropouts cited school-related reasons for leaving school, such as not liking school or being expelled or suspended (Rumberger, 1983). Twenty percent of the dropouts (but 40 percent of the Latino students) cited economic reasons for leaving school. One-third of the female students dropped out for personal reasons, such as pregnancy or marriage.

Most research on dropouts has focused on high school students. One recent study focused on middle school dropouts (Rumberger, 1995). The observed differences in dropout rates among ethnic groups were related to differences in family background—especially socioeconomic status. Lack of parental academic support, low parental supervision, and low parental educational expectations for their adolescents were also related to dropping out of middle school.

To help reduce the dropout rate, community institutions, especially schools, need to break down the barriers between work and school. Many youth step off the education ladder long before reaching the level needed for a professional career, often with nowhere to step next, and left to their own devices to search for work. These youth need more assistance than they are now receiving. Among the approaches worth considering are these (William T. Grant Foundation Commission, 1988):

- Monitored work experiences, such as through cooperative education, apprenticeships, internships, preemployment training, and youth-operated enterprises.
- Community and neighborhood services, including voluntary and youth-guided services.
- Redirected vocational education, the principal thrust of which should not be preparation for specific jobs but acquisition of basic skills needed for a wide range of jobs.
- Guarantees of continuing education, employment, or training, especially in conjunction with mentor programs.
- Career information and counseling to expose youth to job opportunities and career options as well as to successful role models.
- School volunteer programs, not only for tutoring but also for providing access to adult friends and mentors.

CAREER DEVELOPMENT AND WORK

What is the nature of career development in adolescence? Does working part-time while going to school have a positive or negative affect on adolescent development?

Career Development

What theories have been developed to direct our understanding of adolescents' career choices? What roles do exploration, decision making, and planning play in career development? How do sociocultural factors affect career development?

Theories of Career Development

Three main theories describe the manner in which adolescents make choices about career development: Ginzberg's developmental theory, Super's self-concept theory, and Holland's personality type theory.

Ginzberg's Developmental Theory Developmental **career choice theory** *is Eli Ginzberg's theory that children and adolescents go through three career-choice stages: fantasy, tentative, and realistic* (Ginzberg, 1972). When asked what they want to be when they grow up, young children might

answer "a doctor," "a superhero," "a teacher," "a movie star," "a sports star," or any number of other occupations. In childhood, the future seems to hold almost unlimited opportunities. Ginzberg argues that, until about the age of 11, children are in the *fantasy stage* of career choice. From the ages of 11 to 17, adolescents are in the *tentative stage* of career development, a transition from the fantasy stage of childhood to the realistic decision making of young adulthood. Ginzberg believes that adolescents progress from evaluating their interests (11 to 12 years of age) to evaluating their capacities (13 to 14 years of age) to evaluating their values (15 to 16 years of age). Thinking shifts from less subjective to more realistic career choices at around 17 to 18 years of age. Ginzberg calls the period from 17 to 18 years of age through the early twenties the *realistic stage* of career choice. During this time, the individual extensively explores available careers, then focuses on a particular career, and finally selects a specific job within the career (such as family practitioner or orthopedic surgeon, within the career of doctor).

Critics have attacked Ginzberg's theory on a number of grounds. For one, the initial data were collected from middle-class youth, who probably had more career options open to them. And, as with other developmental theories (such as Piaget's), the time frames are too rigid. Moreover, Ginzberg's theory does not take into account individual differences—some adolescents make mature decisions about careers (and stick with them) at much earlier ages than specified by Ginzberg. Not all children engage in career fantasies, either. In a revision of his theory, Ginzberg (1972) conceded that lower-class individuals do not have as many options available as middle-class individuals do. Ginzberg's general point—that at some point during late adolescence or early adulthood more realistic career choices are made—probably is correct.

Super's Self-Concept Theory Career self-concept **theory** *is Donald Super's theory that individuals' self-concepts play central roles in their career choices. Super believes that it is during adolescence that individuals first construct a career self-concept* (Super, 1976). He emphasizes that career development consists of five different phases. First, at about 14 to 18 years of age, adolescents develop ideas about work that mesh with their already existing global self-concept—this phase is called *crystallization.* Between 18 and 22 years of age, they narrow their career choices and initiate behavior that enables them to enter some type of career—this phase is called *specification.* Between 21 and 24 years of age, young adults complete their education or training and enter the world of work—this phase is called *implementation.* The decision on a specific, appropriate career is made between 25 and 35 years of age—this phase is called *stabilization.* Finally, after the age of 35, individuals seek to advance their careers and reach higher-status positions—this phase is called *consolidation.* The age ranges should be thought of as approximate rather than rigid. Super believes that career exploration in adolescence is a key ingredient of the adolescent's career self-concept. He constructed the Career Development Inventory to assist counselors in promoting adolescents' career exploration.

Holland's Personality-Type Theory Personality-type theory *is John Holland's theory that an effort should be made to match an individual's career choice with his or her personality* (Holland, 1987). Once individuals find a career that fits with their personality, they are more likely to enjoy that particular career and stay in a job for a longer period of time than individuals who work at jobs that are not suitable for their personality. Holland believes there are six basic personality types to be considered when matching the individual's psychological makeup to a career:

- *Realistic.* These individuals show characteristically "masculine" traits. They are physically strong, deal in practical ways with problems, and have very little social know-how. They are best oriented toward practical careers such as labor, farming, truck driving, and construction.
- *Intellectual.* These individuals are conceptually and theoretically oriented. They are thinkers rather than doers. Often they avoid interpersonal relations and are best suited to careers in math and science.
- *Social.* These individuals often show characteristically "feminine" traits, especially those associated with verbal skills and interpersonal relations. They are likely to be best equipped to enter "people" professions such as teaching, social work, counseling, and the like.
- *Conventional.* These youth show a distaste for unstructured activities. They are best suited for jobs as subordinates, such as bank tellers, secretaries, and file clerks.
- *Enterprising.* These individuals energize their verbal abilities toward leading others, dominating individuals, and selling people on issues or products. They are best counseled to enter careers such as sales, politics, and management.
- *Artistic.* These youth prefer to interact with their world through artistic expression, avoiding conventional and interpersonal situations in many instances, and should be oriented toward careers such as art and writing.

If all individuals fell conveniently into Holland's personality types, career counselors would have an easy job. But individuals are more varied and complex than Holland's theory suggests. Even Holland now admits that most individuals are not pure types. Still, the basic idea of matching the abilities of individuals to particular careers is

"Your son has made a career choice, Mildred. He's going to win the lottery and travel a lot."

© 1985; Reprinted courtesy of Bill Hoest and Parade Magazine.

an important contribution to the career field (Brown, 1987). Holland's personality types are incorporated into the Strong-Campbell Vocational Interest Inventory, a widely used measure in career guidance.

Exploration, Decision Making, and Planning

Exploration, decision making, and planning play important roles in adolescents' career choices (Michelozzi, 1996; Wallace-Broscious, Serafica, & Osipow, 1994). In countries where equal employment opportunities have emerged—such as the United States, Canada, Great Britain, and France—exploration of various career paths is critical in the adolescent's career development. Adolescents often approach career exploration and decision making with considerable ambiguity, uncertainty, and stress. Many of the career decisions made by youth involve floundering and unplanned changes. Many adolescents do not adequately explore careers on their own and also receive little direction from guidance counselors at their schools. On the average, it has been found that high school students spend less than three hours per year with guidance counselors, and in some schools the average is even less (National Assessment of Educational Progress, 1976). In many schools, students not only do not know *what* information to seek about careers but also do not know *how* to seek it.

Among the important aspects of planning in career development is awareness of the educational requirements for a particular career. In one study, a sample of 6,029 high school seniors from 57 different school districts in Texas was studied (Grotevant & Durrett, 1980). Students lacked knowledge about two aspects of careers: (a) accurate information about the educational requirements of careers they desired, and (b) information about the vocational interests predominantly associated with their career choices. To further evaluate career planning, refer to Critical Thinking About Children's Development.

Sociocultural Influences

Not every individual born into the world can grow up to become a nuclear physicist or a doctor—there is a genetic limitation that keeps some adolescents from performing at the high intellectual levels necessary to enter such careers. Similarly, there are genetic limitations that restrict some adolescents from becoming professional football players or professional golfers. But there usually are many careers available to each of us, careers that provide a reasonable match with our abilities. Our sociocultural experiences exert strong influences on career choices from among the wide range available. Among the important sociocultural factors that influence career development are social class, parents and peers, and schools.

Social Class   The channels of upward mobility open to lower-class youth are largely educational in nature. The school hierarchy from grade school through high school, as well as through college and graduate school, is programmed to orient individuals toward some type of career. Less than a hundred years ago, only eight years of education were believed to be necessary for vocational competence, and anything beyond that qualified the individual for advanced placement in higher status occupations. By the middle of the twentieth century, the high school diploma had already lost ground as a ticket to career success. College rapidly became a prerequisite for entering a higher status occupation. Employers reason that an individual with a college degree is a better risk than a high school graduate or a high school dropout.

Parents and Peers   Parents and peers also are strong influences on adolescents' career choices. David Elkind (1981) believes that today's parents are pressuring their adolescents to achieve too much too soon. In some cases, though, adolescents do not get challenged enough by their parents. Consider the 25-year-old female who vividly describes the details of her adolescence that later prevented her from seeking a competent career. From early in adolescence, both of her parents encouraged her to finish high school, but at the same time they emphasized that she needed to get a job to help them pay the family's bills. She was never told that she could not go to college, but both parents encouraged her to find someone to marry who could support her financially. This very bright girl is now divorced and feels intellectually cheated by her parents, who socialized her in the direction of marriage and away from a college education.

From an early age, children see and hear about what jobs their parents have. In some cases, parents even take their children to work with them on jobs. Recently, when we were building our house, the bricklayer brought his two sons to help with the work. They were only 14 years old, yet were already engaging in apprenticeship work with their father.

Unfortunately, many parents want to live vicariously through their son's or daughter's career achievements. The mother who did not get into medical school and the father who did not make it as a professional athlete may pressure their youth to achieve a career status that is beyond the youth's talents.

Many factors influence the parent's role in the adolescent's career development. For one, mothers who work regularly outside the home and show effort and pride in their work probably have strong influences on their adolescents' career development. A reasonable conclusion is that when both parents work and enjoy their work, adolescents learn work values from both parents. Peers also can influence the adolescent's career development. In one study, when adolescents had friends and parents with high career standards, they were more likely to seek higher career status jobs, even if they came from low-income families (Simpson, 1962).

School Influences   Schools, teachers, and counselors can exert a powerful influence on adolescents' career development. School is the primary setting where individuals first encounter the world of work. School provides an

Imagine that you have been hired as the new director of career development for a school system. How would you get career development to become a more central feature of the school system's curriculum? What would your career education program feature? What developmental considerations would you take into account? By developing guidelines for a career development program for a school system, you are learning to think critically by *applying a developmental framework to understand behavior.*

percent had no established committee to review career information resources. When students talked to counselors, it was more often about high school courses than about career guidance.

School counseling has been criticized heavily, both inside and outside the educational establishment. Insiders complain about the large number of students per school counselor and the weight of non-counseling administrative duties. Outsiders complain that school counseling is ineffective, biased, and a waste of money. Short of a new profession, several options are possible (William T. Grant Foundation Commission, 1988). First, twice the number of counselors are needed to meet all students' needs. Second, there could be a redefinition of teachers' roles, accompanied by retraining and reduction in teaching loads, so that classroom teachers could assume a stronger role in handling the counseling needs of adolescents. The professional counselor's role in this plan would be to train and assist teachers in their counseling and to provide direct counseling in situations the teacher could not handle. Third, the whole idea of school counselors would be abandoned and counselors would be located elsewhere—in neighborhood social service centers or labor offices, for example. (West Germany forbids teachers to give career counseling, reserving this task for officials in well-developed networks of labor offices.)

The College Board Commission on Precollege Guidance and Counseling (1986) recommends other alternatives. It believes that local school districts should develop broad-based planning that actively involves the home, school, and community. Advocating better-trained counselors, the Commission supports stronger partnerships between home and school to increase two-way communication about student progress and better collaboration among schools, community agencies, colleges, businesses, and other community resources. To further evaluate career development in schools, refer to Critical Thinking About Children's Development.

*Adolescents at a job fair seeking information about careers.
Improving adolescents' awareness of career options and educational
requirements is an important agenda for our nation.*

atmosphere for continuing self-development in relation to achievement and work. And school is the only institution in our society presently capable of providing the delivery systems necessary for career education—instruction, guidance, placement, and community connections.

A national survey revealed the nature of career information available to adolescents (Chapman & Katz, 1983). The most common single resource was the *Occupational Outlook Handbook (OOH)*, with 92 percent of the schools having one or more copies. The second major source was the *Dictionary of Occupational Titles (DOT)*, with 82 percent having this book available for students. Less than 30

Gender Roles and Parent-Adolescent
Relationships   Because many females have been socialized to adopt nurturing roles rather than career or achieving roles, traditionally they have not planned seriously for careers, have not explored career options extensively, and have restricted their career choices to careers that are gender-stereotyped (Jozefowicz, Barber, & Mollasis, 1994). The motivation for work is the same for both sexes. However,

females and males make different choices because of their socialization experiences and the way that social forces structure the opportunities available to them.

As growing numbers of females pursue careers, they are faced with questions involving career and family. Should they delay marriage and childbearing and establish their career first? Or should they combine their career, marriage, and childbearing in their twenties? Some females in the last decade have embraced the domestic patterns of an earlier historical period. They have married, borne children, and committed themselves to full-time mothering. These "traditional" females have worked outside the home only intermittently, if at all, and have subordinated the work role to the family role.

> The test for whether or not you can hold a job should not be the arrangement of your chromosomes.
>
> —Bella Abzug,
> Bella! (1972)

Many other females, though, have veered from this time-honored path. They have postponed, and even forgotten, motherhood. They have developed committed, permanent ties to the workplace that resemble the pattern once reserved only for males. When they have had children, they have strived to combine a career and motherhood. While there have always been "career" females, today their numbers are growing at an unprecedented rate.

> Yes, I am wise but it is wisdom for the pain.
> Yes, I've paid the price but look how much
> I've gained. If I have to I can do anything.
> I am strong, I am invincible, I am woman . . .
>
> —Helen Reddy

Work

One of the greatest changes in adolescents' lives in recent years has been the increased number of adolescents who work in some part-time capacity and still attend school on a regular basis. Our discussion of adolescents and work includes information about the sociohistorical context of adolescent work, the advantages and disadvantages of part-time work, and adolescent unemployment.

The Sociohistorical Context of Adolescent Work

Over the past century, the percentage of youth who work full-time as opposed to those who are in school has decreased dramatically. In the late 1800s, fewer than one of every twenty high school age adolescents were in school. Today more than nine of every ten adolescents receive high school diplomas. In the nineteenth century, many adolescents learned a trade from their father or some other adult member of the community.

Even though prolonged education has kept many contemporary youth from holding full-time jobs, it has not prevented them from working on a part-time basis while going to school. Most high school seniors have had some work experience. In a national survey of 17,000 high school seniors, three of four reported some job income during the average school week (Bachman, 1982). For 41 percent of the males and 30 percent of the females, this income exceeded $50 a week. The typical part-time job for high school seniors involves 16 to 20 hours of work per week, although 10 percent work 30 hours a week or more.

In 1940, only one of twenty-five tenth-grade males attended school and simultaneously worked part-time. In the 1970s, the number increased to more than one of every four. And, in the 1980s, as just indicated, three of four combined school and part-time work. Adolescents also are working longer hours now than in the past. For example, the number of 14- to 15-year-olds who work more than 14 hours per week has increased substantially in the last three decades. A similar picture emerges for 16-year-olds. In 1960, 44 percent of 16-year-old males who attended school worked more than 14 hours a week, but by the 1980s the figure had increased to more than 60 percent.

What kinds of jobs are adolescents working at today? About 17 percent who work do so in restaurants, such as McDonald's and Burger King, waiting on customers and cleaning up. Other adolescents work in retail stores as cashiers or salespeople (about 20 percent), in offices as clerical assistants (about 10 percent), or as unskilled laborers (about 10 percent). In one study, boys reported higher self-esteem and well-being when they perceived that their jobs were providing skills that would be useful to them in the future (Mortimer & others, 1992).

Do male and female adolescents take the same types of jobs, and are they paid equally? Some jobs are held almost exclusively by male adolescents—busboy, gardener, manual laborer, and newspaper carrier—while other jobs are held almost exclusively by female adolescents—babysitter and maid. Male adolescents work longer hours and are paid more per hour than female adolescents (Helson, Elliot, & Leigh, 1989).

Advantages and Disadvantages of Part-Time Work in Adolescence

Does the increase in work have benefits for adolescents? In some cases, yes; in others, no. Ellen Greenberger and Laurence Steinberg (1981, 1986) examined the work experiences of students in four California high schools. Their findings disproved some common myths. For example, generally it is assumed that adolescents get extensive on-the-job training when they are hired for work. The reality is that they got little training at all. Also, it is assumed that youths—through work experiences—learn to get along better with adults. However, adolescents reported that they rarely felt close to the adults with whom they worked. The work experiences of the adolescents did help them to understand how the business world works,

John W. Santrock

What are the effects of working and going to school on adolescents' grades and integration into school activities?

how to get and how to keep a job, and how to manage money. Working also helped adolescents to learn to budget their time, to take pride in their accomplishments, and to evaluate their goals. But working adolescents often have to give up sports, social affairs with peers, and sometimes sleep. And they have to balance the demands of work, school, family, and peers.

Greenberger and Steinberg asked students about their grade point averages, school attendance, satisfaction from school, and the number of hours spent studying and participating in extracurricular activities since they began working. They found that the working adolescents had lower grade point averages than nonworking adolescents. More than one of four students reported that their grades dropped when they began working; only one of nine said that their grades improved. But it was not just working that affected adolescents' grades—more importantly, it was *how long* they worked. Tenth-graders who worked more than 14 hours a week suffered a drop in grades. Eleventh-graders worked up to 20 hours a week before their grades dropped. When adolescents spend more than 20 hours per week working, there is little time to study for tests and to complete homework assignments.

In addition to work affecting grades, working adolescents felt less involved in school, were absent more, and said that they did not enjoy school as much as their nonworking counterparts did. Adolescents who worked also spent less time with their families—but just as much time with their peers—as their nonworking counterparts. Adolescents who worked long hours also were more frequent users of alcohol and marijuana.

More recent research confirms the link between part-time work during adolescence and problem behavior (Hansen, 1996). In one recent large-scale study, the role of part-time work in the adjustment of more than 70,000 high school seniors was investigated (Bachman & Schulenberg, 1993). Consistent with other research, part-time work in high school was associated with a number of problem behaviors: insufficient sleep, not eating breakfast, not exercising, not having enough leisure time, and using drugs. For the most part, the results occurred even when students worked 1 to 5 hours per week, but they became more pronounced after 20 hours of work per week. And in another recent study, taking on a job for more than 20 hours per week was associated with increasing disengagement from school, increased delinquency and drug use, increased autonomy from parents, and diminished self-reliance (Steinberg, Fegley, & Dornbusch, 1993). In sum, the overwhelming evidence is that working part-time while going to high school is associated with a number of problem behaviors, especially when the work consumes 20 or more hours of the adolescent's week.

Some states have responded to these findings by limiting the number of hours adolescents can work while they are attending secondary school. In 1986, in Pinellas County, Florida, a new law placed a cap on the previously unregulated hours that adolescents could work while school is in session. The allowable limit was set at 30 hours, which—based on research evidence—is still too high.

Unemployment

In some cases, the media have exaggerated the degree of adolescent unemployment. For example, based on data collected by the U.S. Department of Labor, nine of ten adolescents are either in school, working at a job, or both. Only 5 percent are out of school, without a job, and looking for full-time employment. Most adolescents who are unemployed are not unemployed for long. Only 10 percent are without a job for 6 months or longer. Most unemployed adolescents are school dropouts.

Certain segments of the adolescent population, however, are more likely than others to be unemployed. For example, a disproportionate percentage of unemployed adolescents are African American. The unemployment situation is especially acute for African American and Latino youth between the ages of 16 and 19. The job situation, however, has improved somewhat for African American adolescents: In 1969, 44 percent of African American 16- to 19-year-olds were unemployed; today, that figure is approximately 32 percent.

At this point we have discussed a number of ideas about schools, careers, and work in adolescence. A summary of these ideas is presented in concept table 16.2.

CONCEPT TABLE 16.2

Schools, Careers, and Work in Adolescence

Concept	Processes/Related Ideas	Characteristics/Description
Schools	The controversy surrounding secondary schools	In the 1980s, the back-to-basics movement gained momentum. The back-to-basics movement emphasizes rigorous academic training. Many experts on education and development believe that the back-to-basics movement does not adequately address individual variations among children and adolescents. They also believe that education should be more comprehensive, focusing on social as well as cognitive development.
	Transition to middle or junior high school	The emergence of junior highs in the 1920s and 1930s was justified on the basis of physical, cognitive, and social changes in early adolescence and the need for more schools in response to a growing student population. Middle schools have become more popular in recent years and coincide with puberty's earlier arrival. The transition to middle or junior high school coincides with many social, familial, and individual changes in the adolescent's life. The transition involves moving from the top-dog to the lowest position.
	Effective schools for young adolescents	Successful schools for young adolescents take individual differences in development seriously, show a deep concern for what is known about early adolescence, and emphasize social and emotional development as much as intellectual development. In 1989, the Carnegie Corporation recommended a major redesign of middle schools.
	High school dropouts	Dropping out has been a serious problem for decades. Many dropouts have educational deficiencies that curtail their economic and social well-being for much of their adult life. Some progress has been made in that dropout rates for most ethnic minority groups have declined in recent decades, although dropout rates for inner-city, low-income minorities and Hispanic Americans are still precariously high. Dropping out of school is associated with demographic, family-related, peer-related, school-related, economic and individual factors. Reducing the dropout rate and improving the lives of noncollege youth could be accomplished by strengthening schools and bridging the gap between school and work.
Careers and Work	Career development	Three theories are Ginzberg's developmental theory, Super's self-concept theory, and Holland's personality-type theory. Exploration of career options is a critical aspect of career development in countries where equal employment opportunities exist. Many youth flounder and make unplanned career choice changes. Students also need more knowledge about the education and ability requirements of various careers. Sociocultural influences involve social class, parents and peers, and schools. The channels of opportunity for lower-class youth are largely educational. Many factors influence the parent's role in the adolescent's career development. School counseling has been criticized heavily and recommendations have been made for its improvement. Parents play an important role in their sons' and daughters' career development. Because many females have been socialized to adopt nurturing rather than career or achieving roles, they have not adequately prepared for careers. As growing numbers of females pursue careers, they are faced with questions involving career and family. Parents often have different expectations, give different advice, and provide different opportunities in career development for their sons and daughters.
	Work	Adolescents are not as likely to hold full-time jobs today as their adolescent counterparts from the nineteenth century. There has been a tremendous increase in the number of adolescents who work part-time and go to school, which has both advantages and disadvantages. In some cases, adolescent unemployment has been exaggerated; however, for many minority-group adolescents, unemployment is a major problem.

When we think of the changes that characterize adolescence, we often think of the high drama of puberty or the socioemotional changes of identity and independence. But some impressive cognitive changes also arrive with adolescence.

We began this chapter by exploring the cognitive worlds of adolescents, focusing on Piaget's stage of formal operational thought, adolescent egocentrism, and decision making. Our coverage then turned to values and religion. We also studied schools for adolescents, examining the controversy surrounding secondary schools, the transition to middle or junior high school, health education, and high school dropouts. We read about a number of aspects of career development, including theories of career development, exploration, planning, and decision making, and sociocultural influences. We described the nature of work during adolescence by considering the sociohistorical context of adolescent work, advantages and disadvantages of part-time work, and unemployment.

Remember that you can obtain an overall summary of the chapter by again reading the two concept tables on pages 500 and 510. In the next chapter, we continue our study of adolescence by focusing on socioemotional development.

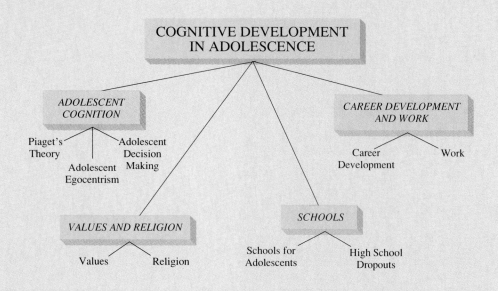

hypothetical-deductive reasoning Piaget's formal operational concept that adolescents have the cognitive ability to develop hypotheses, or best guesses, about ways to solve problems, such as an algebraic equation. 491

early formal operational thought Adolescents' increased ability to think in hypothetical ways which produces unconstrained thoughts with unlimited possibilities. In this early period, the world is perceived too subjectively and idealistically. 493

late formal operational thought A restoration of intellectual balance during which the adolescent accommodates to the cognitive upheaval that has taken place. Adolescents now test out the products of their reasoning against experience and consolidation of formal operational thought takes place. 493

adolescent egocentrism The heightened self-consciousness of adolescents that is reflected in their belief that others are as interested in them as they are in themselves, and in their sense of personal uniqueness. 494

imaginary audience Adolescents' heightened self-consciousness, reflected in their belief that others are as interested in them as they themselves are; attention-getting behavior motivated by a desire to be noticed, visible, and "on stage." 494

personal fable The part of adolescent egocentrism that involves an adolescent's sense of uniqueness. 494

top-dog phenomenon The circumstance of moving from the top position in elementary school to the lowest position in middle or junior high school. 502

developmental career choice theory Ginzberg's theory that children and adolescents go through three career choice stages—fantasy, tentative, and realistic. 504

career self-concept theory Super's theory that individuals' self-concepts play central roles in their career choices. 504

personality-type theory Holland's theory that an effort should be made to match an individual's career choice with his or her personality. 505

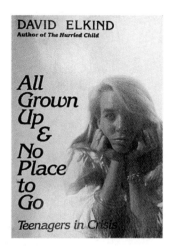

All Grown Up & No Place to Go: Teenagers in Crisis
(1984) by David Elkind.
Reading, MA: Addison-Wesley.

Elkind believes that raising teenagers in today's world is more difficult than ever. He argues that teenagers are expected to confront adult challenges too early in their development. By being pressured into adult roles too soon, today's youth are all grown up with no place to go, hence the title of the book. Elkind believes that the main reason teenagers are pressed into adult roles too early is that parents are more committed to their own self-fulfillment than to their adolescents'. These parents of the "me" generation are often too quick to accept their teenagers' outward sophistication as a sign of emotional maturity. Teens' emotional needs are also neglected by a school system that is up-to-date in computer gadgetry but is bankrupt in responding to adolescents' emotional needs and individual differences, says Elkind. He also believes that the media exploit adolescents by appealing to their vulnerability to peer pressure.

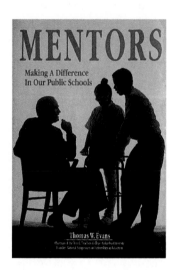

Mentors
(1992) by Thomas Evans.
Princeton, NJ: Peterson's Guides.

This book describes the enriching experience of dozens of motivated individuals—from eye-to-the-future executives to conscientious parents—whose passion for education, especially the education of poor children, has carried them to the classroom and beyond. Author Evans describes how to make a difference in a child's life. The difference consists of becoming involved as a mentor for a child and developing a role as a tutor for students in a one-on-one situation. Evans gives explicit instructions on how to become an effective mentor of a child. Mentoring has helped many children and adolescents become more competent and Evans's book is an excellent overview of the topic.

IMPROVING THE LIVES OF CHILDREN

Improving the lives of children involves providing needed support for adolescents, modifying parental expectations for girls and boys, presenting more educational options, bridging the gap between school and work, and developing better education for bright, gifted girls.

HEALTH AND WELL-BEING

Needed Support for Adolescents

In a recent report on the state of America's children, the Children's Defense Fund (1992) described what life is like for all too many adolescents. When sixth-graders in a poverty-stricken area of St. Louis were asked to describe a perfect day, one boy said he would erase the world, then he would sit and think. Asked if he wouldn't rather go outside and play, the boy responded, "Are you kidding, out there?"

The world is dangerous and unwelcome for too many of America's teenagers, especially those who live in low-income families, neighborhoods, and schools. Many adolescents are resilient and cope with the challenges of adolescence without any major setbacks, but other adolescents struggle unsuccessfully to find jobs, are written off as losses by their schools, become pregnant before they are ready to become parents, or risk their health through drug or alcohol abuse.

Adolescents in almost any era have been risk-takers, testing limits and making short-sighted judgments. But the consequences of choosing a course of risk-taking today are more serious than they have ever been, ranging from single parenthood and extended poverty to AIDS and death by shooting (Lefkowitz, Kahlbaugh, & Sigman, 1994). Three decades ago, adolescents who dropped out of school could usually find a job and anticipate earning enough money to eventually support a family. Today, high school dropouts have only one chance in three of finding a full-time job.

Until the past decade, unprotected sex might have led to pregnancy, but it rarely led to death. Today is a different story. Many young people with AIDS were infected with the fatal disease in adolescence. Adolescents' feelings of invulnerability are causing many of them to ignore the risks of unprotected sex.

Thirty years ago, adolescent boys might get into a fistfight. Today, in some neighborhoods, they shoot each other. Thirty percent of the adolescents living in high-crime neighborhoods of Chicago have witnessed a homicide by the time they are 15 years of age, and more than 70 percent have seen a serious assault.

Each adolescent who reaches adulthood unhealthy, unskilled, or alienated keeps our nation from being as competent and productive as it can be.

John W. Santrock

FAMILIES AND PARENTING

Parents' Different Career Expectations for Girls and Boys

Parents play an important role in their sons' and daughters' career development. In one recent study, 1,500 mothers and their young adolescent sons and daughters were studied to determine the role played by maternal expectations, advice, and provision of opportunities in their sons' and daughters' occupational aspirations (Harold & Eccles, 1990). Mothers were more likely to encourage their sons to consider the military, to expect their sons to go into the military right after high school, and to discuss with their sons the education needed for, and likely income of, different jobs. Expectations of marriage right after high school and discussions of the problems of combining work and family were more common of mothers' interaction with daughters. Also, mothers were more worried that their daughters would not have a happy marriage and were more likely to want their sons to have a job that would support a family.

Findings of the study also indicated that mothers worked more with boys than girls on the computer and provided their sons with more computers, software, and programs than they did their daughters. The mothers bought more math or science books and games

for boys and more often enrolled their sons than their daughters in computer classes. Boys were provided more sports opportunities, whereas girls were given more opportunities in music, art, and dance. Mothers said boys have more talent in math and are better suited for careers involving math, while they believed that girls have more talent in English and are better suited at careers related to English. In sum, the study showed that mothers see and treat their sons and daughters differently—in terms of the advice they give, the opportunities they provide, the expectations and aspirations they hold, and the ability they perceive.

Were advice, opportunities, expectations, and perceived ability associated with adolescents' occupational aspirations in this study? Yes, they were. Mothers tended to provide more math or science books to daughters who aspired to male-typed occupations (nontraditional girls) than to daughters who aspired to female-typed jobs (traditional girls). Mothers talked more about the importance of looking good to their daughters who aspired to more female-type occupations than to their daughters who aspired to male-typed jobs. They

also expected daughters who aspired to more female-typed occupations to be more likely to get married right after high school than their nontraditional counterparts. Further, several of the mothers' and adolescent daughters' values regarding family and work roles were related. For example, the mother's belief that it was better if the man was a breadwinner and the woman took care of the family was related to the adolescent's identical belief. The mother's belief that working mothers can establish just as warm and secure a relationship with their children as nonworking mothers was related to their adolescent's belief that it is OK for mothers to have full-time careers. Nontraditional girls were more likely to endorse the belief that women are better wives and mothers if they have paid jobs. In sum, this research study documented that parental socialization practices in the form of provision of opportunities, expectations, and beliefs are important sources of adolescent females' and males' occupational aspirations. Also in one recent study, teacher support was a key factor in encouraging girls to pursue math and science courses (MacLean & others, 1994).

EDUCATION

Toward More Options

The William T. Grant Foundation Commission (1988) endorsed a mixture of abstract and practical learning opportunities and a combination of conceptual study with concrete applications and practical problem solving. They urged that a new look should be taken at cooperative education, work-study, apprenticeships, internships, service-learning, community service, youth-operated enterprises, on-the-job training, and mentorship. They became convinced that these experience-based educational opportunities can benefit adolescents.

Education does not take place just in a traditional school. It also can take place in the workplace, the media, museums and cultural institutions, public and

nonprofit agencies, youth agencies and community services, field studies and workshops, and community-based organizations in the inner city. Trigonometry learned in the school's machine shop or in the workplace complements learning in the classroom. Botany can be learned in a horticultural laboratory, at a field station, or, perhaps better yet, in both locations.

The commission also agreed with educator John Goodlad (1984) that appropriately conceived vocational technical education, combining hands-on work experience with mastery of academic conceptual ideas, deserves far more attention than it currently enjoys among educators and policymakers. The type of individual who wants to learn

how to apply geometry before and while learning the theorems, or to overhaul a carburetor and valves before and while learning the theories of combustion and energy conversion, is often turned off by an educational system that almost uniformly insists that classroom-taught abstract ideas and theories must precede application.

Educational methods and work experiences need to be better linked. The responsibility of schools is not solely to prepare students for college or work, and cooperative work strategies, experiential learning, and instruction that requires thinking skills instead of rote memorization better prepare adolescents for the complex workplace they will soon have to enter.

Bridging the Gap Between School and Work

How can adolescents be helped to bridge the gap between school and work? For adolescents bound for higher education and a professional degree, the educational system provides ladders from school to career. Most youth, though, step off the educational ladder before reaching the level of a professional career. Often, they are on their own in their search for work. Recommendations for bridging the gap from school to work include the following (William T. Grant Foundation Commission, 1988):

1. Monitored work experiences, including cooperative education, internships, apprenticeships, preemployment training, and youth-operated enterprises, should be implemented. These experiences provide opportunities for youth to gain work experience, to be exposed to adult supervisors and models in the workplace, and to relate their academic training to the workplace.

2. Community and neighborhood services, including individual voluntary service and youth-guided services, should be expanded. Youth need experiences not only as workers but as citizens. Service programs not only expose youth to the adult world, but provide them with a sense of the obligations of citizenship in building a more caring and competent society.

3. Vocational education should be redirected. With few exceptions, today's vocational education does not prepare youth adequately for specific jobs. However, its hands-on methods can provide students with valuable and effective ways of acquiring skills they will need to be successful in a number of jobs. One promising approach is the career academy, which originated in Philadelphia and recently was replicated extensively in California (Glover & Marshall, 1993). At the end of the ninth grade, students at risk for failure are identified and invited to volunteer for a program based on a school-within-a-school format. The students and teachers remain together for 3 years. Students spend the tenth grade catching up on academic course work; computers and field trips are integrated into the curriculum. In the eleventh grade, every student has a mentor from industry who introduces the student to his or her workplace and joins the student for recreational activities at least once a month. By the end of the eleventh grade, the student obtains a summer job with one of the business partners. Students who stay in the program are promised a job when they graduate from high school.

4. Incentives need to be introduced. Low motivation and low expectations for success in the workplace often restrict adolescents' educational achievement. Recent efforts to guarantee postsecondary and continuing education and to provide guaranteed employment, and guaranteed work-related training for students who do well show promise of encouraging adolescents to work harder and be more successful in school.

5. Career information and counseling need to be improved. A variety of information and counseling approaches can be implemented to expose adolescents to job opportunities and career options. These services can be offered both in school and in community settings. They include setting up career information centers, developing the capacity of parents as career educators, and expanding the work of community-based organizations.

6. More school volunteers should be used. Tutoring is the most common form of school volunteer activity. However, adults are needed even more generally—as friends, as mentors for opening up career opportunities, and for assisting youth in mastering the dilemmas of living in a stressful time.

Improving education, elevating skill levels, and providing "hands-on" experience will help adolescents to bridge the gap between school and work. We need to address the needs of youth if we are to retain the confidence of youth who have been brought up to believe in the promise of the American Dream.

The deepest hunger in humans is the desire to be appreciated.
—**William James**

Educating Bright, Gifted Girls

Some of the brightest and most gifted females do not have achievement and career aspirations that match their talents. In one study, high-achieving females had much lower expectations for success than high-achieving males (Stipak & Hoffman, 1980). In the gifted research program at Johns Hopkins University, many mathematically precocious females did select scientific and medical careers, although only 46 percent aspired to a full-time career, compared to 98 percent of the males (Fox, Brody, & Tobin, 1979).

To help talented females redirect their life paths, some high schools are using programs developed by colleges and universities. Project CHOICE (Creating Her Options In Career Education) was designed by Case Western University to detect barriers in reaching one's potential. Gifted eleventh-grade females received individualized counseling that included interviews with female role models, referral to appropriate occupational groups, and information about career workshops. A program at the University of Nebraska was successful in encouraging talented female high school students to pursue more prestigious careers. This was accomplished through individual counseling and participation in a "Perfect Future Day," in which girls shared their career fantasies and discussed barriers that might impede their fantasies. Internal and external constraints were evaluated, gender-role stereotypes were discouraged, and high aspirations were applauded. While these programs have short-term success in redirecting the career paths of high-ability females, in some instances the effects fade over time—6 months or more, for example. It is important to be concerned about improving the career alternatives for all female youth, however, not just those of high ability.

Some of the brightest and most gifted females do not have achievement and career aspirations that match their talents. To help talented females improve their career development choices, some colleges and universities have created career education programs for secondary school students.

Socioemotional Development
in Adolescence

*In case you're worried about what's going
to become of the younger generation, it's
going to grow up and start worrying about
the younger generation.*

—**Roger Allen**

> "Who are you?" said the caterpillar. Alice replied rather shyly, "I—I hardly know, sir, just at present—at least I know who I was when I got up this morning, but I must have changed several times since then."
>
> —Lewis Carroll,
> *Alice in Wonderland*, 1865

IMAGES OF CHILDREN

A 15-Year-Old Girl's Self-Description

How do adolescents describe themselves? How would you have described yourself when you were 15 years old? What features would you have emphasized? The following is a self-portrait of one 15-year-old girl:

What am I like as a person? Complicated! I'm sensitive, friendly, outgoing, popular, and tolerant, though I can also be shy, self-conscious, and even obnoxious. Obnoxious! I'd *like* to be friendly and tolerant all of the time. That's the kind of person I *want* to be, and I'm disappointed when I'm not. I'm responsible, even studious now and then, but on the other hand, I'm a goof-off, too, because if you're too studious, you won't be popular. I don't usually do that well at school. I'm a pretty cheerful person, especially with my friends, where I can even get rowdy. At home I'm more likely to be anxious around my parents. They expect me to get all A's. It's not fair! I worry about how I probably *should* get better grades. But I'd be mortified in the eyes of my friends. So I'm usually pretty stressed-out at home, or sarcastic, since my parents are always on my case. But I really don't understand how I can switch so fast. I mean, how can I be cheerful one minute, anxious the next, and then be sarcastic? Which one is the *real* me? Sometimes, I feel phony, especially around boys. Say I think some guy might be interested in asking me out, I try to act different, like Madonna. I'll be flirtatious and fun-loving. And then everybody, I mean *everybody* else is looking at me like they think I'm totally weird. Then I get self-conscious and embarrassed and become radically introverted, and I don't know who I really am! Am I just trying to impress them or what? But I don't really care what they think anyway. I don't *want* to care, that is. I just want to know what my close friends think. I can be my true self with my close friends. I can't be my real self with my parents. They don't understand me. What do *they* know about what it's like to be a teenager? They still treat me like I'm still a kid. At least at school people treat you more like you're an adult. That gets confusing, though. I mean, which am I, a kid or an adult? It's scary, too, because I don't have any idea what I want to be when I grow up. I mean, I have lots of *ideas*. My friend Sheryl and I talk about whether we'll be stewardesses, or teachers, or nurses, veterinarians, maybe mothers, or actresses. I know I *don't* want to be a waitress or a secretary. But how do you decide all of this? I really don't know. I mean, I think about it a lot, but I can't resolve it. There are days when I wish I could just become immune to myself. (Harter, 1990, p. 352–353)

PREVIEW

The 15-year-old girl's self-description that you just read about exemplifies the increased interest in self-portrayal and search for an identity during adolescence. Later in this chapter we will explore the nature of identity development in adolescence, but before we get to the topic of identity we will examine these aspects of adolescence: families, peers, culture, and rites of passage.

John W. Santrock

FAMILIES

In chapter 14 we discussed how, during middle and late childhood, parents spend less time with their children than in early childhood, discipline involves an increased use of reasoning and deprivation of privileges, there is a gradual transfer of control from parents to children but still within the boundary of coregulation, and parents and children increasingly respond to each other on the basis of labels. Some of the most important issues and questions that need to be raised about family relationships in adolescence are these: What is the nature of autonomy and attachment in adolescence? How extensive is parent-adolescent conflict, and how does it influence the adolescent's development? Does maturation of adolescents and parents influence how adolescents and parents interact?

Autonomy and Attachment

The adolescent's push for autonomy and responsibility puzzles and angers many parents. Parents see their teenager slipping from their grasp. They may have an urge to take stronger control as the adolescent seeks autonomy and responsibility. Heated emotional exchanges may ensue, with either side calling names, making threats, and doing whatever seems necessary to gain control. Parents may seem frustrated because they *expect* their teenager to heed their advice, to want to spend time with the family, and to grow up to do what is right. Most parents anticipate that their teenager will have some difficulty adjusting to the changes that adolescence brings, but few parents can imagine and predict just how strong an adolescent's desires will be to spend time with peers or how much adolescents will want to show that it is they—not their parents—who are responsible for their successes and failures.

The ability to attain autonomy and gain control over one's behavior in adolescence is acquired through appropriate adult reactions to the adolescent's desire for control (Keener & Boykin, 1996; Urberg & Wolowicz, 1996). At the onset of adolescence, the average individual does not have the knowledge to make appropriate or mature decisions in all areas of life. As the adolescent pushes for autonomy, the wise adult relinquishes control in those areas where the adolescent can make reasonable decisions but continues to guide the adolescent to make reasonable decisions in areas where the adolescent's knowledge is more limited. Gradually, adolescents acquire the ability to make mature decisions on their own.

But adolescents do not simply move away from parental influence into a decision-making process all their own. There is continued connectedness to parents as adolescents move toward and gain autonomy. In the last decade, developmentalists have begun to explore the role of secure attachment, and related concepts such as connectedness to parents, in adolescent development. They believe that attachment to parents in adolescence may facilitate the adolescent's social competence and well-being, as reflected in such characteristics as self-esteem, emotional adjustment, and physical health (Allen & Kuperminc, 1995; Black & McCartney, 1995). For example, adolescents who have secure relationships with their parents have higher self-esteem and better emotional well-being. In contrast, emotional detachment from parents is associated with greater feelings of parental rejection and a lower sense of one's own social and romantic attractiveness. Thus, attachment to parents during adolescence may serve the adaptive function of providing a secure base from which adolescents can explore and master new environments and a widening social world in a psychologically healthy manner (Bell, 1995). Secure attachment to parents may buffer adolescents from the anxiety and potential feelings of depression or emotional distress associated with the transition from childhood to adulthood. In one study, when young adolescents had a secure attachment to their parents, they perceived their family as cohesive and reported little social anxiety or feelings of depression (Papini, Roggman, & Anderson, 1990).

> *We cannot build the future for our youth, but we can build our youth for the future.*
>
> —**Franklin D. Roosevelt, 1940**

Secure attachment or connectedness to parents promotes competent peer relations and positive close relationships outside of the family. In one study in which attachment to parents and peers was assessed (Armsden & Greenberg, 1987), adolescents who were securely attached to parents were also securely attached to peers; those who were insecurely attached to parents were also more likely to be insecurely attached to peers. In another study, college students who were securely attached to their parents as young children were more likely to have securely attached relationships with friends, dates, and spouses than their insecurely attached counterparts (Hazen & Shaver, 1987). And in yet another study, older adolescents who had an ambivalent attachment history with their parents reported greater jealousy, conflict and dependency along with less satisfaction in their relationship with their best friend than their securely attached counterparts (Fisher, 1990). There are times when adolescents reject closeness, connection, and attachment to their parents as they assert their ability to make decisions and to develop an identity. But for the most part, the worlds of parents and peers are coordinated and connected, not uncoordinated and disconnected.

Parent-Adolescent Conflict

While attachment and connectedness to parents remains strong during adolescence, the attachment and connectedness is not always smooth. Early adolescence is a time when conflict with parents escalates beyond childhood levels. This increase may be due to a number of factors: the biological changes of puberty, cognitive changes involving increased idealism and logical reasoning, social changes focused on independence and identity, maturational changes in parents, and violated expectations on the part of parents and adolescents. The adolescent compares her parents to an ideal standard and then criticizes the flaws. A 13-year-old girl tells her mother, "That is the tackiest-looking dress I have ever seen. Nobody would be caught dead wearing that." The adolescent demands logical explanations for comments and discipline. A 14-year-old boy tells his mother, "What do you mean I have to be home at 10 P.M. because it's the way we do things around here? Why do we do things around here that way? It doesn't make sense to me."

Many parents see their adolescent changing from a compliant child to someone who is noncompliant, oppositional, and resistant to parental standards. When this happens, parents tend to clamp down and put more pressure on the adolescent to conform to parental standards. Parents often expect their adolescents to become mature adults overnight instead of understanding that the journey takes 10 to 15 years. Parents who recognize that this transition takes time handle their youth more competently and calmly than those who demand immediate conformity to adult standards. The opposite tactic—letting adolescents do as they please without supervision—is also unwise.

Conflict with parents does increase in early adolescence, but it does not reach the tumultuous proportions G. Stanley Hall envisioned at the beginning of the twentieth century (Holmbeck, 1996; Holmbeck, Pitkoff, & Brooks-Gunn, 1995). Rather, much of the conflict involves the everyday events of family life such as keeping a bedroom clean, dressing neatly, getting home by a certain time, not talking forever on the phone, and so on. The conflicts rarely involved major dilemmas like drugs and delinquency.

It is not unusual to hear parents of young adolescents ask, "Is it ever going to get better?" Things usually do get better as adolescents move from early to late adolescence. Conflict with parents often escalates during early adolescence, remains somewhat stable during the high school years, and then lessens as the adolescent reaches 17 to 20 years of age. Parent-adolescent relationships become more positive if adolescents go away to college than if they stay at home and go to college (Sullivan & Sullivan, 1980).

When I was a boy of 14, my father was so ignorant I could hardly stand to have the man around. But when I got to be 21, I was astonished at how much he had learnt in 7 years.

—**Mark Twain**

The everyday conflicts that characterize parent-adolescent relationships may actually serve a positive developmental function. These minor disputes and negotiations facilitate the adolescent's transition from being dependent on parents to becoming an autonomous individual. For example, in one study, adolescents who expressed disagreement with parents explored identity development more actively than adolescents who did not express disagreement with their parents (Cooper & others, 1982). One way for parents to cope with the adolescent's push for independence and identity is to recognize that adolescence is a 10- to 15-year transitional period in the journey to adulthood rather than an overnight accomplishment. Recognizing that conflict and negotiation can serve a positive developmental function can tone down parental hostility, too. Understanding parent-adolescent conflict, though, is not simple.

In sum, the old model of parent-adolescent relationships suggested that as adolescents mature they detach themselves from parents and move into a world of autonomy apart from parents. The old model also suggested that parent-adolescent conflict is intense and stressful throughout adolescence. The new model emphasizes that parents serve as important attachment figures and support systems as adolescents explore a wider, more complex social world. The new model also emphasizes that in the majority of families, parent-adolescent conflict is moderate rather than severe, and that the everyday negotiations and minor disputes are normal and can serve the positive developmental function of helping the adolescent make the transition from childhood dependency to adult independence (see figure 17.1).

It is not enough for parents to understand children. They must accord children the privilege of understanding them.

—**Milton Sapirstein,**
Paradoxes of Everyday Life, 1955

Still, a high degree of conflict characterizes some parent-adolescent relationships. One estimate of the percentage of parents and adolescents who engage in prolonged, intense, repeated, unhealthy conflict is about one in five families (Montemayor, 1982). While this figure represents a minority of adolescents, it indicates that 4 to 5 million American families encounter serious, highly stressful parent-adolescent conflict. And this prolonged, intense conflict is associated with a number of adolescent problems—moving away from home, juvenile delinquency, school dropout, pregnancy and early marriage, joining religious cults, and drug abuse (Brook & others, 1990).

The Maturation of Adolescents and Parents

Physical, cognitive, and socioemotional changes in the adolescent's development influence the nature of parent-adolescent relationships. Parental changes also influence the nature of these relationships. Among the changes in the adolescent are puberty, expanded logical reasoning and increased idealistic and egocentric thought, violated expectations, changes in schooling, peers, friendship and dating, and movement toward independence. Conflict between parents and adolescents is the most stressful during the apex of pubertal growth (Silverberg & Steinberg, 1990).

John W. Santrock

for success. Parents may look to the future and think about how much time they have remaining to accomplish what they want. Adolescents, however, look to the future with unbounded optimism, sensing that they have an unlimited amount of time to accomplish what they desire. Health concerns and an interest in bodily integrity and sexual attractiveness become prominent themes of adolescents' parents. Even when their bodies and sexual attractiveness are not deteriorating, many parents of adolescents perceive that they are. By contrast, adolescents are beginning to reach the peak of their physical attractiveness, strength, and health. While both adolescents and their parents show a heightened preoccupation with their bodies, adolescents' outcomes are probably more positive. To further evaluate parental age, turn to Critical Thinking About Children's Development.

Old model	
Autonomy, detachment from parents; parent and peer worlds are isolated	Intense, stressful conflict throughout adolescence; parent-adolescent relationships are filled with storm and stress on virtually a daily basis

New model	
Attachment and autonomy; parents are important support systems and attachment figures; adolescent-parent and adolescent-peer worlds have some important connections	Moderate parent-adolescent conflict common and can serve a positive developmental function; conflict greater in early adolescence, especially during the apex of puberty

FIGURE 17.1

Old and New Models of Parent-Adolescent Relationships

PEERS

In chapter 14, we discussed how children spend more time with their peers in middle and late childhood than in early childhood. We also found that friendships become more important in middle and late childhood, and that popularity with peers is a strong motivation for most children. Advances in cognitive development during middle and late childhood also allow children to take the perspective of their peers and friends more readily, and their social knowledge of how to make and keep friends increases.

Imagine you are back in junior or senior high school, especially during one of your good times. Peers, friends, cliques, dates, parties, and clubs probably come to mind. Adolescents spend huge chunks of time with peers, more than in middle and late childhood. Among the important issues and questions to be asked about peer relations in adolescence are these: What is the nature of peer pressure and conformity? How important is the nature of peer pressure and conformity? How important are cliques in adolescence? How do children and adolescent groups differ? What is the nature of youth organizations? What is the nature of dating in adolescence?

Parental changes include those involving marital dissatisfaction, economic burdens, career reevaluation and time perspective, and health and body concerns. Marital dissatisfaction is greater when the offspring is an adolescent rather than a child or an adult. A greater economic burden is placed on parents during the rearing of their adolescents. Parents may reevaluate their occupational achievement, deciding whether they have met their youthful aspirations

The parents of many adolescents will be increasingly older in the future because they will delay marriage and childbearing. How do you think this will affect the nature of parent-adolescent relationships? Do you think the parents of adolescents who are in their fifties and sixties will be more strict or more permissive than parents of adolescents who are in their late thirties and forties? By reflecting on age trends in the parents of adolescents and how they might influence parent-adolescent relationships, you are learning to think critically by *creating arguments based on developmental concepts.*

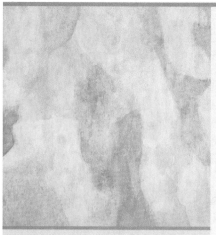

Most adolescents conform to the mainstream standards of their peers. However, the rebellious or anticonformist adolescent reacts counter to the mainstream peer group's expectations, deliberately moving away from the actions or beliefs this group advocates.

Peer Groups

How much pressure is there to conform to peers during adolescence? How important are cliques in adolescents' lives? How are children's and adolescents' groups different?

Peer Pressure and Conformity

Consider the following statement made by an adolescent girl:

Peer pressure is extremely influential in my life. I have never had very many friends, and I spend quite a bit of time alone. The friends I have are older. . . . The closest friend I have had is a lot like me in that we are both sad and depressed a lot. I began to act even more depressed than before when I was with her. I would call her up and try to act even more depressed than I was because that is what I thought she liked. In that relationship, I felt pressure to be like her.

Conformity to peer pressure in adolescence can be positive or negative. Teenagers engage in all sorts of negative conformity behavior—use seedy language, steal, vandalize, and make fun of parents and teachers. However, a great deal of peer conformity is not negative and consists of the desire to be involved in the peer world, such as dressing like friends and wanting to spend huge chunks of time with members of a clique. Such circumstances may involve prosocial activities as well, as when clubs raise money for worthy causes.

During adolescence, especially early adolescence, we conformed more to peer standards than we did in childhood. Investigators have found that around the eighth and ninth grades, conformity to peers—especially to their antisocial standards—peaks (Leventhal, 1994). At this point adolescents are most likely to go along with a peer to steal hubcaps off a car, draw graffiti on a wall, or steal cosmetics from a store counter.

> *Each of you, individually, walkest with the tread of a fox, but collectively ye are geese.*
>
> —Solon, Ancient Greece

Cliques and Crowds

Most peer group relationships in adolescence can be categorized in one of three ways: the crowd, the clique, or individual friendships. The **crowd** *is the largest and least personal of adolescent groups.* Members of the crowd meet because of their mutual interest in activities, not because they are mutually attracted to each other. **Cliques** *are smaller, involve greater intimacy among members, and have more group cohesion than crowds.*

Allegiance to cliques, clubs, organizations, and teams exerts powerful control over the lives of many adolescents (Tapper, 1996). Group identity often overrides personal identity. The leader of a group may place a member in a position of considerable moral conflict by asking, in effect, "What's more important, our code or your parents'?" or "Are you looking out for yourself, or the members of the group?" Such labels as *brother* and *sister* sometimes are adopted and used in the members' conversations with each other. These labels symbolize the bond between the members and suggest the high status of group membership.

One of the most widely cited studies of adolescent cliques and crowds is that of James Coleman (1961). Students from 10 high schools were asked to identify the leading crowds in their schools. They also were asked to identify the students who were the most outstanding in athletics, popularity, and various school activities. Regardless of the school sampled, the leading crowds were composed of athletes and popular girls. Much less power in the leading crowd was attributed to bright students.

Think about your high school years. What were the cliques, and which one were you in? Although the names of cliques change, we could go to almost any high school in the United States and find three to six well-defined cliques or crowds. In one study, six peer group structures emerged: populars, unpopulars, jocks, brains, druggies, and average students (Brown & Mounts, 1989). The proportion of students in these cliques was much lower in multiethnic schools because of the additional existence of ethnically based crowds.

In one study, clique membership was associated with the adolescent's self-esteem (Brown & Lohr, 1987). Cliques included jocks (athletically oriented), populars (well-known students who lead social activities), normals (middle-of-the-road students who make up the masses), druggies or toughs (known for illicit drug use or other delinquent activities), and nobodies (low in social skills or intellectual abilities). The self-esteem of the jocks and the populars was highest, whereas that of the nobodies was lowest. One group of adolescents not in a clique had self-esteem equivalent to that of the jocks and the populars; this group was the independents, who indicated that clique membership was not important to them. Keep in mind that these data are correlational; self-esteem could increase an adolescent's probability of becoming a clique member, just as clique membership could increase the adolescent's self-esteem.

Adolescent Groups Versus Children Groups

Children groups differ from adolescent groups in several important ways. The members of children groups often are friends or neighborhood acquaintances, and their groups usually are not as formalized as many adolescent groups. During the adolescent years, groups tend to include a broader array of members. In other words, adolescents other than friends or neighborhood acquaintances often are members of adolescent groups. Try to recall the student council, honor society, or football team at your junior high school. If you were a member of any of these organizations, you probably remember that they were made up of many people you had not met before and that they were a more heterogeneous group than your childhood peer groups. For example, peer groups in adolescence are more likely to have a mixture of individuals from different ethnic groups than are peer groups in childhood.

As ethnic minority children move into adolescence and enter schools with more heterogeneous school populations, they become more aware of their ethnic minority status. Ethnic minority adolescents may have difficulty joining peer groups and clubs in predominantly White schools. Similarly, White adolescents may have peer relations difficulties in predominately ethnic minority schools. However, schools are only one setting in which peer relations take place; they also occur in the neighborhood and in the community.

Ethnic minority adolescents often have two sets of peer relationships, one at school, the other in the community. Community peers are more likely to be from their own ethnic group in their immediate neighborhood. Sometimes, they go to the same church and participate in activities together, such as Black History Week, Chinese New Year's, or Cinco de Mayo Festival. Because ethnic group adolescents usually have two sets of peers and friends, when researchers ask about their peers and friends, questions should focus on both relationships at school and relationships in the neighborhood and community. Ethnic minority group adolescents who are social isolates at school may be sociometric stars in their segregated neighborhood. Also, because adolescents are more mobile than children, inquiries should be made about the scope of their social networks.

A well-known observational study by Dexter Dunphy (1963) supports the notion that opposite-sex participation in groups increases during adolescence. In late childhood, boys and girls participate in small, same-sex cliques. As they move into the early adolescent years, the same-sex cliques begin to interact with each other. Gradually, the leaders and high-status members form further cliques based on heterosexual relationships. Eventually the newly created heterosexual cliques replace the same-sex cliques. The heterosexual cliques interact with each other in large crowd activities, too—at dances and athletic events, for example. In late adolescence, the crowd begins to dissolve as couples develop more serious relationships and make long-range plans that may include engagement and marriage (see figure 17.2).

Youth Organizations

Youth organizations can have an important influence on the adolescent's development (Snider & Miller, 1993). More than four hundred national youth organizations currently

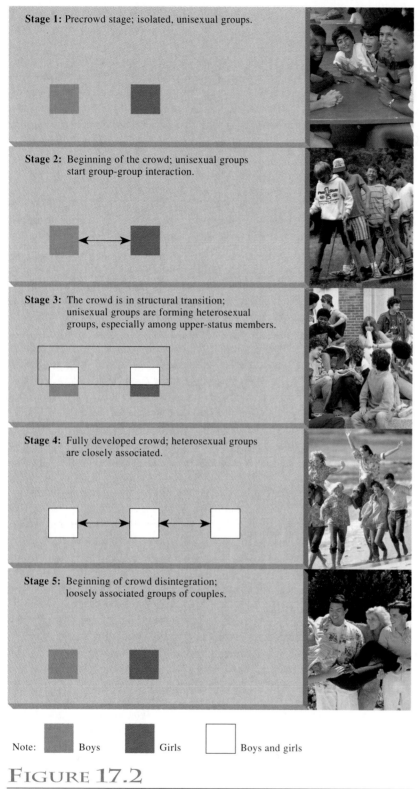

Stage 1: Precrowd stage; isolated, unisexual groups.

Stage 2: Beginning of the crowd; unisexual groups start group-group interaction.

Stage 3: The crowd is in structural transition; unisexual groups are forming heterosexual groups, especially among upper-status members.

Stage 4: Fully developed crowd; heterosexual groups are closely associated.

Stage 5: Beginning of crowd disintegration; loosely associated groups of couples.

Note: ▪ Boys   ▪ Girls   □ Boys and girls

FIGURE 17.2

Dunphy's Progression of Peer Group Relations in Adolescence

of America (Price & others, 1990). They serve approximately 30 million young people each year. The largest youth organization is 4-H with nearly 5 million participants. The smallest are ASPIRA, a Latino youth organization that provides intensive educational enrichment programs for about 13,000 adolescents each year, and WAVE, a dropout-prevention program that serves about 8,000 adolescents each year.

Adolescents who join such groups are more likely to participate in community activities in adulthood and have higher self-esteem, are better educated, and come from families with higher incomes than their counterparts who do not participate in youth groups (Erickson, 1982). Participation in youth groups can help adolescents practice the interpersonal and organization skills that are important for success in adult roles.

To increase the participation of low-income and ethnic minority adolescents in youth groups, Girls Clubs and Boys Clubs are being established in locations where young adolescents are at high risk for dropping out of school, becoming delinquents, and developing substance-abuse problems. The locations are fifteen housing projects in different American cities. The club programs are designed to provide individual, small-group, and drop-in supportive services that enhance educational and personal development. Preliminary results suggest that the Boys and Girls Clubs help to reduce vandalism, drug abuse, and delinquency (Boys and Girls Clubs of America, 1989).

Dating

Dating takes on added importance during adolescence (Feiring, 1995). As Dick Cavett (1974) remembers, the thought of an upcoming dance or sock hop was absolute agony: "I knew I'd never get a date. There seemed to be only this limited set of girls I could and should be seen with, and they were all taken by the jocks." Adolescents spend considerable time either dating or thinking about dating, which has gone far beyond its original courtship function to become a form of recreation, a source of status and achievement, and a setting for learning about close relationships. One function of dating, though, continues to be mate selection.

operate in the United States (Erickson, in press). The organizations include career groups, such as Junior Achievement; groups aimed at building character, such as Girls Scouts and Boy Scouts; political groups, such as Young Republicans and Young Democrats; and ethnic groups, such as Indian Youth

John W. Santrock

These adolescents are participating in Girls Club and Boys Club activities. This type of organization can have an important influence on adolescents' lives. Adolescents who participate in youth organizations on a regular basis participate more in community activities as adults and have higher self-esteem than their counterparts who do not.

He who would learn to fly one day must first learn to stand and walk and climb and dance: one cannot fly into flying.

— **Friedrich Nietzsche,**
Thus Spoke Zarathustra, 1883

Most adolescents have their first date between the ages of 12 and 16. Fewer than 10 percent have a first date before the age of 10, and by the age of 16, more than 90 percent have had at least one date. More than 50 percent of high school students average one or more dates per week. About 15 percent date less than once per month, and about three of every four students have gone steady at least once by the end of high school. Of special concern are early dating and going steady, which in recent studies have been associated with adolescent pregnancy and problems at home and school (Brown & Theobald, 1996; Degirmenciogbu, Saltz, & Ager, 1995).

Female adolescents bring a stronger desire for intimacy and personality exploration to dating than do male adolescents (Feiring, 1996). Adolescent dating is a context in which gender-related role expectations intensify. Males feel pressured to perform in "masculine" ways, and females feel pressured to perform in "feminine" ways. Especially in early adolescence, when pubertal changes are occurring, the adolescent male wants to show that he is the very best male possible, and the adolescent female wants to show that she is the very best female possible.

Dating scripts *are the cognitive models that adolescents and adults use to guide and evaluate dating interactions.* In one recent study, first dates were highly scripted along gender lines (Rose & Frieze, 1993). Males followed a proactive dating script, females a reactive one. The male's script involved initiating the date (asking for and planning it), controlling the public domain (driving and opening doors), and initiating sexual interaction (making physical contact, making out, and kissing). The female's script focused on the private domain (concern about appearance, enjoying the date), participating in the structure of the date provided by the male (being picked up, having doors opened), and responding to his sexual gestures. These gender differences give males more power in the initial stage of a relationship.

The sociocultural context exerts a powerful influence on adolescent dating patterns. Values and religious beliefs of people in various cultures often dictate the age at which dating begins, how much freedom in dating is allowed, whether dates must be chaperoned by adults or parents, and the roles of males and females in dating. For example, Latino and Asian American cultures have more conservative standards regarding adolescent dating than does the Anglo-American culture. Dating may be a source of cultural conflict for many immigrants and their families who have come from cultures in which dating begins at a late age, little freedom in dating is allowed, dates are chaperoned, and adolescent girls' dating is especially restricted.

Thus far, we have discussed a number of ideas about families and peers during adolescence. A summary of these ideas is presented in concept table 17.1.

CULTURE AND ADOLESCENT DEVELOPMENT

Consider the flowers of a garden: though differing in kind, colour, form and shape, yet inasmuch as they are refreshed by the waters of one spring, revived by the breath of one wind, invigorated by the rays of one sun, this diversity increaseth their charm, and addeth unto their beauty. . . . How unpleasing to the eye if all the flowers and plants, the leaves and blossoms, the fruits, the branches and the trees of that garden were all of the same shape and colour! Diversity of hues, form and shape, enricheth and adorneth the garden. . .

— **Àbud'l-Bahá**

We live in an increasingly diverse world, one in which there is increasing contact between adolescents from different cultures and ethnic groups. How do adolescents vary cross-culturally? What rites of passage do adolescents experience? What is the nature of ethnic minority adolescents and their development?

CONCEPT TABLE 17.1

Families and Peers

Concept	Processes/Related Ideas	Characteristics/Description
Families	Autonomy and attachment	Many parents have a difficult time handling the adolescent's push for autonomy, even though this push is one of the hallmarks of adolescent development. Adolescents do not simply move into a world isolated from parents; attachment to parents increases the probability that the adolescent will be socially competent and explore a widening social world in healthy ways.
	Parent-adolescent conflict	Conflict with parents often increases in early adolescence. Such conflict is usually moderate. The increase in conflict probably serves the positive developmental function of promoting autonomy and identity. A small subset of adolescents experience high parent-adolescent conflict that is related to various negative outcomes for adolescents.
	The maturation of the adolescent and parents	Physical, cognitive, and socioemotional changes in the adolescent's development influence parent-adolescent relationships. Parental changes—marital dissatisfaction, economic burdens, career reevaluation and time perspective, and health and body concerns—also influence parent-adolescent relationships.
Peers	Peer groups	The pressure to conform to peers is strong during adolescence, especially during the eighth and ninth grades. There are usually three to six well-defined cliques in every secondary school. Membership in certain cliques—especially jocks and populars—is associated with increased self-esteem. Independents also show high self-esteem. Children groups are less formal, less heterogeneous, and less heterosexual than adolescent groups. Dunphy found that the development of adolescent groups moves through five stages.
	Youth organizations	Youth organizations can have an important influence on the adolescent's development. More than four hundred national youth organizations currently exist.
	Dating	Dating can be a form of mate selection, recreation, a source of status and achievement, and a setting for learning about close relationships. Most adolescents are involved in dating. Adolescent females appear to be more interested in intimacy and personality exploration than adolescent males are. Male dating scripts are proactive, females' reactive. Dating varies cross-culturally.

Cross-Cultural Comparisons and Rites of Passage

Ideas about the nature of adolescents and orientation toward adolescents may vary from culture to culture and within the same culture over different time periods (Whiting, 1989). For example, some cultures (the Mangaian culture in the South Sea islands, for example) have more permissive attitudes toward adolescent sexuality than the American culture, and some cultures (the Ines Beag culture off the coast of Ireland, for example) have more conservative attitudes toward adolescent sexuality than the American culture. Over the course of the twentieth century, attitudes toward sexuality—especially for females—have become more permissive in the American culture.

Early in this century, overgeneralizations about the universal aspects of adolescents were made based on data and experience in a single culture—the middle-class culture of the United States. For example, it was believed that adolescents everywhere went through a period of "storm and stress" characterized by self-doubt and conflict. However, when Margaret Mead visited the island of Samoa, she found that the adolescents of the Samoan culture were not experiencing much stress.

John W. Santrock

These Congolese Kota boys painted their faces as part of a rite of passage to adulthood. What kinds of rites of passage do American adolescents have?

As we discovered in chapter 1, **cross-cultural studies** *involve the comparison of a culture with one or more other cultures, which provides information about the degree to which development is similar, or universal, across cultures, or the degree to which it is culture-specific.* The study of adolescence has emerged in the context of Western industrialized society, with the practical needs and social norms of this culture dominating thinking about adolescents. Consequently, the development of adolescents in Western cultures has evolved as the norm for all adolescents of the human species, regardless of economic and cultural circumstances. This narrow viewpoint can produce erroneous conclusions about the nature of adolescents. One variation in the experiences of adolescents in different cultures is whether the adolescents go through a rite of passage.

Some societies have elaborate ceremonies that signal the adolescent's move to maturity and achievement of adult status. A **rite of passage** *is a ceremony or a ritual that marks an individual's transition from one status to another. Most rites of passage focus on the transition to adult status.* In many primitive cultures, rites of passage are the avenue through which adolescents gain access to sacred adult practices, to knowledge, and to sexuality. These rites often involve dramatic practices intended to facilitate the adolescent's separation from the immediate family, especially the mother. The transformation is usually characterized by some form of ritual death and rebirth, or by means of contact with the spiritual world. Bonds are forged between the adolescent and the adult instructors through shared rituals, hazards, and secrets to allow the adolescent to enter the adult world. This kind of ritual provides a forceful and discontinuous entry into the adult world at a time when the adolescent is perceived to be ready for the change.

Africa has been the location of many rites of passage for adolescents, especially sub-Saharan Africa. Under the influence of Western culture, many of the rites are disappearing today, although some vestiges remain. In locations where formal education is not readily available, rites of passage are still prevalent.

Do we have such rites of passage for American adolescents? We certainly do not have universal formal ceremonies that mark the passage from adolescence to adulthood. Certain religious and social groups do have initiation ceremonies that indicate that an advance in maturity has been reached—the Jewish bar mitzvah, the Catholic confirmation, and social debuts, for example. School graduation ceremonies come the closest to being culture-wide rites of passage in the United States. The high school graduation ceremony has become nearly universal for middle-class adolescents and increasing numbers of adolescents from low-income backgrounds. Nonetheless, high school graduation does not result in universal changes; many high school graduates continue to live with their parents, continue to be economically dependent on them, and continue to be undecided about career and lifestyle matters. Another rite of passage for increasing numbers of American adolescents is sexual intercourse (Halonen & Santrock, 1996). By the end of adolescence, more than 70 percent of American adolescents have had sexual intercourse.

The absence of clear-cut rites of passage make the attainment of adult status ambiguous. Many individuals are unsure whether or not they have reached adult status. In Texas, the age for beginning employment is 15, but many younger adolescents and even children are employed, especially Mexican immigrants. The age for driving is 16, but when emergency need is demonstrated, a driver's license can be obtained at 15. Even at age 16, some parents may not allow their son or daughter to obtain a driver's license, believing they are too young for this responsibility. The age for voting is 18; the age for drinking has recently been raised to 21. Exactly when adolescents become adults in America has not been clearly delineated, as it has been in some primitive cultures where rites of passage are universal in the culture.

Now that we have discussed the importance of a global perspective in understanding adolescence and the nature of rites of passage, we turn our attention to the development of ethnic minority adolescents in the United States.

Ethnicity

First, we will examine the nature of ethnicity and social class; second, we will examine the nature of differences, and diversity; and, third, we will study the aspects of value conflicts, assimilation, and pluralism.

Ethnicity and Social Class

Much of the research on ethnic minority adolescents has failed to tease apart the influences of ethnicity and social class. Ethnicity and social class can interact in ways that exaggerate the influence of ethnicity because ethnic minority individuals are overrepresented in the lower socioeconomic levels of American society. Consequently, researchers too often have given ethnic explanations of adolescent development that were largely due to socioeconomic status rather than ethnicity. For example, decades of research on group differences in self-esteem failed to consider the socioeconomic status of African American and White children and adolescents. When African American adolescents from low-income backgrounds are compared with White adolescents from middle-class backgrounds, the differences are often large but not informative because of the confounding of ethnicity and social class (Scott-Jones, 1995).

Although some ethnic minority youth are from middle-class backgrounds, economic advantage does not entirely enable them to escape their ethnic minority status (Spencer & Dornbusch, 1990). Middle-class ethnic minority youth still encounter much of the prejudice, discrimination, and bias associated with being a member of an ethnic minority group. Often characterized as a "model minority" because of their strong achievement orientation and family cohesiveness, Japanese Americans still experience stress associated with ethnic minority status (Sue, 1990). Even though middle-class ethnic minority adolescents have more resources available to counter the destructive influences of prejudice and discrimination, they still cannot completely avoid the pervasive influence of negative stereotypes about ethnic minority groups.

> In the end, antiblack, antifemale, and all forms of discrimination are equivalent to the same thing—antihumanism.
>
> —Shirley Chisholm,
> Unbought and Unbossed, 1970

Not all ethnic minority families are poor. However, poverty contributes to the stressful life experiences of many ethnic minority adolescents. Thus, many ethnic minority adolescents experience a double disadvantage: (a) prejudice, discrimination, and bias because of their ethnic minority status, and (b) the stressful effects of poverty.

Differences and Diversity

There are legitimate differences between various ethnic minority groups, and between ethnic minority groups and the majority White group. Recognizing and respecting these differences is an important aspect of getting along with others in a diverse, multicultural world. Historical, economic, and social experiences produce differences in ethnic groups (Coll & others, 1995). Individuals living in a particular ethnic or cultural group adapt to the values, attitudes, and stresses of that culture. Their behavior, while possibly different from yours, is, nonetheless, often functional for them. It is important for adolescents, as well as each of us, to take the perspective of individuals from ethnic and cultural groups that are different from ours and think, "If I were in their shoes, what kind of experiences might I have had?" "How would I feel if I were a member of their ethnic or cultural group?" "How would I think and behave if I had grown up in their world?" Such perspective taking often increases an adolescent's empathy and understanding of individuals from ethnic and cultural groups different from their own.

Unfortunately, the differences between ethnic minority groups and the White majority are emphasized by both society and science, with damaging results to ethnic minority individuals. Ethnicity has defined who will enjoy the privileges of citizenship and to what degree and in what ways (Jones, 1990, 1994). An individual's ethnic background has determined whether the individual will be alienated, oppressed, or disadvantaged, all too often humiliating and embarrassing ethnic minority individuals.

Another very important dimension to continually keep in mind when studying ethnic minority adolescents is their diversity, a point we made in chapter 1 but that deserves to be underscored again (Burton & Allison, 1995). Ethnic minority groups are not homogeneous; they have different social, historical, and economic backgrounds. For example, Mexican, Cuban, and Puerto Rican immigrants are all Hispanics, but they migrated for different reasons, came from varying socioeconomic backgrounds in their native countries, and experience different rates and types of employment in the United States. The federal government now recognizes the existence of 511 *different* Native American tribes, each having a unique ancestral background with differing values and characteristics. Asian Americans include the Chinese, Japanese, Filipinos, Koreans, and Southeast Asians, each group having a distinct ancestry and language. As an indication of the diversity of Asian Americans, they not only show high educational attainments but also include a high proportion of individuals with no education whatsoever. For example, 90 percent of Korean American males graduate from high school, but only 71 percent of Vietnamese American males do.

Sometimes well-meaning individuals fail to recognize the diversity within an ethnic group (Sue, 1990). Consider the circumstance of a sixth-grade teacher who goes to a human relations workshop and is exposed to the necessity of incorporating more ethnicity into her instructional planning. Since she has two Mexican American adolescents in her class, she asks them to be prepared to demonstrate to the class on the following Monday how they dance at home. The teacher expected both of them to perform Mexican folk dances, reflecting their ethnic heritage. The first boy got up in front of the class and began dancing in a typical American fashion. The teacher said, "No, I want you to dance like you and your family do at home, like you do when you have Mexican American celebrations." The boy informed the teacher that their family didn't dance that way. The second boy did demonstrate a Mexican folk dance to the class. The first boy was highly assimilated into the American culture and did not know how to dance Mexican folk dances. The second boy was less assimilated and came from a Mexican American family that had retained more of their Mexican heritage.

We all know we are unique individuals, but we tend to see others as representatives of groups.

—**Deborah Tannen**

This example illustrates the diversity and individual differences that exist within any ethnic minority group. Failure to recognize diversity and individual variations results in the stereotyping of an ethnic minority group (Bowser & Hunt, 1996).

Value Conflicts, Assimilation, and Pluralism

Stanley Sue (1990) believes that value conflicts are often involved when individuals respond to ethnic issues. These value conflicts have been a source of considerable controversy. According to Sue, without properly identifying the assumptions and effects of the conflicting values it is difficult to resolve ethnic minority issues. Let's examine one of these value conflicts, assimilation versus pluralism, to see how it might influence an individual's response to an ethnic minority issue.

A faculty member commented that he was glad his psychology department was interested in teaching students about ethnic and cultural issues. He felt that by becoming aware of the cultures of different groups, students would improve their understanding of their own and other cultures. However, another faculty member disagreed. She felt that students' knowledge of ethnic minority issues and different cultures was a relevant concern, but she argued that the department's scarce resources should not be devoted to ethnic and cultural issues. She also believed that if too much attention is given to ethnic and cultural issues, it might actually increase the segregation of students, and even cause friction among ethnic and cultural groups. She commented that we all live in this society and therefore we must all learn the same skills to succeed. In Sue's (1990) perspective, a value conflict involving assimilation and pluralism underlies these opposing views about whether a psychology department should devote increased, or any, funds to teaching students about ethnicity and culture.

Assimilation *refers to the absorption of ethnic minority groups into the dominant group, which often means the loss of some or virtually all of the behavior and values of the ethnic minority group.* Individuals who adopt an assimilation stance usually advocate that ethnic minority groups should become more American. By contrast, **pluralism** *refers to the* *coexistence of distinct ethnic and cultural groups in the same society. Individuals who adopt a pluralistic stance usually advocate that cultural differences be maintained and appreciated.*

For many years, an assimilation approach was thought to be the best course for American society, because it was believed that the mainstream was in many ways the superior culture. Even though many individuals today reject the notion that the mainstream culture is intrinsically superior to ethnic minority cultures, the assimilation approach is currently resurfacing with a more complex face. Advocates of the assimilation approach now often use practical and functional arguments rather than intrinsic superiority arguments to buttress their point of view. For example, assimilation advocates stress that educational programs for immigrant children (Mexican, Chinese, and so on) should stress the learning of English as early as possible in education rather than provide a bilingual education. Their argument is that spending time on any language other than English may be a handicap, particularly because it is not functional in the classroom. By contrast, the advocates of pluralism argue that an English-only approach reasserts the mainstream-is-right-and-best belief. Thus, responses to the ethnic minority issue of bilingual education involve a clash of fundamental values. As Sue asks, how can one argue against the development of functional skills and, to some degree, the support of Americanization? Similarly, how can one doubt that pluralism, diversity, and respect for different cultures is a valid principle? Sue believes that the one-sidedness of the issue is the main problem. Advocates of assimilation often overlook the fact that a consensus may be lacking on what constitutes functional skills, or that a particular context may alter what skills are useful. For example, with the growth in the immigrant population, the ability to speak Spanish or Japanese may be an asset, as is the ability to interact and collaborate with diverse ethnic groups.

> *I am here and you will know that I am the best and will hear me. The color of my skin or the kink of my hair or the spread of my mouth has nothing to do with what you are listening to.*
>
> —Leontyne Price

Sue believes that one way to resolve value conflicts about sociocultural issues is to conceptualize or redefine them in innovative ways. For example, in the assimilation/pluralism conflict, rather than assume that assimilation is necessary for the development of functional skills, one strategy is to focus on the fluctuating criteria defining those skills considered to be functional; another is to consider the possibility that developing functional skills does not prevent the existence of pluralism. For instance, the classroom instructor might use multicultural examples when teaching social studies, and still be able to discuss both culturally universal (etic) and culturally specific (emic) approaches to American and other cultures.

Now that we have considered a number of ideas about the role of culture in the adolescent's development, we turn our attention to one of the most important tasks of adolescence—the development of identity. We will consider the role of adolescence as a critical juncture in the identity development of ethnic minority adolescents as well.

IDENTITY

By far the most comprehensive and provocative story of identity development has been told by Erik Erikson. As you may remember from chapter 2, identity versus identity confusion is the fifth stage in Erikson's eight stages of the life cycle, occurring at about the same time as adolescence. It is a time of being interested in finding out who one is, what one is all about, and where one is headed in life.

> *The thoughts of youth are long, long thoughts.*
> —Henry Wadsworth Longfellow, 1858

During adolescence, worldviews become important to the individual, who enters what Erikson (1968) calls a "psychological moratorium," a gap between the security of childhood and the autonomy of adulthood. Adolescents experiment with numerous roles and identities they draw from the surrounding culture. Youth who successfully cope with these conflicting identities during adolescence emerge with a new sense of self that is both refreshing and acceptable. Adolescents who do not successfully resolve this identity crisis are confused, suffering what Erikson calls "identity confusion." This confusion takes one of two courses: The individuals withdraw, isolating themselves from peers and family; or they may lose their identity in the crowd.

Some Contemporary Thoughts About Identity

Contemporary views of identity development suggest several important considerations. First, identity development is a lengthy process; in many instances it is a more gradual, less cataclysmic transition than Erikson's term *crisis* implies. Second, identity development is extraordinarily complex.

Identity formation neither begins nor ends with adolescence. It begins with the appearance of attachment, the development of a sense of self, and the emergence of independence in infancy, and reaches its final phase with a life review and integration in old age. What is important about identity in adolescence, especially late adolescence, is that for the first time physical development, cognitive development, and social development advance to the point at which the individual can sort through and synthesize childhood identities and identifications to construct a viable pathway toward adult maturity. Resolution of the identity issue at adolescence does not mean identity will be stable through the remainder of one's life. A person who develops a healthy identity is

"Do you have any idea who I am?"

Drawing by Koren; © 1988 The New Yorker Magazine, Inc.

flexible, adaptive, and open to changes in society, in relationships, and in careers. This openness assures numerous reorganizations of identity features throughout the life of the person who has achieved identity.

> *In the beginning was alpha and the end is omega, but somewhere in between occurred delta, which is nothing less than the arrival of man himself into the daylight of . . . being himself and not being himself, of being at home and being a stranger.*
>
> **—Walker Percy, Message in the Bottle**

Identity formation does not happen neatly, and it usually does not happen cataclysmically. At the bare minimum, it involves commitment to a vocational direction, an ideological stance, and a sexual orientation. Synthesizing the identity components can be a long, drawn-out process with many negations and affirmations of various roles and faces (Marcia, 1996). Identities are developed in bits and pieces. Decisions are not made once and for all, but have to be made again and again. And the decisions may seem trivial at the time: whom to date, whether or not to break up, whether or not to have intercourse, whether or not to take drugs, whether to go to college after high school or get a job, which major to choose, whether to study or whether to play, whether or not to be politically active, and so on. Over the years of adolescence, the decisions begin to form a core of what the individual is all about as a person—what is called "identity."

Identity Statuses and Development

Canadian psychologist James Marcia (1980, 1994) analyzed Erikson's theory of identity development and concluded that four identity statuses, or modes of resolution, appear in the theory: identity diffusion, identity foreclosure, identity moratorium, and identity achievement. The extent of an adolescent's commitment and crisis is used to classify the individual according to one of the four identity statuses. **Crisis** *is defined as a period of identity development during which the adolescent is choosing among meaningful alternatives.* Most researchers now use the term *exploration* rather than *crisis*, although in the spirit of Marcia's original formulation, we will use the term *crisis*. **Commitment** *is defined as the part of identity development in which adolescents show a personal investment in what they are going to do.*

Identity diffusion *is Marcia's term for adolescents who have not yet experienced a crisis (that is, they have not yet explored meaningful alternatives) or made any commitments.* Not only are they undecided about occupational and ideological choices, they are also likely to show little interest in such matters. **Identity foreclosure** *is the term Marcia uses to describe adolescents who have made a commitment but have not experienced a crisis.* This occurs most often when parents hand down commitments to their adolescents, more often than not in an authoritarian manner. In these circumstances, adolescents have not had adequate opportunities to explore different approaches, ideologies, and vocations on their own. **Identity moratorium** *is the term Marcia uses to describe adolescents who are in the midst of a crisis, but their commitments are either absent or only vaguely defined.* **Identity achievement** *is Marcia's term for adolescents who have undergone a crisis and have made a commitment.* Marcia's four statuses of identity are summarized in figure 17.3.

Young adolescents are primarily in Marcia's identity diffusion, foreclosure, or moratorium statuses. At least three aspects of the young adolescent's development are important in identity formation: Young adolescents must establish confidence in parental support, develop a sense of industry, and gain a self-reflective perspective on their future.

Some researchers believe the most important identity changes take place in youth rather than earlier in adolescence. For example, Alan Waterman (1992) has found that from the years preceding high school through the last few years of college, an increase in the number of individuals who are identity achieved occurs, along with a decrease in those who are identity diffused. College upperclassmen are more likely to be identity achieved than college freshmen or high school students, Many young adolescents are identity diffused. These developmental changes are especially true for vocational choice. For religious beliefs and political ideology, fewer college students have reached the identity achieved status, with a substantial number characterized by foreclosure and diffusion. Thus, the timing of identity may depend on the particular role involved, and many college students are still wrestling with ideological commitments.

> *As long as one keeps searching, the answers come.*
>
> **—Joan Baez**

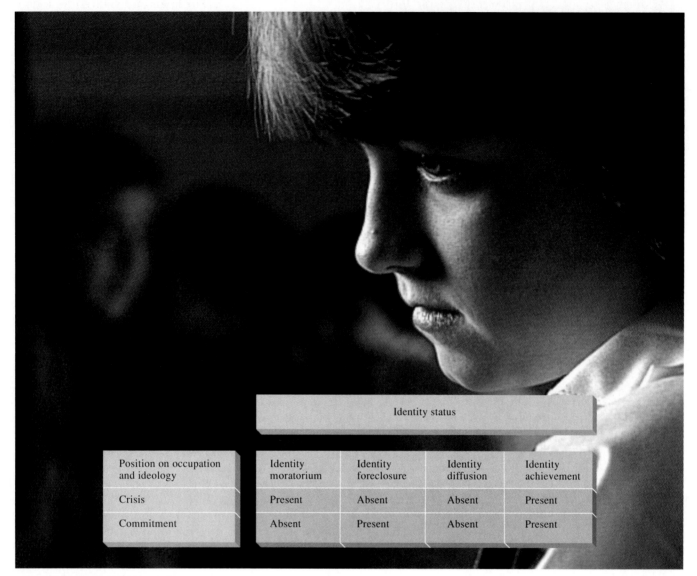

Identity status				
Position on occupation and ideology	Identity moratorium	Identity foreclosure	Identity diffusion	Identity achievement
Crisis	Present	Absent	Absent	Present
Commitment	Absent	Present	Absent	Present

FIGURE 17.3

Marcia's Four Statuses of Identity

Many identity status researchers believe that a common pattern of individuals who develop positive identities is to follow what are called "MAMA" cycles of moratorium-achiever-moratorium-achiever. These cycles may be repeated throughout life. Personal, family, and societal changes are inevitable, and as they occur, the flexibility and skill required to explore new alternatives and develop new commitments are likely to facilitate an individual's coping skills.

Family Influences on Identity

Parents are important figures in the adolescent's development of identity. In studies that relate identity development to parenting styles, democratic parents, who encourage adolescents to participate in family decision making, foster identity achievement. Autocratic parents, who control the adolescent's behavior without giving the adolescent an opportunity to express opinions, encourage identity foreclosure. Permissive parents, who provide little guidance to adolescents and allow them to make their own decisions, promote identity diffusion (Enright & others, 1980).

In addition to studies on parenting styles, researchers have also examined the role of individuality and connectedness in the development of identity. The presence of a family atmosphere that promotes both individuality and connectedness are important in the adolescent's identity development (Cooper & Grotevant, 1989). **Individuality** *consists of two dimensions: self-assertion, the ability to have and communicate a point of view; and separateness, the use of communication patterns to express how one is different from others.* **Connectedness** *also consists of two dimensions: mutuality, sensitivity to, and respect for others' views; and permeability, openness to others' views.* In general, research findings reveal that identity formation is enhanced by family relationships that

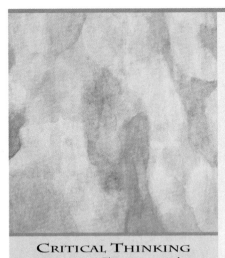

Now that you have read about various aspects of identity development, this is a good time to explore your own identity development. How might you gain insight into your personal self or identity? One way is to list adjectives that describe yourself. You also could ask people who know you well, such as several family members and/or friends, to give you some feedback about how they honestly would describe you. How does their perception match your self-perception? Consider also your interests, attitudes, and hobbies. How did you develop your personal characteristics and interests? Try to trace their origins. Tracing the development of aspects of yourself can help you gain insight into your own identity formation. By exploring your identity development, you are learning to think critically by *applying developmental concepts to enhance personal adaptation.*

have the ability to interpret ethnic and cultural information, to reflect on the past, and to speculate about the future. As they cognitively mature, ethnic minority adolescents become acutely aware of the evaluations of their ethnic group by the majority White culture (Comer, 1988). As one researcher commented, the young African American child may learn that Black is beautiful, but conclude as an adolescent that White is powerful (Semaj, 1985).

Ethnic minority youths' awareness of negative appraisals, conflicting values, and restricted occupational opportunities can influence life choices and plans for the future (Spencer & Dornbusch, 1990). As one ethnic minority youth stated, "The future seems shut off, closed. Why dream? You can't reach your dreams. Why set goals? At least if you don't set any goals, you don't fail."

For many ethnic minority youth, a lack of successful ethnic minority role models with whom to identify is a special concern. The problem is especially acute for inner-city ethnic minority youth. Because of the lack of adult ethnic minority role models, some ethnic minority youth may conform to middle-class White values and identify with successful White role models. However, for many adolescents, their ethnicity and skin color limit their acceptance by the White culture. Thus, many ethnic minority adolescents have a difficult task: negotiating two value systems—that of their own ethnic group and that of the White society. Some adolescents reject the mainstream, foregoing the rewards controlled by White Americans; others adopt the values and standards of the majority White culture; and yet others take the difficult path of biculturalism.

In one study, ethnic identity exploration was higher among ethnic minority than among White American college students (Phinney & Alipura, 1990). In this same study, ethnic minority college students who had thought about and resolved issues involving their ethnicity had higher self-esteem than their ethnic minority counterparts who had not. In another investigation, the ethnic identity development of Asian American, African American, Latino, and White American tenth-grade students in Los Angeles was studied (Phinney, 1989). Adolescents from each of the three ethnic minority groups faced a similar need to deal with their ethnic group identification in a predominantly White American culture. In some instances, the adolescents from the three ethnic minority groups perceived different issues to be important in their resolution of

are both individuated, which encourages adolescents to develop their own point of view, and connected, which provides a secure base from which to explore the widening social worlds of adolescence. To further evaluate identity development, refer to Critical Thinking About Children's Development.

Culture, Ethnicity, and Gender

How do culture and ethnicity influence an adolescent's identity development? How does gender affect the nature of an adolescent's identity development?

Culture and Ethnicity

Erikson is especially sensitive to the role of culture in identity development. He points out that, throughout the world, ethnic minority groups have struggled to maintain their cultural identities while blending into the dominant culture (Erikson, 1968). Erikson says that this struggle for an inclusive identity, or identity within the larger culture, has been the driving force in the founding of churches, empires, and revolutions throughout history.

For ethnic minority individuals, adolescence is often a special juncture in their development (Kurtz, Cantu, & Phinney, 1996; Phinney & others, 1994; Spencer & Dornbusch, 1990). Although children are aware of some ethnic and cultural differences, most ethnic minority individuals consciously confront their ethnicity for the first time in adolescence. In contrast to children, adolescents

Margaret Beale Spencer, shown here talking with adolescents, believes that adolescence is often a critical juncture in the identity development of ethnic minority individuals. Most ethnic minority individuals consciously confront their ethnicity for the first time in adolescence.

of ethnic pride in inner city ethnic youth. Heath and McLaughlin believe that many inner-city youth have too much time on their hands, too little to do, and too few places to go. Inner city youth want to participate in organizations that nurture them and respond positively to their needs and interests. Organizations that perceive youth as fearful, vulnerable, and lonely but also frame them as capable, worthy, and eager to have a healthy and productive life contribute in positive ways to the identity development of ethnic minority youth.

Gender and Identity Development

In Erikson's (1968) classic presentation of identity development, the division of labor between the sexes was reflected in his assertion that males' aspirations were mainly oriented toward career and ideological commitments, while females' were centered around marriage and childbearing. In the 1960s and 1970s researchers found support for Erikson's assertion about gender differences in identity. For example, vocational concerns were more central to the identity of males, and affiliative concerns were more important in the identity of females. However, in the last decade, as females have developed stronger vocational interests, sex differences are turning into sex similarities.

ethnic identity. For Asian American adolescents, pressures to achieve academically and concerns about quotas that make it difficult to get into good colleges were salient issues. Many African American adolescent females discussed their realization that White American standards of beauty (especially hair and skin color) did not apply to them; African American adolescent males were concerned with possible job discrimination and the need to distinguish themselves from a negative societal image of African American male adolescents. For Latino adolescents, prejudice was a recurrent theme, as was the conflict of values between their Latino cultural heritage and the majority culture.

The contexts in which ethnic minority youth live influence their identity development. Many ethnic minority youth in the United States live in low income urban settings where support for developing a positive identity is absent. Many of these youth live in pockets of poverty, are exposed to drugs, gangs, and criminal activities, and interact with other youth and adults who have dropped out of school and/or are unemployed. In such settings, effective organizations and programs for youth can make important contributions to developing a positive identity (Cooper & others, 1996).

Shirley Heath and Milbrey McLaughlin (1993) studied 60 different youth organizations that involved 24,000 adolescents over a period of five years. They found that these organizations were especially good at building a sense

Some investigators believe the order of stages proposed by Erikson are different for females and males. One view is that for males identity formation precedes the stage of intimacy, while for females intimacy precedes identity. These ideas are consistent with the belief that relationships and emotional bonds are more important concerns of females, while autonomy and achievement are more important concerns of males (Gilligan, 1990). In one study, the development of a clear sense of self by adolescent girls was related to their concerns about care and response in relationships (Rogers, 1987).

The task of identity exploration may be more complex for females than for males, in that females may try to establish identities in more domains than males. In today's world, the options for females have increased and thus may at times be confusing and conflicting, especially for females who hope to successfully integrate family and career roles (Archer, 1994).

At this point we have discussed a number of ideas about culture and identity development in adolescence. A summary of these ideas is presented in concept table 17.2.

John W. Santrock

CONCEPT TABLE 17.2

Culture and Identity

Concept	Processes/Related Ideas	Characteristics/Description
Culture and Rites of Passage	Their nature	As in other periods of development, culture influences adolescents' development. Ceremonies mark an individual's transition from one status to another, especially into adulthood. In primitive cultures, rites of passage are often well defined. In contemporary America, rites of passage to adulthood are ill-defined.
	Ethnicity	Much of the research on ethnic minority adolescents has not teased apart the influences of ethnicity and social class. Because of this failure, too often researchers have given ethnic explanations that were largely due to socioeconomic factors. While not all ethnic minority families are poor, poverty contributes to the stress of many ethnic minority adolescents. There are legitimate differences between many ethnic groups, and between ethnic groups and the White majority. Recognizing these differences is an important aspect of getting along with others in a diverse, multicultural world. Too often differences between ethnic groups and the White majority have been interpreted as deficits on the part of the ethnic minority group. Another important dimension of ethnic minority groups is their diversity. Ethnic minority groups are not homogeneous; they have different social, historical, and economic backgrounds. Failure to recognize diversity and individual variations results in the stereotyping of an ethnic minority group. Value conflicts are often involved when individuals respond to ethnic issues. One prominent value conflict involves assimilation versus pluralism.
Identity	Erikson's theory	This is the most comprehensive and provocative view of identity development. Identity versus identity confusion is the fifth stage in Erikson's life-cycle theory. During adolescence, worldviews become important and the adolescent enters a psychological moratorium, a gap between childhood security and adult autonomy.
	Some contemporary thoughts about identity	Identity development is extraordinarily complex. It is done in bits and pieces. For the first time in development, during adolescence, individuals are physically, cognitively, and socially mature enough to synthesize their lives and pursue a viable path toward adult maturity.
	Identity statuses and development	Marcia proposed that four statuses of identity exist, based on a combination of conflict and commitment: identity diffusion, identity foreclosure, identity moratorium, and identity achievement. Some experts believe the main identity changes take place in late adolescence or youth rather than in early adolescence. College upperclassmen are more likely to be identity achieved than freshmen or high school students, although many college students are still wrestling with ideological commitments. Individuals often follow "moratorium-achievement-moratorium-achievement" cycles.
	Family influences	Parents are important figures in adolescents' identity development. Democratic parenting facilitates identity development in adolescence; autocratic and permissive parenting do not. Cooper and her colleagues have shown that both individuation and connectedness in family relations make important contributions to adolescent identity development.
	Culture, ethnicity, and gender	Erikson is especially sensitive to the role of culture in identity development, underscoring how throughout the world ethnic-minority groups have struggled to maintain their cultural identities while blending into the majority culture. Adolescence is often a special juncture in the identity development of ethnic-minority individuals because, for the first time, they consciously confront their ethnic identity. While Erikson's classical theory argued for sex differences in identity development, more recent studies have shown that as females have developed stronger vocational interests, sex differences in identity are turning into similarities. However, others argue that relationships and emotional bonds are more central to the identity development of females than males, and that female identity development today is more complex than male identity development.

As adolescents wend their way from childhood to adulthood they influence and are influenced by people in numerous social contexts, ranging from family to peer to dating to school. And their quest for an identity—of finding out who they are, what they are all about, and where they are going—takes a more central place in their development.

The 15-year-old girl's self-description that began this chapter exemplifies the increasing search for an identity during adolescence. We discussed adolescents and their families, including the nature of attachment and autonomy, parent-adolescent conflict, and the maturation of adolescents and parents. Our coverage of peers focused on peer pressure and conformity, cliques and crowds, adolescent groups compared to children groups, youth organizations, and dating. We also evaluated the role of culture in adolescent development, including cross-cultural comparisons, rites of passage, and ethnicity. And we devoted considerable time to investigating identity, including some contemporary thoughts about identity, the four statuses of identity, developmental changes, family influences, cultural and ethnic aspects, and gender.

Don't forget that you can obtain an overall summary of the chapter by again reading the two concept tables on pages 528 and 537. This chapter on socioemotional development in adolescence is the last one in the book. However, a final part to the book—an epilogue—summarizes some of the main themes of children's development that we have discussed and takes you on a journey through childhood.

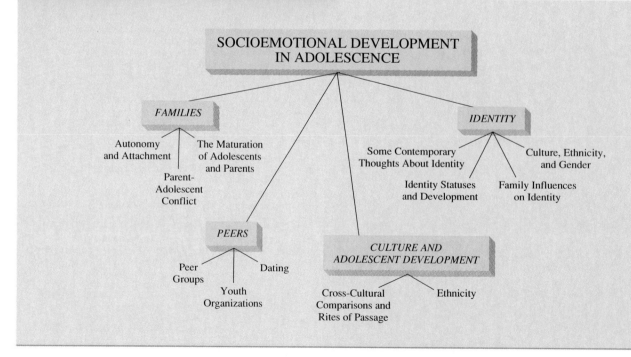

SOCIOEMOTIONAL DEVELOPMENT
IN ADOLESCENCE

FAMILIES

Autonomy and Attachment

The Maturation of Adolescents and Parents

Parent-Adolescent Conflict

PEERS

Peer Groups

Dating

Youth Organizations

CULTURE AND ADOLESCENT DEVELOPMENT

Cross-Cultural Comparisons and Rites of Passage

Ethnicity

IDENTITY

Some Contemporary Thoughts About Identity

Culture, Ethnicity, and Gender

Identity Statuses and Development

Family Influences on Identity

John W. Santrock

KEY TERMS

crowd The largest and least personal of adolescent groups. 524

cliques Smaller groups that involve greater intimacy among members and have more cohesion than crowds. 525

dating scripts The cognitive models that adolescents and adults use to guide and evaluate dating interactions. 527

cross-cultural studies The comparison of a culture with one or more other cultures, which provides information about the degree to which development is similar (universal) across cultures or the degree to which it is culture-specific. 529

rite of passage A ceremony or a ritual that marks an individual's transition from one status to another. Most rites of passage focus on the transition to adult status. 529

assimilation The absorption of ethnic minority groups into the dominant group, which often involves the loss of some or virtually all of the behavior and values of the ethnic minority group. 531

pluralism The coexistence of distinct ethnic and cultural groups in the same society. Individuals with a pluralistic stance usually advocate that cultural differences should be maintained and appreciated. 531

crisis Marcia's term for a period of identity development during which the adolescent is choosing among meaningful alternatives. 533

commitment Marcia's term for the part of identity development in which adolescents show a personal investment in what they are going to do. 533

identity diffusion Marcia's term for adolescents who have not yet experienced a crisis (explored meaningful alternatives) or made any commitments. 533

identity foreclosure Marcia's term for adolescents who have made a commitment but have not experienced a crisis. 533

identity moratorium Marcia's term for adolescents who are in the midst of a crisis, but their commitments are either absent or vaguely defined. 533

identity achievement Marcia's term for adolescents who have undergone a crisis and made a commitment. 533

individuality According to Cooper and her colleagues, individuality consists of two dimensions: self-assertion (the ability to have and communicate a point of view) and separateness (the use of communication patterns to express how one is different from others). 534

connectedness According to Cooper and her colleagues, connectedness consists of two dimensions: mutuality (sensitivity to and respect for others' views) and permeability (openness to others' views). 534

Between Parent & Teenager

(1969) by Dr. Haim G. Ginott.
New York: Avon.

Despite the fact that *Between Parent & Teenager* is well past its own adolescence (it was published in 1969), it continues to be one of the most widely read and recommended books for parents who want to communicate more effectively with their teenagers. Author Haim Ginott was a clinical psychologist at Columbia University who died in 1973. Ginott describes a number of commonsense solutions and strategies. For Ginott, parents' greatest challenge in the teenage years is to let go when they want to hold on—only by letting go can a peaceful and meaningful coexistence be reached between parents and teenagers. Throughout the book, Ginott connects with and educates parents through catchy phrases, such as *Don't collect thorns* (when parents see imperfections in themselves, they often expect perfection on the part of their teenagers) and *Don't step on corns* (adolescents have many imperfections about which they are very sensitive, ranging from zits to dimples; teenagers don't need parents to remind them of these imperfections). The book is very entertaining reading and is full of insightful interchanges between parents and teenagers. Ginott's strategies can make the world of parents and adolescents a kinder, gentler world.

The Adolescent & Young Adult Fact Book

(1993) by Janet Simons, Belva Finlay, and Alice Yang. Washington, DC: Children's Defense Fund.

This book is filled with valuable charts showing the roles that poverty and ethnicity play in adolescent development. Many of the charts display information separately for African American, Latino, and Asian American adolescents. Special attention is given to prevention and intervention programs that work with adolescents from low-income and ethnic minority backgrounds. Topics discussed include families, health, substance abuse, crime, victimization, education, employment, sexual activity, and pregnancy.

IMPROVING THE LIVES OF CHILDREN

Improving the lives of children involves establishing programs to reduce the number of youth gangs, developing strategies for lowering parent-adolescent conflict, creating education programs to benefit low-income ethnic minority adolescents, implementing programs to reduce Latino adolescents' high rate of school dropout, and decreasing the exaggerated masculinity in adolescent males (which is associated with a number of problems).

HEALTH AND WELL-BEING

The Midnight Basketball League

The dark side of peer relations is nowhere more present than in the increasing number of youth gangs. Beginning in 1990, the Chicago Housing Authority began offering youth gang members an alternative to crime—the Midnight Basketball League (MBL) (Simons, Finlay, & Yang, 1991). Most crimes were being committed between 10 P.M. and 2 A.M. by males in their late teens and early twenties. The MBL offers these males a positive diversion during the time they are most likely to get into trouble. There are eight teams in the housing projects and 160 players in all. The year-round program provides top-quality basketball shoes, uniforms, championship rings, all-star games, and awards banquets.

Attitude is considered more important than ability, so most teams consist of

To help combat the participation of youth in gangs, the Midnight Basketball League (MBL) was created in a high-crime neighborhood of Chicago. The comprehensive program not only includes a well-organized basketball league, but also a number of workshops to improve the high-risk youths' life skills and educational orientation. Gil Walker, MBL Commissioner and organizer, is in the first row, far left.

one or two stars and eight or nine enthusiastic, mediocre-to-poor players. Different gang factions are represented on each team.

Basketball, however, is only one component of the MBL. To stay in the league, players must follow rules that prohibit fighting, unsportsmanlike behavior, profanity, drugs, alcohol, radios, and tape players. If they break the rules, they don't play basketball. Practices are mandatory and so are workshops after each game. During the workshops, youth are encouraged to seek drug abuse counseling, vocational counseling and training, life skills advising, basic health care, adult education and GED services, and various social services. The program is funded by the Housing Authority and private donations.

In a recent year, not one of the MBL players had been in trouble and 54 of the 160 participants registered for adult education classes once the season had ended. The program has been replicated in Dallas, Texas; Hartford, Connecticut; Louisville, Kentucky; and Washington, DC. For more information about the MBL, contact: Gil Walker, MBL Commissioner, Chicago Housing Authority, 534 East 37th Street, Chicago, IL 60653, 312–791–4768.

FAMILIES AND PARENTING
Strategies for Reducing Parent-Adolescent Conflict

If parents and adolescents are immersed in conflict, are there ways parents can reduce the conflict? Laurence Steinberg has studied parent-adolescent conflict for a number of years. Steinberg (with Ann Levine, 1990) believes that the best way for parents to handle parent-adolescent conflict is through collaborative problem solving, the goal of which is to discover a solution that satisfies both the parent and the adolescent. The approach works best at a time when neither the parent nor the adolescent will be distracted, when the discussion is restricted to a single issue, and when the adolescent's agreement to try to work out a solution is secured in advance. The collaborative problem-solving approach consists of six basic steps:

1. *Establish ground rules for conflict resolution.* These rules are basically the rules of fighting fairly. Both the parent and the adolescent agree to treat each other with respect—no name-calling or putting each other down, for example—and to listen to each other's point of view. At the beginning of the discussion, the parent should provide a positive note by stating a desire to be fair.

2. *Try to reach a mutual understanding.* Step 2 involves taking turns to reach a mutual understanding, which means that both the parent and the adolescent get the opportunity to say what the real problem is and how they feel about it. In this part of the discussion, it is important to focus on the issue, not on personalities.

3. *Try brainstorming.* Step 3 involves both the adolescent and the parent generating as many solutions to the problem as they can. At this point, no idea should be rejected because it is too crazy, too expensive, or too dumb. A time limit should be set—something like five or ten minutes—for both parent and child to come up with as many ideas as possible for solving the conflict. Write down all of the possibilities.

4. *Try to come to an agreement about one or more solutions.* In step 4 of collaborative problem solving, both the parent and the adolescent select the options they like best. Every option should not be discussed because this can produce endless, sometimes fruitless, debate. In this step, the parent and the adolescent can see where their interests converge. Some give-and-take and some negotiation will probably be needed at this point. Neither the parent nor the adolescent should agree to something they find unacceptable.

5. *Write down the agreement.* While step 5 may sound formal, it should be followed because memories can become distorted. If either the parent or the adolescent breaks the agreement, the written statement can be consulted.

6. *Establish a time for a follow-up conversation to examine the progress that has been made.* Step 6 is just as important as the first five steps. Either the adolescent or the parent may not abide by the agreement, or the solution agreed upon may not be working out as well as was hoped and any new problem that arises will have to be addressed.

The six steps of collaborative problem solving can be applied to a number of parent-adolescent conflicts, including such issues as curfew, choice of friends, keeping a room clean, respect for adults, rules for dating, and so on. In some situations, parents and adolescents will not be able to reach an agreement. When the health and safety of the adolescent is at issue, it may be necessary for the parent to make a decision that is not agreed to by the adolescent. However, adolescents are often far more likely to go along with the direction of a parent's decisions if the adolescent is allowed to participate in the decision-making process and sees that the parent is taking the adolescent's needs and desires seriously.

Education and Ethnic Minority Adolescents

Parents' attitudes and behavior can either improve or detract from adolescents' school performance. In one investigation that controlled for social class, authoritarian and permissive parenting were both associated with poor grades, while authoritative parenting was associated with better grades (Dornbusch & others, 1987). However, more than parenting styles are involved in understanding ethnic minority adolescents' school performance because many Asian American adolescents' parents follow an authoritarian parenting style, yet Asian American adolescents', especially Japanese and Chinese American, often excel in school. A special concern is the large number of African American and Latino adolescents who grow up in single-parent families. For example, half of African American adolescents are likely to remain with a single parent through the end of adolescence, whereas only 15 percent of White American adolescents will. Among ethnic minorities, about 70 percent of African American and Latino adolescents are raised by single mothers. Poor school performance among many ethnic minority youth is related to this pattern of single parenting and poverty.

One program in Washington, D.C., has helped many ethnic minority adolescents do better in school. In 1983, Dr. Henry Gaskins began an after-school tutorial program for ethnic minority students. For 4 hours every weeknight and all day Saturday, 80 students receive one-on-one assistance from Gaskins and his wife, two adult volunteers, and academically talented peers. Those who can afford it contribute five dollars to cover the cost of school supplies. In addition to tutoring in specific subjects, Gaskin's home-based academy helps students set personal goals and commit to a desire to succeed. Many of his students come from families in which the parents are high school dropouts and either can't or are not motivated to help their adolescent sons and daughters achieve in school. In addition, the academy prepares students to qualify for scholarships and college entrance exams. Gaskins recently received the President's Volunteer Action Award at the White House.

Dr. Henry Gaskins, here talking with a high school student, began an after-school tutorial program for ethnic minority students in 1983 in Washington, D.C. Volunteers like Dr. Gaskins can be especially helpful in developing a stronger sense of the importance of education in ethnic minority adolescents.

Parents play an important role in the education of ethnic minority adolescents as demonstrated by this Latino father at his daughter's high school graduation. Many African American and Latino adolescents grow up in low-income, single-parent families and do not receive the support this Latino girl has been given.

El Puente, which means "the bridge," was opened in New York City in 1983 because of community dissatisfaction with the health, education, and social services youth were receiving (Simons, Finlay, & Yang, 1991). El Puente emphasizes five areas of youth development: health, education, achievement, personal growth, and social growth.

El Puente is located in a former Roman Catholic church on the south side of Williamsburg in Brooklyn, a neighborhood made up primarily of low-income Latino families, many of which are far below the poverty line. Sixty-five percent of the residents receive some form of public assistance. The neighborhood has the highest school dropout rate for Latinos in New York City and the highest felony rate for adolescents in Brooklyn.

When the youths, aged 12 through 21, first enroll in El Puente, they meet with counselors and develop a 4-month plan that includes the programs they are interested in joining. At the end of 4 months, youth and staff develop a plan for continued participation. Twenty-six bilingual classes are offered in such subjects as the fine arts, theater, photography, and dance. In addition, a medical and fitness center, GED night school, and mental health and social services centers are also a part of El Puente.

El Puente is funded through state, city, and private organizations and serves about three hundred youth. The program has been replicated in Chelsea and Holyoke, Massachusetts, and two other sites in New York are being developed.

These adolescents participate in the programs of El Puente, located in a predominately low-income Latino neighborhood in Brooklyn, New York. The El Puente program stresses five areas of youth development: health, education, achievement, personal growth, and social growth.

Gender-Role Intensification and Traditional Masculinity in Adolescence

During adolescence, both females and males experience many physical and socioemotional changes that affect their gender role development (Huston & Alvarez, 1990). Especially important is how adolescents incorporate the changes of puberty and emerging sexual interests into their gender makeup. A current debate focuses on whether pubertal and socioemotional changes cause traditional gender roles to intensify during adolescence. In gender intensification during early adolescence, puberty signals that the adolescent is beginning to approach adulthood and, therefore, should begin acting in ways that resemble the stereotypical female or male adult. Also, as girls and boys move through puberty with all of its hormonal and body changes, they are not quite sure how they are going to turn out.

Boys, especially, have strong pressure to act in accordance with a stereotypical male role during adolescence, because many boys believe that if they behave in soft, kind, and sensitive ways they will be perceived as a weak male and possibly even be labeled as a homosexual.

There is a special concern about adolescent boys who adopt a strong masculine role in adolescence because it is increasingly being found to be associated with problem behaviors. Joseph Pleck (1983, 1995) believes that what defines traditional masculinity in many Western cultures includes behaviors that do not have social approval but nonetheless validate the adolescent boy's masculinity. That is, in the male adolescent culture, male adolescents believe that they will be perceived as more masculine if they engage in premarital sex, drink alcohol and take drugs, and participate in illegal delinquent activities.

The idea that male problem behaviors have something to do with "masculinity" has recently gotten the attention of policymakers. U.S. Department of Health and Human Services Secretary Louis Sullivan called for action to address a generation whose manhood is measured by the caliber of gun he carries or the number of children he has fathered. In a similar vein, Virginia Governor Douglas Wilder urged policymakers to get across the message that, contrary to what many of today's youth think, making babies is no act of manhood. Addressing and challenging traditional beliefs about masculinity in adolescent males may have the positive outcome of helping to reduce their problem behaviors.

REVIEW OF CHILDREN'S DEVELOPMENT

Adolescence

—

PHYSICAL DEVELOPMENT

Puberty is a period of rapid skeletal and sexual maturation that occurs mainly in early adolescence. Testosterone plays an important role in male pubertal development, estradiol in female pubertal development. The growth spurt for boys occurs about 2 years later than for girls, with 10½ being the average age of onset for boys, 12½ for girls. Individual maturation in pubertal change is extensive. Adolescents show a heightened interest in their body image. Early maturation often favors boys during early adolescence, but in terms of identity development in adulthood, later maturation is more favorable. Early-maturing girls are vulnerable to a number of problems. At issue is the extent to which puberty's effects have been exaggerated. A number of problems and disorders can appear in adolescence. The United States has the highest rate of adolescent drug use of any industrialized nation. Juvenile delinquency, suicide, and eating disorders are other problems. At-risk adolescents often have more than one problem. Two approaches that have the widest application to improving the lives of at-risk youth are providing individual attention to at-risk youth and developing coordinated community-wide interventions.

COGNITIVE DEVELOPMENT

In Piaget's theory, formal operational thought emerges between 11 and 15 years of age. Formal operational thought is more abstract, idealistic, and logical than concrete operational thought. Piaget believed that adolescents become capable of using hypothetical-deductive reasoning. Some of Piaget's ideas about formal operational thought are being questioned. Changes in social cognition characterize adolescent development in the areas of adolescent egocentrism, implicit personality theory, and social cognitive monitoring. Adolescence is a time of increased decision making, and adolescents need more opportunities to practice and discuss realistic decision making. Adolescence might be a special juncture in religious development. The function of schools for adolescents has been extensively debated. First junior high schools and then middle schools have been developed for educating adolescents. The transition to middle or junior high school is often stressful. A special concern is the number of adolescents who drop out of school, especially Latino adolescents. Career development becomes more important in late adolescence, a time when many adolescents combine school and part-time work.

SOCIOEMOTIONAL DEVELOPMENT

Many parents have a difficult time handling the adolescent's push for autonomy, even though this push is one of the hallmarks of adolescent development. Adolescents do not simply move into a world isolated from parents. Attachment to parents increases the probability that the adolescent will be socially competent and explore a widening social world in competent ways. Conflict with parents often increases in early adolescence, and this likely serves a positive developmental function. Both maturation of the adolescent and maturation of parents affect parent-adolescent relationships. The pressure for peer conformity increases during early adolescence. Children's groups are less formal, less heterogeneous, and more same-sex than adolescent groups. Dating becomes an important aspect of development for most adolescents. In primitive cultures, rites of passage often mark a transition to adult status. In America, rites of passage are poorly defined. An increasing interest focuses on the development of ethnic minority adolescents. Erikson proposed that adolescence is characterized by the stage of identity versus identity confusion. Marcia proposed four statuses of identity. Some experts believe that the most significant changes in identity occur in late adolescence or youth rather than in early adolescence. Parents, culture, ethnicity, and gender likely make important contributions to identity development.

MONET
Poppyfield, detail

EPILOGUE

Children: The Future of Society

As the twenty-first century approaches, the well-being of children is one of our nation's most important concerns. We all cherish the future of our children for they are the future of society. Children who do not reach their full potential, who are destined to make fewer contributions to society than society needs, and who do not take their place as productive adults diminish that society's future.

In the end the power behind development is life.

—**Erik Erickson**

IMPROVING THE LIVES OF CHILDREN

Throughout the book we have discussed many ideas for improving the lives of children. In this regard, we have woven five themes throughout *Children:* health and well-being, families and parenting, education, culture and ethnicity, and gender. To conclude the text, let's think further about what we can do in each of these five domains to improve the lives of children.

Health and Well-Being

Although we have in some ways become a nation far more concerned about health and well-being than previous generations, the health and well-being of America's children and children in many countries around the world raise serious concerns. The AIDS epidemic, malnourished children and parents in Third World countries, the poor quality of health care that many American families receive compared to their counterparts in other industrialized nations, inadequate nutrition and exercise, child abuse, poverty, inadequate parenting, and adolescent drug abuse are among the factors that cause considerable concern about children's health and well-being.

We have woven an interest in children's health and well-being throughout *Children,* highlighting that the ultimate responsibility for our health and well-being, and that of our nation's children, rests in our own hands. Parents, teachers, nurses, physicians, and other adults serve as important models and providers of children's health and well-being.

We need to develop a more passionate concern for the health and well-being of America's children. The health and survival of our country's children compares unfavorably with other Western industrialized democracies. Especially important in improving children's health and well-being is a focus on preventive care. We need to give more attention to our nation's social policy, especially in terms of ways to break the poverty cycle that imprisons more than 20 percent of America's children. Clearly, with such a high percentage of children growing up in poverty, we are not doing nearly enough as a nation to help children reach their full potential.

Families and Parenting

Although many contexts and social agents play important roles in children's development, none are more important than the family and parenting. At a point not too long ago, we heard rumblings about the decreasing influence of the family in children's lives and how the family as we had come to know it was breaking down. The structure of many families has changed as a result of an increasing number of divorced, working mother, and stepparent families, but the family still is the most important socializing force in children's development. Regardless of the type of culture and family structure in which children grow up, they benefit enormously when one or both parents are highly involved in their upbringing, provide them with warmth and nurturance, help them to develop self-control, and provide them with an environment that promotes their health and well-being.

Competent parents are knowledgeable about the nature of children's development, effectively monitor their children's lives, and adapt their behavior as the child grows and matures. The family and parents are fundamentally important to both children's early and later development.

A special concern is that too many of America's children grow up in low-income families and suffer the stressful and burdensome perils of poverty. In a number of places in *Children,* we called attention to family support and parent education programs that can help children get a better start in life. These programs are currently improving the lives of thousands of families, but they need to be expanded to help far more children than are currently being served by them.

For those of you who will become parents someday, or are already parents, I again underscore how important it is for each of you to take seriously the importance of rearing your children. Remember that good parenting takes an incredible amount of time; if you become a parent, you should be willing to commit yourself, day after day, week after week, month after month, and year after year, to providing your children with a warm, supportive, safe, and stimulating environment that will make them feel secure and allow them to reach their full potential as human beings. This is true for fathers as well as mothers. While there has been an increase in the amount of time fathers spend with their children, far too many fathers still do not develop an adequate close relationship with their children.

Education

A third way we can increase the likelihood that children will reach their full potential is by improving their education. The importance of education in children's lives was highlighted throughout *Children.* Although schools are an extremely important context for education and development, children also learn from their parents, siblings, peers, books, television, and computers.

There is widespread agreement that something needs to be done about our nation's schools and the education of our children. We need schools that place a stronger emphasis on education that is developmentally appropriate. This needs to be accomplished at all levels of education, especially in early childhood education, elementary school education, and middle school education.

The information and thinking society of the twenty-first century will no longer be content with products of education who have been trained to merely take in and recycle information handed out by teachers and other authority figures. Today's children who become tomorrow's adults need to experience an education that teaches them to think for themselves and to generate new information. This transformation is occurring in some schools but not in nearly enough.

Sociocultural Contexts

Throughout *Children* we have emphasized the importance of considering the sociocultural contexts in which the child develops. These sociocultural contexts include the cultural and ethnic worlds in which children live and develop. We and our children are not just citizens of the United States or Canada; we are citizens of the world. Global interdependence is no longer a matter of belief or preference. It is an inescapable reality. By increasing our knowledge of the behavior, values, and nature of children's development in cultures around the world, we can learn about the universal aspects of children's development, cultural variations in development, and how to interact with children more effectively to make this planet a more hospitable, peaceful place in which to live.

Understanding our own culture better can also improve children's lives. There is a special sense of urgency in addressing the nature of ethnicity and how it affects children's development because of the dramatic changes in the ethnic composition of America's population. The Asian American, Latino, and African American populations are expected to increase at a much faster pace than the White American population over the foreseeable future. At a point early in the twenty-first century, one-third of the population in the United States will be composed of ethnic minority groups.

To help children of any ethnic heritage reach their full potential, we need to:

- Recognize the diversity within every cultural and ethnic group. Not recognizing this diversity leads to unfortunate, harmful stereotyping.
- Understand that there are legitimate differences among cultural and ethnic groups. Recognizing and accepting these differences are important aspects of getting along with others in a diverse, multicultural world. For too long, differences between ethnic minority individuals and White Americans were characterized as deficits on the part of ethnic minority individuals.

- Recognize and accept similarities among cultural and ethnic groups when differences have been incorrectly assumed. Through much of its history, America has had a White, middle-class bias. The search for legitimate similarities among White Americans and ethnic minority Americans is important because incorrectly assumed differences involve stereotyping and can lead to prejudice.

Gender

Another important dimension of children's lives that needs to be addressed in helping them reach their full potential is gender. Throughout *Children* we emphasized how the world of children and adults has not been a very fair gender world. Not only have ethnic minority children grown up in a world that has confronted them with bias and discrimination, so have girls.

An important goal of this book has been to extensively evaluate the gender worlds of children and to promote gender equity in children's development. I (your author) have two daughters who are now in their twenties. As Tracy and Jennifer were growing up, there were many instances when I felt they experienced bias and discrimination because they were females—in school, in athletics, and in many other contexts of their lives. My wife and I wanted them to have the opportunity to reach their full potential and not be handcuffed by a gender-biased society and authority figures. Our hope was that they not only would develop strengths in traditionally feminine domains, such as relationship skills, but also would acquire a sense of self-assertiveness, a traditionally masculine domain, that would serve them well in their quest to become competent persons. I hope that all children have this opportunity, and that Tracy and Jennifer's children will have fewer gender barriers to break through than they did.

The Journey of Childhood

I hope you can look back and say that you learned a lot about children—
not only other children, but yourself as a child and how your childhood
contributed to who you are today. The insightful words of philosopher Soren
Kierkegaard capture the importance of looking back to understand
ourselves: "Life is lived forward but understood backwards." I also hope
that those of you who become the parents of children or who work with
children in some capacity—whether as teacher, counselor, or community
leader—feel that you have a better grasp of what children's development is
all about.

Future generations depend on our ability to face our children. At some
point in our adult lives, each one of us needs to examine the shape of our life
and ask whether we have met the responsibility of competently and caringly
carving out a better world for our children. Twenty-one centuries ago,
Roman poet and philosopher Lucretius described one of adult life's richest
meanings: grasping that the generations of living things pass in a short while
and, like runners, pass on the torch of life. More than twenty centuries
later, American writer James Agee captured yet another of life's richest
meanings: In every child who is born, the potentiality of the human species
is born again.

As we come to the end of this book, I leave you with the following
montage of thoughts and images that convey the beauty and complexity of
children's development.

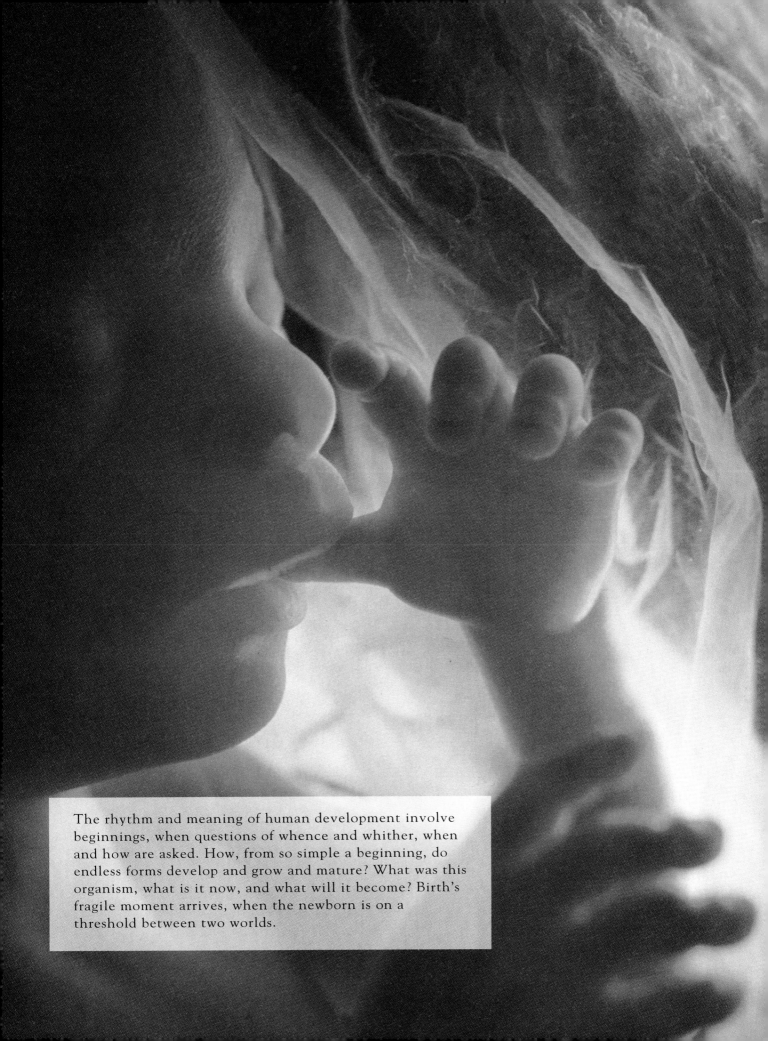

The rhythm and meaning of human development involve beginnings, when questions of whence and whither, when and how are asked. How, from so simple a beginning, do endless forms develop and grow and mature? What was this organism, what is it now, and what will it become? Birth's fragile moment arrives, when the newborn is on a threshold between two worlds.

As newborns, we were not empty-headed organisms. We cried, kicked, coughed, sucked, saw, heard, and tasted. We slept a lot and occasionally we smiled, although the meaning of our first smiles was not entirely clear. We crawled and then we walked, a journey of a thousand miles beginning with a single step. With each forward step we left some ghost of ourselves behind. Sometimes we conformed, sometimes others conformed to us. Our development was a continuous creation of more complex forms and our helpless kind demanded the meeting eyes of love. We split the universe into two halves: "me" and "not me." And we juggled the need to curb our own will with becoming what we could will freely.

In early childhood, our greatest untold poem was being only four years old. We skipped, played, and ran all the day long, never in our lives so busy, busy becoming something we had not quite grasped yet. Who knew our thoughts, which we worked up into small mythologies all our own. While our thoughts and feelings took wings, the blossoms of our heart no wind could touch. Our small world widened as we discovered new refuges and new people. When we said "I" we meant something totally unique, not to be confused with any other.

In middle and late childhood, we were on a different plane, belonging to a generation and feeling properly our own. It is the wisdom of human development that at no other time are we more ready to learn than at the end of early childhood's expansive imagination. Our thirst was to know and to understand. Our parents continued to cradle our lives, but our growth was also being shaped by successive choirs of friends. We did not think much about the future or the past, but enjoyed the present.

In no order of things was adolescence the simple time of
life for us. We clothed ourselves with rainbows and went
brave as the zodiac, flashing from one end of the world to
the other. We tried on one face after another, searching
for a face of our own. We wanted our parents to
understand us and hoped they would give us the privilege
of understanding them. We wanted to fly but found that
first we had to learn to stand and walk and climb and
dance. In our most pimply and awkward moments we
became acquainted with sex. We played furiously at adult
games but were confined to a society of our own peers.
Our generation was the fragile cable by which the best
and the worst of our parents' generation was transmitted to
the present. In the end, there were but two lasting
bequests our parents could leave us—one being roots,
the other wings.

GLOSSARY

A

accommodation Individuals' adjustment to new information. 41

acculturation Cultural change that results from continuous, firsthand contact between two distinctive cultural groups. 362

achievement motivation (need for achievement) The desire to accomplish something, to reach a standard of excellence, and to expend effort to excel. 401

active (niche-picking) genotype-environment interactions The type of interactions that occur when children seek out environments they find compatible and stimulating. 92

activity level The tempo and vigor of movement. 228

adolescence The developmental period of transition from childhood to early adulthood, entered at approximately 10 to 12 years of age and ending at 18 to 22 years of age. 16

adolescent egocentrism The heightened self-consciousness of adolescents that is reflected in their belief that others are as interested in them as they are in themselves, and in their sense of personal uniqueness. 494

adoption study A study in which investigators seek to discover whether, in behavior and psychological characteristics, adopted children are more like their adoptive parents, who provided a home environment, or more like their biological parents, who contributed their heredity. Another form of the adoption study is to compare adoptive and biological siblings. 90

afterbirth The third stage of birth, when the placenta, umbilical cord, and other membranes are detached and expelled. 137

AIDS (acquired immune deficiency syndrome) A syndrome caused by the human immunodeficiency virus (HIV), which destroys the body's immune system. 467

altruism An unselfish interest in helping someone else. 441

amniocentesis A prenatal medical procedure in which a sample of amniotic fluid is withdrawn by syringe and tested to discover if the fetus is suffering from any chromosomal or metabolic disorders. It is performed between the 12th and 16th weeks of pregnancy. 84

amnion The life-support system that is a bag or envelope that contains a clear fluid in which the developing embryo floats. 106

anal stage The second Freudian stage of development, occurring between 1½ and 3 years of age, in which the child's greatest pleasure involves the anus or the eliminative functions associated with it. 38

androgen The main class of male sex hormones. 330

androgyny The presence of desirable masculine and feminine characteristics in the same individual. 433

anger cry Similar to the basic cry, with more excess air forced through the vocal chords (associated with exasperation or rage by mothers). 233

animism The belief that inanimate objects have "lifelike" qualities and are capable of action. 280

anorexia nervosa An eating disorder that involves the relentless pursuit of thinness through starvation. 477

anoxia The insufficient availability of oxygen to the infant. 137

Apgar scale A widely used method to assess the health of newborns at 1 and 5 minutes after birth. The Apgar scale evaluates infants' heart rate, respiratory effort, muscle tone, body color, and reflex irritability. 146

aptitude-treatment interaction (ATI) The interaction between children's aptitudes or characteristics and the treatments or experiences they are given in classrooms. 422

assimilation (Piaget) Individuals' incorporation of new information into their existing knowledge. 41

assimilation (culture) The absorption of ethnic minority groups into the dominant group, which often involves the loss of some or virtually all of the behavior and values of the ethnic minority group. 531

associative play Play that involves social interaction with little or no organization. 322

attachment A close emotional bond between an infant and a caregiver. 221

attention-deficit hyperactivity disorder A disorder characterized by a short attention span, distractibility, and high levels of physical activity; also called hyperactivity. 368

authoritarian parenting A restrictive punitive style in which parents exhort the child to follow their directions and to respect work and effort. The authoritarian parent places firm limits and controls on the child and allows little verbal exchange. Authoritarian parenting is associated with children's social incompetence. 313

authoritative parenting A parenting style in which parents encourage their children to be independent but still place limits and controls on their actions. Extensive verbal give-and-take is allowed, and parents are warm and nurturant toward the child. Authoritative parenting is associated with children's social competence. 313

autonomous morality The second stage of moral development in Piaget's theory, displayed by older children (about 10 years of age and older). The child becomes aware that rules and laws are created by people and that, in judging an action, one should consider the actor's intentions as well as the consequences. 335

autonomy versus shame and doubt Erikson's second stage of development, which occurs in late infancy and toddlerhood (1–3 years). After gaining trust in their caregivers, infants begin to discover that their behavior is their own. 39

B

basal metabolism rate (MBR) The minimum amount of energy a person uses in a resting state. 263

basic cry A rhythmic pattern usually consisting of a cry, a briefer silence, a shorter inspiratory whistle that is higher pitched than the main cry, and then a brief rest before the next cry. 233

basic-skills-and-phonetics approach An approach to teaching reading that stresses phonetics and its basic rules for translating written symbols into sounds. 399

Bayley Scales of Infant Development Scales developed by Nancy Bayley that are widely used in the assessment of infant development. The current version has three components: a mental scale, a motor scale, and an infant behavior profile. 196

becoming parents and families with children The third stage in the family life cycle, in which the adults move up a generation and become caregivers to the next generation. 219

behavior genetics The study of the degree and nature of behavior's heredity basis. 90

behaviorism The scientific study of observable behavioral responses and their environmental determinants. 43

bilingual education Programs for students with limited proficiency in English that instruct students in their own language part of the time while they learn English. 400

biological processes Changes in an individual's physical nature. 15

blastocyst The inner layer of cells that develops during the germinal period. These cells later develop into the embryo. 104

bonding Close contact, especially physical, between parents and their newborn in the period shortly after birth. 148

boundary ambiguity The uncertainty in stepfamilies about who is in or out of the family and who is performing or responsible for certain tasks in the family system. 418

Brazelton Neonatal Behavioral Assessment Scale A test given several days after birth to assess newborns' neurological development, reflexes, and reactions to people. 146

breech position The baby's position in the uterus that causes the buttocks to be the first part to emerge from the vagina. 137

bulimia An eating disorder in which the individual consistently follows a binge-purge eating pattern. 477

C

canalization The process by which characteristics take a narrow path or developmental course. Apparently, preservative forces help to protect a person from environmental extremes. 90

career self-concept theory Super's theory that individuals' self-concepts play central roles in their career choices. 504

care perspective A moral perspective that views people in terms of their connectedness with others and emphasizes interpersonal communication, relationships with others, and concern for others. Gilligan's theory is a care perspective. 440

case study An in-depth look at an individual; it is used mainly by clinical psychologists when the unique aspects of a person's life cannot be duplicated, for either practical or ethical reasons. 52

centration The focusing of attention on one characteristic to the exclusion of all others. 282

cephalocaudal pattern The sequence in which the greatest growth always occurs at the top—the head—with physical growth in size, weight, and feature differentiation gradually working its way down from top to bottom (to neck, shoulders, middle trunk, and so on). 163

cesarean section The surgical removal of the baby from the uterus. 137

child-centered kindergarten Education that involves the whole child by considering both the child's physical, cognitive, and social development and the child's needs, interests, and learning styles. 293

chlamydia A sexually transmitted disease named for the bacteria that cause it. 467

chorionic villus test A prenatal medical procedure in which a small sample of the placenta is removed at a certain point in the pregnancy between the 8th and the 11th weeks of pregnancy. 86

chromosomes Threadlike structures that come in 23 pairs, one member of each pair coming from each parent. Chromosomes contain the genetic substance DNA. 80

chronosystem The patterning of environmental events and transitions over the life course and their sociohistorical contexts. 47

clinical depression This involves being diagnosed as experiencing major depressive disorder or dysthymic disorder. 474

cliques Smaller groups that involve greater intimacy among members and have more cohesion than crowds. 525

cognitive appraisal Lazarus' term for children's interpretations of events in their lives as harmful, threatening, or challenging, and their determination of whether they have the resources to effectively cope with the event. 361

cognitive developmental theory of gender The theory that children's gender typing occurs after they have developed a concept of gender. Once they consistently conceive of themselves as male or female, children often organize their world on the basis of gender. 333

cognitive monitoring The process of taking stock of what you are currently doing, what you will do next, and how effectively the mental activity is unfolding. 385

cognitive processes Changes in an individual's thought, intelligence, and language. 15

cohort effects Effects due to an individual's time of birth or generation but not the individual's age. 57

commitment Marcia's term for the part of identity development in which adolescents show a personal investment in what they are going to do. 533

community rights versus individual rights The fifth stage in Kohlberg's theory of moral development. At this stage, the person understands that values and laws are relative and that standards may vary from one person to another. 438

computer-assisted instruction The teaching strategy that involves using computers as tutors to individualize instruction. Computers are used to present information, give students practice, assess student levels of understanding, and provide additional information when needed. 405

concrete operational stage Piaget's third stage, which lasts from approximately 7 to 11 years of age; children can perform operations, and logical reasoning replaces intuitive thought as long as the reasoning can be applied to specific concrete examples. 42

connectedness According to Cooper and her colleagues, connectedness consists of two dimensions: mutuality (sensitivity to and respect for others' views) and permeability (openness to others' views). 534

conservation The idea that an amount stays the same regardless of how its container changes. 282

constructive play Play that combines sensorimotor/practice repetitive activity with symbolic representation of ideas. Constructive play occurs when children engage in self-regulated creation or construction of a product or a problem solution. 324

constructivist view The view, advocated by Piaget, that the main perceptual abilities—visual, auditory, and tactile, for example—are completely uncoordinated at birth and that young infants do not have intermodal perception. 178

context The settings, influenced by historical, economic, social, and cultural factors, in which development occurs. 11

continuity of development The view that development involves gradual, cumulative change from conception to death. 18

control processes Cognitive processes that do not occur automatically but require work and effort. These processes are under the learner's conscious control and they can be used to improve memory. They are also appropriately called strategies. 384

conventional reasoning The second or intermediate level in Kohlberg's theory of moral development. At this level, the individual's internalization is intermediate. The person abides by certain standards (internal), but they are the standards of others (external), such as parents or the laws of society.   437

convergent thinking Thinking that produces one correct answer and is characteristic of the kind of thinking tested by standardized intelligence tests.   396

cooperative play Play that involves social interaction in a group with a sense of group identity and organized activity.   322

coordination of secondary circular reactions Piaget's fourth sensorimotor substage, which develops between 8 and 12 months of age. In this substage, several significant changes take place involving the coordination of schemes and intentionality.   190

correlational strategy The goal is to describe the strength of the relation between two or more events or characteristics.   54

correlation coefficient A number based on statistical analysis used to describe the degree of association between two variables. The correlation coefficient ranges from −1.00 to 1.00.   54

creativity The ability to think in novel and unusual ways and to come up with unique solutions to problems.   396

crisis Marcia's term for a period of identity development during which the adolescent is choosing among meaningful alternatives.   533

critical period A fixed time period very early in development during which certain behaviors optimally emerge; a period in which there is a learning readiness— beyond this period, learning is difficult or impossible.   46, 201

critical thinking Grasping the deeper meaning of problems, keeping an open mind about different approaches and perspectives, and thinking reflectively rather than merely accepting others' claims or carrying out procedures without significant understanding or evaluation.   387

cross-cultural studies The comparison of a culture with one or more other cultures, which provides information about the degree to which development is similar (universal) across cultures or the degree to which it is culture-specific.   11, 529

cross-sectional approach A research strategy in which individuals of different ages are compared all at one time.   56

crowd The largest and least personal of adolescent groups.   524

cultural-familial retardation Retardation that is characterized by no evidence of organic brain damage, but the individual's IQ is between 50 and 70.   394

culture The behavior patterns, beliefs, and all other products of a group that are passed on from generation to generation.   11

culture-fair tests Tests that are designed to be free of cultural bias.   392

D

dating scripts The cognitive models that adolescents and adults use to guide and evaluate dating interactions.   527

defense mechanisms The psychoanalytic term for unconscious methods used by the ego to distort reality in order to protect itself from anxiety.   37

deferred imitation Imitation that occurs after a time delay of hours or days.   195

Denver Developmental Screening Test A test used to diagnose developmental delay in children from birth to 6 years of age; includes separate assessments of gross and fine motor skills, language, and personal-social ability.   259

dependent variable The factor that is measured in an experiment; it may change because of the manipulation of the independent variable.   55

depressed mood Periods of sadness or unhappy mood that can last for a brief or an extended period of time. They may occur as a result of the loss of a significant relationship or failure on an important task.   474

depression A mood disorder in which the individual is unhappy, demoralized, self-derogatory, and bored. The individual does not feel well, loses stamina easily, often has a poor appetite, is listless, and unmotivated.   364

depressive syndromes A cluster of behaviors and emotions that includes feeling lonely, crying, fear of doing bad things, feeling the need to be perfect, feeling unloved, feeling worthless, nervous, guilty, or sad, and worrying.   474

deprivation dwarfism Growth retardation caused by emotional deprivation; children who are deprived of affection experience stress that affects the release of hormones by the pituitary gland.   256

design stage Kellogg's terms for 3- to 4-year-olds' drawings that mix two basic shapes into more complex designs.   260

development The pattern of change that begins at conception and continues through the life cycle.   15

developmental biodynamics The new perspective on motor development in infancy that seeks to explain how motor behaviors are assembled for perceiving and acting; an outgrowth of developments in the neurosciences, biomechanics, and the behavioral sciences.   167

developmental career choice theory Ginzberg's theory that children and adolescents go through three career choice stages—fantasy, tentative, and realistic.   504

developmentally appropriate practice Education that focuses on the typical developmental patterns of children (age appropriateness) and the uniqueness of each child (individual appropriateness). Such practice contrasts with developmentally inappropriate practice, which ignores the concrete, hands-on approach to learning. Direct teaching largely through abstract, paper-and-pencil activities presented to large groups of young children is believed to be developmentally inappropriate.   294

developmental quotient (DQ) An overall developmental score that combines subscores in motor, language, adaptive, and personal-social domains in the Gesell assessment of infants.   195

difficult child A child who tends to react negatively and cry frequently, who engages in irregular daily routines, and who is slow to accept new experiences.   227

direct-perception view The view that infants are born with intermodal perception abilities that enable them to display intermodal perception early in infancy.   178

discontinuity of development The view that development involves distinct stages in the life span.   18

dishabituation An infant's renewed interest in a stimulus.   193

divergent thinking Thinking that produces many answers to the same question and is characteristic of creativity.   396

DNA A complex molecule that contains genetic information.   80

dominant-recessive genes principle If one gene of a pair is dominant and one is recessive (goes back or recedes), the dominant gene exerts its effect, overriding the potential influence of the recessive gene. A recessive gene exerts its influence only if both genes in a pair are recessive.   88

doula A caregiver who provides continuous physical, emotional, and educational support to the mother before, during, and just after childbirth.   141

Down syndrome A common genetically transmitted form of mental retardation, caused by the presence of an extra (47th) chromosome.   83

dysthymic disorder This occurs when adolescents have a period of at least 1 year in which they have shown depressed or irritable mood every day without more than 2 symptom-free months. Further, dysthymic disorder requires the presence of at least two of the following symptoms: eating problems; sleeping problems; lack of energy; low self-esteem; reduced concentration or decision-making ability; and feelings of hopelessness.   475

E

early childhood   The developmental period that extends from the end of infancy to about 5 to 6 years, sometimes called the preschool years.   16

early formal operational thought   Adolescents' increased ability to think in hypothetical ways which produces unconstrained thoughts with unlimited possibilities. In this early period, the world is perceived too subjectively and idealistically.   493

early-later experience issue   The issue of the degree to which early experiences (especially infancy) or later experiences are the key determinants of the child's development.   19

easy child   A child who is generally in a positive mood, who quickly establishes regular routines in infancy, and who adapts easily to new experiences.   227

echoing   Repeating what a child says, especially if it is an incomplete phrase or sentence.   202

echolalia   An autistic condition in which children echo what they hear.   239

eclectic theoretical orientation   Not following any one theoretical approach, but rather selecting from each theory whatever is considered the best in it.   48

ecological theory   Bronfenbrenner's sociocultural view of development that consists of five environmental systems ranging from the fine-grained inputs of direct interactions with social agents to the broad-based inputs of culture. The five systems in Bronfenbrenner's ecological theory are the microsystem, mesosystem, exosystem, macrosystem, and chronosystem.   46

ectoderm   The outermost layer of cells, which becomes the nervous system, sensory receptors (ears, nose, and eyes, for example), and skin parts (hair and nails, for example).   105

ectopic pregnancy   The presence of a developing embryo or fetus outside the normal location in the uterus.   112

ego   The Freudian structure of personality that deals with the demands of reality.   36

egocentrism   The inability to distinguish between one's own perspective and someone else's (salient feature of the first substage of preoperational thought).   279

embryonic period   The period of prenatal development that occurs 2 to 8 weeks after conception. During the embryonic period, the rate of cell differentiation intensifies, support systems for the cells form, and organs appear.   105

emic approach   The goal is to describe behavior in one culture or ethnic group in terms that are meaningful and important to the people in that group, without regard to other cultures or ethnic groups.   53

emotion   Feeling or affect that involves a mixture of physiological arousal and overt behavior.   231

emotionality   The tendency to be distressed.   228

empathy   Reacting to another's feelings with an emotional response that is similar to the other's feelings.   336

endoderm   The inner layer of cells that develops into digestive and respiratory systems.   105

erogenous zones   Freud's concept of the parts of the body that have especially strong pleasure-giving qualities at each stage of development.   38

estradiol   A hormone associated in girls with breast, uterine, and skeletal development.   460

estrogen   The main class of female sex hormones.   330

ethnic gloss   Using an ethnic label, such as African, Latino, Asian, or Native American, in a superficial way that makes an ethnic group seem more homogeneous than it actually is.   53

ethnic identity   A sense of membership in an ethnic group, based upon shared language, religion, customs, values, history, and race.   11

ethnicity   A characteristic based on cultural heritage, nationality characteristics, race, religion, and language.   11

ethnocentrism   The tendency to favor one's own group over other groups.   428

ethology   A theory that stresses that behavior is strongly influenced by biology, is tied to evolution, and is characterized by critical or sensitive periods.   45

etic approach   The goal in this approach is to describe behaviors so that generalizations can be made across cultures.   53

evocative genotype-environment interactions   The type of interactions that occur when the child's genotype elicits certain types of physical and social environments.   92

evolutionary psychology   A contemporary approach that emphasizes that behavior is a function of mechanisms, requires input for activation, and is ultimately related to survival and reproduction.   76

exosystem   The level at which experiences in another social setting—in which the individual does not have an active role—influence what the individual experiences in an immediate context.   46

expanding   Restating, in a linguistically sophisticated form, what a child has said.   202

experimental strategy   A research strategy that allows investigators to determine behavior's causes by performing an experiment that is a precisely regulated setting in which one or more of the factors believed to influence the behavior being studied are manipulated and all others are held constant.   55

extrinsic motivation   Motivation produced by external rewards and punishments.   402

F

family at midlife   The fifth stage in the family life cycle, an important time of launching children, linking generations, and adapting to midlife changes in development.   219

family in later life   The sixth and final stage in the family life cycle, in which retirement and, for many, grandparenting alter the couple's lifestyle.   221

family structure model   A model according to which any differences in children from different family structures are due to the family structure variations, such as the father's being absent in one set of the families.   318

family with adolescents   The fourth stage in the family life cycle, in which adolescent children push for autonomy and seek to develop their own identity.   219

fetal alcohol syndrome (FAS)   A cluster of abnormalities that appears in the offspring of mothers who drink alcohol heavily during pregnancy.   114

fetal period   The prenatal period of development that begins 2 months after conception and lasts for 7 months, on the average.   107

fine motor skills   Skills that involve more finely tuned movements, such as finger dexterity.   166

first habits and primary circular reactions   Piaget's second sensorimotor substage, which develops between 1 and 4 months of age. In this substage, the infant learns to coordinate sensation and types of schemes or structures—that is, habits and primary circular reactions.   190

formal operational stage   Piaget's fourth and final stage, which occurs between the ages of 11 and 15; individuals move beyond concrete experiences and think in more abstract and more logical ways.   42

fraternal twins   Twins who develop from separate eggs and separate sperm, making them genetically no more similar than ordinary siblings.   90

functional amblyopia   An eye defect that results from not using one eye enough to avoid the discomfort of double vision produced by imbalanced eye muscles; "lazy eye."   256

G

games   Activities engaged in for pleasure that include rules and often competition with one or more individuals.   324

gametes   Human reproduction cells created in the testes of males and the ovaries of females.   80

gender   The sociocultural dimension of being male or female.   12, 330

gender identity The sense of being male or female, which most children acquire by the time they are 3 years old. 330

gender role A set of expectations that prescribe how females or males should think, act, and feel. 330

gender-role transcendence The belief that, when an individual's competence is at issue, it should be conceptualized not on the basis of masculinity, femininity, or androgyny, but rather on a person basis. 434

gender schema A schema that organizes the world in terms of female and male. 334

gender schema theory The theory that an individual's attention and behavior are guided by an internal motivation to conform to gender-based sociocultural standards and stereotypes. 334

gender stereotypes Broad categories that reflect our impressions and beliefs about females and males. 430

generativity versus stagnation Erikson's seventh stage of development, which occurs during middle adulthood. A chief concern is to assist the younger generation in developing and leading useful lives. 39

genes Units of hereditary information composed of DNA. Genes act as a blueprint for cells to reproduce themselves and manufacture the proteins that maintain life. 80

genital stage The fifth and final Freudian stage of development, that occurs from puberty on; a sexual reawakening in which the source of sexual pleasure now becomes someone outside of the family. 38

genotype A person's genetic heritage; the actual genetic material. 88

germinal period The period of prenatal development that takes place in the first 2 weeks after conception. It includes the creation of the zygote, continued cell division, and the attachment of the zygote to the uterine wall. 104

gifted Having above-average intelligence, usually an IQ of 120 or higher, and a superior talent for something. 395

grasping reflex A reflex that occurs when something touches the infants' palms. The infant responds by grasping tightly. 163

gross motor skills Skills that involve large muscle activities such as moving one's arms and walking. 166

H

habituation Repeated presentation of the same stimulus that causes reduced attention to the stimulus. 193

helpless orientation An orientation in which one seems trapped by the experience of difficulty and attributes one's difficulty to a lack of ability. 402

herpes simplex virus II A sexually transmitted disease whose symptoms include irregular cycles of sores and blisters in the genital area. 467

heteronomous morality The first stage of moral development, in Piaget's theory, occurring from approximately 4 to 7 years of age. Justice and rules are conceived of as unchangeable properties of the world, removed from the control of people. 335

holophrase hypothesis The hypothesis that a single word can be used to imply a complete sentence; infants' first words characteristically are holophrastic. 204

hypotheses Assumptions that can be tested to determine their accuracy. 35

hypothetical-deductive reasoning Piaget's formal operational concept that adolescents have the cognitive ability to develop hypotheses, or best guesses, about ways to solve problems, such as an algebraic equation. 491

I

id The Freudian structure of personality that consists of instincts, which are an individual's reserve of psychic energy. 36

identical twins Twins who develop from a single fertilized egg that splits into two genetically identical replicas, each of which becomes a person. 90

identification theory A theory deriving from Freud's view that the preschool child develops a sexual attraction to the opposite-sex parent, then by approximately 5 or 6 years of age renounces this attraction because of anxious feelings, and subsequently identifies with the same-sex parent, unconsciously adopting the same-sex parent's characteristics. 331

identity achievement Marcia's term for adolescents who have undergone a crisis and made a commitment. 533

identity diffusion Marcia's term for adolescents who have not yet experienced a crisis (explored meaningful alternatives) or made any commitments. 533

identity foreclosure Marcia's term for adolescents who have made a commitment but have not experienced a crisis. 533

identity moratorium Marcia's term for adolescents who are in the midst of a crisis, but their commitments are either absent or vaguely defined. 533

identity versus identity confusion Erikson's fifth stage of development, which occurs during the adolescent years. Adolescents are faced with finding out who they are, what they are all about, and where they are going in life. 39

idiographic needs Needs that are important to the individual, not to the group. 59

imaginary audience Adolescents' heightened self-consciousness, reflected in their belief that others are as interested in them as they themselves are; attention-getting behavior motivated by a desire to be noticed, visible, and "on stage." 494

immanent justice The concept that if a rule is broken, punishment will be meted out immediately. 335

implantation The attachment of the zygote to the uterine wall, which takes place about 10 days after conception. 104

imprinting In ethological theory, rapid, innate learning within a limited critical period of time, which involves attachment to the first moving object seen. 46

inclusion Educating children in their natural environments, such as typical kindergarten and elementary school classrooms. 368

independent variable The manipulated, influential, experimental factor in the experiment. 55

individualism and purpose The second stage in Kohlberg's theory of moral development. At this stage, moral thinking is based on rewards and self-interest. 437

individuality According to Cooper and her colleagues, individuality consists of two dimensions: self-assertion (the ability to have and communicate a point of view) and separateness (the use of communication patterns to express how one is different from others). 534

indulgent parenting A style of parenting in which parents are highly involved with their children but place few demands or controls on them. Indulgent parenting is associated with children's social incompetence, especially lack of self-control. 314

industry versus inferiority Erikson's fourth stage of development, which occurs approximately in the elementary school years. Children's initiative brings them into contact with a wealth of new experiences, and they direct their energy toward mastering knowledge and intellectual skills. 39

infancy The developmental period that extends from birth to 18 to 24 months. 16

infantile autism A severe developmental disorder that has its onset in infancy and includes deficiencies in social relationships; abnormalities in communication; and restricted, repetitive, and stereotyped patterns of behavior. 239

infinite generativity An individual's ability to generate an infinite number of meaningful sentences using a finite set of words and rules, which makes language a highly creative enterprise. 197

information processing How individuals process information about their world; how information enters the mind, and how it is stored and transformed, and how it is retrieved to perform such complex activities as problem solving and reasoning. 42

initiative versus guilt Erikson's third stage of development, which occurs during the preschool years. As preschool children encounter a widening social world, they are challenged more than they were as infants. 39

innate goodness view The idea, presented by Swiss-born philosopher Jean-Jacques Rousseau, that children are inherently good. 7

integrity versus despair Erikson's eighth and final stage of development, which occurs during late adulthood. In the later years of life, we look back and evaluate what we have done with our lives. 40

intelligence Verbal ability, problem-solving skills, and the ability to learn from and adapt to the experiences of everyday life. 387

intelligence quotient (IQ) A person's mental age divided by chronological age, multiplied by 100. 389

intermodal perception The ability to relate and integrate information about two or more sensory modalities, such as vision and hearing. 177

internalization The developmental change from behavior that is externally controlled to behavior that is internally controlled. 437

internalization of schemes Piaget's sixth and final sensorimotor substage, which develops between 18 and 24 months of age. In this substage, the infant's mental functioning shifts from a purely sensorimotor plane to a symbolic plane, and the infant develops the ability to use primitive symbols. 190

interpersonal norms The third stage in Kohlberg's theory of moral development. At this stage, the person values trust, caring, and loyalty to others as the basis of moral judgments. 437

intimacy in friendships Self-disclosure and the sharing of private thoughts. 421

intimacy versus isolation Erikson's sixth stage of development, which occurs during the early adulthood years. Young adults face the developmental task of forming intimate relationships with others. 39

intrinsic motivation The desire to be competent and to do something for its own sake. 402

intuitive thought substage Piaget's second substage of preoperational thought, in which children begin to use primitive reasoning and want to know the answers to all sorts of questions (between 4 and 7 years of age). 281

inventionist view The belief that adolescence is a sociohistorical creation. Especially important in the development of the inventionist view of adolescence were the sociohistorical circumstances at the beginning of the twentieth century, a time when legislation was enacted that ensured the dependency of youth and made their move into the economic sphere more manageable. 457

in vitro fertilization Conception outside the body. 81

involution The process by which the uterus returns to its prepregnant size. 147

J

justice perspective A moral perspective that focuses on the rights of the individual; individuals stand alone and independently make moral decisions. Kohlberg's theory is a justice perspective. 440

juvenile delinquent An adolescent who breaks the law or engages in behavior that is considered illegal. 472

K

Klinefelter syndrome A genetic disorder in which males have an extra X chromosome, making them XXY instead of XY. 83

L

labeling Identifying the names of objects. 202

laboratory A controlled setting in which many of the complex factors of the "real world" are removed. 51

Lamaze method A form of prepared childbirth developed by Fernand Lamaze, a pioneering French obstetrician; it involves helping pregnant women cope actively with the pain of childbirth to avoid or reduce medication. 140

language A system of symbols used to communicate with others. In humans language is characterized by infinite generativity and rule systems. 197

language acquisition device (LAD) A biological endowment that enables the child to detect certain language categories, such as phonology, syntax, and semantics. 200

late formal operational thought A restoration of intellectual balance during which the adolescent accommodates to the cognitive upheaval that has taken place. Adolescents now test out the products of their reasoning against experience and consolidation of formal operational thought takes place. 493

latency stage The fourth Freudian stage, occurring between approximately 6 years of age and puberty; the child represses all interest in sexuality and develops social and intellectual skills. 38

learned helplessness Seligman's term for the development of depression in individuals who are exposed to prolonged negative experiences over which they have no control. 365

learning disabilities Disabilities in which individuals with normal intelligence are having academic difficulties in several areas but are not suffering from an overt condition that explains their difficulty. 368

leaving home and becoming a single adult The first stage in the family life cycle, in which the child is launched (or exits his or her family of origin) into adulthood. 219

Leboyer method A birth process, developed by French obstetrician Frederick Leboyer, that intends to make birth less stressful for infants. The procedure is referred to as "birth without violence." 139

longitudinal approach A research strategy in which the same individuals are studied over a period of time, usually several years or more. 56

long-term memory A relatively permanent type of memory that holds huge amounts of information for a long period of time. 384

low-birthweight infant An infant born after a regular period of gestation (the length of time between conception and birth) of 38 to 42 weeks but who weigh less than 5½ pounds. 143

M

macrosystem The culture in which individuals live. 47

major depressive disorder This is present when the adolescent has experienced five or more of the following symptoms for at least a 2-week period at a level that differs from previous functioning: depressed mood or irritable most of the day; decreased interest in pleasurable activities; changes in weight or failure to make necessary weight gains in adolescence; sleep problems; psychomotor agitation or retardation; fatigue or loss of energy; feelings of worthlessness or abnormal amounts of guilt; reduced concentration and decision-making ability; and repeated suicidal ideation, suicide attempts, or plans of suicide. 474

marasmus A wasting away of body tissues in the infant's first year, caused by severe deficiency of protein and calories. 170

mastery orientation An orientation in which one is task oriented and, instead of focusing on one's ability, is concerned with learning strategies. 402

maternal blood test A prenatal diagnostic technique that is used to assess blood alphaprotein level, which is associated with neural-tube defects. This technique is also called the alpha-fetoprotein test (AFP). 86

maturation The orderly sequence of changes dictated by a genetic blueprint. 17

Maximally Discriminative Facial Movement Coding System (MAX) Izard's system of coding infants' facial expressions related to emotions. Using MAX, coders watch slow-motion and stop-action videotapes of infants' facial reactions to stimuli. 233

mean length of utterance (MLU) An index of language development based on the number of morphemes per sentence a child produces in a sample of about 50 to 100 sentences; a good index of language maturity. 204

meiosis The process of cell doubling and separation of chromosomes in which each pair of chromosomes in a cell separates, with one member of each pair going into each gamete. 80

memory A central feature of cognitive development, pertaining to all situations in which an individual retains information over time. 194

menarche First menstruation. 459

mental age (MA) Binet's measure of an individual's level of mental development compared to that of others. 388

mental retardation A condition of limited mental ability in which an individual has a low IQ, usually below 70 on a traditional test of intelligence, and has difficulty adapting to everyday life. 394

mesoderm The middle layer of cells, which becomes the circulatory system, bones, muscles, excretory system, and reproductive system. 105

mesosystem Relationships between microsystems or connections between contexts, such as the connection between family experience and the school experience. 46

microsystem The setting or context in which an individual lives, including the person's family, peers, school, and neighborhood. 46

middle and late childhood The developmental period that extends from about 6 to 11 years of age, approximately corresponding to the elementary school years, sometimes called the elementary school years. 16

Montessori approach An educational philosophy in which children are given considerable freedom and spontaneity in choosing activities and are allowed to move from one activity to another as they desire. 294

moral development Development regarding rules and conventions about what people should do in their interactions with other people. 335

Moro reflex A neonatal startle response that occurs in response to sudden, intense noise or movement. When startled, the newborn arches its back, throws its head back, and flings out its arms and legs. Then the newborn rapidly closes its arms and legs to the center of its body. 163

morphology The study of the rules for combining morphemes; morphemes are the smallest meaningful units of language. 199

motherese The kind of speech often used by mothers and other adults to talk to babies—in a higher pitch than normal and with simple words and sentences. 202

multiple-factor model of divorce Takes into account the complexity of the divorce context and examines a number of influences on the child's development, including not only family structure, but also the strengths and weaknesses of the child prior to the divorce, the nature of the events surrounding the divorce itself, the type of custody involved, visitation patterns, socioeconomic status, and postdivorce family functioning. 318

myelination The process in which the nerve cells are covered and insulated with a layer of fat cells, which increases the speed at which information travels through the nervous system. 256

N

naturalistic observation A method in which scientists observe behavior in real-world settings and make no effort to manipulate or control the situation. 51

natural selection The evolutionary process that favors individuals of a species that are best adapted to survive and reproduce. 75

nature-nurture controversy Nature refers to an organism's biological inheritance, nurture to environmental influences. The "nature" proponents claim biological inheritance is the most important influence on development; the "nurture" proponents claim that environmental experiences are the most important. 18

negative affectivity (NA) Emotions that are negatively toned, such as anger, anxiety, guilt, and sadness. 231

neglected children Children who receive little attention from their peers but are not necessarily disliked by their peers. 419

neglectful parenting A style of parenting in which the parent is very uninvolved in the child's life; it is associated with children's social incompetence, especially a lack of self-control. 313

neo-Piagetians Developmentalists who have elaborated on Piaget's theory, believing that children's cognitive development is more specific in many respects than Piaget thought. 383

new couple The second stage in the family life cycle, in which two individuals from separate families of origin unite to form a new family system. 219

nightmares Frightening dreams that awaken the sleeper. 262

night terrors Sudden arousal from sleep characterized by intense fear, usually accompanied by the physiological reactions such as rapid heart rate and breathing, loud screams, heavy perspiration, and physical movement. 262

nomothetic research Research conducted at the group level in which individual variation is not a major focus. 59

nonnutritive sucking Sucking behavior unrelated to the infants' feeding. 163

nonshared environmental experiences The child's own unique experiences, both within the family and outside the family, that are not shared by another sibling. Thus, experiences occurring within the family can be part of the "nonshared environment." 93

normal distribution A distribution that is symmetrical with most cases falling in the middle of the possible range of scores and a few scores appearing toward the extremes of the range. 389

O

obesity Weighing 20 percent or more above the ideal weight for a particular age and sex. 358

object permanence The Piagetian term for one of an infant's most important accomplishments: understanding that objects and events continue to exist even when they cannot directly be seen, heard, or touched. 190

Oedipus complex In Freudian theory, the young child's development of an intense desire to replace the same-sex parent and enjoy the affections of the opposite-sex parent. 38

onlooker play Play in which the child watches other children play. 322

operations In Piaget's theory, internalized set of actions that allow a child to do mentally what she formerly did physically. 279

oral rehydration therapy (ORT) Treatment to prevent dehydration during episodes of diarrhea by giving fluids by mouth. 267

oral stage The first Freudian stage of development, occurring during the first 18 months of life; the infant's pleasure centers around the mouth. 38

organic retardation Mental retardation that involves some physical damage and is caused by a genetic disorder or brain damage. 394

organogenesis Organ formation that takes place during the first 2 months of prenatal development. 107

original sin view Advocated during the Middle Ages, the belief that children were born into the world as evil beings and were basically bad. 7

oxytocin A hormone that stimulates and regulates the rhythmicity of uterine contractions. It has been widely used as a drug to speed delivery. 138

P

pain cry A sudden appearance of loud crying without preliminary moaning and a long initial cry followed by an extended period of breath holding. 233

parallel play Play in which the child plays separately from others, but with toys like those the others are using or in a manner that mimics their play. 322

passive genotype-environment interactions The type of interactions that occur when parents, who are genetically related to the child, provide a rearing environment for the child. 92

peers Children of about the same age or maturity level. 320

perception The interpretation of what is sensed. 172

performance orientation An orientation in which one focuses on achievement outcomes; winning is what matters most, and happiness is thought to result from winning. 402

personal fable The part of adolescent egocentrism that involves an adolescent's sense of uniqueness. 494

personality-type theory Holland's theory that an effort should be made to match an individual's career choice with his or her personality. 505

perspective taking The ability to assume another person's perspective and understand his or her thoughts and feelings. 426

phallic stage The third Freudian stage of development, occurring between the ages of 3 and 6; its name comes from the Latin word phallus, which means "penis." 38

phenotype The way an individual's genotype is expressed in observed and measurable characteristics. 88

phenylketonuria (PKU) A genetic disorder in which an individual cannot properly metabolize an amino acid. PKU is now easily detected but, if left untreated, results in mental retardation and hyperactivity. 83

phonology The study of a language's sound system. 197

pictorial stage Kellogg's terms for 4- to 5-year-olds' drawings depicting objects that adults can recognize. 261

placement stage Kellogg's terms for 2- to 3-year-olds' drawings that are drawn in placement patterns. 260

placenta A life-support system that consists of a disk-shaped group of tissues in which small blood vessels from the mother and offspring intertwine. 106

play A pleasurable activity that is engaged in for its own sake. 321

play therapy Therapy that allows the child to work off frustrations and is a medium through which the therapist can analyze the child's conflicts and ways of coping with them. Children may feel less threatened and be more likely to express their true feelings in the context of play. 322

pluralism The coexistence of distinct ethnic and cultural groups in the same society. Individuals with a pluralistic stance usually advocate that cultural differences should be maintained and appreciated. 531

polygenic inheritance The genetic principle that many genes can interact to produce a particular characteristic. 88

positive affectivity (PA) The range of positive emotions from high energy, enthusiasm, and excitement to being calm, quiet, and withdrawn. Joy, happiness, and laughter involve positive affectivity. 231

postconventional reasoning The highest level in Kohlberg's theory of moral development. At this level, morality is completely internalized and not based on others' standards. 438

postpartum period The period after childbirth when the mother adjusts, both physically and psychologically, to the process of childbirth. This period lasts for about 6 weeks, or until her body has completed its adjustment and returned to a near prepregnant state. 147

practice play Play that involves repetition of behavior when new skills are being learned or when physical or mental mastery and coordination of skills are required for games or sports. Sensorimotor play, which often involves practice play, is primarily confined to infancy, while practice play can be engaged in throughout life. 323

pragmatics The use of appropriate conversation, and knowledge underlying the use of language in context. 199

precipitate delivery A delivery that takes place too quickly; the baby squeezes through the birth canal in less than 10 minutes. 137

preconventional reasoning The lowest level in Kohlberg's theory of moral development. At this level, the child shows no internalization of moral values—moral reasoning is controlled by external rewards and punishments. 437

prejudice An unjustified negative attitude toward an individual because of that person's membership in a group. 428

prenatal period The time from conception to birth. 16

preoperational stage The second Piagetian developmental stage that lasts from about 2 to 7 years of age; children begin to represent the world with words, images, and drawings. 42

prepared, or natural, childbirth Being informed about what will happen during the procedure, knowing about comfort measures for childbirth, anticipating that little or no medication will be used, and, if complications arise, expecting to participate in decisions made to resolve the problem. 139

pretense/symbolic play Play in which the child transforms the physical environment into a symbol. 323

preterm infant An infant born prior to 38 weeks after conception. 143

primary appraisal Determining whether an event involves harm or loss that has already occurred, a threat of some future danger, or a challenge to be overcome. 361

primary circular reaction A scheme based upon the infant's attempt to reproduce an interesting or pleasurable event that initially occurred by chance. 190

Project Follow Through An adjunct to Project Head Start in which the enrichment programs are carried through the first few years of elementary school. 298

Project Head Start Compensatory education designed to provide children from low-income families the opportunity to acquire the skills and experiences important for school success. 298

proximodistal pattern The sequence in which growth starts at the center of the body and moves toward the extremities. 163

puberty A period of rapid skeletal and sexual maturation that occurs mainly in early adolescence. 459

Public Law 94-142 The federal government's mandate that all children must be given a free and appropriate education. A key provision of the bill is the development of individualized education programs for children with special needs. 368

punishment and obedience orientation The first stage in Kohlberg's theory of moral development. At this stage, moral thinking is based on punishment. 437

Q

questionnaire Similar to a highly structured interview except that respondents read the questions and mark their answers on paper, rather than responding verbally to an interviewer. 52

R

race The term for a system for classifying plants and animals into subcategories according to specific physical and structural characteristics. 77

random assignment The assignment of subjects to experimental and control conditions by chance, thus reducing the likelihood that the results of the experiment will be due to preexisting differences in the two groups. 55

reaction range The range of possible phenotypes for each genotype, suggesting the importance of an environment's restrictiveness or enrichment. 89

recasting Rephrasing something a child has said, perhaps turning it into a question. 202

receptive vocabulary The words an individual understands. 203

reciprocal socialization Socialization that is bidirectional; children socialize parents just as parents socialize children. 218

reciprocal teaching An instructional procedure used by Brown and Palincsar to develop cognitive monitoring; it requires that students take turns leading a study group in the use of strategies for comprehending and remembering text content. 385

reflexive smile A smile that does not occur in response to external stimuli. It happens during the month after birth, usually during irregular patterns of sleep, not when the infant is in an alert state. 233

rejected children Children who are more likely than neglected children to be disruptive and aggressive, and are often disliked by their peers. 419

repression The most powerful and pervasive defense mechanism; it pushes unacceptable id impulses out of awareness and back into the unconscious mind. 37

reproduction The process that, in humans, begins when a female gamete (ovum) is fertilized by a male gamete (sperm). 81

rite of passage A ceremony or a ritual that marks an individual's transition from one status to another. Most rites of passage focus on the transition to adult status. 529

rooting reflex A reflex that occurs when the infant's cheek is stroked or the side of the mouth is touched. In response, the infant turns its head toward the side that was touched, in an apparent effort to find something to suck. 163

S

scaffolding Parental behavior that supports children's efforts, allowing them to be more skillful than they would be if they relied only on their own abilities. 218

schema A cognitive structure, a network of associations that organizes and guides an individual's perceptions. 334

scheme (or schema) The basic unit (or units) for an organized pattern of sensorimotor functioning. 189

scientific method An approach that can be used to discover accurate information about behavior and development (includes the following steps: identify and analyze the problem, collect data, draw conclusions, and revise theories). 35

script A schema for events. 386

secondary appraisal Children's evaluating their resources and determining how effectively they can be used to cope with the event. 361

secondary circular reactions Piaget's third sensorimotor substage, which develops between 4 and 8 months of age. In this substage, the infant becomes more object-oriented or focused on the world, moving beyond preoccupation with the self in sensorimotor interactions. 190

secure attachment The infant uses a caregiver as a secure base from which to explore the environment. Ainsworth believes that secure attachment in the first year of life provides an important foundation for psychological development later in life. 222

self-concept Domain-specific evaluations of the self. 427

self-esteem The global evaluative dimension of the self. Self-esteem is also referred to as self-worth or self-image. 427

Self-Perception Profile for Children A self-concept measure that has five specific domains—scholastic competence, athletic competence, social acceptance, physical appearance, and behavioral conduct—plus general self-worth. 427

self-understanding The child's cognitive representation of self, the substance and content of the child's self-conceptions. 329

semantics The meanings of words and sentences. 199

sensation Sensation occurs when information contacts sensory receptors—the eyes, ears, tongue, nostrils, and skin. 172

sensorimotor play Behavior engaged in by infants to derive pleasure from exercising their existing sensorimotor schemas. 323

sensorimotor stage The first of Piaget's stages that lasts from birth to about 2 years of age; infants construct an understanding of the world by coordinating sensory experiences (such as seeing and hearing) with motoric actions. 42

set point The weight maintained when no effort is made to lose or gain weight. 358

sexual script A stereotyped pattern of role prescriptions for how individuals should behave sexually. 465

shape stage Kellogg's terms for 3-year-olds' drawings consisting of diagrams in different shapes. 260

shared environmental experiences Children's common environmental experiences that are shared with their siblings, such as their parents' personalities and intellectual orientation, the family's social class, and the neighborhood in which they live. 93

short-term memory The memory component in which individuals retain information for 15–30 seconds, assuming there is no rehearsal. 287

sickle-cell anemia A genetic disorder that affects the red blood cells and occurs most often in African American individuals. 83

simple reflexes Piaget's first sensorimotor substage, which corresponds to the first month after birth. In this substage, the basic means of coordinating sensation and action is through reflexive behaviors, such as rooting and sucking, which the infant has at birth. 190

slow-to-warm-up child A child who has a low activity level, is somewhat negative, shows low adaptability, and displays a low intensity mood. 227

sociability The tendency to prefer the company of others to being alone. 228

social identity theory Social psychologist Henry Tajfel's (1978) theory that, when individuals are assigned to a group, they invariably think of that group as an in-group for them. This occurs because individuals want to have a positive image. 428

social learning theory Emphasizes a combination of behavior, environment, and cognition as the key factors in development. 43

social learning theory of gender A theory that emphasizes that children's gender development occurs through observation and imitation of gender behavior, and through the rewards and punishments children experience for gender appropriate and inappropriate behavior. 331

social play Play that involves social interactions with peers. 324

social policy A national government's course of action designed to influence the welfare of its citizens. 12

social smile A smile in response to an external stimulus, which, early in development, typically is in response to a face. 233

social system morality The fourth stage in Kohlberg's theory of moral development. At this stage, moral judgments are based on understanding the social order, law, justice, and duty. 438

sociobiology A view that relies on the principles of evolutionary biology to explain behavior. 76

socioemotional processes Changes in an individual's relationships with other people, emotions, and personality. 15

solitary play Play in which the child plays alone and independently of others. 322

somnambulism Sleepwalking; occurs in the deepest stage of sleep. 262

standardized tests Tests that require an individual to answer a series of written or oral questions. These tests have two distinct features: First, psychologists usually total an individual's score to yield a single score, or set of scores, that reflects something about the individual. Second, psychologists compare the individual's score with the scores of a large group of persons to determine how the individual responded relative to others. 52

stereotype The broad category that reflects our impressions and beliefs about people. All stereotypes refer to an image of what the typical member of a particular group is like. 458

storm-and-stress view Hall's view that adolescence is a turbulent time charged with conflict and mood swings. 457

Strange Situation An observational measure of infant attachment that requires the infant to move through a series of introductions, separations, and reunions with the caregiver and an adult stranger in a prescribed order. 224

stress The response of individuals to circumstances and events, called stressors, that threaten or tax an individual's coping ability. 361

sucking reflex A reflex that occurs when newborns automatically suck an object placed in their mouth. The sucking reflex enables newborns to get nourishment before they have associated a nipple with food. 163

sudden infant death syndrome (SIDS) A condition that occurs when an infant stops breathing, usually during the night, and suddenly dies without apparent cause. 169

superego The Freudian structure of personality that is the moral branch of personality. 36

symbolic function substage Piaget's first substage of preoperational thought, in which the child gains the ability to mentally represent an object that is not present (between 2 and 4 years of age). 279

syntax The ways words are combined to form acceptable phrases and sentences. 199

T

tabula rasa view The idea, proposed by John Locke, that children are like a "blank tablet." 7

telegraphic speech The use of short and precise words to communicate; young children's two- and three-word utterances characteristically are telegraphic. 204

temperament An individual's behavioral style and characteristic way of responding. 227

teratogen From the Greek word tera, meaning "monster." Any agent that causes a birth defect. The field of study that investigates the causes of birth defects is called teratology. 110

tertiary circular reactions, novelty, and curiosity Piaget's fifth sensorimotor substage, which develops between 12 and 18 months of age. In this substage, infants become intrigued by the variety of properties that objects possess and by the multiplicity of things they can make happen to objects. 190

testosterone A hormone associated in boys with the development of genitals, an increase in height, and a change in voice. 460

theory A coherent set of ideas that helps explain data and make predictions. 35

top-dog phenomenon The circumstance of moving from the top position in elementary school to the lowest position in middle or junior high school. 502

toxoplasmosis A mild infection that causes coldlike symptoms in adults but can be a teratogen for the unborn baby. 117

transitional objects Objects that are repeatedly used by children as bedtime companions. These usually are soft and cuddly, and probably mark the child's transition from being dependent to being more independent. 262

triarchic theory Sternberg's theory that intelligence consists of componential intelligence, experiential intelligence, and contextual intelligence. 390

trophoblast The outer layer of cells that develops in the germinal period. These cells provide nutrition and support for the embryo. 104

trust versus mistrust Erikson's first psychosocial stage, experienced in the first year of life; a sense of trust requires a feeling of physical comfort and a minimal amount of fear and apprehension about the future. 39

Turner syndrome A genetic disorder in which females are missing an X chromosome, making them XO instead of XX. 84

twin study A study in which the behavioral similarity of identical twins is compared with the behavioral similarity of fraternal twins. 90

type A babies Infants who exhibit insecurity by avoiding their mother (for example, ignoring her, averting their gaze, and failing to seek proximity). 223

type A behavior pattern A cluster of characteristics (being excessively competitive, hard-driven, impatient, irritable, and hostile) thought to be related to coronary problems. 363

type B babies Infants who use a caregiver as a secure base from which to explore the environment. 223

type C babies Infants who exhibit insecurity by resisting the mother (for example, clinging to her but at the same time kicking and pushing away). 223

U

ultrasound sonography A prenatal medical procedure in which high-frequency sound waves are directed into the pregnant woman's abdomen. 84

umbilical cord A life-support system containing two arteries and one vein that connects the baby to the placenta. 106

universal ethical principles The sixth and highest stage in Kohlberg's theory of moral development. At this stage, persons have developed a moral standard based on universal human rights. 438

unoccupied play Play in which the child is not engaging in play as it is commonly understood and might stand in one spot, look around the room, or perform random movements that do not seem to have a goal. 322

W

whole-language approach An approach to teaching reading that stresses that reading instruction should parallel children's natural language learning. 399

X

XYY syndrome A genetic disorder in which males have an extra Y chromosome. 84

Z

zone of proximal development (ZPD) Vygotsky's term for tasks too difficult for children to master alone, but can be mastered with assistance. 285

zygote A single cell formed through fertilization. 81

REFERENCES

A

Aboud, F., & Skerry, S. (1983). Self and ethnic concepts in relation to ethnic constancy. *Canadian Journal of Behavioral Science, 15*, 3–34.

Abramovitch, R., Corter, C., Pepler, D. J., & Stanhope, L. (1986). Sibling and peer interaction: A final follow-up and comparison. *Child Development, 47*, 217–229.

Abramson, L. Y., Metalsky, G. I., & Alloy, L. B. (1989). Hopelessness depression: A theory-based subtype of depression. *Psychological Bulletin, 96*, 358–372.

Acredolo, L. P., & Hake, J. L. (1982). Infant perception. In B. B. Wolman (Ed.), *Handbook of developmental psychology*. Englewood Cliffs, NJ: Prentice Hall.

Adato, A. (1995, April). Living legacy? Is heredity destiny? *Life*, pp. 60–68.

Adler, T. (1991, January). Seeing double? Controversial twins study is widely reported, debated. *APA Monitor, 22*, 1, 8.

Adolph, K. E., Eppler, M. A., & Gibson, E. J. (1993). Crawling versus walking infants' perception of affordances for locomotion over sloping surfaces. *Child Development, 64*, 1158–1174.

Ainsworth, M. D. S. (1967). Infancy in Uganda: Infant care and the growth of love. In B. M. Caldwell & H. N. Riccuiti (Eds.), *Review of child development research* (Vol. 3). Chicago: University of Chicago Press.

Ainsworth, M. D. S. (1979). Infant-mother attachment. *American Psychologist, 34*, 932–937.

Alan Guttmacher Institute. (1993). *National survey of the American male's sexual habits*. Unpublished data. New York: Author.

Alexander, G. R., & Korenbrot, C. C. (1995). The role of prenatal care in preventing low birth weight. *The Future of Children, 5* (1), 103–120.

Allen, J. P., & Bell, K. L. (1995, March). *Attachment and communication with parent and peers in adolescence*. Paper presented at the meeting of the Society for Research in Child Development, Indianapolis.

Allen, J. P., & Kupermine, G. P. (1995, March). *Adolescent attachment, social competence, and problematic behavior*. Paper presented at the meeting of the Society for Research in Child Development, Indianapolis.

Allen, K. E., & Marotz, L. (1989). *Developmental profiles: Birth-to-six*. Albany, NY: Delmar.

Allen, L., & Majidi-Ahi, S. (1989). Black American children. In J. T. Gibbs & L. N. Huang (Eds.), *Children of color*. San Francisco: Jossey-Bass.

Allen, M., Brown, P., & Finlay, B. (1992). *Helping children by strengthening families*. Washington, DC: Children's Defense Fund.

American Association for Protecting Children. (1986). *Highlights of official child neglect and abuse reporting: 1984*. Denver: American Humane Association.

American College Health Association. (1989, May). *Survey of AIDS on American college and university campuses*. Washington, DC: American College Health Association.

America in Transition. (1989). Washington, DC: National Governors' Association Task Force on Children.

Amsel, E. (1995, March). *The development of causal attributions in two physics domains*. Paper presented at the meeting of the Society for Research in Child Development, Indianapolis.

Anastasi, A. (1988). *Psychological testing* (6th ed.). New York: Macmillan.

Anderman, E. M., Maehr, M. L., & Midgley, C. (1996). *Declining motivation after the transition to middle school: Schools can make a difference*. Unpublished manuscript, University of Kentucky, Lexington.

Anderson, D. R., Lorch, E. P., Field, D. E., Collins, P. A., & Nathan, J. G. (1985, April). *Television viewing at home: Age trends in visual attention and time with TV*. Paper presented at the biennial meeting of the Society for Research in Child Development, Toronto.

Anderson, K. J., & Leaper, C. (1996, March). *The social construction of emotion and gender between friends*. Paper presented at the meeting of the Society for Research on Adolescence, Boston.

Anderson, N. (1996, June). *Socioeconomic status and health*. Paper presented at the meeting of the American Psychological Society, San Francisco.

Archer, S. L. (Ed.). (1994). *Intervention for adolescent identity development*. Newbury Park, CA: Sage.

Argyle, M., & Beit-Hallahmi, B. (1975). *The social psychology of religion*. London: Routledge & Kegan Paul.

Ariès, P. (1962). *Centuries of childhood* (R. Baldrick, Trans.). New York: Knopf.

Armsden, G. C., & Greenberg, M. T. (1987). The inventory of parent and peer attachment: Individual differences and their relationship to psychological well-being in adolescence. *Journal of Youth and Adolescence, 16*, 427–454.

Arnett, J. (1990). Contraceptive use, sensation seeking, and adolescent egocentrism. *Journal of Youth and Adolescence, 19*, 171–180.

Aronson, E. (1986, August). *Teaching students things they think they already know about: The case of prejudice and desegregation*. Paper presented at the meeting of the American Psychological Association, Washington, DC.

Arrendondo, P. (1996). Multicultural counseling theory and Latino/Hispanic-American populations. In D. W. Sue (Ed.), *Theory of multicultural counseling and therapy*. Pacific Grove, CA: Brooks/Cole.

Arroyo, C. G., & Sternberg, R. J. (1993). *Against all odds: A view of the gifted disadvantaged*. Dept. of Psychology, Yale University, New Haven, CT.

Asarnow, J. R., & Callan, J. W. (1985). Boys with peer adjustment problems: Social cognitive processes. *Journal of Consulting and Clinical Psychology, 53*, 80–87.

Astin, A. W., Korn, W. S., Sax, L. J., & Mahoney, K. M. (1994). *The American freshman: National norms for fall 1994*. Los Angeles: UCLA, Higher Education Research Institute.

B

Bachman, J. G. (1982, June 28). *The American high school student: A profile based on national survey data*. Paper presented at a conference entitled, "The American High School Today and Tomorrow," Berkeley, CA.

Bachman, J. G., & Schulenberg, J. (1993). How part-time work intensity relates to drug use, problem behavior, time use, and satisfaction among high school seniors: Are these consequences or just correlates? *Developmental Psychology, 29*, 220–235.

Bahrick, L. E. (1992). Infants' perceptual differentiation of amodal and modality-specific audio-visual relations. *Journal of Experimental Child Psychology, 53*, 180–199.

Bailey, J. M. (1995, March). *Sexual orientation and the multidimensionality of masculinity-femininity*. Paper presented at the meeting of the Society for Research in Child Development, Indianapolis.

Baillargeon, R. (1995). The object concept revisited: New directions in the investigation of infants' physical knowledge. In C. E. Granrud (Ed.), *Visual perception and cognition in infancy*. Hillsdale, NJ: Erlbaum.

Bakeman, R., & Brown, J. V. (1980). Early interaction: Consequences for social and mental development at three years. *Child Development, 51*, 437–447.

Ballou, M. (1996). Multicultural counseling theory and women. In D. W. Sue (Ed.), *Theory of multicultural counseling and therapy*. Pacific Grove, CA: Brooks/Cole.

Baltes, P. B. (1987). Theoretical propositions of life-span developmental psychology: On the dynamics between growth and decline. *Developmental Psychology, 23*, 611–626.

Bandura, A. (1965). Influence of models' reinforcement contingencies on the acquisition of imitative responses. *Journal of Personality and Social Psychology, 1*, 589–595.

Bandura, A. (1977). *Social learning theory*. Englewood Cliffs, NJ: Prentice Hall.

Bandura, A. (1986). *Social foundations of thought and action: A social cognitive theory*. Englewood Cliffs, NJ: Prentice Hall.

Bandura, A. (1994). Social cognitive theory of mass communication. In J. Bryant & D. Zillman (Eds.), *Media effects*. Hillsdale, NJ: Erlbaum.

Banks, E. C. (1993, March). *Moral education curriculum in a multicultural context: The Malaysian primary curriculum*. Paper presented at the biennial meeting of the Society for Research in Child Development, New Orleans.

Barker, R., & Wright, H. F. (1951). *One boy's day*. New York: Harper.

Barkow, J., Cosmides, L., & Tooby, J. (Eds.). (1992). *The adapted mind*. New York: Oxford University Press.

Baron, N. S. (1992). *Growing up with language*. Reading, MA: Addison-Wesley.

Barrett, K. C. (1995, March). *Functionalism, contextualism, and emotional development*. Paper presented at the meeting of the Society for Research in Child Development, Indianapolis.

Barron, F. (1989, April). The birth of a notion: Exercises to tap your creative potential. *Omni*, pp. 112–119.

Bart, W. M. (1971). The factor structure of formal operations. *British Journal of Educational Psychology, 41*, 40–77.

Baskett, L. M., & Johnson, S. M. (1982). The young child's interaction with parents versus siblings. *Child Development, 53*, 643–650.

Bates, A. S., Fitzgerald, J. F., Dittus, R. S., & Wollinsky, F. D. (1994). Risk factors for underimmunization in poor urban infants. *Journal of the American Medical Association, 272*, 1105–1109.

Bates, E., & Thal, D. (1991). Associations and dissociations in language development. In J. Millder (Ed.), *Research on language disorders: A decade of progress*. Austin: Pro-Ed.

Baumrind, D. (1971). Current patterns of parental authority. *Developmental Psychology Monographs, 4*, (1, Pt. 2).

Baumrind, D. (1989, April). *Sex-differentiated socialization effects in childhood and adolescence*. Paper presented at the biennial meeting of the Society for Research in Child Development, Kansas City.

Baumrind, D. (1993). The average expectable environment is not good enough: A response to Scarr. *Child Development, 64*, 1299–1317.

Bayley, N. (1969). *Manual for the Bayley Scales of infant development*. New York: Psychological Corporation.

Bayley, N. (1970). Development of mental abilities. In P. H. Mussen (Ed.), *Manual of child psychology* (3rd ed., Vol. 1). New York: Wiley.

Beagles-Roos, J., & Gat, I. (1983). Specific impact of radio and television in children's story comprehension. *Journal of Educational Psychology, 75*, 128–137.

Beal, C. R. (1994). *Boys and girls: The development of gender roles*. New York: McGraw-Hill.

Beck, A. T. (1973). *The diagnosis and management of depression*. Philadelphia: University of Pennsylvania Press.

Bednar, R. L., Wells, M. G., & Peterson, S. R. (1995). *Self-esteem* (2nd ed.). Washington, DC: American Psychological Association.

Bell, A. P., Weinberg, M. S., & Mammersmith, S. K. (1981). *Sexual preference: Its development in men and women*. New York: Simon & Schuster.

Bell, K. L. (1995, March). *Attachment and flexibility at self-presentation during the transition to adulthood*. Paper presented at the meeting of the Society for Research in Child Development, Indianapolis.

Bell, S. M., & Ainsworth, M. D. S. (1972). Infant crying and maternal responsiveness. *Child Development, 43*, 1171–1190.

Bellinger, D., Leviton, A., Waternaux, C., Needleman, H., & Rabinowitz, M. (1987). Longitudinal analysis of prenatal and postnatal lead exposure and early cognitive development. *New England Journal of Medicine, 316*, 1037–1043.

Belsky, J. (1981). Early human experience: A family perspective. *Developmental Psychology, 17*, 3–23.

Belsky, J. (1989). Infant-parent attachment and day care: In defense of the strange situation. In J. S. Lande, S. Scar, & N. Gunzenhauser (Eds.), *Caring for children: Challenge to America*. Hillsdale, NJ: Erlbaum.

Belson, W. (1978). *Television violence and the adolescent boy*. London: Saxon House.

Bem, S. L. (1977). On the utility of alternative procedures for assessing psychological androgyny. *Journal of Consulting and Clinical Psychology, 45*, 196–205.

Bena, C. R. (1990). *Methods of childbirth* (rev. ed.). New York: William Morrow.

Benelli, C., & Yongue, B. (1995). Supporting young children's motor skill development. *Childhood Education, 72*, 217–220.

Berardo, F. M. (1990). Trends and directions in family research in the 1980s. *Journal of Marriage and the Family, 52*, 809–817.

Bergin, D. (1988). Stages of play development. In D. Bergin (Ed.), *Play as a medium for learning and development*. Portsmouth, NH: Heinemann.

Berk, S. F. (1985). *The gender factory: The apportionment of work in American households*. New York: Plenum.

Berko, J. (1958). The child's learning of English morphology. *Word, 14*, 150–177.

Berlyne, D. E. (1960). *Conflict, arousal, and curiosity*. New York: McGraw-Hill.

Bernard, J. (1972). *The future of marriage*. New York: Bantam.

Berndt, T. J. (1996). Transitions in friendships and friends' influence. In J. A. Graber, J. Brooks-Gunn, & A. C. Petersen (Eds.), *Transitions through adolescence*. Hillsdale, NJ: Erlbaum.

Berndt, T. J., & Perry, T. B. (1990). Distinctive features and effects of early adolescent friendships. In R. Montemayor (Ed.), *Advances in adolescent research*. Greenwich, CT: JAI Press.

Berrueta-Clement, J., Schweinhart, L., Barnett, W., & Weikart, D. (1986). The effects of early educational intervention on crime and delinquency in adolescence and early adulthood. In J. Burchard & S. Burchard (Eds.), *Prevention of delinquent behavior*. Newbury Park, CA: Sage.

Bigler, R. S., Liben, L. S., & Yekel, C. A. (1992, August). *Developmental patterns of gender-related beliefs: Beyond unitary constructs and measures*. Paper presented at the meeting of the American Psychological Association, Washington, DC.

Biller, H. B. (1993). *Father and families*. Westport, CT: Auburn House.

Biller, H. B. (1993). *Fathers and families: Paternal factors in child development*. Westport, CT: Auburn House.

Birren, J. E., & Schaie, K. W. (Eds.). (1996). *Handbook of the psychology of aging* (4th ed.). Orlando, FL: Academic Press.

Black, A. E., & Pedro-Carroll, J. L. (1993, March). *The long-term effects of interpersonal conflict and parental divorce among late adolescents*. Paper presented at the biennial meeting of the Society for Research in Child Development, New Orleans.

Black, K. A., & McCartney, K. (1995, March). *Associations between adolescent attachment to parents and peer interactions*. Paper presented at the meeting of the Society for Research in Child Development, Indianapolis.

Blades, M. (1997). *Individual differences in intelligence*. In P. Scott & C. Spencer (Eds.), *Psychology*. Cambridge, MA: Blackwell.

Blair, C., & Ramey, C. (1996). Early intervention with low birth weight infants: The path to second generation research. In M. J. Guralnick (Ed.), *The effectiveness of early intervention*. Baltimore, MD: Paul Brookes.

Blakemore, J. E. O. (1993, March). *Preschool children's interest in babies: Observations in naturally occurring situations*. Paper presented at the biennial meeting of the Society for Research in Child Development, New Orleans.

Blatt, R. J. R. (1988). *Prenatal tests*. New York: Vintage Books.

Block, J., & Block, J. H. (1988). Longitudinally foretelling drug usage in adolescence: Early childhood personality and environmental precursors. *Child Development, 59*, 336–355.

Blum, B. (1995, August). *Real children, real choices*. Paper presented at the meeting of the American Psychological Association, New York City.

Blumenfeld, P. C., Pintrich, P. R., Wessles, K., & Meece, J. (1981, April). *Age and sex differences in the impact of classroom experiences on self-perceptions*. Paper presented at the biennial meeting of the Society for Research in Child Development, Boston.

Bond, L. A. (1988). Teaching developmental psychology. In P. A. Bronstein & K. Quina (Eds.), *Teaching a psychology of people*. Washington, DC: American Psychological Association.

Bonfenbrenner, U. (1995, March). *Role research has played in Head Start*. Paper presented at the meeting of the Society for Research in Child Development, Indianapolis.

Bonvillian, J. D., Orlansky, M. D., & Novack, L. L. (1983). Developmental milestones: Sign language and motor development. *Child Development, 54*, 1435–1445.

Booth, A., & Dunn, J. F. (Eds.). (1996). The effectiveness of providing social support for families of children at risk. In M. J. Guralnick (Ed.), *The effectiveness of early intervention*. Baltimore, MD: Paul Brookes.

Bornstein, M. H., & Sigman, M. D. (1986). Continuity in mental development from infancy. *Child Development, 57*, 251–274.

Botvin, G. (1986). Substance abuse prevention efforts: Recent developments and future directions. *Journal of School Health, 56*, 369–374.

References

Bouchard, T. J., Lykken, D. T., McGue, M., Segal, N. L., & Tellegen, A. (1990). Source of human psychological differences: The Minnesota Study of Twins Reared Apart. *Science, 250,* 223–228.

Bouchard, T. J., Lykken, D. T., Tellegen, A., & McGue, M. (1996). Genes, drives, environment, and experience. In D. Lubinski & C. Benbow (Eds.), *Psychometrics and social issues concerning intellectual talent.* Baltimore, MD: Johns Hopkins University Press.

Bower, B. (1985). The left hand of math and verbal talent. *Science News, 127,* 263.

Bower, T. G. R. (1977). *A primer of infant development.* New York: W. H. Freeman.

Bower, T. G. R. (1996, January). Personal communication. Program in human development, University of Texas at Dallas, Richardson.

Bower, T. G. R. (1996, January). Personal communication. Program in Psychology and Human Development, University of Texas at Dallas, Richardson.

Bowlby, J. (1969). *Attachment and loss* (Vol. 1). London: Hogarth.

Bowlby, J. (1989). *Secure and insecure attachment.* New York: Basic Books.

Bowlby, J. (1989). *Secure attachment.* New York: Basic Books.

Bowser, B. P., & Hunt, R. G. (Eds.). (1996). *Impacts of racism on White Americans.* Newbury Park, CA: Sage.

Boyce, T. (1991, May). Commentary. In D. Gelman, The miracle of resiliency. *Newsweek* [Special Issue], pp. 44–47.

Boys and Girls Clubs of America (1989, May 12). *Boys and Girls Clubs in public housing projects: Interim report.* Minneapolis: Boys and Girls Clubs of America.

Bracken, M. B., Eskenazi, B., Sachse, K., McSharry, J., Hellenbrand, K., & Leo-Summers, L. (1990). Association of cocaine use with sperm concentration, motility, and morphology. *Fertility and Sterility, 53,* 315–322.

Brazelton, T. B. (1956). Sucking in infancy. *Pediatrics, 17,* 400–404.

Brazelton, T. B. (1983). *Infants and mothers: Differences in development.* New York: Delta.

Brazelton, T. B., Nugent, J. K., & Lester, B. M. (1987). Neonatal behavioral assessment scale. In J. D. Osofsky (Ed.), *Handbook of infant development* (2nd ed.). New York: Wiley.

Bredekamp, S. (1987). *Developmentally appropriate practice in early childhood programs serving children from birth through age 8.* Washington, DC: National Association for the Education of Young Children.

Bredekamp, S. (1993). Reflections on Reggio Emilia. *Young Children, 49,* 13–16.

Brenner, A. (1984). *Helping children cope with stress.* Lexington, MA: D. C. Heath.

Bretherton, I. (1996). Attachment theory and research in historical and personal context. *Contemporary Psychology, 41,* 236–237.

Brewer, W. F. (1996). Children's eyewitness memory research. In N. L. Stein, C. Brainerd, P. A. Ornstein, & B. Tversky (Eds.), *Memory for everyday and emotional events.* Hillsdale, NJ: Erlbaum.

Brislin, R. (1993). *Culture's influence on behavior.* Fort Worth, TX: Harcourt Brace Jovanovich.

Brodzinsky, D., Schechter, M., & Henig, R. (1992). *Being adopted.* New York: Doubleday.

Brodzinsky, D. M., Lang, R., & Smith, D. W. (1995). Parenting adopted children. In M. H. Bornstein (Ed.), *Handbook of parenting* (Vol. 3). Hillsdale, NJ: Erlbaum.

Brodzinsky, D. M., Schechter, D. E., Braff, A. M., & Singer, L. M. (1984). Psychological and academic adjustment in adopted children. *Journal of Consulting and Clinical Psychology, 52,* 582–590.

Bronfenbrenner, U. (1979). Contexts of child rearing: Problems and prospects. *American Psychologist, 34,* 844–850.

Bronfenbrenner, U. (1986). Ecology of the family as a context for human development: Research perspectives. *Developmental Psychology, 22,* 723–742.

Bronfenbrenner, U. (1995, March). *The role research has played in Head Start.* Paper presented at the meeting of the Society for Research in Child Development, Indianapolis.

Bronstein, P., Stoll, M. F., Clausen, J., & Abrams, C. L. (1994). *Fathering after separation or divorce: Which dads make a difference?* Unpublished manuscript, Department of Psychology, University of Vermont, Burlington.

Bronstein, P. A., & Quina, K. (Eds.). (1988). *Teaching a psychology of people.* Washington, DC: American Psychological Association.

Brook, J. S., Brook, D. W., Gordon, A. S., Whiteman, M., & Cohen, P. (1990). The psychological etiology of adolescent drug use: A family interactional approach. *Genetic Psychology Monographs, 116,* no. 2.

Brooks-Gunn, J. (1996, March). *The uniqueness of the early adolescent transition.* Paper presented at the meeting of the Society for Research on Adolescence, Boston.

Brooks-Gunn, J., & Chase-Landsdale, P. L. (1995). Adolescent parenthood. In M. H. Bornstein (Ed.), *Children and parenting* (Vol. 3). Hillsdale, NJ: Erlbaum.

Brooks-Gunn, J., Klebanov, P. K., & Duncan, G. J. (1996). Ethnic differences in children's intelligence test scores: Role of economic deprivation, home environment, and maternal characteristics. *Child Development, 67,* 396–408.

Brooks-Gunn, J., & Matthews, W. S. (1979). *He and she: How children develop their sex-role identity.* Englewood Cliffs, NJ: Prentice Hall.

Brooks-Gunn, J., & Paikoff, R. L. (1993). "Sex is a gamble, kissing is a game": Adolescent sexuality and health promotion. In S. G. Millstein, A. C. Petersen, & E. O. Nightingale (Eds.), *Promoting the health of adolescents.* New York: Oxford University Press.

Brooks-Gunn, J., & Paikoff, R. (in press). Sexuality and developmental transitions during adolescence. In J. Schulenberg, J. Maggs, & K. Hurrelmann (Eds.), *Health risks and developmental transitions during adolescence.* New York: Cambridge University Press.

Brooks-Gunn, J., & Reiter, E. O. (1990). The role of pubertal processes. In S. S. Feldman & G. R. Elliott (Eds.), *At the threshold: The developing adolescent.* Cambridge, MA: Harvard University Press.

Brooks-Gunn, J., & Warren, M. P. (1989). The psychological significance of secondary sexual characteristics in 9- to 11-year-old girls. *Child Development, 59,* 161–169.

Broverman, I., Vogel, S., Broverman, D., Clarkson, F., & Rosenkranz, P. (1972). Sex-role stereotypes: A current appraisal. *Journal of Social Issues, 28,* 59–78.

Brown, A. L., & Palincsar, A. M. (1989). Guided, cooperative learning and individual knowledge acquisition. In L. B. Resnick (Ed.), *Knowing and learning: Essays in honor of Robert Glaser.* Hillsdale, NJ: Erlbaum.

Brown, B. B., & Lohr, M. J. (1987). Peer-group affiliation and adolescent self-esteem: An integration of ego-identity and symbolic-interaction theories. *Journal of Personality and Social Psychology, 52,* 47–55.

Brown, B. B., & Mounts, N. (1989, April). *Peer group structures in single vs. multiethnic high schools.* Paper presented at the biennial meeting of the Society for Research in Child Development, Kansas City.

Brown, B. B., & Theobald, W. (1996, March). *Is teenage romance hazardous to adolescent health?* Paper presented at the meeting of the Society for Research on Adolescence, Boston.

Brown, D. (1987). The status of Holland's theory of vocational choice. *Career Development Quarterly, 36,* 13–24.

Brown, J. L. (1964). States in newborn infants. *Merrill-Palmer Quarterly, 10,* 313–327.

Brown, L., & Allen, D. (1988). Hunger in America. *Annual Review of Public Health, 9,* 503–526.

Brown, L. S., & Brodsky, A. M. (1992). The future of feminist therapy. *Psychotherapy, 29,* 51–57.

Brown, R. (1973). *A first language: The early stages.* Cambridge, MA: Harvard University Press.

Brown, R. (1986). *Social psychology* (2nd ed.). New York: Free Press.

Browne, C. R., Brown, J. V., Blumenthal, J., Anderson, L., & Johnson, P. (1993, March). *African-American fathering: The perception of mothers and sons.* Paper presented at the biennial meeting of the Society for Research in Child Development, New Orleans.

Browne, M. W. (1994, October 16). What is intelligence and who has it? *New York Times Book Review,* pp. 2–3, 41–42.

Brubaker, T. H. (1985). *Later life families.* Newbury Park, CA: Sage.

Bryon, Y. J., Pang, S., Wei, L. S., Dickover, R., Diange, A., and Chen, I. S. Y. (1995). Clearance of HIV infection in a perinatally infected infant. *New England Journal of Medicine, 332,* 833–838.

Buchanan, C. M., Maccoby, E. E., & Dornbusch, S. M. (1992). Adolescents and their families after divorce. Three residential arrangements compared. *Journal of Research in Adolescence, 2* (3), 261–291.

Burchinal, M. R., Roberts, J. E., Nabors, L. A., & Bryant, D. M. (1996). Quality of center child care and infant cognitive and language development. *Child Development, 67,* 606–620.

Burchinal, P., & Sideeck, A. (1996, March). *Math achievement from 8 to 15 years among low income African-American children: Effects of early intervention and family factors.* Paper presented at the meeting of the Society for Research on Adolescence, Boston.

Burton, L., & Allison, K. W. (1995). Social context and adolescence: Alternative perspectives on developmental pathways for African-American teens. In L. J. Crockett & A. C. Crouter (Eds.), *Pathways through adolescence.* Hillsdale, NJ: Erlbaum.

Burts, D. C., Hart, C. H., Charlesworth, R., Hernandez, S., Kirk, L., & Mosley, J. (1989, March). *A comparison of the frequencies of stress behaviors observed in kindergarten children in classrooms with developmentally appropriate and developmentally inappropriate instructional practices.* Paper presented at the meeting of the American Educational Research Association, San Francisco.

Bushnell, E. W., & Boudreau, J. P. (1993). Motor development and the mind: The potential role of motor abilities as a determinant of aspects of perceptual development. *Child Development, 64,* 1005–1021.

Buss, A. H., & Plomin, R. (1987). Commentary. In H. H. Goldsmith, A. H. Buss, R. Plomin, M. K. Rothbart, A. Thomas, A. Chess, R. R. Hinde, & R. B. McCall (Eds.), Roundtable: What is temperament? Four approaches. *Child Development, 58,* 505–529.

Buss, D. M. (1994). *The evolution of desire.* New York: Basic Books.

Buss, D. M. (1995). Evolutionary psychology: A new paradigm for psychological science. *Psychological Inquiry, 6,* 1–30.

Buss, D. M. (1995). Psychological sex differences: Origins through sexual selection. *American Psychologist, 50,* 164–168.

Buss, D. M., & Malamuth, N. (Eds.). (1996). *Sex, power, and conflict.* New York: Oxford University Press.

Buss, D. M., & Schmitt, D. P. (1993). Sexual strategies theory: An evolutionary perspective on human mating. *Psychological Review, 100,* 204–232.

Byrne, R. (1997). Evolution and sociobiology. In P. Scott & C. Spencer (Eds.), *Psychology.* Cambridge, MA: Blackwell.

C

Cairns, E., & Dawes, A. (1996). Children: Ethnic and political violence—A commentary. *Child Development, 67,* 129–139.

Caldwell, M. B., & Rogers, M. F. (1991). Epidemiology of pediatric HIV infection. *Pediatrics Clinics of North America, 38,* 1–16.

Cameron, J. R., Hansen, R., & Rosen, D. (1989). Preventing behavioral problems in infancy through temperament assessment and parental support programs. In W. B. Carey & S. C. McDevitt (Eds.), *Clinical and educational applications of temperament research.* Amsterdam: Swets & Zeitlinger.

Campbell, F. A., & Ramey, C. T. (1994). Effects of early intervention on intellectual and academic achievement: A follow-up study of children from low-income families. *Child Development, 65,* 684–698.

Campbell, F. A., & Taylor, K. (1996). Early childhood programs that work for children from economically disadvantaged families. *Young Children, 51,* 74–79.

Campos, J. (1994, Spring). The new functionalism in emotions. *SRCD Newsletter,* pp. 1, 7, 9–11, 14.

Campos, J. J., Langer, A., & Krowitz, A. (1970). Cardiac responses on the visual cliff in prelocomotor human infants. *Science, 170,* 196–197.

Canfield, R. L., & Haith, M. M. (1991). Young infants' visual expectations for symmetric and asymmetric stimulus sequences. *Developmental Psychology, 27,* 198–208.

Carlson, K. S. (1995, March). *Attachment in sibling relationships during adolescence: Links to other familial and peer relationships.* Paper presented at the meeting of the Society for Research in Child Development, Indianapolis.

Carlson, V., Cicchetti, D., Barnett, D., & Braunwald, K. (1989). Disorganized/disoriented attachment relationships in maltreated infants. *Developmental Psychology, 25,* 525–531.

Carnegie Corporation. (1989). *Turning points: Preparing youth for the 21st century.* New York: Author.

Carnegie Council on Adolescent Development. (1995). *Great transitions.* New York: The Carnegie Foundation.

Carter, B., & McGoldrick, M. (1989). Overview: The changing family life cycle—a framework for family therapy. In B. Carter & M. McGoldrick (Eds.), *The changing family life cycle* (2nd ed.). Boston: Allyn & Bacon.

Carter, D. B., & Levy, G. D. (1988). Cognitive aspects of children's early sex-role development: The influence of gender schemas on preschoolers' memories and preference for sex-typed toys and activities. *Child Development, 59,* 782–793.

Carter-Saltzman, L. (1980). Biological and sociocultural effects on handedness: Comparison between biological and adoptive families. *Science, 209,* 1263–1265.

Case, R. (1987). Neo-Piagetian theory: Retrospect and prospect. *International Journal of Psychology, 22,* 773–791.

Case, R. (1992). *The mind's staircase: Exploring the conceptual underpinnings of children's thought and knowledge.* Hillsdale, NJ: Erlbaum.

Case, R., Kurland, D. M., & Goldberg, J. (1982). Operational efficiency and the growth of short-term memory span. *Journal of Experimental Child Psychology, 33,* 386–404.

Cassell, C. (1984). *Swept away: Why women fear their own sexuality.* New York: Simon & Schuster.

Cauce, A. M. (1996, June). *Culture and ethnicity: Between or within—Which is it?* Informal talk at the Family Research Summer Consortium, San Diego.

CDC National AIDS Clearinghouse. (1993). *Update: Acquired immunodeficiency syndrome—United States, 1992.* Rockville, MD: Author.

Ceci, S. J. (1993, August). *Cognitive and social factors in children's testimony.* Paper presented at the meeting of the American Psychological Association, Toronto.

Chan, W. S. (1963). *A source book in Chinese philosophy.* Princeton, NJ: Princeton University Press.

Chapman, W., & Katz, M. R. (1983). Career information systems in secondary schools: A survey and assessment. *Vocational Guidance Quarterly, 31,* 165–177.

Charlesworth, R. (1996). *Understanding child development* (4th ed.). Albany, NY: Delmar.

Chase-Lansdale, P. L. (1996, June). *Effects of divorce on mental health through the life span.* Informal talk at the Family Research Summer Consortium, San Diego.

Chase-Lansdale, P. L., & Brooks-Gunn, J. (1994). Correlates of adolescent pregnancy and parenthood. In C. B. Fisher & R. M. Lerner (Eds.), *Applied developmental psychology.* New York: McGraw-Hill.

Chase-Lansdale, P. L., & Brooks-Gunn, J. (Eds.). (1996). *Escape from poverty.* New York: Cambridge University Press.

Chasnoff, I. J., Griffith, D. R., Freier, C., & Murray, J. (1992). Cocaine/polydrug use in pregnancy: Two-year follow-up. *Pediatrics, 89,* 284–289.

Chattin-McNichols, J. (1992). *The Montessori controversy.* Albany, NY: Delmar.

Chess, S., & Thomas, A. (1977). Temperamental individuality from childhood to adolescence. *Journal of Child Psychiatry, 16,* 218–226.

Chi, M. T. (1978). Knowledge structures and memory development. In R. S. Siegler (Ed.), *Children's thinking: What develops?* Hillsdale, NJ: Erlbaum.

Children's Defense Fund. (1990). *Children 1990.* Washington, DC: Children's Defense Fund.

Children's Defense Fund. (1992). *The state of America's children., 1992.* Washington, DC: Author.

Children's Defense Fund. (1996). *The health of America's children.* Washington, DC: Children's Defense Fund.

Chodorow, N. J. (1989). *Feminism and psychoanalytic theory.* New Haven, CT: Yale University Press.

Chomitz, V. R., Cheung, L. W. Y., & Lieberman, E. (1995, spring). The role of lifestyle in preventing low birth weight. *The Future of Children, 5,* no. 1, 121–138.

Chomsky, N. (1957). *Syntactic structures.* The Hague: Mouton.

Chow, E. N., Wilkinson, D., & Baca Zinn, M. (1996). *Common bonds, different voices.* Newbury Park, CA: Sage.

Cicchetti, D., Ganiban, J., & Barnett, D. (1991). Contributions from the study of high risk populations to understanding the development of emotion regulation. In J. Garber & K. Dodge (Eds.), *The development of emotion regulation and dysregulation.* New York: Cambridge University Press.

Cicirelli, V. G. (1994). Sibling relationships in cross-cultural perspective. *Journal of Marriage and the Family, 56,* 7–20.

Clark, K. B., & Clark, M. K. (1939). The development of consciousness of self in the emergence or racial identification in Negro preschool children. *Journal of Social Psychology, 10,* 591–599.

Clark, K. B., & Clark, M. P. (1939). The development of self and the emergence of racial identification in Negro preschool children. *Journal of Social Psychology, 10,* 591–599.

Clark, R. D., & Hatfield, E. (1989). Gender differences in receptivity to sexual offers. *Journal of Psychology and Human Sexuality, 2,* 39–55.

Clark, S. D., Zabin, L. S., & Hardy, J. B. (1984). Sex, contraception, and parenthood: Experience and attitudes among urban black young men. *Family Planning Perspectives, 16,* 77–82.

Clarke-Stewart, K. A., Alhusen, V. D., & Clements, D. C. (1995). Nonparental caregiving. In M. H. Bornstein (Ed.), *Handbook of parenting* (Vol. 3). Hillsdale, NJ: Erlbaum.

Clarke-Stewart, K. A., & Fein, G. G. (1983). Early childhood programs. In P. H. Mussen (Ed.), *Handbook of child psychology* (4th ed., Vol. 2). New York: Wiley.

Clifford, B. R., Gunter, B., & McAleer, J. L. (1995). *Television and children.* Hillsdale, NJ: Erlbaum.

Clifton, R. K., Muir, D. W., Ashmead, D. H., & Clarkson, M. G. (1993). Is visually guided reaching in early infancy a myth? *Child Development, 64,* 1099–1110.

Cloninger, S. C. (1996). *Theories of personality* (2nd ed.). Upper Saddle River, NJ: Prentice-Hall.

Coffman, S., Levitt, M. J., & Guacci-Franco, N. (1996). Infant-mother attachment: Relationships to maternal responsiveness and infant temperament. *Journal of Pediatric Nursing, 10,* 9–18.

Cohen, H. J., Grosz, J., Ayooh, K., & Schoen, S. (1996). Early intervention for children with HIV infections. In M. J. Guralnick (Ed.), *The effectiveness of early intervention.* Baltimore, MD: Paul Brookes.

Cohen, R. J., Swerdlik, M. E., & Phillips, S. M. (1996). Psychological testing and assessment (3rd ed.). Mountain View, CA: Mayfield.

Cohen, S. E. (1994, February). *High school dropouts.* Paper presented at the meeting of the Society for Research on Adolescence, San Diego.

Coie, J. D., & Koeppl, G. K. (1990). Adapting intervention to the problems of aggressive and disruptive rejected children. In S. R. Asher & J. D. Coie (Eds.), *Peer rejection in childhood.* New York: Cambridge University Press.

Colby, A., Kohlberg, L., Gibbs, J., & Lieberman, M. (1983). A longitudinal study of moral judgment. *Monographs of the Society for Research in Child Development* (Serial No. 201).

Coleman, J. S. (1961). *The adolescent society.* New York: Free Press.

Coleman, L. (1996, March). *What does it mean to be a Black man or a Black woman?* Paper presented at the meeting of the Society for Research on Adolescence, Boston.

Coleman, M., & Ganong, L. H. (1990). Remarriage and stepfamily research in the 1980s: Increased interest in an old form. *Journal of Marriage and the Family, 52,* 925–939.

Coles, R. (1970). *Erik H. Erikson: The growth of his work.* Boston: Little, Brown.

Coll, C. T. G., Erkut, S., Alarcon, O., Garcia, H. A. V., & Tropp, L. (1995, March). *Puerto Rican adolescents and families: Lessons in construct and instrument development.* Paper presented at the meeting of the Society for Research in Child Development, Indianapolis.

Coll, C. T. G., Meyer, E. C., & Brillion, L. (1995). Ethnic and minority parenting. In M. H. Bornstein (Ed.), *Children and parenting* (Vol. 2). Hillsdale, NJ: Erlbaum.

College Board Commission on Precollege Guidance and Counseling. (1986). *Keeping the options open.* New York: College Entrance Examination Board.

Comer, J. (1993, March). *African-American parents and child development: An agenda for school success.* Paper presented at the biennial meeting of the Society for Research in Child Development, New Orleans.

Comer, J. P. (1988). Educating poor minority children. *Scientific American, 259,* 42–48.

Comer, J. P., & Poussaint, A. E. (1992). *Raising Black children.* New York: Plume.

Compas, B. E., & Grant, K. E. (1993, March). *Stress and adolescent depressive symptoms: Underlying mechanisms and processes.* Paper presented at the biennial meeting of the Society for Research in Child Development, New Orleans.

Conger, J. J. (1988). Hostages to the future: Youth, values, and the public interest. *American Psychologist, 43,* 291–300.

Cooper, C., Lopez, E., Dunbar, N., & Figuera, J. (1996, March). *Identity, relationships, and opportunity structures: African-American and Latino youth in University Academic Outreach programs.* Paper presented at the meeting of the Society for Research on Adolescence, Boston.

Cooper, C. R., & Ayers-Lopez, S. (1985). Family and peer systems in early adolescence: New models of the roles of relationships in development. *Journal of Early Adolescence, 5,* 9–22.

Cooper, C. R., Grotevant, H. D., Moore, M. S., & Condon, S. M. (1982, August). *Family support and conflict: Both foster adolescent identity and role taking.* Paper presented at the meeting of the American Psychological Association, Washington, DC.

Coopersmith, S. (1967). *The antecedents of self-esteem.* San Francisco: W. H. Freeman.

Copeland, A. P., Hwang, H., & Brody, L. R. (1996, March). *Asian-American adolescents: Caught between cultures?* Paper presented at the meeting of the Society for Research on Adolescence, Boston.

Corrigan, R. (1981). The effects of task and practice on search for invisibly displaced objects. *Developmental Review, 11,* 1–17.

Cowan, C. P., Cowan, P. A., Heming, G., & Boxer, C. (1995). *Preventive interventions with parents of preschoolers: Effects on marriage, parenting, and children's school adjustment.* Paper presented at the meeting of the Society for Research on Child Development, Indianapolis.

Cowan, C. P., Heming, G. A., & Shuck, E. L. (1993, March). *The impact of interventions with parents of preschoolers on the children's adaptation to kindergarten.* Paper presented at the biennial meeting of the Society for Research in Child Development, New Orleans.

Crawford, C. (1987). Sociobiology: Of what value to psychology? In C. Crawford, M. Smith, & D. Krebs (Eds.), *Sociobiology and psychology.* Hillsdale, NJ: Erlbaum.

Crick, N. R., & Dodge, K. A. (1994). A review and reformulation of social information-processing mechanisms in children's social adjustment. *Psychological Bulletin, 115,* 74–101.

Crnic, K. (1996). *Children, families, and stress.* Cambridge, MA: Blackwell.

Crnic, K., & Stormshak, E. (1996). The effectiveness of providing social support for families of children at risk. In M. J. Guralnick (Ed.), *The effectiveness of early intervention.* Baltimore, MD: Paul Brookes.

Crockenberg, S. B. (1986). Are temperamental differences in babies associated with predictable differences in caregiving? In J. V. Lerner & R. M. Lerner (Eds.), *Temperament and social interaction during infancy and childhood.* San Francisco: Jossey-Bass.

Cronbach, L. J., & Snow, R. E. (1977). *Aptitudes and instructional methods.* New York: Irvington Books.

Crowder, J. (1969). *Stephanie and the coyote.* Upper Strata, Box 278, Bernalillo, NM 87004.

Crump, A. D., Haynie, D., Aarons, S., & Adair, E. (1996, March). *African American teenagers' norms, expectations, and motivations regarding sex, contraception, and pregnancy.* Paper presented at the meeting of the Society for Research on Adolescence, Boston.

Cummings, E. M. (1987). Coping with background anger in early childhood. *Child Development, 58,* 976–984.

Cummings, L. M., Rebello, P. M., & Gardiner, M. (1995, March). *The UN convention on the rights of the child: A call to child development professionals around the world.* Paper presented at the meeting of the Society for Research in Child Development, Indianapolis.

Cunningham, B. (1994). Portraying fathers and other men in the curriculum. *Young Children, 49,* 4–13.

Curtiss, S. (1977). *Genie.* New York: Academic Press.

D

Daly, M., & Wilson, M. (1995). Evolutionary psychology: Adaptationist, selectionist, and comparative. *Psychological Inquiry, 6,* 34–38.

Damon, W. (1988). *The moral child.* New York: Free Press.

Damon, W., & Hart, D. (1992). Self-understanding and its role in social and moral development. In M. H. Bornstein & M. E. Lamb (Eds.), *Developmental psychology: An advanced textbook* (3rd ed.). Hillsdale, NJ: Erlbaum.

D'Angelo, D. A., & Adler, C. R. (1991). A catalyst for improving parent involvement. *Phi Delta Kappan,* pp. 350–354.

Darling, C. A., Kallen, D. J., & VanDusen, J. E. (1984). Sex in transition, 1900–1984. *Journal of Youth and Adolescence, 13,* 385–399.

Darwin, C. (1859). *On the origin of species.* London: John Murray.

Davis, K. (1996). *Families.* Pacific Grove, CA: Brooks/Cole.

Davis, S. M., Lambert, L. C., Gomez, Y., & Skipper, B. (1995). Southwest Cardiovascular Curriculum Project: Study findings for American Indian elementary students. *Journal of Health Education, 26,* S72–S81.

DeBlassie, A. M., & DeBlassie, R. R. (1996). Education of Hispanic youth: A cultural lag. *Adolescence, 121,* 205–214.

DeCasper, A. J., & Spence, M. J. (1986). Prenatal maternal speech influences newborn's perception of speech sounds. *Infant Behavior and Development, 9,* 133–150.

Degirmencioglu, S. M., Saltz, E., & Aget, J. W. (1995, March). *Early dating and "going steady": A retrospective and prospective look.* Paper presented at the meeting of the Society for Research in Child Development, Indianapolis.

DeLoache, J. S., Cassidy, D. J., & Carpenter, C. J. (1987). The Three Bears are all boys: Mothers' gender labeling of neutral picture book characters. *Sex Roles, 17,* 163–178.

Dempster, F. N. (1981). Memory span: Sources of individual and developmental differences. *Psychological Bulletin, 80,* 63–100.

Denmark, F. L., Russo, N. F., Frieze, I., II., & Sechzur, J. (1988). Guidelines for avoiding sexism in psychological research: A report of the Ad Hoc Committee on Nonsexist Research. *American Psychologist, 43,* 582–585.

Derman-Sparks, L., and the ABC Task Force. (1989). *Anti-bias curriculum.* Washington, DC: National Association for the Education of Young Children.

Derry, P. S. (1996). Buss and sexual selection: The issue of culture. *American Psychologist, 51,* 159–160.

de Villiers, J. (1996). Towards a rational empiricism: Why interactionism isn't behaviorism any more than biology is genetics. In M. E. Rice (Ed.), *Towards a genetics of language.* Hillsdale, NJ: Erlbaum.

Dewey, J. (1933). *How we think: A restatement of the relation of reflective thinking to the educative process.* Lexington, MA: D. C. Heath.

Diaz, R. M. (1983). Thought and two languages: The impact of bilingualism on cognitive development. *Review of Research in Education, 10,* 23–54.

DiPardo, A. (1996). Review of *Writers in the Zone of Proximal Development* by Petrick-Steward. *Contemporary Psychology, 41,* 51–52.

Dishion, T. J., & Spacklen, K. M. (1996, March). *Childhood peer rejection in the development of adolescent substance abuse*. Paper presented at the meeting of the Society for Research on Adolescence, Boston.

Dodge, K. A. (1983). Behavioral antecedents of peer social status. *Child Development, 54,* 1386–1399.

Dolcini, M. M., Coh, L. D., Adler, N. E., Millstein, S. G., Irwin, C. E., Kegeles, S. M., & Stone, G. C. (1989). Adolescent egocentrism and feelings of invulnerability: Are they related? *Journal of Early Adolescence, 9,* 409–418.

Dorn, L. D., & Lucas, F. L. (1995, March). *Do hormone-behavior relations vary depending upon the endocrine and psychological status of the adolescent.* Paper presented at the meeting of the Society for Research in Child Development, Indianapolis.

Dornbusch, S. M., Ritter, P. L., Leiderman, P. H., Roberts, D. F., & Fraleigh, M. J. (1987). The relation of parenting style to adolescent school performance. *Child Development, 58,* 1244–1257.

Doubleday, C. N., & Droege, K. L. (1993). Cognitive developmental influences on children's understanding of television. In G. L. Berry & J. K. Asamen (Eds.), *Children and television.* Newbury Park, CA: Sage.

Dow-Edwards, D. L. (1995). Developmental toxicity of cocaine: Mechanisms of action. In M. Lewis & M. Bendersky (Eds.), *Mothers, babies, and cocaine.* Hillsdale, NJ: Erlbaum.

Downey, G., & Coyne, J. C. (1990). Children of depressed parents: An integrative review. *Psychological Bulletin, 108,* 50–76.

Dreyer, P. H. (1982). Sexuality during adolescence. In B. B. Wolman (Ed.), *Handbook of developmental psychology.* Englewood Cliffs, NJ: Prentice Hall.

Drickamer, L. C., Vessey, S. H., & Miekle, D. (1996). *Animal behavior* (4th ed.). Dubuque, IA: Wm. C. Brown.

Dryfoos, J. G. (1990). *Adolescents at risk: Prevalence and prevention.* New York: Oxford University Press.

Dunn, J., & Kendrick, C. (1982). *Siblings.* Cambridge, MA: Harvard University Press.

Dunphy, D. C. (1963). The social structure of urban adolescent peer groups. *Society, 26,* 230–246.

Durkin, K. (1985). Television and sex-role acquisition: 1. Content. *British Journal of Social Psychology, 24,* 101–113.

Dweck, C. (1975). The role of expectations and attributions in the alleviation of learned helplessness. *Journal of Personality and Social Psychology, 31,* 674–685.

E

Eagly, A. H. (1995). The science and politics of comparing men and women. *American Psychologist, 50,* 145–158.

Eagly, A. H. (1996). Differences between women and men. *American Psychologist, 51,* 158–159.

Eagly, A. H., & Crowley, M. (1986). Gender and helping behavior: A meta-analytic review of the social psychological literature. *Psychological Bulletin, 100,* 283–308.

Early Childhood and Literacy Development Committee of the International Reading Association. (1986). Literacy development and pre-first grade. *Young Children, 41,* 10–13.

East, P., & Felice, M. E. (1996). *Adolescent pregnancy and parenting.* Hillsdale, NJ: Erlbaum.

Ebata, A. T., & Moos, R. H. (1994). Personal, situational, and contextual correlates of coping in adolescence. *Journal of Research in Adolescence, 4,* 99–125.

Eccles, J., MacIver, D., & Lange, L. (1986). *Classroom practices and motivation to study math.* Paper presented at the annual meeting of the American Educational Research Association, San Francisco.

Eccles, J. S., & Midgley, C. (1990). Changes in academic motivation and self-perception during early adolescence. In R. Montemayor, G. R. Adams, & T. P. Gullotta (Eds.), *From childhood to adolescence: A transitional period?* Newbury Park, CA: Sage.

Edelman, M. W. (1992). *The measure of our success: A letter to my children and yours.* Boston: Beacon Press.

Edelman, M. W. (1995). *The state of America's children.* Washington, DC: Children's Defense Fund.

Edelman, M. W. (1996). *The state of America's children.* Washington, DC: Children's Defense Fund.

Egeland, B. (1989, January). *Secure attachment in infancy and competence in the third grade.* Paper presented at the meeting of the American Association for the Advancement of Science, San Francisco.

Ehrhardt, A. A. (1987). A transactional perspective on the development of gender differences. In J. M. Reinisch, L. A. Rosenblum, & S. A. Sanders (Eds.), *Masculinity/femininity: Basic perspectives.* New York: Oxford University Press.

Eiferman, R. R. (1971). Social play in childhood. In R. E. Herron & B. Sutton-Smith (Eds.), *Child's play.* New York: Wiley.

Eiger, M. S. (1992). The feeding of infants and children. In R. A. Hoekelman, S. B. Friedman, N. M. Nelson, & H. M. Seidel (Eds.), *Primary pediatric care* (2nd ed.). St. Louis: Mosby Yearbook.

Eimas, P. (1995). The perception of representation of speech by infants. In J. L. Morgan & K. Demuth (Eds.), *Signal to syntax.* Hillsdale, NJ: Erlbaum.

Eisenberg, A., Murkoff, H., & Hathaway, S. (1989). *What to expect when you're expecting.* New York: Workman.

Eisenberg, A., Murkoff, H., & Hathaway, S. (1991). *What to expect when you're expecting.* (2nd ed., rev.). New York: Workman.

Eisenberg, A., Murkoff, H. E., & Hathaway, S. E. (1989). *What to expect in the first year.* New York: Workman.

Eisenberg, N. (Ed.). (1982). *The development of prosocial behavior.* New York: Wiley.

Eisenberg, N. (1992, Fall). Social development: Current trends and future possibilities. *SRCD Newsletter,* pp. 1, 10–11.

Eisenberg, N., Fabes, R. A., Karbon, M., Murphy, B. C., Wosinski, M., Polazzi, L., Carolo, G., & Juhnke, C. (in press). The relations of children's dispositional prosocial behavior to emotionality, regulation, and social functioning. *Child Development.*

Elkind, D. (1970, April 5). Erik Erikson's eight ages of man. *New York Times Magazine.*

Elkind, D. (1976). *Child development and education: A Piagetian perspective.* New York: Oxford University Press.

Elkind, D. (1978). Understanding the young adolescent. *Adolescence, 13,* 127–134.

Elkind, D. (1981). *The hurried child.* Reading, MA: Addison-Wesley.

Elkind, D. (1988, January). Educating the very young: A call for clear thinking. *NEA Today,* pp. 22–27.

Ellis, L., & Ames, M. A. (1987). Neurohormonal functioning and sexual orientation: A theory of homosexuality-heterosexuality. *Psychological Bulletin, 101,* 233–258.

Emde, R. N., Gaensbauer, T. G., & Harmon, R. J. (1976). Emotional expression in infancy: A biobehavioral study. *Psychological Issues: Monograph Series, 10* (37).

Emlen, S. T. (1984). Cooperative breeding in birds and mammals. In J. R. Krebs & N. B. Davies (Eds.), *Behavioral ecology: An evolutionary approach* (2nd ed.). Oxford: Blackwell Scientific.

Enger, E. D., Kormelink, R., Ross, F. C., & Otto, R. (1996). *Diversity of life.* Dubuque, IA: Wm. C. Brown.

Enright, R. D., Lapsley, D. K., Dricas, A. S., & Fehr, L. A. (1980). Parental influence on the development of adolescent autonomy and identity. *Journal of Youth and Adolescence, 9,* 529–546.

Entwisle, D. R. (1990). Schools and the adolescent. In S. S. Feldman & G. R. Elliott (Eds.), *At the threshold: The developing adolescent.* Cambridge, MA: Harvard University Press.

Epstein, J. (1986). Parent involvement: Implications for limited-English-proficient students. In C. Smith-Dudgeon (Ed.), *Issues of parent involvement and literacy.* Washington, DC: Trinity College.

Epstein, J. L. (1992). School and family partnerships. *Encyclopedia of educational research* (6th ed.). New York: Macmillan.

Epstein, L. H., Klein, K. R., & Wisniewski, L. (1994). Child and parent factors that influence psychological problems in obese children. *Eating Disorders, 15,* 151–158.

Erickson, J. B. (1982). *A profile of community youth organization members, 1980.* Boys Town, NE: Boys Town Center for the Study of Youth Development.

Erickson, J. B. (in press). *Directory of American youth organizations* (2nd rev. ed.). Boys Town, NE: Boys Town.

Erikson, E. H. (1950). *Childhood and society.* New York: W. W. Norton.

Erikson, E. H. (1968). *Identity: Youth and crisis.* New York: W. W. Norton.

Erwin, E. J. (Ed.). (1996). *Putting children first.* Baltimore, MD: Paul Brookes.

Etzel, R. (1988, October). *Children of smokers.* Paper presented at the American Academy of Pediatrics meeting, New Orleans.

Evans, B. J., & Whitfield, J. R. (Eds.). (1988). *Black males in the United States: An annotated bibliography from 1967 to 1987.* Washington, DC: American Psychological Association.

Evans, I. M., Cicchelli, T., Cohen, M., & Shapiro, N. (1995). *Staying in school.* Baltimore: Paul Brookes.

Eyler, F. D., Behnke, M. L., & Stewart, N. J. (1990). *Issues in identification and follow-up of cocaine-exposed neonates.* Unpublished manuscript, University of Florida, Gainesville.

F

Fagot, B. I., Leinbach, M. D., & O'Boyle, C. (1992). Gender labeling, gender stereotyping, and parenting behaviors. *Developmental Psychology, 28,* 225–230.

Falbo, T., & Poston, D. L. (1993). The academic, personality, and physical outcomes of only children in China. *Child Development, 64,* 18–35.

Falbo, T. L., & Romo, H. D. (1994, February). *Hispanic parents and public education: The gap between cultures*. Paper presented at the meeting of the Society for Research on Adolescence, San Diego.

Fantz, R. L. (1963). Pattern vision in newborn infants. *Science, 140*, 296–297.

Fay, A. L. (1995, March). *Factors affecting the content and structure of children's science explanations*. Paper presented at the meeting of the Society for Research in Child Development, Indianapolis.

Fein, G. G. (1986). Pretend play. In D. Görlitz & J. F. Wohlwill (Eds.), *Curiosity, imagination, and play*. Hillsdale, NJ: Erlbaum.

Feiring, C. (1995, March). *The development of romance from 15 to 18 years*. Paper presented at the meeting of the Society for Research in Child Development, Indianapolis.

Feiring, C. (1996). Concepts of romance in 15-year-old adolescents. *Journal of Research on Adolescence, 6*, 181–200.

Feldman, D. H., & Piirto, J. (1995). Parenting talented children. In M. H. Bornstein (Ed.), *Handbook of parenting*. Hillsdale, NJ: Erlbaum.

Feldman, M. A. (1996). The effectiveness of early intervention for children of parents with mental retardation. In M. J. Guralnick (Ed.), *The effectiveness of early intervention*. Baltimore, MD: Paul Brookes.

Feldman, S. S., & Elliott, G. R. (1990). Progress and promise of research on normal adolescent development. In S. S. Feldman & G. Elliott (Eds.). *At the threshold: The developing adolescent*. Cambridge, MA: Harvard University Press.

Feldman, S. S., & Weinberger, D. A. (1994). Self-restraint as a mediator of family influences on boys' delinquent behavior: A longitudinal study. *Child Development, 65*, 195–211.

Ferguson, D. M., Harwood, L. J., & Shannon, F. T. (1987). Breastfeeding and subsequent social adjustment in 6- to 8-year-old children. *Journal of Child Psychology and Psychiatry, 28*, 378–386.

Field, T. (1990). *Infancy*. Cambridge, MA: Harvard University Press.

Field, T. (1992, September). Stroking babies helps growth, reduces stress. *Brown University Child and Adolescent Behavior Letter*, pp. 1, 6.

Field, T., Sandberg, D., Quetel, T. A., Garcia, R., & Rosario, M. (1985). Effects of ultrasound feedback on pregnancy anxiety, fetal activity, and neonatal outcomes. *Obstetrics and Gynecology, 66*, 525–528.

Field, T., Scafidi, F., & Schanberg, S. (1987). Massage of preterm newborns to improve growth and development. *Pediatric Nursing, 13*, 385–387.

Field, T. M. (Ed.). (1995). *Touch in early development*. Hillsdale, NJ: Erlbaum.

Finkel, D., Whitfield, K., & McGue, M. (1995). Genetic and environmental influences on functional age: A twin study. *Journal of Gerontology, 50B*, P104–P113.

Fisher, D. (1990, March). *Effects of attachment on adolescents' friendships*. Paper presented at the meeting of the Society for Research in Adolescence, Atlanta.

Flanagan, A. S. (1996, March). *Romantic behavior of sexually victimized and nonvictimized women*. Paper presented at the meeting of the Society for Research on Adolescence, Boston.

Flavell, J. H. (1992). Cognitive development: Past, present, and future. *Developmental Psychology, 28*, 998–1005.

Flavell, J. H., Green, F. L., & Flavell, E. R. (1995, March). Young children's knowledge about thinking. *Monographs of the Society for Research in Child Development, 60* (Serial No. 143, No. 1).

Flavell, J. H., Miller, P., & Miller, S. A. (1993). *Cognitive development* (3rd ed.). Englewood Cliffs, NJ: Prentice Hall.

Folkman, S., & Lazarus, R. (1991). Coping and emotion. In N. Stein, B. L. Leventhal, & T. Trabasso (Eds.), *Psychological and biological approaches to emotion*. Hillsdale, NJ: Erlbaum.

Fordham, S., & Ogbu, J. U. (1986). Black students' school success: Coping with the burden of acting White. *Urban Review, 18*, 176–206.

Forgatch, M. S., Patterson, G. R., & Ray, J. A. (1996). Divorce and boys' adjustment problems: Two paths with a single model. In E. M. Hetherington & E. A. Blechman (Eds.), *Stress, coping, and resilience in children and families*. Hillsdale, NJ: Erlbaum.

Forrest, J. D. (1990). Cultural influences on adolescents' reproductive behavior. In J. Bancroft & J. M. Reinisch (Eds.), *Adolescence and puberty*. New York: Oxford University Press.

Forshaun, S. (1996, March). *Attributions concerning adolescent suicide: The impact of gender, method, and outcome*. Paper presented at the meeting of the Society for Research on Adolescence, Boston.

Fowler, J. W. (1981). *Stages of faith: The psychology of human development and the quest for faith*. New York: HarperCollins.

Fox, L. H., Brody, L., & Tobin, D. (1979). *Women and mathematics*. Baltimore: Johns Hopkins University, Intellectually Gifted Study Group.

Fraiberg, S. (1959). *The magic years*. New York: Charles Scribner's Sons.

Frankenburg, W. K., Dodds, J., Archer, P., Shapiro, H., & Bresnick, B. (1992). The Denver II: A major revision and restandardization of the Denver Development Screening Test. *Pediatrics, 89*, 91–97.

Fraser, S. (Ed.). (1995). *The bell curve wars: Race, intelligence, and the future of America*. New York: Basic Books.

Freedman, J. L. (1984). Effects of television violence on aggressiveness. *Psychological Bulletin, 96*, 227–246.

Freeman, H. S. (1993, March). *Parental control of adolescents through family transitions*. Paper presented at the biennial meeting of the Society for Research in Child Development, New Orleans.

Freud, A., & Dann, S. (1951). Instinctual anxiety during puberty. In A. Freud (Ed.), *The ego and its mechanisms of defense*. New York: International Universities Press.

Freud, S. (1917). *A general introduction to psychoanalysis*. New York: Washington Square Press.

Fried, P. A., & Watkinson, B. (1990). 36- and 48-month neurobehavioral follow-up of children prenatally exposed to marijuana, cigarettes, and alcohol. *Developmental and Behavioral Pediatrics, 11*, 49–58.

Friedman, H. S., Tucker, J. S., Schwartz, J. E., Tomlinson-Keasey, C., Martin, L. R., Wingard, D. L., & Criqui, M. H. (1995). Psychosocial and behavioral predictors of longevity: The aging and death of the "Termites." *American Psychologist, 50*, 69–78.

Friedman, M., & Rosenman, R. (1974). *Type A behavior and your heart*. New York: Knopf.

Friedrich, L. K., & Stein, A. H. (1973). Aggressive and prosocial TV programs and the natural behavior of preschool children. *Monographs of the Society for Research in Child Development, 38* (4, Serial No. 151).

Furth, H. G., & Wachs, H. (1975). *Thinking goes to school*. New York: Oxford University Press.

G

Gadpaille, W. J. (1996). *Adolescent suicide*. Washington, DC: American Psychiatric Association.

Gage, N. L. (1965). Desirable behaviors of teachers. *Urban Education, 1*, 85–96.

Gaines, K. R. E., Blair, C. B., & Cluett, S. E. (1995, March). *Family environments, cultural diversity, and Head Start: Policy implications*. Paper presented at the meeting of the Society for Research in Child Development, Indianapolis.

Galambos, N. L., & Maggs, J. L. (1989, April). *The after-school ecology of young adolescents and self-reported behavior*. Paper presented at the biennial meeting of the Society for Research in Child Development, Kansas City.

Galambos, N. L., & Sears, H. A. (1995, March). *Depressive symptoms in adolescents: Examining family matters*. Paper presented at the meeting of the Society for Research in Child Development, Indianapolis.

Galambos, N. L., & Tilton-Weaver, L. (1996, March). *The adultoid adolescent: Too much, too soon*. Paper presented at the meeting of the Society for Research on Adolescence, Boston.

Galinsky, E., & David, J. (1988). *The preschool years: Family strategies that work—from experts and parents*. New York: Times Books.

Gallup, G. W., & Bezilla, R. (1992). *The religious life of young Americans*. Princeton, NJ: Gallup Institute.

Galotti, K. M., Kozberg, S. F., & Farmer, M. C. (1990, March). *Gender and developmental differences in adolescents' conceptions of moral reasoning*. Paper presented at the meeting of the Society for Research in Adolescence, Atlanta.

Gandini, L. (1993). Fundamentals of the Reggio Emilia approach to early childhood education. *Young Children, 49*, 4–8.

Gangestad, S. W. (1995). The new evolutionary psychology: Prospects and challenges. *Psychological Inquiry, 6*, 38–41.

Ganzel, A. K., & Jacobs, J. E. (1992, March). *Everyday decision-making by families: A comparison of outcomes and processes*. Paper presented at the meeting of the Society for Research on Adolescence, Washington, DC.

Garbarino, J. (1976). The ecological correlates of child abuse. The impact of socioeconomic stress on mothers. *Child Development, 47*, 178–185.

Gardner, B. T., & Gardner, R. A. (1971). Two-way communication with an infant chimpanzee. In A. Schrier & F. Stollnitz (Eds.), *Behavior of nonhuman primates*. (Vol. 4). New York: Academic Press.

Gardner, H. (1983). *Frames of mind*. New York: Basic Books.

Gardner, L. I. (1972). Deprivation dwarfism. *Scientific American, 227*, 76–82.

Garmezy, N. (1985). Stress-resistant children: The search for protective factors. In J. E. Stevenson (Ed.), Recent research in developmental psychopathology. *Journal of Child Psychology and Psychiatry Book Supplement, 4*, 213–233.

Garmezy, N. (1993). Children in poverty: Resilience despite risk. *Psychiatry, 56,* 127–136.

Garvey, C. (1977). *Play.* Cambridge, MA: Harvard University Press.

Gelman, R. (1969). Conservation acquisition: A problem of learning to attend to relevant attributes. *Journal of Experimental Child Psychology, 7,* 67–87.

Gelman, R. (1972). Logical capacity of very young children: Number invariance rules. *Child Development, 43,* 75–90.

Gelman, R., & Au, T. K. (Eds.). (1996). *Perceptual and cognitive development* (2nd ed.). San Diego, CA: Academic Press.

Gelman, R., & Brenneman, K. (1994). Domain specificity and cultural variation are not inconsistent. In L. A. Hirschfeld & S. Gelman (Eds.), *Mapping the mind: Domain specificity in cognition and culture.* New York: Cambridge University Press.

George, C. M. (1996, March). *Gene-environment interactions: Testing the bioecological model during adolescence.* Paper presented at the meeting of the Society for Research on Adolescence, Boston.

Gerber, P. J., Reiff, H. B., & Ginsberg, R. (1996). Reframing the learning disabilities experience. *Journal of Learning Disabilities, 18,* 98–101.

Gesell, A. (1934). *An atlas of infant behavior.* New Haven, CT: Yale University Press.

Gesell, A. L. (1928). *Infancy and human growth.* New York: Macmillan.

Gewirtz, J. (1977). Maternal responding and the conditioning of infant crying: Directions of influence within the attachment-acquisition process. In B. C. Etzel, J. M. LeBlanc, & D. M. Baer (Eds.), *New developments in behavioral research.* Hillsdale, NJ: Erlbaum.

Gibbs, J. C. (1993, March). *Inductive discipline's contribution to moral motivation.* Paper presented at the biennial meeting of the Society for Research in Child Development, New Orleans.

Gibbs, J. T., & Huang, L. N. (1989). A conceptual framework for assessing and treating minority youth. In J. T. Gibbs & L. N. Huang (Eds.), *Children of color.* San Francisco, CA: Jossey-Bass.

Gibbs, N. (1990, Fall). The dreams of youth. *Time* [Special issue], pp. 10–14.

Gibson, E. G. (1969). *The principles of perceptual learning and development.* New York: Appleton-Century-Crofts.

Gibson, E. J. (1989). Exploratory behavior in the development of perceiving, acting, and the acquiring of knowledge. *Annual Review of Psychology, 39.*

Gibson, E. J., & Spelke, E. S. (1983). The development of perception. In P. H. Mussen (Ed.), *Handbook of child psychology* (4th ed., Vol. 3). New York: Wiley.

Gibson, E. J., & Walk, R. D. (1960). The "visual cliff." *Scientific American, 202,* 64–71.

Gilligan, C. (1982). *In a different voice.* Cambridge, MA: Harvard University Press.

Gilligan, C. (1990). Teaching Shakespeare's sister. In C. Gilligan, N. Lyons, & T. Hammer (Eds.), *Making connections: The relational worlds of adolescent girls at Emma Willard School.* Cambridge, MA: Harvard University Press.

Gilligan, C. (1992, May). *Joining the resistance: Girls' development in adolescence.* Paper presented at the symposium on development and vulnerability in close relationships, Montreal.

Gilligan, C. (1996). The centrality of relationships in psychological development: A puzzle, some evidence, and a theory. In G. G. Noam & K. W. Fischer (Eds.), *Development and vulnerability in close relationships.* Hillsdale, NJ: Erlbaum.

Gilligan, C., & Attanucci, J. (1988). Two moral orientations. In C. Gilligan, J. V. Ward, J. M. Taylor, and B. Bardige (Eds.). *Mapping the moral domain.* Cambridge, MA: Harvard University Press.

Ginzberg, E. (1972). Toward a theory of occupational choice: A restatement. *Vocational Guidance Quarterly, 20,* 169–176.

Gladden, W. G. (1991). *Planning and building a stepfamily.* Huntington, NY: William Gladden Foundation.

Glassman, M. J. (1995, March), *Vygotsky's times: Their times, his times, our times.* Paper presented at the meeting of the Society for Research in Child Development, Indianapolis.

Glover, R. W., & Marshall, R. (1993). Improving the school-to-work transition of American adolescents. In R. Takanishi (Ed.), *Adolescence in the 1990s.* New York: Teachers College Record.

Goldin-Meadow, S. (1979). The development of language-like communication without a language model. *Science, 197,* 401–403.

Goldman, J. A., Fujimura, J. B., Contois, J. H., & Lerman, R. H. (1987, April). *Interactions among preschool children following the ingestion of sucrose.* Paper presented at the biennial meeting of the Society for Research in Child Development, Baltimore.

Goldman, J. A., Lerman, R. H., Contois, J. H., & Udall, J. N. (1986). Behavioral effects of sucrose on preschool children. *Journal of Abnormal Child Psychology, 14,* 565–577.

Goldman, R. (1964). *Religious thinking from childhood to adolescence.* London: Routledge & Kegan Paul.

Goldsmith, H. H. (1994, Winter). The behavior-genetic approach to development and experience: Contexts and constraints. *SRCD Newsletter, 1,* 6, 10–11.

Golombok, S., Cook, R., Bish, A., & Murray, C. (1995). Families created by the new reproductive technologies: Quality of parenting and social and emotional development of children. *Child Development, 66,* 285–298.

Gomby, D. S. (1995, March). *Translating research into the language of policy.* Paper presented at the meeting of the Society for Research in Child Development, Indianapolis.

Goodchilds, J. D., & Zellman, G. L. (1984). Sexual signaling and sexual aggression in adolescent relationships. In N. M. Malamuth & E. D. Donnerstein (Eds.), *Pornography and sexual aggression.* New York: Academic Press.

Goodlad, J. A. (1984). *A place called school.* New York: McGraw-Hill.

Goodman, R. A., Mercy, J. A., Loya, F., Rosenberg, M. L., Smith, J. C., Allen, N. H., Vargas, L., & Kolts, R. (1986). Alcohol use and interpersonal violence: Alcohol detected in homicide victims. *American Journal of Public Health, 76,* 144–149.

Goodnow, J. J. (1995, March). *Incorporating "culture" into accounts of development.* Paper presented at the meeting of the Society for Research in Child Development, Indianapolis.

Gordon, I. (1978, June). *What does research say about the effects of parent involvement on schooling?* Paper presented at the meeting of the Association for Supervision and Curriculum Development, Washington, DC.

Gordon, S., & Gilgun, J. F. (1987). Adolescent sexuality. In V. B. Van Hasselt & M. Hersen (Eds.), *Handbook of adolescent psychology.* New York: Pergamon.

Gorman, K. S., & Pollitt, E. (1996). Does schooling buffer the effects of early risk? *Child Development, 67,* 314–326.

Gottfried, A. E., & Gottfried, A. W. (1989, April). *Home environment and children's academic intrinsic motivation: A longitudinal study.* Paper presented at the biennial meeting of the Society for Child Development, Kansas City.

Gottfried, A. E., Gottfried, A. W., & Bathurst, K. (1995). Maternal and dual-earner employment status and parenting. In M. H. Bornstein (Ed.), *Handbook of parenting* (Vol. 2). Hillsdale, NJ: Erlbaum.

Gottfried, A. E., Gottfried, A. W., & Bathurst K. (1995). Maternal and dual-earner employment status and parenting. In M. H. Bornstein (Ed.), *Handbook of parenting* (Vol. 3). Hillsdale, NJ: Erlbaum.

Gottlieb, D. (1966). Teaching and students: The views of Negro and white teachers. *Sociology of Education, 37,* 345–353.

Gottlieb, G. (1991). Experiential canalization of behavioral development theory. *Developmental Psychology, 27,* 4–13.

Gottman, J. M., & Parker, J. G. (Eds.). (1987). *Conversations of friends.* New York: Cambridge University Press.

Gould, S. J. (1981). *The mismeasure of man.* New York: W. W. Norton.

Gounin-Decarie, T. (1996). Revisiting Piaget, or the vulnerability of Piaget's infancy theory in the nineties. In G. G. Noam & K. W. Fischer (Eds.), *Development and vulnerability in close relationships.* Hillsdale, NJ: Erlbaum.

Graber, J. A., Petersen, A. C., & Brooks-Gunn, J. (1996). Pubertal processes: Methods, measures, and models. In J. A. Graber, J. Brooks-Gunn, & A. C. Petersen (Eds.), *Transitions through adolescence.* Hillsdale, NJ: Erlbaum.

Graham, S. (1986, August). *Can attribution theory tell us something about motivation in Blacks?* Paper presented at the meeting of the American Psychological Association, Washington, DC.

Graham, S. (1990). Motivation in Afro-Americans. In G. L. Berry & J. K. Asamen (Eds.), *Black students: Psychosocial issues and academic achievement.* Newbury Park, CA: Sage.

Grant, J. (1996). *The state of the world's children.* New York: UNICEF and Oxford University Press.

Grant, J. P. (1996). *The state of the world's children.* New York: UNICEF and Oxford University Press.

Grantham-McGregor, S. M. (1995, March). *Studies of the effects of nutrition and stimulation on children's behavioral development in Jamaica.* Paper presented at the meeting of the Society for Research in Child Development, Indianapolis.

Graziano, W. J. (1995). Evolutionary psychology: Old music, but now on CDs? *Psychological Inquiry, 6,* 31–34.

Green, P. (1995, March). *Sesame Street: More than a television show.* Paper presented at the meeting of the Society for Research in Child Development, Indianapolis.

Greenberg, B. S., & Brand, J. E. (1994). Minorities and the mass media. In J. Bryant & D. Zilman (Eds.), *Media effects.* Hillsdale, NJ: Erlbaum.

Greenberger, E., & Steinberg, L. (1981). *Project for the study of adolescent work: Final report.* Report prepared for the National Institute of Education, U.S. Department of Education, Washington, DC.

Greenberger, E., & Steinberg, L. (1986). *When teenagers work: The psychological social costs of adolescent employment.* New York: Basic Books.

Greene, B. (1988, May). The children's hour. *Esquire Magazine,* pp. 47–49.

Grotevant, H. D., & Durrett, M. E. (1980). Occupational knowledge and career development in adolescence. *Journal of Vocational Behavior, 17,* 171–182.

Grunwald, L., Goldberg, J., Berstein, S., & Hollister, A. (1993, July). The amazing mind of babies. *Life,* p. 52.

Gruskin, E. (1994, February). *A review of research on self-identified gay, lesbian, and bisexual youth from 1970–1993.* Paper presented at the meeting of the Society for Research on Adolescence, San Diego.

Guilford, J. P. (1967). *The structure of intellect.* New York: McGraw-Hill.

Gunnar, M. R., Malone, S., & Fisch, R. O. (1987). The psychobiology of stress and coping in the human neonate: Studies of the adrenocortical activity in response to stress in the first week of life. In T. Field, P. McCabe, & N. Scheiderman (Eds.), *Stress and coping.* Hillsdale, NJ: Erlbaum.

Gur, R. C., Mozley, L. H., Mozley, P. D., Resnick, S. M., Karp, J. S., Alavi, A., Arnold, S. E., & Gur, R. E. (1995). Sex differences in regional cerebral glucose metabolism during a resting state. *Science, 267,* 528–531.

Gustafson, G. E., Green, J. A., & Kalinowski, L. L. (1993, March). *The development of communicative skills: Infants' cries and vocalizations in social context.* Paper presented at the biennial meeting of the Society for Research in Child Development, New Orleans.

Gutherie, G. M., Masangkay, Z., & Gutherie, H. A. (1976). Behavior, malnutrition, and mental development. *Journal of Cross-Cultural Psychology, 7,* 169–180.

H

Hack, M. H., Klein, N. K., & Taylor, H. G. (1995, Spring). Long-term developmental outcomes of low birth weight infants. *Future of Children, 5* (1), 176–196.

Haight, W. L., & Miller, P. J. (1993). *Pretending at home.* Albany: State University of New York Press.

Hakim-Larson, J. A. (1995, March). *Affective defaults: Temperament, goals, rules, and values.* Paper presented at the meeting of the Society for Research in Child Development, Indianapolis.

Hakuta, K., & Garcia, E. E. (1989). Bilingualism and education. *American Psychologist, 44,* 374–379.

Hall, C. C. I., Evans, B. J., & Selice, S. (Eds.). (1989). *Black females in the United States.* Washington, DC: American Psychological Association.

Hall, G. S. (1904). *Adolescence* (Vols. 1 & 2). Englewood Cliffs, NJ: Prentice Hall.

Halonen, J. (1995). Demystifying critical thinking. *Teaching of Psychology, 22,* 75–81.

Halonen, J., & Santrock, J. W. (1996). *Psychology: The contexts of behavior* (2nd ed.). Madison, WI: Brown & Benchmark.

Hamilton, M. C. (1991). *Preference for sons or daughters and the sex role characteristics of the potential parents.* Paper presented at the meeting of the Association for Women in Psychology, Hartford, CT.

Hammond, W. R. (1993, August). Participant in open forum with the APA Commission on Youth and Violence, meeting of the American Psychological Association, Washington, DC.

Hans, S. (1989, April). *Infant behavioral effects of prenatal exposure to methadone.* Paper presented at the biennial meeting of the Society for Research in Child Development, Kansas City.

Hansen, D. (1996, March). *Adolescent employment and psychosocial outcomes: A comparison of two employment contexts.* Paper presented at the meeting of the Society for Research on Adolescence, Boston.

Harkness, S., & Super, C. M. (1995). Culture and parenting. In M. H. Bornstein (Ed.), *Children and parenting* (Vol. 2). Hillsdale, NJ: Erlbaum.

Harlow, H. F., & Zimmerman, R. R. (1959). Affectional responses in the infant monkey. *Science, 130,* 421–432.

Harold, R. D., & Eccles, J. S. (1990, March). *Maternal expectations, advice, and provision of opportunities: Their relationships to boys and girls' occupational aspirations.* Paper presented at the meeting of the Society for Research in Adolescence, Atlanta.

Harris, L. (1987, September 3). The latchkey child phenomena. *Dallas Morning News,* pp. 1A, 10A.

Hart, B., & Risley, T. R. (1995). *Meaningful differences.* Baltimore, MD: Paul Brookes.

Hart, C. H., Charlesworth, R., Burts, D. C., & DeWolf, M. (1993, March). *The relationship of attendance in developmentally appropriate or inappropriate kindergarten classrooms to first-grade behavior.* Paper presented at the biennial meeting of the Society for Research in Child Development, New Orleans.

Harter, S. (1982). The perceived competence scale for children. *Child Development, 53,* 87–97.

Harter, S. (1985). *Self-perception profile for children.* Denver: University of Denver, Department of Psychology.

Harter, S. (1989). *Self-perception profile for adolescents.* Denver, University of Denver.

Harter, S. (1990). Processes underlying adolescent self-concept formation. In R. Montemayor, G. R. Adams, & R. P. Gulotta (Eds.), *From childhood to adolescence: A transitional period?* Newbury Park, CA: Sage.

Harter, S. (1990). Self and identity development. In S. S. Feldman & G. R. Elliott (Eds.), *At the threshold: The developing adolescent.* Cambridge, MA: Harvard University Press.

Harter, S., Alexander, P. C., & Neimeyer, R. A. (1988). Long-term effects of incestuous child abuse in college women. Social adjustment, social cognition, and family characteristics. *Journal of Consulting and Clinical Psychology, 56,* 5–8.

Harter, S., & Marold, D. B. (1992). Psychosocial risk factors contributing to adolescent suicide ideation. In G. Noam & S. Borst (Eds.), *Child and adolescent suicide.* San Francisco: Jossey-Bass.

Harter, S., Waters, P., & Whitesell, N. (1996, March). *False self behavior and lack of voice among adolescent males and females.* Paper presented at the meeting of the Society for Research on Adolescence, Boston.

Hartshorne, H., & May, M. S. (1928–1930). *Moral studies in the nature of character: Studies in the nature of character.* New York: Macmillan.

Hartup, W. W. (1983). Peer relations. In P. H. Mussen (Eds.), *Handbook of child psychology* (4th ed., Vol. 4). New York: Wiley.

Hartup, W. W. (1996). The company they keep: Friendships and their developmental significance. *Child Development, 67,* 1–13.

Hawkins, D., & Lam, T. (1986). Teacher practices, social development, and delinquency. In J. Burchard & S. Burchard (Eds.), *Prevention of delinquent behavior.* Newbury Park, CA: Sage.

Hawkins, D., & Lishner, D. (1987). School and delinquency. In E. Johnson (Ed.), *Handbook on crime and delinquency prevention.* Westport, CT: Greenwood Press.

Hawkins, J., Pea, R. D., Glick, J., & Scribner, S. (1984). "Merds that laugh don't like mushrooms." Evidence for deductive reasoning by preschoolers. *Developmental Psychology, 20,* 584–594.

Hawkins, J. A., & Berndt, T. J. (1985, April). *Adjustment following the transition to junior high school.* Paper presented at the biennial meeting of the Society for Research in Child Development, Toronto.

Hazen, C., & Shaver, P. (1987). Romantic love conceptualized as an attachment process. *Journal of Personality and Social Psychology, 51,* 511–524.

Heath, S. B. (1989). Oral and literate traditions among Black Americans living in poverty. *American Psychologist, 44,* 367–373.

Heath, S. B., & McLaughlin, M. W. (Eds.). (1993). *Identity and inner-city youth.* New York: Teachers College Press.

Heinicke, C. M., Beckwith, L., & Thompson, A. (1988). Early intervention in the family system: A framework and review. *Infant Mental Health Journal, 9,* 2.

Helson, R., Elliot, T., & Leigh, J. (1989). Adolescent antecedents of women's work patterns. In D. Stern & D. Eichorn (Eds.), *Adolescence and work.* Hillsdale, NJ: Erlbaum.

Henderson, S. H., Hetherington, E. M., Mekos, D., & Reiss, D. (1996). Stress, parenting, and adolescent psychopathology in nondivorced and stepfamilies: A within-family perspective. In E. M. Hetherington & E. A. Blechman (Eds.), *Stress, coping, and resiliency in children and families.* Hillsdale, NJ: Erlbaum.

Henderson, V. L., & Dweck, C. S. (1990). Motivation and achievement. In S. S. Feldman & G. R. Elliott (Eds.), *At the threshold: The developing adolescent.* Cambridge, MA: Harvard University Press.

Hendry, J. (1986). *Becoming Japanese: The world of the preschool child.* Honolulu: University of Hawaii Press.

Hernstein, R. J., & Murray, C. (1994). *The bell curve: Intelligence and class structure in modern life.* New York: Free Press.

Hess, R. D., Holloway, S. D., Dicson, W. P., & Price, G. G. (1984). Maternal variables as predictors of children's school readiness and later achievement in vocabulary and mathematics in the sixth grade. *Child Development, 55,* 1902–1912.

Hetherington, E. M. (1994, February). *The role of parents, siblings, peers, and schools in the development of behavior problems in nondivorced, divorced, and remarried families.* Paper presented at the meeting of the Society for Research on Adolescence, San Diego.

Hetherington, E. M. (1995, March). *The changing American family and the well-being of children.* Paper presented at the meeting of the Society for Research in Child Development, Indianapolis.

Hetherington, E. M., Cox, M., & Cox, R. (1982). Effects of divorce on children and parents. In M. E. Lamb (Ed.), *Nontraditional families*. Hillsdale, NJ: Erlbaum.

Hetherington, E. M., & Stanley-Hagan, M. M. (1995). Parenting in divorced and remarried families. In M. H. Bornstein (Ed.), *Children and parenting* (Vol. 4). Hillsdale, NJ: Erlbaum.

Hightower, E. (1990). Adolescent interpersonal and familial precursors of positive mental health at midlife. *Journal of Youth and Adolescence, 19,* 257–275.

Hill, C. R., & Stafford, F. P. (1980). Parental care of children: Time diary estimate of quantity, predictability, and variety. *Journal of Human Resources, 15,* 219–239.

Hill, J. P., Holmbeck, G. N., Marlow, L., Green, T. M., & Lynch, M. E. (1985). Pubertal status and parent-child relations in families of seventh-grade boys. *Journal of Early Adolescence, 5,* 31–44.

Hinde, R. A. (1992). Developmental psychology in the context of other behavioral sciences. *Developmental Psychology, 28,* 1018–1029.

Hines, M. (1982). Prenatal gonadal hormones and sex differences in human behavior. *Psychological Bulletin, 92,* 56–80.

Hirsch, B. J., & Rapkin, B. D. (1987). The transition to junior high school: A longitudinal study of self-esteem, psychological symptomatology, school life, and social support. *Child Development, 58,* 1235–1243.

Hirsch-Pasek, K., Hyson, M., Rescorla, L., & Cone, J. (1989, April). *Hurrying children: How does it affect their academic, social, creative, and emotional development?* Paper presented at the Society for Research in Child Development meeting, Kansas City.

Hoagwood, K., Jensen, P., & Fisher, C. (Eds.). (1996). *Ethical issues in mental health research with children and adolescents.* Hillsdale, NJ: Erlbaum.

Hofer, B. K., Carlson, D. M., & Stevenson, H. W. (1996, March). *Gender differences in attitudes and beliefs about mathematics: Correlates of achievement in six countries.* Paper presented at the meeting of the Society for Research on Adolescence, Boston.

Hoff-Ginsburg, E., & Tardif, T. (1995). Socioeconomic status and parenting. In M. H. Bornstein (Ed.), *Handbook of parenting* (Vol. 1). Hillsdale, NJ: Erlbaum.

Hoffman, L. W. (1989). Effects of maternal employment in two-parent families. *American Psychologist, 44,* 283–293.

Hoffman, M. L. (1970). Moral development. In P. H. Mussen (Ed.), *Manual of child psychology* (3rd ed., Vol. 2). New York: Wiley.

Holland, J. L. (1987). Current status of Holland's theory of careers: Another perspective. *Career Development Quarterly, 36,* 24–30.

Holmbeck, G. N. (1996). A model of family relational transformations during the transition to adolescence: Parent-adolescent conflict and adaptation. In J. A. Graber, J. Brooks-Gunn, & A. C. Petersen (Eds.), *Transitions through adolescence.* Hillsdale, NJ: Erlbaum.

Holmbeck, G. N., Paikoff, R. L., & Brooks-Gunn, J. (1995). Parenting adolescents. In M. H. Bornstein (Ed.), *Children and parenting* (Vol. 1). Hillsdale, NJ: Erlbaum.

Holtzman, W. H. (Ed.). (1992). *School of the future.* Austin, TX: American Psychological Association and Hogg Foundation for Mental Health.

Honig, A. S. (1995). Choosing childcare for young children. In M. H. Bornstein (Ed.), *Handbook of parenting* (Vol. 4). Hillsdale, NJ: Erlbaum.

Hoot, J. L., & Robertson, G. (1994). Creating safer environments in the home, school and community. *Childhood Education, 71,* 259.

Horney, K. (1967). *Feminine psychology.* New York: W. W. Norton.

Horowitz, F. D., & O'Brien, M. (1989). In the interest of the nation: A reflective essay on the state of knowledge and the challenges before us. *American Psychologist, 44,* 441–445.

Houston, M., & Wood, J. T. (1996). Difficult dialogues—Communicating across race and class. In J. T. Wood (Ed.), *Gendered relationships.* Mountain View, CA: Mayfield.

Howes, C. (1988, April). *Can the age of entry and the quality of infant child care predict behaviors in kindergarten?* Paper presented at the International Conference on Infant Studies, Washington, DC.

Howes, C. (1992). *The collaborative construction of pretend: Social pretend play functions.* Albany: State University of New York Press.

Huang, L. N., & Gibbs, J. T. (1989). Future directions: Implications for research, training, and practice. In J. T. Gibbs & L. N. Huang (Eds.), *Children of color.* San Francisco: Jossey-Bass.

Huang, L. N., & Ying, Y. (1989). Japanese children and adolescents. In J. T. Gibbs & L. N. Huang (Eds.), *Children of color.* San Francisco: Jossey-Bass.

Hudson, L. M., Forman, E. R., & Brion-Meisels, S. (1982). Role-taking as a predictor of prosocial behavior in cross-age tutors. *Child Development, 53,* 222–234.

Huebner, A. M., Garrod, A. C., & Snarey, J. (1990, March). *Moral development in Tibetan Buddhist monks: A cross-cultural study of adolescents and young adults in Nepal.* Paper presented at the meeting of the Society for Research in Adolescence, Atlanta.

Huesmann, L. R. (1986). Psychological processes promoting the relation between exposure to media violence and aggressive behavior by the viewer. *Journal of Social Issues, 42,* 125–139.

Huesmann, L. R., Eron, L. D., Klein, R., Brice, P., & Fischer, P. (1983). Mitigating the imitation of aggressive behaviors by changing children's attitudes about media violence. *Journal of Personality and Social Psychology, 44,* 899–910.

Hunt, M. (1974). *Sexual behavior in the 1970s.* Chicago: Playboy Press.

Huston, A. C. (1983). Sex-typing. In P. H. Mussen (Ed.), *Handbook of child psychology* (4th ed., Vol. 4). New York: Wiley.

Huston, A. C., & Alvarez, M. (1990). The socialization context of gender-role development in early adolescence. In R. Montemayor, G. R. Adams, & T. P. Gulotta (Eds.), *From childhood to adolescence: A transitional period?* Newbury Park, CA: Sage.

Huston, A. C., McLoyd, V. C., & Coll, C. G. (1994). Children and poverty: Issues in contemporary research. *Child Development, 65,* 275–282.

Huston, A. C., Seigle, J., & Bremer, M. (1983, April). *Family environment and television use by preschool children.* Paper presented at the Society for Research in Child Development meeting, Detroit.

Huttenlocher, J. (1995, March). *Children's language and relation to input.* Paper presented at the meeting of the Society for Research in Child Development, Indianapolis.

Hyde, J. S. (1990). Meta-analysis and the psychology of gender differences. *Signs: Journal of Women in Psychology and Culture, 16,* 55–69.

Hyde, J. S., & Plant, E. A. (1995). Magnitude of psychological gender differences: Another side of the story. *American Psychologist, 50,* 159–161.

I

Infant Health and Development Program Staff. (1990). Enhancing the outcomes of low birthweight, premature infants: A multisite randomized trial. *Journal of the American Medical Association, 263,* 3035–3042.

Inoff-Germain, G., Arnold, G. S., Nottelmann, E. D., Susman, E. J., Cutler, G. B., & Chrousos, G. P. (1988). Relations between hormone levels and observational measures of aggressive behavior of young adolescents in family interactions. *Developmental Psychology, 24,* 124–139.

Intons-Peterson, M. (1996). Memory aids. In D. Hermann, C. McEvoy, C. Hertog, P. Hertel, & M. Johnson (Eds.), *Basic and applied memory research* (Vol. 2). Hillsdale, NJ: Erlbaum.

Izard, C. E. (1982). *Measuring emotions in infants and young children.* New York: Cambridge University Press.

J

Jackson, J. F. (1993). Human behavioral genetics, Scarr's theory, and her views on interventions: A critical review and commentary on their implications for African American children. *Child Development, 64,* 1318–1332.

Jacobs, F. H., Little, P., & Almeida, C. (1993). *Supporting family life: A survey of homeless shelters.* Unpublished manuscript, Department of Child Study, Tufts University, Medford, MA.

Jacobs, J. K., Garnier, H. E., & Weisner, T. (1996, March). *The impact of family life on the process of dropping out of high school.* Paper presented at the meeting of the Society for Research on Adolescence, Boston.

Jacobson, J. L., Jacobson, S. W., Padgett, R. J., Brumitt, G. A., & Billings, R. L. (1992). Effects of prenatal PCB Exposure on cognitive processing efficiency and sustained attention. *Developmental Psychology, 28,* 297–306.

James, W. (1890/1950). *The principles of psychology.* New York: Dover.

Jarrett, R. L. (1995). Growing up poor: The family experiences of socially mobile youth in low-income African-American neighborhoods. *Journal of Adolescent Research, 10,* 111–135.

Jeans, P. C., Smith, M. B., & Stearns, G. (1955). Incidence of prematurity in relation to maternal nutrition. *Journal of the American Dietary Association, 31,* 576–581.

Jensen, L. C., & Kingston, M. (1986). *Parenting.* Fort Worth, TX: Holt, Rinehart & Winston.

Jensen, R. A. (1969). How much can we boost IQ and scholastic achievement? *Harvard Educational Review, 39,* 1–123.

Jiao, S., Ji, G., & Jing, Q. (1996). Cognitive development of Chinese urban only children and children with siblings. *Child Development, 67,* 387–395.

Joesph, C. L. M. (1989). Identification of factors associated with delayed antenatal care. *Journal of the American Medical Association, 81,* 57–63.

Johnson, D. D. L., Swank, P., Howie, V. M., Baldwin, C., & Owen, M. (1993, March). *Tobacco smoke in the home and child intelligence.* Paper presented at the biennial meeting of the Society for Research in Child Development, New Orleans.

Johnston, L., Bachman, J. G., & O'Malley, P. M. (1990). *Monitoring the future.* Ann Arbor: University of Michigan, Institute of Social Research.

Johnston, L., O'Malley, P., & Bachman, G. (1994, January). *Drug use rises among the nation's eighth-grade students.* Ann Arbor: University of Michigan, Institute of Social Research.

Jones, E. R., Forrest, J. D., Goldman, N., Henshaw, S. K., Lincoln, R., Rosoff, J. I., Westoff, C. G., & Wulf, D. (1985). Teenage pregnancy in developed countries: Determinants and policy implications. *Family Planning Perspectives, 17,* 53–63.

Jones, J. M. (1990, August). *Psychological approaches to race: What have they been and what should they be?* Paper presented at the meeting of the American Psychological Association, Boston.

Jones, J. M. (1993, August). *Racism and civil rights: Right problem, wrong solution.* Paper presented at the meeting of the American Psychological Association, Toronto.

Jones, J. M. (1994). The African American: A duality dilemma? In W. J. Lonner & R. Malpass (Eds.), *Psychology and culture.* Needham Heights, MA: Allyn & Bacon.

Jones, L. (1984). White-black achievement differences: The narrowing gap. *American Psychologist, 39,* 1207–1213.

Jones, L. (1996). *HIV/AIDS: What to do about it.* Pacific Grove, CA: Brooks/Cole.

Jones, M. C. (1965). Psychological correlates of somatic development. *Child Development, 36,* 899–911.

Jozefowicz, D. M., Barber, B. L., & Mollasis, C. (1994, February). *Relations between maternal and adolescent values and beliefs: Sex differences and implications for occupational choice.* Papers presented at the meeting of the Society for Research on Adolescence, San Diego.

K

Kagan, J. (1984). *The nature of the child.* New York: Basic Books.

Kagan, J. (1987). Perspectives on infancy. In J. D. Osofsky (Ed.), *Handbook on infant development* (2nd ed.). New York: Wiley.

Kagan, J. (1992). Yesterday's promises, tomorrow's promises. *Developmental Psychology, 28,* 990–997.

Kagan, J., Kearsley, R. B., & Zelazo, P. R. (1978). *Infancy.* Cambridge, MA: Harvard University Press.

Kagan, J., & Snidman, N. (1991). Temperamental factors in human development. *American Psychologist, 46,* 856–862.

Kagitcibasi, C. (1996). *Human development across cultures.* Hillsdale, NJ: Erlbaum.

Kalichman, S. C. (1996). *Answering your questions about AIDS.* Washington, DC: American Psychological Association.

Kamerman, S. B. (1989). Child care, women, work, and the family: An international overview of child-care services and related policies. In J. S. Lande, S. Scarr, & N. Gunzenhauser (Eds.), *Caring for children: Challenge to America.* Hillsdale, NJ: Erlbaum.

Kamerman, S. B., & Kahn, A. J. (Eds.). (1978). *Family policy: Government and families in fourteen countries.* New York: Columbia University Press.

Kandel, D. B. (1974). The role of parents and peers in marijuana use. *Journal of Social Issues, 30,* 107–135.

Katz, L., & Chard, S. (1989). *Engaging the minds of young children. The project approach.* Norwood, NJ: Ablex.

Katz, P. A. (1987, August). *Children and social issues.* Paper presented at the meeting of the American Psychological Association, New York.

Kaufmann, A. S., & Flaitz, J. (1987). Intellectual growth. In V. B. Van Hasselt & M. Hersen (Eds.), *Handbook of adolescent psychology.* New York: Pergamon Press.

Kavale, K. A., & Forness, S. R. (1996). Social skill deficits and learning disabilities: A meta-analysis. *Journal of Learning Disabilities, 24,* 226–337.

Kavin, E. J., & Parcell, S. R. (1977). Sexual aggression: A second look at the offended female. *Archives of Sexual Behavior, 6,* 67–76.

Keating, D. P. (1990). Adolescent thinking. In S. S. Feldman & G. R. Elliott (Eds.), *At the threshold: The developing adolescent.* Cambridge, MA: Harvard University Press.

Keener, D. C., & Boykin, K. A. (1996, March). *Parental control, autonomy, and ego development.* Paper presented at the meeting of the Society for Research on Adolescence, Boston.

Keirouz, K. S. (1990). Concerns of parents of gifted children: A research review. *Gifted Child Quarterly, 34,* 56–62.

Kelder, S. H., Perry, C. L., Peters, R. J., Lytle, L. L., & Klepp, K. (1995). Gender differences in the class of 1989 study: The school component of the Minnesota Heart Health Program. *Journal of Health Education, 26,* S36–S44.

Keller, A., Ford, L., & Meacham, J. (1978). Dimensions of self-concept in preschool children. *Developmental Psychology, 14,* 483–489.

Kellogg, R. (1970). *Understanding children's art: Readings in developmental psychology today.* Del Mar, CA: CRM.

Keltikangas-Järvinen, L., & Raikkonen, K. (1990). Healthy and maladjusted Type-A behavior in adolescents. *Journal of Youth and Adolescence, 19,* 1–18.

Kendler, K. S. (1996). Parenting: A genetic-epidemiologic perspective. *American Journal of Psychiatry, 153,* 11–20.

Kennedy, J. H. (1990). Determinants of peer social status: Contributions of physical appearance, reputation, and behavior. *Journal of Youth and Adolescence, 19,* 233–244.

Kershner, R. (1996). Adolescent attitudes about rape. *Adolescence, 31,* 29–34.

Kessen, W., Haith, M. M., & Salapatek, P. (1970). Human infancy. In P. H. Mussen (Ed.), *Manual of child psychology* (3rd ed., Vol. 1). New York: Wiley.

Kimmel, A. (1996). *Ethical issues in behavioral research.* Cambridge, MA: Blackwell.

King, N. (1982). School uses of materials traditionally associated with children's play. *Theory and Research in Social Education, 10,* 17–27.

Kinsey, A. C., Pomeroy, W. B., & Martin, E. E. (1948). *Sexual behavior in the human male.* Philadelphia: W. B. Saunders.

Kisilevsky, B. S. (1995). The influence stimulus and subject variables on human fetal responses to sound and vibration. In J-P Lecaunet, W. P. Fifer, M. A. Krasnegor, & W. P. Smotherman (Eds.), *Fetal development.* Hillsdale, NJ: Erlbaum.

Klaus, M., & Kennell, H. H. (1976). *Maternal-infant bonding.* St. Louis: Mosby.

Klaus, M. H., Kennell, J. H., & Klaus, P. H. (1993). *Mothering the infant.* Reading, MA: Addison-Wesley.

Klein, A. S., & Starkey, P. (1995, March). *Preparing for the transition to school mathematics: The Head Start family math project.* Paper presented at the meeting of the Society for Research in Child Development, Indianapolis.

Klonoff-Cohen, H. S., Edelstein, S. L., Lefkowitz, E. S., Srinivasan, I. P., Kaegi, D., Chang, J. C., and Wiley, K. J. (1995). The effect of passive smoke and tobacco exposure through breast milk on sudden infant death syndrome. *Journal of the American Medical Association, 293,* 795–798.

Knight, G. P., Virdin, L., & Roosa, M. (1994). Socialization and family correlates of mental health outcomes among Hispanic and Anglo American children. Consideration of cross-ethnic scalar equivalence. *Child Development, 65,* 212–224.

Koenig, W. D., Mumme, R. L., & Pitelka, F. A. (1984). The breeding system of the acorn woodpecker in central coastal California. *Zeitschrift für Tierpsychologie, 65,* 289–308.

Kohlberg, L. (1958). *The development on modes of moral thinking and choice in the years 10 to 16.* Unpublished doctoral dissertation. University of Chicago.

Kohlberg, L. (1966). A cognitive-developmental analysis of children's sex-role concepts and attitudes. In E. E. Maccoby (Ed.), *The development of sex differences.* Palo Alto, CA: Stanford University Press.

Kohlberg, L. (1969). Stage and sequence: The cognitive-developmental approach to socialization. In D. A. Goslin (Ed.), *Handbook of socialization theory and research.* Chicago: Rand McNally.

Kohlberg, L. (1976). Moral stages and moralization: The cognitive-developmental approach. In T. Lickona (Ed.), *Moral development and behavior.* New York: Holt, Rinehart & Winston.

Kohlberg, L. (1986). A current statement on some theoretical issues. In S. Modgil & C. Modgil (Eds.), *Lawrence Kohlberg.* Philadelphia: Falmer.

Kopp, C. B. (1992, October). *Trends and directions in studies of developmental risk.* Paper presented at the 27th Minnesota Symposium on Child Psychology, University of Minnesota, Minneapolis.

Kortenhaus, C. M., & Demarest, J. (1993). Gender role stereotyping in children's literature. An update. *Sex Roles, 28,* 219–230.

Kuhl, P. K. (1993). Infant speech perception: A window on psycholinguistic development. *International Journal of Psycholinguistics, 9,* 33–56.

Kupersmidt, J. B., & Coie, J. D. (1990). Preadolescent peer status, aggression, and school adjustment as predictors of externalizing problems in adolescence. *Child Development, 61,* 1350–1363.

Kurdek, L. A., & Krile, D. (1982). A developmental analysis of the relation between peer acceptance and both interpersonal understanding and perceived social self-competence. *Child Development, 53,* 1485–1491.

Kurtz, D. A., Cantu, C. L., & Phinney, J. S. (1996, March). *Group identities as predictors of self-esteem among African American, Latino, and White adolescents.* Paper presented at the meeting of the Society for Research on Adolescence, Boston.

L

Ladd, G., & Hart, C. H. (1992). Creating informal play opportunities: Are parents' and preschoolers' initiations related to children's competence with peers? *Developmental Psychology, 28,* 1179–1187.

Ladd, G. W., & Le Sieur, K. D. (1995). Parents and children's peer relationships. In M. H. Bornstein (Ed.), *Children and parenting* (Vol. 4). Hillsdale, NJ: Erlbaum.

LaFromboise, T., & Trimble, J. (1996). Multicultural counseling theory and American-Indian populations. In D. W. Sue (Ed.), *Theory of multicultural counseling and therapy*. Pacific Grove, CA: Brooks/Cole.

LaFromboise, T. D. (1993). American Indian mental health policy. In D. R. Atkinson, G. Morten, & D. W. Sue (Eds.), *Counseling American minorities*. Madison, WI: Brown & Benchmark.

LaFromboise, T. D., & Low, D. G. (1989). American Indian children and adolescents. In J. T. Gibbs & L. N. Huang (Eds.), *Children of color*. San Francisco: Jossey-Bass.

Lally, J. R., Mangione, P., & Honig, S. (1987). *The Syracuse University family development research program*. Unpublished manuscript, Syracuse University, Syracuse, NY.

Lamb, M. (1994). Infant care practices and the application of knowledge. In C. B. Fisher & R. M. Lerner (Eds.), *Applied developmental psychology*. New York: McGraw-Hill.

Lamb, M. E. (1977). The development of mother-infant and father-infant attachments in the second year of life. *Developmental Psychology, 13*, 637–648.

Lamb, M. E. (1986). *The father's role: Applied perspectives*. New York: Wiley.

Lamb, M. E., Frodi, A. M., Hwant, C. P., Frodi, M., & Steinberg, J. (1982). Mother- and father-infant interaction involving play and holding in traditional and nontraditional Swedish families. *Developmental Psychology, 18*, 215–221.

Lamb, M. E., & Sternberg, K. J. (1992). Sociocultural perspectives in nonparental childcare. In M. E. Lamb, K. J. Sternberg, C. Hwang, & A. G. Broberg (Eds.), *Child care in context*. Hillsdale, NJ: Erlbaum.

Landesman-Dwyer, S., & Sackett, G. P. (1983, April). *Prenatal nicotine exposure and sleep-wake patterns in infancy*. Paper presented at the biennial meeting of the Society for Research in Child Development, Detroit.

Lane, H. (1976). *The wild boy of Aveyron*. Cambridge, MA: Harvard University Press.

Lapsley, D. K. (1991). The adolescent egocentrism theory and the "new look" at the imaginary audience and personal fable. In R. M. Lerner, A. C. Petersen, & J. Brooks-Gunn (Eds.), *Encyclopedia of adolescence*. New York: Garland.

Lapsley, D. K. (1996). *Moral psychology*. Boulder, CO: Westview Press.

Lapsley, D. K., Enright, R. D., & Serlin, R. C. (1985). Toward a theoretical perspective on the legislation of adolescence. *Journal of Early Adolescence, 5*, 441–466.

Lasko, D. S., Field, T. M., Gonzalez, K. P., Harding, J., Yando, R., & Bendell, D. (1996). Adolescent depressed mood and parental unhappiness. *Adolescence, 121*, 49–58.

Lazarus, R. S. (1993). Coping theory and research: Past, present, and future. *Psychosomatic Medicine, 55*, 234–247.

Leach, P. (1990). *Your baby and child: From birth to age five*. New York: Knopf.

Leach, P. (1991). *Your baby and child: From birth to age five* (2nd ed.). New York: Alfred A. Knopf.

Leboyer, F. (1975). *Birth without violence*. New York: Knopf.

Lecaunet, J-P, Graneir-Deferre, C., & Busnel, M-C. (1995). Human fetal auditory perception. In J-P Lecaunet, W. P. Fifer, N. A. Krasnegor, and W. P. Smotherman (Eds.), *Fetal development*. Hillsdale, NJ: Erlbaum.

Lee, L. C. (1992, August). *The search for universals: Whatever happened to race?* Paper presented at the meeting of the American Psychological Association, Washington, DC.

Leffert, N., & Blyth, D. A. (1996, March). *The effects of community contexts on adolescent adjustment*. Paper presented at the meeting of the Society for Research on Adolescence, Boston.

Lefkowitz, E. S., Kahlbaugh, P. E., & Sigman, M. D. (1994, February). *Adolescent risk-taking and thrill-seeking: Relationship to gender, AIDS beliefs, and family interactions*. Paper presented at the meeting of the Society for Research in Adolescence, San Diego.

Leifer, A. D. (1973). *Television and the development of social behavior*. Paper presented at the meeting of the International Society for the Study of Behavioral Development, Ann Arbor, MI.

Lemery, K. S., & Buss, D. A. (1995, March). *Genetic models of toddler and preschooler temperament*. Paper presented at the meeting of the Society for Research in Child Development, Indianapolis.

Lenneberg, E. (1967). *The biological foundations of language*. New York: Wiley.

Lenneberg, E. H., Rebelsky, F. G., & Nichols, I. A. (1965). The vocalization of infants born to deaf and hearing parents. *Human Development, 8*, 23–37.

Leong, F. (1996). Multicultural counseling theory and Asian-American populations. In D. W. Sue (Ed.), *Theory of multicultural counseling and therapy*. Pacific Grove, CA: Brooks/Cole.

Lepper, M., Greene, D., & Nisbett, R. R. (1973). Undermining children's intrinsic interest with extrinsic rewards. *Journal of Personality and Social Psychology, 28*, 129–137.

Lepper, M. R., & Gurtner, J. (1989). Children and computers: Approaching the twenty-first century. *American Psychologist, 44*, 170–178.

Lerner, R. M., & Karabenick, S. A. (1974). Physical attractiveness, body attitudes, and self-concept in late adolescence. *Journal of Youth and Adolescence, 3*, 307–316.

Lester, B. M., Freier, K., & LcGasse, K. (1995). Prenatal cocaine exposure and child outcome: How much do we really know? In M. Lewis & M. Bendersky (Eds.), *Mothers, babies, and cocaine*. Hillsdale, NJ: Erlbaum.

Lester, B. M., & Tronick, E. Z. (1990). Introduction. In B. M. Lester & E. Z. Tronick (Eds.), *Stimulation and the preterm infant: The limits of plasticity*. Philadelphia: Saunders.

Leventhal, A. (1994, February). *Peer conformity during adolescence: An integration of developmental, situational, and individual characteristics*. Paper presented at the meeting of the Society for Research on Adolescence, San Diego.

Levin, J. (1980). *The mnemonic '80s: Keywords in the classroom*. Theoretical paper No. 86. Wisconsin Research and Development Center for Individualized Schooling, Madison.

LeVine, R. A., & Shweder, R. A. (1995, March). *Culture, pluralism, and the nature-nurture problem*. Paper presented at the meeting of the Society for Research in Child Development, Indianapolis.

Lewis, C. G. (1981). How adolescents approach decisions: Changes over grades seven to twelve and policy implications. *Child Development, 52*, 538–554.

Lewis, M., & Brooks-Gunn, J. (1979). *Social cognition and the acquisition of the self*. New York: Plenum.

Lewis, V. G., Money, J., & Bobrow, N. A. (1977). Idiopathic pubertal delay beyond the age of 15: Psychological study of 12 boys. *Adolescence, 12*, 1–11.

Lewkowicz, D. J. (1988). Sensory dominance in infants: 1. Six-month-old infants' response to auditory-visual compounds. *Developmental Psychology, 24*, 155–171.

Lewkowicz, D. J., & Lickliter, R. (Eds.). (1995). *The development of intersensory perception*. Hillsdale, NJ: Erlbaum.

Liaw, F., Meisels, S. J., & Brooks-Gunn, J. (1994). *Intervention with low birth weight, premature children: An examination of the experience of intervention*. Unpublished manuscript, Dept. of Psychology, Columbia University, New York City.

Lifshitz, F., Pugliese, M. T., Moses, N., & Weyman-Daum, M. (1987). Parental health beliefs as a cause of nonorganic failure to thrive. *Pediatrics, 80*, 175–182.

Lipsitt, L. P., Reilly, B. M., Butcher, M. J., & Greenwood, M. M. (1976). The stability and interrelationships of newborn sucking and heart rate. *Developmental Psychology, 9*, 305–310.

Lipsitz, J. (1983, October). *Making it the hard way: Adolescents in the 1980s*. Testimony presented at the Crisis Intervention Task Force, House Select Committee on Children, Youth, and Families, Washington, DC.

Lipsitz, J. (1984). *Successful schools for young adolescents*. New Brunswick, NJ: Transaction.

Lively, W., & Bromley, D. (1973). *Person perception in childhood and adolescence*. New York: Wiley.

Locke, J. L. (1993). *The child's path to spoken language*. Cambridge, MA: Harvard University Press.

Long, T., & Long, L. (1983). *Latchkey children*. New York: Penguin.

Lorch, E. (1995, March). *Young children's perception of importance in televised stories*. Paper presented at the meeting of the Society for Research in Child Development, Indianapolis.

Lorenz, K. Z. (1965). *Evolution and the modification of behavior*. Chicago: University of Chicago Press.

Lourenco, O., & Machado, A. (1996). In defense of Piaget's theory: A reply to 10 common criticisms. *Psychological Review, 103*, 143–164.

Louv, R. (1990). *Childhood's future*. Boston: Houghton Mifflin.

Luria, A., & Herzog, E. (1985, April). *Gender segregation across and within settings*. Paper presented at the biennial meeting of the Society for Research in Child Development, Toronto.

Luster, T. J., Perlstadt, J., McKinney, M. H., & Sims, K. E. (1995, March). *Factors related to the quality of the home environment adolescents provide for their infants*. Paper presented at the meeting of the Society for Research in Child Development, Indianapolis.

Lynch, E. W., & Hanson, M. J. (1993). *Developing cross-cultural competence: A guide for working with young children and their families*. Baltimore: Paul H. Brookes.

Lyons, N. P. (1990). Listening to voices we have not heard. In C. Gilligan, N. P. Lyons, & T. J. Hanmer (Eds.), *Making connections*. Cambridge, MA: Harvard University Press.

Lyytinen, P., Rasku-Puttonen, H., Poikkeus, A., Laakso, M., & Ahonen, T. (1994). Mother-child teaching strategies and learning disabilities. *Journal of Learning Disabilities, 27*, 186–192.

M

Maccoby, E. E. (1980). *Social development*. San Diego: Harcourt Brace Jovanovich.

Maccoby, E. E. (1984). Middle childhood in the context of the family. In *Development during middle childhood*. Washington, DC: National Academy Press.

Maccoby, E. E. (1987, November). Interview with Elizabeth Hall: All in the family. *Psychology Today*, pp. 54–60.

Maccoby, E. E. (1992). The role of parents in the socialization of children: An historical overview. *Developmental Psychology, 28*, 1006–1018.

Maccoby, E. E. (1992). Trends in the study of socialization: Is there a Lewinian heritage? *Journal of Social Issues, 48*, 171–185.

Maccoby, E. E. (1993, March). *Trends and issues in the study of gender role development*. Paper presented at the biennial meeting of the Society for Research in Child Development, New Orleans.

Maccoby, E. E. (1996). Peer conflict and intrafamily conflict: Are there conceptual bridges? *Merrill-Palmer Quarterly, 42*, 165–176.

Maccoby, E. E., & Jacklin, C. N. (1974). *The psychology of sex differences*. Palo Alto, CA: Stanford University Press.

Maccoby, E. E., & Martin, J. A. (1983). Socialization in the context of the family: Parent-child interaction. In P. H. Mussen (Ed.), *Handbook of Child Psychology* (4th ed., Vol. 4). New York: Wiley.

MacFarlane, J. A. (1975). Olfaction in the development of social preferences in the human neonate. In *Parent-infant interaction*. Ciba Foundation Symposium No. 33. Amsterdam: Elsevier.

MacLean, D. J., Keating, D. P., Miller, F., & Shuart, V. (1994, February). *Adolescents' decisions to pursue mathematics and science: Social and psychological factors*. Paper presented at the meeting of the Society for Research on Adolescence, San Diego.

Maddux, J. E., Roberts, M. C., Sledden, E. A., & Wright, L. (1986). Developmental issues in child health psychology. *American Psychologist, 41*, 24–34.

Mader, S. (1996). *Biology* (5th ed.). Dubuque, IA: Wm. C. Brown.

Magai, C., & McFadden, S. H. (1995). *The role of emotions in social and personality development*. New York: Plenum.

Mahler, M. (1979). *Separation-individuation* (Vol. 2). London: Jason Aronson.

Main, M., & Solomon, J. (1990). Procedures for identifying infants as disorganized/disoriented during the Ainsworth Strange Situation. In M. Greenberg, D. Cicchetti, & E. M. Cummings (Eds.), *Attachment during the preschool years*. Chicago: University of Chicago Press.

Malinosky-Rummell, R., & Hansen, D. J. (1993). Long-term consequences of childhood physical abuse. *Psychological Bulletin, 114*, 68–79.

Malinowski, B. (1927). *Sex and repression in savage society*. New York: Humanities Press.

Mamorstein, N. R., & Shiner, R. L. (1996, March). *The family environment of depressed adolescents*. Paper presented at the meeting of the Society for Research on Adolescence, Boston.

Mandler, J. M. (1992). The foundations of conceptual thought in infancy. *Cognitive Development, 7*, 273–285.

Marcia, J. (1996). Review of *Adolescence*, 7th Ed., by John W. Santrock.

Marcia, J. E. (1980). Ego identity development. In J. Adelson (Ed.), *Handbook of adolescent psychology*. New York: Wiley.

Marcia, J. E. (1994). The empirical study of ego identity. In H. A. Bosma, T. L. G. Graafsma, H. D. Grotevant, & D. J. De Levita (Eds.), *Identity and development*, Newbury Park, CA: Sage.

Mare, R. (1996). Family structure, social change, school outcomes, and educational inequality. In A. Booth & J. F. Dunn (Eds.), *Family-school links*. Hillsdale, NJ: Erlbaum.

Margolin, L. (1994). Child sexual abuse by uncles. *Child Abuse and Neglect, 18*, 215–224.

Marks, I. M. (1987). *Fears, phobias, and rituals*. New York: Oxford University Press.

Marquis, K. S., & Detweiler, R. A. (1985). Does adopted mean different? An attributional analysis. *Journal of Personality and Social Psychology, 48*, 1054–1066.

Martin, D. W. (1996). *Doing psychology experiments* (4th ed.). Pacific Grove, CA: Brooks/Cole.

Martin, J. (1976). *The education of adolescents*. Washington, DC: U.S. Office of Education.

Masten, A. S., & Hubbard, J. J. (1995, March). *Resilient adolescents: Do they differ from competent peers unchallenged by adversity?* Paper presented at the meeting of the Society for Research in Child Development, Indianapolis.

Matas, L., Arend, R. A., & Sroufe, L. A. (1978). Continuity in adaptation: Quality of attachment and later competence. *Child Development, 49*, 547–556.

Matlin, M. W. (1993). *The psychology of women* (2nd ed.). Fort Worth, TX: Harcourt Brace.

Matsumoto, D. (1996). *Culture and psychology*. Pacific Grove, CA: Brooks/Cole.

Mayer, F. S., & Sutton, K. (1996). *Personality*. Upper Saddle River, NJ: Prentice-Hall.

McAdoo, H. P. (Ed.). (1988). *Black families*. Newbury Park, CA: Sage.

McBride, A. B. (1990). Mental health effects of women's multiple roles. *American Psychologist, 45*, 381–384.

McCall, R. B., & Carriger, M. S. (1993). A meta-analysis of infant habituation and recognition memory performance as predictors of later IQ. *Child Development, 64*, 57–79.

McClelland, D. C. (1955). Some social consequences of achievement motivation. In M. R. Jones (Ed.), *The Nebraska Symposium on Motivation*. Lincoln: University of Nebraska Press.

McDonald, K. (1992). Warmth as a developmental construct: An evolutionary analysis. *Child Development, 63*, 753–773.

McDougall, P., Schonert-Reichel, K., & Hymel, S. (1996, March). *Adolescents at risk for high school dropout: The role of social factors*. Paper presented at the meeting of the Society for Research on Adolescence, Boston.

McFarlane, J., Parker, B., & Soeken, K. (1996). Abuse during pregnancy: Associations with maternal health and infant birth weight. *Nursing Research, 45*, 37–47.

McGue, M., & Carmichael, C. M. (1995). Life-span developmental psychology: A behavioral genetic perspective. In L. F. Dilalla & S. M. C. Dollinger (Eds.), *Assessment of biological mechanisms across the life span*. Hillsdale, NJ: Erlbaum.

McHale, J. L., Frosch, C. A., Greene, C. A., & Ferry, K. S. (1995, March). *Correlates of maternal and paternal behavior*. Paper presented at the meeting of the Society for Research in Child Development, Indianapolis.

McIntosh, D. E. (1996). Review of *Implementing early intervention* by Bryant & Graham (Eds.). *Contemporary Psychology, 41*, 135–136.

McLoyd, V. C., & Ceballo, R. (1995, March). *Conceptualizing economic context*. Paper presented at the meeting of the Society for Research in Child Development, Indianapolis.

Medrich, E. A., Rossen, J., Rubin, V., & Buckley, S. (1982). *The serious business of growing up*. Berkeley: University of California Press.

Meltzoff, A. N. (1988). Infant imitation and memory: Nine-month-old infants in immediate and deferred tests. *Child Development, 59*, 217–225.

Meltzoff, A. N. (1992, May). *Cognition in the service of learning*. Paper presented at the International Conference on Infant Studies, Miami Beach.

Meredith, H. V. (1978). Research between 1960 and 1970 on the standing height of young children in different parts of the world. In H. W. Reece & L. P. Lipsitt (Eds.), *Advances in child development and behavior* (Vol. 12). New York: Academic Press.

Meyerhoff, M. K., & White, B. L. (1986, September). Making the grades as parents. *Psychology Today*, pp. 38–45.

Michel, G. L. (1981). Right-handedness: A consequence of infant supine head-orientation preference? *Science, 212*, 685–687.

Michelozzi, B. N. (1996). *Coming alive from nine to five: The career search handbook*. Mountain View, CA: Mayfield.

Miller, G. (1981). *Language and speech*. New York: W. H. Freeman.

Miller, J. G. (1995, March). *Culture, context, and personal agency: The cultural grounding of self and morality*. Paper presented at the meeting of the Society for Research in Child Development, Indianapolis.

Miller, S. A., & Harley, J. P. (1996). *Zoology* (3rd ed.). Dubuque, IA: Wm. C. Brown.

Miller-Jones, D. (1989). Culture and testing. *American Psychologist, 44*, 360–366.

Minnett, A. M., Vandell, D. L., & Santrock, J. W. (1983). The effects of sibling status on sibling interaction: Influence of birth order, age spacing, sex of the child, and sex of the sibling. *Child Development, 54*, 1064–1072.

Minuchin, P. P., & Shapiro, E. K. (1983). The school as a context for social development. In P. H. Mussen (Ed.), *Handbook of child psychology* (4th ed., Vol. 4). New York: Wiley.

Mischel, W. (1973). Toward a cognitive social learning reconceptualization of personality. *Psychological Review, 80*, 252–283.

Mischel, W. (1994, August). *From good intentions to willpower*. Paper presented at the meeting of the American Psychological Association, Los Angeles.

Mischel, W., & Patterson, C. J. (1976). Substantive and structural elements of effective plans for self-control. *Journal of Personality and Social Psychology, 34*, 942–950.

Montemayor, R. (1982). The relationship between parent-adolescent conflict and the amount of time adolescents spend with parents, peers, and alone. *Child Development, 53*, 1512–1519.

Montemayor, R., Adams, G. R., & Gulotta, T. P. (Eds.). (1990). *From childhood to adolescence: A transitional period?* Newbury Park, CA: Sage.

Morgan, J. L., & Demuth, K. (Eds.). (1995). *Signal to syntax*. Hillsdale, NJ: Erlbaum.

Morrison, G. S. (1995). *Early childhood education today* (6th ed.). Columbus, OH: Merrill.

Morrongiello, B. A., Fenwick, K. D., & Chance, G. (1990). Sound localization acuity in very young infants: An observer-based testing procedure. *Developmental Psychology, 26,* 75–84.

Morrow, L. (1988, August 8). Through the eyes of children. *Time,* pp. 32–33.

Mortimer, J. T., Finch, M., Shanahan, M., & Ryu, S. (1992). Work experience, mental health, and behavioral adjustment in adolescence. *Journal of Research on Adolescence, 2,* 24–57.

Mott, F. L., & Marsiglio, W. (1985, September/October). Early childbearing and completion of high school. *Family Planning Perspectives,* p. 234.

Mueller, N., & Silverman, N. (1989). Peer relations in maltreated children. In D. Cicchetti & V. Carlson (Eds.), *Child maltreatment.* New York: Cambridge University Press.

Munroe, R. H., Himmin, H. S., & Munroe, R. L. (1984). Gender understanding and sex role preference in four cultures. *Developmental Psychology, 20,* 673–682.

Murray, V. M. (1996, March). *Sexual and motherhood statuses.* Paper presented at the meeting of the Society for Research on Adolescence, Boston.

Myers, N. A., Clifton, R. K., & Clarkson, M. G. (1987). When they were very young: Almost-threes remember two years ago. *Infant Behavior and Development, 10,* 123–132.

N

NAEYC. (1996). NAEYC position statement: Responding to linguistic and cultural diversity—recommendations for effective early childhood education. *Young Children, 51,* 4–12.

National Assessment of Educational Progress. (1976). *Adult work skills and knowledge* (Report No. 35-COD-01). Denver: Author.

National Association for the Education of Young Children. (1986). Position statement on developmentally appropriate practice in programs for 4- and 5-year-olds. *Young Children 41,* 20–29.

National Association for the Education of Young Children. (1986). *How to choose a good early childhood program.* Washington, DC: Author.

National Association for the Education of Young Children. (1988). NAEYC position statement on developmentally appropriate practices in the primary grades, serving 5- through 8-year olds. *Young Children, 43,* 64–83.

Neighbors, H. W., & Jackson, J. S. (Eds.). (1996). *Mental health in Black America.* Newbury Park, CA: Sage.

Neisser, U., Boodoo, G., Bouchard, T. J., Boykin, A. W., Brody, N., Ceci, S. J., Halpern, D. F., Loehlin, J. C., Perloff, R., Sternberg, R. J., & Urbina, S. (1996). Intelligence: Knowns and unknowns. *American Psychologist, 51,* 77–101.

Nelson, K. E., & Réger, Z. (Eds.). (1995). *Children's language* (Vol. 8). Hillsdale, NJ: Erlbaum.

Neuman, S. B., & Roskos, K. (1993). *Language and literacy learning in the early years.* Fort Worth, TX: Harcourt Brace.

Newacheck, P. W., & Halfon, N. (1988). Access to ambulatory care services for economically disadvantaged children. *Pediatrics, 78,* 813–819.

Newcomb, M. D., & Bentler, P. M. (1989). Substance use and abuse among children and teenagers. *American Psychologist, 44,* 242–248.

Newman, B. S., & Muzzonigro, P. G. (1993). The effects of traditional family values on the coming out process of gay male adolescents. *Adolescence, 28,* 213–226.

Newson, J., Newson, E., & Mahalski, P. A. (1982). Persistent infant comfort habits and their sequelae at 11 and 16 years. *Journal of Child Psychology and Psychiatry, 23,* 421–436.

Nicholls, J. G. (1984). Conceptions of ability and achievement motivation. In R. E. Ames & C. Ames (Eds.), *Motivation in education.* New York: Academic Press.

Nicklas, T. A., Webber, L. S., Jonson, C. S., Srinivasan, S. R., & Berenson, G. S. (1995). Foundations for health promotion with youth: A review of observations from the Bogalusa Heart Study. *Journal of Health Education, 26,* S18–S26.

Ninio, A., & Snow, C. E. (1996). *Pragmatic development.* Boulder, CO: Westview Press.

Nottelmann, E. D., Susman, E. J., Blue, J. H., Inoff-Germain, G., Dorn, L. D., Loriaux, D. L., Cutler, G. B., & Chrousos, G. P. (1987). Gonadal and adrenal hormone correlates of adjustment in early adolescence. In R. M. Lerner & T. T. Foch (Eds.), *Biological-psychological interactions in early adolescence.* Hillsdale, NJ: Erlbaum.

O

Obler, L. K. (1993). Language beyond childhood. In J. B. Gleason (Ed.), *The development of language* (3rd ed.). New York: Macmillan.

O'Connell, K. L. (1996). Attention deficit hyperactivity disorder. *Pediatric Nursing, 22,* 30–33.

O'Donnell, C., Manos, M., & Chesney-Lind, M. (1987). Diversion and neighborhood delinquency programs in open settings. In E. Morris & C. Braukmann (Eds.), *Behavioral approaches to crime and delinquency.* New York: Plenum.

Offer, D., Ostrov, E., Howard, K. I., & Atkinson, R. (1988). *The teenage world: Adolescents' self-image in ten countries.* New York: Plenum.

Ogbu, J. U. (1986). The consequences of the American caste system. In U. Neisser (Ed.), *The school achievement of minority children: New perspectives.* Hillsdale, NJ: Erlbaum.

Ogbu, J. U. (1989, April). *Academic socialization of Black children: An inoculation against future failure?* Paper presented at the biennial meeting of the Society for Research in Child Development, Kansas City.

Olds, S. B., London, M. L., & Ladewig, P. A. (1988). *Maternal newborn nursing: A family-centered approach.* Menlo Park, CA: Addison-Wesley.

Oller, D. K. (1995, February). *Early speech and word learning in bilingual and monolingual children: Advantages of early bilingualism.* Paper presented at the meeting of the American Association for the Advancement of Science, Atlanta.

Olson, H. C., & Burgess, D. M. (1996). Early intervention with children prenatally exposed to alcohol and other drugs. In M. J. Guralnick (Ed.), *The effectiveness of early intervention.* Baltimore, MD: Paul Brookes.

Olweus, D. (1980). Bullying among schoolboys. In R. Barnen (Ed.), *Children and violence.* Stockholm: Adaemic Litteratur.

Oser, F., & Gmunder, P. (1991). *Religious judgment: A developmental perspective.* Birmingham, AL: Religious Education Press.

Osofsky, J. D. (1989, April). *Affective relationships in adolescent mothers and their infants.* Paper presented at the biennial meeting of the Society for Research in Child Development, Kansas City.

Ottinger, D. R., & Simmons, J. E. (1964). Behavior of human neonates and prenatal maternal anxiety. *Psychological Reports, 14,* 391–394.

P

Paloutzian, R. F. (1996). *Invitation to the psychology of religion* (2nd ed.). Needham Heights, MA: Allyn & Bacon.

Paloutzian, R. F., & Santrock, J. W. (1997). The psychology of religion. In J. W. Santrock, *Psychology* (5th ed.). Madison, WI: Brown & Benchmark.

Paludi, M. A. (1995). *The psychology of women.* (2nd ed.). Madison, WI: Brown & Benchmark.

Paneth, N. S. (1995, Spring). The problem of low birth weight. *Future of Children, 5* (1), 19–34.

Papert, S. (1980). *Mindstorms: Children, computers, and powerful ideas.* New York: Basic Books.

Papini, D. R., Roggman, L. A., & Anderson, J. (1990). *Early adolescent perceptions of attachment to mother and father: A test of the emotional distancing hypothesis.* Paper presented at the meeting of the Society for Research in Adolescence, Atlanta.

Parcel, G. S., Simons-Morton, G. G., O'Hara, N. M., Baranowski, T., Kolbe, L. J., & Bee, D. E. (1987). School promotion of healthful diet and exercise behavior: An integration of organizational change and social learning theory interventions. *Journal of School Health, 57,* 150–156.

Parcel, G. S., Tiernan, K., Nadar, P. R., & Gottlob, D. (1979). Health education and kindergarten children. *Journal of School Health, 49,* 129–131.

Parham, T. (1996). Multicultural counseling theory and African-American populations. In D. W. Sue (Ed.), *Theory of multicultural counseling and therapy.* Pacific Grove, CA: Brooks/Cole.

Parham, T. A., & McDavis, R. J. (1993). Black men, an endangered species: Who's really pulling the trigger? In D. R. Atkinson, G. Morten, & D. W. Sue (Eds.), *Counseling American minorities.* Madison, WI: Brown & Benchmark.

Parke, R. D. (1995). Fathers and families. In M. H. Bornstein (Ed.), *Children and parenting* (Vol. 3), Hillsdale, NJ: Erlbaum.

Parke, R. D. (1996, June). *Tracking families across contexts.* Paper presented at the Family Research Summer Consortium, San Diego.

Parker, F. L., Abdul-Kabir, S., Stevenson, H. G., & Garrett, B. (1995, March). *Partnerships between researchers and the community in Head Start.* Paper presented at the meeting of the Society for Research in Child Development, Indianapolis.

Parker, S. J., & Barrett, D. E. (1992). Maternal type A behavior during pregnancy, neonatal crying, and infant temperament: Do type A women have type A babies? *Pediatrics, 89,* 474–479.

Parmalee, A. H. (1986). Children's illnesses: Their beneficial effects on behavioral development. *Child Development, 57,* 1–10.

Parten, M. (1932). Social play among preschool children. *Journal of Abnormal and Social Psychology, 27,* 243–269.

Patterson, G. R. (1991, April). *Which parenting skills are necessary for what?* Paper presented at the biennial meeting of the Society for Research in Child Development, Seattle.

Patterson, G. R., Capaldi, D., & Bank, L. (1991). An early starter model for predicting delinquency. In D. Pepler & K. Rubin (Eds.), *The development and treatment of childhood aggression,* Hillsdale, NJ: Erlbaum.

Patterson, G. R., DeBaryshe, B. D., & Ramsey, E. (1989). A developmental perspective on antisocial behavior. *American Psychologist, 44,* 329–335.

Paulson, S. E., Marchant, G. J., & Rothlisberg, B. (1995, March). *Relations among parent, teacher, and school factors: Implications for achievement outcome in middle grade students.* Paper presented at the meeting of the Society for Research in Child Development, Indianapolis.

Pearson, S. (1978). *Everybody knows that.* New York: Dial.

Pellegrini, A. D. (1996). *Observing children in their natural worlds.* Hillsdale, NJ: Erlbaum.

Perkins, D. N. (1984, September). Creativity by design. *Educational Leadership,* pp. 18–25.

Perris, E. E., Myers, N. A., & Clifton, R. K. (1990). Long-term memory for a single experience. *Child Development, 61,* 1796–1807.

Peskin, H. (1967). Pubertal onset and ego functioning. *Journal of Abnormal Psychology, 72,* 1–15.

Peters, R. D., & McMahon, R. J. (Eds.). (1996). *Preventing childhood disorders, substance abuse, and delinquency.* Newbury Park, CA: Sage.

Petersen, A. C. (1979, January). Can puberty come any faster? *Psychology Today,* pp. 45–56.

Petersen, A. C. (1993). Creating adolescents: The role of context and process in developmental trajectories. *Journal of Research on Adolescence, 3,* 1–18.

Petersen, A. C., Compas, B. E., Brooks-Gunn, J., Stemmler, M., Ey, S., & Grant, K. E. (1993). Depression in adolescence. *American Psychologist, 48,* 155–168.

Petersen, A. C., & Ding, S. (1994, February). *Depression and body image disorders in adolescence.* Paper presented at the meeting of the Society for Research on Adolescence, San Diego.

Peterson, C. C., & Peterson, J. L. (1973). Preference for sex of offspring as a measure of change in sex attitudes. *Psychology, 10,* 3–5.

Peterson, P. L. (1977). Interactive effects of student anxiety, achievement orientation, and teacher behavior on student achievement and attitude. *Journal of Educational Psychology, 69,* 779–792.

Pfeffer, C. R. (1996). *Severe stress and mental disturbance in children.* Washington, DC: American Psychiatric Press.

Phillips, D. A., Voran, K., Kisker, E., Howes, C., & Whitebook, M. (1994). Child care for children in poverty: Opportunity or inequity? *Child Development, 65,* 472–492.

Phinney, J. S. (1989). Stages of ethnic identity development in minority group adolescents. *Journal of Early Adolescence, 9,* 34–49.

Phinney, J. S., & Alipura, L. L. (1990). Ethnic identity in college students from four ethnic groups. *Journal of Adolescence, 13,* 171–183.

Phinney, J. S., Chavira, V., & Williamson, L. (1992). Acculturation attitudes and self-esteem among high school and college students. *Youth and Society, 25,* 299–312.

Phinney, J. S., Dupont, S., Landin, J., & Onwughalu, M. (1994, February). *Social identity orientation, bicultural conflict, and coping strategies among minority adolescents.* Paper presented at the meeting of the Society for Research on Adolescence, San Diego.

Piaget, J. (1932). *The moral judgment of the child.* New York: Harcourt Brace Jovanovich.

Piaget, J. (1952). *The origins of intelligence in children.* New York: International Universities Press.

Piaget, J. (1952a). Jean Piaget. In C. A. Murchison (Ed.), *A history of psychology in autobiography* (Vol. 4). Worcester, MA: Clark University Press.

Piaget, J. (1954). *The construction of reality in the child.* New York: Basic Books.

Piaget, J. (1962). *Play, dreams, and imitation in childhood.* New York: W. W. Norton.

Piaget, J. (1967). *The child's conception of the world.* Totowa, NJ: Littlefield, Adams.

Piaget, J. (1972). Intellectual evolution from adolescence to adulthood. *Human Development, 15,* 1–12.

Piaget, J., & Inhelder, B. (1969). *The child's conception of space* (F. J. Langdon & J. L. Lunzer, Trans.). New York: W. W. Norton.

Pićo, I. (1983). *Machismo y educacion en Puerto Rico* (2nd ed.). Rio Piedras: Universidad de Puerto Rico.

Pillow, D. R., Zautra, A. J., & Sandler, I. (1996). Major life events and minor stressors: Identifying mediational links in the stress process. *Journal of Personality and Social Psychology, 70,* 381–394.

Pipes, P. (1988). Nutrition in childhood. In S. R. Williams & B. S. Worthington-Roberts (Eds.), *Nutrition throughout the life cycle.* St. Louis: Times Mirror/Mosby.

Pleck, J. (1981). *Three conceptual issues in research on male roles.* Working paper no. 98, Wellesley College Center for Research on Women, Wellesley, MA.

Pleck, J. H. (1983). The theory of male sex role identity: Its rise and fall, 1936–present. In M. Lewin (Ed.), *In the shadow of the past: Psychology portrays the sexes.* New York: Columbia University Press.

Pleck, J. H. (1995). The gender-role strain paradigm: An update: In R. F. Levant & W. S. Pollack (Eds.), *A new psychology of men.* New York: Basic.

Plomin, R. (1993, March). *Human behavioral genetics and development: An overview and update.* Paper presented at the biennial meeting of the Society for Research in Child Development, New Orleans.

Plomin, R. (1996, August). *Nature and nurture together.* Paper presented at the meeting of the American Psychological Association, Toronto.

Plomin, R., DeFries, J. C., & McClearn, G. E. (1990). *Behavioral genetics: A primer.* New York: W. H. Freeman.

Plomin, R., Reiss, D., Hetherington, E. M., & Howe, G. W. (1994). Nature and nurture: Contributions to measures of the family environment. *Developmental Psychology, 30,* 32–43.

Poest, C. A., Williams, J. R., Witt, D. D., & Atwood, M. E. (1990). Challenge me to move: Large muscle development in young children. *Young Children, 45,* 4–10.

Pollitt, E. P., Gorman, K. S., Engle, P. L., Martorell, R., & Rivera, J. (1993). Early supplementary feeding and cognition. *Monographs of the Society for Research in Child Development, 58* (7, Serial No. 235).

Pomeroy, C. (1996). Anorexia nervosa, bulimia nervosa, and binge eating disorder. In J. K. Thompson (Ed.), *Body image, eating disorders, and obesity.* Washington, DC: American Psychological Association.

Posada, G., Lord, C., & Waters, E. (1995, March). *Secure base behavior and children's misbehavior in three different contexts: Home, neighbors, and school.* Paper presented at the meeting of the Society for Research in Child Development, Indianapolis.

Posner, J. K., & Vandell, D. L. (1994). Low-income children's after-school care: Are there benefits of after-school programs? *Child Development, 65,* 440–456.

Poulton, S., & Sexton, D. (1996). Feeding young children: Developmentally appropriate considerations for supplementing family care. *Childhood Education, 73,* 66–71.

Premack, D. (1986). *Gavagai! The future history of the ape language controversy.* Cambridge, MA: MIT Press.

Pressley, M. (1996). Personal reflections on the study of practical memory in the mid-1990s. In D. Hermann, C. McEvoy, C. Hertzog, P. Hertel, & M. Johnson (Eds.), *Basic and applied memory research* (Vol. 2). Hillsdale, NJ: Erlbaum.

Price, R. H., Cioci, M., Penner, W., & Trautlein, B. (1990). *School and community support programs that enhance adolescent health and education.* Washington, DC: Carnegie Council on Adolescent Development.

Prinstein, M. M., Fetter, M. D., & La Greca, A. M. (1996, March). *Can you judge adolescents by the company they keep?: Peer group membership, substance abuse, and risk-taking behaviors.* Paper presented at the meeting of the Society for Research on Adolescence, Boston.

Q

Quiggle, N. L., Garber, Jn, Panak, W. F., & Dodge, K. A. (1992). Social information processing in aggressive and depressed children. *Child Development, 63,* 1305–1320.

R

Rabin, B. E., & Dorr, A. (1995, March). *Children's understanding of emotional events on family television series.* Paper presented at the meeting of the Society for Research in Child Development, Indianapolis.

Ramey, C. T., Bryant, D. M., Campbell, F. A., Sparling, J. J., & Wasik, B. H. (1988). Early intervention for high-risk children: The Carolina Early Intervention Program. In R. H. Price, E. L. Cowen, R. P. Lorion, & J. Ramos-McKay (Eds.), *14 ounces of prevention.* Washington, DC: American Psychological Association.

Ramsay, D. S. (1980). Onset of unimanual handedness in infants. *Infant Behavior and Development, 3,* 377–385.

Reilly, R. (1988, August 5). Here no one is spared. *Sports Illustrated,* pp. 70–77.

Reinherz, H. Z., Giaconia, R. M., Silverman, A. B., & Friedman, A. C. (1994, February). *Early psychosocial risks for adolescent suicidal ideation and attempts.* Paper presented at the meeting of the Society for Research on Adolescence, San Diego.

Remafedi, G., Resnick, M., Blum, R., & Harris, L. (in press). The demography of sexual orientation in adolescents. *Pediatrics.*

Rice, M. B. (1991). Preschoolers' QUIL: Quick incidental learning of words. In G. Conti-Ramsden & C. E. Snow (Eds.), *Children's language* (Vol. 7). Hillsdale, NJ: Erlbaum.

Rice, M. L. (Ed.). (1996). *Toward a genetics of language.* Hillsdale, NJ: Erlbaum.

Richards, M., Suleiman, L., Sims, B., & Sedeno, A. (1994, February). *Experiences of ethnically diverse young adolescents growing up in poverty.* Paper presented at the meeting of the Society for Research on Adolescence, San Diego.

Richards, M. H., & Duckett, E. (1994). The relationship of maternal employment to early adolescent daily experiences with and without parents. *Child Development, 65*, 225–236.

Rickel, A. V., & Hendren, M. C. (1993). Aberrant sexual experiences in adolescence. In T. P. Gullotta, G. R. Adams, & R. Montemayor (Eds.), *Adolescent sexuality.* Newbury Park, CA: Sage.

Riddle, D. B., & Prinz, R. (1984, August). *Sugar consumption in young children.* Paper presented at the meeting of the American Psychological Association, Toronto.

Roberts, D., Jacobsen, L., & Taylor, R. D. (1996, March). *Neighborhood characteristics, stressful life events, and African-American adolescents' adjustment.* Paper presented at the meeting of the Society for Research on Adolescence, Boston.

Roberts, W., & Strayer, J. (1996). Empathy, emotional expressiveness, and prosocial behavior. *Child Development, 67*, 471–489.

Roberts, W. L. (1993, March). *Programs for the collection and analysis of observational data.* Paper presented at the biennial meeting of the Society for Research in Child Development, New Orleans.

Rode, S. S., Chang, P., Fisch, R. O., & Sroufe, L. A. (1981). Attachment patterns of infants separated at birth. *Developmental Psychology, 17*, 188–191.

Rodin, J. (1984, December). Interview: A sense of control. *Psychology Today*, pp. 38–45.

Rodin, J., & Ickovics, J. R. (1990). Women's health: Review and research agenda as we approach the 21st century. *American Psychologist, 45*, 1018–1034.

Roff, M., Sells, S. B., & Golden, M. W. (1972). *Social adjustment and personality development in children.* Minneapolis: University of Minnesota Press.

Rogers, A. (1987). *Questions of gender differences: Ego development and moral voice in adolescence.* Unpublished manuscript, Department of Education, Harvard University.

Rogers, C. S., & Morris, S. S. (1986, July). Reducing sugar in children's diets: Why? How? *Young Children*, pp. 11–16.

Rogoff, B., & Morelli, G. (1989). Perspectives on children's development from cultural psychology. *American Psychologist, 44*, 343–348.

Rogosch, F. A., Cicchetti, D., Shields, A., & Toth, S. L. (1995). Parenting dysfunction in child maltreatment. In M. H. Bornstein (Ed.), *Handbook of Parenting* (Vol. 4). Hillsdale, NJ: Erlbaum.

Rohner, R. P., & Rohner, E. C. (1981). Parental acceptance-rejection and parental control: Cross-cultural codes. *Ethnology, 20*, 245–260.

Rose, R. J. (1995). Genetics and human behavior. *Annual Review of Psychology, 46*. Palo Alto, CA: Annual Reviews.

Rose, S., & Frieze, I. R. (1993). Young singles' contemporary dating scripts. *Sex Roles, 28*, 499–509.

Rose, S. A. (1995). From hand to eye: Findings and issues in infant cross-modal transfer. In D. J. Lewkowicz & R. Lickliter (Eds.), *The development of intersensory perception.* Hillsdale, NJ: Erlbaum.

Rose, S. A., Feldman, J. F., McCarton, C. M., & Wolfson, J. (1988). Information processing in seven-month-old infants as a function of risk status. *Child Development, 59*, 489–603.

Rosenblith, J. F. (1992). *In the beginning* (2nd ed.). Newbury Park, CA: Sage.

Rosenthal, D. M., & Sawyers, J. Y. (1996). Building successful home/school partnerships: Strategies for parent support and involvement. *Childhood Education, 72*, 194–200.

Rosenthal, R., & Jacobsen, L. (1968). *Pygmalian in the classroom.* New York: Holt, Rinehart & Winston.

Rosnow, R. L., & Rosenthal, R. (1996). *Beginning behavioral research* (2nd ed.). Upper Saddle River, NJ: Prentice-Hall.

Rossi, A. S. (1989). A life-course approach to gender, aging, and intergenerational relations. In K. W. Schaie & C. Schooler (Eds.), *Social structure and aging.* Hillsdale, NJ: Erlbaum.

Rothbart, M. L. K. (1971). Birth order and mother-child interaction. *Dissertation Abstracts, 27*, 45–57.

Rovee-Collier, C. (1987). Learning and memory in children. In J. D. Osofsky (Ed.), *Handbook of infant development* (2nd ed.). New York: Wiley.

Rubin, K. H., Maioni, T. L., & Hornung, M. (1976). Free play behaviors in middle and lower social class preschoolers: Parten and Piaget revisited. *Child Development, 47*, 414–419.

Rubin, K. N., Fein, G. G., & Vandenberg, B. (1983). Play. In P. H. Mussen (Ed.), *Handbook of child psychology* (4th ed., Vol. 4). New York: Wiley.

Rubin, Z., & Sloman, J. (1984). How parents influence their children's friendships. In M. Lewis (Ed.), *Beyond the dyad.* New York: Plenum.

Rueter, M. A. (1994, February). *Family dysfunction as a mediator in the relationship between parental substance use and adolescent substance use.* Paper presented at the meeting of the Society for Research on Adolescence, San Diego.

Rumberger, R. W. (1983). Dropping out of high school: The influence of race, sex, and family background. *American Educational Research Journal, 20*, 199–220.

Rumberger, R. W. (1995). Dropping out of middle school: A multilevel analysis of students and schools. *American Educational Research Journal, 3*, 583–625.

Rushton, J. P. (1988). Race differences in behavior: A review and evolutionary analysis. *Journal of Personality and Individual Differences, 9*, 1035–1040.

Rutter, M. (1979). Protective factors in children's response to stress and disadvantage. In M. W. Kent & J. E. Rolf (Eds.), *Primary prevention in psychopathology* (Vol. 3). Hanover, NH: University Press of New England.

Rutter, M., & Schopler, E. (1987). Autism and pervasive developmental disorders: Concepts and diagnostic issues. *Journal of Autism and Developmental Disorders, 17*, 159–186.

Ryan, A. M., & Patrick, H. (1996, March). *Positive peer relationships and psychosocial adjustment during adolescence.* Paper presented at the meeting of the Society for Research on Adolescence, Boston.

Ryan, R. A. (1980). Strengths of the American Indian family: State of the art. In F. Hoffman (Ed.), *The American Indian family: Strengths and stresses.* Isleta, NM: American Indian Social Research and Development Association.

Rymer, R. (1992). *Genie.* New York: HarperCollins.

S

Saarni, C. (1988). Children's understanding of the interpersonal consequences of dissemblance of nonverbal emotional-expressive behavior. *Journal of Nonverbal Behavior, 12*, 275–294.

Sadker, M., & Sadker, D. (1986, March). Sexism in the classroom: From grade school to graduate school. *Phi Delta Kappan.* pp. 512–515.

Sadker, M., & Sadker, D. (1994). *Failing at fairness.* New York: Touchstone.

Sagan, C. (1977). *The dragons of Eden.* New York: Random House.

Salk, L. (1992). *Familyhood.* New York: Simon & Schuster.

Sallade, J. B. (1973). A comparison of the psychological adjustment of obese versus non-obese children. *Journal of Psychosomatic Research, 17*, 89–96.

Samaras, A. P. (1996). Children's computers. *Childhood Education, 72*, 133–136.

Sameroff, A. J., Dickstein, S., Hayden, L. C., & Schiller, M. (1993, March). *Effects of family process and parental depression on children.* Paper presented at the biennial meeting of the Society for Child Development, New Orleans.

Sanson, A., & Rothbart, M. K. (1995). Child temperament and parenting. In M. H. Bornstein (Ed.), *Handbook of parenting* (Vol. 4). Hillsdale, NJ: Erlbaum.

Santrock, J. W. (1997). *Life-span development* (6th ed.). Madison, WI: Brown & Benchmark.

Santrock, J. W., & Sitterle, K. A. (1987). Parent-child relationships in stepmother families. In K. Pasley & M. Ihinger-Tallman (Eds.), *Remarriage and stepparenting.* New York: Guilford Press.

Santrock, J. W., & Warshak, R. A. (1986). Development, relationships, and legal/clinical considerations in father custody families. In M. E. Lamb (Ed.), *The father's role: Applied perspectives.* New York: Wiley.

Savage-Rumbaugh, E. S., Murphy, J., Sevick, R. A., Brakke, K. E., Williams, S. L., & Rumbaugh, D. (1993). Language comprehension in ape and child. *Monographs of the Society for Research in Child Development, 58* (3–4, Serial No. 233).

Savin-Williams, R. C., & Rodriguez, R. G. (1993). A developmental, clinical perspective on lesbian, gay male, and bisexual youths. In T. P. Gullotta, G. R. Adams, & R. Montemayor (Eds.), *Adolescent sexuality.* Newbury Park, CA: Sage.

Saxe, G. B., Guberman, S. R., & Gearhart, M. (1987). Social processes in early number development. *Monographs of the Society for Research in Child Development, 52* (2, Serial No. 216).

Scales, P. C. (1992). *A portrait of young adolescents in the 1990s: Implications for promoting healthy growth and development.* Carrboro, NC: Center for Early Adolescence.

Scarr, S. (1984, May). Interview. *Psychology Today*, pp. 59–63.

Scarr, S. (1993). Biological and cultural diversity: The legacy of Darwin for development. *Child Development, 64*, 1333–1353.

Scarr, S. (1996). Best of human genetics. *Contemporary Psychology, 41*, 149–150.

Scarr, S., Lande, J., & McCartney, K. (1989). Child care and the family: Complements and interactions. In J. Lande, S. Scarr, & N. Gunzenhauser (Eds.), *Caring for children: Challenge to America.* Hillsdale, NJ: Erlbaum.

Scarr, S., & Weinberg, R. A. (1980). Calling all camps! The war is over. *American Sociological Review, 45*, 859–865.

Scarr, S., & Weinberg, R. A. (1983). The Minnesota adoption studies: Genetic differences and malleability. *Child Development, 54*, 253–259.

Schaffer, H. R. (1996). *Social development.* Cambridge, MA: Blackwell.

Schaie, K. W. (1994). Developmental designs revisited. In S. H. Cohen & H. W. Reese (Eds.), *Life-span developmental psychology: Methodological contributions.* Hillsdale, NJ: Erlbaum.

Schartz, D., & Mayaux, M. J. (1982). Female fecundity as a function of age: Results of artificial insemination in nulliparous women with azoospermic husbands. *New England Journal of Medicine, 306,* 304–406.

Schiller, M. (1995). An emergent art curriculum that fosters understanding. *Young Children, 50,* 33–38.

Schmitz, S., Saudino, K. J., Plomin, R., Fulker, D. W., & DeFries, J. C. (1996). Genetic and environmental influences on temperament in middle childhood: Analyses of teacher and tester ratings. *Child Development, 67,* 409–422.

Schnorr, T. M., & others. (1991). Videodisplay terminals and the risk of spontaneous abortion. *New England Journal of Medicine, 324,* 727–733.

Schoendorf, K. C., & Kiely, J. L. (1992). Relationship of sudden infant death syndrome to maternal smoking during and after pregnancy. *Pediatrics, 90,* 905–908.

Schorr, L. (1989). Early interventions to reduce intergenerational disadvantage: The new policy context. *Teachers College Record, 90,* 362–374.

Schrag, S. G., & Dixon, R. L. (1985). Occupational exposure associated with male reproductive dysfunction. *Annual Review of Pharmacology and Toxicology, 25,* 467–592.

Schreiber, L. R. (1990). *The parent's guide to kids' sports.* Boston: Little, Brown.

Schunk, D. H. (1983). Developing children's self-efficacy and skills: The roles of social comparative information and goal-setting. *Contemporary Educational Psychology, 8,* 76–86.

Scott, P. (1997). Language. In P. Scott & C. Spencer (Eds.), *Psychology.* Cambridge, MA: Blackwell.

Scott-Jones, D. (1995, March). *Incorporating ethnicity and socioeconomic status in research with children.* Paper presented at the meeting of the Society for Research in Child Development, Indianapolis.

Scott-Jones, D. (1996). Toward a balanced view of family change. In A. Booth & J. F. Dunn (Eds.), *Family-school links.* Hillsdale, NJ: Erlbaum.

Seefeldt, C. (1995). Art—A serious work. *Young Children, 50,* 39–45.

Seligman, M. E. P. (1975). *Learned helplessness.* San Francisco: W. H. Freeman.

Selman, R. L. (1976). Social-cognitive understanding. In T. Lickona (Ed.), *Moral development and behavior.* New York: Holt, Rinehart & Winston.

Selman, R. L. (1980). *The growth of interpersonal understanding.* New York: Academic Press.

Semaj, L. T. (1985). Afrikanity, cognition, and extended self-identity. In M. B. Spencer, G. K. Brookins, & W. R. Allen (Eds.), *Beginnings: The social and affective development of Black children.* Hillsdale, NJ: Erlbaum.

Serbin, L. A., & Sprafkin, C. (1986). The salience of gender in the process of sex-typing in three- to seven-year-old children. *Child Development, 57,* 1188–1209.

Serdula, M., Williamson, D. F., Kendrick, J. S., Anda, R. F., & Byers, T. (1991). Trends in alcohol consumption by pregnant women: 1985 through 1988. *Journal of the American Medical Association, 265,* 876–879.

Sharma, A. R., McGue, M. K., & Benson, P. L. (1996, March). *The emotional and behavioral adjustment of United States adopted adolescents.* Paper presented at the meeting of the Society for Research on Adolescence, Boston.

Shaw, S. M. (1988). Gender differences in the definition and perception of household labor. *Family Relations, 37,* 333–337.

Shields, S. A. (1991). Gender in the psychology of emotion: A selective research review. In K. T. Strongman (Ed.), *International Review of Studies on Emotion* (Vol. I). New York: Wiley.

Shiono, P. H., & Behrman, R. E. (1995, spring). Low birth weight: Analysis and recommendations. *The Future of Children, 5,* no. 1, 4–18.

Shirley, M. M. (1933). *The first two years.* Minneapolis: University of Minnesota Press.

Siegel, L. S. (1989, April). *Perceptual-motor, cognitive, and language skills as predictors of cognitive abilities at school age.* Paper presented at the biennial meeting of the Society for Research in Children, Kansas City.

Siegler, R. S. (1995, March). *Nothing is; everything becomes.* Paper presented at the meeting of the Society for Research in Child Development, Indianapolis.

Siegler, R. S. (1996). *Children's thinking* (3rd ed.). Englewood Cliffs, NJ: Prentice Hall.

Siegman, A. W., & Dembrowsky, T. (Eds.). (1989). *In search of coronary-prone behavior: Beyond Type A.* Hillsdale, NJ: Erlbaum.

Silbereisen, R. K. (1995). How parenting styles and crowd contexts interact in actualizing potentials for development: commentary. In L. J. Crockett & A. C. Crouter, (Eds.), *Pathways through adolescence.* Hillsdale, NJ: Erlbaum.

Silverberg, S. B., & Steinberg, L. (1990). Psychological well-being of parents with early adolescent children. *Developmental Psychology, 26,* 658–666.

Simich-Dudgeon, C. (1993). Increasing student achievement through teacher knowledge about parent involvement. In N. F. Chavkin (Ed.), *Families and schools in a pluralistic society.* Albany: State University of New York Press.

Simkin, P., Whalley, J., & Keppler, A. (1984). *Pregnancy, childbirth, and the newborn.* New York: Simon & Schuster.

Simmons, R. G., & Blyth, D. A. (1987). *Moving into adolescence.* Hawthorne, NY: Aldine.

Simons, J. M., Finlay, B., & Yang, A. (1991). *The adolescent and young adult fact book.* Washington, DC: Children's Defense Fund.

Simpson, R. L. (1962). Parental influence, anticipatory socialization, and social mobility. *American Sociological Review, 27,* 517–522.

Sims, R. (1983). Strong Black girls. *Journal of Research and Development in Education, 16,* 21–28.

Singer, D. G. (1993). Creativity of children in a changing world. In G. L. Berry & J. K. Asamen (Eds.), *Children and television: Images in a changing sociocultural world.* Newbury Park, CA: Sage.

Skinner, B. F. (1957). *Verbal behavior.* New York: Appleton-Century-Crofts.

Skinner, E. A., Wellborn, J. G., & Connell, J. P. (1990). What it takes to do well in school and whether I've got it: A process model of perceived control and children's engagement and achievement in school. *Journal of Educational Psychology, 82,* 22–32.

Slavin, R. E. (1989). Cooperative learning and student achievement. In R. E. Slavin (Ed.), *School and classroom organization.* Hillsdale, NJ: Erlbaum.

Slobin, D. (1972, July). Children and language: They learn the same way all around the world. *Psychology Today,* pp. 71–76.

Smith, B. A., Fillion, T. J., & Blass, E. M. (1990). Orally mediated sources of calming in 1- to 3-day-old human infants. *Developmental Psychology, 26,* 731–737.

Smolak, L., Levine, M. P., & Striegel-Moore, R. H. (Eds.). (1996). *Developmental psychopathology of eating disorders.* Hillsdale, NJ: Erlbaum.

Snarey, J. (1987, June). A question of morality. *Psychology Today,* pp. 6–8.

Snider, B. A., & Miller, J. P. (1993). The land-grant university system and 4-H: A mutually beneficial relationship of scholars and practitioners in youth development. In R. M. Lerner (Ed.), *Early adolescence.* Hillsdale, NJ: Erlbaum.

Snow, C. E. (1996). Interactionist account of language acquisition. In M. E. Rice (Ed.), *Toward a genetics of language.* Hillsdale, NJ: Erlbaum.

Sonenstein, F. L., Pleck, J. H., & Ku, L. C. (1989). Sexual activity, condom use, and AIDS awareness among adolescent males. *Family Planning Perspectives, 2,* 152–158.

Sowers-Hoag, K. W., Thyer, B. A., & Bailey, J. S. (1987). Promoting automobile safety belt use by young children. *Journal of Applied Behavior Analysis, 20,* 133–138.

Spear-Swerling, L., & Sternberg, R. J. (1994). The road not taken: An integrative theoretical model of reading disability. *Journal of Learning Disabilities, 27,* 91–103.

Spelke, E. S. (1991). Physical knowledge in infancy: Reflections on Piaget's theory. In S. Carey & R. Gelman (Eds.), *The epigenesis of mind: Essays on biology and cognition.* Hillsdale, NJ: Erlbaum.

Spence, J. T., & Helmreich, R. (1978). *Masculinity and femininity: Their psychological dimensions.* Austin: University of Texas Press.

Spencer, M. B., & Dornbusch, S. M. (1990). Challenges in studying minority youth. In S. S. Feldman & G. R. Elliott (Eds.), *At the threshold: The developing adolescent.* Cambridge, MA: Harvard University Press.

Sroufe, L. A. (1985). Attachment classification from the perspective of infant-caregiver relationships an infant temperament. *Child Development, 56,* 1–14.

Sroufe, L. A. (1996). *Emotional development.* New York: Cambridge University Press.

Sroufe, L. A., & Waters, E. (1976). The ontogenesis of smiling and laughter: A perspective on the organization of development in infancy. *Psychological Review, 83,* 173–198.

Stallings, J. (1975). Implementation and child effects of teaching practices in Follow Through classrooms. *Monographs of the Society for Research in Child Development, 40* (Serial No. 163).

Stanhope, L., & Corter, C. (1993, March). *The mother's role in the transition to siblinghood.* Paper presented at the biennial meeting of the Society for Research in Child Development, New Orleans.

Stanley, K., Soule, B., & Copans, S. A. (1979). Dimensions of prenatal anxiety and their influence on pregnancy outcome. *American Journal of Obstetrics and Gynecology, 135,* 333–348.

Stapp, J., Tucker, A. M., & VandenBos, G. R. (1985). Census of psychological personnel, 1983. *American Psychologist, 40,* 1317–1351.

Stattin, H., & Magnusson, D. (1990). *Pubertal maturation in female development: Paths through life* (Vol. 2). Hillsdale, NJ: Erlbaum.

Staub, E. (1996). Cultural-societal roots of violence. *American Psychologist, 51,* 117–132.

Staub, E. (in press). Altruism and aggression in children and youth: Origins and cures. In R. Feldman (Ed.), *The psychology of adversity.* Amherst: University of Massachusetts Press.

Stechler, G., & Halton, A. (1982). Prenatal influences on human development. In B. B. Wolman (Ed.), *Handbook of developmental psychology*. Englewood Cliffs, NJ: Prentice Hall.

Steinberg, L., Fegley, S., & Dornbusch, S. M. (1993). Negative impact of part-time work on adolescent adjustment: Evidence from a longitudinal study. *Developmental Psychology, 29*, 171–180.

Steinberg, L., & Levine, A. (1990). *You and your adolescent*. New York: HarperCollins.

Steinberg, L. D. (1986). Latchkey children and susceptibility to peer pressure: An ecological analysis. *Developmental Psychology, 22*, 433–439.

Steiner, J. E. (1979). Human facial expressions in response to taste and smell stimulation. In H. Reese & L. Lipsitt (Eds.), *Advances in child development and behavior* (Vol. 13). New York: Academic Press.

Stenhouse, G. (1996). *Practical parenting*. New York: Oxford University Press.

Stephenson, A. L., Henry, C. S., & Robinson, L. C. (1996). Family characteristics and adolescent substance abuse. *Adolescence, 121*, 59–78.

Stern, D. N., Beebe, B., Jaffe, J., & Bennett, S. L. (1977). The infant's stimulus world during social interaction: A study of caregiver behaviors with particular reference to repetition and timing. In H. R. Schaffer (Ed.), *Studies in mother-infant interaction*. London: Academic Press.

Sternberg, R. J. (1986). *Intelligence applied*. San Diego: Harcourt Brace Jovanovich.

Sternberg, R. J. (1987). Teaching intelligence: The application of cognitive psychology of intellectual skills. In J. B. Baron & R. J. Sternberg (Eds.), *Teaching thinking skills: Theory and practice*. New York: W. H. Freeman.

Sternberg, R. J. (1994, December). Commentary. *APA Monitor*, p. 22.

Sternglanz, S. H., Serbin, L. A. (1974). Sex-role stereotyping in children's television programming. *Developmental Psychology, 10*, 710–715.

Steur, F. B., Applefield, J. M., & Smith, R. (1971). Televised aggression and interpersonal aggression of preschool children. *Journal of Experimental Child Psychology, 11*, 442–447.

Stevenson, H. W. (1995). Mathematics achievement of American children: First in the world by the year 2000? In C. A. Nelson (Ed.), *Basic and applied perspectives on learning, cognition, and development*. Minneapolis: University of Minnesota Press.

Stevenson, H. W., Chen, C., & Lee, S. Y. (1993). Mathematics achievement of Chinese, Japanese, and American Children: Ten years later. *Science, 259*, 53–58.

Stevenson, M. R., & Black, K. N. (1996). *How divorce affects offspring*. Boulder, CO: Westview Press.

Steward, P. (1995). *Beginning writers in the zone of proximal development*. Hillsdale, NJ: Erlbaum.

Stipek, D., Rosenblatt, L., & DiRocco, L. (1994). Making parents your allies. *Young Children, 49*, 4–9.

Stipek, D. J., & Hoffman, J. M. (1980). Children's achievement-related expectancies as a function of academic performance histories and sex. *Journal of Educational Psychology, 72*, 861–865.

Stocker, C., & Dunn, J. (1991). Sibling relationships in adolescence. In R. M. Lerner, A. C. Petersen, & J. Brooks-Gunn (Eds.), *Encyclopedia of adolescence* (Vol. 2). New York: Garland.

Stone, L. (1994). Teaching Sam to enjoy reading. *Young Children, 49*, 76–79.

Stormer, S. M., & Thompson, J. K. (1996). Explanations of body image disturbance: A test of maturational status, negative verbal commentary, social comparison, and sociocultural hypotheses. *International Journal of Eating Disorders, 19*, 193–199.

Strahan, D. B. (1983). The emergence of formal operations in adolescence. *Transcendence, 11*, 7–14.

Strasburger, V. C. (1995). *Adolescents and the media*. Newbury Park, CA: Sage.

Streissguth, A. P., Martin, D. C., Barr, H. M., Sandman, B. M., Kirchner, G. L., & Darby, B. L. (1984). Intrauterine alcohol and nicotine exposure: Attention and reaction time in 4-year-old children. *Developmental Psychology, 20*, 533–541.

Streissguth, A. P., Martin, D. C., Sandman, B. M., Kirchner, G. L., & Darby, B. L. (1984). Intrauterine alcohol and nicotine exposure: Attention and reaction time in four-year-old children. *Developmental Psychology, 20*, 533–543.

Stricker, G., Davis-Russell, E., Bourg, E., Duran, E., Hammond, W. R., McHolland, J., Polite, K., & Vaughn, B. E. (Eds.). (1990). *Toward ethnic diversification in psychology education and training*. Washington, DC: American Psychological Association.

Sue, S. (1990, August). *Ethnicity and culture in psychological research and practice*. Paper presented at the meeting of the American Psychological Association, Boston.

Sullivan, H. S. (1953). *The interpersonal theory of psychiatry*. New York: W. W. Norton.

Sullivan, K., & Sullivan, A. (1980). Adolescent-parent separation. *Developmental Psychology, 16*, 93–99.

Suomi, S. J., Harlow, H. F., & Domek, C. J. (1970) Effect of repetitive infant-infant separations of young monkeys. *Journal of Abnormal Psychology, 76*, 161–172.

Super, D. E. (1976). *Career education and the meanings of work*. Washington, DC: U.S. Office of Education.

Susman, E. J., Murowchick, E., Worrall, B. K., & Murray, D. A. (1995, March). *Emotionality, adrenal hormones, and context interactions during puberty and pregnancy*. Paper presented at the meeting of the Society for Research in Child Development, Indianapolis.

T

Tager-Flusberg, H. (Ed.). (1994). *Constraints on language acquisition*. Hillsdale, NJ: Erlbaum.

Tajfel, H. (1978). The achievement of group differentiation. In H. Tajfel (Ed.), *Differentiation between social groups: Studies in the social psychology of intergroup relations*. London: Academic Press.

Takanishi, R. (1993). The opportunities of adolescence—research, interventions, and policy. *American Psychologist, 48*, 85–87.

Tamarin, R. (1996). *Principles of genetics* (5th ed.). Dubuque, IA: Wm. C. Brown.

Tapper, J. (1996, March). *Values, lifestyles, and crowd identification in adolescence*. Paper presented at the meeting of the Society for Research on Adolescence, Boston.

Tappero, E. (1996). Making choices to ease the stress. *The Journal of Neonatal Nursing, 15*, 5–6.

Tavris, C. (1992). *The mismeasure of women*. New York: Touchstone.

Tavris, C., & Wade, C. (1984). *The longest war: Sex differences in perspective* (2nd ed.). San Diego: Harcourt Brace Jovanovich.

Taylor, H. G., Klein, N. K., & Hack, M. H. (1994). Academic functioning in ≤750 gm birthweight children who have normal cognitive abilities: Evidence for specific learning disabilities. *Pediatric Research, 35*, 289A.

Terman, L. (1925). *Genetic studies of genius: Vol. 1. Mental and physical traits of a thousand gifted children*. Stanford, CA: Stanford.

Terman, L. H., & Oden, M. H. (1959). *Genetic studies of genius: Vol. 5. The gifted group at mid-life*. Stanford, CA: Stanford University Press.

Teti, D. M., Sakin, J., Kucera, E., Caballeros, M., & Corns, K. M. (1993, March). *Transitions to siblinghood and security of firstborn attachment. Psychosocial and psychiatric correlates of changes over time*. Paper presented at the biennial meeting of the Society for Research in Child Development, New Orleans.

Teti, D. M., & Teti, L. O. (1996). Infant-parent relationships. In N. Vanzetti & S. Duck (Eds.), *A lifetime of relationships*. Pacific Grove, CA: Brooks/Cole.

Thelen, E. (1995). Motor development: A new synthesis. *American Psychologist, 50*, 79–95.

Thomas, A., & Chess, S. (1991). Temperament in adolescence and its functional significance. In R. M. Lerner, A. C. Petersen, & J. Brooks-Gunn (Eds.), *Encyclopedia of adolescence* (Vol. 2). New York: Garland.

Thompson, E. T., & Hughes, E. C. (1958). *Race: Individual and collective behavior*. Glencoe, IL: Free Press.

Thompson, J. K. (Ed.). (1996). *Body image, eating disorders, and obesity*. Washington, DC: American Psychological Association.

Thoresen, C. E., Eagleston, J. R., Kirmil-Gray, K., & Bracke, P. E. (1985, August). *Exploring the Type A behavior pattern in children and adolescents*. Paper presented at the meeting of the American Psychological Association, Los Angeles.

Thorton, A., & Camburn, D. (1989). Religious participation and sexual behavior and attitudes. *Journal of Marriage and the Family, 49*, 117–128.

Tobin, J. J., Wu, D. Y. H., & Davidson, D. H. (1989). *Preschool in three cultures*. New Haven, CT: Yale University Press.

Tomlinson-Keasey, C. (1972). Formal operations in females from 11 to 54 years of age. *Developmental Psychology, 6*, 364.

Tomlinson-Keasey, C. (1990). The working lives of Terman's gifted women. In H. W. Grossman & N. L. Chester (Eds.), *The experience and meaning of work in women's lives*. Hillsdale, NJ: Erlbaum.

Tomlinson-Keasey, C. (1993, August). *Tracing the lives of gifted women*. Paper presented at the meeting of the American Psychological Association, Toronto.

Tomlinson-Keasey, C., Warren, L. W., & Elliott, J. E. (1986). Suicide among gifted women: A prospective study. *Journal of Abnormal Psychology, 95*, 123–130.

Torney-Purta, J. (1993, August). *Cross-cultural examination of stages of faith development*. Paper presented at the meeting of the American Psychological Association, Toronto.

Toth, S. L., Manley, J. T., & Cicchetti, D. (1992). Child maltreatment and vulnerability to depression. *Development and Psychopathology 4*, 97–112.

Trankina, F. (1983). Clinical issues and techniques in working with Hispanic children and their families. In G. J. Powell, J. Yamamoto, A. Romero, & A. Morales (Eds.), *The psychosocial development of minority group children*. New York: Brunner/Mazel.

Triandis, H. C. (1994). *Culture and social behavior*. New York: McGraw-Hill.

Trimble, J. E. (1989). *The enculturation of contemporary psychology*. Paper presented at the meeting of the American Psychological Association, New Orleans.

Tubman, J. G., Windle, M., & Windle, R. C. (1996). The onset and cross-temporal patterning of sexual intercourse in middle adolescence: Prospective relations with behavioral and emotional problems. *Child Development, 67,* 327–343.

Tucker, L. A. (1987). Television, teenagers, and health. *Journal of Youth and Adolescence, 16,* 415–425.

Tuckman, B. W., & Hinkle, J. S. (1988). An experimental study of the physical and psychological effects of aerobic exercise on school children. In B. G. Melamed, K. A. Matthews, D. K. Routh, B. Stabler, & N. Schneiderman (Eds.), *Child health psychology*. Hillsdale, NJ: Erlbaum.

Turecki, S., & Tonner, L. (1989). *The difficult child*. New York: Bantam.

Tyack, D. (1976). Ways of seeing: An essay on the history of compulsory schooling. *Harvard Educational Review, 46,* 355–389.

U

Unger, R., & Crawford, M. (1992). *Women and gender* (2nd ed.). New York: McGraw-Hill.

United States Commission on Civil Rights. (1975). *A better chance to learn: Bilingual bicultural education*. Washington, DC: U.S. Government Printing Office.

Urberg, K. A., & Wolowicz, L. S. (1996, March). *Antecedents and consequents of changes in parental monitoring*. Paper presented at the meeting of the Society for Research on Adolescence, Boston.

U.S. Department of Education. (1993). *Violence in schools*. Washington, DC: U.S. Department of Education.

U.S. General Accounting Office. (1987, September). *Prenatal care: Medicaid recipients and uninsured women obtain insufficient care*. A report to the Congress of the United States, HRD-97-137. Washington, DC: Author.

V

Vandell, D. L., & Corasaniti, M. A. (1988). Variations in early child care: Do they predict subsequent social, emotional, and cognitive differences? *Child Development, 59,* 176–186.

Vandell, D. L., & Wilson, K. S. (1988). Infants' interactions with mother, sibling, and peer: Contrasts and relations between interaction systems. *Child Development, 48,* 176–186.

Van den Berghe, P. L. (1978). *Race and racism: A comparative perspective*. New York: Wiley.

van den Boom, D. C. (1989). Neonatal irritability and the development of attachment. In G. A. Kohnstamm, J. E. Bates, & M. K. Rothbart (Eds.), *Temperament in childhood*. New York: Wiley.

Verbrugge, L. M. (1987). Role responsibilities, role burdens, and physical health. *Journal of Community Health, 7,* 262–283.

Vining, E. P. G. (1992). Down syndrome. In R. A. Hoekelman (Ed.), *Primary pediatric care* (2nd ed.). St. Louis: Mosby Yearbook.

Voyer, D., Voyer, S., & Bryden, M. P. (1995). Magnitude of sex differences in spatial abilities: A meta-analysis and consideration of critical variables. *Psychological Bulletin, 117,* 250–270.

Vygotsky, L. S. (1962). *Thought and language*. Cambridge, MA: MIT Press.

W

Waddington, C. H. (1957). *The strategy of the genes*. London: Allen & Son.

Wagner, B. M., Cole, R. E., & Schwartzman, P. (1993, March). *Prediction of suicide attempts among junior and senior high school youth*. Paper presented at the biennial meeting of the Society for Research in Child Development, New Orleans.

Wakschlag, L. S., Chase-Lansdale, P. L., & Brooks-Gunn, J. (1996, March). *Not just "ghosts in the nursery": Contemporaneous intergenerational relationships and parenting in young African American families*. Paper presented at the meeting of the Society for Research on Adolescence, Boston.

Walker, L. J. (1991). Sex differences in moral development. In W. M. Kurtines & J. Gewirtz (Eds.), *Moral behavior and development* (Vol. 2). Hillsdale, NJ: Erlbaum.

Wallace-Broscious, A., Serafica, F. C., & Osipow, S. H. (1994). Adolescent career development: Relationships to self-concept and identity status. *Journal of Research on Adolescence, 4,* 127–150.

Wallerstein, J. S., Corbin, S. B., & Lewis, J. M. (1988). Children of divorce: A 10-year study. In E. M. Hetherington & J. D. Arasteh (Eds.), *Impact of divorce, single parenting, and stepparenting on children*. Hillsdale, NJ: Erlbaum.

Warshak, R. A. (1996, January 15). Personal communication, Department of Psychology, University of Texas at Dallas, Richardson, TX.

Waterman, A. S. (1992). Identity as an aspect of optimal psychological functioning. In G. R. Adams, T. P. Gullotta, & R. Montemayor (Eds.), *Adolescent Identity formation*. Newbury Park, CA: Sage.

Waters, E., Merrick, S. K., Albersheim, L. J., & Treboux, E. (1995, March). *Attachment security from infancy to early adulthood: A 20-year longitudinal study*. Paper presented at the meeting of the Society for Research in Child Development, Indianapolis, IN.

Watson, J. B. (1928). *Psychological care of infant and child*. New York: W. W. Norton.

Weaver, R. F., & Hedrick, P. W. (1996). *Genetics* (2nd ed.). Dubuque, IA: Wm. C. Brown.

Weidner, G., Sexton, G., Matarazzo, J. D., Pereira, C., & Friend, R. (1988). Type A behavior in children, adolescents, and their parents. *Developmental Psychology, 24,* 118–121.

Weikart, D. P. (1982). Preschool education for disadvantaged children. In J. R. Travers & R. J. Light (Eds.), *Learning from experience: Evaluating early childhood demonstration programs*. Washington, DC: National Academy Press.

Weikart, P. S. (1987). *Round the circle: Key experiences in movement for children ages 3 to 5*. Ypsilanti, MI: High/Scope Press.

Weikert, D. P. (1993). [Long-term positive effects in the Perry Preschool Head Start program]. Unpublished data, High Scope Foundation, Ypsilanti, MI.

Weinstein, N. D. (1984). Reducing unrealistic optimism about illness susceptibility. *Health Psychology, 3,* 431–457.

Weiss, B., Dodge, K. A., Bates, J. E., & Pettit, G. S. (1992). Some consequences of early harsh discipline: Child aggression and a maladaptive social information processing style. *Child Development, 63,* 1321–1335.

Weizmann, F., Wiener, N. I., Wiesenthal, D. L., & Ziegler, M. (1990). Differential K theory and racial hierarchies. *Canadian Psychology, 31,* 1–13.

Wellman, H. M. (1990). *The child's theory of mind*. Cambridge, MA: M.I.T. Press.

Werner, E. E. (1979). *Cross-cultural child development: A view from planet earth*. Monterey, CA: Brooks/Cole.

Werner, E. E. (1989). High risk children in young adulthood: A longitudinal study from birth to 32 years. *American Journal of Orthopsychiatry, 59,* 72–81.

Werner, E. E., & Smith, R. S. (1982). *Vulnerable but invincible: A longitudinal study of resilient children and youth*. New York: McGraw-Hill.

Werner, L. A., & Marean, G. C. (1996). *Human auditory development*. Boulder, CO: Westview Press.

Wertheimer, M. (1945). *Productive thinking*. New York: Harper.

White, B., Castle, P., & Held, R. (1964). Observations on the development of visually directed reaching. *Child Development, 35,* 349–364.

White, B. L. (1988). *Educating the infant and toddler*. Lexington, MA: Lexington Books.

Whiting, B. B. (1989, April). *Culture and interpersonal behavior*. Paper presented at the biennial meeting of the Society for Research in Child Development, Kansas City.

Whiting, B. B., & Edwards, C. P. (1988). *Children of different worlds*. Cambridge, MA: Harvard University Press.

Whiting, B. B., & Whiting, J. W. M. (1975). *Children of six cultures*. Cambridge, MA: Harvard University Press.

Wicks-Nelson, R., & Israel, A. C. (1996). *Behavior disorders of childhood* (3rd ed.). Upper Saddle River, NJ: Prentice-Hall.

Wigfield, A., & Eccles, J. S. (1994). Middle grades schooling and early adolescent development: An introduction. *Journal of Early Adolescence, 14,* 102–106.

Wigfield, A., & Eccles, J. S. (1995). Middle school grades schooling and early adolescent development. *Journal of Early Adolescence, 15,* 5–8.

Wilcox, K. J., & Bouchard, T. J. (1996). Behavior genetics. *Encyclopedia of Science and Technology*. New York: McGraw-Hill.

William T. Grant Foundation Commission. (1988, February). *The forgotten half: Non-college-bound youth in America*. Washington, DC: William T. Grant Foundation.

Williams, C. R. (1986). *The impact of television: A natural experiment in three communities*. New York: Academic Press.

Williams, J. E., & Best, D. L. (1982). *Measuring sex stereotypes: A thirty-nation study*. Newbury Park, CA: Sage.

Williams, J. E., & Best, D. L. (1989). *Sex and psyche: Self-concept view cross-culturally*. Newbury Park, CA: Sage.

Williams, M. F., & Condry, J. C. (1989, April). *Living color: Minority portrayals and cross-racial interactions on television.* Paper presented at the Society for Research in Child Development meeting, Kansas City.

Williams, R. A. (1994, April 14). *Anger kills.* Paper presented at the meeting of the American Psychosomatic Society, Boston.

Wilson, E. O. (1975). *Sociobiology: The new synthesis.* Cambridge, MA: Harvard University Press.

Wilson, E. O. (1995, February). *Unity in biodiversity.* Paper presented at the meeting of the American Association for the Advancement of Science, Atlanta.

Wilson, L. C. (1990). *Infants and toddlers: Curriculum and teaching.* Albany, NY: Delmar.

Windle, W. F. (1940). *Physiology of the human fetus.* Philadelphia: Saunders.

Winner, E. (1986, August). Where pelicans kiss seals. *Psychology Today,* pp. 24–35.

Witkin, H. A., Mednick, S. A., Schulsinger, R., Bakkestrom, E., Christiansen, K. O., Goodenbough, D. R., Hirchhorn, K., Lunsteen, C., Owen, D. R., Philip, J., Ruben, D. B., & Stocking, M. (1976). Criminality in XYY and XXY men. *Science, 193,* 547–555.

Wodrich, D. L. (1994). *Attention deficit hyperactivity disorder and your child.* Baltimore: Paul Brookes.

Wolff, P. H. (1969). The natural history of crying and other vocalizations in early infancy. In B. M. Foss (Ed.), *Determinants of infant development* (Vol. 4). London, England: Methuen.

Women on Words & Images. (1972). *Dick and Jane as victims.* Princeton, NJ: Author.

Wood, J. T. (1996). Gender, relationships, and communication. In J. T. Wood (Ed.), *Gendered relationships.* Mountain View, CA: Mayfield.

Woolfenden, G. E. (1972). Florida scrub jay helpers at the nest. *Auk, 92,* 1–15.

Woolsey, S. F. (1992). Sudden infant death syndrome. In R. A. Hoekelman, S. B. Friedman, N. M. Nelson, & H. M. Seidel (Eds.), *Primary pediatric care* (2nd ed.). St. Louis: Mosby Yearbook.

Worell, J., & Todd, J. (1996). Development of the gendered self. In L. Smolak, M. P. Levine, & R. H. Striegel-Moore (Eds.), *Developmental psychopathology of eating disorders.* Hillsdale, NJ: Erlbaum.

Worobey, J., & Belsky, J. (1982). Employing the Brazelton Scale to influence mothering: An experimental comparison of three strategies. *Developmental Psychology, 18,* 736–743.

Worrell, J., & Remer, P. (1992). *Feminist perspectives in therapy.* New York: John Wiley.

Wright, J. C. (1995, March). *Effects of viewing Sesame Street: The longitudinal study of media and time use.* Paper presented at the meeting of the Society for Research in Child Development, Indianapolis.

Wroblewski, R., & Huston, A. C. (1987). Televised occupational stereotypes and their effects on early adolescents: Are they changing? *Journal of Early Adolescence, 7,* 283–297.

Y

Yankelovich, D. (1974). *The new morality: A profile of American youth in the 1970s.* New York: McGraw-Hill.

Yates, M. (1996, March). *Community service and political-moral discussions among Black urban adolescents.* Paper presented at the meeting of the Society for Research on Adolescence, Boston.

Yates, M. J. (1995, March). *Political socialization as a function of volunteerism.* Paper presented at the meeting of the Society for Research in Child Development, Indianapolis.

Yeni-Komshian, G. H. (1995, February). *What happens to our first language when we learn a second language?* Paper presented at the meeting of the American Association for the Advancement of Science, Atlanta.

Yip, R. (1995, March). *Nutritional status of U.S. children: The extent and causes of malnutrition.* Paper presented at the meeting of the Society for Research in Child Development, Indianapolis.

Young, K. T. (1990). American conceptions of infant development from 1955 to 1984: What the experts are telling parents. *Child Development, 61,* 17–28.

Young, S. K., & Shahinfar, A. (1995, March). *The contributions of maternal sensitivity and child temperament to attachment status at 14 months.* Paper presented at the meeting of the Society for Research in Child Development, Indianapolis.

Z

Zambriana, R. E. (Ed.). (1995). *Understanding Latino families.* Newbury Park, CA: Sage.

Zelazo, P. R., Potter, S., & Valiante, A. G. (1995, March). *Effects of fetal cocaine exposure on neonatal information processing.* Paper presented at the meeting of the Society for Research in Child Development, Indianapolis.

Zeskind, P. S., Klein, L., & Marshall, T. R. (1992). Adults' perceptions of experimental modifications of durations and expiratory sounds in infant crying. *Developmental Psychology, 28,* 1153–1162.

Zigler, E. (1987, April). *Child care for parents who work outside the home: Problems and solutions.* Paper presented at the biennial meeting of the Society for Research in Child Development, Baltimore.

Zigler, E., & Styfco, S. J. (1994). Head Start: Criticisms in a constructive context. *American Psychologist, 49,* 127–132.

Zolotow, C. (1972). *William's doll.* New York: Harper & Row.

Zubay, G. L. (1996). *Origins of life on the earth and in the cosmos.* Dubuque, IA: Wm. C. Brown.

Zuckerman, M. (1979). *Sensation seeking: Beyond the optimal level of arousal.* Hillsdale, NJ: Erlbaum.

CREDITS

PHOTOGRAPHS

Prologue

Opener: © Art Institute of Chicago

Section Openers

Section 1: © Ross Whitaker/The Image Bank Chicago; Section 2: © Petit Format/ Photo Researchers, Inc.; Section 3: © Northern Telecom; Section 4: © Shuster/Photo Researchers, Inc.; Section 5: © SuperStock; Section 6: © Lanpher Productions

Chapter 1

Opener: National Gallery, London; 1.1a: © Erich Lessing/Art Resource, New York; 1.1b: © Scala/Art Resource, New York; 1.2: © Courtesy of Nancy Agostini; 1.3a: © Michael Melford/The Image Bank Chicago; 1.3b: © Mark Walker/Picture Cube; p. 14: Courtesy of Marian Edelman; 1.5 top to bottom: © James Shaffer, © Michael Salas/The Image Bank Chicago, © Joe Sohm/Image Works, Courtesy of John Santrock, © L. Shettles; p. 19: © Duka/Photo Network; 1.7: © Lucy Rosenthal/SuperStock; 1.8 top to bottom: © FPG International, © Peter Turnley/Black Star, © Kevin Horan/ Picture Group, Alan Stuart Frank/Photo Researchers, Inc., © Joseph Rodriguez/ Black Star; p. 29: © Renato Rotola/ Gamma Liaison; p. 30 left: Courtesy of Kenneth Clark; p. 30 right: Courtesy of George Sanchez; p. 31 top left: © M. Richards/PhotoEdit; p. 31 top middle: © Fujiphotos/Image Works; p. 31 top right: © Joseph Nettis/Photo Researchers, Inc.

Chapter 2

Opener: Courtesy of James A. Bakker Antiques and Melvin Holmes; p. 35: © Sharon Beals for INSIGHT; p. 36: © Bettmann Newsphotos; p. 37 left: © Shooting Star; p. 37 right: © Stock Montage; p. 39: © Sarah Putnam/Picture Cube; 2.2b: © William Hopkins, Jr.; 2.2c and d: © Suzanne Szasz/Photo Researchers, Inc.; 2.2e: © Mel Digiacomo/The Image Bank Chicago; 2.2f: © Sam Zarember/The Image Bank Texas; 2.2g: © Brett Froomer/ The Image Bank Texas; 2.2h: © Alan Carey/Image Works; 2.2i: © Harold Sund/ The Image Bank Texas; p. 42: © Yves DeBraine/Black Star; p. 44 left: © Bettmann Archives; p. 44 right: Courtesy of Albert Bandura; 2.4: Photo by Nina Leen/Time/Life Magazine © Time Inc.; p. 46: Courtesy of Urie Bronfenbrenner; 2.5: © David Austen/ Stock Boston; 2.6a: © Jerry Alexander/ Tony Stone Worldwide; 2.6b: © James Rowan/Tony Stone Worldwide; 2.6c: © Jacques Jangoux/Tony Stone Worldwide; p. 51: © Ray Stott/Image Works; p. 53: © Anthro-Photo; 2.7: © Jeff Hunter/The Image Bank Chicago; 2.8: © Gary Chapman/The Image Bank Texas; p. 58: Courtesy of Dr. Florence L. Denmark/Photo by Robert Wesner; p. 66: © PhotoEdit; p. 67: © Brian ViKander/ West Light; p. 68 top: Courtesy of Charles Eickelberger; p. 68 bottom: © Robin Smith/SuperStock; p. 69 left: The Bettmann Archive; p. 69 right: Courtesy of Nancy Chodorow

Chapter 3

Opener: Winslow Homer/Worcester Art Museum; p. 74: © Enrico Ferorelli; 3.1a: © John P. Kelly/The Image Bank Chicago; 3.1b: © Michael P. Gadomski/Photo Researchers, Inc.; p. 78 large: Courtesy of United Nations; p. 78 top left: Courtesy of United Nations; p. 78 top right: © Gio Barto/The Image Bank Texas; p. 78 middle: © Elaine Sulle/The Image Bank Chicago; p. 78 bottom left: © Janeart/ The Image Bank Chicago; p. 78 bottom right: © Harvey Lloyd/The Stock Market; 3.2: Regents of the University of California; 3.3 top: © R. Heinzen/ SuperStock; 3.3 bottom: © Elyse Lewin/ The Image Bank Texas; 3.4: © Sundstrom/ Gamma Liaison; 3.5: © Alexandria Tsiaras/Photo Researchers, Inc.; p. 82: © Kelly Wilkinson/Indianapolis Star; 3.6a and b: © Andrew Eccles/Outline; 3.7: © Will and Deni McIntyre/Photo Researchers, Inc.; 3.8: © J. Pavlousky/ SYGMA; 3.9: © Grant A. Hall/Unicorn; 3.10a: © Tim Davis/Photo Researchers, Inc.; 3.10b: © Sandy Clark-Roessler/The Stock Market; p. 90: © Myrleen Ferguson/ PhotoEdit; p. 93: Courtesy of Sandra Scarr; p. 100: © Elizabeth Crews/Image Works; p. 101: © Gabe Palmer/The Stock Market

Chapter 4

Opener: Courtesy of Michael McCormick Gallery; 4.1: Russ Kinne/Comstock; p. 107 all: © Lennart Nilsson; 4.4 large: © Petit Format/Nestle/Photo Researchers, Inc.; 4.4 top: © Lennart Nilsson; 4.4 middle and bottom: © Nestle/Photo Researchers, Inc.; p. 112: © Richard Cash/PhotoEdit; 4.7: Courtesy A.P. Streissguth, University of Washington School of Medicine; p. 114 right: Courtesy of American Cancer Society; 4.8: © Will and Deni McIntyre/ Photo Researchers, Inc.; p. 116: © Chas Cancellare/Picture Group; 4.9b: © Ed Kashi/Discover; p. 122 left: © David Young Wolff/PhotoEdit; p. 122 right: © David Shaefer/PhotoEdit; p. 124: © Mike Malyszko/Stock Boston; p. 132: © Charles Gupton/Stock Boston

Chapter 5

Opener: Scala/Art Resource; p. 139: © Comstock Inc.; p. 140: © Charles Gupton/Tony Stone; p. 141: © Charles Gupton/Stock Boston; p. 142: © Susan Leavines/Photo Researchers, Inc.; p. 143 left: © Stephen McBrady/PhotoEdit; p. 143 right: © David Brownell/The Image Bank Chicago; p. 145: © Charles Gupton/Stock Boston; 5.2: © Comstock/ Comstock, Inc.; p. 148: © Michael Newman/PhotoEdit; p. 149: © James G. White; p. 153: Courtesy of Dr. Tiffany Field; p. 155: Courtesy of Maternity Center Association

Epilogue

Opener: © Art Resource; p. 553: © Lennart Nilsson; p. 554: © Niki Mareschal/The Image Bank Texas; p. 555: © Barbara Feigles/Stock Boston; p. 556: © Sumo/The Image Bank Texas; p. 557: © Upitis/The Image Bank Chicago

---

LINE ART AND TEXT

Prologue

Poem, p. xxix: From the book *Full Esteem Ahead* © 1994 by Diane Loomans with Julia Loomans. Reprinted by permission of H J Kramer, P.O. Box 1082, Tiburon, CA. All rights reserved.

Chapter 1

Figure 1.3 (text): Reprinted with permission from *The State of America's Children Yearbook 1996*. Washington, DC: Children's Defense Fund, 1996.
Lyric, p. 15: THE GREATEST LOVE OF ALL, by Linda Creed and Michael Masser. Copyright © 1977 Gold Horizon Music Corp. and Golden Torch Music. International Copyright Secured. Made in USA. Used by Permission of CPP/Belwin, Inc., Miami, FL 33014. All Rights Reserved.
p. 26: Reprinted with the permission of Simon & Schuster from *Familyhood* by Lee Salk. Copyright © 1992 by Simon & Schuster, Inc.
p. 26: From Marian Wright Edelman, *The Measure of Our Success*. Copyright © Harper Perennial, a division of HarperCollins Publishers. Reprinted by permission.

Chapter 2

Figure 2.1: From *Psychology: A Scientific Study of Human Behavior*, by L. S. Wrightsman, C. K. Sigelman and F. H. Sanford. Copyright © 1979, 1975, 1970, 1965, 1961 by Brooks/Cole Publishing Company, Pacific Grove, CA 93950, a division of International Thomson Publishing Inc. By permission of the publisher.
Poem, p. 38: From *The Poetry of Robert Frost* edited by Edward Connery Lathem. Copyright 1936 by Robert Frost. Copyright © 1964 by Lesley Frost Ballantine. Copyright © 1969 by Henry Holt and Company, Inc. Reprinted by permission of Henry Holt and Company, Inc.
Figure 2.5: C B Kopp/J B Krakow, *The Child*, © 1982 by Addison-Wesley Publishing Company, Inc. Reprinted by permission of Addison-Wesley Publishing Company, Inc.
Excerpt, p. 58: From Florence Denmark, et al., "Guidelines for Avoiding Sexism in Psychological Research: A Report of the

Ad Hoc Committee on Nonsexist Research" in *American Psychologist*, 43:582–585. Copyright 1988 by the American Psychological Association. Reprinted by permission.
p. 65: From Erik H. Erikson, *Identity: Youth and Crisis*. Copyright © 1968 W. W. Norton & Company, Inc., New York, NY. Reprinted by permission.

Chapter 3

Poem, p. 80: From *Verses from 1929 On* by Ogden Nash. Copyright 1940 by Ogden Nash. By permission of Little, Brown and Company.
Figure 3.11: From I. Gottesman, "Genetic Aspects of Intellectual Behavior" in *Handbook of Mental Deficiency*, Norman R. Ellis (ed.). Copyright © 1983 McGraw-Hill, Inc., New York, NY. Reprinted by permission of Norman R. Ellis.
p. 97: From M. D. Brodzinsky, *Being Adopted*. Copyright © 1992 Doubleday & Co., Inc., a division of Bantam Doubleday Dell Group, Inc. Reprinted by permission.
p. 97: From *Prenatal Tests* by Robin J. R. Blatt. Text copyright © 1988 by Robin J. R. Blatt. Illustrations copyright © 1988 by Jackie Aher. Reprinted by permission of Random House, Inc.
p. 97: From Carol Krause, *How Healthy Is Your Family Tree?* COVER COPYRIGHT © 1995 by Todd Radom. Reprinted by permission.

Chapter 4

Figure 4.2: From Charles Carroll and Dean Miller, *Health: The Science of Human Adaptation*, 5th ed. Copyright © 1991 Wm. C. Brown Communications, Inc., Dubuque, Iowa. All Rights Reserved. Reprinted by permission.
Figure 4.4: © 1979, 1984, 1991 by the Childbirth Education Association. Reprinted from *Pregnancy, Childbirth, and the Newborn: The Complete Guide* by Penny Simkin, Janet Whalley, and Ann Keppler with permission of its publisher, Meadowbrook Press, Deephaven, MN.
Figure 4.5: From Moore, K. L., *The Developing Human: Clinically Oriented Embryology*, 4th ed. Copyright © 1988 W. B. Saunders Company. Reprinted by permission.
Figure 4.8: From Queenan and Queenan, *A New Life: Pregnancy, Birth & Your Child's First Year*. Copyright © 1986 Marshall Cavendish Ltd., London, England. Reprinted by permission.
Figure 4.9a: John Karapelou © 1991 *Discover* Magazine.
Figure 4.11: Source: Data from Food and Nutrition Board, "Recommended Nutrient Increases for Adult Pregnancy," National Academy of Sciences, Washington, DC, 1980.

p. 130: *What To Expect When You're Expecting* by Arlene Eisenberg, Heidi E. Murkoff, and Sandee E. Hathaway © 1984, 1988, 1991. Cover reprinted by permission of Workman Publishing Company, Inc. All rights reserved.
p. 130: R. S. Abrams, *Will It Hurt the Baby?* © 1990 by Richard S. Abrams, M.D. Reprinted by permission of Addison-Wesley Publishing Company, Inc.
p. 130: *What To Eat When You're Expecting* by Arlene Eisenberg, Heidi E. Murkoff, and Sandee E. Hathaway © 1986. Cover reprinted by permission of Workman Publishing Company, Inc. All rights reserved.

Chapter 5

Figure 5.1: From Kent M. Van De Graaff and Stuart Ira Fox, *Concepts of Human Anatomy and Physiology*, 3d ed. Copyright © 1992 Wm. C. Brown Communications, Inc. All Rights Reserved. Reprinted by permission.
Figure 5.2: From Virginia Apgar, "A Proposal for a New Method of Evaluation of a Newborn Infant" in *Anesthesia and Analgesia*, 32:260–267. Copyright © 1975 International Anesthesia Research Society. Reprinted by permission of Williams & Wilkins.
Figure 5.3: From: *Cultural Perspectives on Child Development* by Wagner and Stevenson. Copyright © 1982 by W. H. Freeman and Company. Used with permission.
p. 152: Cover of *Methods of Childbirth* by Constance A. Bean. By permission of Avon Books.

Chapter 6

Figure 6.2: Source: National Center for Health Statistics, NCHS Growth Charts, *Monthly Vital Statistics Report*.
Figure 6.3: From Jesse LeRoy Conel, *Postnatal Development of the Human Cerebral Cortex*. Copyright © Harvard University Press, Cambridge, MA. Reprinted by permission.
Figure 6.4: From W. K. Frankenburg and J. B. Dodds, "The Denver Development Screening Test" in *Journal of Pediatrics*, 71:181–191. Copyright © 1967 Mosby-Year Book, Inc. Reprinted by permission.
Figure 6.5: Sources: Data from R. Charlesworth, *Understanding Child Development*, 2d ed., Delmar Press, Albany, NY, 1987; and G. J. Schirmer (ed.), *Performance Objectives for Preschool Children*, Adapt Press, Sioux Falls, SD, 1974.
p. 181: *What To Expect The First Year* by Arlene Eisenberg, Heidi E. Murkoff, and Sandee E. Hathaway © 1989. Cover reprinted by permission of Workman Publishing Company, Inc. All rights reserved.

Chapter 14

Figure 14.3: From Janet S. Hyde, et al., "Gender Differences in Mathematics Performance: A Meta-Analysis" in *Psychological Bulletin*, 107:139–155. Copyright 1990 by the American Psychological Association. Reprinted by permission.

p. 445: Reproduced with permission of publisher American Guidance Service, Inc., 4201 Woodland Road, Circle Pines, MN 55014-1796.

p. 445: From Edward B. Fiske, *Smart Schools, Smart Kids*. COVER COPYRIGHT © 1992 by Simon & Schuster, Inc. Reprinted by permission of Simon & Schuster, Inc.

p. 445: Reprinted with the permission of Simon & Schuster from *Failing at Fairness* by Myra and David Sadker. Coypright © 1994 by Myra and David Sadker.

p. 445: From Lyn Mikel Brown and Carol Gilligan, *Meeting at the Crossroads*. Copyright © 1992 Harvard University Press, Cambridge, MA. Reprinted by permission.

Excerpt, p. 446: From Carle F. O'Neil and Waln K. Brown, "Planning and Building a Stepfamily." Copyright © 1991 The William Gladden Foundation. Reprinted by permission.

Chapter 15

Figure 15.1: From J. M. Tanner, et al., "Standards from Birth to Maturity for Height, Weight, Height Velocity, and Weight Velocity: British Children 1965" in *Archives of Diseases in Childhood*, 41. Copyright © 1966 British Medical Association, London, England. Reprinted by permission.

Figure 15.4: Source: Data from the Alan Guttmacher Institute, 1988.

Figure 15.5: Excerpted from *Adolescents at Risk: Prevalence and Prevention* by Joy C. Dryfoos. Copyright © 1990 by Joy C. Dryfoos. Reprinted by permission of Oxford University Press, Inc.

p. 482: From Laurence Steinberg and Ann Levine, *You and Your Adolescent*. Copyright © 1990 Harper Perennial, a division of HarperCollins Publishers, New York, NY.

p. 482: Jacket design from *Fateful Choices: Healthy Youth for the 21st Century* by Fred Hechinger. Jacket design © 1992 by Meadows and Wiser. Cover photograph © 1992 by Harold Feinstein from *Children of War*. Reprinted by permission of Hill and Wang, a division of Farrar, Straus & Giroux, Inc.

p. 482: Excerpted from *Adolescents at Risk: Prevalence and Prevention* by Joy C. Dryfoos. Copyright © 1990 by Joy C. Dryfoos. Reprinted by permission of Oxford University Press, Inc.

Chapter 16

Figure 16.2: From E. L. Dey, et al., *The American Freshman: Twenty-Five-Year Trends*, 1991; A. W. Astin, et al., *The American Freshman: National Norms for Fall 1991*, 1991; E. L. Dey, et al., *The American Freshman: National Norms for Fall 1992*, 1992; A. W. Astin, et al., *The American Freshman: National Norms for Fall 1993*, 1993; and A. W. Astin, et al, *The American Freshman: National Norms for Fall 1994*, 1994. All works © Higher Education Research Institute, UCLA.

Lyric, p. 508: "I Am Woman." Words by Helen Reddy. Music by Ray Burton. © 1971 IRVING MUSIC, INC. (BMI) & BUGGERLUGS MUSIC CO. (BMI). All Rights Reserved. International Copyright Secured.

p. 513: D. Elkind, *All Grown Up and No Place to Go*, © 1984 by David Elkind. Reprinted by permission of Addison-Wesley Publishing Company, Inc.

p. 513: From Thomas Evans, *Mentors*. Copyright © 1992 Peterson's Guides, Princeton, NJ. Reprinted by permission.

Chapter 17

Excerpt, p. 520: From S. Shirley Feldman and Glen R. Elliott, *At the Threshhold: The Developing Adolescent*, 1990. Reprinted by permission.

Figure 17.2: Source: Data from Dexter C. Dunphy, "The Social Structure of Urban Adolescent Peer Groups" in *Sociometry*, Vol. 26, American Sociological Association, Washington, DC, 1963.

Excerpt, p. 527: Reprinted by permission from *Selections from the Writings of 'Abdu'l-Baha*. Copyright © 1978 by the Universal House of Justice.

p. 540: Avon edition cover, *Between Parent and Teenager* by Dr. Haim Ginott. By permission of Avon Books.

p. 540: From Janet Simons, Belva Finlay, and Alice Yang, *The Adolescent and Young Adult Fact Book*. Copyright © 1993 Children's Defense Fund, Washington, DC. Reprinted by permission.

ILLUSTRATORS

GBR

4.8A

Illustrious, Inc.

1.6, 1.8A, 2.1, 2.5B, 3.3C, 3.9B, 4.6, 4.9A, 4.10, 11.1A, 11.4A, 11.5A, 13.1, 14.1B, 14.4, 15.5, 17.1B, 17.2A, 17.3B

Wilderness Graphics

8.4A, 12.3B, 16.2A, 16.3; text art, pages 24, 62, 95, 128, 151, 179, 206, 241, 270, 302, 338, 371, 408, 443, 480, 511, 538

Name Index

Bigler, R. S., 430
Biller, H. B., 247, 275
Billings, R. L., 116
Bish, A., 82
Black, A. E., 328
Black, K. A., 521
Black, K. N., 318
Blades, M., 388
Blair, C. B., 145, 298
Blakemore, J. E. O., 433
Blass, E. M., 177
Blatt, R. J. R., 98
Block, J., 471
Block, J. H., 471
Blue, J. H., 460
Blum, B., 12
Blum, R., 466
Blumenfeld, P. C., 422
Blumenthal, J., 436
Blyth, D. A., 362
Bobrow, N. A., 463
Bond, L. A., 31
Bonvillian, J. D., 192
Boodoo, G., 392
Booth, A., 7, 46
Bornstein, M. H., 286
Botvin, G., 485
Bouchard, T. J., 74, 392
Boudreau, J. P., 167
Bourg, E., 29
Bower, B., 261
Bower, T. G. R., 172, 184, 192
Bowlby, J., 19, 77, 221, 222, 233, 364
Bowser, B. P., 531
Boxer, C., 217
Boyce, T., 66
Boykin, A. W., 392
Boykin, K. A., 521
Boys and Girls Clubs of America, 526
Bracke, P. E., 364
Bracken, M. B., 82
Braff, A. M., 82
Brakke, K. E., 200
Brand, J. E., 325
Braunwald, K., 239
Brazelton, T. B., 147, 163, 318
Bredekamp, S., 278, 295
Bremer, M., 325
Brenneman, K., 383
Brenner, A., 365, 366
Bresnick, B., 260
Bretherton, I., 223
Brewer, W. F., 384
Brice, P., 326
Brillion, L., 53, 531
Brion-Meisels, S., 427
Brislin, R., 79
Brodsky, A. M., 69
Brody, L., 517
Brody, L. R., 437
Brody, N., 392
Brodzinsky, D., 82, 86
Bromley, D., 426
Bronfenbrenner, U., 46, 51, 298
Bronstein, P., 319
Bronstein, P. A., 29
Brook, D. W., 471, 522

Brook, J. S., 471, 522
Brooks-Gunn, J., 100, 213, 235, 320, 363,
   392, 460, 461, 462, 463, 470, 474,
   522
Broverman, D., 433
Broverman, I., 433
Brown, A. L., 385
Brown, B. B., 525, 527
Brown, J. L., 169
Brown, J. V., 149, 436
Brown, L., 266
Brown, L. S., 69
Brown, P., 28
Brown, R., 202, 203, 204, 290, 447
Browne, C. R., 436
Browne, M. W., 92
Brubaker, T. H., 221
Brumitt, G. A., 116
Bryant, D. M., 100
Bryden, M. P., 421
Bryon, Y. J., 112
Buchanan, C. M., 319
Buckley, S., 419
Burchinal, M. R., 100, 225
Burgess, D. M., 114
Burton, L., 331
Burts, D. C., 295, 300
Bushnell, E. W., 167
Busnel, M. C., 175
Buss, A. H., 228
Buss, D. A., 228
Buss, D. M., 76, 77, 432
Butcher, M. J., 177
Byers, T., 114
Byrne, R., 76

C

Caballeros, M., 315
Cairns, E., 11
Caldwell, M. B., 112
Callan, J. W., 420
Camburn, D., 498
Cameron, J. R., 229
Campbell, F. A., 100, 298
Campbell, R. A., 100
Campos, J., 231
Campos, J. J., 174
Canfield, R. L., 194
Cantu, C. L., 535
Capaldi, D., 35
Carlson, D. M., 404
Carlson, K. S., 315
Carlson, V., 239
Carmichael, C. M., 93
Carnegie Corporation, 503
Carnegie Council on Adolescent
   Development, 459, 503
Carolo, G., 336
Carpenter, C. J., 334
Carriger, M. S., 196
Carter, B., 219
Carter, D. B., 334
Carter-Saltzman, L., 262
Case, R., 47, 287, 383
Cassell, C., 476
Cassidy, D. J., 334

Castle, P., 167
Cauce, A. M., 11
CDC National AIDS Clearinghouse, 467
Ceballo, R., 363, 392, 459
Ceci, S. J., 384, 392
Chan, W. S., 19
Chance, G., 175
Chang, J. C., 169
Chang, P., 149
Chapman, W., 507
Chard, S., 422
Charlesworth, R., 293, 295, 300
Chase-Landsdale, P. L., 319, 320, 363, 470
Chasnoff, I. J., 115
Chattin-McNichols, J., 294
Chavira, V., 362
Chen, C., 404
Chen, I. S. Y., 112
Chesney-Lind, M., 474
Chess, S., 227
Cheung, L. W. Y., 114
Chi, M. T., 384
Children's Defense Fund, 266, 362, 514
Chodorow, N. J., 69
Chomitz, V. R., 114
Chomsky, N., 199, 200
Chow, E. N., 436
Christiansen, K. O., 84
Chrousos, G. P., 460
Cicchelli, T., 503
Cicchetti, D., 238, 239
Cicirelli, V. G., 315
Cioci, M., 526
Clark, K. B., 29, 428
Clark, M. K., 29, 428
Clark, R. D., 432
Clark, S. D., 465
Clarke-Stewart, K. A., 226, 298
Clarkson, F., 433
Clarkson, M. G., 167, 194
Clausen, J., 319
Clements, D. C., 226
Clifford, B. R., 325
Clifton, R. K., 167, 194
Cloninger, S. C., 68
Cluett, S. E., 298
Coffman, S., 222
Coh, L. K., 494
Cohen, H. J., 112
Cohen, M., 503
Cohen, P., 471, 522
Cohen, R. J., 388
Cohen, S. E., 503
Coie, J. D., 320, 419
Colby, A., 438
Cole, R. E., 476
Coleman, J. S., 525
Coleman, L., 436
Coleman, M., 418
Coles, R., 34
Coll, C. G., 226, 363
Coll, C. T. G., 53, 531
College Board Commission on Precollege
   Guidance and Counseling, 507
Collins, P. A., 286
Comer, J. P., 346, 411, 424, 535
Compas, B. E., 474, 475

Condon, S. M., 522
Condry, J. C., 325
Cone, J., 300
Conger, J. J., 470, 495, 496
Connell, J. P., 402
Contois, J. H., 265, 266
Cook, R., 82
Cooper, C., 536
Cooper, C. R., 321, 522
Coopersmith, S., 427, 428
Copans, S. A., 113
Copeland, A. P., 437
Corasaniti, M. A., 226
Corbin, S. B., 318
Corns, K. M., 315
Corrigan, R., 190
Corter, C., 316
Cosmides, L., 77
Cowan, C. P., 217, 306
Cowan, P. A., 217
Cox, M., 47, 318
Cox, R., 47, 318
Coyne, J. C., 365
Crawford, C., 76
Crawford, M., 432
Crick, N. R., 420
Criqui, M. H., 395
Crnic, K., 305
Crockenberg, S. B., 229
Cronbach, L. J., 423
Crowder, J., 309
Crowley, M., 432
Crump, A. D., 463
Cummings, E. M., 232
Cummings, L. M., 14
Cunningham, B., 275
Curtiss, S., 201
Cutler, G. B., 460

D

Daly, M., 77
Damon, W., 329, 336, 441
D'Angelo, D. A., 68
Dann, S., 320
Darby, B. L., 114, 369
Darling, C. A., 463
Darwin, C., 75
David, J., 306, 343, 344
Davidson, D. H., 308
Davis, S. M., 376
Davis-Russell, E., 29
Dawes, A., 11
DeBaryshe, B. D., 472
DeBlassie, A. M., 423
DeBlassie, R. R., 423
DeCasper, A. J., 175
DeFries, J. C., 91, 228
Degirmencioglu, S. M., 527
DeLoache, J. S., 334
Demarest, J., 347
Dembrowsky, T., 363
Dempster, F. N., 287
Demuth, K., 197
Denmark, F. L., 58
Derman-Sparks, L., 309
Derry, P. S., 432

Detweiler, R. A., 82
de Villiers, J., 203
Dewey, J., 387
DeWolf, M., 295
Diange, A., 112
Diaz, R. M., 400
Dickover, R., 112
Dickstein, S., 365
Dicson, W. P., 306
Ding, S., 364, 475
DiPardo, A., 285
DiRocco, L., 306
Dishion, T. J., 419
Dittus, R. S., 131
Dixon, R. L., 116
Dodds, J., 260
Dodge, K. A., 313, 365, 420
Dolcini, M. M., 494
Domek, C. J., 320
Dorn, L. D., 460
Dornbusch, S. M., 319, 424, 509, 530, 535, 543
Dorr, A., 326
Doubleday, C. N., 326
Dow-Edwards, D. L., 115
Downey, G., 365
Dreyer, P. H., 465
Dricas, A. S., 534
Drickamer, L. C., 54
Droege, K. L., 326
Dryfoos, J. G., 474, 478
Duckett, E., 317
Dunbar, N., 536
Duncan, G. J., 392
Dunn, H., 317
Dunn, J., 202, 316
Dunn, J. F., 46
Dunphy, D. C., 525
Dupont, S., 535
Duran, E., 29
Durkin, K., 333
Durrett, M. E., 505
Dweck, C., 413
Dweck, C. S., 402

E

Eagleston, J. R., 364
Eagly, A. H., 432
Early Childhood and Literacy
    Development Committee of the
    International Reading Association,
    293
East, P., 469
Ebata, A. T., 365
Eccles, J., 333
Eccles, J. S., 413, 503, 515
Edelman, M. W., 10, 14, 30, 305
Edelstein, S. L., 169
Edwards, C. P., 319
Egeland, B., 223
Ehrhardt, A. A., 330
Eiferman, R. R., 324
Eiger, M. S., 170
Eimas, P., 197
Eisenberg, A., 101, 149, 154, 185
Eisenberg, N., 228, 336, 441

Elkind, D., 234, 235, 282, 284, 293, 299, 329, 382, 429, 494, 506
Elliot, T., 508
Elliott, G. R., 458, 459
Elliott, J. E., 476
Ellis, L., 466
Emde, R. N., 233
Emlen, S. T., 76
Enger, E. D., 75
Engle, P. L., 209
Enright, R. D., 457, 534
Entwisle, D. R., 424
Eppler, M. A., 168
Epstein, J., 446
Epstein, J. L., 68
Epstein, L. H., 358
Erickson, J. B., 526
Erikson, E. H., 39, 222, 234, 235, 329, 422, 472, 497, 532, 535, 536
Eron, L. D., 326
Erwin, E. J., 12
Eskenazi, B., 82
Etzel, B. C., 233
Etzel, R., 268
Evans, B. J., 436
Evans, I. M., 503
Eyler, F. D., 115
Ey, S., 474

F

Fabes, R. S., 336
Fagot, B. I., 332
Falbo, T., 316
Falbo, T. L., 423
Fantz, R. L., 172
Farmer, M. C., 440
Fay, A. L., 386
Fegley, A., 509
Fehr, L. A., 534
Fein, G. G., 298, 323, 324
Feiring, C., 526, 527
Feldman, D. H., 395
Feldman, J. F., 90
Feldman, M. A., 395
Feldman, S. S., 458, 459, 472
Felice, M. E., 469
Fenwick, K. D., 175
Ferguson, D. M., 170
Ferry, K. S., 224
Fetter, M. D., 320
Field, D. E., 286
Field, T., 113, 153, 154
Field, T. M., 153, 154, 475
Figuera, J., 536
Fillion, T. J., 177
Finch, M., 508
Finkel, D., 93
Finlay, B., 28, 423, 541, 544
Fisch, R. O., 149, 176, 177
Fischer, P., 326
Fisher, C., 57
Fisher, D., 521
Fitzgerald, J. F., 131
Flaitz, J., 493
Flanagan, A. S., 487
Flavell, E. R., 287

Flavell, J. H., 287, 288, 382, 383
Folkman, S., 361
Ford, L., 330
Fordham, S., 411
Forgatch, M. S., 318
Forman, E. R., 427
Forness, S. R., 368
Forrest, J. D., 465, 469
Forshaun, S., 475
Fowler, J. W., 498, 499
Fox, L. H., 517
Fraiberg, S., 166
Fraleigh, M. J., 543
Frankenberg, W. K., 260
Fraser, S., 92
Freedman, J. L., 326
Freeman, H. S., 418
Freier, C., 115
Freier, K., 116
Freud, A., 320
Freud, S., 36
Fried, P. A., 114, 115
Friedman, A. C., 476
Friedman, H. S., 395
Friedman, M., 363
Friedrich, L. K., 326
Friend, R., 364
Frieze, I., II., 58
Frieze, I. R., 527
Frodi, A. M., 225
Frodi, M., 225
Frosch, C. A., 224
Fujimura, J. B., 266
Fulker, D. W., 228
Furth, H. G., 381

G

Gadpaille, W. J., 476
Gaensbauer, T. G., 233
Gage, N. L., 422
Gaines, K. R. E., 298
Galambos, N. L., 419, 459, 475
Galinsky, E., 306, 343, 344
Gallup, G. W., 496
Galotti, K. M., 440
Gandini, L., 278
Gangestad, S. W., 77
Ganiban, J., 238
Ganong, L. H., 418
Ganzel, A. K., 494
Garbarino, J., 238
Garber, N., 365
Garcia, E. E., 400
Garcia, R., 154
Gardiner, M., 14
Gardner, B. T., 200
Gardner, H., 391
Gardner, L. I., 256
Gardner, R. A., 200
Garmezy, N., 365
Garnier, H. E., 503
Garrett, B., 298
Garrod, A. C., 439
Garvey, C., 324
Gat, I., 327
Gearhart, M., 286

Gelman, R., 192, 283, 381, 383
George, C. M., 93
Gerber, P. J., 368
Gesell, A., 195
Gesell, A. L., 167
Giaconia, R. M., 476
Gibbs, J., 438
Gibbs, J. C., 440
Gibbs, J. T., 363, 392, 423
Gibbs, N., 449
Gibson, E. G., 172
Gibson, E. J., 168, 174, 178, 192
Gilgun, J. F., 465
Gilligan, C., 440, 441, 536
Ginsberg, R., 368
Ginzberg, E., 504
Glassman, M. J., 286
Glick, J., 287
Glover, R. W., 516
Gmunder, P., 497
Goldberg, J., 194, 287
Golden, M. W., 320
Goldin-Meadow, S., 200
Goldman, J. A., 265, 266
Goldman, N., 469
Goldman, R., 497
Goldsmith, H. H., 90, 93
Golombok, S., 82
Gomby, D. S., 12
Gomez, Y., 376
Gonzalez, K. P., 475
Goodchilds, J. D., 466
Goodenbough, D. R., 84
Goodlad, J. A., 515
Goodman, R. A., 471
Goodnow, J. J., 11
Gordon, A. S., 471, 522
Gordon, I., 67
Gordon, S., 465
Gorman, K. S., 9, 209
Gottfried, A. E., 8, 317, 402
Gottfried, A. W., 8, 317, 402
Gottlieb, D., 423
Gottlieb, G., 90
Gottlob, D., 268
Gottman, J. M., 420
Gould, S. J., 101
Gounin-Decarie, T., 192
Graber, J. A., 460
Graham, S., 403
Graneir-Deferre, C., 175
Grant, J., 156, 170, 267
Grant, K. E., 474, 475
Grantham-McGregor, S. M., 169
Graziano, W. J., 77
Green, F. L., 287
Green, J. A., 232, 233
Green, P., 325
Greenberg, B. S., 325
Greenberg, M. T., 521
Greenberger, E., 456, 508
Greene, B., 456
Greene, C. A., 224
Greene, D., 402
Greenwood, M. M., 177
Griffith, D. R., 115
Grosz, J., 112

Grotevant, H. D., 422, 505
Grunwald, L., 194
Gruskin, E., 466
Guacci-Franco, N., 222
Guberman, S. R., 286
Guilford, J. P., 396
Gulotta, T. P., 462
Gunnar, M. P., 176, 177
Gunter, B., 325
Gur, R. C., 431
Gur, R. E., 431
Gurtner, J., 405, 406
Gustafson, G. E., 232, 233
Gutherie, G. M., 209
Gutherie, H. A., 209

H

Hack, M. H., 145
Hadrick, P. W., 88
Haight, W. L., 324
Haith, M. M., 163, 194
Hake, J. L., 175
Hakim-Larson, J. A., 231, 232
Hakuta, K., 400
Halfon, N., 272
Hall, C. C. I., 436
Hall, G. S., 457, 458
Halonen, J., 10, 387, 530
Halpern, D. F., 392
Halton, A., 113
Hamilton, M. C., 213
Hammond, W. R., 29, 473
Hans, S., 115
Hansen, D., 509
Hansen, D. J., 239
Hansen, R., 229
Hanson, M. J., 374
Harding, J., 475
Hardy, J. B., 465
Harkness, S., 223
Harley, J. P., 79
Harlow, H. F., 221, 320
Harmon, R. J., 233
Harold, R. D., 515
Harris, L., 419, 466
Hart, B., 202
Hart, C. H., 295, 300, 321
Hart, D., 329, 336, 441
Harter, S., 238, 427, 428, 432, 476, 520
Hartshorne, H., 336
Hartup, W. W., 419, 420
Harwood, L. J., 170
Hatfield, E., 432
Hathaway, S., 101, 149, 154, 185
Hawkins, D., 474
Hawkins, J., 287
Hawkins, J. A., 502
Hayden, L. C., 365
Haynie, D., 463
Hazen, C., 521
Heath, S. B., 212, 536
Heinicke, C. M., 100
Held, R., 167
Hellenbrand, K., 82
Helmreich, R., 433
Helson, R., 508

Heming, G., 217
Heming, G. A., 306
Henderson, S. H., 418
Henderson, V. L., 402
Hendren, M. C., 487
Hendry, J., 308
Henig, R., 86
Henry, C. S., 471
Henshaw, S. K., 469
Hernandez, S., 300
Hernstein, R. J., 91
Herzog, E., 332
Hess, R. D., 306
Hetherington, E. M., 47, 228, 318, 319, 418
Hightower, E., 321
Hill, C. R., 417
Himmin, H. S., 448
Hinde, R. A., 45
Hines, M., 330
Hinkle, J. S., 359
Hirchhorn, K., 84
Hirsch, B. J., 502
Hirsch-Pasek, K., 300
Hoagwood, K., 57
Hofer, B. K., 404
Hoff-Ginsberg, E., 320
Hoffman, J. M., 517
Hoffman, L. W., 317
Hoffman, M. L., 440
Holland, J. L., 505
Hollister, A., 194
Holloway, S. D., 306
Holmbeck, G. N., 522
Holtzman, W. H., 9
Honig, A. S., 227
Honig, S., 306
Hoot, J. L., 268
Horney, K., 69
Hornung, M., 324
Horowitz, F. D., 12
Houston, M., 434
Howard, K. I., 458
Howe, G. W., 228
Howes, C., 226, 227, 324
Howie, V. M., 114
Huang, L. N., 363, 392, 423, 436
Hubbard, J. J., 365
Hudson, L. M., 427
Huebner, A. M., 439
Huesmann, L. R., 326
Hughes, E. C., 79
Hunt, M., 466
Hunt, R. G., 531
Huston, A. C., 226, 325, 330, 332, 333, 363, 545
Huttonlocher, J., 202
Hwang, H., 437
Hwant, C. P., 225
Hyde, J. S., 31, 431, 432
Hymel, S., 503
Hyson, M., 300

I

Ickovics, J. R., 377

Infant Health and Development Program Staff, 100
Inhelder, B., 280
Inoff-Germain, G., 460
Inton-Peterson, M., 384
Irwin, C. E., 494
Israel, A. C., 239
Izard, C. E., 232, 233

J

Jacklin, C. N., 431
Jackson, J. F., 93
Jackson, J. S., 436
Jacobs, F. H., 29
Jacobs, J. E., 494
Jacobs, J. K., 503
Jacobsen, L., 362, 394
Jacobson, J. L., 116
Jacobson, S. W., 116
Jaffe, J., 218
James, W., 172
Jarrett, R. L., 363
Jeans, P. C., 113
Jensen, L. C., 67
Jensen, P., 57
Jensen, R. A., 91
Jiao, S., 316
Jing, Q., 316
Johnson, D. D. L., 114
Johnson, P., 436
Johnson, S. M., 315
Johnston, L., 470, 471, 496
Jones, E. R., 468
Jones, J. M., 79, 392, 531
Jones, L., 392, 468
Jones, M. C., 461
Jonson, C. S., 375, 376
Joseph, C. L. M., 131
Journal of the American Medical Association, 8
Jozefowicz, D. M., 507
Juhnke, C., 336

K

Kaegi, D., 169
Kagan, J., 19, 48, 90, 223, 227
Kagitcibasi, C., 11
Kahlbaugh, P. E., 514
Kahn, A. J., 29
Kalichman, S. C., 468
Kalinowski, L. L., 232, 233
Kallen, D. J., 463
Kamerman, S. B., 29, 246
Kandel, D. B., 472
Karabenick, S. A., 461
Karbon, M., 336
Karp, J. S., 431
Katz, L., 422
Katz, M. R., 507
Katz, P. A., 416
Kaufmann, A. S., 493
Kavale, K. A., 368
Kavin, E. J., 487
Kearsley, R. B., 227
Keating, D. P., 494, 495, 515

Keener, D. C., 521
Kegeles, S. M., 494
Keirouz, K. S., 411
Kelder, S. H., 376
Keller, A., 330
Kellogg, R., 260
Keltikangas-Jarvinen, L., 364
Kendler, K. S., 93
Kendrick, C., 202, 316
Kendrick, J. S., 114
Kennedy, J. H., 419
Kennell, J. H., 141, 149
Keppler, A., 143
Kershner, R., 487
Kessen, W., 163
Ki, G., 316
Kiely, J. L., 114
Kimmel, A., 57
King, N., 324
Kingston, M., 67
Kinsey, A. C., 466
Kirchner, G. L., 114, 369
Kirk, L., 300
Kirmil-Gray, K., 364
Kisilevsky, B. S., 175
Kisker, E., 226
Klaus, M. H., 141, 149
Klaus, P. H., 141, 149
Klebanov, P. K., 392
Klein, A. S., 298
Klein, K. R., 358
Klein, L., 233
Klein, N. K., 145
Klein, R., 326
Klepp, K., 376
Klonoff-Cohen, H. S., 169
Knight, G. P., 362
Koenig, W. D., 76
Koeppl, G. K., 419
Kohlberg, L., 333, 437, 438
Kolbe, L. J., 359
Kolts, R., 471
Kopp, C. B., 143
Korenbrot, C. C., 131, 132
Kormelink, R., 75
Korn, W. S., 495
Kortenhaus, C. M., 347
Kozberg, S. F., 440
Krile, D., 427
Krowitz, A., 174
Ku, L. C., 468
Kucera, E., 315
Kuhl, P. K., 197
Kupermine, G. P., 321
Kupersmidt, J. B., 320, 419
Kurdek, L. A., 427
Kurland, D. M., 287
Kurtz, D. A., 535

L

Laaksa, M., 374
Ladd, G., 321
Ladd, G. W., 321
Ladewig, P. A., 123, 132
LaFromboise, T. D., 436, 437
La Greca, A. M., 320

Lally, J. R., 306
Lam, T., 474
Lamb, M., 8
Lamb, M. E., 19, 224, 225
Lambert, L. C., 376
Lande, J., 226
Landesman-Dwyer, S., 114
Landin, J., 535
Lane, H., 197
Lang, R., 82
Lange, L., 333
Langer, A., 174
Lapsley, D. K., 438, 457, 494, 534
Lasko, D. S., 475
Lazarus, R., 361
Lazarus, R. S., 361
Leach, P., 194, 266
Leaper, C., 433
LeBlanc, J. M., 233
Leboyer, F., 139
Lecaunet, J. P., 175
Lee, L. C., 53
Lee, S. Y., 404
Leffert, N., 362
Lefkowitz, E. S., 169, 514
LeGasse, K., 116
Leiderman, P. H., 543
Leifer, A. D., 326
Leigh, J., 508
Leinbach, M. D., 332
Lemery, K. S., 228
Lenneberg, E., 201
Lenneberg, E. H., 203
Leong, F., 437
Leo-Summers, L., 82
Lepper, M., 402
Lepper, M. R., 405, 406
Lerman, R. H., 265, 266
Lerner, R. M., 461
Le Sieur, K. D., 321
Lester, B. M., 116, 146, 147
Leventhal, A., 524
Levin, J., 384
Levine, A., 484, 542
Levine, M. P., 477
LeVine, R. A., 11
Leviton, A., 116
Levitt, M. J., 222
Levy, G. D., 334
Lewis, C. G., 494
Lewis, J. M., 318
Lewis, M., 235
Lewis, V. G., 463
Lewkowicz, D. J., 178
Liaw, F., 100
Liben, L. S., 430
Lickliter, R., 178
Lieberman, E., 114
Lieberman, M., 438
Lifshitz, F., 183
Lincoln, R., 469
Lipsitt, L. P., 177
Lipstiz, J., 419, 502
Lishner, D., 474
Little, P., 29
Livesly, W., 426
Locke, J. L., 202

Loehlin, J. C., 392
Lohr, M. J., 525
London, M. L., 123, 132
Long, L., 419
Long, T., 419
Lopez, E., 536
Lorch, E., 326
Lorch, E. P., 286
Lord, C., 231, 232, 321
Lorenz, K. Z., 45, 222
Loriaux, D. L., 460
Lourenco, O., 382
Louv, R., 29, 57, 245, 377
Loya, F., 471
Lucas, F. L., 460
Lunsteen, C., 84
Luria, A., 332
Luster, T. J., 470
Lykken, D. T., 74
Lynch, E. W., 374
Lyons, N. P., 441
Lytle, L. L., 376
Lyytinen, P., 374

M

Macadoo, H. P., 346
Maccoby, E. E., 93, 216, 232, 313, 319,
    321, 332, 417, 431
MacFarlane, J. A., 177
Machado, A., 382
MacIver, D., 333
MacLean, D. J., 515
Maddux, J. E., 268
Mader, S., 94
Maehr, M. L., 402
Magai, C., 231
Maggs, J. L., 419
Magnusson, D., 462
Mahalski, P. A., 262
Mahler, M., 235
Mahoney, K. M., 495
Main, M., 239
Maioni, T. L., 324
Majidi-Ahi, S., 428
Malamuth, N., 77
Malinowski, B., 68
Malinowski-Rummell, R., 239
Malone, S., 176, 177
Mammersmith, S. K., 466
Mamorstein, N. R., 475
Mandler, J. M., 192
Mangione, P., 306
Manley, J. T., 239
Manos, C., 474
Marchant, G. J., 402
Marcia, J., 533
Mare, R., 423
Margolin, L., 238
Marks, I. M., 77
Marold, D. B., 476
Marotz, L., 264
Marquis, K. S., 82
Marshall, R., 516
Marshall, T. R., 233
Marsiglio, W., 470
Martin, D. C., 114, 369

Martin, D. W., 51
Martin, E. E., 466
Martin, J., 501
Martin, J. A., 313
Martin, L. R., 395
Martorell, R., 209
Masangkay, Z., 209
Masten, A. S., 365
Matarazzo, J. D., 364
Matas, L., 223
Matlin, M. W., 177, 213, 247
Matsumoto, D., 11
Matthews, W. S., 213
May, M. S., 336
Mayaux, M. J., 113
Mayer, F. S., 45
McAleer, J. L., 325
McBride, A. B., 377
McCall, R. B., 196
McCartney, K., 226, 521
McCarton, C. M., 90
McClearn, G. E., 91
McClelland, D. C., 401
McDavis, R. J., 436
McDougall, P., 503
McFadden, S. H., 231
McGoldrick, M., 219
McGue, M., 74, 93
McGue, M. K., 82
McHale, J. L., 224
McHolland, J., 29
McIntosh, D. E., 305
McKinney, M. H., 470
McLaughlin, M. W., 536
McLoyd, V. C., 226, 363, 392, 459
McMahon, R. J., 471
McSharry, J., 82
Meacham, J., 330
Mednick, S. A., 84
Medrich, E. A., 419
Meece, J., 422
Meisels, S. J., 100
Mekos, D., 418
Meltzoff, A. N., 193, 195
Mercy, J. A., 471
Meredith, H. V., 255
Merrick, S. K., 19, 223
Metalsky, G. I., 365
Meyer, E. C., 53, 531
Meyerhoff, M. K., 345
Michel, G. L., 261
Michelozzi, B. N., 505
Midgley, C., 402, 413
Miekle, D., 54
Miller, F., 515
Miller, G., 199
Miller, J. G., 439
Miller, J. P., 525
Miller, P., 288
Miller, P. J., 324
Miller, S. A., 79, 288
Miller-Jones, D., 392
Millstein, S. G., 494
Minnett, A. M., 316
Minuchin, P. P., 423
Mischel, W., 44, 336
Mollasis, C., 507

Reilly, R., 354
Reinherz, H. Z., 476
Reiss, D., 228, 418
Reiter, E. O., 463
Remafedi, G., 466
Rescorla, L., 300
Resnick, M., 466
Resnick, S. M., 431
Rice, M. B., 203, 292
Richards, M., 363
Richards, M. H., 317
Rickel, A. V., 487
Riddle, D. B., 265
Risley, T. R., 202
Ritter, P. L., 543
Rivera, J., 209
Roberts, D., 362
Roberts, D. R., 543
Roberts, J. E., 225
Roberts, M. C., 268
Roberts, W., 336
Roberts, W. L., 51
Robertson, G., 268
Robinson, L. C., 471
Rode, S. S., 149
Rodin, J., 358, 377
Rodriguez, R. G., 466
Roff, M., 320
Rogers, A., 536
Rogers, C. S., 265
Rogers, M. F., 112
Roggman, L. A., 521
Rogoff, B., 286
Rogosch, F. A., 238
Rohner, E. C., 319
Rohner, R. P., 319
Romo, H. D., 423
Roosas, M., 362
Rosario, M., 154
Rose, R. J., 93
Rose, S., 527
Rose, S. A., 90, 178, 193
Rosen, D., 229
Rosenberg, M. L., 471
Rosenblatt, L., 306
Rosenblith, J. F., 106, 138, 139, 194
Rosenkranz, P., 433
Rosenman, R., 363
Rosenthal, D. M., 68
Rosenthal, R., 51, 68, 394
Roskos, K., 293
Rosnow, R. L., 51
Rosoff, J. I., 469
Ross, F. C., 75
Rossen, J., 419
Rossi, A. S., 221
Rothbart, M. K., 228, 229
Rothbart, M. L. K., 316
Rothlisberg, B., 402
Rovee-Collier, C., 193, 194
Ruben, D. B., 84
Rubin, K. H., 324
Rubin, K. N., 323
Rubin, V., 419
Rubin, Z., 321
Rumbaugh, D., 200
Rumberger, R. W., 503

Rushton, J. P., 79
Russo, N. F., 58
Rutter, M., 239, 366
Ryan, A. M., 320
Ryan, R. A., 436, 437
Rymer, R., 201
Ryu, S., 508

S

Saarni, C., 433
Sachse, K., 82
Sackett, G. P., 114
Sadker, D., 33, 333
Sadker, M., 33, 333
Sagan, C., 75
Sakin, J., 315
Salapatek, P., 163
Sallade, J. B., 358
Saltz, E., 527
Samaras, A. P., 405
Sameroff, A. J., 365
Sandberg, D., 154
Sandler, I., 361
Sandman, B. M., 114, 369
Sanson, A., 228, 229
Santrock, J. W., 10, 16, 316, 319, 418, 496, 530
Saudino, K. J., 228
Savage-Rumbaugh, E. S., 200
Savin-Williams, R. C., 466
Sawyers, J. Y., 68
Saxe, G. B., 286
Scafidi, F., 154
Scales, P. C., 503
Scarr, S., 89, 90, 92, 93, 94, 226, 392
Schaie, K. W., 57
Schanberg, S., 153
Schechter, D. E., 82
Schechter, M., 86
Schiller, M., 261, 365
Schmitt, D. P., 432
Schmitz, S., 228
Schnorr, T. M., 116
Schoen, S., 112
Schoendord, K. C., 114
Schonert-Reichel, K., 503
Schopler, E., 239
Schorr, L., 305
Schrag, S. G., 116
Schreiber, L. R., 374
Schulenberg, J., 509
Schulsinger, R., 84
Schunk, D. H., 402
Schwartz, D., 113
Schwartz, J. E., 395
Schwartzman, P., 476
Schweinhart, L., 474
Scott, P., 199
Scott-Jones, D., 423, 530
Scribner, S., 287
Sears, H. A., 475
Sechzur, J., 58
Sedeno, A., 363
Seefeldt, C., 261
Segal, N. L., 74
Seigle, J., 325

Selice, S., 436
Seligman, M. E. P., 365
Sells, S. B., 320
Selman, R. L., 426, 427
Semaj, L. T., 535
Serafica, F. C., 505
Serbin, L. A., 333, 334
Serdula, M., 114
Serlin, R. C., 457
Sevick, R. A., 200
Sexton, D., 265
Sexton, G., 364
Shahinfar, A., 223
Shanahan, M., 508
Shannon, F. T., 170
Shapiro, E. K., 423
Shapiro, H., 260
Shapiro, N., 503
Sharma, A. R., 82
Shaver, P., 521
Shaw, S. M., 247
Shields, A., 238
Shields, S. A., 431, 433
Shiner, R. L., 475
Shiono, P. H., 131, 145
Shirley, M., 167
Shuart, V., 515
Shuck, E. L., 306
Shweder, R. A., 11
Sideeck, A., 100
Siegel, L. S., 196
Siegler, R. S., 383, 386
Siegman, A. W., 363
Sigman, M. D., 286, 514
Silbereisen, R. K., 321
Silverberg, S. B., 522
Silverman, A. B., 476
Silverman, N., 239
Simich-Dudgeon, C., 446
Simkin, P., 143
Simmons, R. G., 423, 541, 544
Simons-Morton, G. G., 359
Simpson, R. L., 506
Sims, B., 363
Sims, K. E., 470
Sims, R., 347
Singer, D. G., 327
Singer, L. M., 82
Sitterle, K. A., 418
Skerry, S., 426
Skinner, B. F., 202
Skinner, E. A., 402
Skipper, B., 376
Slavin, R. E., 447
Sledden, E. A., 268
Slobin, D., 204
Sloman, J., 321
Smith, B. A., 177
Smith, D. W., 82
Smith, J. C., 471
Smith, M. B., 113
Smith, R., 326
Smith, R. S., 66, 237
Smolak, L., 477
Snarey, J., 439
Snider, B. A., 525
Snidman, N., 19

Snow, C. E., 203, 292
Snow, R. E., 423
Solomon, J., 239
Sonenstein, F. L., 468
Soule, B., 113
Sowers-Hoag, K. W., 273
Sparling, J. J., 100
Spear-Swerling, L., 368, 399
Specklen, K. M., 419
Spelke, E. S., 174, 178, 192
Spence, J. T., 433
Spence, M. J., 175
Spencer, M. B., 424, 530, 535
Sprafkin, C., 334
Srinivasan, I. P., 169
Srinivasan, S. R., 375, 376
Sroufe, L. A., 149, 222, 223, 231, 232, 233
Stafford, F. P., 417
Stallings, J., 298
Stanhope, L., 316
Stanley, K., 113
Stanley-Hagan, M. M., 318
Stapp, J., 30
Starkey, P., 298
Stattin, H., 462
Staub, E., 473
Stearns, G., 113
Stechler, G., 113
Stein, A. H., 326
Steinberg, J., 225
Steinberg, L., 456, 484, 508, 509, 522, 542
Steinberg, L. D., 419
Steiner, J. E., 177
Stemmler, M., 474
Stenhouse, G., 8
Stephenson, A. L., 471
Stern, D. N., 218
Sternberg, K. J., 19
Sternberg, R. J., 368, 387, 390, 392, 399, 411
Sternglanz, S. H., 333
Steur, F. B., 326
Stevenson, H. G., 298
Stevenson, H. W., 11, 53, 404
Stevenson, M. R., 318
Steward, P., 286
Stewart, N. J., 115
Stipek, D., 306
Stipek, D. J., 517
Stocker, C., 317
Stocking, M., 84
Stoll, M. F., 319
Stone, G. C., 494
Stone, L., 293
Stormer, S. M., 477
Stormshak, E., 305
Strahan, D. B., 493
Strasburger, V. C., 326
Strayer, J., 336
Streissguth, A. P., 114, 369
Stricker, G., 29
Striegel-Moore, R. H., 477
Styfco, S. J., 14, 298
Sue, S., 530, 531
Suleiman, L., 363
Sullivan, A., 522
Sullivan, H. S., 421

Sullivan, K., 522
Suomi, S. J., 320
Super, C. M., 223
Super, D. E., 504
Susman, E. J., 53, 460
Sutton, K., 45
Swank, P., 114
Swerdlik, M. E., 388

T

Tager-Flusberg, H., 201
Tajfel, H., 428
Takanishi, R., 483
Tamarin, R., 86
Tapper, J., 325
Tappero, E., 139
Tardif, T., 320
Tavris, C., 31, 157, 334, 432, 433
Taylor, H. G., 145
Taylor, K., 298
Taylor, R. D., 362
Tellegen, A., 74
Terman, L., 395
Terman, L. H., 395
Teti, D. M., 223, 315
Teti, L. O., 223
Thal, D., 199
Thelen, E., 167
Theobald, W., 527
Thomas, A., 227
Thompson, A., 100
Thompson, E. T., 79
Thompson, J. K., 477
Thoresen, C. E., 364
Thorton, A., 498
Thyer, B. A., 273
Tiernan, K., 268
Tilton-Weaver, L., 459
Tobin, D., 517
Tobin, J. J., 308
Todd, J., 477
Tomlinson-Keasey, C., 395, 476, 493
Tonner, L., 229
Tooby, J., 77
Torney-Purta, J., 498
Toth, S. L., 238, 239
Trankina, F., 437
Trautlein, B., 526
Treboux, E., 19, 223
Triandis, H. C., 53
Trimble, J., 436
Trimble, J. E., 53
Tronick, E. Z., 146
Tubman, J. G., 477
Tucker, A. M., 30
Tucker, J. S., 395
Tucker, L. A., 358
Tuckman, B. W., 359
Turecki, S., 229
Tyack, D., 501

U

Udall, J. N., 265
Unger, R., 432

United States Commission on Civil Rights, 400
United States Department of Education, 473
United States General Accounting Office, 131
Urberg, K. A., 521
Urbina, S., 392

V

Valiante, A. G., 115
Vandell, D. L., 218, 226, 316, 419
Vandenberg, B., 323
Van den Berghe, P. L., 79
van den Boom, D. C., 229
VandenBos, G. R., 30
VanDusen, J. E., 463
Vargas, L., 471
Vaughn, B. D., 29
Verbrugge, L. M., 377
Vessey, S. H., 54
Vining, E. P. G., 83
Virdin, L., 362
Vogel, S., 433
Voran, K., 226
Voyer, D., 431
Voyer, S., 431
Vygotsky, L. S., 286, 322

W

Wachs, H., 381
Waddington, C. H., 90
Wade, C., 334, 432, 433
Wagner, B. M., 476
Wakschlag, L. S., 320
Walk, R. D., 174, 178
Wallace-Broscious, A., 505
Wallerstein, J. S., 318
Warren, L. W., 476
Warren, M. P., 460, 461
Warshak, R. A., 83, 319
Wasik, B. H., 100
Waterman, A. S., 533
Waternaux, C., 116
Waters, E., 19, 223, 231, 232, 233, 321
Waters, P., 432
Watkinson, B., 114, 115
Watson, J. B., 233
Weaver, R. F., 88
Webber, L. S., 375, 376
Wei, L. S., 112
Weidner, G., 364
Weikart, D., 474
Weikart, D. P., 209, 258, 298
Weinberg, M. S., 466
Weinberg, R. A., 90, 94, 392
Weinberger, D. A., 472
Weinstein, N. D., 357
Weisner, T., 503
Weiss, B., 313
Weizmann, F., 79
Wellborn, J. G., 402
Wellman, H. M., 287
Wells, M. G., 429
Werner, E. E., 66, 113, 237, 365

Wertheimer, M., 387
Wessles, K., 422
Westoff, C. G., 469
Weyman-Daum, M., 183
Whalley, J., 143
White, B., 167
White, B. L., 345
Whitebook, M., 226
Whiteman, M., 471, 522
Whitesell, N., 432
Whitfield, J. R., 436
Whitfield, K., 93
Whiting, B. B., 53, 319, 433, 529
Whiting, J. W. M., 53
Wicks-Nelson, R., 239
Wiener, N. I., 79
Wiesenthal, D. L., 79
Wigfield, A., 503
Wilcox, K. J., 74
Wiley, K. J., 169
Wilkinson, D., 436
William T. Grant Foundation
      Commission, 504, 507, 515
Williams, C. R., 327
Williams, J. E., 430
Williams, J. F., 325
Williams, J. R., 257
Williams, R. A., 363, 364
Williams, S. L., 200
Williamson, D. F., 114
Williamson, L., 362

Wilson, E. O., 76
Wilson, K. S., 218
Wilson, L. C., 211, 236, 244
Wilson, M., 77
Windle, M., 477
Windle, R. C., 477
Windle, W. F., 177
Wingard, D. L., 395
Winner, E., 280
Wisniewski, L., 358
Witkin, H. A., 84
Witt, D. D., 257
Wodrich, D. L., 368
Wolff, P. H., 232, 233
Wolfson, J., 90
Wollinsky, F. D., 131
Wolowicz, L. S., 521
Women on Words & Images, 347
Wood, J. T., 12, 434
Woolfenden, G. E., 76
Woolsey, S. F., 169
Worobey, J., 147
Worrall, B. K., 53
Worrell, J., 69, 477
Wosinski, M., 336
Wright, H. F., 419
Wright, J. C., 326
Wright, L., 268
Wroblewski, R., 333
Wu, D. Y. H., 308
Wulf, D., 469

Y

Yando, R., 475
Yang, A., 423, 541, 544
Yankelovich, D., 458
Yates, M., 496
Yates, M. J., 496
Yekel, C. A., 430
Yeni-Komshian, G. H., 401
Ying, Y., 436
Yip, R., 169
Yongue, B., 274
Young, K. T., 170
Young, S. K., 223

Z

Zabin, L. S., 465
Zambriani, R. E., 53
Zautra, A. J., 361
Zelazo, P. R., 115, 227
Zellman, G. L., 466
Zeskind, P. S., 233
Ziegler, M., 79
Zigler, E., 14, 227, 298
Zimmerman, R. R., 221
Zolotow, C., 309
Zubay, G. L., 75
Zuckerman, M., 184

SUBJECT INDEX

Behavioral theory
  language development, 202
  view of development, 43
Behavior genetics
  adoption studies, 90
  nature of, 90
  twin studies, 90
Bell curve concept, of intelligence, 91–92
Bem Sex-Role Inventory, 433, 434
Bilingual education, 400–401
  evaluation of, 400–401
  nature of, 400
Biological processes, nature of, 15
Birth defects. See Prenatal hazards
Birth order, 315–316
  firstborns, 315–316
  only children, 316
  same-sex siblings, 316
  and sibling relationships, 316
Birth process
  afterbirth, 137
  childbirth classes, format of, 155
  complications of, 137–138
  doula support, 141
  drugs used during, 138
  eclectic approach to, 139–140
  father participation, 141–142
  Lamaze method, 140–141
  Leboyer method, 139
  low-birthweight infants, 143, 145–146
  neonatal assessment, 146–147
  postpartum period, 147–149
  prepared childbirth, 139
  preterm infants, 143, 145–146
  stages of, 136–137
  standard childbirth procedure, 138–139
Blastocyst, 104, 105
Bonding, mother/infant, 148–149
Boundary ambiguity, and stepfamilies, 418
Brain
  early childhood, 256
  infancy, 166
  myelination, 256
Braxton Hicks contractions, 122
Brazelton Neonatal Behavioral
    Assessment Scale, 146–147
Breast feeding
  versus bottle feeding, 169–170
  and working mothers, 185
Breech birth, 137
Bulimia, 477

C

Canalization, 90
Career development, 504–508
  career self-concept theory, 504–505
  developmental career choice theory, 504
  and gender roles, 507–508
  and parenting, 506, 515
  personality-type theory, 505
  planning in, 505
  school influences, 506–507
  and social class, 506
Career self-concept theory, 504–505
Careers, in child development field, 20,
    22–23
Care perspective, moral development,
    440–441
Carnegie report, on middle schools,
    502–503

Case studies, 52
Centration, Piaget's theory, 282
Cephalocaudal growth, 163
Cesarean section, 137–138
Child abuse, 237–239
  cultural context of, 238
  developmental consequences of, 238–239
  family influences, 238
  risk reduction program, 182
  types of, 238
Childbirth. See Birth process
Childbirth classes, format of, 155
Child-centered kindergarten, 293
Child development, historical view, 7
Child development careers, types of, 20,
    22–23
Child development theories
  behaviorism, 43
  eclectic theoretical orientation, 48–49
  ecological theory, 46–47
  Erikson's theory, 39–40
  ethological theories, 45–46
  Freud's theory, 36–39
  information processing theory, 42
  Piaget's theory, 40–42
  social learning theory, 43–45
Children, reasons for study of, 6–7
China, Olympic training for children, 354
Chlamydia, 467
Chorionic villus test, 86
Chromosomes, 80
Chronosystem, 47
Cigarette smoking
  physical effects on children, 268
  as prenatal hazard, 114–115
Classification, 381
Cliques, 524–525
Cocaine, 471
  as prenatal hazard, 115–116
Cognitive appraisal, 361
Cognitive development
  adolescence, 490–495
  comparison of theories, 397–398
  early childhood, 278–288
  infancy, 189–195
  information processing theory, 42
  Piaget's theory, 40–42
  and play, 322
  and television viewing, 326–327
  Vygotsky's theory, 285–286
  See also specific theories
Cognitive developmental theory, gender
    development, 333–334
Cognitive monitoring, 385
  and reciprocal teaching, 385
Cognitive processes, nature of, 15
Cognitive view, of depression, 364–365
Cohort effects, 57
Commitment, in identity
    development, 533
Community rights versus individual rights,
    moral development, 438
Computers, 405–406
  computer-assisted instruction, 405–406
  in early childhood classes, 307
  and ethnic minorities, 413
  negative influences of, 406
  positive influences of, 405–406
Conceptual development, infancy, 192
Concrete operational thought, 381–382

characteristics of, 381–382
classification, 381
time span of, 42
Conformity, to peer pressure, 524
Connectedness, meaning of, 534
Conscience, 329
  superego, 36–37, 336
Conservation, Piaget's theory,
    282–284, 381
Constructive play, 324
Constructivist view, perception, 178
Context, meaning of, 11
Continuity of development, meaning
    of, 18
Contraception, rating of different
    methods, 133
Control processes, memory, 384
Conventional reasoning, moral
    development, 437–438
Convergent thinking, 396
Conversations, language
    development, 292
Cooperative play, 322
Coping, 365–367
  with death, 366–367
  with stress, 365–366
Correlational research, 54–55
  and causal conclusions, 60
  correlation coefficient, 54–55
Correlation coefficient, 54–55
Creativity, 395–396
  definition of, 396
  and divergent thinking, 396
  snowflake model of, 412–413
  and television viewing, 327
Crisis, in identity development, 533
Critical period
  in language development, 201–202
  meaning of, 46
Critical thinking, 386–387
  elements of, 387
  thinking processes in, 387
Cross-cultural research, 52–53
  aggression, 52
  emic approach, 53
  ethnic gloss, 53
  etic approach, 53
  nature of, 11
Cross-cultural view
  achievement, 404
  of child care policies, 246
  early childhood education, 308
  foreign language learning, 401
  of Freudian theory, 68–69
  gender roles, 448
  illness and health of children, 266–267
  low-birthweight infants, 156
  moral development, 439
  mortality rates for children, 267
  Olympic training for children, 354
  pregnancy, 124–125
  rites of passage, 527–530
  social policy and children, 30–31
  teenage pregnancy, 469
Cross-sectional research, 56
Crowds, 524–525
Crying in infancy
  anger cry, 233
  basic cry, 233
  pain cry, 233
  responding to crying infant, 233

and career development, 507–508
cross-cultural view, 448
definition of, 330
and ethnic minorities, 434–437
future view, 449, 551
gender-role transcendence, 434
male adolescent culture, 545
Gender schema, meaning of, 334
Gender schema theory, gender
    development, 334
Gender stereotypes
and culture, 430
meaning of, 430
pervasiveness of, 430
and television, 333
Generativity versus stagnation, 39, 41
Genes, 79–80
function of, 80
Genetic abnormalities, 83–86
anencephaly, 85
cystic fibrosis, 85
Down syndrome, 83, 85
and genetic counseling, 99
hemophilia, 85
Klinefelter syndrome, 83–84, 85
phenylketonuria (PKU), 83, 85
pyloric stenosis, 85
sickle-cell anemia, 83, 85
spina bifida, 85
Tay-Sachs disease, 85
thalassemia, 85
Turner syndrome, 84, 85
XYY syndrome, 84
Genetic counseling, 99
Genetic principles, 86, 88–90
canalization, 90
dominant-recessive genes principle, 88
genotype and phenotype, 88
polygenic inheritance, 88
reaction range, 89–90
Genetic testing, 84, 86
amniocentesis, 84
chorionic villus test, 86
maternal blood test, 86
ultrasound sonography, 84
Genital herpes, as prenatal hazard, 111
Genital stage, 38
Genotype, 88
Germinal period, 104
Gesell test, 195–196
Giftedness, 395
definition of, 395
females, education of, 517
gifted disadvantaged children, 411
longitudinal study of, 395
parenting issues, 411–412
Grasping reflex, 163
Gross motor skills
early childhood, 257–259
infancy, 166–167
middle and late childhood, 355–356
muscle activities in, 166
Group identity
and ethnocentrism, 428
social identity theory, 428
Guilt, and maternal employment, 318

H

Habituation, 193–194
Handedness, 261–262
development of, 261–262
left-handedness, 261

Health and well-being
and caregiver behavior, 268
child abuse risk reduction program, 182
doctors, role of, 8
elementary school children, health
    problems, 357
fatal disorders in childhood, 266–267
future view, 550
health education programs, 268
Heart Smart program, 375–376
illness/health in world's children, 267
and low-income families, 266, 272
mortality rates for children, 267
prenatal care, 131
prepregnancy planning, 98
preventive services for poor, 272
protective factors for children, 66
puberty, health care in, 462–463
services for parents and children, 28
working parents, stress reduction, 344
Hearing
hearing problems, causes of, 357
infancy, 175
Heart Smart program, 375–376
Height/weight
early childhood, 254–256
infancy, 164
middle and late childhood, 355
Helping behavior, gender differences,
    432–433
Helpless orientation, and
    achievement, 402
Hemophilia, 85
Heredity, 79–86
behavior genetics, 90
chromosomes, 80
and DNA, 80
genes, 79–80
genetic abnormalities, 83–86
and intelligence issue, 91–92
reproduction, 80–83
Heredity-environment interaction, 92–94
active (niche-picking) genotype-
    environment interactions, 92
contemporary issues, 93–94
evocative genotype-environment
    interactions, 92
passive genotype-environment
    interactions, 92
shared and nonshared environmental
    experiences, 93
Heroin, as prenatal hazard, 115
Herpes simplex virus II, 467
Heteronomous morality, 335
High school, 501, 503–504
back-to-basics movement, 501
dropouts, 503–504
historical view, 501
History, view of children, 7
Holophrase hypothesis, 204
Homeless, family policy and, 29
Homosexuality, and adolescents, 466
Hormones
androgen, 330
estrogen, 330, 430, 460
and gender development, 330
in puberty, 460
testosterone, 430–431, 460
Humor, as coping response, 366
Hypotheses, meaning of, 35
Hypothetical-deductive reasoning,
    491–492

I

Id, 36, 37
Identification theory, gender
    development, 331
Identity development
adolescence, 532–536
commitment in, 533
crisis, 533
and culture, 535
and ethnic minorities, 535–536
gender differences, 536
identity achievement, 533
identity diffusion, 533
identity foreclosure, 533
identity moratorium, 533
and parenting, 534–535
as process, 532–533
Identity versus identity confusion, 39, 41
Idiographic needs, 59
Illness, in early childhood, 266–267
Imagery, memory strategy, 384
Imitation
deferred imitation, 195
of gender development, 331
in infancy, 194–195
of parents by child, 67
Immanent justice, moral
    development, 335
Immunization, 170, 171, 266, 267
recommended schedule, 171
Implantation, of zygote, 104
Imprinting, meaning of, 46
Impulsivity, as coping response, 366
Independent variables, 55
Individualism and purpose, moral
    development, 437
Individuality, meaning of, 534
Indulgent parenting, 314
Industry versus inferiority, 39, 40, 429
Infancy
accident prevention, 170–171
attachment, 221–224
brain, 166
cognitive development, 189–195
conceptual development, 192
developmental biodynamics, 167–168
emotional development, 232–233, 236
fine motor skills, 167, 168
gross motor skills, 166–167
growth patterns, 163–164
hearing, 175
height/weight, 164
immunization, 170, 171
infant states, 169
intelligence testing in, 195–197
intermodal perception, 177–178
language development, 197, 201–205
malnutrition in, 170, 209
nutrition in, 169–170, 182–183
personality development, 234–236
physical fitness/swimming classes, 183
reflexes, 162–163
sensory/perceptual development, 172–178
sensory stimulation in, 184
social development changes, 236–237
sudden infant death syndrome (SIDS), 169
time span of, 16
toilet training, 171–172
Infantile autism, 239
causation, 239
characteristics of, 239

Infant testing, 195–197
    Bayley Scales of Infant Development, 196
    developmental quotient (DQ), 195–196
Infertility, 81–83
    and adoption, 82–83
    fertility problems, types of, 82
    in vitro fertilization, 81
    and maternal age, 113
Infinite generativity, language, 197
Information processing theory, 42
    attention, 286–287
    cognitive monitoring, 385
    critical thinking, 386–387
    evaluation of, 397
    habituation/dishabituation, 193–194
    imitation, 194–195
    infancy, 193–195
    memory, 194, 287, 384–385
    scientific reasoning, 386
    scripts, 386
    task analysis, 287
    view of development, 42
Informed consent, research with
        children, 57
Initiative versus guilt, 39, 40, 329
Innate goodness view, of children, 7
Insecure attachment, 223
Integrity versus despair, 40, 41
Intelligence, 387–398
    and creativity, 395–396
    definition of, 387
    and early educational experiences, 100
    giftedness, 395
    and heredity issue, 91–92
    and mental retardation, 394–395
    seven intelligences concept, 391–392
    triarchic theory, 390–391
Intelligence tests
    Binet scale, 388–389
    culture-fair tests, 392–393
    and ethnic minorities, 392–393
    historical view, 388–389
    infant tests, 195–197
    intelligence quotient (IQ), 389
    mental age, 388–389
    misuse of, 380, 394
    Stanford-Binet, 389
    Wechsler scales, 389–390
Intermodal perception
    infancy, 177–178
    meaning of, 177
Internalization of schemes, 190
Interpersonal norms, moral
        development, 437
Interventionist view, adolescence, 457
Intimacy, in friendships, 421
Intimacy versus isolation, 39, 41
Intrinsic motivation, 402
Intuitive thought substage, 280–282
In vitro fertilization, 81
Involution, 147–148

J

Japan, early childhood education, 308
Jigsaw classroom, 447
Junior high school. See Middle school
Justice perspective, moral
        development, 440
Juvenile delinquency, 472–474
    causes of, 472

family influences, 472–473
prevention of, 473–474, 478
violence, 473

K

Kaufman Assessment Battery for Children
        (K-ABC), 393
Keyword method, memory strategy, 384
Kindergarten
    child-centered, 293
    computers in, 307
Klinefelter syndrome, 83–84, 85
Kohlberg's moral development theory,
        437–438
    conventional reasoning, 437–438
    criticism of, 438
    postconventional reasoning, 438
    preconventional reasoning, 437

L

Labeling, 202–203
Lamaze method, 140–141
Language
    infinite generativity of, 197
    morphology, 199
    phonology, 197, 199
    pragmatics, 199
    semantics, 199
    syntax, 199
Language acquisition device (LAD), 200
Language development
    in animals, 200–201
    behavioral view, 202
    bilingualism, 400–401
    biological foundations of, 199–200
    Brown's stages of, 290–291
    conversations, 292
    critical period in, 201–202
    early childhood, 288, 290–292
    echoing, 202
    environmental influences, 202–203
    expanding, 202
    family facilitation of, 202, 210
    grammatical rules, 399
    holophrase hypothesis, 204
    infancy, 197, 201–205
    labeling, 202–203
    language acquisition device (LAD), 200
    in low-income families, 212
    mean length of utterance (MLU), 204,
        290–291
    middle and late childhood, 398–401
    morphological rules, 291
    motherese, 202
    pragmatics, 292
    reading, 399–400
    recasting, 202
    receptive vocabulary, 203–204
    semantics, 292
    syntactical rules, 291–292
    telegraphic speech, 204
    and television viewing, 327
    and thought, 286
    vocabulary, increases in, 398–399
    Vygotsky's theory, 286
    in wild children, 197, 201, 202
Latchkey children, 418–419
    negative effects, 419
Late childhood. See Middle and late
        childhood

Latency stage, 38
Later life family, 221
Latinos
    females, behavioral/psychological
        orientations of, 436
    identity concerns, 536
    males, behavioral/psychological orientations
        of, 436
Learned helplessness, and depression, 365
Learning disabilities, 368
    helping children with, 368
    types of, 368
Leboyer method, 139
Life events, and stress, 361
Life Skills Training program, 485
Literacy programs, in early childhood,
        292–293
Logo, 406
Longitudinal research, 56
    cohort effects, 57
Long-term memory, 384
Low-birthweight infants, 143, 145–146
    African American babies, 145
    age/weight at birth, 143
    cross-cultural view, 156
    long-term outcomes for, 145
    reversing effects of, 145

M

Macrosystem, 47
Malnutrition
    in America, 185
    and cognitive development, 209
    in early childhood, 266, 267
    in infancy, 170, 209
    in low-income families, 266
    as prenatal hazards, 113
Marijuana, as prenatal hazard, 115
Massage, for preterm infants, 153–154
Mastery orientation, and achievement,
        402, 403
Maternal age, and prenatal development,
        112–113
Maternal blood test, 86
    Maternal employment, 317–318
    and breast feeding, 185
    and guilt, 318
    new mother, 154
Mate selection, evolutionary psychology
        view, 77
Math ability, gender differences, 431
Maturation, definition of, 17
Maximally Discriminative Facial
        Movement Coding System
        (MAX), 233
Mean length of utterance (MLU), 204,
        290–291
Media
    and gender development, 333
    portrayal of adolescents, 458
    reporting on research, 58–59
    See also Television viewing
Medicaid, preventive benefits for
        children, 272
Meiosis, 80–81
Memory, 287, 384–385
    control processes, 384
    credibility of children's memories, 384–385
    early childhood, 287
    infancy, 194

Sports, 359–360
    guidelines for parental behavior, 374–375
    positive/negative aspects, 359
    pressures related to, 359–360
Standardized tests, 52
Stanford-Binet intelligence test, 389
Stepfamilies, 418
    and boundary ambiguity, 418
    common problems in, 418, 446–447
    effects of remarriage, 418
    positive actions for, 447
Stereotypes
    adolescents, 458
    definition of, 458
    gender stereotypes, 333, 430
Storm-and-stress view, adolescence,
    457, 458
Stranger anxiety, 236
Strange Situation scale, 224
Stress, 361–364
    acculturative stress, 362
    children's coping strategies, 365–366
    cognitive factors, 361
    definition of, 361
    and life events, 361
    and poverty, 362–363
    as prenatal hazard, 113
    and preschool, 300
    reduction for working parents, 343
    Type A behavior pattern, 363–364
Sublimation, as coping response, 366
Sucking reflex, 163
Sudden infant death syndrome
    (SIDS), 169
Sugar
    consumption and eating behavior, 358
    excessive intake by children, 265–266
Suicide, 475–476
    in adolescence, 475–476
    causes of, 476
    preventive actions, 476
    warning signs, 476
Superego, 36–37, 336
Swimming, classes for infants, 183
Symbolic function substage, 279–280
Syntax, 199
    learning rules of, 291–292
Syphilis, 467
    as prenatal hazard, 111
System of Multicultural Pluralistic
    Assessment (SOMPA), 393

T

Tabula rasa view, of children, 7
Task analysis, early childhood, 287
Taste, infancy, 177
Tay-Sachs disease, 85

Teachers
    expectations and social class of child, 423
    good teachers, characteristics of, 422
    influence on children, 422–423
Teenage pregnancy, 131
    consequences of, 470
    cross-cultural view, 469
    prevention program, 133
Teeth, dental problems of children, 357
Telegraphic speech, 204
Television viewing, 325–327
    and aggression, 326
    average viewing time by children, 326
    and cognitive development, 326–327
    and creativity, 327
    educational television, 325–326, 327
    gender stereotyping, 333
    and language development, 327
    negative/positive influences, 325
    and overweight, 358
    and prosocial behavior, 326
Temperament
    activity level, 228
    and attachment, 223
    consistency of, 228–229
    difficult child, 227, 228, 229
    easy child, 227, 228
    effects on parenting, 229
    emotionality, 228
    meaning of, 227
    siblings and parental treatment, 317
    slow-to-warm-up child, 227, 228
    sociability, 228
Teratology, 110
Terman study, of gifted, 395
Terrible twos, 236
Tertiary circular reactions, 190
Testosterone, 430–431
    in puberty, 460
Thalassemia, 85
Thalidomide, 113
Theory
    nature of, 35
    revising theory, 36
Thought, and language development, 286
Toilet training, 171–172
Top-dog phenomenon, 502
Touch sensation, infancy, 175–176
Toxoplasmosis, as prenatal hazard, 117
Transitional objects, use of, 262
Triarchic theory, of intelligence, 390–391
Trophoblast, 104
Trust versus mistrust, 39, 40, 234
Turner syndrome, 84, 85
Twin studies
    criticisms of, 74
    nature of, 74, 90
Type A behavior pattern, 363–364
Type A/Type B/Type C babies, 223

U

Ultrasound sonography, 84
Unconscious, Freudian view, 37
Undernutrition, 267
Unemployment, and adolescents, 509
Universal ethical principles, moral
    development, 438
Unoccupied play, 322

V

Values, 495–496
    of adolescents, 495–496
    conflicts and ethnic minorities, 531
Verbal ability, gender differences, 431
Violence, and adolescents, 473
VistaKids, 413
Visual disorders
    functional amblyopia, 256–257
    vision problems of children, 357
Visual perception
    depth perception, 174, 256
    early childhood, 256–257
    infancy, 172, 174
Vocabulary, increases in, 398–399
Vygotsky's theory, 285–286
    evaluation of, 286, 397
    language development, 286
    play, 322
    zone of proximal development, 285–286

W

Wechsler intelligence scales, 389–390
Whole-language approach, 399
Wild Boy of Aveyron, 197, 202
Withdrawal, as coping response, 366
Work, 508–509
    part-time, pros and cons of, 508–509
    and school experiences, 515–516
    sociohistorical context, 508
    unemployment, 509
Writing to Read program, 307

X

XYY syndrome, 84

Y

Youth gangs, 473, 541
Youth organizations, 525–526
    and ethnic minorities, 526

Z

Zone of proximal development, 285–286
Zygote, 81

$$11\ 111 \quad {}^{3}32$$

$$\begin{array}{r} 6 \\ 4 \end{array} \qquad .86 \qquad 50\overline{)44.00}$$

$$50\overline{)43.00}$$
$$100$$

$$39.91$$
$$50\overline{)45.00}$$
$$40.0$$
$$\overline{50}$$